State Wildlife Laws Handbook

Funded by:

Federal Aid in Wildlife and Sportfish Restoration Acts

Geraldine R. Dodge Foundation

University of New Mexico School of Law

National Fish and Wildlife Foundation

Francis Seebee Charitable Trust

International Association of Fish and Wildlife Agencies

State Wildlife Laws Handbook

Center for Wildlife Law

at the

Institute of Public Law
University of New Mexico
Albuquerque, New Mexico

Ruth S. Musgrave, J.D. *and* Mary Anne Stein, Ph.D., J.D.

with contributions from

Karen Cantrell, Ph.D., J.D.; Sara Parker, J.D.; *and* Miriam Wolok, J.D.

 Government Institutes, Inc.

Government Institutes, Inc., Rockville, Maryland 20850

98 97 96 95 94 93   5 4 3 2 1

Illustrations appear courtesy of Angela Werneke © 1991, and are reprinted from *The
Golden Cauldron* by Nicki Scully (Bear & Company, 1991).

Library of Congress Cataloging-in-Publication Data

Musgrave, Ruth S .
    State wildlife laws handbook/Center for Wildlife
Law at the Institute of Public Law, University of New
Mexico, Albuquerque, New Mexico; Ruth Musgrave and
Mary Anne Stein; with contributions from Karen
Cantrell...(et al.). -- 1st ed.
        p.   cm.
        Includes bibliographical references.
        ISBN 0-86587-357-7
        1. Wildlife conservation--Law and legislation--United
States--States. I. Stein, Mary Anne. II. University of
New Mexico. Center for Wildlife Law. III. Title.
KF5640.Z95M87 1993
346.78904'69516--dc20
(347.8906469516)
                                        93-23418
                                        CIP

Printed on acid-free paper

Printed in the United States of America

This book is dedicated to

Ruth Hoppe Musgrave
1926-1991

*without whose inspiration and support
the Center for Wildlife Law would not exist*

TABLE OF CONTENTS

TABLE OF CONTENTS

TABLES

APPENDICES

PREFACE

When I began to investigate the possibility of creating the Center for Wildlife Law, I introduced myself to and sought the advice of wildlife law and policy experts around the country. What was expressed to me again and again was the need for some kind of comparison and analysis of our states' wildlife laws. Comparisons concerning certain discreet issues were available, but an all-inclusive survey with a comprehensive analysis of the fish and wildlife laws of the states had yet to be undertaken. In starting the Center for Wildlife Law, it was my intention that projects would make a real contribution to the field of wildlife law and to education about wildlife's present situation, and not merely to duplicate efforts already underway. Thus the concept for this *Handbook* had developed apace with the Center itself. With the documented rise in poaching of wildlife and the increasing attention that is being given to nongame wildlife issues in this country, the need for such a study now appears even more compelling.

Based on other 50-state law surveys that had been accomplished at the Institute of Public Law, we considered that a state wildlife law handbook was achievable. Moving ahead with perhaps more naivety and enthusiasm than wisdom, we initially had no idea how much time and funding it would eventually require. Three years and numerous grant proposals later, this *Handbook* has emerged as the first-ever attempt to explain, summarize and compare the wildlife laws of our nation.

Although we had developed an outline with ten major topics for reviewing states' laws, when we began processing individual state fish and wildlife codes through this system we immediately confronted an almost overwhelming array of complexities, nuances and differences in organization and substance between states' laws. Ultimately, our outline withstood the test and proved to be the best method to review all of the fish and wildlife codes. Our effort to systematize the states' laws illustrated for us a point that has been frequently made by wildlife officials: making state wildlife laws as uniform as possible would aid enforcement and management efforts. We seriously considered reviewing the regulations under each state's codes as well, but finally concluded that a written effort would be unrealistic because regulations are not easy to obtain, are subject to change at any time and are often more voluminous than the statutes themselves.

One of our most important goals was to craft this *Handbook* for a broad audience so that it could provide assistance to the greatest number of people. In the largest section of the book, the summarizing of all fifty states' laws, this proved to be a real challenge because of the need for legal accuracy and readability. Our goal throughout the work has been to write for not only attorneys in private and public practice, but for state fish and wildlife officials, legislators, legislative analysts, environmental and other organizations, and interested individuals. We welcome the comments of our readers, whose input will be a vital part of the evolution and updating process of this *Handbook*.

Ruth Shippen Musgrave
Director
Center for Wildlife Law

ACKNOWLEDGEMENTS

While any project of this scope relies on the efforts of many to reach completion, I would first and foremost like to express my gratitude to the funding entities which not only recognized the need for this *Handbook* but, through a combination of federal, state and private grants, made it possible. Major support was provided by the **U.S. Fish and Wildlife Service Division of Federal Aid**, which administers the Federal Aid in Wildlife and Sportfish Restoration Acts to support projects for better state wildlife management. The **Geraldine R. Dodge Foundation**, the **University of New Mexico School of Law**, the **National Fish and Wildlife Foundation**, and the **Francis Seebee Charitable Trust** provided additional resources and the encouragement to see this project through to completion. Thanks also to the **International Association of Fish and Wildlife Agencies** for assisting with funding for the poaching chapter. Through their show of faith in the newly-established Center for Wildlife Law, the trustees, officers, project directors, committees, and staff of each of those important organizations gave generous and much appreciated support and encouragement.

Very special thanks are due to Mary Anne Stein, Ph.D., J.D., coauthor, who walked into the Center and this project when both were in their infancy, who infused this project with life before it was funded and then gave unstintingly of her time and detailed research once it was underway. Special thanks also to Karen Cantrell, Ph.D., J.D., who helped turn the seemingly impossible into a distinct possibility by developing the outline and questionnaire for summarizing the laws, and for summarizing several states. Thanks to Sara Parker, J.D., and Miriam Wolok, J.D., who interviewed sources extensively and coauthored Chapter 3 in its original version, "Poaching in the U.S." It is very clear that this work would not have been completed without the tireless, eagle-eyed editing, formatting and substantive contributions of both Edwina Crawford, Chief Editor, and Carolyn Byers, keeper of the keys of sanity for the Center, both of the Institute of Public Law, and koalas to Barbara Waxer for her constant creativity and for researching and composing the comparative tables.

This project is remarkable in that I believe it is safe to say that every person who worked on this project donated at least some of their time because they believed in the cause. Special thanks to Dave Warren of the NM Senate Conservation Committee, who dedicated long volunteer hours editing and rewriting, and who heartened and inspired us to produce a useable document for the legislative process. Deepest gratitude also to Karen Fisk, Denise Hogan, and Sue Lowrey, J.D., for volunteering many hours of legal expertise reviewing state laws and charts, and for editing and word processing when we needed it the most. Thanks also to Lori Nelson and Lydia Clark for literally bringing in their expertise from out of town to help bring the final document together.

Thanks to our *Handbook* advisory board, Paul Lenzini, J.D., counsel for the International Association of Fish and Wildlife Agencies; Professor David Favre of Detroit College of Law; Larry Bell of the New Mexico Department of Game and Fish; and to those state fish and wildlife departments who generously reviewed state summary and other drafts and offered suggestions, corrections and updates.

I am also grateful to Paul Nathanson, J.D., Director of the Institute of Public Law, for his leadership and support, and to all of the brilliant and helpful participants at the Institute, especially David Farris, Laura Farris, Victoria Garcia, Joan Gibson, Kathy Grassel, Julia Heller, Larheta Martin and Kate Watson for help in editing, formatting, administration and other tasks, and for guidance in structuring a 50-state legal survey. Joseph Campbell, Albert Graves, Andrew Smith, and Ellen Staley were our indefatigable and helpful law student interns from the University of New Mexico School of Law.

Finally, our heartfelt thanks to artist and designer Angela Werneke, and to her publisher Bear and Company, for their gracious donation of the right to reproduce Angela's beautiful artwork for this book.

PART I

WERNEKE © 1991

OVERVIEW OF WILDLIFE LAWS AND ISSUES

Chapter 1

INTRODUCTION

HOW TO USE THIS HANDBOOK

The *Handbook* is organized into three parts. Part I (Chapters 1-3) provides an overview of wildlife law and current issues of concern. Part II contains the summaries of each of the fifty states fish and wildlife codes. Part III provides a discussion of the states' provisions, recommendations, lists of sample statutes, and charts comparing particular topics among the states. Users of this *Handbook* should read this chapter before continuing with the following chapters.

During two years of research on state wildlife laws, the authors developed a standard questionnaire/outline used to research and compile the summaries of the state wildlife laws. An attempt has been made to fit the summaries of each state into that outline in as uniform a manner as possible. The ten major categories used in the outline, as described in detail in Chapter 2 are: **State Wildlife Policy; Relevant Wildlife Definitions; State Fish and Wildlife Agencies; Protected Species of Wildlife; General Exceptions to Protection; Hunting, Fishing, and Trapping Provisions; Animal Damage Control; Enforcement of Wildlife Laws; Habitat Protection;** and **Native American Wildlife Provisions**. In some instances there is obvious overlap between these major categories, and we have attempted to cross-reference the overlaps if particular provisions could fit equally well into different categories. Because of space restrictions, and because the wording of many provisions includes several topics, clear and unambiguous placement into one outline category or another has not always been possible. For example, provisions for restrictions on taking certain species might fall equally well under the Protected Species of Wildlife heading or the Hunting, Fishing and Trapping Provisions heading, depending upon the wording of the specific statute and the judgment call of the authors. Therefore, the reader is advised to not only check cross-referencing where present, but to read each particular state summary in full, regardless of the specific area or topic of interest.

Statutes are paraphrased and condensed into a ten to twenty page summary due to space restrictions, while every effort has been made to keep the legal meaning intact. Where more detail is given than space would allow, the reader will find editorial comments indicated in brackets [ ] regarding the content of the detail or other provisions. Readers are advised to read carefully the list at the end of this chapter for areas of wildlife laws that are not included in the summaries. Most of these excluded topics are explained in Chapter 2, such that readers will be aware of them and can conduct further research into the statutes should they so desire.

Summaries of states with unusually detailed and comprehensive wildlife statutes, such as California, Louisiana, Montana, Pennsylvania and Texas, are necessarily more condensed than others. The reader is encouraged to go directly to these and other statutes for actual language, provisions, annotations with information of interest concerning statutory history, related legal commentary and sources, and case law that has arisen under the statute, all of which could not be included in the *Handbook*'s summaries.

Charts, tables and other comparative information are provided in Chapter 5, **Tables Comparing State Wildlife Laws**. Because statutory language pertaining to a particular topic differs among states, these charts necessarily are general and the reader is again referred to the specific state summary and the appropriate statute for details. Chapter 6, **Discussion and Recommendations**, contains suggestions for change in state fish and wildlife laws and, although they are not tailored for each state individually, the reader is encouraged to peruse suggested recommendations for their potential applicability to the state in which the reader has an interest.

Chapter 7, **Sample Statutes** is compiled to provide examples of useful or model provisions for those interested in drafting or comparing similar legislation. Since only a small sampling of "unique" or "exemplary" statutes could be included, an attempt has been made to alert the reader to such provisions by the use of the following: a single star (★) delineates statutes that are unusual or unique in some way, or different in their coverage of the issue than that of most other states; double starts (★★) indicate statutes that, in our judgment, could be models for other states, or that are exemplary in their provisions or coverage of an issue.

Only the main section number is cited for each statutory provision; subheadings, numbers or letters within subsections have not been included. Where possible, statutory language has been preserved, and the non-attorney is cautioned to be aware of the nuances of the language used to preserve legal meaning. For example, where a statute specifically directs an agency to perform some act, the word "shall" as used in the statute is preserved, rather than the more permissive "may," such that the legal distinction in the directive is retained.

As wildlife law is changing rapidly, and the authors' research had to terminate at some point, the reader should consult any statutory supplements dated during or after the Spring of 1993. (State legislative session dates and contact information are included in the Appendices.)

The *Handbook* provides an extensive survey of the provisions found in each state's fish and wildlife codes. The reader should be aware that **regulations**, as opposed to **laws** or **statutes**, are not included. Rules, regulations, proclamations and orders are promulgated pursuant to law by fish and wildlife agencies, commissions and departments as authorized by state legislatures. These rules and regulations are often quite voluminous, but they are promulgated or amended more easily and quickly than statute, as changing needs and conditions dictate. For example, a statute may require various types of hunting licenses, or provide for hunting seasons, but the license fees and season dates will be set by rule or regulation. Since license fees, bag limits or season dates may need to be modified yearly, rule or regulation making allows flexibility in meeting changing conditions. These rules and regulations are often summarized and distributed to hunters and fishermen by license vendors when a license is purchased.

There is considerable variation among the states as to what extent the wildlife management structure is governed by statute and how much is delegated by statute to regulation. For example, Maine's requirements for licensing, fees and restrictions on hunting are set forth in statute, while Arizona's statutes leave these details to the Game and Fish Department to establish through regulations. Rules and regulations are not usually promulgated or amended at regular intervals, nor are all states' fish and wildlife regulations found in standard legal reference resources such as law libraries, thus the reader who wants exact details or copies of wildlife regulations should write to the fish and game department of that state. Addresses of fish and wildlife agencies are listed in the Appendices.

TOPICS EXCLUDED FROM STATE SUMMARIES

- ▸ Anything not contained in the fish and wildlife code, other than agency provisions
- ▸ Rules, regulations, proclamations and orders
- ▸ Administrative procedures regarding approval of rules, regulations, etc.
- ▸ Fish, wildlife, animal damage control, health and habitat provisions found in titles within statutes other than natural resources or fish and wildlife codes
- ▸ State "assent" provisions to Federal Aid in Wildlife and Sportfish Restoration Acts
- ▸ Marine fish and wildlife provisions
- ▸ Marine fisheries and commercial fisheries
- ▸ Estuarian and tidal fishing and wildlife provisions
- ▸ Specific provisions relating to locations, regions, refuges, lakes or other areas, and specific state forests, state parks, natural heritage areas, etc.
- ▸ Criminal penalty details when they are enumerated in the state criminal code or other sections of the state laws
- ▸ Definitions, other than those directly defining wildlife species or terms (see Definitions section in *Handbook* Appendices)
- ▸ Agency employment details, including pay, posting of bonds, reimbursement for costs
- ▸ Administrative details of defendant arrest, court appearance, posting bond, hearings, appeal, venue, etc.
- ▸ Fees for hunting, fishing, trapping, guide and other licenses
- ▸ Classes of specific licenses
- ▸ Age and other requirements for licenses
- ▸ Veterans, age, handicapped, military and other special exceptions for licenses
- ▸ Youth hunting, fishing licensing provisions
- ▸ Licensing agents and reporting, accounting and fee and excess license remissions for license sales
- ▸ License application provisions, requirements and qualifications
- ▸ Lotteries, drawings, limits on number of licenses issued

- Hunter harassment provisions (but see Table on "Hunter Harassment Laws")
- Requirements for wearing hunter orange, or florescent clothing while hunting
- Falconry and raptor provisions
- Details of carcass tagging requirements, i.e., name, address, consignor, etc.
- Condemnation proceeding details
- Details of records to be kept and submitted by commercial wildlife business licensees
- Fishing tournament, derby, and free fishing day details
- Commercial licensing for whitewater rafting, dog trainers, troop and camp leaders
- Game transportation details, i.e., common carrier requirements, storage facilities
- Firearm, weapon and ammunition restrictions
- Timber and mineral sales on state lands

Chapter 2

OVERVIEW OF WILDLIFE LAW

INTRODUCTION

For most Americans who do not hunt, the experience of encountering wildlife in a natural setting does not immediately provoke thoughts about laws that govern these ostensibly "free" animals. One might assume that wildlife answers only to a natural law, that of survival. It is, however, laws, or the lack of them, that increasingly determine the survival of wildlife in our various states. Heedless of state and national borders, wildlife move according to patterns established by millions of years of evolution. Pressures on their habitat, more often than not caused by human activities, cause decreases in wildlife populations and stress their abilities to adapt in order to survive. As development encroaches upon habitats, many wildlife species have become threatened, endangered or extinct.

Understanding the laws that both protect and fail to protect wildlife in this country is critically important to implement the measures that will guarantee its sustainability in the future. The three chapters comprising Part I of the *Handbook* address some of the issues that confront the people of the United States in attempting to protect and manage their wildlife.

Unseen but affecting the nation's myriad ecosystems and varying numbers of wildlife species and populations are federal, state and sometimes local wildlife laws that regulate management and protection. At the state level, the laws vary widely in their comprehensiveness, protection of species, considerations of animal welfare, resources for various programs, and hunting and fishing restrictions. For example, bear parts illegally poached in one state may be legally sold across the next state's border. Strict restrictions on taking a species that migrates may be nonexistent in the bordering state into which that animal has historically traveled. Penalties for violations of wildlife laws also run the gamut from the occasional felony with mandatory sentencing to more common discretionary civil penalties of as little as ten dollars.

Despite dawning recognition of the importance of wildlife laws, spurred by the controversy over logging in Pacific Northwest forests that provide the habitat for the Northern spotted owl, the legal community is only now beginning to devote to wildlife issues the same attention as is devoted to other environmental issues such as clean air, clean water, and waste management. Because of this and the complexity and difficulty in managing wildlife and protecting habitat to ensure survival, wildlife law has quickly become one of the most controversial areas of environmental law. Until recently, wildlife law was not even recognized as an active component of what was considered to make up the field of "environmental law" purr se. Though seldom viewed as such by the legal community, wildlife is a resource and a natural heritage with as much need of stewardship as our lands, forests and precious minerals.

Some of the wildlife issues under debate by the environmental legal community that impact wildlife law include: the impending reauthorization of the federal Endangered Species Act; habitat issues related to logging and the preservation of ancient forests; development of dams and water use and rights;

the effects on wildlife of pollution from mining and other extractive industries; and the growing awareness among legislators of the need to consider wildlife in the writing of environmental legislation and other legislation related to development.

Throughout the history of this country, federal and state wildlife legislation has motivated an intricate dance over jurisdiction and the right to manage wildlife. Federal wildlife laws have largely evolved out of the need to protect certain habitats or a certain species or type of animal such as migratory birds. On occasion federal legislation has been passed as an implementation of the terms of an international treaty to protect wildlife, such as the Migratory Bird Treaty Act, which implements treaties with Mexico, Japan, Canada and the Soviet Union,[1] or the Marine Mammal Protection Act, which in part implements the Polar Bear Agreement with the five circumpolar nations.[2]

State wildlife laws have largely developed by the nature of states' "ownership" of the wildlife within its borders in trust for its citizens, with states shouldering the right and duty to manage that wildlife.[3] Federal wildlife laws generally preempt state laws only when it is necessary to manage or conserve wildlife species occurring over several or many states. State laws often expressly include or compliment federal laws such as the Endangered Species Act, whose list of endangered species is usually adopted in full by states in their own legislation regarding endangered and threatened species.

Legislation for management or protection of wildlife has often accumulated in state fish and wildlife codes through accretion, in response to various issues or crises affecting a state or regional areas, rather than from a comprehensive policy. Hence, there is little consistency between states, especially in enforcement of wildlife laws, and there has been no easy method of ascertaining what neighboring states have legislated in order to consider enacting compatible legislation. Adding to the vast complexity of the states' laws themselves are the individual state regulations, local ordinances and Native American wildlife laws, each with their sometimes contradictory or overlapping jurisdiction and management issues.

Despite the complexity of state wildlife laws, many states are aware of the irrefutable fact that wildlife knows no legal boundaries, and states are examining ways to open up the boundaries between states so that effective and consistent legislation can be passed, which should in turn improve interstate cooperation. While some states have enacted specific interstate agreements with their neighbors, many more are needed. Comparing differences in state laws will illustrate how interstate agreements and more consistent legislation can improve wildlife protection and management. Increased habitat protection and nongame wildlife management, poaching issues, habitat loss, and better funding for agencies are other areas where states should compare provisions in other states' legislation.

This overview presents the historic background of development of wildlife law in this country and an outline of federal and state wildlife laws, with a brief discussion of international laws. Later chapters in Part I will examine the critical issues of poaching and illegal taking of wildlife in the United States and make recommendations for legislative change.

An understanding of the history of the development of wildlife laws in this country and elsewhere may be helpful to understanding where the laws have come from, where they stand today, and where they may be going.

HISTORY OF WILDLIFE LAWS

Ancient History

Greek and Egyptian cultures often held wild animals in revered positions, while during the Roman Empire it was believed that they were created for the use and pleasure of man. Under Roman Law, animals were considered the property of no one, but anyone who could catch or kill a wild animal gained its ownership.[4] Ironically, the Romans revealed in their art an appreciation of the graceful beauty of wild animals and traveled great distances to procure exotic mammals such as lions and bears for exhibits, but then saw no contradiction in slaughtering the exhibit animals. Indeed the ancient Romans apparently found a "pleasure in the often hideous sufferings and agonizing deaths of quantities of magnificent and noble creatures."[5]

The Christian concept of dominion over wildlife was set forth in book of Genesis in the Bible: "Then God said, 'Let us make man in our image, in our likeness, and let them rule over the fish of the sea and the birds of the air, over the livestock, over all the earth, and over all the creatures that move along the ground.'"[6] The Jewish faith, also embodied in Genesis and the Old Testament of the Bible, not only abhorred the killing of animals for sport, but passed laws prohibiting cruelty to them and indicating a concern for their wellbeing.[7] Native Americans, in the meantime, had developed over the centuries an elaborate system of traditions, culture, and religion which reflected respect and often sacred status for many wild animals.

Europe in the Middle Centuries

During the Dark and Middle Ages, when the Roman Catholic Church assumed preeminence, the civilized world's relationship to animals was summed up by St. Thomas Aquinas, who wrote, "For by divine providence they are intended for man's use in the natural order. Hence it is no wrong for man to make use of them either by killing or in any other way whatever."[8] This concept of wildlife changed very little in Europe over the ensuing centuries, and it produced the English tradition of "harvesting" wildlife for man's own purposes, a tradition that carried over to North America with the arrival of European settlers.

Europeans found upon arrival in America an almost infinite number and array of wildlife species, from marine mammals packing the shoreline to flocks of birds blackening the sky. Colonial Americans treated wildlife as an endless bounty to be taken at will and used for survival and profit. In the development of wildlife laws, however, there were four goals of English wildlife laws that established precedent and survived as a direct legacy of early English law.

The first goal of early English wildlife law and one of the most difficult to achieve, was the sustainability of the harvest so that wildlife populations could be maintained and continually harvested.[9] While this has also been the purpose of many current wildlife laws, this goal may be no easier to achieve today than it was centuries ago. Populations of game species are now tracked with accuracy, but it is still often difficult to ascertain whether a population of a nongame species is successfully maintained, and if so, in what regions or ranges and under the influence of what variables.

The second goal of wildlife laws was to regulate human behavior by regulating hunting methods, restricting the use of weapons.[10] Often hunting laws in England were concerned with keeping weapons out of the hands of the poor and the dissident. These were called "qualification statutes" and were a blatant attempt by the aristocracy to maintain power and control. Hunting restrictions were also necessary to regulate methods of taking wildlife.[11] Without restrictions, hunters would stoop to all levels to take wildlife, including night hunting, drowning, fires, and other unsportsmanlike taking techniques. Regulation of methods of hunting is still a major goal of modern state wildlife laws.

The third goal of wildlife laws was wealth discrimination.[12] These laws would restrict the classes of people who were allowed to hunt, and would sometimes restrict the types of animals that could be sold or eaten.[13] This goal and the qualification statutes in general do not survive in the United States laws today.

The fourth goal was based upon the idea of the intrinsic right of wildlife to exist. As early as the 16th Century in England, the king had a separate legal jurisdiction called the "Forest Jurisdiction." The Forest Jurisdiction had special officials, special doctrines protecting wildlife, and special courts to handle wildlife violations.[14] This form of wildlife law was not totally altruistic as it was developed largely for the pleasure of the king to have wildlife available to him. This goal is still reflected in some of the state and federal wildlife laws today.

As wildlife laws evolved in England, several forms or methods of management became somewhat more defined. One form, restrictions on the taking of wildlife were accomplished in several ways: hunting could be forbidden during the reproductive or juvenile stages for various species[15]; limits could be put on the apparatus used for taking wildlife (as a modern example, state wildlife laws often restrict the use of types of firearms and other weapons, lights, and various fishing devices such as explosives and certain nets used for taking.); the number of people allowed to hunt could be restricted; and laws could be used to attempt to decrease the value of an animal (by making sale of an animal illegal, it was hoped that the commercial value would fall. This has not been an historically effective method of restriction, however, as black market prices for wildlife even today continue to make illegal taking lucrative.)

A second form of wildlife management was habitat preservation through systems such as the English Forest Jurisdiction mentioned above. This was managed somewhat like a wildlife preserve, but included private lands as well. For example, private lands in England had to retain adequate foliage for wildlife forage and cover. All forest land was subject to an "easement for the benefit of wildlife" during the winter months so that the wildlife could be fed if necessary.[16] In addition, herds of domestic animals had to be limited so that wildlife could successfully compete for food. If the wildlife increased such that they required the use of all the land for forage, the herdsman was out of luck, rather than the wildlife. As a form of compromise by rulers, domestic animals were often allowed to run over public forest ground.[17] Habitat preservation is an active arena for wildlife legislation today, however, modern competition for use of public and private lands for grazing domestic animals has become an area of contention.

A third form of wildlife management that evolved in England was stocking of animals to increase populations and thus the yield of animals.[18] This practice was made common in the United States, where stocking is an important function of fish and wildlife departments.

Early America

Early American colonial wildlife laws were not so much based on aristocracy as they were on survival. Initially, free taking of any and all wildlife was the order of the day, because of the incredible wealth of species found in the New World. Free taking applied even to private lands, such that hunters would pursue their game at will. Undeveloped private lands were open by law to wildlife takers, and land could only be excluded by fencing or developing, such as for agriculture.[19]

Managing wildlife in early America began with regulating the taking of wildlife near the Atlantic seaboard. Many of these wildlife laws sought to maintain maximum sustained yield of wildlife while preventing their depletion.[20] Animals became protected by moratoriums on hunting for periods of time, by protecting animals during breeding periods or during severe winters.[21] Poor people often suffered, but were somewhat protected by the laws allowing taking of wildlife damaging their property, and those allowing taking for subsistence.[22]

In the middle and southern colonies, status privileges were afforded under wildlife laws in a manner similar to the "qualification" statutes of England. Under such laws, slaves and Indians were often not allowed to hunt.[23] Monopolies developed for taking wildlife, especially inland fish.[24] These monopolies were highly regulated, like a utility, and were seen as helpful to commerce.

Enforcement of wildlife laws in colonial times was most difficult. Poachers were hard to find or catch or limits on numbers of game that could be taken, or bag limits, were ignored. The more effective restrictions were in the market place, by illegalizing the sale of certain animals.[25] Systems for rewarding the informer were more successful at obtaining convictions than enforcement by game wardens.[26]

Bounties were used as an attempt to exterminate animals that became a threat to agriculture. Bounty laws assured decimation of nuisance animals. This practice became a popular local practice in various regions, and local governments had to become more and more creative to keep up with the bounty hunters' ingenious methods developed for presenting an animal for bounty more than once.[27]

Decimation of Wildlife

Wildlife populations declined in North America through the nineteenth century. From herds of buffalo on the plains, to the beaver and the passenger pigeon, certain species of wildlife were decimated. This occurred for several reasons, not the least of which was the lack of enforcement of wildlife laws. Other reasons for the decline in wildlife population were the policies of extirpating nuisance species, especially large predators, widespread ignorance of why wildlife was actually disappearing, excesses in taking caused by commercial (usually fashion) demand, blatant excesses in hunting, and loss of habitat because of agriculture, logging and other settlement activities.[28]

MODERN WILDLIFE LAWS

The group that came to the rescue of American wildlife initially was the sportshunters. Hunters had an interest in halting the decline in wildlife populations, and their efforts contributed to passage of laws for protection of wildlife. Laws began to restrict hunting to those who acquired licenses to do so, and funding for wildlife agencies began to come directly from hunting and fishing license fees. Game wardens could then be paid with those funds to enforce wildlife laws. In addition, sportsmen could argue effectively against market hunters because domesticated animals could well supply the food needs of the population.[29] It is still the sportsmen today who provide most of the funding for state fish and wildlife agencies to manage wildlife, acquire habitat, restrict the impact of taking, and enforce the fish and wildlife laws. Fees and taxes from sportsmen also fund some of the programs created under federal laws for conservation and protection of wildlife.

INTERNATIONAL WILDLIFE LAWS

International treaties impact state management of wildlife to the extent that federal legislation implementing the treaty protects or otherwise affects species or types of species of wildlife within the states. Such federal laws usually complement or enhance conservation efforts by state agencies.

International wildlife treaties have developed in large part to aid in the management and protection of specific severely depleted species of wildlife in their international ranges.[30] These treaties can range from bilateral agreements, ratified by two signatory nations, to multilateral treaties, where ratification of the treaty is generally more complex and may include many nations. To become enforceable within a nation, treaties must be implemented by national legislation within that country.[31] Ratification of a treaty by the United States requires the advice and consent of the United States Senate for our nation's participation.[32] In addition, federal legislation must be passed to implement the treaty's terms into enforceable United States law. There are dozens of international environmental and wildlife treaties to which the U.S. is signatory. Nevertheless, international enforcement of treaties is difficult because nonsignatory nations are not bound by them. Signatories are bound only to the extent that they have enacted their own implementing legislation, and to the extent that other nations try to force their compliance. Further, if a nation lodges a formal protest against a requirement, it can exclude itself from enforcement.

Most treaties are species-specific: examples include the International Convention for the Regulation of Whaling Convention,[33] the Polar Bear Agreement;[34] and the Interim Convention on the Conservation of North Pacific Fur Seals.[35] Other treaties are an attempt to attain general cooperation in protection of wildlife or habitat, such as the Convention on International Trade in Endangered Species of Wild Fauna and Flora (CITES),[36] and the Convention Concerning the Protection of the World Cultural and National Heritage.[37]

FEDERAL LAWS RELEVANT TO STATE WILDLIFE MANAGEMENT

There are several general types of federal laws that impact wildlife: Laws to protect specific species or types of species, such as the Endangered Species Act, Bald and Golden Eagle Protection Act, and Marine Mammal Protection Act; federal acts which implement the terms of international treaties regarding wildlife, such as the Migratory Bird Treaty Act; federal legislation such as the Lacey Act Amendments of 1981 to enforce state, Native American, or foreign wildlife laws, in addition to federal laws, and restrict commerce in wildlife; laws specifically to designed assist states in restoration of wildlife resources, such as the Federal Aid in Wildlife Restoration Act and the Federal Aid in Sportfish Restoration

Act; general conservation and environmental protection acts, such as the National Environmental Policy Act, Fish and Wildlife Coordination Act, National Wetlands Act, Clean Air Act and Clean Water Act; and laws to protect specific habitats, such as the National Wildlife Refuge System and the National Wilderness Preservation System.

An explanation of selected federal wildlife laws sets the stage for their interaction with and impact on state wildlife laws which deal with the same issues and/or species. The statutes described below have specific impact on state wildlife laws, which often refer directly to federal laws.

Federal Endangered Species Act of 1973 (ESA), 16 U.S.C. § 1531-1543

The Endangered Species Act of 1973, as it currently stands,[38] is the broadest federal statute ever enacted for protection of wildlife species. The Act protects both animal and plant species that are "endangered," which term is defined under the Act as a species determined to be in danger of extinction throughout all or a significant portion of its range.[39] It also protects "threatened" species, which are species likely to become endangered within the foreseeable future throughout all or a significant portion of its range.[40]

Under Sec. 9 of the ESA, it is prohibited for any person, including private and governmental entities, to "take" an endangered or threatened species. A "taking" is broadly defined: "to harass, harm, pursue, hunt, shoot, wound, kill, trap, capture, or collect, or to attempt to engage in any such conduct."[41] Under the *Palila I and II* cases out of Hawaii, "taking" was found by the federal district and appellate courts to include significant habitat modifications which would injure or kill listed species, and to include actions that would prevent the recovery of the species by affecting essential behavior patterns.[42]

Listing a species as threatened or endangered under the Act may be accomplished under Sec. 4 through the Secretary of Interior, acting through the U.S. Fish and Wildlife Service, or through the Secretary of Commerce (for listing marine species), acting through the National Marine Fishery Service.[43] Private citizens may also petition to list or change the status of a species.[44] The listing shall be based on "the best scientific data available".[45] In 1978, the listing procedure was changed to require designation of a species' critical habitat (the area needed for the species to make a successful recovery) concurrently with the listing.[46] Consideration of economic impacts in critical habitat designation decisions was also permitted.[47] A species thus could not be listed without its critical habitat also being designated. Concurrent designation proved to be onerous to the agencies because of the difficulty of designating critical habitat.

> Linking the listing procedure to critical habitat designation and to economic considerations halted species listing almost entirely. Approximately 2,000 species proposed for listing in 1978 were withdrawn. During the first year of the Reagan Presidency, no species were added to the protected lists.[48]

The 1982 amendments to the ESA changed the concurrent critical habitat designation to the "maximum extent prudent and determinable."[49] In 1988, further amendments required the Secretary to establish a monitoring system for the status of the enormous numbers of candidate species for listing, but as yet unlisted.[50] Emergency listing powers were also enacted to prevent significant risk to the wellbeing of any candidate species.[51]

The affirmative requirement on the Secretaries to prepare recovery plans for the survival of the listed species are also found in Sec. 4 of the Act.[52] Sec. 7 directs federal agencies to ensure that their actions do not jeopardize the continued existence of listed species, or destroy or adversely modify a species' critical habitat.[53] It is under Sec. 7 that the Endangered Species Committee (termed the "God Squad" because of its power to allow elimination of a species) was created to authorize exemptions from the Act.[54] Under Sec. 7, agencies must consult with either the U.S. Fish and Wildlife Service or National Marine Fishery Service if an action is likely to affect a listed species, to insure that any agency action is not likely to jeopardize the continued existence of an endangered or threatened species, or result in the destruction or adverse modifications of its critical habitat.[55]

Exceptions to the Act also exist. An exception to the prohibitions against taking of endangered or threatened species is provided in Sec. 10, which allows for the development and submission of a habitat conservation plan ("HCP") if the taking of the species is incidental to an otherwise lawful activity.[56] Sec. 7 allows an exception for agency action through issuance of an "incidental take statement" as part of the biological opinion required regarding the agency action.[57] The federal Endangered Species Act is expressly referred to in the fish and wildlife codes of almost every state. Most states expressly adopt the federal list of protected species, and provide their own list, and many have modeled their state statutes after the federal ESA.

Lacey Act Amendments of 1981, 16 U.S.C. § 3371, et seq.

The Lacey Act Amendments of 1981 provide broad federal criminal enforcement of federal, state, foreign and Native American wildlife laws. The Act makes it a federal crime for any person to acquire or sell any fish or wildlife taken in violation of state, federal or tribal law.[58] The Lacey Act in effect expands state enforcement authority by allowing federal enforcement of state wildlife laws. (See Chapter 3 for a complete discussion of the Lacey Act.)

Migratory Bird Treaty Act of 1918 (MBTA), 16 U.S.C. § 703-711

The Migratory Bird Treaty Act is the Congressional implementation of a series of international treaties, beginning with the Convention With Great Britain for the Protection of Migratory Birds in 1916.[59] Other treaties regarding conservation of migratory birds include those with Mexico, Japan and the Soviet Union.[60] Each of the treaties recognizes the need for conservation of migratory birds, and establishes fairly specific closed hunting seasons for these birds.[61] The Migratory Bird Treaty Act makes it unlawful to "hunt, take, capture, kill, ... [or] possess" any bird protected by the Convention except as permitted by the Secretary of Interior.[62] The Secretary must determine when and to what extent, if at all, and by what means taking may be allowed as to migratory birds. The Act provides that nothing therein prevents the states from making or enforcing laws or regulations that are consistent with the Conventions or the Act, or that give further protection to migratory birds, their parts, nests or eggs.[63] All states refer to and require that agency and hunter action be in concert with the Act. Many states have incorporated further protection into their wildlife laws, as the state summaries indicate.

Federal Aid in Wildlife/Sportfish Restoration Acts, 16 U.S.C. §§ 669-669i and 777-777k

Virtually every state fish and wildlife code contains assent provisions to the Federal Aid in Wildlife and Sportfish Restoration Acts. Better known as the Pittman-Robertson Act, the Federal Aid in Wildlife Restoration Act was enacted in 1937 to consistently fund state wildlife programs. It provides federal assistance for the restoration, maintenance, and acquisition of wildlife habitat, management of wildlife resources and areas, hunter education programs, introduction of wildlife into suitable habitat, and for surveys of and research into wildlife management problems.[64]

Also provided by the Act was the "federal restoration to wildlife fund," comprised exclusively of excise taxes on firearms, other weapons and ammunition. While a percent of these annual revenues were allocated for administration, the remainder was apportioned among the states, who could apply for funding for up to 75% of wildlife restoration project costs.

Initially the Pittman-Robertson Act resulted in a significant amount of federal control over state wildlife restoration projects because it placed restrictions on types of projects funded and set certain standards for states to meet in order to receive funds. In past decades, however, a series of amendments have increased the flexibility of the states in using Pittman-Robertson funds. The most significant amendments were passed in 1970. The first allocated a portion of revenues from a tax on pistols and revolvers for state hunter safety programs. The second allowed states to submit a "comprehensive fish and wildlife management resource plan" instead of a specific restoration project. The period of the plan submitted must be at least five years, and must "insure the perpetuation of these resources for the economic, scientific, and recreation enrichment of the people."[65]

The Federal Aid in Sportfish Restoration Act, commonly called the Dingell-Johnson Act, has nearly the same provisions for federal aid to states for marine and freshwater fish projects, and boating facilities and aquatic resources education.[66] Funds are obtained through taxes on fishing tackle and other equipment, and motor boat fuel. "Project activities include acquisition and improvement of sport fish habitat, stocking of fish, research into fishery resource problems, surveys and inventories of sport fish populations, and acquisition and development of access facilities for public use."[67]

Marine Mammal Protection Act of 1972 (MMPA), 16 U.S.C. § 1361-1407

The Marine Mammal Protection Act (MMPA) was originally enacted in 1972 in response to the rapid depredation of marine mammal species, including whales, dolphins, seals, sea otters, manatees, walruses, and polar bears.[68] The Act imposes a moratorium on the taking and importation of marine mammals and their products, with some exceptions regarding scientific research purposes and commercial fishing incidental takings.[69] An exemption allows the taking of marine mammals by any "Indian, Aleut, or Eskimo who dwells on the coast of the North Pacific Ocean or the Arctic Ocean."[70] The exemption is only for taking for native subsistence purposes, or for "creating and selling authentic native articles of handicrafts and clothing".[71] Any taking done for subsistence or handicraft purposes may not be done "in a wasteful manner."[72]

Sec. 109 of the Act provides that no state may enforce any state law or regulation relating to the taking of any species of marine mammal.[73] That section does provide a mechanism where the moratorium on taking marine mammals can be waived, and management authority returned to a state which is found to have laws and regulations consistent with requirements of the MMPA. However, the only instance of attempted use of this waiver was in 1975 when the management of the Pacific walrus was returned to the State of Alaska.[74] Alaska also requested return of management of the other marine mammal species within its jurisdiction, but in the meantime was sued by Alaskan natives.[75] The court ruled in favor of the natives, enjoining the federal government from approving any state laws restricting taking by the natives under the MMPA.[76] Alaska then elected to return management authority of marine mammal species to the federal government. Thus, state regulation of marine mammal wildlife has been relinquished to the federal government in all instances.

STATE WILDLIFE LAWS

State Power to Manage Wildlife

"State wildlife laws of this century reflect substantial contributions toward advancing the condition of wildlife."[77] However, state wildlife laws have developed more in response to individual issues and needs of the each of the states than in response to an overall comprehensive wildlife management and protection policy. A tension has always existed between the rights of the states to manage the wildlife within their borders and the right of the federal government to restrict taking or otherwise manage wildlife in the national interest. States attempting to manage wildlife have run up against arguments that their actions conflict variously with the U.S. Constitution's Commerce Clause, the Privileges and Immunities Clause, and the equal protection clause of the Fourteenth Amendment. The extent of the states' right to exercise its police power under the Tenth Amendment to the Constitution has also been challenged.

Federal preemption has been tested with regard to state power to manage wildlife. As early as 1920, the U.S. Supreme Court in *Missouri v. Holland*,[78] found that a federal game warden's enforcement of the Migratory Bird Treaty Act was not an unconstitutional invasion of the Tenth Amendment right of police power of the state. The Court found that protection of migratory birds is a national interest of the first magnitude, and that the federal treaty making power is supreme. And in *New Mexico State Game Commission v. Udall*,[79] the Court found that, under the federal property power, the federal government could kill deer on a national park within New Mexico without a state permit without violating the state's right to manage its own wildlife.

The states' right to affect trade in wildlife and wildlife parts has also brought up consideration of state legislation's impact on interstate commerce and possible violations of the Commerce Clause of the U.S. Constitution. In the 1896 case of *Geer v. Connecticut*,[80] the U.S. Supreme Court found that states have "ownership" of the wildlife within their borders, and that a state has a duty to preserve for its people a valuable food supply. Thus the Commerce Clause was not violated by a Connecticut statute which forbade possession of birds taken within the state for the purpose of transporting them out of state. However, the property interest of the states in wildlife has limitations. In overruling *Geer* almost one hundred years later, the Supreme Court in *Hughes v. Oklahoma*,[81] found that the Commerce Clause had been violated by enforcement of an Oklahoma law forbidding the transporting of minnows raised in Oklahoma to a point outside of the state. The Court found that a state may protect its wildlife only in ways consistent with our nation as one economic unit, and that discrimination against interstate commerce is not allowable when equally nondiscriminatory alternative conservation measures are available.

The Supreme Court found no such Commerce Clause violation in *Maine v. Taylor*,[82] wherein Maine's ban on importation of golden shiner fish was upheld because of Maine's legitimate local purpose in guarding against environmental risks of non-native parasites and disruption of ecology. Thus, a state's wildlife laws that discriminate against or restrict commerce may be allowed if they serve a legitimate state interest, such as protection of the environment, and there are no reasonable alternatives to the action mandated by the statute. Despite these limitations, by and large states still retain the lion's share of the responsibility for the management and protection of the wildlife species that reside in or migrate through, their borders.

Elements of State Wildlife Laws

Current state wildlife laws are almost infinite in their variety of treatment and organization of wildlife management and protection provisions. In attempting to summarize the wildlife laws of each state of the United States, it was found that state wildlife laws generally fit into ten standard categories that can be used to achieve a uniformity of presentation. These are: policy; definitions; agencies; protected species; exceptions to protection; hunting, fishing and trapping provisions; animal damage control; enforcement; habitat protection; and Native American provisions.

As noted in Chapter One there are many topics within the various codes that had to be excluded from the summaries within this *Handbook*. However, some of the many interesting topics which appear in codes deserve some discussion. The following cursory discussion of assorted topics within state wildlife laws is organized according to the ten broad categories above. Where significant, trends and new developments seen in states are mentioned. The reader is referred to Chapter 4 which discusses a myriad of recommendations regarding each of these topics and provides an extensive treatment of favorable and creative legislation for states to consider.

1. State Wildlife Policy

Policy statements by legislatures of the states often speak to the desires of the people to see a program brought into being, a policy enforced, or a trend reversed in loss of wildlife. States such as California have policy statements at the beginning of provisions for almost every fish and wildlife program. Other states have no policy statements. Such statements give a more clear idea of the relevant and pressing issues and concerns of the citizenry of a state.

2. Relevant Wildlife Definitions

Definitions of various species of fish and wildlife, and of other related wildlife terms often differ between states. The definition of "wildlife," for example, can be as broad as Alaska's, where invertebrates and even insects are included, or it may not be defined as in New Mexico wherein the result is that reptiles and amphibians have no protection under the fish and game code. Definitions of endangered and threatened species tend to be quite consistent between states, and are usually based upon the definitions in the federal Endangered Species Act. Interesting differences exist between states' definitions of nongame and game wildlife and nongame and game fish. Relevant wildlife definitions for each of the states (non-wildlife definitions that exist in fish and wildlife codes are not included) can be found in the Appendices of this *Handbook*.

3. State Fish and Wildlife Agencies

Agency Names: There appears to be a growing trend for state legislatures to rename state agencies that were previously termed "Game and Fish Department" to either Wildlife Department, or Fish and Wildlife Department. This appears at first blush to be a somewhat innocuous change, however, it does allow for the scope of authority of these departments to legitimately extend to management of wildlife other than game wildlife that is traditionally hunted, fished or trapped. Departments are having to take on this responsibility of nongame wildlife management, whether or not they are fully funded or given the name to match these duties.

Department Organization: Most states have a fish and wildlife agency separate from other environmental and natural resources departments. Such agencies usually have a director who is responsible for management of the fish and wildlife resources of the state. Often the director is responsible to a commission made up of appointees. Several states, however, merely have a department of natural resources or environment, into which the fish and wildlife management responsibilities fall. Often such a department is headed by a secretary who has oversight and primary responsibility for fish and wildlife resource management.

Department Director and Commissioner Qualifications: Three tables in Chapter 5 outline the various methods of appointment and required qualifications, if any, of the director, commissioner, and commission members of each of the states. Many states have bestowed the authority on the governor to appoint the fish and wildlife department directors and commissioners, who often to serve at the pleasure of the governor as well. This can lead to a politicized commission and department, which may lead to changes in policies with changes in administration. An awkward situation may also arise if a governor-appointed commissioner must oversee a nonpolitical director and department, which can lead to lack of coordination and effectiveness. However, there appears to be a trend toward requirement of various qualifications for department directors and especially for the several commissioners.

Qualification requirements for holding office can vary from none to a requirement of a background in wildlife conservation, to affiliation with a ranching or agricultural organization or association, to a required number of years in wildlife management practice.

Agency Funding Sources: Sources of funding for fish and wildlife departments are becoming increasingly important, with belt-tightening by legislatures in almost all states concurrent with increased responsibility of agencies for nongame wildlife and habitat management. Historically fish and wildlife agencies have been funded through fees derived from sale of hunting, fishing and trapping licenses, fees and permits. State agencies must become more and more creative in seeking out new sources of funding other than license fees and general legislative appropriations. The "Agency Funding Sources" table in Chapter 5 lists most of the creative funds and sources of funding for each of the states. States usually have a "general fund" from which they derive most of their monies for operation of the department, and which is most often funded by license, permit and other fees. Other useful methods of acquiring funds, and which may or may not feed directly into the general fund of the department, include sale of various wildlife stamps and related artwork. Wildlife stamps can be mandatory for taking a certain type of species, or they can be purchased on a voluntary basis. Examples of stamps are habitat protection stamps, duck stamps, and migratory waterfowl stamps. Artwork for various stamps may also be used for sale of posters, prints and other products. Posters and artwork other than stamp-related are also provided for in many states.

One unique and successful form of funding for a fish and wildlife agency is found in the Missouri State Constitution. Under Article IV of the constitution, it is declared to be the policy of the people to preserve and protect wildlife, and that a separate severance tax is therefore issued for funding the department's activities (see Sample Statutes, Chapter 7, for full text of provision).

Funds can also be obtained from fines and penalties collected for violations of the fish and wildlife laws. Some states provide for division of such monies collected between the department and the county in which the fines were imposed, thus enhancing the county's motivation for consistent imposition of adequate penalties.

Often funding is provided directly through state legislative appropriation, for specific programs such as habitat acquisition, or as general annual appropriations. Trends in state legislatures are toward more creative funding sources, and for funding aimed at specific programs or policy directives.

Advisory Boards, Councils and Committees: Many state legislatures have made provisions within fish and wildlife departments for a variety of advisory boards, councils and committees. These various councils are outlined in the table titled "Agency Advisory Councils," wherein a brief description of the roles of each committee are given. Advisory councils usually review and make recommendations to the department, directory or commission regarding a specific topic such as endangered and threatened species or habitat protection. States tend to require that members be qualified in the field for which the committee was created, and some states use many such councils to assist with the responsibilities of the department and commission.

Volunteer programs: Volunteer programs have been developed as a creative way to assist with the problem of adequate funding for state fish and wildlife agencies, as well as a way to enhance citizen awareness and participation in wildlife management, conservation and protection. Some states allow volunteers to train for and become commissioned as temporary state game wardens. Provisions are even made, in Louisiana for example, for commissioning of volunteer retired game wardens.

Other states may provide for a hot line for citizens to call regarding observed or potential fish and wildlife law violations. Reward programs can provide monetary rewards to citizens upon conviction of the violator. Chapter 4 contains examples of excellent volunteer programs, as does the table "Rewards for Assisting with Enforcement Against Violators" in Chapter 5.

4. Protected Species of Wildlife

Nongame Wildlife Provisions: Almost every state makes provision in its game and fish code for protection of nongame, or nonhunted wildlife species. States are more often passing legislation for protection of such species, and protections usually include prohibitions against taking, possession, selling, buying or offering for sale such species. Certain states make specific provisions spelling out protection for a species of particular concern, such as the mountain lion or panther, or the grizzly bear.

Endangered and Threatened Species: Virtually every state except West Virginia has some statutory provision for protection of species determined to be either threatened or endangered under the federal Endangered Species Act in addition to their own list. There appear to be among the states different procedures for listing and delisting species, but a majority of the states have generally adopted the procedure of the federal ESA wherein either the agency or an interested citizen or group of citizens may petition for an addition, deletion or change in the listing of a species. Many provide for public notice and a hearing before listing or delisting, and other provisions are often made for citizen participation in the listing process. Most states seem to rely on the federal standard for listing a species, that is, the best scientific data available. States appear to be maintaining the strength of their endangered species protection provisions, and some states even encourage private landowner participation with incentives and assistance (see Chapter 6 discussion and recommendations regarding protected species of wildlife and habitat protection).

5. General Exceptions to Protection

Exceptions to the protection of otherwise protected species are generally made among the states, for scientific, educational or research purposes. Taking of otherwise protected species can usually occur under permit from the department, which may specify terms and conditions of taking. Types of permits allowed may include taking animals for rehabilitation purposes, keeping animals in captivity as pets or for display or propogation.

Generally states also make exceptions to protection for zoos and other educational institutions which may hold protected animals live in captivity for exhibition and education or research purposes. Such institutions often may also sell or exchange such protected animals under separate permit.

6. Hunting, Fishing, Trapping Provisions

Restrictions on hunting, fishing and trapping often make up the lion's share of fish and wildlife code provisions. Some states go into great detail regarding eligibility for licenses and permits, dates of issue, numbers that may be issued, and fees for each. Many other states deal with such details in their department regulations rather than through legislative mandate. Restrictions on methods of taking and equipment used are universal, such as restrictions on use of spotlights, poisons, dogs, traps, and vehicles. Seasons, bag limits, possession limits and other restrictions on harvest are also detailed within states' statutes.

Licenses and Permits: Many types of licenses and permits, tags, stamps, certificates, applications and reservations may be issued by the state fish and wildlife agencies and/or the commission or commissioner, including recreational hunting licenses for use of firearms, bow and arrow or other weapons for taking wildlife, fishing and sportfishing licenses, and trapping licenses for taking fur-bearing animals. Activities authorized by licenses often require in addition, stamps, tags and other labels. Permits of various types often include reporting requirements to the department or commission.

Commercial taking or businesses involving use of wildlife or parts thereof most often require license and permits as well. Examples are guide licenses, fur-buyer licenses and taxidermy licenses (see "Statutory Regulation of Selected Hunting Businesses" table in Chapter 5).

Qualifications for licenses and permits include an array of requirements, such as age limits, requirements for completion of hunter education courses, resident versus nonresident considerations, along with various exceptions. These exceptions are not summarized in the *Handbook*, but include categories of persons such as senior citizens, handicapped citizens, military, and persons younger than age 12 to 16.

Hunter Education Programs: More states are requiring that applicants for hunting licenses show evidence of completion of a hunter or trapper education course. The "Hunter Education Courses" and "Trapper Education Courses" tables in Chapter 5 give a detailed overview of what requirements exist for the various states in this field. Hunter education can vary from merely firearm safety to hunter ethics and nongame conservation, and even survival techniques. Often states will allow a hunter to receive certification for a hunter education course if they have been so certified in another state or international province or country. Statutes often provide that course and certification may be issued by instructors from organizations with a proven interest in wildlife conservation, hunting and firearm safety. Some states even provide for firearm safety courses to be held in public schools for students.

Hunter Harassment Laws: There is a definite trend among state legislatures to pass hunter harassment laws that make illegal interference with or harassment of hunters or the wildlife that is being hunted. Although not described in each separate state summary, the "Status of Hunter Harassment Statutes" table outlines the states with such laws and some of the provisions and issues. A comprehensive study done in 1991 by the Center for Wildlife Law, "Report on the Constitutionality and Consistency of Hunter Harassment Statutes," comparing the hunter harassment laws of the fifty states, analyzed the constitutional issues surrounding these laws under the First Amendment of the U.S. Constitution.

Private Landowner Considerations: Private landowners are often given special consideration in the fish and wildlife laws, as their lands can be crucial to hunting, fishing and trapping activities. Landowners are often allowed to post their lands against hunting and to require permission before hunting or taking commences, or before entering the land. The tables in Chapter 5, "Permission to Hunt on Private Land" and "Permission to Trap on Private Land" summarize these provisions.

Buying, Selling and Transporting Wildlife: These provisions provide restrictions on commerce in fish and wildlife, including transportation and shipping provisions, and buying and selling wildlife, parts or products. Restrictions on buying, selling and transporting endangered, threatened, and other protected species generally exist in all states, and some states have specific provisions for species that are often poached, such as bears.

Import, Export and Release Provisions: States vary widely in their treatment of importation of wildlife, ranging from no provisions at all, to extensive testing, quarantine and inspection provisions for restricting importation of non-native or even native but diseased, species. The trend in states is toward more restrictive legislation because of the problems presented by the importation of exotic species which may carry diseases or parasites, or which may, like the piranha, prove to be a voracious predator of native species. See discussion and recommendations on this subject in Chapter 6.

7. Animal Damage Control

In many states the majority of animal damage control provisions are not found in the fish and wildlife codes, but rather in state department of agriculture provisions regarding elimination of nuisance or pest animals. Such provisions often provide for state cooperation with the federal animal damage control program of the U.S. Department of Agriculture. The "Animal Damage Control" table outlines provisions that the state fish and wildlife codes do make for control and management of wildlife that is considered to be "nuisance," "pest" or "predatory."

Often a state department of fish and wildlife director or commissioner is specifically empowered to use methods of taking which are otherwise not allowed in order to control the species or the damage that it is causing or about to cause. Destruction of crops or other agricultural interests is a major reason for animal damage control operations. In addition, a landowner is very often expressly allowed to take and destroy animals that are destroying or about to destroy their crops, livestock or other property, usually under department permit. Many states have provisions expressly allowing landowners or others to kill even an endangered species when there is an immediate threat to human life.

Certain states even allow for wildlife depredation and compensation programs, wherein the loss of crops or other property such as livestock may be compensated by the state upon proof of destruction by the landowner. These kinds of programs may become more popular among state legislatures to avoid "takings" issues that may otherwise arise.

Some of the more bizarre provisions for animal damage control include bounty programs, where specific bounties are offered for animals such as wolves, hawks, crows, bobcats, gophers, moles, beavers, and fox. Some provisions even require the skins, paws, heads or other parts of animals to be presented to the department for receipt of the bounty.

8. Enforcement of Wildlife Laws

Enforcement of wildlife laws takes many forms, and enforcement problems and suggested solutions are discussed in detail in Chapter 3, "Poaching in the U.S.". State statutory provisions range from powers delegated to game wardens and other enforcement officers, to the types of criminal and civil penalties and the dollar amount of fines, and jail sentences, if any. Powers accorded fish and game wardens vary between states. Some states give full powers equal to police officers to wardens; some allow wardens to enforce only the provisions of the fish and wildlife code. Many states authorize wardens to search containers and vehicles without a warrant upon probable cause to believe that a violation of the fish and wildlife laws has occurred. The authority to arrest without warrant in the field is also often provided to game wardens.

Penalties for violations of fish and wildlife laws, regulations, rules or orders cover an incredible range between the states. Felony provisions are somewhat rare (see "States with Criminal Felony Provisions" table), but virtually all of the states impose misdemeanors for various violations. Jail terms are sometimes imposed, however many states leave the level of punishment upon conviction (eg. fines and/or jail), if any, to the discretion of the sentencing judge. Fines set forth in the statutes are also generally very low. Restitution made to the state for the value of the animal lost is popular (see "Restitution, Spotlighting and Waste" table), and amounts to be paid are usually in addition to any other fines or penalties imposed. Restitution may be mandatorily imposed, however, for each animal taken. License or permit revocation or suspension is provided for upon conviction of certain fish & wildlife provisions such as spotlighting. Revocation and suspension periods vary, as do their mandatory or discretionary nature. The table titled "License Revocation and Suspension" outlines the differences between states in this area of enforcement.

Seizure, confiscation and forfeiture of illegal devices or of equipment or vehicles used in fish and wildlife provision violations are common enforcement provisions among states. Forfeiture can be a strong detriment to violations, but not all states include valuable vehicles and airplanes as items that are subject to forfeiture.

9. Habitat Protection

As state legislatures have come to realize that the habitat of their state's wildlife is disappearing, more have passed legislation to protect that habitat. Within the habitat protection laws are some of the most creative provisions within the fish and wildlife codes of the states. Habitat protection laws run the gamut from ecological reserves where no taking is allowed of any wildlife, and which are established in large part for the benefit and recovery of endangered and threatened species, to state game refuges, sanctuaries, preserves, and parks, wherein taking is restricted to specific species and dates. Agencies and commissions are generally empowered under these provisions to acquire land or water, or various kinds of interests in that land, for protected habitat.

Other habitat protection measures include prohibitions against pollution or dumping; provision for fishways or fish ladders on dams to ensure free passage of fish; and restrictions on stream bed diversions. Landowner incentives are often provided, such as assistance with planting for habitat; materials and/or assistance with developing habitat on private land; aid in posting lands; and designation of private lands as wildlife refuges. See the recommendations in Chapter 6 on this subject.

10. Native American Wildlife Provisions

Native American rights to hunt, fish and trap and to manage the wildlife within their own reservations has been a source of tension between tribes and state wildlife managers. These rights are generally spelled out in the treaties and court decisions on the subject.[83] Only about a third of the states' wildlife codes have wildlife provisions relating to Native Americans. Most of these provisions relate to the applicability of the state wildlife laws to Native Americans when hunting or fishing off reservations. Some states do not require Native Americans to carry licenses or pay license fees however, as long as they have proof of tribal membership. Taking for ceremonial or subsistence purposes is also provided for in several states. See Chapter 5, "Native American Provisions" table.

ENDNOTES

1. 16 U.S.C. § 703-711 (as amended 1984 and Supp. 1991).
2. 16 U.S.C. § 1361-1407 (1984).
3. See *Geer v. Connecticut*, 161 U.S. 19 (1896), which found that states have a property interest in the wildlife within their borders (overruled in part by *Hughes v. Oklahoma*, 441 U.S. 322 (1979).
4. M. Bean, *The Evolution of National Wildlife Law*, 2nd ed. 1983, p.10.
5. D. Favre, *Wildlife Law*, 1-9 (1991).
6. *Genesis* 1:26-28.
7. G. Horowitz, *The Spirit of Jewish Law*, 105-19 (1953).
8. Favre, *supra* at 1-9, quoting T. Aquinas, *Summa Control Gentiles*.
9. T. Lund, *American Wildlife Law*, Univ. Calif. Press, Berkeley, 1980, p.4.
10. *Id.* at 5.
11. *Id.* at 7.
12. *Id.* at 8.
13. *Id.* at 9.
14. *Id.* at 11.
15. *Id.*
16. *Id.* at 16.
17. *Id.* at 17.
18. *Id.* at 14.
19. *Id.* at 20.
20. Favre, *supra* at 1-11.
21. Lund, *supra* at 29.
22. *Id.*
23. *Id.* at 26-27.
24. *Id.* at 27.
25. *Id.* at 30.
26. *Id.* at 31.
27. *Id.* at 32-34.
28. *Id.* at 57-60.
29. *Id.* at 62-63.
30. Regarding this topic *see* generally, Lyster, *International Wildlife Law* (1985).
31. *Id.*, at 13.
32. *Id.*, at 12.
33. International Convention for the Regulation of Whaling (*Whaling Convention*), Dec. 2, 1946, 161 U.N.T.S. 72.
34. Agreement on the Conservation of Polar Bears, Nov. 15, 1973, 13 I.L.M. 13, 27 U.S.T. 3918.
35. Interim Convention on the Conservation of North Pacific Fur Seals, Feb. 9, 1957, 314 U.N.T.S. 105.
36. Convention on International Trade in Endangered Species of Wild Fauna and Flora, March 6, 1973, 12 I.L.M. 1085, 27 U.S.T. 1087.
37. Convention Concerning the Protection of the World Cultural and Natural Heritage (*World Heritage Convention*), Nov. 16, 1972, 11 I.L.M. 1358; 27 U.S.T. 37.
38. Pub. L. No. 93-205, 81 Stat. 884 (Dec. 28, 1973), current version at 16 U.S.C. § 1531-1543 (1982).
39. *Id.*, § 1532(6), (2).
40. *Id.*
41. *Id.*, § 1532(19).

42. *Palila v. Hawaii Dept. of Land and Natural Resources*, 471 F. Supp. 985 (D. Hawaii 1979), aff'd, 639 F.2d 495 (9th Cir. 1981); *Palila v. Hawaii Dept. of Land and Natural Resources*, 649 F. Supp. 1070 (D. Hawaii 1986), aff'd 852 F.2d 1106 (9th Cir. 1988).

43. 16 U.S.C. § 1533(a).

44. 16 U.S.C. § 1533(b)(3)(A).

45. 16 U.S.C. § 1533(b)(1)(B)(2) and (f).

46. Pub. L. No. 95-632, §§ 11, 13, 92 Stat. 3751 (1978).

47. 16 U.S.C. § 1533(b)(1)(B)(2).

48. Rohlf, *The Endangered Species Act, A Guide to its Protections and Implementation*, Stanford Environmental Law Society (1989), at 27.

49. 16 U.S.C. § 1533(a)(3).

50. Pub. L. No. 100-478, 102 Stat. 2306 (1988), 16 U.S.C. § 1533(b)(3)(C)(iii).

51. *Id.*

52. 16 U.S.C. § 1533(b)(1)(B)(2) and (f).

53. *Id.* at § 1536(a)(2).

54. The "God Squad" was most recently convened to consider granting a BLM exemption for timber harvesting in the Pacific Northwest habitat of the endangered northern spotted owl.

55. *Id.*, at § 1536(c).

56. *Id.*, at § 1539(a)(2). For further discussion of the Sec. 10 HCP exception, see Musgrave, *A Practical Guide to the Endangered Species Act*, New Mexico Natural Resources Law Reporter, 1991.

57. 16 U.S.C. § 1536(b)(4).

58. 16 U.S.C. § 3372(a)(1)(1984).

59. 16 U.S.C. § 703-711 (1984 and Supp. 1991).

60. Convention for the Protection of Migratory Birds and Game Mammals, Feb. 7, 1936, United States-Mexico, 50 Stat. 1311; Convention for the Protection of Migratory Birds and Birds in Danger of Extinction, and Their Environment, Mar. 4, 1972, United States-Japan, 25 U.S.T. 3329; Convention Concerning the Conservation of Migratory Birds and Their Environment, Nov. 19, 1976, United States-USSR, 29 U.S.T. 4647.

61. Ch. 128, Sec. 2, 40 Stat. 755 (1918), 16 U.S.C. § 703.

62. *Id.* § 703.

63. *Id.* § 708.

64. 16 U.S.C. §§ 669-669i, as amended 1989.

65. 16 U.S.C. § 669e(a)(1).

66. 16 U.S.C. §§ 777-77k, as amended.

67. U.S. Department of the Interior, *USFWS Digest of Federal Resource Laws of Interest of the U.S. Fish and Wildlife Service*, April 1992.

68. 16 U.S.C. § 1361-1407.

69. The commercial fishing incidental takings sections has been the focus of the dolphin-tuna controversy wherein millions of dolphins have been caught and drowned in the huge tuna nets, which are set by observation of schools of dolphins swimming with schools of tuna.

70. 16 U.S.C § 1371(b) (1984).

71. 16 U.S.C. § 1371(b)(1) and (2).

72. 16 U.S.C. § 1371(b)(3).

73. 16 U.S.C. § 1379(a).

74. 40 Fed. Reg. 54959 (Dec. 24, 1975).

75. *People of Togiak v. United States*, 470 F. Supp. 423 (D.D.C. 1979).

76. For a complete discussion of this case see M. Bean, *Evolution of National Wildlife Law*, (1983), at 303-304.

77. Lund, *supra* at 79.

78. *Missouri v. Holland*, 252 U.S. 416 (1920).

79. *New Mexico State Game Commission v. Udall*, 410 F.2d 1197, cert. den. sub. nom., 396 U.S. 961 (1961).

80. *Geer v. Connecticut*, 161 U.S. 519 (1986).

81. *Hughes v. Oklahoma*, 441 U.S. 322 (1979).

82. *Maine v. Taylor*, 477 U.S. 131 (1896).

83. R. Musgrave and M. Dow, *Indian Wildlife Resources and Endangered Species Management*, 1991 A.B.A. Sec. SONREEL, paper no. 9.

Chapter 3

WILDLIFE POACHING IN THE U.S.

SCOPE OF THE PROBLEM

For as much as wildlife suffers from human activities causing habitat loss, poaching incidents and commercial operations inflict a damage just as irreparable. Almost nowhere is poaching of wildlife more lucrative, more dangerous and more difficult to control than in the United States, yet the poaching problem in this country seldom receives international attention. The level of poaching has reached a crisis here at home both financially and in loss of numbers of game and nongame wildlife. From the local, state and federal level to international border operations, poaching is causing an irreplaceable depletion of our national wildlife resources that has warranted a separate chapter here to address the issue.

Analysis of the poaching problem should include a review of our state and federal laws which attempt to restrict poaching activities, as well as a preliminary review of cultural and economic factors that currently impact poaching in the United States. Although various federal statutes grant authority to federal agents to protect certain wildlife species, it is primarily the states that regulate the taking of wildlife within their respective borders through their own state fish and wildlife codes. But with poaching on the rise, the effectiveness of both state and federal laws is being questioned. For example, a comparison of states' restrictions, penalties and enforcement powers reveals gaps in consistency and level of enforcement of wildlife protection laws. Poachers can use these gaps between states' laws to their own advantage, trafficking illegally taken wildlife through and out of the country.

This chapter only attempts to scratch the surface of a complex and increasingly difficult national problem. It does not and cannot offer an easy or quick solution to the issue of poaching. In fact, as economic and other pressures make poaching more attractive, methods of dealing with poaching will have to become proportionately more creative and proactive. This preliminary examination includes a survey of factors affecting poaching, a review and comparison of state and federal laws and penalties restricting poaching, interviews with wildlife professionals across the country, and a shopping list of recommendations, proposed deterrents and solutions.

The poaching problem is so immense and complex that even this preliminary examination should be helpful to wildlife managers and decision-makers who want to take affirmative action. We hope this chapter will form the basis for a more in-depth study and analysis of each state's fish and wildlife laws so a determination can be made about what is and is not working in solving the poaching problem in the United States.

THE POACHING PROBLEM IN THE U.S.

In recent years, the media have revealed shocking information about the worldwide depletion of wildlife caused by poaching. Stories making the headlines include African elephant herds decimated for their ivory tusks and primates captured for sale as pets, food and for medical research. In the United States the illegal taking of wildlife, both commercially and non-commercially, is on the rise. U.S. Fish and Wildlife Service (USFW) agent Terry Grosz remarked that poaching is more severe now than at any other time in his 27-year career, and this observation was echoed in other interviews.[1]

For purposes of this chapter, poaching is defined as the illegal "taking" of wildlife. Taking can include hunting, fishing, trapping, seining, netting and other methods of capturing and/or killing wildlife. As will be explained further, poaching in this chapter implies but does not always include taking of wildlife for strictly commercial gain.

The USFW estimates that $200 million is illegally earned each year in the United States from the illegal taking of wildlife.[2] It is also estimated that the total amount of annual imports to and exports from the United States, the largest consumer of wildlife in the world, are valued at approximately $1 billion annually in wildlife and wildlife products.[3] A 1990 article reported that poaching and illegal trafficking networks were active in the United States in at least 17 states.[4] In a single operation, agents from Tennessee, North Carolina and Georgia arrested and convicted over 30 poachers who were fined over $100,000.[5] As early as 1979, U.S. Customs and Fish and Wildlife Service agents confiscated from one operation 17,500 illegally taken furs valued at $1.2 million. Other studies suggest that in certain parts of the country, the illegal taking of wildlife now equals or exceeds the number of animals taken legally.[6]

A 1991 *National Geographic* article revealed startling information about the number of wildlife species from the United States that are included in the national and international illegal trade of wildlife. Among the more lucrative illegal domestic wildlife products are walrus tusks taken for their ivory; bear gallbladders taken for medicinal purposes and as aphrodisiacs; bear paws and bear meat used for soup and exotic foods; paddlefish and sturgeon eggs taken for sale as caviar; eagle feathers taken for use in Southwestern art; elk antlers used for medicinal purposes; bobcats taken for their pelts; seal penises taken for medicinal purposes; redfish, shellfish, trout and salmon taken for their meat; white-tailed deer taken for their antlers and meat; bighorn sheep taken as trophy animals; and snakes taken for their skins.[7] Poaching activity is pervasive across the nation, but western states have especially experienced increased poaching activity in recent years as the popularity of trophy hunting and the proliferation of commercial poaching has soared. Commercial poachers in particular prey on populations of grizzly bears, moose, bighorn sheep, elk, mountain lions, eagles and snakes.[8]

Trophy animals are not the only game animals vulnerable to poaching activities. A 1974 USFW study of 3,600 waterfowl hunters disclosed that 70 percent of individuals admitted to illegal party, or group hunting, 48 percent admitted to shooting before and after legal hours and 39 percent admitted to violating bag limits.[9]

One of the most sensitive poaching issues in the United States is the slaughter of domestic bear species for their parts, namely gallbladders and paws, caused by demand from international markets. One-third of the world still practices traditional Oriental medicine, which uses bear gallbladders for medicinal and aphrodisiac purposes. The demand for bear parts is of particular concern in the United States because of depleted populations of native Asian bear.[10] Between 1985 and 1990, an estimated 80,000 pounds of bear gallbladder were exported from China to Japan, and that amount included gallbladders from the American black bear.[11] A wildlife investigator in New York reported that he had seen 2,000 gallbladders at one time in New York City's Chinatown.[12] Wildlife enforcement officials estimate that nearly 3,000 American black bears are illegally taken nationwide each year--a figure twice the number of legally taken bears.[13]

A 1989 report revealed that some private zoos and game farms in the United States are also involved in laundering schemes involving live black bears that are bred in captivity or illegally trapped for use in the black market trade. A 1981 investigation of the use of dogs to track bears revealed that every single one of the 100 hunters interviewed were involved in illegal commercial activity.[14]

Not all state laws address the bear poaching problem, as some still allow the sale and transport of bear parts (see State Laws section discussion).[15] In any event a further handicap to enforcement efforts is the difficulty of recognizing species or subspecies once parts such as gallbladders are removed from the animals. This species recognition problem has necessitated international protection for the American black bear.[16]

Accurately determining overall depletion of various wildlife populations from poaching is difficult, but several methods have been used to gain more information about the impact of poaching on wildlife. In Wisconsin, law enforcement agents use the black market price for wildlife species to estimate the number and condition of wildlife resources. If the black market price is high, for example, it is perceived that the numbers and taking opportunities of a species are down.[17] Wildlife enforcement officers also use interviews with convicted poachers to determine how many animals have been taken and how many other violators there may be (the accuracy of this method naturally hinges on the honesty of the responses).

Poacher Profiles

Distinguishing between the commercial poacher who violates the law for profit and the noncommercial poacher who violates for other reasons is not necessarily useful for assessing impact on wildlife. Although the media and federal enforcement programs focus primarily on commercial poachers who selfishly destroy endangered and threatened species and other species for profit, commercial poachers are not the only violators contributing to the decline of wildlife populations. Some wildlife professionals argue that the cumulative impact of non-commercial poachers is just as great to wildlife populations because they are more numerous than commercial poachers. The poacher who kills 200 ducks and gives them away to others is ultimately no less culpable than the commercial poacher who kills the same number of ducks for profit. However, distinguishing between the commercial and non-commercial poacher may be helpful to formulate effective deterrents because different motivations govern these two types of poachers.

Profile of the Commercial Poacher

The federal Lacey Act defines any transaction of $350 or more involving wildlife as a "commercial" activity (see Federal Laws section herein regarding Lacey Act).[18] Thus the hunter who pays a guide $500 to assist him in killing a trophy animal out of season is legally culpable as a commercial poacher under the Lacey Act just as the professional poacher who takes 200 gallbladders to sell on the black market.

Studies on commercial poachers, however, reveal that the professional commercial poacher is frequently involved in other illegal activities such as drug trafficking.[19] In fact, with the professional poacher, ties with organized crime are often suspected.[20] Commercial poachers are clearly motivated by economic profit. The monetary value of trafficking in wildlife and wildlife parts is witnessed by profits as high as those for illegal trade in heroin or cocaine. For example, "velvet" elk antlers bring up to $140 per pound. Bear gallbladders are sold for up to $800 per gram. In fact, a World Wildife Fund report estimated that South Korea, which is perhaps the largest nation trading in bear parts, recently set a new price for a single bear gallbladder at $64,000.[21] A cup of bear paw soup sells for as much as $800 in Asian markets.[22] Paddlefish eggs are another lucrative product for commercial poachers. They are sold in Iran as caviar for approximately $500 a pound.[23]

A 1989 report listed the price of teeth from the coyote, raccoon, badger and porcupine to be between 50 cents and $2.50 each.[24] Eagle feathers go for between $50 to $100 each.[25] It should be noted that it is not illegal to harvest and sell the animal parts described above unless a state or federal law specifically restricts or prohibits the activity or the time of harvest. Once restricted, however, what may before been previously legal activity becomes illegal poaching activity if it is pursued nonetheless. Game ranches have become big money enterprises and are legal primarily in the Western United States. A New Mexico state enforcement agent reported pregnant cow elks being sold to elk ranch owners for approximately $16,500 each.[26] Elk antlers are harvested for sale for aphrodisiacs and for medicinal uses. The process is perhaps painful but not fatal to the elk, and depending upon the state, this harvest may or may not be legal.

Profile of the Non-Commercial Poacher

Defining poaching as any illegal taking of wildlife will make many sportspersons uncomfortable. Given the complexity and number of wildlife laws, anyone who spends significant time hunting or fishing is likely to have violated wildlife laws at one time or another, whether intentionally or not. The term "poaching" then should not necessarily be used to suggest equal culpability of all violators. Noncommercial violators do not often fall distinctly into any one category, as often they are influenced by diverse factors or motivations.

Unintentional violators may, for example, misidentify a species or shoot in an area unaware that it is illegally baited with feed. For the most part, these accidental violators are law-abiding hunters. Non-commercial poachers may also intentionally violate the law, however. Non-commercial poachers comprise by all estimates a large group which encompasses a variety of backgrounds and motivations for poaching. One type of non-commercial poacher is the "opportunistic poacher," who risks violating the law because he believes he will not be caught. For example, researchers who witnessed waterfowl hunters violating the law or behaving unethically noted that these hunters also had more opportunities to violate without being seen by authorities.[27] Another profile is the "trophy hunter" who will go to any length to take a trophy animal, even if it means violating the law.

There is also the "slob hunter," who is a serious abuser of wildlife. This type of violator hunts out of sheer greed, indifference to hunting laws and conservation, or ignorance of any laws concerning protection of wildlife. This attitude is illustrated by the story of a man arrested in Montana for allegedly stopping alongside an interstate and killing two trophy elk grazing inside a game reserve. When a local resident told him he had committed a crime, he replied that this was the way they hunt back in New York.[28]

Causes of Poaching

Cultural Influences

Hunting behavior is often shaped by family and community influences. Cultural influence may differ regionally, yet the national impact of cultural values on hunting behavior and on wildlife is significant. For example, USFW Special Agent Dave Hall is convinced that many rural Louisiana hunters are products of the cultural "Robin Hood Syndrome." Hunters intentionally violate wildlife laws as a sign of defiance to state control of wildlife, much like the English folk hero who defied the king's ownership of wildlife.[29] This occurs despite the fact that American wildlife law differs significantly from the English law of Sherwood Forest days. The taking of wildlife in the United States is a right bestowed on all people, not just the gentry, although states have the authority to regulate taking for the benefit of its citizens.

Studies further suggest that cultural influence on poaching is sometimes specific to both economic class and to a geographic region. A Wisconsin study revealed that a high percentage of waterfowl violators were white-collar businessmen, suggesting possible influence from a business ethic that the ends justify the means.[30] A study of convicted deer poachers in Missouri revealed that a high percentage of poachers were unemployed blue-collar workers who lived in the region. The study concludes: "From a sociological viewpoint, it is probable that Missouri deer poachers belong to a subculture from which they derive distinct values and norms."[31]

Misperceptions about Wildlife

Non-commercial and commercial poachers may also harbor misperceptions about wildlife which may include a belief that wildlife resources are unlimited or that wildlife belongs to the hunter and thus the harvest should not be regulated. Another misperception is that the hunter's harvest will not have a marked effect on wildlife populations. Waterfowl hunters in the South often have this misperception because they live near one of the North American waterfowl flyway bottlenecks, which serves as a virtual funnel for migrating waterfowl. Hunters may be inclined to exceed the bag limit because they believe that the multitude of ducks seen in their locale is representative of duck populations nationwide. The hope is that education will eventually deter this illegal hunting behavior (see Solutions in this chapter).

A good example of how poaching mentality can be changed when misperceptions are cleared up occurred in the sport fishing community more than two decades ago. When information was disseminated nationwide about the poor condition of certain fish populations, many tournament and recreational fishermen readily adopted the "catch and release" method of fishing. Furthermore, peer pressure proved to be a forceful tool in altering behavior in that instance.   Another example of how education can change misperceptions was demonstrated when waterfowl hunters were informed about the poor condition of many waterfowl populations. Many hunters refrained from shooting hens by stopping short of their bag limit and by counting cripples as part of their limit.[32]

Subsistence Poaching

There are still hunters who poach for their own subsistence, although their numbers are uncertain. Alaska is known for its numbers of both subsistence hunters and poachers. Residents of rural areas of the country with poor economies are particularly susceptible to continual subsistence poaching. For example, the study of convicted deer poachers in Missouri revealed that the unemployment rate of poachers was over 30 times greater than that of legal hunters.[33] More than 50 percent of poachers convicted for closed-season violations said they killed for the meat, though it is believed that this response may be tainted by an after-the-fact need to justify their illegal behavior to the public.[34]

STATE LAWS

This section of the chapter describes and compares the major provisions of state wildlife statutes pertaining to restrictions on wildlife taking. These laws are the main legal tools available to restrain poaching. Comparisons made between states are the result of a preliminary survey of the 50 states' fish and wildlife codes (see also various tables in Chapter 5). State regulations, which are promulgated by fish and wildlife agencies, often contain the more precise and detailed hunting and taking restrictions. Because of their sheer numbers and   difficulty of access, regulations have not been included here.   This section also highlights various state law provisions, and discusses the effectiveness of some of the laws in practice. Comparisons between states reveals enforcement and protection problems caused by inconsistencies between states. Because most wildlife protection laws have varying penalties, variations in penalties are described in a separate section.

States do not generally have a specific statute addressing "poaching" nor is poaching defined. Rather, laws which are meant to protect against poaching are scattered throughout each state's fish and wildlife codes under various subheadings. Poaching encompasses a wide range of illegal hunting and fishing activities and can be traced further to transporting, selling and buying illegally taken wildlife parts.

Taking Restrictions

States generally prohibit unlawful "taking" of either game or nongame wildlife. Most states define taking as hunting, pursuing, harassing, capturing, possessing, trapping or killing any protected wildlife or the attempt to do so.[35] For example, Illinois broadly defines taking as hunting, shooting, luring, killing, destroying, capturing, using gigs or spears, trapping, ensnaring, and harassing, or attempting to do these actions.[36] Unlawful "taking" does not include illegal selling, purchasing and transporting of wildlife. Instead, taking prohibitions emphasize field enforcement at the point of capturing or killing the animal.

In the great majority of states it is a misdemeanor to take game animals during closed season and/or at night. Many states also ban the luring of game animals to hunting areas with food, recorded calls, decoys, or the like. Baiting, in which poachers stock an area with food so that they have a better chance of attracting game, is a common tactic by poachers to lure waterfowl and big game. One-third of the states prohibit baiting.

Almost two-thirds of the states also prohibit the use of automatic machine guns, poison, explosives, snares, nets and pitfall traps in taking wildlife. Still other state statutes establish vehicular crimes such as hunting from aircraft or having a loaded firearm in the vehicle. Finally, almost all states criminalize the taking or possession of game beyond the legal bag limit.

The penalty for violating a taking law in all states is a misdemeanor. In addition, forfeitures of wildlife, vehicles and weapons can often accompany conviction under such statutes (see section on Penalties in this chapter and "Enforcement" subheading in Chapter 6).[37] A first conviction under South Dakota's laws against taking of big game, for example, results in a misdemeanor plus mandatory hunting license revocation. A second violation for illegally taking big game in South Dakota is a felony.[38]

While these statutes apply only to poaching activities at the taking level as opposed to sale and purchase activities, they are vital to catching both for-profit and other poachers. Such laws give wildlife officers broad authority to enforce wildlife laws before the illegally taken wildlife enter the stream of commerce. A wide range of poaching activities can be prosecuted under these laws, from commercial poaching to hanging a trophy on the wall or putting meat on the table. As a result, some wildlife enforcement officials prefer judicial discretion in sentencing, allowing judges to sentence each violator in accordance with the severity, intent and/or number of wildlife violations committed.

Waste

Waste statutes typically prohibit the taking of wild game while intentionally or knowingly permitting the majority of the carcass or edible portions to go to waste.[39] Theoretically, waste provisions can be extremely useful for intercepting commercial poachers because they target poachers of specific parts such as gallbladders and paws. The purpose is to protect wildlife from wasteful exploitation of certain parts for profit. Some state provisions more precisely prohibit the removal of elk and/or deer antlers from live animals for commercial purposes,[40] or specify other parts that cannot be removed from game carcasses.[41] A few states' waste provisions apply specifically to detaching deer heads without removing the carcasses from the scene of the kill.[42] Over one-third of the states, mostly in the Western United States, prohibit waste (see table comparing waste laws). Alaska's statute makes it a crime to waste wildlife even negligently, to fail to salvage from big game at least the hock, or to possess the horns or antlers of big game without possessing the edible meat as well.[43]

The penalty for wasting wildlife is a misdemeanor under most states' waste laws. Alaska nonetheless imposes steep fines for violations and requires mandatory hunting license forfeiture. Alaska's waste provision allows for defenses such as theft of the carcass, unanticipated weather conditions, unavoidable loss in the field to another wild animal, or the meat having been consumed by humans or delivered (given, sold or bartered) to another person.[44] Colorado makes waste of big game a felony and waste of other wildlife a misdemeanor. Colorado's statute is particularly specific and thorough (see endnote 42 for text of the statute).

Waste statutes should be effective deterrents to commercial poaching, but in practice understaffing of wildlife enforcement personnel and inaccessibility to the latest technology hinder enforcement. State fish and wildlife agencies usually do not have funding to send specimens to the USFW Forensic Lab in Oregon for genetic identification when an officer discovers animal parts in possession of a hunter or wasted remains of an animal in the field. More fundamentally, there are not enough enforcement officers in the field to discover wasted remains, and once a carcass is found with parts missing, it is very hard to discover who is the violator unless he is caught in the act. In addition, it is difficult to establish that the alleged violator had the intent to abandon the edible portions of the carcass. Finally, specific defenses in a statute such as those in Alaska's may be hard to disprove.

Spotlighting Laws

Nearly all states have prohibitions against spotlighting, or hunting with artificial lights at night (see table comparing spotlighting laws). Typical is West Virginia's statute which states that hunters cannot use or take advantage of artificial lights in hunting, locating, attracting, taking, trapping or killing wildlife, or attempting to do so, while possessing or having under control a firearm.[45] Most often spotlighting is used illegally to locate and surprise deer or other big game. Some statutes, as West Virginia's, imply but do not specifically require that the violator have the intent to take wildlife. Others either require specific intent or explicitly exempt from the statute's proscription the normal use of headlights on roads or flashlights not used for the purpose of taking wildlife.

California's spotlighting statute is comprehensive. In that state, it is unlawful to throw rays of any artificial light on any highway, field or forest where game and nongame mammals are commonly found, or while having in possession or control any firearm or weapon with which such mammals could be killed. However, it is lawful to use a flashlight if not affixed to a weapon, lamp or lantern, and headlights of a vehicle operated in a usual manner, if no attempt is made to locate mammals (see Sample Statutes for full text).[46] Delaware's spotlighting law, unlike California's, provides that fines for violators cannot be suspended.[47] It is common among states that the state prosecutor must only show that a violator used an artificial light to hunt big game while possessing a firearm at night, in a place where big game can reasonably be expected to occur.[48]

Spotlighting violations constitute a misdemeanor in all states with spotlighting laws. The amount of fines and jail terms fluctuates widely among the states. In Colorado, for instance, punishment for the first offense is $200 and mandatory hunting license suspension for up to three years.[49] New York's penalty for using an artificial light to take deer is a fine of up to $2,000 and/or jail for up to one year.[50] North Carolina's penalty, on the other hand, is a fine of between $25 and $100 and/or a jail term of 30 days or less.[51] Also, a handful of states require a convicted spotlighter to forfeit the vehicle used to perpetrate the crime.[52]

The effectiveness of spotlighting laws against poachers is debatable, according to wildlife enforcement officers, depending on the severity of the penalty. For example, statutes like North Carolina's probably would not deter illegal spotlighting because the penalty is so light. In addition, state and local judges in some regions who take poaching violations less seriously may suspend violators' punishment or dismiss the spotlighting charges altogether. Delaware's solution to increase the effectiveness of spotlighting statutes is to expressly prohibit judges from suspending punishment.[53] Although such a measure would not preclude judges from dismissing the charges, it could serve as a message to judges to take the crime seriously.

Some spotlighting laws recently have come under constitutional scrutiny. In a few states, statutes have been repealed under the First Amendment as overbroad, when the language is so broad that it fails to put the public on notice of how a violation could occur and gives too much discretion to law enforcers to interpret its meaning. Those spotlighting statutes that would render the normal use of headlights in driving, or a landowner's use of a light to survey his or her property, would be overbroad and therefore unconstitutional. An example of a possibly unconstitutional statute is New York's, which simply makes it a misdemeanor to use artificial lights to take deer.[54]

Sale and Purchase of Wildlife

Most state fish and wildlife codes include a wildlife sale and purchase provision, which typically reads simply that it is illegal to sell or purchase wildlife species or their parts, unless authorized by the state's laws.[55] Additional prohibitions may apply to a single species or category of wildlife such as endangered species. For example, Florida's code makes it a misdemeanor to sell illegally taken alligators or their skins and a felony to sell illegally taken deer or turkey.[56] North Carolina prohibits buying or selling wildlife or selling bears, cougars, eagles or their parts.[57] Other states regulate either the sale or the purchase of wildlife but not both. There is little consistency between states' laws restricting sale and purchase of wildlife because the provisions vary widely regarding the particular types of wildlife protected.

State codes contain various exceptions to wildlife sale or purchase prohibitions. Idaho, for example, prohibits the sale or purchase of any wildlife species or wildlife parts, but specifically exempts the sale of legally taken hides, horns or heads of game animals accompanied by a statement of the lawful taking, and the sale of pelts or other parts of fur-bearers when legally taken.[58] Illinois allows buying, selling and possessing wildlife and their parts when legally imported. These include deer, and their parts; fur-bearers and their parts when legally taken; and inedible parts of game mammals.[59] West Virginia permits the sale of inedible parts of legally taken deer and bear and their organs.[60] Connecticut allows the buying, selling and possessing with the intent to sell or exchange wildlife and their parts, if such wildlife was legally taken in another state and legally imported into the state.[61] Varying exceptions between states can create opportunities for commercial poachers to launder parts illegally taken in one state through other states. Consistency of buying and selling laws among states would be particularly helpful in stemming illegal wildlife trade.

Some states have attempted to enforce wildlife buying and selling restrictions through rigorous penalties. Illinois prohibits the sale or receipt of protected wildlife valued at $300 or more "for profit or commercial purposes," and violation is a felony.[62] In Arizona, it is a felony to sell big game and parts that were unlawfully taken, and to sell any wildlife or parts that were bought or imported illegally.[63] Colorado makes it a felony to unlawfully buy, sell or solicit to illegally take big game, endangered species or eagles for money or commercial gain and makes it a misdemeanor to do so regarding all other wildlife.[64] Most states also provide that the unlawful sale or purchase of each animal and/or each part constitutes a separate crime.[65]

All of the states with selling and/or purchasing restrictions make it a misdemeanor to unlawfully buy or sell wildlife. The punishment for the misdemeanor violation varies with each state, but most carry fines ranging from $10 to $1,000 and/or jail terms not exceeding six months, or both. Many states also permit the state prosecutor or the state fish and wildlife agency to sue for damages in civil court and to collect restitution for the loss of the wildlife. Some agencies also can further order the convicted violator to forfeit the wildlife or parts and any weapons or vehicles seized in connection with the violation (see penalties section of this chapter and table in Chapter 5).

Buying and selling laws are important and necessary to curtail exploitation of finite wildlife populations and to eliminate poacher's profits. They directly address a wide range of poaching activities and hurt the poacher's wallet. Prohibition of sale in wildlife "parts" in the statutes is extremely important because major markets in illegal wildlife trade are in parts such as bear gallbladders and paws, antlers, horns, hides and heads of big game, feathers of birds, and paddlefish eggs.[66] Regulation or outright bans on buying and selling of particular animals like endangered species, birds of prey, bears, and their parts, are also vital. Creating economic disincentives such as fines for each animal or part involved and stacking mandatory jail sentences instead of allowing concurrent serving of sentences, are some of the states' options to tighten their laws.

Transportation Restrictions

Almost every state has restrictions on transportation of wildlife. Wildlife transportation laws target poaching operations, persons attempting to profit from poachers' activities, and all transporters. Provisions usually prohibit transporting or shipping protected wildlife within or without the state unless accompanied by documentation such as shipping permits, affidavits of ownership, or lawful hunting licenses.[67] Provisions such as those of Nevada ban outright the transportation of more than one or two daily bag limits of game.[68] Many states also regulate transportation of wildlife by requiring shipping permits and tags which openly identify the wildlife.[69]

Other states further regulate transportation by specifically regulating the importation and/or exportation of wildlife. Import/export bans can apply to illegally taken or possessed wildlife or their parts.[70] Some states, however, allow the importation of game lawfully taken in other states at all times or during the originating state's open season.[71] Transportation, exportation, and importation bans also exist in some states for particular species of wildlife, alive or dead, such as bears, big game and/or endangered species.[72]

In addition, 19 state statutes directly restrict the activities of common carriers. Some allow common carriers to transport wildlife or wildlife parts only upon proof of its legality.[73] Other states prohibit common carriers from importing protected species taken in the state of origin or without ascertaining that a valid hunting license is in the transporter's possession. Still others prohibit common carriers from transporting game or fish except during the open season for that species.[74] Arkansas gives common carriers the authority to refuse to receive for export packages or baggage suspected of carrying wildlife.[75]

A misdemeanor is the most common penalty for violating a transportation restriction, although Illinois' statute makes it a felony to transport, export or receive protected species for profit or commercial purposes where the value of each animal is at least $300.[76] While most common carriers are subject merely to fines for violating transportation laws, a few states criminalize violations.[77]

As with sale and purchase restrictions, regulation of the transportation, importation and exportation of wildlife parts is an important enforcement tool. Unlike buying and selling laws, however, conviction under a transportation provision almost never requires that the state prove that the violator intended or knew that he or she was transporting wildlife or their parts. Often the state must prove only that the transporter was illegally possessing the wildlife at the time of transportation.

State export restrictions are especially useful for preventing animal parts from entering the stream of commerce, where the animal parts are exported not only from one state to another but also from the United States to foreign countries. Interstate agreements to honor sister states' export laws and to achieve full cooperation between states and federal governments would further boost the effectiveness of state transportation laws (see Solutions for further discussion of interstate agreements).

Agency Enforcement Powers

The powers that the state legislatures confer on wildlife enforcement officers may determine the effectiveness with which they can detect and deter poaching. Police power includes the states' authority to make arrests, searches and seizures, and further includes the power to search and seize evidence without obtaining a warrant, subject to constitutional restrictions. Disparities in the extent of police powers granted to wildlife officers exist among the states, with half of the codes giving wildlife enforcement agents the same powers as peace officers generally and about half the codes expressly limiting their authority. The implication is that wildlife officers in only certain states have the clear authority to conduct warrantless searches of suspected violators and their possessions, or to conduct searches outside of state-owned property.

Some states like Virginia and New York explicitly prohibit wildlife officers from conducting searches without a warrant.[78] Wildlife officers have substantially less enforcement power than other peace officers in these states. On the other hand, one-third of the states give wildlife enforcement officers greater power than other peace officers. Alabama authorizes wildlife officers to search vehicles without a warrant for waterfowl violations, except for vehicles traveling on federal or state highways.[79] Tennessee empowers its wildlife officers to search vehicles without a warrant and to conduct other warrantless searches, subject to constitutional restrictions.[80] Other states either give their wildlife enforcers the power to enforce only the wildlife code (which is interpreted variously among the states as conferring either equal or less power as other peace officers),[81] or they give them general police powers like other peace officers.[82]

Regulation of Hunting Businesses

Fur dealers, taxidermists and hunting guides or outfitters make profits largely from hunters and trappers. Because large volumes of legally and sometimes illegally taken wildlife pass through these businesses, many states regulate them. Many undercover enforcement operations have targeted fur dealing and taxidermy because they are focal points for the illegal taker, seller and buyer of wildlife or their parts.[83] Some hunting guides and outfitters also have been implicated in poaching operations (and thus can be deemed to be poachers themselves) because some poachers rely on them to provide the wildlife and are willing to pay a high price for the assurance that they will obtain the animals they seek.[84]

Almost all states regulate fur dealers (see table in Chapter 5). States regulate fur dealers in several ways. Some states permit fur dealers to buy or sell raw ("green") hides only if they have a fur dealing license.[85] In addition, these states require that fur dealers keep records of and report annually on all their purchases and sales.[86] Taxidermists also must obtain licenses to practice and must report annually on the number and kinds of animals that come through their business in over one-third of the states.[87] About half of the states with fur dealing laws criminalize violations as a misdemeanor; the other half impose civil fines and/or loss of licenses.

One-third of the states regulate guides and outfitters (see table in Chapter 5). These states require that each guide obtain a hunting license, and they provide for the suspension or revocation of that license if the guide commits hunting violations. A few states also require that each licensed guide report annually to the state on his or her guiding activities.[88] Guides and others can be punished in more than one-third of the states for illegal taking not only as hunters, but also for conspiracy to violate the law and/or acting as accomplices (meaning that guides are guilty of the same crime as the poacher if they aid the poacher in committing the crime).[89] In some states the person who hires a guide to violate wildlife laws is guilty of a misdemeanor.[90]

Taxidermy and hunting guide laws are designed primarily to catch illegal trophy hunters. Fur dealers as well as trappers are often rigorously regulated to cut down on legal exploitation of furbearing mammals, but also to eliminate illegal trade in furs.

Penalties

Each state's penalties for violating wildlife protection laws determine to some extent the effectiveness of these laws. Penalties can range from small civil fines to criminal misdemeanors and their varying punishments, to felonies and forfeiture of property (see table in Chapter 5 regarding felonies). Offenses that are punishable by small fines such as $10 to $25 do not deter commercial poachers who often make many times more from the sale of the animal or part than the amount of the fine. Penalties are most effective that dip deeply into the wallet, threaten stiff jail terms, and confiscate property, but only if judges take advantage of the measures available in the statutes.

Misdemeanors and Felonies

The most common penalty for wildlife violations in all states is the criminal misdemeanor. For misdemeanors, most states give the judge discretion in choosing a fine that may vary widely in amount and between states, ranging from ten dollars to thousands of dollars, a jail term anywhere from several days to one year, or both. Nearly one-third of the states consider certain wildlife violations to be especially egregious and therefore make those offenses a felony (see table in Chapter 5 regarding felonies). For example, in Arizona selling big game that are unlawfully taken or assisting another in unlawfully taking big game for financial gain is a felony upon conviction.[91] In Colorado, buying or selling big game, endangered species or eagles is a felony.[92] In Florida, it is a felony to kill a Florida panther, to take or possess alligators unlawfully, and to sell unlawfully taken deer or turkey.[93] West Virginia considers the use of explosives to take wildlife to be a felony.[94] Violation of North Dakota's ban on paddlefish taking is a felony.[95] The threat of a felony conviction is certainly a greater deterrent than a misdemeanor even for hardcore, profit-seeking poachers.

Suspension of Hunting Licenses

All states authorize the court, the fish and wildlife agency, or both, to suspend or permanently revoke hunting licenses for wildlife code violations.[96] A few states have enacted mandatory license suspension. Maine, for example, requires license suspension for at least three years for a habitual violator.[97] In Connecticut, a first conviction under any wildlife law carries a mandatory 30-day to 1-year suspension.[98] License suspension provisions are extremely important to effective enforcement of wildlife laws (see Solutions). Enforcers across the country agree that taking hunting licenses away is one of the best deterrents to poaching.

Forfeiture

Over two-thirds of the states also require convicted wildlife poachers to forfeit vehicles, weapons and/or equipment used in wildlife violations. The validity of vehicle forfeiture laws is highly contested because it involves giving up a big financial investment. Thus far, however, vehicle forfeitures generally have been upheld as valid exercises of the states' power to enforce wildlife laws. These forfeiture provisions, together with mandatory or even discretionary license suspension or revocation, provide strong deterrents to violators.

Various Laws with Stiffer Penalties

Some states impose stiffer penalties for violation of particular laws. In some western states, waste violations carry stiff penalties. In Alaska, the minimum sentence for waste cannot be reduced or suspended, and involves both forfeiture of the wildlife and a mandatory one to five-year suspension of the violator's hunting license.[99] As mentioned, waste of big game, endangered species, or eagles in Colorado is a felony.[100] Virginia requires a license suspension for one year and mandatory vehicle and equipment forfeiture for spotlighting. Connecticut and Tennessee have similar punishments. In Delaware, the judge cannot suspend the fines for spotlighting.[101] Finally, Oregon requires the permanent revocation of licenses for any unlawful taking of wildlife.[102]

Civil Liability

In addition to criminal penalties, over one-third of the states have civil liability provisions of some kind (see table in Chapter 5 on restitution). Violators may be liable for any damages incurred by enforcement officers as well as for damage to the wildlife taken illegally. Although it is difficult to assess the value of wildlife, half the state legislatures have assessed a value of wildlife for civil liability purposes. These states list the value of various important wildlife species and require the violator to pay restitution to the state for the value of each such animal taken. For commercial poachers who deal in large numbers of wildlife, upon conviction restitution amounts to be paid can be high. In Washington, for example, restitution is mandatory and cannot be suspended, waived, modified or deferred. In that state, moose, antelope, mountain sheep and goats, and all endangered species are valued at

$2,000 each; mountain caribou and grizzly bears are valued at $5,000 each; and elk, deer, black bears and cougars are "worth" $1,000 each.[103] Arizona requires a minimum restitution of $750 for each buffalo, elk, bighorn sheep, eagle and endangered species unlawfully taken or possessed.[104] Restitution and imposition of civil damages can be effective financial deterrents to for-profit poaching.

Miscellaneous Unique Penalty Provisions

As can be seen by the discussion above, sentencing and penalty structures vary widely between states and between violations. Overall comparisons are hard to make, but certain state penalty systems are interesting. Colorado, for example, has a point system that is innovative and precise. The statutes set forth how many points are to be assessed for each wildlife violation. When violators accumulate 20 points within five years, their hunting license is suspended.[105]

Pennsylvania's code is interesting in that it does not allow judges to impose community service instead of the usual jail term and/or fine.[106] This may limit opportunities for innovative sentencing, but may at the same time force poachers to pay heavy fines. Texas has a penalty system that allows poachers to pay a civil fine of at least $150 for each day their hunting license would have been suspended instead of actually having their licenses suspended.[107] This loophole could unintentionally cater to commercial poachers who can well afford to pay the civil fines and therefore escape license suspension.

Specific Wildlife Species Protection Laws

Many states have separate provisions that protect certain wildlife species, most notably endangered species and bears. As discussed in the Federal Laws section below, citizens of the various states are also subject to federal wildlife protection laws such as the federal Endangered Species Act. Most states further protect species determined to be endangered within their own borders. States commonly prohibit hunting, possessing, selling, buying, and/or transportation of endangered species. Vermont like many other states has a general prohibition on taking endangered species.[108] In Delaware, for example, there is a separate state ban on killing, possessing or bartering bald eagles.[109]

Less than one-third of the states also specifically regulate the taking and/or selling of bears or bear parts. Maine requires a permit to hunt or transport bears and a hide dealer's license to buy, sell or take the head, hide or gallbladder of bears.[110] Georgia imposes restitution and forfeiture of vehicles and equipment for buying or selling bears or bear parts, possessing, transporting, taking or attempting to take bears during the closed season.[111] Georgia also imposes stiff fines, prison terms, or both. Arkansas bans shipping, exporting, and accepting for export bears and bear parts.[112] Because of the skyrocketing demand for American bear parts and endangered species parts in Asia and elsewhere, strict regulations on taking bears and consistency in regulating between states is increasingly critical.

Particularly Effective State Laws

Several statutes do not fit within any of the above categories but are particularly effective against poachers or specifically address for-profit poaching. Less than one-third of state statutes explicitly allow citizens to recover a reward when they supply wildlife agents with information leading to arrests or conviction or when they apprehend wildlife violators. Hawaii appears to have one of the more generous laws because it requires half of fines collected to go to the person giving information that leads to arrest.[113]

Restrictions on commercial wildlife operations are becoming more common because of the potential for illegal trade and abuse of species harvesting. West Virginia, for example, generally bans commercialization of wildlife except by permit. Utah prohibits the use of wildlife as a commercial venture for financial gain unless authorized by law. In a specific provision, California bans removal of the horns or antlers of live elk for commercial purposes.[114]

State legislatures also sometimes limit available defenses within wildlife poaching laws. In California and Tennessee, it is no defense to a wildlife violation that the defendant is mistaken as to species, sex or size of the animal. If there is more than one defendant on trial for wildlife violations in Texas, joint and several liability is imposed, meaning that each violator is fully liable for all the penalties. Maine requires each district attorney to prosecute all wildlife law violators, regardless of the chances of a successful prosecution.[115] Because these mandates can provide uniformity in prosecution of poaching violations in a state, they can be seen as positive attempts to deal with the breadth of poaching and the problems of judicial enforcement.

Interstate Compacts and Reciprocal Agreements Between States

Compacts and reciprocal law enforcement agreements between states can ensure uniformity and cooperation in enforcement where wildlife violations affect more than one state. For example, the Wildlife Violator Compact of 1989 has been signed by Colorado, Arizona, California, Idaho, Nevada, Washington, Utah and Wyoming. These states have agreed to recognize each other's license suspensions and to communicate with each other regarding wildlife violations and changes in state laws.[116] Other states individually recognize their neighboring states' laws. For example, Oregon's wildlife code mandates the suspension or revocation of hunting licenses in Oregon of persons convicted under another state's laws who fail to comply with sentencing pronouncements.[117] Rhode Island authorizes the Director of the state's wildlife agency to cooperate with fish and wildlife directors from other states.[118] Illinois prohibits common carriers from importing protected species illegally taken in the state of origin.[119]

States that make full use of these reciprocal agreements and pronouncements can have an impact on interstate transport of illegally taken wildlife. Such provisions can also fill the gaps and loopholes in participating states' wildlife laws because, depending upon the terms of the agreement, the more stringent laws will control interstate enforcement where the laws conflict or one is weaker than another.

As this overview of the various states' provisions demonstrates, the lack of uniformity of fish and wildlife laws to catch poachers is nearly as widespread as the poaching problem itself. Presently, interstate agreements or pronouncements to honor sister states' wildlife laws or that foster communication among enforcement officers between different states, or between states and the federal government, are some of the only means of infiltrating poaching operations that cross state borders.

FEDERAL LAWS

There are many federal statutes which have been enacted specifically to protect wildlife in the United States. Apart from the federal wildlife refuge acts, the major pieces of legislation are:

- The Lacey Act, as amended (18 U.S.C. 42; 16 U.S.C. 3371-3378);
- The Migratory Bird Treaty Act, as amended (16 U.S.C. 703-712);
- The Bald and Golden Eagle Protection Act, as amended (16 U.S.C. 668-668c);
- The Endangered Species Act (ESA) of 1973, as amended (16 U.S.C. 1531-1543) and provisions of the Convention on International Trade in Endangered Species of Wild Fauna and Flora (CITES) through the ESA;
- The Migratory Bird Hunting and Conservation Stamp Act (16 U.S.C. 718);
- The Airborne Hunting Act (16 U.S.C. 742j-l);
- The National Wildlife Refuge System Administration Act of 1966 (16 U.S.C. 668dd-668ee);
- The Marine Mammal Protection Act of 1972 (16 U.S.C. 1361-1407);
- The Antarctic Conservation Act of 1978 (16 U.S.C. 2401-2412);
- The African Elephant Conservation Act (16 U.S.C. 4201-4245).

According to a 1991 government report, 65 percent of the investigations that USFW special agents performed during 1987 through 1989 were under suspected violations of four federal statutes: the Lacey Act; the Migratory Bird Treaty Act; the Bald and Golden Eagle Protection Act; and the Endangered Species Act.[120]

All federal USFW personnel interviewed agreed that existing federal laws supplied adequate authority to protect wildlife. However, in a 1991 U.S. General Accounting Office report, federal agents raised two concerns. The first was that the Migratory Bird Treaty Act, unlike other wildlife laws, does not authorize warrantless searches and seizures, which are important to prevent destruction of evidence and to allow flexibility for agents in the field.

The second concern involved enforcement of the Endangered Species Act. Alleged violators often claim that the live wildlife they have captured is not endangered but is a hybrid of the protected species. The ESA does have a provision protecting species that are closely related or similar in appearance to the endangered or threatened species in order to protect the listed species, yet this provision is rarely used.[121] The alternative is to have a live animal destroyed in order to determine whether it is an endangered or threatened species, but obviously this option is not favorably considered.[122]

Passed in 1900, the Lacey Act is perhaps the most commonly used federal statute to protect wildlife. The law prohibits the importation, exportation, transportation, sale, receipt, acquisition, or purchase of fish, wildlife, or plants that are taken possessed, transported, or sold in violation of any federal, state, tribal, or foreign law. The Lacey Act grants agents the power to make warrantless searches and seizures when they suspect violations. A survey of federal agents revealed that when both the Lacey Act and another statute apply to a violation, agents prefer to enforce the Lacey Act because the violation is more likely to be a felony and penalties are more stringent under the Lacey Act. Lacey Act penalties include imprisonment of up to one year and fines of up to $100,000 for misdemeanors, and imprisonment of up to five years and fines of up to $250,000 for felonies. Vehicles, equipment, and illegally obtained wildlife are subject to forfeiture. The 1988 amendments to the Lacey Act added felony provisions to deal with commercial guides who are accessories to wildlife violations. [123]

ENFORCEMENT OF EXISTING LAWS

Law enforcement statistics, such as the number of citations or convictions in a given year, are ineffective as a measure of determining whether wildlife species are being protected. These statistics may reflect the diligence of law enforcement officers, the level of poaching activity in a specific area and the rate at which wildlife cases are prosecuted. However, they do not measure how many violators are relatively unscathed by sentencing after conviction, the numbers of wildlife actually protected as a result of law enforcement efforts, or the depletion of wildlife populations by poaching. Nor do statistics accurately measure the likelihood that poachers will violate wildlife laws again.

Nonetheless, enforcement statistics provide hard evidence that poaching is a real and present problem. Factors to keep in mind when analyzing enforcement statistics are the size of the enforcement staff, the area of the state, average numbers of hunters, and the richness of wildlife resources in the state. State hunter population may not always be relevant because of unlicensed poachers from within and out of state. For example, in 1991 the New Mexico Game and Fish Department reported that nearly 3,000 citations were given for state wildlife law violations. New Mexico, the fifth largest state, has 52 officers in full-time wildlife enforcement with a total of 140 commissioned wildlife officers.[124] In Missouri, on the other hand, with an enforcement staff of approximately 173 field officers and staff supervisors, 21,863 violations were recorded out of 250,778 contacts officers made with sportspersons.[125] Texas, with a Parks and Wildlife Department enforcement staff of over 500 field officers, reported 34,363 citations in 1991.[126]

Law enforcement activities to ensure compliance with wildlife laws is critical. However, many enforcement problems exist. Enforcement efforts can be divided into several levels: field enforcement, prosecutorial enforcement, and judicial enforcement. An analysis of the problems at each level follows.

Field Enforcement

The first level of enforcement is in the field, where federal and state wildlife enforcement agents are the key players. With an estimated 7,000 state wildlife agents and just over 200 federal agents nationwide, effective field enforcement is extremely difficult.[127] According to USFW agent Dave Hall, "New York policemen alone outnumber the conservation officers of all 50 states combined by more than 10 to 1. America's 17 million hunters outnumber conservation officers by approximately 9,000 to 1."[128] One result of this shortage is that wildlife agents are forced to selectively enforce wildlife laws. At the federal level, this means the focus is turned toward commercial poachers or "the worst of the worst," according to USFW agent Terry Grosz.[129] Lack of funding restricts some state enforcement staff to desk work for several months a year. In some states agents are responsible for enforcing other environmental laws as well as wildlife protection laws.[130] Both law enforcement officers and convicted poachers agree that as a consequence many poaching activities go undetected. Some hunters complain that selective enforcement at the state level often means agents spend more time in the field on "technical" violations than on large-scale commercial violations. Covert operations are usually necessary to catch commercial violators and state agents have neither the time, money, nor agents to handle many of these cases. Selective enforcement is further reinforced by a system that measures law enforcement success by numbers of citations.[131] Concentration on smaller violations, however, sometimes causes alienation between the wardens and the sportspersons.[132] In addition, whereas hunters could be effective sources of information about violations, hostility may prevent sportspersons from cooperating with law enforcement efforts. Furthermore, state agents also argue that they spend much of their time simply dealing with telephone complaints about violators. "State agents can't always pick and choose who to go after, they normally just take it as it comes," USFW Agent John Cross stated.[133]

When state agents take on commercial poaching cases, federal violations are usually involved and therefore federal agents are often requested to assist with the investigation. Shortages of personnel and money at the federal level means federal agents cannot always meet this request. Though most state and federal agents work well together, state agents are often frustrated at the lack of federal assistance. In fact, directors of 10 state law enforcement agencies in the Northeast United States advised the USFW that they were not willing to renew cooperative law enforcement agreements with the USFW because of a lack of federal assistance in state covert operations.[134]

Prosecutorial Recognition

The next level of enforcement occurs when wildlife cases are presented to the state or federal prosecutor who brings cases before the court. This level of enforcement has not always been used in favor of wildlife. "We get good sentences once we get to the judge, but the difficult part is getting the U.S. Attorney's office to recognize the importance of wildlife laws," according to Texas USFW Agent Jim Stinebaugh.[135] The problem may be the result of value judgements prosecutors make about wildlife violations as compared to other crimes. Also, state prosecutors may feel that it is not worth the time to prosecute violations when such low penalties are involved. Like judges, prosecutors are also subject to political, community and cultural pressures which can sway decisions whether or not to prosecute or actively pursue wildlife cases.

Judicial Recognition

The last level of enforcement occurs once a case gets into the courtroom. Most of the problems at this level are in the state judicial systems. Federal judges are non-elected life-appointees and thus are not as affected by political and community pressures. State judges, on the other hand, are elected by the public or serve as political appointees. In either case, state judges are subject to pressures which can affect whether poachers are convicted or penalized.

If cases do get heard at the state level, state laws rarely provide for stiff enough penalties to provide an adequate deterrent. Most violators of state wildlife laws are charged with misdemeanors, which may mean a fine as low as $10 to $50. These fines do little to hinder the lucrative activities of the commercial poacher. Second, federal judges have more discretionary power to apply penalties which will more effectively deter wildlife violators. For example, though federal judges must work within federal sentencing guidelines, they may also include forfeiture of vehicles and equipment, loss of hunting privileges and other innovative probationary measures as part of the penalty. State judges may have less innovative penalties available to them. They may suspend sentences, however, and substitute probationary measures in lieu of state penalties. In this way they may also be able to instigate some of the more innovative sentencing techniques.

SOLUTIONS AND RECOMMENDATIONS

Identification of a problem is the first step in solving it. Since the illegal taking of wildlife is being recognized as a critical problem in the United States, the next step is devising solutions to better protect wildlife from poaching. The individuals interviewed for this chapter unanimously called for added enforcement combined with education to increase compliance with wildlife laws. Naturalist Aldo Leopold employed two terms to define this enforcement/education approach which he called the restrictive and incentive methodologies. Restrictive methodology has been described as the judicial system, law enforcement, and wildlife laws and regulations. The incentive methodology involves participation of the hunter, an individual or communal vested interest in wildlife, and self-enlightenment brought about through education.[136]

Restrictive Deterrents

Increase Penalties

Studies indicate that the commercial poacher is likely to be involved in other criminal activities.[137] The severity of the crimes that the commercial poacher perpetrates against wildlife, particularly the taking of endangered and threatened species, suggests a dispassionate and criminal mentality. Judges, prosecutors and wildlife enforcement officers often agree that incarceration, stiff fines, and/or revocation of hunting privileges are therefore the most appropriate remedies for commercial poachers and repeat offenders who have not been deterred by lesser penalties.

Those in the wildlife law enforcement profession seem more optimistic about the likelihood of rehabilitating the first-time convicted poacher or non-commercial poacher. The need for stiff penalties still exists, however. Fines should be steep enough to act as a deterrent to future violations and to convey the seriousness of the violation. Suspension or revocation of hunting privileges should also be applied more readily as a penalty for more serious offenses. Professor Jackson and Agent Hall both reiterate that hunters fear no other penalty as much as license revocation.[138]

Federal Magistrate Michaelle Wynne argues that court appearances should be mandatory at both the state and federal levels. This conveys the severity of the offense and allows judges the opportunity to apply innovative sentencing techniques. Though state judges have less sentencing discretion than federal judges, they can suspend sentences to substitute probationary measures like community service hours spent assisting wildlife programs.

Simplify Laws

The consensus of those interviewed recommended simplifying state wildlife laws and making them more consistent with each other. Some poachers justify their behavior by citing the complexity of current laws and their inability to comprehend them. Enforcement officers also suffer from the complexity and the constantly changing nature of their wildlife laws. If current laws were simplified, a greater willingness to comply with the laws may result. Professor Jackson argues that confusion from complexity of state laws can also be reduced by notifying hunters of changes in law in advance of their implementation.[139]

Increase Law Enforcement Funding

Many agree that increased funding for state and federal wildlife law enforcement agencies is needed to better protect wildlife. The initial need is for more wildlife enforcement agents. As USFW Agent John Cross stated, "All the laws in the world will do no good if you don't have the people to enforce those laws."[140] Currently, there are just over 200 USFW agents and approximately 7,000 state agents in the United States. USFW personnel have estimated that the addition of between 100 and 200 federal agents and approximately 100 wildlife inspectors would adequately equip the federal agency to enforce wildlife laws and protect wildlife.[141]

Increased funding would also allow for more wildlife agents and for updating agency equipment necessary to catch poachers. Law enforcement agencies currently complain that commercial and "hard-core" poachers have the most current equipment, such as aircraft and surveillance equipment, and elude capture because agency equipment is so outdated. Funding increases are naturally difficult to obtain from state legislatures. Fish and wildlife agencies are often funded solely through hunting and fishing license fees, so new sources of funding are sorely needed. Sale of wildlife stamps and emblems are bringing in additional funds, as are tax return check-offs and other programs. (For comparisons, see State Summaries for various states' funding sources, and the table on Agency Funding Sources in Chapter 5.)

Regarding innovative funding sources, Missouri is the only state in the country to capitalize successfully on the support of its citizenry by passage of referendum for a .06 percent sales tax, which funds go to the Missouri Department of Conservation. The law is part of the state constitution; it can only be changed by a majority vote of the people. Among the benefits of the sales tax is that the constant influx of funds allows for long-range planning of programs such as law enforcement and habitat protection.

Increase Law Enforcement Authority

Many states confer full police powers to their wildlife enforcement officers which allows the officer to enforce all state laws as would any police officer. The added authority is particularly beneficial to the lone game warden who is occasionally placed in dangerous situations during the course of his or her work. USFW Agent Stinebaugh stated, "Full police powers enables the wildlife agent to handle any situation that comes up."

Federal USFW agents do not have full police powers under federal law. However, in states where state and federal wildlife agents are cross-credentialed, federal agents are given the same authority as state agents, including full police powers when the state authorizes such powers. Cross-credentialed state agents have authority to enforce federal laws. Both forms of extended authority, full police powers and cross-credentialing powers, facilitate uniform and effective enforcement of wildlife laws and may actually further deter poachers who may be aware of this enforcement authority.

Prioritize Law Enforcement Responsibilities

Thomas Harelson, a wildlife law enforcement supervisor in Wisconsin, divided Wisconsin wildlife statutes into three categories: social, traditional, and laws which protect the resource. An example of the first type is the prohibition against hunting on Sunday. Such statutes can still be found in a number of states. An example of the traditional law is the prohibition against hunting waterfowl with an unplugged shotgun, that is, a gun that does not restrict the number of shells in the chamber. The third type of law directly influences the number of wildlife taken. The bag limit for each game species is an example. According to one study, law enforcement agents would better protect wildlife if they concentrated their time and energy on enforcing this third type of statute.[142]

Regulate or Ban the Commercialization of Wildlife

Some wildlife professionals argue that the only way to effectively curtail the illegal taking of wildlife is to legislate a complete ban on the commercial trade in wildlife. They point to specific national restrictions which were placed on waterfowl and alligators and which proved successful in limiting the taking and the sale of those animals. Others argue that such a ban could be disastrous to certain regions of the country which rely on wildlife trade for their livelihood. Another argument altogether is that the focus should not be placed on the economic value of the sale of animal parts, but rather on the indirect economic benefits that could be derived from protecting wildlife rather than trading in wildlife, through recreational and "watchable wildlife" activities.[143]

Other wildlife professionals feel that better regulation of the wildlife trade would be more effective than total prohibition. Their belief is that a total ban on the sale of wildlife and wildlife parts in the United States will not stop poaching activities but will simply move the business farther into the black market. It is logically argued that when a commercial market for a species exists without controls, pressure to harvest the species will last until wildlife populations are nearly or totally depleted, when the focus will turn to another more plentiful species.[144]

Others support developing uniform state wildlife laws, particularly those which regulate commercial trade in wildlife. As discussed, many states allow the sale of some or all species and their parts, which makes laundering of illegally taken animals and parts through those states a substantial enforcement problem (see State Laws section). Uniformity between states in commercial trade prohibitions would clearly help solve the laundering problem. However, the right of each state to regulate its wildlife has strong historical ties, and individual states must be convinced that it is in their own interest to pass commercial trade laws consistent with other states.

Increase Reward Programs

All states now have established toll-free hotlines where persons may call anonymously to report hunting violations. These programs, such as "Operation Game Thief" in New Mexico, have proven to be a very effective tool in assisting wildlife enforcement efforts. The same two-year study of deer poaching incidents in Missouri discussed previously revealed that informants were responsible for providing information on 83.7% of the poaching violations. Interest in conservation was cited by 83.2% of the informants as the reason for reporting the violation.[145] This also suggests that hunters police their own ranks. Reward programs should prove beneficial to states which have not already adopted such programs. Increased publicity about these programs would serve to educate more of the public, including nonhunters, who in turn may be willing to help law enforcement efforts.

Instigate a National Reporting System

The USFW has plans to implement a National Incident Based Reporting System to improve documentation of reported or suspected crimes and facilitate enforcement efforts nationwide.[146] Though the USFW has a nationally based computer system which records all federal violators, states are not yet linked into this system. Thus state wildlife law violators are not included in the database. Until law enforcement agencies can access information about both state and federal violators, the effectiveness of the system is limited. The USFW has also opened a wildlife forensics lab in Oregon for use primarily in commercial poaching investigations.[147] Due to shortages of resources and personnel, state enforcement departments have limited access to the lab's services. Another benefit of increased funding, then, would be to provide state agencies access to these services.

Instigate a National Permit Assistance Program

Another suggestion from enforcement officials is to create a national center where hunters could get access to hunting and fishing laws and permit requirements of every state.[148] Such a program would almost certainly increase wildlife law compliance among hunters seeking this information. To make sure the hunter is receiving the most current state law, an independent organization could take over the task (and assume legal liability) for a fee. For the time being, the reader is referred to the State Law Summaries in this text and the addresses of each state fish and wildlife agency at the end of the text.

Incentive Methodology

Educate the Judicial System

Most federal wildlife enforcement officers feel that federal statutes provide adequate authority to intercept the wildlife law violators. However, this does not guarantee judicial enforcement. The most often cited recommendation of wildlife experts was educating judges and prosecutors about the importance of supporting wildlife enforcement efforts. Traditionally, judges and prosecutors have not dealt harshly with poachers. An Alaskan federal judge reflected the lax attitude toward wildlife violations when during the sentencing of a defendant who illegally had killed a brown bear he stated, "In my mind these offenses are no more serious than a moderate traffic offense, like speeding."[149] Such attitudes of the judiciary may serve to encourage, not deter, poaching behavior. Through effective judicial education about the rapid depletion of wildlife resources combined with education about the importance of laws to protect wildlife and about innovative sentencing techniques, the attitudes of judges and prosecutors may change.

Enforcement agents also argue that prosecutors should prepare more and better cases against wildlife violators. USFW Agent Jim Stinebaugh recommends having each U.S. Attorney's office designate one person to handle wildlife cases so that enforcement officers do not have to reiterate the importance of prosecuting wildlife law violators to different government attorneys. "This wouldn't overburden the system. It would just involve one person spending more time with wildlife cases," Stinebaugh said.[150]

It has been suggested that mandatory penalties for wildlife violations may solve the problem of community and political pressure affecting state judges and prosecutors. It is also possible, however, that mandatory sentencing could result in judges choosing to impose no convictions at all. Others suggest that, in combination with education, judges must be given greater discretion to assess appropriate penalties. Uniform penalties do not always adequately reflect the crime, and slight penalties do not deter future violations. Federal Magistrate Judge Wynne stated, "In the event of a conviction, sentences should vary with the offense and with the offender. I, personally, do not believe that fines are very effective. The wealthy can afford to pay a fine without much problem, and it is the family of the poor that directly suffers rather than the violator."[151]

Furthermore, Magistrate Wynne has witnessed the benefit of using innovative sentencing techniques to alter attitudes. First, she insists upon mandatory court appearances to establish the severity of the violation in the mind of the poacher. She also uses probationary measures like community service hours to rehabilitate wildlife law violators. Often this includes watching videos and even participating in the making of videos about poaching. According to Wynne, the video program has proven to be an effective tool in Louisiana to educate and rehabilitate all types of poachers into advocates of wildlife conservation.[152]

Improve the Relationship Between Law Enforcement and the Public

Law enforcement is an effective deterrent in itself because it creates incentive among hunters to abide by the law for fear of retribution if they get caught. However, some hunters perceive that certain law enforcement officers are overzealous in their enforcement responsibilities, causing a division between these agents and the sporting community. Educating law enforcement agents about the importance of maintaining a good relationship with the sporting community and increasing agents' involvement with the sporting community can be effective tools in bringing about compliance with wildlife laws.

Post-season interviews with waterfowl hunters revealed that the personality and attitude of the local game wardens were key factors in whether hunters violated the law. "Given respect for the individual, they (waterfowl hunters) choose not to violate. Without respect, violating becomes a way to test and defy the authority."[153] Laurence R. Jahn of the United Conservation Alliance calls this "community policing." Jahn states that this form of enforcement "hinges on the philosophy that a good officer knows the community and knows enough to be able to solve problems, rather than just react to them. An officer's priority task is to involve local people and gain their support for the good of themselves and their communities."[154] Jackson notes that wildlife professionals often alienate sportspersons by not involving them in department programs. He stated, "My point, of course, is that the agency, by denying involvement, is throwing away the most effective strategy we have in developing the stewardship and responsibility that it wants to develop in its citizenry."[155]

Educate the Sporting Community

Studies on convicted poachers reveal that most are experienced sportsmen. Unfortunately, they lack the knowledge or motivation to be good stewards of wildlife. State wildlife agencies are hopeful that incorporating ethics into hunter education programs will help reverse this trend. All states currently have hunter education programs, and nearly all states have made attendance a requisite to obtaining a hunting license (see tables in Chapter 5). Ethics are now part of the educational materials in every state. The importance of emphasizing ethics in these programs is valuable not only as a deterrent to wildlife law violations but also to preserve the integrity of the hunting tradition. Furthermore, statistics show that hunting accidents decrease in states where hunter education programs are mandatory. Though most hunter education programs are available for children 11 or 12 years of age, many children learn to violate wildlife laws at an earlier age. This probably indicates that wildlife protection and hunting education programs must start even earlier (see discussion below).

Hunter education programs have also been advocated under the belief that no time is too late to change attitudes. Professor Jackson wrote, "I often hear calls for programs that will focus all efforts in teaching responsibility on the very young. No way! I have changed as an adult... I changed when my kids said, 'Dad, why do you do that?' I have become a more responsible hunter. So can any adult."[156] It has been recommended that states amend their laws to require **all** hunters to go through hunter education programs.

Educate Youth

Incorporating programs on conservation and hunting ethics into the school systems as early as kindergarten would provide another means to affect attitudes on a broader scale. Even children who will not be hunters should learn to be stewards of wildlife because wildlife belongs to every citizen. Furthermore, an informed public creates peer pressure to compel responsible behavior.

A study done in Nova Scotia illustrates the importance of educating children. In this study the children of known poachers were educated about the importance of conservation and protection of wildlife. Subsequently, the newly formed attitudes of the children profoundly altered their parents' attitudes about wildlife as well. The result of this strategy, among several others, was the increase in seabird populations because of decreases in poaching practice.[157]

Create a Vested Interest

USFW Agent Hall and Professor Jackson both advocate the theory that a person needs to have a "vested" or personal interest in something before he or she will care for it. As our society becomes increasingly urbanized, individuals become more isolated from wildlife. This includes the urban sportsperson who recreates but does not live in proximity to the outdoors. Hall and Jackson believe that by making hunters feel they have a vested interest in the land, they will become more responsible for wildlife resources.[158]

For example, if hunters could become more active in the wildlife regulation process, they not only would feel more informed about the laws but would likely feel an added sense of responsibility in upholding laws they helped to create. "Most people are more likely to abide by a law they believe in and understand than one they don't."[159] African countries have used this incentive methodology to restore and perpetuate healthy populations of wildlife. The propagation of game farms is taking hold throughout the African continent in which private individuals or communities allow regulated hunting of wildlife on the ranges. Turning wildlife into a valuable commodity creates an incentive to preserve and protect species and habitats. This system of creating a vested interest in wildlife, though in Africa it is largely a commercial interest, has been astoundingly effective in supporting populations of wildlife.[160]

Involve the Media

The media can be very effective in educating the public about the role of stewardship that humans must take to protect wildlife resources. The media then are another vehicle for creating a vested interest in wildlife, particularly among the nonhunters. The USFW, in its attempt to educate the public, develops brochures and fact sheets, works with the media in coverage of enforcement efforts, gives presentations, uses direct mailings, creates airport displays, and donates forfeited property to educational programs and museums.[161]

Sporting magazines could also be encouraged to include conservation and ethics material in their literature. Delwin E. Benson of the Colorado State University Department of Fishery and Wildlife Biology discovered that hunters rely heavily on hunter magazines to increase their knowledge about hunting. However, a 1991 study of 193 articles from three major hunting magazines revealed that the majority of articles covered information on species hunted, hunting techniques and places to hunt. Rarely were hunting ethics discussed.[162]

Agent Dave Hall capitalizes on the importance the media can play in changing attitudes in his region of the country. Publicizing the stories of "converted" poachers affects those in the community who consider the poacher to be a folk hero. When poachers confess the error of their ways and make public commitments to abide by the law, they make a significant impact on the attitudes and behaviors of other hunters. Further, Hall believes that once hunters are convinced that wildlife is worth protecting and that laws are necessary to protect wildlife resources, then peer pressure will encourage compliance with the laws.[163]

Similarly, a study of waterfowl hunters revealed that fines do not have much impact on violators, but the possibility that their names might appear in the paper as wildlife violators does create an impact. Peer pressure and public attitudes may be very important deterrents to poaching. "A society is law abiding when citizens take responsibility for each other and become directly involved in demanding legal and ethical behavior of others."[164]

PRIORITIES

The ultimate goal of this chapter has been to provide ideas, comparisons and solutions for managers, wildlife professionals, decision-makers and the public to stem the tide of wildlife poaching that is depleting wildlife populations. The information and state law surveys presented in this chapter are only an initial step toward understanding and improving the poaching situation in the United States. Much more work must be done to eliminate motivations to poach. Priorities include creating legislative and regulatory uniformity among the states, educating judges, prosecutors and the public about the seriousness of the problem, and eliminating trade routes and markets for poachers.

ENDNOTES:

1. Personal communication with Terry Grosz, Regional Director, U.S. Fish and Wildlife Service, by Sara Parker, University of New Mexico Center for Wildlife Law (Summer 1992) (on file with the University of New Mexico Center for Wildlife Law).

2. Constance J. Poten, *A Shameful Harvest*, National Geographic 110 (September 1991); Jessica Speart, *A Poacher's Worst Nightmare*, National Wildlife 26 (April-May 1992); Daniel Glick, *New Killing Fields*, Newsweek 55 (July 23, 1990).

3. Vicki Moeser, *'Scotland Yard' for Animals Thwarts Wildlife Crime*, Smithsonian News Service 2 (September 1990); John Gavitt, U.S. Fish and Wildlife Service, *Unlawful Commercialization of Wildlife Parts* (1989) (citing Ginette Hemley, Director, TRAFFIC, USA, World Wildlife Fund).

4. *Asian Markets Foster Uncontrolled Poaching of Black Bears in the U.S.*, 40 Animal Welfare Institute Quarterly 11 (Summer 1991).

5. *Fur Dealers Go to Prison*, 40 Animal Welfare Institute Quarterly 15 (Summer 1991).

6. John Brinkley, *Wildlife Managers Claim Poaching is out of Control*, Rocky Mountain News (December 16, 1991).

7. Poten, *supra* note 3, at 110.

8. David Favre, *Wildlife Law*, at 1-6 (Lupis Publications, 1991).

9. David L. Hall, Gerald J. Bonnaffons & Robert M. Jackson, *Relationship of Enforcement, Courts and Sentencing to Compliance with Waterfowl Hunting Regulations*, Transactions of the Fifty-fourth North American Wildlife and Natural Resources Conference 342 (1989).

10. Judy A. Mills & Christopher Servheen, *Asian Trade in Bears and Bear Parts*, 84 World Wildlife Fund (1991).

11. Gavitt, *supra* note 4, at 4.

12. Poten, *supra* note 3, at 112.

13. Michael Tennesen, *Poaching, Ancient Tradition, and the Law*, Audubon 97 (July-August 1991).

14. Gavitt, *supra* note 4, at 5.

15. Mills & Servheen, *supra* note 11, at 84.

16. *See* Mills & Servheen, *supra* note 11.

17. Kirk H. Beattie, *Warden Perceptions of Hunter Compliance in the United States from 1986-1991*, Proceedings of the International Conference on Improving Hunter Compliance with Wildlife Laws 118 (1992).

18. The Lacey Act, 18 U.S.C. § 42 (Supp. III 1991); 16 U.S.C. §§ 3371-3378 (1988 & Supp. III 1991).

19. Tennesen, *supra* note 14, at 92.

20. Poten, *supra* note 3, at 110; Speart, *supra* note 3, at 26; Glick, *supra* note 3, at 110.

21. Memorandum from Defenders of Wildlife to members, (May 28, 1992) (on file with the University of New Mexico Center for Wildlife Law).

22. Conger Beasley, Jr., *Live and Let Die*, Buzzworm 33 (July-August 1992).

23. Glick, *supra* note 3, at 55.

24. Gavitt, *supra* note 4, at 3.

25. Tennesen, *supra* note 14, at 93.

26. Personal communication with Larry Bell, New Mexico Game and Fish Department by Sara Parker, University of New Mexico Center for Wildlife Law (Summer 1992) (on file with the University of New Mexico Center for Wildlife Law).

27. George Arimond & Robert M. Jackson, *Educational and Psychological Principles for Improving Hunter Compliance*, Proceedings of the International Conference on Improving Hunter Compliance with Wildlife Laws 144 (1992); Robert M. Jackson, Robert Norton & Ray Anderson, *Improving Ethical Behavior in Hunters*, Proceedings of the North American Wildlife Conference 9 (March 1979).

28. Favre, *supra* note 9, at 1-7.

29. Personal communication with David Hall, U.S. Fish and Wildlife Service, Slidell, Louisiana by Sara Parker, University of New Mexico Center for Wildlife Law (Summer 1992) (on file with the University of New Mexico Center for Wildlife Law).

30. Personal communication with Robert M. Jackson, Professor, University of Wisconsin-LaCrosse, by Sara Parker, University of New Mexico Center for Wildlife Law (Summer 1992) (on file with the University of New Mexico Center for Wildlife Law).

31. Ron Glover, *Sociological Profiles of Missouri Deer Poachers: Management Applications*, Transactions of the Forty-ninth North American Wildlife and Natural Resources Conference 108 (1989).

32. Charles S. Potter, Jr., *Making a Difference for Waterfowl - It is Time for the Thinking Waterfowler*, Proceedings of the International Conference on Improving Hunter Compliance with Wildlife Laws 170 (1992).

33. Glover, *supra* note 32, at 108.

34. *Id.*, at 108.

35. Utah Code Ann. § 23.13.2(38)a (Supp. 1992).

36. Ill. Rev. Stat. ch. 520, § 2.2 (1992 Cum. Ann. Pock. Part).

37. Ga. Code Ann. § 27-3-48 (Michie Supp. 1992); Vt. Stat Ann. tit. 10, § 4503 (Cum. Supp. 1992).

38. S.D. Codified Laws Ann. § 41-8-12 (Rev. 1991).

39. Ariz. Rev. Stat. Ann. § 17-309(A)(5) (Cum. Supp. 1991). Arkansas' statute does not require knowing waste. Ark. Code Ann. § 43-237 (Michie 1987).

40. Cal. Fish & Game Code § 2118.3 (1984).

41. Colo. Rev. Stat. Ann. § 33-6-117 (1990) (it is unlawful to remove, with the intent to abandon the body, only the head, hide, claws, teeth, antlers, horns, internal organs or feathers of any wildlife).

42. Ga. Code Ann. § 27-3-43 (1986); S.C. Code Ann. § 50-11-400 (1976).

43. Alaska Stat. § 16.30.010 (Cum. Supp. 1991).

44. *Id.*

45. W. Va. Code § 20-2-5 (Cum. Supp. 1991).

46. Cal. Fish & Game Code § 2005 (1987).

47. Del. Code Ann. tit. 7, § 723 (Repl. Vol. 1991).

48. Wash. Rev. Code Ann. § 77-16-050 (Cum. Supp. 1992).

49. Colo. Rev. Stat. Ann. § 33-6-127 (1990).

50. N.Y. Envtl. Conserv. Law § 71-0921 (1984).

51. N.C. Gen. Stat. § 113-135 (Cum. Supp. 1991).

52. Minn. Stat. Ann. § 97A.225 (1985).

53. Del. Code Ann. tit. 7, § 723 (Repl. Vol. 1991).

54. N.Y. Envtl. Conserv. Law § 71-0921 (Cum. Supp. 1992).

55. Ga. Code Ann. § 27-1-29 (1986).

56. Fla. Stat. Ann. §§ 372.662, 372.99 (Cum. Supp. 1991).

57. N.C. Gen. Stat. § 113-294 (Cum. Supp. 1991).

58. Idaho Code § 36-501 (Cum. Supp. 1991).

59. Ill. Rev. Stat. ch. 61, § 2.36 (Cum. Supp. 1992).

60. W.Va. Code § 20-2-11 (Repl. Vol. 1989).

61. Conn. Gen. Stat. Ann. § 26-78 (1958).

62. Ill. Rev. Stat. ch. 61, § 2.36 (Cum. Supp. 1992).

63. Ariz. Rev. Stat. Ann. § 17-309 (Cum. Supp. 1991).

64. Colo. Rev. Stat. Ann. § 33-6-113 (1990).

65. S.D. Codified Laws Ann. § 41-14-32 (Rev. 1991).

66. Poten, *supra* note 3, at 100, 117.

67. Ala. Code § 9-11-255 (Cum. Supp. 1991).

68. Cal. Fish & Game Code §§ 2346, 2347 (1984); R.I. Gen. Laws § 20-14-4 (1989).

69. Del. Code Ann. tit. 7, § 717 (Repl. Vol. 1991).

70. Ariz. Rev. Stat. Ann. § 17-309 (Cum. Supp. 1991).

71. Ark. Code Ann. § 44-103 (1987).

72. Ark. Code Ann. § 44-107 (bears, deer or their parts, turkeys); Cal. Fish & Game Code §§ 2118.2 (elk), 2350 (deer, game birds or their parts) (1984).

73. Ala. Code § 9-11-255 (Cum. Supp. 1991).

74. N.D. Cent. Code § 20.1-01-16 (Repl. Vol. 1991).

75. Ark. Code Ann. § 44-106 (1987).

76. Ill. Rev. Stat. ch. 61, § 2.36 (Cum. Supp. 1992).

77. Cal. Fish & Game Code § 2225 (1984).

78. Va. Code Ann. § 19.2-53 (Repl. Vol. 1990); N.Y. Envtl. Conserv. Laws § 71-0907 (1984).

79. Ala. Code § 9-11-303 (1987).

80. Tenn. Code Ann. § 70-6-101 (Supp. 1991).

81. S.C. Code Ann. § 50-3-340 (1976).

82. Tex. Parks & Wild. Code Ann. § 11.019 (1991).

83. Poten, *supra* note 3, at 129.

84. *Id.*, at 124.

85. Ariz. Rev. Stat. Ann. § 17-361 (1956).

86. Idaho Code § 36-603 (Cum. Supp. 1991).

87. Ga. Code Ann. § 27-2-9 (Cum. Supp. 1991).

88. Ariz. Rev. Stat. Ann. § 17-362 (1956).

89.   Pa. Cons. Stat. § 34-924 (Pamp. 1992).

90.   Tenn. Code Ann. § 70-4-201 (Supp. 1991).

91.   Ariz. Rev. Stat. Ann. § 17-309 (Cum. Supp. 1991).

92.   Colo. Rev. Stat. Ann. § 33-6-113 (1990).

93.   Fla. Stat. Ann. §§ 372.662, .671, .99 (Cum. Supp. 1991).

94.   W.Va. Code § 20-2-5 (Cum. Supp. 1992).

95.   N.D. Cent. Code § 20.1-0602 (Repl. Vol. 1991).

96.   R.I. Gen. Laws § 20-2-13 (1989).

97.   Me. Rev. Stat. Ann. tit. 12, § 7079 (Cum. Supp. 1991).

98.   Conn. Gen. Stat. Ann. § 26-61 (Cum. Supp. 1992).

99.   Alaska Stat. §§ 16.30.010, .015 (Cum. Supp. 1991).

100.   Colo. Rev. Stat. Ann. § 33-6-117 (1990).

101.   Va. Code Ann. § 29.1-523 (Repl. Vol. 1992); Conn. Gen. Stat. Ann. § 26-61 (Cum. Supp. 1992); Tenn. Code Ann. § 70-4-110 (Supp. 1991); Del. Code Ann. tit. 7, § 723 (Repl. Vol. 1991).

102.   Or. Rev. Stat. § 497.435 (Supp. 1992).

103.   Wash. Rev. Code Ann. § 77.21.070 (Cum. Supp. 1992).

104.   Ariz. Rev. Stat. Ann. § 17-314 (Cum. Supp. 1991).

105.   Colo. Rev. Stat. Ann. § 33-6-106 (1990).

106.   Pa. Cons. Stat. § 34-925 (Pamp. 1992).

107.   Tex. Parks & Wild. Code Ann. § 12.507 (1991).

108.   Vt. Stat. Ann. tit. 10, § 5403 (1984).

109.   Del. Code Ann. tit. 7, § 747 (Repl. Vol. 1991).

110.   Me. Rev. Stat. Ann. tit. 12, §§ 7110, 7233, 7234, 7237 (1964 & Cum. Supp. 1991).

111.   Ga. Code Ann. § 27-3-26 (Cum. Supp. 1991).

112.   Ark. Code Ann. § 43-229 (1987).

113.   Haw. Rev. Stat. § 183D-11 (Supp. 1989).

114.   W.Va. Code § 20-2-14 (Repl. Vol. 1989); Utah Code Ann. § 23-13-13 (Repl. Vol. 1991); Cal. Fish & Game Code § 2118.3 (1984).

115.   Tenn. Code Ann. § 70-6-105 (Repl. 1987); Tex. Parks & Wild. Code Ann. § 12.304 (1991); Me. Rev. Stat. Ann. tit. 12, § 7902 (1964).

116.   Colo. Rev. Stat. Ann. § 24-60-2501 (1990).

117.   Or. Rev. Stat. § 497.415 (Supp. 1992).

118.   R.I. Gen. Laws § 20-1-17 (1989).

119.   Ill. Rev. Stat. ch. 61, § 4.3 (Cum. Supp. 1991).

120.   United States General Accounting Office, *Wildlife Protection: Enforcement of Federal Laws Could Be Strengthened*, Report to Congressional Requesters 11 (1991)

121.   Endangered Species Act, 16 U.S.C. § 1533e (Supp. III 1991).

122.   United States General Accounting Office, *supra* note 125, at 16.

123.   The Lacey Act, *supra* note 19.

124.   Statistics from the New Mexico Department of Game and Fish, 1992.

125.   Statistics from the Missouri Department of Conservation, 1992.

126.   Personal communication with Harold Oates, Texas Parks and Wildlife Department by Sara Parker, University of New Mexico Center for Wildlife Law (Summer 1992) (on file with the University of New Mexico Center for Wildlife Law).

127.   Poten, *supra* note 3, at 131; Glick, *supra* note 3, at 34-44.

128.   David L. Hall, *Hunter Compliance in North America Past, Present and Future*, Proceedings of the International Conference on Improving Hunter Compliance with Wildlife Laws 26 (1992).

129.   Personal communication with Terry Grosz, Regional Director, U.S. Fish and Wildlife Service by Sara Parker, University of New Mexico Center for Wildlife Law (Summer 1992) (on file with the University of New Mexico Center for Wildlife Law).

130.   John Brinkley, *Losing the War for Wildlife*, Rocky Mountain News (December 15, 1991).

131.   Hall, Bonnaffons & Jackson, *supra* note 10, at 350.

132.   United States Fish and Wildlife Service, *Report of Finding and Recommendation* 18 (June 1992).

133.   Personal communication with John Cross, United States Fish and Wildlife Service, Albuquerque by Sara Parker, University of New Mexico Center for Wildlife Law (Summer 1992) (on file with the University of New Mexico Center for Wildlife Law).

134.   United States General Accounting Office, *supra* note 121, at 5.

135. Personal communication with Jim Stinebaugh, United States Fish and Wildlife Service, Texas by Sara Parker, University of New Mexico Center for Wildlife Law (Summer 1992) (on file with the University of New Mexico Center for Wildlife Law).

136. Hall, *supra* note 129, at 24.

137. Tennesen, *supra* note 14, at 92.

138. Hall, *supra* note 30.

139. Arimond & Jackson, *supra* note 28, at 146.

140. Cross, *supra* note 134.

141. *Congress Looks at Wildlife Law Enforcement,* 41 Animal Welfare Institute Quarterly 11 (Winter 1992).

142. Thomas Harelson, *Streamlining Waterfowl Enforcement,* Proceedings of the International Conference on Improving Hunter Compliance with Wildlife Laws 153 (1992).

143. Gavitt, *supra* note 4, at 10.

144. Gavitt, *supra* note 4, at 10.

145. Ron Glover, *Locations and Timing of Closed-Season Deer Poaching Incidents in Missouri,* Transactions, Missouri Academy of Science 17, 88 (1983).

146. United States General Accounting Office, *supra* note 121, at 30.

147. Brad Knickerbocker, *On the Trail of Wildlife Crime,* Christian Science Monitor 12 (September 11, 1990).

148. United States Fish and Wildlife Service, *Report of Finding and Recommendation,* 19 (June 1990).

149. Hall, Bonnaffons & Jackson, *supra* note 10, at 343.

150. Stinebaugh, *supra* note 136.

151. Michaelle Pitard Wynne, *View from the Judiciary,* Proceedings of the International Conference on Improving Hunter Compliance with Wildlife Laws 56 (1992).

152. *Id.,* at 25.

153. Jackson, Norton & Anderson, *supra* note 28, at 27.

154. Laurence R. Jahn, *Summary: Management and Hunter Compliance,* Proceedings of the International Conference on Improving Hunter Compliance with Wildlife Laws 98 (1992).

155. Arimond & Jackson, *supra* note 28, at 60-61.

156. *Id.,* at 59.

157. Kathleen A. Blanchard, Remarks given to the Environmental Education Workshop, St. Paul, Minnesota (September 24, 1991).

158. Personal communication with David L. Hall & Robert M. Jackson by Sara Parker, University of New Mexico Center for Wildlife Law (Summer 1992) (on file with the University of New Mexico Center for Wildlife Law).

159. F. D. Mike Stone, *Hunter Education in Colorado: A Model for Teaching Compliance,* Proceedings of the International Conference on Improving Hunter Compliance with Wildlife Laws 102 (1992).

160. Marilyn Achiron, *Making Wildlife Pay Its Way* 46-51.

161. United States Fish and Wildlife Service, Division of Law Enforcement, *FY 1990 Annual Report* 3 (1990).

162. Delwin E. Benson, *The Real Problem: Delivery Systems for Advanced Hunter Education,* Proceedings of the International Conference on Improving Hunter Compliance with Wildlife Laws 111 (1992).

163. Hall, *supra* note 30.

164. Robert Jackson & Robert Norton, *Someone is Watching You Hunt* 15.

PART II

STATE WILDLIFE LAWS

Chapter 4

STATE SUMMARIES

In this Chapter, we have attempted to condense each state's wildlife statutes into a relatively short summary of 10 to 20 pages, following an outline of main outline headings and subheadings (see Chapter 1, "How to Use This Handbook" for further details). Although there is unlimited variation in specific statutory details between states, we found that most statutes fit into the following broad outline categories with comparatively little overlap. Where overlap occurs, we have tried to cross-reference to other sections as appropriate. With few exceptions, the statutes for each state have been categorized under the following major headings and subheadings:

STATE WILDLIFE POLICY
RELEVANT WILDLIFE DEFINITIONS
STATE FISH AND WILDLIFE AGENCIES
    Agency Structure
    Agency Powers and Duties
    Agency Regulations
    Agency Funding Sources
    Agency Advisory Boards
PROTECTED SPECIES OF WILDLIFE
GENERAL EXCEPTIONS TO PROTECTION
HUNTING, FISHING AND TRAPPING PROVISIONS
    General Provisions
    Licenses and Permits
    Restrictions on Taking: Hunting and Trapping
    Restrictions on Taking: Fishing
    Commercial and Private Enterprise Provisions
    Import, Export and Release Provisions
    Interstate Reciprocal Agreements
ANIMAL DAMAGE CONTROL
ENFORCEMENT OF WILDLIFE LAWS
    Enforcement Powers
    Criminal Penalties
    Civil Penalties
    Illegal Taking of Wildlife
    License Revocations and Suspensions
    Reward Payments
    Intoxication Testing of Hunters
HABITAT PROTECTION
NATIVE AMERICAN WILDLIFE PROVISIONS

ALABAMA

Sources: Code of Alabama, 1975, Title 9; 1987 Replacement Volume; 1992 Cumulative Supplement.

STATE WILDLIFE POLICY

The title to freshwater fish and to all wild birds and wild animals in the state of Alabama is vested in the state for regulating the use and disposition of the same in accordance with the laws of the state (9-11-81 and -230).

RELEVANT WILDLIFE DEFINITIONS: See Definitions section of Appendices.

See also PROTECTED SPECIES OF WILDLIFE.

STATE FISH AND WILDLIFE AGENCIES

Agency Structure

The **Department of Conservation and Natural Resources** (Department) is an executive and administrative department bringing together under one department effective control over the state's natural resources, parks and monuments and historical sites (9-2-1). The Department is headed by the **Commissioner of Conservation and Natural Resources** (Commissioner), appointed by the Governor, who advises the Governor and the legislature in matters relating to the state's wildlife and natural resources and to the discovery, development, protection and conservation thereof (9-2-5). Within the Department there is a **Game and Fish Division** (Division), headed by the **Director of the Division of Game and Fish** (Director), appointed by the Commissioner with the Governor's approval (9-2-60 and -61). The Commissioner has the power to appoint as many **Game and Fish Wardens** (Wardens) to enforce the game and fish laws (9-2-64).

Agency Powers and Duties

The general functions and duties of the **Department** are to: ▸ protect, conserve and increase the state's wildlife and administer laws relating to wildlife and the protection, conservation and increase thereof; ▸ make surveys and studies concerning state wildlife and publish reports thereon; ▸ maintain, supervise and operate state lands other than those committed to the specific use of another department; ▸ enter into cooperative agreements with federal and state agencies on wildlife restoration projects, developing educational programs, the collection and publication of data on wildlife, state parks and monuments, and enforce regulations relating to agreements; ▸ carry on a program of education and public enlightenment on the wildlife and other natural resources; ▸ report activities to the Governor and make recommendations to the legislature regarding wildlife legislation (9-2-2).

The **Commissioner** has the power and authority to carry out the functions and duties of the Department and enforce and administer laws providing for the preservation, protection, propagation and development of wild birds, wild fur-bearing animals, game fish, saltwater fish, shrimp, oysters and other shellfish, crustaceans and other species of wildlife not in private ownership. The Commissioner is empowered to: ▸ formulate a state wildlife policy; ▸ fix open seasons for the taking of game birds, game and fur-bearing animals, and fix daily and season bag limits; ▸ designate the game fish species; ▸ regulate the manner, means and devices for catching or taking game fishes, game birds, game and fur-bearing animals and the manner, means and devices for catching or taking other species of fish not designated as game fish; ▸ close the season of a species of game in an area or county when necessary to the conservation and perpetuation of the species, and reopen seasons as advisable; ▸ designate by name animals classed as game or fur-bearing animals and the time, manner, means and devices for taking same; ▸ introduce desirable species of game, fish and birds (9-2-6 and -7). With the Governor's approval, the Commissioner may create additional divisions as needed for the Department to carry out its duties (9-2-11).

The **Director** of the Division has the personnel, powers, properties, functions and duties of the Department which pertain to game and fish and those as may be conferred by law, and supervises and directs the Division (9-2-61).

The Director shall: ▸ constantly keep in touch with wardens; ▸ advise them in their work; ▸ see that duties of wardens are performed; ▸ report derelictions of duty to the Commissioner; ▸ assist in the prosecution of Department laws; ▸ perform other duties as directed by the Commissioner (9-2-65).

Game and Fish Wardens have the power to: ▸ enforce laws relating to animals, birds and fish; ▸ execute warrants and search warrants for violation of game, fish and fur laws; ▸ carry firearms as provided by law for enforcement officers; ▸ confiscate game, birds, animals or fish or parts illegally caught, taken, killed or held, shipped or transported, the seized wildlife or parts to be held as evidence and disposed of by written court order; ▸ enter upon land or water in performance of duties; ▸ assist citizens, clubs and groups of sportsmen by furnishing information and other assistance for the construction of fish ponds, establishing feeding grounds for migratory wild fowl, planting fish from state/federal hatcheries; ▸ reclaim stranded fish, and control predators on useful forms of wildlife (9-2-65).

★**Deputy Game and Fish Wardens** are appointed by the Commissioner and enforce laws relative to wild game birds, animals and fish upon privately owned game preserves and refuges, with no state compensation for expenses and no pay. Deputy wardens must pass a written examination with a score of 70%; must execute a $2,000 bond; give proof of good moral character and reputation; must never have been convicted of a felony or misdemeanor involving force, violence or moral turpitude; must have three letters of recommendation from voters in the area proposed to be served; and submit a letter of consent and authorization from the landowner where the deputy will exercise authority. Deputy wardens shall: ▸ exercise authority on the privately owned land described in the letter of consent submitted with the application; ▸ comply with federal, state and local laws and regulations; ▸ enforce laws and regulations relative to wild game birds, animals, and fish upon the privately owned lands, but no deputy warden shall have the power of arrest for the violation of game and fish laws unless they have met the requirements of this section (9-11-17).★

Agency Regulations

The Commissioner is authorized to make and promulgate regulations not in conflict with the game and fish laws for conservation, protection and propagation of wild game, birds, animals, fish and seafood, which rules and regulations shall have the effect of law. ★The Commissioner shall not make or promulgate regulations which will hamper industry or interfere with the operation of an industrial plant or operation, nor which will hamper or interfere with: the construction of dams impounding private waters as defined by the legislature; the catching, marketing, sale or resale of the fish crop or fish caught or taken from private waters; the maximum development of private waters as a source of food, farm income and recreation in Alabama.★ The Commissioner shall publish in pamphlet form all laws and rules and regulations relating to game, birds, fish, fur-bearers, seafood and other matters over which the Commissioner has authority and supervision, the pamphlet to be received as evidence without further proof of rules/regulations in a state court (9-2-8). The Commissioner shall exercise all rule making powers of the Department, with approval by the Advisory Board of Conservation and Natural Resources, and shall have the power to establish and promulgate rules and regulations subject to the provisions of 9-2-15 (9-2-12).

Agency Funding Sources

The **Game and Fish Fund** (Fund) shall consist of all money received from: ▸ state occupational licenses or privilege taxes on a person, firm or corporation for engaging in a business or activity relating to taking, catching, capturing or killing of a fur-bearing or game animal bird or fish; ▸ a tax, license, permit, certificate, fee or other charge pursuant to game and fish laws or regulations; ▸ administration and enforcement of the game and fish laws and regulations; ▸ fines, penalties and forfeitures pursuant to the game and fish laws; ▸ sale of hunting and fishing licenses or permits; ▸ moneys accruing to the Game and Fish Division (9-2-20).

Within the Fund, there is a **Game and Fish Endowment Fund Account**, consisting of proceeds from sales of lifetime hunting, fishing and combination licenses; gifts, grants and contributions to the state designated for use in said fund; and other sources specified by law. This fund is administered by a board of trustees consisting of the director of finance, the secretary-treasurer of the State Employees Retirement System and the Commissioner, with the power to invest fund assets. This endowment fund is declared to be a special trust between the state and the members of the public whose investments contribute to the fund, and the annual income shall be credited to the Fund (9-2-20.1). Within the Fund, there is a **Nongame Wildlife Endowment Account** with assets to consist of proceeds from the sale of reproductions of prints and/or stamps; proceeds of gifts, grants and contributions to the state designated for inclusion in the account; and other sources specified by law. Administration of the account is by the Game and Fish Endowment Fund trustees. Income derived annually from the Nongame Wildlife Endowment Account shall be credited to the Fund and expended exclusively for preserving, protecting, perpetuating and enhancing nongame wildlife (9-2-20.2). The moneys in the Fund and its various accounts shall be expended by the Commissioner in furtherance of the preservation, protection, propagation and development of wild birds, wild fur-bearing animals, game, fish and all other species of wildlife not in private ownership, including Division and Department administrative expenses as provided by legislative appropriation (9-2-22). The Department shall have no power to issue bonds or borrow money (9-2-24). There is an official annual state nongame wildlife print and/or stamp to be sold by the Department which will contract with an artist for the print/stamp (9-2-66 and -67).

Agency Advisory Boards

The **Advisory Board of Conservation and Natural Resources** (Board) consists of the Governor, the Commissioner of Agriculture and Industries, the Director of the Agricultural Extension Service of Auburn University ex officio and ten other members to be appointed by the Governor, one of whom the Governor shall designate as chairperson. Appointed members shall be selected based on their training and experience in Department activities and shall serve six-year terms. The Commissioner shall be ex officio secretary of the Board (9-2-14). The Board's duties are to: ▸ assist in formulating Department policies; ▸ examine rules and regulations promulgated by the Commissioner and recommend amendments or repeals or additional rules or regulations, and by a two-thirds vote and approval of the Governor amend, repeal or promulgate additional rules or regulations; ▸ advise the Commissioner concerning Department functions; ▸ assist in giving publicity to the wildlife and other natural resources and Department work (9-2-15). The Board shall have the power to promulgate rules and regulations having the force and effect of law to regulate, including to prohibit, the use of an airboat on state public waters that are subject to an ebb and flow of the tide of at least two inches. Violation of airboat regulations: Class C misdemeanor (9-2-15.1).

See also GENERAL EXCEPTIONS TO PROTECTION for information on "wildlife exhibition committee."

PROTECTED SPECIES OF WILDLIFE

The following are game fish: ▸ largemouth and smallmouth black bass, commonly called trout or green trout; ▸ bream, crappie or perch and all other members of the sunfish family, including rock bass or goggle eye, calico bass, warmouth, redbreast, white perch, speckled perch, bluegill and coppernose; ▸ walleye pike, sauger or jack salmon, jack fish or pickerel and all other members of the pickerel and pike families; ▸ white lake bass, commonly called striped bass, yellow bass and other members of the bass family; ▸ saltwater striped bass or rock fish when taken in fresh water (9-11-82). The following are commercial fish or nongame fish: drum, buffalo, channel catfish and all members of the catfish family; spotted sucker and all members of the sucker family, including the species known as red horse and black horse (9-11-83).

No person shall collect a protected wild animal or bird or egg for propagation or scientific purposes except under the direction and regulation of the Commissioner who shall issue permits. Violation: fine of $10-25 for each offense (9-11-231). A person, firm association or corporation who takes, catches, kills or has in possession, living or dead, a protected wild bird not a game bird, or who sells or offers for sale, buys, purchases or offers to buy, purchase or exchange the bird for value, or who sells or exposes for sale or buys the plumage, skin or body of a protected bird, or who takes or willfully destroys nests or possesses nests or eggs, except as provided, is guilty of a misdemeanor and shall be fined $10-25 for each offense (9-11-232).

The flattened musk turtle is a reptile unique to Alabama and the legislature finds protection is required for its survival. It is unlawful to hunt, wound, injure, kill, trap, collect or capture a flattened musk turtle, or sell, purchase or ship the turtle, alive or dead, or its parts, or purchase, transport, ship the animal in interstate, intrastate or foreign commerce. The Department shall permit an act otherwise prohibited for scientific or survival research, zoological exhibition, or education. The prohibitions regarding the killing or injuring of a flattened musk turtle shall not apply where the killing or injuring is incidental to, and not the purpose of, activities which are otherwise lawful. Violation: fine up to $5,000; jail up to one year; or both (9-11-269).

GENERAL EXCEPTIONS TO PROTECTION

English sparrows, crows and starlings are not protected and may be killed (9-11-233). Not withstanding other laws, the Commissioner is authorized to open a season in a county, area or section of the state for the hunting, taking, capturing, killing of female deer or unantlered male deer by regulation for biological reasons, or because of crop damage provided approval of the landowner is obtained (9-11-240).

★A sportsman association in Alabama of not less than 25 members incorporated as a nonprofit association or organization shall possess not more than 10 raccoons at one time during a season of the year, to keep caged, and to use for demonstrating to its members and the general public the respective abilities of the raccoon to resist being retrieved or taken from a log in a lake by a dog and the ability of the respective dogs to retrieve raccoons. The association may take, trap or capture raccoons for the purpose of the demonstrations, the raccoons to be taken, trapped, caught or captured during the open season by licensed hunters, or if taken by trap, by licensed trappers (9-11-247). An association desiring to hold a "coon on the log" show or contest shall obtain a permit from the Commissioner at a cost of $1.50, the money to go to the Game and Fish Fund. The permit is to state number of raccoons held, date of proposed show, and time and place (9-11-248). Violation: misdemeanor; fine of $25-50 (9-11-249).★

The Commissioner may issue a permit to an individual, association or corporation owning property in Alabama to engage in the business of raising game birds and game or fur-bearing animals for propagation under Department rules, for stocking private or protected lands under the permittee's ownership or control. The permittee shall not be authorized to dispose of game or fur-bearing animals propagated under this permit. Violation: forfeiture of the permit; fine of $25-100 (9-11-261).

No person shall possess wildlife in captivity for public exhibition except as provided by statute or Commission regulation (9-11-321). ★The Commissioner shall appoint a committee, not to exceed five in number, of recognized experts in the exhibition, conservation, preservation and humane care of public wildlife to study and recommend standards for the care and treatment of captive wildlife for public display, including sanitation standards (9-11-322).★ Recommendations shall be considered by the Commissioner, who shall issue regulations prescribing standards for care of captive wildlife for public display (9-11-323). The Commissioner may issue an annual permit to a person qualified by education or experience in the care or treatment of wildlife to possess wildlife for public exhibition purpose in accordance with applicable laws and regulations; the permit is to include a description of the proposed facilities to keep the wildlife, the permittee's qualifications or education, a statement of the number of species to be covered by the permit, including the source of the wildlife, and a signed agreement that the Commissioner's regulations and standards for wildlife exhibitors will be adopted and adhered to (9-11-324). If a violation of the permit conditions is discovered, after reasonable notice to abate the violation, the Commissioner may bring an abatement action in an appropriate court (9-11-325). Authorized enforcement personnel may, with or without a warrant, arrest a person who violates provisions or standards in their presence, and may, with a search warrant or as incident to a lawful arrest, search for and seize wildlife possessed in violation of law or of the permit provisions (9-11-326). Anyone who knowingly violates the provisions of this article or a permit shall be fined not more than $500, or imprisoned up to 3 months, or both (9-11-327). These provisions shall not apply to a city, county, state or other publicly owned zoo, privately owned traveling zoo or circus or pet shop (9-11-328).

See also PROTECTED SPECIES OF WILDLIFE and HUNTING, FISHING, TRAPPING PROVISIONS.

HUNTING, FISHING, TRAPPING PROVISIONS

General Provisions

It is unlawful, except as to trapping as otherwise provided by law, for a person to take, capture or kill or attempt to do so, a bird or animal protected by state laws between sunset and daylight of the following day, provided that the Commissioner has the authority, by regulation, to allow the taking, catching or killing of raccoons and opossums between sunset and daylight in state counties; and where taking raccoons and opossums is permitted during nighttime hours, the animals may only be legally taken with the use of a light and/or shotgun using shot no larger than number eight, and the hunter must be accompanied by a dog and have written permission of the landowner. First offense violation: misdemeanor; fine of $250 to $500; revocation of license up to one year at the court's discretion. Second or subsequent offense: fine of $500; mandatory revocation of hunting license privileges; mandatory jail term of 3 to 10 days. No provision of this act prohibits the nighttime hunting of foxes with dogs (9-11-235).

It is illegal to take, catch or kill a bird or animal protected by law or regulation by means, aid or use, directly or indirectly, of bait such as shelled, shucked or unshucked corn or wheat or other grain, salt or other feed whatsoever that has been deposited, placed or scattered so as to constitute a lure or enticement, on or over the area where hunters are attempting to kill or take them, provided that birds or animals may be taken under properly shocked corn and standing grain crops where grain is scattered solely as a result of normal agricultural harvesting (9-11-244).

No person shall make use of pitfall, deadfall, baited field, cage, trap, net, pen, baited hook, snare, poison, explosive or chemical for the purpose of injuring, capturing or killing birds or animals protected by law, provided that nothing in this section shall prevent the trapping of classified fur-bearing animals by a licensed fur catcher. Scaffolds are legal for gun deer hunting only, and for bow hunting of all legal game species (9-11-245). Illegal baiting or use of illegal devices: misdemeanor; fine of $25-100. A second violation: fine of $50-250; jail up to 6 months. A third or subsequent conviction: fine of $100-500; jail up to 6 months. Conviction of illegally baiting for deer or turkey: misdemeanor; fine on the first offense of $250-500; and revocation of all hunting privileges for up to 1 year at the court's discretion. Second and each subsequent violation: fine of $500-2,000; the automatic loss of hunting privileges for 1 year; at the court's discretion, jail for 10 to 30 days (9-11-246).

A person who hunts or discharges a firearm from, upon or across a road, highway, logging roads excepted, or railroad is guilty of a misdemeanor and shall be fined not less than $250. A second or subsequent offense: fine of $500; revocation of license for one year (9-11-257). ★If a person hunting deer at night kills a horse, mare, colt or other domestic animal, the person is liable for double damages in a civil action instituted by the owner of the property (9-11-258). ★

Licenses and Permits

Persons between the ages of 16 and 65 who have been residents for at least 90 days, and who are not serving in the US armed forces during a time of war, must procure an annual state hunting license (9-11-44). Persons hunting deer or wild turkey on state operated wildlife management areas shall pay a special annual license fee of $3.00 in addition to the statutory license fee (except for residents over age 65), the moneys to go into the Game and Fish Fund to be expended in the operation of the game and fish program, including acquiring additional conservation officers and expanding public hunting areas. Violation: misdemeanor; fine of not less than three times the license and special license fees cost. Payment of the special deer/turkey management area fee shall be evidenced by a stamp, license, or big game tag system (9-11-45).

Residents of not less than 90 days, between the ages of 16 and 65, shall not take, catch, kill fish in state waters by angling with rod and reel or by use of artificial bait, fly or lure without procuring an annual freshwater fishing license. A resident angling with hook and line in state waters outside their county of residence must have a freshwater fishing license (9-11-53). Landowners and immediate family members need no hunting license to hunt on their own lands (9-11-44). Persons under age 16 need no fishing license. Residents over age 65 need no fishing license if they carry proof of residence and age while fishing. Reciprocal agreement is available with Florida for residents over age 65 to be exempt from license requirement. No fishing license is required for persons or immediate family to fish on their own lands. No license is required to fish with an ordinary hook and line in one's county of residence if carrying proof of residence, nor to fish in commercial fee fishing ponds (9-11-53). Nonresidents age 16 or older must have a fishing license (9-11-55). Lifetime resident hunting, fishing, or hunting/fishing combination licenses are available (9-11-65).

Restrictions on Taking: Hunting and Trapping

It is unlawful to hunt, take, catch or kill a bird or animal protected by state game laws or regulations on land designated as a state or federal game sanctuary or refuge. Violation: misdemeanor; fine of $250-500, the fine amount to be fixed, determined and imposed at the court's discretion (9-11-234). Raccoons or opossums may be legally hunted and taken at night by catching or killing with the use of dogs, a light and a 22 cal. rimfire rifle or pistol or a shotgun using No. 6 shot or smaller size (9-11-235.1). Hunting, pursuing, killing a wild turkey with the aid of a dog is a misdemeanor, and a fine of $25-50 for each offense (9-11-238).

A person who hunts, traps, captures, injures, kills or destroys wild game on the lands of another during the day without the written permission of, or accompanied by, the landowner is guilty of a misdemeanor and shall be fined on the first offense not less than $250, and at the discretion of the court may have all hunting license privileges revoked for up to one year. A second offense: fine of not less than $500; revocation of all hunting license privileges for one year; jail for 10-30 days (9-11-241). The same provisions apply to a person who hunts, traps, captures, injures, kills or destroys wild game on the lands of another during nighttime hours without the landowner's permission, provided that this section does not apply to raccoon and opossum hunting with dogs only nor to fox hunting with dogs exclusively (9-11-242). A person who hunts, traps, captures, injures, kills or destroys a fur-bearing animal on or in a river, creek or pond running through property not the person's own, within 10 feet of the banks thereof, without the written permission of the owner is guilty of a misdemeanor, with a fine of $10-50 for each offense (9-11-243).

It is unlawful to take or catch deer, whether dead or alive, from the public waters or to take, capture or kill deer at night by any means or device, including, but not limited to, the use of any type of light (9-11-250 and -251). Violation: misdemeanor; fine of $500 on the first offense; revocation of hunting license privileges for 1 year; and mandatory jail for 3 to 10 days. A second conviction: misdemeanor; fine of $1,000; revocation of hunting license privileges for 3 years; mandatory jail for 10 to 30 days. A third or subsequent conviction: misdemeanor; fine of $1,000; revocation of hunting license for 5 years; mandatory jail term of 30 to 60 days (9-11-252).

No person using traps for taking fur-bearing animals shall set in one day more than 150 traps. Violation: misdemeanor; fine of $10-25 for each offense (9-11-254). It is unlawful to trap on or from a state highway right-of-way without the permission of adjoining landowners (9-11-265). All traps set in or beneath water must be checked at least once every 72 hours. Other traps must be checked at least once every 24 hours. It is unlawful to hang or suspend bait over or within 25 feet of a steel trap (9-11-266). ★A person shall be strictly liable for civil damages who causes the injury or damage to a person or domestic animal as a result of using a trap or similar device to take, capture or kill protected fur-bearing animals. A person suffering injury or damage to his or her person or domestic animal as a result of the activity shall have an action for civil damages and need not prove negligence (9-11-264).★ Persons licensed to trap fur-bearing animals shall file with the Division report listing by county the number and type of animals trapped during the preceding season and the names and addresses of persons/companies to whom the furs were sold; fur dealers must keep records of from whom furs were bought. Violation of 9-11-265, 9-11-266 and 9-11-267: misdemeanor; fine $50-200 (9-11-267 and -268).

Restrictions on Taking: Fishing

It is unlawful to take, catch or kill game fish by other than ordinary hook and line, artificial lure, troll or spinner in state public waters. Violation: misdemeanor; fine of $25-100 (9-11-87). It is unlawful to take, catch, kill game or nongame fish by use of a gill, trammel or similar type net in certain specified waters. Violation: misdemeanor; fine of $100-500; or jail for 6 months; or both (9-11-88). It is unlawful to use game fish for fish bait (9-11-89). It is lawful to use the following species of the sunfish family for bait: bluegill, redear sunfish, green sunfish and/or other species of bream, provided that no person may have in possession sunfish or bream in excess of the daily creel limit regardless of size (9-11-90). It is unlawful to take, catch or kill fish by use of a seine, net, trap or a similar device which may be used for catching, killing or stunning fish or by the use of hook and line, rod and reel or by use of dynamite or other explosives or by the use of poison, poisonous substance, fishberries, lime or other deleterious matter in a private pond or private lake, except as provided in this section. Violation: misdemeanor; fine of $25-100. Violation for seining, netting, dynamiting or poisoning fish in private bodies of water: fine $200-500; jail or hard labor for the county for not more than 6 months at the court's discretion. These provisions do not apply to the owner of a private pond or lake, the owner's family or agent, nor to a federal or state agent engaged in research, restocking or rescue work, nor a private fish culturist with a written permit from the pond owner. Fine moneys are to go the Department Game and Fish Fund (9-11-91).

It is unlawful for a person to fish or take fish from a fish farm without consent of the owner. A person possessing fishing tackle on the premises of a fish farm shall be rebuttably presumed to be fishing. A motor vehicle, or fishing tackle or other fishing equipment which has been or is used for illegal fishing shall be contraband, and may be forfeited to the county wherein the violation occurred at the court's discretion, the proceeds of the sale of condemned property to go the credit of the county. Violation: misdemeanor; fine of $500-1,000; jail at court's discretion up to 1 year; or both. Subsequent violations: fine $1,000-2,000; mandatory jail term of 30 days to one year (9-11-91.1).

★A person who by means of traps or obstructions other than dams prevents the passage of fish up the waters of a river or creek must be fined not more than $100, but it is not unlawful to erect or maintain a dam on a nonnavigable stream for the impounding of private waters for the production of fish for food and recreation or for the furtherance of a lawful business without providing or maintaining means for the passage of fish up the stream (9-11-92).★ See also Agency Regulations under STATE FISH AND WILDLIFE AGENCIES.

A person who takes, catches or kills or attempts such by depositing in a public stream or public body of water a poison, poisonous substance, fishberries, lime or other deleterious or poisonous matter, or who takes, catches or kills fish by the use of giant powder, dynamite, gunpowder or other explosive substance must be fined not less than $50-200, the fine to go to the Game and Fish Fund (9-11-93). It is unlawful to take, catch, stun or kill game or nongame fish by means other than those allowed by Department law or regulation. Violation: fine $50-500. A second violation: misdemeanor; mandatory fine of $200-500; jail up to 6 months at the court's discretion. Possession on a public stream bank or in a boat of a device capable of taking, stunning or killing fish shall be prima facie evidence that the device is being used illegally (9-11-94). All money arising under the game and fish article from fines, and forfeitures not otherwise provided for shall go into the Game and Fish Fund (9-11-95).

Species of fish designated by law or regulation as game fish which are taken from public impounded waters or navigable streams by the use of commercial fishing gear shall be immediately returned to the waters without injury (9-11-148). Commercial provisions relating to the licensing of setlines, trotlines or snaglines shall not apply to resident fishermen nor to state or federal agencies conducting research on freshwater fish nor to nonresident fishermen with a state sport fishing license (9-11-155).

The spearing of commercial or nongame fish for sport in state waters, both fresh and salt, shall be lawful, provided that spearfishers shall be completely submerged. "Commercial or nongame fish" shall be limited to those freshwater fish designated by the Department and all species of saltwater fish (9-11-170). (See PROTECTED SPECIES OF WILDLIFE.) A license for commercial/nongame spearfishing is required (9-11-171). The Commissioner may open and close spearfishing of commercial or nongame fish by regulation, and may further regulate spearfishing in the interest of conservation (9-11-173). The possession of a spear, spear gun or spearing device in a boat, on the bank of or in a body of public water is prima facie evidence that the person is engaged in spearfishing, unless the person is frog gigging (9-11-175).

★The Commissioner is authorized to promulgate rules authorizing the taking, catching or killing of nongame fish from state public waters by wire baskets having a mesh of one inch or more, but only upon the written petition of all of the state representatives and state senators from the counties in which said regulations shall be effective, the petitions to specify whether wire baskets shall have one or two inch mesh (9-11-190).★ A wire basket license is required and is not to be issued to persons holding a commercial fishing license, and a person is limited to four basket licenses and to fishing with no more than four baskets (9-11-191 through -193). Only nongame fish may be taken, captured or killed by a basket that may become legal for use under the provisions of this article; game fish are to be returned without injury to water (9-11-196). Violation: misdemeanor; fine $25; revocation of all basket licenses for a period of three years (9-11-198).

Commercial and Private Enterprise Provisions

The Commissioner may issue an annual game breeder's license to raise game birds and game or fur-bearing animals for propagating after thorough investigation of the qualifications, responsibility and equipment of the applicant (9-11-30). A licensee may sell live protected game, game birds or their eggs for propagation provided that the purchaser is made known to the Commissioner before the sale or shipment. The Commissioner may cancel or void the license if it is not used in compliance with these provisions (9-11-31).

A person, firm or corporation may engage in the business of propagating pen-raised quail, commonly known as bobwhite quail, for restocking, propagation and other commercial purposes with a commercial quail breeder's license, and may thereafter sell live quail or their carcasses, including sale for food, either within or without the state (9-11-341 and -342). Pen-raised quail have been hatched from eggs laid by quail confined in a pen or coop, and have been wholly raised in a pen or coop by a licensed quail breeder (9-11-340). Carcasses must be marked, and Department specified invoices attached to a packages of carcasses for shipment (9-11-344 and -345). Violation: misdemeanor, to be punished as provided by law (9-11-351).

A person or firm may operate a hunting or shooting preserve commercially on which artificially propagated birds except turkeys may be hunted, taken, captured or killed with a hunting preserve license. Hunting preserves must be a minimum of 100 acres in one tract, and no larger than 1,000 contiguous acres, the boundaries of which are to be fenced or marked (9-11-410 and -411). Game which may be hunted shall be artificially propagated bob-white quail, pheasants, chukar partridge and other species designated by the Commissioner. A minimum stock of 1,000 quail, or 200 of the other listed species of birds shall be released on the licensed hunting area during each hunting period (9-11-412). No more than 80% of the birds released may be taken during the year by the licensee or licensee's guests, but there is no daily bag limit for pen-raised quail. The pen-raised bird season shall be from October 1 through March 31 (9-11-414). The hunting preserve operator must keep records, and released quail must be tagged (9-11-415 and -416). An Alabama hunting license is required for hunting on licensed hunting preserves, and Department game wardens and other law enforcement officers may enforce all game and fish laws and regulations on the preserves and are authorized to enter and inspect the preserves (9-11-417 and -418).

A person may operate a commercial fee fishing pond from which legally permitted freshwater fish, which are private farm or hatchery produced, may be taken, with a commercial fee fishing pond letter permit. Under no circumstances shall a fishing site be operated on state public waters. Site entrances are to be posted. No license is required to fish at the ponds, and creel limits may be set by the pond operator. No fish caught from the fee fishing site shall be sold or traded. Violation: fine of not more than $250 (9-11-450 through -457).

Import, Export and Release Provisions

The Commissioner may prohibit by regulation the importation of a bird, animal, reptile, amphibian or fish. These provisions do not apply to birds, animals, reptiles, amphibians and fish used for display purposes for carnivals, zoos or circuses where provision is made preventing escape or release. Illegal importation of a bird, animal, reptile, amphibian or fish: fine $50-250 for each offense (9-2-13). It is unlawful to release a tame or other turkey into a wild area, except turkeys kept for normal agricultural purposes or personal consumption. The Department may stock wild turkeys for propagation or research purposes. Violation: punishable under the criminal code (9-11-20).

See also Agency Powers and Duties under STATE FISH AND WILDLIFE AGENCIES.

Interstate Reciprocal Agreements

The Commissioner, with the consent of the Board, may establish bag limits, lengths of seasons and license fees for nonresidents residing in states with reciprocal agreements with Alabama. The annual all game nonresident license shall not be less than $99, nor the trip all game license be less than $50 (9-11-49.1). Nonresident Alabama property owners who pay at least $100 ad valorem property taxes per year shall be treated as Alabama residents for purposes of procuring hunting licenses, but may not procure lifetime licenses (9-11-49.2) It is the intent of the legislature that Alabama enter into a reciprocal agreement with Florida exempting persons over 65 years of age from Alabama fishing and hunting license requirements (9-11-53.3). Residents of Georgia, Florida, Louisiana, Tennessee and Mississippi may get license for the same fee as Alabama residents by means of reciprocal agreements between these states (9-11-55).

The Commissioner shall have authority to enter into agreements of reciprocity with Commissioners of other states bordering Alabama whereby Alabama citizens may take fish from other states' waters upon similar agreements whereby nonresidents are allowed to take fish from Alabama public waters regardless of residence (9-11-210). The Commissioner may enter into agreements with Georgia, Florida, Tennessee and Mississippi whereby valid fishing licenses from any state are honored in the bordering waters between the states (9-11-211). Agreements are to apply separately to the waters lying between Alabama and each agreeing bordering state (9-11-212). Nonresidents shall act in accordance with the laws and regulations of Alabama pertaining to the catching of freshwater fish (9-11-213). The Commissioner may enter into agreements of reciprocity with other states bordering Alabama wherein Alabama citizens may be permitted to hunt and take waterfowl from the waters of other states upon similar agreements whereby nonresidents are allowed to take waterfowl from Alabama waters, with similar restrictions as apply to fishing reciprocity (9-11-280 through -283).

ANIMAL DAMAGE CONTROL

Whenever the Commissioner determines that a reduction in the number of beavers is necessary to the public health and welfare, or for species preservation, or to prevent serious damage resulting from the damming or diversion of public streams by beavers, the Commissioner may open or close a season in a county or section for the killing of beavers and provide for the payment of a bounty of $5 for each beaver killed. The Commissioner is to prescribe regulations to implement these provisions and conditions under which the payment shall be made (9-11-262).

See also GENERAL EXCEPTIONS TO PROTECTION.

ENFORCEMENT OF WILDLIFE LAWS

General Provisions

Unless provided, a violation of the provisions of this title or a regulation approved by the Board shall be a misdemeanor (9-1-4). Making a false statement to obtain a hunting, fishing, fur-bearing animal or seafood license or lending, borrowing, selling, renting or using the license of another to hunt, fish, trap, or deal in furs is a misdemeanor with a fine of $25-50 (9-1-1 and -3).

A hunting accident involving a gun or bow and arrow which results in death and when the death is caused by one person against another, upon the recommendation of the Department, shall be investigated by the grand jury of the county in which the death occurs. Accidents shall be reported by law enforcement officers to the Director within 72 hours of a death, by the coroner and sheriff's department of that county (9-11-21).

Nonresident fishing license violation: fine of $50-250 (9-11-55 and -56). Resident fishing license violation: fine of $50-250 (9-11-53). Resident hunting license violation: fine of $10-25 (9-11-51). Nonresident hunting license violation: misdemeanor; fine of not less than three times the cost of the nonresident license (9-11-51). Fishing without a license in fresh waters: misdemeanor; fine of $10-25 (9-11-57). Transporting of furs, skins or pelts taken without a fur catcher's license: misdemeanor; fine of $25-50 (9-11-61). A violation of fur-dealer license provisions: misdemeanor; fine of $50-300 (9-11-63).

Enforcement Powers

The Commissioner, Commissioner's wardens, agents and employees shall be state peace officers with full and unlimited police power and jurisdiction to enforce the provisions of the game and fish laws and the rules and regulations, and may exercise this power in a state county or in/on state waters or within state territorial jurisdiction (9-11-5). The district attorney of a county in which a violation of the game and fish laws/regulations occurs shall appear on behalf of the state and prosecute the offender (9-11-7). Commission enforcement officers and inspectors have the power and authority of deputy sheriffs and shall arrest without warrant and carry before the district court of the county in which an offense is committed a person violating game and fish laws or regulations (9-11-8). Two or more offenses may be charged in the same affidavit, and proof as to a part of a game bird, animal or fish shall be sufficient to sustain a charge as to the whole of it; the violation as to the number of animals, birds or fish of the same kind may be charged in the same count and punished as separate offenses (9-11-11). The district courts shall be given final jurisdiction to convict game and fish law violators, and they shall remit to the Commissioner each month all fines and forfeitures collected, together with a statement of the name of the person, firm or corporation convicted of the violation, time of conviction, the amount of the fine or penalty, and the specific charge for which the defendant was tried (9-11-6 and -10).

Illegal Taking of Wildlife

It is the duty of the Commissioner or wardens to seize prohibited instruments/devices used to trap, capture and kill fur-bearing animals or fish and to hold them as evidence of illegal use. On conviction, the court shall order the instruments/devices forfeited to the Department for destruction or other disposition (9-11-16).

It is unlawful to sell within this state, or ship or transport for sale within or without this state, or to ship into this state game fish caught or taken in the fresh waters, public or private, of this state or any other state. All species of black bass, white bass, yellow bass, saltwater striped bass, bream and pickerel, as well as walleye, sauger, black and white crappie and yellow perch are designated game fish for purposes of this section. This section does not apply to the sale of game fish raised in hatcheries and sold for stocking purposes, nor to the sale of nonnative game fish raised for food, nor to the sale of largemouth bass, shellcracker and bluegill bream raised in farm ponds, but a permit from the Commissioner is required. Private pond owners may charge for game fish caught by fishermen when the charges are based on number of fish caught or the total pounds caught. Violation: misdemeanor; fine $200-500 (9-11-84). All game fish taken must at all times be carried or transported openly. Violation: misdemeanor; fine $20-25. Game fish carried/transported in an illegal manner or taken or killed illegally shall be confiscated and disposed of under Commission regulations (9-11-85). No person, firm or corporation shall carry, ship or transport beyond the boundaries of this state more than one day's creel limit of game fish, and then only for personal use. Violation: misdemeanor; fine $25-50 (9-11-86).

A person who hunts, takes, catches, captures, kills or has in possession, or who attempts to do so, a bird or animal protected by law or regulation except during open season is guilty of a misdemeanor and shall be fined $50-500, and may be jailed up to 6 months. A second violation: misdemeanor; fine of $100-500; jail up to 6 months. A third or subsequent violation: misdemeanor; fine of $250-500; jail up to 6 months. A person who hunts, takes, catches, captures or kills a wild turkey in an illegal manner or during the closed hunting season, or attempts such, or has in possession a wild turkey killed during the closed hunting season or taken in an illegal manner, is guilty of a misdemeanor and shall be fined $250-500, and may be jailed up to 6 months (9-11-236). A person, firm or corporation who sells, offers or exposes for sale, buys, barters or exchanges anything of value for a game bird or game animal or part is guilty of a misdemeanor and shall be fined $250-500 for each offense, provided that licensed catchers of fur-bearing animals may sell to licensed dealers the furs, skins or pelts of fur-bearing animals lawfully taken, captured or killed, provided that licensed catchers of fur-bearing animals may sell or offer for sale for food the dressed carcass of edible fur-bearing animals named by law/regulation. It shall not be a violation of this section to sell, offer or expose for sale, buy, purchase, or exchange anything of value for: lawfully taken "green" or raw untanned deer hides and their hooves; squirrel skins, hides and tails; finished product items such as gloves, shoes, clothing, jewelry, tanned deer hides and similar products (9-11-237).

A motor vehicle, gun, rifle, ammunition or other hunting equipment used for illegal nighttime deer hunting shall be contraband, and, at the court's discretion, may be forfeited to the state. The sheriff or other authorized person who finds a vehicle being used in illegal nighttime hunting shall seize the vehicle and a gun, rifle or ammunition found in the possession of the person. The proceeds of a property condemned and forfeited to the state shall go to the Game and Fish Fund (9-11-252.1).

It is illegal to take, ship or transport within or without the state protected birds or game unless they are in the personal possession of or are carried openly by the owner or killer, who has in possession the proper resident or nonresident license. Violation: misdemeanor; fine $25-50. A person may transport as baggage or by express not more than two days' bag limit of game birds or animals taken legally and properly tagged. Violation: misdemeanor; fine of $25-50 (9-11-255). Common carriers who ship game birds or animals without ascertaining that the person offering same for shipment has a license to possess them are guilty of a misdemeanor and shall be fined $25-50 (9-11-256). All game, birds or animals taken or killed must be carried or transported openly. Violation: misdemeanor; fine of $10-25; confiscation and disposal of game, birds or animals (9-11-259).

HABITAT PROTECTION

The Commissioner may, with the Governor's approval, by lease, gift or otherwise, acquire title to or control over lands within the state suitable for protection and propagation of game and fish or for public hunting and fishing purposes or to be used otherwise as provided by law, to be known as state game lands. The Director may purchase, erect and equip necessary buildings for propagating game, birds and fish (9-11-2). The title to land acquired by gift or otherwise shall be approved by the attorney general; the title shall vest in the state, and supervision over the lands shall be under the control of the Commissioner (9-11-3). The Commissioner may, on the Governor's approval, establish and maintain state game refuges or sanctuaries for the protection, preservation or propagation of game birds, animals or fish on all or a portion of lands or waters held in fee or trust or under lease by the state, and game birds, animals or fish shall not be hunted, pursued, disturbed or molested. The Commissioner may, with the consent of federal authorities, maintain, develop and utilize for hunting state shooting preserves, game refuges and sanctuaries in national forests or other federal owned lands (9-11-4).

★The Commissioner is authorized to propagate game birds, game and fur-bearing animals; to secure by lease, gift or otherwise lands suitable for their propagation; to expend game and fish revenues to procure buildings, equipment and expert assistance in the breeding and propagation of birds and animals (9-11-260). ★

The Department, through the Commissioner, may establish by proclamation wildlife management areas in the public interest and enter into agreements with the USFS, the US Bureau of Biological Survey, the TVA or other land owners to establish wildlife management areas, the agreements to provide for: ▸ the responsibilities of the Department and the cooperating agency for restocking wildlife species; ▸ planting and cultivation of game and fish foods; ▸ protection of the areas from predatory animals and unauthorized hunting or fishing; ▸ work necessary for the management of area wildlife, including provision for harvesting game and fish crops; ▸ collecting special fees for hunting or fishing on the wildlife management areas, up to 50% of which may go to the cooperating party or agency (9-11-300). The Commissioner is to: set up boundaries; make regulations; establish special open and closed seasons on game animals, game birds and fish; establish fee amounts; and require permits and limit their number for hunting or fishing in management areas (9-11-301). The Commissioner is authorized to: close to all hunting and fishing land or water within the boundary of a management area which is not under a cooperative wildlife management agreement with the Department, provided that at least 90% of the said management area is under an agreement (9-11-302); search without warrant a vehicle, hunting sack or hunting coat within a wildlife management area; confiscate a protected bird, animal or fish found killed or held in violation of the game laws (9-11-303). Carrying or possessing firearms within a wildlife management area without a permit is prohibited (9-11-304).

No unleashed dogs are permitted within a wildlife management area; a violation is a misdemeanor (9-11-305). The Commissioner shall impound dogs found running at large within a wildlife management area, the dogs to be held until claimed by owner or destroyed in accordance with this section. Dog owners are to be notified if possible, and notice published in a paper of general circulation in the county in which the management area is located, allowing dog owners to claim dogs within 21 days of notice by paying an impoundment fee (9-11-306). Violation: misdemeanor; fine $25-100; or jail for 30 days to 1 year; or both (9-11-307).

NATIVE AMERICAN WILDLIFE PROVISIONS: None.

ALASKA

Sources: Alaska Statutes, 1987, Titles 16 and 46; 1992 Replacement Volume.

STATE WILDLIFE POLICY

It is the policy of the state to encourage settlement of its land and development of its resources by making them available for maximum use consistent with the public interest. The Legislature shall provide for the utilization, development and conservation of all natural resources belonging to the state, including land and waters, for the maximum benefit of its people. Wherever occurring in their natural state, fish, wildlife, and waters are reserved to the people for common use. Fish, forests, wildlife, grasslands and all other replenishable resources belonging to the state shall be utilized, developed and maintained on the sustained yield principle, subject to preferences among beneficial uses. The Legislature may provide for facilities, improvements, and services to assure greater utilization, development, reclamation, and settlement of lands, and to assure fuller utilization and development of the fisheries, wildlife and waters (Alaska Const. art. VIII, Sections 1-5).

See HABITAT PROTECTION for legislative statement on wildlife refuges and PROTECTED SPECIES OF WILDLIFE for statement on endangered species.

RELEVANT WILDLIFE DEFINITIONS: See Definitions section of Appendices.

STATE FISH AND WILDLIFE AGENCIES

Agency Structure

The **Commissioner of Fish and Game** (Commissioner) is the principal executive officer of the **Department of Fish and Game** (Department), and shall have knowledge of requirements for the protection, management, conservation and restoration of state fish and game resources, appointed for a five-year term (16.05.010).

The **Commissioner** may, with the Governor's approval, establish within the **Department**, a **Division of Commercial Fisheries**, a **Division of Sport Fisheries**, a **Division of Game**, and other divisions. The Commissioner shall establish a departmental **Division of Fisheries Rehabilitation, Enhancement and Development**. There is established in the Department a **Section of Subsistence Hunting and Fishing** (16.05.090).

For purposes of the conservation and development of state fisheries, there is created the **Board of Fisheries**. For purposes of the conservation and development of state game resources, there is created a **Board of Game** (16.05.221). (See Agency Advisory Boards under this section.)

Agency Powers and Duties

The Commissioner shall: ▸ supervise the Department, appoint division heads, enforcement agents and other employees; ▸ manage, protect, maintain, improve and extend the fish, game and aquatic plant resources in the interest of the economy and well-being of the state; ▸ have the power to accomplish the foregoing, including delegation of authority to Department employees (16.05.020).

The Commissioner has, but is not limited to, the following powers and duties to: ▸ assist the USFW in the enforcing of federal laws/regulations pertaining to fish and game; ▸ acquire by gift, purchase, or lease land, buildings, water, rights-of-way or other real or personal property to further Department objectives; ▸ design and construct hatcheries, rearing ponds, fishways and other projects beneficial for fish and game; ▸ accept money from persons under conditions requiring its use for specific purposes in furtherance of the protection, rehabilitation, propagation, preservation, or investigation of the fish and game resources or in settlement of claims for damages to fish or game resources; ▸ collect and disseminate statistics and data to promote the purposes of this title; ▸ capture, propagate, transport, buy, sell or exchange fish or game or eggs for propagating, scientific or stocking purposes; ▸ to provide public facilities to facilitate taking fish or game and to enter into cooperative agreements to effect them; ▸ construct and operate vessels used by the Department; ▸ establish and charge fees equal to the cost of services provided by the Department, including provision of public shooting ranges, broodstock and eggs for private nonprofit hatcheries, Department publications and fees for the use of Department facilities; ▸ permit and regulate aquatic farming to ensure the protection of fish and game resources and improve the economy, health, and well-being of state citizens; ▸ operate state housing and facilities for employees (16.05.050).

This chapter does not limit the power of the Commissioner to open or close seasons or areas or to change weekly closed periods on fish or game by emergency orders when circumstances require. The Commissioner may increase or decrease sport fish bag limits or modify methods of harvest for sport fish by emergency orders under criteria adopted by the Board of Fisheries. An emergency order has the force and effect of law after field announcement by the Commissioner and is not subject to the Administrative Procedure Act in 44.62 (16.05.060). The Commissioner shall extend the time and dates for fish or game registration if conservation of the fish or game resource will not be adversely affected and the failure to apply timely is the result of excusable neglect as defined by statute (16.05.065).

Fish stocks shall be managed consistent with sustained yield of wild fish stocks and may be managed consistent with sustained yield of enhanced fish stocks. In allocating enhanced fish stocks, the Board shall consider the need of fish enhancement projects to obtain brood stock, and regulate contractors who operate state-owned enhancement projects to harvest and sell fish not needed for brood stock (16.05.730). The Commission shall specify the rivers, lakes and streams that are important for the spawning, rearing or migration of anadromous fish (16.05.870 through .895).

The Commissioner shall designate regions for salmon production and develop and amend a comprehensive salmon plan for each region, including provisions for public and private nonprofit hatchery systems. Subject to Commissioner approval, comprehensive salmon plans shall be developed by regional planning teams consisting of Department personnel and representatives of appropriate regional associations formed under 16.10.380 (16.10.375).

The **Division of Fisheries Rehabilitation** shall: ▸ develop and maintain a comprehensive, coordinated state plan for present and long-range rehabilitation, enhancement and development of all aspects of the state's fisheries for the perpetual use, benefit and enjoyment of citizens; ▸ encourage private investment in the technological development and economic utilization of the fisheries resources; ▸ do all things necessary to insure perpetual and increasing production and use of the food resources of state waters and continental shelf areas; ▸ report annually to the Legislature (16.05.092).

★The **Section of Subsistence Hunting and Fishing** shall: ▸ compile existing data and conduct studies to gather information, including data from subsistence users, on all aspects of subsistence hunting and fishing in the lives of state residents; ▸ quantify the amount, nutritional value and extent of dependence on food acquired through subsistence hunting and fishing; ▸ make information available to the public and appropriate agencies; ▸ assist the Department, the Board of Fisheries and the Board of Game in determining what uses of game and fish, and which users and methods, should be termed subsistence uses, users and methods; ▸ evaluate the impact of state and federal laws on subsistence activities, and make recommendations to the Department for changes; ▸ make recommendations to the Board of Game and the Board of Fisheries regarding adoption, amendment and repeal of subsistence hunting and fishing regulations; ▸ participate with other Divisions in preparing statewide and regional management plans that recognize and incorporate the needs of subsistence users of fish and game (16.05.094).★

The Department shall establish a special program for the raising, maintenance, and release of upland game birds in appropriate areas. Such birds are to be harvested only during regular hunting seasons. The Department shall establish a facility for raising and maintenance of such birds, and shall tag birds, compile harvest statistics, and report results annually to the Legislature (16.05.825).

When the Department finds a surplus in buffalo and musk oxen herds under its positive control, it may grant the surplus to persons, groups, associations, partnerships or corporations for raising and breeding the animals as domestic stock for commercial, scientific and educational purposes. Such a person or group must show an intent to raise and breed the animals and must have facilities for maintaining them under positive control (16.40.010). The sale of buffalo or musk oxen meat from these animals or their offspring is authorized (16.40.020). Recipients of animals shall furnish the Department information regarding status of the animals or offspring as requested (16.40.030).

The Department shall assist in developing and coordinating activities with private organizations relating to shooting and firearms, develop a hunting safety program, and establish a program to assist the planning, construction and operation of public shooting ranges (16.55.010). The Department may provide technical assistance to towns and organizations and make grants to develop public shooting ranges and operate programs involving education and training in the safe use of firearms (16.55.020). The Department may impose restrictions on the use of funds granted (16.55.030). (See also Agency Advisory Boards under this section.)

Agency Regulations

Regulations of a Board or the Commissioner, including emergency openings and closures, are admissible as evidence in state courts (16.05.070). Nothing in this chapter authorizes the Department or Board to change the amount of fees or licenses (16.05.080). The Board of Fisheries and the Board of Game have regulation-making powers as set out in the Fish and Game Code (16.05.010 through .950), but do not have administrative, budgetary, or fiscal powers (16.05.241).

Agency Funding Sources

The Department shall annually produce the **Waterfowl Conservation Stamp,** make stamps available for creation of waterfowl conservation limited edition prints, provide for their sale to the public, and provide for the design selection and production of the annual waterfowl conservation stamp (16.05.826).

There is a **Fisheries Enhancement Loan Program** established to promote enhancement of the state's fisheries through grants for organizational and planning purposes to regional associations that have qualified for long-term, low interest loans for hatchery planning, construction and operation, and for planning and implementing enhancement and rehabilitation activities including lake fertilization and habitat improvement (16.10.500).

There is a revolving **Fish and Game Fund** to be used to carry out the purposes and provisions of this title, except 16.51 and 16.52, or other duties delegated by the Legislature; and purposes and objectives as may be directed by the donor of funds (16.05.100). The Fish and Game Fund consists of: ▸ money received from the sale of state sport fishing, hunting and trapping licenses, special permits, and waterfowl conservation tags; ▸ sale proceeds of furs, skins and specimens taken by predator hunters and employees; ▸ money received in settlement of a claim or loss caused by damage to the fish and game resources; ▸ money received from federal, state or private donors for fish and game purposes; ▸ interest earned; ▸ money from any other source (16.05.110).

Except as provided, money accruing from sport fishing, hunting and trapping licenses or permits may be used only for protection, propagation, investigation and restoration of sport fish and game resources and expenses of these Department divisions. Money from waterfowl conservation tag fees may be used only for: ▸ conservation and enhancement of waterfowl; ▸ acquisition of wetlands for waterfowl and public use of waterfowl; ▸ waterfowl related projects approved by the Commissioner; ▸ administration of the waterfowl conservation program; ▸ emergencies as determined by the Governor. The Department shall report annually to the public and Legislature on the use of money from waterfowl conservation tags and limited edition prints. Money from the sale of resident trapping licenses may be used only for fur-bearer management to enhance the fur-bearer population, increase the productivity of fur-bearer habitats; initiate fur-bearer research, and educate trappers consistent with the goal of providing an optimum fur-bearer population. Revenue from the sale of general hunting, trapping and fishing licenses and tags and federal matching funds shall be allocated to programs intended directly to benefit license purchasers (16.05.130).

The Department, subject to Board of Game regulations, may issue one bison harvest permit each year for a bison from the Delta bison herd through a competitive auction or raffle, and may authorize a nonprofit organization, established to promote fish and game law enforcement, to conduct the auction or raffle. Proceeds, minus costs and a fee, shall go into the Fish and Game Fund. The permit is subject to laws relating to the time, place and manner of taking from the Delta bison herd (16.05.343).

There is a **Fisheries Enhancement Revolving Loan Fund** created within the Department of Commerce and Economic Development only for the purposes of 16.10.500 through 16.10.560. This fund shall be used to make loans to qualified regional associations approved for construction and operation of salmon hatcheries, to make grants for qualified regional associations not exceeding $100,000 per region, and to make loans to regional associations for implementation of fisheries enhancement and rehabilitation activities, including lake fertilization and habitat improvement (16.10.510). A loan may not exceed $10,000,000 for a hatchery or rehabilitation activity under permit to a qualified regional association or local nonprofit corporation approved by such association. A loan for any other nonprofit hatchery corporation project may not exceed $1,000,000 (16.10.520). [Extensive details of loan fund operation, repayment, default or foreclosure, and voluntary assessments on salmon sales by members holding permits are given in the statutes, 16.10.500 through 16.10.560.]

Agency Advisory Boards

There is a **Board of Fisheries** composed of seven members appointed by the Governor, subject to legislative confirmation, for the purpose of conservation and development of fishery resources. Members shall be residents, and appointed on the basis of interest in public affairs, good judgment, knowledge and ability in the field of fisheries, and with a view to providing diversity of interest and points of view. Members shall be residents and appointed without regard to political affiliation or location of residence. The Commissioner is not a member but is ex officio secretary. There is a **Board of Game**, appointed in the same manner, and with the same qualifications and experience, consisting of seven members, for purposes of the conservation and development of the game resources. Members of both boards serve three-year terms. The Boards have regulation-making powers but no administrative, budgeting or fiscal powers (16.05.221 and .241).

The **Board of Fisheries** may adopt regulations to: ▸ set apart fish reserve areas, refuges and sanctuaries in state waters subject to legislative approval; ▸ establish open and closed seasons and areas for fish taking, and restricted areas/seasons for those over age 60 to participate in sport, personal use, or subsistence fishing; ▸ set quotas, bag limits, harvest levels, sex and size limits for fish; ▸ establish means and methods for pursuit, capture, transport of fish; ▸ establish marking and identification requirements for fish; ▸ classify as commercial fish, sport fish, guided sport fish, personal use fish, subsistence fish, or predators or other categories essential for regulatory purposes; ▸ improve watershed and habitat, management protection, and stocking of fish; ▸ investigate the extent and effect of disease, predation and competition among fish and exercise control measures; ▸ prohibit/regulate the live capture, possession, transport or release of native/exotic fish or eggs; ▸ establish seasons and harvest methods for aquatic plants; ▸ regulate license/permit issuance; ▸ regulate commercial, sport, guided sport, subsistence and personal use fishing; ▸ regulate observers on board fishing vessels. Consistent with sustained yield, regulations must provide a fair and reasonable opportunity for taking fish for personal use, sport and commercial purposes. If the Board denies a petition or proposal to amend, adopt or repeal a regulation, it shall, upon written request of the petition sponsor, furnish a written explanation. The Board may allocate fishery resources among personal use, sport, guided sport and commercial fisheries and shall adopt criteria for allocation of these resources, including factors such as: ▸ history of each type of fishery; ▸ number of residents/nonresidents participating in the past; ▸ importance of each fishery for providing residents opportunities to obtain fish for personal/family consumption; ▸ importance of each fishery to regional and local economy; ▸ availability of alternative fisheries resources; ▸ recreational importance; ▸ adoption of a policy for management of mixed stock fisheries consistent with sustained yield of wild fish stocks (16.05.251). The Board may require a person operating a stationary fishing net at a beach or riparian site to be physically present when the fishing gear is in operation (16.05.253).

The **Board of Game** may adopt regulations to: ▸ set aside game reserve areas, refuges and sanctuaries in/on state lands or waters subject to legislative approval; ▸ establish open and closed seasons, areas, means and methods for taking game, including allowance for hunters with physical disabilities; ▸ set quotas, bag limits, harvest levels, and age, sex, and size limitations on game taking; ▸ classify game as game birds, song birds, big game animals, fur-bearing animals, predators or other categories; ▸ set methods, means and harvest levels to control predation and competition among game; ▸ improve watershed and habitat, and manage, conserve, protect, and stock game; ▸ prohibit the live capture, possession, transport or release of native/exotic game or their eggs; ▸ set times and dates for license/permit issuance; ▸ regulate sport hunting and subsistence hunting as needed for game conservation and utilization. The Board of Game must follow similar procedures as the Board of Fisheries when denying a petition to amend, adopt or repeal a regulation. ★Regulations must provide that, consistent with 16.05.258, taking of moose, deer, elk, and caribou by residents for personal or family consumption has preference over taking by nonresidents (16.05.255).★ (See also Licenses and Permits under HUNTING, FISHING, TRAPPING PROVISIONS.)

★★Except in nonsubsistence areas, the Boards shall identify the fish stocks and game populations that are customarily and traditionally taken for subsistence, with recommendations from the Commissioner. The appropriate Board shall: ▸ determine whether a portion of a fish stock or game population so identified can be harvested consistent with sustained yield, and if so, the amount necessary for subsistence uses, and then adopt regulations providing for reasonable opportunities for subsistence uses; ▸ determine opportunities for other uses; ▸ allocate the resources fairly according to statutory guidelines, which include social, economic, population, and cultural considerations (16.05.258). [Extensive details are given for procedure of implementation.]★★

★The Boards may adopt regulations establishing **advisory committees** at places designated by the individual Boards, consisting of persons well informed on fish or game resources of the locality. The Boards shall set the number and terms of each of the advisory committee members, delegate the chairs and give them authority to hold public hearings on fish or game matters.★ Advisory committee recommendations shall be forwarded to the appropriate Board for consideration, which Board shall inform the committee of its reasons if a decision is made to not follow those recommendations. ★The Commissioner shall delegate authority to advisory committees for emergency closures of established seasons, reserving the power to declare such closures null and void (16.05.260).★ The Boards may delegate authority to the Commissioner to act on their behalf for administering regulations, and if there is a conflict between a Board and the Commissioner on proposed regulations, public hearings shall be held, with a final decision to rest with the Governor (16.05.270).

The Commissioner shall assist in and encourage the formation of **regional associations** for enhancing salmon production. A regional association is qualified if the Commissioner determines that it: ▸ is comprised of associations representative of commercial fisherman in the region; ▸ includes representatives of other user groups interested in fisheries within the region; ▸ possesses a board of directors that includes no less than one representative of each member user group. "User group" may include sport fishing, processor, commercial fishing, and subsistence fishing groups and representatives of local communities. A qualified regional association, when it becomes a nonprofit corporation, is established as a service area in the unorganized borough for providing salmon enhancement services (16.10.380). (See also Commercial and Private Enterprise Provisions under HUNTING, FISHING, TRAPPING PROVISIONS.)

An **Advisory Committee on Hunting and Firearm Safety**, consisting of five members appointed by the Commissioner, is established in the Department to advise it in fulfilling responsibilities related to hunting and firearm safety (16.55.040).

PROTECTED SPECIES OF WILDLIFE

The Legislature recognizes that, due to growth and development, certain species or subspecies of fish and wildlife are now, and may be in the future, threatened with extinction. The **Endangered Species Act** establishes a program for their continued conservation, protection, restoration and propagation (16.20.180). On land under their respective jurisdictions, the Commissioner and the Commissioner of Natural Resources shall take measures to preserve the natural habitat of species or subspecies of fish and wildlife that are recognized as threatened with extinction (16.20.185). A species or subspecies is considered endangered when the Commissioner determines that its numbers have decreased such that its continued existence is threatened. The Commissioner shall consider: ▸ the destruction, drastic modification or severe curtailment of its habitat; ▸ its overutilization for commercial or sporting purposes; ▸ the effect on it of disease or predation; ▸ other natural or man-made factors affecting its continued existence. The Commissioner shall publish a list of the species/subspecies that are endangered, and review the list every two years to determine what changes have occurred. Consideration of existing species or subspecies of fish and wildlife for listing shall be made on a continuing basis. The review of listed species shall be submitted in writing to the Governor and Legislature and made available to the public. In making the species list determination and review, the Commissioner shall seek the advice and recommendation of interested persons and organizations, including, but not limited to, ornithologists, ichthyologists, ecologists and zoologists (16.20.190). An endangered species/subspecies of fish or wildlife may not be harvested, captured or propagated except under a special permit issued by the Commissioner for scientific or educational purposes, or for propagation in captivity for preservation (16.20.195).

A person who, without such permit, harvests, injures, imports, exports or captures an endangered species of fish or wildlife is guilty of a misdemeanor (16.20.200). "Fish or wildlife" in this article includes birds (16.20.210).

GENERAL EXCEPTIONS TO PROTECTION

The Commissioner may issue a permit to collect fish and game, including fur animals, for scientific, propagative or educational purposes. The Commissioner shall issue permits for collecting wild fur animals for improving the genetic stock of fur farm animals. Permits shall be in accordance with current sustained yield management practices for such species (16.05.340).

HUNTING, FISHING, TRAPPING PROVISIONS

Licenses and Permits

Whenever necessary so that the opportunity for residents to take big game can be reasonably satisfied in accordance with sustained yield principles, the Board of Game may, through permits, limit taking of big game by nonresidents and aliens (16.05.256).

Except as otherwise permitted, without having the appropriate license/tag in actual possession a person may not engage in: ▸ sport fishing, including taking razor clams; ▸ hunting, trapping or fur dealing; ▸ farming of fish, fur or game; ▸ taxidermy. The Board may adopt regulations for subsistence permits for areas, villages, communities or individuals to regulate the subsistence harvest of fish and game when the subsistence preference requires a reduction of such harvest by nonsubsistence users. ★★A person may not receive a sport fishing, hunting or trapping license or other permit or tag if that person's right to obtain or exercise the privileges granted by a sport fishing, hunting, or trapping license is suspended/revoked in another state (16.05.330).★★

★Reduced license fees are available to residents who have received federal or state welfare assistance during the previous six months. Nonresident and nonresident alien big game tags issued but not used for an animal may be used to satisfy the tagging requirement for another species for which the tag fee is of equal or less value.★ The Board of Game may eliminate the resident brown/grizzly bear or musk oxen tag and fee for all or a portion of a game management unit for a maximum of one year. The Board by regulation shall exempt the requirement of a waterfowl conservation tag for waterfowl hunting in areas not likely to benefit from waterfowl habitat or management programs. A nonresident may not engage in sport fishing for king salmon without a king salmon tag, nor hunt for waterfowl without a waterfowl tag in actual possession (16.05.340). The Commissioner may require reports by licensees concerning the time, manner, and place of taking fish and game, the kinds and quantities taken, and other information for administering fish and game resources (16.05.370).

★Subject to regulations of the Boards, a resident may take fish or game harvested primarily for food on behalf of another person by proxy, including for those who are over age 65, blind, or physically disabled, if the person is licensed for sport or personal use fishing or game. Such person may also simultaneously fish or hunt for the person's own use; the person may not take fish or game by proxy for more than one person at a time (16.05.405).★

Restrictions on Taking: Hunting and Trapping

It is unlawful for a nonresident to hunt, pursue or take brown bear, grizzly bear, mountain goat or sheep unless accompanied by a licensed guide-outfitter or Class A assistant guide-outfitter or assistant guide outfitter, or by a resident over age 19 who is a spouse of or related to the nonresident, including the second degree of kindred by marriage or blood. A nonresident big game tag applicant shall furnish an affidavit showing that the applicant will be accompanied while hunting under the above criteria. Violation: misdemeanor; jail up to one year; or fine up to $5,000; or both (16.05.407). Nonresident alien hunters must be accompanied by a licensed marine mammal guide-outfitter to take marine mammals, and by a guide-outfitter as designated above to hunt, pursue or take a big game animal as defined by the Board of Game. Similar affidavits and permits to hunt on state, federal or private land shall be presented to the Department for nonresident hunters (16.05.408).

The taking of antlerless moose in a game management unit is prohibited except under Department regulations based on biological evidence and after a majority of local advisory committees for that unit have recommended an opening for that year (16.05.780).

★It is a class A misdemeanor, except as provided, to take a brown or grizzly bear within one-half mile of a solid waste disposal facility. In addition to the penalty imposed by law, the court shall order forfeiture of the hide and skull of the bear, but if these are not salvaged and delivered to the Department, the court shall impose an additional fine of up to $10,000. Self defense of life or property is an affirmative defense if the defendant shows by a preponderance of the evidence that the necessity for taking was not brought about by harassment or provocation of the bear; nor by negligent disposal of garbage creating an attractive nuisance; and the person exhausted all other practicable means to protect life and property. The Department may authorize taking a problem brown or grizzly bear within one-half mile of a solid waste disposal facility, if necessary to protect the public and consistent with sound game management principles (16.05.782).★

Unless otherwise permitted, a person may not take, possess, transport, sell, or purchase fish, game, or parts, or nests or eggs. A person may not knowingly disturb, injure, or destroy Department equipment used in the administration or enforcement of this title, or a poster or notice concerning title provisions, or boundary markers of areas closed to hunting, trapping or fishing, or interfere with a tag issued for a skin or carcass of fish or game (16.05.920). Violation is a Class A misdemeanor (16.05.925).

Restrictions on Taking: Fishing

A person may not waste salmon intentionally, knowingly, or with reckless disregard for the consequences. "Waste" means the failure to utilize the majority of the carcass, excluding viscera and sex parts, of a salmon intended for: ▸ sale to a commercial buyer/processor; ▸ consumption by humans or domesticated animals; ▸ scientific, educational or display purposes. The Commissioner, upon request, may authorize other uses of salmon consistent with maximum and wise use of the resource. Violation: fine up to $10,000; or jail up to 6 months; or both. In addition, the person is subject to a civil action by the state for the cost of replacing the salmon wasted (16.05.831).

Fish traps, including but not limited to floating, pile-driven, or hand-driven traps, may not be operated nor erected on or over state land, tideland, submerged land, or water. This does not prevent the operation of small hand-driven fish traps of the type ordinarily used on rivers that are legally operated in or above the mouth of a stream (16.10.070 and .100). Violation: misdemeanor; fine up to $5,000; and/or jail up to one year (16.10.090 and .110). These provisions may not be construed to violate provisions of the Alaska Statehood Act which constitutes a compact between the US and Alaska, under which the state disclaims all right and title to land or other property (including fishing rights), which right or title may be held by Indians, Eskimos, or Aleuts, or which is held by the US in trust for these Natives (16.10.080).

Commercial and Private Enterprise Provisions

★Elk may be raised and bred as domestic stock for commercial purposes, including the sale of meat, by a lawful owner of elk who holds a Game Mammal Farming License. The Department may issue a license to a person who shows an intent to raise and breed elk, and who possesses facilities for maintaining the elk under positive control. An additional license or permit is not required to import, export or possess elk for elk farming. A live elk may not be captured from, or released into, the wild without an appropriate license/permit. Elk imported, exported, or possessed for elk farming are subject to regulations for domestic animals and livestock to the extent that they are made applicable to elk by the Commissioners of Natural Resources or Environmental Conservation (16.40.050).★

A person may not, without a permit from the Commissioner, construct or operate an aquatic farm or a hatchery for supplying aquatic plants or shellfish to an aquatic farm. An Aquatic Farm and Hatchery Permit authorizes the permittee to acquire, purchase, possess, sell and transfer stock and aquatic farm products that are used or reared at the hatchery or aquatic farm, and to sell shellfish to the Department or to aquatic farms or hatcheries outside of the state. The Commissioner may set conditions to protect natural fish and wildlife resources, and may not issue a permit for farming or hatchery operations involving Atlantic salmon (16.40.100). The Commissioner shall deny or restrict a permit on finding that the proposed harvest will impair sustained yield of the species or disrupt established uses of the resources by commercial, sport, personal use or subsistence users. Otherwise, the Commissioner shall issue a permit if: ▸ wild stock is needed to meet the initial needs of a farm/hatchery; ▸ there are technological limitations on the propagation of culture stock for the species sought; and ▸ the wild stock sought is not fully utilized by sport, subsistence, commercial or other uses/fisheries (16.40.120). The Department shall order the quarantine or destruction and disposal of diseased hatchery stock to protect wild stock, and a permittee shall inform the Department of an outbreak of disease within aquatic farm stock within 48 hours after discovery (16.40.150). Violations of permit provisions are class B misdemeanors (16.40.170).

A person may not grow or cultivate finfish in captivity for commercial purposes. This does not restrict: ▸ fishery rehabilitation, enhancement or development activities of the Department; ▸ ability of a nonprofit corporation that holds a salmon hatchery permit under 16.10.400 to sell salmon returning from the natural water of the state as authorized, or surplus salmon eggs as authorized; ▸ rearing and sale of ornamental finfish for aquariums or ornamental ponds provided that the fish are not reared in or released into state waters. "Ornamental finfish" are commonly known as "tropical fish," "aquarium fish," or "goldfish" and are imported, cultured or sold customarily for viewing in aquaria, and not customarily used for sport fishing or human consumption (16.40.210).

The Commissioner may issue a permit to a nonprofit corporation organized for construction and operation of a salmon hatchery. A qualified regional association, which has become a nonprofit corporation, has a preference to a permit if the proposed hatchery is provided for in the region's comprehensive plan and the fresh water source exceeds one cubic foot per second minimum flow. The stream must be classified as suitable for enhancement purposes by the Commissioner, who must determine that the hatchery will result in substantial public benefits and will not jeopardize natural stocks (16.10.400). Public hearings must be held at least 30 days before permit issuance, and the Department shall respond within 10 days after the hearing to specific objections offered at the hearing (16.10.410). The Department shall require in a permit that: ▸ salmon eggs must be from the Department or an approved source; ▸ salmon eggs or fry may not be placed in state waters unless specifically designated in the permit; ▸ salmon eggs may not be resold or otherwise transferred; ▸ salmon may not be released by the hatchery before Department approval and examination for disease; ▸ adult salmon may be harvested only under Department regulations; ▸ the hatchery be located where reasonable segregation from natural stocks occurs, but, where feasible, in an area where returning hatchery fish will pass through traditional salmon fisheries; ▸ surplus eggs from salmon returning to the hatchery be made available for sale first to the Department and then to other authorized hatcheries (16.10.420). [Extensive statutory details are given regarding released hatchery fish, egg sources, Department assistance, and sale of salmon and eggs from hatcheries, including quality controls, use of proceeds, hatchery inspections, record keeping, annual reports, and contracts for the operation of state hatcheries in sections 16.10.430 through 16.10.480.]

See also Agency Powers and Duties under STATE FISH AND WILDLIFE AGENCIES and Import, Export and Release Provisions under HUNTING, FISHING, TRAPPING PROVISIONS.

Import, Export and Release Provisions

See also Agency Advisory Boards under STATE FISH AND WILDLIFE AGENCIES and Commercial and Private Enterprise Provisions under HUNTING, FISHING, TRAPPING PROVISIONS.

A program of stocking state lands with valuable game and fur-bearing animals that do not at present occur on the land is adopted. The Department is responsible for establishing priorities on species of animals to be stocked and the area for stocking. Priorities shall be based on habitat requirements of the species, the population of native game animals present, and other factors that will effect the successful establishment of the species (16.25.010).

★A person may not import, possess, transport or release in the state live venomous reptiles or their eggs, or live venomous insects or their eggs except by permit. A permit may only be granted if the Commissioner determines that there is a valid educational purpose for seeking the permit, including display in educational institutions and in zoos (16.05.921). Violation: Class A misdemeanor (16.05.925).★ This chapter does not prevent the collection or exportation of fish and game or parts, or a nest or egg of a bird for scientific or educational purposes, or for propagation/exhibition under a permit. Sections 16.05.920 and 16.05.921 do not prohibit rearing and sale of fish from private ponds, the raising of wild animals in captivity for food or the raising of game birds for recreational hunting on game hunting preserves, under regulations of the appropriate Board. In this subsection, "animals" includes all animal life, including insects and bugs. Nondomestic animals may not be transferred or transported from the state unless approved by the Board of Game. Animals transferred or transported must be certified by the Department to be surplus and unnecessary to the sustained yield management of the resource. Each application shall be accompanied by a statement prepared by the Department examining the probable environmental impact of the action. This chapter does not prevent the traditional barter of fish and game taken by subsistence hunting or fishing, except that the Commissioner may prohibit such barter by regulation, emergency or otherwise, if a determination on the record is made that the barter is resulting in a waste of the resource, damage to fish stocks or game populations or circumvention of fish or game management programs. A permit may not be required for possessing, importing or exporting mink and fox for fur farming purposes. Licensing requirements do not apply to activities authorized by aquatic farm and hatchery permits or to a person or vessel employed in an activity authorized by such a permit (16.05.930).

ANIMAL DAMAGE CONTROL

A department, state agency or person may not use poison to kill predatory animals without written consent of the appropriate Board (16.35.200).

See also Agency Advisory Boards under STATE FISH AND WILDLIFE AGENCIES and Restrictions on Taking: Hunting and Trapping under HUNTING, FISHING, TRAPPING PROVISIONS.

ENFORCEMENT OF WILDLIFE LAWS

Enforcement Powers

The following are state peace officers who shall enforce this title, except 16.51 and 16.52: employees authorized by the Commissioner; State Police Officers; a person authorized by the Commissioner (16.05.150). Each peace officer shall arrest violators of title provisions or regulations committed in the officer's presence/view and issue a warning citation or take the person for trial before an officer or court of competent jurisdiction (16.05.160). ★The Supreme Court shall specify by rule those misdemeanors that are appropriate for disposition without court appearance and shall establish a schedule of bail amounts. The officer may use discretion to issue a citation under those guidelines. Before establishing the schedule of bail amounts, the Supreme Court shall consult with an advisory committee consisting of two officers of the Department of Public Safety's Division of Fish and Wildlife Protection, two Department representatives, two district court judges, and the chairpersons of the House and Senate Judiciary Committees of the Legislature.★ The maximum bail amount for an offense may not exceed the maximum fine specified by law for that offense. A person cited for a misdemeanor for which a bail amount has been established may pay, within 15 days of citation, such bail to the court clerk who shall enter a judgment of conviction (16.05.165).

Peace officers may execute a warrant issued by a court, and may search any place at any time with such warrant issued showing probable cause (16.05.170). Peace officers may search without a warrant any thing or place if the search is reasonable or is not protected from searches and seizures without warrant within the meaning of Alaska State Constitution article I, Section 14, which specifically enumerates "persons, houses and other property, papers and effects." Before a search without warrant, the officer shall submit to the property owner a written statement of the reason for the search, and shall give a written receipt for property seized (16.05.180).

Guns, traps, nets, fishing tackle, boats, aircraft, automobiles or other vehicles, sleds and paraphernalia used in violation of this chapter or a Department Regulation may be seized under a valid search, and all fish and game, or parts, nests or eggs taken, transported or possessed illegally shall be seized by a peace officer, and on conviction forfeited to the state and disposed of as directed by the court. If sold, proceeds go into the General Fund. Guns, traps, nets, vehicles and other equipment seized, unless forfeited by court order, shall be returned after completion of the case and payment of a fine (16.05.190). Equipment used in violation of this title, and all fish and game held, taken or transported illegally may be forfeited upon conviction in a criminal proceeding, or upon judgment of a court that an item was used in aid of a violation, regardless of whether items were seized before the forfeiture action. An action for forfeiture may be joined with an action for damages brought by the state to recover the value of fish and game or parts, nests or eggs taken, transported or possessed illegally. It is no defense that the person in possession of the item at the time of its use and seizure has not been convicted or acquitted in a criminal proceeding arising out of its use. Items subsequently sold to an innocent purchaser in good faith may not be forfeited. Items forfeited shall be disposed of at the discretion of the Department. ★Before disposing of an aircraft, the Department shall consider transfer of the aircraft to the Alaska Wing, Civil Air Patrol (16.05.195).★

An employee or special hunter of the Department may not receive a bounty for killing a predator, or transfer the scalp or other part to another to collect a bounty (16.05.210).

In a prosecution for taking fish or game in violation of a statute or regulation, it is not a defense that the taking was done for subsistence uses (16.05.259).

A net, seine, lantern, snare, device, or contrivance while in use, kept and maintained for catching, taking, killing, attracting or decoying fish or game illegally is a public nuisance and is subject to abatement (16.05.800). The possession of fish or game or a part, nest or egg during a time that taking is prohibited is prima facie evidence that it was taken, possessed, bought or sold in violation; the burden of proof is on the possessor to overcome the presumption of illegal possession. This does not apply during the first 10 days after the close of a season, or if the fish or game is in a preserved condition, whether frozen, smoked, canned, salted, pickled or otherwise (16.05.810).

Illegal Taking of Wildlife

It is a class A misdemeanor for a person who kills a big game animal or a wild fowl species intentionally, knowingly, recklessly, or with criminal negligence to fail to salvage for human consumption the edible meat. On conviction of failure to salvage at least the hindquarters as far as the distal joint of the tibia-fibula (hock), the court shall impose jail of a minimum seven days and a fine of at least $2,500; the minimum sentence may not be suspended or reduced (16.30.010). It is a class A misdemeanor to possess the horns or antlers of a big game animal, taken during the open season, without possessing the edible meat. A person may not be arrested for a violation unless the arresting officer determines that there is probable cause to believe that the edible meat of the big game animal from which the horns/antlers were taken has not been salvaged (16.30.012). Persons convicted of 16.30.010 shall surrender to the Department all salvaged portions of the animal or fowl; forfeit their hunting licenses; be ineligible to hold a hunting license for the remainder of that year and the following year, and for five years, if they fail to salvage at least the hindquarters of a big game animal (16.30.015). These provisions do not apply to animals that the Board exempts by regulation (16.30.020). It is a defense to a criminal charge that failure to salvage edible meat was due to circumstances beyond the control of the person charged, including: ▸ theft of the animal/fowl; ▸ unanticipated weather conditions or acts of God; ▸ unavoidable loss in the field due to another wild animal; ▸ the meat was consumed by human beings or delivered to another person (sold or bartered legally) (16.30.017). For waste provisions, "big game animal" means moose, caribou, mountain sheep, mountain goat, feral reindeer, deer, elk, bison, walrus or musk-ox. ★"Edible meat" is the meat of the ribs, neck, brisket, front and rear quarters as far as the distal joint of the knee or hock, and that portion of the big game animal between the front and hindquarters; in the case of fowl, the meat of the breast. "Edible meat" does not include meat of the head; meat made inedible or damaged by the method of taking; bones, sinew and incidental meat lost due to boning or close trimming of the bones; or viscera. "Wild fowl" is a species of wild fowl for which seasons or bag limits have been established by state or federal law (16.30.030).★

License Revocations and Suspensions

Upon conviction of a first violation of 16.05.330 to 16.05.340 (relating to licensing), or of a federal or state law or regulation for protection of sport fish and game, the court may revoke the person's license, in addition to the penalty imposed by law. On a subsequent conviction, the court shall revoke the license for two to three years. These provisions do not apply when the offense is a misdemeanor for which a forfeitable bail amount has been set, unless the person is convicted during a two-year period of two or more such misdemeanor offenses, when a peace officer may file a civil action in district court to revoke the license. The court shall hold a non-jury hearing and shall hear evidence regarding the nature and seriousness of the offenses, the time period involved, the potential effect of the person's actions upon the preservation of the resource and other circumstances. If the court finds that the person's actions demonstrate a disregard for the preservation of the state's fish or wildlife resources, the court may revoke the person's license for one to three years (16.05.410).

A false statement of a material fact in a license/tag/permit application voids such license, tag or permit, and the person may be guilty of unsworn falsification under 11.56.210. It is illegal to alter, change, transfer or loan to another person a license or tag (16.05.420). Violation of license provisions or regulations is a misdemeanor, with a fine up to $1,000, jail up to 6 months, or both. Fine proceeds go into the state General Fund (16.05.430).

HABITAT PROTECTION

The Commissioner may require that every dam or other obstruction built across a stream frequented by salmon or other fish have a fishway and a device for efficient passage downstream. The fishway shall be maintained in the place, form and capacity the Commissioner approves, and kept open, unobstructed and supplied with sufficient water to allow free passage of fish (16.05.840). ★If construction of a fishway is impracticable in the Commissioner's opinion because of cost, the owner of the dam has the option to: ▸ pay an acceptable lump sum to the Fish and Game Fund; ▸ convey to the state a site of satisfactory size, at a place mutually satisfactory, and erect a fish hatchery and other facilities and give sufficient bond to furnish water, lights and money to operate and maintain a hatchery and rearing ponds; and ▸ enter into an agreement with the Commissioner, secured by bond, to pay to the Fish and Game Fund the initial money and annual payments necessary to expand, maintain and operate additional facilities at existing hatcheries within a reasonable distance of the dam or obstruction (16.05.850).★ Failure to comply with the above provisions within a reasonable time specified by written notice from the Commissioner is a misdemeanor, fine up to $1,000, with each day of noncompliance a separate offense. In addition, the dam or obstruction is a public nuisance and is subject to abatement (16.05.860).

A person may not: ▸ obstruct, divert or pollute state waters, either fresh or salt, utilized by salmon for propagation, by felling trees or timber in those waters, casting, passing, throwing, or dumping tree limbs, foliage, stumps, rubbish, earth, stones, rock or other debris, or passing or dumping sawdust, planer shavings, or other waste or refuse in those waters; ▸ erect a dam, barricade or obstruction to retard, conserve, impound, or divert waters to prevent free ingress/egress of salmon in the natural spawning process; ▸ render waters inaccessible or uninhabitable for salmon for spawning or propagation without a permit or license which sets forth the purpose, plans, waters and location, and persons for which the application is made (16.10.010). ★If the Department determines that the purpose is to develop power, obtain water for civic, domestic, irrigation, manufacturing, mining or other purposes tending to develop state natural resources, it may grant the permit or license and may require the applicant to construct and maintain adequate fish ladders, fishways or other means by which fish may pass over, around or through the obstruction in the propagation/spawning process (16.10.020). Violation: misdemeanor; fine $100-500 (16.10.030).

The Legislature recognizes that: ▸ the state has jurisdiction over all fish and game in the state except in those areas where it has assented to federal control; ▸ the state has not assented to federal control of fish and game in those areas which were set apart as National Bird and Wildlife Refuges while the state was a US territory; ▸ special recognition of the value to the state and the nation of areas of unspoiled habitat and the game characteristic to it will be demonstrated by designating as state game refuges those federal lands which were National Bird and Wildlife Refuges or Ranges at the time Alaska achieved statehood. The purpose of the State Game Refuge provision [16.20.010 through 16.20.080] is to protect and preserve the natural habitat and game population in certain designated areas (16.20.010 and .020). State Game Refuges are established (16.20.030 through 16.20.041).

[A large number of land areas are described and given refuge, range or sanctuary names in the statutes, including regulations for specified refuges, restrictions governing land acquisitions in such refuges, and agencies responsible for managing each designated area, with specific management goals and requirements (16.20.010 through 16.20.360). Only a few unusual refuges are mentioned here by name.]

Where the use, lease or disposal of real property in state game refuges is under state control/jurisdiction, through federal permit or state ownership, the responsible state agency shall notify the Commissioner before initiating use, lease or disposal of real property (16.20.050). The Commissioner shall require the person/agency to submit full plans for the anticipated use, construction work, protection of fish and game, and proposed construction date, and shall require written approval from the Commissioner before construction is commenced. ★The Commissioner shall abide by the principle that recognizes preferences among beneficial uses as forth in article VIII of the state constitution (16.20.060). The Board shall adopt regulations governing taking game on state game refuges for conservation and protection purposes (16.20.075).★

The Commission shall specify the rivers, lakes and streams that are important for the spawning, rearing, or migration of Anadromous fish (16.05.870). ★If a person or governmental agency desires to construct a hydraulic project or use, divert, pollute or change the natural flow or bed of a river, lake or stream, or use wheeled or tracked excavation or log-dragging equipment in the bed, the Commissioner shall be notified. Upon request, the person shall submit information on the full plans of the proposed construction, complete plans for proper protection of fish and game, and the approximate date work will begin. If such plans are determined to be insufficient for protection of fish and game, the Commissioner shall notify the person or agency who may request a hearing within 90 days (16.05.870). Construction on a project for which notice is required without approval of plans for proper protection of fish and game is a misdemeanor, and continued work on such project is a public nuisance and subject to abatement. The cost of restoring a river, lake or stream to its original condition shall be borne by the violator and shall be in addition to the penalty imposed by the court (16.05.880).★ Failure to notify the Commissioner of construction or use that causes material damage to the spawning beds or prevents migration of anadromous fish, or by neglect or noncompliance with the Commissioner's plans and specifications causing such damage is a class A misdemeanor (16.05.895 and .900).

The Boards, where appropriate, shall adopt regulations for conservation and protection governing taking fish and game in these critical habitat areas (16.20.510). Before the use, lease or other disposal of land under private ownership or state jurisdiction and control, within state fish and game critical habitat areas, the person or responsible agency shall notify the Commissioner (16.20.520). When a Board determines that information is required, it shall instruct the Commissioner to require the person/agency to submit: plans for anticipated use; full plans and specifications for proposed construction work; complete plans for protection of fish and game; date on which construction is to begin. The Board shall require the person or agency to obtain the Commissioner's written approval as to the sufficiency of the plans before construction is commenced (16.20.530). Critical habitat areas and allowed public uses are established (16.20.550 through .625). The Commissioner shall submit a list of additional critical habitat areas to the Legislature annually (16.20.690).

Three State Game Sanctuaries are established to protect concentrations of walrus, brown bear and other wildlife (16.20.090 through .162). The boards may adopt regulations governing entry, development, construction, hunting, fishing and other uses or activities for preserving the natural habitat and fish and game (16.20.094); except that, oil and mineral exploration and development is permitted on the Walrus Islands (16.20.096).

There are established State Range Areas for management of bison, moose and other wildlife (16.20.300 through .360).

Wherever occurring in a natural state, the water is reserved to the people for common use and is subject to appropriation and beneficial use and to reservation of instream flows and levels of water, as provided by law (46.15.030). A government agency or a person may apply to the Commissioner to reserve sufficient water to maintain a specified instream flow or level of water on a stream or body of water for four uses, including protection of fish and wildlife habitat, migration and propagation (46.15.145).

See Agency Powers and Duties under STATE FISH AND WILDLIFE AGENCIES for Departmental acquisitions of habitats and PROTECTED SPECIES OF WILDLIFE for endangered species habitat provisions.

NATIVE AMERICAN WILDLIFE PROVISIONS

See HUNTING, FISHING, TRAPPING PROVISIONS.

ARIZONA

Sources: Arizona Revised Statutes, 1958, Title 17; 1992 Cumulative Pocket Part.

STATE WILDLIFE POLICY

Wildlife, both resident and migratory, native or introduced, found in this state, except fish and bullfrogs impounded in private ponds or wildlife and birds reared or held in captivity under permit from the Commission, is property of the state and may be taken as provided by law or rule of the Commission (17-102).

RELEVANT WILDLIFE DEFINITIONS: See Definitions section of Appendices.

STATE FISH AND WILDLIFE AGENCIES

Agency Structure

The **Game and Fish Department** (Department) administers the wildlife laws of the state. Control of the Department is vested in the **Game and Fish Commission** (Commission), consisting of five members, appointed by the Governor. Not more than three members shall be members of the same political party, and no two members may be residents of the same county. Members shall be well informed on the subject of wildlife and its conservation. Terms are for five years (17-201). The Commission shall appoint a **Director** of the Game and Fish Department to serve a term of five years. The Director shall be selected on the basis of administrative ability and knowledge of wildlife management. ★The Commission shall prepare an examination for post of Director to establish an active list of eligible applications, and the Director shall be selected from those scoring satisfactory grades and having other desirable qualities (17-211).★ ★An auxiliary body, the **Arizona Game and Fish Department Reserve**, may be established by the Commission to consist of volunteers who shall assist the Department and perform duties in the areas of education, conservation and enforcement as prescribed by Commission rule, and may serve in the same manner and with the same powers as Game Rangers and Wildlife Managers if the Director so designates, but without compensation (17-214).★

Agency Powers and Duties

The **Director** will appoint employees in accordance with procedures and qualifications established by the Commission. The Director shall have general supervision and control of activities, functions and employees of the Department and enforce provisions of this title, conduct searches, inspect wildlife taken or transported, seize illegal devices, and generally exercise peace officer powers (17-211). The Director and Department employees are prohibited from taking active part in political campaigns (17-213).

The **Commission** shall: ► make rules and establish services to carry out provisions of this title; ► establish broad policies and long range programs for wildlife management, preservation and harvest; ► establish hunting, trapping and fishing rules and prescribe the manner and methods for taking wildlife; ► enforce laws for wildlife protection; ► distribute wildlife information to the public; ► prescribe rules for expenditure of funds arising from appropriation, licenses, gifts or other sources. The Commission may: ► conduct investigations or hearings; ► establish game management units or refuges for wildlife preservation and management; ► construct and operate game farms, fish hatcheries or other facilities for wildlife preservation or propagation; ► expend funds for safe firearm handling; ► remove from public or private waters fish which hinder propagation of game or food fish; ► purchase, sell or barter wildlife for stocking public or private lands and waters and take wildlife for research, propagation and restocking or for use at a game farm and declare wildlife saleable when in the public interest; ► enter into agreements with federal and state governments for management purposes; ► prescribe rules for the sale, trade, importation, exportation or possession of wildlife; ► expend monies for producing wildlife publications for sale to public; ► contract for design and production of wildlife artwork and sell or distribute the same; ► consider adverse, beneficial, short and long-term economic impacts of policies and programs for the management, preservation and harvest of wildlife on resource dependent communities, small businesses and the state by holding a public hearing (17-231). The

Commission shall coordinate with Arizona Water Resources regarding water development and use projects, the abatement of pollution injurious to wildlife, and shall have jurisdiction over fish and wildlife activities of projects constructed for the state pursuant to the jurisdiction of the Arizona water resources (17-231).

In addition, the Commission ▸ may, with the Governor's approval, enter into reciprocal agreements with adjoining states regarding licenses in joint waters (17-232); ▸ may purchase, sell, barter or give away buffalo or buffalo meat to public institutions (17-233); ▸ shall by order open, close, alter seasons and establish bag, possession limits for wildlife (17-234); ▸ shall prescribe seasons, bag limits, possession limits and other regulations for migratory bird taking in accordance with the Migratory Bird Treaty Act (17-235); ▸ is authorized to bring suit against a person or corporation to restrain or enjoin discharge or dumping into state waters of any substance deleterious to wildlife (17-237); ▸ may adopt regulations and issue licenses for conduct of field trials, shooting preserves, private wildlife farms, zoos and personal use and possession of wildlife, and may issue scientific taking permits for wildlife to accredited representatives of public education or scientific institutions (17-238); ▸ may, with the Governor's approval, acquire by purchase, lease, exchange, gift or condemnation lands for use as fish hatcheries, game farms, firing ranges, reservoir sites or rights of way to fishing waters, and may lease, exchange, or sell the lands, reserving to the state all mineral rights, with money from sale or lease of land to go into the Fish and Game Fund (17-241); ▸ shall establish a procedure by rule to permit the possession of certified triploid white amur and evaluate potential sites for stocking in closed aquatic systems with at least one public hearing considering hydrologic factors and risk of severe damage to the aquatic habitat in other bodies of water (17-317). ★The Commission may also contract with the state Department of Corrections for the use of inmate labor, including juveniles, in constructing, operating or maintaining game and fish facilities (17-249).★

Agency Funding Sources

The **Game and Fish Fund** consists of money from licenses or other source under this title. The fund is appropriated to the Commission in carrying out provisions of this title to match federal grants for wildlife restoration (17-261). The Legislature shall, in its general appropriation, make an appropriation for operation of the Commission and Department payable from the Game and Fish Fund (17-264).

The **Permanent Game and Fish Revolving Fund** consists of $30,000 for making cash outlays for postage, travel or other minor disbursements (17-261). The **Game and Fish Federal Reclamation Trust Fund** consists of all payments made by the Commission for the assessments or charges from irrigation assessments (17-242), which monies shall not revert to the general fund (17-265). The **Land and Water Conservation and Recreation Development Fund** consists of monies to be used to pay for recreation benefits in connection with fish and wildlife restoration and as matching funds for federal restoration acts. Monies are subject to annual appropriations by legislature (17-267). The **Game, Non-game, Fish and Endangered Species Fund** is to be used by the Commission for game, non-game, fish and endangered species purposes. Monies are subject to annual legislative appropriation; interest earned remains in the fund (17-268).

The **Game and Fish Publications Revolving Fund** consists of monies received from the sale of publications under 17-231. Monies are appropriated to the Department to produce and distribute Department publications and information. Sums in excess of $20,000 revert to the Game and Fish Fund (17-269). The **Waterfowl Conservation Fund** consists of monies received from selling waterfowl stamps and artwork and from gifts, grants and other contributions. Monies are used by the Commission for developing migratory waterfowl habitat and associated research and management to increase the number of state waterfowl. The Commission may expend monies to match contributions from any other source for these purposes, but funds may not be used for salaries, and interest earned stays in fund (17-270). The **Wildlife Endowment Fund** is to be used by the Commission for wildlife conservation and management and consists of: revenues from lifetime hunting and fishing licenses under 17-335.01; designated gifts, grants and contributions; and interest and income. Wildlife Endowment Fund monies are subject to annual appropriation by the legislature and exempt from lapsing. The Commissioner shall administer the fund (17-271).

The **Conservation Development Fund** is held and administered by a fiscal agent designated by the Commission. Monies in fund are not subject to appropriation or budget laws of the state, and no legislative action is needed to expend funds (17-282). The Commission, with legislative budget committee approval, may issue bonds for game and fish facilities, bonds to be payable solely from monies in the Conservation Development Fund. The funds are to be used to construct game and fish facilities and establish reserves of funds to secure payments due on bonds (17-

282 and -283). There is a related **Capital Improvement Fund** to be administered by a fiscal agent, with funds similarly expended (17-292). The aggregate amount of bonds that may be issued under this article shall not exceed $7,500,000 (17-295). The **Arizona Game and Fish Commission Heritage Fund** consists of monies deposited from the state lottery fund pursuant to Section 5-522 and interest earned. The fund is to be administered by the Game and Fish Commission and is not subject to appropriation, and expenditures are not subject to outside approval regardless of a statutory provision to the contrary. All monies in the fund shall be spent by the Commission for purposes set forth below. The Commission shall not use rights of eminent domain to acquire property to be paid for with money from this fund (17-297). Five percent of the fund shall be spent on public access; 60% on identification, inventory, acquisition, protection and management of sensitive habitat; 40% on acquisition of sensitive habitat utilized by endangered, threatened and candidate species; 15% on habitat evaluation or habitat protection; 15% on urban wildlife and urban wildlife habitat protection; and 5% on environmental education (17-298).

★Through 1998, the Department shall issue lifetime hunting and fishing licenses and trout stamps in several hunting and fishing categories according to age groups for lifetime fee computation. Except for the Resident Lifetime Wildlife Benefactor license, the fees from lifetime licenses are distributed as follows: an amount equal to the fee for an equivalent annual license/stamp to the Game and Fish Fund; an amount equal to two times the maximum fee for the equivalent annual license to the Conservation Development Fund; the remaining monies to the Wildlife Endowment Fund. The Resident Lifetime Wildlife Benefactor license, valid for hunting and fishing, costs $1,000, and the difference between $1,000 and the fee the licensee would otherwise pay for a resident lifetime class F license (resident ordinary lifetime hunting and fishing license) is considered a donation to the state for continued management, protection and conservation of the state's wildlife and is credited to the Wildlife Endowment Fund (17-335.01).★

See ENFORCEMENT OF WILDLIFE LAWS for information on the Wildlife Theft Prevention Fund.

PROTECTED SPECIES OF WILDLIFE

See RELEVANT WILDLIFE DEFINITIONS for listed animals.

Except as provided, no persons shall take wildlife unless they have a license on their person (17-331). It is unlawful to take or injure a bird, to harass a bird upon its nest, or to remove its nests or eggs, except as may occur in normal horticultural/agricultural practices or as authorized by Commission order. Such birds may be taken for scientific purposes under Commission permits (17-236).

GENERAL EXCEPTIONS TO PROTECTION

See ANIMAL DAMAGE CONTROL.

HUNTING, FISHING, TRAPPING PROVISIONS

Licenses and Permits

Except as provided, no persons shall take wildlife unless they have a license on their person (17-331). It is unlawful to apply for or obtain more than one original big game license per year (17-332). Persons over age 16 must have a state waterfowl stamp to take or possess a duck, goose, or swan (17-333.01). Taxidermists and fur dealers for hire must be licensed and keep transaction records (17-363 and -364). ★The Commission may issue special big game license tags to incorporated nonprofit organizations which are dedicated to wildlife conservation.★ No more than two special big game license tags may be issued for each big game species in a license year. The organization may sell/transfer these tags if the proceeds of sale are used for Arizona wildlife management (17-346).

A trapping license holder may trap predatory, nongame and fur-bearing mammals under Commission regulations. All traps are to be identified and on file with the Department. All traps are to be inspected daily. It is unlawful to disturb the trap of another unless authorized by the owner. Detailed records are to be kept on number and disposition of each kind of mammal taken and filed with the Department (17-361). ★★Trapping license applicants must complete a trapping education course approved by the Department. The Department shall conduct or approve a course of instruction in responsible trapping and environmental ethics, trapping laws, techniques in safely releasing nontarget animals, trapping equipment, wildlife management, proper catch handling, trapper health and safety, and considerations and ethics intended to avoid conflicts with other public land users. Persons born prior to 1967, or those who have completed, between December 31, 1987, and March 1, 1993, the voluntary trapper education course conducted in cooperation with the Department are exempt from the above provisions (17-333.02). ★★

Restrictions on Taking

It is unlawful to enter a game refuge or area closed to hunting and take or drive wildlife from the area (17-303). Wildlife, except aquatic wildlife, may be taken only during daylight hours unless the Commission states otherwise. No species of wildlife is to be taken by aid of a jacklight or spotlight or illegal device. No discharging of a firearm is allowed upon or across a roadway. No taking of wildlife, except aquatic wildlife, or discharging of firearms from a motor vehicle, including automobile, aircraft, train, or powerboat, is allowed except by permit. Fish are to be taken only by angling, with line constantly attended, and lure, fly or hook must be used so that fish voluntarily take it in their mouths (17-301). It is unlawful to carry, transport or possess devices for taking game within a game refuge except by Commission's written consent (17-305). The carcass or parts of wildlife lawfully obtained may be possessed, placed in storage, given as gifts or prepared in public eating places for hunter and guests. Wildlife lawfully produced by a commercial wildlife breeding business may be sold in the state (17-307). ★It is unlawful to camp within one-quarter mile of a natural or manmade watering facility so that wildlife or domestic stock will be denied access to the only reasonably available water (17-308). ★

Unless otherwise prescribed by this title, it is unlawful to: ▸ violate a provision of this title or rule prescribed under this title's provisions; ▸ take, possess, transport, buy, sell wildlife except as expressly permitted by this title; ▸ destroy, injure, molest livestock, crops, signboards while hunting, trapping, fishing; ▸ discharge a firearm within one-quarter mile of occupied farmhouse, cabin, etc., while taking wildlife without permission of owner or resident; ▸ take a game bird, mammal or fish and knowingly permit an edible portion to go to waste; ▸ take big game, except bear or mountain lion, with aid of dogs; ▸ make more than one use of shipping permit issued by Commission; ▸ obtain a license or take wildlife while one's license has been revoked or suspended; ▸ litter hunting and fishing areas while taking wildlife; ▸ possess while hunting any contrivance designed to silence or muffle a firearm's report; ▸ take wildlife during closed season; ▸ take wildlife in an area closed to taking; ▸ take wildlife by an unlawful method; ▸ take wildlife with an unlawful device; ▸ take wildlife in excess of bag limit; ▸ take or possess wildlife in excess of possession limit; ▸ possess or transport wildlife or parts which were unlawfully taken; ▸ possess or transport carcass of big game without attached tag; ▸ use edible parts of a game mammal or bird or nongame bird as bait; ▸ possess or transport carcass of a wildlife which cannot be identified as to species; ▸ take game animals, birds or fish with explosive, poison or other deleterious substance; ▸ import into or export from the state the carcass or parts of wildlife unlawfully taken or possessed; ▸ conduct fishing events or contests on public waters that award prizes and require registration of entrants without a permit from the Department (17-309).

There is a duty to report shooting accidents resulting in injury or death and a duty to assist the victim (17-311). It is unlawful while taking wildlife to handle or discharge a firearm while intoxicated or in a careless/reckless manner or with wanton disregard for human or property safety (17-312). A carcass of a big game animal killed by accidental collision on maintained road may be possessed by the vehicle driver by permit. Use of the permit by fraud is a class 1 misdemeanor (17-319).

Import, Export and Release Provisions

No person shall import into the state or sell, trade or release within the state or possess live wildlife except as authorized by the Commission (17-306).

ANIMAL DAMAGE CONTROL

★A person suffering property damage from wildlife may exercise reasonable measures to alleviate the damage except that reasonable measures shall not include injuring or killing game mammals, game birds or wildlife protected by federal law or regulation unless authorized by the Commission.★ The person is to file a written report of damage and species causing damage, and the Director shall order investigation by an employee trained in wildlife depredation. The Department shall provide technical advice and assist in the necessary anti-depredation measures recommended, including trapping, capturing and relocating animals. If harvest of animals is found to be necessary to relieve damage, the Commission may establish special seasons, bag limits and reduced license fees to crop the wildlife, or issue special permit to landowner suffering damage, with edible portions to go to a public institution or charity. A person suffering depredations may appeal the Commission decisions regarding conduct of depredation alleviation measures to superior court if dissatisfied (17-239). A landowner/lessee suffering depredations on livestock by bear or mountain lion may exercise measures to prevent further damage, including taking of animals by leg-hold traps without teeth, leg snares, firearms or other legal hunting weapons or devices. All traps are to be inspected within 72 hours, and nontarget animals released and target animals dispatched immediately. A livestock operator taking a lion or bear shall notify the Department within five days of setting traps or initiating pursuit, including information on the number and kind of livestock killed, and the operator shall provide evidence of having livestock recently killed by bear or lion. Dogs may be used to facilitate pursuit of depredating bears and lions. No license or tag is required, but report of taking must be filed within ten days, detailing the number/type of stock killed and the number of lions/bears taken. No portion of an animal taken pursuant to this section shall be retained or sold by a person nor held in captivity except by Commission authorization (17-302).

The Arizona Game and Fish Department shall offer non-financial assistance in eradicating existing populations of diploid white amur and in restocking other previously existing fish species (17-317). ★The Department shall test all cloven-hoofed wildlife it introduces or imports into the state or releases in the state for presence of diseases that can be transmitted to livestock, and shall conduct wildlife immunization against domestic diseases if possible (17-318).★

ENFORCEMENT OF WILDLIFE LAWS

General Provisions

★★Arizona is a member of the Wildlife Violator Compact (17-501 through -503). ★★ See Model Statute Section of Handbook for full provisions of the compact.

County, city, and town peace officers are ex officio special game rangers and are required to carry out the duties of this title (17-104).

Wildlife seized under this title may be disposed of as the Commission or court may prescribe, but edible portions are to go to charity or public institutions. Devices, excepting firearms, which are unlawful for wildlife taking and being illegally used may be seized and destroyed, with notice given to offender. Other devices, including firearms seized under this title, shall be returned to the person after final disposition of case. Records of wildlife and devices seized are to be kept by the Department, and money derived from the sale of devices is to go to the Game and Fish Fund (17-240).

Criminal Penalties

Unless specifically prescribed, violations of provisions of this title or a lawful order or rule of the Commission is a class 2 misdemeanor. Taking big game during a closed season or knowingly possessing, transporting or buying big game which was unlawfully taken during a closed season is a class 1 misdemeanor. It is a class 6 felony violation to: ▸ barter, sell or offer wildlife or their parts unlawfully taken during a closed season, imported or purchased in violation of title or Commission regulation, or taken unlawfully; and ▸ assist another person for monetary gain with unlawful taking of big game. A peace officer who knowingly fails to enforce a rule of the Commission or this title is guilty of a class 2 misdemeanor (17-309).

Civil Penalties

The Commission and enforcement officers, if so directed by the Commission, may bring civil action in the name of the state against a person unlawfully taking, wounding, killing, possessing the following wildlife or their parts and seek to recover the following minimum sums as damage: each turkey or javelina - $150; each bear, mountain lion, antelope or deer - $450; each buffalo, elk, bighorn sheep, eagle or endangered species - $750; each beaver - $75; each goose or raptor - $40; each duck, small game animal or small game bird - $15; each nongame bird or game fish - $10. No verdict or judgment shall be for less than the mandatory sum fixed in this section. Action for damages may be joined with an action for possession and recovery had for both actions. The pendency or determination of an action for damages or payment of a judgment, or pendency or determination of criminal prosecution for the same taking is not a bar to the other, nor does either affect the right of seizure under a game and fish laws. Funds recovered go into the Wildlife Theft Prevention Fund (17-314).

License Revocations and Suspensions

Upon conviction and in addition to other penalties prescribed by this title, the Commission, after public hearing, may revoke or suspend a license issued to a person and deny the right to secure another license to take wildlife for a period not to exceed five years for: ▸ unlawful taking or possession of wildlife; ▸ careless use of firearms which has resulted in injury or death of a person; ▸ destroying, injuring, molesting livestock or damaging or destroying crops, personal property, notices or signboards; ▸ littering public hunting or fishing areas while taking wildlife; ▸ knowingly allowing another to use their game tag. The Commission may suspend a license to take wildlife on receiving a report from the licensing authority of a state which is a party to the Wildlife Violator Compact (Chapter 5, this title) that a resident of Arizona has failed to comply with the terms of a wildlife citation in that other state. The Director shall notify the person within 180 days after conviction to show cause why the license should not be revoked, suspended or denied. The Commission shall furnish to license dealers the names and addresses of persons whose licenses have been revoked or suspended and the periods for which they have been denied the right to secure a license. Taking wildlife at a time when the privilege to do so is suspended, revoked or denied is a class 1 misdemeanor, and the Commission may extend the period of suspension or revocation for up to an additional five years. A license to take wildlife which is obtained by fraud or misrepresentation is void, and violation is a class 3 misdemeanor (17-340 and -341).

Reward Payments

This fund shall consist of monies received from damage assessments pursuant to 17-314, donations, appropriated funds, and monies received as fines, forfeitures and penalties collected for violations of this title. Funds are to be expended only for: ▸ financing of reward payments to persons other than peace officers responsible for information leading to the arrest of a person for unlawfully taking, wounding, killing, selling, etc., wildlife and attendant acts of vandalism, the Commission establishing a schedule of rewards to be made; ▸ financing of a statewide telephone reporting system named "Operation Game Thief," to be established by the Director under the guidance of the Commission; ▸ promoting public recognition and awareness of the wildlife theft prevention program; ▸ investigating unlawful commercial use of wildlife. Monies shall not lapse, but a balance in excess of $50,000 is to revert to the Game and Fish Fund (17-315). Fines, forfeitures, and penalties collected for violations of this title shall be credited to the Wildlife Theft Prevention Fund (17-313).

HABITAT PROTECTION

See Arizona Game and Fish Commission Heritage Fund under Agency Funding Sources, STATE FISH AND WILDLIFE AGENCIES.

★When the Commission determines that the operation of motor vehicles within a certain area, except private land, is or may be damaging to wildlife reproduction, management or habitat, the Commission, with the concurrence of the land management agency involved and after public hearing, may order the area closed to motor vehicles for not more than one year, provided that all roads in the area shall remain open unless specifically closed.★ The Commission may recommend that particular areas of land be set aside for use of recreational vehicles. The Commission may enter into agreements with landowners and agencies controlling the areas, stipulating the restrictions and permitted uses of motor vehicles in the areas and the duties of the Commission and landowners relating to enforcement of the agreements (17-452). The areas shall be posted and publicized, giving prohibitions and permitted uses of closed areas (17-453). No person shall drive a motor operated vehicle cross-country on public or private lands where driving is prohibited by regulation or posting (17-454). Exceptions are for state agency personnel, utilities personnel, emergency situations, hunters entering solely to pick up big game animals legally killed, and allowed camping on open roads in closed areas when the vehicle is parked within 300 feet of road (17-455).

The Commission may expend general appropriation funds to: ▸ conduct surveys of actual or possible wildlife habitat damage by motor vehicles and the areas to be recommended for recreational vehicle use; ▸ post restricted areas; ▸ provide maps; ▸ provide educational programs on wildlife habitat preservation and restoration; ▸ enforce restrictions

(17-456). All peace officers of the state, counties, cities and other authorized state and federal employees shall enforce wildlife habitat protection provisions (17-457). Violation of this article or regulations regarding closed areas is a class 3 misdemeanor (17-458). Landowners or lessees of private land desiring to prohibit hunting or shooting on their lands shall post lands using plainly legible wording on signs of specified size. State or federal lands, including those under lease, may not be posted except by Commission consent. Posting is to be at one-quarter mile intervals or less. No action for trespassing may lie unless lands have been posted as provided (17-304).

NATIVE AMERICAN WILDLIFE PROVISIONS: None.

ARKANSAS

Sources: Arkansas Code of 1987 Annotated, Title 15; 1991 Cumulative Supplement.

[NOTE: Under Arkansas Constitution Amendment 35, adopted in 1945, the Arkansas Game and Fish Commission was created and given full and complete authority to administer the laws and to promulgate rules and regulations necessary for the control, management, restoration, conservation and regulation of all wildlife resources of the state. Courts have held that the Commission has complete and exclusive authority to manage and regulate birds, fish, game and wildlife resources under the provisions of the constitutional amendment, i.e, *W.R. Wrape Stave Co. v. Arkansas Game and Fish Commission*, 219 SW2d 948 (Ark. 1949). The powers reserved to the General Assembly are powers to set license fees and appropriate funds from the Game Protection Fund. The reader, therefore, is advised to refer to the Game and Fish Commission Code of Regulations.]

STATE WILDLIFE POLICY

All game and fish except fish in private ponds, found in the limits of this state, are declared to be the property of the state. The hunting, killing, and catching of the game and fish are declared to be privileges (15-43-104).

The General Assembly declares that it is the public policy of the State of Arkansas to promote sound management, conservation, and public awareness of Arkansas' high diversity of native plants and nongame animals. Many of these species, subspecies, or populations of animals and plants are rare, threatened, endangered or are of special significance to the state, and it is in the state's interest to provide for their conservation for present and future generations. It is also in the state's interest to provide for the protection of natural areas harboring significance or having unusual importance to the survival of Arkansas' native animals and plants in their natural environments. It is the purpose of the Wildlife Preservation subchapter and 26-51-434 to provide a means by which the protection of nongame species of animals and native plants may be financed in part through a voluntary checkoff designation on state income tax return forms, whereby an individual taxpayer may designate a portion or all of the individuals's income tax refund to be withheld and contributed for the purposes set forth above. It is the intent of the General Assembly that this program of income tax checkoff is supplemental and in no way is intended to take the place of funding that would otherwise be appropriated for this purpose (15-45-301).

RELEVANT WILDLIFE DEFINITIONS: None.

STATE FISH AND WILDLIFE AGENCIES

Agency Structure

The Commission appoints the number of **Game Wardens** necessary to enforce state wildlife laws. Wardens must meet Commission qualifications and be 21 years of age. The Commission may deputize citizens interested in wildlife conservation as **Deputy Wardens** who shall have the authority held by regular wardens, but shall serve without pay except for regular fees allowed sheriffs and police officers except when doing special work under the Commission's supervision. Regular and deputy wardens shall be paid from the Game Protection Fund (15-41-201 and -202).

Agency Powers and Duties

The **Director of the Arkansas State Game and Fish Commission** (Director) has the authority to act for the Commission in enforcing or administering the provisions of this section and 15-41-103 and 15-42-206 (15-41-101).

The **Arkansas Game and Fish Commission** (Commission) shall: ▸ provide itself with a seal; ▸ keep a complete record of acts done by the Commission or under its authority; ▸ report annually to the Governor and make recommendations to the general assembly; ▸ let to the lowest bidder the contract for license blank printing, to be paid out of the Game Protection Fund as are other Commission expenses; ▸ adopt ways to conserve and propagate the game, fish, fur-bearing animals, and other wildlife of the state. The Commission may: ▸ expend surplus from funds derived, after payment of salaries and expenses, in importing, raising and distributing game, fish, and fur-bearing animals for propagation in the state; ▸ establish regulations governing the propagation of game, fish, and fur-bearing animals in captivity upon private premises and authorize the sale or exportation from the state with permits; ► by regulation, permit game, fish, and fur-bearing animals to be shipped from the state for propagation purposes; ► emphasize programs for migratory waterfowl and issue permits to responsible persons permitting the collection, possession, buying, and selling of migratory birds and other game birds and animals for scientific and propagative purposes (a migratory bird permittee must also have a USDA permit); ► enter into cooperative agreements with the US, or any agency, establish hunting and fishing areas within national forests and close them to hunting and fishing for necessary periods, and prescribe the season for hunting or fishing therein; ► fix the amount of fees required for special hunting and fishing permits; ► issue hunting and fishing permits and prescribe the number, size and sex of game, fish and birds that shall be taken from national forests; ► promulgate the rules prescribed in and under the cooperative agreements. A violation of Commission rules or seasons in national forests: fine of $25-100; jail 10-30 days; or both (15-41-103 through -107).

Game Wardens, sheriffs, constables and other state peace officers, shall have the right to apprehend persons violating wildlife laws, and to take offenders before a court with jurisdiction in the county where the offense was committed. They shall report monthly to the Commission the name and character of the offenses reported to various state peace officers (15-41-201).

Agency Funding Sources

No funds accruing to the state from license fees paid by hunters and fishermen shall be used for any other purpose than the administration of the Commission (15-41-111). ★Commission members may request free state railroad transportation (15-41-112).★

The State Treasurer shall compute monthly the average daily balance of the **Game Protection Fund** or other funds administered by the Commission, and shall transfer to the Game Protection Fund interest on the average daily balances (15-41-110). Twenty-five cents of the additional fee derived from the sale of each annual resident hunting license shall be set aside by the Commission into a special account within the Game Protection Fund to be known as the **Beaver Control and Eradication Account** to be used for control and eradication of beavers destroying private property. Fifty percent of all remaining funds derived from the increase in resident hunting and fishing licenses shall be expended by the Commission exclusively for the acquisition and development of public hunting and fishing areas (15-42-125).

Moneys contributed for the **Nongame Preservation Program** through the state income tax refund check-off system and interest earned shall be expended for protecting, preserving, and restoring the nongame resources, including development and implementation of management programs, land acquisition, public education, or other purposes upon appropriation by the General Assembly. State agencies may apply to the Nongame Preservation Committee for a grant from the fund to effectuate nongame preservation. No expenditure shall be made without the Governor's approval on recommendation of the Nongame Preservation Committee. Funds may be used for restoring and protecting nongame animals and plants, both terrestrial and aquatic, but the highest priority shall be accorded to state rare, endangered, or threatened native organisms or organisms of special interest. Balances in the Nongame Preservation Program shall be carried forward each year so that none shall revert to the state's General Fund (15-45-303 and -305).

See also STATE WILDLIFE POLICY for nongame wildlife tax return checkoff provisions.

Agency Advisory Boards

★There is an **Appraisal Board** in each county composed of the game wardens of that county and two farmers who are landowners in the county appointed by the county judge and county agent. This board is to investigate and determine the amount of damages payable to the owner, lessor or tenant owning agricultural crops within or near game refuges where crops have been damaged by wildlife in a game reservation. All moneys appropriated by the General Assembly to be expended from the Game Protection Fund for damages to agricultural crops caused by wildlife shall be approved by the Appraisal Board before payment (15-45-209).★

The **Nongame Preservation Committee** consists of five members including the Director of the Commission, the Director of the State Parks Division of the Department of Parks and Tourism, the Director of the Arkansas Natural Heritage Commission, and two members appointed by the Governor for three-year terms from nominations from private conservation organizations within the state (15-45-302). See also Agency Funding Sources under STATE FISH AND WILDLIFE AGENCIES and STATE WILDLIFE POLICY.

PROTECTED SPECIES OF WILDLIFE

The entire state is designated, and shall constitute, a sanctuary for wild fowl of all species except black birds, crows and starlings. No person shall catch, kill, injure, pursue, or have in possession, either dead or alive, or purchase, sell, transport, or ship within or without the state, or receive or deliver for transportation wild fowl except black birds, crows and starlings unless authorized to do so by a Commission regulation or a federal regulation constitutionally adopted and imposed. Sparrows and pigeons shall be excluded from the provisions of this section, except for Birmingham roller pigeons. Nothing herein shall prohibit collecting wild birds or their nests or eggs, except birds protected by federal or state game laws, for scientific study, school instruction, or other educational uses. Scientific collecting permits for birds, nests or eggs are issued by the Commission, and shall state the interest and need of the applicant in collection and the species and number desired to be collected. Permit holders must keep and submit records annually of the number and species of birds, nests or eggs collected. Violation: misdemeanor; fine up to $50 (15-45-210).

Areas embraced within the limits of state parks are designated and established as bird sanctuaries. It is unlawful to trap, hunt, shoot or molest a bird or wild fowl, or to rob bird nests in these areas. ★If starlings or similar birds are congregating in numbers that in the opinion of the Arkansas Department of Health constitutes a nuisance or menace to health or property, officials after three days notice shall meet with representatives of the Audubon Society, bird club, garden club, or humane society, or with as many of those clubs as exist in the state, to discuss possible solutions to the problem. If no satisfactory alternative is found to abate the nuisance, the birds may be destroyed under Arkansas State Police supervision. Violation: misdemeanor; fine up to $100; or jail up to 30 days (15-45-211).★

GENERAL EXCEPTIONS TO PROTECTION

The Commission may contract with manufacturers and commercial fishermen to supply gar fish, turtles and other uneatable fish; to designate the type of all tackle to be used to take uneatable fish and turtles; and to designate the season and the waters from which uneatable fish are to be taken. Work shall be done under Commission supervision. The Commission shall provide for the removal of predatory species such as gar, turtles, carp, buffalo, drum and other nongame fish from state waters, to be done on a percentage basis under Department supervision which shall see that game fish such as trout, bass, crappie and perch are immediately and carefully returned to the waters and that all gar, grinnel and turtles are destroyed. No seining of a live stream shall be done. Violation: fine of $50-500 (15-43-326 and -327). (See also PROTECTED SPECIES OF WILDLIFE, Restrictions on Taking: Fishing under HUNTING, FISHING, TRAPPING PROVISIONS and ANIMAL DAMAGE CONTROL.)

HUNTING, FISHING, TRAPPING PROVISIONS

General Provisions

Any person owning/operating cultivated farm lands (excluding forests), commercial fish farms, private water storage reservoirs, fruit orchards/pecan groves or fenced lands may post the lands and give notice in a newspaper of general circulation to prevent hunting/fishing thereon. It is unlawful to ride, range, hunt, fish, or trespass on posted lands. Violation: misdemeanor; fine on first offense minimum $500, $1,500 for a second/subsequent offense. Possession of firearms in fields, forests or any location known to be game cover is prima facie evidence of hunting. Possession of tackle, nets, spears or other devices usually used in fishing in the vicinity of lakes and streams is prima facie evidence of fishing. It is lawful to possess a game bird or animal lawfully killed during the open season for 10 days following the open season, during the open season and for a 30-day period following the open season when animal is tagged and placed in cold storage (15-43-101 through -106).

Licenses and Permits

A resident who hunts or fishes without a license is guilty of a misdemeanor, with a fine of $10-200. Each person licensed under the provisions of 15-42-104 and 15-42-110 shall disclose all information or knowledge they may have relating to violations of game and fish laws upon the request of a game warden, Commission member, constable or sheriff. Failure to do so results in license forfeiture for one year in addition to other penalties. No license issued under this chapter shall authorize the holder to kill, take, or catch any game, fish, or fur-bearing animal during the closed seasons or in violation of chapter provisions (15-42-102 through -103). Counterfeiting or altering a license, permit, tag or stamp is a misdemeanor and a fine not less than $50 (15-42-119). ★No person shall be licensed to hunt who: ▸ has been convicted twice of violations of this section; ▸ is an habitual drunkard; ▸ has been convicted of grand larceny. The prosecuting attorney is allowed for each conviction or guilty plea in violation of this section a fee of $25 for costs in the case, and an additional fee of $10 if the conviction is sustained, and shall report twice yearly to the Commission the names of all persons prosecuted under this section, those convicted, acquitted, and cases still pending. Failure by the attorney to so report, after request by the Commission, is a fine of $100 to go to the Game Protection Fund, to be recovered in a civil action by the Commission (15-42-121).★

It is unlawful to take fish with artificial bait/lures without a resident fishing license, and unlawful for a resident over age 16 to take fish with net seines or gigs without a resident fishing license (15-42-106). Nonresidents must have a nonresident fishing license. Violation: fine $10-50 (15-42-107).

It is unlawful for a resident over age 16 to hunt without a hunting license, provided that residents of any age may take rabbits, squirrels and predatory animals without a license. Violation: misdemeanor; fine $25-200 (15-42-109). Nonresidents who hunt game birds, game or fur-bearing animals except deer, bear, elk, or turkey must be licensed, and licensed separately to take deer, bear, elk or turkey. Violation: misdemeanor; fine $50-250 (15-42-111). ★It is unlawful for the Commission to issue a permit to a person or firm in a state bordering Arkansas for nonresident hunting and fishing licenses unless the other state allows Arkansas persons to do the same. Violation: Class A misdemeanor, and violator shall be removed from office and not be eligible for reemployment, election or appointment to a state office for three years (15-42-122).★ It is unlawful to take with snare, traps, or deadfalls any fur-bearing animals where more than 12 traps or deadfalls are used without a license. Violation: misdemeanor; fine $10-200 for each offense. Violations by resident dealers is fine of $25-100; for nonresident dealers $100-500; and each day of violation is a separate offense. A nonresident who hunts or takes fur-bearing animals for commercial purposes, or who sells their pelts without a license shall be fined not less than $100. A fur dealer license is required for residents/nonresidents (15-42-203 through -206). Shipments of pelts originating in Arkansas must be marked with the name and address of the shipper, license number, date and "fur pelts," and may be made only during the legal period if the pelts are in green condition. This does not apply to legally obtained pelts from outside the state consigned directly to a licensed dealer (15-42-209). ★It is unlawful to hunt, pursue, chase or take a deer, wild turkey, wild duck, quail, snipe, woodcock or other wild fowl or game bird with an unlicensed dog. Violation: fine $10-200 (15-42-302). The Commission shall license dogs to hunt. It is prima facie evidence of intent to steal a Commission-licensed dog to keep it more than 10 days and fail to advertise the dog in 5 public places or in a newspaper with at least 500 subscribers. Violation: felony theft. (15-42-303).★

Restrictions on Taking: Hunting and Trapping

It is unlawful to shoot, maim, wound, chase, take or possess buck deer except during open season, or to establish camp for deer hunting more than 48 hours before the season opens. Violation: misdemeanor; fine $50-300. It is unlawful to take a buck deer with antlers less than two and one-half inches long, or to possess/transport a carcass not having natural evidences of its sex. Violation: misdemeanor; fine $25-200. During open season for buck deer, it is unlawful to kill or possess more than one buck deer, or to shoot at, kill or possess a doe deer. Violation: misdemeanor; fine $50-300. ★Fifty or more qualified electors residing within an area designated by Commission regulation as a doe killing area may petition the county court for an election to be held to determine whether or not the area shall remain a doe killing area.★ ★The General Assembly has become aware of the fact that many persons hunting deer allow their firearms to be discharged without proper care, thereby endangering the life, limb, and property of others. It is the intent of this section to deter the negligent use of firearms by deer hunters by imposing a fine of $100-1,000, jail for 30 days to 6 months, or both for negligence.★ It is unlawful to allow a dog to pursue or run deer between January 15 and November 1 or at season unless the person accompanies the dog. Violation: misdemeanor; fine $15-25 (15-43-201 through -207).

It is unlawful to hunt, maim, wound, take or possess a wild turkey gobbler except during open season, and hunting camps may not be established more than 48 hours in advance of the season. Feeding or baiting to lure wild turkeys and construction of blinds for hunting wild turkeys is prohibited. Violation: misdemeanor; fine $50-300. The bag/possession on turkey gobblers is two birds. Violation: misdemeanor; fine $10-200. It is unlawful to shoot, hunt or possess a wild turkey hen. Violation: misdemeanor; fine $100-300. See also ENFORCEMENT OF WILDLIFE LAWS. It is unlawful to possess or transport the carcass of a wild turkey unless it has thereon the natural evidences of its sex. Violation: misdemeanor; fine $25-200. A special bow and arrow season for buck deer and turkey gobblers is seven days preceding the regular seasons, during which time bow and arrow must be exclusively used, and the use of dogs in hunting, chasing or disturbing deer during this period is prohibited. Persons qualified and licensed to hunt buck deer or wild turkey gobbler with firearms may also hunt with bow and arrow under the same license. Persons taking one buck deer or two turkey gobblers during the special bow and arrow season may not take additional deer or turkey until the next annual open season. Game taken by bow and arrow must be tagged (15-43-208 through -214).

The seasons for taking, killing and possessing beaver, otter, bear, elk and buffalo are the same as for deer. The season for taking, killing or possessing prairie chickens, pheasants, Hungarian partridges, chukar partridges or other introduced game bird is set in statutes, as are bag limits. Violation: misdemeanor; fine not less than $25. Quail, partridge and bobwhite quail season and bag limits are set in statute. Bird dogs may be field trained for 45 days preceding the season; the Commission may not issue a permit authorizing shooting bobwhite quail out of season. Violation: misdemeanor; fine $25-500. Seasons and bag limits are set by statute for wild goose, wild duck, brant, coot, gallinule, Wilson snipe, jack snipe, black-bellied and golden plover, yellowlegs, woodcock, rail, mourning and turtle dove. Violation of hunting season, misdemeanor, fine $25-200; violation of bag limit, fine $10-200. It is unlawful to use or display more than 12 live, dead or artificial duck decoys at one stand, blind or shooting place. Violation: misdemeanor; fine minimum $25. Legal gun sizes are specified for quail and turkey; violation, misdemeanor, fine $25-100. Guides may not carry guns when accompanying persons hunting migratory birds; birds killed by the guide with the client's gun count toward the bag limit. Violation: misdemeanor, fine minimum $50 (15-43-217 through -225).

It is unlawful: ▸ for an operator of a hunting camp, club or other place where migratory birds are shot, to place food or bait to attract ducks or other migratory birds (violation: misdemeanor; fine minimum $50); ▸ for a person, other than the owner, to kill, molest, detain or shoot an Antwerp, messenger or homing pigeon (violation: misdemeanor; fine up to $10; or jail up to 60 days); ▸ to hunt, chase, kill or possess squirrels except during the open season, nor to take more than eight squirrels per day (violation: misdemeanor; fine $10-200); ▸ to shoot upon or over state waters more than 30 minutes before sunrise or after sunset, or to shoot or kill a wild duck or goose more than 30 minutes before sunrise or after sunset; ▸ to hunt, capture or kill a migratory game bird by or with the use of an airplane, machine gun, powerboat, sailboat, or a towed floating device; ▸ to use a powerboat or sailboat for flushing birds and driving them toward a blind or battery and to shoot squirrels from a boat (violation: misdemeanor; fine $25-250); ▸ to net, trap, snare, or catch a wild bear, deer, wild turkey, wild pheasant, grouse, prairie chicken, partridge or quail, turtle dove or robin redbreast (violation: misdemeanor; fine $10-200 for each offense) (15-43-226 through -230).

It is unlawful: ▸ to hunt, kill or possess fur-bearing animals except during the open season, or have in possession their pelts except during the 10 days after the close of the open season, except that wolves, bobcats, coyotes and rabbits are excluded, and fur-bearing animals actually found destroying crops, poultry, or livestock may be killed and persons holding a permit may raise fur-bearing animals on private property (violation: misdemeanor; fine $25-250); ▸ to take or kill a fur-bearing animal by the use of poisons, explosives or chemicals, or to destroy or cut a den tree on another's land without the landowner's written permission (violation: misdemeanor; fine minimum $10); ▸ to use, set, possess or tend a snare, trap or deadfall except smooth jawed steel traps, to set a trap in a path commonly used by persons, domestic animals, poultry or dogs, and not to visit steel traps at least once each day, Sunday excepted, except authorized persons may possess and use traps usually used in taking wolves, bobcats and other predatory animals (violation: misdemeanor; fine minimum $25). All foxes shall be classified as fur-bearing animals, and they and their pelts may be taken, possessed, sold or traded in the open season provided for taking all other fur-bearing animals. ★Foxes may be chased for pleasure and may be destroyed when destroying poultry or livestock, but pelts taken during closed seasons must be surrendered to the Commission.★ All license requirements/regulations for taking of all other fur-bearing animals and the penalties provided shall also apply to the taking, possessing and selling of foxes or their pelts. It is unlawful to trap, kill or take a muskrat within 10 feet of a muskrat house, defined as a structure built by muskrat as a place in which to live, rest, sleep, feed or play. Violation: misdemeanor; fine minimum $25 (15-43-231 through -235).

The Commission may promulgate and publish regulations making the time, manner, bag limits or possession limits of all hunting, taking, possession or shipment of migratory birds, game birds, game or fur-bearing animals within the boundaries of federally owned areas conform to changes in federal regulations, the regulations to become state law. Violation: misdemeanor; fine minimum $25. It is unlawful to permit to go to waste the edible portion of game or fish at any season of the year; destroy, rob or disturb the nest or eggs of a game bird; chase, take or molest the young of a game or fur-bearing animal except during the open season and in the manner prescribed by law; shoot, kill or harm a songbird or insectivorous bird not classified as a game bird or vermin. English sparrows, crows, hawks and owls are excluded from these provisions. Violation: misdemeanor; fine $10-200. A person who acts as a guide for another person shall be equally responsible with the person for a violation of game and fish laws unless the guide reports violations to the Commission, and persons employing guides are equally responsible with the guide for violations. Violation: misdemeanor; fine minimum $25 (15-43-236 through -239).

★★The General Assembly finds and determines that: ▸ management of the state's wildlife and regulation of hunting and hunters is the primary responsibility of the Game and Fish Commission; ▸ properly regulated and controlled hunting is one of the most important single game management tools available; ▸ untrained and improperly trained hunters account for a great percentage of the loss of game in the state; ▸ the number of hunting accidents is increasing annually due primarily to the lack of training or improper training of hunters; ▸ the establishment of a hunter training and safety program would greatly improve and facilitate hunter safety and game management programs; ▸ the intent of this section is to authorize the Commission to establish and operate a hunter safety and training program and to designate the Commission as the agency to receive federal funds; ▸ the Commission is authorized and encouraged to establish, maintain and operate hunter training and safety program, consisting of, but not limited to, safe and proper handling of firearms, suitability and effectiveness of types of firearms for hunting various game, effective range and killing power, the best placement of shots on large game to assure clean kills and related matters; ▸ the Commission is designated as the state agency to receive, distribute and disburse all federal funds available under PL 91-503 and related congressional acts and may use funds in the Game Protection Fund to match federal funds; ▸ the Commission may adopt and enforce rules and regulations necessary to carry out the purposes and intent of this section (15-43-238).★★

Restrictions on Taking: Fishing

★It is unlawful to fish with artificial bait from March 15 to May 15. Violation: misdemeanor; fine $10-200.★ It is unlawful to fish with artificial bait or to sell artificial bait having more than nine hooks, but new, unused baits having more than nine hooks may be possessed and sold by retailers and wholesale dealers. Violation: misdemeanor; fine minimum $10. [Minimum fish lengths for small and large black bass; white, striped, bar bass; crappie, white perch, calico bass; walleyed pike, jack, jack salmon are given in statutes.] Violation: misdemeanor; fine minimum $10. [String limits are set in statutes for large or smallmouth black bass; striped, white or calico bass, crappie or white perch; bream, black, goggle-eyed, sun or other perch; trout, pike, jack or jack salmon. Seasons, lengths and string limits are set for trout. There are closed seasons on black bass and on all minnows.] Violation: misdemeanor; fine $10 minimum. Minnow seines not exceeding 20 feet in length and 4 feet deep may be used to take true species of minnows during the open season. Any fish except gar or grinnel caught in minnow seines must be carefully returned to the waters. Violation: misdemeanor; fine minimum $50. It is unlawful to: ▸ use more than six hooks on any one line, and no person shall use more than four lines at a time in fishing for buffalo, carp, drum and red or black horse fish (violation: misdemeanor; fine $10-50); ▸ possess, use, build, erect or control a wire net, wire basket, fish trap, fish basket or other device of similar kind with which a fish may be caught or trapped (violation: misdemeanor; fine $10-500), there being an open season to grabble by use of hands and by hogging for personal use rough fish, buffalo, carp, catfish, drum, or suckers (violation: misdemeanor; fine $10-50); ▸ take fish by use of a gig or spear except during the open season (violation: misdemeanor; fine minimum of $10); ▸ use, possess, or transport an electrical device for the purpose of stunning, stupefying or taking fish from state waters (violation: misdemeanor; fine minimum $1,000; jail up to one year; or both); ▸ shoot fish with a gun, or to throw, drop or explode dynamite or other explosive in state waters, except for work undertaken by lawful authority, or use in trying to raise bodies of drowned persons (violation: misdemeanor; fine $100-1,000; jail 5-60 days); ▸ deposit, throw, drop or discharge in state waters any substance, liquid or gas or anything else that will/does intoxicate, stupefy or injure fish, whether done to take fish or not (violation: felony; prison term 1-12 months) (15-43-302 through -317).

★Seines and trammel nets not exceeding 100 feet in length may be used in season by two or more families fishing for their own use on picnics or fish fries. Each family using legal picnic seines is entitled to carry to their homes specified quantities and kinds of fish that may be caught and are surplus to the quantities that are to be prepared, cooked and eaten at the place where caught. Fish caught in excess of the permitted amounts must be prepared, cooked and eaten where caught or immediately released. Persons desiring to use nets must apply to the Commission for the proper metal tags. Violations as to net/mesh size shall be punished as commercial violations, not less than $50 fine and license and tackle forfeiture. Only the picnic seine/net owner must have a resident fishing license, and one license is required for each seine or net used. Helpers in the operation of a picnic net need no license (15-43-321).★ [Commercial gill, trammel and seine nets, trotlines, snag lines, set hooks; hoop, barrel and pond nets, as well as license requirements, are specified by statutes (15-43-318, -323, -324 and -325).] Only the Ameriurdae species of catfish, commonly known as brown, yellow and black bullhead, or buffalo fish, over 16 inches in length may be sold in the state. Violation: misdemeanor; minimum fine $15 (15-43-321). Commercial fishermen must return game fish to the waters, including trout, bass, crappie, bream, perch, goggle-eye, jack salmon, pike or other fish, the sale of which is prohibited. Fish that cannot be sold legally in the state may not be displayed or held in live boxes at a commercial business. Violation: misdemeanor; minimum fine $25 (15-43-322). Taking of fish from an enclosed or artificial lake without the consent of the owner is a misdemeanor; fine $100; or jail up to 30 days. Artificial pond owners must give public notice within the precinct of their intent to breed fish (15-43-329). It is unlawful to take fish from or to fish in a fish farm without the consent of the owner. Persons possessing fishing tackle on fish farm premises are rebuttably presumed to be fishing, and the tackle shall be confiscated and sold at public auction, the proceeds to be deposited in the county general fund. Violation: misdemeanor; fine $500-1,000; jail 90 days to six months on first offense. Subsequent offense: fine $1,000-2,000; jail six months to one year (15-43-330). [Mussel and shell taking, licensing, boat licensing and enforcement of mussel taking operations shall be regulated by the Commission (15-43-401 through -407).]

It is unlawful to withdraw water from a public body of water without screening the intake pipes against entry of any fish, or to lower the natural state of water to a point whereby fish existence is endangered. Violation: misdemeanor; fine $50-500 (15-44-111). Persons owning/controlling a dam or other obstruction across a watercourse are required to keep the dam open sufficiently to admit the free and easy passage of all fish during designated seasons. This does not apply to dams constructed for the accumulation of water power for mills and manufactories, but owners must construct a fish runway over the dams. Violation: misdemeanor; fine $10-500 (15-44-110).

Commercial and Private Enterprise Provisions

Any person, firm, club or organization who owns, leases or controls a tract of land or body of water operated as a hunting or fishing place and charges fees for daily permits or memberships to hunt or fish must be licensed by the Commission with records and premises open to inspection. Violation: fine $250-500 (15-42-112). Persons engaged in taking, transporting, possessing or selling of true species of minnows as a business, for use as bait, must have a license. The Commission may, after determination that minnow taking for commercial purposes in a river, lake or body of water is detrimental to the supply of game fish, commercial fish, or minnows therein, close the body of water to minnow taking for commercial purpose after giving notice in a general circulation newspaper. Violation: misdemeanor; fine $25-100 (15-43-311).

It is unlawful to serve quail or other protected game animals or birds in a public dining room, dining car or cafe. The serving of bobwhite quail at a banquet or social gathering is expressly prohibited. Provided, customers may have their own game cooked and served at hotels, cafes or other public dining rooms. Violation: misdemeanor; fine $25-250 for first offense; minimum $500 for second offense (15-44-109).

It is unlawful to buy, sell, barter, trade or exchange or offer such, or to possess after buying in this state a game animal or bird or part protected under the state laws. This applies to game or game birds raised in captivity on private premises unless the owner obtains a permit for the raising in captivity and sale. The Commission may issue game or game bird breeder permits to raise game birds, game fish or animals for sale, within or without the state, such shipments to be legally tagged. Permittees shall report monthly an itemized inventory of all game animals, game birds or fur-bearing animals held. The Commission may issue scientific or propagative permits allowing holders to hold, possess and raise protected species of game birds, game and fur-bearing animals for scientific investigation or propagation, but they shall not be sold. The sale of deer, bobwhite quail, black bass and crappie for other than restocking or propagation is expressly prohibited. No permit can be issued whereby deer, bobwhite quail, black bass and crappie can be sold in this state for use as food. Violation: fine $25-300; second offense, an amount not less than $500 (15-44-101). Storage plant operators who allow the storing of game animals or birds therein shall keep a complete list of animals and owners' names, the animals to be tagged. Violation: misdemeanor; fine $25-500 (15-44-108). At the close of each season, fur dealers must furnish the Commission with an itemized list of all furs purchased, giving the number and kinds and from whom obtained (15-44-113).

Import, Export and Release Provisions

It is unlawful to export from Arkansas any of the true species of minnows. This does not prohibit the importing of minnows or the exporting of goldfish. Violation: misdemeanor; fine $25-50 (15-43-309). It is unlawful to ship, take, transport or export out of the state bullfrogs or parts, except for commercial bullfrog production operations on private property. Violation: misdemeanor; fine minimum $25 (15-44-112).

★It is unlawful to ship, export or carry, or accept for shipment, export or carriage, or permit to be shipped in a vehicle out of the state a wild bear or deer or part, wild turkey or part, wild pheasant, grouse, prairie chicken, partridge or quail, wild duck or other wild fowl, squirrel, or game of any description, dead or alive, or game fish known as trout, black bass, striped bass, rock bass, crappie, or white perch except as provided.★ Violation: misdemeanor; fine $50-500 for each offense. Each shipment is a separate offense (15-44-107).

See Agency Powers and Duties under STATE FISH AND WILDLIFE AGENCIES.

ANIMAL DAMAGE CONTROL

The Commission may: ▸ devise ways and means for reduction and control of predatory birds, animals and fish; ▸ capture, propagate, transport, buy, sell or exchange any species of game, bird, fish or fur-bearing animal needed for propagation or stocking, or remove and dispose of undesirable species; ▸ control predatory species such as hawks, owls, wolves and bobcats; ▸ cooperate with the Department of Predatory Animal Control of the USDA; ▸ expend money appropriated from the Game Protection Fund in paying bounties or otherwise carrying on the work (15-46-101). A county court may pay a bounty for each wolf killed within the county upon satisfactory proof of the killing. The state shall pay a bounty in a matching amount to that paid by the county. Payment shall be from the Game Protection Fund, but may not exceed $15 for each old wolf and $5 for each wolf under six months of age. Nonresidents may not get a bounty, nor may state or federal employees (15-46-102). A county desiring to exterminate bobcats (wildcats), gophers and wolves shall, through the quorum court, provide in a general levy a fund to be designated "Bobcat Fund" to be used for extermination of bobcats or wildcats, gophers and wolves in the jurisdiction of the quorum courts. The fund shall be in the custody of the county judge, to be paid out to a person who shall catch and destroy or kill bobcats, gophers and wolves, and upon presenting to the county judge as evidence the scalp of each bobcat destroyed or killed. The bounty shall be $3 per animal killed. The evidence showing the number of animals destroyed shall be kept by the judge for audit purposes twice a year, and the clerk preparing the audit shall receive $1 per audit (15-46-103).

A county desiring to exterminate hawks or crows shall, through a quorum court, provide in a general levy for current expenses a fund to be designated "Hawks and Crow Fund," to be used for the extermination of hawks and crows. The head of each hawk or crow destroyed is to be presented to the county judge as proof of extermination. Bounty is to be $.25 per hawk or crow. The catching and killing of hawks and crows shall be by trapping or shooting or any practical method (15-46-104). [Exactly the same provisions apply for the "Gopher and Mole Fund."] Evidence of destruction is to be the two front paws of each gopher or mole destroyed, and the bounty is $.10 per animal; catching shall be by trapping or any practicable method (15-46-105). Upon the request of a farmer with demonstrated damage to an agricultural crop from wildlife, the game warden shall implement a control program to relocate or eradicate wildlife causing injury to the crop. The program may authorize the farmer limited nighttime hunting of the specific wildlife. A program developed by the warden shall be exempt from the hunting laws of Arkansas, except federal and state laws which prohibit destruction of endangered or protected species (15-44-114).

See also Restrictions on Taking: Hunting and Trapping under HUNTING, TRAPPING, FISHING PROVISIONS, Agency Funding Sources under STATE FISH AND WILDLIFE AGENCIES, PROTECTED SPECIES OF WILDLIFE and GENERAL EXCEPTIONS TO PROTECTION.

ENFORCEMENT OF WILDLIFE LAWS

Enforcement Powers

★The General Assembly declares that a Commission employee enforcing or attempting to enforce the existing Commission regulations with respect to dogs running at large shall immediately, upon conviction, be discharged from employment and shall be ineligible for reemployment by the Commission. In addition, an employee or official of the Commission attempting to enforce the regulation in violation of this section shall be subject to a fine of $500-5,000, or jail 30 to 90 days, or both. Each violation is a separate offense and is to be punished accordingly (15-41-113).★

A game warden or other officer with authority to enforce state game laws may search a person, train, boat, business or public carrier to ascertain if the game laws are being violated. It is the duty of a justice of the peace, on information received of game law violations, to issue a warrant of arrest ordering that the offender be arrested and held for trial. ★Prosecuting attorneys who are present and assist in prosecutions for violations shall receive a fee of $10 for each conviction, to be taxed as other case costs.★ ★A peace officer or warden who fails/refuses to arrest a person known by the officer to have violated any state laws protecting game, fish, fur-bearing animals, fresh water mussels and other wildlife, or where authentic reports are made of the violations, is guilty of a misdemeanor and fined not less than $100 and shall be removed/suspended from office (15-41-203 through -205).★

Game wardens shall confiscate all unlawful shipments and game and fish unlawfully caught or killed and use the same for charitable purposes; failure to comply results in the warden's dismissal. Any game, fish, fresh water mussel shells, fur-bearing animals or pelts confiscated under state wildlife laws shall be disposed of by the confiscating officer and proceeds paid into the Game Protection Fund. Fur-bearing animals shall be liberated in the community where confiscated. Pelts confiscated during closed seasons shall be held until the open season if possible, and game or fish, the sale of which is prohibited by law, shall be donated to a charitable organization. All guns, tackle, nets, boats, motors of every kind, and equipment used in willful violation by persons taking, transporting or selling game birds, game or fur-bearing animals or fish are declared contraband, and the title to them forfeited to the state, and it is the duty of the Commission or its agents to seize the contraband and deliver it to the trial court. The offender may possess the contraband goods, except devices whose use is expressly prohibited in the taking of game birds, game, fur-bearing animals or fish, on filing of bond fixed by the court. On conviction, the court shall order the sheriff to sell the seized property at public auction within 20 days, proceeds to go to the Game Protection Fund (15-41-206 through -208).

Criminal Penalties

Fines collected from violations of the game laws shall be paid to the county where the fine is assessed and forwarded to the Game Protection Fund. No warden shall collect fees/costs for the warden's own use or benefit, but in cases of convictions for game law violations, fees and costs provided by law for sheriffs shall be taxed and paid to a local peace officer assisting the warden in the arrest/case, or into the county common school fund in the absence of the officer. Convicted persons failing to pay fines/costs shall be dealt with the same as persons convicted of violations of other state criminal laws. Violations of this act, not otherwise provided herein, are misdemeanors, with a fine of $5-300 (15-41-209 through -211).

Illegal Taking of Wildlife

It is unlawful to sell or offer to sell black, striped or white bass, or rock, war-mouth or calico bass, crappie, bream, perch, pike or jack salmon. The Commission may issue a permit for the sale of game fish raised in a private hatchery. Violation: misdemeanor; fine $25-300; and forfeiture of permit (15-44-102).

It is lawful at all times to bring into and possess in this state game, animals or birds and fish lawfully taken in another state. Nonresidents properly licensed may carry/ship out of the state game animals or birds not exceeding one day's legal kill at a time. The license holder must accompany the game animals/birds carried out of the state, and the game must bear a tag bearing hunter's name, package contents and license number. Not more than three days' legal kill of game animals or birds shall be carried out during the period covered by a nonresident license, nor more than two days' legal kill during carried out during one week. Violation: misdemeanor; fine $50-500 (15-44-103 and -104).

A permit issued by the Commission, deputy or regular warden, sheriff or justice of the peace is required to ship a specimen of game or fish or any part, legally taken, outside the state for the purpose of having it mounted, tanned or converted into wearing apparel, the permit to state the species, body part, and shipper's name. Violation: misdemeanor; fine minimum $25. Common carriers may refuse to receive a package they suspect contains fish or game designed for export and may open the package (15-44-105 and -106).

See also Agency Powers and Duties under STATE FISH AND WILDLIFE AGENCIES; HUNTING, FISHING AND TRAPPING PROVISIONS.

Reward Payments

Upon conviction for violation of the terms of 15-43-208 through 15-43-210 (turkey hunting provisions), the officer collecting the fine is authorized to pay to the party furnishing the information responsible for the conviction $25 out of each fine collected (15-43-211).

HABITAT PROTECTION

★★The General Assembly recognizes the importance of preserving the environment of the state and is aware of the provisions of Arkansas Constitution, Amendment 35, which created the Commission and granted it broad authority to manage and regulate the fish and wildlife resources of the state. It is the intent of this section to establish reasonable procedures whereby the Commission, in the management of the fish and wildlife resources of the state, shall perform the functions and duties in accordance with sound principles of environmental preservation. Before the Commission shall undertake the cutting of timber on its lands, including selective cutting, the Commission shall: cause an environmental impact statement to be made; prepare a written environmental impact statement in regard to the proposed timber cutting; and file such with the **Natural Heritage Commission** which shall hold hearings according to statutory requirements and file its evaluation of the proposed timber cutting. This does not apply to the cutting or sale of salvageable timber for construction of levees, structures, public access routes, boating ramps or roads. A citizen may bring an action within the county of the proposed timber cutting to enjoin timber cutting until the environmental impact statement is made and properly filed, heard by the public, and the Natural Heritage Commission's recommendations are received (15-41-108).★★

★The Commission may apply to the Commissioner of State Lands for transfer of state-owned land, or land which has reverted to the state due to delinquent taxes, and which is desirable for game or fish refuge areas or public hunting or fishing areas or other development of wildlife resource purposes and that is not suitable for agricultural or industrial uses; the land is to be transferred to the Commission on receipt of sufficient proof of the nature of land desired and of the Commission's need for the land, the transfers to operate as an appropriation of the land for game or fish refuge areas, public hunting and fishing areas or other uses. The transfer shall be a bar to grants by this state of the land or interest in the land; provided that land so acquired cannot be sold by the Commission, but shall revert to the state if not developed within two years of acquisition or when it is no longer desired by the Commission (15-41-109).★

To encourage wildlife habitat conservation on private lands, the Commission shall enter into licensing agreements for not less than 10 years for approved projects on privately owned lands, the agreements to detail the landowner's responsibilities. Expenditures by private landowners for these approved wildlife habitat conservation projects shall be considered contributions for the use of the state (15-45-101). Violation: misdemeanor; fine minimum $25; or jail up to 30 days; or both (15-45-201). Owners of suitable lands totalling not less than 640 acres desiring to have lands set apart as a refuge for game and wild birds or other wildlife may petition the Commission stating their consent to vest in the state all rights to prohibit hunting on the lands and agreeing that they and their families and tenants shall not hunt on the lands, and that they will make every effort to help protect the refuge from hunting or other violations. Agreements shall be for a minimum of five years. On approval of the refuges, the Commission shall post the lands against trespass and shall publish notice to the public as specified by statute. The game refuge shall then be deemed a public state game refuge (15-45-202 and -203).

The Governor may set aside and designate as game, fowl and fish refuges state lands for the protection of game. Refuges shall contain not less than 5,000 contiguous acres and only lands unfit for agriculture and which are nonmineral-bearing shall be included. Whoever shall hunt, catch, trap, willfully destroy, disturb or kill a game animal, game or nongame bird, or fish or their eggs or spawn on the lands except under regulations and laws shall be fined up to $100, or jailed up to 30 days, or both. The Commission may: ► accept or acquire through gift or purchase suitable lands for the creation of game refuges, to be designated and regulated as prescribed by statute, title in fee, including timber and mineral rights, to be vested in the state; ► accept or acquire watered areas and adjacent lands for fish refuges subject to the same provisions as for game refuges, but the areas need not amount to 640 acres if suited to fish propagation; ► formulate and post regulations regarding the protection of game birds and game animals, songbirds and insectivorous birds and other wildlife on the refuge, such regulations, published by posters, to become the law of the state controlling the game refuge. Lands designated by the Governor as a game refuge are not subject to redemption, sale, donation, homestead or disposal under a state law until the General Assembly abolishes the game refuge (15-45-204 through -208). Money spent by the Commission in procuring, improving, or policing a state game or fish refuge shall be paid out of the Game Protection Fund (15-45-212).

When the purchase of lands by state agencies is considered an appropriate strategy for protection of certain nongame species, the lands considered shall be restricted to: natural communities, both terrestrial and aquatic, that exhibit the highest degree of integrity and least evidence of disturbance; habitats of Arkansas' rarest and most severely endangered or threatened native organisms. Decisions for land purchase under this program will take into account the availability and preservation status of all Arkansas lands known to represent whatever particular value may be under consideration. In accordance with the same system of priorities, funds from the Nongame Preservation Program may be used for restoring and protecting natural communities, both terrestrial and aquatic, and populations of rare, endangered, or threatened native organisms (15-45-304). (See also STATE WILDLIFE POLICY and STATE FISH AND WILDLIFE AGENCIES for additional information on nongame preservation.)

NATIVE AMERICAN WILDLIFE PROVISIONS: None.

CALIFORNIA

Sources: West's Annotated California Codes, 1957; Fish and Game Code, Sections 1 to 16541; 1992 Cumulative Pocket Part.

STATE WILDLIFE POLICY

[California has many statements of policy at the beginning of statutes delineating various programs. The following is a mere sampling of statements of policy found throughout the fish and wildlife laws.]

It is state policy to encourage preservation, conservation, and maintenance of wildlife resources. Policy objectives include: ► maintain sufficient populations of all species of wildlife and habitat necessary; ► provide for beneficial use and enjoyment of wildlife; ► perpetuate all species for intrinsic and ecological values, and direct benefits to people; ► provide for aesthetic, educational, and nonappropriative uses of various wildlife species; ► maintain recreational uses of wildlife, including hunting, as uses of designated species, subject to regulations for healthy, viable wildlife resources, public safety, and a quality outdoor experience; ► provide economic return through regulated management, consistent with maintenance of thriving wildlife resources and public ownership; ► alleviate economic losses or public health or safety problems caused by wildlife. Such resolution shall be designed consistent with economic and public health considerations and the objectives above; ► it is not intended that this policy shall provide power to regulate natural resources or other activities, except as the Legislature provides (1801).

The Legislature finds many species and subspecies of birds, mammals, fish, amphibia, and reptiles are endangered because habitats are threatened with destruction, drastic modification, or severe curtailment, or because of commercial exploitation through exports and imports of birds, mammals, fish, amphibia, and reptiles, or because of disease, predation, or other factors (2050). The Legislature finds: ► certain species of fish, wildlife, and plants have become extinct as a result of man's activities, untempered by adequate concern and conservation; ► other species are threatened with extinction because they or their habitats are threatened with destruction, adverse modification, severe curtailment, overexploitation, disease, predation, or other factors; ► these species are of ecological, educational, historical, recreational, esthetic, economic, and scientific value, and the conservation, protection, and enhancement of these species and their habitat is of statewide concern (2051).

★★The people find: ► protection, enhancement, and restoration of wildlife habitat and fisheries are vital to maintaining quality of life; ► as population increases, there is an urgent need to protect the rapidly disappearing wildlife habitats; ► much of the important deer winter ranges have been destroyed or are increasingly subject to incompatible land uses, a major threat to the survival of many migratory deer herds; ► deer, mountain lion, and other wildlife habitat is disappearing rapidly; ► small and often isolated wildlife populations depend upon these shrinking habitats; ► natural habitat must be preserved to maintain the genetic integrity of California's wildlife; ► officials shall implement this chapter to preserve, maintain, and enhance the diverse wildlife and habitats (2780). ★★

★★The people find that wildlife and fisheries conservation is in the public interest and necessary to keep certain lands in natural condition to protect significant environmental values of wildlife and native plant habitat, riparian and wetland areas, native oak woodlands, and other open-space lands, and provide opportunities to visit natural environments and wildlife. Additional funds are needed to protect fish, wildlife, and native plant resources and the Legislature should provide those funds through appropriate sources (2781). ★★   See also Agency Funding Sources under STATE FISH AND WILDLIFE AGENCIES.

RELEVANT WILDLIFE DEFINITIONS: See Definitions section of Appendices.

STATE FISH AND WILDLIFE AGENCIES

Agency Structure

There is in the Resources Agency the **Fish and Game Commission** (Commission) created by Section 20 of Article IV of the Constitution (101). The president of the Commission may be a member ex officio of the Migratory Bird Conservation Commission created by the federal Migratory Bird Conservation Act (357).

There is in the Resources Agency a **Department of Fish and Game** (Department) administered through the Director (700). The Director and Deputy Director are appointed by and serve at the pleasure of the Governor. The Deputy Director has duties assigned by and is responsible to the Director (701 and 701.3).

The provisions of this Code shall be administered and enforced by the Department (702). General policies for the Department shall be formulated by the Commission. The Director is responsible to the Commission for Department administration (703).

Agency Powers and Duties

The **Commission** is granted the power to regulate the taking or possession of birds, mammals, fish, amphibia, and reptiles, but not the power to regulate the taking, possessing, processing, or use of fish, amphibia, kelp, or other aquatic plants for commercial purposes (200).

The **Department:** ▸ shall expend funds for biological research and collection of information on the conservation, propagation, protection, and perpetuation of birds, nests and eggs, and of mammals, reptiles, and fish (1000); ▸ shall submit periodic reports to the Governor and the Legislature on selected freshwater and ocean fisheries, which may include historical population trends, potential problems facing species, the effects of toxics in the environment on those species, problems relating to disease, and other relevant considerations [details provided] (1000.5); ▸ may accept donations of money and services for educational material; ▸ may charge for the use of such materials (1005); ▸ may accept personal property if the donor is a county and it is purchased with fish and game violation fines (1005.5); ▸ may import, propagate, and distribute birds, mammals, or fish; ▸ shall investigate all diseases of birds, mammals, or fish, and establish and maintain laboratories; ▸ may obtain rights of way for access for hunting or fishing, except by eminent domain; ▸ with Department of General Services approval, may sell grazing permits or products produced on Department lands (1007 through 1010); ▸ shall determine the extent to which salmon and steelhead resources will be protected from damage and how project plans will increase those resources, and advise the Commission of such (1015).

★★It is policy to anticipate and resolve conflicts between management, conservation, and protection of fish and wildlife resources, their habitat, and activities that may affect them by using informal consultative procedures prior to formal action. Fees charged by a mediator are a proper charge against funds available to the Department (1017).★★

The Department shall establish procedures for application and award of hunting license tags for fundraising [procedures for licensing agents are contained in 1055 through 1060] (1054.8). The Department, under Commission policies may provide for feeding of game birds, mammals, or fish (1502), and shall provide feeding of deer where natural forage is unavailable due to snow. Feeding upon private land requires owner consent (1503). The Department may protect [certain listed] spawning areas on state-owned lands to protect fishlife [with exceptions, including commerce and navigation, flood control projects, etc.]. Exceptions shall not extend to depositing or dredging materials, other than as necessary for structures (1505). For propagating, feeding and protecting birds, mammals, and fish, and establishing wildlife management areas or public shooting grounds, the Department, with Commission approval, may: ▸ accept donations of birds, mammals, and fish, and money; ▸ acquire and occupy, develop, maintain, use and administer, land, water, and water rights for state game farms, wildlife management areas, or public shooting grounds (1525).

The Department shall conduct a biological and physical inventory of all trout streams and lakes to determine regulations, management as a wild trout fishery, or if trout should be planted (1726.4). [Details of trout inventory and management are described.] The Department has jurisdiction over the conservation, protection, and management of fish, wildlife, native plants, and habitat for sustainable populations of those species (1802).

The Commission may authorize the taking of tule elk pursuant to Section 332. The Department shall relocate tule elk and shall cooperate with federal and local agencies and landowners. When economic or environmental damage occurs, emphasis shall be placed on managing each herd through relocation, sporthunting, or other appropriate means [details regarding Owens Valley provided]. The Department shall complete management plans for high priority areas, to include: ▸ area boundaries; ▸ characteristics of the herds; ▸ habitat conditions and trends; ▸ factors affecting the tule elk population, including conflicts with other land uses; ▸ management activities. The Director shall submit a report on the status of tule elk to the Commission, the Governor and to the Legislature every two years [details of report provided] (3951).

Agency Regulations

The Commission shall exercise its powers by regulations made and promulgated pursuant to this article (202). Any Commission regulation relating to resident game birds, game mammals, fur-bearing mammals, fish, amphibia or reptiles may apply to any areas, districts, or portions, and may do the following as to any species or subspecies: ▸ establish, extend, shorten, or abolish seasons, bag and possession limits, and territorial limits; ▸ prescribe the manner of taking; ▸ [for game birds, game and fur-bearing mammals only] establish, change, or abolish restrictions based upon sex, maturity, or other physical distinctions (203 and 205). ★★Commission regulations shall consider populations, habitat, food supplies, and welfare of individual animals (203.1).★★ The Commission cannot authorize or permit taking: ▸ any bird or mammal in any refuge; ▸ elk or antelope, regulated pursuant to sections 332 and 331; ▸ spike buck or spotted fawn (204).

[Regular annual Commission meetings revising regulations for various types of wildlife are described in sections 206-210, including notice and publication of meeting dates and times and publication of regulations.] Any regulation adopted pursuant to this article may supersede any section of this code, if specifically provided in the regulation. A regulation shall be valid only if it makes changes to this code under one of the following circumstances: ▸ it is necessary for the protection of fish, wildlife, and other natural resources; ▸ the Commission determines that an emergency exists or will exist. The regulation shall be supported by written findings, and remain in effect not more than 12 months (219) [other details for adding or changing regulations are provided in 220]. The Commission may, after at least one hearing, adopt or repeal an emergency regulation for the immediate conservation, preservation, or protection of birds, mammals, reptiles, or fish, nests or eggs or for immediate preservation of the public peace, health and safety, or general welfare (240).

Agency Funding Sources

★★The Legislature declares that the Department has not been properly funded, because of fixed revenues in contrast to rising inflation, which has prevented proper planning and manpower allocation, and has required the Department to restrict warden enforcement and defer essential repairs to facilities. The lack of secure funding for fish and wildlife activities other than sport and commercial fishing and hunting has resulted in inadequate nongame fish and wildlife protection programs (710). With revenues declining, the Department's responsibilities have been expanding into numerous new areas. Limitations on Department revenues have resulted in its inability effectively to provide all of the programs and activities required and to manage the wildlife resources held in trust. The Department has been largely supported by fees paid by those who utilize the resources held in trust. The Department should continue to be funded by user fees, which should more accurately reflect all costs associated with these resources. (710.5).★★ To ensure adequate funding for the Department, the Legislature declares: ▸ the cost of nongame fish and wildlife programs and free hunting and fishing license programs shall be provided in the Budget Act by appropriating money from sources other than the **Fish and Game Preservation Fund**; ▸ the costs of commercial fishing programs shall be provided solely out of revenues from commercial fishing taxes, license fees, reimbursements and federal funds; ▸ the costs of hunting and sportfishing programs shall be provided solely out of hunting and sportfishing revenues, reimbursements and federal funds and shall not be used to support commercial fishing, free hunting and fishing license, or nongame fish and wildlife programs; ▸ costs of managing lands and wildlife shall be supplemented out of revenues in the Native Species Conservation and Enhancement Account in the Fish and Game Preservation Fund; ▸ the Department shall review its programs at least every five years; ▸ license fees shall be adjusted annually; ▸ a substantial increase in hunting and sportfishing programs shall be reflected by appropriate amendments to the code that establishes the base sport license fees (711).

★★The Department of Finance shall include in the Governor's budget sufficient moneys from the General Fund and sources other than the Fish and Game Preservation Fund to fund the Department's nongame programs, including those for protection and enhancement of nongame fish and wildlife and their habitat, the free hunting and fishing license programs, and special repairs and capital outlay. Funds shall not provide for any program or project not related to protection or propagation of fish and game (712). The Department shall, at least every five years, analyze fees for permits, licenses, stamps, and tags, and recommend adjustments (713). ★★

The Department shall maintain within the Fish and Game Preservation Fund a **Native Species Conservation and Enhancement Account** to permit separate accountability for donations for support of nongame and native plant conservation and enhancement programs (1760), and take all appropriate measures to encourage donations to the account, including public information concerning the status of threatened native species (1763). The Department may offer for sale a **native species stamp**, promotional materials, and nature study aids (1766).

The Department shall maintain within the Fish and Game Preservation Fund an **Endangered and Rare Fish, Wildlife, and Plant Species Conservation and Enhancement Account**, for programs for endangered and rare species, related conservation and enhancement programs, and programs for candidate species for endangered or rare designation; may encourage donations to this account through the tax return checkoff system, and may disseminate information concerning the status of endangered and rare species (1770 through 1772).

The **Animal Trust Fund** is established in the State Treasury. Upon appropriation, 5% of the fund is available to the Department to make grants (2201). The Department may seek grants and accept donations for the fund (2202). The Director, with the advice of the committee established pursuant to Section 2150.3, shall adopt regulations to administer a grant program for facilities which care for and shelter mammals (2203).

All money deposited in the **Fish and Wildlife Habitat Enhancement Fund** shall be available for appropriation by the Legislature for: ▸ [specific dollar amounts are set forth] expenditure by the Wildlife Conservation Board for acquisition, enhancement, or development of lands outside the coastal zone for preservation of resources and management of wildlife and fisheries [monies are divided between acquisition, enhancement or development of lands for marsh or aquatic environment or waterways]; ▸ habitat for rare, endangered and fully protected species [only habitat subject to destruction, drastic modification, or severe curtailment of habitat values (2624)]; ▸ grants to local public agencies, for expenditures by the conservancy for purposes authorized; ▸ expenditure by the Wildlife Conservation Board for acquisition, enhancement, or development inside the coastal zone of marshlands and adjacent lands for habitat for wildlife benefitted by a marsh or aquatic environment (2620). Bonds may be issued to provide a fund for carrying out the purposes of this chapter (2640). Bond proceeds shall be deposited in the Fish and Wildlife Habitat Enhancement Fund, which may be expended only as specified in this chapter and pursuant to appropriation (2643). [Provision for withdrawal of amounts not exceeding the amount of unsold bonds is made in section (2644).] For authorizing the issuance and sale of bonds, the **Wildlife Habitat Enhancement Program Finance Committee** is created, consisting of the Controller, Director of Finance, and the Treasurer (2647).

Moneys available for this chapter pursuant to Chapter 4 (commencing with Section 5930) of the Public Resources Code shall be deposited in a **Wildlife and Natural Areas Conservation Fund** (2720). See also HABITAT PROTECTION.

The **Fisheries Restoration Account** is created in the Fish and Game Preservation Fund, for construction, operation, and administration of projects in accordance with the Salmon, Steelhead Trout, and Anadromous Fisheries Program Act, and projects to restore and maintain fishery resources and their habitat that have been damaged by past water diversions and projects and other development. Proposals for projects must be submitted to the Joint Committee on Fisheries and Aquaculture and to the Joint Legislative Budget Committee and shall have as their primary objective the restoration of fishery resources and may include acquisition of lands, restoration of habitat, restoration or creation of spawning areas, construction of fish screens or fish ladders, stream rehabilitation, and installation of pollution control facilities. Priority shall be given to projects that employ fishermen, fish processing workers, and others unemployed or underemployed by elimination of a commercial fishing season due to restrictions imposed by federal regulations (2762).

The **Habitat Conservation Fund**, shall be used for acquisition of habitat: ▸ including native oak woodlands to protect deer and mountain lions; ▸ to protect rare, endangered, threatened, or fully protected species; ▸ to implement the Habitat Conservation Program commencing with Section 2721; ▸ for acquisition, enhancement, or restoration of: ▸ wetlands aquatic habitat for spawning and rearing of anadromous salmonids and trout resources and riparian habitat (2786). ★★In areas where habitats are or may become isolated or fragmented, preference shall be given to projects which will serve as corridors linking otherwise separated habitat so that genetic integrity of wildlife populations will be maintained (2789).★★ Each agency receiving money from the fund shall report to the board [limitations on amounts of funds to be spent detailed] (2790). The state or local agency that manages lands acquired shall prepare, with public participation, a management plan to reduce possible conflicts with neighboring land use and landowners, including agriculturists. The plans shall comply with the California Environmental Quality Act (2794).

The Controller shall annually transfer 10% of the funds in the Unallocated Account in the Cigarette and Tobacco Products Surtax Fund to the Habitat Conservation Fund (2795). The Controller shall annually transfer $30,000,000 from the General Fund to the Habitat Conservation Fund, less any amount transferred to the Habitat Conservation Fund from the various accounts and funds [specific accounts and funds named]. This does not limit the amount of funds which may be transferred to the Habitat Conservation Fund or which may be expended for fish and wildlife habitat protection from the Fund or other sources (2796).

It is the policy of the state to encourage biologically sound management of fish and other wildlife resources on lands administered by the Department of Defense (3450). The Department may coordinate and cooperate with all branches of the US military, for developing fish and wildlife management plans and programs to provide optimum fish and wildlife resource management and use compatible with military use of those lands (3451).

The **California Waterfowl Habitat Preservation Account** is in the Fish and Game Preservation Fund. The proceeds of investment shall be available, upon appropriation, for expenditure pursuant to this article, not more than 7% for administrative costs of the Department (3467). All funds from sale of **upland game bird stamps** shall be deposited in the Fish and Game Preservation Fund and expended solely for purposes specified in Section 3685 (3684). Funds shall be available for programs, projects, and land acquisitions to benefit upland game bird species, and for related hunting opportunities and public outreach (3685).

All funds from sale of state duck stamps and related items shall be deposited in the **State Duck Stamp Account** in the Fish and Game Preservation Fund, not more than 6% used for administration and implementation of the federal Migratory Bird Harvest Program (3701). Funds shall be used for protecting, preserving, restoring, enhancing, and developing migratory waterfowl breeding and wintering habitat, evaluating habitat projects, and conducting waterfowl resource assessments and related research. Funds may be used to reimburse nonprofit organizations for completed habitat projects, or for grants or contracts for carrying out this article (3702). $2.25 from each state duck stamp sold shall be allocated for the North American Waterfowl Management Plan in those areas of Canada from which come substantial numbers of migratory waterfowl. These funds shall be matched with federal or private funds. The available balance of the funds shall be used for any project authorized pursuant to Section 3702. Lands acquired in California with those funds shall be open to waterfowl hunting as a public shooting ground or wildlife management area (3704). Before allocating funds outside the state or the US, the Commission shall secure evidence of its acceptability to the government agency having jurisdiction (3705).

The Director shall appoint a nine member **Striped Bass Stamp Advisory Committee** to provide recommendations regarding allocation of funds from **striped bass stamps**. Members shall be selected from names submitted by striped bass fishermen and their associations and shall serve at the discretion of the Director. The advisory committee shall annually recommend to the Department projects and budgets. All projects proposed for funding shall be reviewed by the advisory committee (7362).

Revenue from the **steelhead trout catch report-restoration card** may be expended to monitor, restore, or enhance steelhead trout resources, and to administer the catch report-restoration card program. The Department shall submit proposed expenditures to the **Advisory Committee on Salmon and Steelhead Trout** for review and comment. The Department shall report to the Legislature regarding the program, projects, benefits, and its recommendation as to whether the catch report-restoration card requirement should be continued (7381).

The **Fish and Wildlife Pollution Cleanup and Abatement Account** in the Fish and Game Preservation Fund [designation of source of funds is detailed] shall be expended for the following: ▸ abatement, cleanup, and removal of pollutants from the environment; ▸ response coordination, planning, and program management; ▸ resource injury determination; ▸ resource damage assessment; ▸ economic valuation of resources; ▸ restoration or rehabilitation at sites damaged by pollution. Funds in the account in excess of $1,000,000 as of July 1 may be expended for the preservation of plants, wildlife, and fisheries. Funds may be expended for cleanup and abatement if effort has been made to have the responsible party pay cleanup and abatement costs, and funds are not available from the emergency reserve account of the Hazardous Substance Account (12017).

Agency Advisory Boards

There is in the Department the **Wildlife Conservation Board** (Board), consisting of the president of the Commission, the Director and the Director of Finance (1320). Three members of the Senate, appointed by the Committee on Rules, and three members of the Assembly, appointed by the Speaker, shall meet with the Board and participate to the extent not incompatible with their positions in the Legislature (1323). The Members of the Legislature shall constitute an interim investigating committee on this chapter (1324). The Board shall: ▸ investigate and determine what areas are most essential for wildlife production and preservation, and will provide recreation; ▸ ascertain lands for game propagation, game refuges, bird refuges, waterfowl refuges, game farms, fish hatcheries, game management areas, and streams and lakes for fishing, hunting, and shooting; ▸ ascertain what lands are suitable for providing cover for propagating and rearing waterfowl, shore birds, and upland birds, and possibilities of acquiring easements; ▸ determine what areas, lands, or rights should be acquired for a coordinated and balanced program for maximum restoration of wildlife and maximum recreational advantages; ▸ authorize acquisition of such real property, rights in real property, water, or water rights to carry out this chapter, by gifts, purchases, leases, easements, transfer or exchange of property, transfers of development rights or credits, and purchases of development rights, conservation easements, and other interests. The Board may also authorize the Department to engage in various real estate transactions (1345 through 1348).

The Department: ▸ shall construct facilities for purposes for which real property or rights in real property or water, or water rights were acquired; ▸ may accept federal grants, and receive gifts, donations, and other public or private support for fish and wildlife habitat enhancement, including riparian habitat restoration. Funds from those sources shall be deposited in the Wildlife Restoration Fund. The Board may award grants or loans to nonprofit organizations, local, federal and state agencies for habitat restoration, enhancement, management, protection and improvement of riparian resources, and for development of compatible public access facilities (1350). The money in the Wildlife Restoration Fund is available for expenditure under any provision of this chapter. Federal moneys for projects authorized by the Board shall be deposited in that fund (1352). The Board may authorize acquisition of such lands or rights for furnishing access for fishing, hunting and shooting (1354).

There is within the Department an **Aquaculture Coordinator** who shall: ▸ promote aquaculture among public agencies and the public; ▸ propose methods of reducing the negative impact of public regulation on the industry; ▸ provide information on regulatory compliance to the industry; ▸ provide needed advice to aquaculturists on facility site and design (15100). The Director shall appoint an **Aquaculture Industry Advisory Committee** of at least 12 members, representing all sectors of the fresh and salt water aquaculture industry (15700), to advise the Director on matters pertaining to aquaculture, and to assist in developing and implementing a state aquaculture plan, identifying opportunities for regulatory relief, developing research and development priorities and criteria to assure that pilot programs are compatible with industry needs, and identifying other opportunities for industrial development (15702).

The Director shall appoint an **Interagency Committee for Aquaculture Development** (15800). The Committee shall advise the Director on matters pertaining to aquaculture and coordinate agencies (15803).

See Agency Funding Sources under this section for Striped Bass Stamp Advisory Committee and Advisory Committee on Salmon and Steelhead Trout.

PROTECTED SPECIES OF WILDLIFE

It is state policy to conserve, protect, restore, and enhance any endangered or threatened species and its habitat and it is the intent of the Legislature to acquire lands for habitat for these species. No person shall import, or take, possess, or sell, any bird, mammal, fish, amphibia or reptile, or any part or product, that the Commission determines to be endangered or rare, except as provided (2052). ★★Cooperation of owners of land identified as habitat for endangered and threatened species is essential, and it is state policy to foster and encourage that cooperation. An owner of property on which an endangered, threatened or candidate species lives shall not be liable for civil damages for injury to employees or persons under contract with the Department if they are injured while conducting survey, management, or species recovery efforts (2056).★★

The Commission shall establish a list of endangered and a list of threatened species, and add or remove species as warranted (2070). [Listing procedures are detailed in 2071 through 2074.4.] The Department promptly shall commence a review of the species' status. Within 12 months of publication of a notice, the Department shall report to the Commission, based upon the best scientific information available, indicating whether the petitioned action is warranted, including a preliminary identification of essential habitat, and recommending actions for management activities (2074.6).

This article imposes no duty, obligation or requirement on the Commission or Department to undertake independent studies or assessments when reviewing a petition (2074.8). At the meeting for final consideration the Commission shall find the petitioned action is not warranted and the petitioned species shall be removed from the list of candidate species, or the action is warranted and it shall publish a notice of that finding and the proposed rulemaking to add or remove the species from the lists (2075 and 2075.5). A finding pursuant to this section is subject to judicial review (2076). The Commission may adopt an emergency regulation adding an endangered or threatened species if it finds a significant threat to the continued existence of the species. The Commission shall notify affected or interested persons of the regulation (2076.5).

The Department shall review listed species every five years to determine if the conditions for original listing are still present, based on the best scientific information available. The Department shall report to the Commission the results of its five-year review (2077). The Department shall report annually summarizing the status of listed endangered, threatened, and candidate species to the Commission, Legislature, Governor, and interested individuals (2079). No person shall import or export, or take, possess, purchase, or sell, any species, part or product, determined to be endangered or threatened, or attempt any of those acts, except as provided (2080). This article does not apply to a candidate species if notice has been given pursuant to Section 2074.4 (2085).

[Detailed provisions are made for state agency consultation with the Department to ensure that any action funded, authorized or carried out by the agency is not likely to jeopardize an endangered or threatened species. Provisions follow the consultation procedures required by Section 7 of the federal Endangered Species Act (2053 through 2055, and 2909 through 2095).]

The provisions of this article do not apply to candidate species. Upon a request from a lead agency or a project proponent, the Department shall grant an informal consultation on any proposed project which may affect such species. It is the intent of the Legislature to facilitate resolution of potential conflicts between candidate species and proposed projects on the basis of information available at the time, and not to require the alteration of project processing schedules pending final determination of any candidate species' status (2096).

It is unlawful to: ▸ take, possess, or destroy needlessly a bird's nest or eggs, except as provided (3503); ▸ take, possess, or destroy birds, nests or eggs in Falconiformes or Strigiformes orders (birds-of-prey), except as provided (3503.5); ▸ take, sell, or purchase an aigrette or egret, osprey, bird of paradise, goura, numidi, or any parts (3505). Fully protected birds or parts may not be taken or possessed and no provision of this code or other law shall authorize issuance of permits or licenses to take a fully protected bird. No such permits or licenses heretofore issued shall have any force or effect, except the Commission may authorize collecting species for scientific research and may authorize live capture and relocation under a permit for protection of livestock. Legally imported, fully protected birds or parts may be possessed under Department permit [protected birds are listed] (3511). Except as provided in the Migratory Bird Treaty Act and regulations, it is unlawful to take or possess a migratory nongame bird (3513). All birds occurring naturally in California which are not resident game birds, migratory game birds, or fully protected birds, are nongame birds, and it is unlawful to take any nongame bird, except as provided in this code or regulations (3800). [The Department's duties regarding California condors are provided in 3850 through 3853, 3855 and 3857.]

★+Notwithstanding Section 3950 or other code provision, the mountain lion (genus Felis) shall not be listed as a game mammal by the Department or the Commission. Neither the Commission nor the Department shall adopt a regulation that conflicts with or supersedes this section (3950.1).★+ Mammals occurring naturally in California which are not game mammals, fully protected mammals, or fur-bearing mammals, are nongame mammals, which may not be taken or possessed except as provided in this code or regulations (4150). A house cat found within the limits of a fish and game refuge is a nongame mammal, unless in its owner's residence or on grounds adjacent to such residence (4151). It is unlawful to kill, wound, capture, or possess an undomesticated burro (a wild burro or a burro not tamed for three years after its capture), except as provided (4600 and 4601).

Fully protected mammals or parts may not be taken or possessed at any time and no provision of this code or other law shall authorize issuance of permits or licenses to take a fully protected mammal. The Commission may authorize collecting of species for scientific research. Legally imported, fully protected mammals or parts may be possessed under Department permit. The following are fully protected mammals: Morro Bay kangaroo rat; bighorn sheep, except Nelson bighorn sheep; ring-tailed cat; salt-marsh harvest mouse; and wolverine [marine mammals also listed] (4700).

The mountain lion is a specially protected mammal. It is unlawful to take, injure, possess, transport, import, or sell any mountain lion, part or product, except as provided. This does not prohibit sale or possession of a mountain lion, part or product when the owner can demonstrate that it was in possession on June 6, 1990. Violation is a misdemeanor punishable by jail up to one year, or a fine up to $10,000, or both. It is not a violation if it is demonstrated that in taking or injuring a mountain lion the individual was acting in self-defense or in defense of others. Neither the Commission nor the Department shall adopt any regulation that conflicts with or supersedes provisions of this chapter (4800).

It is unlawful to sell, purchase, harm, take, possess, or transport a tortoise or parts, or to shoot a projectile at a tortoise, unless authorized by the Department (5000). This does not prohibit possession when the owner can demonstrate legal possession before the effective date of this section, such tortoise to be marked or otherwise identified, and shall not be transferred without Department approval (5001). It is unlawful to take diamond-back terrapin (5020). Fully protected reptiles and amphibians or parts may not be taken or possessed and no provision shall authorize the issuance of permits or licenses to take a fully protected reptile or amphibian and no such permits or licenses shall have any force or effect, except for collecting of species for scientific research. Legally imported fully protected reptiles or amphibians or parts may be possessed under Department permit. The following are fully protected reptiles and amphibians: Blunt-nosed leopard lizard, San Francisco garter snake, Santa Cruz long-toed salamander, Limestone salamander, and Black toad (5050). The Commission shall establish rules and regulations for the commercial take, sale, transport, export, or import of native reptiles (5061). No permit shall be issued or renewed for the operation of a farm for alligators or any species of the family crocodilidae if the animals are kept for the use and sale of the meat or hides (5062).

Fully protected fish or parts may not be taken or possessed and no provision of this code or other law shall authorize the issuance of permits or licenses to take them, except for collecting for scientific research. Legally imported fully protected fish or parts may be possessed under permit. Fully protected fish are: Colorado River squawfish, Thicktail chub; Mohave chub, Lost River sucker, Modoc sucker, Shortnose sucker, Humpback sucker, Owens River pupfish, Unarmored threespine stickleback, rough sculpin (5515).

GENERAL EXCEPTIONS TO PROTECTION

The Department may take, for scientific or propagation purposes, fish, amphibia, reptiles, mammals, birds, and nests and eggs, or any other plant or animal life. The Department may issue permits, under Commission restrictions and regulations, to take or possess for scientific, educational, or propagation purposes. Permits may be issued for banding of birds and the exhibition of live or dead wildlife specimens by public zoological gardens, scientific, or educational institutions; or to a regularly enrolled student in, or faculty member teaching, commercial fishing. Permittees need not have a sportfishing or hunting license for scientific collecting. Plants and animals taken under permit may be shipped or transported anywhere with prior written Department approval and permittee information attached (1001 through 1003).

Through permits or memorandums of understanding, the Department may authorize individuals, agencies or organizations to import, export, take, or possess endangered, threatened or candidate species for scientific, educational, or management purposes. This does not prohibit the possession or sale of any endangered or threatened species, parts or products, when the owner can demonstrate that it was in possession before the listing or prior to January 1, 1985 listing as endangered or rare, and does not prohibit its sale if it was originally possessed for the seller's own use. It is unlawful to sell a species, part or product, if that sale would have been unlawful in any event. The Commission may authorize taking a candidate species, or taking a fish by hook and line for sport that is endangered, threatened, or candidate (2081 through 2084). Upon Department recommendation, the Commission may authorize, pursuant to Section 2084, the taking of any candidate species or any identified species whose conservation, protection, restoration, and enhancement is provided for in an approved natural community conservation plan consistent with Section 2825 (2830 and 2835).

Except as provided in this division and in Section 3202, it is unlawful to possess or confine a live cat, except a house cat. [Authorized actions regarding cats other than house cats are found in 3005.9, 3005.91 and 3005.92.]

It is unlawful to: ▸ take a bird or mammal, except a nongame mammal (unless regulations are adopted), between one-half hour after sunset and one-half hour before sunrise except as provided (3000); ▸ take pheasant within 300 yards of a vehicle from which pheasants are being released; ▸ take bear with iron or steel-jawed or any type of metal-jawed traps, and no provision of this code or other law shall authorize such use; ▸ use recorded or electrically amplified bird or mammal calls or sounds or imitations to assist in taking a bird or mammal, except nongame birds and mammals as permitted by Commission regulations (3010 through 3012). English sparrows and starlings are nongame birds that may be taken and possessed, except as provided in Section 3000 (3801). Nongame birds not covered by the Migratory Bird Treaty Act found to be injuring growing crops or property may be taken by the owner or tenant, or officers or employees of the Department of Food and Agriculture or by federal or county officers or employees (3801.5)   See also ANIMAL DAMAGE CONTROL. Permits may be granted by the Department of Food and Agriculture for capture and domestication of undomesticated burros as pets or for use as beasts of burden (4602). The Department may issue permits, subject to Commission terms and conditions, for possession of any tortoise, part or product by an educational or scientific institution or a public zoological garden (5002).

HUNTING, FISHING, TRAPPING PROVISIONS

General Provisions

★★When adopting regulations, the Commission shall annually determine whether to continue, repeal, or amend regulations establishing hunting seasons for black bears, including a review of factors which impact the health and viability of the black bear population (302).★★

When an area is closed because of extreme fire hazard, the Commission may establish a hunting or fishing season, to commence upon or after the termination of such closure and to correspond as nearly as possible to the length of time of closure (306). When after investigation, the Commission finds that game fish, resident or migratory birds, game or fur-bearing mammals, or amphibia have decreased in numbers in any areas, districts, or portions so that a scarcity exists, it may reduce the daily bag and possession limit, for a specified period or until new legislation becomes effective. Such regulation shall be published twice in any county affected (307).

For the preservation, protection and restoration of mountain sheep and other birds and mammals in arid regions, the Commission, in cooperation with the agency authorized to manage the land, may prohibit any activity, including camping, in the vicinity of waterholes, springs, seeps, and other watering places on public lands (308.5). The Commission at any time may close an area to taking a species or subspecies of bird or mammal newly stocked by the Department with resident or migratory game birds or game or fur-bearing mammals, or an area where added protection is needed to conserve birds or mammals, for a specified time, or until new legislation becomes effective (314).

The Commission annually may promulgate regulations pertaining to migratory birds to conform with or to restrict further the Migratory Bird Treaty Act rules and regulations (355). Migratory game birds may be taken in conformity with federal laws and regulations and Commission regulations. In the event no federal regulations are prescribed,

Commission rules and regulations may determine and fix areas, seasons and hours, species, bag and possession limits during open season, and have the same effect as if enacted by the Legislature (356).

With regard to any bird, mammal, fish, reptile or amphibian or parts, it is unlawful to: ▸ take such except as provided in this code or regulations; ▸ possess such in or on the fields, forests, or waters, or while returning with fishing or hunting equipment, and possession is prima facie evidence of taking; ▸ possess such during the open season and 10 days thereafter, and not more than one daily bag limit after season close; ▸ possess such taken in violation of any of the provisions of this code, or regulations; ▸ offer a prize or reward for taking in a contest [permits provided]; ▸ while taking, cause or assist in causing damage to real or personal property, or leave gates or bars open, or break down, destroy, or damage fences, or tear down or scatter piles of rails, posts, stone, or wood, or to injure livestock; ▸ set, cause to be set, or place a trap gun; ▸ use or possess a shotgun larger than 10-gauge, or capable of holding more than six cartridges; ▸ possess a loaded rifle or shotgun in a vehicle or conveyance on a public highway or other way open to the public; ▸ use an artificial light to assist in taking, except where night fishing is permitted; ▸ throw or cast rays of a spotlight, headlight, or other artificial light on any highway, field, woodland, or forest where game, fur-bearing, or nongame mammals are found while possessing a firearm or weapon; ▸ use or possess an infrared or similar light with a sniperscope in hunting. This does not apply: ▸ to hand held flashlights; ▸ if motor vehicle headlights are operated in a usual manner and there is no attempt to locate a game, fur-bearing or nongame mammal; ▸ landowners or controllers of agricultural land, on their land; ▸ other Commission authorized uses (2000 through 20007, and 2010).

Taking, mutilating or destroying a bird or mammal, lawfully possessed by another is a misdemeanor (2011). Licenses, license tags, and the wildlife taken or otherwise dealt with under this code, and any device or apparatus designed and capable of use to take birds, mammals, fish, reptiles, or amphibia shall be exhibited upon demand of an authorized person (2012). It is unlawful to enter lands under cultivation or enclosed by a fence, belonging to, or occupied by, another, or to enter any uncultivated or unenclosed lands, including lands temporarily inundated by waters, where signs forbidding trespass are displayed, to discharge a firearm or take or destroy a mammal or bird, without written permission from the owner, agent, or possessor (2016). It is unlawful to take a mammal or bird or to discharge a firearm on land posted with "Private Property No Hunting" signs. This applies to all persons, including the landowner or the possessor, and a person obtaining permission, written or oral, from the owner or lawful possessor. The owner or agent may take nonprotected mammals or birds on the land (2017). The Commission may designate wild animals which may be possessed without a permit (2118.5).

This article applies to all dead wild birds, mammals, fish, and amphibia, and live mollusks and crustaceans transported for purposes other than placement in waters of this state. It does not apply to animals imported for aquaculture. It is unlawful: ▸ for a common carrier to transport for, receive for transportation from, or offer to transport for more than the bag limit of birds, mammals, fish, or amphibia which may legally be taken and possessed, a package containing such animals or parts to be labeled [details provided]; ▸ to ship any animal by parcel post, except smoked, cured, or dried fish other than trout; ▸ to transport or carry out of this state a deer or game bird, or parts, except by the nonresident hunting licensee or under Department permit; ▸ for a common carrier to transport a protected nongame bird, or a resident or migratory game bird for which there is no open season, except as permitted (2345 through 2350, and 2352).

Birds, mammals, fish, reptiles, or amphibia may be brought into this state and possessed if legally taken and possessed outside of this state and a declaration is submitted at or immediately prior to entry, in the form and manner prescribed by the Department. A declaration is not needed if the shipment is handled by a common carrier under a bill of lading or as supplies as food for passengers [migratory game bird importation must be allowed pursuant to federal regulations](2353). Deer may be transported into this state only in accordance with the law of the state where taken an this state's laws (2355). It is unlawful to import for commercial purposes a salmon of smaller size than can be legally taken under regulations of either the Pacific Fishery Management Council or the state of landing. This does not apply to domestically reared salmon (salmon which have returned to a hatchery or licensed artificial collection facility), which may be imported under Commission regulations (2361). Striped bass, sturgeon, shad or parts legally taken in another state, which permits the sale of that fish, may be imported under Commission regulations after public hearing (2363).

Common carriers may transport carcasses or parts of domesticated game birds and mammals with a domesticated game breeder's tag. A tag or label shall also be affixed to every package (2400). Carcasses or parts of domesticated game birds raised outside of this state may be imported and transported, sold, or possessed. A label shall be affixed to every package [details provided] (2401).

It is unlawful to: ▸ shoot at a game bird or mammal, from a powerboat, sailboat, motor vehicle, or airplane (3002); ▸ pursue, drive, or herd a bird or mammal with any motorized vehicle, except on private property to drive or herd game mammals to prevent damage, under Department permit or in the pursuit of agriculture (3003.5); ▸ other than owners, possessors, or one with their express permission, to hunt or to discharge while hunting, a firearm or deadly weapon within a 150 yard ("safety zone") of an occupied dwelling house, residence, or other building (3004); ▸ take birds or mammals with a net, pound, cage, trap, set line or wire, or poisonous substance, or to possess such, which must show evidence of taking other than by these methods, or it is prima facie evidence of violation of this section [lawful exceptions listed] (3005); ▸ capture a game mammal, game bird, nongame bird, nongame mammal, or fur-bearer, or to possess or confine such alive except as provided, and such animals are to be seized [provisions made for temporary confinement if injured or diseased] (3005.5); ▸ use a powerboat, vehicle, or airplane to drive a game bird toward another with the intent that the other shall take the bird (3501); ▸ use a mammal (except a dog) or an imitation of a mammal as a blind in approaching or taking game birds (3502); ▸ sell or purchase any game bird or nongame bird or part, except domestically raised game birds (3504); ▸ capture or destroy a deer and detach or remove from the carcass only the head, hide, antlers, or horns, or leave through carelessness or neglect a game mammal or bird, or portion of the flesh usually eaten, to go to waste needlessly (4304).

Licenses and Permits

Licenses, certificates, permits, and license tags authorized by this code shall be issued by the Department, and the terms, conditions, fees and form determined by the Commission (1050). With regard to licenses, tags, stamps, permits, applications or reservations, it is unlawful to: ▸ transfer, use or possess such when obtained by fraud or fake forms; ▸ use or possess fake or counterfeit licenses; ▸ predate, postdate, alter, mutilate, deface or duplicate such (1052). A license stamp is valid only if affixed to the license (1052.5). It is unlawful to make a false statement when obtaining a license or license tag, and such obtained in violation of this section is void (1054). Licensees must have licenses, tags, stamps or permits in possession while taking (1054.2).

Applicants for hunting licenses shall first satisfactorily complete a hunter safety equivalency examination and obtain a certificate as provided by Commission regulations, or show proof of completion of a hunter safety training course, or a previous year's hunting license (1053.5). No hunting license shall be issued without: ▸ evidence of a previous hunting license; ▸ a certificate of completion of a course in hunter safety, conservation, and sportsmanship, with a hunter safety instruction validation stamp; ▸ a certificate of successful completion of a hunter safety course in another state with a California hunter safety instruction validation stamp affixed; ▸ evidence of completion of a course in hunter safety, conservation, and sportsmanship, which the Commission may require (3050). The Department shall provide for a course of instruction in hunter safety, principles of conservation, and sportsmanship, and may cooperate with any reputable association or organization with those objectives. Hunting license applicants shall obtain a hunter safety instruction validation stamp, affixed to the certificate of completion. Resident applicants shall also obtain a hunter safety instruction validation stamp (3055).

Trapping designated fur-bearing or nongame mammals or selling raw furs requires a trapping license. The Department shall develop standards to ensure competence and proficiency of applicants, and must pass a test of knowledge and skill in this field. Persons taking mammals in accordance with Section 4152 or 4180 are not required to procure a trapping license, but no raw furs so taken may be sold (4005). A trapping license shall not be issued to a nonresident if the nonresident's state does not provide for nonresident trapping licenses for California residents. A nonresident issued a license may take or possess only that quantity of a species which a resident of California may take or possess under a nonresident trapping license or permit in the nonresident's state (4006). Trapping licenses shall not be reissued without a sworn record of previous activity (4008).

Restrictions on Taking: Hunting and Trapping

If the Commission finds that game mammals, other than deer, and fur-bearing mammals and resident game birds have increased in areas other than a refuge or preserve so that a surplus exists, or there is overgrazing, or the animals are damaging property, it may regulate a special hunting season, increased bag limits or removal of sex restrictions (325). The Commission may determine and fix areas, seasons and hours, bag and possession limits, and sex and total number of antelope and elk that may be taken under Commission regulations [restrictions on eligibility for licenses provided]. Taking of tule elk may be authorized if the statewide population estimate exceeds 2,000, or the Legislature determines that suitable areas cannot be found to accommodate that population in a healthy condition (331 and 332).

The Department shall designate deer herd management units and a manager for the units, and develop plans for restoration and maintenance of healthy deer herds and for high quality and diversified use of deer. [Plans shall include programs enumerated in 452 through 457 and 459.] Plans shall be reviewed annually. The Department shall report biennially to the Legislature and Commission on progress toward the restoration and maintenance of deer herds [details of report provided] (452 through 457, and 459). [Detailed provisions are made for Department recommendations to the Commission regarding hunting seasons, conditions of herds, taking of antlerless deer, and quota units in 460.]

To provide added protection for landowners and lessees and to provide greater access to hunt, the Department may contract with landowners or lessees for the establishment of cooperative hunting areas. Cooperative hunting areas operated for other than waterfowl shall be at least 5,000 acres, and for waterfowl hunting, at least 1,000 acres. The Department shall enforce trespass provisions (1570 and 1571).

Game birds or mammals may be possessed other than the open season if tagged under Commission regulations. This section shall not apply to possession of deer or deer meat. Meat tagged in conformity with Section 3081 may be possessed at any time. Nothing authorizes possession of game birds, carcasses or parts contrary to Migratory Bird Treaty Act regulations. It is unlawful to possess deer, elk, bear, or antelope meat except during the open season and 15 days after, or at any time if marked pursuant to Commission regulations (3080 and 3081). [Provisions pertaining to practice dogs and domesticated game birds are in 3508 through 3510.]

It is unlawful to: ► possess the carcass, such that the sex or species cannot be easily determined, of any pheasant while in the field, forest or while upon any highway, vehicle or other conveyance when returning from any hunting trip with gun or other hunting equipment (3660); ► take an upland game bird without an upland game bird stamp affixed to the hunting license, unless licensed under Section 3031 (3682); ► take a migratory game bird, except jacksnipe, coots, gallinules, western mourning doves, white-winged doves, and band-tailed pigeons, without an open edition or a Governor's edition state duck stamp in possession (3700); ► possess the carcass, skin, or parts of a nongame bird, except as provided, and such shall be seized by the Department and delivered to a scientific or educational institution (3801.6). [Sections 3960 and 3961 specify dog hunting laws.]

Fur-bearing mammals may be taken November 16 to February 28, and may be taken only with a trap, a firearm, bow and arrow, or poison under a permit, or with dogs. It is unlawful to: ► use poison to take fur-bearing mammals without a Department permit; ► use a trap with saw-toothed or spiked jaws; ► use or sell leghold steel-jawed traps with a spread of 5 1/2 inches or larger without offset jaws; ► use steel-jawed traps larger than size 1 1/2 or with a spread larger than 4 7/8 inches for muskrat; ► set or maintain traps which do not bear identifying marks; ► fail to visit and remove all animals from traps at least once daily; ► use a steel leghold trap with a spread exceeding 7 1/2 inches or killer-type trap of the conibear type that is larger than 10 inches by 10 inches; ► set or maintain steel leghold traps within 30 feet of bait placed so that it may be seen by any soaring bird; ► set or maintain steel leghold traps with a spread of 5 1/2 inches or larger without a tension device (4001 through 4004); ► remove or disturb the trap of a licensee while in use on public land or on land where the licensee has permission to trap, except for a Department employee performing official duties (4009). The Commission may adopt regulations to regulate the taking and sale of fur-bearing mammals or nongame mammals taken under a trapping license (4009.5). This does not apply to, or prohibit propagation of, fur-bearing mammals confined under Commission regulations (4010).

It is unlawful to take a deer without a deer license tag or permit in possession, the tag to be attached to the deer upon taking (4330 and 4336). A person convicted of a violation of a provision of this code, or rule, regulation, or order relating to deer shall forfeit deer license tags, and none may be issued during that license year. License tags shall be countersigned by one in authority before transporting deer (4340 and 4341). Open seasons for deer have an archery season for taking deer with bow and arrow. The Commission shall prescribe the season for each area, with a minimum interposing interval of three days immediately preceding the regular open season. No person taking or attempting to take deer during the archery season shall carry or control a firearm (4370).

The Department shall prepare a wild pig management plan, wherein the status and trend of wild pig populations shall be determined and management units designated [details of plan provided]. A license tag is required to take wild pig. A resident age 12 or older with a hunting license may procure wild pig tags. Revenues received shall be deposited in the Fish and Game Preservation Fund, to be expended solely for wild pig management. Wild pig license tags shall be in possession while hunting [details of tagging provided] (4651 and 4652, and 4654 through 4657).

It is unlawful to take a bear with firearm, trap, or bow and arrow without a proper license tag, but no type of metal-jawed trap shall be used to take a bear. Licensees may procure the number of bear tags corresponding to the number of bear that may legally be taken, and shall carry, fill out and attach the tag upon taking. Possession of an untagged bear shall be a violation (4750, 4751 and 4753). One convicted of a violation relating to bears shall forfeit bear license tags for the current license year. A person legally killing a bear shall have the license tag countersigned by an authorized person before transporting. Except as provided, it is unlawful to use dogs to hunt, pursue, or molest bears. One dog per hunter is permitted for bear hunting during open season for deer in the area affected; or more than one per hunter during the open season on bears, except during open archery deer or regular deer seasons. If bear is taken, hunters must retain during the open season, and 15 days thereafter, the skin and portion of the head with the ears, and must produce such upon demand of an officer (4754 through 4757). ★★Subject to provisions permitting sale of domestically raised game mammals, it is unlawful to sell or purchase, or possess for sale, the meat, skin, hide, teeth, claws, or other parts of any bear in this state. The possession of more than one bear gall bladder is prima facie evidence that the bear gall bladders are possessed for sale. Nothing in this section prohibits a sale authorized pursuant to Section 3087.★★ The skin, hide, teeth, claws, or other parts of a bear lawfully taken and possessed for the period provided in Section 4757 may be tanned or utilized for personal use only, or donated to veterans' organizations or service committees. The donor shall obtain a receipt. ★★Chapter provisions relating to possession of bear apply to bear taken outside this state and transported into this state (4758 through 4760).★★ Chapter provisions do not apply to taking of bear when otherwise authorized to protect livestock, land, or property from damage or threatened damage (4763).

It is state policy to encourage the preservation, restoration, utilization, and management of California's bighorn sheep. The Department shall determine the status and the trend of bighorn sheep populations by management units, and a plan shall be developed for each. ★No license tag shall be valid without completion of a prehunt hunter familiarization and orientation and demonstration to the Department of familiarity with requisite equipment for hunting bighorn rams.★ Revenue from fees shall go to the Fish and Game Preservation Fund to be spent solely for the bighorn sheep program [details provided]. The Department shall annually report to the Legislature regarding management plans, data, tags issued, unlawful takings, relocations, and environmental impacts of hunting (4900 through 4904).

Restrictions on Taking: Fishing

The Commission may designate salmon spawning areas, in which it is unlawful to take salmon, or within 250 feet of a salmon spawning station (310). The Commission may close a stream, lake, or other inland waters to taking of a species or subspecies of fish to protect and conserve the fish, except under commercial fishing license, for a designated time, or until new legislation (315). Such waters may be opened, when new facts are presented to the Commission, for a designated time or until new legislation may become effective (315.3).

The Commission shall establish fish hatcheries for state stocking waters. The Department shall maintain and operate such hatcheries (1120). The Department may purchase and import spawn or ova of fish suitable for food, and stock state waters (1123). It is unlawful to take fish in a pond or reservoir belonging to or controlled by the Department for propagating, protecting, or conserving fish (1124). County boards of supervisors may establish and maintain fish hatcheries (1150). A nonprofit organization may construct and operate an anadromous fish hatchery only if it has the financial capability to construct and operate the hatchery and will diligently conduct the operation. No permit will be issued which may tend to deplete the natural runs of anadromous fish, result in waste or deterioration of fish, or when the proposed operation is located on waters below a state or federal fish hatchery or egg-taking station (1170 through 1172). [Permit requirements, alterations to permits to mitigate adverse effects, and permit termination details are provided] (1174). The Department is authorized to enter into agreements with counties, nonprofit groups or private entities for management and operation of rearing facilities for salmon and steelhead, under Commission policies and Department criteria, to provide additional fishing resources and to augment natural runs (1200). Fish handled or released under authority of this article are state property and may be taken only after release and under a sport or commercial fishing license (1202). Release shall be under Commission policies (1203). The Department shall make available appropriate fish size and species for such facilities (1205).

To provide for a diversity of angling experiences, the Commission shall maintain the existing wild trout program, and develop catch and release fisheries in the more than 20,000 miles of trout streams and approximately 5,000 lakes containing trout (details of this program provided] (1727). The Department's black bass management program is described in 1743. The Department may implement the Adopt a Lake Program to facilitate volunteer efforts of private groups and associations to rehabilitate and improve fisheries, fish habitat, and resources, and shall prepare and periodically update a plan for the volunteer efforts. The plan shall be prepared cooperatively by the Department, the private group and the public agency with jurisdiction over the affected inland water (2003.6).

It is unlawful to: ▸ offer for shipment, ship, or receive for shipment, or transport from this state trout taken in this state, except that a nonresident angling licensee, or a person on active military duty may transport not more than one daily bag limit of trout; ▸ carry trout into a closed season area without a filed affidavit; ▸ ship trout into a closed season area without a written statement [details provided]. Except as provided, no striped bass may be transported or carried out of or into this state, unless taken from the Colorado River by sportfishing licensees lawfully taking fish from the Arizona shore who may transport or carry such fish into California, or an Arizona resident or nonresident sportfishing licensee lawfully taking such fish on the waters or from the California shore who may transport or carry such fish into Arizona. Black bass and spotted bass lawfully taken may be carried or transported into and possessed in closed season areas (2356 through 2360).

It is unlawful to: ▸ use explosives in waters inhabited by fish, except under Department permit and Commission terms and conditions, or except in case of emergency, to remove an accidental obstruction to water flow [the Department's decision to grant or deny a permit may be appealed] (5500); ▸ take fish within 250 feet of a fishway, within 150 feet of the lower side of a dam, or within 150 feet of the upper side of a fish screen (5502); ▸ take fish solely to remove its eggs, except for developing a brood stock for aquaculture pursuant to Commission regulations, and the Commission shall determine ownership and regulate distribution of progeny taken from wild brood stock; ▸ possess, except at home, a fish spear or gaff within 300 feet of a lake or stream when spearing is prohibited, but this does not apply to possession of a gaff as an accessory while angling (5507); ▸ possess on a boat or bring ashore a fish in such condition that its size or weight cannot be determined [Commission regulations may establish sizes or weights for cleaned or otherwise cut fish] (5508); ▸ possess on a boat or bring ashore a fish such that its species cannot be determined, except as provided by Commission regulations (5509). Mollusks, crustaceans, and amphibia may be used for bait or released in the waters where taken (5505). Commission regulations may prevent deterioration and waste of fish taken for purposes other than profit, and regulate disposal of the offal of such fish (5510). Except under Department permit, it is unlawful to carry on a fish cultural operations on a stream above where water is diverted to a state fish hatchery (5511). A body of water restricted by the Commission to fishing by use of artificial flies or artificial lures shall be posted at places of entry (5516). [Restrictions and permitted activities of dam owners are found in 5939 through 5948.]

It is unlawful to take shellfish used or intended to be used for human consumption from any area from which it is be determined that taking does or may constitute a menace to the lives or health of human beings [extensive details for examination and posting of contaminated shellfish and mollusks provided in sections 5671 through 5702] (5670). It is unlawful to take frogs by the use of firearms of any caliber or type (6854).

The natural production of salmon and steelhead trout has declined dramatically, primarily as a result of lost stream habitat. Protection of, and increase in, natural spawning must be accomplished primarily through stream habitat improvement. The Department's successful program of contracts with local government, nonprofit agencies and private groups have attracted substantial citizen effort. A comprehensive salmon, steelhead trout, and anadromous fisheries plan, program, and government organization is needed to protect and increase such resources (6901). The Department shall consult with public agencies whose policies or decisions may affect the goals of this program (6920). [Identification, evaluation and recommendations are specified for the plan in 6922.]

This part applies to the taking and possession of fish for any purpose other than commercial (7100). It is unlawful to: ▸ possess more than one daily bag limit of fish taken under sport fishing license (7120); ▸ sell or purchase fish or amphibia taken in or brought into state waters, except as provided; ▸ buy, sell, or possess in any place of business where fish are bought, sold, or processed, fish or amphibia taken on a boat, barge, or vessel which carries sport fishermen, except for canning or smoking such under Commission regulations (7121). Except as provided, persons over age 16 who take fish, reptile, or amphibia for any purpose other than profit shall obtain and possess a license (7145). The owner or operator of a boat or vessel licensed under Section 7920 shall not permit fishing without a sportfishing license and any required license stamp (7147). A sportfishing license to take any fish, reptile, or amphibia for other than profit shall be issued [details for eligibility provided] (7149). A sportfishing license is not required for residents to take rattlesnakes (7149.3). Offal from a fish taken under a sportfishing license which is delivered to a fish canner or processor may be processed, used, or sold by that fish canner or processor. A fish canner or processor may not purchase from a sportfishing licensee any fish or portion taken (7232).

A person taking striped bass shall have affixed to the sportfishing license a striped bass stamp (7360). Except as provided, it is unlawful to buy, sell or possess striped bass or parts, in any place or conveyance where fish are bought, possessed for sale, or sold, or where food is offered for sale, except in a restaurant when brought by the licensee for immediate consumption (7364). The Department may operate hatchery facilities to research striped bass and other fish (7366). Except as provided, it is unlawful to buy or sell, offer to buy or sell, or possess, a whole sturgeon, or part including eggs in any place or conveyance where fish are bought, possessed for sale, or sold, or where food is offered for sale (7370). A person taking steelhead trout in inland waters shall possess a sportfishing license, applicable license stamp, and a steelhead trout catch report-restoration card. Regulations shall include procedures to obtain steelhead trout management information and a requirement that the card explain potential uses of the funds (7380).

Commercial and Private Enterprise Provisions

It is unlawful to engage in the business of guiding or packing, or to act as a guide for any consideration or compensation without a guide license. An employee of a licensee who acts as a guide only in connection with, and within the scope of employment is exempt under certain circumstances (2536).

A grazing permit is required if the licensee operates with pack or riding animals in an area in which such permit is required. A licensee shall not guide clients on lands under jurisdiction of the USDI or DOA where permits are required without a federal agency permit (2539). Commission regulations shall govern the conduct and qualifications of guides to ensure safety and welfare, including knowledge of basic first aid and rescue operations (2542). The Commission may require guides to maintain and submit records. A license may be refused or revoked upon a showing that the applicant failed to fulfill responsibilities to a client, violated this code or a regulation, or knowingly permitted a client or member of a party being guided to violate this code or a regulation when the licensee had the authority and means to prevent the violation. An applicant denied a guide license may request a Commission hearing (2542 through 2546).

It is unlawful to capture or transport for sale, or sell wild rodents knowingly, except as provided (2576). Except as provided, it is unlawful to sell or purchase a species or part of bird or mammal found in the wild. Products or handicraft items made from fur-bearing and nongame mammals, their carcass or parts, lawfully taken under trapping license, may be purchased or sold at any time. Shed antlers, or antlers from domestically reared animals that have been manufactured, or cut into blocks to be handcrafted or manufactured may be purchased or sold. However, complete antlers, whole heads with antlers, antlers mounted for display, or antlers in velvet may not be sold or purchased at any time, except as authorized by Section 3087. Inedible parts of domestically raised game birds may be sold or purchased at any time. A person who illegally takes a bird or mammal for profit or personal gain by engaging in an activity authorized by this section is subject to civil liability pursuant to Section 2582 (3039). Persons who prepare, stuff, or mount the skin of a fish, reptile, bird, or mammal for another shall keep records of taxidermy activities [details provided]. When a taxidermist has prepared, stuffed, or mounted a skin and the person does not pay or take delivery, the taxidermist may sell the skin only under Commission regulations [details of potential regulations provided] (3087).

Raising or importing, or keeping in captivity domesticated game birds or mammals which normally exist in the wild in this state requires a domesticated game breeder's license if the birds or mammals are kept more than 30 days. No license is required of: ▸ licensed pheasant clubs; ▸ licensed domesticated migratory game bird shooting areas; ▸ keepers of hotels, restaurants, boardinghouses, or clubs serving birds or mammals for actual consumption; ▸ retail meat dealers selling such meat for actual consumption.; ▸ public zoological gardens possessing those birds or mammals for exhibition or sale, exchange, or donation to other zoological gardens. Selling the carcass of a domesticated game bird or mammal requires a domesticated game breeder's license. Licenses may be revoked for sufficient cause. A Class 1 domesticated game breeder's license authorizes the licensee to engage in domesticated game breeding activities, except not more than 175 Chinese ringneck or Mongolian ringneck pheasants, or both, or hybrids thereof, may be sold. A Class 2 license allows selling of more than 175 such birds (3200 through 3202). Carriers for hire may carry within the state live domesticated game birds and mammals upon Commission terms and conditions (3205). No domesticated game bird or mammal shall be transported or sold dead unless each quarter and loin of each large mammal, the carcass of each bird and small mammal is tagged with a domesticated game breeder's tag or seal (3206). Licensees must report each year (3208).

The keeper of a restaurant, boardinghouse, club or a retail meat dealer may sell such portions or carcasses for actual consumption on the premises with no license, and may be inspected. All such game shall be tagged under Section 3206 (3212 and 3213). Domesticated game breeders or others holding domesticated game mammals in captivity shall confine the mammals in escape-proof cages or enclosures [procedures and costs in event of escape are outlined] (3214). Licenses may be revoked by the Commission upon conviction of violation of a code provision, and may not be reissued during the same license year (3218). Domesticated reindeer may be imported and sold only in accordance with Commission regulations (3219).

A person in possession or control of property who imposes an entry fee or use permit for the privilege of taking birds or mammals shall procure a commercial hunting club license [details on license are provided] (3240.5 and 3246). A person who owns or controls the shooting rights on a tract of land may apply for a licensed pheasant club license or game bird club license under this article and Commission regulations (3270). Wherever pheasant is used in this article as applied to game bird clubs, it means any game bird, including pheasants and Indian chukars, authorized to be taken on such clubs, except that the area, season, and bag limit of Indian chukars shall be as provided in Section 3517 and Indian chukars planted on such clubs may be taken during the season planted (3270.5). [Provisions on licensed pheasant clubs are extensive and can be found at 3272 through 3273, 3275, 3280, 3281, 3284, and 3287 through 3291A.]

A revocable, nontransferable license is required to raise and/or release domesticated migratory game birds for shooting for pay. Migratory game birds held live in captivity are domesticated migratory game birds, unless released before attaining six weeks of age. Applications shall show area size and location, and if approved, the licensee shall post boundaries. The Commission may prescribe additional regulations for release and shooting and shall set the season and areas for taking. Violation of this article or regulations may cause license cancellation or revocation after notice and Commission hearing. The licensee shall provide proper care and sanitary conditions and allow inspection. The licensee shall raise or use a minimum of 500 birds per annual license. All domesticated migratory game birds at time of release for shooting shall be at least 14 weeks, capable of strong and sustained flight, fully feathered, and able to survive in the wild. Shooting shall be confined to blinds limited to three shooters [other details provided]. The licensee shall not permit shooting or taking within 500 feet of release. ★★Birds killed or injured shall be retrieved without delay, and injured birds shall be dispatched humanely. The licensee shall not permit injured birds to remain on a pond or feeding area, or knowingly permit their subsequent release. To prevent the loss of dead or injured birds, the licensee shall provide a retrieving dog, without cost (3300 through 3307).★★ It is unlawful to shoot such birds on a licensed area without a hunting license. The licensee shall comply with all federal laws or regulations for releasing and shooting of domesticated migratory game birds (3310 and 3311). Exotic nonresident game birds may be released only with Commission approval, and regulations may govern the release, taking, and possession of exotic nonresident game birds and inspection of resident game birds imported (3515 and 3316).

It is unlawful to take any cross fox, silver fox, or red fox for profit (4012). A person engaging in the business of buying, selling, trading or dealing in raw furs of fur-bearing or nongame mammals shall procure a fur dealer license, except for a licensed trapper selling raw furs, or a domesticated game breeder selling raw furs of raised animals (4030). A fur dealer license authorizes buying, selling, barter, exchange, or possession of raw furs or parts of fur-bearing and nongame mammals (4034). Licenses shall be shown upon request to authorized persons (4035). It is unlawful for a fur dealer to purchase raw fur from a seller without a trapping, fur dealer or fur agent license. Fur dealers shall maintain detailed records of any transfer of raw furs, which may be inspected at any time by the Department (4036 through 4038). Fur dealers shall submit an annual report to the Department (4040). The Commission may regulate the fur dealer business of buying, selling, trading, or dealing in raw furs, or parts (4042). A license may be revoked by the Commission upon the licensee's conviction of a violation of this article (4043).

Subject to provisions permitting sale of domestically raised game mammals, it is unlawful to sell, purchase, or transport for sale, deer meat whether fresh, smoked, canned or preserved, unless imported from a foreign country for processing (manufacturing) and selling venison or deer jerky or venison or deer salami, for human consumption. All such deer meat shall meet sanitary and inspection requirements [other details, including requirement for bill of lading provided]. A person taking deer shall retain during the open season and for 15 days after, the portion of the head which in adult males bears antlers, to be produced upon demand. The skin or hide of any deer lawfully taken may be sold, purchased, tanned, or manufactured into articles for sale, or donated to veterans' organizations or service committees (4301 through 4303).

Except as provided in this code or regulations, it is unlawful to take or possess a frog for commercial purposes (6851). A person conducting a business where frogs are sold to the public for food, or who takes or possesses frogs for sale to, or for use by, educational or scientific institutions for scientific purposes may possess only the number legally obtained (6852). Except as provided, the Commission shall establish rules for commercial take, sale, transport, export, or import of native amphibians (6896).

Fees may be assessed on aquaculturists (15003). When necessary to protect native wildlife, the Commission may regulate the transportation, purchase, possession, and sale of aquaculture products, and require [detailed] documents (15005). [Provisions for aquaculture are specified in detail in 15101 through 15103, 15200 through 15202, 15300, 15301, 15402 through 15414, 15500 and 15501.] The Director, in consultation with the Aquaculture Industry Advisory Committee and the Interagency Committee for Aquaculture Development, shall appoint an 11-member Aquaculture Disease Committee (15502). The Aquaculture Disease Committee may recommend regulations to the Commission to safeguard wild and cultured organisms from the list of harmful organisms compiled pursuant to Section 15500 (15503). [Detailed provisions are made for the Director to act upon finding of disease or parasites in any area in 15512.] No live aquatic plant or animal may be imported by a registered aquaculturist without Department approval pursuant to Commission regulations (15600). The Department shall report to the Legislature on the importation, spawning, incubation, rearing, and sale of anadromous fish listed in Section 2118 (15603). A registered aquaculturist may be granted a permit, under Commission terms and conditions, to release and capture anadromous fish reared in an aquaculture facility, after public hearing in the counties affected. Permits may not be issued which may deplete natural runs of anadromous fish, result in waste or deterioration of fish, or when the proposed operation is located below a state or federal fish hatchery or egg-taking station. Such fish released are state property and may be taken under a sport or commercial fishing license (15900 through 15903). [Provisions are made in detail for conditions that must be in permits, in 15905.]

Import, Export and Release Provisions

The importation, transportation, and possession of wild animals shall be regulated to protect their health and welfare, to reduce depletion of wildlife, to protect native wildlife and agricultural interests against damage, and to protect the public health and safety (2116.5). It is unlawful to import, transport, possess, or release alive, except under a revocable, nontransferable permit, a wild animal of the following species [scientific names provided]: ▸ cuckoos, larks, crows, jays, magpies; ▸ thrushes, European blackbird, mistle, starlings and mynas (mynahs), except hill myna, Gracula religiosa, weavers; ▸ Spanish sparrow, Italian sparrow, European tree sparrow, Cape sparrow, weaver, Baya weaver, Hawaiian rice bird, Red-billed quelea, Red-headed quelea, sparrows, finches, buntings, Yellowhammer; ▸ all primates, except sloths, anteaters, armadillos; ▸ marsupials and pouched mammals; ▸ shrews, moles, hedgehogs; ▸ gliding lemurs; ▸ bats; ▸ spiny anteaters, platypuses; ▸ pangolins, scaly anteaters; ▸ pikas, rabbits, hares; ▸ all rodents, except domesticated races of rabbits; ▸ rodents, except domesticated golden hamsters (Syrian hamsters), domesticated races of rats or mice (white or albino, trained, dancing or spinning, laboratory-reared), and domestic strains of guinea pig (2118); ▸ carnivores, except domestic dogs and cats; ▸ aardvarks; ▸ elephants; ▸ hyraxes; ▸ dugongs, manatees; ▸ horses, zebras, tapirs, rhinoceroses; ▸ all species of swine, peccaries, camels, deer, elk, except elk which are subject to Section 2118.2, moose, antelopes, cattle, goats, sheep, except domestic swine, American bison, and domestic cattle, sheep and goats; ▸ big-horned sheep now or formerly indigenous to this state. Mammals of the orders Primates, Edentata, Dermoptera, Monotremata, Pholidota, Tubulidentata, Proboscidea, Perissodactyla, Hyracoidea, Sirenia and Carnivora are restricted for the welfare of the animals, except animals of the families Viverridae and Mustelidae in the order Carnivora are restricted because such animals are undesirable and a menace to native wildlife, the agricultural interests of the state, or to the public health or safety (2118).

It is unlawful to import, transport, possess, or release alive, except under a revocable, nontransferable permit, a wild animal of the following species [scientific names provided]: ▸ frogs, toads, salamanders, Giant toad or marine toad; ▸ lampreys; ▸ bony fishes, White perch, herring, Gizzard shad, croakers, Freshwater sheepshead, characins, Banded tetra; ▸ all species of piranhas; ▸ gars, bowfins; ▸ snakes, lizards, turtles, alligators; ▸ crustaceans; ▸ all species of crayfishes; ▸ slugs, snails, clams; ▸ other classes, orders, families, genera, and species of wild animals which may be designated by the Commission in cooperation with the Department of Food and Agriculture, when the class, order, family, genus, or species is proven to be undesirable and a menace to native wildlife or the agricultural interests of the state, or to provide for the welfare of wild animals. Classes, families, genera, and species in addition to those listed may be added to or deleted from time to time by Commission regulations in cooperation with the Department of Food and Agriculture (2118).

It is unlawful to import any elk. The Department may import elk if it issues written findings justifying the need and purpose of the importation. This does not apply to USDA certified zoos (2118.2). ★★No part of an elk horn or antler shall be removed from a live elk for commercial purposes (2118.3).★★ The Department shall seize any elk illegally imported (2118.4). The Department shall publish from time to time as changes arise, a list of animals which may not be imported or transported into this state (2119). The Commission, in cooperation with the Department of Food and Agriculture, shall promulgate regulations governing entry, transportation, keeping, confinement, or release of wild animals which will be or have been imported, and possession of other wild animals. No person with possession or control over any wild animal legally imported shall intentionally free, or knowingly permit their escape or release except under Commission regulations. Regulations shall be promulgated for guidance of enforcing officers, including a list of the wild animals for which permits will be refused, and disposition of animals illegally imported. Except as authorized, it is unlawful to possess, transport, import, export, propagate, purchase, sell, or transfer any live mammal listed under Section 2118 for the purposes of maiming, injuring, or killing for gain, amusement, or sport; and the buyer of such mammal shall not resell it to another buyer who has intent (2120 through 2124).

The Department or an eligible local entity, in cooperation with the Department of Food and Agriculture, may issue a permit to import, possess, or transport any wild animal enumerated in Section 2118, upon a determination that the animal is not detrimental or potentially damaging to agriculture, native wildlife, public health or safety, or the welfare of the animal. Federally licensed exhibitors or dealers may only sell or transfer animals to those with this permit (2150).

★★The Director shall appoint a committee to advise on humane care and treatment of wild animals. The committee shall make recommendations to the Director regarding: ▸ standards of performance for administration and enforcement; ▸ frequency of inspections needed for possession, handling, care, or holding facilities; ▸ memorandums of understanding with eligible local entities (2150.3). ★★ The Department or an eligible local entity shall inspect the wild animal facilities of permittees and collect an inspection fee (2150.4). The Department shall establish and keep current, policies and procedures to implement animal housing, possession, importation, and transportation requirements. [Extensive provisions on importation, transportation and receipt of live animals are found in 2150.5, 2151, 2153, 2156, and 2185 through 2190.],

Except as provided, it is unlawful: ▸ for a common carrier to transport a live protected nongame bird or resident or migratory game bird for which there is no open season (2225); ▸ to import, transport or possess any live muskrat [in various specific locations], a county agricultural commissioner, fish and game deputy, or state plant quarantine officer being able to enter lands or waters where muskrats exist unlawfully, and remove or destroy them (2250); ▸ to receive, bring, or cause to be brought into this state for propagation, any fish, reptile, amphibian, or aquatic plant from any place wherein any infected, diseased, or parasitized fish, reptile, amphibia, or aquatic plants are known to exist (2270).

No live aquatic plant or animal may be imported without written Department approval under Commission regulations. This section does not apply to the following plants or animals unless they are in state waters: ▸ mollusks; ▸ crustaceans; ▸ ornamental marine or freshwater plants and animals not utilized for human consumption or bait and maintained in closed systems for personal, pet industry, or hobby purposes; ▸ live aquatic plants or animals imported by a registered aquaculturist (2271). Live aquatic plant or animal containers shall bear a tag [details provided] (2272). The eggs and fry of golden trout shall not be transported out of the state (2273). It is unlawful to place or plant such in state waters, or cause such, a live fish, fresh or salt water animal, or aquatic plant, taken outside of or within the state, without inspection and with written Department permission (6400).

Interstate Reciprocal Agreements

The Commission may negotiate the terms of a compact between Arizona and California with Arizona officials in relation to reciprocal privileges and licenses for hunting and fishing. The negotiations shall include, but shall not be limited to, provisions relating to sport fishing and hunting migratory waterfowl in, on, or along the Colorado River. It is the purpose of this section to provide a method whereby the hunting and fishing opportunities afforded by the Colorado River may be enjoyed mutually by the residents of Arizona and California despite the fact that the state boundary line is the middle of the channel of the Colorado River (375). Subject to Attorney General approval, the Commission may enter into reciprocal agreements with corresponding state or county official agencies of adjoining states for establishment of a basis whereby sport fishing licenses issued by parties to the reciprocal agreements may be used by their licensees within the jurisdiction of either (390). In conformity with Commission regulations, the Department may issue special Colorado River hunting licenses when the Commission finds and determines that under the laws of the State of Arizona substantially similar licenses are authorized to be issued to licensees of the State of California upon substantially the same terms and conditions as are provided for in this article as to the issuance of licenses to licensees of the State of Arizona (3060). A special Colorado River hunting license may be issued to a person holding an Arizona hunting license (3061). Arizona Colorado River special use stamps shall be sold under Department supervision in the same manner as sport fishing licenses, and California sport fishing licenses and Colorado River special use stamps shall be sold by Arizona license dealers under Arizona Game and Fish Commission supervision (7182). This article remains effective so long as substantially similar Arizona licenses are authorized to be issued to California licensees upon substantially the same terms and conditions (7185).

ANIMAL DAMAGE CONTROL

★★It is unlawful for a person, including state, federal, county, and city officials or their agents, to authorize, offer or pay a bounty for any bird or mammal. This does not apply to taking a bird or mammal on one's private property (2019).★★

In cooperation with the State Department of Food and Agriculture, the Department shall furnish material concerning the wild animals enumerated in Section 2118, as well as explanatory material regarding such animals designated as undesirable and a menace to native wildlife or to agricultural interests, for guidance of enforcing officers (2123). The Department may enter into cooperative contracts with the USFW for control or eradication of predatory birds, and may take any bird unduly preying upon a bird, mammal, or fish (3802 and 3803). In order to aid in relieving widespread waterfowl depredation of agricultural crops, licenses may be issued to permit the feeding of migratory game birds (3806).

Fur-bearing, game and nongame mammals involved in dangerous disease outbreaks may be taken by federal and state officers (4011). Nongame mammals and black-tailed jackrabbits, muskrats, and red fox squirrels found injuring growing crops or other property may be taken at any time or in any manner by the landowner or tenant, except leghold steel-jawed traps must be used in accordance with Section 4004. They may also be taken by county, state or federal officers in their official capacities. Traps shall be inspected and all animals removed at least once daily. The Department may enter into cooperative agreements with any state or federal agency for controlling harmful nongame mammals, and may take a mammal unduly preying upon a bird, mammal, or fish. The Department may enter into cooperative contracts with the USFW for control of nongame mammals and use funds to that end (4152 through 4154).

Fur-bearing mammals injuring property may be taken in any manner, except leghold steel-jawed traps shall be used in accordance with Section 4004, and inspected daily (4180). It is unlawful to use snares, hooks, or barbed wire to remove from the den, or fire to kill in the den, any immature depredator mammal. Fire-ignited gas cartridges or other products registered or permitted under the Federal Insecticide, Rodenticide, and Fungicide Act are not prohibited (4180.1). Except as provided, any owner or tenant of property being damaged or destroyed or is in danger of such by elk, bear, beaver, wild pig, or gray squirrels, may apply for a permit to kill such mammals. Upon evidence, the Department shall issue a revocable permit under Commission regulations. Mammals so taken shall not be sold or shipped from the premises except under Department instructions. ★★No metal-jawed trap shall be used to take any bear. No poison may be used to take a gray squirrel. The Department shall designate the type of trap to be used to insure the most humane method to trap gray squirrels. The Department may require trapped squirrels to be released in parks or nonagricultural areas.★★ It is unlawful to violate the terms of a permit issued under this section. ★★The permit for taking bears shall contain: ‣ why the permit was necessary; ‣ what efforts were made to solve the problem without killing the bears; ‣ what corrective actions should be implemented to prevent reoccurrence.★★ The Department shall provide applicants for a depredation permit to take wild pigs, with written information describing options for wild pig control, including depredation permits, allowing periodic access to licensed hunters, and holding special hunts (4181).

A bear or wild pig encountered inflicting injury to, molesting, or killing livestock may be taken by the livestock owner or employee if the taking is reported the next working day and the carcass is made available to the Department. Nothing prohibits federal, state, or county trappers from killing or trapping bears killing or molesting livestock, but no person shall use metal-jawed traps to take bear (4181.1). A owner or tenant of land or property that is being damaged or destroyed or is in immediate danger of such by deer may apply for a permit to kill deer. Upon satisfactory evidence, the Department shall issue a revocable permit not to exceed 60 days under Commission regulations, which shall include provisions concerning allowable weapons [statute details restrictions on weapons]. The Department shall issue tags [details for use provided]. Permits may be renewed only after a finding that further damage has occurred or will occur without renewal (4181.5).

When it is demonstrated that beavers are damaging or threatening to damage agricultural lands, crops, levees or other irrigation structures, the Commission shall establish a beaver control area with defined boundaries to permit taking beavers under regulations allowing marketing of pelts until actual or threatened damage is abated (4182). Landowners or tenants, or one authorized in writing, may take cottontail or brush rabbits upon damage to crops or forage. When transporting rabbits from such property, persons other than the owner or tenant shall possess written authority from the owner or tenant. Rabbits taken under this provision may not be sold (4186). An owner or tenant of land or property that is being damaged by burros may apply to the Department of Agriculture for a permit to kill such burros. Burros so taken shall not be sold, nor shipped from the premises, except under Department of Agriculture instructions (4187). When a landowner or tenant applies for a permit under Section 4181 for wild pigs, or Section 4181.5 for deer, the Commission may issue permits to hunting licensees to take deer or wild pigs in sufficient numbers to stop the damage or threatened damage. The Department first shall investigate and determine the number of permits, the territory involved, the dates of the proposed hunt, the manner of issuing the permits, and the fee (4188). The Department shall tag, brand, or otherwise identify in a persistent and distinctive manner large depredatory mammals relocated by, or with the approval of, the Department for game management purposes (4190).

The Department may remove or take any mountain lion, or authorize an appropriate local agency with public safety responsibility, that is perceived to be an imminent threat to public health or safety. A person, employee or agent, whose livestock or other property is being or has been injured, damaged, or destroyed by a mountain lion may report to the Department and request a taking permit. The Department or authorized animal damage control officer shall confirm depredation not more than 48 hours after receiving the report, and promptly shall issue a permit. The permit shall: ‣ expire 10 days after issuance; ‣ authorize the holder to begin pursuit not more than one mile from the depredation site; ‣ limit pursuit to within a 10-mile radius from the reported damage or destruction. Oral authorization may be given if it will assist materially in the pursuit. Taking shall be reported within 24 hours by telephone or five days in writing, and arrangements made to turn the carcass in to the Department. A mountain lion encountered pursuing, inflicting injury to, or killing livestock, or domestic animals, may be taken immediately by the landowner or employee or agent, and reported within 72 hours. The Department shall investigate and recover the carcass and issue a permit confirming that requirements have been met. Mountain lions authorized to be taken shall be taken by the most effective means available, except by poison, leg-hold or metal-jawed traps, and snares (4801 through 4807, and 4809).

The Department may take a fish unduly preying upon a bird, mammal, or fish. The Commission may prescribe permit terms to take fish harmful to other species of fish (5501). The Department is authorized to enter at any time any car, warehouse, depot, ship, or growing area where any fish, amphibia, or aquatic plants are held or stored, for examination for infection, disease, or parasites. Except as provided, all fish, amphibia, or aquatic plants found to be infected, diseased, or parasitized are a public nuisance and shall be destroyed. [Further details provided in 6301 through 6306, 6400.5 and 6855.]

ENFORCEMENT OF WILDLIFE LAWS

Enforcement Powers

★★Subject to Attorney General approval, the Department may enter into reciprocal agreements with federal or county agencies, or agencies in other states, to exchange information on fish and wildlife law enforcement, including the records of persons involved in, or suspected of involvement in, a violation of this code or regulations. This information shall be confidential, and the records shall not be public, except when used for the purpose of prosecution (391).★★

A deputy appointed to enforce code provisions is a peace officer, with the powers and authority of peace officers to make arrests for violations of this code, and may serve processes and notices throughout the state (851). ★The Director may deputize Department employees to check persons for licenses and to enforce section 7145, after satisfactory completion of a training course comparable to the training for "level III reserve" under regulations of the Commission on Peace Officer Standards and Training. Such person is not a peace officer. The Department shall report on the effectiveness of the program (853).★ Department employees designated by the Director as deputized law enforcement officers are peace officers, which authority extends to any place as to a public offense committed or which there is probable cause to believe has been committed within the state [additional requirements for peace officers provided] (856).

County boards of supervisors may appoint a fish and game warden for their county (875). The county warden shall enforce the state laws relating to the protection of fish and game, with peace officer powers and authority (878). [Provisions for reporting and appointment of deputies made in 879 and -880.] The Department may inspect boats, markets, stores and other buildings, except dwellings, and all receptacles, except the clothing actually worn at the time of inspection, where birds, mammals, fish, reptiles, or amphibia may be stored, placed, or held for sale or storage, and boxes and packages containing such held for transportation by a common carrier (1006).

Criminal Penalties

California provides infractions, misdemeanors and felonies for specified violations. Increased fines, jail terms and mandatory suspension of licenses, permits or stamps are provided for second or subsequent violations. [Space does not permit the listing of these extensive provisions in the text. Interested readers need to refer to the original statutes for specific information on penalties. See sections 12000 through 12003, 12006 and 12008.]

Killing or injuring another person by a firearm, bow and arrow, spear, slingshot, or other weapon or device used while taking a bird or mammal and knowingly abandoning the person or failing to render all necessary aid possible is a felony (3009). Except as expressly provided, a violation of this code, or rule, regulation, or order under this code, is a misdemeanor. Taking a bird or mammal in violation of an order issued pursuant to Section 12150 is a felony. Unless provided, the punishment for a misdemeanor violation of this code is a fine up to $1,000, jail up to six months, or both.

The maximum punishment relating to an endangered, threatened, or fully protected bird-of-prey is a fine of $5,000, or jail up to one year, or both. The maximum punishment for a violation relating to any bird-of-prey taken from the wild and reported as having been bred in captivity is a fine of $5,000, or jail up to one year, or both (12010).

In addition to any other penalty, anyone responsible for polluting, contaminating, or obstructing state waters, or depositing or discharging materials threatening to pollute, contaminate, or obstruct state waters, to the detriment of fish, plant, bird, or animal life, shall be required to remove any material which can be removed, that caused the prohibited condition or to pay the costs of the removal by the Department. The Department shall make a reasonable effort to have the person responsible remove, or agree to pay for the removal of, the substance [details provided for alternative actions and funding for cleanup] (12015). In addition to any other provision, a person who discharges or deposits any substance deleterious to fish, plant, bird, or animal life or their habitat, or which threatens to enter, state waters of this state is liable civilly to the Department for all actual damages to such animal life or their habitat, and for reasonable costs of cleaning up or abating, or both (12016).

Whenever a person, while taking a bird or mammal, kills or wounds a person and that fact is ascertained by the Department, the Department shall notify the district attorney, who may bring an action in the municipal or justice court to determine the cause. Such proceedings shall be conducted in the same manner as an action to try a misdemeanor. ★★If it is found that such person did the killing or wounding but that it was not intentional or negligent, the court shall dismiss the proceeding. If it is found that the killing or wounding was intentional, by an act of gross negligence, or while under the influence of alcohol, the court shall permanently prohibit the person from taking any bird or mammal. If simple negligence is found, the court shall prohibit taking any bird or mammal for up to five years (12150).★★

Whenever a person, while taking a bird or mammal, kills or wounds any domestic animal belonging to another [language is identical to provision above] and it is found that the killing or wounding was intentional or negligent, the court shall prohibit taking any bird or mammal for five years (12151). A person who, while hunting, kills or wounds or witnesses the killing or wounding of a human being or domestic animal belonging to another, shall within 48 hours forward a complete written report to the Department (12151.5). [Records to be kept by courts and Department are described in 12152.]

Civil Penalties

Violation of Section 1603 regarding diversion or obstruction of water flow is a civil penalty with up to $25,000 for each violation. This penalty is separate, and in addition to, any other civil penalty imposed pursuant to this section or other law. In determining the amount of civil penalty, the court shall consider the nature, circumstance, extent, and gravity of the violation, and may consider the degree of toxicity and volume of the discharge, whether the effects may be reversed or mitigated, ability to pay, ability to continue in business, voluntary cleanup efforts undertaken, prior history of violations, the gravity of the behavior, the economic benefit, if any, resulting from the violation, and other matters. Every such civil action shall be brought by the Attorney General upon complaint by the Department, or by the district or city attorney [details provided for cases involving injunctions]. Fifty percent of the civil penalties collected go to the county fish and wildlife propagation fund, and half to the Fish and Game Preservation Fund (1603.1).

The state may recover damages in a civil action against a person or local agency which unlawfully or negligently takes or destroys any bird, mammal, fish, reptile, or amphibian protected by state law. The measure of damages is the amount which will compensate for all the detriment proximately caused by the animal's destruction. The State Water Resources Control Board may join in any such action involving unlawful discharge of pollutants into state waters or other violation of the Water Code. This section does not apply to persons or local agencies engaged in agricultural pest control, to the destruction of fish in irrigation canals, or birds or mammals killed while damaging crops. Any recovery or settlement section shall be deposited in the Fish and Wildlife Pollution Cleanup and Abatement Account in the Fish and Game Preservation Fund (2014).

In addition to any other penalty provided by law, a person who illegally imports wildlife is subject to a civil penalty of $500-10,000 for each violation. The Attorney General or the city, district or county attorney, may bring a civil action to recover the civil penalty and the costs of seizing and holding the animal listed in Section 2118. Reasonable costs of investigation, attorney's and expert witness' fees may also be recovered (2125).

The Department may impose civil liability upon a person pursuant to this chapter for any of the acts enumerated in 2582, committed by a person for profit or personal gain. Except as provided, a person who violates this code or its regulations, and, with the exercise of due care, should have known that the birds, mammals, amphibians, reptiles, or fish, or the endangered or threatened species, or the fully protected birds, mammals, or fish were taken, possessed, transported, imported, received, purchased, acquired, or sold in violation of, or in a manner unlawful under, this code, may be assessed a civil penalty up to $10,000 for each bird, mammal, amphibian, reptile, or fish, or for each such animal. This civil penalty may be in addition to any other penalty provided in this code or otherwise by law (2583).

Commission regulations shall adopt guidelines to assist the Director and the Department in ascertaining the amount of civil penalties to be imposed pursuant to Section 2582 or 2583, including amounts or ranges that are adequate to deter illegal actions and partially compensate for losses to the fish and wildlife resources. If the violation involves birds, mammals, amphibians, reptiles, or fish with aggregate value (retail market value, potential monetary gain to the accused or, for commercial species, the established retail market value) less than $400 and involves only transportation, taking, or receipt, the guidelines shall provide that the civil penalty shall not exceed the maximum criminal fine provided for the violation, or $10,000, whichever is less. The guidelines shall include consideration of the nature, circumstances, extent, and gravity of the prohibited acts, and the degree of culpability of the violator, including the effect upon the resources (500).

The Department shall consult with the appropriate district attorney as to the appropriate civil or criminal remedy, and shall seek Attorney General concurrence before proceeding with a civil action. [Details of Director investigation, hearing and referee or hearing board, and assessment of penalty are provided.] The decision of the Director assessing the civil penalty is final (2584). The civil penalties imposed under this chapter are in addition to any forfeiture of equipment pursuant to Section 12157 or forfeiture of birds, mammals, amphibia, reptiles, or fish pursuant to Section 12159 (2585). An action to recover civil penalties imposed under this chapter shall be commenced within three years after discovery of the offense (2587).

It is unlawful to deposit in, permit to pass into, or place where it can pass into state waters any poisonous or polluting substance (5650.1).

License Revocations and Suspensions

Upon the third conviction of a violation of any provision relating to taking or possession of fish, reptiles, or amphibia, or parts, or the violation of a provision relating to the taking or possession of birds or mammals or parts, in any five-year period, and upon any conviction subsequent to the three convictions during five years, that person shall be prohibited from taking any fish, reptiles, or amphibia, or birds or mammals, for three years from the last conviction. (12154 and 12155). A person, whose license was revoked may appeal to the Commission for license reissuance and termination of the prohibition, which the Commission may do if it finds at a hearing sufficient mitigating circumstances (12155.5).

No person licensed or required to be licensed pursuant to Section 4005 and who is convicted of a violation of any provision of Section 4000 or Section 4150 shall take a fur-bearing or nongame mammal for three years [details provided]. The Commission shall revoke a trapping license for the period of prohibition, and it is illegal to obtain, or attempt to obtain, such license during prohibition (12156). Upon conviction of a code or regulation violation, a guide may have the privilege to hunt, fish, or guide revoked for up to three years, and it is unlawful to obtain such license during revocation. Neither the disposition of the criminal action other than by conviction nor refusal of the judge to order revocation impairs the right of the Department to commence proceedings to order revocation of a guide license (12156.5).

Upon conviction of a code provision or regulation, a court may order forfeiture of any device or apparatus used to take birds, mammals, fish, reptiles, or amphibia. If the offense is punishable under Section 12008 of this code or the Penal Code, the judge shall order forfeiture of any device or apparatus used in committing the offense, including any vehicle or snowmobile. A device forfeited shall be sold, used, or destroyed, proceeds to be paid into the Fish and Game Preservation Fund. If the lienholder is a conspirator, it is not a valid lien. Neither the disposition of the criminal action other than by conviction nor refusal of the judge to order forfeiture impairs the right of the Department to commence forfeiture proceedings of fish nets or traps pursuant to Section 8630 (12157). The sport fishing or hunting license may be suspended or revoked upon conviction of a violation for purposes other than profit, in addition to any fine or other punishment. Obtaining a hunting or fishing license during suspension or revocation is a misdemeanor (12158). A plea of nolo contendere is treated a conviction (12158.5).

Birds, mammals, fish, reptiles, or amphibia, or parts illegally taken, possessed, sold, imported, or transported shall be seized, and notice of seizure given (12159). Upon conviction of a violation that prohibits taking an endangered species, threatened species, or fully protected bird, mammal, reptile, amphibian, or fish, the court may order forfeiture of any proceeds from taking that animal (12159.5). Birds, mammals, fish, reptiles, or amphibia, or parts, seized, the sale of which is not prohibited, which have a market value of $100 or more, shall be put to economical use immediately upon seizure, at the prevailing market price, proceeds to go to the Fish and Game Preservation Fund (12160), or they may be donated to a state, county, city, or charitable institution, or destroyed (12161 and 12162). Upon conviction of trespassing, in addition to any other fine or forfeiture imposed, the court shall confiscate a bird or mammal or parts taken while trespassing, and shall order it donated or destroyed. A guide convicted of violating

California

or permitting violation may have the guide license revoked. Obtaining another guide license within two years after revocation is a misdemeanor (12164 and 12165).

Reward Payments

The Director may pay a reward for furnishing information which led to an arrest, criminal conviction, assessment of a civil penalty, or forfeiture of property. The amount shall be designated with advice of the CalTIP Award Board (2586).

Intoxication Testing of Hunters

It is unlawful to take birds or mammals with firearms or bow and arrow when intoxicated (3001).

HABITAT PROTECTION

[There are many provisions throughout the game and fish code for protection of fish and wildlife habitat. The following provisions are summarized and shortened substantially; the reader is advised to review the statutes for further details].

When the Department determines that an oil sump is hazardous and either does or may present immediate and grave danger to wildlife, the State Oil and Gas Supervisor shall be notified to have the condition abated. The Commission shall promulgate regulations for implementation and definition of "hazardous" and "wildlife" (1016).

★★The **California Riparian Habitat Conservation Program**, administered by the Wildlife Conservation Board, is to protect, preserve, and restore riparian habitats by acquisition of interests and rights in real property and waters (1387). Preservation and enhancement of riparian habitat shall be a primary concern of the Board, the Department, and state agencies whose activities impact riparian habitat [included Departments are listed] (1389).★★

The **Inland Wetlands Conservation Program**, administered by the Wildlife Conservation Board, is to carry out the programs of the Central Valley Habitat Joint Venture. The board may engage in several listed functions regarding wetland habitat acquisition. The board shall report to the Governor and the Legislature (1410 through 1422). The **Inland Wetlands Conservation Fund** is created in the Wildlife Restoration Fund, to carry out this program (1430).

With approval of the Commission and the Department of General Services, the Department may sell or exchange any portion of property within any area or range [specific areas and ranges listed] for property within or contiguous to such area or range, provided that no exchange or sale shall reduce the total area (1500). The Department may: ► expend funds to improve property, including nonnavigable lakes and streams, riparian zones, and upland, to restore, rehabilitate, and improve fish and wildlife habitat. Improvement may include removal of barriers to migration and improvement of hatching, feeding, resting, and breeding places; ► undertake habitat improvement on lands without acquiring an interest in the property (1501); ► contract for habitat preservation, restoration, and enhancement (1501.5). Except under regulations, it is unlawful to enter wildlife management areas or public shooting grounds, or to take a bird, nest, eggs, or any mammal (1530).

The policy of the state is to protect threatened or endangered native plants, wildlife, or aquatic organisms or specialized habitat types, both terrestrial and aquatic, through establishment of ecological reserves (1580). [Details provided in 1583 through 1585.]

Plans for a construction project on behalf of a state or local governmental agency or public utility shall be submitted if the project will: ► divert, obstruct, or change the natural flow or the bed, channel, or bank of any designated river, stream, or lake in which there is an existing fish or wildlife resource or benefit; ► use streambed material; ► result in the deposition of debris, waste, or material containing crumbled, flaked, or ground pavement where it can pass into such river, stream, or lake. If a fish or wildlife resource may be affected adversely by construction, the Department shall notify the agency or utility and propose reasonable modifications. [Details of proposals and negotiations provided.] Construction shall not begin until the Department has found no substantial adverse impact or until the Department's modifications have been incorporated into the project (1601). [Provisions for review of modifications and/or arbitration are given in 1602. Similar provisions apply if there will be a substantial diversion or obstruction of the natural flow or changing of the bed, channel or bank of such river, stream or lake, in 1603.] The Director may establish a schedule of fees to pay costs (1607).

A Significant Natural Areas Program will be administered by the Department, which shall access the most recent natural resources information [details provided], considering alternative approaches, including alternatives to fee acquisition such as incentives, leasing, and dedication. The Department shall provide coordinating services to aid in the maintenance and perpetuation of significant natural areas (1932). The Fish and Wildlife Habitat Enhancement Fund is created to provide the financial means to correct the most severe deficiencies in fish and wildlife habitat in California through acquisition, enhancement, and development of habitat areas most in need of conservation and management (2620). (See Agency Funding Sources under STATE FISH AND WILDLIFE AGENCIES.)

This chapter provides the financial means to correct the most severe deficiencies in habitat and in the areas designated for preservation of natural diversity through acquisition, enhancement, restoration, and protection (2701). (See Agency Funding Sources under STATE FISH AND WILDLIFE AGENCIES.) The Wildlife and Natural Areas Conservation Fund shall be used to acquire, enhance, restore, or protect lands on which specific criteria naturally exist [details provided in 2721 through 2725, 2810, 2810 and 2825].

★★It is the policy of the state actively to ensure the improvement of habitat on private land to encourage propagation, utilization, and conservation of fish and wildlife resources. The Commission and the Department may develop a Private Wildlife Habitat Enhancement and Management Program (3400). The Commission may authorize the Department to issue licenses for wildlife habitat enhancement and management areas (WHEMA) on private lands. Such licensed private lands shall have public access without landowner consent. The Commission shall authorize hunting during the deer rut only in a WHEMA when consistent with management plans (3401).★★ [Extensive details are provided for license issuance, posting, taking of species, tagging after taking, and Department reporting, in Sections 3402 through 3409.]

The Director may contract with private owners to utilize land for conservation of waterfowl and habitat, with priority to contracts with the greatest potential for restoring, enhancing, and protecting high quality waterfowl habitat, especially that subject to destruction, drastic modification, or significant curtailment of habitat values (3460). [Details of contracts, management plans and payment requirements are provided, in 3461.]

The US shall file with the Commission a separate application for dams it proposes to construct or enlarge. [Details of US application provided in 5904] (5903). The Department shall examine dams naturally frequented by fish (5930). If in the opinion of the Commission, there is not free passage for fish, the Department shall cause plans to be furnished for and the owner provide a fishway (5931 and 5933). [Details of obligations of dam owners for maintenance of fishways are provided in Sections 5932 through 3937.] If it is impracticable to construct a fishway, the owner of the dam may be ordered to equip a hatchery, together with dwellings, traps for taking fish, and other equipment, according to Department plans and specifications, which the Department shall operate without owner expense (5938).

[Provisions for prevention of introduction of aquatic nuisance species from vessel ballast water are made in Sections 6430 through 6433.]

[Detailed game refuge laws are set out in 10500 through 10504, 10506, and 10512 through 10514.]

Upon Commission approval, people consent to acquisition by the US of land and water for migratory bird reservations; reserving to the state full and complete jurisdiction and authority and rights, privileges, and immunities over such areas not incompatible with the administration, maintenance, protection, and control by the US under the Act (10680). State consent is conditioned on US conformity with state water laws (10683). With Commission approval, the people also consent to the declaration, withdrawal, or determination of any national forest or power site, and to the condemnation of any lands below 230-feet below sea level, as a migratory bird reservation (10685).

Except as provided, it is a misdemeanor to take, possess, harm, molest, harass, or interfere with any burro in the burro sanctuary described in Section 10930, except persons lawfully on sanctuary lands raising cattle (10931).

California

NATIVE AMERICAN WILDLIFE PROVISIONS

Registered members of the Yurok Indian Tribe may take fish, for subsistence only, from the Klamath River between its mouth and the junction of Tectah Creek, exclusive of tributaries, under the following conditions: ▸ upon application the Department shall issue a renewable, nontransferable permit to take fish, using hand dip nets and hook and line only, for one calendar year. A Yurok Indian while taking fish shall possess and display on request a permit. Daily limits are three trout, salmon or combination, and one sturgeon. There is no bag limit on any other fish. While fishing, no Yurok Indian may be accompanied by a person without a permit. It is unlawful for that person to accompany any such Yurok Indian. Sale of fish is cause for permanent revocation of the permit (7155).

Irrespective of any other provision of law, the provisions of this code are not applicable to enrolled California Indians, while on the reservation and under circumstances where the code was not applicable [prior to 1953 federal provision]. No such Indian shall be prosecuted for violation in the places and under the circumstances referred to. This does not restrict prosecution of any Indian for violation of this code prohibiting the sale of any bird, mammal, fish, or amphibia (12300).

[Provisions are made for a pilot project for Indian subsistence fishing by the Covelo Indian Community (confederated tribes of the Round Valley Indian Reservation) under agreement with the Department and approved by the Commission in Sections 16000 to 16011. Similar provisions are made for the Yurok and Hoopa Valley Reservations for commercial fishing on the Klamath and Trinity Rivers in Sections 16500 to 16541].

COLORADO

Sources: Colorado Revised Statutes, Annotated, 1985, Title 33; 1990 Replacement Volume; 1992 Cumulative Pocket Part.

STATE WILDLIFE POLICY

It is the policy of the state that wildlife and their environment be protected, preserved, enhanced, and managed for the use, benefit, and enjoyment of the people of the state and its visitors. There shall be a comprehensive program to offer the greatest possible variety of wildlife-related recreational opportunities, with continuous planning, acquisition, and development of wildlife habitats and facilities for wildlife-related opportunities. All wildlife not lawfully acquired and held by private ownership is declared to be the property of the state. Right, title, interest, acquisition, transfer, sale, importation, exportation, release, donation, or possession of wildlife shall be permitted only as provided in this title or in any rule of the Wildlife Commission. To foster the welfare of its inhabitants, the state shall protect and encourage full development of absolute and conditional water rights created under state law and develop and maximize the beneficial use of the waters to which Colorado and its citizens are entitled under interstate compacts. The state shall utilize hunting, trapping, and fishing as the primary methods of effecting necessary wildlife harvests (33-1-101). (See HABITAT PROTECTION.)

It is the policy of the state that the natural, scenic, scientific, and outdoor recreation areas be protected, preserved, enhanced, and managed for the use, benefit, and enjoyment of the people of this state and visitors. It is further state policy that there shall be a comprehensive program of outdoor recreational opportunities. The state shall: ▸ develop state parks and state recreation areas suitable for camping, picnicking, hiking, horseback riding, environmental education, sightseeing, hunting, boating, fishing, swimming, and other water sports, and other recreational activities; ▸ advise citizens and visitors of the location of these areas; ▸ charge fees for the use of any state park or state area; ▸ allow sport hunting, trapping, and fishing as a wildlife management tool and as the primary method of effecting a necessary wildlife management (33-10-101).

RELEVANT WILDLIFE DEFINITIONS: See Definitions section of Appendices.

STATE FISH AND WILDLIFE AGENCIES

Agency Structure

The **Division of Wildlife** (Division) under the jurisdiction of a **Wildlife Commission** (Commission), consisting of eight members appointed by the Governor, with consent of the Senate. One member is selected from each of five designated districts and three from the public at large for four-year terms. No district may supply more than two members. Members must be residents of the state and of the district from which appointed. One member shall be appointed from each of the following categories: livestock producers, agricultural or produce growers, sportsmen or outfitters, wildlife organizations, and boards of county commissioners; three members from the public at large. Not more than four members shall be members of the same political party (33-1-103). The Commission shall appoint the **Director of the Division of Wildlife** (Director) who shall possess qualifications as established by the Commission, the **Executive Director of the Department of Natural Resources** (Executive Director), and the state personnel board. The Director is the head of the Division under the direction and supervision of the Commission and the Executive Director and has supervisory control of and authority over all activities, functions, and employees of the Division (33-1-109 and -110).

Agency Powers and Duties

The **Commission** is responsible for all wildlife management, licensing requirements, and promulgation of rules, regulations, and orders concerning wildlife programs. The Commission shall establish objectives within state policy, to enable the Division to develop, manage, and maintain sound programs of hunting, fishing, trapping, and other wildlife-related outdoor recreational activities. The Commission shall report to the Executive Director as required.

Publications of the Commission circulated in quantity outside the Division shall be subject to approval and control of the Executive Director (33-1-104).

The Commission has power to: ▸ acquire by gift, transfer, devise, lease, purchase, or long-term operating agreement land and water necessary for wildlife or its preservation or conservation; ▸ lease, exchange, or sell property, water and land, including oil, gas, and other organic and inorganic substances; ▸ construct or establish public facilities and conveniences on land in which the Commission holds an interest, and operate, maintain, provide services, and make reasonable fees for use, or enter into contracts for maintenance or operation; ▸ capture, propagate, transport, buy, sell, or exchange species of wildlife for stocking state lands or waters; ▸ enter into cooperative agreements with state and other government agencies, educational institutions, corporations, clubs, landowners, associations, and individuals for development and promotion of wildlife programs; ▸ receive and expend grants, gifts, and bequests, including federal funds; ▸ enter into agreements with landowners for public hunting and fishing areas (33-1-105).

In order to provide an adequate, flexible, and coordinated statewide system of wildlife management and to maintain adequate populations of wildlife species, the Commission shall have authority, through regulations, to: determine under what circumstances, when, in which localities, by what means, what sex, and in what numbers wildlife may be taken; ▸ shorten, extend, or close seasons when necessary; ▸ provide for disposal of usable portions of wildlife confiscated, abandoned, or unclaimed at meat processing and storage facilities; ▸ control the exportation, importation, transportation, release, possession, sale, transfer, and donation of wildlife; ▸ establish requirements for those in the business of buying, selling, processing, or handling wildlife for keeping records and making them available for inspection; ▸ provide for issuance of licenses for hunting, fishing, trapping, taking, or possession of wildlife. ★In no event shall the Commission adopt regulations concerning taking black bears in conflict with the provisions of section 33-4-101.3 (33-1-106).★

The **Director** shall ▸ exercise all powers and perform all functions of the Commission in the interim between its meetings, subject to Commission ratification; ▸ perform duties prescribed by the Commission, Executive Director, or by law, except making rules or regulations; ▸ prepare reports as the Executive Director requires from the Commission or Director; ▸ with Commission approval, authorize scientific studies and collect, classify, and disseminate statistics, data, and information which will accomplish the objectives of this title and state policy. The Director and the Executive Director shall consult with the Commission on the Division's budget and expenditures of moneys. The Director shall appoint **District Wildlife Managers** and may appoint **Special District Wildlife Managers** to serve without pay. A Special District Wildlife Manager shall not be commissioned until submission of an application setting forth qualifications. The Director may revoke any Special District Wildlife Manager Commission (33-1-110).

★Neither the Commission nor Division shall enter into mitigation agreements with any federal agency relating to transfer or exchange of land or water condemned by the federal government without express consent of the general assembly. The Commission or Division may enter into agreements with a federal agency pertaining to stocking fish or management of wildlife on federally owned lands. The programs of the Commission and Division, including listing of threatened and endangered species, shall not supersede, abrogate, or impair any water right. "Impair" means requiring water users to forego water to which they are entitled under a water right (33-1-120). It is the duty of the Division to maintain records of wildlife migration areas, and to furnish wildlife migration area information to requesting persons (33-3-105).★

Agency Regulations

Rule-making procedures are prescribed in Title 24, except as provided in this title (33-1-108). The Commission shall adopt rules for administration, protection, and maintenance of land and water acquired by the Commission. The Commission shall have power to adopt rules or regulations for: ▸ maintenance, enhancement, or management of property, vegetation, wildlife, signs, markers, buildings or other structures, and any objects of scientific value or interest in such areas; ▸ restriction, limitation, or prohibition concerning time, manner, permitted activities, or numbers of people in such areas; ▸ sanitation, health, and safety measures. Rules that apply to any particular area shall be published and prominently posted at the area. ★Absence of posting shall not relieve responsibility to comply with applicable published rules or regulations (33-1-107).★

Agency Funding Sources

Except as provided, moneys received from wildlife license fees and other wildlife sources, and interest earned, shall be credited to the **Wildlife Cash Fund**. These moneys shall be utilized for authorized expenditures for wildlife activities and functions, and for financing impact assistance grants pursuant to Title 30. Moneys in the Wildlife Cash Fund shall not be deposited or transferred to the state's general fund or any other fund. A **Stores Revolving Fund** shall acquire stock for warehousing and distributing supplies to operating units of the Division. The fund shall not be used for operating expenses but shall be maintained as a revolving fund of $800,000 composed of: cash, accounts receivable, and inventory supplies. The purpose of the fund is to provide better budgetary control. The Director, with consent and approval of the Executive Director, is authorized to establish an adequate system of accounting for records of: ▸ moneys received and from what sources; ▸ all moneys expended and for what purposes; ▸ licenses issued. In the annual budget request to the Governor, the Executive Director shall clearly show fund allocations for wildlife purposes among operations, land acquisition, capital construction and other purposes. The cost of nongame programs established under this title shall be borne by the **General Fund**, the **Nongame and Endangered Wildlife Cash Fund**, the Wildlife Cash Fund, and other sources deemed appropriate by the general assembly (33-1-112).

★★The Commission is authorized to accept grants and donations for a **Wildlife for Future Generations Trust Fund**. Moneys deposited in the fund shall not be appropriated but shall be accrued and maintained intact. Only interest earned may be expended on wildlife projects. The fund is under the control of and to be administered by the Commission, which shall submit an annual report of moneys expended from the fund and matters accomplished by such expenditures to the general assembly. Moneys and interest shall not be deposited or transferred to any other fund (33-1-112).★★

The **Habitat Partnership Cash Fund** consists of moneys annually appropriated to the Division for the partnership program and gifts, donations, and reimbursements to the program from other sources. Fund moneys shall be used in accordance with the duties of the Habitat Partnership Council. All interest earned from the fund shall be credited to the fund, and balances remaining at fiscal year end shall remain in the fund. The Council shall submit an annual report to the Commission, the senate and house agriculture committees, the Executive Director, and the general assembly stating the items and purposes for which it has expended fund moneys. If the Council ceases to exist, all moneys in the fund shall revert to the Wildlife Cash Fund (33-1-112).

★★The **Search and Rescue Fund** is the sole source of funds for any state agency or political subdivision for costs incurred in search and rescue activities involving persons holding hunting or fishing licenses or vessel, snowmobile, or off-highway vehicle registrations. Reimbursable costs are limited to actual operational expenses, including related training and equipment other than vehicles. A surcharge of twenty-five cents shall be assessed on each hunting and fishing license and each vessel, snowmobile, and off-highway vehicle registration, to be deposited in the Fund. All state agencies and political subdivisions have the right to make a claim on the fund for reimbursement of costs incurred in performance of search and rescue activities. The moneys in the Fund shall be subject to annual appropriation by the general assembly for costs of administration of this section. Any balance in the fund over $300,000, after claims and administrative costs have been paid, shall be transferred to the Wildlife Cash Fund. Moneys remaining in the fund and appropriated for search and rescue expenses, after claims and administrative costs have been paid, shall be divided among counties which have applied for year-end grants. The Commission shall establish rules and regulations for applying for year-end grants (33-1-112.5).★★

The Division is authorized to distribute a conservation magazine on a paid subscription basis, with revenues to be credited to the **Colorado Outdoors Magazine Revolving Fund** for publication and distribution, and additional funds, if necessary, will be included in the Division's annual budget of Wildlife Cash Funds. The magazine may be sold by the Division or by designated individuals who may receive up to ten percent of moneys collected for sale of a subscription and ten cents for each copy sold. Any surplus in the revolving fund over $50,000 shall revert to the Wildlife Cash Fund (33-1-114).

Certain revenues and earnings derived from properties purchased and operated jointly by the US and Colorado under the provisions of sections 33-1-116 to 33-1-119, the provisions of the acts of Congress referred to in this article, and the regulations of the US Department of the Interior shall be deposited in a **Federal Aid Projects Income Fund**. Such revenues and earnings shall be limited to specific revenues and earnings to which each has a right under cooperative agreements (33-1-119).

See also licenses and permits under HUNTING, FISHING, TRAPPING PROVISIONS for mountain sheep and mountain goat raffle.

Agency Advisory Boards

★★The Director, with Commission approval, shall appoint nine persons to act as the **Habitat Partnership Council** (Council) with statewide responsibility and authority. The Council shall consist of: ▸ two sportspersons who purchase big game licenses on a regular basis in Colorado; ▸ two persons representing livestock growers; ▸ one person from the US Forest Service; ▸ one from the US Bureau of Land Management; ▸ one from the Colorado State University Range Extension Program; ▸ one person representing agricultural crop producers; ▸ one person from the Division of Wildlife. All shall be state residents. Members who will represent livestock growers and agricultural crop producers shall be chosen by the Director from persons nominated by the local Habitat Partnership Committees. Terms of the members representing sportspersons and livestock growers are four years. The terms of members representing the various agencies shall be at the discretion of the respective agencies. Council duties are to: ▸ advise local Habitat Partnership Committees; ▸ assist in dissemination of information concerning the habitat partnership program; ▸ review draft plans for compliance with program guidelines established by the Commission and recommend Commission action; ▸ monitor program effectiveness and propose changes in guidelines and land acquisition planning and review; ▸ certify to the state treasurer that payment vouchers submitted by local Habitat Partnership Committees are consistent with approved distribution management plans; ▸ report to the Commission and general assembly (33-1-110).★★

★★The Director, with Commission approval, shall have authority to appoint a **Habitat Partnership Committee** (Committee) where conflicts between wildlife and rangeland managers exist. The Committee shall consist of the following members: ▸ one sportsperson who purchases big game licenses on a regular basis in Colorado; ▸ three persons representing livestock growers in that area; ▸ one person from each of the federal agencies that has land management responsibilities in that state area; ▸ one person from the Division of Wildlife. All shall be state residents. Committee duties are to: ▸ develop big game distribution management plans to resolve rangeland forage and fence conflicts; ▸ monitor program effectiveness and propose to the Council changes in guidelines and land acquisition planning and review; ▸ request annually funds from the Council consistent with the distribution management plan; ▸ expend funds allocated by the Council or from other sources to implement distribution management plans; ▸ make an annual report of expenditures and accomplishments to the Council; ▸ nominate a representative of agricultural livestock growers or crop producers to the Council for the relevant state area; ▸ procure from land owners, land managers, or other providers, agricultural materials or services for carrying out activities (33-1-110).★★

There is established in the Division a **Fish Health Board**, with five members: one who is not a commercial aquaculturist and who may be a Department of Agriculture employee, appointed by its Commissioner; one who may be a Division employee, appointed by the Director; two who are engaged in private aquaculture and shall represent the various segments of the aquaculture industry and geographic areas of the state, appointed by the Commissioner of Agriculture; and one member who is a USFW employee, appointed by the Regional Director. Terms shall be three years and members shall be eligible for reappointment. The Commissioner of Agriculture and the Director shall be ex officio nonvoting members. The Board shall meet at least once each year (33-5.5-101). The **Fish Health Board** shall review or initiate and consider every proposed rule relating to fish health, the spread of aquatic disease in private aquaculture facilities or cultured aquatic stock, or the importation or distribution of any exotic aquatic species. The Board shall vote to approve or disapprove any proposed rule. The Commission shall either adopt or decline to adopt the rule [details of approval or disapproval of proposed rules included]. Nothing herein shall diminish or supersede Division or Commission authority to regulate or manage wild aquatic organisms in state waters or in facilities controlled by the Division or by USFW. The Board shall review any orders for destruction of aquatic organisms or quarantines of aquaculture facilities which last beyond thirty days, and all orders require the Board's approval, except destruction orders may be approved by the Director if a situation exists which threatens imminent danger to existing aquatic populations or to human health and safety, and no more reasonable means of control exist. Destruction of aquatic organisms or quarantines shall be in accordance with Division regulations. The Board shall periodically review regulations and recommend changes to the Commission (33-5.5-101 and -102).

See also GENERAL EXCEPTIONS TO PROTECTION.

PROTECTED SPECIES OF WILDLIFE

The open season for all state migratory game birds shall be the same as that fixed by the Federal Migratory Bird Treaty Act. Any changes or new rulings under the Act applicable to the state shall be in effect and be enforced by the Division. The term "migratory birds" includes birds defined as such under the administrative provisions and regulations of the Act. The Commission shall issue regulations and licenses to permit possession of raptors for falconry and captive breeding and to encourage individual efforts to propagate the species. ★It is the intent of the general assembly for the Commission to make the rules and regulations of this state conform to or be more stringent than the provisions of the Migratory Bird Treaty Act and the Endangered Species Act. These regulations may include, but not be limited to, captive breeding and the use of domestic captive-bred raptors and purchase, sale, transportation, importation, exportation, or exchange of raptors with persons having like licenses (33-1-115).★

The General Assembly declares that: ▸ it is the policy of this state to manage all nongame wildlife, recognizing the private property rights of individual property owners, for human enjoyment and welfare, for scientific purposes, and to insure their perpetuation as members of ecosystems; ▸ species or subspecies of state indigenous wildlife found to be endangered or threatened within the state should be accorded protection to maintain and enhance their numbers; ▸ the state should assist in the protection of species or subspecies of wildlife endangered or threatened elsewhere; ▸ adequate funding be made available to the Division annually by appropriations from the general fund. "Management" means collection and application of biological information to increase the number of individuals within species of wildlife to the optimum carrying capacity of their habitat and maintaining such levels. The term includes the entire range of activities that constitute a modern, scientific resource program including, but not limited to, research, census, law enforcement, habitat acquisition and improvement, and education. Also included is the periodic or total protection of species, and may include artificial propagation to maintain threatened or endangered species, in concert with water rights, and may also include restriction of stocking of species in competition with threatened or endangered species for available habitat (33-2-102 and -103).

The Division shall establish programs including acquisition of land or aquatic habitat for management of nongame, endangered, or threatened wildlife, and may enter into agreements with federal agencies, political subdivisions or private persons for administration and management of any area established under this section or utilized for management of nongame, endangered, or threatened wildlife (33-2-106 and -107).

The Division shall conduct investigations on nongame wildlife to develop information relating to population, distribution, habitat needs, limiting factors, and other biological and ecological data to determine management measures. On the basis of such determinations, the Commission shall issue regulations and develop management programs. Regulations shall set forth species or subspecies of nongame wildlife in need of management. The Commission shall conduct ongoing investigations of nongame wildlife and may amend regulations by adding or deleting species or subspecies. The Commission shall by regulation establish limitations on the taking, possession, transportation, exportation, processing, sale or offering for sale, or shipment to manage nongame wildlife. Except as provided, it is unlawful to take, possess, transport, export, process, sell or offer for sale, or ship nongame wildlife in need of management and unlawful for any common or contract carrier knowingly to transport or receive for shipment such nongame wildlife (33-2-104).

On the basis of investigations of nongame wildlife and other available scientific and commercial data and after consultation with appropriate state and federal entities and other interested persons and organizations, the Commission shall by regulation establish a list of species and, where necessary, subspecies of wildlife indigenous to the state determined to be endangered or threatened. At least once every five years, the Commission shall review all species included in the state lists of endangered or threatened species and determine whether any species should be: ▸ removed from such list; ▸ changed in status from endangered to threatened; ▸ changed in status from threatened to endangered. Except as provided, it is unlawful to take, possess, transport, export, process, sell or offer for sale, or ship and for any common or contract carrier knowingly to transport or receive for shipment any species or subspecies of wildlife appearing on the list of wildlife indigenous to this state determined to be threatened or endangered (33-2-105). The Commission shall issue necessary regulations to carry out the purposes of this article (33-2-107).

★★It is the intent of the voters of Colorado to prohibit the taking of black bears when females are rearing their cubs. It is their further intent to promote the concept of fair chase in the taking of black bears by eliminating the use of bait and dogs. During March 1 through September 1, it is unlawful to take a black bear by any means including firearm or bow and arrow. It is unlawful to take a black bear with the use of bait, or with dogs at any time. If a dog accidentally chases a black bear while the owner or person in control of such dog is in legal pursuit of other game, such owner or person in control shall not be charged with illegal taking of a black bear if the dog is called off as soon as the mistake is realized and the bear is not injured or killed. This section shall not apply to Division employees or to field agents of the US Department of Agriculture acting in their official capacity, nor to a person who lawfully takes a black bear in defense of life or property, or to a person who traps, kills, or otherwise disposes of a black bear in accordance with statutory exceptions. "Bait" means to place, expose, deposit, distribute, or scatter salt, minerals, grain, animal parts, or other food so as to lure, attract, or entice black bears on or over any area where hunters are attempting to take black bears. Violation: Class 1 misdemeanor punished as provided in 18-1-106; and license privileges suspended for five years. Persons convicted of a second or subsequent offense shall have their wildlife license privileges suspended permanently (33-4-101.3).★★

GENERAL EXCEPTIONS TO PROTECTION

The Commission may permit, under regulation terms and conditions, the taking, possession, transportation, exportation, or shipment of species or subspecies of wildlife which appear on the state lists of endangered or threatened species for scientific, zoological, or educational purposes, for propagation in captivity, or for other special purposes. Upon good cause shown and to alleviate damage to property or to protect human health, endangered or threatened species may be removed, captured, or destroyed but only under Division permit and, where possible, under the supervision of a Division agent and under Commission regulations (33-2-106).

HUNTING, FISHING, TRAPPING PROVISIONS

General Provisions

A person who hunts, traps, fishes, or possesses wildlife for any purpose shall produce all applicable licenses, firearms, records required to be maintained, wildlife, and personal identification documents when requested to do so by a District Wildlife Manager or other peace officer. Refusal to permit inspection is a misdemeanor; fine of $50; and 5 license suspension points. The Division is authorized to establish check stations to aid in management of wildlife and enforcement of statutes and regulations. Persons who encounter check stations, whether in possession of wildlife or not, shall stop and produce Division licenses, firearms, and wildlife for inspection. Violation: misdemeanor; fine of $100; 5 points. Failure to void a license or carcass tag as required is a misdemeanor; fine of $50; 10 points. It is unlawful to elude or attempt to elude by any means a District Wildlife Manager or other peace officer after having received a visual or audible signal directing the person to stop. Violation: misdemeanor; $100-1,000 fine; 10 points. In addition, the court shall require payment for damages caused to public or private real or personal property while eluding an officer (33-6-111).

Unless otherwise permitted, it is unlawful willfully to damage or destroy any wildlife den, nest or eggs or to harass any wildlife. Violation: misdemeanor; fine of $100; 10 points. However, nothing shall prohibit the removal of wildlife dens or nests to prevent damage to property or livestock or while trapping. Unless allowed by regulation, it is unlawful to allow or direct knowingly or negligently a dog under a person's control to harass wildlife, whether or not the wildlife is actually injured. Violation: misdemeanor; fine of $200. A District Wildlife Manager or other peace officer may capture or kill a dog harassing wildlife. This subsection shall not apply to dogs under the direct personal control of a person. It is unlawful to remove, damage, deface, or destroy real or personal property or wildlife habitat under Division control, or to use Division property in violation. Violation: misdemeanor; and the court may require the defendant to reimburse the Division for damages (33-6-128 and -129).

Unless otherwise permitted, it is unlawful to use toxicants, poisons, drugs, dynamite, explosives, or stupefying substances for taking or harassing wildlife. Violation: misdemeanor; fine of $200; 20 points. The Division shall cooperate with the Department of Agriculture in developing policies for Department issuance of permits for the use of poison by livestock owners or operators (33-6-130).

Licenses and Permits

The Division is authorized to issue resident and nonresident licenses and special licenses and collect fees as provided [details of fee reductions, increases and replacement of licenses provided]. Aquaculture facility permittees may charge a fee for fishing at the production facility; no state fishing license is required. Several satellite stations of a fish production facility may operate under one aquaculture license if all stations are listed on such license (33-4-102).

A State Migratory Waterfowl Stamp is required before hunting or taking migratory waterfowl. The Commission may contract with a nonprofit waterfowl conservation organization for providing the form and design. All moneys received from the Stamp shall be used for migratory waterfowl habitats and subject to an annual appropriation (33-4-102.5). ★Colorado landowners are entitled to landowner preference for licenses to hunt deer, elk, or antelope when: ▸ the applicant is an owner of agricultural land of 160 acres or more; ▸ the land was inhabited by the species during the greater portion of the year before the application; ▸ application for a license preference is made concurrent with license application; ▸ the applicant submits no more than one application per species per calendar year; ▸ all licenses permitting firearm hunting are limited in number by Commission regulation in the area where the land is located. Landowners receiving licenses pursuant to this section shall allow hunting on their land by licensed hunters, subject to a limitation of numbers (33-4-103).★

The Division is authorized to issue up to two male rocky mountain big horn sheep licenses, and two male or female rocky mountain goat licenses each year through a competitive auction or raffle, under Commission regulations. Nonprofit organizations involved in the conservation of these species may be authorized to conduct the license auction or raffle, and may retain up to 10% of proceeds to cover expenses. All remaining proceeds shall be used for the benefit of rocky mountain goat or big horn sheep research and/or habitat development, and proceeds shall be in addition to any other funds used for management of these animals. The Commission shall report to the general assembly each year concerning use of the proceeds from auctions or raffles (33-4-116).

Restrictions on Taking

★The Commission may establish by regulation requirements for preserving the evidence of sex and\or species of wildlife taken under statutory provisions and it is unlawful to possess any wildlife or considerable portion in violation. Evidence of species or sex may be one or more of the following: head, antlers, horns, testes, scrotum, udder, spurred leg, wing, skin, or plumage in sufficient amount to allow species or sex to be determined by ordinary inspection.★ Violation: misdemeanor; for big game, $100 fine; 10 points. With respect to other wildlife, $50 fine; 5 points (33-6-112).

It is unlawful to take from another without permission wildlife lawfully acquired and possessed. Violation: misdemeanor; $100-500 fine; 20 points. A person having wildlife taken unlawfully shall be entitled to compensation ordered by the court. It is unlawful to interfere with, disturb, remove, or tamper with a trap, snare, or device that has been legally set. Violation: misdemeanor; $200 fine; 10 points (33-6-115).

It is unlawful to enter upon private land or lands under control of the State Board of Land Commissioners to take wildlife by hunting, trapping, or fishing without first obtaining permission from the owner or person in possession. It is unlawful to post, sign, or indicate that public lands not held under an exclusive control lease are privately owned. Violation: misdemeanor; $100 fine; 20 points (33-6-116).

★★Except as is provided, it is unlawful to take or solicit another to take wildlife and detach or remove, with the intent to abandon the carcass or body, only the head, hide, claws, teeth, antlers, horns, internal organs, or feathers or parts, or to kill and abandon any wildlife. Violation, with respect to big game, eagles, and endangered species is a class 5 felony and shall be punished as provided in 18-1-105, and in addition, a $1,000-20,000 fine. The fine shall be in an amount within the presumptive range set out in 18-1-105(1). Upon conviction, the Commission may permanently suspend all license privileges. Violation, with respect to all other wildlife species, is a misdemeanor, and a $100-1,000 fine; or jail up to one year; or both; and 20 points. The purpose and intent of this section is to protect the wildlife of this state from wanton, ruthless, or wasteful destruction or mutilation for their heads, hides, claws, teeth, antlers, horns, internal organs, or feathers or any of the foregoing (33-6-117).★★ Except as provided, it is unlawful for a person who wounds or may have wounded game wildlife to fail to make a reasonable attempt to locate the wildlife and take it into possession. Violation: misdemeanor and for big game, a fine of $100, and 15 points. With respect to small game, a fine of $50, and 15 points. If wounded game goes onto private property, the person who wounded the game shall make a reasonable attempt to contact the landowner or person in charge before pursuing the wounded game. Except as provided, it is unlawful to fail immediately to dress or care for and provide for human consumption the edible portions of game wildlife. Violation: misdemeanor for big game, a fine of $300 and 15 points; other game wildlife, a fine of $100 and 10 points. It is unlawful to use wildlife as bait unless otherwise provided. Violation: misdemeanor; fine of $100; 10 (33-6-119). It is unlawful to take wildlife outside of the established season or in an area closed by regulation. Violation: misdemeanor; fine of $100; 10 points (33-6-120).

★★It is unlawful to advertise, conduct or offer to conduct, or otherwise promote or participate in any contest or competition involving monetary payment or awarding of any prize when the object of the contest involves killing big game or the display for comparison of big game or any part. Certificates issued by organizations solely for registration and recognition of animals legally taken are not prohibited. Violation: misdemeanor; fine of $500; 20 points (33-6-118).★★

Unless otherwise permitted, it is unlawful to take or harass wildlife from or with a motor vehicle. It is unlawful to spot or locate wildlife from an aircraft and communicate the location to a person on the ground as an aid to hunting or pursuing wildlife.   ★It is unlawful for such airborne person or person on the ground receiving such communication to pursue or take game on the same day or the day following such flight.★ Violation: misdemeanor; a fine of $200; 15 points (33-6-124).

It is unlawful for a person, except if authorized by law or the Division, to possess or have under control a firearm, other than a pistol or revolver, in or on a motor vehicle unless the chamber is unloaded, and a person shall allow a peace officer to inspect the chamber of a rifle or shotgun in the motor vehicle. A "muzzle-loader" shall be considered unloaded if it is not primed. Violation: misdemeanor; fine of $50; 15 points (33-6-125). It is unlawful for a person to discharge a firearm or release an arrow from, upon, or across a public road. Violation: misdemeanor; fine of $50; 5 points (33-6-126).

Unless provided, and except for persons owning or leasing land, members of their family, or their agents, it is unlawful to utilize artificial light as an aid in taking wildlife. Possession of a loaded firearm or a strung bow, unless cased, while attempting to project an artificial light into areas where wildlife may be found is prima facie evidence of violation. Violation: misdemeanor; fine of $200; 20 points (33-6-127).

Import, Export and Release Provisions

The State Agricultural Commission shall review Division regulations concerning captive wild ungulates, make recommendations, and approve such regulations. If the Commission makes possession of red deer unlawful, the Division shall compensate a person who owns or possesses same for the cost to replace them with legal elk of the same sex and comparable age. For purposes of this section, "captive wild ungulates" means wildlife which are ungulates lawfully acquired and confined for breeding for agricultural purposes, production of meat, or other animal products, not including wildlife held or used for hunting. Captive wild mammals which have escaped may be removed from the wild by the Division at the owner's expense, but not sooner than 72 hours after the Division has given the owner actual notice of the escape, or the owner has notified the Division. The amount the Division may charge an owner is limited to actual costs incurred for removal, subject to the following maximum caps: ▸ for native wildlife and nonnative or exotic wildlife, $1,000 per animal not to exceed $5,000 per incident; ▸ for prohibited species, no maximum cap per animal or per incident (33-1-106).

It is unlawful, except as provided, to: transport or export any wildlife or portion within or from the state; import live wildlife unless an importation license is obtained, and a health certificate accompanies each shipment; release, or knowingly allow the escape of, any live native, nonnative or exotic wildlife in the state. This does not apply to the transportation, importation, exportation, and release of live native or nonnative fish or viable gametes (eggs and sperm) governed by 33-6-114.5. Violation: misdemeanor; fine of $50 for violations involving native wildlife; $250-1,000 for violations involving nonnative or exotic wildlife. In addition, for violations involving native, nonnative or exotic wildlife, five points per incident may be assessed, (33-6-114).

It is unlawful to: ▸ possess, transport, import, or export live native or nonnative fish or viable gametes (eggs or sperm) except in accordance with Commission regulations; ▸ possess live native or nonnative fish or viable gametes infected with a disease designated by the Commission as detrimental to existing fish populations or habitats unless the Division is notified within two business days after the discovery of the presence of the disease, or which are of a species designated by regulation as detrimental to existing fish populations or habitats; ▸ import live native or nonnative fish or viable gametes without an importation license and health certificate; ▸ release live native or nonnative fish or viable gametes; ▸ transport, import, export, or release live native or nonnative fish or viable gametes in violation of any quarantine order or disposition plan. Violation: Class 1 misdemeanor; $500-5,000 fine; liability for damages and costs, including, but not limited to, the costs of eradication or removal. ★As an alternative punishment, violation of this section or any regulation relating to fish health, the spread of aquatic diseases, or importation or distribution and management of exotic aquatic species may be punished as follows: in any first administrative proceeding, $100-1,000 fine; in any subsequent administrative proceeding against the same person, $500-5,000 fine, plus liability for damages and costs, including, but not limited to, the costs of eradication or removal of organisms, disease agents, or both (33-6-114.5). ★

ANIMAL DAMAGE CONTROL

★★The state is liable for certain damages caused by wildlife (33-3-102). The state shall not be liable for: ▸ damage to livestock caused by coyotes, bobcats, or dogs, the Division to use whatever means are available to minimize depredation to livestock by coyotes and bobcats; ▸ damage to motor vehicles caused by wildlife; ▸ injury to or the death of a person caused by wildlife; ▸ damages, if the Division has furnished to the claimant sufficient and appropriate damage prevention materials and the claimant has refused to accept or use them, and if the provisions of this section have been complied with; ▸ damages, if the claimant has willfully failed to maintain damage prevention materials throughout the normal life of such materials, and such materials have not been damaged or destroyed by wildlife; ▸ damages caused by wildlife if the claimant has unreasonably restricted hunting or access across land under claimant's control, if the restriction has significantly and adversely reduced a necessary wildlife harvest; ▸ damages caused by wildlife, if claimant charges in excess of $100 per person, per season for big game hunting access on or across claimant's property (33-3-103). The Division shall be responsible for providing to landowners sufficient and appropriate damage prevention materials if the claimant has given at least a thirty-day notice to the Division in writing. The Division shall deliver such materials to the specific sites as directed by the claimant. When agreed upon, the Division may construct permanent stockyards or orchard fencing in areas of high wildlife damage potential within the limitations of appropriations for that purpose. If the Division does not provide sufficient and appropriate damage prevention materials by September 1 upon request, the Division shall have the sole responsibility to supply and erect such materials. If the Division fails to supply such materials by said date, or has also failed to supply and erect sufficient and appropriate damage prevention materials upon request, it shall not refuse to pay any wildlife damages caused by the lack of such materials. When erecting damage prevention materials, the Division may use Division employees, individuals under contract or voluntary workers (33-3-103). ★★

The state shall be liable only for: ▸ damages to real or personal property caused by bear and mountain lion; ▸ damages to real or personal property when caused by wildlife that is being moved or is otherwise under the direct control of Division personnel; ▸ damage to real or personal property caused by the use of damage prevention materials if the use of such materials or equipment is under the control of a personnel under Division direction at the time; ▸ damages caused by species enumerated in section 33-1-102(2), to orchards, nurseries, crops under cultivation, and harvested crops, damages to fences exceeding 10% of the fence's value, and damages to livestock forage in excess of 10% of historic use levels for privately owned and fenced ranch or farm units which are limited to hay meadows, pasture meadows, artificially seeded rangelands, and grazing land which is deferred to seasonal uses. Full damages to aftermath on alfalfa shall be paid without regard to historic numbers of wildlife [details of arbitration options provided]. If the Commission has not promulgated rules relating to damage by wildlife, the Division shall not refuse to pay a claim for wildlife damage. Reimbursement for wildlife damages shall be reduced by the amount of any insurance claim awarded (33-3-104).

Where wildlife is causing excessive damage to property, as determined by the Division, a permit may be issued to the property owner or other person to kill a specified number of wildlife. Any wildlife killed shall remain the property of the state, be field dressed promptly, and be reported to the Division within 48 hours. Nothing in this section shall make it unlawful to trap, kill, or otherwise dispose of bears, mountain lions, or dogs to prevent them from inflicting death or injury to livestock or human life, or dogs to prevent them from inflicting death or injury to other big game and to small game, birds, and mammals. ★The Division may bring a civil action against the owner of a dog inflicting death or injury to any big game other than bear or mountain lion and to small game, birds, and mammals for the value of each animal. The minimum value of each animal shall be as set forth in section 33-6-110.★ It shall not be necessary to obtain any permit for taking bears, mountain lions, coyotes, bobcats, or dogs. No dog shall be killed within the city limits of any town, city, or municipality or while in the possession of or under the control of a person unless otherwise permitted. All bears and mountain lions taken or destroyed under this section shall be reported to the Division within five days (33-3-106).

When a person has sustained damages to property caused by wildlife, the person shall notify the Division within ten days after discovery. In the case of recurring damage, the Division shall be notified within ten days after the discovery of each new or different occurrence. Proof of loss forms shall be filed within 90 days, and the Division, within 30 days, shall investigate the alleged loss and attempt to settle the claim. The Commission may review settlement agreements and disapprove any unreasonable settlement. The Commission shall review all claims recommended for denial and those which are unable to reach a settlement [provisions detailed for proceeding directly to small claims court]. If the claimant disagrees with a determination or refuses to accept the Commission's offer, the claimant may file an action for damages [details provided] (33-3-107 and -108).

ENFORCEMENT OF WILDLIFE LAWS

Enforcement Powers

Every District Wildlife Manager or other commissioned Division officer shall enforce the provisions of this title and every other peace officer may assist. Each officer has full power and authority to arrest when there is probable cause to believe a person is guilty of a violation of this title, and, in accordance with the constitutions and laws of the US and Colorado, to open, enter, and search all places of concealment where there is probable cause to believe wildlife held in violation is to be found or where other material evidence relating to a violation of this title is to be found and to seize the same. Each officer shall have the authority to secure and execute search or arrest warrants. Any peace officer empowered with enforcing the wildlife statues has the authority to go onto any lands or waters, public or private, to demand of a person, who the peace officer has reason to believe has exercised any license benefits, immediate production of such license and any wildlife in possession for inspection. ★When protection of public health, safety, or welfare requires, any such authorized officer has authority to make use of any motor vehicle or other means of transportation, whether privately or publicly owned, to aid in performance of duties. Reasonable compensation shall be made for the use of motor vehicles (33-6-101).★

Every motor vehicle, vessel, firearm, seine, net, trap, explosive, poisonous or stupefying substance, or other personal property illegally used in taking or harassing of wildlife is declared to be a public nuisance, and subject to seizure, confiscation, and forfeiture or destruction as provided, unless the possession of the property is not unlawful, the owner was not a party to the violation, and would suffer undue hardship by the sale, confiscation, or destruction of the property. A personal property subject to seizure, confiscation, and forfeiture or destruction, for which disposition is not provided by another statute, shall be disposed of as provided. Any property illegally possessed, which in the opinion of the court is not properly subject to sale, may be destroyed under a court warrant for destruction of personal property. The court shall stay the execution of any such warrant while the property is used as evidence in any pending criminal or civil proceeding. Except as otherwise provided, the court may order such property sold by the Division in the manner provided for sales on execution. The proceeds of the sale shall be applied as follows: ▸ to the fees and costs of removal and sale; ▸ to the payment of the state's costs; ▸ the balance, to the Wildlife Cash Fund. Instead of being deposited in the Wildlife Cash Fund, such balance or any portion may be transmitted, upon court order: to the seizing agency, if the court finds that the proceeds can be used by such agency; upon petition, to a person who suffers bodily injury or property damage as a result of the violation (33-6-102).

It is unlawful to take wildlife in a careless manner or to discharge a firearm or release an arrow in a careless manner which endangers human life or property, failing to exercise the degree of reasonable care that would be exercised by a person of ordinary prudence under all the existing circumstances considering the probable danger of injury or damage. Violation: misdemeanor; $100-1,000 fine; or by jail up to one year; or both; and 20 points (33-6-122).

Criminal Penalties

★If the possession, use, importation, exportation, transportation, storage, sale, or offering or exposing for sale of wildlife is prohibited or restricted by statute or regulation, the prohibition, where not otherwise specifically provided, shall include every part of such wildlife, and violations as to each animal or part is a separate offense. Two or more offenses may be charged in the same complaint, information, or indictment, and proof as to part of an animal is sufficient to sustain a charge as to the whole animal. Violations as to any number of animals of the same kind may be charged in the same count and punished as a separate offense as to each animal (33-6-103).★

Violation of the wildlife provisions of this title or regulation that does not have a specific penalty is a misdemeanor punishable by a fine of $50 and an assessment of five points. At the time that a person is charged with violating any misdemeanor provisions, the officer shall issue a summons and complaint or, in the case of a violation for which a fixed fine is prescribed, may give the alleged offender an opportunity voluntarily to pay the fine in the form of a penalty assessment. Penalty assessments shall not be issued for violations for which minimum and maximum fines have been established [details of penalty assessments and procedures provided] (33-6-104).

Except as provided, no person shall procure or use more than one license of a certain type in any one calendar year. Violation: misdemeanor; for wildlife other than big game, a fine of $50, 10 points; for big game, fine of $200, 15 points. Making a false statement in applying for a license, or any license agent knowingly accepting false information in selling or issuing a license, is a misdemeanor; fine of $200; 15 points. All licenses obtained with false information are void. Except as provided, a person who takes wildlife shall have in possession a license when exercising its benefits. Violation: misdemeanor; with respect to wildlife other than big game, a fine of $50, 10 points; for big game, a fine of $250, 15 points (33-6-107).

A person who possesses live wildlife and who is required to have a license for such possession shall have the license at the site where the wildlife is kept. Violation: misdemeanor; fine of $50; 10 points. A person 15 or older who fishes shall have a fishing license in possession. Violation: misdemeanor; fine of $50; 10 points. It is unlawful to transfer, sell, loan, or assign a license to another person. Violation: misdemeanor; fine of $200; 15 points; and any licenses so used are void (33-6-107).

It is unlawful unless born before January 1, 1949, to purchase a hunting license without successful completion of a Division certified hunter education course, the certificate to be in possession while hunting. The Division shall recognize a temporary Division hunter education certificate, and may recognize hunter education programs of other states or countries for purchasing a hunting license. Violation: misdemeanor; fine of $50; 10 points (33-6-107).

Any landowner, lessee, family members or agents may take black-billed magpies, common crows, starlings, English or house sparrows, common pigeons, coyotes, bobcats, red foxes, raccoons, jackrabbits, badgers, marmots, prairie dogs, pocket gophers, Richardson's ground squirrels, rock squirrels, thirteen-lined ground squirrels, porcupines, crayfish, tiger salamanders, muskrats, beavers, and common snapping turtles on lands owned or leased without licenses when such wildlife is causing damage. ★A person may take skunks or rattlesnakes when necessary to protect life or property.★ Wildlife taken under this subsection may be sold by purchasing an appropriate small game or fur-bearer license (33-6-107).

The possession of wildlife shall be prima facie evidence that the person is or has been engaged in hunting, fishing, or trapping (33-6-108). It is unlawful to take or have in one's possession wildlife that is state property, except as permitted by this title or by Commission regulation. It is unlawful to possess wildlife, as defined by the state or country of origin, that was acquired, taken, or transported from such state or country in violation of the laws or regulations thereof. This section does not apply to illegal possession of live native or nonnative fish or viable gametes (eggs or sperm) governed by 33-6-114.5. Violation is a misdemeanor and shall be punished by a fine and license suspension points [in parentheses], according to the wildlife involved, as follows: ► each eagle, endangered species, rocky mountain goat, moose, rocky mountain bighorn sheep, or lynx, $1,000 (20); ► each elk or threatened species: $700 (15) ► each antelope, deer, black bear, or mountain lion, $500 (15); ► each raptor not otherwise covered and each wild turkey, $200 (10); ► one illegal animal or bird, $50 (10); ► each additional illegal animal or bird of a multipossession offense, $25 (1); ► one illegal fish, $35 (10); ► each additional illegal fish of a multipossession offense, $10 (1) (33-6-109).

It is unlawful to possess nonnative or exotic wildlife except in accordance with Commission regulations. Violation: misdemeanor; $250-1,000 fine; in addition, ten suspension points per incident for possessing an animal on the prohibited species list and five suspension points per incident for any other nonnative or exotic wildlife species (33-6-109).

Civil Penalties

All moneys collected for fines shall go to the state treasurer, who shall credit one-half to the general fund and one-half to the Wildlife Cash Fund or the Nongame and Endangered Wildlife Cash Fund. For offenses involving nongame wildlife, such half shall be credited to the Nongame and Endangered Wildlife Cash Fund, and for all other wildlife offenses, such half shall be credited to the Wildlife Cash Fund. When an arrest has been made or citation for any wildlife offense issued by an officer of the Division of Parks and Outdoor Recreation, the state treasurer shall credit one-half to the Parks and Outdoor Recreation Cash Fund and one-half to the general fund (33-6-105).

★★Every court clerk must notify the Division of amount and disposition of fines collected. No fine, penalty, or judgment assessed or rendered under the provisions of this title shall be suspended, reduced, or remitted otherwise than as expressly provided by law. All moneys collected by the Division as surcharges on penalty assessments pursuant to section 33-6-104 shall go to the court administrator for credit to the victims and witnesses assistance and law enforcement fund established in that judicial district (33-6-105).★★

Illegal Taking of Wildlife

The Division may bring a civil action in the name of the people of the state to recover possession and/or value of wildlife taken in violation of this title. A writ of replevin may issue in such an action without bond. No previous demand for possession is necessary. If costs or damages are adjudged in favor of the defendant, they shall be paid out of the Wildlife Cash Fund. Neither the civil action nor a criminal prosecution for the same taking is a bar to the other, nor shall this section affect the right of seizure under other provisions of this title. The following shall be the minimum value of wildlife unlawfully taken or possessed and may be recovered in addition to recovery of the wildlife itself: ▸ each eagle, endangered species, rocky mountain goat, moose, rocky mountain bighorn sheep, or lynx, $1,000; ▸ each elk or threatened species or subspecies, $700; ▸ each antelope, deer, black bear, or mountain lion, $500; ▸ each raptor not covered above and each wild turkey, $200; ▸ each nongame or small game species or subspecies not covered above, $100; ▸ each game fish not covered above, $35. ★No verdict or judgment recovered by the state shall be for less than the sum fixed in this section, but may be for such greater sum as the evidence may show the value of the wildlife to have been when living and uninjured (33-6-110).★

★★Except as otherwise provided, it is unlawful to sell or purchase, or offer to do so, wildlife, or to solicit another in the illegal taking of wildlife for monetary or commercial gain or profit. Violation, with respect to big game, endangered species, or eagles, is a class 5 felony and shall be punished as provided in 18-1-105, and in addition, shall be punished by a fine of $1,000-20,000. The fine shall be in an amount within the presumptive range set out in 18-1-105(1). Upon conviction, the Commission may permanently suspend all wildlife license privileges. Violation, with respect to all other wildlife, is a misdemeanor and shall be punished by a fine of $100-1,000, or jail up to one year, or both, and 20 points (33-6-113).★★

See Licenses and Permits under HUNTING, FISHING, TRAPPING PROVISIONS for aquaculture provisions.

License Revocations and Suspensions

The Commission has authority to suspend the privilege of applying for, purchasing, or exercising benefits conferred by any Divisions license for a period up to three years, if a person: ▸ has been convicted of violations of this title totalling twenty or more points in any consecutive five-year period; ★ ▸ has been convicted of wildlife violations of another state, province, territory, or federal agency for which similar charges exist in this state; ▸ has been convicted of any violation of Title 18, committed while hunting, trapping, fishing, or engaging in a related activity; ▸ is found to meet the requirements for suspension as provided in a compact with another state, territory, or province; ▸ has been convicted of any violation of 33-6-114. Payment of a penalty assessment, a court conviction, a plea of no contest, imposition of a deferred or suspended sentence, or forfeiture of bail shall be deemed a conviction. Persons considered for suspension, including permanent suspension, shall be given notice and opportunity

to appear and show cause why license privileges should not be suspended [details of notice and hearing provided].
★For license suspension of a resident pursuant to provisions of a compact with another state, territory, or province for failure to comply with a summons, complaint, penalty assessment notice, or other official notice of an alleged wildlife violation issued in such other state, territory, or province, the Commission shall have the authority to suspend the resident's privileges until satisfactory evidence of compliance with the terms of the legal document has been furnished to the Division. ★ Notice of suspension shall be sent to the person and to license agents and other persons who should be notified (33-6-106). A person whose license privileges have been suspended may not purchase, apply for, or exercise the benefits conferred by any license until suspension has expired. Violation: misdemeanor; fine of $500, and an automatic two-year extension of the existing suspension (33-6-106).

Intoxication Testing of Hunters

It is unlawful for a person under the influence of alcohol, controlled substance, or other drug to a degree which renders the person incapable of safely operating a firearm or bow and arrow to take any wildlife. Violation: misdemeanor; $100-1,000 fine; or by jail up to one year; or both; and 20 points (33-6-123).

HABITAT PROTECTION

The Director of USFW and the Director's authorized agents have the right to conduct fish hatching and fish culture activities and other connected operations. Nothing herein shall be construed as granting jurisdiction over or right to interfere with Division activities or facilities, nor as contravening any state laws relating to public health, pollution, or water rights (33-1-116).

It is declared to be the policy of this state that its fish and wildlife resources, and particularly the fishing waters within the state, are to be protected and preserved from the actions of any state agency to the end that they be available for all time and without change in their natural existing state, except as may be necessary and appropriate after due consideration of all factors involved (33-5-101). ★★No state agency (applicant), shall obstruct, damage, diminish, destroy, change, modify, or vary the natural existing shape and form of any stream or its banks or tributaries by any type of construction without first notifying the Commission of such plan. Notice shall be on Commission forms submitted not less than 90 days prior to commencement of planned construction, and shall include detailed plans and specifications of the project as may or will affect any stream. The Commission shall promptly examine all plans submitted, and if determined that the plans and specifications are technically inadequate to accomplish the purposes set forth in 33-5-101, it may aid in preparing adequate plans and specifications. Within thirty days the Commission shall notify the applicant if the planned construction or project will adversely affect the stream involved, and if so will provide recommendations or alternative plans which will eliminate or diminish such adverse effect (33-5-102 through -104).★★ The applicant within fifteen days shall notify the Commission if it refuses to modify its plans. The Commission shall then determine if it desires to have the matter arbitrated. Within ten days after an affirmative decision and after notice to the other agency or agencies involved, the Commission shall notify the Governor. No further action shall be taken on planned construction until the Governor issues a written decision within thirty days which shall be binding on all parties concerned, with no judicial review (33-5-105).
★These provisions shall not operate or be construed to impair, diminish, or divest existing or vested water rights, nor shall they apply in emergency situations, or to irrigation projects (33-5-106 and -107).★

See also PROTECTED SPECIES OF WILDLIFE.

NATIVE AMERICAN WILDLIFE PROVISIONS: None.

CONNECTICUT

Sources: Connecticut General Statutes Annotated, 1990, Title 22, 23 and 26; 1992 Cumulative Pocket Part.

STATE WILDLIFE POLICY

The General Assembly declares it to be the policy of the state to manage wildlife to insure their continued participation in the ecosystem and to accord special protection to endangered species or subspecies of wildlife indigenous to the state in order to maintain and enhance their numbers. The Commissioner of Environmental Protection shall establish a conservation program for species not traditionally harvested which shall include provisions for: ▸ resource inventory; ▸ habitat conservation; ▸ monitoring of environmental impacts; ▸ endangered and threatened species conservation; ▸ wildlife recreation management; ▸ wildlife conservation education; ▸ private landowner assistance; ▸ urban wildlife conservation; ▸ problem animal management; ▸ scientific research, planning, administration and development (26-107f). The Commissioner shall report annually to the joint standing committee of the General Assembly which deals with environment matters on the progress of this program, how allocated funds were expended and the program's future, including a response to recommendations made by the Citizens' Advisory Board for Nonharvested Wildlife (26-107g and -107h).

The general assembly finds certain species of wildlife and plants have been rendered extinct as a consequence of man's activities and other species are threatened with extinction, or have been reduced, because of destruction, modification or severe curtailment of their habitats, exploitation for commercial, scientific, educational, or private use, or disease, predation or other factors. Such species are of ecological, scientific, educational, historical, economic, recreational and aesthetic value to the people of the state, and the conservation, protection and enhancement of them and their habitats are of state-wide concern. Therefore, the general assembly declares it is a policy of the state to conserve, protect, restore and enhance any endangered or threatened species and essential habitat (26-303).

RELEVANT WILDLIFE DEFINITIONS: See Definitions section of Appendices.

STATE FISH AND WILDLIFE AGENCIES

Agency Structure

There is a **Department of Environmental Protection** (Department) with jurisdiction over matters relating to preservation and protection of air, water and natural resources of the state, under the direction of a **Commissioner of Environmental Protection** (Commissioner), appointed for a four-year term by the Governor subject to Senate confirmation (22a-2). Each Department head (including the Commissioner) shall be qualified by training and experience (4-8). [Details of Governor's appointments to some boards and commissions are given in 4-9a to 4-15, and of state agency organization in chapter 48.]

The **Commissioner** shall appoint **Conservation Officers** for execution of Department duties, and may appoint Department employees as Special Conservation Officers or patrolmen. All officers shall complete a police training course at the state police training school or equivalent course approved by the Public Safety Commissioner (26-5). ★The chief executive authority of a town, city or borough, with the consent of the Police Commission or Police Chief, may appoint special officers, designating them **Constables for Fish and Game Protection**, with duties limited to enforcing the town, state, and local fish and game laws and Commission regulations, and local ordinances relating to hunting, fishing and trapping, and other provisions as specified. The Commissioner shall cooperate with local officials in instructing the Constables, and conduct a training seminar annually prior to entering office. Constables can be removed from office by the local Police Commission or Chief of Police. The Commissioner shall request that the town's chief executive authority appoint Constables upon receiving written reports of hunting regulation violations in proximity to buildings occupied by persons or domestic animals, or used for flammable materials storage, or shooting towards persons, buildings or animals (26-6a).★ ★★The Commissioner may appoint citizens in each community as Volunteer Assistants, without compensation, with the same authority as regular Department members except the power of enforcement or arrest (26-7). ★★

Agency Powers and Duties

The **Commissioner** shall: ‣ carry out state environmental policies; ‣ promote and coordinate management of water, land and air resources; ‣ provide for protection and management of plants, trees, fish, shellfish, wildlife and other animal life, including endangered species; public forests, parks, open areas and natural area preserves; and inland, marine and coastal water resources; ‣ provide for pollution abatement, pest control, solid and liquid waste disposal, storage of pollutant materials and chemicals; and mining standards [details are given for these latter topics] (22a-5). The Commissioner may adopt, amend or repeal environmental standards and procedural regulations to carry out powers and duties, after a public hearing. The Commissioner may: ‣ enter into contracts with a person or firm; ‣ hold hearings and take testimony; ‣ require, issue, renew, revoke or deny permits; ‣ enter public/private property to investigate possible violations of the above; ‣ make studies and surveys to accomplish duties [details (22a-6).

The Commissioner shall establish a system of natural area preserves, be responsible for selection, care, control, and management, and maintain them in a natural and wild state consistent with educational and scientific purposes. ★In establishing such systems, it shall be a priority to acquire areas identified as essential habitats of endangered and threatened species, and the Commissioner may inventory potentially worthy areas for inclusion and promulgate regulations to manage (23-5c). ★ [Details about preserve establishment and alienation are given in 23-5d through 23-5h.] The Commissioner shall: ‣ enforce all laws relating to wildlife, fish, crustacea, game and nongame birds, waterfowl, and game and fur-bearing animals, and possess all powers to fulfill duties prescribed by law, and to bring actions in state courts to enforce laws, orders and regulations; ‣ supervise hatcheries and retaining ponds and the introduction, propagation, securing and distribution of fish and game adapted to state waters and lands; ‣ have jurisdiction of all fish and game matters on state land and regulation of hunting, fishing, trapping and use of waters on the land; ‣ cooperate with USFW and the fish and game commissioners of other states; ‣ establish proper boundaries by agreement with owners of adjoining properties. The Commissioner shall not grant to a conservation officer, appointee or other, special privileges to hunt, fish, trap or use waters on such (26-3).

The Commissioner may: ‣ close inland water fishing areas to provide spawning beds; ‣ take fish, crustacean, bird or animal for scientific and educational purposes, public health and safety, or propagation and dissemination; ‣ erect buildings upon state land subject to approval of the public works commissioner and the State Properties Review Board; ‣ assign persons to occupy Department-owned property; ‣ employ special assistants; ‣ acquire by gift, lease, or purchase, lands for fish hatcheries and game preserves, with the Governor's approval; ‣ grant easements and rights-of-way for public utilities, state or federal agencies; ‣ exchange land with property owners and execute deeds to establish property boundaries, with the Attorney General's approval; ‣ provide for importation of game birds, game, and fur-bearing animals, and for their protection, propagation and distribution; ‣ locate, construct, and maintain nurseries and rearing ponds where fish may be planted, propagated and reared, and liberate and distribute them; ‣ acquire by gift, purchase, capture or otherwise any fish, game birds or animals for propagation, experimentation, or scientific purposes, and destroy and dispose of undesirable/diseased species; ‣ enter into cooperative agreements with educational institutions and state, federal or other agencies to promote wildlife research and to train persons for wildlife management and education projects; ‣ enter into cooperative agreements with a group or landowners to develop management and demonstration projects for game, birds, fish or fur-bearing animals; ‣ allocate and expend state funds collected and appropriated for protecting, restoring, preserving and propagating fish, crustacea, game and fur-bearing animals, and game and nongame birds, (26-3). The Commissioner may acquire by purchase, lease, gift, or condemnation, easements for maintenance and remodeling of state-owned dams (26-3a).

The Commissioner may acquire by gift, lease, purchase or agreement, fishing, hunting, trapping or shooting rights on state land or water, with rights of access; or with the Governor's approval, purchase land or water. By regulation, the Commissioner may: ‣ govern the number of persons or boats that may use state land or waters; ‣ require an entry permit and reports on fish or wildlife taken; ‣ prescribe the use of the lands and waters; ‣ prescribe open and closed seasons, method of taking, legal sizes and creel/bag limits; ‣ furnish for a fee boats or facilities for fishermen or hunters. Portions of lands and waters may be posted as closed. No person over age 16 shall fish, hunt or trap on such land or water without a license. If an owner in fee of land or water conveys to the state hunting, fishing, trapping or shooting rights by gift, lease or agreement, the owner and the family may sport fish, hunt or trap during the open seasons without a license. Violation of regulations under this section is an infraction. By agreement with the landowner, the Commissioner may cancel a short-term lease of fishing or hunting rights in the event of the sale or transfer of the property (26-16 and -17).

The Commissioner may declare a closed season for hunting or fishing in inland waters due to fire danger, except for licensed shooting preserves, authorized field trials sanctioned by the American Kennel Club or American Field, or for sport fishing from boats, docks, floats or bridges in lakes and ponds specified. The Commissioner may reopen the season after the fire danger, and may extend the open season for a period equal to the closed period. When the harvest level for a species exceeds or fails to meet the harvest level for its efficient management, the Commissioner may close or extend the open season for taking such species. ★Notice of a closed season or its reopening shall be published in the *Connecticut Law Journal* (26-25). In accordance with chapter 54, the Commissioner may adopt regulations prohibiting or restricting feeding wildlife on state-owned property, including restricted areas, to become effective after public notice and comment. A conservation officer may enforce such regulation; violations are infractions (26-25a).★ To control waterfowl hunting, the Commissioner may establish and define zones to distinguish open coastal waters beyond outer harbor limits where certain species of waterfowl may be taken during the open season (26-77). A schedule describing the date and location of stocking/release of fish or animal into the wild shall not be disclosed until after stocking/release has taken place unless in the best interest of fish or wildlife management (26-25b). ★No person, nonprofit organization, firm or corporation, including the state and its political subdivisions, shall [knowingly] release, organize the release, or intentionally cause to be released into the atmosphere ten or more helium or other lighter-than-air gas balloons within a 24-hour period. Violation: infraction (26-25c).★

Agency Regulations

The Commissioner may adopt regulations governing the taking of wildlife that: ▸ establish modifiable open and closed seasons; ▸ establish hours, days or periods during open seasons when hunting specific species is not permitted; ▸ establish legal hours; ▸ prescribe legal methods, including type, kind, gauge and caliber of weapons, ammunition, and long bows; ▸ prescribe the sex of wildlife that may be taken; ▸ establish daily and seasonal bag limits; ▸ establish the maximum number of persons that may hunt on designated areas during a 24-hour period; ▸ require a landowner or Commission issued permit to enter upon designated hunting areas, with an accurate report of all wildlife taken, time spent, and other data as specified; ▸ establish areas to be restricted for hunting with long bow or other specified weapons, or for hunting exclusively by the physically handicapped; ▸ establish requirements for tagging and reporting birds or animals taken by hunting or trapping. ★★In the interest of public safety, to prevent abuses by hunters, and to control hunters, the Commissioner may issue regulations to: ▸ prohibit carrying loaded firearms or their discharge, and hunting within specified distances of buildings, persons, and livestock; ▸ prohibit hunting on roads adjacent to state parks, forests, or premises used for breeding or holding wildlife in captivity; ▸ establish minimum distances between fixed position, floating and drift blinds for waterfowl hunting; ▸ prohibit crossing over cultivated lands/lawns, and property damage to livestock and crops; ▸ prohibit training and running of dogs on designated areas during specified periods; ▸ prohibit operation and parking of vehicles on specified parts of public and private roads, rights-of-way and fields; ▸ prohibit littering; ▸ control launching from, mooring to, and abandonment of boats on Commission controlled lands; ▸ regulate wearing of fluorescent orange clothing (26-66). The Commissioner may issue regulations based upon accepted standards of wildlife conservation, concerning: ▸ scientific and factual findings of a biological nature; ▸ availability of the species involved; ▸ unusual weather conditions and special hazards; ▸ available supply of food and natural cover; ▸ general condition of woods and streams; ▸ control of a species; ▸ number of permits issued; ▸ area available; ▸ rights and privileges of sportspersons, landowners and the general public; ▸ a sound program of wildlife management and recreation (26-67).★★ In an emergency, the Commissioner may declare a closed season on a species threatened with undue depletion, and close an area, stream or lake, or portions of it, to hunting and trapping (26-68).

After notice and hearing, the Commissioner may issue regulations governing taking of fur-bearing animals by traps which may: ▸ establish open and closed seasons; ▸ establish legal hours; ▸ prescribe legal methods, including sizes, types of traps, baits and lures; ▸ designate places for setting traps, and conditions; ▸ establish daily and season bag limits; ★▸ assess a fee or develop an equitable plan for season trapping rights on state property (26-72).★ (See Restrictions on Taking: Hunting and Trapping under HUNTING, FISHING, TRAPPING PROVISIONS.) After notice and hearing, the Commissioner may issue regulations governing fishing and taking of bait species in the inland district which may: ▸ establish open and closed seasons and number of days; ▸ establish hours, days or periods during open seasons when fishing is not permitted in designated waters; ▸ prescribe legal methods of taking, legal lengths, daily and season creel and possession limits; ▸ restrict or prohibit wading and fishing from boats or canoes;

▸ establish number of persons that may use an area of water for fishing, and number of boats, canoes and other devices; ▸ require a permit to enter designated premises for fishing, and require reports; ▸ restrict the use of crafts other than manually propelled. ★★To protect public and private interests and prevent abuses by persons who fish, and control their actions and behavior, the Commissioner may issue regulations to: ▸ provide that entrance and exit from streams and ponds be restricted to designated rights-of-way, or with landowner consent; ▸ establish distances from banks of streams, lakes and ponds and prohibit trespass thereon; ▸ prohibit crossing over cultivated lands/lawns; ▸ prohibit damage to property, livestock and crops; ▸ prohibit swimming and picnicking in designated areas; ▸ prohibit operation or parking of vehicles on designated roads, fields and lots; ▸ prohibit littering; ▸ control boat launching from, anchoring and storage on Commission controlled lands (26-112).★★ [Fisheries management regulations provided, in 26-113.]

Agency Funding Sources

Funds accruing from fishing license fees shall be used for protection, propagation, preservation and investigation of fish and game and Department administration (26-14). There shall be appropriated each fiscal year a sum not less than the total estimated receipts from fishing, hunting and trapping licenses, which the Department shall supplement from annual apportionments under federal acts, and shall annually report to the General Assembly Joint Standing Committee the federal fund amounts received and expended, and purposes of expenditures (26-15a). The Commissioner may establish a program for sale of wildlife stamps, prints, posters, calendars, and publications, with revenues deposited in the general fund and allocated to the program for conservation of nonharvested wildlife (26-107f and -107i).

Agency Advisory Boards

There is a **Citizens' Advisory Board for Nonharvested Wildlife** of seven appointed members, of which one each shall be appointed by the Governor, the minority and majority leaders of the House and Senate, the president pro tempore of the Senate, and the House Speaker. Members shall represent organizations in wildlife conservation and environmental education. The Board advises the Commissioner on administration of the program established under 26-107f and makes recommendations (26-107g). (See also STATE WILDLIFE POLICY.)

There is a **Natural Area Preserves Advisory Committee** of seven members. Three shall be Department members serving at the Commissioner's pleasure, one of whom shall chair the committee. Four members are appointed by the Governor from persons with an interest in preservation of lands in natural condition for scientific and educational purposes. Members serve four-year terms, meet at least semiannually, and have experience or training in ecological, biological or natural sciences, or environmental education, or be representatives of institutions with experience in natural area research, education or preservation. The Committee shall advise the Commissioner relative to the administration of 23-5a to 23-5i, and cooperate with the Commissioner in: ▸ establishing standards for acquisition, designation, maintenance and operation of natural area preserves; ▸ periodic state-wide surveys to determine the availability of land to be designated as such preserves; ▸ recommending acquisition of specific lands or interests; ▸ preparing and disseminating informational literature; ▸ consulting and cooperating with conservation and naturalist groups to acquire and maintain natural area preserves; ▸ recommending the acquisition of lands with Natural Heritage Trust Program funds or other funds; ▸ preparing management plans for specific preserves; ▸ recommending the revocation of such preserves (26-314).

PROTECTED SPECIES OF WILDLIFE

★The Commissioner may appoint as custodians persons who possess injured, sick or immature birds or quadrupeds until they can be released, may issue permits authorizing possession of legally acquired wild birds or quadrupeds as pets or for training dogs, and may regulate the number and species of the birds or animals and type and size of confinement pens for their care and feeding. In the interest of protecting other game, domestic birds, quadrupeds, or public health and safety, or for a violation of regulations under which the permit was granted, the Commissioner may revoke the permit, confiscate and destroy birds or animals possessed. Possession of a bird or quadruped without authorization shall be a fine of up to $100 (26-54).★ No person shall catch, kill, purchase, sell, or possess a living or dead wild bird, or part or plumage other than a game bird, except as provided. No person shall take, needlessly destroy, or possess a nest or egg of a wild or game bird. English sparrows, starlings, and, when destroying corn, crows and red-winged and crow blackbirds, shall not be protected. A Conservation Officer or other officer with authority to serve criminal process shall have the same powers to enforce this section as are conferred by 26-6 (26-92). (See also RELEVANT WILDLIFE DEFINITIONS.)

A person who disturbs, molests, harasses, hunts, takes, or kills a bald eagle, or species of swan, shall be fined up to $100, jailed up to 30 days, or both. No person shall trap, net or snare a bird during a closed season or which is protected by statute, or set, bait, place or use a net, trap snare or other device to take a bird, except for traps on poles eight feet high or more for taking predatory birds not protected by law. The Commissioner may issue permits prescribing methods for taking nuisance birds damaging property, poultry, domestic animals and agricultural crops. No permit is required by USFW agents to trap birds for banding and release, but the Commissioner may require a permit to trap a bird listed as endangered, threatened or of special concern. No person shall keep, expose, let loose, or allow to escape a bird or fowl to have it shot at for sport, gain, marksmanship, or other purpose. No person shall shoot at a bird or fowl that has been kept or freed for such a purpose. This does not prohibit release of legally propagated game birds to be shot during open season (26-93 through -96).

A program is established for protection of endangered and threatened species. The Commissioner may conduct investigations of wildlife population, distribution, habitat needs, limiting factors, essential habitats and other biological and ecological data to determine conservation and management measures necessary to sustain the species successfully (26-305). The Commissioner shall establish procedures for determining whether a native species is endangered, threatened or of special concern, which consider: ▸ destruction/threatened destruction, modification or curtailment of habitat; ▸ overutilization for commercial, recreational, scientific, educational or private purposes; ▸ disease, predation or competition; ▸ inadequacy of existing regulatory mechanisms for continued existence of the species; ▸ other natural or man-made factors. The Commissioner shall adopt regulations listing native wildlife and plants endangered, threatened or of special concern, and to identify, where biologically feasible, essential habitats for endangered and threatened species. ★The Commissioner shall adopt regulations to establish criteria to be included in a petition pursuant to 4-174 to add/remove a species from the lists, or to add/remove an area identified as an essential habitat (26-306).★ Lists shall be reviewed at least every five years to determine whether to add/remove a species, or an area from the essential habitats list. The review of endangered species listed by the USDI shall be conducted in conjunction with the periodic year review process of the USDI pursuant to the Endangered Species Act. The Commissioner may adopt regulations to treat a species not listed as endangered or threatened under 26-306 as an endangered or threatened species when: ▸ the species so closely resembles a listed species that enforcement personnel would have substantial difficulty in differentiating them; ▸ this difficulty presents an additional threat to the listed species; ▸ treatment of the unlisted species as endangered or threatened would substantially facilitate enforcement and further the policy of 26-303. ★The regulations may include a provision to allow conducting an activity which affects a species that resembles an endangered or threatened species if the person can demonstrate to the Commissioner that the activity does not affect the listed species (26-307 and -308).★ (See also HABITAT PROTECTION.)

★★In consultation with the Commissioner, each state agency shall conserve endangered and threatened species and their essential habitats, and ensure that agency action authorized, funded or performed does not threaten the continued existence of a listed species, or result in the destruction or adverse modification of essential habitat, unless the agency has been granted an exemption as provided. Agencies responsible for primary recommendation/initiation of actions on land or in aquatic habitats which may significantly affect the environment shall ensure that those actions are consistent with endangered species provisions, and shall take all reasonable measures to mitigate adverse impact on the species or essential habitat. The Secretary of the Office of Policy and Management shall consider the consistency of proposed actions with statutory provisions in determining whether an environment impact evaluation satisfies requirements. If a proposed action would be in violation, and there are no feasible and prudent alternatives, the agency may apply to the Commissioner for an exemption, which may be granted after considering the following: ▸ the agency did not make an irreversible commitment of resources after consultation with the Department that forecloses such alternatives; ▸ the action's benefits clearly outweigh alternative actions, consistent with conserving the species or its habitat, and the action is in the public interest; ▸ the action is of regional or state-wide significance; ▸ the agency plans to take reasonable mitigation measures to minimize adverse impacts upon the species or habitat, including, but not limited to, live propagation, transplantation, and habitat acquisition and improvement. If it is determined that a proposed action would not appreciably reduce the likelihood of survival or recovery of an endangered/threatened species, but would result in its incidental taking, the Commissioner shall provide the agency with a written statement specifying: ▸ the impact of incidental taking on the species; ▸ measures and alternatives to ensure the action does not appreciably reduce the likelihood of species recovery; ▸ terms, conditions and reporting requirements to ensure compliance with this section. Taking in compliance with measures and alternatives specified herein shall not be prohibited by 26-303 to 26-312 (26-310).★★

Except as otherwise provided, it is unlawful for: ▸ a person to take willfully endangered or threatened species on or from public property, state waters, or property of another without written permission of the owner; ▸ a person, including a landowner on whose land an endangered/threatened species occurs, to take willfully such species to sell, offer to sell, transport for commercial gain or export; ▸ any state agency to destroy or adversely modify essential habitat designated under 26-306 to reduce the habitat's viability to support such species, or so as to kill or injure the species, or appreciably reduce its likelihood of survival. Nothing herein shall prohibit: ▸ performing legal activities on one's own land that may result in incidental taking of endangered/threatened species or species of special concern; ▸ action pursuant to an exemption or permit under the federal Endangered Species Act or regulation, nor permit action prohibited by such act or regulation; ▸ transportation through the state of such species in accordance with terms of permit issued under another state's laws if the possessor can prove legal possession. In an emergency, the Commissioner may prohibit the taking of a state species of special concern threatened with undue depletion from overutilization for commercial, recreational, scientific, educational or private purposes. If the Commissioner finds that a person is conducting an activity or maintaining a facility or condition in violation of the above, a written order by certified mail shall be issued to cease immediately or to correct such facility. A hearing shall be held within 10 days to show cause why the order should not remain in effect, and within 10 days of the hearing the person shall be notified that the order remains in effect, is modified, or withdrawn. ★★Notwithstanding other statutory provisions, the Commissioner may withhold from disclosure maps and records of the location of essential habitat or of threatened/endangered or special concern species, if the disclosure would create an unacceptable risk of destruction of, or harm to, such habitat or species. Prior to disclosure, the Commissioner may impose conditions including that the receiver of such information must furnish security sufficient to guarantee that they shall not destroy or harm, a habitat or species. The person shall be afforded opportunity for a hearing to challenge a refusal to disclose, or unreasonableness of an imposed condition or amount/kind of security required in accordance with provisions of chapter 54 (26-311 through -313).★★

★★If the Commissioner determines that trade in Connecticut of raw elephant ivory, or products manufactured or derived from same, contributes to extinction or endangerment of elephants, regulations shall be adopted in accordance with provisions in chapter 54 to regulate such trade (26-315).★★

GENERAL EXCEPTIONS TO PROTECTION

In the interest of fisheries management, the Commissioner may use chemical, electrical or mechanical means to remove undesirable plants or animals from state waters or may add substances to increase the production of fish food organisms (26-22). The Commissioner may grant a permit to collect fish, crustaceans and wildlife and their nests and eggs, for scientific and educational purposes only, and not for sale, exchange, shipment or removal from the state without consent. The Commissioner may determine the number and species which may be taken, and collection area and method. Detailed reports of collections are required. Violation: $10-200 fine; jail up to 60 days; or both; and permit is voided (26-60). ★★The Commissioner may authorize conservation officers to take rabbits by use of ferrets for restocking and redistribution. Taking a rabbit with a ferret, except as authorized, is a fine of $10-50, or jail up to 30 days, or both, for each rabbit taken and possessed (26-87).★★

Under regulations in accordance with chapter 54, the Commissioner may permit transfer, sale, offering for sale, or delivery of threatened/endangered species, or an activity otherwise prohibited under 26-303 to 26-312, for scientific, educational, biological or zoological purposes, and for propagation of captive species for preservation, unless prohibited by federal law or regulation (26-40d). (See also ENFORCEMENT OF WILDLIFE LAWS, PROTECTED SPECIES OF WILDLIFE, ANIMAL DAMAGE CONTROL, and Commercial and Private Enterprise Provisions under HUNTING, FISHING, TRAPPING PROVISIONS.

HUNTING, FISHING, TRAPPING PROVISIONS

General Provisions

No person shall transport within or out of the state any fish, bird, quadruped, reptile or amphibian for which a closed season exists without a permit, except as provided. No such animal shall be transported unless each unit, package or container is tagged as specified. Any such animal addressed for shipment outside the state without a tag received by a common carrier within the state is prima facie evidence of a violation. No permit is required to transport within or without the state fish, bird or other animals legally taken, bred, propagated or possessed under a proper license, registration or permit, or by persons legally exempt from license requirements as specified. Violation: $10-200 fine; or jail up to 60 days; or both (26-57). No person shall hunt or take from the wild a wild game bird, wild quadruped, reptile or amphibian, or attempt or assist in such, except as authorized by statute and regulation, and each animal so taken or possessed is a separate offense (26-70). Violation: fine up to $200; jail up to 60 days; or both (26-71). Sunday is a closed season except for trapping as specified. Possession in the open air on Sunday of a hunting implement is prima facie evidence of illegal hunting. Designated artificially propagated birds may be shot on Sundays on licensed private shooting preserves subject to regulations and local town permission (26-73).

No person shall buy, sell or exchange, or possess with such intent, a wild or game bird, wild quadruped, reptile or amphibian, alive or dead, or parts, including plumage, except as provided, except that such animal or part, except plumage, legally taken and transported into this state from another state or country which does not prohibit its sale or exportation, may be bought or sold in this state under Commissioner regulations. Any such animal or bird, or parts possessed contrary to this section or regulation shall be seized by a Department agent, and disposed of by sale, destruction or gift to an educational institution, museum, zoological park or other suitable place. This does not prohibit possession, sale or exchange of heads, hides or pelts of legally acquired deer and fur-bearing animals, or possession and mounting of legally acquired animals and birds. Each wild or game bird, wild quadruped, reptile or amphibian, or part, or each package of plumage, possessed contrary to this section is a separate offense. Violation: $200 fine; jail up to 60 days; or both (26-78). (See also Import, Export and Release Provisions under this section.)

Licenses and Permits

Except as otherwise provided, no person shall take, hunt or trap a wild bird or mammal, and no person over age 16 shall take fish or bait species in inland waters, without a license. A resident landowner and family may hunt, trap or fish without a license on owned/leased land where domiciled and which is not used for club fishing or hunting. A person operating a boat for fishermen needs no fishing license. Residents participating in a fishing derby authorized by the Commissioner need no license if no fees are charged, the derby is one day or less, is sponsored by a nonprofit civic service organization, and is limited to once a year (26-27). Resident licenses for firearms or archery hunting, trapping or fishing, or combination licenses, shall be issued to qualified applicants. No application shall contain a false statement (26-30). The Governor may issue complimentary hunting and fishing licenses to nonresidents (26-33).

★The Commissioner shall formulate conservation courses in safe trapping, hunting and archery practices, and the handling and use of traps and hunting implements, including bow and arrow, for first-time license applicants and for minors who hunt with adults, and shall designate competent persons or organizations to give instruction.★ A materials fee may be charged for the trapping course, no fee for the hunting/archery courses. No firearms hunting, archery hunting, or trapping license shall be issued without proof of having held a similar resident license from any state or country within five years from application, or a certificate of completion of a safety course or equivalent approved by the Commissioner. A person using false information or a fraudulent certificate to obtain a license shall be fined $25-100, and such license revoked and not reissued for one year. Conservation education/firearms safety instructors, and students, may possess, transport and discharge shotguns and rifles on Sunday on state or private property with permission of the agency or landowner. There is an annual Department appropriation of $50,000 to purchase materials to carry out these provisions. A person who has been refused a certificate of completion may appeal to the Commissioner for a final determination. ★The Commissioner shall formulate a Fishing Education and Urban Angling Program in fishing techniques, designate competent persons or groups to give instruction, and issue without fee a certificate of successful program completion (26-31a).★

★All licenses shall be carried as designated by the Commissioner and produced upon demand by a Conservation Officer or other person authorized to make arrests, or the agent or landowner of any land/water upon which the licensee is found.★ A licensee may be required to surrender a license when entering a wildlife management study area. Each licensee shall annually report to the Commissioner as required. A firearms hunting or combination license shall not authorize carrying or possession of a pistol or revolver (26-35).

★A hunting organization or individual owning and using for hunting a pack of 10 or more hounds or beagles may hunt foxes or rabbits for sport during the open season if licensed. Firearms may not be carried in such hunts (26-39).★ A person with a hunting license may train hunting dogs in the field during closed season, except for closures due to forest fire hazard (26-49). A field dog trial permit may be issued by the Commissioner and revoked at any time. The Commissioner may issue a permit to hold field dog trials on approved land at which legally possessed and liberated game birds, waterfowl and pigeons may be shot [details as to tagging, regulation of liberating, taking, species and sex, locations, seasons are given] (26-51 and -52).

The Commissioner may adopt standards for the management of salmon, pheasant and turkey, including permits, tags or stamps to be issued to holders of licenses to hunt or fish, and fees to be charged (26-48a). A permit to hunt deer or small game with bow and arrow is issued only to valid archery license holders and qualified applicants (26-86c).

Making a material false statement or signing the name of another on a deer or other quadruped-related permit application, or signing the wrong name on a deer-taking report, unless otherwise specified, is a fine of $25-200, jail up to 60 days, or both, and the possession of each quadruped or part is a separate offense. A weapon, ammunition, or device used, and found by a trial court to have been in possession of a person charged, may be seized and forfeited upon conviction, and disposed of, sold or used as the Commissioner determines, any proceeds to the general fund (26-90).

Restrictions on Taking: Hunting and Trapping

To develop a wildlife program for all wild birds and quadrupeds, encourage landowner participation, and develop public hunting on public and private lands and waters, the Commissioner may regulate hunting as provided (26-65). (See Agency Regulations under STATE FISH AND WILDLIFE AGENCIES for regulatory powers and topics covered.)

No person shall use silencers on firearms when hunting. No person while in a motor vehicle, snowmobile or ATV, or by aid or use of light(s) carried or attached, shall hunt or take a wild bird, quadruped, reptile or amphibian. This does not affect the statutes relating to jacklighting for deer. Violation: fine up to $200; jail up to 30 days; or both. During open or closed seasons, the possession limit for game birds, wild quadrupeds, reptiles and amphibians, shall not exceed the season bag limits, except for USFW set possession limits for migratory game birds, and for licensed game and fur breeders or persons authorized to possess such animals. Each animal, bird, or part shall constitute a separate offense. Violation of possession limits: fine up to $200; jail up to 60 days; or both (26-74 through - 76).

No person shall set a trap upon another's land without possessing the written permission of the landowner or agent, nor set a trap not tagged with their name; provided the landowner or agent may set a legal steel trap within a radius of 100 feet of a permanent building located on such land. Traps must be visited every 24 hours. No person shall set a snare, net or similar device capable of taking or injuring an animal. The pelt of a legally taken fur-bearing animal may be possessed, sold or transported at any time. Upon demand of an officer having authority to serve criminal process or Department representative, a person shall furnish satisfactory evidence that the pelt was legally taken or acquired. These provisions do not prohibit an agricultural landowner, or the owner of a game or fur-bearing breeding farm who has a game breeder's or fur breeder's license, from pursuing, trapping and killing at any time a fur-bearing animal, except deer, which is injuring property. No person shall molest, injure or disturb a muskrat house or den. A trap illegally set and a snare, net or similar device found in violation shall be seized and, if not claimed within 24 hours, the Commissioner may order it destroyed, sold or retained for Department use. Violation: fine up to $200, up to 60 days jail; or both. If a person is convicted, forfeits a bond, or receives a suspended sentence for trapping violations, all traps used in violation may be forfeited by trial court order and retained for Department use, or sold or destroyed, the proceeds to go to the general fund (26-72). (See also Commercial and Private Enterprise Provisions under HUNTING, FISHING, TRAPPING PROVISIONS.)

The Commissioner shall regulate deer management standards, and methods, areas, bag limits, season and permit eligibility for hunting deer with bow and arrow, muzzleloader and shotgun, except no hunting is permitted on Sunday. No person shall hunt, pursue, wound or kill a deer by firearm without a deer permit and a hunting license, and the permit may be revoked for violation of a statutory provision or regulation ["muzzleloader" is defined]. The Commissioner shall issue without fee a private land deer permit to the owner of 10 or more acres, and to specified relatives, provided no person shall be issued more than one permit per season, and it is used with permitted weapons. Deer may be hunted on state land as designated by the Commissioner, and on private land with the landowner's signed consent, which must be carried when hunting. The owner of 10 acres or more may allow the use of a rifle to hunt deer during the shotgun season. The Commissioner shall determine the number of consent forms issued for a regulated area, and provide a fair method for random selection of applicants for shotgun and muzzleloader permits. No person shall hunt, wound or kill deer with a bow and arrow without both a bow and arrow permit and a hunting license ["bow and arrow" is defined]. Taking a deer without a permit is a $200-500 fine, jail 30 days to six months, or both, for the first offense; each subsequent offense is a $200-1,000 fine, jail up to one year, or both. The Commissioner shall issue tags to be attached to a deer carcass until it is dressed, butchered and packaged for consumption. A person shall report a deer kill within 24 hours to the Commissioner (26-86a and -86b).

No person shall hunt, pursue, wound or kill a deer, or sell or possess flesh of a deer captured or killed in this state or from another state or country, unless it is tagged as required by such state or country, except as provided herein. (See also ANIMAL DAMAGE CONTROL.) No person shall make, set or use a trap, snare, salt lick, bait or other device for taking, injuring or killing deer, nor hunt, pursue or kill deer being pursued by a dog, whether or not the person owns/controls the dog, except that no motor vehicle operator shall be guilty of a violation when a deer is struck by the vehicle. No person in charge of a dog shall allow it to hunt, pursue or kill deer. Violation: $200-500 fine, jail 30 days to six months, or both, for first offense; for each subsequent offense, a $200-1,000 fine, jail up to one year, or both (26-82). After inspection by local police or a conservation officer, and after issuance of a deer kill incident report, a deer killed or seriously wounded as the result of a collision with a motor vehicle may become the property of the vehicle operator or other person if the operator declines possession (26-86). The Commissioner may issue regulations prohibiting hunting, wounding, killing or possession of doe deer on a described area basis when necessary to preserve adequate breeding stock. No person shall hunt, wound, kill or remove from the wild a fawn deer, except that deer found wounded may be removed with due care from the wild for treatment, but shall be turned over within 24 hours to a Department agent for disposition (26-86e and -86f). (See also ENFORCEMENT OF WILDLIFE LAWS for illegal jacklighting provisions.)

It is illegal to take a gray squirrel, rabbit or other protected fur-bearing animal, by use of gunpowder, dynamite, other explosive compound, or by fire, smoke, brimstone, sulphur, gas or chemical, or by digging it from a hole or den, but this does not prevent shooting a gray squirrel, rabbit or fur-bearing animal. It is illegal to cut down a tree or to use fire, smudge or smoke for taking a raccoon. Violation: fine up to $200 (26-88 and -89). The closed season, daily bag limit and possession limit for migratory game birds and the methods of taking shall be at least as stringent as the USFW regulations under federal migratory bird acts. Nothing shall affect the right to kill or possess wild ducks, geese and brant to be sold, which were propagated by a domestic breeder. Violation: fine up to $50; jail up to 30 days; or both; each bird or part possessed is a separate offense (26-91). Violation of regulations or statutes relating to taking birds for which no other penalty is provided, making material false statements in procuring a permit: fine of $10-200; jail up to 30 days; or both; each bird or part taken/possessed illegally is a separate offense (26-98).

Restrictions on Taking: Fishing

[Provisions relating to recreational taking of shellfish and marine life for personal use in coastal or tidal waters are in chapters 490, 491, and 492, Commercial Fisheries, State Shell Fisheries, Local Shell Fisheries. Connecticut is a member of the Atlantic States Marine Fisheries Commission and, with the states of Massachusetts, New Hampshire and Vermont, a member of the Connecticut River Atlantic Salmon Compact.]

★Notwithstanding any taking or purchase made for highway purposes by the Commissioner of Transportation, the fishing rights in a flowing stream which crosses a highway shall run with the land of the abutting owner, condemnee or grantor, unless just compensation for the rights has been determined and paid, and the deed conveying title expressly transferred the rights. The Commissioner may prohibit, regulate or curtail the exercise of such rights by the owner from a bridge under the Commissioner's control (26-140).★ A violation of sport fishing provisions for which no other penalty is provided is a fine up to $100; jail up to 30 days; or both. Each fish taken/possessed in violation is a separate offense (26-141).

★★After notice and hearing, the Commissioner may determine the location of a line across waters and streams designated in the statutes which shall be "inland water" and below which shall be "marine district"; notice shall be published at least twice in a general circulation newspaper in the county affected (26-108 and -109). The Commissioner may establish a line at the outlet and inlet of an artificial or natural lake or pond dividing such water from a stream or river flowing into or out of it. On one side of the line statutory provisions relating to fishing in lakes and ponds shall apply, and on the other side statutory provisions relating to fishing in rivers or streams shall apply. The line shall be fixed by posts marked and set upon opposite banks of such lake, pond, river or stream (26-110). In the interest of developing a sound program of sport fisheries management for all warm water, cold water and anadromous fish species, and all bait species, to encourage landowner participation and to develop public fishing in state waters, the Commissioner may regulate fishing and taking of all bait species in a lake, pond, stream, and in all other waters in the inland district as defined by established boundary lines (26-111).★★ (See also Agency Regulations under STATE FISH AND WILDLIFE AGENCIES.)

No fish or bait species shall be taken except as authorized. A species taken during the closed season, or of less than legal length, or in excess of the daily, season or possession limits shall be immediately returned without avoidable injury to the waters from whence taken. Each fish/bait species illegally taken is a separate offense. No person shall buy, sell or exchange, offer for sale, or possess with intent to sell, any species of trout, any species of salmon specified, black bass, calico bass or crappie, chain pickerel, great northern pike or pike perch, wall-eyed pike or bait species except as provided by law or regulation. Each fish or bait species sold, purchased or exchanged illegally is a separate offense (26-114).

No person shall take fish from a lake, pond or reservoir used for domestic purposes without written permission from the official controlling same. Fish shall not be taken by means of explosive. Except for mining or mechanical purposes, no dynamite or other explosive shall be used in state waters or possessed upon a shore or island of inland waters, and possession is prima facie evidence of illegal possession. No person shall place in any waters lime, creosote, cocculus indicus or other drug or poison injurious to fish; provided the persons supplying water to town residents may apply copper sulfate to the waters of a lake, pond or reservoir under their control within limits set by the State Department of Health Services, and the Commissioner may issue permits for addition of chemicals to inland water to control vegetation, fish or other aquatic organisms (26-118 and -119). [Special provisions regarding fish taking methods and seasons are listed for designated waters within the state.] A fish, crustacean, or part, illegally taken/possessed shall be seized by the Commissioner, Department employee, or conservation officer and sold or otherwise disposed of, with sale proceeds to go to the general fund (26-126). A boat, seine, net, spear, torch, fishing tackle or other device used in taking fish or crustaceans in violation of statute or regulation shall be forfeited. Upon complaint alleging that such device was being used in violation, the court may order it to be forfeited, to be sold or destroyed at the Commissioner's discretion, with sale proceeds to go to the general fund. The person using or in charge of a device used in violation of any provision is considered the owner for condemnation or forfeiture of such device when the owner is unknown to the informer or prosecuting officer. Aggrieved parties may appeal within 15 days to the superior court in the judicial district in which judgment was rendered, and the appellate court may proceed as in any in rem (property) proceeding (26-129).

Commercial and Private Enterprise Provisions

No person, association, or corporation shall possess more than one live specimen of or breed or propagate any of the following wild game bird or game quadruped species without a game breeder's license: all ducks, geese and swans; all quail, partridge and Blackneck, Chinese, English, Formosan, melanistic mutant and Mongolian or a cross-breed of pheasants (all other pheasants are considered domestic fowl); ruffed grouse; turkeys except domestic strains; sika and white tail deer; raccoon; otter; beaver; all species of Leporidae except domestic strains [other scientific names are given]. Upon application, a person, corporation or association may be licensed by the Commissioner to possess, breed, propagate and sell birds or mammals specified herein, under regulations. Records must be kept and an annual report made of the number of birds and mammals procured, possessed and propagated, and date and to whom sold. Each package containing birds or mammals specified, or parts, so propagated and offered for transportation shall be plainly labeled. The Commissioner may revoke a license granted. ★No person may breed, propagate or sell a skunk or raccoon, except with the Commissioner's approval such animals may be kept in a zoo, nature center, museum, laboratory or research facility. In no instance shall such animals be accessible to handling by the general public. No person may possess a skunk purchased in any state retail establishment.★ Violation: fine up to $90 for each offense. No person shall possess a potentially dangerous animal, defined as: lion, leopard, cheetah, jaguar, ocelot, jaguarundi cat, puma, lynx, bobcat, wolf, coyote, black bear, grizzly and brown bear, or a member of these families [scientific names are given]. An animal illegally possessed may be seized and disposed of as the Commissioner determines. Violation: up to $100 for each offense. These provisions do not apply to municipal parks, zoos, nature centers or research facilities, or to persons possessing such animals legally before May 23, 1983 (26-40 and -40a).

A fur-bearing animal legally taken alive may be possessed by the person taking it, provided the Commissioner is notified in writing of its species and sex, the date taken, name of the town where taken, and the specific address where it will be kept. A Department representative may inspect the animal and its facilities, and inquire about its diet and care. Absent proper care, it may be seized and disposed of as the Commissioner determines. Fur-bearing animals taken alive shall not be sold or exchanged, provided persons who legally possess fur-bearing animals may apply for a game breeder's license, or to the Department of Agriculture's Livestock Division for a fur-breeder's license, to breed the animals and their progeny; fur-bearing animals that are three generations removed from the wild may be sold or exchanged dead or alive (26-72). No person shall engage in the business of buying raw furs produced in this state without a license, which may be revoked for failure to report as specified. A conservation, special conservation, or recreation officer may examine premises used or records maintained by a licensee. Records shall be confidential except for release of information for wildlife research, management or development. The Commissioner may adopt regulations concerning buying and selling of raw furs, reporting procedures, and tagging requirements. Violation: fine $100-250; or jail up to 10 days; or both (26-42). A licensed resident fur dealer or other person who sells raw furs to an unlicensed nonresident fur dealer within state boundaries, or who aids an unlicensed nonresident dealer in buying raw furs within state boundaries shall be fined $100-250, jailed up to 10 days, or both, and shall forfeit the fur dealer's license for one year (26-43).

No person shall possess for sale, sell, or offer for sale any bait species without a bait dealer's license, except for commercial hatchery license holders. Licensees may possess and sell bait species authorized by regulations, provided live carp and goldfish shall not be possessed on premises used by licensed bait dealers. Records must be kept, and failure to file reports as required may result in refusal to reissue such license. Authorized persons may enter bait dealer premises to inspect records and bait species possessed and to detect violations, and may confiscate and dispose of fish illegally possessed. Violation: $10-100 fine; jail up to 30 days; or both (26-45).

The Commissioner may issue permits authorizing regulated private shooting preserves which do not conflict with reasonable prior public interest. A hunting license is not required on such preserves. The Commissioner shall regulate the size of the preserves, methods of hunting, species and sex of birds that may be taken, open and closed seasons, tagging of birds, and the release, possession and use of legally propagated game birds, and may require reports concerning operation. A permit may be revoked for violation of any statute or rule relating to such preserves (26-48). ★The Commissioner may authorize the establishment and operation of regulated hunting dog-training areas and may issue a permit to a private shooting preserve permittee, licensed game breeder, or commercial kennel licensee which authorizes liberation of artificially propagated game birds and pigeons, legally possessed and tagged. Only in the course of training hunting dogs may the birds be shot if approved by local town officials, by persons authorized by the permittee. A hunting license is required to train a dog on regulated dog-training areas, whether or not birds are to be shot. The Commissioner may regulate the size and posting of areas, number of birds to be released in ratio to number of hunters/dogs, method of liberation and retrapping of pen raised birds, species, sex and condition of birds, tagging method, and reporting of all activities. Violation: $25-100 fine; possible revocation of permit for up to one year (26-49).★

No person shall practice taxidermy for profit without a license. A licensee shall permit a law enforcement officer to examine the premises and may receive a bird or animal legally killed in the state or legally imported for tanning, curing or mounting. Annual reports are required. Violation: $1-100 fine; jail up to 30 days; or both; and license may be revoked or suspended for cause (26-58). The Commissioner may regulate tanning, curing and mounting of all species and permit issuance. Possession of a bird or animal for taxidermy, unless authorized, is a fine up to $100, and the animal shall be seized and disposed of as determined by the Commissioner (26-59).

★Owners of private waters desiring to fish therein shall apply for a certificate of registration. Owners of registered waters may take, or permit guests to take, a species of fish at any season, without a license, provided the waters were not stocked at state expense, and the Commissioner may regulate methods of taking and conditions under which such fish may be removed, possessed and transported. Violation of certificate provisions is a fine up to $200, and the

Commissioner may suspend or revoke such certificate (26-131). ★ Upon request by an association controlling the fishing rights in a stream or pond stocked by them, the Commissioner may regulate the open and closed seasons, creel limits and legal lengths for all species taken from such waters, provided no public interest is adversely affected and no weir, dam or other obstruction erected to stop the free passage of fish. Violation: fine up to $100, and the Commissioner may revoke or suspend the license (26-132).

Import, Export, Release Provisions

No person shall import or introduce into the state, or possess or liberate, a live fish, wild bird, wild quadruped, reptile or amphibian without a permit from the Commissioner, and under regulations as to numbers of certain species which may be imported, possessed, introduced or liberated. By regulation, the Commissioner may exempt certain species or live fish from permit requirements, and may determine which species must meet permit requirements, and may totally prohibit importation, possession, introduction or liberation of certain species determined to be a potential threat to humans, agricultural crops or established species of plants and animals. The Commissioner may exempt from permit requirements zoos, research laboratories, universities, public nonprofit aquaria or nature centers. A fish, bird, quadruped, reptile or amphibian illegally imported or possessed shall be seized by a Department representative and disposed of as the Commissioner determines. Violation: infraction; importation, liberation, or possession of each fish, bird, quadruped, reptile or amphibian in violation is a separate offense. Each day of violation is a separate offense. The Department shall evaluate each site where diploid grass carp are present, and those in a "contained environment" (no outlet, or screened to prevent fish migration) as of June 6, 1989, may remain. The Department shall publicize statutes and regulations pertaining to importation, possession and liberation of diploid grass carp (26-55 and -55a).

No person shall transport into this state a wild hare or rabbit, or liberate same, without a permit, except that snowshoe rabbits or variant hares may be imported without a permit from a New England state, the Province of Quebec, or Canadian maritime provinces, and liberated, subject to regulations. The Commissioner may quarantine, confiscate, destroy or otherwise dispose of a wild hare or rabbit other than a snowshoe rabbit, and may regulate its importation and liberation. Violation: fine up to $100; jail up to 30 days; or both (26-56).

The Commissioner may regulate importation, exportation, possession, sale and exchange of protected and unprotected species of live wild birds, wild quadrupeds, reptiles and amphibians legally acquired. The Commissioner may order such bird or animal impounded at the time and place, and in the manner determined, to allow its examination for disease or parasite infection, and may order its destruction in the public interest. Violation: $200 fine; jail up to 60 days; or both. These provisions do not apply to snapping turtles. The Commissioner may regulate importation, transportation, purchase, sale or exchange of wild or game bird plumage (26-78). (See also Restrictions on Taking: Hunting and Trapping under this section.) A person who transports out of this state a bait species taken from state waters, or who takes bait species, assists or attempts such shall be fined $50-200; jailed up to 30 days or both. No provision herein shall prevent the exportation of bait species propagated in private waters registered with the Board, or in licensed commercial hatcheries (26-127). No person shall sell, offer for sale, transport, transfer, possess or use carp or goldfish for bait fish purposes, nor introduce them into inland waters without a permit from the Commissioner. Violation: $100 fine; jail up to 30 days; or both (26-128).

See also Commercial and Private Enterprise Provisions under this section.

Interstate Reciprocal Agreements

If and when Rhode Island, Massachusetts or New York enacts a similar law for arrest and punishment for fish and game law violations of this state or that state, committed by a person fishing in boundary waters lying between such state and Connecticut, a game protector, conservation officer, game warden or other person authorized to make arrests for violations of either state may make arrests on borderline waters, and take the arrested person to the state in which the violation was committed for prosecution (26-26). Nonresidents residing in one of the New England states or New York may obtain hunting/fishing licenses for the resident fee if their state allows the same to Connecticut residents (26-28). If and when New York, Massachusetts or Rhode Island enacts similar laws granting reciprocal privileges to Connecticut residents, persons licensed to fish in those states may fish in borderline waters or in waters as negotiated by the states, without a nonresident license, provided they shall be subject to all other statutory provisions and regulations relating to fishing in lakes and ponds (26-46).

ANIMAL DAMAGE CONTROL

When shown to the Commissioner's satisfaction that wildlife is causing unreasonable damage to agricultural crops at night and that damage control is impracticable during daylight, the Commissioner may issue permits for taking wildlife to control damage by appropriate methods, including the use of lights at night, upon application of the landowner/lessee. These provisions shall not apply to deer. No person shall engage in the business of controlling nuisance wildlife without a license and under regulations which define the scope and methods for such and establish criteria and procedures for license issuance. A person who violates license provisions or conditions shall be fined $25-200, jailed up to 60 days, or both, and such permit or license shall be revoked and not reissued for as long as the Commissioner determines. Permits or licenses shall not authorize the taking of deer (26-47). ★An owner of land used for agricultural purposes may apply to the Commissioner of Agriculture for a permit to use approved types of noise-making devices to scare or repel marauding birds or other wildlife to prevent damage to crops and other property. No permit shall be issued for use of such device for use on any parcel of land not less than five acres, or for use within 500 feet of a human dwelling, without written consent of all occupants over age 18 presented to the Commissioner, who shall regulate such devices to insure public safety (26-47a). ★

★★A landowner, lessee, agent, spouse or lineal descendant who possesses a damage permit may use a shotgun or rifle to kill deer, provided such person has not been convicted for a violation of sections 26-82, 26-85, 26-86a and b, or 26-90 (relating to the taking of deer) within three years preceding the date of application. Upon receipt of an application from a landowner who has actual or potential gross annual income of $2,500 or more from commercial production of grain, forage, fruit, vegetables, flowers, ornamental plants or Christmas trees, and who is experiencing actual or potential loss of income because of severe damage by deer, the Commissioner shall issue up to six damage permits without fee. The application shall be notarized and signed by all landowners. The permit may specify the hunting implement or shot size, or both, which shall be used, and the time period. ★★ The Commissioner may revoke such permit for violation of any statute or regulation, or upon the applicant's request. The Commissioner may issue a permit to an approved landowner, agent, lessee or spouse to use a jacklight for taking deer when it is shown that such deer is causing damage which cannot be reduced during the daylight hours. The Commissioner may require notification as specified on the permit prior to its use. A deer killed under these provisions shall be the property of the landowner, but shall not be sold, bartered, traded or offered for sale, and the deer must be tagged and reported, upon receipt of which the Commissioner shall issue an additional damage permit. A deer killed otherwise than under these conditions shall remain state property and may be disposed of to a state institution, or sold, the proceeds to be applied to the general fund. No person, except the Commissioner, shall retail, sell or offer for sale the whole or part of such deer (26-82).

See also PROTECTED SPECIES OF WILDLIFE, GENERAL EXCEPTIONS TO PROTECTION and Restrictions on Taking: Hunting and Trapping under HUNTING, FISHING, TRAPPING PROVISIONS.

ENFORCEMENT OF WILDLIFE LAWS

Enforcement Powers

Conservation officers, special conservation officers, and patrolmen shall enforce the provisions of Titles 23 and 26 and other chapters, statutes and regulations as specified herein. Without warrant they may make arrests for violation of any of the provisions specified. A full-time conservation officer shall have the same powers to enforce laws as do sheriffs, police officers or constables in their respective jurisdictions, and incident to a lawful arrest, have the same powers as those officers with respect to criminal matters and related law enforcement. A conservation officer, special conservation officer or patrolman may examine contents of a boat, automobile, vehicle, box, basket, creel, game bag or other package when there is probable cause to believe that a fish, crustacean, bird or quadruped is being kept in violation of any statutory provision, Commission-issued regulation, or USFW-issued regulation under 26-91, and shall have the same authority as police officers to obtain and execute search warrants. A conservation officer, special conservation officer or patrolman may be appointed a Special Police Officer under 29-18 (26-6).

A person who, upon request of a conservation or special conservation officer, fails to stop and allow inspection of a container, or who disposes of a fish or crustacean, container, or its contents before the officer has inspected it, shall be fined $50-500 or jailed up to 90 days, or both (26-6b). A weapon, article or implement, usable for taking, catching or holding a fish, crustacean, wild or game bird, wild or game quadruped, reptile or amphibian, which is abandoned or discarded in an attempt to destroy or conceal evidence or to prevent apprehension, may be seized by a conservation officer. If the owner fails to claim such article within one year, it shall be forfeited to the state and may be retained by the Commissioner, sold at public auction, or destroyed, the proceeds to be paid into the general fund (26-23). A hunting, fishing, or trapping weapon, device or article seized and held as evidence by the Commissioner and not claimed within one year may be similarly retained or sold as provided (26-24).

An officer or agent authorized by the Commissioner or a state/town police officer has authority to execute a warrant to search for and seize goods, merchandise or threatened or endangered species possessed, sold or offered for sale in violation of 26-311, or property used in connection therewith. Items shall be held pending court proceedings, and upon conviction shall be forfeited and retained by the Commissioner, offered to a recognized institution for scientific or educational purposes, or destroyed, with costs assessed against the violator (26-40c). A person violating these provisions relating to endangered or threatened species shall be fined up to $1,000, jailed up to one year, or both. The illegal taking of each endangered or threatened plant or wildlife species or specimen or part shall be a separate offense (26-40f). (See also EXCEPTIONS TO PROTECTION.)

Criminal Penalties

A person who makes a false statement in an application concerning the use of fish, fish fry, fingerling fish, game, game bird or egg, or who makes use of same other than was specified in the application shall be fined up to $100, or jailed up to 30 days, or both (26-18). A person who violates license or permit provisions, or who makes a material false statement in procuring a license or permit, shall be fined $10-200, or jailed up to 60 days, or both (26-64). (See also HUNTING, FISHING, TRAPPING PROVISIONS.)

Illegal Taking of Wildlife

A bird, quadruped, reptile or amphibian, or part, illegally taken or possessed, or used illegally in pursuit of same shall be seized and disposed of or sold (26-80). (See also ENFORCEMENT POWERS under this section.)

★No person shall use, attempt to use, or possess a jacklight for taking deer. A jacklight is artificial light used in conjunction with a rifle larger than a twenty-two, or with a shotgun and ball shells or shot larger than no. 2 shot, or with a bow and arrow or cross bow, in an area frequented by deer or where deer are known to be present, or in a deer habitat. Possession of such articles in such place or on an adjacent road, by a person during nighttime hours as defined, is prima facie evidence of violation. A person who kills a deer with a firearm using artificial light during the defined night hours is subject to these provisions. Violation: $200-500 fine; jail 30 days to six months; or both for the first offense. Each subsequent offense is a $200-1,000 fine; jail up to one year; or both.★ A firearm, shell, cartridge, other weapon, portable lights, batteries and other devices used by, and found by the trial court to have been in the possession of, a person charged with a violation of this section, upon conviction or bond forfeiture, shall be forfeited to the state. By court order, the articles shall be turned over to the Commissioner to be retained for use, assigned to another agency, sold at public auction, or destroyed, proceeds to be credited to the general fund. ★★If a motor vehicle was used to transport such person to, toward or away from the place where the illegal act was committed, the person's operator's license, or the privilege to obtain such license, shall be suspended by Motor Vehicles for one year from the date of conviction. The Commissioner, after hearing, may issue the person a restricted, limited operator's license if it is required to earn a livelihood, but it shall be suspended for the remainder of the original suspension period if used for purposes other than those set by that Commissioner (26-85).★★

License Revocations, Suspensions

★★Upon the complaint of a person concerning an alleged violation of a provision of this chapter, regulation of the Commissioner or of the USFW relating to migratory birds, or other provisions as specified, after notice and hearing, the Commissioner may suspend a license, registration or permit issued or the right to obtain such for up to one year. The license or permit shall be surrendered. Upon conviction for a violation specified above or forfeiture of any bond, for a first offense, a license or permit and the right to obtain such shall be surrendered for 30 days to one year, except that for jacklighting for deer, such permit or license or privilege, shall be suspended for at least one to two years. For a second violation, the Commissioner may suspend a permit or license up to two years, except that for jacklighting deer the suspension shall be two to five years. A third violation is a suspension up to three years; for jacklighting deer, a minimum of five years, and may be an indefinite period. For a fourth violation within 10 years, a permit or license may be suspended for an indefinite period. Upon conviction for a violation of a regulation concerning hunting in proximity to buildings occupied by persons or domestic animals, or used for storage of flammable materials, or of a regulation regarding shooting towards persons, buildings or animals, the Commissioner shall suspend a hunting license for one year; for a second conviction within five years, a minimum of two years. A person whose license or permit is voided or suspended may apply to the Commissioner who may hear such application and may restore or reinstate same. A person who procures a permit or license to which they are not entitled or engages in fishing, hunting or trapping with a suspended license shall be fined $100-300; when such license is suspended for an indefinite period, the fine is a minimum of $200, jail up to 60 days, or both. For a subsequent violation on an indefinite suspension, the fine is $200-500, jail up to one year, or both. These provisions do not apply to infractions (26-61).★★   A person who injures or causes the death of a person, or domestic animal, or damages the property of another with a weapon or instrument used in hunting shall be given a hearing by the Commissioner, who may suspend for cause the hunting license or privilege to hunt for such period as deemed advisable. A person may apply to the Commissioner for restoration of hunting privileges (26-62).

See also Agency Powers and Duties under STATE FISH AND WILDLIFE AGENCIES and HUNTING, FISHING, TRAPPING PROVISIONS.

HABITAT PROTECTION

[A program for the protection, preservation, acquisition and improvement of tidal wetlands is established, details of taking by eminent domain and for unpaid municipal property taxes (26-17a).] The Commissioner shall post rights-of-way to each state owned/leased pond or stream clearly indicating its location and limits, and destruction of notices or Department property is a fine of $10-200, jail up to 60 days, or both (26-20 and -21).

The Department may establish state fish and game refuges and lease a tract of land, stream, lake, or pond suitable for propagation and preservation of fish and game, and may accept gifts of interest in a land, stream, lake, pond or personal property to be used for same upon agreed conditions, subject to Attorney General approval. The Commissioner may exercise the authority of a property owner for such purposes. The donor may exercise all rights incident to ownership of such property, except as limited by the conditions of the gift. The Commissioner shall post the boundary lines of fish and wildlife refuges, closed areas, management areas, fish hatcheries, fish rearing pools and retaining ponds forbidding entrance, but destruction of such notices shall not be a defense in a prosecution. The Commissioner may establish wildlife refuges, closed areas and safety zones on public lands and waters, and with the owner's consent, on private lands and waters, and close them to hunting, trapping, fishing and trespassing. Violation: up to $200 fine; jail up to 60 days; or both (26-99 through -101). Fish spawning areas and refuges may be established on waters or lands, and the Commissioner has emergency authority to declare a closed season on a species of fish threatened with depletion, and may suspend commercial fishing activity or close waters to fishing for limited periods (26-102). [Certain islands, rivers, marshes, and sanctuaries are listed and statutory restrictions on hunting, fishing and other activities are detailed in 26-103 through 26-106.]   ★★[Connecticut has a good policy statement on the preservation of tidal wetlands, and Chapter 440 covers permitted activities and the Commissioner's regulation of such areas.]★★

Unless authorized by the Commissioner, no person shall prevent the passing of fish in a stream by means of a rack, screen weir or other obstruction, or fail to remove such obstruction within 10 days after service of a Commissioner order (26-134).   ★★Upon petition of 10 or more persons owning property above a dam or artificial obstruction in existence on October 1, 1982, the Commissioner shall determine whether the dam shall be provided with a fishway by the person, firm or municipality owning or controlling the dam. Upon receipt of an application for a permit to construct or repair a dam, the Commissioner shall require a fishway if necessary to protect fisheries resources by providing access to natural spawning or nursery areas or to prevent the loss of a fishery from the dam area. Fishways shall be constructed and maintained subject to the Commissioner's approval and shall be kept open for fish passage. No person shall take a fish, except lamprey eels, during open season, within 250 feet of a fishway except as provided (26-136 and -137).★★   ★★Whenever a state dam impounds, affects the flow, or diverts the waters of a river or stream stocked with state trout, the Commissioner may regulate and set standards concerning stream flow. After consultation with state agencies, and after recognizing and providing for the needs and requirements of public health, flood control, industry, public utilities and water supply, stream and river ecology, aquatic life requirements, natural wildlife and public recreation, and after considering the natural flow into an impoundment, and after notice in the *Connecticut Law Journal* and to all parties having a direct interest, the Commissioner shall hold a public hearing, and promulgate regulations establishing instantaneous minimum flow standards and regulations for all stocked river and stream systems. These regulations shall: ▸ apply to all river and stream systems necessary to keep a sufficient flow of water to protect and maintain fish pursuant to the Commissioner's stocking program; ▸ preserve and protect the natural aquatic life; ▸ preserve and protect the natural and stocked wildlife dependent upon the flow of the water; ▸ promote and protect the water for public recreation; ▸ be consistent with needs and requirements of public health, flood control, industry, public utilities, water supply, public safety, agriculture and other lawful uses of such waters. After the promulgation of these minimum flow standards, no person, firm or corporation shall maintain a dam impounding or diverting water except in accordance with same. If a violation occurs, the Commissioner shall issue an order to comply, including a time schedule. If the person, firm or corporation fails to comply with the minimum flow standards, the Commissioner may request the Attorney General to bring an action in the Superior Court to enjoin restricting the water flow (26-141a through -141c).★★

No persons shall enter a state wildlife refuge or closed area to hunt, take, trap, snare, net, pursue, kill or destroy wildlife, nest or egg, or attempt such, nor permit their dogs to enter such refuge, nor do such in a lane, road or highway adjacent to a wildlife refuge or closed area; provided the Commissioner may take, hunt, kill or trap a fox, skunk, raccoon, wildcat, muskrat, mink, weasel, hawk, owl or other predacious bird or animal in state wildlife refuge or closed area. The detection of a person with a firearm, bow and arrow, trap, snare, net or dog upon such area shall be prima facie evidence of a violation; fine up to $100 (26-107).

The Commissioner may engage in wildlife management practices and expend federal aid funds to establish and maintain wildlife propagation installations and experimental stations on state land and water, and perform work related to the establishment, restoration, and protection of wildlife habitats, and for public ingress/egress from areas under its control (26-69). The Commissioner may engage in fisheries management practices and expend federal aid funds to establish, construct and maintain fish cultural installations, stream and pond improvement and control structures, experimental stations, and public facilities on Commission-controlled land and waters, and with a landowner's consent, on private land and water. Inland fisheries provisions do not apply to commercial fishing and do not affect any statute regulating fishing in a lake, pond or reservoir used for domestic water supply, nor shall any action be taken which will unreasonably interfere with management of a public water supply system. Violation: fine up to $200; jail up to 60 days; or both. Each fish taken or possessed illegally is a separate offense (26-115 through -117). (See also Restrictions on Taking: Fishing, under HUNTING, FISHING, TRAPPING PROVISIONS.)

No fish shall be furnished by the state for stocking a stream, river or lake in which fishing is prohibited by the owner, except that if the state has on hand more fish than required for stocking streams and other waters, the Commissioner may sell surplus fish at cost to a person for use for stocking state waters, whether or nor open to public fishing. ★To encourage landowners to engage in fish management practices, the Commissioner may sell at cost to landowners from stock on hand fish foods, chemicals, and compounds used in fisheries management, lake and pond bottom contour maps and related commodities.★ The Commissioner may sell surplus disease-free fish or fish eggs to commercial hatcheries at a cost competitive to commercial hatcheries, the proceeds to go into the general fund (26-130). ★★No person, firm or municipality shall intentionally drain water from a stream, lake, pond, reservoir or other impoundment for taking fish, or any other purpose, to the point where the fish is endangered unless 48-hour notice has been given so that Department agents may enter such property to determine whether salvage of fish is necessary, and to carry out same. The person issuing an order to drain such waters is deemed responsible, and their name and title must be registered upon request of the Commissioner. Violation: fine up to $200 (26-138 and -139).★★

The Commissioner may acquire for the state essential habitat, for conservation of endangered, threatened or species of special concern by gift, devise, purchase, exchange, condemnation or other method. Agreements may be entered with federal agencies, state political subdivisions, other states, individuals or private organizations, for administration and management of programs established for the conservation of endangered and threatened species and for management of essential habitat areas for such species under 26-306 (26-309).

See also HUNTING, FISHING, TRAPPING PROVISIONS and Agency Advisory Boards under STATE FISH AND WILDLIFE AGENCIES.

NATIVE AMERICAN WILDLIFE PROVISIONS: None.

143   *Connecticut*

DELAWARE

Sources: Delaware Code Annotated, 1974, Title 7; 1991 Replacement Volume; 1992 Supplement.

STATE WILDLIFE POLICY

The General Assembly finds and declares: It is in the best interest of the state to preserve and enhance the diversity and abundance of nongame fish and wildlife, and to protect the habitat and natural areas harboring rare and vanishing species of fish, wildlife, plants and areas of unusual scientific significance or unusual importance to the survival of Delaware's native fish, wildlife and plants in their natural environments. Rare and endangered species are a public trust in need of active, protective management, and it is in the broad public interest to preserve and enhance such species. Historically, fish and wildlife conservation programs have focused on the more recreationally and commercially important species and, consequently, have been financed largely by hunting and fishing license revenues and by federal assistance based on excise taxes on certain hunting and fishing equipment. These traditional financing mechanisms are neither adequate nor fully appropriate to meet the needs of all fish and wildlife. It is the policy of the state to enable and encourage taxpayers voluntarily to support nongame fish and wildlife, nongame habitat and natural areas preservation programs, including rare plants protection, through contributions designated on state income tax forms (7-201). (See also RELEVANT WILDLIFE DEFINITIONS and Agency Funding Sources under STATE FISH AND WILDLIFE AGENCIES.)

RELEVANT WILDLIFE DEFINITIONS: See Definitions section of Appendices.

STATE FISH AND WILDLIFE AGENCIES

Agency Structure

There is a **Department of Natural Resources and Environmental Control** (Department) and a **Secretary** of the Department (7-101). [Under title 29, the Secretary appoints with Governor approval and assigns duties to the **Director** of the **Division of Fish and Wildlife** (29-8003). The **Division** is responsible for all powers and duties heretofore vested in the Board of Game and Fish Commissioners under title 7 (29-8005). The **Council on Game and Fish** is also established to advise the Director (29-8006).] The **Secretary** shall employ wardens and other necessary employees, who shall have the power to arrest without warrant for all violations of the game laws of the state (7-102). The Department shall appoint a suitable person as **Chief Game and Fish Warden** (Warden), to serve at the pleasure of the Secretary. All sheriffs, deputy sheriffs, constables and policemen, or other peace officers of the state shall be ex officio **Deputy Game Wardens** (7-306).

Agency Powers and Duties

The **Department** shall: ▸ protect, conserve and propagate all forms of protected wildlife and enforce the law relating thereto; ▸ authorize studies as necessary, and collect, classify and preserve such statistics, data and information as will tend to promote the objects of Parts I and II of this title; ▸ prescribe the form of licenses; ▸ collect license fees and all fines and forfeitures imposed for violations of the game and fish laws; ▸ have authority to arrest without warrant for all game and fish law violations; ▸ issue a permit to any recognized sportsmen's club to hold field trials on liberated game or liberated artificially propagated game legally possessed, and take such game by shooting. Game taken shall be tagged for identification and then may be possessed, transported, bought and sold at any time (7-102).

The Department may take any game birds, animals or fish in or out of season in any way for strictly propagating and restocking purposes (7-115).

The **Warden** shall protect, propagate and distribute game and fish throughout the state, enforce the game and fish laws, and perform other work required by the Department. ★Rabbits, quail and pheasants shall be distributed by the Warden throughout the state except in the city of Wilmington; the number allotted to each county shall be distributed equally among the districts of that county.★ ★The Warden may arrest persons violating the laws relating to fish and fisheries and may call for aid from any person, boat or vessel, with the crew as a posse comitatus in the enforcement of the laws (7-302 through -304).★

Agency Regulations

The **Department** may: ‣ promulgate regulations; ‣ make expenditures necessary to fix and regulate seasons as to length; ‣ regulate bag limits on any protected wildlife or freshwater fish, except muskrat, in any locality after public hearing, when necessary to assure their conservation and the maintenance of an adequate supply thereof, or to limit the supply when conditions warrant; ‣ establish and close to hunting, fishing or trapping such wildlife refuges or lake, stream or pond to conserve any species of wildlife or fish. The Department may acquire by purchase, lease, gift or devise, lands, marshes or waters suitable to: ‣ provide fish hatcheries and game farms; ‣ provide lands or waters suitable for upland game, waterfowl, fish, fur-bearing animal propagation and protection; ‣ provide public hunting, fishing or other recreational grounds or waters; ‣ extend and consolidate lands, marshes or waters suitable for these purposes by exchange of other lands or waters; ‣ capture, propagate, transport, buy or exchange any species of protected wildlife needed for stocking any lands, marshes or waters of the state. The Department may establish rules and regulations concerning any species of protected wildlife or freshwater fish except muskrat in any specified localities necessary or advisable for the protection and conservation of wildlife or freshwater fish. The Department shall give notice of proposed changes to regulations in statewide newspapers and hold public hearings at least 60 days prior to changing any rule or regulation. All rules and regulations of the Department shall have the effect of law and shall be published at least 30 days prior to the effective date, except in emergencies when it shall give such advance notice as it deems necessary. The Department is not authorized to change any penalty for violating any game or fish law, change license fee amounts, issue any license not lawfully authorized, or extend any open season or bag limit beyond federal law or regulation limits (7-103).

Agency Funding Sources

There is a **Nongame Fish and Wildlife, Nongame Habitat and Natural Areas Preservation Fund** of the Treasury of the state. All moneys from the voluntary contribution system shall be deposited in the fund. The General Assembly shall make no appropriation into the fund, but individuals may make contributions to the fund. The fund moneys shall be transferred to the Department for the purposes of this chapter, and the distribution of moneys among Department subdivisions shall be determined by the Secretary. The Department shall periodically submit a detailed report of revenues, expenditures and program measures to the Delaware State Clearinghouse Committee. The Division of Revenue shall provide space on the Delaware income tax return form for voluntary designation of a contribution to the Fund, to be deducted from the individual's tax refund. The Department, with the Division of Revenue, shall provide adequate educational information and instructions on the tax form (7-203 and 7-204).

All funds from hunting and trapping licenses shall be deposited by the Department with the state Treasurer to be used for matching and securing money allotted to Delaware under federal-state cooperative wildlife restoration projects, with any surplus to go to the propagation of upland game, including cottontail rabbits. All funds from the issuance of fishing licenses shall be set aside by the state Treasurer to match federal-state fish restoration monies, with any balance to be expended for coordinated fish management projects (7-107 and 7-108).

All funds from the **Migratory Waterfowl Stamp** shall be set aside as the **State Duck Stamp Account**. Of collected revenues, 50% shall be contracted to a nonprofit organization for the development of waterfowl propagation areas in Canada approved by appropriate agencies and 50% shall be used for protection, preserving, restoring, enhancing and developing waterfowl habitat in Delaware. The Division shall establish, by regulation, the method for selecting the design for the stamp (7-518).

The Department shall issue annually a distinctive **Delaware Trout Fishing Stamp** for fresh water trout fishermen. Moneys from sale of the trout stamp shall be used only for the purchase of trout for restocking and improving state waters for trout fishing (7-1124 and -1128).

There is a **Wildlife Theft Prevention Special Fund** consisting of moneys received from fines imposed by chapters 1, 5, 6 and 7 of this title, donations to the fund and moneys appropriated by the General Assembly. Moneys from the fund shall be spent only for financing of rewards to persons, other than peace officers, Department personnel or their families, responsible for information leading to the conviction of any person for unlawfully taking, wounding, carrying, possessing, transporting or selling wildlife or trapping, attempting to trap or illegally setting traps for catching wildlife. The Division shall: ▸ establish a schedule of rewards for information received, and payment shall be made from available funds, rewards to not exceed $1,000; ▸ finance a statewide telephone reporting system called "Operation Game Theft;" ▸ promote public recognition and awareness of the Wildlife Theft Prevention Special Program; ▸ develop regulations to preserve the confidentiality of informants' identities (7-1312).

PROTECTED SPECIES OF WILDLIFE

No person shall take or needlessly destroy the nests or eggs of any wild bird, nor have such nests or eggs in possession (7-742).

★Any person who disturbs, destroys, or in any manner damages a bald eagle's nest or aerie shall be fined up to $500, plus costs, and/or jailed 50 days. Any person shooting, killing or attempting to kill a bald eagle or who attempts to remove eggs or eaglets from their nest shall be fined $1,000, plus costs, and/or jailed 100 days. Any person who barters, trades or possesses any bald eagle, bald eagle eggs or eaglets shall be fined $1,000, plus costs, and/or jailed 100 days (7-747).★

Whoever takes or destroys any terrapin eggs found or collected on or near the shore of any bay, river or stream where the water is salt, or upon any salt marsh or beach, shall be fined $10. Anyone possessing such eggs shall be deemed to have taken them there unless the person proves the contrary (7-781). (See also Restrictions on Taking: Hunting and Trapping under HUNTING, FISHING AND TRAPPING PROVISIONS for other terrapin provisions.)

No person shall catch, kill, possess (living or dead), purchase, sell, transport or ship any wild bird other than a game bird, or any part of the plumage, skin or body of such bird, or any game bird except as expressly permitted by law; but house sparrows and starlings may be killed, sold or shipped by any person in any manner and at any time (7-741).

All state lands, except as otherwise provided, and state, county and municipal parks in Delaware shall be state game refuges, and no person shall hunt, kill or injure any game therein at any time. Any person may shoot and kill, during the open season for game, wild duck, wild geese, brant and snipe on state lands bordering on Delaware Bay, Atlantic Ocean, Indian River and Assawoman Bay. All wildlife refuges created under this title are under the jurisdiction of the Department and subject to regulations, including those covering the right to hunt and fish (7-743).

See also RELEVANT WILDLIFE DEFINITIONS.

GENERAL EXCEPTIONS TO PROTECTION

The Division may issue a permit, revocable at the Director's discretion, to take, capture, possess or transport wild birds, nests or eggs, game animals or fish for scientific or propagating purposes. Permits may establish any conditions and/or restrictions deemed desirable. No wild birds, game animals or fish held in captivity shall be confined under inhumane or unsanitary conditions. Permittees must file with the Division a report of their operations prior to permit renewal, including number of wildlife taken, list of species taken and disposition (7-571).

The woodchuck or groundhog may be hunted, trapped, caught, shot, killed, sold, shipped or otherwise disposed of, by any person at any time (7-812). The animal known as woodchuck or groundhog shall not be protected wildlife (7-811).

The crow may be hunted in accordance with federal regulations (7-748). Sections 7-741, 7-742, and 7-743, relating to sale and transport of wild birds, protection of nests and eggs and state game/wildlife refuges, shall not apply to any person holding a scientific license to take birds and their nests and eggs (7-745).

See also PROTECTED SPECIES OF WILDLIFE for sparrows and starlings.

HUNTING, FISHING, TRAPPING PROVISIONS

General Provisions

Open seasons for pheasant, frogs, migratory birds and waterfowl, mink, muskrat, opossum, otter, quail, rabbit or hare, raccoon, red fox and squirrel are set in statutes, and according to location or county for some species. There are special seasons for hunting foxes with dogs (no shooting). No red fox may be shot during a time when it is lawful to take deer with a firearm, nor when being pursued by a pack of hounds (7-703).

No dog owner shall permit such dog to injure, destroy or disturb any muskrat den, trap, lead or house, or any poultry or livestock (7-1705). The owner of any bird, rabbit, raccoon or fox dog may train at specified seasons of the year, day or night. If the dog owner exercises reasonable precautions to keep dogs under control, and if a dog during training wanders off and out of control, it shall not be deemed to be running at large. An owner of any dog that kills protected game during the closed season while training shall be fined $2-5 for each offense. No person shall carry a gun while dog training in a closed game season. Special permits are available to retriever dog trainers for training at any time of year provided no game is used in the training. A permittee may possess artificially reared game and hunt with a shotgun, but such game must be hand-liberated during dog training (7-1706). Unlicensed dogs running at large at any time may be killed by any police officer, constable or Game Warden. Any unlicensed dog entering any field constitutes a public nuisance, and the landowner may kill such dog without liability while it is in the field. Any person may kill any unlicensed dog which the person sees worrying or wounding livestock or attacking human beings (7-1708). It is unlawful for any person, except a police officer or Game warden, to kill, injure or poison any licensed dog unless it attacks a human being. No persons, except police officers or Game Wardens, shall place any kind of poison in any place on their premises, or elsewhere, where it may be easily found and eaten by dogs (7-1709 and 1710). Dog field trials require a permit from the Department, which may be granted to bona fide field trial clubs under regulations to safeguard the interests of the game (7-1713). Any dog found running at large contrary to any of these provisions may be impounded and disposed of under regulations after five days written notice to the owner, if such can be determined (7-1712). Violations of dog provisions are a fine of $5-50 and costs for each offense, and jail up to 10 days for failure to pay fine (7-1714).

★Upon application of any club having 20 or more members, the Department may issue a license for a special dog training area wherein dogs may be trained at any time during the year. The area shall be 100 to 250 acres in size, and no more than four permits for dog training areas may be issued for any one county (7-1721). The licensees shall, from time to time, during each year stock each such area with 25 pieces of game per 100 acres at their own expense under Department supervision, unless the area is already adequately stocked. Licensees may at any time train their own dogs or those of permitted others on such areas. No person shall hunt or trap at any time within the area, except the licensees may trap vermin and predators on such area (7-1722).★ Boundaries of special dog training areas must be posted, and destruction of boundary fences or posters is a fine of $10 for each offense, and in default of payment, jail up to 5 days (7-1724). The Department shall establish a Department of Dog Law Management and hire dog control officers or dog wardens to carry out these provisions (7-1725).

Licenses and Permits

Every resident, except as otherwise provided, shall obtain a general license before hunting, trapping and/or fishing in this state. Residents born after January 1, 1967, shall also have satisfactorily completed not less than ten hours of instruction, which includes, but is not limited to, the safe and proficient use of hunting equipment, hunter responsibility, principles of wildlife management, wildlife identification, and, to the degree practical, a live firing experience before applying for a hunting license. After July 1, 1986, every resident shall obtain a trapping license before trapping any animals regulated by this title. During any deer season, the Department may issue an additional permit to kill a single deer under Department criteria, in addition to the general hunting license. Nonresidents, except as otherwise provided, must be licensed before hunting, trapping or fishing, and must have completed a similar hunter education course. Similar exceptions to license requirements exist for nonresidents. No nonresident or alien shall have any protected game or wildlife in possession who does not hold a hunting, trapping or fishing license unless such game or wildlife has been lawfully killed out of the state and may be lawfully possessed in this state. This does not apply to a nonresident who owns and resides on a farm of at least 20 acres and is engaged in husbandry, or to the lawful interstate transportation of protected wildlife (7-501, -504, -506, -507, and -515).

Forgery, alteration or misuse of license is illegal. Violation: $10-50 plus costs for residents; minimum $50 for nonresidents; and forfeiture of license (7-516). Hunting, fishing or trapping without a license, or unlawful hunting, fishing or trapping, or carrying a firearm if an unnaturalized foreigner is a fine of $10-50 and costs for each offense; for aliens the fine is a minimum of $50 plus costs for each offense. Aliens may lawfully hunt, fish or trap on their own land of 20 acres or more if they reside on and engage in husbandry on such farm. Unnaturalized foreigners convicted of hunting, fishing or trapping in violation of law, in addition to other penalties imposed, shall forfeit any or all hunting, fishing or trapping equipment, firearms and ammunitions in possession at the time of arrest, such equipment to be disposed of by the Department (7-722).

Except as otherwise provided, no person may hunt or take any migratory waterfowl without first procuring a migratory waterfowl stamp and having it in possession while hunting. Persons exempt from hunting license requirements and those under age 16 need not have a waterfowl stamp (7-518).

The Department shall furnish each licensee a tag or button bearing the license number, to be displayed on an outer garment (7-513). No person shall set any kind of metal trap whatsoever, except for taking muskrats, without tagging such trap with the owner's license number. Using an untagged trap is a fine of $10-50, costs for each offense, and forfeiture of each trap so set (7-514).

Restrictions on Taking: Hunting and Trapping

★No person shall make use of any pitfall, deadfall, scaffold, cage, snare, trap, net, pen, baited hook, lure, urine, baited field, or any other similar device, or any drug, poison, chemicals or explosives for the purpose of injuring, capturing or killing birds or animals protected by the laws of this state, except muskrats, raccoon, opossum, minks, snapping turtles and otters, and otherwise expressly provided.★ Landlords, tenants and their children may take rabbits in traps and snares during the open season on their own land. The unlawful setting of any of these devices is an offense, and such devices shall be seized and disposed of as the Department sees fit. No person shall shoot at, or kill any bird protected by state law with any device, swivel or punt gun or with any gun other than one fired from the shoulder. Possession of such illegal device or gun while hunting shall be prima facie evidence of violation. No person shall use shotgun shells with lead larger than No. 2 shot, except ammunition permitted for deer hunting during the open season therefor. No person shall use dogs for hunting/pursuing deer with intent to kill deer at any time. Violation: $50-100 for each offense. Muzzle-loading rifles and ammunition of specified sizes may be used in the pursuit or taking of protected wildlife during designated primitive weapon seasons established by the Department (7-704).

★Pens or cages located adjacent to waterfowl shooting blinds which are used for live decoys must be of specified construction to prevent entrance of wild waterfowl. Violation: fine $50-100 and costs for each offense, in addition to other penalties for unlawful hunting or capturing of wild waterfowl. ★ Traps, except for muskrats, must be visited at least once in each 24-hour period. Violation: $10-50 for each offense. No person shall needlessly destroy, break or interfere with any nest, den or lair of any protected bird or animal, or set fire to, or in any way mutilate, any tree, living or dead, stump or log on another's lands without the owner's express consent (7-705 through -707).

It is illegal to shoot at or kill any protected bird or animal with any firearm at any time or place from any motor vehicle, motor/sail boat or farm machinery. Violation during daylight hours is a fine of $25-50 for each offense; during night hours a fine of $50-100 for each offense, and up to 30 days jail for failure to pay. No person shall have a loaded shotgun or rifle in possession in, against or on any automobile, other vehicle, piece of farm machinery or boat under power, or have ammunition in such weapon unless hunting crippled migratory birds. No person shall take any migratory bird except within permitted hours, nor take any protected animal including muskrats during nighttime hours, except frogs, muskrats, raccoons, opossums, skunks, minks, otter and foxes. Using a silencer on a gun is a $20 fine for each offense. Use of an automatic or hand-loading shotgun not properly plugged for only three shells is a fine of $10-50 per offense, and jail up to 30 days for failure to pay. ★No person shall hunt any protected bird or animal except muskrats, minks and otters while there is snow upon the ground in such condition that any such bird or animal may be tracked therein, or track any bird or animal in the snow. Violation: $20 for each bird or animal.★ No person shall hunt or pursue any game birds or game animals with any dog or any killing implement on Sundays, except for trapping, training dogs, or hunting red foxes with dogs. It is illegal to fire any woodlot, forest or other wild land, other than brush in clearing land, without the consent of the owner, or to fire marshlands except during the permitted season. Violation: fine of $25-100 and costs for each offense, and/or jail 30 to 90 days, in addition to damages caused by setting unlawful fires (7-708 through -715).

No person shall kill, in any one day, more migratory birds or fowl than permitted by federal law, or more than eight birds of any other species, and four animals, or have such birds or animals in possession for more than 30 days after the close of the season, except for animals habitually trapped for their pelts, snipe, plover and reed birds, and animals and birds stored in refrigeration for food (7-716).

Hunting license holders may ship within or out of the state in one week not more than 50 reed birds, 50 rail birds, 20 birds of other species, and 10 animals of each species, except muskrats. Such game shall be carried/shipped openly for inspection and counting, and the person shall make affidavit, before one duly authorized to administer oaths, that the birds/animals have been lawfully killed by the affiant, and are not being shipped for purposes of sale, one copy of which shall be given to the common carrier receiving game for transportation. Violation: $10-50 and costs, plus liability for perjury for swearing falsely to a material fact in an affidavit. Common carriers who ship game birds or animals without meeting these provisions shall be fined $50-100 and costs for each offense. Residents, gunning for their own sport, may take, carry or ship within the borders of the state any protected birds or animals, lawfully killed, that do not exceed the numbers prescribed in 717 and which are carried or shipped openly and not for purposes of sale (7-717 through -719).

One who enters on another's lands with gun and dog, or with gun alone, for shooting any kind of birds or game without first obtaining the landowner's permission shall be fined $30. ★Failure to pay shall result in forfeiture of the gun for 30 days while the fine is paid, after which time the gun shall be publicly sold (7-720).★

Bullfrogs, lawfully taken, may be sold, bought and possessed in any quantity (7-797). No person shall take or kill more than 24 bullfrogs in any one day or have the same in possession for more than 5 days after the season's close except when held alive for scientific or propagating purposes. Violation: fine $5-10. A fishing licensee may take 10 bullfrogs in any one day or night during the open season (7-796 and -797).

No person shall at any time shoot or wound any red fox except in designated counties. No red fox may be shot during time when it is lawful to take deer with a firearm; provided further, no red fox may be shot that are being pursued by a pack of hounds, and no person shall take or kill more than four red foxes. Owners of poultry may take foxes in the act of killing or carrying away poultry. Violation: $100-500, and in default of payment of fine and costs, jail up to 30 days. The fine shall not be suspended. No red fox or hide thereof shall be sold, possessed or exposed for sale or shipped or carried outside the state, except for live foxes in animal exhibitions owned by the state or political subdivisions thereof. Violation: $100-500 or jail up to 30 days; penalty shall not be suspended. ★No person shall dig out or in any manner take from any den or kill a female fox, or her young whelps, during the time in which she is suckling them. Violation $10-50, or jail up to 10 days for every female fox or whelp dug or taken out of any den, or killed. A poultry owner may take such fox in the act of killing poultry within a reasonable time after the killing or carrying away of such poultry.★ ★★A Department permit may be issued for taking, possessing and raising of red fox whelps between April 1 and August 15 by persons possessing at least five foxhounds kept for chasing mature red foxes. Whelps may be taken only with the landowner's permission, and must be released prior to each August 15 (7-793 through -795A).★★

It is a fine of $25-50 to frighten or harass migratory birds while at rest on the property of another with a firearm, or to take or kill an otter, other than by trap and other than during the open season for muskrat (7-723 and 724). Anyone who sets, tends or possesses a killer, body-gripping trap with a jaw spread in excess of five inches shall be fined $250-500 for the first offense; $500-1,000 for each subsequent offense; such fines shall not be suspended (7-728).

No person shall have more than two times the daily bag or creel limit of any game bird, game animal or game fish when such possession is lawful except for rabbits lawfully killed outside of the state, or muskrat lawfully taken, or terrapin lawfully taken and of lawful size, when it is lawful to have these animals, their meat and skins in possession. Violation: fine of $25-100 and costs, for each offense, and an additional $5 fine for each game bird, game fish and game animal caught or killed illegally, purchased or sold or possessed in excess of the bag limit. No person shall possess any game fish during the closed season therefor, whether taken within or without the state, nor sell or buy any protected game birds, game animals or game fish, except the muskrat, snapping turtle and diamond back terrapin may be traded during lawful season, and trading is allowed at any and all times in muskrat and other skins and in terrapin lawfully taken of legal size. Food establishments and clubs may offer pheasants and quail for food from licensed game breeders only. No person shall knowingly possess any game birds, animals or fish which have been unlawfully killed. Violation: fine $25-100 and costs for each offense, and an additional fine of $5 for each game bird, game fish and game animal caught or killed illegally, purchased or sold, or found in possession in excess of the bag limit (7-721).

No person, except in lawful self defense, shall discharge any firearm while on or within 15 yards of a public road unless it is within an area open to hunting or trapping, nor shoot at any wild bird or animal while it is on a public road, nor shoot across a public road at such bird or animal. Violation: fine of $100-300, and/or jail up to 90 days; justices of the peace have jurisdiction for these offenses (7-726). Permits to shoot from a stationary vehicle are available for disabled persons under specified conditions (7-727). No person, except the owner/occupant, shall discharge a firearm within 100 yards of an occupied dwelling or barn while hunting or trapping. The area shall be a "safety zone," and it is unlawful to shoot at or attempt to trap any wild bird or wild animal while it is within such safety zone without specific advance permission of the owner/occupant. Violation: fine $25-100 (7-730).

No person shall hunt at nighttime any species of wild bird or animal with a light or headlights of any vehicle. Possession of any firearms or other killing implements while in a motor vehicle, loaded or unloaded, exposed within immediate reach, while using artificial lights shall be prima facie evidence of the use of such firearms or other implements for hunting. Raccoons or opossums may be hunted on foot or horseback at night during open season with the use of a dog or light or both. Frogs may be hunted on foot at night with a light during open season. No person shall make use of any artificial light emanating from a vehicle and directed toward woods, field livestock, wild animals or birds, dwellings or buildings, except for normal headlights on traveling vehicles on public roads, or a landowner checking on the landowner's own land or livestock. Violation: fine $100-250 for the first offense; $250-500 for each subsequent offense; such fines shall not be suspended (7-729).

No person shall catch, pursue or possess (living or dead) any deer, or purchase, sell, transport or ship any such deer or any part. Any person may possess a deer lawfully killed in another state with proof of lawful killing/possession. It is lawful to possess deer within an enclosure in a public zoo or park. A daytime violation is a fine of $100 for each offense. A night violation using artificial lights is a fine of $150-250 and costs. Failure to pay is a jail term up to 60 days unless sooner paid (7-792).

★The habitat of a muskrat shall be a marsh of any size, ordinarily subject to rise and fall of tide, a ditch, a stream, or land not suited to cultivation of crops due to marshy conditions. A trap set or found at any place other than such habitat shall be considered as having been set for game animals other than muskrats. No person shall take, kill or capture, by any means whatever, any muskrat during the time of any flood or freshet, when a muskrat may leave its usual and accustomed place of shelter and protection.★ No person shall take, catch or kill any muskrat with a dog. Violation for each offense is a fine of $5, and in default of payment and costs, jail up to 20 days. No person shall take, capture or kill, at any time, any muskrat by the method commonly known as "nailing;" or dig into, tear down, remove, interfere with, or damage any muskrat house, nest, den or refuge. Violation: fine $25-100 for each muskrat house, nest, den dug into, damaged or destroyed in any way, and in default of the payment of the fine and costs, jail for one day for each dollar of the total fine. Entering/trespassing upon the marshes or lands of another without consent of the owner for taking, trapping, capturing or killing muskrat in any manner whatsoever is illegal. Violation: fine $50-100, plus costs for each offense, and in default of payment, jail up to 30 days. The party injured has a right to a civil action for damages as in cases of trespass (7-761 through 7-765).

No person shall take, capture or kill any muskrat on any public road or highway. Violation: $25-50 for each offense, and in default of payment, jail up to 30 days, or both. No person shall take or kill, at any time, any muskrat with a diving or box trap. Setting any such trap in any muskrat den or runway shall be prima facie evidence of an offense. Violation: $25-50 for each offense, and in default of the payment, jail up to 30 days (7-767 and -768).

No person shall hunt, take, kill or destroy any rabbit or hare with a ferret, or have a ferret in possession while hunting. A special license is not required to sell rabbits received from without the state, in accordance with 7-772. No person shall receive from without the state any European or San Juan rabbit or rabbit from an endemic state or area listed by the US Public Health Service; nor receive any rabbit unless it has a disease free certificate from the state Board of Health. Violation: $100-1,000. Rabbits exposed for sale, which were received from without the state, must be labeled as "shipped rabbits" and show the state of origin. Bills of lading for rabbits must be shown to any Game Warden or police officer to satisfy such officer that the rabbits were not killed or shipped from within this state. Violation of 774 or 775: fine $10-20 (7-771 through -776).

The taking of terrapins is restricted by size of shell, method, and location in the state, with fines ranging from $5-20 for each offense (7-782 through 784).

No person shall catch, kill or posses, except for strictly scientific or propagating purposes, any diamond back terrapin from March 15 to September 15. No person shall catch, kill, or possess, except for scientific or propagating purposes, any heifer diamond back terrapin measuring less than 5 1/2 inches in length on the bottom shell. Violation: $5-25 for each terrapin caught or killed, and in default of payment, up to 10 days jail. Any person may raise terrapin in a private pond (7-785 and -786).

No person shall kill any raccoon or opossum, or needlessly destroy or interfere with any den of any raccoon or opossum, or set fire to or otherwise mutilate any tree, living or dead, stump or log to kill any such animal at any time of the year during daylight hours. Any person may trap, hunt with dogs or otherwise take raccoons from any lands during periods defined by Department regulations. Raccoon and opossum may be legally trapped statewide in a box type trap operated so as to not harm the animal. Any person may trap or hunt raccoons with dogs, with permission of the landowner, from any lands in designated counties at any time of year (except Sundays) (7-791).

Restrictions on Taking: Fishing

It is illegal to fish for any freshwater fish in nontidal state waters unless it meets these provisions: ▸ hook and line may be used, each to have no more than three hooks or three separate lures with hooks; ▸ except for ice fishing, no more than two hooks and lines may be used by one person; ▸ dip nets may be used to land fish; ▸ the Director may issue a permit to landowners or tenants to fish in their own ponds for freshwater finfish with any fishing equipment or by any method not otherwise authorized, except they may not use any chemical, poison and/or electrical equipment to fish for freshwater finfish; ▸ upon a landowner's request, Division employees may be authorized by the Director to use such chemicals or electrical equipment to fish in said owner's pond for fish management purposes; ▸ carp may be taken by bow and arrow or spear unless such equipment is otherwise restricted by Department regulations (7-1103). No person shall sell, trade or barter any freshwater finfish unless authorized by Director's permit (7-1105). The Secretary and Department shall enforce fishing provisions and regulations, violations to be punished under 7-1304 for permit and statutory violations and under 7-103(7-e) for violation of any Department regulation regarding freshwater finfish (7-1106).

A trout fishing stamp is required to take trout during the open season in a manner permitted by law from fresh waters stocked with trout by the Department. Persons exempt from purchasing a fishing license are also exempt from purchasing a trout stamp, as is a landowner whose land is traversed by trout-stocked waters (7-1126 and 1127). It is illegal to: ▸ alter a trout stamp; ▸ loan a stamp to another person for use in trout-stocked waters; ▸ furnish false information on an application for a trout stamp; ▸ take trout from any Department stocked waters without having purchased a trout stamp; ▸ refuse to exhibit a stamp on the demand of a Game Warden (7-1129).

Commercial and Private Enterprise Provisions

A person must obtain a **Raw Fur Dealer License** before purchasing or receiving raw furs or pelts for commercial purposes. Violation is $100-500 and costs for each offense. No fine imposed shall be suspended (7-551 and 554). A fur dealer licensee shall keep detailed records, to be open to inspection, of purchases, sales, kinds and numbers of furs dealt in. Violation: fine $150-350 and costs for each offense; fine shall not be suspended. This section shall not apply to pelts or furs of muskrats (7-555).

A **Game Breeder License** is required before engaging in the business of breeding game animals or game birds. This does not apply to birds or animals raised by or for the Department, or to any person engaged in breeding of animals or birds not exceeding 25 (7-561). A permit from the Department is required to sell any game animals or game birds before shipping out of the state. Violation is $10 for each offense (7-563 and 564).

Persons, clubs or associations may obtain annual licenses to operate **Restricted Experimental, Propagation and Shooting Preserves** for experimental propagating, holding, raising, releasing and shooting of rabbits and game birds, including, but not limited to, grouse, pheasant, quail and partridge, referred to as game. The Department must be satisfied that such experimental game preserve will not conflict with any reasonable public interest and will result in a general improvement in the quality and quantity of game in other areas of the state, due to the travel and movement of game from heavy stocking of the restricted area. Preserve/restricted area lands must be 300 to 1,000 acres, and must have sufficient cover and feed adequately to support game in numbers which will be beneficial to other areas outside the reservation. External boundaries of restricted areas shall be posted and clearly defined by natural boundaries or fences (7-582 through -584).

To stimulate an increase in the quantity of game released upon reservations, the licensee or guests, when properly licensed, may liberate upon the reservation propagated game, and may kill up to two-third of the total number of each species liberated. The licensees must submit monthly reports during the shooting season, itemizing all game released and killed. The Department may temporarily reduce the number of game birds or rabbits killed to the proportion released, but not to less than one-half the total number of each species released. The licensee shall cooperate with the Department and assist in conducting experimental breeding, propagating, feeding and care of game, and keep records. All game released shall be banded, and then may be transported from the premises by the licensee or guests. Shooting seasons shall conform to regular open seasons for such game, November 15 to December 31. Total liberations will be made a ratio of not less than one male to five females of each species, except quail, with a ratio of one male to each female. All activities on such preserves shall be subject to the game laws and regulations of the state, except as they may be in conflict with this chapter. Trespassers on such preserves shall be fined $100-200 for each offense. ★The owner of a restricted preserve and the owner's authorized agents may be authorized by the Department to make arrests (7-585 through -589).★

Import, Export and Release Provisions

The Director may permit the importation of any species or subspecies of fish or wildlife listed in the chapter on endangered species for zoological, educational, and scientific purposes and for the propagation of such fish or wildlife in captivity for the preservation of a species, unless such importation is prohibited by federal law or regulation (7-604).

The importation, transportation, possession or sale of any endangered species of fish or wildlife, or hides or parts, or the sale or possession with intent to sell any article made in whole/part from the skin, hide or other part of any endangered species of fish or wildlife is prohibited except under Division of Fish and Wildlife permit. Endangered species shall mean species of fish and wildlife designated by the Division as seriously threatened with extinction. Such list shall include, but not be limited to, endangered species designated by the Secretary of the Interior (7-601). No part of the skin or body, raw or manufactured, of the following species or the animal itself may be sold or offered for sale by any individual, firm, or partnership within the state: all endangered species designated by the US Department of the Interior; leopard; snow leopard; clouded leopard; tiger; cheetah; alligator, crocodile or caiman; vicuna; red wolf; polar bear; harp seal (7-602). Any officer or agent authorized by the Secretary or Director, or any police officer of the state or municipality, has authority to execute any warrant in search for and seizure of any goods, merchandise or wildlife sold in violation of endangered species provisions, the same to be forfeited upon conviction (7-603). No live skunks or raccoons shall be sold or possessed in this state or transported into this state for any purpose without a Division permit (7-799).

See also Restrictions on Taking: Hunting and Trapping under HUNTING, FISHING, TRAPPING PROVISIONS for rabbit importation restrictions.

ANIMAL DAMAGE CONTROL

When information is furnished to the Department that any species of protected wildlife has become, under extraordinary conditions, seriously injurious to agriculture or other interests in any community, the Department shall investigate the nature and extent of the injury, whether the wildlife alleged to be doing the damage should be killed or captured, and if so, by whom, when, and by what means, and shall issue an order to that effect (7-113).

When the Department receives information from a landowner that any one or more species of protected wildlife are detrimental to crops, property or other interests on the landowner's land, with a statement of the land's location, the nature of the crops or property being damaged/destroyed, the extent of the injury and the species of protected wildlife involved, the Department shall investigate. If it is determined the injury is substantial and can be abated only by killing or capturing the protected wildlife, a permit to kill or capture any number or all of such wildlife shall be issued, specifying the time, means, methods and persons by whom the wildlife may be killed or captured, and the disposition to be made thereof, with other restrictions the Department deems necessary (7-114).

ENFORCEMENT OF WILDLIFE LAWS

Enforcement Powers

The Secretary, the Chief Warden and Game Wardens may search and examine without warrant any person, conveyance, vehicle, game bag or other receptacle for protected wildlife, and, in the presence of an occupant of any camp or tent, may search the camp without warrant for protected wildlife, when there is reason to believe, and the occupant is told the reasons for believing, laws have been violated, and may seize and possess any protected wildlife illegally in possession. A search warrant is required to enter a dwelling house (7-111).

★★Every person holding a license for hunting or fishing may arrest, without warrant, violators of fish and game laws. Any freeholders or leaseholders or members of their families or employees may arrest, without warrant, any person who commits any violation of fish and game laws upon such land (7-1301 and 1302).★★

The Department shall confiscate all game and fish unlawfully taken or possessed and dispose of it by destruction or distribution to charitable institutions (7-1303).

Criminal Penalties

Whoever violates any rule or regulation of the Department except those pertaining to deer shall be fined $10-50 and costs for each offense, or jailed up to 30 days or both. Whoever violates any rule or regulation pertaining to deer shall for a first offense be fined $50-150 and costs, or jailed 30 days, or both; for a second offense, $150 and/or jail not less than 30 days; for subsequent offenses, not less than $500 and/or jail not less than 60 days for each offense (7-103).

Any person convicted of violating any provision of Part I of this title (Game, Wildlife and Dogs) which does not specifically prescribe a penalty shall be fined not less than $50 nor more than $250 plus costs, and/or jailed up to 30 days. ★No penalty imposed by this section shall be suspended.★ Any officer or warden who fails to perform any act, duty or obligation under this title shall be fined $50-100 and costs for each offense. Courts shall, within 20 days of trial or dismissal thereof of any prosecution, report in writing the result, the amount of fine/forfeiture collected, and the disposition to the Department, and remit all money collected (7-1304 through -1307).

Proof as to a part of a bird, animal or fish shall be sufficient to charge a violation for the whole of it. Violation as to a number of animals may be charged in the same count, and punished as a separate offense as to each animal, bird or fish. The justices of the peace have jurisdiction of all offenses unless another court is given exclusive jurisdiction (7-1308 and -1309).

See also Restrictions on Taking: Hunting and Trapping under HUNTING, FISHING AND TRAPPING PROVISIONS for additional fines for exceeding bag limits.

Illegal Taking of Wildlife

No person shall hunt, chase or pursue with intent to kill or possess any deer (7-living or dead) except those taken during the open season and during lawful hours in each county. All evidence, including weapons, ammunition, lights, communication systems, and/or instrumentalities, including motor vehicles, used in violation of this subsection may be seized and retained as evidence, and forfeited according to Superior Court jurisdiction and procedures. Violation of this subsection is a fine of $100-500, and/or jail up to 60 days, and loss of hunting privileges for two years. A subsequent offense is a fine of $500-1,000, and/or jail at least 6 months, and loss of hunting privileges for 5 years. Hunting in violation of license revocation is a fine of $100-500 (7-103).

License Revocations and Suspensions

The Department may revoke any hunting, fishing or trapping license, or any other license, and deny the right to secure such license or to hunt, fish or trap for a period within its discretion, but in no case longer than one year, if: ‣ the person has been convicted of violating any game or fish law; ‣ the person has been convicted in any court of having defaced, mutilated or carried away notices posted by a leaseholder, freeholder or the Department, or personal property or crops; ‣ the licensee has been convicted of an offense involving carelessness in the use of firearms while hunting and caused injury to any person, poultry or livestock; ‣the person has been convicted of an offense involving unlawful setting of forest, marsh or grass fires; ‣ it is established to the Department's satisfaction that the person, while hunting with firearms, was intoxicated.   ★The Department may revoke any hunting or trapping license for a period of three to five years if the licensee has been convicted of illegally possessing, tending or setting a killer, body-gripping trap.★   To revoke a license, the Department shall send a written notice to the licensee and shall furnish to license agents the names and addresses of all persons whose licenses have been revoked (7-512). Trapping during a period of license revocation is illegal with a fine of $1,000; the fine shall not be suspended (7-519).

Reward Payments

There is a **Wildlife Theft Prevention Special Fund** and an **Operation Game Theft** statewide telephone hotline to provide rewards for those who give information leading to the conviction of any person for unlawfully taking, possessing, shipping or selling wildlife (7-1312). (See Agency Funding Sources under state FISH AND WILDLIFE AGENCIES for details of this program.)

HABITAT PROTECTION

See Agency Funding Sources under state FISH AND WILDLIFE AGENCIES.

NATIVE AMERICAN WILDLIFE PROVISIONS: None.

DISTRICT OF COLUMBIA

Sources: District of Columbia Code Annotated, 1981, Titles 6, 16 and 22; 1989 Replacement Volume; 1992 Cumulative Supplement.

STATE WILDLIFE POLICY

While regulating against water pollution and except as required to protect against nuisance, the Mayor shall protect aquatic animals and shall preserve and restore aquatic life in District of Columbia (District) waters for aesthetic enjoyment, recreation, and industry (6-923).

RELEVANT WILDLIFE DEFINITIONS: See Definitions section of Appendices.

STATE FISH AND WILDLIFE AGENCIES

Agency Powers and Duties

The **District Council** is authorized to restrict, prohibit, regulate, and control hunting and fishing and the taking, possession, and sale of wild animals in the District, provided that: nothing herein shall authorize the Council to impose any requirement for a fishing license or fee of any nature whatsoever; nothing herein shall authorize the Council to prohibit, restrict, regulate, or control the killing, capture, purchase, sale, or possession of migratory birds as defined in regulations issued pursuant to the Migratory Bird Treaty Act and taken for scientific, propagating, or other purposes under permits issued by the Secretary of the Interior; and nothing herein shall authorize the Council to prohibit, restrict, regulate, or control the sale or possession of wild animals taken legally in any state, territory or US possession or in any foreign country, or produced on a game farm, except as may be necessary to protect the public health or safety (22-1628).

The **Secretary of the Interior** and the **Mayor** are authorized to delegate any of the functions to be performed by them under the authority of District game and fish laws (22-1632). The Mayor may enter into agreements with state and federal agencies to manage and protect aquatic life (6-923). The District Council is authorized to make such regulations as may be necessary to carry out the District's game and fish laws, provided that any regulations so issued shall be subject to the approval of the Secretary of the Interior insofar as they involve any District areas or waters under the Secretary's administrative jurisdiction (22-1632). Nothing in District game and fish law or in any regulation promulgated by the District Council under authority of the game and fish laws shall in any way impair the existing authority of the Secretary of the Interior to control and manage fish and wildlife on District land and waters under the Secretary's administrative jurisdiction (22-1633).

Agency Funding Sources

Revenues from a licensing regulatory scheme for protection of aquatic life shall be used only for protecting and managing aquatic life (6-923).

PROTECTED SPECIES OF WILDLIFE

No person shall own or keep five or more mammals, larger than a guinea pig and over the age of four months, without obtaining an animal hobby permit, except that this section shall not apply to a licensed pet shop, licensed veterinary hospital, circus or traveling exhibition. An owner applying for an animal hobby permit shall fully describe the kind and number of mammals to be maintained and the premises where the mammals are to be kept. No animal hobby permit shall be issued to an owner who maintains mammals for commercial purposes. For purposes of this section, "commercial purposes" shall not include the sale of offspring if such sales are occasional and are not the primary purpose for maintaining the mammals (6-1009).

GENERAL EXCEPTIONS TO PROTECTION

The District Mayor may protect against aquatic life which creates a nuisance in the District (6-923).

HUNTING, FISHING, TRAPPING PROVISIONS

General Provisions

The District Mayor shall study the number and well-being of aquatic plants and animals, and shall determine the need to license or otherwise limit fishing and other forms of hunting, sports or industry which take or destroy aquatic life or habitat. The mayor shall consider the economic impact upon the various segments of the public before establishing fees for licenses. The Mayor may establish fishing seasons and other seasons for hunting, sports or industry, which take or destroy aquatic life or the aquatic habitat (6-923).

Import, Export and Release Provisions

No person shall import into the District, display, offer for sale, trade, barter, exchange, or adoption, or give as a household pet any live fox, raccoon, skunk or ferret, except a person may offer these species to a public zoo, park, museum, or educational institution for educational, medical, scientific, or exhibition purposes (6-1008).

ANIMAL DAMAGE CONTROL

See GENERAL EXCEPTIONS TO PROTECTION.

ENFORCEMENT OF WILDLIFE LAWS

Enforcement Powers

Prosecutions for violations of the game and fish laws or regulations shall be conducted in the name of the District by the Corporation Counsel (22-1631). Authorized US or District government officers and employees are empowered, during business hours, to inspect any building or premises in or on which any business, trade, vocation or occupation requiring a license or permit is carried on, or any vehicle, boat, market box, market stall or cold-storage plant. No person shall refuse to permit any such inspection (22-1629).

Penalties

Any person convicted of violating any game and fish law, or any regulation made pursuant thereto, shall be fined not more than $300 or imprisoned not more than 90 days, or both (22-1631).

Illegal Taking of Wildlife

All rifles, shotguns, ammunition, bows, arrows, traps, seines, nets, boats, and other devices of every nature or description used by any person within the District when engaged in killing, ensnaring, trapping, or capturing any wild bird, wild mammal or fish contrary to District game and fish laws or regulations shall be seized by any police officer upon the arrest of such person on a charge of violating District laws or regulations, and be delivered to the Mayor. If the person so arrested is acquitted, the property seized shall be returned; if the person is convicted, the property shall, in the discretion of the court, be forfeited to the District, and sold at public auction, the proceeds to be deposited in the Treasury to District credit (22-1630).

HABITAT PROTECTION

Except as provided, no person shall discharge a pollutant into District waters (6-922).

NATIVE AMERICAN WILDLIFE PROVISIONS: None.

FLORIDA

Sources: Florida Statutes Annotated, 1990, Chapter 372; 1991 Cumulative Pocket Part.

STATE WILDLIFE POLICY

The legislature recognizes that the State of Florida harbors a wide diversity of fish and wildlife and that it is the policy of this state to conserve and wisely manage these resources, with particular attention to those species defined by the Game and Fresh Water Fish Commission, the Department of Natural Resources, or the US Department of the Interior as being endangered or threatened. As Florida has more endangered and threatened species than any other continental state, it is the intent of the legislature to provide for research and management to conserve and protect these species as a natural resource (372.072). (See also RELEVANT WILDLIFE DEFINITIONS.)

The legislature recognizes the value of maintaining ecologically healthy and stable populations of a wide diversity of fish and wildlife species and recognizes the need for monitoring, research, management, and public awareness of all wildlife species in order to guarantee that self-sustaining populations be conserved. ★The legislature further recognizes that research and management for game species traditionally have been supported by licenses and fees collected by the Commission for consumptive uses of wildlife and that no support mechanism is available for species not commonly pursued for sport or profit. It is the intent of the legislature that the funds provided herein be spent to identify and meet the needs of nongame wildlife as a first priority with the ultimate goal of establishing an integrated approach to the management and conservation of all native fish, wildlife and plants (372.991).★ (See Agency Funding Sources under STATE FISH AND WILDLIFE AGENCIES.)

★★The legislature finds that the release of large numbers of balloons inflated with lighter-than-air gases poses a danger and nuisance to the environment, particularly to wildlife and marine animals. It is unlawful to intentionally release within a 24-hour period 10 or more lighter than air balloons except for meteorological/scientific government agency balloons, hot air balloons recovered after launching, balloons released indoors, or balloons which are biodegradable or photodegradable, as determined by rule of the Marine Fisheries Commission, and which are closed by a hand-tied knot without string, ribbon or other attachments. Violation: noncriminal infraction; fine $250. Persons may petition the circuit court to enjoin the release of 10 or more balloons within their county (372.995).★★

The legislature finds that commercial and recreational fishing constitute activities of statewide importance and their continuation will benefit the health and welfare of the people. The legislature further finds that commercial and recreational fishing operations conducted in developing and urbanizing areas are potentially subject to curtailment by local government zoning and nuisance ordinances which may unreasonably force the closure of the productive fishing operations. It is the purpose of this act to prevent the curtailment or abolishment of fishing operations solely because the area in which they are located has changed in character or the operations are displeasing to neighboring residents. As used in this act, "commercial fishing operation" means any type of activity conducted on land, requiring location or storage of commercial fishing equipment such as fishing vessels, fishing gear, docks, piers, landing areas, cold storage facilities, including an activity necessary to prepare finfish or shellfish for refrigeration; it does not include operations with the sole or primary function of processing seafood. No commercial or recreational fishing operation shall be declared a public or private nuisance solely because of a change in ownership, or change in the character of the property around the locality of the operation. No local governing authority shall adopt an ordinance that declares commercial or recreational fishing operation to be a nuisance solely because of its nature, or a zoning ordinance that unreasonably forces its closure. Local governments may regulate to prevent, ameliorate, or remove nuisance conditions pursuant to local zoning codes by declaring such operation to be a nonconforming use. This act shall not be construed to permit an existing operation to change to a larger operation with regard to emitting more noise or odor, where the change violates local ordinances or regulations or creates a nuisance (372.993).

RELEVANT WILDLIFE DEFINITIONS: See Definitions section of Appendices.

STATE FISH AND WILDLIFE AGENCIES

Agency Structure

The **Game and Fresh Water Fish Commission** (Commission) consists of five members appointed by the Governor, confirmed by the Senate, for staggered terms of five years. A chairperson is selected by the members annually and may be removed by a majority vote. The Commission shall appoint, fix the salary of, and at pleasure remove, a suitable person, not a Commission member, as **Director** (372.01 and .04).

Agency Powers and Duties

The **Director** shall: ▸ keep minutes of Commission meetings; ▸ employ assistants; ▸ have full authority to represent the Commission in dealings with other state departments and federal agencies; ▸ report actions taken to the Commission; ▸ visit each county in the state at least once a year; ▸ appoint assistants and other employees; ▸ have other powers and duties as may be prescribed by the Commission in pursuance of its duties under Section 9, Article IV of the State Constitution (372.05).

The **Commission** may exercise powers, duties and authority granted by Section 9, Article IV of the Constitution of Florida by adoption of rules, regulations and orders in accordance with chapter 120 (372.021). The Commission, with the Governor's approval, may acquire lands and waters for the protection and propagation of game, fish, nongame birds or fur-bearing animals, or for hunting purposes, game farms, by purchase, lease, gift or otherwise to be known as state game lands. No lands shall be purchased at a price to exceed $10 per acre, nor be exempt from state, county or district taxation (372.12). The Commission is authorized to make and enforce all rules and regulations for the protection, control, operation or development of lands or waters owned by, leased by, or otherwise assigned to the Commission for fish or wildlife management, including the right of ingress and egress. Before rules are adopted, other than relating to wild animal life or freshwater aquatic life, the Commission shall obtain the consent in writing of the owner or custodian thereof (372.121).

★The Commission may authorize the establishment of citizen support organizations to provide assistance, funding and promotional support for Commission programs. Citizen support organizations are nonprofit and organized to: ▸ conduct programs and activities; ▸ raise funds; ▸ request and receive grants, gifts and bequests of money; ▸ acquire, receive, invest securities, funds or real/personal property; ▸ make expenditures for the Commission's benefit, but may not receive Commission funds unless authorized by the legislature, approved in writing by the Commission.★ The Commission may permit a citizen support organization to use Commission property, facilities and personnel free of charge within certain restrictions, and the groups shall provide an annual audit. Donors to groups may remain anonymous (372.0215). The Commission may arrange private publication of Commission-approved information brochures, pamphlets, videotapes and related materials for distribution in return for vendor advertising rights (372.0222).

The Commission is responsible for research and management of freshwater and upland species; the **Department of Natural Resources** (Department) for research and management of marine species. Recognizing that citizen awareness is a key element in the success of this plan, the Commission, the Department and the Office of Environmental Education are encouraged to work together to develop a public education program with emphasis on, but not limited to, both public and private schools. ★The Department of Natural Resources, the Marine Fisheries Commission or the Commission, in consultation with other agencies, may establish reduced speed zones along roads, streets and highways to protect endangered or threatened species (372.072).★ The Commission's **Division of Fisheries** is to regulate the promotion, marketing, quality control, processing, documentation standards, and scientific and economic study of commercial freshwater organisms (372.0225).

The Commission is directed to develop, manage and enforce laws on certain recreational sites in the water conservation areas of the Everglades from funds to be appropriated by the legislature when it can be accomplished without endangering the water quality and quantity and where environmental impact will be minimal, where extensive uncontrolled use of the interior regions of the everglades can be discouraged, and where there is potential for nature trails, bird study, fishing, hunting and target shooting (372.025). In an alligator management and trapping program that the Commission shall establish, it shall have the authority to adopt all rules necessary for full implementation, and may: ▸ regulate the marketing and sale of alligators, their hides, eggs, meat and byproducts, including development of a state-sanctioned sale; ► regulate the handling and processing of alligators, their eggs, hides, meat and byproducts for lawful and sanitary handling and processing; ► regulate commercial alligator farming operations for the captive propagation and rearing of alligators and their eggs; ► provide hide-grading services and certification of hide graders under Commission rules; ► provide public notice of state-sanctioned sales; ► market alligator hides or products obtained as a result of law enforcement actions or its nuisance alligator program (372.6672). The Commission shall conduct studies of all areas which it intends to open to alligator collection permits, including individual wet areas, lakes and rivers, and shall determine the safe yield of alligators for which permits may be issued. Studies shall be based upon biological information that indicates the number of alligators which can be removed from the system without long-term adverse impacts on population (372.6678).

The Commission may enter into cooperative agreements with the USFS for the development of game, bird, fish, reptile or fur-bearing animal management and demonstration projects, and may make, adopt, amend and repeal rules/regulations in cooperation with that agency for better control of hunting, fishing, and wildlife in national forests; may shorten or extend seasons, reduce bag limits, or close seasons on a species of game, bird, fish, reptile or fur-bearing animal within Florida law in national forests; and may set fees over and above the license fees for hunting in forests (372.74).

Agency Funding Sources

★★Within the Commission there is an **Endangered and Threatened Species Reward Trust Fund** to be used exclusively for rewards for providing information leading to the arrest and conviction of persons illegally killing or wounding or wrongfully possessing endangered and threatened species on the official list of species maintained by the Commission, or of persons who violate 372.667 (baiting of alligators) or 372.671 (killing Florida panthers). The fund shall be credited with money collected pursuant to 372.72 (fines, forfeitures, penalties collected relating to endangered species), donations from individuals and organizations and from legislative appropriations. The reward program is administered by the Commission which sets a schedule of rewards. Fund proceeds are to be spent only for rewards for information or for the promotion of the endangered and threatened species reward program (372.073).★★

The funds from the operation of the Commission and administration of laws and regulations pertaining to birds, game, fur-bearing animals, fresh water fish, reptiles and amphibians, together with other funds specifically provided for such purposes constitute the **State Game Trust Fund** and shall be used by the Commission only for carrying out the provisions hereof. The Commission may not obligate itself beyond the current resources of the fund unless authorized by the legislature (372.09).

The Commission shall expend the revenues generated from the sale of the **Florida Waterfowl Stamp** or that pro rata portion of a license that includes waterfowl hunting privileges as follows: a maximum of 5% of the gross revenues for administrative costs; a maximum of 25% for waterfowl research; and a maximum of 70% for projects, in consultation with the Waterfowl Advisory Council, for protecting and propagating migratory waterfowl and for the development, restoration, maintenance and preservation of wetlands. The intent of this section is to expand waterfowl research and management and increase waterfowl populations without detracting from other programs. The Commission shall document the use of these funds annually to the Governor, Speaker of the House, and the President of the Senate (372.5712). The Commission shall use revenue from the sale of the **Turkey Stamp** or that pro rata portion of a license that includes turkey hunting privileges for research and management of wild turkeys; however, a maximum of 5% may be spent on administrative costs. The intent of this section is to expand wild turkey research and management and to increase wild turkey populations without detracting from other programs. The Commission shall report annually to the Governor and legislature (372.5715). The Commission shall use revenue from the sale of the **Management Area Stamp** or that pro rata portion of a license that includes management area privileges as follows: 30% for the purchase of lands for public hunting, fishing and other outdoor recreation, and 70% for the lease, management and protection of lands for such purposes (372.573).

Within the Commission, the **Florida Panther Research and Management Trust Fund** is to be used exclusively to: ► manage and protect existing Florida panther populations by increasing panther food sources where food is a limiting factor; ► determine conflicts between public use and panther survival, and maintain sufficient genetic variability in existing populations; ► educate the public concerning the value of the panther and the necessity for panther management; ► reestablish Florida panthers into areas of suitable habitat by assessing the necessity of a captive breeding program for reintroduction of the panthers; ▸ select reintroduction sites and investige human sociological aspects; ▸ assess the potential for panther habitat acquisition. The Commission is authorized to receive donations for the fund (372.672).

The **Wildlife Law Enforcement Trust Fund** is to provide moneys for Commission law enforcement activities to operate programs for conservation, enhancement and regulation of wildlife and freshwater aquatic resources and to conduct programs to educate the public about the enforcement of wildlife laws and regulations. Moneys that accrue to the fund by law and donation must be deposited into the fund (372.9906). Within the Commission is a **Nongame Wildlife Trust Fund**, to be credited with moneys collected pursuant to 319.32(3) and 320.02(8), legislative appropriations and donations from individuals and organizations. Proceeds shall be used for: documentation of population trends of nongame wildlife and assessment of wildlife habitat in coordination with the data base of Florida natural areas inventory; establishment of conservation, management and regulatory programs for nongame wildlife of the state; public education programs. The Commission may enter into cooperative agreements with related agencies to coordinate nongame programs (372.991). The **Fish and Wildlife Habitat Trust Fund** is to be used for acquiring and managing lands for conservation of fish and wildlife. Title to acquired lands is in the Board of Trustees of the **Internal Improvement Trust Fund**. The Commission shall manage the lands for the primary purpose of maintaining and enhancing their habitat value for fish and wildlife, or other uses. Land acquisition shall be voluntary, negotiated acquisition. Moneys which accrue to the trust fund may include, but not be limited to, donations, grants, development-of-regional-impact wildlife mitigation contributions, or legislative appropriations (372.074).

The **Lifetime Fish and Wildlife Trust Fund** is to be used for supporting fish and wildlife conservation programs. The principal of the fund shall be derived from gifts, grants and contributions specifically designated for inclusion in the fund and proceeds from the sale of lifetime licenses issued under 372.57, with the exception of the saltwater portion of the license. The trust is derived from a contractual relationship between the state and the public whose investments contribute to the fund, making it subject to the following restrictions: ▸ no expenditures from the principal of the fund; ▸ interest income from fund investments shall be spent to further the Commission's regulatory and executive powers with respect to the management, protection and conservation of wild animal life and freshwater aquatic life; ▸ no expenditures from the interest income from sale of lifetime licenses shall be made until license holders attain the age of 16; ▸ limitations specified by the donors on the uses of the interest income shall be respected but shall not be binding; ▸ no repeal or modification of this chapter or section 9, Article IV of the State Constitution shall alter the fundamental purposes to which the fund may be applied; ▸ dissolution of the Commission shall not invalidate a lifetime license issued (372.105). There is also a **Dedicated License Trust Fund**, to be credited with moneys collected pursuant to 372.57 and 370.0605 for five-year licenses (372.106).

Agency Advisory Boards

The **Waterfowl Advisory Council** consists of three members, one each appointed by the Governor, the Speaker of the House, and the President of the Senate. Members may be representative of appropriate state agencies, private conservation groups or private citizens and shall possess knowledge and experience in waterfowl management and protection, serve four-year terms and be eligible for reappointment. The Council shall advise the Commission regarding administration of revenues generated by sale of the Florida Waterfowl Stamp, and regarding the establishment and operating of projects for protection and propagation of migratory waterfowl and the development, restoration, maintenance and preservation of wetlands (372.5714).

The **Florida Panther Technical Advisory Council** within the Commission consists of five members with technical knowledge and expertise in the research and management of large mammals. Two members shall represent state or federal agencies responsible for management of endangered species; two members, with specific experience in the research and management of large felines/mammals, shall be appointed from universities/colleges; one member, with similar expertise, shall be appointed from the public at large. Members serve four-year terms. The Council: ▸ advises the Commission on technical matters concerning the Florida panther recovery program and advises specific actions needed to accomplish the purposes of this act; ▸ reviews and comments on research and management programs and practices to identify potential harm to the Florida panther population; ▸ provides a forum for technical review and discussion of the status and development of the Florida panther recovery program (372.673).

There is a **Nongame Wildlife Advisory Council** consisting of nine members appointed by the Governor: one representative each from the Commission, the Department of Natural Resources and the USFWS; the Director of the Florida Museum of Natural History; one from a professional wildlife organization; one from a private wildlife institution; one from a Florida university/college who has expertise in nongame biology; and two members from conservation organizations. Members serve four year-terms and are eligible for reappointment. The Council recommends to the Commission policies, objectives and specific actions for nongame wildlife research and management (372.992).

PROTECTED SPECIES OF WILDLIFE

It is unlawful to kill an "endangered species" known as the Florida panther (*Felis concolor coryi*), or to kill a member of the species of panther (*Felis concolor*) occurring in the wild. Unlawfully killing a Florida panther or a member of the species of panther occurring in the wild, is a felony of the third degree, punishable as provided in 775.082, 775.083 and 775.084 (372.671). It is unlawful intentionally to kill or wound a fish or wildlife designated by.the Commission as endangered, threatened, or of special concern, or intentionally to destroy the eggs or nest of the fish or wildlife, except as provided for in rules of the Commission, the Department of Natural Resources, or the Marine Fisheries Commission. A violation is a felony of the third degree, punishable as provided in 775.082, 775.083 and 775.084 (372.0725).

No person or firm shall keep, possess, or exhibit a poisonous or venomous reptile without a permit. The permit is to be issued only when assured that all provisions of 372.86 through 372.91 and other Commission regulations will be fully complied with in all respects and is subject to revocation for violation of a Commission regulation relating to the keeping, possessing and exhibiting of reptiles. No person shall exhibit to the public, with or without charge, a poisonous or venomous reptile without posting a bond in the penal sum of $1,000 conditioned that the exhibitor will indemnify and save harmless all persons from injury or damage from reptiles and shall comply with all Commission regulations. All persons licensed to keep/exhibit poisonous reptiles shall provide safe, secure housing in a manner approved by the Commission. Poisonous reptiles may be transported only in cloth sacks in ventilated boxes with "danger" label as specified. No person except the licensee or the licensee's authorized employee shall open a pit, cage or other container which contains poisonous or venomous reptiles. The Commission may prescribe other rules necessary to prevent the escape of poisonous and venomous reptiles (372.86 through .92). Reptiles are subject to inspection by Commission officers to determine if they are securely housed, and deficiencies must be remedied within 30 days or the license is subject to revocation (372.901). All persons sponsoring and conducting an organized poisonous reptile hunt for whatever purpose shall comply with the above provisions, and hunts must be registered with the Department of State and with the Commission (372.912).

See also RELEVANT WILDLIFE DEFINITIONS; HUNTING, FISHING, TRAPPING PROVISIONS; and ENFORCEMENT OF WILDLIFE LAWS.

GENERAL EXCEPTIONS TO PROTECTION

It is unlawful to possess wildlife as defined in this act, whether indigenous to Florida or not, without a permit. Class 1 wildlife, as classified by the Commission, is wildlife which, because of its nature, habits or status, shall not be possessed as a personal pet. Class 2 wildlife is considered to present a real or potential threat to human safety, and a permit fee is $100. The Commission shall promulgate rules defining Class 1 and 2 types of wildlife and formulate regulations to ensure that permits are granted only to persons qualified to possess and care for wildlife and maintain them in sanitary surroundings and appropriate neighborhoods. Permitted wildlife exhibitors are exempt from these provisions. Violators shall be punished under 372.83 (372.922). (See also ANIMAL DAMAGE CONTROL and HUNTING FISHING, TRAPPING PROVISIONS.)

In order to provide humane treatment and sanitary surroundings for wild animals kept in captivity, no person or firm shall possess in captivity for public display, with or without charge, or for public sale any wildlife, specifically birds, mammals and reptiles, whether indigenous to Florida or not, without a Commission permit; however, this does not apply to wildlife not protected by law or Commission regulations. Applicants for a permit must state the place, number and species of wildlife to be held in captivity and show when, where and in what manner the applicant came into possession of the wildlife, such sources not to be revealed by the Commission except in connection with a violation of this section or when required as evidence. The Commission may inspect premises where captive wildlife are held and may confiscate or release specimens of wildlife when unsanitary, unsafe conditions are found or there is evidence of maltreatment or neglect after warning the owner in writing of the unsatisfactory conditions and affording a 30-day period for remedy. These provisions do not apply to municipal, county, state or other publicly owned wildlife exhibit, nor to a traveling zoo, circus or exhibit licensed under chapter 205 (372.921).

HUNTING, FISHING, TRAPPING PROVISIONS

Licenses and Permits

No person, except as provided herein, shall take game, freshwater fish, or fur-bearing animals without a license or stamp (372.57). Making false statements on a license application or entering false information on a license in order to avoid prosecution is a second degree misdemeanor, and the license shall be null and void (372.58 and .581). The Commission shall establish the form for the licenses and stamps (372.561).

It is unlawful for a person born on or after June 1, 1975, to take wild animal life with a firearm, gun, bow or crossbow without completing a hunter safety course and having a certificate in possession. The Commission shall coordinate a statewide hunter safety course which shall be offered in every county and consist of 12-16 hours of instruction in safe handling of firearms, conservation and hunting ethics. This section does not apply to persons hunting in their county of residence on their homestead or the homestead of their spouse or minor child, or to minor children on parent's homestead. Violation: misdemeanor of the second degree (372.5717).

Restrictions on Taking

No person may throw or place dynamite, lyddite, gunpowder, cannon cracker, acids, filtration discharge, debris from mines, Indian berries, sawdust, green walnuts, walnut leaves, creosote, oil or other explosives or deleterious substance into state fresh waters. Nothing herein may be construed as preventing the release of water slightly discolored by mining operations or water escaping from such operations as the result of providential causes (372.75). It is unlawful to cause dyestuff, coal tar, oil, sawdust, poison or deleterious substance to be thrown, run or drained into state fresh running waters in quantities sufficient to injure, stupefy or kill fish at or below the point of substance discharge, provided that a person or firm engaged in a mining industry may cause water handled or used in a branch of such industry to be discharged on the surface of land where the industry is being carried on under precautionary measures as the Commission approves. Violation: misdemeanor of the second degree for the first offense; misdemeanor of the first degree for a second/subsequent offense, punishable under 775.082 and 775.083 (372.85).

No game fish taken from, or caught in, a lake with an area in excess of 500 square miles shall be sold for consumption unless it is tagged according to Commission rules. Bass or pickerel taken by a method other than hook and line shall be returned immediately to the water. Trawls and haul seines shall not be operated within one mile of rooted aquatic vegetation. No freshwater game fish shall be taken from a lake less than 500 square miles in area other than with pole and line; rod and reel; or plug, bob, spinner, spoon, or other artificial bait or lure, nor offered for sale or sold (372.653).

Restrictions on Taking: Alligators

It is unlawful to engage in the business of a dealer or buyer in alligator skins or green or dried furs or purchase the skins within the state without a license, and reports showing number and kind of hides bought and the name of the trapper must be made each two weeks during open season (372.66).

No person shall intentionally feed an wild American alligator (*Alligator mississippiensis*) or American crocodile (*Crocodylus acutus*) except those in protected captivity under Commission permit for educational, scientific, or commercial purposes. Violation: misdemeanor of the second degree punishable under 775.082 and 775.083 (372.667). It is unlawful to use the word "gator" or "alligator" in connection with the sale of a product derived or made from the skins of crocodilia or in connection with their sale. Violation: misdemeanor (372.665).

No person shall take or possess an alligator or its eggs without a trapping license authorizing the licensee to take the same and to sell, possess, and process an alligator and its hide and meat in accordance with Commission rules. In order to assure the optimal utilization of the estimated available alligator resource and to ensure adequate control of the alligator management and harvest, the Commission may limit the number of persons taking alligators or eggs from the wild. No person who has been convicted of illegal taking of alligators under 372.663 or 372.664 or Commission rules relating to taking crocodilian species shall be eligible for a license for five years subsequent to conviction. If conviction involves the unauthorized taking of an endangered crocodilian species, no license shall be issued for ten years after the conviction. No person shall take or possess an alligator egg occurring in the wild without an alligator egg collection permit in addition to the alligator farming license. The Commission may assess up to $5 per egg on the permit for taking. The Commission shall adopt criteria by rule for appropriate qualifications for alligator collectors who receive permits (372.6673). No person shall take or possess an alligator occurring in the wild unless it is tagged as required by Commission rule. One-third of the revenue from hatchling tags shall be expended for alligator husbandry research. Hide validation tags are required for wild alligator hides. The number of tags available shall be determined so as to equal the safe yield of alligators pursuant to 372.6678 (372.6674). (See also Illegal Taking of Wildlife under ENFORCEMENT OF WILDLIFE LAWS.)

Commercial and Private Enterprise Provisions

Any person who operates a private hunting preserve commercially or otherwise shall have a license for each preserve, provided that during the open seasons established for wild game a private individual may take artificially propagated game up to the bag limit for the species without payment of the license fee, and if the individual charges a fee for taking game, the individual shall pay the license fee and comply with Commission rules relative to private hunting preserve operations. A commercial hunting preserve license is available only to those private hunting preserves operated exclusively for commercial purposes, open to the public, and for which a uniform fee is charged to patrons for hunting privileges, and patrons are exempt from other state licensure requirements (372.661).

Any private landowner may, after obtaining a license from the Commission, establish and operate a private preserve and farm, not exceeding 640 acres, for the protection, preservation, propagation, rearing and production of game birds and animals for private and commercial purposes, provided that no two game preserves shall join each other or be connected. Game preserves must be fenced so that domestic game may not escape, nor wild game enter, and equipped so as to provide sufficient food and humane treatment for the game. Game produced on private game preserves is considered domestic game and private property and may be sold or disposed of. Live game may be purchased, sold, shipped for propagation and restocking purposes only. Game may be sold for food only during the open season for game. All game must be killed by means other than shooting, except during the open season, and must be tagged according to Commission rule. Violation: misdemeanor of the second degree; a subsequent violation, misdemeanor of the first degree. Violation: license forfeiture for one year (372.16).

Import, Export and Release Provisions

No person shall import or place in the fresh waters of the state a freshwater fish of a species, or import for sale or use, or release a species of the animal kingdom not indigenous to Florida without a permit from the Commission, which is authorized to issue or deny the permit upon completion of studies of the species to determine any detrimental effect it might have on the ecology of the state. Violation: misdemeanor of the first degree, punishable as provided in 775.082 and 775.083 (372.26 and .265). No person shall release, permit to be released or be responsible for the release of any *Myocastor coypu*, commonly known as nutria. No person shall have in possession for sale or otherwise any nutria without a license from the Commission and nutria must be housed according to Commission rules. Violation: misdemeanor of the second degree and confiscation of the nutria (372.98). The Commission shall promulgate regulations to control the importation of caiman (372.981).

ANIMAL DAMAGE CONTROL

Any person cultivating agricultural crops may apply to the Commission for a permit to take or kill deer on land currently being cultivated. When demonstrated to the Commission that taking deer is justified because of crop damage, it may issue a limited permit to take/kill deer (372.99).

ENFORCEMENT OF WILDLIFE LAWS

Enforcement Powers

The Commission, the Director and the Director's assistants, and each wildlife officer are constituted peace officers with the power to make arrests for violations of state laws when committed in the presence of the officer or when committed on lands under the management of the Commission. Laws applicable to arrests by peace officers are applicable to these persons, who may enter upon state land or waters to perform their lawful duties without committing trespass. Officers have the power and authority to enforce throughout the state all laws relating to game, nongame birds, fresh water fish, and fur-bearing animals and all Commission rules/regulations relating to wild animal life and fresh water aquatic life and the power to: ▸ go upon all premises, posted or otherwise; ▸ execute warrants and search warrants; ▸ serve subpoenas; ▸ carry firearms, concealed or otherwise; ▸ arrest upon probable cause without warrant a person found in the act of violating the laws and to examine any person, boat, vehicle, game bag, camp, or tent in the presence of any person belonging to the camp or tent when the officer has reason to believe any law has been violated; ▸ secure and execute search warrants and enter any building or car and break open and examine the contents of any apartment, chest, locker or other container and examine the contents; ▸ seize and take possession of wild animal life or fresh water aquatic life illegally taken or possessed by any person (372.07).

The prosecuting officers of the several courts of criminal jurisdiction shall investigate and prosecute all violations relating to game, freshwater fish, nongame birds and fur-bearing animals (372.70). Persons who fail to respond to the citation shall be charged with a misdemeanor, in addition to the charge relating to wildlife or freshwater fish (372.701). All moneys collected from fines or forfeitures of bail shall be deposited in the county of the convictions, except for moneys from violations of the rules, regulations or Commission orders concerning endangered/threatened species, or of violations of 372.662, 372.663, 372.667, or 372.671 (offenses relating to illegal taking of alligators and/or Florida panther) which shall be deposited in the Endangered and Threatened Species Reward Trust Fund (372.72).

Any certified law enforcement officer of the Department or Commission, upon receiving information from any law enforcement officer stationed on the ground, on the water or in the air, that a driver or occupant of any vehicle, boat or airboat has violated any section of chapter 327, 328, 370 or 372 may arrest the person when there is proper identification of the vehicle, boat or airboat and probable grounds to believe that the person has committed or is committing an offense (372.071). A search warrant may be issued by a Commission officer to search private dwellings used for unlawful sale or purchase of wildlife or freshwater fish being kept unlawfully therein, the warrant to be issued only upon probable cause supported by sworn affidavit of some creditable witness (372.761).

Criminal Penalties

In all cases of arrest and conviction for the use of illegal nets, traps or fishing devices, such devices are declared to be a nuisance and shall be seized; the court shall order illegal devices forfeited to the Commission immediately after trial conviction. When ownership of illegal devices is unknown, the officer shall obtain a court order forfeiting them to the Commission, which may destroy them. Devices used illegally shall be seized and forfeited (372.31). All sums received from sale or other disposition of seized property shall be paid into the county fine and forfeiture fund (372.319). The legislature deems that the sections above are necessary for more efficient and proper enforcement of the statutes prohibiting the illegal use of nets, traps or fishing devices and a lawful exercise of the police power of the state for protection of the public welfare, health, and safety of the people of the state; all provisions of this law shall be liberally construed for the accomplishment of these purposes (372.321). All game and freshwater fish seized shall, upon conviction, or sooner if the court so orders, be forfeited and given to a charitable institution. All furs or hides seized shall, upon conviction, be forfeited to the Commission which shall sell them and deposit the proceeds into the State Game Trust Fund. (372.73). (See also Illegal Taking of Wildlife in this section.)

It is a misdemeanor of the second degree, punishable as provided in 775.082 and 775.083, to violate Commission rules, regulations or orders that: ▸ specify season or time periods for the taking of freshwater fish or wildlife; ▸ specify bag limits or restrict methods of taking freshwater fish or wildlife; ▸ relate to the sale, possession for sale, purchase, transfer, transportation or importation of freshwater fish or wildlife; ▸ prohibit public access for specified periods to wildlife management areas; ▸ require a fee to obtain a permit to possess captive wildlife or keeping of records relating to captive wildlife; ▸ violate any other Commission rule, regulation or order. Unless otherwise provided, a first offense is misdemeanor of the second degree; a second or subsequent offense, a misdemeanor of the first degree, punishable as provided in 775.082 or 775.083. The court may order suspension or revocation of license or permit if the person commits a criminal offense specified in this chapter or a noncriminal infraction specified in this section (372.83).

Civil Penalties

★It is a noncriminal infraction, punishable as provided in 372.711, to violate any rules, regulations or orders relating to: ▸ the filing of reports or other documents required of licensees/permittees; ▸ fish management areas; ▸ quota hunt permits, daily use permits, hunting zone assignments, camping restrictions, use of alcoholic beverages, vehicle use, and check station requirements within wildlife management areas; ▸ requirement of permits to possess captive wildlife for personal use; ▸ establishment of size or slot limits for freshwater game fish; ▸ rules, regulations or orders regulating vessel size or registration of off-road vehicles or airboats operated on state lands; ▸ section 372.57, hunting, fishing, trapping licenses; ▸ section 372.988, hunter orange requirements for deer hunters. Failure to pay the civil penalty specified in 372.711 within 30 days after being cited for a noncriminal infraction is a misdemeanor of the second degree punishable as provided in 775.082, 775.083, and 775.084 (372.83), and forfeiture of any license or permit. If violation occurs in the open season, relating to game, no license or permit shall be issued to the person during the remainder of the open season; if during closed season, no permit or license may be issued to the person for the next open season (372.84).★

The civil penalty for any noncriminal infraction involving the license and stamp requirements of 372.57 is $50 in addition to the cost of the license or stamp involved in the infraction. The civil penalty for any other noncriminal infraction is $50, except as otherwise provided. Persons cited may pay the civil penalty within 30 days of the citation or forfeit bond by not appearing. Persons electing to appear before the county court are deemed to have waived the limitations on the civil penalty, and the court, after a hearing, may impose a civil penalty not to exceed $500 (372.711).

Illegal Taking of Wildlife

It is unlawful intentionally to kill, injure, possess, or capture, or attempt to do such to an alligator or other crocodilian, or their eggs, unless authorized by Commission rules. Violation: a felony of the third degree, punishable as provided in 775.082, 775.083 or 775.084 in addition to other punishment provided by law. Any equipment, including but not limited to, weapons, vehicles, boats and lines, used in the violation of any law, rule, regulation or order relating to alligators, other crocodilia or their eggs shall, upon conviction, be confiscated and disposed of according to Commission regulations (372.663). Except as otherwise provided by Commission rule for limited collection of alligators in designated areas, display or use of a light where alligators might be known to inhabit, in a manner capable of disclosing the presence of alligators, together with the possession of firearms, spear guns, gigs and harpoons customarily used for taking alligators, one hour after sunset and one hour before sunrise is prima facie evidence of an intent to violate the provisions of law regarding the protection of alligators (372.664). It is unlawful to sell any stuffed baby alligator or other baby crocodilia product. No person shall sell any alligator product manufactured from a species declared endangered by the USFW or the Commission. Violation: misdemeanor of the first degree (372.6645). (See also Licenses and Permits under HUNTING, FISHING, TRAPPING PROVISIONS.) Whenever the sale, possession, or transporting of alligators or alligator skins is prohibited by state law or Commission regulation, a violation is a misdemeanor of the first degree, punishable as provided in 775.082 and 775.083 (372.662). (See also PROTECTED SPECIES OF WILDLIFE.) Whoever takes/kills any deer or wild turkey, or possesses a freshly killed deer or wild turkey, during the closed season, or whoever takes or attempts to take deer or wild turkey using gun and light in or out of closed season, is guilty of a misdemeanor of the first degree, punishable under 775.082 and 775.083, and shall forfeit issued license or permit. A license may not be obtained for three years following violation on a first offense. Any person guilty of a second or subsequent violation shall be permanently ineligible for a license or permit. The display or use of a light where deer might be found, together with possession of firearms/other weapons customarily used in taking deer, between one hour after sunset and one hour before sunrise, is prima facie evidence of an intent to violate these provisions. Whoever takes or kills any doe deer, fawn or baby deer, or deer, male or female, which does not have one or more antlers at least five inches in length except as provided by Commission rule during the open season, is guilty of a misdemeanor of the first degree, and may be required to forfeit any license or permit for three years on the first offense. A second/subsequent violation makes a person permanently ineligible for a license or permit. Possession for sale or sale of deer or wild turkey taken in violation of this chapter or Commission regulations is a felony of the third degree, punishable under 775.082, 775.083, or 775.084. Entering upon private property and shining lights without the express permission of the owner and with the intent to take deer by utilizing shining lights is a misdemeanor of the second degree (372.99).

Any vehicle, vessel, animal, gun, light or other hunting device used in the commission of an offense prohibited by 372.99 shall be seized and delivered to the Commission, with details of facts and circumstances under which it was seized and the reason that it was seized. Upon conviction, the property shall be forfeited, and proceeds of sale of the property shall be paid into the State Game Trust Fund, and if not sold, delivered to the Director of the Commission (372.9901).

Whoever possesses, moves, or transports any black bass, bream, speckled perch or other freshwater game fish in commercial quantities in violation of law or Commission rules is guilty of a misdemeanor of the first degree. "Commercial quantities" is a quantity of game fish of 150 or more pounds, and the possession, movement, or transportation of freshwater game fish in excess of the weight is prima facie evidence of possession/transportation for commercial purposes (372.9903). Any vehicle, vessel or other transportation device used, except common carriers, shall be seized, and on conviction, shall be forfeited (372.9904).

Reward Payments

The Commission is authorized to offer rewards of up to $500 to any person furnishing information leading to the arrest and conviction of any person who has inflicted or attempted to inflict bodily injury upon any wildlife officer engaged in the enforcement of the provisions of this chapter or Commission rules (372.911). See also Agency Funding Sources under STATE FISH AND WILDLIFE AGENCIES for information on the Endangered and Threatened Species Reward Trust Fund.

HABITAT PROTECTION

See Agency Funding Sources under STATE FISH AND WILDLIFE AGENCIES.

NATIVE AMERICAN WILDLIFE PROVISIONS

No recreational site will be developed on any Indian reservation as created by chapter 285 (in Florida Everglades water conservation areas) without first obtaining written approval from the Indians of the reservation lands affected (372.025).

GEORGIA

Sources: Official Code of Georgia, 1986, Titles 12 and 27; 1992 Cumulative Supplement.

STATE WILDLIFE POLICY

The ownership of, jurisdiction over, and control of all wildlife, as defined in this title, are declared to be in the State of Georgia, in its sovereign capacity to be controlled, regulated and disposed of in accordance with this title. To hunt, trap, fish, possess or transport wildlife is declared to be a privilege to be exercised only in accordance with the laws granting such privilege, and every person exercising this privilege does so subject to the right of the state to regulate (27-1-3). (See also Import, Export and Release Provisions under HUNTING, FISHING, TRAPPING PROVISIONS and Illegal Taking under ENFORCEMENT OF WILDLIFE LAWS.)

The General Assembly finds it is the best interest of the state to provide for the conservation of nongame wildlife species for the benefit and nonconsumptive use of Georgia citizens. Historically, wildlife conservation programs have been focused on the more recreationally and commercially important game species. As a consequence, such programs have been largely financed by hunting and fishing license revenues and federal assistance based on excise taxes on hunting and fishing equipment. These traditional financing mechanisms are neither adequate or fully appropriate to meet the needs of nongame wildlife conservation and habitat acquisition (12-3-600).

RELEVANT WILDLIFE DEFINITIONS: See Definitions section of Appendices.

STATE FISH AND WILDLIFE AGENCIES

Agency Structure

There is a **Board of Natural Resources** (Board) consisting of one member from each state congressional district, four members from the state at large and one member each from six specified counties. The members are appointed by the Governor, confirmed by the Senate and serve for seven years. Members shall be representative of all areas and functions within the **Department of Natural Resources** (Department) (12-2-21).

Conservation Rangers are a unit of peace officers within the Department. Rangers include, but are not limited to, the Commissioner and other supervisory personnel. The Commissioner has the power to appoint the number of Rangers necessary to carry out assigned duties. **Deputy Conservation Rangers** are appointed by the Board and must have duties relating to the protection of natural resources, and have all or part of the powers and duties of Conservation Rangers. If Deputy Rangers are not Department employees, they shall receive no compensation and must post $5,000 bond. The Board has the power to adopt rules and regulations concerning qualifications, appointments and other matters pertaining to the Deputy Conservation Rangers (27-1-16 and -17).

Agency Powers and Duties

The **Board of Natural Resources** (Board) has the power to: ▸ establish general policies to be followed by the Department under this title; ▸ promulgate rules and regulations for administration of this title, including rules to regulate times, places, numbers, species, sizes, manner, methods, ways, means, and devices of killing, taking, capturing, transporting, storing, selling, using, or consuming wildlife, and to carry out this title and rules and regulations requiring daily, season or annual use permits for hunting and fishing in designated streams, lakes, and game management areas; ▸ promulgate rules and regulations to protect wildlife, the public and state natural resources in the event of fire, flood, disease, pollution or other emergency situation without complying with Title 50 of the Georgia Administrative Procedure Act. Except as specifically provided, all rules and regulations under this title shall be promulgated pursuant to Chapter 13 of Title 50, Georgia Administrative Procedure Act (27-1-4 and -5).

The **Department of Game and Fish** (Department) has the power to: ▸ acquire by purchase, condemnation, lease, agreement, gift, or devise lands or waters for purposes enumerated here and develop, operate and maintain the same

Georgia

for fish hatcheries, nursery ponds, game farms, sanctuaries, reservations, refuges; wildlife restoration, propagation, protection, preservation, research or management; and public hunting, fishing, or trapping areas, for use in accordance with the law and regulations; ▸ capture, propagate, transport, purchase, sell, band, or release a wildlife species for propagation, research or stocking purposes, to safeguard habitats, and to exercise control measures of nuisance or destructive species; ▸ enter into cooperative agreements with educational institutions and state, federal and other agencies to promote wildlife management, conservation and research; ▸ publish and distribute magazines, pamphlets, books or literature to inform and educate the public concerning the wildlife resources and the Department's functions and duties; ▸ contract with private landowners for managing and operating public hunting and fishing areas on their property; ▸ develop, issue and reproduce an official waterfowl stamp for promoting, supporting, or otherwise assisting any waterfowl program, including public education, research, and acquisition of wetlands (27-1-6). (See also Agency Funding Sources under STATE FISH AND WILDLIFE AGENCIES.)

Conservation Rangers have the power and authority to: ▸ enforce state laws on Department controlled and owned property; ▸ enforce laws pertaining to Department functions, or any law violated in conjunction with a violation of such; ▸ enforce any law upon order of the Governor or to protect life or property; ▸ assist upon request the Department of Public Safety and Georgia Bureau of Investigation; ▸ cooperate with and render assistance to any law enforcement agency, or other state political subdivision, in prevention, detection or arrest of persons who violate criminal laws of Georgia or other states. Conservation and Deputy Rangers, when authorized by the Board, may arrest persons accused of violating any law or regulation which officers are empowered to enforce. The powers of Conservation Rangers shall include, but not be limited to: ▸ enforcing all wildlife laws, rules and regulations; ▸ executing all warrants and search warrants for the violation of wildlife laws; ▸ serving subpoenas issued for all offenses against wildlife laws, rules and regulations; ▸ arresting without warrant persons found violating wildlife laws; ▸ seizing and taking possession of wildlife or parts illegally caught, killed, captured, possessed, controlled or shipped or about to be shipped; ▸ carrying firearms; ▸ seizing as evidence without warrant a device other than a boat, vehicle or aircraft, when they have cause to believe its possession or use is in violation of wildlife laws or regulations; ▸ entering and inspecting a commercial cold storage facility; ▸ exercising full authority of peace officers while in performance of duties. Conservation Rangers and other peace officers shall seize wildlife taken or possessed illegally, to be disposed of as the Commissioner directs unless the possessor files a civil action against the state. If an action is filed, items shall be held unless perishable or unable to be stored; items then may be disposed of and the proceeds held in escrow until final disposition. Items with no marketable value may be donated to a charitable institution (27-1-18 through -21).

Agency Funding Sources

A special fund to be known as the **Nongame Wildlife Conservation and Wildlife Habitat Acquisition Fund** is established for nongame wildlife conservation programs and habitat acquisition, to consist of money contributed through the income tax return contribution mechanism, Departmental fund raising or promotional programs and other contributions to the fund and interest thereon. All fund balances shall be deposited in an interest-bearing account and carried forward each year so that no part of the fund may be deposited in the general treasury. The Department shall administer the fund and prepare an accounting of funds for the Board and for the public on request (12-3-602).

All funds resulting from the operation of the Department, excluding fines, but including license fees, shall be paid into general funds and appropriated to the Department each year. ★★The Department may accept grants and donations, monetary or real property, for purpose of creating and maintaining state natural resources conservation camps. Surplus money made by the camps shall be used for the camps.★★ Moneys from operation of wildlife management areas and refuges and public fishing areas shall be used for their operation and maintenance. Proceeds from fines and forfeitures arising from criminal prosecutions, except as otherwise specified, shall be applied to payment of fees of the trial court officers and court costs. Remaining moneys go to the county treasurer for deposit in the general funds of the county (27-1-13 and -14). The **Waterfowl Stamp Fund** (Fund) consists of all moneys paid to the Department as royalties derived from the sale of official waterfowl stamps and contributed to the Fund. Fund balances shall be deposited in an interest-bearing account and carried forward each year so that no part thereof may be deposited in the general treasury (27-1-6).

PROTECTED SPECIES OF WILDLIFE

Except as provided, it is unlawful to hunt, trap, fish, take, possess, or transport a nongame species of wildlife, except that the following species may be taken by any method except those prohibited by law or regulation: rats, mice, coyotes, armadillos, groundhogs, beaver, fresh-water turtles, poisonous snakes, frogs, spring lizards, fiddler crabs, fresh-water crayfish, fresh-water mussels and nutria. Nothing in this section authorizes taking of a species protected under the federal Endangered Species Act or under a state law which protects endangered or threatened species. It is unlawful to: ▸ hunt or take a bear except during open season; ▸ buy sell, barter or exchange a bear or bear part; ▸ possess or transport a freshly killed bear or bear part except during open season. Violation: misdemeanor of a high and aggravated nature; fine $500-5,000; or jail up to 12 months; or both. The court may order restitution be paid to the Department of not less than $1,500. Equipment used illegally, excluding motor vehicles, is declared to be contraband and forfeited to the state. Hunting and fishing privileges shall be suspended for three years. It is unlawful to use bait to concentrate the bear population in an area or to lure them to give a hunter an unnatural advantage. Violation: misdemeanor of a high and aggravated nature; fine $500-5,000; or jail up to 12 months; or both (27-3-26 through -28).

"Protected species" means a species the Department has designated as subject to the protection of this article, the "Endangered Wildlife Act of 1973." The Department shall identify and inventory species of animal life which are rare, unusual or in danger of extinction, which shall then become protected. The Board shall issue rules and regulations for the protection of protected species and enforcement of this article. ★These rules and regulations shall not affect rights in private property or in public or private streams, nor impede construction, and shall be limited to the regulation of the capture, killing or selling of a protected species and the protection of its habitat on public lands.★ Violation: misdemeanor (27-3-130 through -132). It is unlawful to possess, transport or trap a Golden Eagle (27-2-17). (See also GENERAL EXCEPTIONS TO PROTECTION.)

GENERAL EXCEPTIONS TO PROTECTION

★It is unlawful to take, possess, or transport state wildlife, or the plumage, skin, body, nests or eggs of such, for scientific purposes without a scientific collecting permit. The Department shall issue a permit only if it has determined the proposed activities are in the best interest of wildlife resources (27-2-12).★ The Department is authorized to take, transport, possess, purchase, sell, band, and release wildlife at times, by methods, and in quantities designated (27-1-22). It is unlawful to hunt, trap, take, possess, sell, purchase, ship or transport a hawk, eagle, owl, or other bird or part, nest or egg, except for the English or European house sparrow, the European starling, feral pigeons and domestic fowl, except as otherwise permitted (27-3-22). It is lawful to sell the tails of legally taken squirrels (27-3-23) and the antlers, hides and tails of legally taken deer (27-3-50).

Unless otherwise provided in 27-5-5, without a license or permit it is unlawful to import, transport, transfer, sell, purchase or possess a wild animal listed or specified by regulation. Wild animal licenses will be issued only to persons engaged in the wild animal business or exhibiting wild animals to the public. Wild animal permits will be issued only for scientific or educational purposes or to a pond owner for grass carp. Federal, state, city, county or municipal governments and transient circuses with wild animal exhibitions, which can demonstrate that 10 percent of exhibition proceeds go to state charitable purposes, are required to obtain a wild animal license, but at no charge. If a wild animal is listed in this section as inherently dangerous, each licensee or permittee shall have a liability insurance policy which covers claims for damage to persons or property. Wild animals for which a license or permit is required are listed in 27-5-5. It is unlawful to import, transport, sell, transfer or possess a wild animal without meeting code specifications for humane handling, care, confinement and transportation (27-5-4 and -6). Peace officers may seize as contraband a wild animal for which a permit or license is required and not obtained (27-5-8). (See Restrictions on Taking under HUNTING, FISHING, TRAPPING PROVISIONS; PROTECTED SPECIES OF WILDLIFE.)

HUNTING, FISHING, TRAPPING PROVISIONS

General Provisions

It is unlawful to hunt, trap or fish except: ▸ during an open season; ▸ in compliance with bag, creel, size and possession limits, by legal methods and weapons, and at times and places established by law or regulations (27-1-3).

It is unlawful to: ▸ refuse to allow inspection of a license, permit or stamp; ▸ refuse to provide identification; ▸ make false statements to obtain a license or permit; ▸ counterfeit, change, or alter a license or permit, or attempt to do so; ▸ collect funds for an issued license or permit except for collection by authorized Department personnel (27-2-28).

The Board is authorized to promulgate rules and regulations establishing open seasons and bag limits based on sound wildlife management principles, those for migratory game birds to be promulgated in accordance with federal law. There are closed and open seasons for quail, grouse, turkey, deer, bobcat, opossum, rabbit, raccoon, fox, bear, alligators and migratory game birds. The season is closed for sea turtles and their eggs and for cougar. There are no season bag limits for quail, grouse, bobcat, opossum, rabbit, raccoon, squirrel and fox. Bag limits for alligator are set by Board. Open and closed season for taking by falconry are set for quail, grouse, rabbit and squirrel, with no bag limits during season. The Department shall report to the General Assembly on or before the fifth day of February each year the estimated number of deer killed, by sex, in the preceding season (27-3-15).

Licenses and Permits

It is unlawful to hunt, fish, trap or possess wildlife without required licenses, stamps, or permits, except on landowners' premises, or when otherwise directed by the Department, or as provided by law and interstate agreements (27-2-1). Persons born after January 1, 1961, may not procure a hunting license unless they have a certificate of completion from a Board prescribed hunter education course. A nonresident applying for a season hunting license may have a hunter education certificate from the nonresident's state if the course has been approved by the Georgia Board. Nonresidents applying for a ten-day hunting license are not required to exhibit a hunter education certificate. Violation: misdemeanor (27-2-5).

It is unlawful for a resident age 16 or over, or for any nonresident, to fish in trout waters without a trout stamp, to hunt or possess big game without a big game license and a hunting license, or to hunt ducks, geese, or swans without a waterfowl stamp and a hunting license. No resident is required to obtain a trout stamp, Georgia waterfowl stamp or big game license to hunt, fish, or trap on premises owned by the resident or immediate family. A visitor to a state park is not required to obtain a trout stamp when fishing in impounded waters on lands owned or leased by the Department (27-2-6). A nonresident and immediate family owning 50 acres of land in Georgia may hunt game on the land without a hunting or big game license and may hunt ducks, geese, or swans on the land without purchasing a Georgia Waterfowl Stamp (27-2-1 and -6).

It is unlawful to trap, take, transport, or possess raptors for falconry without a falconry permit and a hunting license. It is lawful for a nonresident to transport or possess raptors for falconry purposes if the person has a nonresident hunting license and a falconry license from the state of residence, if that state meets federal falconry standards. It is unlawful to trap, transport, or possess a Golden Eagle. Only American kestrels and great-horned owls may be taken when over one year old, except that a raptor taken under a depredation (or special purpose) permit, other than endangered or threatened species, may be used for falconry (27-2-17).

It is unlawful to hunt brant, ducks, geese, and swans without a federal migratory bird hunting and conservation stamp. Field and retriever trial permits are required to conduct a field or retriever trial. Species of wildlife specified on the permit may be pursued by dogs, but may not be taken except during the open season for such species of wildlife. An appropriate hunting license is required (27-2-20 and -21).

Restrictions on Taking: Hunting and Trapping

It is unlawful to hunt upon the lands of another without permission from the landowner or lessee, except for family members of the landowner or lessee. Violation: misdemeanor; first offense, minimum $250 fine; second or subsequent offense within two years, minimum $500 fine and revocation of hunting license for one year. The minimum fines and revocation periods do not apply to an offender who is age 17 or younger (27-3-1).

On a wildlife management area it is unlawful to: ▸ possess a firearm during a closed hunting season unless unloaded; ▸ possess a loaded firearm in a motor vehicle during a legal open season; ▸ be under the influence of drugs and intoxicating beverages; ▸ hunt within 50 yards of a maintained road; ▸ target practice; ▸ drive a vehicle around a closed gate; ▸ hunt within a posted safety zone; ▸ camp or drive upon a permanent pasture or crop area;

▶ kill a female bear with cubs or a cub weighing less than 75 pounds; ▶ fail to report the killing of a deer, bear, or turkey in the manner specified by the Department; ▶ hunt small game during a managed deer, turkey or bear hunt; ▶ hunt from a tree stand except a portable or natural one; ▶ trap without a permit (27-3-1.1). It is unlawful to: ▶ hunt game birds or animals at night except raccoons, opossums, foxes and bobcats, and these may not be hunted with lights exceeding six volts; ▶ hunt migratory game birds at night and during daylight hours except during hours designated for a particular migratory game bird (27-3-2 and -3).

It is unlawful to: ▶ possess a firearm while hunting with a bow and arrow during archery season for deer; ▶ hunt while under the influence of drugs or intoxicating beverages; ▶ make use of a pitfall, deadfall, catch, snare, trap, net, salt lick, blind pig, baited hook, or other device for taking a game animal or bird or other wildlife, except as otherwise provided; ▶ scatter grain or other feeds to entice a game bird or animal to where hunters are or will be hunting; except as otherwise provided, it is unlawful to hunt a game bird or animal upon or near such place for ten days following complete removal of the feed or bait; ▶ hunt wildlife upon a public road and discharge a weapon across a public road, violation of which is a misdemeanor and a maximum $1,000 fine and imprisonment up to 12 months; ▶ hunt game animals or birds by means of drugs, poisons, chemicals, smoke, gas, explosives, or recorded or amplified calls or sounds and use electronic communications equipment to facilitate their pursuit; ▶ hunt wildlife or feral hog from boats, aircraft or motor vehicles, violation of which is a misdemeanor; ▶ kill or cripple a game bird or animal without making a reasonable effort to retrieve it (27-3-1-6 through -14).

It is unlawful to: ▶ take game while training dogs except during lawful open seasons; ▶ hunt deer with dogs except during special open seasons as designated (27-3-16 and -17). Except as provided in 27-3-15, it is unlawful to hunt alligators. Violation: misdemeanor; minimum $500 fine; imprisonment up to 12 months; and revocation of hunting privileges for not less than two years. It is unlawful to possess, buy or sell untanned hides or skin or alligator productions of illegally taken alligators. It is unlawful to take rabbits or hares except during lawful hunting season. Persons under 16 may trap and sell rabbits in rabbit boxes (27-3-19 and -20). During season, it is permissible for a landowner, family and tenants to trap rabbits upon the owner's land without a permit or license. The Director may issue a permit for of trapping or capturing rabbits or hares to sell for use at time trials approved by the American Kennel Club (27-3-66 and -67). It is unlawful to hunt feral hogs: ▶ upon the lands of another or posted land without permission; ▶ upon baited land constituting a lure to feral hogs, except that bait may be used to hunt feral hogs by means other than a firearm or bow and arrow; ▶ from within a vehicle; ▶ at night with a light, except with a light not exceeding six volts or a fuel-type lantern (27-3-24).

It is unlawful to: ▶ hunt deer unless under direct adult supervision if the hunter is under age 16; ▶ take a deer that is in a lake, stream or pond; ▶ remove the head of a deer until the carcass is processed; ▶ kill a deer unless the deer has visible antlers, provided that the Board may authorize an antlerless or either-sex season; ▶ remove a deer carcass from the place of killing without affixing a tag which is to remain on the deer until it has been processed for consumption; ▶ fail to report a taken deer to the Department within five days after the close of the season; ▶ fail to notify immediately the nearest Conservation Ranger or sheriff's office if a person kills a deer in a motor vehicle collision; ▶ hunt deer at night, conviction to be a misdemeanor with a minimum $500 fine, jail up to 12 months, and suspended hunting privileges of not less than two years; conviction of two or more violations to be a misdemeanor of a high and aggravated nature with a $1,500-5,000 fine and jail up to 12 months. It is the duty of every Conservation Ranger to kill a dog pursuing or killing deer in any locality other than that prescribed by law. It is unlawful for a person other than a Conservation Ranger or peace officer to kill a dog wearing a collar when the dog is or has been pursuing or killing deer. It is lawful for a person to kill a dog without a collar doing such (27-3-41 through -49).

Except as provided, it is unlawful to trap wildlife between March 1 and November 19, and between November 20 and February 29, except if a portion of that period is designated an open trapping season for a fur-bearing animal. ★It is lawful to trap beaver, rats and mice.★ It is unlawful to trap raccoons in certain areas at any time. Violation: misdemeanor. The Board may regulate open seasons for trapping locally or statewide (27-3-62). It is unlawful for a fur dealer to dispose of carcasses or parts of fur-bearing animals or alligators except pursuant to a written plan of disposal approved by the Department. Violation: misdemeanor; administrative license revocation, suspension, denial and refusal (27-3-73). It is unlawful to: ▶ trap wildlife upon the right of way of a public road; ▶ trap wildlife upon the land or in the waters adjoining land of any other person, except during open trapping season and with written owner permission; ▶ trap wildlife without inspecting traps once each 24-hour period; ▶ trap wildlife using a trap without the trapper's identification number etched on it; ▶ remove the raw or undressed hide, fur, pelt or skin of a fur-bearing animal from the state without first reporting to the Department; ▸ fail to carry a weapon of .22 caliber rimfire while tending traps to dispatch a fur-bearing animal found in a trap; ▸ fail to carry a choke stick while tending traps to release trapped domestic animals; ▸ set on land a trap with a jaw opening larger than 5 3/4 inches; ▸ sell the fur, hide or pelt of a domestic dog or cat caught by a trap; ▸ sell the raw, undressed fur, hide, skin or pelt of a fur-bearing animal without a commercial trapping or fur dealer license; ▸ set a body-gripping trap of a size in excess of 9 1/2 inches square, except in water or on land within ten feet of water. Violation: misdemeanor (27-3-63).

It is unlawful to: ▸ use a firearm to kill or injure mink or otter or possess or sell one killed by a firearm, except a mink or otter found in a trap or destroying or damaging a person's crops or domestic fowl may be dispatched (27-3-64); ▸ remove a legally set trap, except for a landowner, or remove lawfully trapped wildlife without the permission of owner (27-3-65); ▸ transport within or beyond state borders wildlife taken in the state unless the wildlife was taken by and is in the possession of a person with a license or permit (27-3-90); transport wildlife or parts for propagation or scientific purposes without a scientific collecting permit (27-3-93).

Except as specifically provided, it is unlawful to: ▸ sell or purchase game species or parts; ▸ use or possess wildlife or parts which the person reasonably should have known had been taken or possessed illegally, or conceal the taking or possession of wildlife; hire another to take or possess wildlife illegally; ▸ enter upon or hunt, trap, or fish on a public fishing or wildlife management area owned or operated by the Department, except in compliance with applicable wildlife laws and regulations, and to do so without a wildlife management area stamp, violation of which is an offense of criminal trespass (27-1-29 through -33).

See also GENERAL EXCEPTIONS TO PROTECTION.

Restrictions on Taking: Fishing

It is unlawful to: ▸ fish in the waters or from the lands of another without permission from the owner, provided that nothing in this section applies to the taking of fish, other than oysters, clams and other shellfish, in the salt-water creeks, streams, or estuaries leading from the Atlantic Ocean or the sounds, rivers or bays surrounding the islands of the state and that no person shall interfere with the right of a person to fish in these salt-waters (27-4-2); ▸ fish for game fish, except American and hickory shad, or flathead and channel catfish, by other than a pole and line, and take fish in state fresh waters by other than a pole and line, sport trotlines, set hooks, jugs, bow and arrow, spears, bow nets, and seines, it being lawful to use seines, nets and chemicals in a pond, except oxbow lakes, if all the owners desire such and a local Conservation Ranger is notified at least two hours in advance; ▸ take game or nongame fish or American eels by minnow seines, except fish under five inches in length and not for sale, and where waters are not trout waters; ▸ use a gill net, except licensed fishermen may use such nets in taking shad and sturgeon; ▸ use a firearm, battery, generator or similar device or dynamite, explosives or destructive substances to catch fish (27-4-5 through -8). It is unlawful to throw, dump, drain or allow to pass into state waters being utilized by the Department for fish propagation any sawdust, dyestuff, oil, chemicals, or other deleterious substances which will injure, destroy, or drive away fish or aquatic organisms. The Department may recover damages in a civil action, the measure of damages being the amount which will compensate for all the detriment proximately caused by the destruction or injury of the fish or aquatic organism (27-4-4). Possession in a boat upon state waters of nets or devices capable of taking shad during the time such is prohibited is prima-facie evidence the person is guilty of taking shad. Creel and possession limits are set for numerous species in the statutes, along with size limits for largemouth and shoal bass, and mountain and brook trout in certain waters (27-4-9 through -11).

On a public fishing area it is unlawful to: ▸ possess a firearm during a closed hunting season unless it is unloaded and stored in a motor vehicle so as not to be readily accessible; ▸ possess a loaded firearm in a motor vehicle during an open hunting season; ▸ be under the influence of drugs or intoxicating liquors; ▸ fish in a pond or lake which has been posted "closed"; ▸ take in one day more than creel limits for bream, sunfish, bass and channel catfish; ▸ fish with gear other than a pole and line, with exceptions made for certain public fishing areas; ▸ fish at night; ▸ use live bait (27-4-11.1).

The owner of a private pond, and the owner's family or tenants, are permitted to fish within the bounds of the pond without a fishing license; all other persons must have licenses unless the fish are domestic fish. The owner of a catch-out pond may purchase a catch-out pond license where residents and nonresidents may fish without a license and without complying with creel and size limits and seasons (27-4-30 and -31).

It is unlawful to: ▸ use sport trotlines unless they are marked with the owner's name and address, have visible buoys, are submerged at least three feet below the surface of the water, are attended regularly and are removed after a completed fishing trip; ▸ spear game fish and all species of catfish in fresh waters, it being lawful to spear other nongame fish solely for sport if the person is completely submerged; ▸ take nongame fish by bow and arrow unless the person has a fishing license and arrows are harpoon type, or use arrows with poisonous or exploding heads; ▸ use more than two poles and lines and use bow nets less than 3 1/2 inches stretched mesh when sport shad fishing; ▸ not use an artificial-lure in an artificial lure stream (27-4-32 through -36). It is unlawful to: ▸ fish for trout in fresh waters other than by using one pole and line held in hand, use live fish for bait in waters designated in sections 27-4-52 and 27-4-53, or move trout from state fresh waters to other fresh waters (27-4-50); ▸ fish in state trout waters except during designated trout fishing hours set forth (27-4-51). It is unlawful to take, capture or kill diamondback terrapins with any device except gill nets, with a 5 1/2 inch stretched mesh, between April 1 and August 1 of each year (27-4-116).

Commercial and Private Enterprise Provisions

A taxidermist license is required to engage in the business of taxidermy. It is lawful for a taxidermist to mount and sell legally taken fur-bearers, deer, and squirrel, or parts. It is unlawful for a taxidermist to possess or mount a game species for which there is no open season or an endangered, rare, threatened or unusual species without a permit from the Department. A licensed taxidermist may mount and sell legally taken fur-bearers or alligators and alligator products without a fur dealer's license. An alligator farming license is required to propagate or possess live alligators or to sell or export alligator hides. Without a permit it is unlawful to acquire a live alligator or a hide, except by propagation of live alligators lawfully possessed, or to sell, exchange or loan a live alligator. The Board ha the authority to adopt and promulgate rules and regulations relative to commercial alligator farming, including care, treatment and marketing. A game-holding permit is required to hold a game animal or bird for propagation or as a pet. This section does not authorize the holding of the progeny of a game bird or animal under the permit under which a parent is held, unless specifically stated on the game-holding permit (27-2-9 through -11). A wildlife exhibition permit is required to keep, hold, or possess wildlife in captivity for display or exhibition. Educational institutions, zoos or transient circuses are not required to procure such a permit, but exhibitors must comply with all regulations regarding housing, feed, and sanitation of captive wildlife. ★A liberation-of-wildlife permit is required to liberate wildlife within the state. A wildlife storage permit is required for a commercial facility to store wildlife or parts, and the facility must require the person delivering wildlife to exhibit a license authorizing possession of the wildlife. A permit is not required to store fish.★ A commercial quail breeder permit is required to engage in the business of propagating quail for food or other commercial purposes, unless the quail are pen raised (27-2-13 through -16).

A wildlife rehabilitation permit is required to keep, hold or possess in captivity a sick or injured wildlife, except fish. Such permit shall be issued only to qualified persons for specified terms and conditions (27-2-22).

It is unlawful to trap and sell live foxes without first a commercial trapping license. Live foxes may be taken from the wild only during trapping season and may be sold only to licensed commercial fox hunting preserves or breeders. A commercial fox hunting preserve license is required to own or operate an area utilized for running, taking, or hunting penned foxes for a fee. A commercial fox breeder license is required to engage in the business of propagating or breeding foxes for sale, restocking, propagation, or other commercial purposes. Nonresidents may procure a nonresident hunting preserve license. A permit is required to receive or possess a fox shipped, transported, or removed from outside of the state (27-2-22.1).

It is unlawful to engage in business as a trapper without a commercial trapping license. A landowner or member of the landowner's family may obtain a license at no charge: Violation: misdemeanor (27-3-60). A nonresident commercial trapping license requires a cash bond of $2,500 (27-3-60 and -61).

★Without a raccoon fur seller's license it is unlawful to sell the raw, undressed fur, hide, skin, or pelt of a raccoon lawfully taken by means other than trapping. A person who purchases or sells raw, undressed furs, hides, skins, or pelts of raccoons taken by trapping and other means is considered a fur dealer (27-2-23.1).★ It is unlawful to engage in business as a fur dealer or agent without a fur dealer's license, and a forfeiture bond of $5,000 must be posted or obtained (27-3-69 and -70).

It is unlawful for a carrier to ship, transport or receive for shipment or transportation wildlife without having ascertained that the person shipping the wildlife has a license or permit, or without receiving from the person a sworn statement showing the wildlife was lawfully taken and is not for sale (27-3-94).

Except as provided, it is unlawful to: ▸ sell or purchase game fish; ▸ sell fish from a commercial fish hatchery unless the hatchery is licensed; ▸ sell fish from a commercial fish hatchery which the Department has determined to have diseases or parasites which would be harmful to native fish populations; ▸ engage in the wholesale or retail fish dealer business without a wholesale or retail fish dealer license; a commercial fish hatchery is not required to have such a license. A nonresident may sell and transport fish and fish eggs into the state without a wholesale fish dealer license when the sale and shipment are made to a licensed wholesale fish dealer (27-4-74 through -76).

It is unlawful to: ▸ release pen raised game birds without a commercial or private shooting preserve license; ▸ remove an untagged game bird from a shooting preserve and release a mallard or black duck unless pen raised; ▸ hunt on a shooting preserve during daylight hours, except between October 1 and March 31; ▸ exceed season bag limits, there being no bag limits for pen raised birds; ▸ hunt on a preserve except during open season for a bird or animal, except for bobwhite quail and pen raised game birds; ▸ propagate, possess or release on a shooting preserve a bird or animal except bobwhite quail, chukar or red-legged partridge, octurnix or Japanese quail, pheasant, mallard and black duck, without prior written Department approval. The importation of a bird or animal on a shooting preserve shall conform with requirements of this title. Except as otherwise provided, wildlife laws and regulations are in full force and effect on licensed shooting preserves (27-3-110 through -114). (See also GENERAL EXCEPTIONS TO PROTECTION.)

Import, Export and Release Provisions

The Board may prohibit or limit the importation, possession, or sale of live fish or fish eggs harmful to endemic fish populations or which might introduce or spread disease or parasites. Violation: confiscation of fish so imported, purchased or acquired (27-4-76).

The importation, transportation, sale, transfer and possession of wild animals are privileges not to be granted unless it can be clearly demonstrated such actions can be accomplished in a manner that does not pose unnecessary risk to Georgia's wildlife, other natural resources or citizens of and visitors to the state. For these reasons, the General Assembly finds and declares only certain wild animals may be held for scientific or educational purposes, public exhibition and/or as pets. The Board has the authority to regulate the importation, transportation, sale and possession of wild animals when there is a possibility of: ▸ harmful competition for wildlife; ▸ problems of enforcement of wildlife laws and regulations; ▸ danger to wildlife or other natural resources; ▸ danger to the physical safety of human beings. The Board is authorized to supplement the list of wild animals for which a permit or license is required. The Department is authorized to: ▸ prescribe the form and contents for license and permit applications; ▸ issue a cease and desist order to a violator; ▸ quarantine or dispose of a wild animal with a contagious or infectious disease or infested with a harmful parasite; ▸ determine if standards are met for public safety and humane handling, care, confinement and transportation of the wild animal for which an application for license has been received; ▸ capture and contain a wild animal regulated by this section which has escaped or been released if it poses a risk to wildlife, citizens or visitors (27-5-1 through -3).

It is unlawful to import wildlife other than fish and pen raised duck, turkey and quail without a wildlife importation permit, to be issued by the Department only in the best interest of state wildlife (27-2-19). Importation of a bird or animal on a shooting preserve must conform to the requirements of this title (27-3-113). (See also Commercial and Private Enterprise Provisions, and License and Permits, under HUNTING, FISHING, TRAPPING PROVISIONS.)

ANIMAL DAMAGE CONTROL

The Department may issue permits to kill deer causing damage to crops to persons who cultivate crops. Permits shall include restrictions and conditions relative to the property on which deer may be killed, persons authorized to kill deer, crops which may be protected, and number and sex of deer which may be killed (27-2-18). With permission from the landowner, the owner of a beehive has the right to kill a bear constituting a threat to the owner's property (27-3-21). ★Upon request of a city, county, or combination thereof, the Department is authorized to provide assistance in the control or elimination of wild or abandoned dogs running at large (27-1-7).★ (See also Agency Powers and Duties under STATE FISH AND WILDLIFE AGENCIES.)

ENFORCEMENT OF WILDLIFE LAWS

Enforcement Powers

When the Department believes a violation of a wildlife law or regulation has occurred or is occurring, it may issue an administrative order requiring corrective action, and authorizing the seizure of wildlife taken, imported, sold, transferred, or possessed illegally. Orders must be supported by an affidavit stating the affiant has personal knowledge that immediate irreparable injury is likely to occur to wildlife or other natural resources, to wild animals, or to human beings. An administrative order is not required to seize contraband or wildlife. Violation: misdemeanor (27-1-37 and -38). ★In a prosecution for violation of wildlife laws, it is not a defense that the person taking, possessing, transporting, or storing wildlife was mistaken as to the species, sex, age, size or other fact regarding such wildlife or that the person lacked criminal intent, as it is one of the purposes of the wildlife laws to penalize recklessness (27-1-34).★

Civil Penalties

★As an alternative to criminal enforcement, the Department may employ one or combination of the following methods: ▸ A violator of provisions of this title shall be liable civilly for a penalty of up to $1,000, for each and every violation. ▸ The Commissioner may issue an administrative order imposing a civil penalty not to exceed $1,000 for the violation. The violator has the right to an administrative hearing. All civil penalties recovered by the Department shall be paid into the state treasury (27-1-36).★

Illegal Taking of Wildlife

Any commercial fishing gear or trap, net, seine, basket or similar device for taking fish being used illegally shall be confiscated, and if not claimed within a reasonable time and the owner is unknown, the gear shall become Department property and disposed of as ordered by the Commissioner (27-4-73). (See Agency Powers and Duties under STATE FISH AND WILDLIFE AGENCIES.)

License Revocations and Suspensions

The General Assembly has declared hunting is a privilege to be exercised with due care and hunting privileges may be suspended if a person refuses or fails to exercise due care. If a person engaged in hunting kills or injures another person, the person shall notify a law enforcement officer; failure to do so is a misdemeanor. If the Department determines after an investigation that negligence was the cause of death or injury, the person's hunting privileges may be suspended for up to ten years. Hunting during suspension shall be a misdemeanor of a high and aggravated nature and punished by a fine up to $5,000, or imprisonment up to 12 months, or both. This shall be in addition to, and not in lieu of, any civil or criminal action provided for by law. Pursuant to Board procedure, the Department may revoke or cancel any license, certificate, stamp, card or permit when it is determined the holder was not entitled to issuance or obtained such fraudulently. Violation: misdemeanor. In lieu of revocation, suspension, denial or refusal to renew a license or permit, with written consent of the affected party, the Commissioner or Board may impose a penalty not to exceed $1,000 for each violation, the moneys to be paid into the general fund (27-2-25.1, -26 and -27).

See also HUNTING, FISHING, TRAPPING PROVISIONS.

HABITAT PROTECTION

The Department shall establish nongame wildlife conservation and habitat acquisition programs and educational and promotional activities to enhance the protection of nongame wildlife and the nonconsumptive use by Georgia citizens

(12-3-602). (See Agency Funding Sources under STATE FISH AND WILDLIFE AGENCIES for information on the Nongame Wildlife Conservation and Wildlife Habitat Acquisition Fund.)

Except as otherwise provided, it is unlawful to disturb, mutilate, or destroy the dens, holes, or homes of wildlife, to blind wildlife with lights, to use explosives, chemicals, electrical or mechanical devices or smokers to drive wildlife other than poisonous snakes out of habitats (27-1-30).

The Department is authorized to provide for free passage of fish in state fresh-water streams for spawning and propagating and to erect or cause to be erected fish ladders or other passageways. Should a private person restrict free passage of fish in fresh-water streams and refuse to provide a fish ladder or passageway, the Department shall provide such, assessing the cost against the private person (27-1-8).

NATIVE AMERICAN WILDLIFE PROVISIONS: None.

HAWAII

Sources: Hawaii Revised Statutes Annotated, 1988, Title 12; 1992 Cumulative Supplement.

STATE WILDLIFE POLICY

Chapter 195D, Conservation of Aquatic Life, Wildlife, and Land Plants, has a finding and declaration of necessity: "Since the discovery and settlement of the Hawaiian islands by man, many species of aquatic life, wildlife, and land plants that occurred naturally only in Hawaii have become extinct and many are threatened with extinction, primarily because of increased human use of the land and disturbance to native ecosystems. Indigenous species of aquatic life, wildlife, and land plants are integral parts of Hawaii's native ecosystems and comprise the living heritage of Hawaii, for they represent a natural resource of scientific, cultural, educational, environmental, and economic value to future generations of Hawaii's people. To insure the perpetuation of indigenous aquatic life, wildlife, and land plants, and their habitats for human enjoyment, for scientific purposes, and as members of ecosystems, it is necessary that the state take positive actions to enhance their prospects for survival." (12-195D-1)

All fishing grounds appertaining to government land or otherwise belonging to the government, except ponds, are forever granted to the people, for free and equal use by all; except that the Department of Land and Natural Resources may manage and regulate taking of aquatic life (12-187A-21).

RELEVANT WILDLIFE DEFINITIONS: See Definitions Section of Appendices.

STATE FISH AND WILDLIFE AGENCIES

Agency Structure

The department ultimately responsible for wildlife is the **Department of Land and Natural Resources** (Department) (12-183D-2).

Officials responsible for determining the programs of the Department are on the **Board of Land and Natural Resources** (Board) (12-26-15). The **Board** is composed of six members, appointed by the Governor, by and with the advice and consent of the senate (12-171-4). The Board has police powers and may appoint and commission enforcement officers within the conservation enforcement program who will have the authority of police officers and will enforce all state and county laws and rules; their primary duty is enforcement of Title 12 (12-199-4). The Board appoints an **Administrator of Forestry and Wildlife**, who has charge and control over all matters relating to forestry and wildlife management (12-183-3). The Board appoints an **Administrator of Aquatic Resources**, who has charge and control of all matters relating to aquatic resource management, conservation, and development activities under Title 12, and other matters as the Board may direct. The appointee shall be trained and educated in natural resource management (12-187A-4).

The Board shall establish within the Department a **Conservation and Resources Enforcement Program** for enforcement of chapters, rules and regulations under Title 12, "Conservation and Resources," and shall employ or appoint: A **Department Chief of Enforcement**, who shall be head of the enforcement program and shall have charge, direction and control, subject to Board direction, of enforcement of state conservation and resource laws, rules and regulations and other matters as the Board may direct, and shall be experienced in conservation and resources law enforcement, management, and personnel and shall appoint program enforcement officers, including but not limited to voluntary officers (12-199-1). The Board may delegate authority for enforcement of state conservation and resource laws, rules and regulations (12-199-2). (See also Enforcement Powers under ENFORCEMENT OF WILDLIFE LAWS.)

Agency Powers and Duties

The powers and duties of the **Department** are to: ▸ manage and administer the wildlife and wildlife resources of the state; ▸ enforce all laws relating to the protecting, taking, hunting, killing, propagating, or increasing the wildlife within the state and the waters subject to its jurisdiction; ▸ establish and maintain wildlife propagating facilities; ▸ import wildlife for the purpose of propagating and disseminating the same in the state and the waters subject to its jurisdiction; ▸ distribute game to increase the state food supply, provided that when in the discretion of the Department the public interest will not be materially interfered with, the Department may propagate and furnish wildlife to private parties, upon reasonable terms, conditions, and prices; ▸ ascertain, compile, and disseminate, free of charge, information and advice as to the best methods of protecting, propagating, and distributing wildlife in the state and waters subject to its jurisdiction; ▸ gather and compile information and statistics concerning the area, location, character, and increase and decrease of wildlife in the state; ▸ gather and compile information concerning wildlife recommended for release in different localities, including the care and propagation of wildlife for protective, productive, and aesthetic purposes; ▸ manage and regulate all lands set apart as game management areas, public hunting areas, and wildlife sanctuaries; ▸ destroy predators harmful to wildlife, pursuant to section 12-183D-65; ▸ formulate, and recommend to the Governor and legislature, additional legislation necessary or desirable to implement the objectives of Title 12 (12-183D-2).

Pursuant to chapter 187A-2, the Department shall: ▸ manage and administer the aquatic life, aquatic resources, and aquaculture programs of the state; ▸ establish and maintain aquatic life propagating stations; ▸ establish, manage, and regulate public fishing areas, reefs, fish aggregating devices, refuges and other areas pursuant to Title 12 [marine references are excluded]; ▸ import aquatic life for propagating and disseminating, subject to Title 12; ▸ distribute aquatic life to increase the state food, and if not materially interfering with the public interest, propagate and furnish aquatic life to private parties on terms and conditions; ▸ gather and compile information and statistics concerning the habitat and character of, and increase and decrease in, aquatic resources, including the care and propagation for protective, productive and aesthetic purposes, and other useful information; ▸ enforce all laws relating to the protection, taking, killing, propagation, and increasing of aquatic life within the state and waters subject to its jurisdiction; ▸ formulate, and recommend to the Governor and legislature, additional legislation to implement the objectives of Title 12 (12-187-3).

The Department may establish, maintain, manage, and operate game management areas, wildlife sanctuaries, and public hunting areas on land under its control and enter into agreements for taking control of privately owned lands for those purposes (12-183D-4). The Department may: ▸ expend appropriations made for the purpose of effectuating Title 12; ▸ expend proceeds in the wildlife revolving fund without appropriation; ▸ use lands set apart for its use by the Governor; ▸ accept gifts and contributions of property or service or enter into contracts for furtherance of purposes of chapters 183D-7 and 187A-7; ▸ conduct investigations on aquatic life, wildlife and land plants to develop information relating to their biology, ecology, population, status, distribution, habitat needs, and other limiting factors to determine conservation measures for their continued ability to sustain themselves successfully; ▸ adopt rules relating to the taking, possession, transportation, importation, exportation, processing, selling, offering for sale, or shipment of a species of aquatic life, wildlife and land plant for the purpose of saving them (12-195D-3). (See also HABITAT PROTECTION PROVISIONS regarding conservation program authority.)

Agency Regulations

Subject to chapter 91, the Department shall adopt, amend, and repeal rules: ▸ concerning the preservation, protection, regulation, extension, and utilization of, and conditions for entry into wildlife sanctuaries, game management areas, and public hunting areas; ▸ protecting, conserving, monitoring, propagating, and harvesting wildlife; ▸ concerning size limits, bag limits, open and closed seasons, and specifications of hunting gear; ▸ setting fees for permitted activities, unless otherwise provided for by law. The rules may vary from county to county or in any part of the county and may specify days of the week or hours of the day in designating open seasons. All rules shall have the force and effect of law (12-183D-3). The Department shall adopt, amend and repeal rules for the protection and propagation of introduced and transplanted aquatic life, or the conservation and allocation of the natural supply of aquatic life in any area. Rules may include: ▸ size limits; ▸ bag limits; ▸ open and closed fishing seasons; ▸ specifications and numbers of fishing or taking gear which may be used or possessed; ▸ the kind and amount of bait; ▸ conditions for entry into areas for taking aquatic life (12-187A-5).

Agency Funding Sources

Moneys collected for hunting and fishing permits or licenses, or under the provisions of any law relating to the importation, taking, catching, or killing of aquatic life, game, wildlife, and their products, shall be credited to the General Fund. They shall be expended by the Department, in accordance with appropriations authorized by the legislature, for the importation, management, preservation, propagation, and protection of aquatic life, game or wildlife in the state, and for expenses of prosecution of game, aquatic life and wildlife law offenders (12-187A-11).

A **Wildlife Revolving Fund** in the Department consists of: ▸ hunting license fees; ▸ attendance fees for hunter education programs; ▸ fees for use of public target ranges; ▸ moneys collected under provisions relating to importation, taking, catching or killing of game, wildlife and products thereof; ▸ fines or bail forfeitures collected under this chapter other than informers' fees under section 12-183D-11. Revolving Fund expenditures are limited to: ▸ programs and activities to implement or enforce this chapter or chapter 195D concerning wildlife conservation; ▸ acquisition, development or maintenance of trails for reserves, game management, public hunting and other areas; ▸ research programs and activities concerning wildlife conservation and management; ▸ importation, management, propagation and protection of wildlife. The fund shall not be used as security or pledge for bonds or other instruments of indebtedness. Nothing prohibits general funds or other funding to implement or enforce this chapter or 195D concerning wildlife conservation. An annual report on the fund must be submitted to the legislature (12-183D-10.5).

A **Natural Area Reserve Fund** is established to implement the purposes of chapter 195, the Natural Area Reserves System, including identification, establishment and management of natural area reserves, for acquisition of private lands for reserves, and for the heritage program. The fund shall consist of all moneys received from public or private sources. It shall be held separate from other treasury funds, and investment earnings of the fund shall become part of the assets of the fund (12-195-9).

Agency Advisory Boards

★A **Natural Area Reserves System Commission** is part of the Department. There are 11 members, 6 possessing scientific qualifications evidenced by an academic degree in wildlife or marine biology, botany, forestry, ecology, resource management, biogeography, zoology, or geology. Ex officio voting members are the Chairman of the Board, the Superintendent of Education, Director of the Office of State Planning, Chairman of the Board of Agriculture, and President of the University of Hawaii, or their designated representatives. The Governor shall appoint the chairman from among the members.★ The Natural Area Reserves System Commission shall: ▸ establish criteria to be used in determining whether an area is suitable for inclusion in the reserves system; ▸ conduct studies of areas for possible inclusion; ▸ recommend suitable areas to the Governor and Department; ▸ establish policies and criteria regarding the management, protection, and permitted uses of reserve areas; ▸ advise the Governor and Department on any matter relating to the preservation of Hawaii's unique natural resources; ▸ develop ways and means of extending and strengthening presently established preserves, sanctuaries, and refuges within the state; ▸ advise the Department and other public agencies managing state-owned land or natural resources regarding areas which may be appropriate for designation; ▸ in carrying out the above duties, consult the most comprehensive up-to-date compilation of scientific data on the communities of natural flora and fauna of Hawaii (12-195-6 and -7).

★★An **Animal Species Advisory Commission** is established within the Department to advise the Board on proposals for the deliberate introduction of aquatic life and wildlife into a habitat within the state. The commission may also advise the Board on matters affecting the taking and conservation of aquatic life and wildlife, including proposed rules. The commission may hear persons and acquire information and shall communicate findings and recommendations to the Board (12-197-2).★★ ★★In each state county there is established an **Aquatic Life and Wildlife Advisory Committee**, composed of Board members representing the county, serving ex officio and nonvoting, and five members appointed by the Governor, who must be knowledgeable in taking and conservation of aquatic life and wildlife. The committee shall meet on matters affecting the taking and conservation of aquatic life and wildlife within the county, including proposed rules and their enforcement. Findings and recommendations shall be communicated to the Department (12-197-4).★★

PROTECTED SPECIES OF WILDLIFE

See HUNTING, FISHING, TRAPPING PROVISIONS regarding various restrictions on taking of species.

No person other than the owner shall shoot, maim, kill, or detain an Antwerp, messenger, or homing pigeon (12-183D-33). Except as provided in 12-183D-61, no person shall intentionally or recklessly take, catch, injure, kill, or destroy, or attempt such, or keep or possess a wild bird, dead or alive, or damage or destroy a nest of a wild bird. Except as in 12-183D-61, no wild bird shall be kept in captivity unless lawfully imported or bred in captivity from birds lawfully imported. No wild bird may be transported from any part of the state except under scientific or educational permit (12-183D-62 through -64).

Except as permitted by Department rules, it is unlawful to take, possess, transport, export, process, sell, offer for sale, or ship a species of aquatic life, wildlife, or land plants in need of conservation (12-195D-3). A species determined to be endangered under the Endangered Species Act shall be deemed an endangered species under this chapter and an indigenous species determined to be threatened under the Endangered Species Act shall be deemed to be threatened under this chapter. The Department may determine that a threatened species is an endangered species throughout all or a portion of its range within the state. In addition to those species, the Department may determine an indigenous species to be endangered or threatened because of any of these factors: the present or threatened destruction, modification, or curtailment of its habitat or range; overutilization for commercial, sporting, scientific, educational, or other purposes; disease or predation; inadequacy of existing regulatory mechanisms; or other natural or manmade factors affecting its continued existence within Hawaii (12-195D-4).

The Department shall make the above determinations on the basis of all available scientific, commercial and other data, after consultation as appropriate with federal agencies, other interested state and county agencies, and interested persons and organizations. The Department shall issue rules containing a list of endangered and threatened species. Each list shall contain the scientific, common and Hawaiian names, and shall specify over what portion of its range it is endangered or threatened. Except for species listed under the Endangered Species Act, the Department shall on its own, or upon petition of three interested persons who have presented substantial evidence which warrants review, conduct a review of any listed or unlisted indigenous species proposed to be removed from or added to the lists published. With respect to an endangered species of aquatic life, wildlife, or land plants, except as provided for licensing for scientific purposes or for enhancement or propagation of species, it is unlawful to: ▸ export such species from this state; ▸ take such species within this state; ▸ possess, process, sell, offer for sale, deliver, carry, transport, or ship such species; ▸ violate a rule pertaining to conservation of the species or to a threatened species listed pursuant to this section and adopted by the Department (12-195D-4).

GENERAL EXCEPTIONS TO PROTECTION

Notwithstanding the provisions of any other law, the Department may take wildlife or aquatic life for scientific, educational, or propagation purposes. The Department may also issue permits to take wildlife or to fish or use fishing gear for scientific, educational, or propagation purposes, except as prohibited by chapter 195D and subject to Department rules. Wildlife or aquatic life so taken shall be accompanied by a permit while being taken or transported and shall be exempt from seizure (12-183D-6 and 187A-6). Regarding aquatic life, a permit may be revoked for an infraction of the permit terms and conditions, and anyone whose permit has been revoked is not eligible for a permit until one year from revocation (12-187A-6).

The Department may adopt rules pursuant to chapter 91 authorizing: ▸ taking and collection of wild birds, game birds and game mammals for scientific and educational purposes, or to distribute wild birds to different localities in the state pursuant to this title; ▸ keeping wild birds in captivity for protection, treatment for injury or disease, propagation and other similar purposes consistent with preservation, protection and conservation of wild birds; ▸ taking and destruction of those wild birds, game birds and game mammals found after investigation to be destructive to crops or other game birds and mammals or otherwise harmful to agriculture or aquaculture, or to constitute a nuisance or health hazard; ▸ destruction within a district of wild birds, game birds and game mammals generally destructive to crops or otherwise harmful to agriculture or aquaculture, or constituting a nuisance or health hazard (12-183D-61).

The Board may issue permits for use of fine meshed traps or nets other than throw nets for taking marine or freshwater nongame fish for aquarium purposes, upon proof that applicants possess facilities for maintaining fish alive and in reasonable health (12-188-31). The Department may issue temporary licenses to allow taking, export, possession and other proscribed acts, of endangered species for scientific purposes or to enhance the propagation or survival of the affected species. The Department may issue permits for taking, possession, transportation, or exportation of indigenous aquatic life, wildlife, or land plants on the endangered species list for scientific purposes and for propagation of the captive species for preservation purposes (12-195D-4 and -5).

HUNTING, FISHING, TRAPPING PROVISIONS

Licenses and Permits

No one shall hunt, pursue, kill, or take a game bird or game mammal without a hunting license (12-183D-21).

The Department shall establish a hunter education training course in hunter safety, principles of conservation and sportsmanship. A hunter education certificate is required for hunting license eligibility, unless the person was born before January 1, 1972, and previously held a hunting license, or unless satisfactory proof is shown of completion of a hunter education and safety course approved by the Hunter Education Association and meeting USFW Federal Aid Manual requirements, in which case a written exemption for life is issued. A hunter education office position may be established, and the Department may operate public target ranges for the program (12-183D-28).

It is unlawful, except for children below nine years of age, to fish, take or catch introduced fresh water game fish without a license. The Department may adopt rules for chapter 188 pertaining to fishing rights and regulations, and set fees for fresh water game fishing. Licenses may be revoked for infractions, and may not be reissued for one year after revocation (12-188-50).

Restrictions on Taking: Hunting and Trapping

The Department may declare by rule any bird introduced into the state to be propagated for hunting purposes to be a game bird. Taking, stalking, pursuing or killing a game bird which is domesticated or legally controlled by another or otherwise prohibited is illegal. No one shall intentionally or recklessly take, kill, pursue, or have in possession a game bird except during designated open seasons. It is not unlawful to possess under refrigeration for five days legally killed game birds not in excess of the daily bag limit (12-183D-31 and -32).

The following mammals living in a wild or feral state not under domestication are designated as game mammals: deer, pronghorn, goat, sheep, cattle, pig, and any other mammal that may be or has been introduced into the state and released for hunting and for which a hunting season has been established. Nothing shall permit taking, catching, pursuing, or killing a mammal in the legal possession or control of a person or where otherwise prohibited (12-183D-51).

No one shall enter upon land belonging to, held, or occupied by another to hunt or take wildlife without permission from the owner, but there will be no prosecution except upon a sworn complaint by the owner (12-183D-26). No one shall take or pursue a game bird or game mammal, wild bird or wild mammal at night on privately owned lands except as authorized by the Department (12-183D-27).

Restrictions on Taking: Fishing

It is unlawful to possess or use on or near state waters explosives, blasting fuse caps, electrofishing devices, or any source of electrical energy for introduction of electricity into the water for taking aquatic life, except the Department may issue permits with terms and conditions for electrofishing devices and explosives. It is unlawful to deposit in, permit to pass into, or place where it can pass into the state waters for the purpose of taking aquatic life: ▸ petroleum, coal or oil tar, lampblack, aniline, asphalt, bitumen, or residuary product or petroleum or carbonaceous material or substance; ▸ hypochlorous acid or its salts, including bleaches commonly sold under trade names, and bleaching powder; ▸ preparations containing rotenone, tephrosin, or plant materials from Barringtonia asiatica, Cocculus ferrendiandus, Hura crepitans, Piscidia erythrina, Tephrosia purpurea, Wikstroemia; ▸ any other substance or material deleterious to aquatic life, except under terms and conditions of a Department permit. A permit for possession may be issued for legitimate purposes if the amounts are too small to harm aquatic life. Possession of these substances without a permit by anyone on or near the water where fish can be taken is prima facie evidence of violation. Permits may be revoked for violation of terms and conditions, and cannot be reissued for one year from revocation (12-188-23).

No one shall pursue, take, or kill with firearms a turtle, crustacean, mollusk, aquatic mammal or fish except caught and gaffed tuna and billfish and sharks. No one shall pursue, take or kill a crustacean (except introduced freshwater prawns), turtle, or aquatic mammal with a spear. Species taken, killed or offered for sale in violation of this section shall be confiscated and offered as evidence. No one shall take a fish by the use of spears, or possess a speared fish smaller than state limits, and first time violators will receive a citation. Subsequent violations are punishable under 12-188-70, although the first subsequent violation is treated as a first violation under 12-188-70 (12-188-25).

Nets and traps for taking aquatic life are limited in size to a stretched mesh of less than two inches, with some exceptions for pond owners, aquarium fish collectors, scuba divers, sport fishers and for taking some small species of fish and shrimp (12-188-29). ★★It is unlawful to discard or otherwise dispose of a fishing net, trap, or gear with netting, or parts thereof in state waters (12-188-29.1).★★ It is unlawful to possess in or near the water throw nets of less than 1.5 inches mesh; after December 31, 1994, it is unlawful to possess, sell or offer to sell 2-inch mesh or less throw nets (12-188-30). ★★It is unlawful to possess or use a drift gill net in state waters (12-188-30.5).★★ Aquarium fish permits are allowed for taking fish alive with fine mesh nets for aquarium purposes (12-188-31).

The Department shall adopt rules to monitor the aquarium fish catch and export and shall require reports of quantities of species taken (12-188-31.5). [Provisions excluding fishing in certain specific canals, bays and areas are not included.] Fishing is allowed even in restricted areas with one line and not more than two hooks, and under license a fish pond owner or operator may take pua or other small fish for stocking the pond; all licenses can be revoked if necessary to preserve the stock of fish in the canals or waters (12-188-35). Possession with intent to sell, or offering to sell, certain species of fish below a minimum length or weight is prohibited (species listed in 12-188-40).

Commercial and Private Enterprise Provisions

Private and commercial shooting preserves, game bird farming, and domestication and propagation of game birds is encouraged, and licenses may be issued to a resident for $1. The Department may authorize any government agency to breed and sell the birds, and any person to possess lawfully obtained birds (12-183D-34). A resident who holds a private or commercial shooting preserve license may bring within the state and have custody of a game bird except those prohibited by 12-150A-6. A game bird brought within the state or reared in captivity in the state may be sold or transported for propagation, food or other purposes, if properly tagged as provided in 12-183D-36 (12-183D-35). Licensees must submit quarterly reports to the Department. Licensees may obtain game birds with permit from state game farms or other jurisdictions, may dispose of game bird eggs for propagation only, shall hold game birds as their exclusive property, and must submit to inspections (12-183D-39 through -42).

The keeper of a hotel, restaurant, boarding house, club or a retail dealer in meats may sell carcasses or parts obtained from a licensed game farm for actual consumption, after securing a $5 license. A common carrier may transport tagged game bird carcasses or parts, but every coop or package must be labeled in detail as to licensees and contents (12-183D-37 and -38).

Import, Export and Release Provisions

★★No aquatic life or wildlife may be deliberately introduced by the Department into a state habitat, whether from without into the state or from one state area to another unless introduction is recommended by the Department and authorized by its rules. In determining whether to introduce a species the Department shall make the following findings: ▸ factors which limit the distribution and abundance of the species in its native habitat have been studied and its probable dispersal pattern appraised; ▸ whether in the area where the species is proposed to be introduced there is or had been stock of desirable, ecologically comparable indigenous species which can be increased or rehabilitated by reintroduction or by encouraging extension of its range; ▸ whether the species would threaten the existence and stability of an indigenous species as predator, competitor for food, cover, or breeding sites, or in any other way arising from its characteristics and ecological requirements; ▸ the availability of socially acceptable methods of eliminating the species or keeping it under control in the area where it is proposed to be introduced and adjoining areas; ▸ the extent to which the species will enhance the economic and aesthetic values of the area where it is proposed to be introduced; ▸ the individuals to be introduced are free of communicable diseases and parasites and that there is no reason to believe that a communicable disease or parasite constitutes an important factor in the control of the population; ▸ there is no foreseeable risk of conflict with land use policies in the area or in adjoining areas to which the species might spread. Before a species is introduced into a habitat, the suitability of the introduction should be tested, if there is available an experimental area which can be fully controlled with a habitat typical of the proposed area. When a species is deliberately introduced, and until it becomes established on a stable basis, the Department shall conduct studies of its rate of spread and impact on the habitat (12-197-3).★★ (See also Agency Powers and Duties and Agency Advisory Boards under STATE FISH AND WILDLIFE AGENCIES; PROTECTED SPECIES OF WILDLIFE; GENERAL EXCEPTIONS TO PROTECTION; Commercial and Private Enterprise Provisions under this section.

ANIMAL DAMAGE CONTROL

★★On a game management area, public hunting area, or forest reserve or other lands under the jurisdiction of the Department, predators harmful to wildlife may be destroyed by the Department. Where predators are dogs and methods of destruction may endanger pets or hunting dogs, all major points of entrance into the predator area shall be posted with warning signs. A predator may be destroyed in a posted area whether or not the predator is the property of some person (12-183D-65).★★ (See also GENERAL EXCEPTIONS TO PROTECTION.)

ENFORCEMENT OF WILDLIFE LAWS

Enforcement Powers

An authorized officer or agent has authority to conduct searches as provided by law, and may seize equipment, business records, merchandise, aquatic life, wildlife, or land plants taken, possessed, transported, sold, offered for sale, or used illegally. Anything seized shall be held by the Department or may direct the transfer of specimens seized to a qualified ichthyological, zoological, botanical, educational, or scientific institution for safekeeping. Upon conviction the items shall be forfeited to the state for disposition as the Department sees fit (12-195D-8; similar provision at 199-7, which also mandates that a list of equipment and vehicles be published in the Department's annual report).

With respect to all state lands, including public lands, state parks, forest reserves, forests, aquatic life and wildlife areas, the conservation and resources enforcement officers shall: ▸ enforce Title 12 and chapter 6E, and their rules; ▸ investigate complaints, gather evidence, conduct investigations, and conduct field observations and inspections; ▸ cooperate with enforcement authorities of the state, counties and federal government in developing programs and agreements for conservation and resources enforcement activities; ▸ cooperate with established federal and county search and rescue agencies in developing search and rescue plans, programs and mutual aid agreements; ▸ check and verify all Department leases, permits, and licenses; ▸ enforce firearms, ammunition and dangerous weapons laws; ▸ enforce rules to control and manage state owned or controlled boating facilities, ocean waters and navigable streams and activities thereon, beaches with public easements, and rules regulating vessels and their use; ▸ carry out other duties and responsibilities as the Board directs. Every state and county officer charged with enforcement of laws and ordinances shall enforce Title 12 and chapter 6E, and their rules (12-199-3).

Criminal Penalties

Violations of chapter 188, except 188-23, or any rule adopted pursuant thereto, are petty misdemeanors and punishable as follows: ▸ first conviction, up to $500 fine, and/or jail not more than 30 days; ▸ second conviction within five years, $100-500 fine; and/or jail not more than 30 days; ▸ third or subsequent conviction within five years of the first two or more convictions, $300-500 fine, and/or jail not more than 30 days. Violation of 12-188-23 regarding use of prohibited fishing devices is a misdemeanor punishable as follows: ▸ first conviction, up to $1,000 fine, and/or jail not more than one year; ▸ second conviction within five years, $250-1,000 fine, and/or jail not more than one year; ▸ third or subsequent conviction within five years of the first two or more convictions, $500-1,000 fine, and/or jail up to one year. In addition to the above penalties, for the first conviction a fine of up to $25 may be levied for each specimen of aquatic life taken; for every subsequent conviction within five years, a fine of up to

$25 shall be levied for each specimen taken (12-188-70). A violation of the provisions of chapter 187A regarding aquatic resources, or a rule adopted thereunder for which a penalty is not provided, is a petty misdemeanor punishable under 12-188-70 (187A-13).

A Department employee or agent with police officer powers, and a county police officer has authority to enforce provisions of this chapter concerning conservation (12-195D-7). Violation of a section of chapter 195D, Conservation of Aquatic Life, Wildlife, and Land Plants, is a misdemeanor with a $250-1,000 fine, and/or jail of not more than one year; for subsequent convictions within five years, $500-1,000 fine, and/or jail of not more than one year. In addition to the above penalties, a $500 fine for each threatened species and a $1,000 fine for each endangered species intentionally, knowingly or recklessly killed or removed shall be levied (12-195D-9). Violation of the provisions or rules under chapter 197 relating to aquatic resources and wildlife, is a petty misdemeanor punishable as provided by law (12-197-5).

Reward Payments

★★One-half of fines imposed and collected through conviction under chapters 187A, 188, 189 except part II, and 191, shall be paid to the person giving the information leading to the arrest of the violator; except if the informer is a regular salaried sheriff, deputy sheriff, police officer, warden, constable, or officer or agent of the Department (187A-14).★★

HABITAT PROTECTION

For the purposes of managing, preserving, protecting, conserving and propagating introduced freshwater fishes, and other freshwater or marine life, the Department may establish, maintain, manage, and operate freshwater or marine fishing reserves, refuges and public fishing areas in areas under its control and may enter into agreements for the taking of control of privately owned waters, lands, or fisheries. The Department may make, adopt, and amend rules and may issue permits for managing the fish reserves, refuges, public fishing areas, and other state waters or lands. It is unlawful to enter the area without a Department permit, if required, or to violate any rule governing same. Permits may be revoked for infraction of terms and conditions, and may not be reissued for one year from revocation (188-53).

The Department shall conduct research on indigenous aquatic life, wildlife, and land plants, and on endangered species and their ecosystems, and shall utilize the land acquisition and other authority to carry out programs for the conservation, management, and protection of the species and their associated ecosystems. The Department is also authorized to acquire by purchase, donation or otherwise lands or interests therein needed to carry out conservation programs. The Governor's office shall review other programs administered by the Department and, to the extent practicable, utilize those programs in furtherance of the conservation purposes. The Governor or the Governor's representative shall also encourage other state and federal agencies to do the same by carrying out programs for the protection of endangered species and by taking action to insure that actions authorized, funded or carried out by them do not jeopardize the continued existence of the endangered species (12-195D-5).

In carrying out the programs authorized by section 195D, the Department may enter into agreements with federal agencies and counties for administration and management of areas established under 195D, or utilized for conserving, managing, enhancing, or protecting indigenous aquatic life, wildlife, land plants and endangered species. ★Priority shall be given to conservation and protection of endangered species and their ecosystems, whose extinction within the state would imperil or terminate, respectively, their existence in the world.★ The Department may permit taking, possession, transportation, or exportation of an indigenous endangered species for scientific purposes and for propagation in captivity for preservation purposes. The Department shall initiate amendments to the conservation district boundaries consistent with section 205-4 in order to include high quality native forests and habitat of rare native species of flora and fauna within the conservation district. The Department may seek assistance from appropriate public, private and nonprofit agencies and may employ consultants (12-195D-5.1). Rules shall be adopted to carry out the conservation purposes of 12-195D (12-195D-5, -5.1 and -6). (See also Agency Powers and Duties under STATE FISH AND WILDLIFE AGENCIES for establishment of wildlife sanctuaries.)

NATIVE AMERICAN WILDLIFE PROVISIONS: None.

IDAHO

Sources: Idaho Code, 1977, Title 36; 1992 Cumulative Pocket Supplement.

STATE WILDLIFE POLICY

All wildlife, including all wild animals, birds, and fish, within Idaho, is declared to be the property of the state. It shall be preserved, protected, perpetuated, and managed. It only shall be captured or taken at such times or places, under such conditions, or by such manner, as will preserve, protect, and perpetuate the wildlife, and provide for the citizens of the state, and as by law permitted to others, continued supplies of wildlife for hunting, fishing and trapping (36-103).

Because changing conditions affect the preservation, protection, and perpetuation of Idaho wildlife, the methods of administering the state's policy must be flexible and dependent on facts which from time to time exist and fix the needs for regulation and control of fishing, hunting, trapping, and other activity relating to wildlife. Because it is inconvenient and impractical for the Legislature to administer such policy, it shall be the duty of the Fish and Game Commission to administer and carry out the policy of the state in accordance with the provisions of the Idaho Fish and Game Code. The Commission is not authorized to change the policy, but only to administer it (36-103).

★The Legislature declares that it would be for the public good to authorize and empower the Boards of Commissioners of the respective counties to raise moneys through taxation to be expended for artificial propagation of game fish and in distribution and planting of the fish within their counties within the limitations prescribed in the code (36-1701).★

See Commercial and Private Enterprise Provisions under HUNTING, FISHING, TRAPPING PROVISIONS for outfitters and guides policy statement.

RELEVANT WILDLIFE DEFINITIONS: See Definitions section of Appendices.

See Agency Powers and Duties under STATE FISH AND WILDLIFE AGENCIES for Commission wildlife classification system and list of predatory animals.

STATE FISH AND WILDLIFE AGENCIES

Agency Structure

There is a **Department of Fish and Game** (Department) which, for the purposes of section 20, article IV of the Idaho Constitution, is an executive department of state government. The Department is under the supervision, management and control of the **Idaho Fish and Game Commission** (Commission). The Commission consists of six members appointed by the Governor, and selected solely upon consideration of the welfare and best interests of fish and game in the state, and members must be well informed about, and interested in, wildlife conservation and restoration. No more than three members may be of the same political party, and each must be a US and Idaho citizen and a resident of the district from which appointed. Six geographic districts are designated, and one Commissioner selected from each for a six-year term. The Commission shall appoint a **Director** of the Department (Director) who shall have knowledge and experience in the requirements for protection, conservation, restoration and management of the state wildlife resources. The Director serves as Commission Secretary (36-101, -102 and -106).

Agency Powers and Duties

The **Commission** selects a chairman annually for a one-year term, and is to hold quarterly meetings and special meetings. The Commission is authorized to: ► investigate and find facts regarding the status of wildlife populations to give effect to state wildlife policy; ► hold hearings and consider evidence to determine when the supply of any state wildlife will be injuriously affected by taking, or to determine when open seasons may be declared; ▸ make an order stating when, under what circumstances, where, by what means, what sex, and in what numbers wildlife may be taken, if longer or different seasons, different bag limits, or new seasons are needed; ▸ declare by written order, in emergency, for protection or management of wildlife, that affected areas or streams be closed to hunting, fishing or trapping, or impose needed restrictions; ▸ declare open seasons on game preserves for game management; ▸ authorize controlled hunt permits and lotteries, and issue controlled hunt permits to landowners in controlled hunt units where permits for deer, elk or antelope are limited, and charge a special fee for hunters selected to participate in controlled hunts; ▸ adopt rules pertaining to importation, exportation, release, sale, possession or transportation into, within or from the state live, native or exotic wildlife or eggs; ▸ acquire lands or waters by purchase, condemnation, lease, agreement, or gift after first making a good faith attempt to obtain a conservation easement before purchasing or condemning lands to be used for fish hatcheries, game bird and animal farms, game, bird, fish or fur-bearing animal restoration, propagation or protection, or for public hunting, fishing and trapping areas; ▸ enter into cooperative agreements with educational institutions and state, federal or other agencies to promote wildlife research and train students for wildlife management and to develop wildlife rearing, propagating, protection, management and demonstration projects; ▸ capture, propagate, transport, buy, sell or exchange a wildlife species needed for propagation or stocking purposes, or to control undesirable species; ▸ adopt rules for a lifetime license certificate program; ▸ adopt rules governing permits for fishing contests. Nothing in this title shall authorize the Commission to change any penalty prescribed by law or to change the amount of license fees (36-104).

★★The Commission may enter into agreements with landowners who have restricted the operation of motor-propelled vehicles upon their lands after public hearing and consultation with other potentially affected landowners, and if requested by at least ten residents of a county in which the land is located, may cooperate with the landowners to enforce those restrictions when they protect wildlife or wildlife habitat. The Commission shall not enter into agreements for lands which lie outside of or are not adjacent to adjoining proclaimed boundaries of national forests in Idaho. The landowners, with the assistance of the Department, shall post restrictions on roads entering the restricted areas. The Commission may make additional rules to enforce and administer the agreements (36-104). ★★

★With the exception of predatory animals, the Commission is authorized to define by classification or reclassification all state wildlife, the classifications and definitions to include: game animals; game birds; game fish; fur-bearing animals; migratory birds; threatened or endangered wildlife; protected nongame species; unprotected wildlife. Predatory wildlife shall include coyote, jackrabbit, skunk, weasel and starling (36-201).★

The **Director** has general supervision of Department employees and control of Department activities under Commission supervision, and shall enforce the wildlife laws and regulations, and shall appoint classified employees to enforce the laws and to properly implement management, propagation and protection programs. The Director may establish and maintain fish hatcheries, and shall supervise matters pertaining to propagation and distribution of wildlife, and may: ▸ take wildlife, dead or alive, or import the same for inspection, cultivation, propagation, distribution, scientific or other purposes deemed to be of interest to the fish and game resource; ▸ obtain by purchase or otherwise, needed wildlife suitable for state distribution; ▸ introduce new species, close seasons when species are threatened with excessive taking or during emergencies by written order; ▸ with Commission authority, declare an open season on a species to protect property from damage, detailing when, how, where, by what means, and in what amounts, numbers, and sex such wildlife may be taken; ▸ sell publications and materials (36-106).

The Director, with the Governor's approval, is authorized to employ special counsel for the Department and to pay reasonable attorneys' fees incurred in the conduct of Department business, or prosecution of violations civilly or criminally, the fees to be charged against the Game and Fish Fund (36-121).

The **Board of County Commissioners** in a county shall have the power to construct and operate fish hatcheries, rearing ponds and other facilities for the propagation and distribution of game fish within its own county according to authorized tax levies and expenditures (36-1702).

Agency Regulations (effective July 1, 1993)

All rules, regulations and orders adopted pursuant to this title shall be made in accordance with chapter 52, Title 67, and publicized as the Commission deems desirable. Rules, regulations and orders have the force of law, and violations are to be punished as set forth in 36-1401 and 36-1402. Proper notice procedures to be followed when adopting, repealing, or amending a rule relating to the setting of a season or limit on numbers, size, sex or species of wildlife classified as game animals, game birds, fur-bearers and resident fish, and for salmon, steelhead, or migratory birds include publication in the Idaho Administrative Bulletin at least 14 days before the effective date, and with concurrent notice to legislative counsel (36-105).

Agency Funding Sources

The Director shall transmit to the state treasurer moneys received from hunting, fishing, and trapping licenses, tags and permits, or from another source connected with administration of the Fish and Game Code or a wildlife law or regulation, including moneys from the sale of predatory animal furs for deposit into the **Fish and Game Account**. These moneys, and interest earned, are to be used as directed by the Commission only in carrying out the purposes of the Fish and Game code for protection of wildlife. ★★The state auditor shall annually deposit $100,000 from the Fish and Game Account to the University of Idaho Caine Veterinary Teaching and Research Center for disease research regarding the interaction of disease between wildlife and domestic livestock, the moneys to be expended on projects agreed upon by the Center and the state wildlife veterinarian.★★ Two dollars from each fishing license shall be used for the construction, repair or rehabilitation of fish hatcheries, fishing lakes or reservoirs. Up to $1.50 from each resident deer and elk tag and $5 from each non-resident deer or elk tag may go to the Department's Big Game Landowner-Sportsman's Relations Program (36-107).

The Director may receive on the Department's behalf any money or real or personal property donated, bequeathed or conditionally granted to the Department, and moneys from the sale of the property shall go into the **Fish and Game Expendable Trust Account** to carry out the terms of the donations, or to carry out Fish and Game Code policies and not for other purposes. There is a **Fish and Game Nonexpendable Trust Account** which is identical in funding to the Expendable Trust Account, but the principal amount of the moneys is not subject to appropriation, while interest can be spent as above according to the terms of the donation. Moneys received from the federal government for administration of an aspect of the fish and game laws shall be deposited in the **Fish and Game Federal Account**, and are subject to investment and appropriation (36-108 through -110).

There is a **Fish and Game Set-Aside Account** consisting of: ▸ $3 of each steelhead trout or anadromous salmon permit to be used for acquisition and maintenance of parking areas, access sites, boat ramps and sanitation facilities in salmon and steelhead fishing areas, for management of these species, and for technical assistance with litigation concerning these species originating in Idaho; ▸ $2 from each combination hunting and fishing license, or each hunting license, with certain exceptions, to be used for acquiring access to and rehabilitating and acquiring big game ranges and upland bird and waterfowl habitats, it being the intent of the Legislature that the Commission negotiate lease arrangements instead of outright purchase of private property; ★ ▸ $1.50 from each antelope, elk and deer tag for winter feeding of these species, control of depredation of private property by them, and control of predators and rehabilitation of winter range affecting these species;★ ▸ moneys from upland game permits, to be used as provided by 36-414 to acquire and manage upland game habitat; ▸ moneys from the sale of migratory waterfowl stamps to be used as provided in 36-414 for waterfowl projects and land acquisition for waterfowl habitat and management; ▸ moneys designated by individuals in accordance with 63-3067A(c)(i) and from fees paid under 49-417 to be used for a nongame management and protection program under the Commission's direction. The state auditor shall annually transfer $50,000 from the Fish and Game Account into the **Animal Damage Control Account**, the moneys subject to appropriation to the State Animal Damage Control Board established by 25-128 for control of predatory animals and birds, the Board to give priority to proposed actions on predatory animals or birds forwarded by the Department by the same date (36-111 and -112).

★The state auditor shall annually transfer $200,000 from the Fish and Game Account into the **Big Game Primary Depredation Account**, the moneys subject to appropriation for the purposes in 36-1108 regarding control of damage by elk, deer or moose on private lands, to be used only to honor payment agreements or to make depredation payments, or to reimburse expenses for Advisory Committee members. Interest earned and unexpended balances at fiscal year's end revert to the Fish and Game Account. Payment for damages is limited by the following conditions: ▸ the Director may order not more than one-third of the amount to be paid from this account to be paid immediately, the remainder to be paid along with other damage claims if there is a sufficient amount to pay fully all claims at fiscal year's end. Otherwise, each claimant will receive a proportionate share. The Director shall encumber the balance of the moneys in the account, or moneys sufficient to pay the approved claims, whichever is less; ▸ each claimant must submit a statement of total damages per occurrence, and $1,000 must be deducted from the total, which is a net loss to the landowner, and will not be compensated from either the Big Game Primary Depredation Account or the Secondary Depredation Account. The total amount that may be paid per approved claim is $9,000. Approved claims in excess of this amount shall be processed under the provisions of the Big Game Secondary Depredation Account, as shall approved claims that involve damage to livestock by black bear or mountain lion). or approved claims of an amount that involve damage to forage by antelope, deer, elk or moose. The Director must certify that statutory requirements leading up to approval for payment have been met and that the claimant will accept the approved amount as payment in full for the claim submitted (36-114).★

In addition to moneys appropriated to the account from other sources, the state auditor shall transfer the earned interest not to exceed $250,000 from the Fish and Game Account to the **Big Game Secondary Depredation Account** each fiscal year until a total of $1,250,000 has been transferred. The money is to be spent for the purposes in 36-1108(c) (crop damage by elk, deer, moose and antelope), 36-1109 (damage by black bear and mountain lion, and 36-1110 (damage to forage by grazing wildlife). Only interest earned on the account is available for appropriation. If the balance in the account ever exceeds $3,000,000, interest earnings that exceed the amount appropriated for a fiscal year shall be transferred into the Fish and Game Set-Aside Account for habitat rehabilitation (36-115). [The procedure for payments of approved claims is similar to that for the Big Game Primary Depredation Account (36-114), but there are different conditions of payment according to the type of damage and the animal species involved (36-115).]

A **State Migratory Waterfowl Stamp** is required for persons over age 16. There is a **Migratory Waterfowl Art Committee** consisting of seven members; one appointed by the Governor and four members by the Director who are knowledgeable about waterfowl management, one appointed by the Idaho Commission on the Arts who is knowledgeable about fine art reproduction, and one appointed by the Director of the Department of Agriculture to represent farming interests. The Department's four members shall represent a statewide conservation organization, a group with a major interest in migratory waterfowl conservation, and northern and southern sports groups. Members serve three years and are responsible for selection of the annual migratory waterfowl stamp design, and arranging for sale of prints. Moneys from sale of prints, stamps and related artwork shall be deposited in the Fish and Game Set-Aside Account, and net funds shall be expended 20% to a nonprofit entity or wildlife conservation agency to develop migratory waterfowl propagation within Alberta and British Columbia in Canada, and 80% to acquire and develop waterfowl propagation projects within Idaho (36-414).

From Fish and Game Fund moneys the Commission shall budget an amount to match cooperative grants of the federal government, the amounts to be placed in two separate funds, the **Wildlife Restoration Project Section** and the **Fish Restoration and Management Project Section** of the Department, to be used by the Commission in cooperative activities in wildlife and fish restoration projects. The money shall be used in the selection, restoration, rehabilitation and improvement of areas of land or water adaptable as feeding, resting, or breeding places for wildlife and fish, and the construction thereon of necessary facilities, including research into problems of wildlife management and fish restoration. Wildlife restoration projects moneys may also be used in establishment of a hunter safety program and the acquisition and operation of public outdoor target ranges as part of such a program. The moneys set aside by the Commission from the Fish and Game Fund and grants-in-aid income under provisions of the Wildlife Restoration Projects Act shall be transferred to the Wildlife Restoration Projects Fund to be used as a revolving fund for the above purposes only (36-1803 through -1805).

See Licenses and Permits for auction and lottery of special bighorn sheep tags and disposition of moneys, and lifetime license provisions, and Commercial and Private Enterprise Provisions for Outfitter's and Guide's Fund; both sections under HUNTING, FISHING, TRAPPING PROVISIONS. See also ANIMAL DAMAGE CONTROL and Civil Liability under ENFORCEMENT OF WILDLIFE LAWS.

Agency Advisory Boards

The **Fish and Game Advisory Committee** consists of 12 members, 6 appointed by the Director to represent wildlife interests, and 6 appointed by the Director of the Department of Agriculture to represent agricultural interests. The Directors shall alternate in appointing the chairperson annually. Terms are for four years. The Advisory Committee shall have authority to: ▸ act as a liaison between the Commission, the Department, landowners, the Department of Agriculture, and wildlife, outdoor recreation and sportsmen's organizations; ▸ act as an independent resource to give advice and recommendations on administration of the programs regarding compensation for damage by antelope, deer, elk, moose, black bear and mountain lion (36-122). (See Agency Funding Sources under STATE FISH AND WILDLIFE AGENCIES for the Migratory Waterfowl Art Committee. See Commercial and Private Enterprise Provisions under HUNTING, FISHING, TRAPPING PROVISIONS for the Idaho Outfitters and Guides Licensing Board.)

PROTECTED SPECIES OF WILDLIFE

Except for English Sparrows and starlings, no person shall take a game, song, rodent killing, insectivorous or other innocent bird, except as provided by regulation, nor intentionally disturb or destroy the eggs or nests of the birds. No person shall hunt, take or possess migratory birds except as provided by law, nor take the waterfowl unless possessing a Federal Migratory Bird Hunting Stamp. The Commission is authorized to establish a falconry program and make rules governing same (36-1102). No person shall take wild animals or wild birds in a state wildlife preserve except as provided otherwise by law or regulation (36-1902). (See also Agency Powers and Duties under STATE FISH AND WILDLIFE AGENCIES.)

GENERAL EXCEPTIONS TO PROTECTION

No person shall engage in propagation or hold in captivity a species of big game animal found wild in this state except by license or permit. All other species of mammals, birds or reptiles found in the wild and are not species of special concern or threatened or endangered species, may be held in captivity without permit if the possessor retains proof that the wildlife was lawfully obtained. No license or permit is required for a public zoo or wildlife exhibit or for a traveling circus, menagerie or trained animal act not permanently located within the state, nor for pet stores or fur farms with lawfully acquired wildlife (36-701).

★★Since wolf/dog hybridizations are known to exist within Idaho and are not protected by the US Endangered Species Act (ESA), a biological evaluation shall be required of the animal to determine species priority before the Department may take action in accordance with the ESA. The Department shall not be authorized to expend funds or enter into a cooperative agreement with any US agency or entity concerning wolves unless expressly authorized by state statute, except that the Department is authorized to provide a representative to participate on the Northern Rocky Mountain Wolf Recovery Team and to participate in activities regarding nuisance wolves. If a wolf is sighted, the burden of proof concerning its reported presence within Idaho shall rest with the observer and the Department shall take no action to enforce the ESA in absence of that proof. From April 8, 1992 through May 13, 1993, the Department is authorized to cooperate with the US government to receive and expend federal funds in the preparation of an environmental impact statement regarding wolf recovery for Idaho (36-715).★★

See also Agency Powers and Duties under STATE FISH AND WILDLIFE AGENCIES.

HUNTING, FISHING, TRAPPING PROVISIONS

General Provisions

Idaho is a member of the Pacific Marine Fisheries Compact. The three commissioners from Idaho shall be the Director or other officer charged with the conservation of the state's anadromous fisheries resource, and two members appointed by the Governor, one from the Commission and one from the Legislature (36-2001 and -2003).

Licenses and Permits

The Director shall have copies of applicable fish and game laws and regulations printed and supplied to license vendors for distribution to the public and license purchasers. The Director shall determine the form of various licenses, tags and permits and select license vendors. It is a misdemeanor for the Director, a Department employee or license vendor to issue an honorary or temporary permit or license permitting a person to hunt, fish or trap, but the Director may issue scientific collecting permits under 36-106(e) (36--301, -302, -303 and -305). No person shall hunt, trap, fish or take a wild animal, bird or fish without a license. There are exceptions for children under age 14 to fish, children under age 12 to take predatory or unprotected birds and animals by means other than with firearms and to trap muskrats, for residents over age 70, blind, disabled, military, Boy Scouts, and certain institutional inmates. Nothing shall prevent state citizens from carrying arms for protection of life and property. The six licenses available allow a person to take wildlife as authorized by the license, subject to statutory and regulatory provisions promulgated (36-401 and -402).

The Commission is authorized to: ▸ prescribe the number and kind of wildlife that may be taken under the several types of tags and permits, and the manner in which tags and permits shall be used and validated; ▸ establish a limit annually on the number of each kind and class of licenses, tags or permits to be sold; ▸ limit the number or prohibit entirely, the participation of non-residents in controlled hunts. ★When the Commission sets a limit on the number of non-resident deer and elk tags, it shall set aside annually a maximum of 25% of the tags to be sold on a first-come, first-served basis, only to persons that have entered into an agreement for that year to utilize the services of a licensed outfitter. In order to utilize this Outfitters Set-Aside, the person's outfitter must submit an application with the proper fees to the Department. Non-resident deer or elk tags unsold by July 1 of the set-aside year may be sold to general public non-residents (36-408).★

★★The Commission is authorized to issue two special bighorn sheep tags per year. One is to be auctioned off to the highest bidder by an incorporated nonprofit organization dedicated to wildlife conservation selected by the Commission. Money raised from the tag auction shall be used for bighorn sheep research and management. No more than 5% of the money for the tag may be retained by the organization. The other special bighorn sheep tag will be disposed of by lottery and marketed by the Department or a nonprofit organization dedicated to wildlife conservation. No more than 25% of the gross revenue can be retained for administrative costs by the organization. Net proceeds for the lottery tag shall be remitted to the **Bighorn Sheep Account** created in the dedicated fund, the moneys to be used in solving problems between bighorn sheep and domestic sheep, or between wildlife and domestic animals, or to improving relationships between sportsmen and private landowners by being utilized in the veterinarian program (36-106), and may be expended by appropriation. The two bighorn tags shall be taken from the non-resident bighorn sheep tag quota. Moneys raised from the auction or lottery may not be used to transplant additional bighorn sheep into the state, nor for litigation or environmental impact statements involving bighorn sheep. No transplants of bighorn sheep accomplished with moneys raised pursuant to this subsection shall occur until hearings are conducted in the area (36-408).★★ Residents who have purchased a license to hunt are eligible to receive a game tag to hunt a moose, bighorn sheep, mountain goat, elk, deer, antelope, mountain lion, bear or turkey in accordance with law or regulation. Archery and muzzleloader permits are available at an additional fee for designated controlled hunts. Failure to have a tag or to tag properly a carcass for which a tag is required is a misdemeanor. Until July 1, 1995, an Upland Game Permit may be issued by the Commission for persons over age 16 prior to hunting upland game, provided that no permit is required to hunt forest grouse (blue, ruffed or spruce), sharp-tailed grouse, sage grouse, mourning dove, turkey, cottontail rabbit, pygmy rabbit or snowshoe hare. Proceeds from the sale of this permit go for acquisition of lands and management of upland game habitat. ★A person using a dog for hunting or taking big game or fur-bearing animals must have a Hound Hunter Permit (36-409).★

In addition to the proper fishing or combination license, a permit is required to take either steelhead trout or anadromous salmon. Non-residents must have a permit, or, if under 14, fish with a permit holder, their catch to count as part of the licensed permit holders' creel limit (36-410).

Persons born after January 1, 1975, must have a certificate of completion of a hunter education course or must have previously held a hunting license in this or another state. The Commission shall prescribe and administer a hunter education program for the safe handling of lawful hunting weapons and instruction on wildlife and natural resources conservation, respect for the rights and property of others, and survival in the outdoors. The Department shall recruit and train competent volunteer instructors, and may enter into agreements with public or private agencies to carry out the provisions of the Hunter Education Program. Lifetime licenses are available for payment of 20 to 35 times the regular annual license fee for different age categories: one day through one year; two years through 50 years; 51 years and older. Moneys from lifetime licenses go to the Fish and Game Trust Account to be expended for the protection of wildlife only (36-411 through -413). A State Migratory Waterfowl Stamp is required for persons over age 16 to hunt migratory waterfowl. (See Agency Funding Sources under STATE FISH AND WILDLIFE AGENCIES.)

Restrictions on Taking: Hunting and Trapping

It is a misdemeanor for a person to: ▸ allow the waste through carelessness or neglect of a game bird, game animal or game fish or an edible portion; ▸ capture or kill a game animal, except a carnivore, and detach or remove from the carcass only the head, hide, antlers, horns or tusks and leave the carcass to waste. To fail to dress properly and care for a game animal except carnivores killed and, if the carcass is reasonably accessible, to fail to transport same to one's camp within 24 hours is prima facie evidence of a violation (36-1202).

It is unlawful, except as otherwise provided by law or Commission regulation, for a person to take game animals, birds or fur-bearing animals of this state. It is unlawful to: ▸ hunt from motorized vehicles game animals or birds unless by handicapped hunter permit as defined by statute and under permit restrictions; ▸ use a motorized vehicle to molest, stir up, rally or drive game animals or birds; ▸ use aircraft to spot or locate game animals, game birds or fur-bearing animals from the air and communicate their location by signals, whether radio, visual or otherwise, to persons on the ground; ★ ▸ use a helicopter in the taking of game or loading, unloading hunters, game or hunting gear except at recognized airports or airplane landing fields, or at heliports previously established on private land or by a department or agency of the federal, state or local government or in the course of emergency or search and rescue operations; ★ ▸ hunt an animal or bird except raccoon by the aid of a spotlight, flashlight or artificial light. The casting after sunset of a light, six volts or more, upon a field, forest or other place by a person while having in possession an uncased firearm or device capable of killing an animal or bird shall be prima facie evidence of hunting with artificial light. This does not prevent the hunting of unprotected or predatory wildlife with the aid of artificial light for protecting property or livestock if done by a landowner on the landowner's property, or on public lands under the Director's permit. It is unlawful to use a dog to pursue, take or kill big game animals except as provided by regulation. Anyone owning, possessing or harboring a dog found running at large and which is actively tracking, harassing, or attacking, or which injures or kills deer or other big game animal, is guilty as provided under 36-1401. It is no defense that the dog was pursuing big game animals without the aid or direction of the owner. A dog found running at large and which is actively tracking, attacking or killing deer or other big game animals may be destroyed by the Director or a peace or law enforcement officer (36-1101).

No person shall trap or take wild fur-bearing animals or pelts except as permitted by law or regulation. No person shall: ▸ use a part of a game bird, game animal or game fish for bait in trapping or taking of wildlife; ▸ destroy, disturb or remove the traps of a licensed trapper, except that the Director may seize and sell illegal or unclaimed traps, the moneys to go to the Fish and Game Fund; ▸ trap in or on, or destroy or damage, a muskrat house, except that a "push-up" is not a muskrat house in the sense of the law pertaining to trapping in or on muskrat houses. A special tag must be attached to the hide of bobcat or lynx legally taken within the state and exported. When the Commission declares an open season on beaver, it may regulate the issuance of special beaver tags to licensed trappers, including the maximum number to be issued to one person. Once legally tagged, the beaver pelt shall become the property of the trapper and may be sold, transferred or shipped in ordinary trade. Illegally taken beaver or untagged pelts may be confiscated and sold by the Director, the proceeds to go into the Fish and Game Fund. Licensed trappers must make an annual written report as to the number and kinds of wild animals caught, killed and pelted during the open season, where the pelts were sold, and the amount of income derived from their sale. A trapper failing to report shall be refused a trapping license for the ensuing year (36-1103 through -1105).

It is a misdemeanor to: ▸ discharge a firearm from or across a public highway; ▸ have in the possession of children under age 12 a firearm while in fields, forests, tents, camps, or vehicles in Idaho; ▸ cut an opening larger than ten inches in diameter through the ice for fishing except on Bear Lake for dip netting Cisco (36-1508 and -1509). No person shall enter the enclosed, posted, or cultivated lands of another to hunt, fish or trap with a dog or weapon without first obtaining permission from the owner or occupant (36-1602 and -1603).

Restrictions on Taking: Fishing

No person shall take or possess fish from state waters except as permitted by law and regulation. Except as otherwise permitted, no person shall: ▸ deposit, throw, place or allow to pass into state waters a deleterious drug, toxicant, chemical, poisonous substance, explosive, electrical current or other material which may tend to destroy, kill, disable or drive away fish, or operate a sawmill, reduction works or quartz mill upon a natural stream course or lake without first constructing a proper settling dam (violation: minimum $150; and/or jail up to six months); ▸ attempt to catch or kill a species of fish in state waters with a seine, net, spear, snag hook, weir, fence, basket, trap, gill net, dip net, trammel net or other contrivance (violation: fine not less than $50 and/or jail up to six months); ▸ take, transport, use or have in possession minnows, fish or young of a fish or parts for bait or to release live minnows, fish or the young of a fish into state waters except in connection with fishing in the Kootenai River; ► deposit or distribute a substance not attached to a hook for attracting fish (chumming). Salmon eggs may be used for bait only when attached to a hook on a line [penalty for chumming or minnow use provided in 36-1402]. Under the Director's permit and supervision, whitefish may be taken with seine for local consumption where they are found to be of sufficient number or quantity. It is a misdemeanor to keep other game fish caught by seining whitefish (36-901, -902 and -904).

No person shall place fish racks or traps or other obstructions across a stream of the state without a permit, or tamper with an authorized trap. No person shall construct a dam or other obstruction without a Director approved fishway installed at the owner's expense. No person shall operate a mill, factory, power plant or other manufacturing concern run by water power, or operate a ditch, flume or canal taking water from a state stream without first installing a suitable fish screen under Director specifications. The Director shall order in writing the construction of screens or fishways, specifying the type, design and location thereof, and installation shall occur between 30 days to 6 months of the order. The Director may order removal of abandoned structures which are detrimental to the fishery resource . Violations relating to fish racks, fishways, fish ladders or screens are misdemeanors, with a separate offense for each day of violation (36-905, -906 and -909).

Commercial and Private Enterprise Provisions

Classified personnel employed at state game farms and fish hatcheries shall not engage in the operation of a fish hatchery, public or private, unless ordered by the Director and shall not be entitled to have a holding in or own private fish ponds, lakes or streams of this state, nor shall they engage in the selling or disposal of wildlife, except in the duties of their office and as directed by the Director (36-120).

A person who desires to mount, preserve, or prepare for preservation dead bodies of wildlife or parts not taken personally must have a Taxidermy License. A person who engages in the business of buying hides, skins or pelts of fur-bearers must have a Fur Buyer's license. Such persons shall keep written records for two years of all transactions of taxidermy or fur buying or sale. Failure to keep required records relating to the transportation, possession or sale of wildlife, in addition to other penalties, shall be grounds for license revocation for up to 12 months. The Director shall seize and confiscate wildlife or skins, hides, pelts, horns or antlers or other parts in the possession of a fur buyer or taxidermist who fails to produce satisfactory record of lawful origin and proof of ownership (36-601, -603, -604 and -606).

No person shall obtain, possess, preserve, or propagate a species of big game animal found wild in this state for the purpose of selling without a Commercial Wildlife Farm license. The farm must be entirely on private property and may not be constructed so as to contain land where wild big game animals naturally abound. The farm must be enclosed to prevent escape of commercial animals and entry of the same species of publicly owned big game animals, and farm boundaries must be posted. Records must be kept for two years of each sale, purchase or shipment of animals. No person shall capture or possess wildlife owned/held in trust by the state except as provided by law. It is unlawful to take fish or wild animals or birds from a county, state, federal or private fish hatchery, fish trap, or wildlife farm. No person shall establish and maintain a private park or pond, nor obtain, possess, propagate or process fish or big game animals found wild in the state without a permit. A separate permit is required for each location, and must satisfy conditions set by the Director regarding dams, water inlet screening, and fencing and posting of lands. No person shall maintain a private park or pond without a permit, nor sell or purchase fish or big game animals found wild in the state which are possessed or propagated in such private park or pond. The Commission is authorized to regulate standards of sanitation, humane treatment, proper care and maintenance of big game animals held in captivity under license or permit for private or commercial farms. Licensees shall allow reasonable inspection of facilities and wildlife held on private or commercial game farms, and records must be kept for five years of sources of wildlife and purchase or sale dates. Violation may result in license revocation up to 12 months and confiscation of wildlife. Regulation of breeding, raising, producing or other phase of the production or distribution of domestic fur-bearing animals is vested in the Department of Agriculture (36-703 through -711). (See RELEVANT WILDLIFE DEFINITIONS.)

★A wolf that is captured alive for later release, or which is born or held in captivity, must be reported within three days of the capture or commencement of captivity to the Department. Violation: up to $1,000 fine for each animal possessed and not reported. Each reported animal shall be permanently tattooed in a manner that will provide positive identification, unless the animal is subject to a permanent identification process by another state or federal agency. A person holding a wolf in captivity shall immediately report its death, escape, release, transfer of custody or other disposition to the Department. A canine exhibiting primary wolf characteristics shall be classified as a wolf for identification purposes and shall be tattooed, registered and licensed by the Department (36-712). The Department shall maintain records of each reported animal, including by whom captured, the location of the capture/captivity, the date tattooed, the purpose of the captivity or capture, and a death, release, transfer of custody or other disposition (36-713).★ (See also ANIMAL DAMAGE CONTROL for other wolf provisions.)

★★The natural resources of the state are an invaluable asset to every community in which they abound. Every year, in rapidly increasing numbers, Nevada residents and non-residents are enjoying the benefits of Idaho's recreational opportunities. The tourist trade is of vital importance, and the recreational value of Idaho's natural resources is such that the number of persons participating in their enjoyment is steadily increasing. The intent of the Outfitters and Guides Act is to promote and encourage residents and non-residents to participate in the enjoyment and use of the deserts, mountains, rivers, streams and other natural resources, and the fish and game therein, and to that end to regulate and license those persons who undertake for compensation to provide equipment and personal services to such persons, for the explicit purpose of safeguarding the health, safety, welfare and freedom from injury or danger of such persons, in the exercise of the police power of this state. It is not the intent of this legislation to interfere with livestock operations, nor to prevent pack animal owners from using same to accommodate friends where no consideration is involved for the use thereof, nor to interfere with the right of the general public to enjoy the recreational value of Idaho's natural resources when commercial outfitters and guides are not utilized (36-2101).★★

It is a misdemeanor to engage in the business of or act in the capacity of an outfitter or guide unless licensed (36-2104). Violation is a $300-1,000 fine; and/or jail up to 90 days, if not a corporation (36-2117). License fees collected shall go to the **Idaho Outfitters and Guides Board Fund**, for conducting Board operations (36-2111). A person holding a outfitter's license may act as a guide without a guide's license if the person possesses the qualifications of a guide as determined by the Board (36-2112). The prosecuting attorney of each county shall prosecute, in the county where the violation occurs, a violation of 36-2104 or 36-2116. Violation is a misdemeanor with $100-5,000 fine; and/or jail up to 90 days, if not a corporation. Fines shall be paid 50% to the Outfitters and Guides Board Account, and 50% in accordance with 19-4705. The court shall send notice to the Board of the nature of the offense, the fine and sentence imposed, and names of violators (36-2117). The Board may prosecute in district court a civil enforcement action against alleged violators of a statute or rule within two years of time the Board had notice of the violation. The civil penalty shall not be less than $100 nor more than $5,000 for each separate violation. Moneys collected shall be credited 50% to the Outfitters and Guides Board Account, and 50% to the general account in the state operating fund (36-2117A).

There is created in the Department of Self-Governing Agencies the **Idaho Outfitters and Guides Licensing Board** (Board), consisting of four members appointed by the Governor with Senate approval, and one member appointed by the Commission. One shall be a Commission member or a designee, and one from the public. Three shall be qualified and licensed outfitters and guides with at least five years of experience. Terms are for three years, and the Board shall meet at least quarterly. The Board has the power to: ► conduct examinations to ascertain the qualifications for outfitter or guide licenses; ► prescribe rules to carry into effect the provisions of the outfitter's act including qualifications of training, experience, knowledge, type of equipment, examinations to be given applicants; ► conduct hearings to suspend, revoke or restrict outfitter/guide licenses for due cause; ► enforce the outfitter's act provisions and to make and enforce rules to safeguard the health, safety, and welfare of persons utilizing outfitter/guide services and for conservation of wildlife and range resources; ► cooperate with federal and state agencies regarding the outfitting/guide business in the state; ► request witness attendance and production of books, records and papers at a hearing before it; ► request a district court to issue a subpoena for a witness or a subpoena duces tecum to compel the production of records; ► appoint an executive director of the board; ► hire enforcement agents to conduct investigations. Agents certified by the Idaho Peace Officer Standards and Training Advisory Council have the power of peace officers limited to enforcement of this chapter's provisions and responding to express requests from other law enforcement agencies for aid in enforcing other laws for singular violations. The Board shall annually report to the Director on the number of each species of big game taken in each management unit by clients of licensed outfitters during the prior fiscal year. In January each year, each non-resident licensee, permittee or tagholder shall provide to the Department a report showing the number of each species of big game taken in each management unit during the previous calendar year, and if a licensed outfitter or guide was used, the name and license number of the outfitter. [Extensive statutory details are given concerning license applications, qualifications and bond requirements, as well as the territorial limits of operation of each outfitter.] The Board shall not issue a license to a person who is not competent and of good moral character, less than 18 years of age, and who does not possess a working knowledge of state game and fish laws and US Forest Service regulations, or who has violated the provisions of this chapter. The operating area as set forth on the license shall be the limit of the operations for each licensee, but the Board may adjust the territorial scope of operations of a licensee for reasons of game harvest, where territorial conflict between the big game operations of outfitters exists, or for the safety of clients (36-2105 through -2110).

Every outfitter/guide license shall be subject to suspension, revocation or restriction by the Board for: ▸ supplying false information or other fraud in the license application procedure; ▸ fraud in advertising; ▸ conviction of a felony; ▸ conviction of or two or more forfeitures of deposits of money with a court for violation of regulations of the US Forest Service or the BLM; ▸ unethical or unprofessional conduct as defined by Board rules; ▸ breach of contract with a client; ▸ wilfully operating in an area for which the licensee is not licensed or engaging in an unlicensed activity; ▸ employment of an unlicensed guide; ▸ inhumane treatment of an animal used in the conduct of business; ▸ failure to provide animals with proper food, drink and shelter or subjecting the animal to needless abuse or cruel and inhumane treatment; ▸ failure to serve the public by limiting services or not offering services; ▸ violation or noncompliance with the Outfitters' Act, or violation of rule, regulation or order of the Board. Any of these violations is a misdemeanor, to be punished as provided in 36-2117. In lieu of suspension or revocation, the Board may impose an administrative fine up to $5,000 for each violation of the provisions of this chapter (36-2113 and -2116).

A person may make a written accusation to the Board which shall make a preliminary investigation of all facts in connection with the charge. The Board may decide to take no further action, or may initiate proceedings to suspend/revoke the outfitter/guide license, giving notice of hearing date to the alleged violator no later than 180 days after the filing of accusations. After full, fair and impartial hearing, if the majority of the Board finds the accused guilty of the violations alleged, the Board may suspend the license for up to one year, or may order the license revoked. An applicant denied application for an outfitter's/guide's license by the Board has 20 days to submit a written request for a hearing before the Board to review the action (effective July 1, 1993). For certain misdemeanor violations enumerated under 36-2113, the Board may prefer a complaint before a court with jurisdiction. No person acting in the capacity of an outfitter or guide shall bring an action for the collection of compensation for outfitting/guide services without alleging and proving that they were a duly licensed guide/outfitter at the time the alleged cause of action arose (36-2114, -2116 and -2118).

It is the intent of the Legislature to provide for and control the establishment and operation of Shooting Preserves in a manner in the best public interest. The Director is authorized to issue shooting preserve licenses to permit shooting privately owned upland game birds on private premises under Commission regulations. During the shooting preserve season, hunting upland game birds on preserves shall be open to a holder of a license of the proper class upon payment of the shooting fee established by the licensed shooting preserve operator (36-2201). The Director shall inspect the proposed shooting preserve premises and facilities, and if requirements are met, issue operating permits. Each shooting preserve shall contain a minimum of 160 acres but not more than 1,600 acres, and must meet statutory requirements. Boundaries shall be clearly defined and posted. Only artificially propagated upland game birds may be hunted. A minimum of 200 marked or banded birds of each species must be released during the shooting preserve season. An upland game bird license or a special shooting preserve license is required. The shooting season shall be from August 15 to April 15, and the total number of birds taken during the season shall not exceed 85% of the total number of each species released during the license year. Operators may set their own sex and bag limits, and 100% of exotic species not classified as game birds in this state may be taken. Birds taken outside preserve boundaries are subject to state game laws. Detailed records must be kept by the preserve operator, and Commission rules adhered to that relate to care and sanitary provisions. Only birds killed by shooting and properly tagged may be removed from the premises, and it is unlawful to sell or attempt to buy the birds thereafter. The Director may suspend or revoke a shooting preserve license for noncompliance with statutory provisions or rules (36-2201 through -2215).

Import, Export and Release Provisions

★A deer, elk, antelope, moose, bighorn sheep or bison imported or transported by the Department shall be tested for communicable diseases that can be transmitted to domestic livestock as determined by agreement between the Department and the Department of Agriculture. A comprehensive health program for deer, elk, antelope, moose, bighorn sheep or bison imported into, transported, or resident within the state shall be implemented, and the Department of Agriculture shall employ at least one veterinarian whose duties shall include addressing wildlife disease issues and coordinating disease prevention work between the two departments, and whose salary is to be shared between the two departments. In order to monitor and evaluate the disease status of wildlife and to protect Idaho's livestock resources, a suspicion by Department personnel of a potential communicable disease process in wildlife shall be reported within 24 hours to the Department of Agriculture (36-106). ★ No person shall import into this state or release in the wild a species of wildlife except by Director permit. Except for inspection provisions (36-709), these provisions do not apply to domestic fur farm, tropical fish or other aquaria, or ornamental fish which the Commission determines does not pose a threat to native fish if released into public waters (36-701). (See also STATE FISH AND WILDLIFE AGENCIES.)

Interstate Reciprocal Agreements

There are reciprocal agreements between Idaho, Oregon and Washington for fishing, hunting, and trapping in the Snake River or its islands in order to avoid the conflict, confusion and difficulty of an attempt to find the exact locations of state boundaries, but residents of other states may not fish, hunt or trap on the shoreline, sloughs or tributaries on the Idaho side of the Snake River except by reciprocal agreements in 36-1003 (36-1001). Similar reciprocal agreements exist for reciprocal licensing rights recognition for Washington, Oregon and Utah on Bear Lake. Violation of reciprocal agreement provisions is a misdemeanor. Cooperative agreements with Utah and Wyoming for development, construction and maintenance of the Bear Lake watershed fishing resource are authorized (36-1003 through -1005).

★★To avoid conflicts in recognizing state boundary lines, the right to hunt big game in herd units where the herd unit incorporates the boundary line between a contiguous state and Idaho is recognized. The Director is authorized to enter into reciprocal agreements with the departments of contiguous states for recognizing license rights for hunting in herd units which incorporate boundary lines between states. For enforcement purposes, the courts of this state sitting in counties which incorporate boundary herd units, and law enforcement officers shall have jurisdiction over the entire boundary herd unit, and concurrent jurisdiction therein with the court and enforcement officers of contiguous states over said boundary herd units is recognized and established (36-1006).★★

ANIMAL DAMAGE CONTROL

If a wolf held in, or escaped from, captivity causes damage to the personal property of another, damage compensation shall be paid by the person holding the animal in captivity. This does not apply to animals captured and released as part of a game management program or ongoing predator control program, or as part of a scientific, educational or research program, unless the animals have been involved in livestock killing (36-714). A person may control, trap, and/or remove wild animals or birds or may destroy the houses, dams or other structures of fur-bearing animals to protect property from depredations (36-1107).

Except for antelope, elk, deer or moose, when wildlife protected by statute is damaging or destroying property, or is likely to do so, the landowner may make complaint and report the facts to the Director who shall investigate, and if the complaint is well-founded, and property damage has occurred or is likely to occur, the Director may: ▸ send a representative to control, trap and/or remove protected wildlife as will stop the damage, the animals to remain state property; ▸ grant properly safeguarded permission to the landowner to control, trap and/or remove the protected wildlife or to destroy houses or dams erected by said animals or birds; ▸ when in the public interest, authorize or cause the removal of a dam, house, structure erected by fur-bearing animals; ▸ issue a permit to a landowner/lessee of property which is being actually and materially damaged by fur-bearing animals to trap or kill the animals on landowner's own lands, the permit to specify the number of animals that may be trapped, the animals to become the property of the taker, except for beaver which are covered in 36-1104. Muskrats may be taken in or along the banks of irrigation ditches, canals or dams by landowners or those in charge of the facilities. Black bears, mountain lions and predators may be disposed of without a permit by livestock owners/employees when they are molesting livestock, but mountain lions so taken shall be reported to the Director. ★Livestock owners may take steps necessary to protect their livestock (36-1107).★

★★Prevention of depredation is a priority management objective of the Department, and it is the obligation of landowners to take steps to prevent property loss from wildlife or to mitigate damages by wildlife.★★ When antelope, elk, deer or moose are damaging or destroying property, or are likely to do so, the landowner may make complaint to the Director, who shall within 72 hours, investigate, and if the complaint is well-founded, the Director may: ▸ send a representative onto the premises to control, trap and/or remove the animals as will stop the damage, the animals to remain state property; ▸ grant properly safeguarded permission to the landowner to control, trap or remove the animals, which remain state property; ▸ make an agreement with the landowner to allow continued use of the lands by the animals where damage has occurred to stored, growing or matured crops on private property after other attempts to resolve the problem have failed. The agreement may provide for financial compensation under 36-114, and the payments shall not be in addition to payments for crop losses from another source. Compensation under this section shall be available for damage done to private lands, whether owned or leased, if the owner/lessee allowed hunters reasonable access to or through the property to public lands for hunting during the preceding hunting season. If there is no agreement made, then persons suffering crop damages on private lands caused by antelope, deer, elk or moose must notify the Department's regional office within 72 hours, giving written description of damages and a claim for damages attested under oath of at least $1,000. The Department shall review the claim, and if approved, pay it as provided in 36-114 or 36-115. Failure to allow on-site access shall negate the claim. The Department may pay the amount as claimed, or make a counter offer in a lesser amount. If this offer is refused, or if the Department finds that no damage occurred, the matter shall be referred to arbitration within five days. ★The arbitration panel shall consist of the Director (or designee), the landowner/lessee (or designee), and one member selected by those two. The panel shall have the same power to make on-site inspections, and shall select either the owner's claimed amount or the Department's assessed amount of damages, and this decision shall be binding on the owner and the Department (36-1108).★

[Similar provisions concerning landowner responsibility for mitigating damage from black bears, mountain lions, and grazing wildlife apply (36-1109 and -1110).] The Director will consult with appropriate land management agencies and land users before transplanting or relocating a black bear or mountain lion. Complaints about bear or mountain lion damage are made to the US Department of Agriculture Animal Plant and Health Inspection Services/Animal Damage Control, which shall investigate, and present to the Director a final, binding report on the extent of physical damage. Claims for compensation shall be for a minimum of $5,000 per occurrence, and similar arbitration procedures apply as for ungulate damage under 36-1108 (36-1109). If damage is being done by grazing wildlife, the owner shall report to the Director for investigation within 72 hours. If well-founded, the landowner shall, at landowner's own expense, contract with a qualified range management consultant to prepare an estimate of depredation. Claims shall be limited to loss of forage on private lands, and shall be processed under 36-1108(c), with approved claims paid under 36-115(f) (36-1109 and -1110). (See Agency Funding Sources under STATE FISH AND WILDLIFE AGENCIES and Criminal Penalties under ENFORCEMENT OF WILDLIFE LAWS.)

ENFORCEMENT OF WILDLIFE LAWS

General Provisions

Idaho is authorized to become a member of the multi-state **Wildlife Violator Compact** for the purposes of cooperating with those states for promotion of interstate cooperation with the enforcement of wildlife laws (36-2301 through -2303). (See also License Revocations, Suspensions under ENFORCEMENT OF WILDLIFE LAW.)

Enforcement Powers

The Director, conservation officers and other classified Department employees, and sheriffs, deputy sheriffs, forest supervisors, marshals, police officers, state forest department officers and national forest rangers shall have statewide jurisdiction and shall have the duty to enforce the provisions of the Fish and Game Code. Conservation officers with certification from the Peace Officer Standards and Training Advisory Council shall have the authority given by statute to state peace officers. All other classified employees appointed by the Director shall have the power of peace officers limited to: ▸ enforcing Title 36 and Commission regulations promulgated pursuant thereto; ▸ arresting persons possessing domestic animals unlawfully; ▸ responding to requests from other law enforcement agencies for aid in enforcing a particular and singular violation of law; ▸ other peace officer powers as designated by statute. Arrests pursuant to Title 36 provisions may be effected by taking the offender into custody for immediate appearance before a state magistrate; or issuing a citation to the offender to appear before the magistrate, the citation to contain the information required in this section. Failure to appear at the time and place specified in the citation is cause for issuance of an arrest warrant. Actions shall be in the name of the state and prosecuted by the county attorney having jurisdiction (36-1301 and -1302).

Officers are vested with authority and have the duty to: ▸ inspect depots, cars, cold storage facilities, restaurants, air terminals and baggage where they have probable cause to believe the contents are in violation of title provisions; ▸ search, with or without a warrant, tents, wagons, autos, boats, aircraft (private or chartered), camp trailers, baggage or packs when there is probable cause to believe possession of unlawfully taken wildlife or equipment or substances used to take the wildlife. The Director and enforcement officers are authorized to seize and hold as evidence any powder, explosives, lime, drugs, toxicants, spears, traps, snares, guns, tackle, nets, seines or other hunting, fishing or trapping equipment used in violation of a law or regulation, provided that all lawful traps, guns, spears, tackle, nets and seines taken from an accused violator and held as evidence shall not be subject to confiscation but returned to the person when no longer needed as evidence. If evidence indicates that the powder, explosive, lime, toxicant, drug or other unlawful means or device was used for unlawful taking or killing of wildlife, the magistrate shall order the same confiscated and sold by the Director at public sale, the proceeds to go to the Fish and Game Account. Any guns, fishing tackle, nets, traps used in taking wildlife unlawfully and for which no lawful owner can be determined, or unclaimed within six months following final case disposition, shall become Department property after written notice to the lawful owner. Unlawfully taken or unclaimed wildlife shall be seized and given to charitable institutions or sold, the proceeds to go into the Fish and Game Account (36-1303 and -1304).

Criminal Penalties

A person convicted of a violation of the provisions of this title, or Commission rules or regulations, except where an offense is expressly an infraction or felony, is guilty of a misdemeanor (36-1401). Unless a higher penalty is prescribed, a misdemeanor is a $25-1,000 fine, and/or jail up to six months (36-1402). (See also Illegal Taking of Wildlife under ENFORCEMENT OF WILDLIFE LAWS.)

It is an infraction to: ▸ take, transport or possess bait fish under 36-902; ▸ engage in chumming; ▸ hunt waterfowl without a federal and state migratory waterfowl stamp; ▸ hunt upland game birds without a permit; ▸ trap in, destroy or damage a muskrat house; ▸ cut a hole larger than ten inches diameter for ice fishing; ▸ store fish without required tags; ▸ own, possess or harbor a dog found running loose and tracking, harassing or attacking a big game animal; ▸ fish without a license if a non-resident under age 14 unless accompanied by a licensed person; ▸ fish with a motor where prohibited; ▸ use illegal hooks or tackle; ▸ exceed bag limits by two fish; ▸ fail to have heads and tails on possessed fish; ▸ snag fish and fail to release them, except anadromous fish; ▸ fail to leave sex/species evidence on game birds; ▸ fail to comply with mandatory check and report requirements; ▸ use lead shot in a steel shot zone; ▸ fail to release nontarget trapped animals; ▸ fail to complete required reports on trapped fur-bearers; ▸ fail to tag traps or bait traps illegally; ▸ fail to present required fur-bearer/fish parts for inspection. Infraction violations shall be punished in accordance with provisions of the Idaho infractions rules. The minimum fine, per animal, fish or bird, for illegal taking, possession or waste of the following animals is: bighorn sheep, mountain goat and moose, $500; elk, $300; deer and pronghorn antelope, $200; wild turkey, swan and sturgeon, $200; Chinook salmon, $100 (36-1401 and -1402).

The following offenses are felonies: ▸ intentionally selling or offering for sale or purchasing wildlife or parts unlawfully killed, taken or possessed; ▸ releasing into the wild without a permit from the Director, any ungulates, bears, wolves, large felines, swine or peccaries, whether native or exotic; ▸ unlawfully killing, possessing or wasting any combination of numbers or species of wildlife which has a single or combined reimbursable damage assessment of more than $1,000 as provided in 36-1404; ▸ conviction within five years of three or more violations of the provisions of this title, penalties for which include either or both a mandatory license revocation or a reimbursable damage assessment. A person found guilty of a felony under this title shall be punished in accordance with 18-112, Idaho Code. The judge hearing the case shall revoke for life, the hunting, fishing or trapping license and privileges of a person who, within a five year period is found guilty of three or more felony violations of this title's provisions (36-1401 and -1402).

Conviction of violation of provisions of this title with respect to methods of taking, seasons or limits relating to mountain lion is a fine of $100-1,000 for each offence; and/or jail up to six months. A violation relating to the protection of buffalo and caribou is a $150-1,000 fine; and jail up to six months. Other violations of animal damage control provisions for which no specific penalty is given are subject to the penalties of 36-1402 (36-1111).

Civil Liability

In addition to the penalties for violating the provisions of Title 36, a person convicted of illegal killing, possession or waste of game animals, birds or fish shall reimburse the state as follows for the value of each animal illegally killed, possessed or wasted: elk, $500; caribou, bighorn sheep, mountain goat and moose, $1,000; deer, pronghorn antelope, wild turkey, swan and sturgeon, $200; Chinook salmon, $100. In every conviction or plea of guilty, the court shall order the defendant to reimburse the state as set forth including postjudgment interest. Two or more defendants convicted of illegal possession, killing or wasting are jointly and severally liable. The court may allow installment payments not to exceed two years from the date of judgment. ★In addition to the fines imposed in 36-1402 and 36-1404, there is imposed an additional fine of $7.50 against each person convicted as provided in those sections to be deposited directly to the credit of the **Search and Rescue Account** in 67-2903 (36-1404 and -1405).★

Illegal Taking of Wildlife

★★It is unlawful to import, export, transport, sell, receive, acquire, purchase or possess wildlife that is taken, possessed or sold after July 1, 1991, in violation of a US law or regulation, an Indian law or regulation, or a law or regulation of another state or a foreign country. Each violation is a separate offense and shall be deemed to have been committed not only in the location where the violation first occurred, but also in a location in which the defendant may have been in possession of the wildlife within Idaho. Such wildlife is subject to the effect of Idaho law to the same manner as though it had been produced in Idaho. Violations shall be punished in accordance with chapter 14, Title 36 provisions (36-504).★★ No person shall sell or buy wildlife or parts except: ► legally taken species of wildlife classified as unprotected by law; ► legally taken hides, horns or heads of game animals, when detached from the carcass, and mounted wildlife, where sale is not specifically prohibited by federal/state law and when accompanied by statement showing lawful taking; ► pelts and parts of fur-bearers legally taken; ► confiscated, abandoned or unclaimed wildlife under 36-1304; ► commercially raised or harvested wildlife by licensed operations. Purchases or sales shall be made under Commission conditions and reporting requirements, and the Commission may permit the sale of other wildlife parts when the sale will not injuriously affect the species (36-501). (See also NATIVE AMERICAN WILDLIFE PROVISIONS.)

No person shall possess, transport, or ship or accept for shipment wildlife unless it is accompanied by the proper licenses, tags, or validation as to legality of the taking, and the packages are plainly labeled designating numbers, sex and species, and name/address of hunter, consignor, or donee. No person may lawfully claim ownership of more game animals, birds or fish than allowed by Commission possession limits. Storage/processing facilities must keep records as prescribed by the Commission (36-502 and -503.

Except as otherwise provided, possession of wildlife during closed season shall be prima facie evidence of unlawful taking (36-1305). No person shall refuse to allow inspection of wildlife in the person's possession or to stop and report at a wildlife check station when directed to do so by Department personnel on duty, or to carry the proper license and produce it for inspection when requested. No person shall be convicted of failure to have a license in possession if the person produces in court a license valid at the time of arrest (36-1202).

License Revocations and Suspensions

The Department shall suspend immediately the hunting, fishing or trapping license of a person upon receiving notice from a state court that the person has failed to pay the penalty for a fish and game infraction judgment after opportunity for notice and hearing. The suspension shall continue and the person may not hunt, fish or trap nor purchase a new license until the fine is paid (36-505). A court with jurisdiction has authority to revoke a hunter's license and deny the right to secure a new license for the periods herein indicated, certified notice of the revocation to be submitted to the Director within 30 days of the order. Upon revocation of a hunting license, the Director shall notify the licensee to surrender the license (36-1504 through -1506). [An appeal procedure from a revocation order is provided (36-1507).]

A person convicted of violating title provisions or who fails to comply with citation requirements, may in addition to another penalty assessed, have hunting, fishing, or trapping privileges revoked for a court determined period of time, not to exceed three years. ★The court shall revoke privileges for not less than one year for convictions of the following offenses: ► taking/possessing upland game birds, migratory waterfowl, salmon, steelhead, sturgeon or a big game animal during closed season; ► exceeding daily bag or possession limits of upland game birds, migratory waterfowl or big game animals; ► taking fish by unlawful methods set forth in 36-902; ► unlawfully purchasing, possessing or using a license, tag or permit under 36-405; ► trespassing in violation of warning signs under 36-1603; ► engaging in unlawful sale or purchase of wildlife under 36-501; ► taking a game animal with a firearm during an archery only season.★   ★In cases of multiple convictions, the revocation periods may run consecutively. In cases of convictions involving taking big game animals during closed season or exceeding daily bag/possession limits of big game, the magistrate shall revoke the hunting, fishing or trapping privileges for not less than one year for each big game animal illegally taken/possessed.★   It is a misdemeanor for a person to hunt, fish or trap or purchase a license during the period the license is revoked. Violation: $100-1,000 fine; and/or jail up to six months; plus extension of the revocation period for a time equal to the original revocation period. For purposes of the Wildlife Violator Compact, the Department shall suspend a violator's license for failure to comply with terms of a citation from a party state or revoke the license for a conviction in a party state. Records of all revocations of fishing and/or hunting privileges shall be submitted to the Department by the magistrate and a list of revocations compiled and sent to conservation officers and license vendors (36-1402 and -1403).

★The Director shall revoke the license of a person and deny the person the right to secure a hunting license for the following acts, for the periods specified, and may hold a hearing, receive evidence and subpoena witnesses in cases where the person is alleged to have: ► carelessly handled a gun that caused accident/injury to person or property; ► carelessly injured a human being by gunfire; ► caused accidental injury or death to a person by gunfire and fled or failed to render assistance; ► caused injury or death to a person by gunfire and not furnished proof to the Director of release from all medical and other expense liability from the injured person or heirs; ► caused damage to livestock by gunfire, and not furnished proof to the Director of release from all liability by the livestock owner (36-1501). A person may prefer charges on the above grounds in writing, against a hunting licensee, and the Director shall hear the charges within 60 days in either the county of the defendant's residence or the county of the offense. Personal service on the defendant at least 15 days prior to the hearing is required (36-1502).★   Upon finding violation of the acts specified above, the Director is required to revoke the license of the offender and to deny the right to hunt for up to five years for the first offense, and five years for each additional offense (36-1504).

HABITAT PROTECTION

Wildlife preserves are created for the protection of wild animals and birds, for establishment of breeding places and for species preservation. No person shall take wild animals or birds in a state wildlife preserve except as provided or by regulation. Predatory animals may be taken within a wildlife preserve by conservation officers when causing damage. Other wildlife causing damage within private inholdings within the preserve shall be controlled in accordance with 36-1107 (36-1901 through - 1903).

NATIVE AMERICAN WILDLIFE PROVISIONS

A person holding a wholesale or retail steelhead trout buyer's license may buy or sell steelhead trout in Idaho that have been taken by an Indian lawfully exercising fishing rights reserved by federal statute, treaty or executive order, provided that the Indian is an enrolled member of the tribe holding the rights and the tribal code authorizes the sales. No license is required for a person buying steelhead trout for personal consumption from Indians who are lawfully exercising their fishing rights under federal statute, treaty, executive order, or tribal code or regulation (36-501). (See Illegal Taking of Wildlife under ENFORCEMENT OF WILDLIFE LAWS regarding violation of Indian law or regulation.)

ILLINOIS

Sources: Smith-Hurd Illinois Annotated Statutes, 1985, Chapters 56, 61 and 520; 1992 Cumulative Annual Pocket Part.

[NOTE: Fish and Aquatic Life statute citations are preceded by [56]; Wildlife statute citations are preceded by [61]; Endangered Species Act statute citations are preceded by [520]. Also, Illinois habitat protection statutes cited as [61] through [61] in this summary were changed as this Handbook was going to press and are now cited as [520]20-2 through [520]20-16.]

STATE WILDLIFE POLICY

The title to all wild birds and wild mammals, and all aquatic life within the state is in the state, and no wild birds or wild mammals or aquatic life shall be taken or killed, in any manner or at any time, unless the person so doing consents that the title is in the state for regulating taking, killing, possession, use, sale, and transportation. Taking or killing wild birds, wild mammals, or aquatic life at any time, in any manner, by a person, shall be deemed a consent that title is in the state for regulating the possession, use, sale and transportation ([56]5-5); ([61]2.1). The Fish and Aquatic Life Code shall apply to aquatic life or parts in any lakes, rivers or other state waters or over which Illinois has concurrent jurisdiction with any other state, or which may be brought into Illinois ([56]5-10).

★The General Assembly declares that wildlife species which are not commonly pursued, killed or consumed either for sport or profit, referred to in this Act as "non-game wildlife" have need of special protection and that it is in the public interest to preserve, protect, perpetuate and enhance non-game wildlife and native plant resources of the state through preservation of a satisfactory environment and an ecological balance. The General Assembly specifically recognizes that such non-game wildlife includes protected wildlife and wildlife of specialized habitats -- both terrestrial and aquatic types -- and mollusks, crustaceans and other invertebrates under the jurisdiction of the Department of Conservation. This Act provides a means by which such protection may be financed through a voluntary check-off designation on state income tax return forms.★ The General Assembly's intent is that this income tax check-off is supplemental to any funding and is not intended to take the place of funding that would otherwise be appropriated for this purpose ([61]402). Each taxpayer required to file a return desiring to contribute to the Illinois Non-Game Wildlife Conservation Fund may do so by stating the amount of such contribution (not less than $1) on each return ([61]403).

RELEVANT WILDLIFE DEFINITIONS: See Definitions section of Appendices.

See also listings under PROTECTED SPECIES OF WILDLIFE.

STATE FISH AND WILDLIFE AGENCIES

Agency Structure

The Wildlife Code and the Fish and Aquatic Life Code shall be administered by the **Department of Conservation** (Department) ([56]1-5); ([61]1.1 and 1.2).

Agency Powers and Duties

The **Department** shall: ► take all measures necessary for the conservation, distribution, introduction and restoration of birds and mammals; ► bring actions in the name of the state to enforce the provisions of this Act, including rules; ► recover fines and penalties. Nothing in this Act authorizes the Department to change any penalty prescribed by law for a violation of its provisions, or to change license fees. The Department is authorized to cooperate with the federal government, other state agencies and educational institutions in conducting surveys, experiments or work of joint benefit ([61]1.10).

The Department shall use modern conservation methods to manage wildlife on state lands/waters for propagation of wildlife. ★The Department may cooperate with a person desirous of managing wildlife on private lands/waters by furnishing trees, shrubs, seeds or other materials where necessary, and providing labor, equipment and technical supervision to plan and assist the landowner in wildlife habitat development ([61]1.12).★

★★The Department may establish **Conservation Training Schools** and employ technicians to teach conservation methods to Department employees and other interested groups to carry out provisions. In order to educate the state's citizens in modern trends of conservation, the Department shall disseminate conservation information and provisions through lectures, movies, exhibits, news items and other media. The Department may publish a bulletin/magazine with information on the Department's work, conservation and propagation of wildlife, hunting and fishing and other information ([56]1-155) and ([61]1.11).★★

Agency Regulations

The Department is authorized to make rules and regulations for carrying out, administering and enforcing provisions, to be called "administrative rules" (rules). Rules shall be promulgated in accordance with the Illinois Administrative Procedures Act ([56]l-125 and [61]1.1).

Agency Funding Sources

No funds accruing to the state from fishing license fees shall be diverted for any other purpose than the administration of the Department ([56]30-15) and ([61]134).

All fees, fines, bond forfeitures, and income of any kind derived from hunting and fishing activities on lands or waters under the Department's control, and all penalties collected shall be deposited in the state treasury and set apart in a **Wildlife and Fish Fund**, except that fees derived solely from the sale of salmon stamps, and related art contests and reprints, and gifts, donations, grants and bequests of money for the conservation/propagation of salmon shall be put into the **Salmon Fund** to be used solely for the conservation and propagation of salmon, including construction of a cold water hatchery and for payment of costs of the salmon stamp, reprint and design costs. Fees from the sale of state waterfowl stamps and gifts, donations and bequests of money for the conservation/propagation of waterfowl shall be deposited into the **State Migratory Waterfowl Stamp Fund**. Fees derived from State Fur-bearer Stamp sales, State Pheasant Stamp and related art work sales, or gifts and donations go to the **State Fur-bearer Stamp Fund** and the **State Pheasant Stamp Fund**. Wildlife and Fish Fund appropriations shall be for: ► purchasing and maintaining land for fish hatcheries, wildlife refuges, preserves and public shooting and fishing grounds; ► purchasing and distributing wild birds and eggs, and wild mammals; ► rescuing, restoring and distributing fish; ► feeding and care of wild birds, wild animals and fish ([56]1-230) and ([61]1.28).

State Migratory Waterfowl Stamp Fund moneys shall be appropriated to the Department as follows: 50% for conservation and propagation of waterfowl, waterfowl attracting projects and improving public migratory waterfowl areas, and waterfowl stamp, art and reprint costs. These projects may include repair, maintenance and operation of public migratory waterfowl areas only in emergencies as determined by the Duck Stamp Committee, but no money shall be used for administrative expenses. Twenty-five percent of the funds go to non-profit organizations for the development of waterfowl propagation areas in Canada or the US that specifically provide waterfowl for the Mississippi Flyway; and 25% of the funds go to non-profit organizations to implement the North American Waterfowl Management Plan for development of waterfowl areas within the US or Canada that provide waterfowl for the Mississippi Flyway. These projects shall be investigated by the Department and must be acceptable to appropriate government agencies of the US and Canada ([61]1.29).

★State Pheasant Stamp Fund moneys shall be allocated as follows: 50% from the Pheasant Stamp, 100% from related artwork, and all gifts and donations for the conservation of wild pheasants shall be used for wild pheasant conservation and for stamp printing, reprint, and art design costs. Pheasant conservation projects may include land acquisition, pheasant habitat improvement on public or private land, pheasant research, and public education. The Department shall present project plans to the Pheasant Stamp Committee for approval. No money shall be used for administrative expenses. Fifty percent of the pheasant stamp fund monies shall go to non-profit organizations for wild pheasant conservation, to be used for projects similar to those enumerated above, after committee approval ([61]1.31).

★**State Fur-bearer Stamp Fund** moneys shall be expended as follows: 50% from the sale of stamps and 100% of all gifts and donations for the conservation of fur-bearing mammals, for projects for improving public fur-bearing mammal habitat management areas. On an emergency basis, the State Fur-bearer Stamp Committee may include projects for repair, maintenance and operation of mammal habitat management areas, but no moneys shall go for administrative expenses. Thirty-five percent shall be allocated to non-profit groups for conducting surveys concerning the biology, ecology and management of state fur-bearing mammals; and 15% of all funds shall go for educating hunters, trappers, and the public concerning the role of hunting and trapping in fur-bearer management, harvest laws, hunting and trapping techniques, and conservation, management and ecology. Committee approved projects may include the promotion of products made from wild fur-bearing mammals ([61]1.32).★

See STATE WILDLIFE POLICY for income tax write-off for the Non-Game Wildlife Conservation Fund.

Agency Advisory Boards

The **State Duck Stamp Committee** consists of the State Waterfowl Biologist; Division Chiefs from Wildlife Resources, Land Management, and Technical Services; and two or more at-large representatives appointed by the Director from statewide waterfowl organizations. The Committee shall review and recommend all Duck Stamp Projects and Migratory Waterfowl Stamp Fund expenditures, giving consideration to waterfowl projects that are readily available to stamp holders. The **State Pheasant Stamp Committee** consists of Division Chiefs from Wildlife Resources, Land Management, and Technical Services; one person appointed by the Director from a non-profit institution, corporation or state university actively engaged in research pertaining to game birds, especially pheasants; two or more persons appointed by the Director from statewide pheasant organizations. The Committee shall review and recommend all State Pheasant Stamp Fund allocations ([61]1.31). The **State Fur-bearer Stamp Committee** shall consist of the State Fur-bearer Biologist; Division Chiefs from Wildlife Resources and Land Management; one person from a non-profit institution, or state university actively engaged in wildlife research pertaining to game or fur-bearing mammals; two or three at-large representatives appointed by the Director from statewide fur-bearing mammal hunting and trapping organizations. The Committee shall review and recommend all State Fur-bearer Stamp Fund projects and expenditures ([61]1.32).

The **Endangered Species Protection Board** duties include listing, delisting, or change of listing status of species, in consultation with and upon written approval of the Department. The Board shall also advise the Department on methods of assistance, protection, conservation and management of endangered and threatened species and their habitats, and on related matters. The Board shall be composed of nine persons appointed by the Governor, and the Director as a non-voting member. At least six appointed members shall be recognized as naturalists by training, avocation or vocation; two shall be zoologists, one a botanist, and two ecologists. The Governor shall consider conservation groups' recommendations for appointments. Terms shall be three years, and the Governor shall fill vacancies for the unexpired term. Meetings shall be at regular set intervals, on Department request, or upon written notice of at least five members, but no less than quarterly. Members shall not be compensated but shall be reimbursed for actual expenses. The Board shall select a chairman and other officers, and may name an Executive Committee to which it may grant specific powers. The Board shall review and revise the endangered/threatened list as warranted, but no less frequently than every five years, and shall report accomplishments biennially ([520]10.6).

PROTECTED SPECIES OF WILDLIFE

This Act shall apply only to the wild birds and parts (nests and eggs), and wild mammals and parts, including green hides, in the state, or which may be brought into the state, which are defined as follows [scientific names are given]: ▸ all game and nongame birds except the house sparrow, European starling, and rock dove and domestic pigeon; ▸ game birds, including the ruffed grouse, sharp-tailed grouse, bobwhite quail, Hungarian Partridge, chukar partridge, ring-necked pheasant, greater prairie chicken, wild turkey; ▸ migratory game birds, including the brant, wild duck, goose, swan, rail, gallinule, coot, dove, wild pigeon, crow, snipe, and woodcock; ▸ resident and nonmigratory birds, including the loon, grebe, pelican, cormorant, heron, bittern, egret, ibis, spoonbill, stork, vulture, kite, hawk and eagle, osprey, falcon (including peregrine), crane, rail, gallinule, gull, tern, cuckoo, owl, whip-poor-will and nighthawk, swift, hummingbird, kingfisher, woodpecker, kingbird and flycatcher, lark, swallow, martin, crow, magpie, jay, chickadee and titmouse, nuthatch, creeper, wren, mockingbird, catbird and thrasher, robin, bluebird and thrush, gnatcatcher and kinglet, pipit, waxwing, shrike, vireo, warbler, European tree sparrow, blackbird, meadowlark, oriole, tananger, cardinal, grosbeak, finch, towhee, dickcissel, sparrow, junco, bunting, longspur, and all shorebirds of specified families; ▸ game mammals, including the woodchuck, gray and fox squirrel, white-tailed jackrabbit, Eastern cottontail, swamp rabbit, white-tailed deer; ▸ fur-bearing mammals, including the muskrat, beaver, raccoon, opossum, least and long-tailed weasel, mink, river otter, striped skunk, badger, red and gray fox, coyote, and bobcat; ▸ other mammals, including the flying and red squirrel, Eastern woodrat, golden mouse, rice rat, and bat ([61]2.2).

It shall be unlawful at any time to take, possess, sell or offer for sale, any such wild birds (dead or alive) and parts, including nests and eggs, wild mammals (dead or alive) and parts, including green hides contrary to provisions. This does not prohibit public or state scientific, educational or zoological institutions from receiving, holding and displaying wildlife specimens that were salvaged or legally obtained ([61]2.2). (See also Import, Export, and Release Provisions, and Restrictions on Taking, under HUNTING, FISHING, TRAPPING PROVISIONS.) Birds of prey include all species of owls, falcons, hawks, kites, harriers, ospreys and eagles. It is unlawful to take or possess a bird of prey, or to propagate them without a license or permit from the Department. A scientific collectors permit may be obtained for scientific, educational or zoological purposes. No person may have in their possession bald eagle, osprey, or barn owl. All captive-held birds must be permanently marked as provided by rule. Birds of prey may be used to hunt game birds, migratory birds, game mammals and fur-bearing mammals during falconry seasons ([61]2.4). It is unlawful to take or possess hen pheasants at any time except as provided ([61]2.6). It is unlawful to take ruffed, sharp-tailed, and pinnated grouse (prairie chicken) at any time ([61]2.8).

Endangered/Threatened/Rare Animals

No person shall take or possess any of the aquatic life listed in the Illinois Endangered Species Protection Act or rules, except as provided in that act ([56]10-55).

It is unlawful to possess, take, transport, sell, offer for sale, give or otherwise dispose of any animal or the product thereof of any species on the Board's list of endangered or threatened species [restrictions regarding plants included]([520]10.3).

Any species/subspecies designated as endangered or threatened by the Secretary of the Interior pursuant to the Federal Endangered Species Act, shall be automatically placed on the Illinois List by the Board without notice or public hearing. The Board may list species which have reproduced in or otherwise significantly used, as in migration or overwintering, the area which is now Illinois, if there is scientific evidence that the species qualify as endangered or threatened as defined in this Act. The Board may delist any non-federally-listed species for which it finds satisfactory scientific evidence that its wild or natural populations are no longer endangered or threatened. Listing, delisting or change of status shall be made only after a public hearing. Notice of hearing shall be published seven days before in a statewide newspaper and mailed to a person requesting notice. All persons represented at a hearing, and requesting notice, shall be given a written summary of any action taken. Upon listing, delisting or change of status, the Director shall file a certified copy of the action with the Secretary of State ([520]10.7).

Any Department authorized officer/agent, state police officer, or local government unit, may execute a warrant to search for and seize goods, merchandise or animals, plants, or animal/plant products sold or offered for sale in violation of this Act, or any property or item used in a violation, or examine a premises for determination of actions in violation of this Act. Seized goods, merchandise, animals, plants or their products shall be held pending proceedings in the circuit court. Upon conviction, seized items shall be forfeited and offered to a recognized institution for scientific or educational purposes, or destroyed if a suitable depository is not located ([520]10.8).

Violation of any provision of this Act is a Class A misdemeanor ([520]10.9).

The **Endangered and Threatened Species Program** shall be within the Department of Conservation. All fines collected under this Act shall be paid to the state treasurer and deposited in the Nongame Wildlife Conservation Fund ([520]10.10).

★★With Board advice, the Department shall actively plan and implement a program for conservation of endangered and threatened species, by means including published data search, research, management, cooperative agreements with other agencies, identification, protection and acquisition of essential habitat, support of beneficial legislation, issuance of grants from appropriated funds, and public education. It is the public policy of all state agencies and local governments to utilize their authorities to further the purposes of this Act by evaluating through Department consultation whether actions authorized, funded, or carried out by them are likely to jeopardize the continued existence of Illinois listed endangered and threatened species or are likely to result in the destruction or adverse modification of the designated essential habitat of such species. The policy shall be enforceable only by writ of mandamus; and where a state or local agency does consult in furtherance of this public policy, it shall be deemed to have complied with its obligations, provided the agency action shall not result in killing or injuring any listed species. This shall not apply to any state agency project on which a biological opinion has been issued (in accordance with Section 7 of the Federal Endangered Species Act) prior to the effective date of this Act stating that the action proposed will not jeopardize the continued existence of any federal endangered or threatened species. The Department shall have authority to adopt rules as are reasonable and necessary to implement the provisions of this Act ([520]10.11).★★ (See also HUNTING, FISHING, TRAPPING PROVISIONS.)

GENERAL EXCEPTIONS TO PROTECTION

The Department may take, purchase or propagate, any mammals, birds, aquatic life, or eggs for propagation and stocking purposes, and may stock them in parts of the state where a scarcity of such birds, mammals, or aquatic life exists ([56]1-135) and ([61]1.6). The Department is authorized to produce such mammals, birds, aquatic life or eggs, and to distribute them to anyone having suitable land or means for their breeding, hatching or further propagation and shall have authority to enter into agreements with distributees for the propagation or purchase of mammals, birds, or eggs produced by such distributees [56]1-140) and ([61]1.7). The Department may remove and dispose of any aquatic life from state waters to maintain the biological balance of aquatic life, or contract with a person to remove/dispose of aquatic life on Department terms ([56]1-135). The Department may issue a permit to capture, band or collect (including nests, eggs, or young) any protected fauna, or of any fish, reptiles, mussels, crayfish, frogs or amphibians for strictly scientific purposes. The Department may grant permits for other aquatic species by rule. A salvage permit may be granted to salvage dead or crippled protected wildlife species for permanent donation to bona fide public or state scientific, educational or zoological institutions or to rehabilitate and subsequently release them to the wild. Reports must be kept of kinds of specimens taken, from whom received, and disposition of same ([56]20-100) and ([61]3.22).

Upon proper application and approval, the Department may issue to any qualified person a permit to allow taking, possession, transport, purchase, or disposal of specimens or products of an endangered or threatened species for justified purposes, that will enhance the species' survival for zoological, botanical or educational or for scientific purposes only. Department rules for permits shall be promulgated after consultation with and written approval of the Board. The Department shall upon notice and hearing, revoke a permit upon finding that the person is not complying with the permit terms or is knowingly providing incorrect or inadequate information, the activity covered by the permit is placing the species in undue jeopardy, or for other cause ([520]10.4). Upon proper application and approval, the Department may issue a limited permit authorizing possession, purchase or disposition of animals or animal products of endangered or threatened species, to a person possessing prior to the effective date of this Act such an item, or obtaining the item legally out-of-state. Such permit shall specifically name and describe each item and shall be valid only for possession, purchase or disposition. The Department may require proof that acquisition of items was made before the effective date of this Act. The Department may also issue a limited permit authorizing the possession, purchase or disposition of live animals or items to one to whom the permit holder gives, sells, or transfers the item named in the permit. Limited permits shall be valid only as long as the item remains in the possession of the person to whom the permit was issued. The permit shall be revoked if the Department finds that the holder received it on the basis of false information, is not complying with its terms, or for other cause ([520]10.5).

HUNTING, FISHING, TRAPPING PROVISIONS

General Provisions

★The seasons for taking wildlife and protected aquatic life, and daily bag and possession limits, are based upon a proper biological balance being maintained for each species in each zone and shall remain in effect as long as the population is adequate to maintain such balance. This balance exists for any species when its population is replaced by natural reproduction or by artificial replacement, replenishment or stocking. If the Department finds, or the

Conservation Advisory Board so advises after investigation, that the number of each sex of any wildlife species is not adequate to maintain the biological balance of such species, it shall, by rule, shorten or close the season or decrease the bag/possession limit. The Department may not provide for a longer season, bag or possession limit than is provided in this Act.★ Migratory waterfowl seasons shall be adjusted within the limits of federal migratory bird regulations. The Department may use the services of the Illinois State Natural History Survey Division in the Department of Energy and Natural Resources for making wildlife population investigations. The Department shall modify existing provisions when necessary, including open seasons, size and bag limits and methods of taking fish from the waters of Lake Michigan in order to fulfill agreements/compacts between Canadian and US governments regarding the best interests of the fisheries resources and the general public ([56]1-120) and ([61]1.3).

Except as provided, it is lawful to ship or transport within the state any protected birds or wild mammals only if the container is properly tagged showing the species, name/address/license of consignor and name/address of consignee. It is unlawful to carry or transport as baggage on any conveyance more than one package containing more than the possession limit of birds or mammals as the Act provides, such baggage to be labeled as required ([61]4.1). It is unlawful for a nonresident to transport from the state any protected wild mammals or birds except when they are carried in the owner's personal possession and open to inspection. Migratory game birds may be transported/shipped according to federal regulations ([61]4.2). ★It is unlawful for common carriers knowingly to transport into the state any protected wild bird or mammal taken and shipped contrary to any laws or rules of the state of origin ([61]4.3).★

The Department shall authorize its personnel or certified volunteer instructors to conduct courses of at least eight hours in firearms and hunter safety, which may include bow and arrow safety, and cooperate in establishing courses with any organization promoting safety in firearm/bow and arrow handling. ★Funds for conducting firearms and hunter safety courses shall be taken from fees charged for Firearm Owners Identification Cards ([61]3.2).★

★The Department shall authorize courses in trapping techniques and ethical trapping behavior, at least eight hours in length, set up similar to the hunting safety courses under [61]3.3. In offering such courses, the Department may cooperate with associations which promote ethical use of legal fur harvesting devices and techniques.★ Landowners/tenants and families actually residing on their lands need no trapping license, but must comply with state trapping seasons and permitted devices ([61]3.3). Trappers of fur-bearing mammals shall report annually all hides taken, sold, or shipped during the open season, with names of consignees. Failure may result in denial of a trapping license for the next year ([61]3.4).

Persons in accidents involving serious personal injury resulting from hunting with a firearm or bow and arrow, or in trapping, shall: ▸ render assistance to others affected by the accident; ▸ file a Department Accident Report Form with the Department within five days. Reports are for confidential use of the Department and shall not be used as evidence in any trial ([61]3.40).

Before trapping any protected mammals for which there is an open season, a person shall procure a trapping license. No traps shall be placed in the field set or unset, prior to the opening day of the trapping season. Persons age 16 through 64 must have a State Fur-bearer Stamp in addition to a trapping license. Traps used in taking fur-bearers shall be tagged with the owners' name; absence thereof is prima facie evidence that such trap is illegally used and the trap shall be confiscated and disposed of. No trapping license shall be issued to a person under 18 years of age unless he has a certificate of competency for trapping ([61]3.3).

Each licensee of any devices or boats named in the code, other than a hook and line, must attach a Department issued tag, and the Department may furnish hook and line licensees (as well as hunting licensees and Migratory Waterfowl Stamp holders) with an insignia as evidence of license possession, to be exhibited according to Department rule ([56]20-65) and ([61]3.2). Persons holding any license, stamp or permit issued shall have it in possession for inspection by wardens or other officers upon request, except at sites requiring all hunters to deposit such licenses or Firearm Owner's Identification Card at their check station upon entering the hunting area ([61]3.2).

Licenses and Permits

Owners or tenants residing on or members of private clubs that control lands which encompass artificial lakes of less than 30 acres fed by springs or surface drainage of intermittent streams may take any protected fish except largemouth, smallmouth or spotted bass, with any size mesh hoop nets up to 100 yards in length, wire nets, baskets or traps from these ponds without a license, but only for fish management purposes ([56]20-25).

The Department is authorized to issue a public hunting grounds for waterfowl daily usage stamp for duck and Canada goose hunting areas, and a public hunting grounds for pheasants daily usage stamp. The stamp(s) shall be attached to a person's permit card under Department rules for operating State Public Hunting Grounds. The Department shall set rules for operating public hunting areas, and may permit harvest of both male and female hand-reared pheasants ([61]1.13).

A valid hunting license is required for taking any protected species for which there is an open season. Persons over age 16 must have a State Migratory Waterfowl Stamp before taking migratory waterfowl, including coots. Owners/tenants residing on lands may hunt protected species on their own lands during lawful seasons, using lawful methods ([61]3.1). Residents and nonresidents pay the same fee for State Pheasant Stamps, State Fur-bearer Stamps, and State Migratory Waterfowl Stamps and must have these stamps in addition to any applicable license or permit ([61]3.2).

Restrictions on Taking: Hunting and Trapping

It is unlawful to take cock pheasants, bobwhite quail or Hungarian partridge except with shotgun or bow and arrow during open seasons, and unlawful to possess more than the daily limit of these birds as set by rule. Dogs may be used in hunting these birds. It is unlawful to remove plumage or heads of pheasants in the field or when dressed for storage ([61]2.6, 2.7 and 2.13).

It is unlawful to take or possess wild turkey except during the statutory open season, or without a valid wild turkey hunting permit. Exceptions are Illinois landowners, including nonresidents, who own at least 40 acres and hunt on their own land, resident tenants, or shareholders of a corporation holding such acreage who may obtain one permit for each 40 acres. Turkeys may be taken only with shotguns or bows and arrows of specified sizes/gauges during specified daylight hours. It is unlawful to take wild turkey by use of dogs, horses, automobiles, aircraft or other vehicles or by the use of bait, or to exceed the statutory bag/possession limit of four turkeys per year ([61]2.9 through 2.11).

It is unlawful to possess at any time any net or trap for netting or trapping any game birds ([61]2.15). It is unlawful to sell, barter, or offer such of any game birds, whether taken within or without the state, except as provided ([61]2.16). It is unlawful to take, possess, or transport migratory game birds except during the time and in the manner and numbers permitted by federal law and state regulations ([61]2.18). It is unlawful to sell or barter, or offer to sell or barter, or buy any game mammals, whether taken in this state or imported except as provided ([61]2.29).

★It is lawful for the holder of required licenses, permits and stamps for taking migratory waterfowl to use either lead or steel shotgun pellets, in lieu of other authorized ammunition, at any location where hunting is authorized, except at sites where there are documented cases of lead poisoning of waterfowl and all alternative methods of alleviating lead poisoning (such as dewatering, flooding and/or tillage) have proved unsuccessful in preventing lead poisoning losses of waterfowl. At such sites non-toxic pellets, such as steel, shall be used. These sites may be designated by the Department after statewide public hearings have been held and the results reviewed. The Department is authorized to designate, by rule, areas limited to the use of non-toxic pellets, provided authorization is only for areas which the federal government has mandated shall be closed to all waterfowl hunting unless the state agrees to prohibit the use of toxic shotgun pellets. No state agency shall issue or make any rule or agreement in conflict with this section ([61]2.18-1).★

It is unlawful to use a floating blind (watercraft or floating structure that is camouflaged or altered in appearance to conceal a hunter) for taking migratory waterfowl unless the blind is anchored in a stationary position when in use. A scull boat may be used except where prohibited by rule ([61]2.19). It is unlawful to take waterfowl or any species of wildlife in any area managed by the Department except as provided by rules ([61]2.20).

It is unlawful to use a floating blind (watercraft or floating structure that is camouflaged or altered in appearance to conceal a hunter) for taking migratory waterfowl unless the blind is anchored in a stationary position when in use. A scull boat may be used except where prohibited by rule ([61]2.19). It is unlawful to take waterfowl or any species of wildlife in any area managed by the Department except as provided by rules ([61]2.20).

It is unlawful to take or possess deer except as provided by statute or rule. ★It is unlawful to knowingly take any white whitetail deer at any time ([61]2.24).★   Deer may be taken only with a shotgun or muzzle-loading rifle during the open season set by the Director. It is unlawful to take deer except with a bow and arrow, or by crossbow for handicapped hunters, during the archery season, or to take deer except with a muzzle-loading rifle or bow and arrow/crossbow during muzzle-loading rifle season. The Director shall set bag, possession limits, and counties where there will be an open season. The Department may set separate harvest periods for gun hunting only at specific sites to harvest surplus deer that cannot be taken during the regular deer season ([61]2.25).

A deer hunting permit is required for taking deer, with similar exceptions for landowners for pheasant hunting. Standards and specifications for use of guns and bow and arrow for deer hunting shall be established by rule. Deer may be taken only during daylight hours, and other firearms may not be carried when taking deer by shotgun, bow and arrow or muzzle-loading rifle. It is unlawful to take deer by use of dogs, horses, vehicles aircraft, or by the use of salt or bait of any kind. An area is considered baited during the 10-day period following bait removal. It is unlawful to possess/transport any wild deer which has been injured or killed on a highway except by rule. ★It is unlawful for a person having taken the legal limit of deer by bow and arrow or gun to further participate with same in any deer hunting party.★   Guns/bows and arrows must be made inoperable by unloading or unstringing, or by locking device, during hours when deer hunting is unlawful. The Department may prohibit upland game hunting during the gun deer season by rule. Violation: Class B misdemeanor ([61]2.26).

It is unlawful to take cottontails, jack and swamp rabbits, or fox and gray squirrels except with a gun or bow and arrow during the open season. Dogs may be used. Season, bag and possession limits are set by statute. White or red squirrels may not be taken at any time. The state may be divided into management zones by rule for the purpose of taking squirrels ([61]2.27 and 2.28).

It is unlawful to take wild birds or wild mammals along, upon, across or from any highway or public right-of-way, or to molest or destroy any feed bed, nest, den, house or cavity of any protected wild mammal except as provided in [61]2.37. A feed bed is a mound, pile or mat of branches, cattails or other vegetation gathered and piled by muskrats or beaver ([61]2.31 and 2.32).

It is unlawful to: ▸ trap or hunt with gun, dog, or bow and arrow any gray fox, red fox, raccoon, weasel, mink, muskrat and opossum except during the open season; ▸ take bobcat, badger or river otter at any time; ▸ trap beaver except during the open season. Coyote and striped skunk may be taken by trapping only during open seasons for each species, but may be taken by hunting at any time. For taking fur-bearing animals, the state may be divided into management zones. Dogs may not be used to hunt any fur-bearing mammal during the night-time hours for 10 days preceding and following the raccoon hunting season, except for Department field trial permits.   ★A nonresident from a state with more restrictive fur-bearer pursuit regulations than Illinois has for a particular species may not pursue that species except during the time period Illinois residents are allowed to pursue that species in the nonresident's state.★   ★Department approved fenced fox hound training enclosures are exempt from these provisions ([61]2.30).★

Except as provided, it is unlawful to: ▸ carry or possess any gun in any state refuge; ▸ use/possess any snare, deadfall, net or pit trap to take any species; ▸ take a protected wild mammal from its den by means of a mechanical device, spade, smoke or gases; ▸ use a ferret to drive any mammal from its den; ▸ use any recording or electronic calling device to attract any protected birds or animals; ▸ use spears, gigs, hooks to take any protected species; ▸ use poisons, chemicals or explosives to take any protected species;   ★ ▸ hunt adjacent to or near any peat, grass, brush or other inflammable substance when it is burning;★   ▸ use larger than a 10 gauge shotgun to take protected species; ▸ use a crossbow without a handicapped permit; ▸ take game birds, migratory game birds or migratory waterfowl with a rifle, pistol, revolver or airgun; ▸ fire any firearm over or into state waters, including frozen waters; ▸ discharge a firearm or bow and arrow along, upon, across or from any public highway; ▸ use a silencer to muffle a firearm ([61]2.33).

It is unlawful to: ► take, pursue or harass any wild birds or mammals by use of any vehicle/conveyance, or its lights, in any area where wildlife may be found, except that striped skunk, opossum, red fox, gray fox, raccoon and coyote may be taken during open season by use of a small light that is hand-held or worn on the body by a person on foot; ► carry a loaded, uncased firearm in a vehicle, or a bow that is not unstrung except for blank cartridge firearms carried on horseback at field trials; ► trap or hunt, or allow a dog to hunt, on another's land without permission and being able to so demonstrate to a field officer. ★The officer must receive notice from the landowner to enforce this provision, and statements made shall be exceptions to the hearsay rule.★ It is unlawful to: ► knowingly or wantonly allow one's dog to pursue, harass or kill deer; ► hunt between sunset and sunrise except by rule for fur-bearing mammals, deer, wild turkey and waterfowl; ► remove fur-bearing mammals from or disturb the traps of another without permission ([61]2.33).

It is unlawful to discharge a firearm, hunt, trap, or allow a dog to hunt within 300 yards of an inhabited dwelling without the owner's permission; a 100 yard limit applies on federal, Department, Migratory Waterfowl Hunting Area lands and on licensed game breeding and hunting preserve areas. It is unlawful to: ★ ► take any protected game bird (except turkey), migratory game birds or migratory waterfowl when not flying, except that crippled birds may be retrieved within 200 yards of a blind immediately upon downing the bird;★ ► use or possess a tree climbing or cutting device while hunting fur-bearing animals; ► have in possession any freshly killed species during the closed season; ► take any protected species and retain it alive; ► possess any rifle in the field during gun deer season; ► kill or cripple any protected species without making a reasonable effort to retrieve and include such species in the bag limit. Species or parts, legally taken in and transported from other states/countries may be possessed. Protected aquatic life, birds and mammals (except deer and fur-bearers) may be taken from a non-camouflaged boat not propelled by sail or mechanical power ([61]2.33).

When trapping, it is unlawful to: ► fail to visit and remove animals from traps at least once a day; ► fail to use the size and type of traps, and place traps as prescribed by statute; ► use any trap with saw-toothed, spiked or toothed jaws; ► destroy or disturb dams, lodges, burrows or feed beds of beaver or to set a trap inside a muskrat or beaver house; ► set traps closer than 10 feet from a game or fur-bearing mammal hole; ► trap any fur-bearing mammal with any colony, cage, box or stove-pipe trap designed to take more than one animal at a single setting; ► place traps during the closed season, or place a leghold trap within 30 feet of bait that is not completely covered; ► have the green hides of fur-bearing mammals in possession except during open season and for 10 days thereafter; ► use a snare trap except as specified ([61]2.33a).

Dogs of any breed may be trained year round. During closed seasons, firearms with blank cartridges must be used. Organized field trials or training grounds approved by the Department are exempt, and the Department may designate training areas and grant permits for field trials in which reared game birds are released. Field trial or dog training permit applicants must have the landowner's consent. Permit holders for designated dog training areas must have a wild game breeder's or game breeding and hunting preserve area permit and may use live bird recall devices on such areas. A dog can be used in taking squirrel during the open season. Hand-reared game released and shot at field trials shall be properly tagged before release or removal from the field trial area ([61]2.34).

Migratory game birds may be possessed only in accordance with federal regulations. It is unlawful to possess wild game birds, game mammals or parts except during open season and for the time period following such season as specified in statute. ★Each hunter shall maintain his bag of animals separately from those of other hunters for species with a daily bag/possession limit.★ Failure to establish proof of legal possession in another state or country and of importation into Illinois, is prima facie evidence that the animal or parts were taken within the state ([61]2.35).

It is unlawful to buy, sell or barter, or offer to do such, or to possess any protected wild birds, wild mammals or parts or eggs except as provided; the same must be properly labeled, or otherwise accounted for as to origin. ★Inedible parts of game mammals may be held, possessed, and sold when legally taken in Illinois, or when legally taken, possessed and transported in from other states or countries ([61]2.36).★

Restrictions on Taking: Fishing

The Department shall take all measures necessary for the conservation, distribution, introduction and restoration of aquatic life. If after investigation it is found that there is imminent danger of loss of aquatic life, the Director may authorize the taking of aquatic life from any area and specify other reasonable limits, methods and devices for salvage. ★Nothing here shall permit the Department to take action that hinders the operation of an electric generating station of an electric supplier.★ The Department shall bring actions in the name of the state to enforce the code, including administrative rules, and to recover any and all fines and penalties. The Department is not authorized to change any penalty prescribed by law or to change the amount of license fees. The Department is authorized to cooperate with the federal government, state agencies, and educational institutions in conducting surveys, experiments or work of joint interest/benefit ([56]1-150).

All state waters including boundary waters shall be fish preserves. Hook and line or sport fishing up to 50 hooks, except as provided by Code or rule, are the only lawful means of taking fish. The Department has the authority to prohibit all sport fishing or certain sport fishing devices in designated waters and to allow commercial fishing in designated waters by regulating commercial fishing devices used in the interest of the total management of the fishery resource ([56]25-5).

A person taking salmon shall obtain a salmon stamp in addition to any other required license. Individuals not required to obtain a fishing license need no salmon stamp ([56]20-10). Nonresidents over age 16 must be licensed to fish and must have a salmon stamp to take salmon ([56]20-20).

A person taking or attempting to take any fish, including minnows, for commercial purposes, or turtles, mussels, crayfish or frogs by any means in state waters shall first obtain a license, and shall do so only during lawful seasons ([56]20-5). Landowners or tenants and their immediate families may take with hook and line fish from waters on or flowing over their lands without a license. This does not apply to club lakes or lake developments ([56]20-15).

Aquatic life or parts shall be taken only with devices and in the manner permitted by Code, and terms shall apply to aquatic life when smoked, frozen or otherwise processed ([56]5-15). Persons taking aquatic life on private lands shall first obtain the landowner's consent ([56]5-20).

If a person causes any waste, sewage, thermal effluent or other pollutant to enter into any state waters, or causes or allows pollution of same, so as to kill aquatic life, the Department may bring an action to recover the value (and related costs in determining the value) of the aquatic life destroyed; money recovered goes into the Wildlife and Fish Fund. Placing any wire, can, bottle, glass, paper, trash, boxes, trees, brush, or animal or vegetable material into state waters, or on the banks where it may be washed into the waters, is a pollution violation. Violation: petty offense, and the Court shall order the violator to remove the debris within a specified time. Failure to comply is a Class B misdemeanor ([56]5-5).

It is unlawful to take any aquatic life by: ► use of electricity or any electrical device; lime, acid, medical, chemical or mechanical compound; ► fishberry, dynamite, giant powder, nitro glycerine, or other explosives; ► snare, treated grain, firearms, air gun wire basket, wire seine, wire net, wire trotline or limb lines of any kind ([56]10-80). [Daily bag limits, size limits, and/or methods of taking are specified in statute for bass, trout, salmon, northern pike, pickerels, walleye, sauger, bass (all varieties), sunfish, bluegill, crappie, muskellunge and hybrids, bullfrogs, smelt, shad and turtles ([56]10-5 through -60).]

It is illegal to take turtles or bullfrogs by commercial fishing devices, including hoop nets, traps or seines, or by the use of firearms or airguns ([56]10-60). Turtles may be taken only by hand or hook and line, unless modified by rule ([56]10-115). ★Unless otherwise provided, snakes may be taken by the owners/tenants of lands residing on their lands and their families ([56]10-65).★ Carp, buffalo, suckers, gar and bowfin may be taken by means of a pitchfork, underwater spear gun, bow and arrow, spear or gig by persons with valid sport fishing licenses. No other fish may be taken in this state by these means ([56]10-110). Mussels may not be taken by basket dredges, or mechanical or suction devices ([56]10-120). It is unlawful to troll for fish with more than three poles, and lines with more than two hooks or lures attached to each device ([56]10-130). It is unlawful to use, set, or place any snag line or snag pole to drag hooks through the water for catching fish by drawing the hooks into its body, except as provided

([56]10-90). Ice fishing holes may not exceed 12 inches in diameter, and no more than two poles and lines or two tipups, two hooks per line, may be used. Ice fishing shelters must be tagged with owner's name ([56]10-85). A sport fishing license holder may seine for minnows not to be sold for bait, and dip nets for non-commercial smelt fishing may be used as provided. Any sport fishing device, including trot lines, bank poles, or buoyed ganging devices left unattended must be tagged with the owner's name and exposed to public view at all times. Licensed sports fishermen may use pole and line, bank pole and line, throw line, trotline, buoyed ganging devices or other legal devices not exceeding 50 hooks in the aggregate, provided any individual at any one time may use only two untagged sports fishing devices; additional devices must be tagged with the owners name/address ([56]10-95). Licensed sports fishermen may use a dip net to take carp, buffalo, carpsuckers or shad for personal consumption except within 100 feet of the base of any dam. The taking of game fish by dip net without a commercial license is a petty offense with a minimum fine of $100, plus confiscation of illegally used equipment ([56]10-140).

Aquatic life taken into actual possession, unless immediately released unharmed, shall be included in the daily bag limit ([56]10-70). Any aquatic life taken at any time except during an open season, or below legal size, shall be immediately returned, without unnecessary injury, to the waters from which taken ([56]10-75).

Commercial and Private Enterprise Provisions

Aquatic products, as defined by the Aquaculture Development Act, that are bred, hatched, or propagated by the owner of a body of water, under an aquaculture permit in permitted aquaculture facilities, are the property of that person. Ownership of aquatic products reverts to the state upon revocation or expiration of an aquaculture permit ([56]5-5).

Nonresident and resident fish dealers must be licensed and shall maintain records of aquatic life bought, sold or shipped. Nonresidents buying fish for sale solely outside the state need no license if they buy from a licensed resident wholesale or retail fish dealer [extensive other details apply] ([56]20-70).

Before receiving or buying mussels, mussel dealers must have a Department license. Violation: business offense, fine $1,000-5,000 ([56]20-75).

A person who sells live minnows to wholesalers or retailers or for consumption, from within or without the state, is an intrastate wholesale minnow dealer and must be licensed. Persons selling live minnows for stocking only, or selling live minnows they legally caught, to a licensed wholesale minnow dealer are exempt from this section. Only residents are permitted to transport live minnows obtained in Illinois across any state borders, and they must have an interstate minnow license. Minnow dealers may sell any frog species for bait, but these must be obtained only from an aquaculture permit holder, from states where it is legal to obtain frogs for shipment to Illinois, or from frogs taken legally during the open season. Violation: business offense; fine $1,000-5,000 ([56]20-80).

Taxidermy businesses must obtain a Department license. Records must be kept of employees, date aquatic life was received, number and species, fishing licenses, and other required information. Mounted specimens must be tagged for shipment ([56]20-85).

Breeding, hatching, propagating or raising aquatic life, whether indigenous or non-indigenous, requires a Department permit. Such aquatic life may be transported and sold for food or stocking purposes, and permittees are exempt from having a fish or minnow dealer license. Records must be kept for two years and made available on request. Permittees may not take wild aquatic life contrary to Code provisions. Department permission is required to import or receive live, non-indigenous aquatic life for aquaculture or stocking purposes. Violation: business offense; $1,000-5,000 fine ([56]20-90).

Persons owning or operating a fee fishing water area must have a Department license. After inspecting the area, as to size, source and species of fish for stocking, and the applicant's ability to supervise such area, the Department may issue a permit. Seasonal operation records shall be submitted. The Department may refuse to issue, refuse to renew, suspend or revoke any license for non-compliance, but shall allow a hearing unless the cause is the protection of public health and safety ([56]20-95).

All aquatic life dealers, including minnow dealers, fish dealers, mussel dealers, and breeders, upon purchasing or receiving any protected aquatic life, shall issue a numbered receipt to the person from whom the aquatic life was purchased which shows pounds, kind of aquatic life, purchase date, price paid, and names, addresses and license numbers. Receipts, reports and records must be available for inspection. Failure to comply shall bar the licensee from obtaining a license/permit for the following year, and is a Class B misdemeanor ([56]20-125).

Except as provided in [56]l-130, [61]20-85 and [61]20-90, any common carrier before receiving protected aquatic life for shipment shall require a valid fish dealer license. Every box, barrel, or crate containing aquatic life must be tagged, showing species, number of pounds of each variety, name and business address, and the wholesale fish dealer license number. It is unlawful to carry or transport as baggage on any commercial conveyance more than the possession limit of aquatic life, and such package must be labeled. It is unlawful for common carriers to knowingly transport into Illinois any aquatic life protected under this code that was illegally taken and shipped contrary to any laws or rules of the state of origin ([56]25-20).

★Persons who commercially control land or water for the taking of migratory waterfowl must have a Department permit entitling them to possess blinds, pits or similar legal devices of concealment. Such persons "commercially control" when they directly or indirectly receive compensation in exchange for allowing hunters to enter the land/water ([61]3.6). Persons controlling land or water for commercial purposes for the taking of wild ducks or wild geese shall obtain a migratory waterfowl hunting area permit (commercial) and pay a fee for each blind or pit on the area. The Department shall issue such permits on the basis of principal use. Permittees may harvest either wild ducks or wild geese.★ The permittee shall: ▸ require all hunters to register daily prior to hunting; ▸ require each hunter to report daily the migratory waterfowl taken; ▸ exhibit the daily registers and make them available to inspection; ▸ ensure compliance with provisions by the permittee, guests or employees; ▸ report at the end of the season the number and species of birds taken in the permit area ([61]3.7).

On any property operated under a migratory waterfowl hunting area permit (commercial) where the principal use is to take wild geese, the permittee must ensure: ▸ no person takes wild geese except from a blind or pit; ▸ no person uses any blind or pit for taking wild geese within 200 yards of any other blind or within 100 yards of the property boundaries; ▸ no person uses any blind within 200 yards of any wildlife refuge boundary or public road adjacent to any state or Federal waterfowl refuge; ▸ not more than three persons occupy a blind or pit at the same time; ▸ no person takes geese in designated counties except during specified hours and under statutory conditions for taking geese ([61]3.8).

Resident wholesale fur buyers, retail fur buyers, and fur tanners must have a Department permit to deal in green hides of protected fur-bearing or game mammals, and to possess, transport and ship green hides of legally taken animals. Proper records and certificates of transactions must be kept available for Department inspection. Any manufacturer, converter or consumer who purchases green hides of fur-bearing or game animals for dressing and fabricating them into fur garments or products shall purchase such hides only from licensed fur buyers or breeders and require an invoice. Green hides shall not be offered for resale. Failure to produce valid certificates of purchase or invoices shall be prima facie evidence that green hides are contraband ([61]3.11 through 3.16). Nonresident fur dealers must have a Department permit ([61]3.18). All dealers of green hides of any sort must have a valid permit in possession at all times when receiving, buying, selling green hides or accepting the same for dressing, dying or tanning. Persons conducting organized and established auction sales of green hides are exempt from these provisions ([61]3.19). All fur buyers shall issue a numbered receipt to the hunter or other person from whom furs are received ([61]3.20). Taxidermists must be licensed, keep written records of all transactions according to all provisions, and must properly tag and label all specimens possessed or shipped ([61]3.21).

One of several types of Department permits is required to hold, possess, or engage in the raising of protected game mammals, game birds or migratory game birds, depending on whether the birds or animals will be sold or not. No person shall breed, raise, or sell ferrets without a commercial or noncommercial game breeder permit, but such permit does not authorize the sale of ferrets for taking any protected wild birds or mammals. Holders of Wild Game or bird breeder permits may import game mammals, game birds or migratory game birds into the state, but may not release them without the Director's permission. Special provisions apply to bobwhite quail, pheasants and chukar partridges as to release, hunting, sale to field trial groups, and dog training ground operators. Permittees do not have authority to take game mammals, game birds or migratory game birds in their wild state. Records must be kept, and all birds or game mammals tagged before import, sale, export as carcasses. Failure to keep such records or certificates shall be prima facie evidence that the animals or birds are contraband. Organized clubs and associations approved by the Department that engage in raising for release only and without profit any protected game mammals and game birds are exempt from these provisions ([61]3.23). (See also Import, Export and Release Provisions under this section.)

Persons engaged in breeding or raising protected live fur-bearing mammals must have a fur-bearing mammal breeder permit from the Department to hold, possess, breed, raise or sell such animals. Permittees may import fur-bearing mammals, but may release the same only after health and disease prevention requirements have been met. Breeding, raising and producing in captivity, and marketing by the producer, of mink, red fox, or arctic fox as live animals or as pelts or carcasses shall be deemed an agricultural pursuit, and such animals are subject to state laws relating to domestic animals, and such breeders are farmers for statutory purposes and are exempt from the fur-bearing mammal breeder permit requirements if 20% of their gross income is generated from selling these animals. No fur-bearing mammal breeder permit will be issued to hold, possess or breed striped skunks or coyotes ([61]3.25).

A person holding for at least five years any contiguous tract of land of 200-1,280 acres with at least 100 acres of suitable wildlife habitat may apply for a game breeding and hunting preserve license from the Department. Every licensee shall release not less than 250 bobwhite quail or pheasants each season. Such areas must be posted and boundaries clearly defined after Department inspection and approval ([61]3.27). The licensee may authorize to be taken, within the designated season, 100% of the released, hand reared pheasants, bobwhite quail, Hungarian partridges, chukar partridges, coturnix and wild turkeys, and mallard ducks (mallards may be released at any time of year). All released birds must be in full plumage and at least 16 weeks of age ([61]3.28). The licensee shall keep detailed records of the number and kind of game birds released and propagated yearly and their disposition. Department tags shall be used to band birds released, such tags to remain until prepared for final consumption ([61]3.29). A hunting license is required on such hunting preserves, and the Department shall designate the open seasons ([61]3.30). ★The Department may designate any preserve operator as a special representative of the Department with power to enforce the game laws and to prevent trespassing upon the preserve, subject to Department rules.★ No more than two such persons may be designated per preserve area ([61]3.31). The Department, after 15 days notice and opportunity for hearing, may suspend, revoke, or refuse to license any preserve not in compliance with Department rules ([61]3.33). Misuse of tags or transfer of tags to another preserve operator, or use of tags on wild birds/animals is a Class B misdemeanor ([61]3.35).

Import, Export and Release Provisions

It is unlawful to bring into the state for holding, releasing, propagating or selling, any living wild animal not covered by this Act without a permit from the Director upon proof that the specific animals to be imported are free of communicable disease, will not become a nuisance, and will not cause damage to any existing wild or domestic species. These provisions do not apply to animals imported to be confined and exhibited in any zoo or other public display of animals, nor to such animals or groups that the Department may exempt by rule ([61]2.2). It is unlawful to release from captivity any protected live species, except as provided in [61]2.34, 3.23 and 3.29, without the Department's permission ([61]2.3).

Importing wild or semi-domestic mammals from other states or foreign countries for hunting with bow and arrow or gun, with or without dogs, requires an exotic game hunting area permit. The annual fee shall be $1,000, and the area must be from 640 to 2,560 acres, must be fenced in a manner capable of holding the mammals released, and the permittee must obtain a $10,000 bond to cover damages from escapees. The mammals must be certified disease-free by an Illinois veterinarian, and the area inspected by the Department. Violation: business offense; $500-1,000 ([61]3.34).

It is unlawful, except for licensed game breeders, to import, carry into or possess alive, any species of wildlife taken outside of the state without the Director's permission ([61]2.33). No person shall release, hold, possess or engage in raising San Juan (European) rabbits or finn raccoons (raccoon dogs) and no permit shall be issued. No person shall release or propagate for release any nutria and monk parakeet in the state at any time ([61]3.23).

Live fish, viable fish eggs or viable sperm of any species or hybrid of salmon or trout may be imported only with a fish importation permit and other required permits. Such permit shall be issued only if the source hatchery is inspected and found free of diseases designated by Department rule, or of other diseases that may be detrimental to the state fishery resource. Permits are valid for up to six months from the date the source hatchery is certified as disease-free, and may be canceled upon diagnosis of a disease at the source hatchery. Salmon or trout in transit through the state which will not be released from their containers need no permit. Failure to comply is grounds for revocation of the aquaculture or fish dealer license/permit ([56]10-105). It is unlawful to release any fish into state waters without the Department's permission except that landowners may release fish that are indigenous to the state into waters wholly upon their lands. The Department may promulgate rules regulating the possession, transportation and shipping of non-indigenous aquatic life. All fish may be released into waters from which taken ([56]10-100).

See also Commercial and Private Enterprise Provisions.

Interstate Reciprocal Agreements

The Department may enter into reciprocal fishing agreements with Missouri, Iowa, Wisconsin, Kentucky and Indiana to permit persons licensed, or legally exempt from being licensed, by those states to fish in boundary waters between those states and Illinois if those states extend a similar privilege to Illinois residents, subject to Department conditions and restrictions ([56]20-60).

ANIMAL DAMAGE CONTROL

Upon written permission from the Department, landowners/tenants may remove or destroy any wild bird or wild mammal, other than a game bird or migratory game bird, that is destroying property on the land. Upon receipt of information from the owner that any wildlife is damaging dams, levees, ditches or other property, together with a statement of location of the damages, their nature and extent, and the particular species doing damage, the Department shall investigate. If damage exists and can be abated only by removing or destroying such wildlife, the Department shall issue a permit to remove/destroy the species. The permit shall be for up to 90 days, and shall specify the means, methods, persons, disposition of the wildlife taken, and other restrictions. When possible, specimens shall be given to a scientific, educational or zoological institution. The permittee shall advise the Department in writing within ten days after permit expiration of the number of individual species taken and disposition made ([61]2.37).

The Department may grant an individual, corporation or government body the authority to control wildlife under an Administrative Order and may require reports listing numbers and species taken and dates. Drainage districts have authority to control beaver, but must notify the Department in writing that a problem exists and of their intention to trap the animals at least seven days before trapping begins, and must identify traps with tags, must use specified sizes of traps (except during open season for the species), and must set traps as required. No beaver or other fur-bearer taken outside of the dates for the fur-bearer trapping season may be sold, but must be given to a Conservation Officer within 48 hours of being caught. The District must report annually as to animals caught, and must show all species taken ([61]2.37).

ENFORCEMENT OF WILDLIFE LAWS

Enforcement Powers

All authorized employees of the Department shall be peace officers and shall have the power to enforce the Act's provisions and rules, and may carry such weapons necessary to arrest a person resisting arrest ([56]1-160) and ([61]1.14).

All authorized Department employees, USFW officers, and all sheriffs, deputy sheriffs and other peace officers shall be empowered to arrest a person violating any Act provisions or rules. Complaints shall be filed with Circuit Courts having jurisdiction. Accredited officers and Department employees may serve warrants and render assistance in prosecutions ([56]1-165). ★Officers may operate without vehicle lights at night in order to lawfully arrest violators when the public safety will not be endangered ([61]1.15).★ State attorneys shall enforce the provisions of this act in their respective counties and prosecute persons charged with violations upon the Department's request ([56]1.16 and [61]1-170). All such prosecutions shall commence within two years from the time of the offense ([56]1-175) and ([61]1.17). The Circuit Court Clerk shall submit to the Department all fines collected, names of the persons fined, arresting officers, fine amounts and conviction dates ([56]1-180) and ([61]1.18).

Authorized Department employees are empowered to enter all lands and waters to enforce the Act's provisions, and may examine all buildings, private or public clubs (except dwellings), fish markets, cold storage facilities, cars, vessels, and boats, tents, game bags, and to open packages possessed by common carriers which they have reason to believe contain any wild birds, wild mammals or parts taken, bought, sold, shipped or possessed contrary to law or rule ([56]1-185) and ([61]1.19). The possession of any wild bird, wild mammal or aquatic life protected under this Act is prima facie evidence that the same is subject to the Act's provisions. When the contents of any container consists partly of contraband and partly of legal species, the entire contents is subject to confiscation. Wild birds or wild mammals possessed in excess of the legal bag/possession limits are subject to confiscation ([56]1-190) and ([61]1.20).

When authorized Department employees or peace officers have reason to believe that a person or institution has illegal possession of any wild birds, mammals or aquatic life, they may execute search warrants and return to a Circuit Court an inventory of all wildlife or parts held illegally. If the court determines that the wildlife was held, possessed or transported illegally, a judgment shall be entered against the owner/party found in possession for costs of the proceeding and disposition of the seized property ([56]1-195) and ([61]1.21). Contraband aquatic life, wild birds, wild mammals, fur-bearing mammals, or parts seized and confiscated shall be disposed of as the Department directs ([56]1-210) and ([61]1.24).

Criminal Penalties

A person who for profit or commercial purposes knowingly captures, kills, possesses, sells, barters, buys, ships, exports, imports, receives or attempts or causes any of these things to any aquatic life, in part or whole, of any of the species protected by this Code, contrary to its provisions, and that aquatic life, in whole or part, is valued in excess of a total of $300, commits a Class 3 felony. Possession of aquatic life, in whole or part, captured or killed in violation of this Code, valued in excess of $600 shall be considered prima facie evidence of possession for profit or commercial purposes ([56]5-25).

For purposes of this section, the value of all protected species, whether dressed or not dressed, is as follows: ► each muskellunge or hybrid, northern pike, walleye, striped bass or hybrid, sauger, largemouth bass, smallmouth bass, spotted bass, trout (all species), salmon (all species other than chinook as specified), and sturgeon of one pound or more, $4 for each pound or fraction of fish; ► each of these species of less than one pound, $4 per fish; ► parts of fish processed past the dressed state, $8 per pound; ► processed turtle parts, $6 for each pound or fraction; ► non-processed turtles, $8 each; ► frogs, toads, salamanders, lizards and snakes, $2 per animal in whole or in part; ► all species of goldeye, mooneye, carp, carpsuckers, suckers, redhorse, buffalo, freshwater drum, skipjack, shad, alewife, smelt, gar, bowfin, mussels, chinook salmon as specified and all other protected aquatic life, $1 per pound, in part or in whole ([56]5-25).

Except as prescribed in [56]5-25 (illegal taking of fish for profit), any violation of provisions and rules of the Fish and Aquatic Life Code is a petty offense. Violation of [56]10-80 (illegal taking of protected fish) is a Class B misdemeanor. Violation of [56]10-55 (taking endangered species) or [56]10-1-200 (obstruction of officer), or violation of any Fish Code provisions during the five years following license revocation under [56]20-105 is a Class A misdemeanor. ★Any violation of [56]5-25 (illegal taking of fish for profit) is a Class 3 felony ([56]20-35).★

★A person who for profit or commercial purposes knowingly captures, kills, possesses, sells, barters, purchases, ships, exports, imports or offers or causes any of these, or who causes to be carried or receives for shipment or exports any animal or parts of any species protected by this Act, and such animals, in whole or in part, are valued in excess of $300, commits a Class 3 felony.★ Possession of animals, in whole or in part, captured or killed in violation of this Act, valued in excess of $600, shall be prima facie evidence of possession for profit or commercial purposes. The values of protected species are: bald eagle, $200; whitetail deer and wild turkey, $145; fur-bearing mammals, $25; game birds (except turkey), migratory game birds, resident and migratory non-game birds (except bald eagle and falcons), game mammals (except whitetail deer), and non-game mammals, $10; eagles, owls, hawks, falcons, kites, harriers and ospreys, $125 ([61]2.36a).

Any violation of [61]2.36a (illegal taking for profit) is a Class 3 felony. Violation of [61]1.22, [61]2.4, [61]2.36 and [61]2.38 (resisting an officer, killing a raptor, license falsification, illegal commercial sale/possession) is a Class A misdemeanor; subsequent violation of [61]2.4 or [61]2.36 is a Class 4 felony. Any violation during a period of license revocation is a Class A misdemeanor [Other offenses are either petty offenses or Class B misdemeanors, as specified in this section.] ([61]3.5).

Civil Penalties

In addition to any fines imposed, or as otherwise provided, a person found guilty of unlawfully taking or possessing any aquatic life protected by the Fish Code or hunting or trapping provisions of the Wildlife Code shall be assessed a civil penalty for that aquatic life in accordance with the values prescribed in [56]5-25 of the Code. This civil penalty shall be imposed at the time of the conviction by the Circuit Court of the county where the offense was committed. All penalties provided in this section shall be remitted to the Department in accordance with the provisions of [61]1.18 of the Wildlife Act ([56]1-180) and ([61]3.5). (See Other Enforcement Provisions under this section.)

Other Enforcement Provisions

Every hunting or trapping device, vehicle or conveyance, seine, net, trap, watercraft, aircraft, or electrical device used illegally in taking, transporting or holding any wild bird, wild mammal, or aquatic life contrary to law is a public nuisance and subject to seizure by any authorized Department employee. That employee shall file a complaint before the Circuit Court and a summons requiring the alleged violator to appear and show cause why the property should not be forfeited. If the court determines the property was illegally used, it may order the property forfeited to the Department. The owner may have a jury determine the illegality of the property's use and has right of appeal. Forfeiture does not affect prosecution and assessment of penalties otherwise provided. The Department shall make reasonable efforts to notify owners entitled to possession of abandoned, lost or stolen property which was illegally possessed or used, who may claim such property within six months before its sale at public auction after reimbursing the Department for expenses of custody. Any forfeited property, including guns, may be publicly auctioned, with proceeds to the Wildlife and Fish Fund ([56]1-215) and ([61]1.25).

Each protected wild bird, wild mammal or fish, or any part, including nests and eggs taken, shipped, transported, bought, sold or bartered or possessed, and each green hide of game mammals or fur-bearing mammals held, bought or sold contrary to law, and each trap, snare, net or other device, including ferrets used, in violation of the Act's provisions constitutes a separate offense ([56]1-220) and ([61]1.26). A person who aids or contributes in any manner to a violation is individually liable, as a separate offense, for the penalties imposed on person who committed the violation ([56]1-225) and ([61]1.27).

License Revocations and Suspensions

Whenever any license/permit holder is guilty of misrepresentation in obtaining such license/permit or of violating any Code provisions, the Department may revoke the license/permit, and suspend the person from engaging in the permit/license activity, and no new license will be issued for up to five years, according to revocation procedure rules. Violation of any provisions during the revocation period is a Class A misdemeanor ([56]20-105) and ([61]3.36).

HABITAT PROTECTION

The Department shall provide and maintain management and habitat development on state lands/waters used in propagating or breeding aquatic life to conform with the most modern conservation methods, and may cooperate with a person propagating or breeding aquatic life on private lands/waters ([56]1-155). When deemed feasible for the conservation of mussels, the Department by rule may prescribe waters to be known as mussel preserves from which mussels shall not be taken for any purpose during any periods to restore a supply of mussel life ([56]25-10).

The Department may establish and maintain refuges or public hunting areas upon any lands or waters owned by the federal government by mutual consent of federal and state governments and may designate by rule refuges upon any lands owned/leased by the state with approval of the controlling agency. It is unlawful to take any species of wildlife on any wildlife refuge except as provided in [61]2.25. The Department shall post the boundaries of refuges and publish legal notices ([61]1.8).

The Department has the power to acquire by purchase, lease, donation or eminent domain: ▸ suitable lands for breeding, hatching, propagation and conservation of birds, mammals, and aquatic life; ▸ lands/waters for public hunting/fishing grounds; ▸ lands/waters for wildlife refuges; and to construct buildings, roads, bridges and other facilities necessary for full public utilization of such areas ([56]1-150) and ([61]1.9).

★★To cooperate with private landowners and others who desire to aid in conservation of game and other wildlife, the Department may create and maintain Wildlife Habitat Management Areas on lands owned by individuals, corporations or municipalities. Hunting rights shall be controlled by the property owners in mutual agreement with the Department for five years or more. The Director may cancel such agreements upon 60 days notice if: ▸ use of the lands is no longer needed; ▸ the owners desire to sell the property and the sale cannot be consummated under the agreement and the object of such sale is not to convert hunting rights to private use; ▸ the lessor becomes dissatisfied with the project and files a written request. Areas shall comprise at least 600 acres of contiguous farm lands or a combination of tillable land and woodlots suitable for the protection and propagation of small game species normally found on such lands. Not more than 1/3 of the total acreage of such a project may be set apart as State Game Refuges wherein no hunting shall be permitted. These areas and safety zones contained therein shall be posted. Two-thirds of the land shall be open to hunting and trapping. The Department has the right to develop and improve area game food and habitat conditions, without interfering with normal operations on the tract. The Department shall formulate, adopt, and enforce rules for management of the areas. It is unlawful to shoot within safety zones within 150 yards from buildings, or to hunt, pursue, disturb or chase any wild animal or bird within a safety zone. The Department shall aid in protecting the lands, fences, livestock and other property of the cooperator during the hunting season and enforce safety zone restrictions. If deemed desirable to remove surplus game from the property for stocking elsewhere, the cooperator has preference as a Department agent to trap surplus game for, and be paid a price per head as agreed. If the cooperator is willing to leave a strip(s) of grain or hay stand in place for game food, nesting, cover or travel lanes, or to delay mowing of hay, the Department may reimburse him/her at a price mutually agreed upon in advance of the harvest period. The cooperator or family may go upon such area any time of the year in connection with the normal and customary management of the farm, without dog, firearm, or bow and arrow providing no attempt is made to drive or disturb game. Hunters shall be limited to a number agreed upon as reasonable with respect to the game population. Hunters shall at all times respect the rights of cooperating farmers and shall not injure or destroy their livestock or property. Trees or shrubs shall not be cut, nor shall berries, nuts or fruits be picked within such refuge area except with the owner's permission. Streams shall not be contaminated/polluted in any manner. Dogs entering a refuge area inadvertently may be recovered by the owner entering without firearms or other weapons. Wounded game birds or animals entering a refuge area may be recovered by a hunter after reporting to a warden who may investigate and go with the unarmed hunter to recover the animal ([61]219 through 233).★★

★Until clearly evident that rigid supervision is no longer needed, each cooperative area will have at least one Director appointed supervisory officer on duty at a conveniently located telephone on or adjacent to the area. Participating farmers will be given the officer's location and number. Parking areas will be posted to inform hunters. Check-in stations may be located with these officers, and the stations used to control the number of hunters on a cooperative area and to collect a nominal fee. In lieu of other charges, a fee in addition to the regular license fee may be charged by cooperators for a permit to hunt on cooperative areas. Surplus funds collected over the program's cost are to be used for farmer-hunter benefit (directly or indirectly to the hunter) by benefiting the farmer and creating good will for the hunting program. It is unlawful for a person, except by Department permission, to enter a Wildlife Habitat Management Area Refuge Safety Zone during any open season for hunting game, or to enter with firearms, bows and arrows, traps or dogs, or to permit dogs to enter the refuge. The Department by rule may prohibit persons from entering such refuge. Wardens or Department agents may enter such areas unarmed at any time for official duties. A violation is a petty offense, and resisting arrest for violation of property damage laws or any state law intended to protect farm livestock or human life is unlawful ([61]234 through 239).

NATIVE AMERICAN WILDLIFE PROVISIONS: None.

INDIANA

Sources: Burns Indiana Statutes Annotated, Title 14, 1990; 1992 Cumulative Supplement.

STATE WILDLIFE POLICY

The **Department of Natural Resources** has the authority and responsibility to protect and properly manage the fish and wildlife resources of the state. Any and all wild animals, except those legally owned or held in captivity under license or permit or as otherwise excepted in this article, shall be the property of the people of the state and the protection, reproduction, care, management, survival, and regulation of the wild animal population shall be entrusted to the **Division of Fish and Wildlife** of the Department (14-2-1-2). (See also Agency Funding Sources under STATE FISH AND WILDLIFE AGENCIES.)

RELEVANT WILDLIFE DEFINITIONS: See Definitions section of Appendices.

STATE FISH AND WILDLIFE AGENCIES

Agency Structure

There is an overall **Department of Natural Resources** (Department) with a **Head Director,** appointed by the Governor, who supervises all Department work and that of each of the divisions. The Head Director has direct charge of the **Conservation Officers** in the enforcement of penal provisions of this article or of the rules of the **Natural Resources Commission** (Commission), and may, with Commission approval, cooperate with any other state government department in enforcement, and assign deputies to aid in the prevention or detection of crime (14-3-1-1 and -3-4). The Department consists of the Commission, the Head Director, two deputy directors and other personnel necessary to carry out the Department's duties (14-3-3-2). The Department is concerned with all state natural resources, including the culture and preservation of forests, fish and game (14-3-1-3). Within the Department are Divisions of Geology, Entomology and Plant Pathology, Forestry, Land and Waters, Engineering and Fish and Game (14-3-1-8).

There is within the **Department of Natural Resources** (Department) a **Division of Fish and Wildlife** (Division) which shall administer for the Department the provisions of this article (14-4-14). The chief administrative officer of the Division is the **Director of the Division of Fish and Wildlife of the Department of Natural Resources** (Director), and shall be appointed as provided by law to administer this article's provisions (14-2-3-1). Division chiefs (Directors) and all assistants, inspectors and employees shall be chosen solely for fitness for the position, professional or practical, as the position demands, irrespective of political beliefs or affiliations, which fitness may be determined by examination or otherwise as the Commission shall determine (14-3-1-2).

Each division chief is responsible for the work of the division (14-3-1-9). [Additional details are given concerning bureaus, agencies and divisions of the Department, including advisory councils for various bureaus, and various reorganization details and transfers of power in the recent change from Department of Conservation to Department of Natural Resources.]

The **Commission** consists of 12 members, of whom seven are ex-officio members as follows: Commissioners of the Departments of Transportation and of Environmental Management; Directors of the Departments of Commerce and Natural Resources; Chairmen of the Advisory Council on Water and Mineral Resources and of Land, Forest, and Wildlife Resources; and the Indiana Academy of Science President. The remaining five members shall be citizens appointed by the Governor for three years, and at least two must have knowledge, experience or education in the environment or in natural resource conservation. The Commission shall have at least four meetings a year. ★The Commission shall appoint administrative law judges; a person not appointed by the Commission shall not act as an administrative law judge (14-3-3-3).★ The Commission is the ultimate authority of the Department (14-3-3-21). The Commission may issue a notice of violation to a person who violates a law which is a misdemeanor or infraction penalty. If the person fails to abate the violation within 15 days, the Commission may impose a charge that does not exceed the maximum amount that may be assessed by a court for the violation (14-3-3-22).

The **Law Enforcement Division** is a Division of the Department of Natural Resources separate from the Division of Fish and Wildlife (14-3-4-1). The Director is appointed by the Governor, selected on the basis of training and experience, and shall have had at least five years experience in a supervisory capacity in a law enforcement agency closely associated with conservation (14-3-4-2). The Law Enforcement Director shall organize and conduct a required training school for officer candidates and other employees. Examinations will test applicants in the qualifications required for the rank, grade or position (14-3-4-6). (See also ENFORCEMENT OF WILDLIFE LAWS.)

Agency Powers and Duties

The Department may cooperate with any public or private institution, individuals, societies or associations in making scientific investigations, and compiling reports the Commission deems necessary (14-3-1-4).

A member of the Commission or a Division Director may administer oaths and subpoena witnesses (14-3-1-5). The Commission may cause to be prepared technical and nontechnical literature and information relating to the work of the Department or any Division, and shall disseminate the same (14-3-1-7).

The Commission has the power of eminent domain as necessary for carrying out this chapter's provisions under specified procedures (14-3-1-19).

The **Director** shall: ▸ provide for the protection, reproduction, care, management, survival and regulation of wild animal populations on public or private properties and organize and pursue research and management of wild animals that will serve the best interests of the resources and the people; ▸ write and issue any licenses/permits required by this article; ▸ enter any private or public property (except dwellings, barns and other buildings) for the purpose of managing and protecting any wild animal or for the purpose of killing or removing any wild animal which may be a nuisance or detrimental to overall populations (14-2-3-2); ▸ adopt rules to open, close, suspend or shorten seasons; ▸ adopt bag, sex and size limits; ▸ limit the numbers of hunters and fishermen; ▸ establish methods, means and time of taking, chasing, transporting, selling or so attempting, of any wild animals, with or without dogs; ▸ set aside lands or waters owned or controlled by the state for conservation purposes as a public hunting and fishing ground under appropriate conditions and limitations; ▸ establish other necessary rules to administer this chapter and properly manage wild animals (14-2-3-3). The Director may designate and set aside any waters containing state-owned fish, state waters, and boundary waters for the purpose of improvement and propagation of the wild animal population, and shall post area borders. It is unlawful to take, catch, kill or pursue any wild animal from any such designated area (14-2-6-9).

The **Attorney General** has concurrent power with the several prosecuting attorneys of the state, and it is the duty of all of these to attend to rigid enforcement of all provisions of this chapter (14-3-1-23).

Agency Regulations

The Director shall adopt rules only after thorough investigation, based upon data relative to the welfare of the particular wild animal, its relationship to other animals, and the welfare of the people. Necessary rules shall: ▸ clearly describe and set forth any applicable changes; ▸ be periodically reviewed; ▸ be included in each official compilation of the Fish and Wildlife Laws. The Director may modify or suspend a rule up to one year (14-2-3-3). ★Any and all rules or restrictions incorporated in or attached to any license or permit shall be construed to mean and include only such rules or restrictions as may be necessary and proper for adequate protection or propagation of wild animals or to promote the general purpose of this article (14-2-7-27).★

Agency Funding Sources

The Division, with the Director's approval, may engage in revenue-raising projects, including: ▸ sale of items made by Department employees, purchased for resale, or taken on consignment for sale; ▸ sale of right/authority to market items, devices or artwork owned/controlled by the Department; ▸ solicitation of gifts; ▸ sale of nonmonetary gifts. All money raised shall be deposited in the Fish and Wildlife Fund (14-2-3-11).

The Department shall determine the form of and distribute for sale the **Migratory Waterfowl Stamp** (14-2-4.5-2). The Department shall contract annually with a nonprofit organization to utilize 50% of the revenue for development of waterfowl propagation areas. The Department shall obtain evidence that the project is acceptable to the agency having jurisdiction over the lands and waters affected by the project. The Department shall spend 50% of the stamp revenues for the acquisition or development of wetlands or to participate in joint funding of North American waterfowl management plans (14-2-4.5-4).

The Department shall determine the form of the **Game Bird Habitat Restoration Stamp** and distribute them for sale (14-2-4.6-2). Proceeds go into the **Game Bird Habitat Restoration Fund** to be expended by the Director solely for the purpose of restoring the habitat of the various game birds (14-2-4.6-4). (See also HABITAT PROTECTION.)

★Four dollars from the cost of every nonresident license to hunt game for any period in any manner shall be used by the Department to increase the upland game bird population. Twenty dollars from the cost of every nonresident license to hunt deer shall be deposited in the Deer Research and Management Fund and forty dollars used to increase the upland game bird population. To encourage donations to the Fish and Wildlife Fund, the Department may issue on a distinctive form a limited number of any licenses authorized under 14-2-7-5(a). Including the license fee plus a donation, the charge may not be less than $50. Money collected in excess of the regular license fee amount goes to the Fish and Wildlife Fund (14-2-7-5).★

Money received from the sale of **Lifetime Hunting and Fishing Licenses** shall be deposited in the **Lifetime Hunting and Fishing License Trust Fund** (14-2-7-5.7). Administered by the Department, the fund may accept gifts, and proceeds shall be deposited in the fund, along with any interest earned. Annually, all accumulated earnings in the fund, plus 2.5% times the amount of money in the fund (less accumulated earnings) shall be transferred to the Fish and Wildlife Fund, and may be used for no other purpose (14-3-1-16.5).

The **Nongame Fund** is a dedicated fund administered by the Department. In recognition of the importance of preserving the natural heritage of Indiana, it is the intent of the General Assembly to provide a fund to be used exclusively for protection, conservation, management and identification of nongame and endangered species primarily through acquisition of their natural habitat. Therefore, the money in the fund may be expended exclusively for the preservation of nongame and endangered species. No portion of the fund shall revert to the general fund at the end of the fiscal year (14-2-8.5-15). If the Natural Resources Commission establishes entrance fees for admission to fish and wildlife areas, the fees shall be deposited in the Nongame Fund; however, holders of hunting or fishing licenses may not be charged a fee for admission to fish and wildlife areas (14-2-8.5-16).

Each court which collects money due the Department for violation of any of the fish and wildlife laws shall remit it to the Department, which shall remit it to the state auditor monthly, who shall remit it to the State Treasurer. The money paid to the State Treasurer, together with other sums as may be appropriated or set apart for that purpose, shall constitute a special revenue fund, the **Fish and Wildlife Fund**, which shall be used for the purpose of propagating game, fish and birds in the state and paying the operational expenses of the Division and Law Enforcement Division. Money in the fund attributable to amounts deposited under 33-19-7-5 shall be used to administer the **Turn In A Poacher** program and reward system established under 14-3-4-13 (14-3-1-16).

The **Conservation Officers Fish and Wildlife Fund**, administered by the Department, is exclusively for special law enforcement investigations of fish and wildlife violations. Any excess over $35,000 in the fund at the end of a fiscal year shall be transferred into the Fish and Wildlife Fund (14-3-4-11).

There is a **Deer Research and Management Fund**, administered by the Department, the moneys to be used for deer research and management (14-3-19-1 through -4).

The purpose of the **Indiana Heritage Trust Fund** and related program is the acquisition of real property that: ▸is an example of outstanding natural features and habitats; ▸has historical and archaeological significance; ▸provides areas for conservation, recreation and restoration of native biological diversity. The program will acquire property for new and existing state parks, state forests, nature preserves, fish and wildlife areas, wetlands, trails and river corridors, ensuring that Indiana's rich natural heritage is preserved/enhanced for succeeding generations (14-3-20-1). Within the fund are a number of accounts, including the Fish and Wildlife Account, which moneys may be used only to purchase property for fish or wildlife management purposes (14-3-20-28).

Agency Advisory Boards

★★[The Indiana Heritage Trust Program (chapter 20 and 14-3-20-1 through -30), within which are wildlife interests, funds and provisions, has both a **Trust Committee** and a **Program Committee**, and membership includes various Department Division Directors (forestry, nature preserves, state parks, fish and wildlife) and members from academic, organized hunting and fishing, environmental and other groups. Extensive details are given concerning this program and its committees and their operation and duties, along with that of the **Indiana Natural Resources Foundation** and its related fund (discussed in chapter 17 and 14-3-17-1 through -15), and these details are worthy of review by those seeking to establish similar programs. (See also Agency Funding Sources.)]★★

PROTECTED SPECIES OF WILDLIFE

Except as provided in the Director's regulations, it is unlawful to take, possess, transport, export, process, sell or ship nongame species deemed by the Director to be in need of management, or for any common carrier knowingly to transport nongame species in need of management (14-2-8.5-4). The Director shall conduct investigations on nongame species to determine which species are in need of management and shall issue regulations setting forth those nongame species. The Director may consider information relating to population, distribution, habitat needs, limiting factors and other biological and ecological data. The Director shall issue proposed regulations to develop management programs designed to insure the continued perpetuation of nongame species in need of management. Investigations shall be ongoing and regulations may from time to time be amended (14-2-8.5-2). The Director shall by regulations establish limitations on taking, possession, transportation, exportation, use, processing, sale or shipment of nongame species deemed necessary to manage them (14-2-8.5-3).

On the basis of investigations and other available scientific and commercial data, and after consultation with other state wildlife agencies, federal agencies and other interested persons and organizations, the Director shall, by rule, list those species/subspecies of wildlife indigenous to the state (14-2-8.5-5). This list shall be reviewed and amended at least every two years, and the Director shall submit to the Governor a summary report of the data used in support of all amendments to the list during the preceding biennium (14-2-8.5-6).

Except as otherwise provided, it is unlawful to take, possess, transport, export, process, ship, sell (or for any common carrier to ship) any species or subspecies of wildlife appearing on the list of state indigenous wildlife determined to be endangered, the US list of endangered wildlife, or the state list of endangered species developed under 14-2-8.5-8. Any species on any of the foregoing lists which enters the state from another state or country and which is transported across the state destined for a point beyond the state may be transported without restriction in accordance with federal or other state permits (14-2-8.5-7). If the Director determines that any species should be designated endangered and has not been by the federal government, the Director by rule may make such addition binding whether or not such species are indigenous to the state (14-2-8.5-8). The Director shall establish such programs, including acquisition of land or aquatic habitat, deemed necessary for management of nongame species and shall utilize all authority vested in the department for this purpose, and may enter into agreements with agencies or private persons for administration and management of areas utilized for management of nongame species. The Governor shall utilize other programs in furtherance of these purposes to the extent practicable, and shall encourage other state and federal agencies to do likewise (14-2-8.5-9). ★The costs of programs established herein for endangered species and nongame species in need of management shall not be borne by funds dedicated to fish and game purposes.★ (See also ANIMAL DAMAGE CONTROL and GENERAL EXCEPTIONS TO PROTECTION.)

GENERAL EXCEPTIONS TO PROTECTION

This article does not apply to groundhogs (14.2.2.2). It is lawful for a person who possesses land, or another person designated in writing by that person, to take coyotes on that land at any time (14-2-4-8).

The Department may issue to a properly accredited individual a Scientific Collector's License, authorizing collection and possession of wild birds, nests and eggs, or other wild animals, for scientific purposes only, under rules adopted under 4-22-2. The application shall bear signatures of two persons qualified to attest to the accomplishments and fitness of the applicant (14-2-7-17).

The Director may permit, under conditions prescribed by rule, the taking, possession, transportation, exportation or shipment of wildlife species designated as in need of management or endangered (on any list) for scientific, zoological or educational purposes, for propagation in captivity of such wildlife, or for other special purposes (14-2-8.5-10). (See also PROTECTED SPECIES OF WILDLIFE amd ANIMAL DAMAGE CONTROL.)

See also Licenses and Permits under HUNTING, FISHING, TRAPPING PROVISIONS.

HUNTING, FISHING, TRAPPING PROVISIONS

General Provisions

It is unlawful to: fish, hunt, trap, chase, or shoot with firearms upon private land without first securing the landowner's consent (14-2-6-1); kill or cripple any wild animal without making a reasonable effort to retrieve the animal and include it in the daily bag limit (14-2-6-8).

Licenses and Permits

It is unlawful to take or chase, with or without dogs, any wild animal without a license, except for: a resident or nonresident participating in a sanctioned field trial; a landowner or lessee residing on the land, and the spouse and children, who may hunt, fish and trap on their own land. These exceptions do not apply to any commercial license issued under this article (14-2-7-1).

In addition to other requirements for obtaining a hunting license, a person born after 1986 must have successfully completed a course of instruction in hunter education as specified in 14-2-10-1. ★If a hunting license applicant requests that such course be offered in the applicant's county of residence, the Department shall offer a course in that county not more than 92 days after receiving a request (14-2-7-2.5).★ The Department shall provide for a course of instruction in hunter safety, principles of conservation and sportsmanship, and may cooperate with any association promoting hunter safety, conservation and sportsmanship. The Director shall designate a Conservation Officer as administrator of this program. The Department may construct and operate public outdoor and indoor target ranges, and shall prepare reports as required to seek federal assistance in developing hunter safety programs (14-2-10-1). ★★The Department shall establish a trapper training program including a course of instruction in trapping wild animals that emphasizes methods, laws, ethics, responsibilities, natural history, wildlife management and other matters associated with trapping. The program shall be administered and developed in the same manner as the hunter education program (14-2-10-2).★★

Every person must have a hunting, fishing or trapping license in possession when doing any of these activities except as otherwise provided. Every person must have a valid Trout-Salmon Stamp in possession to fish for or take trout or salmon in waters containing state-owned fish. When a special hunting, trapping, or fishing license is issued, a regular license is not required (14-2-7-3). (See also Agency Funding Sources under STATE FISH AND WILDLIFE AGENCIES for uses of certain license funds.)

Lifetime licenses are available to residents according to a detailed schedule of fees based on regular license fees and whether the applicant is over or under age 50. Such licenses may be suspended or revoked for the same causes that resident yearly licenses to hunt or fish may be suspended or revoked (14-2-7-5.7).

No person may hunt or take any migratory waterfowl (wild goose, brant, wild duck) without a Migratory Waterfowl Stamp from the Department in possession while hunting (14-2-4.5-2). No person may take any game bird (pheasant, quail, grouse, wild turkey and Hungarian partridge) without a Game Bird Habitat Restoration Stamp from the Department in possession while hunting. These stamps are in addition to hunting licenses (14-2-4.6-2). No person may practice falconry in the state without a Falconry License issued by the Department (14-2-7-17.5).

Dog field trials require a permit from the Department. It is unlawful to conduct a field trial whereby wild animals are being pursued out of season except in such areas and at such times as the Department approves. A nonresident may not train, work or exercise a dog at any time that Indiana residents are not permitted to do the same in the nonresident's state. Permits shall not be issued unless the field trial is sanctioned under a national or regional hunting dog association approved by the Department (14-2-7-19).

Falsely claiming to be a resident of Indiana when applying for a license or permit shall result in any license or permit to be void. It is unlawful to fail to carry one's license or permit while engaging in the permitted activity, or to falsify, change or alter any license or permit (14-2-7-28 and -29).

Restrictions on Taking: Hunting and Trapping

It is unlawful to take, possess, sell, purchase, ship or receive for shipment beyond the limits of the state any migratory bird designated in this article, or any part, nest, or egg thereof, except as otherwise permitted by law. It is unlawful to possess for any purpose whatsoever, during the closed season, migratory birds, nests, eggs or increase, without the proper permit or license issued by the Director or by an authorized department of the US government (14-2-4-1).

It is unlawful to: ▸ remove any fur-bearing animal from any trap not one's own without the owner's permission, or to fail to tend or visit one's own trap within each 24-hour period; ▸ use any snare for trapping animals except on one's own land or with the owner's permission, or to use a snare exceeding 15 inches in circumference; ▸ knowingly throw or cast the rays of any spotlight or other artificial light not required by law on a motor vehicle, in search of or upon any wild bird or wild animal, from a vehicle while having in possession any firearm, bow, or crossbow, whereby any wild bird or wild animal could be killed even though the animal is not killed, injured, shot at, or pursued; ▸ take any wildlife, except fur-bearing mammals, with the aid of illumination of any spotlight, searchlight or other artificial light; ▸ shine a spotlight, searchlight or other artificial light for the purpose of taking or attempting to take a deer; ▸ use a silencer on a firearm or possess such device while hunting; ▸ hunt, shoot at or kill any animal or shoot at any object from within, into, upon or across any public highway; ★▸ shoot at, hunt or kill any animal or shoot into or across any state waters or boundary waters except in the lawful pursuit of wild animals;★ ▸ sell, buy, or trade, or offer such, any wild bird or mammal, live or dead, or its meat, whether taken within or without the state except as otherwise provided, or for any hotel, or eating house to serve such meat, except during open season a guest and family may be served any bird or mammal lawfully taken by such guest. It is lawful to trap fur-bearing animals with an underwater box trap during trapping season (14-2-4-2 through -7).

★The season for taking raccoons is closed to nonresidents, except the Director may open the season to nonresidents during the same days and hours of raccoon open season in the nonresident's state. A nonresident shall not take raccoons in Indiana when the season is closed in Indiana even if the season is open in the nonresident's state (14-2-7-1.5).★

US laws, US migratory bird treaties with other countries, and rules issued by any department of the US government concerning migratory birds have the force and effect of law. It is unlawful to hunt, shoot, take, kill, possess, sell, purchase, or ship any migratory bird in violation of federal law. The Director may establish a season and bag limit for migratory birds identical to that established by federal law and give notice by publication as specified by statute (14-2-8-1.1). In order to promote fish culture and the increase of useful food and game fishes in state lakes and streams, full authority is granted to the US Bureau of Sport Fisheries and Wildlife to conduct fish hatching and related operations at any time considered necessary, other fish and game laws to the contrary notwithstanding (14-2-8-3).

Restrictions on Taking: Fishing

Except as otherwise provided, it is unlawful to take from waters containing state-owned fish or from state waters or boundary waters any fish by means of any weir, electric current, dynamite or other explosive, net, seine or trap or any other substance to stupefy or poison fish. It is unlawful to take any fish from state owned or stocked waters by means of any firearm or crossbow or by means of the hands alone. Otherwise prohibited devices/methods may be used under special permit issued by Director regulations (14-2-5-1). It is unlawful to ice fish through a hole greater than 12 inches in diameter, and any ice house shall be labeled with the owner's name and removed before the ice leaves (14-2-5-2). It is unlawful to use any trotline, set line, throw line, net, trap or seine, except legal minnow seines or dip nets, within 300 yards of any dam in the state or its boundary waters (24-2-5-3). It is unlawful for any bait dealer to transport or hold any live minnows and/or live crayfish for any purposes in a manner causing unnecessary loss and death of same. Violation is sufficient cause for the Division to revoke and seize the bait dealer's license. It is unlawful to transport beyond the state limits more than 100 minnows and/or 100 crayfish in any 24-hour period, except for commercial minnow raising for sale in private waters (14-2-5-4).

★All offal or filth of any description, accruing from the catching, curing, cleaning or shipping of fish in or near the waters of Lake Michigan shall be burned, buried or otherwise disposed of in a sanitary manner so as not to pollute the waters nor become a danger to public health (14-2-5-6).★

It is unlawful to sell, barter, exchange, purchase any protected fish taken within or without the state, except as otherwise provided. During open season, restaurants may prepare and serve to a guest and family any fish lawfully taken by such guest. These provisions do not apply to the sale of fish produced in private ponds for sale or for breeding and stocking purposes under permits from the Director. Hatchery reared fish or fish legally taken outside the state under a valid commercial fishing license, dead or alive, may be sold under state health agency regulations if properly tagged as specified (14-2-5-7).

It is unlawful to place any obstruction, other than a dam, across any waterway of the state or its boundary waters, that prevents fish from ascending or descending a waterway. Any person controlling any dam whose impounded water is withdrawn for municipal, industrial, electrical, agricultural, mining or other use, across any state waterway whose watershed is greater than 50 square miles, may be required to incorporate into such structure sufficient water storage head to maintain during periods of minimum stream flow a downstream discharge equal to the upstream inflow and to maintain sufficient water above the dam to support fish life. This does not apply to existing municipal or fire protection impoundments which have not impounded sufficient waters for such release. Any owner of a dam whose watershed is greater than 50 square miles may be required to construct and maintain fish ladders and may be required to construct and maintain a passageway around and over the dam sufficient to allow the upstream and downstream hand-carrying of small boats. The Director shall prescribe the materials and construction manner of fishways or fishladders. Violation: Class C infraction, and each day of violation is a separate offense (14-2-5-9).

It is unlawful to chemically treat aquatic vegetation in public waters without a permit from the Department setting conditions therefor by rule. This does not apply to a privately owned lake, farm pond or public or private drainage ditch, or to landowners adjacent to public waters who chemically treat aquatic vegetation in the immediate vicinity of a boat landing or bathing beach on or adjacent to the real estate of those landowners. The area within which aquatic vegetation is to be treated chemically must not exceed one-half acre or 50% of the aquatic vegetation, whichever is less (14-2-5-10).

Private pond owners may obtain a permit to possess and use otherwise illegal fishing devices on their own waters under the Director's rules. It is unlawful to use, set or discharge dynamite or other explosives in any state waters without a permit from the Director, and under rules prescribed for protection of fish (14-2-7-25 and -26).

Commercial and Private Enterprise Provisions

No person may engage in the business of buying fur-bearing animals, untanned hides or furs without a Department license. Purchases direct from trappers may be made only during the open season on such fur-bearing animals and the grace period thereafter. Within 60 days of the close of the fur-bearer season, every licensed fur dealer shall report to the Department all purchases of skins, hides or furs made during the season (14-2-7-7).

The Department may issue a Game Breeder's license to propagate in captivity, and to possess, buy or sell for such purposes only, protected game birds, game mammals or fur-bearing mammals. Such licenses shall authorize the sale of nonmigratory game birds, game mammals or fur-bearing mammals for breeding or release, and nonmigratory game birds for food purposes. Any person who acquires any live game bird, game mammal or fur-bearing mammal legally in open season, or purchases the same from a licensed game breeder, may apply for a Game Breeder's license within five days of acquiring such animal or bird. Otherwise the animal or bird is to be released. Animals raised domestically by out-of-state breeders may be imported and sold for food purposes with proof of their out-of-state origin. The breeding, raising and producing in captivity, and marketing of marten, nutria, mink, chinchilla, domesticated rabbits, except cottontail and swamp rabbits, is deemed an agricultural pursuit, and all such animals

Indiana

deemed domestic animals so that a Game Breeder license is not required, but such breeders shall, upon request, register with the Department and report annually the number of animals held and sold (14-2-7-8).

Wild animals not protected by state law may be possessed for taxidermy purposes without a license. The Department may issue a license to possess for taxidermy purposes protected wild animals, hides or skins thereof, during the closed season for that animal, under rules adopted under 4-22-2. Wild animals lawfully taken in open season and mounted may be possessed by any person at any time (14-2-7-9).

A person owning or leasing for not less than five years a contiguous tract of land containing 100 to 640 acres, who desires to establish a licensed shooting preserve (preserve) for propagating or hunting captive reared and released pheasant, quail, chukar partridges, properly marked mallard ducks, and other game species as the Department may add, shall apply to the Division for a license. The Department shall inspect the proposed preserve and facilities, cover, and capabilities of the applicant, and may issue a license. The licensee shall post the licensed area and clearly define the boundaries. A preserve may not be established within five miles of a state-owned game refuge or state public hunting ground. Duck shooting may not be permitted where wild duck, geese or other migratory game birds frequent the area where captive reared birds are to be held, released and flighted for shooting. Persons taking captive birds on a preserve must have a hunting license; nonresidents must have a special shooting preserve license. Shooting is allowed only during September through April. The licensee shall issue a bill of sale for all birds taken from the preserve, and must keep a daily register showing the number of wild animals and species released and taken each day, and the number of hunters, to be submitted to the Department annually. Failure to comply is sufficient cause for license revocation for one year. Conviction of falsification of required reports is grounds for refusal to issue any new license (14-2-7-10).

A license is required to take mussels or mussel shells, or to take, ship, sell, buy or export them. Any person in the business of taking, catching, selling or bartering live minnows and crayfish for bait shall obtain a Bait Dealer's License, including those raising and hatching their own stock. Possession at any one time of more than 500 live minnows and/or live crayfish not intended for sale as bait requires a permit (14-2-7-15 and -16).

Import, Export and Release Provisions

It is unlawful to import and sell any live species of fish which has not been approved by the Director, without a permit from the Director. It is unlawful to stock any fish in waters containing state-owned fish, state waters or boundary waters except as otherwise provided (14-2-5-7 and -8).

See also Commercial and Private Enterprise Provisions under this section.

No person may bring into the state for the purpose of release or selling for release, any living fish or fry or wild animal, without a permit issued by the Department, to be granted only upon satisfactory proof that the specific animals are free of any communicable disease that could harm any native wild or domestic species. These provisions do not apply to animals imported for the purpose of being confined and exhibited in any zoo or other public display of animals or to such other animals as the Department may designate (14-2-7-20).

The Director may issue a permit to: possess a wild animal protected by statute or rule; possess a wild animal that may be harmful or dangerous to plants or animals, each of which requires a separate permit. This does not apply to licensed commercial animal dealers, zoological parks, circuses or carnivals. If an emergency exists, the Director may summarily suspend a permit and/or seize and hold an animal for which a permit is required pending the outcome of the proceedings if: a permit has not been issued to possess the animal; and even though a permit has been issued, the Director believes that the animal is in a position to harm another animal or the life/health of the animal is in peril. A hearing shall be held as specified by statute. Rules under this section must provide for the safety of the public and the health of the animals (14-2-7-21).

Persons who take others sport fishing for hire on Indiana waters, waters containing state-owned fish, or boundary waters must have a Charter Fishing Boat license issued by the Director. The licensee shall record each day's catch and other required information, even if no fish are caught. Violation: Class C infraction (14-2-7-31).

Interstate Reciprocal Agreements

The Director may enter into an interstate agreement or compact with one or more of the other states bordering on boundary waters whenever necessary for the better protection of wild animals in such boundary waters. The agreement/compact may establish uniform open seasons on such animals in such waters, uniform restrictions on type and amount of gear, method of use, weights or size of wild animals taken, and any other restrictions necessary for the better protection of wild animals in the areas (14-2-6-10).

The Director may enter into interstate agreements with Kentucky for fishing in boundary waters, so that license holders in each state may fish in the border waters, and for reciprocal hunting or trapping licenses on the main stem of the Ohio River (14-2-7-24).

ANIMAL DAMAGE CONTROL

The Director may issue to any owner of property being damaged by any protected wild animal a free permit to take, kill, or capture the wild animal in such manner, for such time, and under such rules as the Director prescribes, such conditions to be incorporated or attached to the permit. The Director may investigate any complaint that wild animals are causing damage, and if it is found that the damage has not been caused by wild animals, or that the person would abuse the privileges, the permit shall be denied. Any protected wild animals taken under permit during the closed season shall be disposed of as the Director deems necessary (14-2-7-23).

Upon good cause shown, and where necessary to alleviate damage to property or to protect human health, endangered species or species in need of management may be removed, captured or destroyed but only by permit issued by the Director, and where possible, under the supervision of the Department; provided, that endangered species or species in need of management may be removed, captured or destroyed without permit in emergency situations involving an immediate threat to human life. Provisions for removal, capture or destruction of nongame species for damage control shall be set forth in rules issued by the Director (14-2-8.5-11).

ENFORCEMENT OF WILDLIFE LAWS

Enforcement Powers

A law enforcement officer has all necessary police powers to enforce the natural resources laws, and without warrant to arrest for violation of those laws when committed in the officer's presence. Conservation officers shall detect and prevent violations of natural resources laws, enforce these laws and perform other related duties as may be imposed upon them by law. A conservation officer has the same power with respect to natural resources matters and enforcement of laws relating to natural resources laws as have law enforcement officers in their respective jurisdictions. All uniformed conservation officers shall carry arms, and nonuniformed conservation officers may carry arms. Conservation officers are law enforcement officers, and have the power to enforce state laws and to arrest without warrant for any violations when committed in the officer's presence. A conservation officer is a "police officer" under 9-13-2-127 and has the power of law enforcement officers to arrest. Conservation officers may exercise all powers granted by law to state police officers, sheriffs and members of police departments. It is a Class C misdemeanor to knowingly obstruct or interfere with the Director, a conservation officer, or Division of Fish and Wildlife employee in lawful discharge of duty in the enforcement of wildlife laws. The Law Enforcement Division shall cooperate with state law enforcement officers in detecting violations of natural resources laws and shall conduct investigations to secure evidence for convicting alleged violators of such laws (14-3-4-9 and -10). (See also Agency Funding Sources under STATE FISH AND WILDLIFE AGENCIES.)

Courts may issue warrants to search any house or place for seines, fishnets, fish traps, fish-spears or any implement or device used for unlawfully taking wild animals, fish, frogs, mussels or game, or any wild animals or parts, the possession of which is unlawful (14-2-3-4 and -9-4). The Attorney General is granted concurrent power with the several prosecuting attorneys of the state to enforce any and all of the provisions of this article including the power to approve and file any affidavit charging any violation of law (14-2-3-7). The Director and conservation officers have the power and authority to search any boat, vehicle, fish box, game bag or other receptacle in which game may be carried and may enter upon any private or public property for such purposes when there is good reason to believe that evidence of a violation will be secured of any of this article's provisions. Private property does not include dwelling houses. (14-2-9-1). Conservation and police officers shall seize any wild animals, remains or hides or furs taken in violation of this article. Upon conviction, items seized are forfeited to the state and shall be disposed of at the Director's discretion. Officers shall seize all equipment, devices or machinery used to take a wild animal or to store or transport carcasses, hides or furs in violation of this article, such devices to be forfeited to the state and disposed of upon conviction (14-2-9-2).

The Director or any conservation officer may execute and serve all warrants and processes issued by a court. Conservation officers may issue a summons for violations committed within their view if the defendant promises to appear by signing the summons. Failure to appear is contempt of court and a fine up to $20, and the court shall issue an arrest warrant (14-2-9-3).

The Director may authorize a person who is not a conservation officer to enforce the fish and wildlife laws for up to 90 days under specified conditions enumerated in the statutes, and may authorize Indiana conservation officers to work temporarily with law enforcement agencies in this or another state or in Canada for up to 30 days under specified conditions (14-3-4-14).

Criminal Penalties

A person may not take, chase or possess a wild animal except as provided by statute or rule adopted under 4-22-2 to implement this article. Except as otherwise provided, a violation of this article is a Class C misdemeanor. A person who takes a deer or a wild turkey in violation commits a Class B misdemeanor. The offense becomes a Class A misdemeanor if the person has a prior conviction under this subsection. Violation of 14-2-7-3 (hunting without a license) is a Class C infraction. Taking, catching, killing, possession or transportation of each animal or part, or the possession of each fishing, hunting or trapping device in violation of this article is a separate offense. Each day's possession of any animal or illegal device is a separate offense (14-2-3-8).

★A person who knowingly or intentionally sells or ships wild animals, nests, or eggs protected which have an aggregate market value of less than $500 commits a Class C misdemeanor. If the value is $500 to $5,000, the violation is a Class D felony. Illegal shipment of protected wild animals, nests or eggs with an aggregate market value of over $5,000 is a Class C felony (14-2-3-10).★

Civil Penalties

A person who: unlawfully takes or possesses a deer or wild turkey; takes or possesses a deer or wild turkey by illegal methods or with illegal devices; sells, purchases or offers such of a deer or wild turkey or any part, shall for the first violation reimburse the state $500; for the second and each subsequent violation the sum of $1,000, to be deposited in the Conservation Officers Fish and Wildlife Fund. This penalty is in addition to any other penalty prescribed by law. A person who takes or possesses a wild animal, except deer or turkey, in violation of any provision of this article, shall reimburse the state $20; for second or subsequent convictions the sum of $35 will be deposited in the fund (14-2-3-9).

Illegal Taking of Wildlife

The title to any and all wild animals illegally taken or accidentally killed in violation of this article shall remain in the state and such wild animal shall be seized, forfeited and confiscated by the Director and sold or disposed of, the proceeds to go to the Fish and Wildlife Fund (14-2-6-6).

★★Any person, whether or not they have a permit, license or other document of approval under this article or any other state law, who discharges, sprays or releases any waste materials, chemicals or other substances, either accidently, negligently or willfully, in such quantity, concentration or manner into any state waters or onto any public or private lands, so that wild animals are killed as a result, shall be responsible for such kill and the Director shall recover damages from such person. If no settlement is reached within a reasonable time, the Attorney General shall bring civil action in the county where the discharge of material took place. The proceeds shall be used to replace, insofar as possible, in whatever manner the Director deems proper, the wild animal population or habitat in the water or lands in question. Where improvement of the wild animal population is not possible, the proceeds shall be deposited into the Fish and Wildlife Fund (14-2-6-7).★★

License Revocations and Suspensions

Any license or permit may be revoked by the Director at any time without refund for failure to comply with, or violation of, the terms, conditions, rules or restrictions incorporated in the license/permit when issued, or for violation of any provision of this article. When a license has been revoked, the person may request in writing to the Director a hearing, to be held within 15 days. The Director shall keep a record of all evidence presented, and may rescind or affirm revocation. Every court having jurisdiction of any offense committed in violation of any of the laws for the protection of wildlife, at its discretion, may revoke the license of the offender for 30, 60 or 90 days, or one year, and after the revocation shall forward to the Division the record of the conviction and the license (14-2-7-30).

Reward Payments

A **Turn in a Poacher** program is established within the Law Enforcement Division to encourage citizen participation in deterring the unlawful taking or possession of game, fish or nongame wildlife. The Department shall: ►provide a toll free telephone service; ►develop and conduct a publicity campaign; ►conduct investigations initiated through citizen participation in the enforcement of game, fish and nongame wildlife laws; ►approve and coordinate reward payments (14-3-4-13).

HABITAT PROTECTION

★The Department shall contract for the development of game bird habitats in the state. Each contract shall be for a minimum of three years and provide a plan for development of habitat for one or more species of game birds. The Department may seek cooperation from federal agencies such as the Soil Conservation Service in plan development and compensation not to exceed $100 per acre per year, and each contract may provide that the site be open for regulated public game bird hunting. The Department may purchase from willing sellers land for the development of game bird habitats (14-2-4.6-5).★

See also PROTECTED SPECIES OF WILDLIFE and Agency Funding Sources under STATE FISH AND WILDLIFE AGENCIES.

NATIVE AMERICAN WILDLIFE PROVISIONS: None.

IOWA

Sources: Iowa Code Annotated, 1984, Sections 107, 109, 110, 111 and 455A; 1992 Cumulative Annual Pocket Part.

[NOTE: On May 24, 1993, the Code Editor changed the Iowa cites for Code 1993. Due to publishing constraints, these cites were not changed in this statutory summary. The cite changes are: Section 107 to Section 456A, 109 to 481A, 110 to 483A and 111 to 461A. Section 455A was not changed.]

STATE WILDLIFE POLICY

The title and ownership of all fish, mussels, clams, and frogs in state public waters and ponds, sloughs, bayous, or other land and waters adjacent to public waters stocked with fish by overflow of public waters, and of wild game, animals, and birds, including their nests and eggs, and other wildlife, whether game or nongame, native or migratory, except deer in parks and in public and private preserves, the ownership of which was acquired prior to April 19, 1911, are hereby declared to be in the state, except as otherwise provided in this chapter. The title and ownership of all fish in private fish hatcheries shall be in private persons (109.2).

RELEVANT WILDLIFE DEFINITIONS: See Definitions section of Appendices.

STATE FISH AND WILDLIFE AGENCIES

Agency Structure

The Director of the **Department of Natural Resources** (Department) must provide overall supervision, direction and coordination of the functions of the administrators under the wildlife conservation and protection, game and fish chapters, except as provided and subject to rules adopted by the Natural Resources Commission and Environmental Protection Commission. The Director shall adopt necessary and desirable rules for organization or reorganization of the Department, and report to the Natural Resources Commission and general assembly every five years on: ▸ classification of state parks and preserves and recommendations for reclassification; ▸ methods of maintaining diversity of animal and plant life; ▸ options for controlled deer hunting to prevent overpopulation of deer; ▸ prevention of economic damage to private property adjacent to state parks and preserves. The Director is appointed by the Governor subject to senate confirmation. Appointment shall be based on training, experience, capabilities and knowledge in the general field of natural resource management and environmental protection (455A.3 and .4).

Within the Department is created a **Fish and Wildlife Division** (Division) which is responsible for programs relating to wildlife, law enforcement, fisheries, and land acquisition and management. The Director shall appoint an Administrator of the Division who is responsible for administering the assigned programs, and who is under the general direction and supervision of the Director (455A.7).

There is created a **Natural Resources Commission** (Commission) consisting of seven citizens who are interested in and have substantial knowledge of the subjects embraced in this chapter and the Executive Director of the Department of Water, Air and Waste Management or the Director's designee who shall be a nonvoting member. Not more than four of the seven citizen members shall belong to the same political party, nor during their term hold any other state or federal office (107.1). The Commission shall: ▸ establish policy and adopt rules to provide for effective administration of the wildlife, fish and game chapters; ▸ hear appeals regarding actions taken by the Director under those chapters; ▸ approve/disapprove the Director's proposals for acquisition or disposal of state lands and waters relating to state parks and wildlife programs; ▸ approve the Director's budget requests on wildlife, fish and game matters; ▸ adopt by rule a schedule of fees for permits and administration of the permits (455A.5).

Agency Powers and Duties

The **Director** shall employ assistants to carry out Commission duties and shall appoint full-time officers and supervisory personnel to enforce state laws and Commission rules and regulations, these personnel having the powers of peace officers in the enforcement of state laws. "Full-time officer" means a person appointed by the Director to enforce state laws (107.13).

The Director may appoint temporary officers for a period not to exceed six months and may adopt minimum physical, educational, mental, and moral requirements. Temporary officers have all the powers of peace officers in the enforcement of wildlife and trespass laws. Appointees and employees may be removed by the Director at any time with Commission approval (107.14 and .15).

The **Department** shall protect, propagate, increase, and preserve the state's wild mammals, fish, birds, reptiles, and amphibians and enforce the laws, rules, and regulations relating to them. The Department shall collect, classify, and preserve all statistics, data, and information tending to promote the objects of this chapter, conduct research in improved conservation methods, and disseminate conservation information to residents and nonresidents (107.23).

The Department is authorized and empowered to: ▸ expend moneys accruing to the Fish and Game Protection Fund; ▸ acquire by purchase, condemnation, lease, agreement, gift, and devise lands or waters, and rights of way thereto, and maintain the same for public hunting, fishing, trapping grounds and waters and for hatcheries, fish nurseries, game farms, and wild mammal, fish, bird, reptile, and amphibian refuges; ▸ extend and consolidate lands or waters suitable for the above purposes by exchange for other lands or waters and to purchase, erect and maintain buildings; ▸ capture, propagate, buy, sell, or exchange any species of wild mammal, fish, bird, reptile, and amphibian needed for stocking state lands or waters, and to feed, provide for, and care for them; ▸ adopt and enforce Departmental rules to carry out the provisions of this chapter and other laws the enforcement of which is vested in the Department; ▸ adopt, publish and enforce administrative orders pertaining to restrictions on taking, prohibited acts and special licenses; ▸ pay the salaries, wages, compensation, travelling and other expenses of the Commissioners, Director, officers and other Department employees, expend money for supplies and equipment, and make other expenditures for the purposes of this chapter; ▸ control by shooting or trapping any wild mammal, fish, bird, reptile, and amphibian to prevent destruction of or damage to private or public property, not going upon private property without consent of owner or occupant; ▸ provide for protection against fire and other destructive agencies on state and privately owned forests, parks, wildlife areas, and other property under its jurisdiction, and cooperate with federal and state agencies in protection programs; ▸ provide conservation employees uniforms, equipment, arms, and supplies; ▸ adopt rules authorizing officers and Department employees who are peace officers to issue warning citations for wildlife violations (107.24).

The **Commission** may not: ▸ change any penalty for violating any game law or regulation; ▸ change the amount of any license established by the legislature; ▸ promulgate open season on any fish, animal or bird contrary to the laws; ▸ extend, except as provided chapter, open season or bag limit on any kind of fish, game, fur-bearing animals or birds prescribed by state or federal laws or regulations; ▸ contract indebtedness or obligation beyond the funds to which they are lawfully entitled (107.26).

To promote conservation, the Commission may alter, limit or restrict the methods or means employed and the instruments or equipment used in taking wild mammals, birds subject to section 109.48, fish, reptiles, and amphibians, or, when it is found there is imminent danger of loss of fish through natural causes, authorize the taking of fish to salvage imperiled fish. The Commission shall adopt a rule permitting cross bows to be used by handicapped individuals physically incapable of using a bow and arrow. If the number of hunters licensed or the type of license should be limited or further regulated, the Commission shall conduct a drawing to determine which applicants shall receive a license and the type of license. The Commission is designated the sole agency to determine whether biological balance does or does not exist, and shall by administrative rule, extend, shorten, open, or close seasons and set, increase, or reduce catch, bag, size and possession limits, or territorial limitations, or further regulate taking conditions (109.38 and .39).

The Commission shall observe, administer, and enforce this chapter. The Commission may: ▸ remove or cause to be removed any aquatic species judged to be an underused renewable resource or to have a detrimental effect on other aquatic populations, proceeds from sale of aquatic organisms to be credited to the Fish and Game Protection Fund; ▸ issue a permit or license authorizing a person to take, possess, and sell underused, undesirable, or injurious aquatic organisms; ▸ authorize the Director to enter into written contracts for removal of these organisms; ▸ designate any body of water as protected habitat and restrict, prohibit, or regulate taking commercial fish, turtles, and mussels in these areas (109B.1). The Commission may adopt rules designating game, commercial and rough fish (109.69).

Agency Funding Sources

The **Fish and Game Protection Fund**, except as otherwise provided, consists of all moneys accruing from license fees and all other sources of Fish and Wildlife Division revenue. Interest or earnings on the Public Outdoor Recreation and Resources Fund shall be credited to those funds respectively. The **Conservation Fund**, except as otherwise provided, consists of all other funds accruing to the Department for the purposes embraced by this chapter. The **Administrative Fund** shall consist of an equitable portion of the gross amount of the State Fish and Game Protection Fund and the State Conservation Fund, to be determined by the Commission, sufficient to pay the administrative expense. The **Public Outdoor Recreation and Resources Fund** and the **County Conservation Board Fund** consist of all moneys credited to them by law or appropriated by the general assembly (107.17).

Receipts, refunds and reimbursements related to activities funded by administration funds are appropriated to the Administration Fund. All refunds and reimbursements relating to activities of the Fish and Game Protection Fund are credited to that Fund. The Director shall return monthly to the state treasurer all moneys belonging to the five funds. All funds of the Fish and Game Protection Fund are to be spent only for Fish and Wildlife Division activities, expenses to be authorized by the general assembly [details of expenditures provided] (107.17 through .19).

A person filing a state income tax return may designate any amount to be deposited to the Fish and Game Protection Fund and used for habitat development. The revenue may be used for matching of federal funds and acquisition or leasing of land to use as wildlife habitats. Not less than 50% of the funds derived from the check-off shall be used for preserving, protecting, perpetuating and enhancing nongame wildlife, including species which are endangered/threatened or not commonly pursued or killed for sport or profit. The land acquired is subject to property taxes to be paid from those revenues. In addition, the revenues may be used for the development and enhancement of wildlife lands and habitat areas and for research and management necessary to qualify for federal funds (107.16). The revenue received from nonresident deer and wild turkey hunting license fees shall be used to employ and maintain as many additional full-time conservation officers as possible (110.30). (See also Licenses and Permits under HUNTING, FISHING, TRAPPING PROVISIONS for various wildlife stamps and revenue uses.)

Agency Advisory Boards

The Director shall establish a **Farmer Advisory Committee** for providing information to the Department regarding crop and tree damage caused by deer, wild turkey, and other predators. The Committee shall serve without compensation or reimbursement for expenses (109.10A).

The **State Advisory Board for State Preserves** is composed of seven members, one of whom will be the Director and six appointed by the Governor. The Commission, the Conservation Committee of the Iowa Academy of Science and the State Historical Society shall submit to the Governor a list of possible appointments. Members shall be selected from persons with a demonstrated interest in the preservation of natural lands and waters and historic sites (111B.3).

There is created a **County Conservation Board** (Board), consisting of five county residents, to serve without compensation, and counties are authorized to: acquire, develop, maintain, and make available to county residents, public museums, parks, preserves, parkways, playgrounds, recreational centers, county forests, wildlife, and other conservation areas; promote and preserve the health and general welfare of the people; encourage the orderly development and conservation of natural resources; and cultivate good citizenship by providing adequate programs of public recreation (111A.1). ★The Board shall have the custody, control and management of all real and personal property acquired by the county for public museums, parks, preserves, parkways, playgrounds, recreation centers, and county forests, wildlife areas, and other conservation and recreation purposes and is authorized and empowered to: ► study and ascertain the need for county museums, parks, preserves, parkways, recreation and other conservation facilities, and the extent to which needs are being met, and to prepare and adopt a coordinated plan of areas and facilities; ► acquire by gift, purchase, lease, agreement, exchange or otherwise suitable real estate within or without the territorial limits of the county; ► plan, develop, preserve, administer and maintain all such areas, places and facilities, and construct, reconstruct, alter and renew buildings and other structures, and equip and maintain the same; ▸ accept gifts, bequests, contributions and appropriations of money and other personal property for conservation purposes; ▸ employ and fix the compensation for an executive officer who shall be responsible to the Board for the carrying out of its policies; ▸ charge and collect fees. The Board shall file with and obtain Commission approval on all proposals for acquisition or exchange of land and all general development plans. The Board may make, alter, amend or repeal regulations for the protection, regulation, and control of all property under its control, conforming with state laws (111A.4 and .5).★

PROTECTED SPECIES OF WILDLIFE

See RELEVANT WILDLIFE DEFINITIONS for protected nongame species.

No person, except as otherwise provided, willfully shall disturb, pursue, shoot, kill, take or attempt to take or have in possession any of the following game birds or animals except in open season: gray or fox squirrel, bobwhite quail, cottontail or jack rabbit, duck, snipe, pheasant, goose, woodcock, partridge, coot, rail, rugged grouse, wild turkey, pigeons, or deer. Seasons, bag limits, possession limits and locality are established by the Department or Commission. The Commission may adopt rules for taking and possession of migratory birds, including designated raptors and crows, subject to the Migratory Bird Treaty Act and Migratory Bird Stamp Hunting Act. The Commission shall establish methods for taking pigeons, including trapping, chemical repellents or toxic perches (109.48).

It is unlawful for a nonresident or alien to take turtles or crayfish by any means or method, except from the Missouri, Mississippi and Big Sioux Rivers. It is a simple misdemeanor to take a predominantly white deer; this applies to whitetail deer only (109.121 and .124).

The Commission shall cooperate with the federal government in the conservation, protection, restoration and propagation of endangered and threatened species. The Director shall conduct investigations on fish, plants, and wildlife to develop information on population, distribution, habitat needs, limiting factors, and other biological and ecological data to determine management measures. Using these determinations and available scientific and commercial data, the Commission shall issue a rule listing state endangered or threatened species of fish, plants, and wildlife, the list being reviewed at least every two years, and the Commission may amend the list. The Director shall establish programs, including acquisition of land or aquatic habitat, for the management of endangered or threatened species. The Commission may treat any species as endangered or threatened, even if not on the list, if it finds that it closely resembles in appearance a listed species, and enforcement personnel would have substantial difficulty in differentiating between the listed and unlisted species (109A.2 through .6).

GENERAL EXCEPTIONS TO PROTECTION

★This chapter does not forbid selling or shipping parrots, canaries, or any other cage birds imported from other countries or not native to any part of the US (109.20).★   ★A person shall not keep or use any live pigeon or other bird as a target, to be shot at for amusement or as a test of marksmanship, or shoot at a bird kept or used for such purpose, or be a party to such shooting, or lease any building, room, field, or premises for that purpose. This section does not prevent shooting at live pigeons, sparrows, and starlings when training hunting dogs (109.21).★

This chapter shall not prohibit importation of a lawfully taken trophy animal under a permit which is not for resale and taking a threatened species when the Commission has determined that its abundance justifies a controlled harvest not in violation of federal laws or regulations (109A.9). Except as otherwise provided, it is unlawful to buy or sell any protected bird or animal or part, but this does not apply to fur-bearing animals, and the skins, plumage, and antlers of legally taken game, and does not prohibit purchasing jackrabbits from outside the state. A person shall not purchase, sell, barter, or offer to do so, for millinery or ornamental use, feathers or mounted specimens of migratory game birds (109.55).

The Director may issue a scientific collector's license or wildlife salvage, educational project, or wildlife rehabilitation permits. A scientific collector's license authorizes collection for scientific purposes any birds, nest, eggs, or wildlife. A wildlife salvage permit authorizes the salvage for educational purposes any birds, nests, eggs, or animals according to Department rules. An educational project permit authorizes collection, keeping, or possession for educational purposes birds, fish, or wildlife which are not endangered, threatened or otherwise specially managed under Department rules. A wildlife rehabilitation permit authorizes possession for rehabilitation only any orphaned or injured wildlife according to Department rules. A licensee or permittee shall not dispose of any birds, nests, eggs, or wildlife or their parts except upon written permission of the Director. Licenses may be revoked at any time for cause (109.65). The Director may permit taking, possessing, purchasing, selling, transporting, importing, exporting or shipping of endangered or threatened listed species for scientific, zoological, or educational purposes, or for propagation in captivity to ensure their survival (109A.7). See also Agency Powers and Duties under STATE FISH AND WILDLIFE AGENCIES and PROTECTED SPECIES OF WILDLIFE.

HUNTING, FISHING, TRAPPING PROVISIONS

General Provisions

It is unlawful to offer for transportation or to transport by common carrier or any vehicle, within or without the state, for purposes of sale, any fish, game, animals or birds, taken, caught or killed within the state and to ship, carry or transport in any one day these species, except fur-bearers, in excess of the legal possession number (109.23 and .26). It is lawful to possess fish or game lawfully taken outside and brought into the state, but the possessor has the burden of proving lawful taking and transportation. A violation is presumed if a person has: unlawfully taken wildlife in possession; wildlife in possession at an unlawful time or place of taking; prohibited equipment or devices or at a place where taking is unlawful. It is unlawful to take, pursue, kill, trap, or ensnare, buy, sell, possess, transport, or attempt to do so, any game, protected nongame birds, fur-bearing animals or their fur or skin, mussels, frogs, spawn or fish or any part, except as set forth herein and in administrative rules, or as provided by the code. Means and equipment for taking wildlife may be altered in the interests of conservation (109.31, .37 and .38).

Rifles may not be shot on or over any state public waters or highways or railroad rights-of-way. A person shall not shoot a shotgun with a slug load, pistol, or revolver on or over a public roadway. This section does not apply to peace officers or military personnel when performing official duty (109.54). It is unlawful to discharge a firearm within 200 yards of a building inhabited by people or domestic livestock or within 200 yards of a feedlot, without owner or tenant permission (109.123). No person except as permitted by law shall have or carry a gun in or on a vehicle on a public highway, unless the gun is taken down or totally contained in a securely fastened case, and its barrels and magazines unloaded. No person shall use a swivel gun or other firearm, except those commonly shot from the shoulder or hand in hunting of game, and no gun shall be larger than 10 gauge (110.36 and .37).

Licenses and Permits

Owners or tenants of land, and their juvenile children, may hunt, fish or trap on such lands and shoot by lawful means ground squirrels, gophers, or woodchucks on adjacent roads without a license, but special licenses to hunt deer and wild turkey are required. The Department shall issue annually a deer or wild turkey hunting license, or both, to the owner, family member, or tenant who applies, valid only for hunting on the farm upon which the licensee resides. Residents actively engaged in operation of farm units are also eligible for a free deer and a wild turkey license to hunt on the farm (110.24).

A person with a dog entered in a licensed field trial is not required to have a hunting license or fur-harvester license to participate or to exercise the dog on the area on which the field trial is to be held. No person is required to have a special wild turkey license to hunt wild turkey on a licensed game breeding and shooting preserve. A lessee of a camping space may fish on a private lake or pond on the campground without a license if the lease confers an exclusive right to fish in common with the owner and other lessees (110.24).

A person with a hunting license may train a bird dog on game birds and one with a fur-harvester license may train a coon hound, fox hound, or trailing dog on fur-bearing animals at any time including closed seasons; however, the animals, when pursued to a tree or den, shall not be further chased or removed. A licensee may train a dog on coyote or groundhog. Only a gun shooting blank cartridges shall be used while training dogs during closed season. Pen-raised game birds may be used and shot in training bird dogs, if the bird is banded. The Commission may adopt rules prohibiting training any hunting dog on any game bird, game animals, or fur-bearing animal in the wild at any time if training might have an adverse effect on populations of these species. A person lawfully possessing game or fur-bearing animals or pelts may hold them not more than 30 days after close of season, except with a Department permit (109.56 and .57).

No person shall fish, trap, hunt, pursue, catch, kill or take in any manner or possess, sell, transport all or any portion of any wild animal, bird, game, or fish, without first procuring a license or certificate. A resident or nonresident required to have a hunting, fur-harvester or fur, fish and game license shall carry a wildlife habitat stamp. All revenue from sale of wildlife habitat stamps shall be used for habitat development and be deposited in the Fish and Game Protection Fund, except that up to 60% of revenue is to be used for agreements with county conservation boards or other public agencies, and may be credited to the Wildlife Habitat Bond Fund. The revenues and any matching federal funds shall be used for acquisition or leasing of land, or obtaining easements from willing sellers for wildlife habitats (110.1 and .3).

A resident hunting wild turkey must have a resident hunting license or combined hunting and fishing license or fur, fish and game license and a wildlife habitat stamp in addition to the wild turkey hunting license. A nonresident wild turkey hunter is required to have only a nonresident wild turkey license and a wildlife habitat stamp and must exhibit proof of completing a hunter safety and ethics education program. To hunt deer, a resident must have a hunting license or combined hunting and fishing license, or a fur, fish and game license and a wildlife habitat stamp, in addition to the deer hunting license, and a tag which shall be dated on the day a deer is taken. A nonresident deer hunter must have only a nonresident deer license and a wildlife habitat stamp and must exhibit proof of completing a hunter safety and ethics education program (110.7 and .8).

Licenses, certificates or permits must be exhibited upon request to any peace officer or the owner or person in lawful control of the land or water when hunting, fishing or trapping. Failure to carry, show or exhibit a license, certificate or permit is a violation. Licenses for bait dealers or for fishing, hunting, or trapping shall not be issued to residents of states that do not sell similar licenses or certificates to residents of Iowa. However, the licensing of nonresident bait dealers who sell at wholesale to licensed dealers in Iowa for resale is permitted (110.19 and .20).

A person may possess not more than two game birds or fur-bearing animals as pets without a game breeder license and shall not be allowed to increase, kill or sell such stock. Confined game birds or animals must be obtained from a licensed game breeder or a legal source outside of the state (110.23). Persons born after January 1, 1967, may only obtain a hunting license after satisfactorily completing a hunter safety and ethics education course approved by the Commission. A certificate of completion from an approved course issued in this state since 1960, by another state or province of Canada, is valid. A certificate of completion shall not be issued to persons who have not satisfactorily completed a minimum of 10 hours of training in an approved hunter safety and ethics education course. The Department shall provide manuals and certify instructors. A certificate may be issued to a person who has not completed the course but meets the criteria established by the Commission. Failure to carry or refusal to exhibit the certificate is a misdemeanor (110.27).

No person 16 or older shall hunt or take any migratory waterfowl without first procuring a state migratory waterfowl stamp and having such stamp in possession while hunting. The Commission shall determine the stampform and furnish the stamps for issuance or sale in the same manner as hunting licenses. Revenue shall be used for projects to protect and propagate migratory waterfowl and for acquisition and maintenance of wetlands (110B.2 and .4).

Restrictions on Taking: Hunting and Trapping

A person shall not throw or cast the rays of a spotlight, headlight, or other artificial light on a highway, in a field, woodland, or forest to spot, locate, or take or attempt to take or hunt a bird or animal, except raccoons or other fur-bearing animals when treed with the aid of dogs, while having in possession or control any firearm, bow, or other implement or device whereby a bird or animal could be killed or taken (109.93). ★★A person shall not intentionally kill or wound, or attempt to do so, or pursue any animal, fowl, or fish from aircraft in flight or self-propelled vehicles designed for travel on snow or ice (109.120).★★

No person except those under authority of the Director shall capture or take, or attempt to do so, with any trap, snare or net, any game bird, or use a poison or any medicated or poisoned food or any other substance for killing, capturing or taking of any game bird or animal (109.58). ★Hunters shall not use a mobile radio transmitter to communicate the location or direction of game or fur-bearing animals or to coordinate the movement of other hunters. This does not apply to hunting coyotes January 1 through March 31 (109.24). ★ A person possessing any game bird or animal or part shall upon request exhibit it to the Director or officer. It is unlawful to possess while hunting any ferret, device or substance for chasing animals from their dens (109.52 and .53).

Except as otherwise provided, no person shall take, capture, kill, or have in possession a fur-bearing animal or parts, except during the open season and where killing, trapping, or ensnaring is for the protection of public or private property. All fur-bearing animals so taken shall be relinquished to the Commission. Within 10 days after the close of the season, a person may apply to the Commission to hold hides or skins of fur-bearing animals for a longer time than specified. A person shall not molest or disturb any den, lodge, or house of a fur-bearing animal or beaver dam except by written permission of an officer appointed by the Director. This does not prohibit destroying a den to protect an owner's property (109.87, .89 and .90).

No person shall kill with shotgun or spear any beaver, mink, otter, or muskrat, or have in possession animals, carcasses, skins or parts that have been so killed (109.91). Except as otherwise provided, a person shall not use or attempt to use colony traps in taking, capturing, trapping, or killing game or fur-bearing animals. Box traps capable of capturing more than one animal at each setting are prohibited. A valid hunting license is required for box trapping cottontail rabbits and squirrels. All traps and snares must have a metal tag with user's name and address and be checked once every 24 hours. Except as otherwise provided, a person shall not use chemicals, explosives, smoking devices, mechanical ferrets, wire, tools, instruments, or water to remove fur-bearing animals from their dens. ★Humane traps, or traps designed to kill instantly, with a jaw spread exceeding eight inches are unlawful except when placed entirely under water (109.92). ★ A fur-harvester license or fur, fish and game license is required to hunt and or trap a fur-bearing animal. A hunting license is not required when hunting fur-bearers with a fur-harvester license; however, coyote and groundhog may be hunted with a hunting, a fur-harvester or a fur, fish and game license (110.5).

Restrictions on Taking: Fishing

It is unlawful to take, capture or kill, or take in excess of the daily limit, fish, frogs, or turtles, except during the open season. It is unlawful to use more than three tip-up fishing devices in the Mississippi River and its connected backwater. A person cannot use more than three hooks on the same line. The tip-up device is also prohibited for fishing within 300 feet of a dam or spillway or in a part of the river closed or posted against use of the device (109.67 and .68). It is illegal to take from waters of the state any fish except with hook, line and bait, to use more than two lines or two hooks on each line and to leave lines unattended. Not more than 5 tagged lines shall be used with not more than 15 hooks, and all shall be properly tagged (109.73 and .74).

It is unlawful to use on or in the waters of the state any grabhook, snaghook, net, seine, trap, firearm, dynamite or other explosives, or poisonous or stupefying substances such as lime, ashes, or electricity, in taking or attempting to take fish, except that gaffhooks or landing net may be used to land fish. It is unlawful to take or kill, or attempt to do so, a fish by hand fishing, except carp, buffalo, quill back, gar, sheepshead, dogfish, and other rough fish designated by the Commission to be taken by hand fishing, snagging, spear, bow and arrow, day or night with artificial light (109.76). Frogs may be used for bait or food, but no more than four dozen frogs may be taken in one day or more than eight dozen possessed. Transportation of frogs out of state is prohibited. It is unlawful to take any aquatic or biological life from state fish hatcheries, nurseries or other areas operated for fish production (109.84 and .85). To fish for trout, a person must have a fishing license and a trout stamp. Proceeds from sale of the stamp shall be used to restock trout waters designated by the Commission. The Commission may grant a permit to a community event in which trout will be stocked in water which is not designated trout water, for catching and possessing of trout without a special trout stamp (110.6).

Reciprocal fishing privileges are contingent upon a grant of similar privileges by another state to Iowa residents. The Commission may designate one period of the year of not more than three days as free fishing days, during which residents may fish and possess fish without a license. It is unlawful for a person, firm or corporation to place, erect, or cause to be placed or erected, any dam, other device or contrivance in such manner as to hinder or obstruct free passage of fish up, down, or through such waters, except as otherwise provided (109.14).

Commercial and Private Enterprise Provisions

It is unlawful to raise or sell protected game or fur-bearing animals, except rock doves and pigeons, without a game breeder's license. The Commission may adopt rules to ensure that all game birds, game animals and fur-bearing animals are given humane care and treatment (109.60).

A person owning, holding or controlling for five or more years any contiguous tract of land containing 320 to 1,280 acres, providing that there shall be no more than one area in any township and that not more than 3% of the area of any county shall be so licensed, may apply to the State Conservation Commission for a license to establish a game breeding and shooting preserve area to propagate, preserve, and shoot game birds. The Commission shall inspect the area and issue a license if: ▸ the area meets requirements for the operation of such property; ▸ the game birds propagated or released are not likely to be a menace to other game; ▸ the proposed area will not interfere with the normal activities of migratory birds; ▸ the operation of such preserve will not work a fraud upon persons who may be permitted to hunt thereon; ▸ the license will be in the public interest. The licensee may take, or authorize to be taken within the designated season, game in such numbers as herein provided (110A.1 and .3). Records of birds released and taken shall be kept, and special tags used for game birds to designate birds taken from licensed areas. Tags shall be affixed and remain until the bird is prepared for consumption. Game birds may only be taken upon a game breeding and shooting preserve area between September 1 and March 31. Waterfowl may not be shot over water areas where pen-reared birds might be live decoys for waterfowl. Persons taking game birds upon such licensed preserve areas shall secure a hunting license, except a nonresident may secure a license for shooting preserve areas only (110A.4, .5 and .6).

The Commission may designate any licensed game breeding and shooting preserve area operator, agent or employee as a special representative with power to enforce the game laws, to prevent trespassing and to hunt and trap rodents and other mammals or birds destroying or likely to destroy the game birds raised or liberated there. The special representative is subject to Commission rules and regulations and shall serve without compensation. Any licensee or other person who wilfully and intentionally transfers or permits the transfer of the tag issued to the operator of one licensed preserve area to the operator of another, or to any other person, or who affixes such tags to game birds not taken from a preserve area or not taken from any area other than the area for which such tags were issued, is guilty of a simple misdemeanor (110A.7 and .9).

A licensed game breeder who obtains original stock from a lawful source may possess any game bird, game animal, or fur-bearing animal, or their parts. Fur-bearing animals cannot be acquired for breeding or propagating from any source unless pen-raised for at least two successive generations. A game breeder may not possess, breed, propagate, sell or dispose of any endangered or threatened species unless the species is listed on the license; when listed, it is subject to all applicable state and federal statutes. A licensed game breeder shall not acquire protected live game animals, game birds, their eggs, or fur-bearing animals taken from the wild within this state (109.61).

Import, Export and Release Provisions

It is unlawful to bring into the state for propagating or introducing, or to place or introduce into state inland or boundary waters, fish or spawn that are native to such waters, or introduce or stock any bird or animals without a written Commission permit (109.47). It is unlawful to use, sell or offer for sale or introduce into inland waters carp, quillback, gar or dogfish or minnows of these species. These fish may be returned to waters where caught. Live fish may not be stocked or introduced without Director permission (109.82 and .83). Except as provided, a person shall not take, possess, transport, import, export, process, buy, or offer to do so, nor shall a common or contract carrier transport or receive for shipment, any species of fish, plants, or wildlife appearing on the following lists: state list of endangered or threatened fish, plants, and wildlife; US list of endangered or threatened plants or foreign fish and wildlife. A species of fish, plant, or wildlife appearing on any of the lists entering the state from another state or from outside the US may enter, be transported, possessed and sold in accordance with a federal permit (109A.5).

Interstate Reciprocal Agreements

★A person licensed by Illinois, Minnesota, Missouri, Wisconsin, Nebraska, or South Dakota to take fish, game mussels, or fur-bearing animals from or in the waters forming the boundary between these states and Iowa may take them from waters within the jurisdiction of this state without an Iowa license, if the laws of these states extend similar privileges to Iowa licensees (109.19).★ (See also GENERAL EXCEPTIONS TO PROTECTION and Restrictions on Taking: Fishing, under this section.)

ANIMAL DAMAGE CONTROL

The owner or operator of any fish hatchery may kill or take any pied-billed grebe, gull or tern, American bittern, black-crowned night heron, merganser, great blue heron, or kingfisher, within the bounds of such hatchery with a permit from the Commission. No part of the plumage, skin or body of any protected bird shall be sold or possessed for sale, whether captured or killed within or without the state, unless provided (109.49 and .50). Upon good cause shown and where necessary to reduce damage to property or to protect human health, listed endangered or threatened species may be removed, captured, or destroyed, pursuant to permit issued by the Director (109A.8). (See also PROTECTED SPECIES OF WILDLIFE.)

ENFORCEMENT OF WILDLIFE LAWS

Enforcement Powers

The Director or any peace officer shall seize with or without warrant any fish, furs, birds, or animals, or mussels, clams, or frogs, held in possession or under control, which have been caught, taken, or killed, offered for shipment, or illegally transported in the state or beyond its borders, in a manner contrary to the code (109.12).

★Any device, contrivance or material used to violate any regulation or provision of this chapter is declared to be a public nuisance and shall be seized without warrant or process and delivered to a magistrate, provided that no automobile shall be construed to be a public nuisance (110.32).★ The magistrate may order the same to be confiscated and destroyed or placed at the disposal of the Director, who may either use or sell the same, depositing the proceeds of sale in the Fish and Game Protection Fund (110.34). Violation: a simple misdemeanor; $10 fine for each cited offense (110.42). In shipping fish, game, animals, birds, or furs, whenever a container includes one or more fish, game, animals, birds, or furs that are contraband, the entire contents of the container shall be deemed contraband and seized by the Director's officers (109.30). ★★It is the duty of the attorney general when requested by the Director to have an opinion in writing upon any question of law arising under this chapter; and it shall be the duty of all county attorneys when requested by the Director or any officer appointed by the Commission to prosecute all criminal actions brought in their respective counties for violations of the provisions of this chapter. Nothing in this chapter shall be construed as prohibiting a person from instituting legal proceedings for the enforcement of any of the provisions herein (109.35).★★

Criminal Penalties

Whoever shall take, catch, kill, injure, destroy, have in possession, buy, sell, ship, or transport any frogs, fish, mussels, birds, their nests, eggs, or plumage, fowls, game or animals or their fur or raw pelt in violation of the provisions of this chapter or of Commission rules, or whoever shall use any prohibited device, equipment, seine, trap, net, tackle, firearm, drug, poison, explosive, or other substance or means, or use the same at a time, place or in a manner or for a purpose prohibited, or do any other act for which no other punishment is provided, is guilty of a simple misdemeanor and shall pay a minimum fine of $10 for each offense, and each act shall be a separate offense. Conviction of taking a deer, antelope, moose, buffalo, or elk with a prohibited weapon is a fine of $100 for each offense (109.32). Violation of the provisions of the chapter on endangered and threatened species is a simple misdemeanor (109A.10). Violation of any of the provisions of the chapter on migratory waterfowl is a simple misdemeanor (110B.6). ★A common carrier which violates any of the provisions of this chapter or regulations relating to receiving, having in possession, shipping, or delivering any fish, fowl, birds, bird nests, eggs, or plumage, fur, raw pelts, game, or animals, and any agent, employee, or servant of a common carrier violating such provisions is guilty of simple misdemeanor (109.34).★

Illegal Taking of Wildlife

In addition to other penalties, a person convicted of unlawfully selling, taking, catching, killing, injuring, destroying, or having in possession any animal, shall reimburse the state for the value of each animal as follows: ► elk, antelope, buffalo, or moose, $2,500; ▸ each wild turkey, $200; ▸ bird or animal or its raw pelt or plumage, for which damages are not otherwise prescribed, $50; ▸ fish, reptile, mussel, or amphibian, $15; ▸ beaver, mink, otter, red fox, gray fox or raccoon, $200; ▸ animals classified by the Commission as an endangered or threatened species, $1,000; ▸ deer, $750 (109.130). ★In addition to other civil and criminal penalties for illegally taking or possessing elk, antelope, buffalo, or moose, the court shall revoke the hunting license (110.21).★

If two or more persons who have acted together are convicted of unlawful taking, catching, killing, injuring, destroying or having possession of any fish, game or fur-bearing animal, judgment shall be entered against them jointly. Any liquidated damages received shall be remitted to the state treasurer and credited to the Fish and Game Protection Fund. If the fish, game or fur-bearing animal is returned uninjured to the place it was unlawfully caught or possessed or to any other place approved by the Commission, damages will be discharged. Civil suits for collection of judgments may be prosecuted by the attorney general or by county attorneys (109.131). A person who is assessed damages shall immediately surrender all licenses, certificates, and permits to hunt, fish, or trap, and they shall remain suspended until assessed damages and any accrued interest are paid or a payment schedule is established by the court. Upon payment of damages and any accrued interest, the suspension shall be lifted (109.133).

License Revocations and Suspensions

A person who pleads guilty or is convicted of a violation of wildlife provisions while the person's license or licenses are suspended or revoked is guilty of a simple misdemeanor, if the person has no other violations within the previous three years while the person's license has been suspended or revoked. It is a serious misdemeanor if the person has one other violation within the previous three years which occurred while the license or licenses have been suspended or revoked, and an aggravated misdemeanor if the person has had two or more convictions within the previous three years while the license or licenses have been suspended or revoked (109.135).

Upon conviction of any violation of wildlife provisions on conservation and license requirements, or any Commission administrative order, the magistrate may as a part of the judgment, revoke or suspend the license for any definite period. The magistrate shall revoke the license or suspend the privilege of procuring a hunting license for one year of anyone who has been convicted twice within a year of trespassing while hunting. If the hunting privileges of a combined hunting and fishing license are revoked, the fishing privileges shall be valid. The violator shall not be allowed to procure a hunting license for the next two calendar years. The Commission may refuse to issue a new license to a person whose license has been revoked (110.21 and .22).

HABITAT PROTECTION

The Commission may establish state game refuges or sanctuaries on any state land to preserve biological balance for the protection of public parks, public health, safety and welfare, or to effect sound wildlife management. ★In emergency situations, the Director may establish temporary state game refuges by posting notices in conspicuous places around the refuge. Establishment shall be effective until five days after the next meeting of the Commission or longer as necessary (109.5).★ The Commission may establish a game management area upon any public lands or waters, or upon any private lands or waters with the consent of the owner, to maintain a biological balance or to provide for public hunting, fishing, or trapping. When a game management area is established, the Commission, with the consent of any owner, shall have the right to post and prohibit, and to regulate or limit the lands or waters against trespassing, hunting, fishing, or trapping (109.6). The Commission may also set aside portions of state water for spawning grounds, and notice must be posted in conspicuous places. Violation: misdemeanor (109.9).

It is unlawful to hunt, pursue, kill, trap, or take any wild animal, bird, or game on any state game refuge at any time, and no one shall carry firearms thereon, providing that predatory birds and animals may be killed or trapped under authority and direction of the Director. The Commission may specify the necessary distance from a state game refuge where shooting is prohibited and shall post notice at such distance in conspicuous places. This prohibition shall not apply to owners or tenants hunting on their own land outside of a state game refuge (109.7).

NATIVE AMERICAN WILDLIFE PROVISIONS: None.

KANSAS

Sources: Kansas Statutes Annotated, 1986, Chapters 21, 32, 58 and 79; 1992 Cumulative Supplement.

STATE WILDLIFE POLICY

It shall be the policy of the state of Kansas to protect, provide and improve outdoor recreation and natural resources in this state and to plan and provide for the wise management and use of such resources, thus contributing to and benefiting the public's health and its cultural, recreational and economic life. For these purposes, the Secretary, the Commission and the Department are vested with the duties and powers hereinafter set forth. The ownership of and title to all wildlife, both resident and migratory, in the state, not held by private ownerships, legally acquired, shall be, and are hereby declared to be in the state (32-702 and -703).

RELEVANT WILDLIFE DEFINITIONS: See Definitions section of Appendices.

STATE FISH AND WILDLIFE AGENCIES

Agency Structure

There is within the executive branch of government the **Department of Wildlife and Parks** (Department) (formerly the Fish and Game Commission), which is administered by the **Secretary of Wildlife and Parks** (Secretary) (formerly the Director of the Fish and Game Commission) who is appointed by the Governor with the consent of the senate. The Secretary shall be qualified by education, training and experience in wildlife, parks or natural resources or a related field, have the ability to discharge the duties of the office and serve at the pleasure of the Governor (32-801).

There is within the Department the **Wildlife and Parks Commission** (Commission) composed of seven members appointed by the Governor who shall consider the appointment of licensed hunters, fishermen and fur-harvesters, park users, nonconsumptive users of wildlife and park resources and geographic balance among Commission members. No more than four members shall be of the same political party. Members shall serve four years; the Governor may remove a Commissioner after opportunity for hearing (32-805).

Agency Powers and Duties

The **Commission** shall have the powers and duties prescribed by law. Other than Department personnel regulations, the Secretary shall submit to the Commission all proposed rules and regulations for approval, modification or rejection and shall adopt rules and regulations so approved. Fees established for licenses, permits, stamps and other Department issues shall be subject to approval of the Commission. It shall be the duty of the Commission to serve as advisor to the Governor and the Secretary in the formulation of policies and plans (32-805).

The **Secretary** shall have the power to: ► adopt rules and regulations to implement, administer and enforce the wildlife and parks laws; ► enter into contracts and agreements; ► employ consultants; ► sue, be sued, plead and be impleaded in the Department's name; ► purchase, lease, accept gifts or grants of or otherwise acquire water, water rights, easements, facilities, equipment, moneys and other real and personal property and interests therein, and maintain, improve, exchange and dispose of the property; ► acquire, establish, develop, construct, maintain and improve state parks, recreational grounds, wildlife areas and sanctuaries, fish hatcheries, natural areas, physical structures, dams, lakes, reservoirs, embankments for impounding water, roads, landscaping, habitats, vegetation and other property, improvements and facilities for wildlife management, preservation of natural areas and historic sites and providing recreational or cultural opportunities and facilities to the public to carry out the intent and purposes of wildlife and parks laws; ► operate and regulate the use of state parks, lakes, recreational grounds, wildlife areas and sanctuaries, fish hatcheries, natural areas, including setting facility, commercial and boat use fees, historic sites and other lands, waters and facilities under the jurisdiction of the Secretary; ► have exclusive administrative control over state parks, lakes, recreational areas, wildlife areas and sanctuaries, fish hatcheries, natural areas and other lands, waters and facilities under the jurisdiction of the Secretary; ► apply for, receive and accept federal grants; ► control natural resource conservation pertaining to forests, woodlands, public lands, submarginal lands, prevention of soil erosion, habitats and utilization of waters, including all lakes, streams, reservoirs and dams, except that this subsection shall not prohibit a political subdivision of the state or private corporation from having full control of a lake now constructed and owned by it; ► conduct research and disseminate wildlife information; ► publicize the state's natural resources and recreational facilities; ► develop public recreation related to natural resources and implement a recreational plan (32-807).

The Secretary shall provide for the preservation, protection, introduction, distribution, restocking and restoration of wildlife, and its public use, including but not limited to the: ► establishing of open seasons; ► number of wildlife which may be taken by a person; ► legal size limits of fish and frogs which may be taken; ► conditions, procedures and rules under which a person may sell, purchase, buy, deal or trade in wildlife; ► capturing, propagating, transporting, selling, exchanging, giving, or distributing of wildlife needed for stocking or restocking state lands or waters, except that the power to capture wildlife shall not apply to private property except by permission of the owners thereof, or in the case of an emergency threatening public health or welfare; ► establishing of the period of time a license, permit, stamp or other Department issue shall be in effect; ► doing of other acts necessary to protect, conserve, control, use, increase, develop and provide for the enjoyment of the state's natural resources (32-807).

The **Department** is the official state agency to apply for, accept, administer and disburse federal assistance and benefits under the provisions of the Land and Water Conservation Fund Act of 1965 and is the designated agency to procure aid from the federal government to develop natural resources pertaining to the control and utilization of waters, prevention of soil erosion and flood control (32-824 and -827).

The Secretary shall organize a **Wildlife and Parks Conservation Service** and appoint conservation officers, deputy conservation officers, and temporary law enforcement officers to assist the Service. All deputy conservation officers shall receive a minimum of 40 hours of training prior to certification (32-808).

The Department shall cooperate and coordinate its activities with the state Department of Economic Development and all other state agencies, and with municipal, county and township planning boards and commissions concerned with matters under Department supervision. The Department may also cooperate and coordinate its activities with federal agencies and other states. The Department is authorized to cooperate with and assist non-profit citizen-support organizations and may authorize the use of Department facilities or property to further Department objectives (32-831 and -832).

The Secretary may exercise the right of eminent domain to acquire lands, water and water rights necessary to: carry out the wildlife and parks laws and for Department purposes; protect, add to and improve state parks, lakes, recreational areas, wildlife areas and sanctuaries, natural areas, fish hatcheries and other lands, waters and facilities. ★★The taking or appropriating of property authorized for protecting lands, waters and facilities and their environs, and preserving the view, appearance, light, air, health and usefulness thereof by reselling with deed restrictions to protect the property is declared the taking, using and appropriating of property for public use. ★★ The Secretary is authorized to lease lands under the Secretary's control, the title of which is vested in the state, for the production of oil, gas or other minerals. The lessee is liable for damages to the surface property caused by a negligent act or omission of the lessee (32-840, -850 and -852).

The Secretary is authorized to issue Department negotiable bonds in anticipation of the collection of revenues of a specific project or a dedicated revenue source, to construct, acquire, reconstruct, improve, better or extending properties which the Secretary is authorized to acquire, maintain or operate (32-857). [Extensive details on issuance and restrictions on bonds and procedures are given in the statute.]

The Secretary shall determine whether a species of wildlife indigenous to the state is a threatened or endangered species in the state because of the following factors: ► present or threatened destruction, modification or curtailment of its habitat or range; ► overutilization for commercial, sporting, scientific, educational or other purposes; ► disease or predation; ► inadequacy of existing regulatory mechanisms; ► presence of other natural or manmade factors affecting its continued existence within the state. The Secretary shall adopt rules and regulations which contain lists of all endangered and threatened species indigenous to the state. Each list shall refer to the species by scientific and common name and specify the portion of the range of each species in which it is threatened or endangered (32-960).

The Secretary shall adopt rules and regulations prescribing the form and content of and the requirements for applications for resident and nonresident licenses, permits, stamps and other Department issues and the issuance procedures. The Secretary is authorized to adopt rules and regulations fixing the amount of fees for licenses, permits, stamps and other Department issue, subject to statutory limitations (32-980 and -988).

Agency Funding Sources

The Secretary shall supervise the **Wild-Trust Program** which shall be responsible for the receipt and expenditure of moneys through gifts and donations. No moneys from fees paid for hunting, fur-harvester or fishing licenses, permits or stamps shall be used for any purpose other than Department administration and protection, propagation, preservation, management and investigation of wildlife. The rentals, delay rentals, bonuses, royalties and proceeds from mineral leases and production shall be credited to the **Wildlife Fee Fund** or the **Park Fee Fund**, as directed by the Secretary (32-802, -828, -829 and -854).

All moneys derived from the sale of bonds shall be credited to a special account for Department use to pay the cost of the specific public improvement or project for which the bonds were issued (32-858). The Secretary shall prescribe and collect rates, fees, tolls or charges for services, facilities and commodities rendered and provided at each Department project, the revenues of which have been pledged to the payment of bonds issued by the Department. ★★On any land under its control, the Department may erect and operate or lease cabins, hotels, lodges, restaurants and other facilities for the public. In conjunction with bonds issued for the erection, extension or improvement of lodges, hotels, cabins, restaurants or other facilities relating to a specific project, the Secretary may secure leases which will provide for rental incomes sufficient to meet the requirements of principal, interest, insurance and maintenance of the property to be constructed (32-860).★★ [Extensive details regarding bond issuance are provided in subsequent sections.]

For the purposes of paying the principal and interest on revenue bonds issued and sold by the Department, the Secretary shall issue and sell hatchery stamps which shall be affixed to all fishing licenses issued. The Secretary is authorized to issue and sell Department revenue bonds to pay all or part of the cost of acquiring a site, constructing, reconstructing, improving, expanding, equipping and stocking a fish hatchery (32-877 and -878).

Unless otherwise directed by law, all moneys received from licenses, permits, stamps and other Department issues to take, propagate, rehabilitate, collect, possess, sell, import, export, transport or deal in wildlife, or parts, and all moneys from sources related thereto or allied recreational pursuits, shall be remitted at least quarterly to the state treasurer and credited to the **Wildlife Fee Fund**. All Department costs and expenses shall be paid from this fund. No moneys derived from the sources listed herein shall be used for any purpose other than wildlife as provided by law (32-990). All license fees from the sale of lifetime hunting, fishing or combination hunting and fishing licenses shall be remitted at least quarterly to the state treasurer and an amount equal to the amount obtained by multiplying the number of lifetime licenses issued by the current fee for an annual fishing, hunting or combination license credited to the Wildlife Fee Fund, and the remaining balance credited to the **Wildlife Conservation Fund** (32-992).

All moneys received from sale of the migratory waterfowl habitat stamp shall be credited to the **Migratory Waterfowl Propagation and Protection Fund**. No expenditure shall be made from this fund except for projects approved by the Secretary for protecting and propagating waterfowl, including the acquisition, by purchase or lease, of state migratory waterfowl habitats, and for development, restoration, maintenance or preservation of waterfowl habitats. All moneys received as bequests, donations or gifts by the Department shall be credited to the **Wildlife and Parks Private Gifts and Donation Fund** (32-993 and -994).

Each state individual income tax return form shall contain a checkoff designation for donations to the nongame wildlife improvement program. The Director of Taxation shall determine annually the total amount designated for the nongame wildlife improvement program and credit it to the **Nongame Wildlife Improvement Fund**. When donations are made pursuant to 79-3221d, the Director shall remit the entire amount to the state treasurer who shall credit it to the fund. All moneys deposited in the fund shall be used solely to preserve, protect, perpetuate and enhance nongame wildlife (79-3221d and -3221e).

PROTECTED SPECIES OF WILDLIFE

The Secretary shall conduct ongoing investigations on nongame species to develop information relating to population, distribution, habitat needs, limiting factors and other biological and ecological data to determine conservation measures necessary for their continued ability to sustain themselves successfully. On the basis of such information, the Secretary shall adopt rules and regulations which contain a list of nongame species in need of conservation and develop conservation programs to insure the continued ability of nongame species to perpetuate themselves successfully. The Secretary shall adopt rules and regulations which establish limitations for taking, possessing, transporting, exporting, processing, selling, offering for sale or shipping in order to conserve nongame species (32-959).

★Except as otherwise provided, a permit is required to perform wildlife rehabilitation services.★ If the Secretary determines that the applicant possesses adequate facilities for and knowledge of wildlife rehabilitation, the Secretary may issue a rehabilitation permit, setting necessary terms. These provisions do not apply to licensed veterinarians (32-953).

Whenever a species indigenous to the state is listed by the Secretary as a threatened species, the Secretary shall adopt rules and regulations to provide for the conservation of the species. By rules and regulations the Secretary may prohibit for a listed threatened species an act prohibited for an endangered species. Except as otherwise provided, a special permit is required for a person subject to state jurisdiction to: ► export from the state an endangered species; ► possess, process, sell, offer for sale, deliver, carry, transport, or ship an endangered species; ► act in a manner contrary to a rule and regulation pertaining to endangered and threatened species. The Secretary may issue special permits to authorize a proscribed act for scientific purposes or to enhance the propagation or survival of an affected species. Threatened or endangered species may be captured or destroyed without a permit in an emergency situation involving an immediate and demonstrable threat to human life (32-961).

Except as provided in rules and regulations, it shall be unlawful for a person to take, possess, transport, export, process, sell or offer for sale or ship nongame species in need of conservation and for a common or contract carrier knowingly to transport or receive such species for shipment. Except as provided, the intentional taking of a threatened or endangered species indigenous to the state, and included in a list of such species, shall constitute unlawful taking of a threatened species (32-1009 and -1010).

GENERAL EXCEPTIONS TO PROTECTION

A hunting license is not required to hunt moles or gophers (32-919). A permit is required to collect protected wildlife for scientific, educational or exhibition purposes. Protected wildlife may be possessed by a person holding a scientific, educational or exhibition permit and may be shipped or transported within or without the state by permission of the Secretary (32-952).

HUNTING, FISHING AND TRAPPING PROVISIONS

General Provisions

Except as provided, a fur-harvester license is required to fur-harvest in the state or to sell, ship or offer for sale or shipment a fur-bearing animal or its raw fur, pelt, skin or carcass, except that a license is not required for fur-harvesting by: a person or a member of a person's immediate family living on land owned, leased or rented for agricultural purposes; a state resident less that 14 years of age and accompanied by a person holding a fur-harvester license; a nonresident participating in a field trial for dogs. ★No person born on or after July 1, 1966, shall fur-harvest on land other than the person's own land without a fur-harvester certificate of competency. The Secretary shall prescribe a course of instruction of not less than six hours concerning the ethical, humane, safe and selective fur-harvesting and handling of fur-bearing animals and coyotes (32-911 through -913).★

Except as otherwise provided, a hunting license is required to hunt in the state, except a license is not required for: ► a person, or immediate family member living on land owned, leased or rented for agricultural purposes; ► a state resident less that 16 or more than 65 years of age; ► a nonresident participating in a field trial for dogs; ► a person hunting only moles or gophers. A hunting license is valid throughout the state, except the Secretary may issue a special controlled shooting area license valid only for licensed controlled shooting areas. The Secretary may issue a 48-hour waterfowl hunting permit, the purchase of which shall not affect the requirement for a federal migratory bird hunting and conservation stamp or state migratory waterfowl habitat stamp. No persons born on or after July 1, 1957, shall hunt in the state except on their own land unless they have a certificate of completion of an approved hunter education course. The Secretary shall prescribe a course of instruction of not less than a total of 10 hours in hunter education (32-919 through -921).

Except as otherwise provided and in addition to any other license, permit or stamp required, a big game permit and game tags are required to take big game, the permit and tags being valid throughout the state or such portions thereof as provided by rules and regulations. ★Fifty percent of the big game permits authorized for a regular season in a management unit shall be issued to landowners (a resident owner of a farm or ranch of 80 acres or more) or tenants, provided that a limited number of big game permits have been authorized and landowner or tenant hunt-on-your-own-land big game permits for that unit have not been authorized.★ The Secretary may issue permits for deer or turkey to nonresident landowners, but the permits shall be restricted to hunting only on lands owned by the permittee. The Secretary may issue turkey hunting permits to nonresidents in turkey management units with unlimited turkey hunting permits available (32-937).

The Secretary may issue deer hunting permits to nonresidents, except: ★▸ no nonresident deer permit shall be issued for a deer season commencing on or after July 1, 1993; ▸ nonresident deer permits shall only permit hunting of does; ▸ the total number of nonresident deer firearm permits issued in a management unit shall not exceed 2% of the total number of such permits for the season; ▸ the total number of nonresident deer archery permits issued in a management unit shall not exceed 1% of the total number of such permits for the season.★ No big game permit issued to a person under 14 years of age shall be valid until the person reaches 14 years of age, except that a wild turkey firearm permit may be issued to an individual who is age 12 or older but is under age 14, if the individual has been issued a certificate of completion of an approved hunter education course. The turkey firearm permit shall be valid only while the individual is hunting under the immediate supervision of an adult who is age 21 or older. A big game permit shall state the species, number and sex of the big game which may be killed by the permittee (32-937). Except as otherwise provided and in addition to any other license, permit or stamp required, a state migratory waterfowl habitat stamp is required to hunt migratory waterfowl (32-939).

If hatchery stamps have been issued by the Secretary, no person required to purchase a fishing license shall fish without first procuring a hatchery stamp and having it in possession while fishing (32-877). Except as otherwise provided, a fishing license is required to fish or to take a bullfrog, except a license is not required for fishing by: ▸ a person, or immediate family member, on land owned, leased or rented by the person; ▸ state residents under 16 years of age or 65 or more years of age; ▸ nonresidents under 16 years old; ▸ a person fishing in a private water fishing impoundment; ▸ a resident of an adult care home; an inmate in an honor camp; ★▸ a resident of the state of Texas who is 65 or more years of age if the state of Texas permits residents of Kansas who are 65 or more years of age to fish in Texas without having to obtain a Texas fishing license;★ ▸ a person under an institutional group fishing license. The Secretary shall issue an annual institutional group fishing license to each facility operating under the jurisdiction of, or licensed by, the Secretary of Social and Rehabilitation Services and to any state Veterans Administration medical center (32-906).

Licenses and Permits

Except as provided, a person may secure a license, permit, stamp or other Department issue upon application and payment of the fee (32-982). The Secretary is authorized to issue to a resident a lifetime fishing, hunting or combination hunting and fishing license. Whenever a disabled person is unable to hunt and fish in the normal manner, the Secretary may issue a handicapped hunting and fishing permit, permitting the person to hunt and fish from land or water vehicles, but the permit shall not authorize a person to shoot from a highway. A person having a permanent disability who cannot use a conventional long bow or compound bow shall be authorized to take deer or antelope with a crossbow (32-930 through -932). It is unlawful for a person to participate in an activity requiring a license, permit, stamp or other Department issue without having it in possession or to refuse to allow examination thereof (32-1001).

Restrictions on Taking

It is unlawful for a person, unless otherwise provided, to: ▸ take game or fur-bearing animal from a motorboat, airplane, motor vehicle or other water, air or land vehicle, unless the person holds a handicapped hunting and fishing permit; ▸ provide or receive information concerning the location of a game or fur-bearing animal by radio or other mechanical device in order to take the animal;　★▸ use sodium fluoroacetate, commonly called formula 1080, except as permitted by rules and regulations;★　▸ use poison, poisonous gas, smoke or ferrets, or a smoke gun or other device for forcing smoke or other asphyxiating or deadly gas or liquid into the holes, dens, runways or houses of wildlife, except as otherwise permitted; ▸ fish by placing in or upon a lake, pond, river, creek, stream or other state water any deleterious substance or fishberries; ▸ place or explode dynamite, giant powder, lime, nitroglycerine or other explosive in state waters with the intent to take or stun fish; ▸ throw or cast the rays of a spotlight, headlight or other artificial light on a highway, or in a field, grassland, woodland or forest, to spot, locate or take an animal, except fur-bearing animals when treed with the aid of dogs, while having in possession a rifle or pistol larger than a rifle or pistol using .22 rimfire cartridges, shotgun, bow or other implement whereby wildlife could be taken (32-1003).

It is unlawful to take, buy, sell or offer to sell migratory birds and waterfowl except as authorized and permitted by federal regulations (32-1008).　It is unlawful to: destroy a muskrat house, beaver dam, mink run or hole, den or runway of a fur-bearing animal, or cut down or destroy a tree that is the home, habitat or refuge of a fur-bearing animal; place erect, or cause to be, a seine, screen, net, weir, fish dam or obstruction in or across state waters which will obstruct the free passage of fish (32-1015).

Commercial and Private Enterprise Provisions

The owner or tenant having possession and control of a private water fishing impoundment and desiring to use it for the propagation or raising of fish for private or commercial use may do so without securing or holding a state license, permit or stamp and without being limited as to numbers, time or manner of taking fish from the impoundment (32-974).

Except as otherwise authorized, a commercial harvest permit is required, in addition to any other license, permit or stamp required by law, to take state wildlife on a commercial basis.　A person acting within the scope of a fur-harvester or fur dealer license or a person fishing in a private water fishing impoundment does not require a commercial harvest permit.　The Secretary may adopt rules and regulations necessary to implement, administer and enforce the provisions.　Except as otherwise provided, a fur dealer license is required to buy, purchase or trade in raw furs, pelts, skins or carcasses of fur-bearing animals (32-941 and -942).

A person owning, holding or controlling, by lease or otherwise, for a term of five or more years, a contiguous tract of land having an area of not less than 160 acres nor more than 1,280 acres, who desires to establish a controlled shooting area to propagate and shoot game birds shall make application for a license to operate the area.　Every person hunting on a controlled shooting area shall possess a hunting license or controlled shooting area hunting license, if required by law.　The Secretary may issue to the licensee of a private membership licensed controlled shooting area special permits and game tags for the taking of deer for purchase by persons who are permitted by the licensee to hunt such an area (32-944, -946 and -947).

A game breeder permit is required to engage in the business of raising and selling game birds, game animals, fur-bearing animals or other wildlife as required by the rules and regulations.　A person who desires to engage in game breeding as a business may apply to the Secretary for a game breeder permit.　If the Secretary determines that the application is made in good faith and that the premises are suitable for engaging in the business, the Secretary may issue such permit (32-951).　★A field trial permit or commercial dog training permit is required to use wild or pen-raised game birds, game animals, coyotes, fur-bearing animals or other wildlife in a field trial or in training dogs on a commercial basis (32-954).★

A commercial guide permit is required to provide commercial guide services in the state.　Upon application to the Secretary, a commercial guide permit or an associate guide permit may be issued if the applicant possesses adequate knowledge of: state wildlife and parks laws; rules and regulations; hunting and fishing skills.　A written or oral examination may be required.　Unless otherwise exempt, a commercial guide permittee shall be required to possess a hunting and fishing license to conduct hunting and fishing activities (32-964).

Import, Export and Release Provisions

To prohibit certain wildlife from state waters and lands, the Secretary shall adopt rules and regulations which shall contain a list of prohibited wildlife, provide for certain exemptions for experimental, scientific or display purposes and provide for the issuance of wildlife importation permits (32-956).

ANIMAL DAMAGE CONTROL

★A wildlife damage control permit is required to use sodium fluoroacetate, commonly called formula 1080.★ No permit shall be issued until the extension specialist in wildlife damage control approves and recommends the use of 1080. The Secretary may, by regulations, require wildlife damage control permits for wildlife damage control by use of poison, poisonous gas, smoke or ferrets or by use of a smoke gun or other device for forcing smoke or other asphyxiating or deadly gas or liquid into holes, dens, runways or houses of wildlife (32-955). It is lawful for a person who holds a license to hunt or fur-harvest to take coyotes, except it is unlawful to take a coyote during the time period designated as an open season for the hunting of deer by firearm. It is lawful for a person to take moles or gophers in this state at any time (32-1006).

See also Illegal Taking of Wildlife under ENFORCEMENT OF WILDLIFE LAWS.

ENFORCEMENT OF WILDLIFE LAWS

Enforcement Powers

The Secretary shall organize a Wildlife and Parks Conservation Service and employ conservation officers. The Secretary may appoint permanent officers and employees of the Department as deputy conservation officers, and may appoint law enforcement officers temporarily assigned to the Department to assist the Wildlife and Parks Conservation Service. All deputy conservation officer appointments shall be on a voluntary basis and shall expire on December 31 following the date of appointment. The Department shall provide a minimum of 40 hours of internal law enforcement training prior to certification of deputy conservation officers. Conservation officers, deputy conservation officers and any other law enforcement officers shall have the authority to enforce the wildlife and parks laws and rules and regulations. A conservation officer who has completed the required course of instruction for law enforcement officers may assist in the making of an arrest and may arrest a person when in possession of a warrant commanding that the person be arrested when the conservation officer has probable cause to believe the person is committing or has committed a felony or misdemeanor, or a felony or misdemeanor is being committed in the conservation officer's view. If the conservation officer makes an arrest without the presence of an officer of a law enforcement agency, the conservation officer shall cause the arrested person to be delivered to the sheriff, chief of police or a designee in the jurisdiction where the arrest is made. Conservation officers shall have the authority to serve warrants and subpoenas, and to carry firearms or weapons, concealed or otherwise, in the performance of duty, but only if the officer has completed the required course of instruction for law enforcement officers (32-808).

Conservation officers, deputy conservation officers and other law enforcement officers shall have the power to arrest persons found violating wildlife and parks laws and rules or regulations without warrants, and with warrants where not found violating such laws and rules or regulations, and to bring the person before the nearest proper judge of the district court of the county within which the violation occurred (32-1048). It shall be the duty of all conservation officers, deputy conservation officers and law enforcement officers to inquire diligently into and prosecute all violations of the wildlife and parks laws of this state and rules and regulations (32-1051).

★★The court hearing the prosecution of a child age 16 or 17 charged with a violation of the wildlife and parks laws or rules and regulations may impose any fine authorized by law for the offense and may order that a child be placed in a juvenile detention facility (32-1040). ★★

Criminal Penalties

Unlawful hunting is fishing, or shooting, hunting or pursuing a non-wounded bird or animal upon posted land of another, or from a traveled public road or railroad right-of-way that adjoins occupied or improved premises, without having first obtained permission of the owner or person in possession of such premises. Violation: class C misdemeanor (21-3728 and 32-1013). Unless otherwise provided, violation of the wildlife and parks laws or rules and regulations is a class C misdemeanor. Violation of the wildlife and parks laws or rules and regulations relating to big game permits and game tags is a misdemeanor punishable by a $250-1,000 fine; or by jail up to six months; or by both (32-1032). Unlawful taking of an endangered species is a class A misdemeanor (32-1031 through -1033).

Illegal Taking of Wildlife

It is unlawful for a person to: ‣ possess a carcass of a big game animal, taken within the state, unless a game tag is attached to it; ‣ possess wildlife unlawfully killed or otherwise unlawfully taken outside the state; ‣ cause to be shipped within, from or into the state illegally taken or possessed wildlife; ‣ intentionally import into the state, or possess or release, prohibited species of wildlife; ‣ refuse to allow a conservation officer, deputy conservation officer or law officer to inspect devices or facilities used in taking, possessing, transporting, storing or processing wildlife subject to the wildlife and parks laws or rules and regulations (32-1004).

Except as permitted by law or rules and regulations, it is unlawful for a person to: ‣ hunt, fish, fur-harvest or take wildlife by any means or manner; ‣ possess wildlife, dead or alive, at any time or in any number; ‣ purchase, sell or offer for sale any wildlife; ‣ possess a seine, trammel net, hoop net, fyke net, fish gig, fish spear, fish trap or other device, contrivance or material for the purpose of taking wildlife; ‣ take or use a game bird, game animal, coyote or fur-bearing animal, whether pen-raised or wild, in a field trial or for training dogs; ‣ buy, sell, barter, ship, or offer for sale, barter or shipment, or possess, alive or dead, any wildlife. These provisions do not apply to animals sold in surplus property disposal sales of Department exhibit herds or animals legally taken outside the state, do not prevent a person from taking starlings or English and European sparrows, or prevent owners or legal occupants of land from killing animals found in or near buildings on their premises or when destroying property, subject to all federal and state laws and regulations governing protected species. It is unlawful to use, or possess with intent to use, an animal so killed unless authorized by regulations, and owners or legal occupants shall make reasonable efforts to alleviate their problems with animals before killing them (32-1002).

★★Commercialization of wildlife is knowingly committing any of the following, except as permitted by statute or rules and regulations: ‣ capturing, killing or possessing for profit or commercial purposes; ‣ selling, bartering, purchasing, or offering to do so, for profit or commercial purposes; ‣ shipping, exporting, importing, transporting or carrying, or delivering or receiving to do so; ‣ purchasing, for personal use or consumption, all or part of wildlife listed. Protected wildlife and the minimum value thereof are: ‣ eagles, $500; ‣ deer or antelope, $200; ‣ elk or buffalo, $500; ‣ fur-bearing animals, $25; ‣ wild turkey, $75; ‣ owls, hawks, falcons, kites, harriers or ospreys, $125; ‣ game birds, migratory game birds, resident and migratory nongame birds, game and nongame animals, $10 unless a higher amount is specified above; ‣ fish, the value for which shall be not less than the value listed in the guidelines of the American Fisheries Society; ‣ turtles, $8 each for unprocessed turtles or $6 per pound or fraction of a pound for processed turtle parts; ‣ bullfrogs, $2 whether dressed or not; ‣ threatened or endangered wildlife, $200 unless a higher amount is specified above; ‣ other wildlife not listed above, $5. Possession of wildlife, in whole or in part, captured or killed in violation of law and having an aggregate value of $500 or more, as specified above, is prima facie evidence of possession for profit or commercial purposes. Commercialization of wildlife having an aggregate value of $500 or more is a class E felony. Commercialization of wildlife having an aggregate value of less than $500 is a class A misdemeanor. In addition to any other penalty provided by law, a court convicting a person of the crime of commercialization of wildlife may confiscate all equipment used in the commission of the crime and revoke for a period of up to 10 years all licenses and permits issued to the convicted person and order restitution to be paid for the wildlife taken, in an amount not less than the aggregate value of the wildlife. These provisions shall apply only to wildlife illegally harvested and possessed by a person having actual knowledge that the wildlife was illegally harvested (32-1005). ★★

★★It is unlawful for a person to display publicly the carcass of a coyote, except at a fur market or for education or training purposes (32-1007).★★

★A landowner may post land stating that hunting, trapping or fishing shall be by written permission only. ★ It is unlawful for a person to take wildlife on posted land, without having in possession the written permission of the landowner (32-1013). The Department is empowered and directed to seize and posses wildlife taken, possessed, sold or transported unlawfully, and a steel trap, snare or device or equipment used in taking or transporting wildlife unlawfully or during closed season. The Department is authorized to sell the seized item and remit the proceeds to the state treasurer for credit to the Wildlife Fee Fund or retain the seized item for educational, scientific or Departmental operational purposes (32-1047).

License Revocations and Suspensions

Upon the first conviction of violating wildlife laws or regulations, and in addition to a sentence imposed by the court, the court may order the person to refrain from an activity for which convicted and forfeiture of any relevant license, permit, stamp or other Department issue, other than a lifetime license, for a one-year period; upon a subsequent conviction, the court shall order the person to refrain from any related activity and forfeiture of any relevant license, permit, stamp or other Department issue for a one-year period. Upon the first conviction of violating wildlife laws or regulations by a person who has a lifetime hunting or fishing license, and in addition to a sentence imposed by the court, the court may order a one-year license suspension, and upon a subsequent conviction of such a person, in addition to a sentence imposed, the court shall order a one-year license suspension. If a convicted person has been issued a combination hunting and fishing license or a combination lifetime license, only that portion of the license pertaining to the activity for which a person is convicted shall be subject to forfeiture or suspension (32-1041).

A judge, upon a finding of multiple, repeated or otherwise aggravated violations by a defendant, may order forfeiture or suspension of a license, permit, stamp or other Department issue for a period longer than otherwise provided and may order the defendant to refrain from any activity, legal or illegal, related to that for which convicted, for a period longer than otherwise provided (32-1041).

HABITAT PROTECTION

The Secretary shall establish programs, including acquisition of land or aquatic habitat, necessary for the conservation of nongame, threatened and endangered species (32-962).

★★"Conservation easement" means a non-possessory interest of a real property holder imposing limitations or affirmative obligations for retaining or protecting natural, scenic or open-space values of real-property, assuring its availability for agricultural, forest, recreational or open-space use, protecting natural resources, maintaining or enhancing air or water quality, or preserving historical, architectural, archeological, or cultural aspects of real property. Conservation easements may be created by grants to both governmental entities and charitable corporations. A conservation easement may be created only by the record owner of the surface of the land. Except by court action and unless the instrument creating it otherwise provides, a conservation easement shall be limited in duration to the lifetime of the grantor and may be revoked (58-3810 and -3811).★★

NATIVE AMERICAN WILDLIFE PROVISIONS

★★The Secretary shall issue, free of charge, a permanent license to hunt, fish and fur-harvest to a person residing in the state who is at least 1/16 Indian by blood and who is enrolled as an American Indian on a tribal membership roll maintained by the Bureau of Indian Affairs, or who has been issued a certificate of degree of Indian blood by the Bureau of Indian Affairs. Any such person shall be subject to the provisions of all rules and regulations relating to hunting, fishing or fur-harvesting in the state (32-929).★★

KENTUCKY

Sources: Kentucky Revised Statutes Annotated, 1986, Title 12; 1991 Replacement Volume

STATE WILDLIFE POLICY

The policy of Kentucky is to protect and conserve wildlife to insure a permanent and continued supply of state wildlife resources for furnishing sport and recreation for present and future residents; to promote the general welfare; to provide for the prudent taking and disposition of wildlife; to protect the food supply of this state; and to insure the continuation of an important part of the state's commerce which depends upon the existence of its wildlife resources. It is further the declared policy that an adequate and flexible system be installed to accomplish the aforesaid purposes (150.015).

RELEVANT WILDLIFE DEFINITIONS See Definitions section of Appendices.

STATE FISH AND WILDLIFE AGENCIES

Agency Structure

The **Department of Fish and Wildlife Resources** (Department) consists of a **Commissioner**, a **Fish and Wildlife Resources Commission** (Commission) and conservation officers and other agents and employees. The Department enforces wildlife laws and regulations and exercises powers incident thereto. Powers conferred by this chapter upon the Department, Commission, or the Commissioner are exercised subject to Chapters 42, 45, 45A, 56, and 64. The Commission consists of nine members, one from each wildlife district, as set out by the Commissioner with Commission approval, with not more than five of the same political party. The Governor appoints members for four-year terms. Vacancies are filled by appointment by the Governor from a list of five names submitted by the sportsmen of each wildlife district. When a member's term expires, the Commissioner shall call a meeting of the sportsmen in that district who shall submit to the Governor a list of five citizens of the district who are well informed on wildlife conservation and restoration, following which the Governor shall appoint a successor within 60 days (150.021). The Governor may remove a member for inefficiency, neglect of duty, or misconduct in office; but shall deliver a copy of all charges and afford an opportunity of public hearing [details of record provided]. "Sportsman" means a resident hunter or fisherman licensed in Kentucky for each of the past two years (150.021 and .022). The Commission appoints a Commissioner of the Department, with knowledge of and experience in protection, conservation and restoration of state wildlife resources. The Commissioner shall: ▸ have supervision or control of Department activities, functions and employees; ▸ enforce laws relating to wild animals, birds, fish and amphibians; ▸ exercise all powers not specifically conferred on the Commission; ▸ submit an annual report of receipts and disbursements to the Secretary of State (150.061).

Agency Powers and Duties

The **Commission** meets quarterly, or as necessary. The Commission keeps a watchful eye upon the Department, and advises the Commissioner to take action beneficial to the Department and in the interest of wildlife and conservation of natural resources. The **Commissioner**, with Commission approval, authorizes scientific and other studies and collects, classifies and disseminates statistics, data and information to promote the objects of this chapter, and has exclusive power to expend for protection, conservation, propagation, restoration, taking and harvesting of wildlife funds acquired from licenses, gifts or otherwise. The **Department** has the right to acquire property to carry out the purpose of this chapter, and the right of eminent domain (150.023 and .024).   ★After considering the public recreation, sport, and economic value and breeding habits of a wildlife species, if the Commissioner, with Commission concurrence, finds that the supply has become depleted or finds that, because of adverse weather, floods, disease, fire, inadequate food supply, breeding conditions, lack of cover, unequal distribution, excessive destruction or widespread violations of fish and wildlife laws, or other reason, there is serious danger that the supply may be depleted, the Department shall adopt regulations to restore supply or prevent further depletion (150.025). ★

Agency Regulations

The Department may: ▸ fix, close, terminate, shorten or divide open seasons, or make open seasons conditional; ▸ regulate bag or creel and possession limits; ▸ regulate buying, selling or transporting; ▸ regulate the size or type of devices used for taking, and method of taking; ▸ regulate or restrict places where taking is permitted; ▸ regulate taking, or opening or closing of seasons, in waters where the Department is conducting experiments or making improvements to promote conservation of wildlife and increase its supply; ▸ make regulations to implement the purposes of this chapter (150.025). Immediately after filing, the Commissioner shall cause every regulation to be published once in two newspapers having statewide circulation, and mail two copies to the county clerk of each county in which the regulation is applicable, one to be posted on the courthouse door or bulletin board (150.025).

Agency Funding Sources

Except as provided, moneys from sales of licenses or other sources from administration of this chapter are deposited in a **Game and Fish Fund** (fund). The fund is used to carry out the purposes of this chapter and wildlife laws or regulations for protection of wildlife. Funds remaining at the close of each calendar year go to the Department's general fund (150.150). Fines imposed for violations of this chapter are paid into the fund (150.160). There is a special **Nongame Fish and Wildlife Fund** (fund) under the Commission's control for protecting and preserving nongame fish and wildlife and their habitat. The fund consists of monies transferred to it under 141.465, appropriations, donations, federal funds, other revenues designated for the fund, and earned interest. Fund monies are deemed a trust and an agency account and are appropriated continuously for the purposes specified in this section. The Commission has access to and control of the monies, but shall expend them only to protect and preserve nongame fish and wildlife and their habitat (150.165). The Secretary of the Revenue Cabinet shall transfer 50% of the funds designated in 141.460 to the Nongame Fish and Wildlife Fund and 50% to the **Kentucky Nature Preserves Fund** created by 146.520 and reduce the amount of the income tax refund by the amount designated (141.465).

★With Commission approval, the Commissioner may call for issuance of revenue bonds for establishing public shooting areas, waterfowl or other wildlife refuges, public fishing lakes or other projects in the interest of fish and game, and may unite all revenue pledged by the Commissioner into one project. The united revenues shall be used for payment of principal and interest of bonds issued [details provided] (150.610).★

PROTECTED SPECIES OF WILDLIFE

No person shall import, transport, possess for resale or sell endangered species, hides, skins, or parts, or articles made from same of a species designated as endangered by the Department's regulations, except as provided in this section. As used in this section, "endangered species" means a species seriously threatened with worldwide extinction or in danger of being extirpated from Kentucky. The regulations promulgated shall include, but not be limited to, all species designated as endangered by the US Secretary of the Interior on January 1, 1973. The Department may permit, with conditions, the importation, transportation, possession, or sale of a species otherwise prohibited pursuant to this section for zoological, educational, or scientific purposes, and for propagation of such wildlife in captivity for preservation, except as prohibited (150.183).

No person shall: ▸ take a wild bird, except game birds or live raptors for which there is an open season, either under Department laws and regulations or US laws, but this chapter does not protect or limit taking of crow, starling, or English sparrow by a person with a hunting license; ▸ take, disturb or destroy the nest or eggs of wild birds, except raptors as prescribed by regulation; ▸ take, pursue, possess, transport, purchase or sell or attempt to do so, migratory birds, except as authorized by the Migratory Bird Treaty Act and regulations. No person age 16 or older shall hunt waterfowl unless, in addition to a hunting license and waterfowl stamp, the person possesses a migratory bird hunting stamp as required by the Migratory Bird Hunting Stamp Act (150.320 and .330).

GENERAL EXCEPTIONS TO PROTECTION

The Commissioner may issue to a qualified person a permit, for a specified time period, to take and transport wildlife for commercial nuisance wildlife control, scientific, or educational purposes. By regulation, the Commission may set fees for permits authorized by this section (150.275). No person shall propagate or hold protected wildlife without a permit within 10 days after the wildlife is acquired. The Commissioner shall make and publish regulations governing such activity. The application shall be in writing, addressed to the Commissioner, signed by the applicant, and shall describe the land or waters owned or leased to be used and contain such other facts as required. The Commissioner may issue a permit, for a fixed term unless revoked for cause, upon payment of a permit fee and fees for tagging. A fish and game club which enters into an agreement with the Department to operate such a farm for carrying out the Department's program may be issued a permit without a fee. A permit may be revoked for a violation of a state law or regulation (150.280).

HUNTING, FISHING, TRAPPING PROVISIONS

General Provisions

No person shall enter another's lands to shoot, hunt or fish without consent of the owner or tenant, nor enter to trap fur-bearers or to hunt deer or turkey without the written consent of the owner or tenant. Upon written complaint of the owner or tenant, a conservation officer shall arrest a person violating this section, if the officer is already on the land to enforce other provisions of this chapter. Whether or not an officer is already on the land to enforce other provisions of this chapter the officer may arrest for a violation of a provision of this section, but the officer is not required to make an arrest unless already on the land. A person who enters upon another's lands to shoot, hunt, trap or fish shall not damage buildings, fences, crops, livestock or domestic animals, machinery, or other property. Nothing in this section limits the existing powers of peace officers (150.092).

★Except as provided, and subject to regulations adopted under this chapter, no person shall buy, or sell, or attempt to buy, or sell, barter, exchange, or trade, or possess for selling, bartering, or trading protected wildlife or a part, raw fur or processed wildlife, no matter where or when caught or killed (150.180).★

If in legal possession: ► mussels and fish, other than designated sport fish, and all fish raised by licensed propagation permittees may be bought, sold and transported; ► raw furs may be sold, transported, or shipped by a licensed trapper or hunter to a licensed fur buyer, and by a licensed fur buyer to a licensed fur processor or to another fur buyer. Raw furs may be possessed by a trapper or hunter for 20 days and a fur buyer for 30 days after close of the season. A fur processor may hold raw furs or sell to another licensed fur processor at any time. Subject to regulations, a person who has been issued and carries a license may transport anywhere as personal baggage protected wildlife legally taken, not in excess of the number that the law or regulation permits. A person who has taken protected wildlife legally in another state may transport same in this state as personal baggage during the open season for the species in the state in which taken or within 10 days after the close of such season. A person may ship dead game or fish taken subject to the laws of the state in which taken and US laws and regulations (150.180).

Subject to regulations and except as provided, no person shall possess wildlife protected by this chapter, or a raw fur, except during the open season for the species, unless the person holds a permit issued pursuant to section 150.275 or 150.280. A person who has taken wildlife legally may possess same in cold storage, and the package must be marked if it is stored in a commercial locker plant. Legally imported wildlife may be similarly held. Federal regulations govern possession of migratory wild birds. To facilitate enforcement of this section, the Commissioner or a designee has authority to inspect all commercial frozen food lockers at such intervals as the Commissioner determines. No search warrant or other legal process is required for the inspections (150.305).

With Commission approval, the Commissioner has authority to: ► regulate the taking of waterfowl within the state and to establish waterfowl refuges and shooting grounds, regulate distance of pits and shooting from refuges, on public or private lands; ► build shooting pits or blinds and charge for their use; ► control or improve conservation or hunting of waterfowl not contrary to federal regulations. It is unlawful for commercial purposes to hold or control land and water, for the taking of migratory waterfowl, or have the privilege of taking migratory waterfowl without applying to the Department and paying an annual permit fee to possess and build blinds or pits. The permit holder shall keep a daily register and kill survey. No landowner, immediate family member, or resident tenant residing on the owned land or water is required to secure a permit for hunting migratory waterfowl (150.600).

Licenses and Permits

Except as provided and subject to regulations, without a license or permit no person shall do an act authorized by a license or permit, or assist a person in doing such. It is the purpose of this chapter to prohibit taking or pursuing of wildlife, protected or unprotected, or fishing in water, public or private, without a license except as provided. The resident owner or tenant of farmlands, spouse, and dependent children, have the right to fish or hunt without a license during the open season, except for trapping, on farmlands they own. Persons observing and participating in Department authorized field trials may do so without a hunting license if game is not taken. Resident landowners, tenants, spouses, and dependent children who kill or trap wildlife causing damage to their lands or personal property are not required to have a hunting or trapping license. Destruction of wildlife shall be reported to the Department or the resident conservation officer for disposition of the carcass (150.175).

Licenses and tags authorized by this chapter, and acts authorized to be performed under them are as follows: ▸ statewide resident sport fishing licenses authorizing taking fish by angling, or crayfish by a minnow seine, or by hand, taking minnows by the use of a minnow seine, minnow trap or dip net, or taking fish by grabbing, gigging, snagging, snaring, jugging, and bow and arrow, and taking frogs and turtles from waters open for such purposes and subject to this chapter and additional Department limitations, but not to sell fish; ▸ short-term sport fishing licenses for nonresidents to perform acts authorized by a statewide sport fishing license and subject to the same limitations or prescribed regulations; ▸ commercial fishing licenses for acts authorized by a sport fishing license, taking rough fish as prescribed, and selling rough fish, other than those protected by regulation; ▸ [commercial fishing gear tag detailed]; ▸ live fish and bait dealer's licenses for selling bait and live fish; ▸ musseling licenses for taking mussels for commercial purposes as prescribed; ▸ statewide resident hunting licenses authorizing taking or pursuit of wild animals, birds, frogs and turtles with gun, bow and arrow, dog or falcon, or participation in a fox-hunting party to hunt or pursue foxes with dogs for sport, according to Department laws and regulations; ▸ trapping licenses for taking wild animals by trapping upon personally owned lands or upon another's lands with written consent (150.170).

Other licenses include: ▸ commercial and noncommercial taxidermist licenses, to prepare, stuff, and mount skins of wildlife; ▸ a commercial guide's license, to guide hunting and fishing parties according to Department laws and regulations; ▸ a fur buyer's license, to buy raw furs from licensed trappers and hunters and to sell raw furs; ▸ a fur processor's license, to be issued to a resident, or a state partnership, firm, or corporation, to buy raw furs; ▸ a nonresident sport fishing license; ▸ a nonresident annual hunting license; ▸ shoot-to-retrieve field trial permits for government-owned lands, but not required for licensed shooting preserves [details provided]; ▸ a special license for nonresidents to hunt on licensed hunting preserves [details provided]. The Commissioner, with the approval of the Commission, may establish and regulate hunting preserves, private or commercial by issuing: ▸ big game permits which, with hunting licenses, authorize holders to take or pursue deer, bear, or wild turkey, during the open season; ▸ combination hunting and fishing licenses, to perform acts under sport fishing or hunting licenses; ▸ trout stamps, which with fishing licenses, authorize holders to take trout by angling as prescribed; ▸ commercial waterfowl permits, to establish and operate commercial waterfowl hunting preserves; ▸ short-term hunting licenses (nonresident), except for hunting big game species for which an annual nonresident hunting license is required; ▸ joint statewide resident sport fishing licenses issued to husbands and wives; ▸ a Kentucky waterfowl stamp; ▸ pay lake licenses, to operate privately owned impounded waters for fishing for which a fee is charged (150.660).

With Commission approval, The Commissioner may adopt license designs and forms and make regulations for them [details provided]. No person shall make a false statement or provide false information when securing a license, nor alter or falsify a license or permit. [Details of issuance of licenses by Department or county provided.] A commercial guide's license, fur buyer's license, and fur processor's license are issued directly by the Department. A commercial guide's license applicant is required to present proof of qualification to act as a commercial guide. A fur processor's license applicant is required to present proof that the person has sufficient equipment and facilities for the business of processing, manufacture, and storage of raw furs. A live fish and bait dealer's license is issued directly by the Department (150.190).

No person: ▸ shall perform an act authorized by a license without carrying it, except a fur processor may have the license posted in a conspicuous place on the licensed premises; ▸ may permit another to carry the holder's license; ▸ shall present another's license to a conservation officer for inspection while hunting or fishing; ▸ having a license privilege revoked or suspended shall possess the kind of license that would otherwise permit the act during suspension. No nonresident shall perform an act under this chapter without the proper nonresident license (150.235).

A person required to possess a hunting license who takes or attempts to take wild ducks or geese must have affixed to the license a **Kentucky Waterfowl Stamp**, which is not transferable, must be signed by the bearer, and is to be carried while hunting. The Commission shall determine the stamp's form and administer revenues from its sale. Revenue shall be expended for waterfowl research projects protecting and propagating migratory waterfowl and for development, restoration, maintenance, and preservation of wetlands. The intent is to expand waterfowl research and management and increase waterfowl populations in the state without detracting from other programs. The expenditures of funds generated shall be included in the Commissioner's annual report (150.603).

Restrictions on Taking: Hunting and Trapping

No person shall take more wildlife in one day than the bag or creel limit prescribed. A person who has hunted two or more days in succession may transport not more than twice the bag limit set by regulations. Federal and state regulations apply to migratory birds and waterfowl (150.340). ★No person shall use ferrets in hunting, nor keep a ferret without a ferret permit which must be obtained within ten days after acquisition of a ferret. One permit entitles a holder to keep any number of ferrets. If a ferret owner uses a permit in violation, the Commissioner may revoke it and confiscate all ferrets. Each use of a ferret in hunting is a separate offense (150.355).★

No person shall: ▸ take wildlife, whether or not protected by this chapter, except by trapping, snaring, gig, crossbow, bow and arrow, hook and line, nets, gun, gun and dog, dog, falconry, or as prescribed by regulation, and shotguns shall not be larger than 10-gauge and fired from the shoulder; ▸ take wildlife, except deer, with an automatic loading or hand-operated repeating shotgun; ▸ take or attempt to take wildlife from a vehicle, unless prescribed by regulation, and boats may be used, except as prohibited by state or federal regulation; ▸ discharge a firearm, bow and arrow, crossbow or other similar device, upon, over, or across a public roadway; ▸ take wildlife, except opossum, raccoon, fish and frogs, with lights or means designed to blind wildlife or make it visible at night; ▸ take wildlife as a result of a fire, or with any type of explosive, or with the aid of mechanical, electric or hand operated sonic recording devices, except as specified; ▸ use smoke or gas, or molest or destroy the den, hole or nest of wildlife, nor burn a field for driving game, except Department employees or agents carrying out investigative, research or improvement projects (150.360 and .365).

No person shall take wildlife, except during the open season for the species as prescribed. This section does not apply to persons who hunt red fox at night with dogs for sport and not to kill, and who exercise and train, during daylight or night, rabbit dogs, raccoon dogs, bird dogs and retrievers, but not to kill. The Department may: ▸ regulate training seasons [for various hunting dogs]; ▸ permit meets held by organized clubs, regardless of a hunting season, with the prior approval of the Department. The possession of raw fur during closed season for the species is prima facie evidence that the animal was taken out of open season, but this does not apply to possession of fur by a trapper or hunter during the open season and for 20 days thereafter, or by a fur buyer during the open season and 30 days thereafter (150.370). No person shall possess, take, pursue, or attempt to take or pursue or otherwise molest a deer, wild turkey or bear contrary to provisions of this chapter or regulations. No person shall use a dog to chase or molest deer. A conservation officer, peace officer, sheriff or constable may take steps to stop, prevent, or control any dog(s) found chasing or molesting deer (150.390).

★No person or group may deliberately cast the rays of a spotlight or other artificial light, with intent to poach, into a field, pasture, woodlands, or forest where wildlife or domestic livestock may be expected to be located. This section does not apply to: ▸ headlights of vehicles engaged in a normal course of travel; ▸ Department employees or agents on official business; ▸ peace officers in the line of duty; ▸ those engaged in legitimate agricultural activities; ▸ anyone involved in activities legitimate to the person's business, occupation, or circumstances including lawful hunting activities, or a landowner, immediate family, or paid employee working on the land. A violator shall be fined $300-1,000 (150.395).★

A trap set, used, or maintained in violation of the provisions below is subject to confiscation except that a trap set, used, or maintained without a required tag is declared contraband (150.399). ★★No person shall set, use or maintain for taking wildlife a steel trap unless the size and type of trap has been approved by regulation. The Commissioner may approve by regulation a commercially manufactured trap designed to take wildlife alive and unhurt or to kill instantly. Subject to provisions, it is lawful to use snares, deadfalls, wire cage or box traps, but no person shall set, use or maintain a snare large enough to take deer, elk or bear. A manufacturer designing a new trap may send to the Commissioner a sample for approval (150.400).★★ No person shall set, use, or maintain a trap for taking wildlife without a metal tag giving the person's name and address. Each person who sets a trap shall visit it at least once every 24 hours and remove wildlife. No person shall set a trap so as to endanger the life or safety of a domestic animal (150.410).

Restrictions on Taking: Fishing

★The open season and creel limit for taking rough fish by gigging, grabbing, snaring and snagging shall be prescribed by Department regulation (150.440).★ No person shall take fish other than by pole and line in hand, for 200 yards below a dam on or across a stream except as provided by regulation (150.445). The Department shall promulgate regulations governing taking minnows and crayfish, and prescribing the type of gear to be used and the minnows and crayfish that may be taken and their usedd [commercial fishing license and gear provisions detailed] (150.450).

★★No person, firm or corporation shall place or cause to be placed in public waters a substance that might injure, interfere with, or cause the waters to be unfit for support of wildlife. Such an act committed in the course of employment by an employee of a person, firm or corporation is prima facie evidence of the guilt of both the employee and the employer, and one or both may be punished as provided. Each day of violation is a separate offense.★★ Except for fish-finding devices, no person shall use, or attempt to use an electrical device such as a telephone, or electrical leads from a magneto, battery, motor, or other electrical equipment, in a stream or body of water. ★★No person shall place willfully or attempt to place in public waters a substance which has a poisonous or intoxicating effect upon wildlife. No person shall kill, injure, shock, or stun fish, or attempt to do so, using an explosive agent, firearm, or other device. These provisions do not apply to Department employees or agents acting in an official capacity (150.460). No person shall take or possess in one day more fish than the creel or possession limit prescribed, nor take or possess fish smaller than the size limit prescribed (150.470).

Commercial and Private Enterprise Provisions

A breeder may sell and transport live wildlife for propagation, and for food purposes, or minnows for bait, during seasons prescribed by the Commission. Such wildlife shall be identified either by marking the container or by individual tagging as the Commissioner may prescribe. No breeder shall sell wildlife not procured from a licensed propagation farm (150.290). No person shall: ► enter without the Commissioner's permission a propagation farm, game farm or game refuge or fish hatchery and take wildlife; ► enter a pond and take wildlife without the owner's consent, or foul its waters with a substance injurious to life or growth of wildlife, or destroy a dam, reservoir or embankment or divert the waters or willfully damage the farm or pond; ► go upon the premises of a propagation farm, state game farm, game refuge or fish hatchery with a dog while carrying firearms, except employees in the line of duty; ► mar, deface, destroy or damage, a sign or posted notice, or attempt same, on a game farm, game or wildlife refuge or fish hatchery (150.300).

Every licensed taxidermist shall keep a record for five years of each wildlife species mounted and the person for whom the mounting was done. Legally taken wildlife may be mounted, provided it bears identification until it is mounted. A fish and wildlife disposal permit must be attached to wildlife taken other than during a legally open hunting season. Such permit will substitute for the identification required in this section (150.411). A person may sell inedible parts of legally taken wildlife to a licensed taxidermist for mounting. A licensed taxidermist may buy or sell inedible parts of legally taken wildlife for mounting, except as prohibited by federal law. A licensed taxidermist may buy or sell a legally mounted specimen. Within 10 days after the end of each month, a licensed taxidermist shall send to the Department a report of each species purchased and name and address of the person from whom it was purchased (150.4111).

No commercial guide shall participate in taking wildlife protected by this chapter beyond the bag limit or creel limit. Every licensed fur buyer shall issue a receipt to the trapper or hunter from whom the buyer has purchased furs, setting forth the number and kind of furs, the date, the price and the trapper's or hunter's license. The buyer shall make out a duplicate receipt and obtain the signature and address of the trapper or hunter from whom the furs were purchased. Not later than March 15, every licensed fur buyer shall submit a complete report of all furs purchased, with total number and value of each type of fur. Failure to comply with this section shall bar the licensee from obtaining a license for the following year. Every licensed fur processor, within 15 days after January 1 and July 1, shall file with the Department an inventory of furs, and shall issue receipts for the number of furs purchased from fur buyers. Duplicates shall be sent to the Department with the inventory report. In a prosecution of a nonresident for buying raw fur without a buyer's license, proof that such person was in the company of a resident fur buyer at the time the latter purchased a raw fur is prima facie evidence of engaging in buying raw furs without a license (150.412, and .415 through .417).

No person shall sell live crayfish, mud eels, spring lizards, fish, aquatic invertebrates or amphibians for bait in taking fish, nor live fish for stocking or fishing without a live fish and bait dealer's license from the Department (150.485). On or before December 31 of the year in which a musseling license or mussel buyer's license is issued, the holder shall make a written report stating the total weight of mussel shells taken, the names and locations of the waters from which the mussels were taken and the amount received. Upon the failure to make a report, the Commissioner shall not issue another license until such report is made (150.510). The Department shall make regulations governing the taking of mussels. To prevent depletion of mussel beds and to insure propagation of mussels, the Department may close beds to operators during which time no one shall take mussels. When an order is issued closing a mussel bed, notice shall be published (150.520). No person may engage in buying mussel shells or mussels in the shell without a license (150.525) .

No person shall violate a law or regulations relating to licensed shooting or hunting preserves. An owner or operator who permits hunting on a licensed shooting preserve without the required license may have such license canceled or revoked by the Commissioner (150.630). A person may establish a pay lake subject to the approval of the Commissioner, who shall have authority to approve or reject the establishment of pay lakes and issue to the owners or lessees of lakes a license. All pay lakes shall be stocked at least twice per calendar year with not less than 500 adult fish per surface acre of water. When a pay lake is licensed, the Commissioner shall issue consecutively numbered permits, without cost, to pay lake patrons. No person, except those exempted in this chapter, shall fish in a licensed pay lake without possessing a valid special pay lake permit or a valid statewide fishing license. No owner or operator of a licensed pay lake shall allow a patron to fish who is not properly licensed or permitted. A pay lake licensee that fails to comply with laws or regulations may have the operator's license revoked (150.660). (See Licenses and Permits under this section.)

Import, Export and Release Provisions

No person shall import or receive shipment from outside the state live fish or wildlife without a written fish or wildlife transportation permit. If such fish or wildlife are not a menace and are free from disease and undesirable physical characteristics, the Commissioner shall issue a permit for a fee to be determined by the Commission by regulation, pursuant to Chapter 13A. A fish transportation permit shall be valid for one year, and a wildlife transportation permit shall be valid for dates indicated on the permit. No person may stock fish in public waters of the Commonwealth without a permit. This section does not interfere with transportation of fish or wildlife by authorized Department personnel. Federal and state regulations shall govern transportation of migratory wild birds (150.180).

See PROTECTED SPECIES OF WILDLIFE; and Commercial and Private Enterprise Provisions under this section.

Interstate Reciprocal Agreements

If a reciprocal agreement is entered into between the Commissioner, with the approval of the Commission, and ratified by the General Assembly and the similar authorities of Missouri, Tennessee, Virginia, West Virginia, Indiana, Ohio, or Illinois, holders of resident or nonresident fishing or hunting licenses issued in these states shall be permitted to perform the acts authorized by the license upon certain contiguous waters and land areas. A resident shall purchase a proper Kentucky license to conform with the reciprocal agreement (150.170). Kentucky cedes to the US criminal jurisdiction concurrent with that of Kentucky, solely for the purposes of section 13 of Title 18 of the United States Code and enforcement proceedings pursuant thereto, over those portions of Trigg and Lyon Counties that lie within the boundaries of the Kentucky portion of Land Between The Lakes [specifically described] (150.680).

ANIMAL DAMAGE CONTROL

Notwithstanding other provisions, the Commissioner, with the approval of the Commission, may authorize conservation officers or other persons to destroy or to control a wild animal, fish or wild bird, protected or unprotected which is causing damage to persons, property or other animals, fish or birds or spreading diseases (150.105).

Upon adoption of a resolution by the fiscal court that beaver exist within a county in quantities that present a threat to the preservation of farmland, trees, and other property, the fiscal court may request the Department to pay a bounty on beaver. Upon receipt of the resolution, a bounty on each beaver of $10 shall be paid in the following manner. For the tail of a beaver, a conservation officer shall issue a receipt to the presenter. The Department shall redeem the receipts by paying $10 for each receipt. The redemption of receipts shall be paid only from funds especially appropriated, and it is expressly provided that no bounty shall be paid from regular receipts, funds, or appropriations of the Department. The Department may charge a maximum of $1 against the appropriation for bounties for each bounty paid as reimbursement for administering the bounty program. No bounty shall be paid when funds, personnel, or equipment of a governmental unit are used in capturing and killing beaver. Upon receipt of an adopted resolution from a fiscal court stating that beaver no longer present a threat to property within the county, the Department shall cease paying the bounty (150.425).

ENFORCEMENT OF WILDLIFE LAWS

Enforcement Powers

Conservation officers appointed by the Commissioner shall have full powers as peace officers for enforcement of state laws, except that they shall not enforce laws other than this chapter and its administrative regulations or serve process unless so directed by the Commissioner in life threatening situations or when assistance is requested by another law enforcement agency. The Commissioner may appoint other persons to enforce only the provisions of this chapter and regulations. Such persons shall have the power to make arrests or issue citations only for violations of this chapter and its regulations. All other peace officers and their deputies shall enforce the provisions of this chapter and its regulations. Persons charged with enforcement of this chapter and regulations shall have the right to go upon private or public land for conducting research or investigation of game or fish or habitat conditions or engage in restocking game or fish, or work incident to game and fish restoration projects or their enforcement, or enforcement of laws or orders of the Department. They may enter upon, cross over, be upon, and remain upon privately owned lands for such purposes, and shall not be subject to arrest for trespass, and may arrest on sight, without warrant, a person detected violating the provisions of this chapter. They shall have the same rights as sheriffs to require aid in arresting with or without process a person found violating a provision of this chapter and may seize without process anything declared by this chapter to be contraband. No liability shall be incurred by a person charged or directed in the enforcement of this chapter. Conservation officers and other officers charged with enforcement of this chapter, shall have authority to call for and inspect the license or tag, bag or creel of a person engaged in an activity for which a license is required, and shall have authority to take proper identification of a person, hunter, fisherman who is actually engaged in any of these activities, and to call for and inspect firearms and devices that may be used in taking wildlife and is in the possession of a person so engaged. No person shall resist, obstruct, interfere with or threaten or attempt to intimidate or in any other manner interfere with an officer in the discharge of duties under provisions of this chapter. This subsection shall not apply to a criminal homicide or an assault upon such officer. An assault upon such officer shall be deemed an offense under Chapter 507 or 508 (150.090).

Conservation officers are authorized to keep and bear arms in the same manner as all other peace officers, and to use arms as necessary in the discharge of their duties. The Commissioner may authorize conservation officers and other Department personnel to use sirens and visible flashing lights on their vehicles (150.095). The Commissioner, all Department personnel and officers and other persons appointed by the Commissioner may execute a process issued by a court, enforcing the provisions of this chapter or a law relating to propagation or protection of fish and wildlife in the same manner as a constable or sheriff, and may call a peace officer or other person to their aid (150.100).

The Commissioner and conservation officers may arrest without warrant anyone violating the provisions or rules and regulations for protection of mussels. They may inspect mussels in a warehouse, boat, store, car or receptacle with good cause to believe that there has been a violation. This authority does not include the right to enter a dwelling without a search warrant. When officers find mussels in the possession of anyone in violation of this chapter, they shall be confiscated and sold as provided for sale of confiscated wildlife (150.110). The Commissioner, conservation officers, persons appointed by the Commissioner, and peace officers and their deputies shall seize all furs, wildlife, guns, dogs, instruments, boats or devices which have been taken, used, transported or possessed contrary to a law or regulation adopted under this chapter. Upon complaint showing probable cause for believing protected wildlife is kept illegally in a building, car or receptacle, a court having jurisdiction may issue a search warrant and cause same to be searched. Wildlife, furs, guns, dogs, instruments, or devices seized in accordance with this section shall be impounded by the arresting officer and taken before the court trying the person arrested. Upon conviction, the court shall have the discretion of determining whether items seized shall be declared contraband. Any wildlife, fur or dog taken, and a device used or possessed contrary to the provisions of this chapter or regulations, is subject to being declared contraband. When so declared, the court shall enter an order accordingly. A copy of the order shall be forwarded to the Commissioner and contraband placed in the custody of the arresting officer, to be delivered to the Commissioner. The Commissioner may sell to residents, at the highest market price obtainable, with approval of the Governor and the finance and administration cabinet all contraband under the order of a court, or which has been seized and declared to be contraband under a law relating to fish or wildlife. All proceeds shall be paid into the game and fish fund. A record of the sale, including the purchaser and the price paid, shall be kept by the Commissioner. A device or contrivance, which is not expressly recognized and sanctioned by the provisions of this chapter for taking wildlife, is an illegal device. No person shall possess an illegal device or other thing prohibited by law or regulation adopted under this chapter (150.120). All county attorneys and commonwealth's attorneys shall enforce the provisions of this chapter and regulations adopted hereunder (150.130).

★Each circuit clerk responsible for the court before whom a prosecution, may be commenced or shall go on appeal, within 10 days after the end of each month, shall report in writing to the Commissioner the result of the prosecution, the amount of fine collected or penalty imposed. Fines or penalties go to the game and fish fund (150.140).★

Criminal Penalties

Each bird, fish, or animal taken, possessed, bought, sold, or transported and each device used or possessed contrary to the provisions of this chapter or regulation adopted by the Commission is a separate offense. A violator of the provisions of this chapter or regulations, in addition to the penalties provided in this section, may forfeit the license, or if that person is license exempt, may forfeit the privilege authorized by the license, and shall not be permitted to purchase another license during the same license year. ★No fines, penalty, or judgment assessed or rendered under this chapter shall be suspended, reduced, or remitted other than expressly provided by law.★ A violator of a regulation which has been or may be adopted by the Commission under provisions of this chapter is subject to the same penalty as is provided for the violation of provisions of this chapter. Violation of provisions relating to propagation of wildlife; taking birds; ferrets; traps; tagging traps; fur buyers; fur processing; waterfowl stamps; entry on land; licenses; migratory birds; fish creel and size limits, or provisions or regulations of this chapter adopted by the Commission for which no penalty is fixed, is a fine of $25-200. Violation of provisions relating to breeder sale and transportation of wildlife; poaching; taking a dog or gun upon a propagation farm, refuge or hatchery or defacing signs; bag and creel limits; restrictions on taking wildlife; types of guns; discharge of weapon from a vehicle or across a public road; taking fish near dams; required fish and bait dealer's license; taking of waterfowl; licensed shooting or hunting preserves; pay lakes; taking of minnow or crayfish; possession and creel limit for fish; and establishment of pay lakes is a fine of $25-200, or jail up to 6 months, or both. Also, a violator of provisions of 150.300 relating to hunting on propagation farms, refuges or hatcheries, damaging property thereon, taking a dog or gun or defacing signs thereon, shall be assessed treble damages as provided in 150.690 or 150.700, relating to wrongful entry of an elk, buffalo or deer park or enclosed ground, or hunting or killing thereon; or damaging private ponds. Violation of sections 150.190, 150.411, 150.412, or 150.417 relating to conservation officers; taxidermy records and mounting; restrictions on guide taking; or nonresident accompanying fur buyers, is a fine of $100-500 (150.990).

Violations relating to importing, possessing or transporting endangered species; possession of wildlife or raw fur out of season; use of fire or other unlawful means to take; open seasons; taking, transporting and selling migratory birds; use of another's license; nonresident licenses; or possession of revoked licenses is a fine of $100-500, or jail up to

6 months, or both. Violation of provisions relating to use of illegal devices, is a fine of $100-500, or jail up to 6 months, or both. In addition, a violator is liable for an amount necessary to restock fish or replenish wildlife killed or destroyed. Violation of provisions of 150.180, 150.510, 150.520, 150.525, or regulations relating to buying, selling or transporting protected wildlife; reports, regulation and licensing of musseling is as follows: ▸ first offense, a fine of $100-1,000; ▸ second offense, a fine of $500-1,500; ▸ subsequent offense, a fine of $2,000. Violation of provisions relating to mussels or regulations thereunder, if it relates to methods of taking mussels, is punishable by jail for: ▸ a first offense, up to 30 days; ▸ a second offense, up to 6 months; ▸ a subsequent offense no, more than 1 year. Violation of 150.4111, 150.640, or (2) or (3) of 150.450 relating to sale of illegally taken wildlife; depredation while hunting; or use, operation and possession of fishing gear is a fine of $100-1,000. Violation of provisions of 150.390, or subsection (3) of 150.092, relating to restrictions on hunting deer, turkey or bear; or entry on land without consent, is a fine of $100-1,000, or jail 30 days-1 year, or both. In addition, the violator shall forfeit the license or, if license exemption, the privileges authorized by the license for 1-3 years and shall be liable in an amount reasonably necessary to replace a deer, wild turkey, or bear taken in violation of 150.390 and subsection (3) of 150.092 and shall be liable to the landowner or occupant for reasonable compensation for damages. Violations of provisions of 150.090 relating to conservation offers, other than a criminal homicide or assault against an officer enforcing the provisions of this chapter or regulations shall be guilty of a Class A misdemeanor. A person who commits a criminal homicide or an assault against an officer enforcing the provisions or regulations of this chapter shall be subject to the penalties specified for such offense under Chapter 507 or 508, as appropriate. A person shall be guilty of a Class B misdemeanor upon the first violation of 150.710, relating to hunter harassment. A subsequent violation shall be a Class A misdemeanor (150.990).

Civil Penalties

A person who wrongfully breaks or enters a park or other enclosed grounds used for keeping deer, elk or buffalo, or hunts, drives, chases, takes out, maims or kills a deer, elk or buffalo, in addition to any other penalty, also shall pay to the person aggrieved treble damages sustained (150.690). A person who breaks or cuts down, cuts out or destroys a head or dam of a pool, pond, moat, slew, stagnet or pit wherein fish are or will be put or stored by the owner or person in possession, in addition to any other penalty, shall pay the party aggrieved treble damages sustained (150.700).

License Revocations and Suspensions

See Criminal Penalties under this section.

HABITAT PROTECTION

The Commissioner, with approval of the Commission, may contract with a landowner for a specified term of years, to set aside and maintain land as a game refuge. The Commissioner may issue permits for public or commercial shooting areas, and shall adopt regulations governing same (150.240). The Department, with approval from the secretary of the finance and administration cabinet and the Governor, may enter into a contract with the US, or a department or agency, or individual for the preservation, protection and propagation of wildlife (150.250).

To encourage and develop public interest in wildlife and carry out the policy of Chapter 150, the Commission is authorized to acquire lands by purchase, condemnation or lease from the State Property and Buildings Commission or others, and to establish, maintain and operate public shooting and fishing grounds and related recreational facilities, and to pay for such purchase or condemnation, maintenance and operation expenses, and may use funds available for that purpose. The payments under each lease may be secured by a pledge and made from the funds under control of the Department including the Game and Fish Fund, as may be provided and specified in the lease. The Commissioner, with approval of the Commission may sublease lands and improvements acquired under this chapter for agricultural and for any purpose incidental or beneficial to the maintenance and operation of the balance of the lands and improvements. The Commission may impose and enforce special regulations in the maintenance and operation of the facilities and lands acquired and charge rates deemed fair and reasonable for the use and participation of the public (150.620).

★The Department of Highways is authorized to construct fills, necessary for road construction, to impound water. The Department and the Department of Highways shall decide whether creation of a lake in any spot is reasonable and beneficial. The Department shall do everything necessary to insure good fishing and may regulate boating and other recreation. Interested local parties may obtain title to excess land required and deed it to the Commonwealth for creation of a public fishing lake (150.625).★ ★Areas controlled by the Department of Parks and designated as camping, hiking or other family oriented recreation areas are designated wildlife sanctuaries for affording protection to the wildlife natural, integrated, interrelated, ecological communities. No unauthorized person shall enter a wildlife sanctuary and take, damage, injure, kill, destroy or unduly disturb the wildlife except as provided. The Department may issue a permit for the scientific collection of wildlife provided the applicant for such permit holds a current state scientific collecting permit issued by the Department. This section does not apply to fish taken pursuant to chapter 150 and rules and regulations promulgated by the Department of Parks and the Department of Fish and Wildlife Resources. The Departments may cooperate to remove, destroy or disturb wildlife in the course of operating and administering the parks; and in so doing shall consider the ecological impact on the sanctuary as a whole (148.029).★

★[Chapter 146 provides for a Kentucky Nature Preserve System and a commission and fund to protect and preserve natural areas and features by acquiring real property for dedication as nature preserves. Chapter 146 also provides for a Heritage Land Conservation Fund for acquisition of land, in part for habitat for rare and endangered species and for migratory birds.]★

NATIVE AMERICAN WILDLIFE PROVISIONS: None.

LOUISIANA

Sources: Louisiana Statutes Annotated, 1987, Titles 36 and 56; 1992 Cumulative Annual Pocket Part.

STATE WILDLIFE POLICY

Ownership and title to wild birds, wild quadrupeds, fish and other aquatic life, the beds and bottoms of rivers, streams, bayous, lagoons, lakes, bays, sounds, and inlets bordering on or connecting with the Gulf of Mexico within the state, including oysters, shellfish and parts grown thereon, either naturally or cultivated, are and remain the property and in the title of the state, and shall be under the exclusive control of the Wildlife and Fisheries Commission except as provided and for the purpose of regulating and controlling the use and disposition thereof (56:3).

The Legislature finds: that it is the policy of this state to conserve wildlife for human enjoyment and scientific purposes, and to insure their perpetuation; that wildlife found to be threatened or endangered should be accorded protection to enhance their numbers; the state should assist in protection of threatened or endangered species pursuant to the Federal Endangered Species Act, as concurred in by the Commission, by prohibiting or regulating their taking, possession, transportation, exportation, processing, sale or offer for sale or shipment. Exceptions may be permitted for enhancing conservation. Funding for conservation may be made available to the Department by appropriations. Other sources may be utilized, and the Department may enter into agreements with the US, issue and promote the sale of endangered species stamps or utilize methods appropriate to accomplish this Part (56:1901).

RELEVANT WILDLIFE DEFINITIONS: See Definitions section of Appendices.

STATE FISH AND WILDLIFE AGENCIES

Agency Structure

Control and supervision of state wildlife, including aquatic life, is vested in the **Louisiana Wildlife and Fisheries Commission** (Commission), consisting of seven members appointed by the Governor, subject to Senate confirmation. Three members are electors of the coastal parishes and representatives of the commercial fishing and fur industries, and four are electors from the state at large and not from those industries. No member who has served six years or more is eligible for reappointment. The Commission's functions, duties, and responsibilities are provided by law (L.S.A. Const. Art. 9, sec. 7; also 36:601 and 56:1).

The **Department of Wildlife and Fisheries** (Department) controls and supervises all wildlife, including fish and aquatic life, and executes laws enacted for control and supervision of programs relating to the management, protection, conservation, and replenishment of state wildlife, fish, and aquatic life, and regulation of shipping of wildlife, fish, furs, and skins. The Department is responsible for conservation and management of renewable resources on wildlife management areas, wildlife refuges, scenic rivers, and wildlife preserves that it may own or lease; and shall exercise powers and functions as required by law. ★Leasing of nonrenewable state-owned resources is permissible on wildlife management areas, refuges, preserves and scenic rivers only with Department concurrence and after regulations have been adopted to minimize damages to fish and wildlife habitat.★ The Department is composed of the Executive Office of the Secretary, the Offices of Management and Finance, Wildlife, Fisheries, and other offices created by law. When the Secretary determines that administration may be performed more efficiently by eliminating, merging, or consolidating offices or establishing new offices, a plan shall be presented to the Legislature for approval by statute (36:602).

The **Secretary of Wildlife and Fisheries** (Secretary) is appointed by the Governor with Senate consent, who serves at the Governor's pleasure. The Secretary serves as executive head and chief administrative officer and has responsibility for Department policies, except as otherwise provided, and for administration, control, and operations, provided that the Secretary shall function under the general control and supervision of the Governor (36:604). A **Deputy Secretary** may be appointed by the Secretary with Senate consent, who serves at the Secretary's pleasure, with duties and functions determined by the Secretary (36:606). The **Undersecretary of the Department** is appointed by the Governor with Senate consent to serve at the Governor's pleasure, who directs the Office of Management and Finance within the Department, and is responsible for accounting and budget control, procurement and contract management, data processing, management and program analysis, personnel, and grants management for the Department. The Undersecretary shall exercise authority subject to the overall direction of the Secretary (36:607). Each office within the Department, except the Office of Management and Finance, is under immediate supervision and direction of an **Assistant Secretary**, appointed by the Governor with consent of the Senate, to serve at the pleasure of the Governor. Except as expressly provided, the duties and functions of each office and its Assistant Secretary are determined by and under the direct supervision of the Secretary (36:608).

The **Commission** is a policy-making and budgetary-control board, with no administrative functions. The Commission has authority to establish management programs and policies and to approve all contracts. It conducts studies and investigations, and formulates policies, plans, rules, regulations and proceedings. No appointed member may prescribe the conduct of the Commission or the Director or a subordinate member unless first authorized by the Board in a public meeting. The Commission shall not take any action except by vote in meeting, and shall hold an open meeting at least once each month (56:2).

Agency Powers and Duties

The **Secretary** shall: ▸ represent the public interest in the administration and be responsible to the Governor, the Legislature, and the public; ▸ determine Department policies, except as otherwise provided; ▸ make, alter, amend, and promulgate rules and regulations for administrative functions, except as otherwise provided; ▸ organize, plan, supervise, direct, administer, and execute Department functions and programs; ▸ advise the Governor on problems concerning administration; ▸ act as sole agent of the state, or designate one office within the Department or its Assistant Secretary to cooperate with the federal government and other agencies in matters of mutual concern and in the administration of federal funds; ▸ report annually to the Governor and the Legislature, including recommendations for effective structure and administration, upon request by the Governor, the Legislature, or any committee or member; ▸ provide for consolidation of agencies and functions transferred to the Department and report to the Governor and the Legislature. The report shall contain a statement of the reorganization and consolidation plan (36:605).

Except as provided, the Secretary has authority to: ▸ employ, appoint, remove, assign, and promote personnel for the executive office of the Secretary; ▸ appoint, subject to gubernatorial approval, advisory councils, boards, and commissions for Department administration; ▸ accept and use gifts, grants, bequests, and endowments and meet conditions for acceptance; ▸ enforce laws, rules and regulations relative to wildlife and fisheries, including illegal hunting, fishing, and trapping, boating safety regulations, and prohibited methods, times, or seasons, and locations, including illegal transportation, shipping, and sale of wildlife, fish, aquatic life, fur-bearing animals, and alligators, including illegal possession of same. Not less than 25 **wildlife agents** shall be appointed, whose entire time shall be devoted to performance of their official duties. Notwithstanding 40:5, the Secretary has authority to enforce laws specifically assigned to the Department of Health and Hospitals, and rules or regulations for harvesting, processing, or distribution of molluscan shellfish. The Secretary may appoint and remove special or cooperative officers, designated as special wildlife agents (36:605).

★★The Secretary may commission **auxiliary agents** to supplement the efforts of wildlife agents to protect the state's wildlife and fishery resources. At no time shall there be more than 50 active commissioned auxiliary agents. The Secretary shall develop procedures for implementing, administering, and managing the auxiliary law enforcement program directing that each auxiliary agent: ▸ perform under the supervision of a wildlife agent; ▸ be evaluated annually; ▸ perform duties at least 24 hours per month; ▸ provide for insurance coverage (56:69.3). Applicants shall be commissioned as **wildlife volunteers** while in training. Failure to attend and participate in training is grounds to revoke a volunteer commission. Training may be waived if the auxiliary agent was certified by the Louisiana Council on Peace Officer Standards and Training (POST), completes a refresher course, and passes the examination. No wildlife volunteer shall perform enforcement duties until successful completion of training. The Secretary shall develop training standards for the auxiliary program. Standards shall minimally include: ▸ fish and wildlife laws, regulations, and rules; ▸ firearms qualification; ▸ arrest, search, and seizure; ▸ use of force; ▸ officer survival; ▸ first aid; ▸ investigation and evidence; ▸ civil liability of peace officers; ▸ reports and court testimony (56:69.5).★★ [Details of Commission renewal provided in 56:69.7, and revocation of Commission outlined in 56:69.8.] A former wildlife enforcement agent who retired or left in good standing and maintained certification, or a peace officer who has maintained certification, may be commissioned as a reserve agent, and function as a wildlife agent (56:69.9).

The **Office of Wildlife** shall: ▸ be responsible for programs, including research, relating to wild birds, game, non-game species, threatened and endangered species, certain wildlife management areas and game preserves, including law enforcement, and river basin evaluations, including but not limited to recommending seasons, bag and possession limits, establishing rules and regulations for taking and protection of wild birds and game and non-game birds and protected quadrupeds, and regulation of persons who breed, propagate, sell, kill, or transport wild birds and wildlife; ▸ perform administration, operation, and law enforcement of programs, including research, related to the Louisiana Natural Areas Registry, natural and scenic rivers, water pollution control and prevention, review and monitoring of activities occurring in the coastal zone and wetland areas delegated to the Department; ▸ maintain and operate wildlife management areas, refuges, and sanctuaries, responsibilities to include law enforcement and administration of programs for research on marsh wildlife, including fur-bearing animals, alligators and waterfowl, and including licensing and payment of taxes by trappers, alligator hunters, commercial buyers, and dealers (36:609). The **Office of Fisheries** shall perform administration, operation, and law enforcement of programs relating to freshwater fisheries and other aquatic life, including regulation of sport and commercial fishing, domestic fish farming, noxious aquatic weed control, operation, maintenance, and management of fish hatcheries, fish preserves, and boat ramps (36:609). [Functions are described relating to saltwater fisheries, water bottoms and seafoods, in 36:609.]

The **Commission** may sue and be sued and exercise all authority and power prescribed by law for the prior Commissioner of Conservation and the Commissioner of Wildlife and Fisheries in relation to wildlife, including wild game and nongame quadrupeds or animals, game, oysters, fish, and other aquatic life. Any function or authority vested to prior Commissioners of Conservation and Wildlife and fisheries concerning resources under jurisdiction of the Director of the Wildlife and Fisheries Commission, and all records, equipment, funds, and assets relating to such resources, are transferred to the Wildlife and Fisheries Commission. The Commission shall adopt rules and regulations to protect natural resources other than fish and wildlife, especially such resources as standing trees otherwise protected by law but which have no provision for enforcing protection (56:5).

The Commission shall: ▸ have supervision and control over employees, and employ certified scientists to study the life, habits, and productivity of land and aquatic wildlife; ▸ represent the Commission and discharge the obligations and duties that were before upon the Conservation Commission, the Department of Conservation, the Commissioner of Conservation and the Department of Wildlife and Fisheries; ▸ collect, classify, and preserve such data and information as will promote this Part; ▸ make and execute all contracts; ▸ adopt bylaws for the Commission and its employees; ▸ adopt rules and regulations for the control of birds, shellfish, finfish, and wild quadrupeds; ▸ protect and propagate, when possible, all species of birds and game and establish, maintain and operate preserves and hatcheries; ▸ enforce laws relative to bedding, fishing, selling, shipping, and canning oysters, and to protection, propagation, and selling birds, game and fish; ▸ have full power and control over birds, animals, fish, diamond-back terrapins, shrimp, and oysters within the state or its waters; ▸ assist in protection of private fish ponds; ▸ protect and post state game preserves used for propagation or resting places of birds and game; ▸ assist in developing natural resources under the Commission's jurisdiction. The Commission may: ▸ employ an attorney to represent it; ▸ fix the compensation and pay expenses of Commission employees; ▸ acquire land in any wilderness area; ▸ submit a report annually to the Legislature on the red drum, including a biological profile of the species and stock assessment, a total allowable catch with probable allocation scenarios, and a recommendation as to whether game fish status should be continued (56:6).

On behalf of the Department and the state, the Secretary: ▸ may execute documents for property acquisition; ▸ shall promulgate rules and regulations for dredging of fill sand and fill material; ★▸ shall promulgate rules and regulations to set seasons, times, places, size limits, quotas, daily take, and possession limits, based upon biological and technical data, for wildlife and fish. Objectives shall be sound conservation, preservation, replenishment, and management of species for maximum continuing social and economic benefit. A season, time, place, size, quota, daily take or possession limit currently set by law shall be superseded upon promulgation of new rules and regulations concerning a particular species.★ Aquaculturally raised fish are exempt from these provisions. Penalties for violation shall be established by law. The authority to determine game fish or commercial status of a particular species shall be retained by the Legislature. This section shall not amend, supersede, or repeal any other provision of the law pertaining to fish (56:6). The Commission shall promulgate rules and regulations to allow the Secretary to close in an emergency a flooded area to the hunting of quadrupeds. A closure shall be effective upon issuance for not more than 14 days (56:6.1). The Commission is authorized to acquire by purchase, gift, eminent domain, or otherwise, property for its use; and funds from fishing license fees shall be for administration of the Divisions of Fish and Game and for protection, propagation, preservation, and investigation of fish and game (56:26 and :645).

The Commission is authorized to fix, approve, and adopt seasons, bag limits, and possession limits and to establish other rules and regulations for hunting, taking, possession, or protection of wild quadruped and wild birds. Rules and regulations shall have the same force and effect as statutory laws, and violation is a class two violation, unless a penalty is provided by some other provision. [Provisions are made for handicapped and disabled hunting seasons (56:115).] The Commission shall conduct scientific researches into the habits of nongame quadrupeds and, when practicable, give full publicity to such biological findings (56:264). Exclusive control of fish having a game or commercial value is vested in the Commission. The Department shall enforce provisions regulating them. Fish taken, possessed, or transported contrary to this Subpart shall be confiscated (56:313).

Agency Funding

The Commission shall report to the Governor annually on its operations, the amount and sources of money received, money expended and for what purposes, a proposed expenditures estimate, prospective revenues and recommendations for legislative action. At each regular session the Legislature shall appropriate funds for the Commission. Subject to the exception in Article VII, Section 9(A) of the Constitution, all funds collected by the Commission shall be credited to the **Bond Security and Redemption Fund**. After an amount is allocated to pay all obligations secured by the state, prior to placing remaining funds in the state general fund, the treasurer shall: ▸ pay annually into a **Wildlife Stamp Research Fund** funds specifically appropriated; ▸ pay into a **Conservation Fund** an amount equal to the total funds paid into the treasury by the Commission, except other funds herein; ▸ pay annually into a **Duck Stamp Fund** all amounts received pursuant to the Duck Stamp Program, and other funds appropriated by the Legislature. The Wildlife Stamp Research Fund shall be used for the programs associated with the wildlife stamp research program in amounts appropriated to the Commission. The Duck Stamp Fund shall be used solely for the programs associated with the Duck Stamp Program in amounts appropriated to the Department. The Commission shall keep accounting books. All unexpended and unencumbered moneys in the Wildlife Stamp Research Fund, the Duck Stamp Fund, and the Conservation Fund shall remain in the respective funds. The moneys shall be invested by the treasurer, and interest shall be deposited in the respective funds. The state treasurer shall report quarterly to the Department (56:10).

There is established the **Louisiana Wildlife and Fisheries Conservation Fund** (Conservation Fund). Out of the funds remaining in the Bond Security and Redemption Fund, after a sufficient amount is allocated to pay all obligations secured by the state, the treasurer shall pay into the Conservation Fund the following, except as provided in Article VII, Section 9(A), and except for the amount provided in 56:10(B)(1)(a) as that provision existed on the effective date of this section: ▸ all revenue from the types and classes of fees, licenses, permits, royalties, or other revenue; ▸ all funds or revenues donated expressly to the Conservation Fund. The moneys in the Conservation Fund shall be appropriated by the Legislature to the Department, or its successor, and shall be used solely for conservation, protection, preservation, management, and replenishment of the state's natural resources and wildlife, including land acquisition or federal matching fund programs and for the operation and administration of the Department and the Commission, or their successors (56:10).

★★To promote the wildlife and fisheries laws by providing monetary incentives for reporting information that aids in apprehension and prosecution of violators, to promote public involvement in stopping serious violations, to reduce the number of violators, and to create and maintain a reward fund for these purposes, the **Louisiana Help Our Wildlife Fund** (Fund) is created within the Department (56:70.2). The Fund shall be composed of: ▸ legislative appropriations; ▸ moneys paid as a cost levied on class violations as provided by 56:70.3(C); ▸ federal moneys available to the state for enforcement of anti-poaching laws. In addition to other costs imposed by law, and not withstanding any provision of law to the contrary, $5 for any class violation as provided in 56:31 through 56:37 is levied in each criminal action which results in conviction or a guilty plea. After complying with the requirements of the Bond Security and Redemption Fund, the treasurer annually shall pay the same amount of funds as was paid into the state treasury pursuant to 56:70.3 into the Fund. Funds shall be used solely for the purposes set forth in this Subpart and in amounts appropriated each year by the Legislature; unexpended and unencumbered moneys at fiscal year end shall remain in the Fund to be invested by the treasurer, and interest shall be deposited therein. The Fund may be used solely for: ▸ rewards for information leading to the arrest and conviction of poachers; ▸ a promotional and educational campaign to inform the general public of the harm and danger of poaching; ▸ toll free telephone numbers; ▸ expenses to implement these provisions. The Secretary or designee shall determine which informants are to be granted rewards, specify reward amounts ranging from $200-1,000, and direct payment from the Fund. No amount in excess of that available in the Fund is payable, and no reward may be granted to a person who is, or an immediate family member of, a peace officer, game warden, prosecutor, Department employee, or member of the judiciary (56:70.3 and :70.4). ★★

The **Wildlife Stamp Research Program** is created to fund wildlife research, and shall be administered by the Secretary or a designee, assisted by an advisory council. An artist shall be selected to create a wildlife stamp and print, with sale proceeds used for wildlife research (56:91). The selection process shall not restrict entrants by residence. The stamp shall be purchased on a voluntary basis. The Department shall have exclusive stamp ownership and production rights; the reproduction, distribution, and marketing of the wildlife print is the responsibility of the artist with a minimum royalty per print guaranteed to the state. The Department shall determine price and royalty per print (56:94). Start-up funding shall derive from legislative appropriations. The Secretary may receive funds from other sources, public or private. After sales of the first wildlife research stamp and print, moneys for the program shall derive from the Wildlife Stamp Research Fund. Stamp Fund moneys shall be used solely for administrative costs of implementation of the stamp research program and financing wildlife research projects and programs (56:96).

★Ten percent of fees from the sale of hunting licenses shall be dedicated to development and preservation of breeding grounds for migratory waterfowl, the funds to be expended through Ducks Unlimited, Inc. or at the Commission's discretion. An additional 10% of each such fee shall be dedicated to development and rejuvenation of the quail, dove, and rabbits populations, the funds to be expended through a rejuvenation program. Not less than 25% of the funds from hunting license fees shall be deposited monthly into the Wildlife Habitat and Natural Heritage Trust, as provided for in 56:1923, and shall be expended solely for land acquisition for wildlife management areas, including lands for upland game purposes (56:104). ★

To protect and preserve the hunting of migratory waterfowl, the **Louisiana Duck Stamp Program** is created for funding approved projects through sale of the duck stamp and print. No person between age 16 and 60 shall hunt migratory waterfowl without a duck stamp. The Department shall issue signed duck stamps, provide the stamp form and design, and the manner for artist selection. The Department shall provide for the reproduction, distribution, and marketing of prints of the duck stamp design and may use a contracted publisher. Such contract shall not exceed three years with a three-year renewal option. Minimum royalties shall be guaranteed to each artist whose work is selected in accordance with regulations. After costs are paid, remaining moneys shall be paid into the Duck Stamp Fund (56:150 through :153). Funds received from sale of stamps and prints shall be placed in the Duck Stamp Fund. Subject to appropriation, moneys shall be used to: ▸ acquire lands for conserving, restoring, and enhancing migratory waterfowl habitat; ▸ carry out migratory waterfowl habitat restoration and enhancement projects on Department lands; ▸ accomplish the above when feasible and when in coastal areas, to contribute to the protection of coastal areas and enhance the productivity of coastal marshes; ▸ acquire lands for wildlife and game management. Moneys may be used to: ▸ make grants, not to exceed 10% of program revenues, to the North American Waterfowl Habitat Conservation Plan for acquiring, developing, or maintaining migratory waterfowl; ▸ cover administrative costs of the Duck Stamp Program, not to exceed 5% of revenues. The Department may negotiate a reciprocal agreement with a neighboring state, if that state has a similar duck stamp requirement and fee, which may permit a resident of that state to hunt migratory waterfowl in Louisiana without a Louisiana duck stamp if the person possesses a reciprocal waterfowl stamp. A violator of these provisions is subject to a class one violation (56:155 through :157).

★★Recognizing that the fur and alligator industry is vital to Louisiana's coastal economic base; that fur markets and prices have been depressed creating hardships for trappers, coastal landowners, fur buyers, and fur dealers; that world trends question consumptive utilization of wildlife; that these conditions can impact the industry; that trapping of certain species is the only means effectively to manage coastal wetlands and protect adjacent agriculture; that the state alligator industry is growing; and that research must be conducted; the Legislature establishes the **Louisiana Fur and Alligator Public Education and Marketing Fund**. Goals are to: ▸ educate the public about trapping as a wildlife management tool and about fur-bearing species and alligators as renewable resources; ▸ identify the consumers of products, marketing problems, obstacles, and other issues; ▸ strengthen and develop markets; ▸

develop an international advertising campaign; ▸ make recommendations concerning the industry; ▸ enhance the industry; ▸ make recommendations regarding the Alligator Resource Fund (56:266).★★

★★Recognizing that the alligator industry is vital to Louisiana's economic base and that markets and prices have expanded recently, the Department has provided the impetus for the alligator conservation program. Recognizing the influence of crocodilian conservation worldwide, the world trends questioning the consumptive use of wildlife species, and recognizing the need to educate the public, to support research and development, and to provide adequate personnel, the **Louisiana Alligator Resource Fund** is established in the Wildlife and Fisheries Conservation Fund to help fund alligator programs within the Department's Fur and Refuge Division. The goals of the Fund are to: ▸ provide technical and non-technical positions; ▸ assist law enforcement activities for the alligator farm industry ▸ assist marketing; ▸ fund research and enhance the industry; ▸ fund proper management. Revenues from tag fees and other alligator related fees shall be credited to the Alligator Resource Fund from the Bond Fund. Out of funds remaining in the Bond Security and Redemption Fund, the treasurer shall pay into the Louisiana Alligator Resource Fund an amount equal to the revenues generated from other sources. The Department shall report to the Legislature each fiscal year, with a summary of revenues received, expenditures made, and achievement of goals (56:279).★★

Proceeds from recreational licenses issued are dedicated to the Conservation Fund and are for maintaining fish hatcheries, sanctuaries, and law enforcement [saltwater finfish references] except that proceeds from freshwater trout licenses are for management of the freshwater trout program by the Freshwater Fish Division (56:301.7). To enforce conservation laws, rules and regulations of the Commission in operation and development of wildlife management areas, wildlife refuges, public shooting grounds and outdoor recreation areas, revenues from trapping leases, fur sales, mineral leases or mineral resources are to be used (56:631). Recognizing the importance of conserving wildlife resources, and the desires of citizens to make a lifetime contribution to preserve wildlife resources for future generations, the Legislature establishes the Lifetime License Endowment Program [details provided] (56:649 through :650.1).

The Commission is authorized to issue and promote the sale of endangered species commemorative stamps. Proceeds from sales shall be deposited in the **Endangered Species Fund** (56:1906).

Agency Advisory Boards

The **Little River Commission**, the **Louisiana Artificial Reef Development Council**, and the **Louisiana Fur and Alligator Advisory Council** are within the Department and shall exercise and perform powers, duties, functions, and responsibilities in the manner provided for agencies transferred in accordance with this title (36:610).

★★The **Louisiana Fur and Alligator Advisory Council** is created within the Department to approve programs for the Fur and Alligator Public Education and Marketing Fund and the Alligator Resource Fund. Appointees shall represent a cross section of trappers, alligator hunters, coastal landowners, and alligator farmers. Members shall serve four-year terms. Revenues from trapper and alligator hunter licenses are credited to the Bond Security and Redemption Fund. After allocation to pay all obligations, $20 of each $25 trapping and alligator license is credited to the Louisiana Fur and Alligator Public Education and Marketing Fund. At the end of the calendar year, the Department of Wildlife and Fisheries shall report to the Legislature a summary of revenues, expenditures, and goals achieved (56:266).★★

PROTECTED SPECIES OF WILDLIFE

The Commission may prohibit taking any species of fish for not more than three years (56:22).

The Department is authorized to conserve resident species of wildlife, and state or federal threatened or endangered species, and to formulate conservation programs for review by the Secretary of Interior. The Department is authorized to conduct investigations relating to populations, distribution, habitat needs, limiting factors and other biological, economic, and ecological data to determine conservation measures necessary for wildlife to sustain themselves successfully. The Commission may issue regulations to assist the continued ability of wildlife to perpetuate themselves. The Commission may establish programs, including acquisition of land or aquatic habitat or interests therein, for conservation of threatened or endangered species (56:1903). A species determined by the

Secretary to be endangered or threatened pursuant to the Federal Endangered Species Act shall be deemed to be endangered or threatened under the provisions of this Part. In addition, the Commission may determine whether any species in this state is endangered or threatened because of any of the following: ▸ the present or threatened destruction, modification or curtailment of its habitat or range; ▸ overutilization; ▸ disease or predation; ▸ inadequacy of existing regulatory mechanisms; ▸ other natural or man-made factors. The Secretary may make determinations based on the best scientific, commercial, and other data available after consultation with federal or state agencies, other states, and interested persons and organizations. The Secretary may not add nor remove species unless the Secretary has first published a notice and allowed at least 30 days for comment. Where an emergency exists involving the existence of such species as a viable component of the state's wildlife, the Department may add the species if it has published a public notice of the emergency situation (56:1904).

In determining whether a species is endangered or threatened, the Department shall take into consideration those actions carried out by the federal government, other states, other state agencies or political subdivisions, or by any other person. The Commission may issue a list of all endangered or threatened species, and over the portion of range it is so declared. Except with respect to the Federal Endangered Species Act, the Commission may conduct a review of listed or unlisted species proposed to be removed from or added to the lists, but only if it publishes a public notice that substantial evidence warrants a review. If a species is listed, the Commission shall issue regulations to provide for its conservation. With respect to any endangered species, except as provided, it is unlawful to: ▸ export or take such species; ▸ possess, process, sell or offer for sale, deliver, carry, transport or ship such species; ▸ violate a regulation adopted pursuant to this section provided that an endangered species which enters and is being transported beyond this state may do so without restriction under federal or other state permit. The Department may issue permits for any act otherwise prohibited for scientific purposes, regulated taking, or to enhance the propagation or survival of the affected species. Any law, regulation or ordinance of a state political subdivision is void to the extent that it may not permit what is prohibited, or prohibit what is authorized pursuant to an exemption or permit by this Part. This Part shall not be construed to void any law, regulation or ordinance of any state political subdivision intended to conserve wildlife (56:1904). These provisions shall not: ▸ apply retroactively; ▸ prohibit lawful importation of wildlife into the US; ▸ apply to wildlife lawfully taken and removed from another state; ▸ prohibit lawful entry into this state, or possession, transportation, exportation, processing, sale or offer for sale or shipment of wildlife endangered or threatened in this state but not in the state where taken it was lawfully taken and removed. This section does not apply to species listed pursuant to the Federal Endangered Species Act, except as permitted (56:1905). Violation of provisions regarding processing, delivery, carrying, transportation or shipment of threatened or endangered species is a class four violation. Failure to procure a permit or violation of permit terms is a class six violation (56:1907).

GENERAL EXCEPTIONS TO PROTECTION

The Director may take, or write permits to take, fish for science and cultivation and distribution, and permit fish to be introduced into any waters. After a hearing, the Director may set apart for ten years or less waters for propagation or for the USFW (56:17). Upon petition of the governing authority of a parish, the Director may stock fish best suited to such waters, and prescribe and enforce fishing regulations for not more than three years (56:21).

The Department may issue to a public park, museum, educational or scientific institution, or federal or state government, or scientist or responsible person, a permit to take, possess, and transport within and from this state wild birds or the plumage, skins, nests, eggs, or young and wild quadrupeds, their skins or young, for scientific, educational, experimental, or breeding purposes. The permittee is obligated to deliver within 60 days after taking, and before removal from the state, a detailed inventory of the wild birds, wild quadrupeds, and other things taken (56:105). No person shall take a wild bird or quadruped imported by the state or federal government or by a person for experimentation or propagation except under supervision and consent of the Secretary (56:113). The Department may take or issue permits to take, during open or closed season, fish for scientific or educational purposes and for propagation and distribution. The Department shall have the authority to regulate importation or introduction of live fish or fish eggs, and to regulate goldfish and aquarium fish. No person shall introduce live fish or fish eggs without a permit (56:318). (See also Import, Export and Release Provisions under HUNTING, FISHING AND TRAPPING PROVISIONS.)

HUNTING, FISHING, TRAPPING PROVISIONS

General Provisions

★To protect wild birds and quadrupeds and to prevent destruction of feeding and breeding grounds, no person willfully shall set fire to a wild woodland, marshland, or prairie land. This does not apply to a landowner setting fires to clear or prepare enclosed land for agricultural or pastoral purposes or for improving food conditions for wildlife. Burning shall not be done during the wild bird breeding season (56:107).★ The governing authority of a parish may apply for the right to close or curtail the open season for up to one year, so that the game bird or quadruped may restock by natural breeding (56:114).

No person shall sell or offer to sell, or purchase, a game quadruped, or part, or a wild bird, or the plumage, aigrettes, skin, or body. Each sale, offer, or purchase of each animal or part is a separate offense. The sale of legally taken deer hides to licensed fur buyers and dealers is allowed if within ten days of the deer season end. Fur buyers shall dispose of deer hides within 30 days of season close. A dealer possessing deer hides after the close of the season shall file a complete report within 30 days, and at 60-day intervals thereafter. Violation by selling, offering to sell, or purchasing wild deer is a class three violation. Violation of the provisions of 56:124 is a class two violation. The sale of tails or hides of legally taken squirrels to licensed fur buyers, dealers, and other buyers is allowed if within ten days of end of the squirrel hunting season. Fur buyers shall dispose of squirrel tails or hides within 30 days of the close of the season [details of reports required]. No person shall: ▸ possess a wild quadruped, game bird or part, or disturb or destroy a nest, egg, or young, except as expressly provided; ▸ possess a wild game quadruped or wild game bird in a manner contrary to 56:104 or 56:171 through 56:181; ▸ possess illegally taken bear, deer, or turkey; ▸ possess between the place taken and the domicile of the possessor more than the game limit unless such is properly tagged. Violation is a class two violation, except possession of illegally taken bear, deer, or turkey is a class four violation. No person shall take or hunt fur-bearing animals at night with artificial light, except licensed hunters with dogs may hunt raccoons or opossums at night with lights [limits on firearms set]. Farmers may hunt raccoons or opossums with a .22 caliber rifle if such are destroying crops (56:124).

Licenses and Permits

A person dealing in wildlife, fish, and game in a territory for which a license is required must possess a license. The Assistant Secretary and employees of the Office of Forestry, the Secretary, commissioned wildlife agents, commissioned wildlife employees of divisions other than enforcement, the various sheriffs, deputy sheriffs, constables, deputy constables, marshals, and other police officers may without warrant arrest a person violating any of the laws or regulations and immediately take the person into custody and serve and execute a warrant or other process issued by an officer or court (56:54). A license is required to hunt, take, possess, or cause to be transported a wild bird or wild quadruped [provisions made for special big game licenses and muzzleloader licenses]. A license shall be effective during the open season, and shall not be assigned or transferred to, or used by, another person. ★Every officer authorized shall take a violator's license and deliver it to be canceled (56:103).★ In addition to all other licenses, a special bow license is authorized for hunting during bow hunting season (56:105).

[Dog field trials are provided for in 56:106.]

★Upon conviction under a provision governing the hunting or taking of wild birds or wild quadrupeds, other than by trapping, the court, in addition to any fine or penalty, may order the offender to participate in a firearm and hunter education course (56:699).★ No person born on or after September 1, 1969, shall procure a hunting license without a certificate of satisfactory completion of an approved firearm and hunter education course (56:699.1).

General Fishing License Provisions

Persons taking fish recreationally or commercially, and persons involved in the fish industry must be licensed and must show such license upon demand. Violation: class one violation. Licenses are not transferable and violation causes cancellation (56:301.1). A recreational fishing license is required to use: ▸ hook and line; ▸ bow and arrow; ▸ barbless spear; ▸ a castnet with a radius not to exceed six feet; ▸ frog gigs or catchers; ▸ scuba gear. Taking fish for sale or in excess of a recreational limit requires a commercial fisherman's license, commercial gear license, and vessel license if applicable. A person fishing recreationally for freshwater trout in a designated area must have a freshwater trout license to possess such. The Department shall post signs around areas designated for freshwater trout fishing (56:302). Violation of 56:302 is a class three violation (56:308).

The Commission shall adopt rules to regulate the taking of mullet, including zones, seasons, permits, fees, and other provisions (56:333). Residents, nonresidents and foreign corporations are prohibited from seining for and catching menhaden or other species not ordinarily used for human consumption, to be transported out of state for rendering and processing, unless that state offers the same privilege to Louisiana residents (56:339).

Restrictions on Taking: Hunting and Trapping

During the open season, a licensee may possess no more than the two-day bag limit of migratory and resident game birds. Such fact is prima facie evidence of violation. Without a special permit, no licensee shall transport, cause or attempt to transport, or deliver for transportation game birds beyond the state. A nonresident licensee may take beyond state limits an aggregate of no more than the two-day bag limit. No common carrier or agent shall receive for transport any migratory or resident game birds without tags (56:117). Except as provided, no person shall possess a migratory or resident game bird other than during open season. Legal limits of game birds and quadrupeds may be possessed during the closed season, if legally taken during open season (56:119). [Requirements for storage and warehousing of game birds and quadrupeds are in 56:120.] Except as otherwise provided, a trap, cage, snare, net, or device may not be used for taking wild birds. Such devices may be confiscated and destroyed and wild birds found may be liberated. Blackbirds destroying crops on private property may be trapped by the property owner (56:121). No person shall use a hook or set a trap with teeth for taking wild quadrupeds, except alligators may be taken with hook and line (56:121.1). No person, other than the owner, shall kill, wound, catch, or possess, living or dead, a banded racing pigeon. Violation: $25-100 fine; or jail for 10-30 days; or both (56:122).

[Open season dates for various game species are fixed in 56:123.] The Commission may declare closed seasons or restrict hunting in the interest of wildlife management. The open season for migratory game birds, the bag limit and other rules and regulations shall conform to federal regulations under the US-Great Britain treaty. No person shall take a greater number of migratory game birds than specified under federal and state regulations. Game and outlaw quadrupeds and birds may be taken in open season with or without dogs except on state-owned or leased wildlife management areas or refuges [except where prohibited and only at certain times and with certain equipment] (56:123).

The Commission may establish special bow and arrow and muzzleloader deer hunting seasons [details provided]. Violation: class three violation. Hunting or taking of turkeys from one-half hour after official sunset to one-half hour before official sunrise, or hunting or taking of illegal deer, turkeys, or bear in open season shall be punishable as follows: first offense, fine of $500-1,000, or jail up to 90 days, or both; second offense, fine of $1,000-1,600, and jail of 60-90 days; third offense, fine of $1,500-2,000, and jail 90-120 days. The above penalties for the second and third offenses include forfeiture of anything seized in connection with the violation. Violation of taking of deer, turkeys, or bear in closed season shall be punishable as follows: first offense, fine of $1,000-1,500, or jail up to 120 days, or both; second offense, fine of $1,500-6,000, and jail of 90-180 days; third offense, fine of $2,000-10,000, and jail of 180 days to 2 years. The above penalties in all cases shall include forfeiture of anything seized in connection with the violation. Violation by hunting or taking of deer from one-half hour after official sunset to one-half hour before official sunrise shall be punishable as follows: first offense, fine of $1,500-2,000, or jail up to 120 days, or both; second offense, fine of $2,000-6,500, and jail of 90-180 days; third offense, fine of $2,500-10,500, and jail of 180 days-2 years. The above penalties in all cases shall include forfeiture of anything seized in connection with the violation and the person may lose all hunting privileges for a period not more than five years. Violation by hunting rabbits at illegal times of day: first offense, fine of $25-250, or jail of 30 days, or both; second offense, fine of $100-400, or jail of 30-60 days, or both; third offense, fine of $200-500, or jail up to 90 days. Violation by hunting or taking of wild game animals, migratory or resident wild game birds or protected animals other than deer or turkey, shall result in fine or jail, or both, as prescribed in 56:139 (56:123).

No person shall: ▸ hunt deer on or across a highway or road right of way, or stand, loiter, hunt, or shoot game quadrupeds or birds on such; ▸ hunt or take game quadrupeds or game birds from a moving land vehicle or aircraft; ▸ take swimming deer while the person is in a boat with motor in operating position; ▸ take or possess spotted fawn or parts, except as provided. Antlerless deer may be taken only in accordance with and subject to Commission rules and regulations. No person shall: ▸ take or kill a wild game quadruped or wild game bird with a firearm fitted with a silencer, or infrared or electrically operated sight, a night vision device, or an automatic loading or hand operated repeating shotgun [details provided for requiring shotgun be plugged]; ▸ take or kill a wild game quadruped or bird with archery equipment with an infrared or laser sight or similar sighting device; ▸ take or kill, during the open season, a greater number of birds, or animals than specified in rules and regulations; ▸ sell wild rabbits taken in the state. The sale of wild rabbits and hares brought into the state shall not be prohibited; however, the seller must produce an invoice, bill of lading, or express receipt, upon request, and failure is prima facie evidence that they were taken in Louisiana. Each taking in excess of the limit or in closed season is a separate offense (56:124).

There shall be no bag limit during the open trapping season; however, the Commission shall establish a bag limit otherwise. No person shall pelt or sell skins or carcasses taken during the open season without a license for trapping and hunting. Carcasses of raccoons and opossums taken the last day of season may be pelted or sold on the next day. It shall be legal for a licensed hunter to take raccoon or opossum during daylight hours during the open squirrel season, but not from a boat or vehicle. Violation: class two violation. ★No person shall take a rabbit or game quadruped behind a rail or other object driven or pulled by a vehicle. Violation: class two violation. ★ No person shall hunt with firearms or with bows and arrows from one-half hour after sunset to one-half hour before sunrise. This shall not affect night hunting of raccoons or opossums. Violation shall be punished as follows: first offense, fine of $75-200; second offense, fine of $150-350; third or subsequent offense, fine of $250-500, and jail for 30 days. No person shall hunt, trap, or take turkey by baiting. "Baiting" shall mean placing, exposing, depositing, distributing, or scattering shelled, shucked, or unshucked corn, wheat or other grain, salt, or other feed to lure turkeys to hunters; such area is designated baited for 15 days following complete removal of all such feed. Wildlife agents shall close the area and place a sign designating the closed zone and dates of closure. This shall not prohibit taking turkey where baits are found as the result of normal agriculture planting or harvesting; or as a result of manipulation of a crop or other feed on the land where such is grown for wildlife management purposes. Violation: class two violation. No person shall: ▸ hunt or take turkey by the use of recorded or electrically amplified recorded or imitated bird calls or sounds; ▸ hunt or take quadrupeds in an area under a floodwater closure order. Violation: class two violation (56:124).

Possession of more than the limit is prima facie evidence of violation unless each is properly tagged. Evidence of sex, including the head, shall remain on a deer, or on a turkey taken during a special gobbler season when killing of turkey hens is prohibited, if the animal is in camp or field, is in route to the domicile, or is divided at a cold storage facility. If the animal is divided in camp or field each portion shall be identified (56:125).

It is unlawful to trap or kill foxes or bobcats, except that foxes and bobcats may be included in the open season for taking nongame quadrupeds. It is not unlawful to allow dogs to chase foxes or bobcats at any time, except on wildlife management areas and refuges [exceptions provided] (56:140). [Training of dogs during closed season and taking of certain pen-raised birds for field trials and hunting dog training is provided in 56:141.]

The open season for taking nongame quadrupeds shall be fixed by the Commission. Trapping may be regulated in any area. The Commission shall set seasons, methods and hours for taking alligators. Nongame quadrupeds may be taken only by trapping in the open season with a license [methods of driving animals out are prohibited]. Landowners and lessees may kill without a license nutria and beaver as pests on agricultural or forest lands or in residential areas, waterways and on banks adjacent to those lands, except a license is required during open trapping season [restrictions on methods of taking outlined]. No pelting or sale of fresh meat of nongame quadrupeds during the closed trapping season shall be permitted. [Provisions for holding quadrupeds in captivity during open season are set forth.] Violation: class two violation. Traps capable of taking nongame quadrupeds may not be set more than one day either side of open trapping or alligator season. Traps shall be run daily and must be removed the last day of open season. Violation: class two violation. Taking and possession of alligators or eggs is restricted by Commission rules. Alligators and skins must be tagged, and cannot be taken or sold without a special permit if they are less than four feet in length. Violation: class 7-A violation (56:259 through :261).

No person shall: ▸ go upon marsh, low prairie lands, or swamplands without the owner's consent; ▸ capture, catch, trap, take, shoot, or ensnare an alligator, mink, muskrat, nutria, otter or raccoon, or attempt such; ▸ aid or conspire with another to commit or to attempt any such act. Violation: class two violation (56:265).

Restrictions on Taking: Fishing

The Director may exchange fish roe or fish eggs for a percent of the young fish hatched or produced at state fish hatcheries (56:19). Private fish pond owners are not subject to the usual limitations on taking fish, other than game fish, but are subject to Commission rules (56:27).

When fish in any waters have been depleted or fishing is detrimental, the Secretary may declare a closed season after giving public notice by publication three consecutive times in the official journal of each parish affected (56:317). Freshwater and saltwater game fish may be taken by rod, fishing pole, hook and line, trolling line, handline, bait casting, fly casting apparatus, yo-yo or trigger device, bow and arrow, recreational hoop net, recreational slat trap, standard skin diver spearing equipment, recreational pipe, recreational bucket, recreational drum, tire, and can [restrictions on methods for taking bass, crappie and bream provided]. Crawfish may be taken with approved traps and nets [other restrictions detailed]. Crabs may be taken with any legal crab trap, crab dropnet, trawl, trotline, handline, bushline, dip net, cast net, seine, trammel net, or gill net. Dredges shall not be used. No person shall take fish by spears, poisons, stupefying substances, explosives, guns, tree-topping devices, lead nets [exception], electricity, or any instrument or device capable of shocking fish. It is unlawful to possess a prohibited instrument, weapon, substance, or device with the intent to take fish. ★★ The Commission may provide by rule or regulation that no seines or gill nets shall be left unattended, except as otherwise provided. ★★ It is unlawful to use or employ aircraft in the taking of finfish, except menhaden and herring-like fish. In addition to the penalty prescribed in 56:355, an aircraft, boat, or vessel and equipment utilized in taking finfish and fish taken or possessed shall be subject to confiscation. Taking of freshwater and saltwater gamefish by illegal methods is a class four violation. [Provisions made to outlaw fishing interference or harassment.] No person shall take fish by means of or set a trotline above the water surface. Such action is prima facie evidence of negligence in a civil action for damages (56:320 and :321).

The described boundary line easterly from the Texas to the Mississippi state line shall be used in dividing the state into predominantly saltwater and predominantly freshwater areas [details of demarcation and restrictions on taking methods for commercial freshwater fish are provided]. [Daily limits of taking listed species of fish are provided in 56:325.] The Commission may amend by rule the size, daily take, possession limits, seasons, and times set by law for freshwater game fish, which may vary between waterbodies based on biological data or for research or experimentation (56:322). The Commission may set by rule size limits for freshwater and saltwater game fish and commercial fish for which no limits have been set by law (56:326.1). The Commission may set possession limits, quotas, places, seasons, times, size limits, and daily take limits for freshwater and saltwater finfish in state waters. Violation: class two violation (56:326.3). No person shall purchase, sell, exchange, or offer for sale or exchange, or possess or import with such intent [listing of specific bass species included]. Fishing operations shall be conducted such that nests of fish or natural hiding places of young fish or shrimp are not destroyed. Nets shall not be hauled upon the shore such that illegal fish cannot be returned to the waters without injury. All vegetation hauled up, except those condemned as detrimental, shall be removed carefully and returned to the waters so as not to injure fish eggs, small fish, or fish foods. No person knowingly shall import or cause to be imported, without a written permit, noxious aquatic plants [12 species listed]. Violation is a class one violation, and the plants shall be confiscated and destroyed. (See also Import, Export and Release Provisions.) No person shall obstruct the free passage of fish in streams, lakes, bayous, or in any body of water, including crevasses, coulees, and canals in marsh and swamp areas by any means, except for water control structures or dams for conservation [details provided] (56:327 through :329). (See also HABITAT PROTECTION.)

Frogs may be taken with a jacklight or other visible light, and with frog catchers, gigs and spears. No person shall possess a firearm while hunting at night. A person may take small frogs for scientific, educational, or propagating purposes, but not for food or sale. Bullfrogs and lagoon frogs may be taken, except during April and May. No person shall take diamondback terrapin with traps, or turtle eggs, except mobilian turtle eggs, nor ship diamondback terrapin out of state between April 15 and June 15. All diamondback terrapin caught during that period shall be returned to the water alive or held in captivity under natural conditions so that they may deposit their eggs (56:330 through :331).

Commercial and Private Enterprise Provisions

Raising and/or selling the following animals or their parts on private breeding farms or propagating preserves requires a license: ▸ domesticated elk, domestic white-tailed deer, or other domesticated deer native to North America; ▸ squirrels, rabbits, or other wild game quadrupeds; ▸ pheasants, quail, doves, or other domesticated wild game birds; ▸ domesticated wild waterfowl, resident or migratory. For wild migratory game and other birds, the applicant shall have a federal government license under the Migratory Bird Treaty Act (56:171). Licensees may kill or sell such animals or birds, except that domesticated species of wild game birds or wild waterfowl killed by shooting shall not be bought, sold or traded. Wild nongame quadrupeds may be taken for their pelts only in open seasons. Special parish closed seasons do not apply. A tax shall be paid before raw pelts are shipped out of the state. Licensees with a shipping permit may ship live specimens outside the state for breeding, scientific, or educational purposes, and may possess or sell such animals or birds for food (56:172). [Tagging requirements for breeder licensees' shipping or offering for sale are detailed in 56:173 through 56:175. Details of reports required for licensees are in 56:176.]

A farm or preserve used for breeding elk or deer shall be surrounded by a fence not less than seven feet high. Whoever trespasses, catches, takes, or molests such animals or birds when the area has been posted or fenced shall be punished subject to the common property rights of the state (56:177 and :178). The Secretary may revoke the license of a violator, and no similar license shall be issued. Violation of a provision of this Subpart for which a punishment has not otherwise been provided is a fine of $25-100, jail up to 30 days, or both (56:180 and :181).

[License fees for fur trappers, alligator hunters, fur buyers and fur dealers, as well as possession limit for nonresident alligator hunter, deposit as guarantee of payment of severance tax, and penalties are detailed in 56:251. Requirements for tags and labels and for shipping raw furs, alligators, alligator skins, and alligator parts out of state, are outlined in 56:253. Requirements for shipping raw furs and alligator skins within state, and tags and labels required, are outlined in 56:254. Complete records of purchases and sales of alligator hides and skins required are in 56:255. There is a severance tax on all skins or hides taken from fur-bearing animals or alligators within the state payable in amounts set forth in 56:256 and 56:257.] Every dealer shall maintain complete records of furs and skins purchased and shipped. Violation: class two violation (56:258). Engaging in the business of raising and/or exhibiting nongame quadrupeds (imported or native mink, raccoon, opossum, skunk, muskrat, otter, nutria, bobcat, coyote, beaver, fox, alligator), requires a nongame quadruped exhibitor license. A nongame quadruped breeder license is required to breed, propagate, exhibit, and sell such animals alive or sell their parts; and to kill, transport, and sell their pelts, skins, or carcasses. [Alligator farm and fur animal farm are defined.] Violation: class 7-A violation. Licensees shall report as specified by the Department. [Tagging and sale requirements are detailed.] The Department may issue a permit to a licensed breeder to take wild animals for use as breeding stock. [Provisions for property rights and trespass are as in section 56:178.] The Department may revoke the license of a person violating this section. All other rules and regulations pertaining to breeding, propagation, and sale of nongame quadrupeds shall be determined by the Commission. Except as otherwise provided, violation is a class three violation. An alligator parts dealer license is required for alligator parts retailers and restaurants selling prepared alligator meat. Violation: class two violation (56:262 and :263).

A person buying, acquiring, or handling fish for resale, including bait, must purchase a wholesale/retail dealer's license, including owners or operators of a fish factory, platform, or processing plant, or a person shipping fish out of or into the state (56:306). [Details of wholesale/retail dealers buying from other dealers, commercial fishermen and others is provided in 56:306.3. Requirements of records provided in 56:306.4.] Operators and drivers of any commercial transport, except common carriers, who are handling fish shall possess at least one of the following: ▸ commercial fisherman's license; ▸ wholesale/retail dealer's license; ▸ transport license [crawfish and catfish transport excluded] (56:307). A person transporting fish under a transport license is prohibited from buying or selling any species of fish (56:307.2). Common carriers are exempted from these licensing provisions, but must comply with 56:307.7 (56:307.6). [Requirements for labeling and registering shipments of fish are detailed in 56:307.7.] A wholesale or retail dealer buying fish from anyone other than a licensed wholesale/retail dealer, and any commercial fisherman, shall report to the Department. Violation: class two violation (56:345). No person shall waste fish, meaning harvesting for commercial purposes which results in excessive killing [penalties provided] (56:409.1).

It is unlawful to propagate, produce, transport, and possess fish, including hybrid striped bass, or minnows raised or produced in private artificial earthen reservoirs, except with a Department certificate. In the sale or transportation of fish or minnows over the highways of the state, a bill of lading shall accompany each shipment. Undesirable species of fish or minnows are prohibited. A domestic fish farmer is excepted from the provisions of 56:306, and shall be entitled to sell domesticated hybrid striped bass, catfish, carp, drum, and buffalo fish of any size, quantity, or limit without restriction, provided the farmer notifies the Department prior to each shipment. No person may use public water to propagate, raise, feed or grow a finfish species. Harvest and sale of fish, minnows, or gold fish produced in private artificial earthen reservoirs is allowed with seines or tackle. Commercial fish farmers may transport equipment without restriction, except electric fish shocking devices, for harvesting domesticated fish produced in privately owned waters. Violation of this Subpart is a class two violation (56:412 through :414).

A person may apply for a license to establish, maintain or operate a hunting preserve, and may propagate, possess, and release for shooting on the preserve pen-raised quail and pen-raised mallard, and may import, propagate, possess, and release for taking any foreign game bird, if approved (56:651 and :652). The following conditions apply for a hunting preserve license: ▸ the preserve shall be 100-2,000 acres in size and owned or leased by the applicant; ▸ if leased, it shall be for at least one year from date of application, and subject to inspection and approval by the Commission; ▸ only pen-raised mallard or black ducks, at least two generations removed from the wild, or pen-raised quail may be used for preserve hunting; ▸ open-raised quail and pen-raised mallard shall be banded; game birds taken must be tagged. A record shall be furnished to the Commission within 60 days after the close of the season. The Commission has authority to regulate hunting preserves. All laws, and regulations pertaining to hunting or game prevail on hunting preserves, except as provided. Hunters must have regular hunting licenses, except that the Commission may provide for a special resident or non-resident license from any hunting preserve. Violation of any laws or regulations as to hunting preserves may result in immediate revocation of the license [appeal procedures detailed] (56:654 through :657). Violation: class two violation (56:659).

Import, Export and Release Provisions

No animal, fowl, or fish, pen-raised or wild, from outside the state, nor pen-raised turkey or pheasant, shall be liberated, except upon written permission of the Secretary. No wild animal or fowl shall be transported intrastate for restocking purposes, except in accordance with Commission rules and regulations. Violation: class four violation (56:20). No person, firm, or corporation shall possess, sell, or cause to be transported into this state, without written permission of the Secretary, any of these species of fish: carnero catfish, the family clariidae, freshwater electric eel, carp (except those taken in state waters and dead when in possession, common carp and goldfish), rudd, and all species of tilapia [details of annual permits and requests for permission provided]. Violation: class three violation. No person shall possess or sell a piranha or Rio Grande Tetra, except at the Aquarium of the Americas, New Orleans, special Department permit. Violation: class four violation (56:319). The Department has authority to regulate or prohibit the possession, sale, or transportation of fish into Louisiana (56:319.1). [Provisions for aquaculture of saltwater game "cultured" fish are in 56:327.1.]

Interstate Reciprocal Agreements

A Mississippi hunting license holder shall have the same rights and privileges upon islands in and waters of the Mississippi River, between Louisiana and Mississippi, as the holder of a Louisiana hunting license. This shall take effect only when Mississippi grants reciprocal privileges to Louisiana license holders (56:104). [Provisions for reciprocal fishing and hunting license agreements with any other state are made in 56:671 and 56:672. Provisions are made for reciprocal agreements with Arkansas, Mississippi, and Texas pertaining to rules and regulations for taking or protection of fish or other aquatic life and any species or sex of wild quadrupeds or wild birds in areas forming the common boundary between Louisiana and the reciprocating state are in 56:673 and 56:674.] A reciprocal agreement shall become effective when ratified by the Commission and the authorities of the reciprocating state and shall remain in effect until 90 days after it has been rescinded in writing by either authority (56:671). The Commission may enter into reciprocal agreements with Alabama, Arkansas, Mississippi, and Texas regarding all regulations pertaining to taking or protection of any species or sex of fish, other aquatic life, wild quadrupeds, or wild birds in any area within those states. Where the Commission fails to enter into a reciprocal agreement, residents of that state shall be granted or sold licenses equal to privileges and licenses granted or sold to Louisiana residents by the nonresident's state (56:675 and :676).

ANIMAL DAMAGE CONTROL

If a species of protected wild bird or wild quadruped becomes so destructive of private property as to be a nuisance, the Secretary may direct an authorized person to take and dispose of it under conditions specified (56:112).

★[Provisions are made in 56:281 for a program of cost-sharing with the Department and the Wetlands Conservation and Restoration Authority for economic incentives to trappers and coastal landowners to control nutria. Program details are outlined in 56:282 through 56:284, including economic incentives to trappers and cost-sharing for the program with coastal landowners.]★

See also Restrictions on Taking: Hunting and Trapping under HUNTING, FISHING AND TRAPPING PROVISIONS.

ENFORCEMENT OF WILDLIFE LAWS

Enforcement Powers

Commissioned Department employees may carry weapons concealed or exposed while performing their duties (56:53). Each auxiliary agent shall have the same enforcement powers as a wildlife agent, limited only to wildlife and fisheries enforcement on land, and may carry weapons concealed or exposed while performing duties (56:69.10).

When there is probable cause to believe a violation has occurred, with or without a search warrant, the Secretary or a commissioned wildlife agent may visit and inspect records, or any cold storage plant, warehouse, boat, or a receptacle, or place of deposit, for wild birds, wild quadrupeds, fish or aquatic life, or parts. Without search warrants, commissioned wildlife agents frequently may visit or inspect records, and cold storage plants, bait stands, warehouses, or places where wildlife or parts may be kept and offered for sale. They also shall inspect establishments for commercial licenses to retail and/or wholesale commercial and bait fish. The Department may institute proceedings in any court of competent jurisdiction for violation of laws or regulations under its jurisdiction (56:55). Commissioned or authorized wildlife officers, and agents who have graduated from accredited law enforcement training programs, shall be vested with the same authority as other state law enforcement officers. Their qualification and annual requalification for firearms must be established with respect to criminal offenses observed during the performance of their normal duties, including arson, litter, theft, or burglary, conduct constituting resisting arrest, and assault or battery of a commissioned wildlife officer [powers during riot or natural disaster provided]. All Department divisions are authorized to seek, accept, and expend state or federal funds, or both, available for such purposes (56:55.2).

An enforcing officer may seize the following, if taken, used or possessed contrary to the provisions of this chapter: ▶ wild birds and wild quadrupeds or parts possessed, transported, sold, offered for sale, or purchased; ▶ deer, bears, or wild turkey or parts possessed which are not tagged or identified as required; ▶ fish and other aquatic life, taken, possessed, transported, sold, offered for sale, or purchased illegally; ▶ traps, nets, cages, snares, explosives, guns and other devices placed, set, or otherwise used or possessed for taking wild birds or quadrupeds illegally; ▶ tackle, seines and other nets, trawls, tongs, dredges, and other equipment and devices used in taking fish, shrimp, oysters, or other aquatic life illegally; ▶ oysters, shrimp, and hides and pelts of fur-bearing animals and nongame quadrupeds subject to an unpaid tax imposed by this chapter or which are taken illegally; ▶ tackle, dredges, and scrapers possessed or operated in an illegal manner, or not licensed or tagged as required, or taken illegally; ▶ tackle, including gear listed in 56:302, 56:302.5, or 56:305, used to take seafood for sale without a commercial fisherman's license (56:56). Possession or operation of a prohibited device is prima facie evidence of the violation (56:54.1).

An enforcing officer shall seize vessels, airplanes, vehicles, and other means of transport and equipment used or employed illegally (56:57). Where a license has been obtained by fraud or subterfuge, the vessels and equipment used under that license shall be forfeited as provided (56:57.1). Items seized under 56:56 that are not confiscated and are not perishable shall be held as evidence in a prosecution. If the penalty includes forfeiture, upon conviction, they are forfeited to the Department and shall be disposed of as provided in 56:61 (56:58). Vessels, airplanes, vehicles, and other means of transport and equipment seized under 56:57 may be released upon furnishing bond as fixed and approved by the judge or court. If the penalty includes forfeiture, upon conviction the court shall order forfeiture and sale at public auction [details provided, as well as details of suspension of operation activity]. The guilty parties are guilty of a class three violation (56:59). The Commission shall adopt rules and regulations concerning disposition of items seized and forfeited (56:60). [Details of disposal are provided in 56:61 through 56:64.] Neither the Department nor an enforcing officer shall incur liability for a search, arrest, seizure, or other act done in the good faith performance of duties. The attorney general may defend an employee in a civil action when defense is required to protect state interests [defense also may be provided by Department attorney] (56:65). ★Judgments on civil demands may be enforced according to law. No license shall be issued to the defendant until judgment is satisfied (56:67).★ Every authorized officer shall confiscate and hold for evidence any trap, snare, explosive, gun, or other material evidence found placed or set illegally, and confiscate and hold quadrupeds, pelts, skins, and parts found to have been taken or possessed illegally (56:127).

Criminal Penalties

★★The Director shall report criminal law violations to the district attorney with jurisdiction who shall prosecute such actions and report prosecutions to the Director. The judges of any judicial district, or in the parish of Orleans, the judges of the criminal district court, with the consent of the district attorney, may adopt a schedule of fines, penalties and costs for violations of wildlife and fisheries laws as may be found in Title 56 and regulations, within penalty limits set by law, except that the schedule shall not include violations punishable by mandatory imprisonment (56:9).★★

The following are penalties for: ▸ a class two violation: first offense, fine of $100-350, or jail of 60 days, or both; second offense, fine of $300-550, and jail of 30-60 days; third and subsequent offenses, fine of $500-750, and jail of 60- 90 days, plus forfeiture of anything seized in connection with the violation (56:32); ▸ a class three violation: first offense, fine of $250-500, or jail of 90 days, or both; second offense, fine of $500-800, jail of 60-90 days, and forfeiture of anything seized in connection with the violation; third and subsequent offenses, fine of $750-1,000, jail of 90-120 days, plus forfeiture of anything seized (56:33); ▸ a class four violation: first offense, fine of $400-450, or jail of 120 days, or both; second offense, fine of $750-3,000, and jail of 90-180 days; third and subsequent offenses, fine of $1,000-5,000, and jail of 180 days-2 years, plus forfeiture of anything seized in connection with the violation (56:34).

The following are penalties for: ▸ a class 5-A violation: first offense, fine of $500-750, and jail of 15-30 days; second offense, fine of $750-1,000, and jail of 60-90 days; third and subsequent offenses, fine of $750-1,000; and jail of 90-120 days; ▸ a class 5-B violation: first offense, fine of $350-500, and jail of 30 days; second offense, fine of $500-1,000, and jail of 60 days; third and subsequent offenses, fine of $1,000-2,000, and jail of 90 days. In addition to the above fines and jail sentences, and for both classes 5-A and 5-B violations, the license shall be revoked for its period plus one year. The above penalties in all cases shall include forfeiture of anything seized in connection with the violation (56:35).

The following are penalties for: ▸ a class six violation: for each offense, fine of $1,000-2,000, or jail up to of 120 days, or both, and forfeiture of anything seized in connection with the violation (56:36); ▸ a class 7-A violation: for each offense, fine of $5,000-7,500, or jail of 1 year, or both; ▸ a class 7-B violation: for each offense, fine of $5,000-7,500, and jail for 1 year, and forfeiture of anything seized in connection with the violation (56:37); ▸ a class eight violation: for each offense, fine of $5,000-7,000, and jail of 60 days-6 months (56:37.1). In addition to all other penalties, violators subject to the provisions of 56:31 through 56:37 shall upon conviction forfeit any quadrupeds, birds, or fish seized in connection with the violation (56:39).

★★ Violators of provisions of this Subpart, where no fine or imprisonment has been otherwise specifically provided, shall be fined $25-75, or jailed up to 30 days, or both, for a first offense; fined $100-200, or jailed up to 6 months, or both, for a second offense; fined $200-500, and jailed 60-90 days for a third offense, and the license shall be revoked for its period plus one year. Jail sentences shall be mandatory except for first and second offenses, and no sentence or fine shall be suspended or diminished for any cause.★★ Upon conviction for an offense under this Subpart, and in addition to such penalty, the court may suspend or revoke the license and privileges to hunt or fish, not to exceed the period for which the license was issued plus one year (56:139). Penalties for violation of a provision of this Subpart shall be as prescribed in Part II of this chapter. Violation is a class one violation except where a higher class of violation is specified (56:144). Possession or operation on fishing grounds of illegal, unlicensed, or improperly tagged tackle is prima facie evidence of a violation. Such tackle is a public nuisance and

STATE WILDLIFE LAWS HANDBOOK

shall be confiscated and turned over to the Commission (56:314). Violators of the sport fishing provisions for which no penalty has been otherwise provided shall be fined $25-100 or jailed 10-60 days, or both; for a second or subsequent conviction, fined $100-300, or jailed 30-90 days, or both, and tackle used may be disposed of on order of the court. Upon conviction and in addition to such penalty, the court may suspend or revoke the license and privileges to hunt or fish [details are provided in 56:139] (56:336). Penalties for violation of a provision of this Subpart shall be as prescribed in Part II of this chapter. Violation is a class one violation, except where a higher class of violation is specified (56:355).

Civil Penalties

Violators of provisions of this Part for which a penalty has not been otherwise specifically provided shall be fined $25-100, or imprisoned 30 days, or both (56:23). Class one violations shall be adjudicated and civil penalties assessed after a hearing and a decision by the Secretary or a designated hearing officer. The following civil penalties shall be imposed for a class one violation: first offense, $50; second offense, $100; third offense and subsequent offenses, $200 (56:31). [Details of citation procedure and posting and forfeiture of bond provided.] In any adjudicatory hearing in which civil penalties are assessed, the person also shall be liable for all costs of the hearing. The Secretary may institute civil proceedings in district court to enforce rulings. Either party may appeal from a final judgment. Revenues generated from class one violations shall be deposited in the Conservation Fund to be used for hiring and equipping additional enforcement agents, providing a uniform cleaning allowance for field personnel, and administering the class one civil penalty program. Failure to pay penalties and costs assessed shall result in immediate revocation of all recreational hunting and fishing licenses. Such revocation shall continue and no new licenses shall be issued while penalties and costs remain unpaid. Obtaining a hunting or fishing license during revocation shall be a class three violation (56:31.1).

★★A person who kills, catches, takes, possesses, or injures any fish, wild birds, wild quadrupeds, other wildlife, and aquatic life in violation of this title or its regulations, or a federal statute or regulation governing fish and wildlife, or who, through the violation of any other state or federal law or regulation, kills or injures any such animals, is liable to the state for the value of each animal unlawfully killed, caught, taken, possessed, or injured (56:40.1). The Commission shall adopt rules for determining the value of injured or destroyed fish, wild birds, wild quadrupeds, and other wildlife and aquatic life and values based upon recommendations of staff and other relevant factors (56:40.2). The Commission shall assess civil penalties equivalent to the values determined. Such penalties shall be assessed by the Commission or hearing officer after hearing; the defendant has the option to waive the hearing upon payment of the penalties. In any adjudicatory hearing in which civil penalties are assessed, the person shall be liable for hearing costs. The Secretary may institute civil proceedings to enforce the rulings of the Commission (56:40.3). The attorney for the Department, attorney general, or the district attorney of the parish in which the violation occurred may bring a civil suit to recover civil penalties for the value as determined (56:40.4). [Details of venue and procedure are provided in 56:40.5.] Each defendant against whom judgment is rendered is jointly and severally liable for the recovery (56:40.6). The recovery amount is in addition to any other penalty imposed under any other provision of law (56:40.7). The pendency or determination of a suit brought under this Subpart or of a criminal prosecution for the same does not bar the other action; provided that civil restitution paid under the Code of Criminal Procedure shall bar civil penalties or action to recover penalties under this Subpart (56:40.8). Any recovery of civil penalties shall be deposited in the Department Conservation Fund. In any civil action brought by the district attorney under 56:40.4, the office of the district attorney shall receive 40% of the amount collected (56:40.9). The district courts shall have original jurisdiction of the trial of persons charged under this chapter (56:45).★★

License Revocations and Suspensions

In addition to other penalties provided for a violation of this chapter, in accordance with classes 1, 2, 3, 4, 6, and 7, upon conviction the violator's license may be revoked for the period of issuance (56:38).

Reward Payments

See Agency Funding Sources under STATE FISH AND WILDLIFE AGENCIES for Louisiana Help Our Wildlife Fund.

HABITAT PROTECTION

★The Commission may contract with a private landowner for use of lands for at least 25 years for establishing wildlife management areas, and may agree that the lands shall be relieved of state, parish, and district taxes (56:24).★ The Commission may establish, maintain, and manage any state wildlife management area, wildlife refuge, public hunting ground, or outdoor recreation area. With the Governor's approval, it may lease, buy, or accept donation of lands and establish, maintain, and operate them. The public shall be notified by publication of a proclamation by the Governor. The Commission shall cause signs to be placed along the boundaries and at roads and entrances. The Commission shall be the sole authority and establish rules and regulations for propagation, protection and harvesting of all wildlife species, existing, propagated or released upon wildlife management areas, wildlife refuges, public hunting grounds or outdoor recreation areas. No person knowingly shall take, attempt to take, disturb, or destroy a wild bird or wild quadruped, or its nest, egg, or young on wildlife management areas and wildlife refuges, or possess or keep while on the lands, any firearm, trap, snare, or other device capable of taking or disturbing the birds or quadrupeds, unless authorized by permit. The Department shall direct the owner or operator of a Deer Management Assistance Program area to post signs. No person knowingly shall take, attempt to take, disturb, or destroy a wild bird or wild quadruped, or its nest, egg, or young on land so designated, or possess or keep, a device capable of taking or disturbing birds or quadrupeds, unless authorized by a permit from the owner (56:109 and :110).

★★The cooperative environmental action program to save wildlife cover and provide abundant game for future generations is "Louisiana Acres for Wildlife." Its purpose is to supplement the Commission's efforts to protect, conserve, and foster wild birds and game in wildlife management areas, refuges and recreation areas through sound wildlife management practices by providing recommendations to private landowners or lessees producing and maintaining suitable food, water, and cover conditions to support, replenish, and propagate wildlife. The Secretary shall employ personnel funded by the Legislature to carry out this program. Biologists shall administer Louisiana Acres for Wildlife by supplying assistance to qualified landowners or lessees to improve habitat. This assistance may include providing seed packages and plant bundles for planting and instruction and wildlife habitat evaluation surveys, and material to guarantee that certain land be utilized for wildlife habitats. The program shall use its resources to: ▸ instruct and train qualified personnel to administer the program; ▸ supply personnel, farmers, landowners, lessees, and cooperating agencies with information about management techniques and applications; ▸ prepare wildlife management recommendations; ▸ develop a close working relationship with other agencies having similar programs. Participants shall have at least one acre of land utilized as farmland, wetland, woodland, or pasture. This program is voluntary, and participants shall agree that plots shall be maintained and management practices continue for at least one year. Land where wildlife management has already been implemented is ineligible. Qualification for participation shall be determined by rules and regulations (56:191 through :193).★★

The Commission independently, or jointly with a parish game and fish commission, may set aside suitable locations in waters and operate and maintain hatcheries, sanctuaries, and propagating places for maintaining and restocking fish. Such areas shall be closed zones, fishing shall be restricted, and the Commission may purchase lands, build dams, expropriate property and do anything necessary to carry out these provisions (56:315). The Commission independently, or jointly with a parish game and fish commission, may construct or place fish ladders in lakes subject to Department of Public Works approval (56:315.1). The Secretary shall build, operate, and maintain fish hatcheries and may expropriate by law lands lying adjacent to Department owned or controlled property. (56:581). The Secretary shall distribute hatchery fish to all suitable sections of the state (56:582). ★A biologic station for the investigation of problems affecting Louisiana fish and fisheries is created on the Gulf coast [details are provided in 56:612 and 56:613] (56:611).★

For its use, the Commission may acquire property by purchase, gift, expropriation, or otherwise. It may prescribe methods for taking wildlife and fix seasons and bag limits or close seasons on a species to assure an adequate supply of wildlife (56:702). The state may enter into cooperative agreements with the US [details provided] (56:703 and 56:711 through 56:741). ★★A parish may establish, maintain, and operate game and fish preserves. The parish may appoint a game and fish commission composed of three citizens and taxpayers of the parish. The parish commission may: ▸ make rules and regulations for the government, regulation, and control of the preserve; ▸ provide open and closed seasons; ▸ let the right to seine or net non-game fish under rules and regulations and charge therefor; ▸ conserve, protect, and propagate game and fish in the preserve. Levee boards and school boards owning land in the bed of nonnavigable streams, which are annually overflowed, may sell the lands to establish a preserve.

The governing authority of a parish may build dikes or dams, dig canals, or excavate lake or stream beds to create and establish such preserves, and may appropriate and expend necessary money (56:721 through :724). [Details of parish preserves are provided in 56:725 through 56:728.]★★

Vacant and unappropriated public lands belonging to the state on or after December 9, 1921, are perpetually dedicated as game preserves and public hunting grounds. The Commissioner shall adopt rules and regulations controlling such an area. No person shall trap, hunt, or fish on the preserve except under Commission rules and regulations. Violators of this Subpart or its rules and regulations, for each offense, shall pay the cost of prosecution and a fine of $25-500, or be jailed for 10-180 days, or both (56:751 through :754). Except in accordance with rules and regulations, no person shall kill, snare, pursue with intent to kill, take, or possess a wild animal or bird upon a state wildlife refuge, wildlife management area, or public hunting ground. Each killing or pursuing is a separate offense. This section does not prohibit the Secretary from killing noxious animals on lands under the Secretary's supervision, or from catching or snaring wild animals or birds for propagation, restocking, or scientific investigation. No person shall catch, kill, snare, or pursue a wild animal or bird imported by the federal government, or authorized Commission agent, for experimentation or propagation. The Commission may accept lands or waters for wildlife refuges, wildlife management areas, and public hunting grounds, designate and set these apart, and provide rules and regulations for conservation of birds, quadrupeds, and fish thereon. Violation of 56:761, 56:762, or 56:763 is a class two violation (56:761 through :764).

The Commission shall select state-owned lands, and may lease from private persons or corporations lands, for establishment of wildlife refuges, wildlife management areas, public hunting grounds, upland game preserves, and wildlife sanctuaries and may manage them for protection and management of wild game and wild animal life. The Department shall post signs and stock the areas. When a tract of state-owned land has been so selected notice shall be given to the state land office, or other Departments. The Commission may contract with owners of land acquired or accepted under reforestation projects for establishment of such areas, providing notice shall be published. The Commission may make rules and regulations for the protection of wildlife and may fence, equip, or maintain the areas. Once an area becomes dedicated as a wildlife refuge, wildlife management area, public hunting ground, upland game preserve, or wildlife sanctuary, no person shall trespass upon such land or hunt, trap, snare, or take wild animal life or game or destroy or deface fencing or signs. A violator may be arrested on sight by a wildlife agent or other authorized officer. Violation of this Subpart is a class two violation (56:781 through :787).

Except as provided, and in accordance with rules and regulations, no person shall kill, snare, or pursue with intent to take or kill, or possess a wild animal or bird from or upon school land or a school section located within, contiguous to, or adjoining the boundaries of a wildlife refuge, wildlife management area, or public hunting ground. Each wild animal or bird so taken or possessed on such land or section is a separate offense. A violator of this Subpart shall be fined $5-100, with costs of suit, for each offense. Violation of a provision of this Subpart is a class two violation. The Secretary may kill or have killed obnoxious animals on any such land or ensnare or have ensnared a wild animal or bird for propagation, restocking, educational purposes, or scientific investigation (56:791 and :792).

NATIVE AMERICAN WILDLIFE PROVISIONS: None.

MAINE

Sources: Maine Revised States Annotated, 1964, Title 12; 1992 Supplementary Pamphlet.

STATE WILDLIFE POLICY

The legislature finds that various species of fish or wildlife have been and are in danger of being rendered extinct within the state, and that these species are of aesthetic, ecological, educational, historical, recreational and scientific value to the people of the state. The legislature declares that it is state policy to conserve, by according such protection as is necessary to maintain and enhance their numbers, all species of fish or wildlife found in the state, as well as the ecosystems upon which they depend (12-7751).

RELEVANT WILDLIFE DEFINITIONS: See Definitions section of Appendices.

STATE FISH AND WILDLIFE AGENCIES

Agency Structure

The **Department of Inland Fisheries and Wildlife** (Department) is established to preserve, protect and enhance the inland fisheries and wildlife resources; to encourage wise use of these resources; to ensure coordinated planning for future use and preservation of these resources; and to provide for effective resource management. The Department consists of a Commissioner of Inland Fisheries and Wildlife (Commissioner); Deputy Commissioner; Bureau of Administrative Services; Bureau of Resource Management; Bureau of Warden Service; and includes the Advisory Board for the Licensing of Guides, the Junior Maine Guides and Trip Leaders Curriculum Board and other designated state agencies. The Department is under the control and supervision of the Commissioner (12-7011).

The following bureaus are within the Department, each administered by a director immediately responsible to the Deputy Commissioner who possesses full authority for administering all the powers and duties of the bureau, subject to the direction of the Commissioner. Each of the bureaus is equal in organizational level and status with other major organizational units within the Department (12-7012).

The responsibilities of the **Bureau of Administrative Services** include: Department financial accounting; administration and issuance of Department licenses, stamps and permits and registration of snowmobiles, watercraft and all-terrain vehicles; acquisition and development of land for protection, preservation and enhancement of inland fisheries and wildlife resources. The responsibilities of the **Bureau of Resource Management** include: ▸ wildlife and fisheries management; ▸ fish propagation; ▸ habitat management; ▸ management of wildlife sanctuaries and wildlife management areas; ▸ data collection and research; ▸ animal damage control coordination; ▸ rules governing effective management of inland fisheries and wildlife resources. The **Bureau of Warden Service** Director is the Game Warden Colonel. Bureau responsibilities include: ▸ enforcement of laws and Department rules collection of data for management and protection of inland fisheries and wildlife resources; ▸ registration and operation of snowmobiles, watercraft and all-terrain vehicles; ▸ coordination and implementation of search and rescue operations; ▸ administration of programs for hunter safety and safe operation of snowmobiles and watercraft; ▸ other areas specified by law. The **Division of Planning** shall develop short- and long-term plans for preservation, protection, enhancement and use of inland fisheries and wildlife resources. The **Division of Public Information and Education** is responsible for administering programs to increase public knowledge and understanding of inland fisheries and wildlife resources and their management. Responsibilities include public education, promotion of wildlife resources and dissemination of information (12-7012 through -7016).

The **Commissioner** is appointed by the Governor, subject to review by the joint standing committee of the legislature, with jurisdiction over fisheries and wildlife matters and confirmation by the legislature. Candidates for Commissioner shall have a record of demonstrated support for, and understanding of, the basics of modern wildlife and fisheries management and shall have experience in hunting, fishing or trapping (12-7031).

Agency Powers and Duties

The Commissioner shall: ► appoint a Deputy Commissioner, qualified by training and experience in fisheries and wildlife management and conservation law enforcement; ► supervise administration and enforcement of inland fisheries and wildlife laws and manage all inland fish and wildlife in the state; ► investigate the status and needs of inland fisheries and wildlife species; ► provide information on natural resources to municipalities and political subdivisions and the US Government; appoint an Assistant to the Commissioner for Public Information, and a Game Warden Colonel from among Department Game Wardens; ► prepare a written code of the operating procedure of the Warden Service; ► control administrative expenses; ► report annually to the governor; ► furnish town clerks abstracts of the inland fisheries and wildlife laws for distributing with every license. ★The Revisor of Statutes, with the assistance of the Commissioner, shall issue a biennial revision of all laws relating to inland fisheries and wildlife as soon as practicable after the legislature adjourns (12-7034).★

The Commissioner shall appoint Game Wardens who have met written code qualifications and have been approved by the Director of Human Resources, and may appoint temporary assistant game wardens who may hold no other compensated governmental office and are not compensated (12-7051 and -7052).

The Commissioner: ► shall perform search and rescue operations; ► may enter into written agreements with other agencies allowing partial search and rescue within specified areas, and may terminate a rescue operation when all reasonable efforts have been exhausted; ► shall sell all arms and ammunition held or confiscated for violation of inland fisheries and wildlife laws; ► shall establish a program for training in the safe handling of firearms; ★★► shall review what other states have done to develop good relationships between hunters and landowners and implement a program of landowner relations fostering public use of private land for hunting and fishing and promoting high standards of courtesy and responsibility for private lands, such program to be submitted to the joint standing legislative committee on fish and wildlife matters prior to implementation★★ (12-7035).

The Commission has the power to make studies, undertake research, publish and disseminate information and implement programs, enter into contracts or other arrangements with public agencies and private parties, and receive and expend funds from any source, public or private, subject to state laws. Any funds are placed into a nonlapsing, separate account by the State Treasurer, to be expended by the Commission for these purposes. Subject to other state laws, the Commission may acquire, install, construct, operate, manage, sell and convey real and personal property interests, including lands, dams, buildings, facilities, structures, flowage rights, mill privileges, easements and rights of way, except prior rights of municipalities are not affected (12-6252-A).

Agency Regulations

With the advice and consent of the Advisory Council and conforming to the Administrative Procedure Act, the Commissioner may adopt, amend and repeal rules to administer, implement, enforce and interpret any provision of law the Commissioner is charged to administer. Such rules have the full force and effect of law and are effective upon filing with the Secretary of State, unless a later date is required or specified. No municipality or political subdivision may enact any ordinance, law or rule regulating hunting, trapping or fishing, or operation, registration or numbering of watercraft or snowmobiles. The Commissioner may: ► take and destroy wildlife whenever necessary; ► fix a price, sell and deliver publications and materials, and sell or lease the Department's photographs or negatives; ► implement a program to promote fisheries and wildlife to attract sportspersons to the state. The Commissioner shall maintain a coyote control program as follows: qualified persons may serve as agents for coyote control who shall be trained in animal damage control techniques and deployed to control coyotes during winter months, and who may be used to benefit agricultural interests provided that the Department is reimbursed annually for those efforts by the Department of Agriculture, Food and Rural Resources from funds appropriated (12-7035).

The Commission may adopt and amend regulations to promote conservation and propagation of Atlantic sea run salmon in the same manner and with the same limits for the conservation and propagation of marine organisms under other sections. Commission regulations have the same effect, bear the same penalty and are proved and enforced the same as regulations of the Commissioner of Marine Resources. Regulation proof is effected by certified copy and statement of either the Commissioner of Marine Resources or of Inland Fisheries and Wildlife. Any marine patrol officer of the Department of Marine Resources, warden of the Department of Inland Fisheries and Wildlife and any other law enforcement officer may enforce the regulations (12-6252-A).

Agency Funding Sources

All proceeds from Atlantic Salmon licenses shall be paid to the Atlantic Sea Run Salmon Commission for conservation and management of Atlantic salmon resources (12-6255). The Commissioner shall deposit funds from license and stamp sales and any unencumbered balances in the state treasury as undedicated revenue to the General Fund. Funds from sale of licenses or permits under this chapter shall be used only for: Department administration; fish and wildlife protection, preservation, promotion and investigation; conservation education; other expenses incident to these functions (12-7074).

The **Maine Endangered and Nongame Wildlife Fund** consists of all money deposited by the State Treasurer, and earnings are for management of nongame wildlife and necessary administrative and personnel costs. The Commission shall report on the Fund to the Governor and the fish and wildlife joint standing committee. Grants may be awarded from the Fund for research and nongame wildlife activities (12-7757).

Agency Advisory Boards

For purposes of undertaking projects in research, planning, management, restoration and propagation of the Atlantic Sea Run Salmon, the **Atlantic Sea Run Salmon Commission** is established. Members are: the Commissioner of Marine Resources or designee; the Commissioner of Inland Fisheries and Wildlife or designee; and three public members, state residents, appointed by the Governor for four years. One public member shall be chosen from each congressional district and one appointed at-large. The Commissioner of Inland Fisheries and Wildlife is permanent chairman and shall have sole authority over Commission administrative and financial matters (12-6251-A).

The **Inland Fisheries and Wildlife Advisory Council** (Advisory Council) consists of 10 members representing the 16 counties, appointed by the Governor, for three-year terms. The Commissioner is a nonvoting ex officio member, but may vote to break a tie. An employee of the Department, legislators, and former legislators may not serve as members except as specified (12-7033-A).

The Advisory Council provides information and advice to the Commissioner concerning administration of the Department, carries out duties delegated by statute and holds regular meetings with the Commissioner as specified. Meetings shall be in a meeting place convenient for the public, with public notice in a newspaper, and public comments accepted (12-7033-A).

See also Commercial and Private Enterprise Provisions under HUNTING, FISHING, TRAPPING PROVISIONS for Guide Licensing Advisory Board and Advisory Board for the Licensing of Taxidermists.

PROTECTED SPECIES OF WILDLIFE

Except as otherwise provided by fish and wildlife laws or rules, there is a perpetual closed season on hunting or trapping any wild bird or animal (12-7401 and -7431).

The Commissioner may conduct investigations to develop information on population size, distribution, habitat needs, limiting factors and other biological and ecological data relating to survival of resident species of fish or wildlife, endangered or not, and may develop programs to enhance or maintain these populations. The Commissioner shall designate a species as endangered or threatened whenever one of the following is found: ► present or threatened destruction, modification or curtailment of its habitat or range; ► overutilization for commercial, sporting, scientific, educational or other purposes; ► disease or predation; ► inadequacy of existing regulatory mechanisms; ► other natural or manmade factors affecting its continued existence within the state. The Commissioner may: ► establish programs to bring any endangered or threatened species to the point where it is no longer endangered or threatened, including habitat acquisition, propagation, trapping, transplanting and regulated taking; ► designate essential areas as habitat and develop guidelines for species protection; ► enter into agreements with government agencies or persons to establish and maintain endangered or threatened species conservation programs; ► receive federal funds (12-7752 through -7755).

★A state agency or municipal government shall not permit, license or fund projects that will significantly alter endangered species identified habitat or violate Commissioner protection guidelines. Variances may be granted if the Commissioner certifies that the proposed action would not pose a significant risk to such species, and a public hearing is held (12-7755-A).★ It is illegal to: misuse, export, hunt, trap, possess, process, sell, offer for sale, deliver, carry, transport or ship any endangered or threatened species, or feed, set bait for or harass them. Exceptions will be made for educational or scientific purposes, to enhance the propagation or survival of an endangered/threatened species, and for transportation through the state by federal or state permit under conditions set by the Commissioner (12-7756).

GENERAL EXCEPTIONS TO PROTECTION

The Commissioner may under prescribed conditions permit acts prohibited by rule for educational or scientific purposes or to enhance propagation or survival of endangered/threatened species, and permit such species entering the state and being transported to a point outside the state to be transported in accordance with the terms of any federal or state permit. No Department biologist or warden may trap wild animals for profit while on duty (12-7036).

The Commissioner may issue a wildlife exhibit permit to: ▸ keep wildlife in captivity for exhibition for attracting trade; ▸ purchase, sell and transport any wildlife kept under this section; ▸ purchase moose and caribou from the Commissioner, who may capture and sell them to holders of a wildlife exhibit permit. No permit may be granted until housing and caring for the wildlife and protecting the public are adequate and in accordance with Commissioner rules (12-7231). ★The Commissioner may issue a written permit to a holder of a wildlife exhibit permit, permitting the holder to: take from within or import into the state live moose and caribou for the holder's wildlife exhibit; transport moose and caribou for display purposes; breed and sell moose, caribou and bear or their offspring (12-7232, -7233 and -7234).★

The Commissioner may issue a license to any person permitting breeding, rearing or possessing wild birds or animals; or selling, transporting or killing for sale any wild bird or animal raised by virtue of this section. No license is required to raise domestic rabbits or chinchillas, or wild birds or animals owned by the department (12-7235). The Commissioner may issue a permit to take and transport within state limits, fish and wildlife taken in the state for breeding or advertising purposes, or to hunt, trap, possess, band and transport wild animals and birds for scientific purposes. Permittees shall report annually to the Commissioner as required (12-7241 and -7242). Except as otherwise provided, it is lawful to train dogs on wild birds and animals. Any person may train dogs on foxes, rabbits and raccoons from July through March, and train up to four dogs at a time on bear from August 1 to the first day of the open season on bear, except in certain areas (12-7861).

See also HUNTING, FISHING, TRAPPING PROVISIONS and ANIMAL DAMAGE CONTROL.

HUNTING, FISHING, TRAPPING PROVISIONS

General Provisions

Any resident or nonresident over age 10, not mentally ill, may obtain a license from the Commission or agent to hunt wild birds or animals (12-7101). [Various license fees for hunting, trapping and fishing are set in the statutes. Licenses must be kept in possession and exhibited upon request while hunting.]

★Persons guilty of the following offenses are not eligible for any Department license or permit: burglary or criminal trespass of a building within the unorganized territories; theft of trapping, hunting or fishing equipment; theft of any animal in possession or control of the taker. If a first conviction, the person is not eligible for any license or permit for two years (12-7071).★ A person convicted of disturbing traps is not eligible to obtain any license for three years from conviction of a first offense and five years for a second or subsequent offense. Any licenses in effect at the time of conviction shall be revoked and surrendered to the Commissioner. Any person applying for a firearms license, other than a juvenile license, shall submit proof of having successfully completed a hunter safety course, or satisfactory evidence of having previously held an adult license to hunt with firearms in this or another state, province or country, in any year beginning with 1976 (12-7071). (See License Revocations, Suspensions under ENFORCEMENT OF WILDLIFE LAWS.)

★Affixed to all hunting and fishing licenses shall be: "Notice: This license does not give the holder the right to enter upon private property against the wishes of the property owner. Please seek landowner permission before hunting or fishing on someone else's land (12-7071)." (Printed on the back of deer or bear tag portions of a nonresident or alien license shall be: "This deer or bear was shot in the state of Maine.")★

Persons 16 or older may obtain an archery hunting license. Archery deer tags shall be issued like regular deer tags; taking a deer with bow and arrow during the open season on deer precludes further deer hunting during that year. Deer may be taken under this section only by handbow and broad head arrow, and not crossbow or set bow, or with arrows with poisonous or explosive tips. No firearms of any kind may be carried while hunting with a bow and arrow during the special archery season on deer, except one who also holds a license to hunt with firearms may carry a handgun. ★Applicants, other than for junior licenses, shall submit proof of successful completion of an archery hunter education course. The Commission shall establish such a program, similar to the hunter training program (12-7102).★

The Commissioner shall issue a pheasant hunting permit in the form of a stamp, which must be in possession and exhibited upon request while hunting (this section is repealed June 30, 1993, and a report with recommendations is due to the legislature) (12-7106-A). Muzzle-loading license stamps may be issued to those possessing a valid big game license, and provisions regarding deer hunting apply (12-7107-A). Persons with a valid hunting license may obtain a permit to hunt coyotes at night from January 1 to April 30, except those convicted of illegal hunting within five years of application. ★Hunters must possess electronic hand-held or mouth-operated predator calling devices.★ Any hunting license of a person convicted of a violation of this section shall be revoked, and the person shall not be eligible to obtain any hunting license for one year from conviction (12-7108).

The Commissioner shall issue a migratory waterfowl hunting permit stamp permitting hunting or possession of migratory waterfowl. The Commissioner shall provide for reproduction, sale, distribution and design of the stamp. All proceeds go to a special account to be used for waterfowl habitat acquisition and management activities. In addition to a big game license, a permit is required to hunt for bear from the first Monday before September 1st to the day before the open firearm season on deer. This section does not apply to bear trapping (12-7109 and -7110). ★Trapping licenses require proof of completion of a trapper education program established by the Commissioner or evidence of previous trapping licenses.★ No more than two traps may be set for bear at any one time (12-7133).

A resident landowner and immediate family member over age 10 may hunt without a license, on any plot of land in excess of 10 acres which they own, live on, and use exclusively for agriculture. A resident and immediate family member may trap for wild animals, except beaver, or fish without a license in open inland waters, on land they own, live on, and use exclusively for agriculture. Alewives, cusk, eel, hornpout, suckers and yellow perch may be fished for without a license for consumption. This shall not apply to domestic rabbits and chinchillas, or to migratory game birds, partridge, grouse or pheasant owned by the Department. A person who lawfully registers a deer may sell its skin and head (12-7377).

Licenses and Permits

It is unlawful to fish for Atlantic salmon from [indicated] areas, or to take, possess, ship or transport them without an Atlantic salmon license, except as provided. Only one license shall be issued per person per year. Any Atlantic salmon taken from inland or coastal waters shall be immediately tagged. It is unlawful to possess, sell, give away, accept as a gift, offer for transportation or transport an Atlantic salmon not lawfully tagged. It is unlawful to possess, buy or sell Atlantic salmon unless each fish is clearly identified by tags, or bills of sale. Individuals licensed for aquaculture of Atlantic salmon are exempt from restrictions of possessing, buying, or selling, but shall report the number, weight and locations sold to, of all salmon. ★The first person in a season presenting a salmon for shipment to the President, in cooperation with the Commission or the Marine Resources or Inland Fisheries and Wildlife Departments, is entitled to take one additional salmon and be issued one additional tag.★ It is unlawful to possess any part of an Atlantic salmon taken from inland or coastal waters, unless each part is plainly labeled as to person who registered the fish, except fish properly identified in section 12-6255 (12-6255 and -6256).

Restrictions on Taking: Hunting and Trapping

Prohibited acts include: ▸ hunting or possessing wild animals or birds during the closed season (taking deer or bear is a class D crime); ▸ hunting without possessing or exhibiting the license; ▸ hunting while under the influence of intoxicating liquor or drugs, or failing to submit to a test; ▸ hunting on Sunday; ▸ hunting wild birds or animals, except as provided, from sunset to one-half hour before sunrise (class D crime); ▸ hunting at twilight; ▸ hunting from a paved way or from within the right-of-way of any controlled access highway; ▸ hunting from a motor vehicle or motorboat or having a loaded firearm in or on a motor vehicle; ▸ hunting from or having a loaded firearm in or on railways; ▸ possessing wild animals or birds taken in violation of the above except as otherwise provided (class D crime); ▸ shooting with a firearm at or near any wildfowl decoy of another; ▸ shooting with a firearm within an area encompassed by another person's wildfowl decoys including 50 yards from the outer perimeter of the decoys; ▸ discharging a firearm within 100 yards of a residential dwelling, without permission of the owner or adult occupant of the dwelling; ▸ intentionally, knowingly, recklessly or negligently shooting and wounding or killing any domestic animal, including a dog, cat or domestic bird; ▸ failing to aid an injured person (class C crime); ▸ failing to report a hunting accident; ▸ abusing another's property while hunting; ▸ using or possessing prohibited implements or aids, such as automatic firearms, auto-loading firearms with capacity for more than five cartridges, silencers, tracer bullets, explosive bullets, shotguns holding more than three shells, use of crossbows; ▸ use of dogs to hunt deer or moose; ▸ use of artificial lights, snares, traps, swivels, pivots, or set guns to hunt deer or moose, or hunting by any other than the usual methods (12-7406).

A person may hunt migratory waterfowl from a motorboat in accordance with federal regulations; persons with a valid Maine permit to carry a concealed weapon may have in or on a motor vehicle or trailer the permitted loaded pistol or revolver; paraplegics and single or double amputees of the legs may hunt from motor vehicles not in motion (12-7406).

★★Due to large numbers of Maine citizens and visitors hunting during season, the continued decline of unpopulated areas, the widespread use of powerful weapons in the pursuit of wild animals and birds, and the growing presence of nonhunters engaged in nonhunting activities in the state's woods during the hunting season, the legislature finds that sufficient risk of serious bodily injury or death is posed to make it necessary and prudent to provide guidance to hunters on proper target identification. While hunting, a hunter may not shoot at a target without being certain it is the wild animal or bird sought. The target-determining process is that which a reasonable and prudent hunter would observe in the same situation [many additional safety elements discussed] (12-7406-A).★★

Except as otherwise provided, there is a perpetual closed season on trapping (12-7431). It is illegal to: ▸ trap or possess out of season wild animals or birds; ▸ fail to check traps at least once every calendar day or once every five days if trapping in any unorganized or deorganized place using killer-type traps or water sets, except under ice watersets for beaver and muskrat; ▸ fail to remove an animal or bird caught in the trap; ▸ trap without first obtaining written consent of the land's owner or occupant; ▸ trap within one-half mile of the built-up portion of a city (except for water sets); ▸ disturb or take a trap not one's own; ▸ rig a trap with auxiliary teeth or to fail to label a trap; ▸ abuse another's property while trapping; ▸ use or possess for trapping a snare, swivel, pivot or set gun; ▸ deposit any poisonous or stupefying substance for taking any wild animal or bird; ▸ ★sell, advertise, give notice of sale, or keep for sale any swivel, pivot, set gun or poisonous substance for taking any animal (12-7432).★

Open seasons on deer are set [by dates and places] and may be closed if necessary due to weather or severe hunting pressure. Taking of antlerless deer may be regulated by rules and by deer registration stations. The Commissioner may shorten or terminate the open season on deer at any time in any areas, and may extend the open season in sections of the state (12-7457). It is illegal to: ▸ possess more than one deer during open season or hunt deer after killing or registering one deer during the season, except as otherwise provided (class D crime for these two provisions); ▸ buy or sell deer, offer for sale or barter or aid in same for any deer; ▸ fail to register a deer; ▸ keep or possess an unregistered deer; ▸ fail to attach a tag or falsely register a deer; ▸ entice a deer with bait; ▸ drive deer while hunting for deer; ▸ transport deer when the deer is not open to view or the deer tag is not securely attached and filled out, or the person who killed the deer is not accompanying the deer, unless otherwise provided. The head, antlers, feet and hide of deer may be sold and the meat processed, bought and sold for food in accordance with law. Exceptions exist for lawfully possessing an unregistered deer and for transporting registered deer or parts with transportation tags or by use of licensed transportation companies (12-7458).

★The Commissioner may at any time take and transport live hares or rabbits by purchasing from local trappers when necessary for their proper distribution and conservation (12-7461).★ For wild hares and rabbits, it is illegal to: ▸ set or use any snares, traps or other devices in hunting them (except that trappers may take them by box traps solely for sale to the Commissioner); ▸ hunt them in any manner, except the ordinary methods of shooting or falconry; ▸ transport them out of state if they are destined beyond state limits; ▸ possess or transport them out of season (12-7462).

To hunt moose a resident or nonresident must have a valid Maine hunting and/or big game license and a moose permit. [Moose hunting districts and zones are set.] Subpermittees may participate in the hunt. Up to $25,000 of the permit revenues may be used for moose research. The bag limit for moose is one. The moose must be registered with an agent and a moose tag attached if transported. It is illegal to: ▸ possess moose parts unless labeled as authorized; ▸ buy, sell, offer to sell, barter, aid in or counsel others to do such, unless authorized; ▸ drive and hunt moose at the same time; ▸ move or transport any moose or part for transportation that is not tagged and accompanied by the hunter; ▸ fail to or falsely register or to tag moose; ▸ possess, buy or sell moose, except the head, antlers, feet and hide may be sold (12-7463 and -7464).

Wild turkey zones and seasons may be set. The Commissioner may establish the number of wild turkey permits and rules for protection. The bag limit is one bearded turkey per season; the time to hunt is one-half hour before sunrise to 11 AM. Wild turkeys taken must be registered and tagged. A person is guilty of transporting wild turkeys if the turkey or parts is transported or moved without a correct tag or not accompanied by the hunter. A person is guilty of buying or selling a wild turkey if the person buys, sells or offers for sale or barter, aids or counsels in such. A person is guilty of using illegal hunting methods who: ▸ uses a dog in any manner while hunting wild turkeys; ▸ uses electronic calling devices; ▸ engages in any organized drive; ▸ uses any bait, trap or other device intended for capturing or ensnaring wild turkeys. The penalty for buying or selling wild turkeys is a class E crime with a fine not less than $500, not suspendable, plus $500 for each turkey illegally possessed, not suspendable (12-7468 and -7469 and -7901).

Open seasons on hunting and trapping bear and using dogs in bear hunting are set by statute. The Commissioner may shorten or terminate the season at any time in any part of the state if necessary due to adverse weather conditions or severe hunting or trapping pressure. Rules shall be promulgated for bear registration stations. Black bears can be baited subject to restrictions [details in statute]. It is illegal to: ▸ use more than four dogs at a time to hunt bear; ▸ hunt with a dog and not employ, and hunt with, a resident Maine guide if a non-resident; ▸ possess more than one bear in any calendar year; ▸ fail to register the bear taken (violation is class D crime, jail for not more than 180 days, and fine not less than $1,000, not suspendable); ▸ kill or wound a bear treed or held at bay by another's dogs; ▸ bait a bear; ▸ trap and allow another person to kill a bear except as provided; ▸ exceed the bag limit; ▸ fail to register or tag a bear; ▸ transport without a tag and accompanying the bear; ▸ hunt, trap, molest or harass bear, or release dogs to hunt bear, within 200 yards of dumpsites; ▸ leave a bear after it is killed. Except where authorized, it is illegal to buy, sell, or offer for sale or barter any bear, or aid or counsel in such, or to transport any bear beyond state limits. Penalty for buying or selling bear is a class D crime, jail for not less than 10 days for the first offense and not less than 20 days for succeeding offenses, and fine not less than $1,000, fine and jail not suspendable. ★The head, teeth, gallbladder, claws and hide of any bear may be sold; bear or parts may be transported by licensed transportation companies, including common carriers. A bear or parts may be transported in or out of state when a bear transportation tag is attached. A nonresident transportation permit is needed if transported by other than a Maine licensed transportation company (12-7451, -7452 and -7901).★

The open season for raccoons shall be uniform in the state (12-7467). Nonresidents may not trap beaver in this state (12-7454). Snares or conibear traps may be used to trap beaver during open season, subject to rules (12-7453-A). It is illegal to hunt or possess caribou except in accordance with other provisions. Penalty is a fine of $2,000 to $10,000; jail 30 days to 6 months, not suspendable (12-7456-B and -7901). [Open season is declared for hunting partridge in various Wildlife Management Units (12-7455).]

It is illegal to: ▸ hunt, possess, transport, buy, or sell any migratory game bird, except as permitted by the Federal Migratory Bird Treaty Act or by Commissioner rules; ▸ hunt or possess any wild bird, except English or European house sparrow and European starling, except as provided; ▸ sell or possess for sale any wild bird, except as provided. A person may sell the plumage of lawfully taken wild birds if sale does not violate Federal Migratory Bird Treaty Act regulations. Penalty for selling wild birds is a class D crime; jail no less than 10 days for first offense and not less than 20 days for each succeeding offense; fine not less than $1,000, fine and jail not suspendable. It is illegal to take, possess or needlessly destroy the nest or eggs of any wild bird, except the English or European house sparrow and European starling (12-7456 and -7901).

Any resident may transport a wild animal or bird legally possessed, if licensing and all other requirements have been met. Nonresidents may transport or have transported to their home by common carrier any wild animal or bird killed and legally possessed if licensing and all other requirements have been met. A nonresident hunting license entitles the hunter to have any wild animal or wild bird legally killed, and transported to their home without fee. Any wild animal or bird transported or offered for transportation shall be open to view and accompanied by the person who killed it, except that transportation for nonresidents by common carrier need not be accompanied by the owner if all other requirements are met. Any common carrier accepting any wild animal or wild bird for transportation shall check license, affix tags and make required returns to the Commissioner (12-7531 through -7534). Permits may be issued to take and transport fish and wildlife within the state for breeding or advertising purposes (12-7241).

Restrictions on Taking: Fishing

For Atlantic Salmon, it is unlawful to: ▸ take or possess such less than 14 inches long; ▸ take them from coastal waters by other than hook and line with a single hook from May 1 to October 15, salmon taken by any other means to be released immediately; ▸ take salmon from coastal waters by any means from October 16 to April 30; ▸ take more than one in one salmon day from inland waters or coastal waters; ▸ annually take more than five salmon per person from all state waters; ▸ sell or offer for sale salmon taken from inland or coastal waters of the state, except those lawfully raised by aquaculture (12-6553).

It is unlawful to fish for or take striped bass except by hook and line, and except for personal use (12-6555 and -6556). The Commissioner may issue permits to fish for or possess alewives, cusk, eel, hornpout, suckers and yellow perch by means of eel puts, traps, spears or nets in inland waters under rules, provided these permits do not interfere with other rights granted (12-7153). Fish and wildlife laws relating to fish of all varieties and fishways apply to the state's inland waters. Any person on foot may engage in any activity on the great ponds not inconsistent with any other state or local law or regulation. Ponds of 10 acres or less, formed on brooks, streams or rivers, are governed by the same fishing laws that apply to the brook, stream or river on which they are situated, whether the pond is natural or artificial. This section does not apply to private ponds with a license to cultivate or harvest fish commercially (12-7551).

Except as provided in Commission rule, open seasons for fishing in waters free of ice are set by statute for lakes and ponds, rivers above tidewater, brooks and streams and on boundary waters between Maine and New Brunswick. The Commissioner may establish an annual opening date as the last Saturday of April on waters reclaimed by the removal of rough fish. Except as provided, the area within 150 feet of any fishway dam, except certain designated areas, are closed at all times, and all waters within 200 feet of a fish hatchery or rearing station are closed. Alewives and smelts may be taken as provided under laws regulating marine resources (12-7552 and -7553).

All inland waters of the state are closed to ice fishing except those opened by Commissioner rule. Unless otherwise provided, a licensee may fish through ice in the daytime with not more than five lines set or otherwise, which shall be supervised, in any waters so opened. A licensee may fish in the nighttime for cusk in waters opened for ice fishing with not more than five lines. All lines must be visited at least once every hour by the person setting them. Black bass may be taken through the ice during the period for taking salmon or trout (12-7571 and -7572). ★It is illegal to add substances containing ethylene glycol or other antifreeze agents to the waters of this state (12-7573).★ Except as provided, it is illegal to: ▸ ice fish from one-half hour after sunset to one-half hour before sunrise; ▸ allow a shack to remain on the ice more than three days after waters are closed to ice fishing; ▸ place a shack on the ice more than three days before the waters are opened; ▸ fail to paint on the shack in two-inch letters the owner's name and address; ▸ violate any ice fishing restriction in the statutes (12-7626 through -7629).

It is illegal to: ▸ fish or possess fish during closed season; ▸ fish in inland waters closed to fishing, except if fishing for alewives or smelts; ▸ fish for Atlantic salmon in violation of statutes and Commission rules (penalty is $500 fine per fish, not suspendable, and up to $1,000 per violation); ▸ violate the number, amount, weight or size limits set by rule; ▸ introduce fish or fish spawn raised by the Department into a private pond; ▸ except as provided, sell, offer for sale, use or possess for use as bait any species of fish not listed in the statutes as baitfish, or fail to label baitfish traps; ▸ disturb baitfish traps or baitfish holding boxes without owner consent; ▸ jig for fish in inland waters; ▸ use or possess an illegal implement or device such as fish spawn, grapnel, spear, spear gun, trawl, weir, gaff, seine, gill net, trap, or set lines for fishing, or any electronic or battery powered device for luring or attracting fish, except that suckers, eels, hornpout, alewives, yellow perch, and cusk may be taken with a permit and as otherwise provided (12-7601 through -7609).

It is illegal to: ★ ▸ use a helicopter for transporting sports fisherman or fish to or from any pond under 10 acres or any beaver flowage;★ ▸ fish with more than two lines; ▸ import live bait, including smelts and other live fish; ▸ take, buy or transport any hellgrammites for use beyond state limits; ▸ purchase or sell black bass, landlocked salmon, pickerel, togue, trout or white perch either directly or indirectly; ▸ import or sell fresh or frozen salmon, or brook, brown, rainbow or lake trout or any of the family salmonidae whose source is outside the continental US, Canada or Alaska or their adjacent waters; ▸ use dynamite or any other explosive, poisonous or stupefying substance to take or destroy fish; ▸ fish other than using the single baited hook and line, and artificial flies, lures and spinners, except smelts in accordance with rules; ▸ use or possess a gill net; ▸ deposit any meat, bones, dead fish, or parts, or other food for fish for the purpose of luring fish; ▸ troll a fly in inland waters restricted to fly fishing; ▸ abuse another's property while fishing on their land by tearing down or destroying any fence or wall, leaving gates open or trampling any crop; ▸ fail to label black bass, salmon, togue or trout being kept at any sporting camp, hotel or public lodging place with the name and address of the person who caught the fish (12-7610 through -7625). It is lawful to take baitfish from all inland waters when these waters are open to fishing, and the Commissioner may grant permits to take baitfish from certain waters at any time (12-7630).

Commercial and Private Enterprise Provisions

The Commissioner may issue licenses for establishment and operation of commercial shooting areas. The land must be in a county with less than two such areas, five miles from another such area, and encompass 200-400 contiguous acres. Special commercial shooting area hunting licenses may be issued for such areas (12-7104 and -7105).

Any resident or nonresident is eligible for a live bait retailer's license permitting possession of live smelts, Osmerus mordax, and baitfish for resale or sale. A baitfish wholesaler's license permits taking and possessing live baitfish for resale or sale; a smelt wholesaler's license permits taking and possessing live smelts for resale or sale (12-7171).

No person may act as a guide without a valid license. Applicants must be at least 18, be currently certified through completion of any standard first-aid course that meets Commission criteria, and meet all requirements established by Commission rule [classes, hunting and fishing privileges, and fees for guide licenses are set forth] (12-7311). ★★Guide license applicants must pass an examination, and if carrying passengers for hire, must also be certified in watercraft safety. The Commissioner determines the form, content and locations for the examination, and may require reexamination if upon receiving a written complaint it appears that the guide no longer meets qualifications. The Commissioner shall approve a curriculum of practical skills, fisheries and wildlife laws and other aspects to prepare persons for guide examinations (12-7313 and -7313-A). The Commissioner shall establish safety standards to provide guide clients reasonable protection from hazards. The Commissioner may: ▸ require applicants to state whether they use alcohol or drugs which would interfere with their competence; ▸ require previously licensed guides to certify they have not failed to provide services as agreed; ▸ establish competency standards; ▸ establish standards for watercraft use by a guide; ▸ establish general and specialized classifications of guide licenses; ▸ establish rules in any other necessary area (12-7314).★★

The Commissioner or Administrative Court may revoke, suspend, refuse to issue or renew a guide license for failure to meet standards of competency, failure to meet guide license qualifications and guide incompetence or negligence in guiding activities (12-7315). No person may knowingly hire a person as a guide with knowledge that the person does not hold a valid guide license. A guide who knows of a violation by a client of any of the fish and game laws shall, within 24 hours, or as soon as safely possible, inform a person authorized to enforce these laws. A guide shall not take a party of more than 12 people out on any lake, stream or waterway (12-7317 through -7319).

★The Commissioner may issue a commercial hide dealer's license to buy, sell, barter, or take in exchange for any services rendered any raw, untanned wild animal hide or head, or bear gall bladder; and aid or assist another in buying, selling or bartering raw, untanned hides or heads of wild animals or bear gall bladders. Licensees shall keep complete records. A person who lawfully possesses any deer, moose, bear, or any fur-bearing animal may sell the hide, head or gall bladder. The Commissioner may issue a special hide dealer's license to one in the business of butchering wild animals, permitting a licensee to sell or barter commercially the heads or untanned hides of deer or moose that are butchered in the place of business. Licensees shall keep complete records (12-7352 and -7352-A). ★

The Advisory Board for the Licensing of Guides, consisting of seven members [details of qualifications given], shall provide advice and consent on Commissioner rules, conduct oral examinations of applicants at the Commissioner's request, and advise on granting and revoking guide licenses (12-7320).

Taxidermy license holders may possess, transport, sell, and train in taxidermy on fish and wildlife specimens lawfully taken. Licensees must keep records, and the Commissioner shall adopt standards of competency and may adopt other rules. The Advisory Board for the Licensing of Taxidermists is created to advise the Commissioner regarding taxidermy practice, rules and examinations. A license is required for commercial practice of taxidermy, and applicants must show qualifications and be examined as the Commissioner determines. Complaints shall be investigated and licenses may be revoked, suspended or not renewed on the basis of fraud, lack of competency, negligence or neglect, or failing to provide services as contracted, and hearings may be provided (12-7354 through -7357).

See Agency Advisory Boards under STATE FISH AND WILDLIFE AGENCIES and GENERAL EXCEPTIONS TO PROTECTION for game breeding and wildlife exhibit licenses.

Import, Export and Release Provisions

The Commissioner may issue all of the following permits and licenses: ▸ licenses to sell commercially grown or imported fish; ▸ permits to introduce, import, or transport live freshwater fish or eggs or to possess such; ▸ permits to introduce fish of any kind into any inland waters or private pond; ▸ permits to introduce or import wildlife into the state, to receive or possess such wildlife, or to release into the wild captive or imported wild birds and animals; ▸ importation permits for moose and caribou, permitting one who has legally killed moose or caribou outside Maine to possess or import it into the state, possession and importation being allowed for consumption, but not for sale; ▸ permits to import live mallard ducks, quail and Chukar partridge, with proper metallic legbands, to operators of commercial shooting areas; ▸ permits to allow importation of pheasants, alive, dead or dressed, with certification that the birds are free of infectious or contagious diseases (12-7201 through -7204 and 12-7237 through - 7240).

A license to cultivate or harvest fish commercially in private ponds allows a landowner to construct, within property limits, a dam across a nonnavigable brook, stream or river to create a private pond for cultivating or harvesting fish, and the proprietor may fish for, possess, sell, transport or have transported these cultivated fish as specified. These fish may be taken regardless of regulations as to manner, time, season, bag or length limit or fishing license requirements (12-7205).

See also HABITAT PROTECTION

Interstate Reciprocal Agreements

Residents 16 or older may purchase a resident fishing license; nonresidents 12 or older may purchase nonresident fishing licenses. When similar legislation is enacted by New Hampshire, fishing licenses issued by this state or New Hampshire shall be recognized when used on any lake or pond partly in both the states (12-7151).

ANIMAL DAMAGE CONTROL

Landowners or family members may use gas cartridges on their own land for woodchuck control. ★A person may sell and advertise rodenticide for orchard mouse control and gas cartridges for woodchuck control (12-7432). ★ Except as provided, any person may lawfully kill or cause to be killed any wild animals night or day found attacking, worrying or wounding that person's domestic animals or destroying that person's property. One who kills a wild animal by authority of this section shall report the incident to a game warden as provided (12-7501). Except as provided, the cultivator, owner, or authorized agent of any orchard or growing crop, except grass, clover and grain fields, may take or kill deer or other wild animals night or day when they are doing substantial damage to the orchard or crop. The warden shall immediately investigate and may give a certificate of ownership of the carcass to the landowner (12-7502). Section 12-7502 shall not prohibit taking or killing bear found doing damage to blueberry land. The Commissioner may issue a permit to any licensed beekeeper to protect beehives from damage by bear. Beaver and wild birds may not be taken or killed under 12-7501 and -7502. The Commissioner may cause Department personnel to take nuisance beaver at any time without landowner consent. Coyotes may be taken at any time and in any manner prescribed by the Commissioner (12-7504). (See also Agency Powers and Duties under STATE WILDLIFE AGENCIES.)

★Whenever deer are doing damage to orchards and crops, including legumes, except grass, the Department shall furnish to the owner or agent of the orchards and crops suitable repellents without cost. The Department may pay for half the cost of fencing young orchards to keep deer out.★ A game warden may kill any dog outside the enclosure or immediate care of its owner or keeper upon finding the dog chasing, killing, wounding or pursuing moose, caribou, deer, or elk at any time, or any other wild animals in closed season, or worrying, wounding or killing any domestic animal, livestock or poultry. An owner may kill any dog found killing or attacking the owner's livestock, poultry or domestic animals [details of notice, warrants and hearings before killing dogs given]. The Commissioner may declare an open season on muskrats polluting water supplies or damaging property if the owner makes written complaint, suspend the game laws relating to raccoons and bears in restricted localities for periods of time to relieve excessive damage to sweet corn or other crops and make exceptions for using dogs to hunt raccoons and bears, if dogs are under the owner's supervision at all times (12-7504).

ENFORCEMENT OF WILDLIFE LAWS

Enforcement Powers

Game Wardens shall enforce the state fish and game laws, Commissioner rules, the US Migratory Bird Treaty Act and its rules and regulations and may arrest and prosecute violators thereof. If in uniform and having a reasonable and articulable suspicion that a motor vehicle or other conveyance or its operator is or has been involved in, or may contain evidence of, a violation of Title 12, Game Wardens may stop the vehicle to check its registration and vehicle identification, request personal identification of the operator and question the operator about the violation. Game Wardens may: ► stop any watercraft to inspect the craft, its equipment and certificates, and order any watercraft ashore to correct a violation or protect the safety of its occupants; ► stop and examine any all-terrain vehicle or snowmobile to ascertain whether it is operated in compliance with the statutes; ► do anything otherwise prohibited if necessary to carry out their duties and powers. In addition to their specified duties and powers, wardens have the same duties and powers as sheriffs in their respective counties. Wardens may act as agents of the Commissioner (12-7053).

Sheriffs, deputy sheriffs, police officers, constables, marine patrol officers, wardens of the Penobscot Indian Nation within their Territory, and US Department of Interior law enforcement personnel shall have the powers of Game Wardens. The Commissioner shall grant the powers of Game Wardens outside the Penobscot Indian Territory to wardens of the Indian Nation who have qualified under the Commissioner's written code and have been approved by the Commissioner of Personnel. All law enforcement personnel of the state, including all harbormasters except those whose authority is restricted, and all foresters, wardens of the Bureau of Forestry and supervisors and rangers of the state Bureau of Parks and Recreation, have the same powers and duties as Game Wardens (7055 and 7056). District Attorneys shall prosecute all violators of fish and game laws occurring within their districts when so requested by the Commissioner, a Game Warden or other law enforcement officer (12-7902).

Whenever a violation of the marine resources or fish and game laws of New Hampshire or Maine is committed or attempted by persons fishing in any waters between these states, any warden or other person authorized to make arrests for violations of the wildlife laws of New Hampshire may make arrests on any part of the waters between New Hampshire and Maine or their shores and take the person for prosecution to the state in which the violation was committed (12-7057).

It is illegal to fail or refuse to stop a motor vehicle, watercraft, snowmobile, all-terrain vehicle, or other conveyance immediately upon request or signal by any officer in uniform whose duty is to enforce fish and game laws. It is illegal to impersonate or falsely represent oneself as a game warden. A person is guilty of nonfeasance if the person fails to perform any act, duty or obligation enjoined by the fish and game laws (12-7060 through -7062).

Criminal Penalties

Violation of a closed season for deer is a class D crime. Failure to aid an injured person or report a hunting accident is a Class C crime (12-7901). "Habitual violator" means any person having three or more convictions under the fish and game laws within the previous five years, provided that, whenever more than one prohibited act is violated at the same time, multiple convictions are considered as one offense. Violation: fine not less than $500; jail not less than three days; no suspension of penalties (12-7001). Except as provided, a person is guilty of a license or permit violation each day of violation of any restriction of a license or permit, violation of the terms of any special privilege, or failure to have a valid license or permit (12-7371). Violation: class E crime; minimum fine of $50 plus an amount two times the license fee; fine cannot be suspended. Violators may also be subject to forfeiture of not less than $1,000 nor more than $10,000 (12-7901). Licensed guides commit violations if they knowingly assist a client in violating any of the provisions of fish and wildlife laws, have knowledge and fail to report that the client has violated provisions, and take more than 12 people out on any lake, stream or waterway at any time (12-7371-A). Persons who hunt wild animals or birds have a duty to submit to a blood or breath blood-alcohol level test if there is probable cause to believe they are hunting under the influence of intoxicating liquor (12-7408). Violation of any prohibited act of the fish and wildlife laws is a class E crime, except as otherwise provided. Violation of an act prohibited in the fishing statutes is a class E crime, except that in addition to any penalty which the court might impose, a convicted person shall be fined up to $20 for each fish illegally possessed, fine not suspendable. Conviction of illegal fishing of Atlantic salmon shall include a fine of $500 per fish and up to $1,000 per violation, not suspendable (12-7901).

Civil Penalties

★★Upon a violation of the state endangered species laws, any rule adopted pursuant thereto, or any license or permit granted, the Attorney General may institute injunctive proceedings to enjoin any further violation, a civil or criminal action, or any appropriate combination of proceedings. The court may order restoration of any area affected by violations, and shall order restoration with willful violations, unless it would threaten public health and safety, or result in environmental damage or substantial injustice (12-7758).★★

Illegal Taking of Wildlife

All fish or wildlife hunted, trapped, fished, bought, sold, carried, transported or found in possession of any person in violation of the fish and game laws is contraband and subject to seizure by any officer authorized to enforce these laws (12-7907). Upon conviction, such items are subject to disposal or sale, or return if not illegally possessed (12-7909).

It is illegal to keep a wild animal in captivity for any purpose, except as provided or if purchased or obtained originally from a dealer, pet shop or licensed wildlife exhibit, or to hunt on a state game farm or in a licensed wildlife exhibit at any time (12-7736).

See also HUNTING, FISHING, TRAPPING PROVISIONS.

License Revocations and Suspensions

The Commissioner may bring a complaint in the Administrative Court to revoke or suspend the hunting license, or the privilege to obtain same, of any person reasonably believed to have killed, wounded or recklessly endangered the safety of another human while hunting. The Court shall revoke or suspend the license or privilege up to five years if it finds that the person so acted and public safety will be endangered by retention of the license or privilege. Any person whose hunting license has been revoked or suspended, or whose right to hunt or to obtain a hunting license for a period not to exceed five years has been denied, may petition the Commissioner for privilege restoration after one year. If the petition is disallowed, the petitioner may appeal to the Advisory Council (12-7101). Upon conviction of violation of any provision of fish and game laws, the Commissioner may revoke or refuse to grant a license or permit for three months to five years. Upon conviction of violation of any provision of Title 17-A while on a hunting or fishing trip or in the pursuit of wild animals, birds or fish, the Commissioner may revoke the license or permit for up to five years, unless killing or wounding of a human has occurred, in which case the Commissioner may revoke the license or permit for not less than five years. Any person whose license or permit has been revoked may request a hearing by the Commissioner and the license or permit may be reinstated (12-7077).

If a person convicted of a violation of any provision of the fish and game laws does not hold a valid license or permit, the Commissioner may refuse to issue a related license or permit for up to five years following conviction, except when the killing or wounding of a human has occurred in which case the Commissioner may revoke the license or permit for not less than five years (12-7078). If a habitual violator (three or more convictions in five years) is convicted of a fish and wildlife violation, the Commissioner shall revoke all licenses and permits. No license may be granted for a period of not less than three years from revocation. Within 30 days of revocation, the person may petition for a hearing before the Commissioner. A petitioner who denies any facts in the record has the burden of proof (12-7079).

See also Licenses and Permits under HUNTING, FISHING, TRAPPING PROVISIONS.

HABITAT PROTECTION

★The Commissioner shall establish criteria for identification of deer wintering areas, notify appropriate municipalities or plantation officials and property owners of existence of the areas, and provide information to those persons as to actions which may be taken to protect the deer (12-7037).★

★Upon written consent of landowners, the Commissioner may create sanctuaries not to exceed 1,000 acres from any lands in the state for the purpose of liberating tame deer. All or any part of such lands may be released from the restrictions of a sanctuary whenever deemed expedient.★ The Commissioner may promulgate rules regulating hunting, fishing, trapping or public use of any wildlife management area or wildlife sanctuary, except that no landowner shall be prohibited from operating any vehicle on domiciled land. The Commissioner may harvest and sell natural products of and on lands owned by the Department. The Commissioner may regulate trapping wild animals on wildlife sanctuaries or closed territories. It is illegal to hunt, trap or possess hunting implements in wildlife sanctuaries except as provided (12-7651 through -7654).

The Commissioner may purchase lands and erect buildings for operating state game farms to propagate wild animals and birds for restocking woods and forests of the state; and take or import wild animals or birds, dead or alive, for inspection, cultivation, propagation, distribution or for scientific or other purposes (12-7735). The Commissioner may acquire by gift or bequest and may purchase, lease or take real and personal property to establish, erect and operate fish hatcheries or feeding stations. Owners of property taken are entitled to damages equal to the reasonable value of the property, the county commissioners to determine the value, and aggrieved parties may appeal to the Superior Court. Screens may be authorized, spawning areas designated and safe salmon stock accepted for release (12-7671, -7672, and -7675). To conserve and restore anadromous and migratory fish, fishways may be required to be erected, maintained, repaired or altered by persons in control of dams or other obstructions [extensive details of fishway and adjudicatory proceedings given] (12-7701-A). A fish kill resulting from improper operation of fishways may result in a fine equivalent to the value of fish killed but no more than $10,000 per day of violation (12-7701-C). Tampering with a fishway or dam includes closing to migration, damaging or introducing foreign objects into a fishway or dam (12-7702).

NATIVE AMERICAN WILDLIFE PROVISIONS

Members of Maine's Indian tribes are exempt from fees for Atlantic salmon licenses (12-6255). Without any charge or fee, the Commissioner shall issue hunting, trapping and fishing licenses to any Indian age 10 or older of the Passamaquoddy, Penobscot, Maliseet or Micmac Tribes, providing a certificate from the respective reservation governor is presented, the Aroostook Micmac Council or the Central Maine Indian Association, stating that the person is an Indian and a member of that Tribe. License holders are subject to fish and wildlife laws (12-7076). It is unlawful to fish in ponds or portions of rivers or streams subject to the Maine Indian Tribal-State Commission in violation of Commission rules or regulations (12-7655).

See also ENFORCEMENT POWERS.

MARYLAND

Sources: Annotated Code of Maryland, 1989 Replacement Volume, Natural Resources Article, Titles 1, 4, 9 and 10; 1992 Cumulative Supplement.

STATE WILDLIFE POLICY

The General Assembly finds that: ▸ it is the policy of the state to conserve species of fish and wildlife for human enjoyment and scientific purposes, and to insure their perpetuation as viable components of ecosystems; ▸ species of fish and wildlife normally occurring within the state found to be threatened or endangered within the state should be accorded protection to maintain and enhance their numbers; ▸ the state should assist in the protection of fish, wildlife and plants determined to be threatened or endangered elsewhere pursuant to the Endangered Species Act by prohibiting their taking, possession, transportation, exportation, processing, sale or shipment within the state of endangered species and by carefully regulating these activities with regard to threatened species. Exceptions to these prohibitions for the purpose of enhancing species conservation may be permitted as set forth (10-2A-02).

The General Assembly finds that it is in the public interest to insure the conservation, preservation and condition of wildlife native to Maryland, by strictly regulating the possession, importation, exportation, breeding, raising, protection, rehabilitation, hunting, killing, trapping, capture, purchase or sale of certain wildlife which pose a possibility of: ▸ harmful competition to native wildlife; ▸ introduction of a disease or harmful pest; ▸ problems of enforcing wildlife laws and regulations; ▸ threatening native wildlife or other natural resources (10-901) (See also Import, Export and Release Provisions under HUNTING, FISHING, TRAPPING PROVISIONS.) [An overall natural resources environmental protection statement of policy covering all Natural Resources Department agencies, and environmental protection duties thereof, appears in 1-302.]

RELEVANT WILDLIFE DEFINITIONS: See Definitions section of Appendices.

STATE FISH AND WILDLIFE AGENCIES

Agency Structure

There is a **Department of Natural Resources** (Department), established as a principal department of the state government, the head of which is the **Secretary of Natural Resources** (Secretary), appointed by the Governor with advice and consent of the Senate. The Secretary shall have administrative ability, and by reputation and experience demonstrate interest in the field of natural resources. The Secretary serves at the pleasure of, and is directly responsible to, the Governor and shall advise and counsel on matters assigned to the Department and is responsible for carrying out the Governor's policies in natural resources research and development, management and administration [additional overall powers of appointment of the Secretary and responsibilities of the Attorney General's office in relation to the Department are given] (1-101). Every right, power, duty, and function previously conferred upon or exercised by the Department of Game and Inland Fish or the Fish and Wildlife Administration is transferred to the Department, and reference to those agencies in statute, ordinance, regulation, etc. means the Department (4-203 and 10-203). The Secretary is responsible for conservation and management of state wildlife and wildlife resources (10-202).

Agency Powers and Duties

The **Secretary** shall provide for a statewide system of assistance to, and agreements with, local political subdivisions regarding disposition of wild animals, including field services, training, or payment for wildlife control (10-202). The Secretary is responsible for enforcement of all natural resource laws, including any rules adopted pursuant to this article (1-202). The Secretary shall appoint **natural resources police officers** for administration of the **Natural Resources Police Force**, appointments to be made from a list of eligible persons prepared by the Secretary of Personnel or Department. Natural resources police officers appointed for training prior to a regular assignment shall remain on probation for two years (1-203). [A large number of general overall duties and responsibilities of the Secretary with regard to all state natural resources are covered in 1-103 and 1-104.]

★In planning sampling methods and compilation of estimates of wild waterfowl in the state, the **Department** shall take advantage of other organizational surveys, including the Grant National Waterfowl Hunt, Inc. and the Maryland Outfitters Association (10-210).★ The Department may: ▸ acquire and equip vessels for its work; ▸ contract for research or scientific investigation; ▸ conduct demonstrations to improve fisheries and import fish or other organisms for experiment; ▸ inspect fish caught or sold and enforce cull laws not interfering with inspections by the Department of Health and Mental Hygiene; ▸ inspect state waters to stock with food fish; ▸ negotiate agreements with other states concerning catching fish, fish sizes and seasons; ▸ establish by rule boundaries of tidal and nontidal waters; ▸ propose separate fisheries resource management programs for listed water and tributaries (4-205).

Agency Regulations

Having due regard for the distribution, abundance, economic value and breeding habits of fish in non-tidal waters and wildlife, the Secretary may adopt regulations to enlarge, extend, restrict or prohibit angling, hunting, possessing, selling, purchasing, shipping, transporting or exporting wildlife. In addition to any other penalty provided, a person convicted of violating a regulation shall be fined $5 for each bird, mammal, fish, amphibian or reptile illegally caught, hunted or possessed, but this additional penalty does not apply to game birds and mammals. A second or subsequent conviction within a year results in suspension of license, and no new hunting or angling license the following calendar year (4-602 and 10-205).

Agency Funding Sources

There is a **State Wildlife Management and Protection Fund** in the Department. Money from license, stamp, or permit fee shall be credited, unless otherwise provided, to this fund and used for the scientific investigation, protection, propagation and management of wildlife. Clerks of courts shall transmit to the Department monthly all moneys received for hunting licenses and stamps, the Treasurer to credit to the fund (10-209 and -304).

There is a **State Fisheries Management and Protection Fund** consisting of money from a fish and fisheries license, stamp, permit or fee to be used for the scientific investigation, protection, propagation and management of nontidal finfish. Clerks of courts shall transmit such moneys monthly to the Department. There is a **Fisheries Research and Development Fund** consisting of moneys from commercial licenses, permits, taxes and royalties from oyster and clam shells removed from tidal waters, plus certain fines and forfeitures, for replenishing fisheries resources, research, and to match federal funds for fisheries (4-208 and-209).

★★There is a **Birdwatcher's Fund**, administered by the Secretary, consisting of revenue the Department derives from birdwatcher's stamps and decals, private contributions, grants, and donations, to be expended for preservation of nongame wildlife species and threatened and endangered species. "Birdwatcher" means a person who engages in "birdwatching," which means identifying, studying and recording the presence of wild birds in their natural surroundings, but does not include incidental viewing of wild birds. The purpose of the fund is: ▸ dissemination of information pertaining to nongame wildlife, and threatened and endangered species conservation, management and values; ▸ scientific investigation and survey for better protection and conservation; ▸ propagation, distribution, protection and restoration of such species; ▸ research and management; ▸ habitat development; ▸ matching of funds available to the Department under federal programs for such projects and activities (10-2A-06.1).★★

There is a **Chesapeake Bay and Endangered Species Fund** consisting of the net proceeds from contributions under the income tax checkoff system and donations to the fund, administered by the Secretary. Moneys expended from the fund are supplemental to funding that would otherwise be appropriated to the Department. The Secretary may distribute no more than 5% of the net proceeds of the fund to a promotional account to promote further donations to the fund. ★★The remainder shall be distributed 50% to the **Chesapeake Bay Trust** established under 8-1901, to be used as provided herein, and 50% to an Endangered Species Account, to be used to conserve nongame, threatened and endangered species. The trust shall use its funds to provide grants to nonprofit organizations, community associations, civil groups, schools or public agencies for citizen involvement projects that will enhance or promote: ▸ public education concerning Chesapeake Bay; ▸ preservation or enhancement of water quality and fishery or wildlife habitat; ▸ restoration of aquatic or land resources; ▸ reforestation projects; ▸ publication or production of educational materials on the Chesapeake Bay; ▸ training in environmental studies or enhancement. The Secretary shall use the funds credited to the Endangered Species Account to promote conservation, propagation and habitat protection of nongame, threatened or endangered species, including: ▸ acquisition through absolute purchase, or purchase of easements, of habitats to conserve, protect or propagate nongame, threatened or endangered species; ▸ monitoring, surveying and protection of nest sites of bald eagles, Delmarva fox squirrels, peregrine falcons and piping plovers; ▸ promotion of voluntary protection of habitat for threatened and endangered species by management assistance to private landowners; ▸ initiation of surveys and recovery programs, including habitat restoration or protection, for other threatened or endangered species; ▸ protection of threatened or endangered species in natural heritage areas; ▸ surveying of nongame birds, mammals, reptiles, and amphibians not currently receiving review, particularly species whose population status is questionable such as the bog turtle; ▸ development and implementation of an urban wildlife program; ▸ development of a public education and information program. In developing wildlife conservation programs, the Secretary shall solicit the advice and recommendations of the Threatened and Endangered Species Committee and the Department Heritage Program. The Secretary shall report annually to the General Assembly on the administration of the fund, including: ▸ the gross amount of donations; ▸ costs of administration of the income tax checkoff system; ▸ description of promotional efforts undertaken; ▸ a detailed accounting of use by the Chesapeake Bay Trust for wildlife conservation (1-701 through -706).★★

The Department shall use $1 from the sale of each consolidated hunting license and all money from the sale of **Bow and Arrow** and **Black Powder Deer Stamps** as follows: up to 40% to: ▸ provide bow hunter education; ▸ acquire, construct and maintain public archery ranges; ▸ perform studies to evaluate programs related to bow or muzzle-loading hunting. The remaining percentage shall be used to: ▸ establish an effective deer checking system during the bow and muzzle-loading seasons; ▸ acquire additional hunter access by opening more state-owned lands and purchasing rights-of-way to reach areas not open; ▸ acquire additional muzzle loader and bow hunting lands; ▸ administer a permit system applicable to newly opened areas; ▸ police hunting lands during seasons and provide additional law enforcement personnel. All revenues accruing to the Wildlife Management and Protection fund from sales of the **State Migratory Wild Waterfowl Stamp** shall be expended as follows: ▸ 50% for propagation, purchase, distribution of hand reared ducks and operation of hatchery facilities; ▸ 50% for waterfowl projects to create, develop, maintain, manage, preserve and enhance waterfowl habitat on public lands (10-308 and -308.1). (See also HABITAT PROTECTION.)

Agency Advisory Boards

There is a **Wildlife Advisory Commission** [in addition to numerous other commissions], composed of nine members appointed by the Governor, who shall solicit nominations that promote the future of hunting and the preservation of state wildlife, with geographical distribution being a prime consideration in filling vacancies. There shall be representation from the farming community. Members shall be knowledgeable in the area of interest of the advisory commission. In addition to an advisory body established by law, the Secretary, with the Governor's approval, may create an advisory unit (1-102).

There is a **Sport Fisheries Advisory Commission** to provide advice on recreational fisheries, consisting of nine members appointed and serving in accordance with 1-102, who serve four year terms and represent state diversified angling interests and waters (4-204). ★★There is a **Captive Wildlife Advisory Committee** composed of seven members appointed by the Director, of which one each shall represent the: ▸ pet industry; ▸ falconers; ▸ shooting preserve industry; ▸ game breeding industry; ▸ humane society; members from the general public. The Committee shall review proposed regulations, give recommendations to the Director and advise on captive wildlife (10-910)★★.

See HABITAT PROTECTION for the Department's advisory committee on propagation and distribution of wild ducks and habitat conservation.

PROTECTED SPECIES OF WILDLIFE

Except for unprotected birds and game birds hunted during open season, a person may not hunt, destroy or possess a wild bird. Except for the sale of captive-bred birds of prey, person may not sell, purchase, barter or exchange, or offer, the plumage, skin or body of nongame bird, nor possess a game bird for sale, whether caught within or without the state. A person may not take or destroy or attempt to do so, the nest or eggs of a wild bird, or possess same, nor hunt or take nest or egg of birds regulated under the Migratory Bird Treaty Act, except in the manner and by the means prescribed by USDI regulations, except for scientific purposes under a USDI permit and a Department certificate (10-401 and -402).

The Secretary shall conduct investigations of fish and nongame wildlife to develop information on population, distribution, habitat needs, limiting factors and other biological and ecological data to determine conservation measures necessary for their continued ability to sustain themselves successfully. On the basis of these determinations the Secretary shall issue proposed regulations and develop conservation programs. The Secretary shall conduct ongoing investigations of nongame wildlife, and by regulation, shall adopt limitations on taking, possession, transportation, exportation, processing, sale or shipment to conserve fish and nongame wildlife. Except as otherwise provided, a person may not take, possess, transport, export, process, sell or ship fish or nongame wildlife in need of conservation, nor may a common or contract carrier knowingly transport or receive such for shipment (4-2A-03 and 10-2A-03).

There are both a state Endangered Species of Fish Conservation Act and a Nongame and Endangered Species Conservation Act (4-2A-01 *et seq.* and 10-2A-01 *et seq.*). A species endangered or threatened pursuant to the federal Endangered Species Act shall be deemed an endangered or threatened species. The Secretary may determine that a threatened species is endangered throughout all or a portion of its range within the state. In addition, the Secretary, by regulation, shall determine whether a species normally occurring within the state is endangered or threatened due to any of the following factors: ► the present or threatened destruction, modification or curtailment of its habitat or range; ► overutilization for commercial, sporting, scientific, educational or other purposes; ► disease or predation; ► inadequacy of existing regulatory mechanisms; ► other natural or manmade factors affecting its continued existence within the state. In determining whether a species is endangered or threatened, the Secretary shall take into consideration actions by the federal government, other states, other agencies of this state, or by a person which may affect the species. Except with respect to species determined to be endangered or threatened herein, the Secretary may not add a species to nor remove a species from any list published unless the Secretary first: ► publishes a public notice of the proposed action; ► furnishes notice of the proposed action to the Governor of any state sharing a common border with the state and in which the subject species is known to exist; ► allows at least 30 days following publication for comment from the public and other interested parties. If the Department determines that an emergency situation exists involving the continued existence of the species, the Department may add the species to the lists, if it publishes a public notice of such emergency situation with a summary of facts supporting this determination. The Secretary shall adopt regulations containing a list of all endangered and threatened species normally occurring within the state, and specifying over what portion of its range it is endangered or threatened. ★★For a species of fish that the Secretary has determined endangered or threatened, and on which the Secretary has declared a moratorium on catching, sale or possession, the Secretary shall make an annual status report to the General Assembly and the Governor, containing: ► field studies on spawning stock size; ► measurement of egg deposition on spawning grounds; ► measurements of mortality rates of fish eggs, larvae and juveniles on spawning grounds, nursery areas and spawning rivers; ► bioassays on eggs and larvae collected from spawning fish; ► measurements of heavy metals, PCBs, acid rain leachates, sediments and other distresses to the habitat; ► studies on acid rain, studies on the role of fish diseases, trend analyses and recommendations for future management actions and a recommendation to continue for one year or to discontinue the moratorium (4-2A-04 and 10-2A-04).★★

Except for endangered or threatened species pursuant to the Endangered Species Act, the Secretary, upon the petition of an interested person, shall conduct a review of listed or unlisted species proposed to be removed from or added to the lists published, if the Secretary publishes public notice that the person has presented substantial evidence which warrants a review. When a species is listed as threatened within the state, the Secretary shall adopt regulations to provide for its conservation, and may prohibit any act as follows. Except as otherwise provided, with respect to an endangered species, a person may not: ► export the species from the state; ► take the species within the state; ► possess, process, sell or transport; ► violate a regulation pertaining to the species' conservation or to a threatened species listed and adopted by the Secretary. Except as otherwise provided, with respect to an endangered species of fish, wildlife, or plant, a person may not: ► export the species; ► possess, process, sell, transport or ship the species by any means; ► violate a regulation pertaining to the species or to any threatened species. An endangered species of fish or wildlife which enters the state from another state or from a point outside the US and which is transported to a point within or beyond the state may enter and be transported in accordance with the terms of a federal or other state permit. The Secretary may permit any act otherwise prohibited herein for scientific purposes or to enhance the propagation or survival of the affected species, and after January 1, 1990, for aquaculture involving the affected fish species in nontidal ponds, lakes or impoundments (4-2A-05 and 10-2A-05). These provisions do not prohibit importation into the state of fish or wildlife which may be lawfully imported into the US or lawfully taken and removed from another state, or entry into the state or possession, transportation, exportation, sale or shipment of fish or wildlife designated an endangered or threatened species in this state but not in the state where originally taken, if the person presents substantial evidence that the fish or wildlife was lawfully taken and removed from the origin state. This section does not permit the possession, transportation, sale or shipment within the state of fish or wildlife species listed pursuant to the Endangered Species Act (4-2A-08 and 10-2A-08). Special provisions may apply to striped bass or rockfish, including hybrids, if listed as threatened or endangered, or if raised in aquaculture facilities as specified (4-2A-08). (See also Agency Funding Sources under STATE FISH AND WILDLIFE AGENCIES and ENFORCEMENT OF WILDLIFE LAWS.) The Department shall prepare a comprehensive management plan for harvesting striped bass or rockfish, white perch and yellow perch including sustainable harvest rates and indicators that would trigger tightening or loosening of harvest restrictions, and shall present this plan to legislative committees for review, along with recommendations for legislation, or other regulation (4-2A-05.2 and -06). The Department shall adopt regulations allowing the catching of hybrids of striped bass under certain conditions in freshwater impoundments as long as, during the time a moratorium on the taking and sale of striped bass is in effect under the Endangered Species of Fish Conservation Act, the regulations also prohibit the sale of the hybrids of striped bass caught under the authority of the regulations (4-2A-08.1).

A person may not enter a state wildlife refuge without the Department's consent or that of the person in charge of an area, nor allow dog, domestic stock, or poultry to enter. The Department may grant a special permit, subject to revocation at any time, to a person regularly residing thereon to have trap, dog or gun on the refuge; however these may not be used in hunting wildlife unless under permit for propagating purposes. The Department by written permission may grant the right to hunt for vermin and use dog and gun on state wildlife refuges, and to hunt wildlife to be used for propagation purposes (10-807). (See HABITAT PROTECTION.)

GENERAL EXCEPTIONS TO PROTECTION

The Secretary may grant certificates to an accredited person permitting the collection of fish, fish eggs, crustaceans or mollusks for scientific purposes. On proof that the permittee has captured or killed fish, fish eggs, crustaceans or mollusks for other than scientific purposes, the certificate is void (4-212). The Secretary may issue a scientific collecting permit to an accredited person to collect wildlife, nests or eggs for scientific or educational purposes, and may adopt regulations. Such permit becomes void on proof that the permittee has captured or killed wildlife, taken nests or eggs for other than scientific/educational purposes, taken wildlife or nests or eggs not authorized, or violated terms of the permit (10-909).

An accredited person desiring to assist the Department in the control of wildlife injurious to agriculture or other interests, or to provide care and treatment of sick or injured wildlife for rehabilitation and release shall obtain a wildlife cooperator permit. Such person must have adequate training in the capture, handling and care of wildlife and own or lease facilities of sufficient size and design to maintain the wildlife in captivity (10-908).

See PROTECTED SPECIES OF WILDLIFE.

HUNTING, FISHING, TRAPPING PROVISIONS

General Provisions

The Department shall set annually by rule the daily creel, possession and size limits for game and freshwater fish and shall establish and publish open seasons to catch: bass (largemouth, smallmouth); pike, pickerel; walleye; rockfish (striped bass); trout (brook, brown, rainbow); shad, hickory shad and herring; suckers, catfish, carp, eel, gudgeon; all species of sunfish including bluegills, rock bass (commonly known as redeye) fallfish, crappie, perch (white and yellow) (4-603 and -615).

A person may not knowingly ship, transport or carry a fur or pelt of wild quadruped outside the state without a special shipping tag attached. Licensed fur dealers need no special tags if they attach their license number. Common carriers may not knowingly receive a fur or pelt for shipment outside the state unless it is tagged (10-509 and -511).

Licenses and Permits

★To provide a fund to pay the expense of protecting and managing wildlife, and preventing unauthorized persons from hunting, a person may not hunt during open season game birds and mammals without a hunter's license. A permanent resident of a government reservation may obtain a resident hunter's license.★ No license is required for a farmland owner, spouse, children, or tenant thereof and family hunting on farmland and residing thereon, residents in the Armed Forces, or unarmed persons participating in organized foxhunts. ★The applicant shall sign a statement acknowledging the illegality of hunting on private property without the owner's permission.★ [A large number of license types and fees are listed.] ★★Upon issuing a hunting license, the Department shall furnish the licensee with a list of the names and addresses of every state general hospital which offers emergency medical treatment.★★ When the Department has adequate computer capability, it shall compile statistics annually concerning the sale of hunting licenses, and statistics as to counties, ages, and types of licenses sold (10-301). ★There is a patron's hunting license, issued on a yearly basis, for a $500 fee, to hunt game birds or mammals during open season without any other license except the federal and Maryland migratory wild waterfowl stamps (10-301.2).★ A person shall possess a hunter's license while hunting and exhibit it on demand of a natural resources or other law enforcement officer or the landowner or agent thereof on whose property the person is hunting (10-306). ★A violator of this provision who presents to the court a license within five days of conviction may appeal to determine whether the person held the license prior to arrest and the violation was due to inadvertence, and the court may reduce by one-half any penalty (10-311).★

In addition to the basic hunting license, a deer stamp and/or a state migratory waterfowl stamp is required except for resident landowners and tenants and their families, or unless otherwise excepted (10-308 and -308.1). (See Agency Funding Sources under STATE FISH AND WILDLIFE AGENCIES.) Nonresidents desiring to trap fur-bearers, except otter or beaver, must have a nonresident trapper license in addition to any other required license, which shall be issued only to residents of states which grant the same trapping privileges to Maryland residents. A nonresident may not hunt or trap beaver or otter in this state (10-502 and -503).

After 1977, a person, regardless of age, may not procure a hunting license without producing a certificate of competency, a hunting license issued prior to 1977, or affidavit that such license was held. ★This section does not apply to nonresidents who purchase a hunting license to hunt wild waterfowl.★ The Department shall prescribe a course of instruction in conservation and in competency and safety in firearm handling, designate persons or agencies to give the course, and issue certificates of competency and safety. The Department shall institute and coordinate a statewide course of instruction in conservation, competency and firearm safety, and may cooperate with any political subdivision or organization having as one of its objectives the promotion of competency and safety in firearm handling. A similar certificate issued outside the state by a governmental agency shall be accepted, if the privileges are reciprocal for Maryland residents. Presentation of a fictitious certificate or fraud in obtaining same shall result in revocation of hunting privileges for up to one year. One refused a certificate of competency may appeal to the Secretary (10-301.1).

A gunning rig license is required for residents to hunt wild waterfowl from a boat or raft not under power, including a body booting rig, boat or floating blind, bushwack rig, canoe, rowboat, skiff or sneakboat. Nonresidents may not hunt from such rigs unless accompanied by a licensed resident co-owner, and nonresidents may not obtain such license. A law enforcement officer may confiscate the license of a gunning rig being used unlawfully (10-607 and -608). A blind site license is required to erect stationary blinds for riparian landowners owning at least 500 contiguous yards of shoreline unless otherwise excepted (10-612). [Extensive details are given for application for blind site licenses and issuance in order of rotation, depending on county, conflicts between applicants, required distances between blind sites and other details.]

Angler's licenses provide a fund for protecting and managing game and freshwater fish. A person age 16 or older shall secure an angler's license to fish in state nontidal waters during the open season. No license is required of a landowner, tenant or immediate families who fish in nontidal water adjoining their land [other exceptions]. License applicants must sign a statement acknowledging that fishing on private property without permission may subject them to a fine. License moneys shall be credited to the State Fisheries Management and Protection Fund (4-604 and -608).

A person shall exhibit an angler's license on demand of a natural resources police officer, other law enforcement officer, or landowner (4-610). If a person convicted of violating this provision presents an angler's license to the court within five days after conviction, the court may reduce by half any penalty originally imposed if it finds inadvertence. A license may be confiscated if it is used unlawfully by a person other than the licensee. In addition to any other penalty, conviction of fishing without a license in possession or using another's license results in confiscation of the license and no license issued for the following year. Except for a holder of a consolidated senior sport fishing license, a person over age 16 may not fish in special catch-and-return trout management areas and may not possess trout while fishing in nontidal waters without a trout stamp in addition to an angler's license. No stamp is required in a private pond stocked with trout artificially propagated by commercial hatcheries or purchased from persons licensed to sell fish, or any fee fishing lake or pond operated under 4-622 (4-612 through -614). A consolidated senior sport fishing license may be issued to persons over age 65 which allows angling and trout fishing on nontidal waters without a trout stamp, and finfish angling in Chesapeake Bay without a special license (4-216). [Chesapeake Bay sport fishing licenses apply to tidal waters of the Bay and its tributaries. See 4-745.]

Restrictions on Taking: Hunting and Trapping

It is illegal to: purchase, sell or exchange a game bird except as provided; hunt or possess a game bird in excess of state or federal limits; hunt game birds on land or in waters within the boundaries of a migratory bird refuge unless otherwise permitted. ★★It is illegal to hunt or possess a game bird or mammal except during open season, whether hunted in this or in another state or country.★★ A person may possess dead game birds or mammals, fresh or frozen, for the number of days specified by statute. A person may bring into the state by express or baggage a game bird or mammal the person legally killed in any other state if licensed in that state, but such may not be sold or offered for sale. A person may not sell, purchase, barter or exchange, or offer to do such, a game bird or game mammal taken from the wild except the meat, pelt or carcass of muskrat, raccoon, mink, otter, nutria, opossum, beaver, fox, long-tail weasel, fisher or skunk, whether caught in this or another state. The Department by regulation shall set the open season, excepting Sundays, to hunt forest and upland game birds and mammals, and if the normal number of days is reduced due to emergency, it may extend the season. Except during the hunting and trapping season, a person may not hunt or trap a fur-bearing mammal or possess the meat or pelt of same, whether hunted/trapped within the state or in another state. Meat of muskrat or otter may be possessed up to 10 days after the season's close to dispose of the meat for food, or by permit for storage. A person may hunt or trap and possess the pelt or meat of raccoon or opossum within the seasons and bag limits established by the Department. Before establishing the open season for ducks, geese and swan, the Department shall conduct public hearings in certain counties, and shall annually establish and publish the open season, excepting Sundays, for doves, mergansers, woodcock and wetland game birds, including wild waterfowl, in conformity with federal law and regulations. The Department shall regulate the means or weapons for hunting designated wildlife and shall set forth restrictions relating to weapons, including the amount and size of ammunition for designated game birds or mammals, and make same available for distribution with each hunting license purchased. ★This does not authorize the Department to restrict the use of firearms except in the exercise of hunting license privileges (10-403 through -408).★

A person may not hunt muskrat, beaver or otter except by trapping, nor dig into, or molest or destroy, any part of their den or house, nor possess the hide or skin of such animal which has been caught in any way except by trapping, and any such hide which has been punctured by a hole which appears to be a bullet hole shall be prima facie evidence that the animal was killed illegally. A person may not use a light to hunt muskrats, beaver or otter at night, and possession of same shall be prima facie evidence that the light was intended for this purpose. ★A landowner or lessee shall have the exclusive right to trap for muskrats down to the mean low watermark on marsh land adjacent to the landowner's land, and a person may not enter upon or place traps upon such land without the written consent of the landowner (10-504).★ A person may not set snares, body-gripping, or leghold traps within 150 yards of a permanent human residence, except on state, federal or private wetlands, or as otherwise excepted. Body-gripping traps with jaw spread of less than six inches may be placed completely under water, and snap-type rat and mouse traps may be used (10-408.1). The Department shall establish and publish annually the bag limits per day for game birds and mammals, and the bag limits for ducks, geese, brant, railbirds, woodcock, mergansers, doves and snipe may conform to the federal migratory bird rules (10-409). A person may not export from the state a game bird or mammal, except wild waterfowl and fur-bearing mammals, but a licensed hunter may take as personal baggage during the open season only the possession limit set by regulation. An express company or common carrier may not knowingly accept a game bird or mammal except the above for shipment within or outside the state. One desiring to export wild waterfowl shall ship them in the open, tied by head or feet and tagged, or in a slatted container, and may only export in one week the prescribed bag limit. Common carriers may not ship, carry, take or transport a nongame bird within or outside the state (10-417).

A person may not hunt a game bird or mammal on Sundays except: ▸ with state certified raptors used to hunt game during open season; ▸ in an organized fox chase; ▸ using a regulated shooting ground to hunt pen-reared game birds, including pheasants, bobwhite quail, chukar, partridge, mallard ducks, wild turkeys and grouse, with permission of the landowner. A person may not: ▸ hunt game bird or mammal, except raccoon and opossum, at nighttime; ▸ hunt from an aircraft, violation of which is a misdemeanor and a fine of up to $1,000, jail up to 6 months, or both; ▸ carry a firearm to hunt wild bird, mammal, amphibian or reptile while under the influence of alcohol or a narcotic drug; ▸ dig in or drive a motor vehicle on a cleared field while hunting without the owner's permission or park a vehicle so as to block roads on another's land; ▸ shoot at wildlife on, from or across a paved highway or shoulder thereof, or on or from unpaved roads in designated counties; ▸ shoot at wildlife from an automobile or other vehicle except as otherwise provided, or possess in or on same a loaded weapon with ammunition in the magazine. If the vehicle has more than one occupant, and it cannot be determined which is the violator, the owner, if present, is presumed to be responsible for the violation, or if not present, the vehicle operator is presumed responsible. A person may not: ▸ pursue wildlife with an off-road vehicle [detailed definition of "off-road vehicle" included]; ▸ hunt with a ferret or weasel; ▸ kill or attempt to kill wildlife or domestic poultry by poison; ▸ smoke, burn, injure, hunt or molest game birds or mammals in a den or damage or destroy the den; ▸ use steel jaw leghold traps in designated counties except for owners of farmland where set or for Wildlife Service personnel engaged in wildlife control; ▸ use snare traps, pole snares, hanging snares, neck snares except as provided for in designated counties; ▸ shoot or discharge a firearm or deadly weapon within 150 yards ("safety zone") of a dwelling or other building or camp occupied by humans, or shoot at a wild bird or mammal within this area without the specific permission of the owner/occupant, nor hunt or chase within the safety zone without advance permission (10-410).

★In specified counties, a person may cast the rays of an artificial light from a vehicle on woods, fields, orchards, livestock, wild animals or wild birds for the sole purpose of observing or photographing wildlife until 9:00 p.m.★ Such person has the burden of establishing that the light was for observation or photography purposes. If a person casting artificial light, or anyone accompanying the person, has a firearm or bow in possession, the person shall be presumed to be in violation. Otherwise, a person, or two or more persons, may not hunt or attempt such at nighttime a wild bird or quadruped with a light, including vehicle headlights, nor cast the rays of an artificial light when the rays emanate from a vehicle on woods, fields, orchards, livestock, wild animals or birds, dwellings or buildings, except for normal headlight use on public or private roads, or for landowners on their own lands using artificial lights to check their land, crops, livestock or poultry. Raccoons, fox or opossum may be hunted on foot at nighttime during open season with the use of a dog or light or both (10-410).

Except as otherwise provided, a person may not hunt on lands of another without the landowner's or agent's permission, and the landowner is not liable for injury or damage to the person, whether or not permission was given. ★In the counties specified, a person may not hunt on private lands without the written permission of the landowner, and is liable for damages caused to such property. In designated counties, a person may not enter or trespass on private land to hunt deer with gun, rifle, bow and arrow or other means without written permission, to be exhibited to a natural resources police officer or other law enforcement officer or landowner or agent upon request. Such officer shall arrest a person hunting without written permission upon private land upon the request of the landowner/agent. Violation in designated counties on first offense is a fine up to $1,000, and up to $2,000 for a subsequent offense (10-411).★

A person may not possess a live raccoon or opossum without a Department permit, and any reduced to possession by a hunter or trapper shall be killed immediately. A person may not cut a tree to hunt or dislodge a raccoon or opossum without the consent of the tree's owner (see also ANIMAL DAMAGE CONTROL) (10-414). A person may not hunt wetland and upland game birds, except quail and pheasant, by baiting, or on or over a baited area, except for standing crops, flooded crops, flooded harvested croplands, or grain crops properly shocked in the field, or grains scattered solely as the result of normal agricultural planting, or crop manipulation on lands where grown for wildlife purposes, or for pen-raised mallard ducks released on a shooting ground (10-412).

★★A law enforcement officer may destroy, and any other person may destroy, a cat found hunting a game bird or mammal or protected bird or mammal and no cause of action for damages can be maintained for this act.★★ The Department may issue permits for retriever dogs to be trained at any time, and the permittee may, shoot with a shotgun an artificially reared game bird, liberated by hand and tagged. A dog owner may run or train the dog on woodcock, pheasants or imported species, ruffed grouse, rabbit, hare and quail at any time if a person accompanies the dog, has a hunting license, and does not carry firearms, nor permit the dog to kill game birds or mammals except during open season (10-413). While engaged in hunting or pursuing wildlife, a person may not carelessly or negligently shoot, wound or kill another person or intentionally or willfully destroy or damage real or personal property or farm livestock of another (10-424).

There are bow hunting, firearms, and muzzle-loader deer seasons. Every person killing a deer shall report with the deer to a designated checking station within 24 hours. One additional antlered deer permit may be applied for by state residents, or holders of a consolidated hunting license. The Department may regulate the type and number of deer stamps issued to control the deer harvest in various areas, and second deer stamps may be purchased by licensed hunters. ★A person may not remove the head, hide or any part from deer, except internal organs, or cut up the meat until the deer has been checked by the Department, and such removal shall be prima facie evidence of illegal taking, and each separate deer or part found illegally in possession is a separate offense.★ Deer accidentally killed by vehicles may be given to the taker on approval of a natural resources or other officer. A person may not hunt a deer while it is taking refuge in, or swimming through, water (10-415 and -420). A person may not hunt deer: ▸ with automatic firearms; ▸ with full metal-jacketed, incendiary or tracer bullets; ▸ with a firearm holding an ammunition clip holding more than eight bullets; ▸ with a dog or take a dog into the woods. Dogs found pursuing deer may be killed in designated counties unless they have broken away while engaged in fox hunting. It is illegal to cast the rays of a spotlight, headlight, artificial light or other device on highway or in field, forest or woodland while possessing a firearm or other deer-killing device, even though the deer is not shot at, injured or killed. Violation of spotlighting provisions is a misdemeanor; fine up to $2,000; jail up to 6 months; or both; costs at the court's discretion; license revocation for two to five years; every spotlight, firearm, bow and arrow or killing device shall be confiscated and disposed of by the Secretary (10-416). ★A person may hunt deer with a handgun with ammunition and barrel length as specified in hunting areas where a high-powered rifle is allowed (10-420.1).★ ★On the first day of the firearms deer hunting season, a person may not hunt an animal other than deer except for certain waterfowl as specified (10-421).★

★★A person may not hunt wild waterfowl at nighttime as defined by the US Secretary of the Interior, nor possess at nighttime a gun or light used for hunting in or near the vicinity of feeding and resting grounds, and a gun or light found in possession shall be prima facie evidence of intention of a violation and the light shall be confiscated (10-602).★★ A person may not: ▸ shoot wild waterfowl resting on land or water; ▸ hunt from a position more than 10 feet in the air; ▸ use a floating device towed by a power or sail boat; ▸ use a live decoy. Wetland game birds may be hunted with the aid of a dog or with an artificial decoy (10-603, -603.1 and -605). [Restrictions on firearms described.] ★A longbow and arrow are permitted; crossbows are not, when hunting wild waterfowl.★ A natural resources or other law enforcement officer shall confiscate an illegal crossbow or shotgun, rifle or pistol found in the vicinity of wild waterfowl. ★Any law to the contrary notwithstanding, the Secretary and any other Department official may not adopt a regulation banning or limiting the use or possession of lead shot ammunition while hunting wild waterfowl, and a regulation which bans or limits the use or possession of lead shot ammunition is declared null, void and of no effect. The State and any agency or Department may not request that the federal government enforce any federal rule or regulation regarding a ban or limit on the use or possession of lead shot ammunition except for nontoxic shot zones as classified by the USFW (10-604).★ (See also Licenses and Permits under this section.)

A person may not hunt or purposely or unnecessarily disturb wild waterfowl from a boat; however bushwhacking, sneakboating, retrieval of wounded or dead waterfowl by boat, and use of boats on state or federal hunting areas if permitted are allowed. ★The owner of a boat with sail or engines may not use or permit the boat's use for prohibited acts, nor loan or hire the boat without making inquiry into the purpose for the boat's use and ascertaining the boat will not be used illegally and not equipped with guns or ammunition for shooting wild waterfowl. The following shall be prima facie evidence of intentional violation: ▸ location of a power boat propelled by sail or engine having guns or other equipment used for hunting wetland game birds in or near waters used by same; ▸ the firing of shots from a boat in or near waters used by waterfowl; ▸ moving a boat in the direction of waters inhabited by wild waterfowl to cause them to fly (10-606).★ In general, a boat or floating blind not anchored or tied at a licensed blind site may not be permitted closer than 800 yards off privately owned shoreline or within 500 yards of a licensed blind, blind site, gunning rig, or body booter, except as otherwise provided. A person may not use a sneakboat or bushwack rig within 500 yards of a licensed blind or blind site or other rig licensed for hunting wild waterfowl (10-610). [Waterfowl hunting provisions, blind site licensing provisions and application procedures, distance requirements for hunting blinds from shorelines, other blind sites, and dwellings, use of particular boat types as defined in 10-601 (sneakboats, bushwack rigs, body booting, gunning rig), exceptions for particular counties or state waters are detailed; see 10-601 through 10-624 for additional information and statutory requirements on wild waterfowl hunting.] ★A person may not use an electronic device on a boat in state waters or on aircraft, or use aircraft to detect the presence of finfish, except for the use of depth finders from boats. A person may not use a device that may lure finfish by electrical impulses. Violation: misdemeanor; fine up to $1,000; or jail up to one year; or both; with costs imposed at the court's discretion (4-509).★

See ENFORCEMENT OF WILDLIFE LAWS for black bear provisions.

Restrictions on Taking: Fishing

A person may not place, throw or use dynamite or other explosive substance in state waters, except for engineering, milling or mining purposes. Violation: misdemeanor; fine up to $300; jail up to 3 years; or both; with costs at the court's discretion (4-503). ★A person may not whip or beat state waters with a pole, stick, or any other thing in order to drive fish into a device for catching fish (4-504). A person may not fish within 500 yards of a stationary blind or blind site which is occupied and being used for hunting migratory waterfowl (4-512).★ A speargun may be used in state waters only under Department regulations (4-510). A person may not catch or possess game and freshwater fish except during the period and in the manner provided in this subtitle (4-627). Between 8:00 p.m. and 5:30 a.m., a person may not fish for or catch fish in nontidal water which the Department has stocked with trout, except as otherwise provided (4-615). A nonresident may not fish in state nontidal waters with nets (4-618). Except when fishing through ice, a person may not angle with more than three rods and lines with two hooks to each line. Artificial lures with multiple or gang hooks are considered one unit. A slat basket may not be used to catch eels. Licensed anglers may use dip nets to take fish in specified waters. Only a licensed resident may use a bush-bob or bank pole, which may not exceed a total of 25 in total, and one hook to a pole or bob in waters as specified. Bush-bobs or bank poles may not be used on streams stocked with trout. A bush-bob or bank pole which has been baited with scale or live bait may not be used to catch suckers, catfish, carp, eels, gudgeons and every species of sunfish, including bluegills and rock bass, nor used except between sunset and sunrise. The Department may regulate, supervise and control ice-fishing. White shad, hickory shad and herring may be caught or taken only by angling, unless otherwise provided. A person may catch large or small mouth black bass from nontidal waters only by angling, and an artificial lure is legal (4-617).

Except as otherwise provided, a person may not use a gig, gig iron, net, seine, fish pot or other fishing rig, and if found in possession of such devices while catching fish, it is prima facie evidence of violation. Under Department supervision or regulation, a person may catch carp with bow and arrow and by gig, and may catch carp or eels in designated waters. A dip net or seine of specified size may be used to catch bait fish, but not within 50 yards of the mouth of a river or base of a dam. Fish may not be snagged by hooks. Fish pots of specified construction may be used in designated waters, but bass may not be caught from fish pots (4-619 and -620). In addition to any other penalty, persons convicted of a second violation of Department regulation regarding nontidal fishing shall have their license suspended if it occurs within 12 months of violation of the same rule or regulation (4-626). [Fishing restrictions are set for certain counties and specified waters therein in 4-714 through 4-731.] Legal sizes of certain fish, including varieties of catfish, bass, yellow perch, croakers or hardheads, pike or walleyed pike, weakfish, spotted sea trout striped bass, sturgeon, Taylor or bluefish, summer flounder, red drum or channel bass, are set herein. During the open season, a person may not catch by rod or hook and line more than five black bass, and may not sell or purchase any black bass, or offer to do so (4-734 and -735). Methods for catching snapping turtles shall be regulated by the Department. The Department shall regulate sturgeon catching in state waters and the possession and sale of same, such rules to become effective only after a public hearing (4-738 and -739). ★If a person who owns, controls, or erects an artificial pond on land the person owns, puts fish, eggs or spawn in the pond for breeding and cultivating purposes, and gives notice by written or printed handbills in public places near the pond, no other person may enter the premises to fish without the owner's consent (4-11A-22).★

A violation of fishing provisions is a misdemeanor; fine up to $500; with costs optional with the court, unless otherwise provided. A second or subsequent violation of a provision is a fine up to $1,000; jail up to one year; or both; and costs at the court's discretion (within two years of a prior violation). In addition to any administrative penalty, violation of a rule or regulation is a misdemeanor punishable as provided above. A common carrier transporting fish who is not the buyer, seller or catcher is not subject to penalty under this section for transporting fish unlawfully caught or of unlawful size provided that the carrier has a bill of lading stating the origin, shipper, destination and receiver of the fish and does not know, or have reason to know, that the fish were unlawfully caught or of unlawful size. Fine moneys shall be paid to the Fisheries Research and Development Fund (4-1201 and -1202). A local or general state law which regulates minimum and maximum sizes of fish, or the sale of fish, applies whether the fish are caught in state waters or elsewhere and brought into this state. A fine or penalty prescribed for violation of these laws applies to the same extent (4-102).

Commercial and Private Enterprise Provisions

A taxidermist and fur-tanning license is required to practice commercially the art of taxidermy or to mount or preserve legally acquired finfish or wildlife. ★An applicant shall apply on Department forms and provide recent work samples for examination, and must also pass an examination.★ Licensees shall keep a detailed ledger; failure is cause for license revocation up to five years. The licensee shall allow inspection by law enforcement officers of the premises of finfish, records, and holding facilities. Violation: fine of $5 for each specimen of finfish or animal mounted or possessed for mounting, in addition to any other penalty provided (4-211, 10-512 and 10-513). A person desiring to buy, sell, ship or store fur or pelt of a wild quadruped taken within or outside the state must obtain a fur dealer's license, except for: ▸ a person who buys furs or pelts for personal use and not for barter, exchange or sale; ▸ a tanner or taxidermist who possesses furs legally owned by another and which are being held solely for processing; ▸ a person who sells or possesses to sell fur from a fur-bearing mammal or nutria legally taken from the wild by that person; ▸ a person who butchers a deer for another and retains its hide because the hunter did not want it; ▸ a person who can prove that furs or pelts possessed were bought from a licensed fur dealer in this or another state and processed into a finished product but not resold. Licensees shall carry licenses on their persons, and allow law enforcement officers to enter premises at reasonable hours to inspect. Fur dealers shall keep ledgers with detailed information, and shall submit the ledger annually to the Department (10-506 through -508).

A person desiring to provide services as a fishing guide shall obtain a license. No services may be provided as a fishing guide which require operating a boat or vessel without obtaining appropriate federal licenses. All appropriate federal and state licenses must be carried on the guide's person when performing services. Monthly reports are required from commercial guides (4-210).

A master hunting guide license is required for receiving compensation for outfitting or guiding hunters to hunt wild waterfowl, and each agent, employee or helper used shall be registered. A "master hunting guide" is one who owns or is responsible for the operation of a commercial hunting guide organization that outfits or guides hunters to hunt wild waterfowl and receives monetary consideration. Licensing procedures must be followed and an oath sworn to before obtaining such license. A licensee shall report monthly to the Department. e Secretary and Department may not adopt a regulation concerning the licensing of agents, employees or helpers of a master hunting guide, nor request the federal government to enforce a federal rule concerning the licensing of same.★ A licensee may not outfit or guide a waterfowl hunter unless the hunter possesses a proper hunter's license (10-309).

★★A person may not conduct a waterfowl processing operation without a license. A waterfowl processing operation may not receive or have in custody wild waterfowl unless it is tagged as required, must keep detailed records and submit such records annually to the Department, and must allow inspection of premises and records by any law enforcement officers at any reasonable hour. In addition to other penalties, the Department may suspend or revoke the license for violation (10-425)★★.

A club or association may not hold a dog field trial during a closed hunting season without a permit. The Secretary may grant such permit to hold field trials with raccoon, opossum, bird or rabbit dogs any time during the closed season under regulations adopted to safeguard wildlife interests. Such club holding a field trial during closed hunting season may not shoot a game bird or mammal or protected bird, except that game birds bred, raised or purchased in captivity may be shot in flight immediately upon release at retriever trials (10-701 and -702).

A game husbandry license may be issued to raise, breed, protect or sell game birds or mammals, such license to specify: ▸ species of game birds and mammals which may be bred, raised, protected or sold and for what purpose; ▸ the type of fencing or other requirements to prevent undesirable mixing of native wildlife and the captive game birds or mammals; ▸ any other condition to ensure adequate protection of native wildlife. Game birds or mammals raised in captivity must be identified before shipping or removal, and must be accompanied by bill of sale. Licensees shall keep a ledger, and shall allow the Department to enter and inspect the records and premises at reasonable hours. The Secretary may prescribe by regulation the conditions under which a person may possess and sell game birds and mammals intended for human consumption which have been purchased from a licensed game breeder (10-905).

A regulated shooting ground requires a permit and the written permission of the landowner if other than the applicant. The Department shall determine that the establishment does not conflict with any reasonable prior public interest before issuing the permit, and by regulation shall govern and prescribe the size of the area, the method of hunting, open and closed seasons, the release, possession and use of propagated wildlife and required reports. Persons hunting on a regulated shooting ground shall first obtain a special license unless they already hold a resident/nonresident hunting license. Before a noncommercial regulated shooting area is used for hunting pen-raised game birds on Sundays, the operator shall comply with boundary posting requirements that apply to commercial regulated shooting areas (10-906).

Aquaculture operations may only be conducted in nontidal ponds, lakes or impounds, under Department regulations which ensure that operations do not adversely impact wild fish stocks, including measures for identifying fish as products of the operation, and no permit for raising of nonnative species, including hybrids of striped bass or nonnative stocks, may be issued unless the aquaculture operation is constructed so that nonnative stocks are precluded from entering tidal waters or contaminating state native species. Provisions and regulations applicable to the taking, possession, sale and transport of finfish do not apply to finfish in or from aquaculture operations in nontidal ponds, lakes or impounds (4-11A-02). Live bait dealers may sell only minnows, chubs under six inches in length, killifishes and mad toms procured from Potomac River waters, and may not possess more than 750 bait fish at one time. Bait boxes shall be open for natural resources police officer inspection at a reasonable time. A dealer may not sell more than 35 bait fish to a person in a day. A licensee may not transport or sell bait fish out of the county where purchased, but purchasers may do so if such bait fish are not resold (4-11A-19).

The Department may issue a permit to establish and operate an artificial or man-made pond or lake where fishing is permitted for fee, and in which artificially propagated fish are stocked. The Department shall regulate the size of the area, method of fishing, open and closed seasons and the catching of fish by furnishing tags, and shall regulate the release, possession and use of legally propagated game and freshwater fish, and may require reports. Permits may be revoked for violation of a provision or regulation relating to fee-fishing lakes. These provisions do not apply to privately-owned recreational areas if: ► the fee payment to the area owner is not exclusively for the privilege of fishing in ponds or lakes; ► the lakes are privately stocked with privately owned fish; ► activities other than fishing are provided for users. The owner and users of privately-owned recreational areas are not required to display fishing licenses (4-11A-20).

The Department may issue a fish breeder's permit to breed, propagate and sell a species of game and freshwater fish protected by law in ponds or lakes which the permittee owns or leases. The Department shall regulate the release, possession, sale, shipment and identification of fish bred, and may require reports. A permit may be revoked for a violation of this section or regulation (4-11A-21).

Import, Export, and Release Provisions

A person desiring to possess, import, export, breed, raise, protect, rehabilitate, hunt, kill, trap, capture, purchase or sell wildlife native to Maryland, shall obtain a permit or license. The Secretary shall establish by regulation: ► types and classes of permits/licenses to be issued; ► species of wildlife exempt from the permit/license requirement; ► sanitary housing or other conditions for humane, safe and healthy possession of wildlife; ► conditions under which captive wildlife may be hunted or released to the wild; ► recordkeeping requirements. (See also STATE WILDLIFE POLICY and Commercial and Private Enterprise Provisions under HUNTING, FISHING, TRAPPING PROVISIONS.) The Secretary may adopt regulations prohibiting or restricting importation, exportation, sale, release or possession of wildlife not native to Maryland on a finding that the wildlife is harmful to native wildlife or to natural ecosystems. The Secretary shall coordinate with federal and local governments regarding permits, facility inspection and enforcement of pertinent laws and regulations. Local governments may enact stricter requirements regarding housing and sanitation conditions or other health and safety requirements (10-902 through -904).

Interstate Reciprocal Agreements

★When there has occurred on Maryland waters a violation of this article, or there has occurred on Virginia waters a violation enforceable under 28.1-185 or 28.185.1, Code of Virginia, the authorities of the state in which the offense was committed may pursue the offender up to and across the Maryland-Virginia Boundary into the state in which the offender flees. If a capture is made in continuous pursuit under the authority herein, the offender, vessel, and property shall be dealt with as authorized by the state laws in which the offense was committed. This section shall be in effect for so long as Virginia has in force similar legislation authorizing Maryland authorities to pursue and make arrests in Virginia for violations of Maryland laws (1-210).★

Special nonresident angler's licenses may be issued to residents of West Virginia, District of Columbia or Virginia for fishing in the Potomac River in nontidal waters of the river itself, but not in its tributaries, if the other state maintains similar reciprocal agreements with Maryland. Pennsylvania residents may fish in certain reservoir waters without obtaining a Maryland angler's license, if the two states enter a reciprocal agreement. If a state fails to maintain the reciprocal fishing privileges in accordance with an approved agreement, the Secretary may revoke such privileges to licenses of that state by publishing a notice of revocation in the Maryland Register and notifying the licensing agency head of that state (4-606).

ANIMAL DAMAGE CONTROL

The Department may reduce the wildlife population in a state area after investigation reveals that protected wildlife is seriously injurious to agricultural or other interests. The method is at the Department's discretion, except that trapping is preferred whenever feasible. The Department shall dispose of wildlife so taken as it deems advisable (10-206). ★★The Department may not pay bounties for wildlife (10-207).★★ To manage wildlife, the Secretary may issue a permit to trap game on state property, or on property where permission is obtained from the owner (10-313). A landowner or agent may shoot hawks or owls to protect poultry or game birds or mammals from destruction. The Department may control birds or mammals which have become obnoxious in nature or habit or are damaging wildlife on state lands (10-401).

The Department shall establish by regulation the maximum open season for hunting crows permissible under federal law, and shall include provisions permitted under federal law for control of crows when found to be committing or about to commit depredation upon ornamental or shade trees, agricultural crops, livestock or wildlife, or when concentrated in such numbers as to constitute a health hazard or other nuisance. A muskrat damaging an embankment or impoundment may be destroyed by the landowner at any time. Persons may hunt or trap on their land a fox or skunk that is damaging or destroying personal or real property (10-405 and -406). A landowner or agent may set steel traps or similar devices at any time to trap raccoon or opossum damaging property. ★The owner of a marsh may hunt a raccoon which destroys a muskrat or its home in a marsh area at any time (10-414)★.

See GENERAL EXCEPTIONS TO PROTECTION

ENFORCEMENT OF WILDLIFE LAWS

Enforcement Powers

Maryland is a member of the Atlantic States Marine Fisheries Compact (4-301, *et seq.*), and with Virginia, a member of the Potomac River Compact (4-306, *et seq.*).

In addition to other powers conferred by this title, the Secretary and every natural resources officer shall have all the powers conferred upon state police officers, and such powers may be exercised anywhere within the state. The natural resources police force is charged with enforcing the state natural resource laws, and shall perform duties the Secretary designates (1-204). Every sheriff and law enforcement officer has the powers of a natural resources police officer. Whenever the Secretary or a natural resources police officer requires advice and assistance of the state's attorneys, sheriffs or a law enforcement officer, these officers shall render the required assistance as in other state cases, except for the Sheriff of Baltimore County (1-208).

A person may not willfully refuse or fail to comply with a lawful or reasonable order of a natural resources police officer or law enforcement officer enforcing any provisions of law. Violation of this subtitle or regulation thereunder is a misdemeanor; fine up to $500; or jail up to three months; or both; with costs at the court's discretion (1-209).

A natural resources or other law enforcement officer with probable cause to believe that a person possesses any fish, bird, mammal, amphibian or reptile or device in violation of this title shall go before a District Court judge of that county and make affidavit to that fact, and if found legally sufficient, the judge shall issue a search warrant commanding the officer to search for the fish, bird, mammal or device and seize the same and hold until further order (4-1203 and 10-1103). If such officer has probable cause to believe that wildlife or a device is possessed in violation of this title and it is not feasible to secure a search warrant in time to seize same, then the officer may examine any boat, railway car, box, package or game bag without a warrant. In this event, a natural resources police officer, in uniform or accompanied by a uniformed police officer, may stop and search an automobile, vehicle or trailer for examining game bags and to determine whether the person is appropriately licensed. A dwelling house may not be entered without a search warrant (4-1204 and 10-1104). A natural resources or other law enforcement officer, upon arrest shall seize every fish, bird, mammal, reptile and amphibian unlawfully caught, sold, transported, possessed or offered for sale, and may dispose of same at the Department's discretion (4-1205 and 10-1105). A natural resources or other officer, upon arrest may seize any device, equipment, conveyance, or property unlawfully used, and if the owner is convicted, the court may declare the same forfeited, in addition to any other penalty provided, to be disposed of at the Department's discretion, unless the owner was not a consenting party or privy to a violation (10-1106 and 4-1206).

Criminal Penalties

★The Chief Judge of the District Court of Maryland may establish, by administrative regulation, a schedule of prepayable fines for first offense misdemeanor violations. A prepayable fine amount may be no more than the maximum and no less than the minimum criminal penalty established by the General Assembly. By paying a fine in lieu of appearing for trial, a person is voluntarily accepting a conviction for the offense charged (1-801).★

★★Each game bird or mammal taken illegally, purchased, sold, bartered or exchanged in excess of the bag limit or possessed illegally is a separate offense. A person who violates any title provision is guilty of a misdemeanor on first offense, and unless another penalty is specifically provided, subject to a fine up to $1,500 plus costs at the court's discretion. Unless another penalty is provided, a second or subsequent violation, within two years of a prior violation and which arises out of a separate set of circumstances, is subject to a fine up to $4,000, jail up to one year, or both, plus costs at the court's discretion. In addition, the license shall be suspended for 12 months from the second conviction. In addition to any administrative penalty provided, violation of Department regulation is a misdemeanor and punishable as provided above. This section does not apply to a violation of 10-424 (careless negligent shooting of a human; intentional destruction of property or livestock) (10-1101).★★

Illegal Taking of Wildlife

A person who violates any provision of 4-2A-05 or 10-2A-05 regarding endangered or threatened species, or fails to procure a required permit or who violates a permit's terms shall be fined up to $1,000, or jailed up to one year, or both. A natural resources or law enforcement officer may conduct searches and execute a warrant to search for and seize equipment, business records, or fish or wildlife taken, used or possessed in connection with a violation of endangered/threatened species provisions, and may, without warrant, arrest a person the officer has probable cause to believe is violating, in the officer's presence or view, such provisions, regulations or permit. Such officer who has made an arrest may search the person, premises or business records at the time of arrest and may seize any fish, wildlife, plants, records or property taken or used. Equipment, merchandise, wildlife, plants or records seized shall be held pending case disposition, after which they shall be forfeited for destruction or disposition as the Secretary determines. Prior to forfeiture, the Secretary may direct the transfer of fish or wildlife so seized to a zoological, botanical or scientific institution for safekeeping, costs assessable to the defendant (4-2A-07 and 10-2A-07). (See also PROTECTED SPECIES OF WILDLIFE.)

★If a person is convicted of violating a provision of this title and the violation causes or results in the injury, death or destruction of wildlife, including a protected species, in addition to any other penalty provided in this title, the court may order the person to pay restitution to the state for the resource value of the wildlife, as determined by the court, taking into account Department regulations. Department regulations shall establish a schedule of resource values for individual species or describe a system that a court may use in determining the resource value for the species, and may use, but not be limited to, known values to replace lost species, or may ascribe to a species a value which the individual wildlife provides to the greater public good for Maryland citizens. If two or more defendants are convicted for the same violation causing or resulting in injury, death or destruction of protected species, the court may impose restitution against them jointly and equally. Restitution shall be paid within the time prescribed by the court. In each instance, the court shall order the restitution paid to be credited to the Department to be used only for replacement, habitat management or enforcement programs for injured, killed or destroyed wildlife or protected animal species (10-1107).★

Except for an individual who kills or wounds a black bear in defense of the person's own life, lives of others, or the lives of animals on the person's property, if the Secretary adopts a regulation, including an emergency regulation, to prohibit the hunting, possessing, selling, purchasing, shipping transporting or exporting of black bears, a violation is: first offense, fine up to $1,500, jail up to 6 months or both, and license suspension up to two years; a second or subsequent offense, fine up to $2,000, jail up to one year, or both, and license suspension up to four years (10-423). A person may not possess, buy, sell, transport or export, or offer such fur or pelt of a wild quadruped, or part which has been unlawfully hunted, trapped, possessed or transported. Possession of a green pelt during closed season is prima facie evidence that same was taken and possessed illegally. In addition to any other penalty, a violator shall have their fur dealer or taxidermist and fur tanner's license revoked for up to five years (10-505).

License Revocations, Suspensions

A natural resources police officer or law enforcement officer shall confiscate hunter's license used or presented by a person other than to whom it was issued. In addition to any penalty provided in this title, if a person is convicted of hunting without a license in possession, or using another's license, the license shall be confiscated, and that person and the licensee may not procure a hunter's license the following year, except for a licensee who does not knowingly give the license to another (10-312). In addition to other penalties, the Secretary may revoke or suspend a license, permit or certificate if the Secretary finds violations of its terms and conditions, or of a regulation. Wildlife for which a license or permit is required and for which such is not obtained shall be considered a nuisance and contraband, and subject to seizure (4-1207 and 10-911). In addition to any other penalty, a court may suspend the hunting license of a person convicted of violating a title provision, or regulation for up to five years. If a person whose hunting license is suspended passes another hunting safety course after the suspension has expired, they may reapply for a hunting license. A person whose hunting license is suspended under this section may not hunt on lands where a hunting license is required or purchase or attempt to do so during the suspension period (10-1108).

See also HUNTING, FISHING, TRAPPING PROVISIONS

HABITAT PROTECTION

★Consistent with license requirements issued by the Federal Energy Regulatory Commission, a person who owns or operates a dam on state waters used for the generation of electric power and the Secretary shall cooperate to assure the release of a sufficient flow of impounded water to maintain both water quality and aquatic habitat below the obstruction (4-513).★ An obstruction may not be placed at the mouth of a creek, cove or inlet or across a stream so as to prevent fish free passage unless fish ladders are maintained (4-501). Every owner of a dam on state waters shall construct and keep repaired at least one fish ladder if the Department deems it necessary. Every fish ladder shall be constructed to allow anadromous fish free passage at all times. A person intending to build a dam shall file an application with the Department containing sufficient information to enable it to make a decision on the necessity of a fish ladder and to approve the plans for same. ★If the dam owner entered into an agreement prior to 1955 to pay the state an annual periodic sum instead of being required to erect a fish ladder, such provisions remain in effect. The amount of money paid to the state each year may not be less than 4 1/2% of the estimated cost to erect the ladder, but may not exceed $4,000 per year. Money paid to the Department shall be used to manage, rear and distribute the fish placed in the water and to acquire a facility for these purposes. Funds from dams across certain waters shall be credited to the Fisheries Management and Protection Fund. On application of the Department, the circuit court for any county, sitting in equity, may enforce by injunction a provision herein. The Department shall investigate every violation of this section, and serve notice in writing requiring the violator to make or repair the fish ladder, and specifying the penalty for failure to act within a time limit. Notice violation is a misdemeanor; fine up to $300; jail up to three years; or both. Each day of violation is a separate offense (4-501 and -502).★

The Secretary shall establish programs, including acquisition of land or aquatic habitat or interests therein for the conservation of nongame, threatened or endangered species of fish, wildlife or plants, and shall use all vested authority to carry out these provisions. The Secretary shall consult with the State Secretary of Agriculture and other states having a common interest in particular species of nongame, endangered or threatened species, and may enter into agreements with federal agencies, other states or individuals to conserve such species, including agreements for administration and management for conservation of nongame, endangered or threatened species. ★The Governor shall review other state programs and utilize same in furtherance of these purposes. All state departments and agencies, in consultation with the Secretary, shall utilize their authorities in furtherance of these purposes by carrying out programs for the conservation of state endangered and threatened species, and insure that actions authorized, funded or carried out by them do not jeopardize the continued existence of the species or result in the destruction or modification of habitat deemed critical (4-2A-06 and 10-2A-06).★ (See also PROTECTED SPECIES OF WILDLIFE.)

★★After 1990, the Department shall use funds generated by the increase in fees charged for certain resident hunting licenses only for feeding state game birds and mammals. The Department may enter into contracts with state farmers to reimburse for planting and leaving grains, grasses and legumes, including clover, alfalfa and soybeans, unharvested in the fields in order to provide feed for state game birds and mammals (10-301).★★

★★To encourage waterfowl conservation on private lands, the Department shall implement a ten-year licensing agreement for projects on privately owned lands detailing the landowner's responsibilities. Expenditures by private landowners on private land for these waterfowl projects approved by the Department and covered by the licensing agreement shall be considered a contribution to the state. The Governor shall appoint an advisory committee of 13 members, including 9 who have a practical knowledge in raising wild ducks and 4 who have a practical knowledge of waterfowl habitat conservation. The committee shall advise the Department of: the propagation or purchase and distribution of mallard or other ducks to be released; Department regulations to effectuate this program; waterfowl habitat conservation projects (10-308.1).★★

The Department may acquire, by purchase, lease, condemnation or gift, title or control of state land or water suitable to protect, propagate or manage wildlife or for hunting purposes, such areas to be known as wildlife management areas. The Department may purchase or erect structures for wildlife management and may purchase or lease land or water excluding the ownership of and the right to drill any mineral, oil or gas. The title to land or water acquired shall be taken in the state's name for the Department and the entire control of the area shall be under the state's direction. The Secretary may expend from the Wildlife Management and Protection Fund amounts to purchase or condemn such areas. The Department may, if the Governor consents, exchange land or water for privately owned land or water equal to or greater in value than the area exchanged and adapted for wildlife refuge and management, or sell a Department-owned area to the highest bidder. Acquired land or water may be used to create and maintain state wildlife refuges, and for wildlife management and hunting grounds. The Department may cut and remove and sell or permit cutting and selling of timber on such lands, the proceeds to be credited to the Wildlife Management and Protection Fund, and may appoint caretakers and grant rights-of-way, if such does not affect adversely wildlife protection, management and propagation. The Department may establish and maintain state wildlife refuges where wildlife may not be hunted, disturbed or molested, and upon the consent of the Governor and the superintendent in charge, may locate a wildlife refuge on federal or state-owned land or water. Boundaries of each wildlife refuge shall be clearly marked and posted "State Wildlife Refuge - Hunting Unlawful" (10-801 through -805).

★A person who owns/controls land or water who desires to have it set aside for a refuge may apply to the Department giving a description of the area, a map, nature of area, and the location of improvements. The Department may examine the area and determine if it is suitable for wildlife protection and management, and if so, the person shall sign a lease, vesting the state with every hunting right in the area, and providing that the owner and family or agents or other persons may not hunt on the area, and that the person will make every effort to protect the refuge from forest fires, hunting or a violation of state conservation laws. The lease agreement shall continue in force for at least five years. The Department or the owner may rescind any lease upon 90-day notice by any party (10-806). (See also PROTECTED SPECIES OF WILDLIFE.)

★★In order to aid the relief of crop depredations and to provide further protection to wild waterfowl, a person or group, individually or collectively, may apply to the Department for a license to feed waterfowl upon land owned or operated by the person or group, or in waters within 300 yards of a shoreline so owned or operated, in accordance with policies and guidelines herein and regulations adopted by the Secretary. It is the purpose of this subtitle to encourage the placement of feed to supplement the dwindling supply of natural feed available to wild waterfowl and to regulate feeding so that it is not a means of attracting wild waterfowl to, on or over hunting areas [details of applications provided]. The Department may refuse to issue a license if shooting blinds on the applicant's or adjacent property are so placed in relation to the feeding zones that wild waterfowl would have to pass within shooting range of hunters, or it may cancel a license. A licensee may not establish a feeding zone within 400 yards of a building or exterior property line without permission from the adjoining land owner [other details of location on or offshore are given]. Within 10 days of notice of license approval, each zone shall be marked with signs and prior to the opening of the waterfowl hunting season, each licensed shooting blind shall be posted. Every club member, guest and permittee of the applicant is presumed to have knowledge of the location of a feeding zone where shooting is prohibited. Feeding shall commence on and continue through the date the Secretary designates. Prior to hunting season, feeding may be done anywhere on the licensed area, if all food put out other than in the designated feeding zone is consumed or removed at least 10 days prior to the season opening date. After that time, feed may only be placed in the designated feeding zones. Feeding does not include salt blocks, properly shucked corn, standing crops including aquatics, or grains scattered solely as a result of normal agricultural practices. Hunting is not allowed within 400 yards of a licensed feeding zone, but dead or crippled birds may be retrieved within that area. A person may not shoot or hunt from any site in the licensed area except the licensed shooting blinds. Violation by the licensee or an agent or guest is grounds for immediate feeding license revocation. A blind located within 200 yards of any licensed feeding zone shall be rendered incapable of use. The licensee shall submit reports as required. Licensed areas shall be open to inspection at all times by Department or USFW representatives. If defects are found in license compliance, the licensee shall be given written notice and five days to make the necessary changes. If, upon a second inspection, the requirements have not been met, the license may be revoked. Licensees shall be advised in writing of the findings and results of every inspection. Counties, cities and federal and state agencies are authorized to feed without such license. ★★ A person may feed wild waterfowl without applying for or obtaining a license in an area where waterfowl hunting is not done or contemplated, or if such hunting is done, the feeding shall cease and all food put out shall have been consumed or removed at least 10 days prior to the opening of the waterfowl season and the feeding may not be resumed until one day after the season's close (10-1002 through -1008).

NATIVE AMERICAN WILDLIFE PROVISIONS

See Licenses and Permits under HUNTING, FISHING, TRAPPING PROVISIONS.

MASSACHUSETTS

Sources: Massachusetts General Laws Annotated 1991, Chapters 21, 131, 131A; 1992 Cumulative Annual Pocket Part.

STATE WILDLIFE POLICY: None.

RELEVANT WILDLIFE DEFINITIONS: See Definitions section of Appendices.

STATE FISH AND WILDLIFE AGENCIES

Agency Structure

The **Department of Environmental Management** (Department) has the duty to exercise general care and oversight of the natural resources of the commonwealth and its adjacent waters; to make investigations and to carry on research; and to propose and carry out measures for the protection, conservation, control, use, increase and development thereof. The Department is under the control of a **Board of Environmental Management** (Board), with seven members with seven-year terms, appointed by the Governor with regard to geographical distribution. The boards of the Massachusetts Audubon Society, Sierra Club, Appalachian Mountain Club, and the Trustees of Reservations shall nominate three candidates for the seventh member, to be appointed by the Governor. The **Commissioner of Environmental Management** (Commissioner) is executive director and administrative officer of the Department, and shall exercise supervision and control over all divisions of the Department, including appointment of directors of the several divisions [including Fisheries and Wildlife] (21-1 through -3).

The **Division of Fisheries and Wildlife** (Division) is within the Department of Fisheries, Wildlife and Law Enforcement in the Executive Office of Environmental Affairs and is under the supervision and control of the **Fisheries and Wildlife Board** (Board), consisting of seven members to be appointed by the Governor for five-year terms. Five are appointed from each of the five fish and game districts and hold commonwealth sporting licenses. Four of these five represent fishing, hunting and trapping interests, and at least one has been engaged in farming on land owned by the member for not less than five years. Two are appointed at large and have particular interest in propagation, protection, research and management of wild birds, mammals and endangered species, and one shall be a wildlife biologist (21-7).

The **Director of the Division of Fisheries and Wildlife** (Director) is appointed and may be removed by the Board. With approval of the Board, the Director may appoint an Assistant Director for Nongame and Endangered Species and may assign appropriate duties for protection and management. The Director and Assistant Director are qualified by training and experience to conduct duties assigned to them. Under control of the Board, the Director directs and supervises Division matters, and carries out Board policies, prepares and files the annual budget, and makes a complete report of activities, revenue and Division expenditures to the Board, General Court, Governor and Council. In the Division there is a **Bureau of Wildlife Research and Management** headed by a **Superintendent**, appointed by the Director with Board approval, and qualified by training and experience. The Superintendent shall: ‣ provide for all beneficial forms of wildlife; ‣ cooperate with the University of Massachusetts and federal agencies in wildlife research and management matters; ‣ supervise and manage all wildlife sanctuaries under Division control; ‣ conduct scientific studies and collect, classify and designate studies, data and information that will promote objects of the Bureau. ‣A **State Ornithologist** in the Bureau is appointed by the Director with Board approval, to consult with the Superintendent concerning avifauna (21-7F through -7H).‣ The **Division of Law Enforcement** is within the Department of Fisheries, Wildlife and Environmental Law Enforcement in the Executive Office of Environmental Affairs [details regarding **Director of Law Enforcement** and duties of Division provided] (21-6).

Agency Powers and Duties

The **Director** may: ‣ take or authorize taking and possession of fish, fish spawn, birds, nests or eggs, mammals, reptiles or amphibians for observation, research, control or management, subject to federal law and regulations;

▶ investigate questions relating to reptiles, amphibians, fish, birds or mammals and institute and conduct inquiries and biological research to conserve, improve and increase their supply; ▶ occupy not more than four great ponds within the commonwealth at any one time for scientific study or experiment; make rules and regulations for fishing on said waters; ▶ periodically close or open such waters, or a part for fishing; ▶ suspend by order closed seasons on a fish species having destructive proclivities, and regulate the number and length that may be lawfully taken or possessed, if the presence of the fish in a great pond or in public fishing grounds constitutes a hindrance to the promotion and development of fishing; ▶ establish restricted areas, with approval of the riparian owners and persons owning any right of fishing in the waters affected, in a nonnavigable brook or stream, or portion, or in a pond other than a great pond, for breeding fish, and make rules and regulations for taking fish within such area (131-4).

The Director may: ▶ screen ponds, brooks and streams not used as water supply by cities and towns for protection of fish; ▶ cause a great pond to be stocked with fish, and prescribe and enforce fishing regulations, but this does not apply to ponds used as public water supply; ▶ manage a natural or artificial pond, brook or stream by reclaiming and stocking with fish, in privately owned ponds with the written consent of the owner and with the owner agreeing in writing that the waters shall be open for public fishing; ▶ salvage fish for distribution from inland waters where their loss is apparent, and, with Environmental Protection Commissioner approval, remove fish periodically from a reservoir used as public water supply, for stocking or restocking inland waters; ▶ enter upon and pass through or over private lands in the performance of duties, and authorize agents in writing, and remedy conditions caused by wildlife, resulting or likely to result in property damage; ▶ conduct information and promotion programs in wildlife conservation; ▶ conduct investigations into nongame species relating to population, distribution, habitat, limiting factors, and biological and ecological parameters, and promulgate rules and regulations, listing species determined to be endangered, such list to include, but is not limited to, the US List of Endangered and Threatened Wildlife and Wild Plants (131-4).

If the presence of anadromous fish in inland waters is essential for management of fish, birds or mammals, the Director may: ▶ seize and remove at the expense of the owner of or person using and maintaining same, all illegal obstructions, except dams, mills or machinery; ▶ examine dams and obstructions to passage in brooks, rivers and streams, where fishways are needed; ▶ determine whether existing fishways are sufficient for passage of fish; ▶ prescribe by written order changes or repairs to be made and where, how and when a new fishway shall be built, and times it shall be kept open [details of enforcement of orders and department or private payment for work provided]. After consultation with the Division of Law Enforcement Director, the Director may issue an order prohibiting possession or use of a rifle larger than 22 ammunition, from October 1 to April 1, in a place where birds or mammals may be found. Violation: fine of $100-500; or jail up to 6 months (131-4).

With Board approval, the Director may: ▶ acquire by gift, lease, easement, purchase, exchange or license, or accept by transfer, fishing rights and privileges or lands or interests, for providing public fishing grounds; ▶ acquire by gift, lease, easement, purchase, exchange or license or accept by transfer, properties or interests for fish and wildlife management and propagation; ▶ acquire by gift, purchase, lease or easement, or without consideration obtain by license or permit the use of lands or waters for public shooting grounds; ▶ make rules and regulations relative to the public rights, privileges and use of lands, waters and properties. Nothing in this chapter prohibits the Director from disposing, through sale or exchange, of mammals, birds, fish, eggs or vegetable products of such lands in connection with propagation or management (131-6). The Director shall administer the nongame wildlife program and promulgate rules and regulations, including criteria for purchase of lands critical to nongame wildlife and endangered species, and for use of land for protection and enhancement of nongame wildlife and encouragement of compatible wildlife uses (131-5B).

Agency Regulations

The Director shall declare an open season on fish, birds, reptiles, amphibians or mammals in a county, and may make rules and regulations relating to its time and length, bag limits, possession limits, methods of taking, time and methods of reporting and other matters, and may suspend or modify the open season. Rules and regulations are subject to Board approval of at least three members and the Director, after public hearing. The Director without hearing, but with Board approval, may adopt emergency regulations for immediate management or control for not longer than 90 days. Except as provided in rules and regulations and as otherwise provided, a person shall not fish, hunt or trap or possess a fish, bird, reptile, amphibian, mammal or carcass or part, but this does not prohibit hunting, taking or possession of an English sparrow, crow, jay, starling, chipmunk, fox, flying squirrel, red squirrel, porcupine, skunk, weasel, wildcat or woodchuck when otherwise lawful (131-5).

Agency Funding Sources

Moneys from license fees, permit fees and sources pertaining to inland fishing, hunting and trapping permit fees, authorized sales, reimbursements received from the federal government, grants in aid or other receipts, are credited to the **Inland Fisheries and Game Fund** except that sums received for nongame programs are credited to the **Natural Heritage and Endangered Species Fund**, and $1 from each sporting, fishing, trapping and hunting license is credited to the **Wildlands Acquisition Account**. Unexpended balances at fiscal year end are appropriated only for developing, maintaining, managing, operating and administering the Division. Subject to appropriation, the fund is used for: ▸ payment of general administrative expenses of the Division; ▸ acquiring, maintaining or leasing public fishing rights on inland streams and ponds, including stream management and creation of new ponds; ▸ acquiring, maintaining or leasing public hunting rights on land within the commonwealth; ▸ biological surveys of the inland waters; ▸ propagation of game birds and fish; ▸ salvaging and distributing game birds and fish; ▸ acquisition and maintenance of wildlife sanctuaries and fish and wildlife management areas; ▸ maintaining water resources to provide an adequate water supply for wildlife; ▸ maintaining sources of food for game birds; ▸ general Division purposes; ▸ payment not to exceed one-half of the amount necessary for personal services and other expenses for enforcement of laws relating directly to game and inland fisheries (131-2).

★There is within the Inland Fisheries and Game Fund, a **Wildland Acquisition Account** which are moneys from sale of wildland conservation stamps, the portion of the fees for sporting, fishing, trapping and hunting licenses to be credited under the provisions above, contributions and grant moneys from public and private sources. The account, subject to appropriation, is used to purchase land containing wildlife habitat and for administration of the wildlands stamp program. Acquisition of such lands is made with the advice and consent of the Board. Such lands are acquired exclusively for protection and management of wildlife habitat and are available for fishing, trapping, and hunting (131-2A).★

Fines, penalties and forfeitures recovered in prosecutions relative to fish, birds and mammals are divided equally between the county of prosecution and the city/town where the offence is committed; if the complaining officer received compensation from the commonwealth, moneys are credited to the Inland Fisheries and Game Fund (131-3). (See also Licenses and Permits under HUNTING, FISHING, TRAPPING PROVISIONS.)

Agency Advisory Boards

The Commissioner appoints, subject to Board approval, a **Nongame Advisory Committee** (Committee) of seven members to advise the Director regarding nongame wildlife and wild plants. One member has interest in endangered species. Three members have technical training and experience, at the Commissioner's discretion, in the fields of ornithology, mammalogy, herpetology, ichthyology, and botany, and three are knowledgeable in natural history. The Committee selects a chairperson annually, and meets at least quarterly and at the request of the Director or Committee chairperson. Terms are three years (131-5B).

PROTECTED SPECIES OF WILDLIFE

A person, except the owner or authorized agent, shall not detain, hunt, injure or interfere with a homing or carrier pigeon, or remove an identification mark, band or other thing (131-84).

Except as otherwise provided, no person may take, possess, transport, export, process, sell or offer for sale, buy or offer to buy, nor shall a common or contract carrier knowingly transport or receive for shipment, a plant or animal listed as endangered, threatened or of special concern or listed under the Federal Endangered Species Act. Except as otherwise provided in this chapter, no person may alter significant habitat (131A-2).

The Director shall conduct investigations and consult with the Nongame Advisory Committee to determine if a species constitutes an endangered or threatened species or species of special concern. Criteria for determining such status shall be based on biological data including, but not limited to: ▸ reproductive and population status and trends; ▸ whether the species is native or has been introduced; ▸ vulnerability, determined by threats to the species or its habitat; ▸ specialization, determined by unique habitat requirements; ▸ restricted distribution, determined by limited or disjunct geographic range; ▸ rarity, determined by a limited number of occurrences or numbers. The Director shall list endangered, threatened and special concern species and review the list at least once every five years for listing or delisting. The burden of proof for delisting species is on the person requesting such change in status. The establishment of the list and proposed changes shall be by regulation after a public hearing and subject to the provisions of Chapter 30A. By regulation the Director shall designate significant habitats of endangered or threatened species populations, after a public hearing, and subject to provisions of Chapter 30A, after taking into consideration the following criteria: ▸ current and foreseeable threats to the population or its habitat; ▸ population size; ▸ potential benefits of designation to the population and to the status and welfare of the species generally; ▸ current and foreseeable uses of the land. The Director shall review yearly and designate significant habitats and may revise them by regulation (131A-4).

★★The location of designated significant habitats shall be marked on maps, and affected record owners shall be notified by certified mail not less than 30 days before public hearing. Upon designation, the Director shall record a document identifying the location of each habitat, together with a list of the owners of such lands, in the proper registry of deeds and shall send notification by certified mail to each record owner. Significant habitat maps shall be made available to local zoning boards, planning boards and conservation commissions, or to the local board of selectmen or mayor and city council, in communities where such habitats occur. Local zoning or planning boards or conservation commissions shall notify the Director in writing, within 21 days of filing, of petitions, requests or applications for permits, orders or approvals regarding proposed activity within significant habitats. Record owners of lands or interests in land containing significant habitat may appeal a designation to the Secretary of the Office of Environmental Affairs within 21 days. The Secretary shall hold a hearing no later than 120 days from designation, make a determination within 60 days, and reverse the decision only upon a finding that such decision was without substantial basis in fact. In addition to the appeal, owners of land containing significant habitat may petition the Director to consider purchasing such habitat. After a public hearing and in accordance with procedures in Chapter 30A, the Division shall adopt regulations to implement this chapter, to be promulgated with the advice and assistance of a Technical Advisory Committee of nine persons appointed by the Director. This committee shall consist of: ▸ two university or college professors, with expertise in endangered species biology; ▸ a member of a Massachusetts environmental organization; ▸ a member from the Nongame Advisory Committee; ▸ a member of the sporting community; ▸ a utilities industry representative; ▸ a real estate development industry representative; ▸ a Department of Highways staff member; ▸ an agricultural representative. Regulations shall include, but not be limited to: ▸ criteria to be applied in determining which activities will reduce the viability of significant habitat to support endangered or threatened species; ▸ criteria to further define alteration of a significant habitat; ▸ regulations to carry out the purposes of this chapter. This provision does not affect existing regulations listing species. Agencies, departments, boards, commissions and authorities shall utilize their authorities in furtherance of this chapter and determine the impact on listed species of their works, projects or activities and use all practicable means and measures to avoid or minimize damage to such species (131A-4).★★

See HABITAT PROTECTION for alteration of significant habitat.

GENERAL EXCEPTIONS TO PROTECTION

Commercial license requirements do not apply to zoos approved by the US Department of Agriculture. Natural history associations and museums, or zoos not so approved which are operated by the commonwealth or a political subdivision may be exempted from those provisions. Nothing in this section permits zoos, natural history associations or museums to transfer protected fish, spawn, birds, nests, eggs or mammals by sale, exchange, barter, gift, donation or otherwise unless authorized in writing by the Director (131-29).

A person may transport, possess, or sell, in accordance with the terms of a state and federal permit, a listed species which enters the commonwealth from another state or from outside the US [details of lawful possession of endangered/threatened plants provided]. The Director may permit: ▸ taking, possession, purchase, sale, transportation, exportation or shipment of an endangered or threatened species or species of special concern for scientific or educational purposes, or for or from propagation in captivity; ▸ taking of special concern species for falconry pursuant to regulations; ▸ removal, capture, or destruction of a listed species to protect human health, when a public health hazard exists (131A-3).

See also Agency Regulations under STATE FISH AND WILDLIFE AGENCIES.

HUNTING, FISHING, TRAPPING PROVISIONS

General Provisions

Whoever knowingly counsels, aids or assists in a violation of a provision of this chapter, or of a rule or regulation, or knowingly shares in the proceeds of a violation by receiving or possessing fish, birds or mammals, is guilty of such violation. Taking or having in possession a fish, bird or mammal includes taking or possessing a part or portion thereof. The provisions of this chapter and regulations, unless otherwise provided, shall apply only to fish and fisheries in or on inland waters. Provisions do not prohibit a resident who has lawfully taken, killed or possessed dead bodies or carcasses of fish, birds or mammals for personal use and not for sale, unless prohibited by federal law or regulation; the burden is on the resident to prove lawful possession. Provisions do not prohibit bringing into this commonwealth the dead bodies or carcasses of fish, birds or mammals lawfully taken or killed in another state, province or country, or from possessing them, if before importing they are tagged or marked and within limits in accordance with the laws of the other state, province or country and with federal laws relative to interstate commerce; the burden is on the person to prove lawful possession (131-1).

Nothing in section 131-4 or 131-11 through 131-16 affects general laws relating to trespass, or authorizes hunting, fishing or possession of birds, mammals or fish contrary to law, or trapping mammals contrary to law; nor prohibits a legal resident or immediate family member from hunting on land owned or leased, or from trapping on such land, or from fishing in inland waters bordered by such land, if actually domiciled thereon and the land is used principally for agricultural purposes; the burden of proof is upon the person claiming such exception. A person shall not hunt deer during the exclusive archery season on deer, nor during the exclusive primitive firearm season, without a hunting or sporting license. A person shall not hunt migratory waterfowl during the open season without carrying a nontransferrable waterfowl stamp signed by the bearer. Except as provided, no person shall fish, trap, or hunt without a wildlands conservation stamp (131-13 and -13A).

Notwithstanding the provisions of sections 131-22 through 131-24, the Director, with Board approval, may make, alter, amend and rescind rules and regulations for disposition of deer killed by other than sport hunting. Rules and regulations shall include, but not be limited to, procedures for acquiring and possessing deer, categories of persons authorized to acquire and possess such deer, and procedures and time limits for administration. The Director is authorized to issue permits to possess deer, each such deer or carcass to be tagged with an official seal as the Director prescribes. Fees accrued go to the Inland Fisheries and Game Fund. A deer killed by other than sport hunting and not acquired by an individual shall be disposed of by the Director of Law Enforcement by, including, but not limited to, donations to civic associations, sportsmen's clubs, and churches (131-22A). Except as provided, a person shall not possess a live bird or mammal other than those named in section 131-5, or a live reptile or amphibian. Birds and mammals possessed under a dealers or propagator's license may be sold; if sold for food, they shall be killed and tagged with a numbered tag. Every package containing birds or mammals killed under authority of this section, or parts, shall be labelled. Carcasses or parts shall remain entire and unplucked until prepared for consumption. Reptiles and amphibians possessed under a license issued under section 131-23 may be sold. Nothing herein permits possession of a live bird, mammal, reptile or amphibian, other than those named in section 131-5 and those on the special exemption list, by a person purchasing or receiving such a bird, mammal, reptile or amphibian from a holder of a propagator's or dealer's license, without a license authorizing possession. Accounts of all dealings subject to this section shall be kept by licensees, and records shall be open for inspection by the Director and agents, the Director of Law Enforcement and Deputy Directors, enforcement chiefs and deputy chiefs, and environmental police officers. A person licensed under section 131-23 shall not transfer a live bird, or eggs, or a live mammal, reptile or amphibian, by sale, gift, donation or otherwise, unless licensed (131-25).

A person shall not fish, hunt or trap on private land without permission of the owner or tenant, after notices have been posted bearing the owner's name and stating that fishing, hunting or trapping is prohibited (131-36). A person while hunting, fishing or trapping shall not deposit or cause to be deposited garbage, paper, refuse, bottles, cans, rubbish or trash on public or private property without permission of the property owner, tenant or lessee (131-44).

Except as prohibited or limited by federal legislation or regulation, a nonresident sporting, hunting, fishing or trapping licensee may carry from the commonwealth lawfully taken fish, reptiles, amphibians, birds or mammals, but no person shall transport or cause to be transported into or out of the commonwealth fish, reptiles, amphibians, birds or mammals protected by this chapter which have been unlawfully taken or killed, nor transport or cause to be transported into the commonwealth fish, reptiles, amphibians, birds or mammals taken, killed or possessed contrary to the laws of a state or foreign nation (131-85). (See also Commercial and Private Enterprise Provisions.)

Licenses and Permits

A person shall not fish in inland waters, nor hunt or trap except as otherwise provided without a sporting, hunting, fishing or trapping license [classes of persons eligible, licenses and fees detailed]. The state treasurer shall forward upon request of the Director, $1 of the fee for each waterfowl stamp issued to Ducks Unlimited, Inc., pursuant to agreement. Such funds are to be used exclusively for waterfowl management in the Atlantic provinces of Canada. Ducks Unlimited, Inc., shall submit annually a report to the Division setting forth projects, activities and expenses realized from the commonwealth's contribution. The state treasurer shall forward up to $3 of the fee for each stamp to the National Fish and Wildlife Foundation of Washington, D.C. for fulfillment of the North American Waterfowl Management Plan pursuant to agreement or to another nonprofit, waterfowl conservation and management organization whose purpose is to acquire, enhance, develop, or protect waterfowl habitat. Such funds are to be used exclusively for waterfowl management in the Atlantic provinces of Canada and the northeastern US. A report shall be submitted annually by the National Fish and Wildlife Foundation and/or other organization receiving funds, setting forth projects, activities and expenses realized. An unexpended balance shall be credited to the Inland Fisheries and Game Fund. A person shall not kill or possess a game bird or mammals for which a permit is required without paying the established fee. A fee shall accompany each bear and antlerless deer permit, except for a farmer or landowner antlerless deer permit. Upon application for a sporting, hunting, fishing or trapping license and upon payment of the fee, [a qualified person] shall be issued a license [limited to conditions on the license]. A license holder shall carry and wear the license in a visible manner (131-11 and -12).

Licenses, permits and certificates shall not be loaned or transferred. They must be produced for examination upon demand of the Director of Law Enforcement or authorized officers qualified to serve criminal process, the Director of Fisheries and Wildlife and agents, or the owner or lessee of land upon which the license, permit or certificate privileges are being exercised. A person shall not make a false representation or statement to procure a license, permit or certificate. Licenses, permits or certificates, except hunting, fishing, sporting or trapping licenses, after notice and a hearing, may be suspended or revoked for cause. A person shall not alter, forge or counterfeit a license, permit, application, certificate, tag or seal issued, nor possess, procure, use such, or attempt to do so, nor loan or allow another person to use such license (131-32 and -33).

Restrictions on Taking: Hunting and Trapping

Every Sunday is a closed season. Except as otherwise provided, on Sunday a person shall not hunt a bird or mammal or carry a rifle, shotgun or bow and arrow or, unless otherwise permitted, a pistol or revolver, in a place where birds or mammals might be found. It is lawful to: ▸ possess or carry a rifle, shotgun, pistol, revolver or bow and arrow, for use on a skeet, trap or target range, or for use for sport target shooting at artificial targets by an owner or lessee, or a guest, upon the owner's property, or by members or guests of clubs or associations on supervised firing ranges; ▸ take mammals by traps; ▸ train falcons or protected species (131-57).

A person shall not discharge a firearm or release an arrow upon or across a state or hard surfaced highway, or within 150 feet of such highway, or possess a loaded firearm or hunt on the land of another within 500 feet of a dwelling in use, except as authorized by the owner or occupant (131-58). A person shall not use a firearm, bow and arrow or other weapon or article in a careless or negligent manner so as to cause bodily injury or death to another while hunting or target shooting. A person who causes such injury or death and a person having knowledge of such immediately shall report to the state or local police who shall submit a copy to the Director of Law Enforcement. A person found guilty of careless or negligent injury or death or failing to make the report required shall lose any hunting or sporting license held and no other license shall be granted for five years (131-60). ★★A person shall not use a firearm, bow and arrow or other weapon or article in a careless or negligent manner so as to cause damage to another's property or livestock while hunting, fishing, trapping or target shooting. Violators are liable in tort to the owner for the loss of such property or livestock for the amount of the damage, in addition to any other penalty imposed by law (131-61).★★

Except for the Director of Law Enforcement or an officer authorized to enforce this chapter or charged with protection of persons or property while discharging duties, a person shall not possess or control in or on a motor vehicle, aircraft, or motor boat a loaded shotgun or rifle, unless authorized in regulations relating to hunting migratory waterfowl; upon demand of an officer, a person shall display a such shotgun or rifle for inspection, except an owner upon land owned or occupied by the owner. A person shall not use for hunting any type of full automatic firearm, machine gun or submachine gun, or a crossbow or other bow drawn, held or released by mechanical means, nor use a tracer or incendiary ammunition for hunting or outdoor target shooting except on a skeet, trap or target range (131-63 and -64).

Except as otherwise provided, a person shall not: ▸ hunt a bird or mammal by use of a motor vehicle, including a snowmobile, helicopter or other aircraft; ▸ hunt a bird by use of a boat or floating device propelled by sail, steam, naphtha, gasoline, electricity, compressed air or similar motive power, unless such boat or floating device is beached, resting at anchor, or fastened or tied immediately alongside of a fixed hunting blind; ▸ take or kill a wild bird by placing or causing to be placed grain upon the shores or foreshores of, in or upon waters. Nothing in this section prohibits shooting wounded or crippled migratory game birds from powered craft in coastal waters seaward of the first upstream bridge, or picking up or retrieving dead or injured migratory game birds by motorboat, sailboat or other water craft (131-65). A person shall not: ▸ use or possess, where birds or mammals may be found, a rifle chambered larger than 22 long rifle ammunition, or revolver or pistol larger than 38 caliber ammunition between one-half hour after sunset to one-half hour before sunrise; ▸ hunt a bird or mammal, except raccoon or opossum, by use of artificial light, or hunt a bird with a swivel or pivot gun. A weapon or equipment used in hunting by a person convicted of a violation of this section shall be confiscated and forfeited and disposed of by the Director of Law Enforcement, and a motor vehicle as defined, or other vehicle, boat or canoe used may be seized and libeled. A person shall not carry or use a bow and arrow while hunting unless it meets rules and regulations of the Director prescribing general design, weight of pull, and type of bows and arrows, and conforms to accepted standards for bows and arrows used for hunting [provisions for handicap use of mechanical bows] (131-67 through -69).

During the open season for deer with a shotgun, a person shall not hunt a bird or mammal with a rifle, revolver or pistol or by the aid of a dog, or possess or control a dog in a wood or field. Nothing prohibits use of dogs to hunt waterfowl in coastal waters and salt marshes during the open season on migratory waterfowl. Notwithstanding this section, the Director may authorize use of primitive firearms with a rifled bore for hunting during the primitive season under the rules and regulations in accordance with section 131-5 (131-70). A deer tag shall remain attached to each hunting or sporting license until affixed to a deer and becomes void if detached for any other purpose. A person possessing a detached deer tag not affixed to a deer shall surrender the tag to an officer empowered to enforce the provisions of this chapter. Immediately upon taking a deer into possession by hunting in open season, the tag shall be affixed to the deer. A person shall not possess or have under control in a motor vehicle or transport a deer carcass except as provided in rules and regulations. Possession of a deer carcass, except as tagged or authorized, is prima facie evidence of unlawful taking. Proceedings under a rule or regulation under this section or section 131-5 pertaining to tagging or reporting may be begun in the district court within the judicial district where the deer is found or the defendant lives (131-72).

A person shall not hunt a moose. A person shall not take, disturb or destroy a nest or eggs of a bird except an English sparrow, crow, jay or starling. ★A city, town, county or private organization shall not offer or pay bounties for killing or taking of a bird. Except as provided, a person shall not hunt or possess a wild turkey or take, molest, disturb, destroy or possess its nest or eggs. The holder of a special permit or license issued by the Director shall not hunt or possess a bird of prey. No person shall take, molest, disturb, destroy or possess the nest or eggs of a bird, unless authorized by the Director. For the purposes of this section, "bird of prey" includes: eagle, osprey, hawk, owl, kite, falcon or vulture (131-73 through -75A).★

Except as provided, a person shall not remove or attempt to remove a mammal from a hole in a tree or in the ground, stonewall, or from within or under a ledge, stone or log, provided that one authorized by the landowner may remove a chipmunk, fox, flying squirrel, red squirrel, porcupine, skunk, weasel, wildcat or woodchuck (131-76). Except as provided, a person shall not take or attempt to take a bird or mammal by use of a ferret or a fitchew (fitch); nor possess or use a ferret or fitchew without a permit from the Director, who may revoke such permit with reason to believe ferrets or fitchews are kept or used for hunting. Ferrets or fitchews used or possessed illegally shall be forfeited to the commonwealth and disposed of by the Director of Law Enforcement (131-77).

Except as provided, a person shall not erect, set, use, locate, repair, tend or maintain a trap, net or snare for taking or killing a bird or mammal, nor, except as provided, take a bird or mammal by such means. A person shall not place, set, maintain, possess, or tend on the land of another, a trap, unless registered in accordance with this section. The Director shall provide by regulation, approved by the Board, that the registration number and owner name shall be affixed to each trap [details of sale of registered traps and partnerships for trapping provided]. The Director shall furnish periodically to the Director of Law Enforcement a list of all holders of registration certificates (131-79 and -80). ★★No person shall use, set, place or maintain a steel jaw leghold trap on land for fur-bearing mammals except in or under buildings on land owned, leased or rented by the person. The steel jaw leghold trap may be used to capture fur-bearing mammals in water only if set in such a manner that all reasonable care is taken to insure that the mammal dies by drowning in a minimum length of time. No other device set in such a manner that it will knowingly cause continued suffering to a mammal caught, or which is not designed to kill a mammal at once or take it alive unhurt shall be used, set, placed or maintained for the capture of fur-bearing mammals, provided a person may apply for a special permit to use such traps on property owned by the person. Issuance of special permits is governed by rules and regulations, including but not limited to, the applicant or an agent must apply to the Director in writing stating that there exists on the applicant's property an animal problem which cannot be abated reasonably by traps other than those prohibited, not including the steel jaw leghold trap. For up to 90 days, the Director may authorize the use, setting, placing or maintenance of such traps and procedures for obtaining a special permit. Violation of this section, or a rule or regulation, is a fine of $50-100, or jail up to 30 days, or both (131-80A). ★★

Whenever it appears that by reason of extreme drought there is danger of fire from hunting, trapping, fishing or other cause, the Governor may: ▸ suspend by proclamation the opening or continuance of open seasons or authorized extensions, and proclaim a closed season on birds, fish or mammals, for such time as the Governor may designate, and prohibit hunting, trapping, fishing and possession of firearms on property of another during that time; ▸ proclaim that sections of the woodlands where danger of fire might exist shall be closed for such time as the Governor may designate to hunters, trappers, fishermen and other persons, except owners or tenants of such property and their agents and employees, or persons with written permission from such owner or tenant to enter for a lawful purpose other than hunting, trapping or fishing. As soon as the fire hazard is over, the Governor may extend an open season for a time not to exceed the suspension time. If such open season coincides with another open season so as to cause conflict in the laws, such season may be postponed. Every such proclamation shall take effect as stated, and shall be published or posted under Department direction as the Governor may order (131-81).

A person owning, keeping or possessing a dog shall not permit or consent to such dog chasing, hunting, molesting, attacking or killing a deer. The Director of Law Enforcement is authorized to issue an order to restrain all dogs from running at large in a city or town to prevent dogs from chasing, hunting, molesting, attacking or killing deer. Such order shall be in effect 48 hours after publication in the city or town; when no longer necessary, the order shall be rescinded by publication. The Director and other authorized law enforcement officers may destroy a dog found chasing, hunting, molesting, attacking or killing a deer, without liability. When no such order is in force, those enforcement officers and members of the metropolitan district commission police in areas over which they have jurisdiction may destroy a dog found chasing or hunting a deer if it is doing so with the knowledge or consent of the owner. Whenever a dog has been found chasing, hunting, molesting, attacking or killing a deer and the owner or keeper has been notified by the Director, and the dog is thereafter found doing the same, it is prima facie evidence that it was with the knowledge or consent of the owner or keeper (131-82).

A person shall not enter without right a posted building, structure, or area of land, flats or water, used under authority of the Director for scientific experiments or investigations or for propagation, or fish in such waters, and shall not injure or deface such a building or structure or a notice posted, or property used, or otherwise interfere (131-86).

Restrictions on Taking: Fishing

Except as otherwise provided in this section and chapter, every great pond not actively being used as a water supply of a town, fire district or public institution, and not subject to provisions of section 160 of chapter 111, shall be public for hunting or boating, and notwithstanding any special fisheries law, shall be open for fishing. A city or town in which all or a portion of a great pond not exceeding 500 acres is situated, as to the part located within its boundaries, may make and enforce rules and regulations relative to hunting, fishing and boating. A boating rule or regulation may include: ▸ speed limit; ▸ limit on engine horsepower; ▸ prohibition of internal combustion engines; ▸ ban on water skiing and other high speed uses; ▸ a limitation to certain areas and times. Rules or regulations authorizing hunting or fishing shall be subject to the Director's approval, and if they authorize other use, they shall be subject to the approval of the Commissioner of Environmental Protection [other restrictions are subject to the Director of Law Enforcement]. Notwithstanding other provisions, a city or town in which is situated all or part of a great pond, as to that part within its boundaries, make and enforce rules and regulations for the use and operation of aircraft equipped with floats or other means of transportation on water, to be approved by the Massachusetts Aeronautics Commission (131-45).

Except in emergency, a person shall not drain a pond, reservoir or other body of water, unless it is used for irrigation, insect control, flooding cranberry bogs, or public water supply, to an extent dangerous to fish life, unless at least ten days prior the Director shall be notified in writing to enable the salvage of fish prior to such draining (131-48).

Except as otherwise permitted, a person shall not take or attempt to take fish in inland waters other than by angling; but cities and towns may permit use of nets and seines for taking herring and alewives, and the use of pots for taking eels in ponds having direct openings to the sea. This section does not prohibit spearing or taking by bow and arrow eels, carp or suckers, provided no arrows shall be released within 150 feet of any state or hard surfaced highway for taking such fish; nor does this section apply to ponds or waters leased from the Department (131-50).

Each person licensed to fish may take for bait, but not for sale, shiners, minnows, killifish, sculpin, sticklebacks, and suckers in inland waters by means of a single fish trap with openings not over 1 inch, by a single circular or hoop net not exceeding 6 feet in diameter, or by a rectangular net with not more than 36 square feet of net surface. Shiners and suckers may be taken by residents licensed to fish, for sale as bait, in inland waters except great ponds and waters which in whole or in part are leased or licensed as public fishing grounds, by means of up to 10 fish traps with openings not over 1 inch, by a single circular or hoop net not exceeding 6 feet in diameter, or by a net containing up to 200 square feet of net surface, if the operator is licensed by the Director. Live fish taken by such net or trap, other than those permitted to be taken by this section, must be returned immediately to the waters. A person shall not fish with floats (toggle fishing) in inland water. A "float" is a device floating with a line and hook, baited with natural or artificial bait and not under the hand control of the person fishing. Except as otherwise permitted, a person shall not draw, set, stretch or use a fish trap, or gill, drag, set or purse net, seine or trawl, or set or use more than two hooks for fishing, or, in the case of ice fishing, five hooks, in inland water, or aid in so doing. This section does not affect corporate rights of a fishing company. The possession, except as permitted, by a person in or upon inland waters or their banks of any seine, net, trap, trawl or other device adapted for fishing is prima facie evidence of violation. Such devices used illegally, and fish taken in violation, shall be forfeited and disposed of by the Director of Law Enforcement (131-52 through -55).

Commercial and Private Enterprise Provisions

Except as provided, a person shall not buy, sell, barter, exchange, offer or expose for sale or possess for sale, or in a way deal in or trade trout, salmon, horned pout, yellow perch, pickerel, white perch, great northern pike or muskellunge, wall-eyed pike, pike perch or sunfish, taken from commonwealth waters, or black bass taken from waters within or outside the commonwealth, or the bodies of dead or living birds or mammals, or parts, except as provided, or the bodies of dead or living reptiles or amphibians; but a person who has lawfully killed a deer during open season, and has reported as required, may sell the head and hide to a licensed fur buyer, or licensed taxidermist, and may sell the hoofs and shinbones to a person. Nothing in this section prohibits sale of white perch taken from coastal waters, Dukes or Nantucket Counties, or waters held under lease from the Department (131-22).

★★Except as otherwise provided, a person shall not engage in propagation, cultivation, or maintenance of, or dealing in, fish, birds, mammals, reptiles, or amphibians, or parts, without a propagator's or dealer's license. Birds, mammals, reptiles and amphibians refers to undomesticated animals wild by nature. Nothing herein shall prohibit propagation, disposition, sale, possession or maintenance of domesticated species. After a public hearing, the Director shall make, alter, amend, or repeal rules and regulations governing possession, propagation, maintenance, disposition, purchase, exchange, sale or offering for sale of fish, birds, mammals, reptiles or amphibians, or parts, protected by this chapter, and may issue licenses. The Director shall draw up a special exemption list of fish, birds, mammals, reptiles and amphibians which meet the following criteria: ► accidental release of the animal will not result in an adverse effect on the ecology of the commonwealth; ► the animal in captivity, or escaped therefrom, poses no substantial danger to man by injury or disease; ► proper care of the animal is not significantly more demanding than proper care of common domestic animals; ► trade in the animal has no significant adverse effect on the wild population in its natural habitats. No animal listed in the International Union for Conservation of Nature and Natural Resources' Red Data Books shall be listed; no animal protected by either federal endangered species law or by section 131-26A shall be listed. The special exemption list may be altered by the Director after a public hearing. An individual may possess as a pet, without a license, an animal on the special exemption list, and may continue to do so in case of its subsequent removal from the list, for its lifetime, contingent upon evidence of acquisition while so listed. Each license shall specify the degree to which the animals or its parts may be propagated, cultivated, maintained, disposed of, or dealt in, and the section of law with respect to which such license is issued. For an individual license for an animal that is not on the special exemption list, the applicant shall satisfy the Director that the animal can be maintained in good health, properly confined and protected. If depletion of the wild population of the species is an issue, proposed acquisition of a captive-bred animal or acquisition by a person whose ownership is likely to benefit the species shall be given preference. A person, club or association operating under a license shall not sell for food a fish of a size prohibited (131-23). ★★

★The following classes of licenses may be issued: ► a special propagator's license for an individual to possess, propagate and maintain fish for the individual's personal use, or the use of immediate family or guests, or for a club or association and its members or guests to possess, propagate and maintain fish to be fished within waters under the control of the club or association for the personal use of members and guests; ► a special propagator's license for an individual, club or association to possess, propagate and maintain fish for liberation into public waters; ► a propagator's license for an individual, club or association to possess, propagate, maintain, buy, sell or dispose of fish at any season; ► a propagator's license for an individual to possess, maintain, buy, sell, offer for sale or possess for sale, birds, mammals, reptiles or amphibians; ► a special propagator's license for an individual, club or association to possess birds or mammals to propagate for liberation into covers open to public hunting; ► a dealer's license for an individual to possess, buy, sell, or offer for sale, fish, birds or mammals lawfully taken or propagated outside the commonwealth or lawfully propagated within the commonwealth; ► a license for an individual to possess but not to sell except under Director permit, a bird or mammal as a pet, or for training dogs, or a reptile or amphibian; ► a license for an individual to possess, liberate and recapture, but not to sell except under Director permit, up to 25 quail for training dogs; ► a raptor breeding license to possess and propagate birds of the families Accipitridae, Falconidae, Tytonidae, and Strigidae; ► a raptor salvage license to possess, transport, rehabilitate and release to the wild, transfer to a falconry permittee, or other authorized use, birds of the order Falconiformes, except species prohibited by federal regulations [details provided]. An animal possessed, propagated, cultivated, maintained, sold, or offered for sale illegally may be seized and shall be disposed of by the Director of Law Enforcement (131-23). ★

The Director may issue a dealer's license for engaging in the business of buying, selling or offering for sale, for food, the carcasses, or parts, of protected fish, birds or mammals tagged as provided, and as to fish, in accordance with rules and regulations. A propagator's licensee may sell or offer for sale, birds or mammals, alive or dead, or parts, in accordance with section 131-23 without a dealer's license. A person licensed to propagate, cultivate, maintain, sell, or offer for sale, alive or for food, any fish may do so without a dealer's license. No license is required to purchase from a licensed person a fish, bird or mammal, or part, for personal use for food (131-24).

The Director is authorized to issue a taxidermist's license. Licensees may: ► practice taxidermy commercially and may receive and keep indefinitely a fish, bird or mammal lawfully taken or propagated, and sell or dispose of an unclaimed specimen for a tanning, curing, mounting or preserving charge only; ► mount, or acquire and sell a fish, bird or mammal raised under a propagator's license. A permit is required before a specimen is sold, shipped or transported to a nonresident. A taxidermist shall not receive, mount, tan, cure or preserve a fish, bird or mammal or part, not lawfully taken, until the customer presents a permit. The taxidermist shall report within 24 hours an animal unlawfully taken to the Director of Law Enforcement. Taxidermists shall keep detailed records, which shall be open for inspection. Taxidermists may ship from, or remove or permit removal out of the commonwealth of a specimen or part lawfully taken or possessed by a nonresident and shipped or delivered for mounting, tanning, curing or preserving, provided there is attached a label or tag. A licensee may ship from the commonwealth, or remove or permit removal out of the commonwealth, of a specimen or part to a person lawfully engaged in fur dressing, tanning, curing or taxidermy in another state for return to the licensee (131-27).

A person shall not purchase or receive the skins or pelts of fur-bearing mammals without a fur buyer's license [classes of licenses provided]. Except as authorized, no common carrier shall receive within the commonwealth skins or pelts unless marked as required. A person shall not willfully remove, mutilate or destroy a tag or identification attached to a container in which skins are being shipped. Nothing in this section prevents shipment of mammal skins out of the commonwealth by the holder of a license under this section or section 131-23, if the license number and package contents are plainly marked; nor does it prohibit purchase of such from a licensed fur dealer, hunter or trapper for personal use. A skin or pelt used in violation of this section shall be forfeited and disposed of by the Director of Law Enforcement. Licensees shall keep accurate records [of sales, tags or licenses], to be filed with the Director each year. Records shall be open for inspection (131-28).

Notwithstanding other provisions, the Director may issue permits for netting carp and suckers for sale, and subject to Board approval, make rules and regulations governing size and type of nets, method and place of taking (131-30).

The Director may issue commercial shooting preserve permits if: ▸ the proposed preserve is a single parcel of 100 to 500 acres; ▸ the applicant produces evidence of ability to raise or purchase for liberation at least 200 pheasants, quail or nonnative game birds for each 100 acres; ▸ the operation of the preserve does not conflict with the public interest. A permit to operate a commercial shooting preserve entitles its holder and guests to kill and take, by shooting only, pheasants, quail, Chukar partridges, Hungarian partridges, domestic ducks as defined by the USFW, or other nonnative game birds without regard to sex or bag limits from September 15 to March 31. Permits issued under this section are subject to the following conditions: ▸ each commercial shooting preserve must be posted conspicuously not more than 150 feet apart; ▸ the applicant shall release not less than 200 birds per 100 acres of shooting preserve annually between September 15 and March 31; ▸ the number of birds authorized to be taken by shooting shall not exceed 75% of the total number of birds released; ▸ every person hunting on a preserve or participating in a shoot held under a preserve permit shall possess a hunting or sporting license or a nonresident three-day hunting license; ▸ the permittee shall maintain daily records and make the record available upon request; ▸ before a propagated or released bird killed under this section is consumed on the premises or removed, the permittee shall attach a tag, to remain attached until the bird is prepared for consumption; ▸ the Director and agents shall be permitted to enter the premises for inspection or scientific investigation. With approval of the Board, the Director may establish rules and regulations for commercial shooting preserves. A permit may be revoked by the Director for violation of a provision of this section or a rule or regulation (131-31).

Import, Export and Release Provisions

A person shall not put into the inland waters a species of fish or spawn without a license or written approval of the Director. A person shall not bring or cause to be brought into the commonwealth a protected live fish or viable eggs without a permit, applications to be received not less than 15 nor more than 30 days prior to shipment. A permit may be issued if the importation is not detrimental to inland fisheries and if the immediate source of fish or eggs is certified to be free of infectious diseases and parasites. Fish or viable eggs imported under permit shall be subject to inspection by agents of the Director, including taking fish or egg samples for biological examination. The cost of inspection shall be paid by the permittee. Fish or viable eggs brought into the commonwealth in violation of this section, or found upon inspection to be diseased, may be confiscated and shall be forfeited and disposed of (131-19).

A person shall not bring or cause to be brought into the commonwealth a protected live bird or mammal, or a member of the family sciuridae of the order rodentia, or a member of the order lagomorpha or other member of the group vertebrata, wild by nature, without a permit, provided that licensed dealers show evidence of securing a licensed purchaser, or other such vertebrate, which are not excluded from licensing provisions, and which are not on the special exemption list provided for in section 131-23. A person shall not liberate a bird or mammal or other such vertebrates, nor import into or transport within the commonwealth live foxes except in accordance with permit provisions. The Director may issue a permit and include conditions as to importation, inspection, transportation, and liberation of birds and mammals and other vertebrates if the importation is not detrimental to resident wildlife populations, and the animal being imported may be required to be certified to be free of infectious disease or parasites. Permit application shall be filed with the Director not later than ten days before importation, who may for cause revoke a permit, and make, alter, amend, or repeal rules and regulations for issuance and for importation, inspection, transportation and liberating of birds and mammals and other vertebrates. Nothing in this section shall allow liberation into the wild of a pheasant or quail unless certified by the Department of Food and Agriculture that it has been individually tested within the preceding six months, or that the parent stock has been tested within one year, and found free of salmonella pullorum or of any transmissible poultry disease by the University of Massachusetts Veterinary Department, or so certified by a corresponding official of another state. The Department of Food and Agriculture shall supply the Director with the names and addresses of persons whose individual birds, or their parent stock, have met the requirements, which shall be eligible for release if they have not been confined with untested birds or poultry. A bird, mammal or vertebrate brought into the commonwealth in violation of this section, or which is found to be diseased, may be confiscated and shall be forfeited and disposed of (131-19A).

Upon examination of a fish, bird, mammal, reptile or amphibian possessed by persons required to be licensed under section 131-23, except dealers licensed both under 131-23(4) and section 39A of chapter 129 or persons exempted, and with reason to believe that the animal has a contagious or infectious disease or parasite, the Director immediately may cause the animal to be quarantined or isolated for at least ten days upon the premises of the owner, or person in whose charge it is found, or in a designated place. The Director shall take other sanitary measures to prevent the spread of such disease or parasite, and deliver to the owner or person in charge, or to a person having an interest, a written order or quarantine notice which shall set forth conditions, including but not limited to restrictions on maintenance, propagation, cultivation, sale or transportation [details of service provided]. Such fish, bird, mammal, reptile or amphibian shall remain in quarantine until further order of the Director. The expense of quarantine shall be paid by the owner or person in charge, and the commonwealth shall not be liable for expenses, nor for cancellation of orders, loss of income or other loss attributable to the quarantine. If the Director has imposed a quarantine and the public good requires that protection of the commonwealth's animal resources is necessary or that the interest of other propagators are jeopardized, the animal may be destroyed without liability. Orders for destroying shall be in writing by the Director to the owner, person having an interest, or person in charge of the animal and shall contain directions as to examination, disposal, and cleansing and disinfection of the premises. Destruction and disposal shall be in a manner determined by and conducted under the direct supervision of the Director or a designee. A fish, bird, mammal, reptile or amphibian quarantined or isolated by order or notice shall be deemed to be afflicted with a contagious or infectious disease or parasite. The following actions shall be punishable by a fine of $100-500, or jail up to six months, or both: ▶ knowingly breaking or authorizing the breaking of a quarantine, or knowingly removing an animal contrary to an order or notice, or authorizing or causing it to be removed from where it is quarantined or isolated; ▶ placing or causing or authorizing to be placed another animal within a building, place or enclosure where an animal is quarantined; ▶ concealing, selling, removing or transporting, or knowingly authorizing such, an animal one has reasonable cause to believe is afflicted with a contagious or infectious disease or parasite; ▶ authorizing or permitting such animal to go at large or be released to the wilds; ▶ bringing or authorizing or permitting to be brought from another country, state, district or territory into the commonwealth, a fish, bird, mammal, reptile or amphibian which is afflicted with or has been exposed to a contagious or infectious disease or parasite (131-25A through -25C).

Fish, birds, mammals, reptiles or amphibians lawfully taken or propagated without the commonwealth may be purchased by a licensed dealer if: ▶ the export and sale is lawful in the state, province or country in which the animals are taken or from which they are exported; ▶ the import is not in violation of sections 131-19 and 131-19A or rules or regulations; ▶ shipments have the names, content, tag, license or permit number, or identification required by the other state, province or country; ▶ such sale, transportation or export is not contrary to federal legislation or regulation. The burden of proof that skins of mammals and reptiles were lawfully taken shall be upon the person possessing them. Every dealer before offering birds or mammals for sale shall attach to the body or part a numbered tag. Every fish dealer shall attach identification tags to each container. A fish, bird, mammal, reptile or amphibian possessed, shipped, transported or delivered illegally may be seized and disposed of by the Director of Law Enforcement (131-26).

Interstate Reciprocal Agreements

[Reciprocal fishing privileges are outlined for ponds situated both in the commonwealth and in another state, with provisions for rules and regulations and uniformity of regulating the whole pond (131-49).]

ANIMAL DAMAGE CONTROL

★An owner or tenant of land, an immediate family member, or a permanent employee upon the owner's land may: ▶ kill or attempt to kill by other than poisoning or trapping a wild bird damaging property, including domesticated animals, poultry and game on game-rearing farms or preserves, not contrary to a federal law, rule or regulation; ▶

hunt or take by other means, except by poison or snare, a mammal found damaging property except grass growing on uncultivated land. No such owner or tenant shall authorize a person without a trapping permit, other than an immediate family member or a permanent employee, to place traps on the property other than during the open season without a Director's permit. All deer so killed shall be turned over to an environmental police officer and disposed of by the Director of Law Enforcement [details of required written reports provided]. Notwithstanding other provisions, the Director may grant a permit to a farmer to trap live and destroy birds that are destroying agricultural crops or endangering the health of livestock, poultry or fur-bearing animals. The farmer shall mark each trap and check it twice daily. The Director shall issue rules and regulations for the type of traps and kinds of birds which may be trapped, and rules and regulations for protection of song and game birds. The Director and agents may enter upon or pass through or over private property to inspect traps (131-37 and -38).★

★★Whoever owns or leases land devoted to agricultural or horticultural uses as defined, and suffers loss by the eating, browsing or trampling of fruit, ornamental trees, vegetables, produce or crops by deer or moose may notify the Director, declaring the estimated amount of damage. Within 15 days of notice, the Director shall determine whether the damage was inflicted by such deer or moose. If so, an appraisal shall be made under oath by three persons, one designated by the owner of the damaged property, one by the Director, and the third by the trustees for county aid to agriculture or of the agricultural school of the county in which the damage occurred. If the amount of damage declared does not exceed $200, the Director may designate an agent to make an appraisal. Within ten days after the appraisal, the appraiser shall return to the Director a certificate of the damages. Within 30 days, the Director shall approve a claim to the comptroller. If doubt exists, the Director may summon the appraisers and interested parties, make an examination, and cause a review, or new appraisal by other appraisers [details of appraiser compensation provided]. A tree appraised as totally damaged, for which compensation has been paid, may be removed by the Director. No compensation for damage shall be paid to an owner or lessee of land who, within one year prior, has posted such land, other than an orchard, or land surrounding the house, barn or other outbuildings to prevent deer hunting (131-39).★★

★★A person shall not place poison in any form to kill a mammal or bird, except pursuant to a permit issued under the this section. This section does not prohibit a person from placing poison in the person's orchard or in or near the dwelling house, barn or other buildings to destroy rats, woodchucks or other pests, or from placing with like intent under the surface carbon disulfide or other poison applied in a similar manner. The Director is authorized to make rules and regulations and to issue permits to owners or agents of forest plantations or orchards to place poison for extermination of rats, mice and other pests and to employees of municipal, state and federal governments and other qualified persons to place poison elsewhere, for control of animals and birds, public health, wood tick suppression and control, propagation and protection of wild birds and mammals, and similar purposes, or to place poison within an area specified in the permit for killing birds which may lawfully be killed and whose numbers constitute a public nuisance or endanger health or safety. Possession of the raw fur of a mammal or the body of a bird killed by poison, except rats, mice, woodchucks or other pests, is facie evidence of violation of this section unless a government agency employee with a permit (131-43).★★

Officers in charge of public buildings in cities and officers appointed by selectmen in towns may take such reasonable means and use such appliances, except poison, as will effectively exterminate English sparrows and starlings, but nothing authorizes an officer to enter on private property without consent. A person shall not resist willfully officers engaged in such duties or knowingly interfere with the means used by them (131-83).

ENFORCEMENT OF WILDLIFE LAWS

Enforcement Powers

★★Except a commercial dealer or propagation license, a license, permit, or certificate issued under this chapter shall be void and surrendered to an authorized officer if a person is found guilty of, or assessed in any manner after a plea of no contest, or penalized for, a violation of section 131-4(15) (rifle larger than .22 caliber), or sections 131-11 through 131-13, 131-16, 131-32, 131-33, 131-72 (general licensing provisions), 131-54 (certain fishing apparatus), 131-57, 131-58, 131-61 through 131-68, 131-70 (general prohibited acts with hunting weapons), 131-73 (moose), 131-75 (turkey), and 131-80 (registration and identification of traps, or a rule or regulation thereunder, or for fishing, hunting or trapping outside the season, or for unlawful taking or possession of a deer). A violator shall not receive that license for one year from conviction. Every license, permit, or certificate issued under this chapter, held by a person found guilty or assessed on three or more separate occasions for violations of a provision of this chapter, or regulation, shall be void and surrendered, and a violator shall not eligible for such license for one year. No fee for a void license, permit, or certificate shall be refunded. Loss of license or permit shall not apply to a holder of a sporting, hunting, fishing or trapping license who fails to wear such license in a visible manner on outer clothing while fishing, hunting or trapping, upon furnishing proof that the person holds a license. If the holder of such license fails to carry it and wear it in a visible manner, the first offence shall be reported to the Director of Law Enforcement; upon a second offence, the license shall be surrendered and suspended for 30 days; and upon a subsequent offence the license shall be subject to voiding. A person shall surrender such license on demand of an officer empowered to enforce this chapter (131-34 and -35). ★ ★

The Director, deputy directors, chiefs and deputy chiefs of Law Enforcement, environmental police officers and deputies, wardens and state police with jurisdiction, and other officers qualified to serve criminal process may arrest without warrant a person found violating a provision of this chapter or an ordinance, rule or regulation under authority thereof, or other general or special law relating to fish, birds, mammals or dogs, and may seize fish, birds or mammals unlawfully taken or held, to be forfeited and disposed of for the best interest of the commonwealth. Wardens shall enforce the laws relating to fish, birds and mammals. Persons authorized to arrest without a warrant, in performance of their duties, may enter upon and pass over private lands. The Director of Law Enforcement and other authorized officers may request a person reasonably believed to be engaged in hunting, fishing, or trapping; to possess unlawfully fish, birds or mammals; to possess fish, birds or mammals unlawfully taken; or to possess unlawful equipment or ammunition, to display for inspection fish, birds, mammals, equipment or ammunition in possession, and may arrest without warrant a person refusing or failing to comply (131-87 and -88).

Fish, birds or mammals unlawfully taken or held, or equipment, possession or use of which is prohibited by a law relating to inland fisheries and game, may be the subject of a search warrant, which may be issued to the Director of Law Enforcement or an authorized officer. Fish, birds, mammals and equipment described in the warrant may be seized and shall be forfeited. This section does not apply to fish, birds, mammals or equipment passing through the commonwealth under authority of US laws. Fish, birds or mammals so seized shall be preserved when proper facilities exist, until the necessity for preservation ceases, at which time the animals or equipment may be disposed of for the best interest of the commonwealth (131-89). Actions and prosecutions under this chapter, unless otherwise provided, shall be commenced within two years after the cause of action accrued or the offence was committed (131-91).

Criminal Penalties

[Each penalty set forth below is for violation of the provisions of the statutory section as well as for violation of the rules, regulations or orders made under authority of that section.] Violation of provisions relating to: ► open season; ► nature preserves; ► license requirements and fees; ► permits for netting of carps and suckers; ► license expiration, loan, or transfer; ► carrying or displaying license; ► fishing, hunting or trapping on posted, private land; ► farmers permit to trap and kill birds; ► riparian proprietors; ► fishing ponds on state boundaries; ► methods of taking fish; ► trout taking in coastal waters; ► fishing with floats and toggle fishing; ► fish traps, seines and nets, hooks; ► taking on Sunday; ► shooting across highways, near dwellings; ► reservations, parks, public lands, hunting, state forests; ► weapons, intoxicating liquor, drugs; ► bows and arrows; ► orange clothing; ► deer tags; ► registration and identification of traps; ► dogs, sparrows and starlings, pigeons, transportation of fish: fine of $50-100, jail up to 30 days, or both. In addition, for each fish, bird or mammal, other than a deer, bear or turkey unlawfully killed, taken, held or possessed, or for each nest or egg unlawfully taken, molested, distributed or destroyed - fine of $10-50; for each deer, bear or turkey unlawfully killed, or unlawfully possessed - fine of $100-1,000, jail up to 6 months, or both (131-90).

Violation of provisions relating to moose: fine of $300-1,000, jail up to 6 months, or both. Violations relating to: ► loss or destruction of license; ► fur buyer's license; ► prohibited acts, licenses, permits, etc.; ► draining of ponds or reservoirs; ► negligent use of weapons; ► damage to property; ► loaded weapon in vehicle; ► automatic firearms; ► or hunting with firearms or dogs: fine of $50-100, jail up to 60 days, or both. Violations relating to: ► license records, payments, bonds; ► license to put-and-take or import fish, live birds, or mammals; ► negligent use of weapons causing injury; ► artificial light, pivot, or swivel gun; ► trap, net, or snare: fine of $100-500, jail up to 6 months, or both. Violation relating to sale of fish and game: fine of $50-100 for each fish, bird or mammal, other than a deer, bear, or moose, unlawfully bought, sold, bartered, exchanged, offered or exposed for sale, or possessed for sale; for a deer, bear, or moose, fine of $300-1,000 (131-90).

Violation of provisions relating to: ▸ protection of fisheries from waste, pollution, alteration of flows and poisons, fine of $100-5,000, jail up to 2 years, or both. Violation relating to: ▸ hunting from vehicles; ▸ shotgun shells, load; ▸ caliber of firearm; ▸ scientific experiments, fine of $50-100, jail up to 1 year, or both. Violation relating to: ▸ failure to keep open or maintain a fishway as prescribed by the Director, fine of $50 for each day of failure. Violation relating to: ▸ nests and eggs; ▸ taking mammal from hole, lodge, or other, fine of $20-50, jail up to 30 days, or both, for each bird or mammal taken, killed or removed, and for each nest or egg taken, disturbed, molested or destroyed. Violation relating to: ▸ ferrets or fitchews, fine up to $100, jail up to 30 days, or both (131-90).

Violation relating to turkey is a fine of $100-500, jail up to 6 months, or both, for each wild turkey knowingly and unlawfully possessed, and for each nest or egg taken, molested, disturbed or destroyed, or unlawfully possessed. Violation relating to birds of prey is a fine of $100-500, jail up to 6 months, or both; and such person, subject to section 131-34, shall not be issued a license or permit or certificate under this chapter for three years. Violation relating to a dam or obstruction for passage of anadromous fish or refusing or neglecting to keep open or maintain a fishway as prescribed by the Director is a fine of $50 for each day of such refusal or neglect. Unless the context otherwise requires, a violation of a provision of this chapter, or rule or regulation, for which no other penalty is provided, shall be punished by a fine of $20-50, jail up to 30 days, or both. A net, snare, trap, jacklight or other similar device used in violation of a provision, and a bird or mammal taken in violation of said chapter, or a rule or regulation, upon conviction shall be forfeited to the commonwealth and disposed of (131-90).

Illegal Taking of Wildlife

In addition to the penalties provided for in this section for violating provisions of chapter 131 or rule or regulation, a person convicted of illegal taking or possession of animals, birds, fur-bearing animals and fish, resulting in injury, death or destruction, may be required to make restitution to the commonwealth for the value of each animal, bird, fur-bearing animal or fish as follows: ▸ deer and bear, $300; ▸ wild turkey, fisher, bobcat and otter, $200; ▸ fox, coyote and beaver, $50; ▸ mink, muskrat, raccoon, wild rabbit, hare and gray squirrel, $25; ▸ ruffed grouse, pheasant, quail, woodcock and migratory waterfowl, $25 per bird; ▸ fish, $5 per fish; ▸ endangered species, $2,000; ▸ threatened species, $1,000; ▸ species of special concern, $500; ▸ other animals or birds, $10 each. In every conviction involving illegal taking or possession of animals, birds, fur-bearing animals and fish, the court may order reimbursement in a sum to exceed the amounts above, to be paid directly to the court. If two or more defendants are convicted of illegal taking or possession, the reimbursement shall be declared against them jointly and severally. A person failing to make a damage assessment payment ordered by the court shall be guilty of contempt and shall not be eligible to purchase a license until all assessments are paid in full. Violation of section 131-5C: fine of $100-500, jail up to 14 days, or both (131-90).

A person who violates the provisions of 131A-2 (threatened or endangered species), or rules and regulations promulgated thereunder, shall be punished by a fine of not less than $500, or jail up to 90 days, or both; a second or subsequent conviction is punishable by a fine of $5,000-10,000, or jail up to 180 days, or both. A person who violates the provisions of 131A-2 (habitat protection), or rules and regulations thereunder, shall be punished by a fine of $1,000-10,000, or jail up to 90 days, or both; a subsequent conviction is punishable by a fine of $10,000-20,000, or jail up to 180 days, or both. In addition or as an alternative to such penalties, a person may be ordered to restore the significant habitat to its prior condition. Commission of prohibited acts against each individual animal, plant or part, constitutes a separate violation (131A-6).

License Revocations and Suspensions

★★A person whose privilege to hunt, trap, or fish has been suspended or revoked in a jurisdiction of the US or Canada shall not be licensed for such activity in the commonwealth, or if licensed at the time, such license shall be suspended, during the period of suspension or revocation if, after notice and hearing, the Director determines that the offence would constitute a violation of section 131-10, 131-13, 131-22, 131-61, 131-62 through 131-65, 131-68, 131-69, 131-73 through 131-80A, or 131-82. The license shall be returned immediately to the Division of Fisheries and Wildlife. Violation: fine of $50-200 (131-90A).★★

Intoxication Testing of Hunters

While under the influence of intoxicating liquor or drugs a person shall not hunt or carry a firearm, bow and arrow or other weapon while hunting or target shooting (131-62).

HABITAT PROTECTION

For the purpose of protecting a species of useful fish, birds or mammals and for aiding propagation, the Director may acquire in fee by purchase, gift or devise, or may lease, or with the consent of the owners may control land, water or shore, or the right to use, as a wildlife sanctuary. With the approval of the Governor, the Director may receive in trust for the commonwealth any grant or devise of land or a gift or bequest of personal property for aiding in the propagation and protection of useful fish, birds or mammals. Unless approved by the general court, no obligation shall be imposed on the commonwealth to expend more than the income of the trust property, or more than the income and principal thereof. In respect to a territory mentioned in section 131-7 or 131-59, with the consent of the appropriate authorities, the Director may make use of the land, water or shore for improving the feeding and nesting environment of birds or mammals, and may make rules and regulations which when approved by the Governor have the force of law. The Director with like consent may liberate birds within territories, and when advisable, cooperate with landowners in experiments in propagation of birds and mammals. If the Director establishes a wildlife sanctuary, a copy of the order shall be published once a week for two successive weeks, and the order shall be posted within the cities and towns, and also within the limits of the territory itself. If a great pond or part, or a seashore is included within the territory, a copy of the order shall be filed in the office of the clerk of each bordering city and town, and with the state secretary. Orders shall take effect when posted, and shall contain a full description of the territory and the period. Whenever a wildlife sanctuary has been established, except as authorized by the Director, no person shall hunt, trap or take a bird or mammal; nor enter with a firearm, trap, snare, or other device for killing, taking or injuring birds and mammals; nor take, molest, disturb or destroy a nest, eggs or young or mammals or remove eggs or young from the nest (131-7 through -10).

★★The Executive Office of Environmental Affairs, the Department or Department division may designate as a nature preserve real property owned by the commonwealth and under the care and control of one of these offices. After a determination that the parcel qualifies as a nature preserve, the Division shall hold a public hearing, and shall file with the Executive Office of Environmental Affairs a statement dedicating a nature preserve which includes why the parcel qualifies as a nature preserve and a plan for its preservation and protection. A nature preserve shall be monitored and maintained as nearly as possible in its natural condition, and shall be used in a manner and under limitations consistent with its status, without impairment or artificial development, for present or future scientific research and education, for providing a habitat for plant and animal species, communities and other natural objects, and preservation of areas representative of significant habitats and ecosystems of the commonwealth (131-10A). A Nature Preserve Council (Council) shall consist of seven members appointed by the Secretary of the Executive Office of Environmental Affairs: four shall be members of the Nongame Advisory Committee; two shall be trained in plant ecology, and represent colleges, universities, outdoor education programs, primary and secondary schools, science museums, and arboreta; and one shall be knowledgeable in natural history and represent the general public. Terms are three years and members are eligible for reappointment. Duties include advising the Division on policies and rules and regulations concerning nature preserves, consulting regarding nomination of potential nature preserves, assisting in preparation of such plans, and advising the Division on related budgetary matters. The Council shall submit a biennial report to the Governor, describing the condition of each nature preserve, outlining actions taken by the Council, and making recommendations related to the nature preserve program (131-10B). In consultation with another department or division within the Executive Office of Environmental Affairs which has control of such parcel, the Division shall consider the public interest in conservation and preservation of the preserve, and any federal, state or local program in furtherance thereof, any state, regional or local comprehensive land use or development plan affecting said parcel, and a proposal by a governmental body for its use. The Division shall promulgate rules and regulations to effectuate the nature preserve program (131-10D).★★

★★No person shall remove, fill, dredge or alter a bank, fresh water wetland, coastal wetland, beach, dune, flat, marsh, meadow or swamp bordering on the ocean or on an estuary, creek, river, stream, pond, or lake, or land under said waters or land subject to tidal action, coastal storm flowage, or flooding, other than in the course of maintaining, repairing or replacing, but not substantially changing, an existing lawfully located structure or facility used to serve the public and to provide electric, gas, water, telephone, telegraph and other telecommunication services, without filing written notice of intention to act, including plans describing the proposed activity and its effect on the environment and without receiving and complying with an order of conditions [terms of filing of notice, receipt, copies and fees provided]. No such notice shall be sent before all permits, variances, and required approvals have been obtained, except that the notice may be sent after the filing of an application(s) for such permits, variances, and approvals. The notice shall include information describing the effect of the proposed activity on the environment. Within 21 days of receipt by a conservation commission of a written request, the Commission shall make a written determination as to whether this section is applicable to any land or work thereon. The conservation commission, selectmen or mayor receiving notice shall hold a public hearing on the proposed activity within 21 days of receipt of notice [details of time and place of hearing given]. The conservation commission and its agents, officers and employees and the Commissioner of Environmental Protection and agents and employees, may enter upon private land to perform their duties under this section. No conditions shall be imposed, nor a determination be rendered by a conservation commission without a quorum. If after the hearing the conservation commission, selectmen or mayor, determines that the area on which the proposed work is to be done is significant to public or private water supply, groundwater supply, flood control, storm damage prevention, prevention of pollution, protection of land containing shellfish, protection of wildlife habitat or protection of fisheries, they shall by written order within 21 days impose conditions, and all work shall be done in accordance therewith. If it is determined that the proposed activity does not require such conditions, the applicant shall be notified within 21 days after the hearing. If a conservation commission within 21 days has failed to hold a hearing; or after such hearing has failed to issue an order; or upon a written request by a person to determine whether this section is applicable to any work, has failed to make said determination; or where an order does issue; the applicant, an aggrieved person, or owner of land abutting the land, or ten residents of the city or town in which the land is located, within 10 days may request the Department of Environmental Protection to determine whether the area is significant to public or private water supply, groundwater supply, flood control, storm damage prevention, prevention of pollution, protection of land containing shellfish, the protection of wildlife habitat or the protection of fisheries. The Commissioner of Environmental Protection or a designee also may request such a determination within 10 days [further details provided]. As used in this section "wildlife habitat" shall mean those areas subject to this section which, due to their plant community composition and structure, hydrologic regime or other characteristics, provide important food, shelter, migratory or overwintering areas, or breeding areas for wildlife (131-40). For preservation and promotion of the public safety, private property, wildlife, fisheries, water resources, flood plain areas and agriculture, the Commissioner of Environmental Protection shall adopt, amend or repeal orders regulating, restricting or prohibiting dredging, filling, removing or otherwise altering or polluting inland wetlands. In this section, "inland wetlands" includes the definition of "freshwater wetlands" and that portion of a bank which touches inland waters of a freshwater wetland, and freshwater wetland subject to flooding (131-40A). ★★

★★If fisheries in inland waters are of sufficient value to warrant prohibition or regulation of the discharge of waste or other material from any source, which may directly or indirectly injure such fisheries, the Director may give written notice to the Director of the Division of Water Pollution Control, who shall take appropriate action (131-41). A person shall not put, throw, discharge or permit to be discharged or to escape into inland waters waste or other material in violation of section 131-40 or of the Massachusetts Clean Water Act, which may directly or indirectly injure or kill fish or fish spawn, nor shall a person alter or manipulate or permit to be altered or manipulated the flows or water levels in inland waters to the extent that directly or indirectly injures or kills the fish or spawn, except as provided in section 131-48. This section does not apply to agents or persons authorized to use any method for sampling, eradication or management of fish and fish habitat, nor does it prohibit the use of explosives for engineering, construction, fish sampling and public welfare providing the appropriate permit has been given by US, state or municipal government. This section does not apply to providing water for public water supply purposes. Contrary to a provision of this section, except as otherwise provided, whoever does or allows an act that directly or indirectly injures or kills or causes damage to fish or spawn in inland waters is liable in tort, in twice the amount of the damage done, to the commonwealth through its Division of Fisheries and Wildlife. The Director shall establish the value of injured, killed or damaged fish or spawn employing current commercial values. In determining the remuneration for injured, killed or damaged fish or spawn the Director may negotiate a settlement of the amount of such remuneration. If such settlement cannot be negotiated to the Director's satisfaction, the superior court shall upon petition of the Director establish the value of fish or spawn (131-42). ★★

No riparian proprietor of a natural pond other than a great pond, or of an artificial pond or nonnavigable stream, shall enclose waters within those premises without furnishing a suitable passage for anadromous fish naturally frequenting such waters to spawn; nor shall a riparian proprietor enclose the waters for artificial propagation, cultivation and maintenance of fish, except shiners as authorized, without a propagator's license. Without written consent of the proprietor/lessee of a natural pond which is not a great pond, or of an artificial pond or nonnavigable stream, where fish are lawfully propagated or maintained under a license, a person shall not take or attempt to take, fish (131-47).

A person shall not hunt, molest or destroy a bird or mammal within the boundaries of a reservation, park or common, or land owned or leased by the commonwealth or political subdivision, or land held in trust for public use. Authorities or persons having control of such reservations, parks, commons or other lands may permit hunting within the boundaries during open season. Authorities having control of reservations, parks, commons or land owned or leased or held for public use; the Director, deputy directors, chiefs and deputy chiefs of Law Enforcement; environmental police officers and deputies; wardens and state police in areas over which they have jurisdiction; and officers qualified to serve criminal process shall enforce this section. This section does not apply to state forests, or to state parks and reservations under control of the Division of Forests and Parks of the Department of Environmental Management. Nothing in this section prohibits an agency of the commonwealth or its political subdivisions from permitting hunting during open season, in an area owned or leased by it, or from entering into agreements with the Director to establish wildlife management areas (131-59).

★★Before a person alters a significant habitat, except as provided, the person shall submit to the Director the following: ▸ full plans and a complete description of the project and the anticipated use; ▸ alternatives to the proposed project and anticipated use; ▸ impacts of the proposed project and anticipated use on the subject species; ▸ full plans for protection of endangered or threatened species present and mitigation measures to be taken to provide amelioration of the impact; ▸ the potential economic effects of the proposed project on the person and the community. No alteration of a significant habitat may commence without a written permit issued by the Director. The Director shall render a decision within 45 days of receiving all required information. A permit shall be granted only upon a finding that the proposed action will not reduce the viability of the significant habitat to support the endangered or threatened species population involved (131A-5). ★★ (See PROTECTED SPECIES OF WILDLIFE for other significant habitat provisions.)

Any work, project or activity for which a final environmental impact report has been issued and certified by the Secretary of Environmental Affairs as complying with the provisions of Chapter 30, or for which an environmental notification form has been filed and the Secretary has certified that an environmental impact report is not required, and for which the Natural Heritage and Endangered Species Program has reviewed the project and made recommendations, and for which the project proponent has incorporated such measures, shall be issued a permit by the Director, except that the permit may be conditioned upon implementation of the measures. Failure of the program to make recommendations within the following time periods is equivalent to the issuance of a permit by the Director: ▸ if an environmental impact report is not required, 90 days after the Secretary issues a notice of the receipt of an environmental notification form; ▸ if an environmental impact report is required, prior to certification by the Secretary that the final report complies with Chapter 30. Record owners of lands or interests in lands aggrieved by a decision of the Director or by the Director's failure to act may appeal to the Secretary by sending, by certified mail, a notice of appeal within 21 days of such decision. The Secretary shall hold a hearing no later than 120 days from the date of decision, shall consider the information and testimony presented, and shall make a determination within 60 days. The Secretary shall reverse only upon a finding that the decision was without substantial basis in fact, but shall examine fully on the merits an appeal involving the Director's failure to act. This section does not apply to work performed in the normal maintenance or improvement on land in agricultural or aquacultural use. In addition to appeal, a landowner aggrieved by a decision of the Director may file an action in superior court to determine whether such decision constitutes a taking requiring compensation under the US Constitution (131A-5).

NATIVE AMERICAN WILDLIFE PROVISIONS: None.

MICHIGAN

Sources: Michigan Compiled Laws Annotated, 1984, Chapters 259, 299, 300 through 305, 307, 316 and 750; 1993 Cumulative Annual Pocket Parts.

STATE WILDLIFE POLICY

All animals, resident, migratory, native or introduced, found in this state are the property of the people of the state and their taking is regulated by the Commission of Natural Resources and the Department of Natural Resources (300.256). All fish, reptiles, amphibians, mollusks, and crustaceans found in this state are state property and may be taken only at such times and in such manner as provided by law (301.2). (See also HABITAT PROTECTION.)

RELEVANT WILDLIFE DEFINITIONS: See Definitions section of Appendices.

STATE FISH AND WILDLIFE AGENCIES

Agency Structure

There is a **Department of Natural Resources** (Department) (formerly the Department of Conservation), the general administration of powers and duties of which is vested in a **Commission of Natural Resources** (Commission) (formerly the Commission of Conservation), composed of seven members appointed by the Governor, subject to Senate confirmation. A member of the Commission is selected with special reference to training and experience related to at least one principal line of activity vested in the Department and ability. Two members shall reside in the Upper Peninsula. The term of office is six years. The Commission appoints and employs a **Director of the Department of Natural Resources** (Director). With Commission approval, the Director appoints a Deputy Director and assistants and employees. Each member of the Commission and the Director shall qualify by taking and subscribing to the constitutional oath of office, and by filing it with the Secretary of State (299.1).

The Governor, with Senate advice and consent, appoints three state residents to be a **Board of Fish Commissioners** (Board), for six-year terms. The Board selects locations to establish and maintain fish-breeding establishments for propagation and cultivation of whitefish and food fish for stocking state waters (300.51 and .52). The Board may take, or cause to be taken, fish for fish culture or scientific observation. They shall discharge duties required of them by law for fishing interests or enforcement of laws relating to protection of state fish and fisheries (300.54).

Agency Powers and Duties

Powers and duties previously vested in the Public Domain Commission, the State Game, Fish, and Forest Fire Commissioner, and the State Board of Fish Commissioners, the Geological Survey, and the State Park Commission are transferred to and vested in the **Department**. The Commission may: ▸ promulgate rules governing its organization and procedure; ▸ promulgate and enforce rules concerning use and occupancy of lands and property under its control; ▸ provide and develop facilities for outdoor recreation; ▸ conduct investigations for administration of its duties; ▸ remove and dispose of forest products; ▸ require the payment of fees for permits to hunt and take waterfowl on public hunting areas. Except as provided by law, the Commission may enter into contracts for the taking of coal, oil, gas, and other mineral products from state-owned lands, and money received is used to defray expenses, except money received from lands acquired through the Game and Fish Protection Fund. Money received from service charges by persons using areas managed for waterfowl is credited to the Game and Fish Protection Fund (299.2). [Other permitted contract provisions for the Great Lakes are given in 299.2.]

The Department shall: ▸ protect and conserve state natural resources; ▸ provide and develop outdoor recreation facilities; ▸ prevent destruction of timber and other forest growth by fire or otherwise; ▸ promote reforesting of forest lands; ▸ prevent and guard against pollution of lakes and streams, and enforce laws for that purpose; ▸ foster and encourage protection and propagation of game and fish. On behalf of the state, the Commission may accept gifts and grants of land and other property and has authority to buy, sell, exchange or condemn land and other property.

The Department may accept from the federal government funds, moneys or grants for development of salmon and steelhead trout fishing. The Department may lease its lands which have been designated for recreational use to state legal units, or to national or state recognized groups devoted to development of character, citizenship training and physical fitness of youth (299.3).

The Commission or Department, in pursuing the state's policy of propagating fish to stock streams and lakes, shall not refuse to accept federal fish stock, and shall apply for all federal fish stock programs which do not commit the state to future expenditures. The Department shall provide a listing to the legislature of all federal fish stock programs by April 15 of each year (299.3b). Department or Commission writings shall be made available to the public. In years in which a regular session of the legislature is held, the Director shall make a report covering Department operation for the preceding biennial period to the Governor and the legislature (299.4).

The Department shall develop and implement a long-range plan for management of state nongame fish and wildlife resources, to be reviewed and updated every five years. The plan shall be written with the assistance of an advisory committee (299.155 and .156). The Department shall implement a public information program to present the values and benefits of nongame fish and wildlife and their habitats to society, including the means by which citizens can observe and enjoy nongame fish and wildlife; and to inform the public of how the nongame fish and wildlife fund is utilized to meet long-range management goals for nongame fish and wildlife, and about the existence and purpose of the Nongame Fish and Wildlife Fund (299.158).

The **Commission** is authorized and directed to perform acts to conduct and establish wildlife restoration, management, and research projects and areas in cooperation with the federal government (299.201). The Commission is authorized to perform acts to conduct and establish fish restoration, management, and research projects and areas in cooperation with the federal government (300.151). The Commission shall perform acts for the conservation, protection, restoration, and propagation of endangered and threatened species of fish, wildlife, and plants in cooperation with the federal government. The Director shall conduct investigations on fish, plants, and wildlife in order to develop information relating to population, distribution, habitat needs, limiting factors, and other biological and ecological data for determining management measures for their continued ability to sustain themselves successfully. On the basis of these determinations and other scientific and commercial data, the Commission shall promulgate a list of fish, plants, and wildlife species endangered or threatened within the state. The Commission shall conduct a review of the state list every two years, and may amend the list by additions or deletions. The Director may establish programs, including the acquisition of land or aquatic habitat, for management of endangered or threatened species, and may enter into cooperative agreements with government entities or private persons to carry out such programs (299.223 through .225). The Commission may plan the establishment of fish hatcheries for the propagation and cultivation of pickerel, trout and whitefish for restocking the Great Lakes (307.251).

The Commission has power to regulate the taking or killing of fish, game and fur-bearing animals and game birds protected by state laws, and may suspend or abridge the open season and may promulgate regulations to do so (300.1). If the Commission determines that fish, game, or fur-bearing animals, or game birds are in danger of depletion or extermination and require additional protection in designated waters or a state area, it may suspend or abridge the open season on such birds or animals or regulate their taking or killing. The length of time during which the order shall remain in force shall not exceed five years. The public shall be notified of orders changing the rules pertaining to hunting, fishing or trapping. Whenever the Commission determines that conditions no longer require additional protection of a species of fish, game, or fur-bearing animal, it may rescind or modify the order. A person who takes or kills a fish, game, or fur-bearing animal or game bird contrary to these provisions is guilty of a misdemeanor and upon conviction, for the first offense, shall be punished by a fine up to $100, or jail up to 60 days; and for the second or subsequent offense, shall be punished by a fine of $50-250 and jail 20-90 days (300.3 through .5).

A person shall not take, release, transport, sell, buy, or possess game or a protected animal, living or dead, except as provided for in the Wildlife Conservation Act or by Commission order or an interim order of the Director. This does not enhance the Commission's powers to establish an open season for an animal that is not game or give it power to designate a species as game (300.257). Only the legislature may designate a species as game, and only it may establish the first open season for that animal. After the legislature authorizes the first open season, the Commission may issue orders pertaining to that animal (300.261).

The Commission shall manage animals in this state, and may: ▸ recommend animals to be added to or deleted from the category of game; ▸ determine the animals that may be taken; ▸ determine the animals that are protected; ▸ establish open seasons for taking or possessing game, except as provided; ▸ establish lawful methods of taking game; ▸ establish lawful methods of taking game for handicapped persons; ▸ establish bag limits; ▸ establish geographic areas where certain regulations may apply to taking animals; ▸ determine conditions under which permits may be issued by the Director; ▸ establish fees for the issuing of permits; ▸ regulate the hours during which animals may be taken; ▸ require that a person involved in a chase of an animal possess a license; ▸ establish conditions under which animals taken or possessed outside this state may be imported; ▸ regulate buying and selling of animals and parts; ▸ establish methods of taking animals taken primarily because of the value of their pelts (300.258).

The Director may modify a Commission order by issuing an interim order consistent with federal regulations or when animals are at risk of being depleted or extirpated, or are threatening public safety, or inflicting damage to horticulture, agriculture or other property (300.259). The Director may issue a permit to handicapped or disabled persons to use special methods in taking game as specified in this section. The Director may issue permits authorizing: ▸ taking and possession of animals for the purpose of rehabilitating animals; ▸ taking animals to prevent or control damage and nuisance; ▸ collection, transportation, possession, or disposition of animals, and parts, for scientific purposes; ▸ public exhibition of animals; ▸ taxidermy; ▸ disposition of accidentally or unlawfully taken or injured animals, or animals that are unlawfully possessed. Such permits may be suspended, revoked, annulled, withdrawn, recalled, canceled, or amended. If the permittee is convicted of violating these provisions, the permit or license may be revoked and an animal and parts in possession disposed of in a manner approved by the Director. Fees for permits and licenses shall be credited to the Game and Fish Protection Fund (300.264). The Director may establish a quota on the number of each kind of license that may be issued (316.507).

Agency Regulations

The Commission promulgates rules for protection of the lands and property under its control against wrongful use or occupancy, but may not promulgate a rule that applies to commercial fishing except as otherwise provided. A person who violates a Commission rule is guilty of a misdemeanor, punishable by jail up to 90 days or community service up to 30 days; a fine up to $500; or both. After the Civil Procedures Act is enacted into law, a violator is responsible for a civil infraction and subject to a civil fine up to $500 (299.3a).

The Department promulgates rules for administration of the Hunting and Fishing License Act (316.901). The Commission may issue orders to protect public interest and to provide for administration of game breeders and dealers. The Director, with Commission approval, may promulgate rules designating certain game that do not require protection under provisions relating to game breeders and dealers and which may be possessed, propagated, purchased, or sold without a license (317.80)

Agency Funding Sources

The **Nongame Fish and Wildlife Trust Fund** may receive appropriations, money or other things of value. The interest and earnings of the trust fund not otherwise retained are expended for management of the state's nongame fish and wildlife resources. The Department determines which projects should be funded with money from the trust fund (299.153, .154 and .157).

★The Department may issue for sale to the public a stamp, decal, medallion, or other item of personal property to signify the purchaser's interest in contributing to wildlife preservation. Net proceeds from sales of items are used by the Department exclusively for wildlife research and habitat improvement for nongame wild animals or designated endangered species, or designated plant species (299.211 and .212).★

★★In prosecutions for violation of game and fish law, the sentencing court shall assess, as costs, the sum of $10, to be known as the judgment fee, and which shall be paid to the Game and Fish Protection Fund (300.18).★★

The **Game and Fish Protection Trust Fund** consists of: ▸ gifts, grants, or bequests conveyed to the trust fund, or income derived therefrom; ▸ funds transferred to the Game and Fish Protection Fund; ▸ certain royalties from the Kammer Recreational Land Trust Fund Act; ▸ bonuses, rentals, royalties, and other revenues collected or reserved under provisions of leases or direct sale contracts permitting extraction of minerals, coal, oil, gas, or other resources from state owned lands, if these revenues accrue from lands acquired by the state using revenues derived from the Game and Fish Protection Fund, the Kammer recreational land trust fund act, or related state or federal funds. The interest and earnings from the trust fund shall be deposited in the Game and Fish Protection Fund (300.213 and .214). Moneys collected from the sale of license and stamps as provided by the Sportsmen Fishing Law go to the credit of the **Game and Fish Protection Fund** to be used for protection, propagation, and distribution of fish and game, and as otherwise provided (305.10). The Department shall provide license agents with conservation law enforcement stamps enabling the purchaser to contribute to the **Wildlife Resource Protection Fund** (316.501). (See also Reward Payments under ENFORCEMENT OF WILDLIFE LAWS.)

Except as provided, the Director shall transmit money received from the sale of passbooks and licenses to the State Treasurer. The **Game and Fish Protection Fund** is created as a separate fund, and except as provided by law, its money shall be paid out for: ► services rendered by the Director and the Director's assistants, together with expenses incurred in the enforcement and administration of state game, fish, and fur laws; ► propagation and liberation of game, fur-bearing animals, birds, or fish as the Director determines; ► conducting investigations and compiling and publishing information relative to the propagation, protection, and conservation of wildlife; ► delivering lectures, developing cooperation, and carrying out educational activities relating to state wildlife conservation. The Director may make direct grants from the fund to state colleges and universities to conduct fish or wildlife research (316.601).

From each firearm deer, bow and arrow deer, and resident sportsman's hunting license fee, $1.50 shall be used for improving and maintaining a deer habitat and for land acquisition for deer habitat management (316.602). From each zone III hunting license fee, $.35 shall be used for acquiring and administering hunter access leases on private land and for habitat development on the leased land. Participating landowners have authority to control hunter access according to the terms of the lease agreement, including requiring a hunter to obtain verbal or written permission to hunt on the participating landowner's land, and the leased land shall be posted with signs provided by the Department. The Department may promulgate rules governing the administration and operation of a hunting access program (316.605).

★★The Department may sell license application lists or information filed with the Department pursuant to law and related Department publications. The Department shall establish the price of the lists, information, and publications and sale proceeds are credited to the Game and Fish Protection Fund (316.606).★★ From March 1, 1989 to February 28, 1990, lifetime hunting or fishing licenses may be purchased by residents as provided in the Game and Fish Lifetime Trust Fund Act. The **Game and Fish Lifetime License Trust Fund** is created to assist in providing adequate long-term funding for the Game and Fish Protection Fund. Moneys received from sales of lifetime hunting and fishing licenses are credited to the trust fund (316.1003 and 316.1005). Moneys received from sales of fur dealers licenses go to the credit of the Game Protection Fund and are used for protection, propagation and distribution of game and fur-bearing animals as provided by law (317.6). Moneys received from game breeder and dealer licenses go to the Game Protection Fund (317.82). Moneys received from licenses and tags or seals for private shooting preserves are credited to the Game Protection Fund (317.311).

Agency Advisory Boards

★★A Hunting Area Control Committee is established, composed of representatives of the Department and the Department of State Police, the township supervisor or a representative selected by the township board, and representatives of county sheriff departments. For public safety, this committee is empowered to regulate and prohibit hunting, and discharge of firearms and bows and arrows, on areas established under these provisions where such actions may or are likely to kill, injure or disturb persons. Areas may be closed for part or all of the year, and designated where hunting is permitted only by prescribed methods and weapons. The Director may authorize firearms use to prevent or control depredations of birds and animals where significant damages are being caused by wildlife. Violation: a misdemeanor (317.331, .332, .335 and .336).★←

PROTECTED SPECIES OF WILDLIFE

Except as provided, a person shall not take, possess, transport, import, export, process, sell or offer for sale, buy or offer to buy, nor shall a common carrier or contract carrier transport or receive for shipment, a species of fish, plants, or wildlife appearing on: ► the state list of endangered or threatened indigenous fish, plants, and wildlife; ► the US list of endangered or threatened native fish and wildlife; ► the US list of endangered or threatened plants; ► the US list of endangered or threatened foreign fish and wildlife. A species of fish, plant or wildlife appearing on these lists which enters the state from without may be transported, possessed, and sold in accordance with the terms of a federal permit or a permit issued under the laws of another state. The Commission by rule may treat a species as an endangered or threatened species even though it is not so listed if it finds any of the following: ► the species so closely resembles in appearance a listed species that enforcement personnel would have substantial difficulty in attempting to differentiate between the two species; ► the effect of the substantial difficulty in differentiating between a listed and an unlisted species is an additional threat to an endangered or threatened species; ► the treatment of an unlisted species will substantially facilitate the enforcement and further intent of the Endangered Species Act. These provisions do not prohibit importation of a trophy under a lawful permit or the taking of a threatened species when the Commission has determined that the abundance of the species in the state justifies a controlled harvest not in violation of federal law. A law enforcement officer, police officer, sheriff's deputy, or conservation officer shall enforce the state Endangered Species Act and the rules promulgated under the act. Violation of a provision of the act or failure to procure a permit issued under this act is a misdemeanor; fine of $100-1,000, or jail up to 90 days, or both (299.226 through .228).

No person shall hunt, pursue, trap, capture, kill or destroy, or attempt to do so, a deer, moose, elk, caribou, badger, beaver or muskrat, or a pheasant, grouse, partridge or swan, within two miles from a city public park containing over 200 acres of which 150 or more is woodland. Violation: misdemeanor; fine up to $100, or jail up to 90 days, or both (317.121 and .122).

The species of birds known as the snowy heron and the American egret are protected in this state and their killing and purchase and sale of plumes or feathers is forbidden. Violation: misdemeanor; fine of $10-50 and prosecution costs; in default of payment confinement in jail until fine and costs are paid or up to 30 days (317.131 and .132). No person shall hunt, take, pursue, capture, wound, kill, maim or disfigure another's homing pigeons. Violation: for a first offense, a fine of $25-100 and prosecution costs, or jail up to 90 days, or both (317.141 and .143).

★★A person who owns, possesses, keeps or uses a bull, bear, dog or other animal for the purpose of fighting or baiting, or as a target to be shot at as a test of skill in marksmanship and who is a party to or causes the fighting, baiting, or shooting of a bull, bear, dog or other animal is guilty of a felony punishable by jail up to four years, or a fine up to $5,000, or both (750.49).★★

GENERAL EXCEPTIONS TO PROTECTION

The Director may permit the taking, possession, purchase, sale, transportation, exportation, or shipment of species of fish, plants, or wildlife which appear on the state list of endangered or threatened species for scientific, zoological, or educational purposes, or for propagation in captivity to insure their survival (299.226).

The Director may issue permits for removing dogfish, carp, garfish, sheepshead, and other noxious fish from state waters with seines, nets, spears, or in any other manner (305.8). It is unlawful to take fish from state inland waters for fish culture or scientific investigation without a permit from the Director, except persons who operate private fish ponds may take fish from their own ponds. The Director may: ► issue permits to possess live game fish in public or private ponds, pool, or aquariums under Commission rules; ► cause to be taken from inland waters any fish species to obtain spawn for fish culture for scientific investigations or for protection of inland waters from ecological damage or imbalance; ► cause to be taken from inland waters fish species not required to maintain fishery resources of the inland waters (305.9). Without a permit from the Director, it is unlawful to take mussels from state inland waters for culture or scientific investigation (307.60).

HUNTING, FISHING, TRAPPING PROVISIONS

Licenses and Permits

A person shall not: ► if over age 17, fish in state waters or possess fish without a license, nor hunt, trap, or possess a wild animal or wild bird without a license as provided; ► buy or sell an otter or bobcat pelt, or attempt such, without a Department seal attached to the pelt; ► carry or transport without a license a firearm, slingshot, or bow and arrow while in an area frequented by wild animals or birds; ► transport or possess a shotgun with buckshot, slug load, ball load, or cut shell, or a rifle other than a .22 caliber rim fire, during the open season for taking deer or elk with a firearm, other than the muzzle-loading deer season, unless the person possesses a license to hunt deer or elk with a firearm; ▸ carry a firearm or bow and arrow, without a turkey license, during the spring wild turkey hunting season while in an area open for wild turkey. A person may carry, transport, or possess a firearm or bow and arrow without a hunting license while at, or going to and from, a rifle or target range, trap or skeet shooting ground, or archery range if it is enclosed and securely fastened in a case or locked in the trunk of a motor vehicle (316.201 through .205).

A resident, spouse, and children may: ▸ hunt small game without a license upon the enclosed farmlands where domiciled, as permitted by law, but they must obtain a waterfowl hunting stamp for hunting geese, ducks, or mergansers and a federal migratory bird hunting stamp; ▸ fish without a license in water wholly within the limits of their enclosed farmlands or other enclosed lands upon which domiciled, as permitted by law. The Director may issue a permit authorizing a mentally retarded person or a resident of a home for the aged to fish without a license if accompanied by a licensed adult (316.206 and .207).

The holder of a hunting, fishing, or fur harvester's license when hunting, fishing, trapping or in possession of firearms or related apparatus in an area frequented by wild animals, wild birds, and fish, shall carry the license and exhibit it on demand of a law enforcement officer, or the owner or occupant of the land on which the person is hunting, fishing, or trapping. A person who is hunting shall wear a Department back tag displaying the number of the license or passbook. During firearm deer season, without a firearm deer license with an unused kill tag issued in the person's name, the license holder shall not carry afield a: ▸ shotgun with buckshot, slug loads, or ball loads; ▸ bow and arrow; ▸ muzzle-loading rifle or black powder handgun; ▸ centerfire handgun or centerfire rifle. The unused kill tag shall be exhibited on the request of a law enforcement officer, or the owner or occupant of the land on which the person is hunting. A parent or legal guardian of a minor child shall not allow the child to hunt under the authority of a license issued on land on which the parent or guardian is not domiciled unless accompanied by the parent, guardian, or other authorized person age 17 or older (316.208 and .209). To obtain a hunting, trapping, fishing, or sportsman's license, an applicant shall: ▸ submit proof of residency; ▸ provide information required on the license application; ▸ pay the license fee; ▸ possess a passbook. A person shall not be issued a hunting, trapping, fishing, or sportsman's license if a court order prohibits the person from obtaining a license (316.302).

Subject to other requirements, the Director may issue a hunting license to a minor child on application of the parent or legal guardian, if the child is accompanied by the parent, guardian or other authorized person, age 17 or older, when hunting on lands on which the child's parents are not domiciled. A license to hunt deer, bear, or elk with a firearm shall not be issued to a person younger than age 14. A license to hunt shall not be issued to: ▸ a person who is younger than age 12; ▸ a person born after January 1, 1960, without proof of a previous hunting license or a hunter safety training course certificate issued by this state, another state, a province in Canada, or another country. If an applicant does not have proof of a previous license or hunter safety training certification, the applicant may submit a signed affidavit stating the applicant has completed a hunter safety course or has possessed a hunting license previously (316.303). The Director shall issue a license and a passbook if the applicant satisfies the license requirements and pays the license fee. Each license shall be affixed to the passbook and shall authorize the person named in the license or passbook to hunt, fish, or trap as prescribed. Instead of individual licenses, the Director may issue a sportsperson's license which confers the combined rights and privileges of resident licenses for: ▸ firearm deer; ▸ small game; ▸ fish; ▸ archery deer; ▸ trout and salmon stamp (316.304 and .304a).

Except as provided, a person shall not hunt small game without a license, except for animals or birds which require a special license. A nonresident may purchase a three-day small game license. A small game license is void between sunset and sunrise. A licensed nonresident hunter may take from the state as open hand baggage the number of birds and animals permitted at one time. Wild turkey may be taken during the open season with a wild turkey hunting license. Applications for a license to hunt wild turkeys shall be entered into a lottery designed and run by the Department. Fees collected are used for scientific research, biological survey work on wild turkeys, and wild turkey management (316.305 and .306).

A person age 16 or older shall not hunt wild geese, ducks or mergansers without a state waterfowl hunting stamp, in addition to a small game license and federal migratory bird hunting stamp. Without an annual or daily managed waterfowl area permit and other required license, permit, or passbook, a person shall not hunt waterfowl or deer where deer hunting is regulated by permit in a managed waterfowl area. Following a lottery among applicants for hunting privileges in managed waterfowl areas, successful applicants who wish to accept permit privileges are required to purchase a daily or annual managed waterfowl area permit. Waterfowl hunting stamp fees are used to acquire managed waterfowl areas. Annual or daily managed waterfowl area permit fees are used to operate, maintain, and develop managed waterfowl areas (316.307).

A person shall not hunt deer during the firearm deer season without a firearm deer license. With Commission authorization, a person may purchase a second firearm deer license in one season. The Commission may designate the kind of deer which may be taken, and may limit the issuance of a second firearm deer license in areas to manage deer. The Director shall issue a tag with each license, bearing the license number and including information on the date and month of killing the animal, its sex, and antler size. The tag is part of the license. A person who kills a deer shall attach the tag to the deer immediately. A deer shall not be offered for shipment, shipped, or received for shipment by a common carrier unless the tag is attached to the animal. The tag shall remain with the animal until the carcass is disposed of. The carcass of a deer or elk may not be received for transportation or possessed at the initial billing station more than 48 hours immediately following the closing of the season. A person shall not possess or transport a deer or part without an attached tag. A nonresident may possess and transport a deer outside the state if the tag is attached to the deer or part as required. A person shall not hunt deer with a bow and arrow during the bow and arrow deer season without a license. With Commission authorization, a person may purchase a second bow and arrow license in one season. The Commission may designate the kind of deer which may be taken, and may limit the issuance of a second bow and arrow deer license in areas to manage deer. With each bow and arrow license, the Director shall issue a tag which must be attached to the deer in the same manner prescribed for a firearm deer license. A person shall not affix a device to a bow which aids in the cocking or holding of a bow string in a drawn position, except for a hand held device to release the bow string. This provision does not apply to a permanently disabled person who holds a special permit (316.308 and .309).

A person shall not: ► hunt bear without a bear hunting license, nor trap or poison a bear; ► hunt elk without an elk hunting license, there being a nonrefundable application fee and a tag which must be attached to the elk immediately after the kill, remain attached until disposal of the carcass, and the elk may not be possessed or transported unless the tag is attached; ► hunt small game on licensed shooting preserves without a small game license, or a special shooting preserve license; ► trap or hunt a fur-bearing animal without a fur harvester's license, which is not required if hunting of that animal is not restricted by law. A licensee may hunt fur-bearing animals during the open season for fur-bearing animals with firearms and may trap them during trapping open season. A fur harvester licensee may carry a .22 caliber rimfire firearm while hunting or checking a trap line during the open season (316.310, .311, .313, and .314). The Department shall charge a nonrefundable application fee for each person who applies for a wild turkey hunting license, an antlerless deer permit, or a permit to hunt in a managed waterfowl area (316.328a).

A person age 17 or older shall not fish in state waters without a license. The annual fishing license entitles the licensee to take fish other than trout or salmon. An annual fishing license holder may procure a trout and salmon stamp to take trout and salmon as prescribed by law. The purchaser of a salmon snagging stamp is not required to purchase a trout and salmon stamp to snag salmon, but after the 1993 open season, the Department will no longer sell salmon snagging stamps (316.315).

A resident age 65 or older may obtain a: ► senior citizen hunting license which confers the combined rights and privileges granted by a resident small game license, a firearm deer license, a bow and arrow deer license, a bear license, and a fur harvester's license; ► senior citizen fishing license, and a license for the resident's spouse at no additional charge, which confers the combined rights and privileges granted by a resident annual fishing license and trout and salmon stamp. A resident declared legally blind is eligible to purchase a senior citizen fishing license. A resident who has been determined by the Veterans Administration to be permanently and totally disabled, for a disability other than blindness, is eligible to purchase a senior citizen hunting or fishing license, or both (316.317, .318 and .320).

Restrictions on Taking: Hunting and Trapping

Transported game shall be tagged as required and its sex and species identifiable, unless cleaned at a hunting preserve and tagged as required. These provisions do not apply to skins, pelts, or hides of game lawfully taken and legally possessed. Except as provided, a person shall not: ► take an animal from in or upon a vehicle; ► transport or possess a firearm in or upon a vehicle, unless it is unloaded and enclosed in a case, or carried in the trunk; ► hunt or discharge a firearm within 150 yards of an occupied building, dwelling, house, cabin, or barn or other building used in connection with a farm operation without written permission of the owner, renter, or occupant of the property (300.260 and .262).

Except as provided, a person shall not: ► use artificial light in taking game or in an area frequented by animals, or cast rays of a spotlight, headlight, or other artificial light in a field, woodland, or forest while having a bow or firearm or other weapon, except a licensed hunter may use artificial light one hour before and one hour after shooting hours while carrying an unloaded firearm or bow and traveling afoot to and from a hunting location (violation: misdemeanor; jail 5-90 days, or a $100-500 fine, or both, prosecution costs, and the person shall not secure a license to hunt during the remainder of the year in which convicted and the next calendar year); ► throw or cast artificial light rays, or cause same, to locate animals, from December 1 to October 31, between 11:00 p.m. and 6:00 a.m., nor use a spotlight, headlight, or other artificial light from November 1 to November 30, to locate animals, except as provided. These provisions do not apply to: ► a peace officer while in performance of duty; ► a person operating an emergency vehicle in an emergency; ► a public or private utility employee while working in the scope of employment; ► a person operating a vehicle with headlights in a lawful manner on a street, highway, or roadway; ► a person using an artificial light to identify a house or mailbox number; ► the use of artificial lights to conduct a census by the Department; ► a person using an artificial light on the person's own property from November 1 to November 30. Violation: misdemeanor; jail up to 90 days, or a $50-500 fine, or both, and prosecution costs. The operator of a vehicle from which the rays of an artificial light have been cast in a clear attempt to locate game shall stop the vehicle immediately on request of a uniformed peace officer, or when signaled by a peace officer with a flashing signal light or siren from a marked patrol vehicle. Violation: misdemeanor; jail 5-90 days, and a $100-500 fine, and prosecution costs (300.263 and .267).

During the period provided for taking deer by bow and arrow, presence of a dog in the woods, hunting camp, or clubhouse is not prima facie evidence of unlawful use of the dog (316.801). A person shall not: ► carry a pistol, revolver, or other firearm while bow hunting during open season for hunting deer with bow and arrow; ► pursue, hunt, kill, or capture a deer or bear which is in the water, or use a dog to hunt deer; ► transport or possess in an area frequented by deer a rifle or shotgun with buckshot, slug load, ball load, or cut shell during the five days preceding opening of the earliest season for taking deer with firearms, except a person may transport an unloaded rifle or shotgun to or from a hunting camp if locked in the trunk of a motor vehicle or otherwise inaccessible; ► transport or possess a bow and arrow, a shotgun with buckshot, slug load, ball load, or cut shell, or a rifle larger than a .22 caliber rim fire, in an area frequented by deer, between sunset and sunrise during the open season on small game and the season closed to taking deer with firearms, except a bow and arrow may be transported if locked in the trunk of a motor vehicle, or if no trunk, inside the vehicle when unstrung or enclosed securely in a case; ► carry or transport a firearm, slingshot, or bow and arrow between sunset and sunrise in an area frequented by wild animals or birds during the closed season on small game (316.802, and .804 through .807).

A dealer who desires to ship or transport out of state fur-bearing animals, their raw skins, or parts, or the plumage, skins or hides, or parts of protected game birds and animals legally taken or killed in the state during the open season shall procure a Department permit. Shippers of fur-bearing animals, their raw skins, or parts, or of the plumage, skins or hides, or parts of protected game birds and animals must label all packages offered for shipment. No one shall transport or receive for transportation, or sell or offer to sell fur-bearing animals legally taken, or their parts, or the plumage, skins or hides, or parts of game birds and animals, except as specifically provided in these provisions under penalty of confiscation and disposal of as provided by law. Within 10 days after the close of open seasons for taking fur-bearing animals, game birds and game animals, holders of fur dealers permits must report to the Director the number and kinds of furs, hides or pelts of each fur-bearing animal, and plumage, skins or hides, or parts of protected game birds and animals in possession on the last day of the open season. On or before the tenth day of every month fur dealing licensees must report to the Director the number and kinds of raw furs, hides or pelts of fur-bearing animals, or plumage, skins or hides, or parts of protected game birds and animals purchased or sold during the preceding month, and the names and addresses of persons from whom purchased and to whom sold (317.3 through .5).

★Except to retrieve a hunting dog, a person shall not enter or remain on another's lands, other than farm lands or connected farm wood lots, to hunt; fish in a private lake, pond, or stream; or operate a motorized vehicle without written consent of the owner, lessee or agent if the lands are fenced or enclosed and maintained in a manner to exclude intruders, and posted in a conspicuous manner against entry. Except to retrieve a hunting dog, a person shall not enter farm lands or connected farm wood lots without written consent of the owner, lessee or agent. On fenced or posted lands or farm lands, a fisherman wading or floating a navigable, public stream of a length greater than 15 miles, without consent, may enter on the upland within clearly defined banks of the stream or walk a route as closely proximate to the clearly defined bank as possible to avoid a natural or artificial hazard or obstruction or other exercise of ownership by the riparian owner (317.172).★ A person shall not discharge a firearm within the right of way of a public highway adjoining or abutting platted property; fenced, enclosed, or posted lands; or farm lands or connected wood lots without the written consent of the owner, lessee or agent of the abutting lands (317.173). [For specific public shooting and hunting grounds, see 317.271 through 317.297.]

Restrictions on Taking: Fishing

In state waters, a person shall not take, catch, or kill a fish, or attempt such, by use of: ▸ a spear or grab hook, snag hook, gaff gook; ▸ a jack or artificial light; ▸ a set or night line, or a net; ▸ a firearm; ▸ an explosive substance or combination of substances to kill or stupefy fish; ▸ other means or device other than a hand held or controlled single line, or a single rod and line, with hook(s) attached and baited with a natural or artificial bait when used for still fishing, ice fishing, casting, or trolling for fish. A hook is considered to be a single, double, or treble pointed hook; and a hook attached to a manufactured artificial bait is counted as one hook. The Director may designate waters where a treble hook and an artificial bait or lure having more than one single pointed hook shall not be used during designated periods. In smelt waters, any number of hooks, attached to a single line, may be used for taking smelt. A person shall not set or use a tip-up, paddle, or other similar device to take fish through the ice unless the name and address, in English, of the owner is marked on the device and securely fastened to it by a plate or tag (302.1).

A spear or bow and arrow may be used as specified to take carp, suckers, redhorse, mullet, dogfish, and garpike in state rivers and streams. The Director may designate a county, stream or portion of a stream, in which a jack or artificial light may be used for taking fish with a spear or bow and arrow only. A person shall not use or possess a spear or bow and arrow in, upon, or along a trout stream, except one designated by the Director for the taking of carp, suckers, redhorse, mullet, dogfish, and garpike. A person may spear carp, suckers, mullet, redhorse, sheepshead, lake trout, smelt, northern pike, muskellunge, whitefish, ciscoes, pilot fish or Menominee whitefish, sturgeon, catfish, bullheads, dogfish, and garpike through the ice during the months of January and February in inland waters not otherwise closed to spearing (302.1). [Additional spear, bow and arrow, and net fishing provisions and locales, seasons, and restrictions for various species are detailed.]

★Reptiles, amphibians, mollusks, and crustaceans may be taken only in a manner and during those times prescribed by the Director. Persons taking, trapping, catching, or fishing for turtles or frogs for their personal use shall have a fishing license. A person shall not take, trap, catch, or fish for reptiles or amphibians for commercial purposes without a commercial reptile and amphibian license (302.1c).★

It is unlawful to: ▸ fish with seines or nets within 100 feet of a dam or to frighten or hinder fish from free passage of a fish chute or ladder, or to place an obstruction or device in or across any race, stream or river to obstruct the free passage, except as provided by law; ▸ fish within 100 feet up or down a stream from lamprey control weirs installed by the Department or USFW as designated by the Director; ▸ destroy, or interfere with, an artificial dam or barrier placed in trout streams under the direction of the Director. Provisions relating to fishing devices do not prohibit use of a gaff, except on or along trout streams, or landing net to assist in landing fish by a lawful device; nor do they apply to persons engaged in the business of propagating fish; nor to fish caught by a device for which a permit or license is obtained. A person shall not use or possess a landing net more than 5 1/2 feet in circumference, or with a handle exceeding 14 inches in length, on a trout stream April through June (302.2, .2a, .3 and .4).

It is unlawful to possess a net, set lines, jack or other artificial light, dynamite, giant powder or other explosive substance or combination of such, hook and line or other device, for taking fish illegally. Such property, contrivance, or device, found in a person's possession, or found in a boat, boathouse, or other place on state waters, or along the shores, shall be confiscated and disposed of as provided by law. On or along a state trout stream, it is unlawful for a person to possess a gaff, or to use, except from June 1 to Labor Day, a single hook or a kind that is more than 3/8 inches between the point of the hook and the shank. These provisions do not prohibit use or possession of minnow seines, minnow traps or dig nets as provided by law, nor use and possession of seines, nets, spears or artificial lights for which a permit or license has been issued. It is not unlawful to possess an artificial light to use for taking white bass. In prosecutions for violations, and in proceedings for confiscation of such property, possession of such property, contrivance or device, or the presence of such property in a boat, boathouse, or other place on state waters, or along shores, is prima facie evidence that it is owned, possessed or used to violate these provisions. The possession of such property, contrivance, or device on state waters closed to all fishing, or during the closed season, is prima facie evidence that it is owned, possessed or used to violate these provisions. These provisions do not apply to Department fisheries management or control of aquatic vegetation by individuals under permit issued by the Director (302.5).

It is unlawful to: ▸ catch fish, or attempt such, in a lake, stream or pond, or such portion thereof used by the state or federal government for propagation of fish, except where designated by the Director as open to fishing; ▸ catch a game or nongame fish in a lake, stream, pond or in the Great Lakes to remove its eggs (302.5a and .5b); ▸ take, catch or kill fish, or attempt such, in a trout stream or in an inland lake designated as a trout lake, except from the last Saturday in April through the second Sunday in September, or except as otherwise provided. The Director may designate certain trout streams, or portions of them, in which nongame fish and game fish other than trout occur, as open to hook and line fishing throughout the year for taking fish on which the season is not closed. Inland lakes, other than lakes designated as trout lakes, are open to fishing throughout the year for taking fish on which the season is not closed. Non-trout streams, the Great Lakes, and connecting waters are open to fishing throughout the year for taking fish for which the season is not closed (303.1).

It is unlawful to take, catch, kill fish of the species listed in these provisions, or attempt such, except during prescribed open seasons [in 303.1a, regulating open seasons by species of fish and location] (303.1a). The Director may establish a closed season on a spawning bed when it appears that spawning or guarding does not coincide with the time of the closed season as provided. It is unlawful to operate a boat, floating device or other contrivance propelled by or using as motive power, steam, gas, naphtha, oil, gasoline or electricity upon a posted spawning bed. The Director may open to fishing waters in which an excessive mortality of fish occurs or is threatened (303.2). Except as provided, a person shall not in one day catch, kill, or possess at one time, more than the number of fish indicated herein [numerous species, allowable pounds or numbers, and locales are specified] (303.4).

A fishing license holder may carry as open hand baggage up to one day's legal catch of fish, and may obtain one permit from the Director authorizing shipment of one day's legal catch of any species of game fish or combination thereof. The catch of two or more licensed fishermen may be combined into a single package, with each permit attached. For fish taken on a sport fishing license or fish taken without a commercial fishing license, it is unlawful to purchase, buy or sell them, or attempt such, or to transport them to a point outside of the state, or to possess them during periods in which their taking or catching is prohibited. Lawfully taken fish may be possessed for 60 days after close of the open seasons. A nonresident fishing licensee may take from this state a day's legal catch of fish in accordance with license provisions. Nothing shall interfere with the possession, sale or transportation of fish taken legally under state commercial fishing laws and regulations (303.5 and .6).

The Director is authorized to designate the lakes and streams from which cisco, whitefish, suckers, and carp may be taken by spear and artificial light. Whitefish or cisco so taken shall not be bought or sold (305.7). It is unlawful to take, attempt to take, or to possess a grayling taken from state waters (303.7). Catching of coho (silver) salmon and chinook salmon is lawful only during open seasons, in specific locations, and by specified manner or method. On or after October 16, 1992, snagging of fish is illegal in the state. Requirements for permits, licensing, and fees, and limits on the number which may be caught, killed, or in possession pursuant to these provisions shall be the same as provided in the Hunting and Fishing License Act. In addition, a person taking salmon pursuant to these provisions shall obtain an annual salmon snagging stamp. Stamp sale proceeds are credited to the Game and Fish Protection Fund (303.11).

★In the state's navigable or meandered waters where fish have been or may be propagated, planted or spread by this state or the US, people have the right to catch fish with hook and line during seasons and in waters not prohibited by state laws. No legal action shall be maintained against persons entering on such waters to fish by the owner, lessee, or persons having right of possession of adjoining lands, except for actual damage done. In such an action, the defendant under a proper notice may dispute at trial the plaintiff's right to either title or possession of the land claimed to be trespassed upon (307.41 and .42). ★ No person shall take fish from inland lakes where fish are planted by the state, from which waters the public is excluded from taking fish. These provisions do not apply to inland lakes covering less than 250 acres in which fish may be planted without written consent of persons who together own in fee simple the submerged acreage. Violation: misdemeanor; upon conviction a $10-100 fine, or jail up to 30 days, or both (307.71 and 307.72).

It is unlawful to take or kill species of frogs, except during specified times. It is unlawful to spear frogs with the aid of artificial light. This does not prevent the purchase, sale, or possession of frogs or their parts legally taken or shipped in from outside the state. The Director may issue permits to take frogs for scientific or experimental purposes (307.101 through .103). Violation: misdemeanor; upon conviction, a fine up to $50 and prosecution costs; or jail up to 90 days; or both (307.106). [For provisions regulating fishing in specific waters of the state, see 307.151 through 307.172.]

Commercial and Private Enterprise Provisions

★Except as provided, a person shall not purchase, sell, or exchange anything of value for raw or unprocessed salmon eggs, unless the person is licensed pursuant to commercial fishing law [308.26a], and their sale, purchase or exchange is made with another person so licensed. The operator of a fish cleaning station shall not: ► accept raw or unprocessed salmon eggs except from whole salmon or eggs salvaged from salmon cleaned in the station; ► operate a fish cleaning station that sells raw or unprocessed salmon eggs without a permit; ► buy, barter, or exchange anything of value for raw or unprocessed salmon eggs; ► buy or sell salmon carcasses taken by a person licensed under the Hunting and Fishing License Act. A person issued a permit to operate a fish cleaning station shall comply with the following: ► raw or unprocessed salmon eggs only may be collected and stored at the location of the fish cleaning station specified in the permit; ► the station shall be licensed in accordance with law only when the salmon eggs, salmon, or both, are sold or given to another for human consumption; ► disposal of offal and unwanted salmon carcasses is in a manner approved by the local health department; ► a permit holder whose fish cleaning station is located on state-owned land must provide free access to the station facilities to fishermen to clean their own salmon catch. If the Department finds that a person is in violation of a permit, it may issue an order requiring compliance. In addition to penalties provided by law, the Director or another person may seek injunctive relief for a violation of a permit (303.6a).★

A person shall not take, possess or import minnows, wigglers, or crayfish for commercial purposes without a license. Except a fishing license, a license is not required to take minnows, wigglers, or crayfish for individual use for bait. A person shall not set or use minnow traps for taking minnows, wigglers, or crayfish, unless the user's name and address is on the trap, nor transport out of this state minnows, wigglers, or crayfish, dead or alive, taken either in or outside the state. The Director may issue a permit to a resident licensed as a minnow dealer enabling that person to transport minnows, wigglers, or crayfish outside this state. A person shall not use or attempt to use live goldfish or carp for bait in fishing, or offer for sale or use lamprey for bait, or take, possess, or transport minnows, wigglers, or crayfish for commercial purposes unless the taker is a resident and holds a permit or license as required. The Director may designate the lakes and streams from which minnows, wigglers, and crayfish may be taken for commercial purposes and may make rules and regulations for their taking, possession, and transport. A person shall not take or attempt to take minnows, wigglers, or crayfish for commercial purposes from waters not designated by the Director or violate rules. Except as provided, minnow seines not to exceed 125 feet in length and 16 feet in width may be used in the Great Lakes and their connecting waterways, and in state inland lakes, streams, and rivers. Minnows may be taken only from trout streams during open season with glass or wire traps. Minnow seines shall not be used in trout streams at any time. Hand nets not exceeding 8 feet square without sides or walls, minnow traps not exceeding 2 feet in length, minnow seines not exceeding 12 feet in length and 4 feet in width, and hook and line may be used for taking minnows for personal use in waters designated by the Director. However, a person shall not take minnows in trout streams with hand or dip nets (304..2 through .4).

The Director may issue a variety of commercial minnow licenses for residents and nonresidents. Crayfish shall not be imported for commercial purposes without a special permit from the Director. Minnows and wigglers not native to the state shall not be imported. On demand of a conservation officer or other peace officer, a person found taking, collecting, possessing, or transporting live or fresh minnows, wigglers, or crayfish for commercial purposes must display a license or identification card. Equipment utilized in the handling of minnows, wigglers, and crayfish and the tanks or ponds where they are held shall be open to inspection (305.6).

It is unlawful to take, catch, or kill mussels in state inland waters without being registered with and licensed by the Director. A licensee may operate no more than one boat in taking, catching or killing mussels (307.51 and .55). [Additional restrictions are detailed for commercial mussel taking and reporting, in 307.55 through 307.58.]

No one shall engage in the business of buying, selling, dealing or the tanning and dressing of raw furs, hide or pelts of beaver, otter, fisher, marten, muskrat, mink, skunk, raccoon, opossum, wolf, lynx, bobcat, fox, weasel, coyote, badger, deer or bear, or the plumage, skins, or hides of protected game birds and animals without a license. The holder of a fur dealers license may buy furs, hides, pelts and the plumage, skins or hides, or parts of protected game birds and animals legally taken. ★No fur dealer licensee is eligible to hold a license to trap beaver.★ The Commission may designate the plumage and skin of those game birds and game animals which may not be bought or sold. The plumage, skins, or parts of migratory game and nongame birds may be bought and sold only in accordance with federal law or rule. Fur dealers licenses may be revoked by the Director for a violation relating to the buying, selling or dealing in furs, hides or pelts of fur-bearing animals and the plumage, skins or hides of protected game birds and game animals, and the person shall not secure another license except at the Director's discretion (317.1 and .2).

The Director issues licenses to authorize possession for propagation, dealing in, and selling game. A license shall not be granted to an applicant who is not the owner or lessee of the premises to be used for the license purposes. A person shall not maintain in captivity, propagate or sell game without a license, except as provided. A public zoological park is not required to secure a license. A license is not required of a person who purchases a carcass, product, or part of game sold by a licensed person. A licensee may possess, propagate, use, buy, sell, trap, kill, consume, ship, or transport the stock designated in the license, and their offspring, products, carcasses, pelts, or other parts as provided. Enclosures used for propagation shall be of a character and in a location satisfactory to keep in complete and continuous captivity the stock covered by the license, and shall be so constructed to prevent the entrance of wild stock of the same species. Deer that cannot be flushed from land to be enclosed and are covered by a license shall be purchased from the state. When wild, state-owned game animals are present on land covered by a license, the applicant may purchase the state-owned game and secure title thereto. The price to be paid for the game is fixed by the Director, subject to Commission approval, but shall not exceed the market value of the game for breeding purposes. The price of deer is $250 each. Game covered by a license may be taken or killed in any manner and at any time, except that game birds covered by a license may not be shot except by a license holder in special situations when the Commission authorizes their shooting. Wild turkey or wild turkey hybrids covered by a license shall have one wing pinioned within 14 days of hatching. Game, including parts or products, may be removed from licensed premises only when identified as required. Live game may be removed only by licensed game breeders, shooting preserve operators, or persons holding permits authorizing the possession of game. Wild turkeys or wild turkey hybrids shall not be removed unless pinioned. Fertile eggs from wild turkeys or wild turkey hybrids shall not be removed from licensed premises (317.71, .72 and .74 through .78). Game released or escaped from the premises of a licensee becomes state property. No game birds shall be released without written permission of the Director (317.81).

★★It is unlawful for a person or association to acquire or enclose in one tract land exceeding 15,000 acres for the preservation or propagation of game or fish, or for use for hunting, fishing or other sporting purpose. It is unlawful for a person or association to acquire for such purposes land located within two miles of other land acquired for such purposes. Violation: $50 for each day the violation continues (317.261 through .263).★★

The Director may issue licenses authorizing private shooting preserves which may allow hunting on Sundays notwithstanding the provisions of local ordinances or regulations. Each shooting preserve shall contain 80 to 640 acres of leased or owned land, except that preserves whose operations are confined to ducks may contain a minimum of 50 acres. The exterior boundaries of each preserve shall be defined clearly with signs. Shooting preserves involving animals not native or commonly found in the wild in this state shall be adequately fenced and maintained to keep the animals in complete and continuous captivity. Birds hunted under a shooting preserve license are limited to artificially propagated wild turkeys and wild turkey hybrids and other artificially propagated species as prescribed. A licensee may propagate and sell the birds, carcasses or products in addition to releasing the birds for hunting by adhering to requirements in 317.71 to 317.84 and Commission rules. Wild turkey or wild turkey hybrids authorized under a license shall have one wing pinioned and be fenced and released in compliance with Department regulations. Private shooting preserve licenses entitle the holder, lessees and licensed hunters to take the percentage of each species released on the premises each year as the Director determines. Each bird shot under authority of a shooting preserve license shall have affixed to the carcass or wrapper a stamp-mark, band, tag, or seal as designated. No wild bird or animal other than permitted to be hunted under authority of the license shall be hunted or killed on a shooting preserve except in accordance with state laws governing the hunting of such species. Each operator of a shooting preserve shall maintain a record of persons who hunted on the preserve, dates they hunted, and number of each species taken. The operator shall maintain an accurate record of the total number, by species of birds propagated, reared or purchased, and the date and number of each species released. The Director, subject to Commission approval, may establish an open season for shooting preserves that shall not be less than 120 days, and may promulgate rules governing administration of these provisions. Violation: misdemeanor; a $100 fine and prosecution costs; or jail up to 90 days; or both. In addition, a license may be suspended or revoked when a licensee fails to maintain or submit accurate reports or upon conviction of a violation. Birds and animals held under a license that is suspended or revoked shall be disposed of only in a manner approved by the Director (317.301 through .306, .308, .310 and .312).

Import, Export, Release Provisions

No person shall import or bring live game fish or viable eggs of a game fish from outside the state except under Director permit. No person shall plant spawn, fry or fish in state waters without a permit from the Director (305.9). (See PROTECTED SPECIES OF WILDLIFE.)

Interstate Reciprocal Agreements

In order to provide uniform fishing regulations in a river or a Great Lake forming a common boundary with an adjoining state and the inland lake(s) bisected by such boundary, the Commission may enter into a reciprocal agreement with the adjoining state to establish minimum sizes of fish, daily limits, open seasons, and methods for taking. An agreement shall set forth clearly waters to be included and the period during which it shall be in effect. An order promulgated hereunder supersedes other conflicting laws and regulations governing fishing in such waters. Regulations contained in the orders shall be included in the annual digest of fishing laws, rules and regulations published and distributed by the Department. Violation: misdemeanor; a $100 fine and prosecution costs; or jail up to 90 days; or both (300.101 through .103).

ANIMAL DAMAGE CONTROL

Upon good cause shown and to alleviate damage to property or to protect human health, endangered or threatened species on the state list may be removed, captured, or destroyed, pursuant to a permit issued by the Director. Carnivorous animals on the state list may be removed, captured, or destroyed by a person in emergency situations involving an immediate threat to human life, but their removal, capture, or destruction shall be reported to the Director within 24 hours of the act (299.226).

★It is unlawful to have a ferret, ferrets or fitchew in possession, except that the Department may keep or raise ferrets or fitchew for ridding sections of fruit growing territory from rabbits and other rodents. The Department shall grant permits to use ferrets or fitchew to: ► persons suffering damage to nursery stock or fruit trees on their premises from rabbits; ► persons suffering damage from rats on farms; ► merchants suffering damage to stock or merchandize; ► storage companies suffering damage to goods in storage.★ Violation: fine of $5-25 and prosecution costs; or jail 10-20 days; or both (317.151 and .152). (See also Agency Advisory Boards under STATE FISH AND WILDLIFE AGENCIES.)

ENFORCEMENT OF WILDLIFE LAWS

Enforcement Powers

It is the duty of the Director and of any officer appointed by the Director to: ► enforce state laws for protection, propagation or preservation of wild birds, wild animals, and fish; ► enforce the provisions of other state laws pertaining to the powers and duties of the Director and Commission; ► cause to be prosecuted actions and proceedings for punishing a person for violation of statutes or laws (300.11)

★★The Director, or any officer appointed by the Director, may make complaint and cause proceedings to be commenced against a person for a violation of the statutes in 300.11, without the sanction of a prosecuting attorney, and may appear for the people in a court of competent jurisdiction in cases for violation of statutes, and prosecute in the same manner and with the same authority as the prosecuting attorney.★★ When officers have probable cause to believe statutes have been or are being violated by a person, they have power to search, without warrant, any boat, conveyance, vehicle, automobile, fish box, fish basket, game bag, game coat, or other receptacle or place, except dwellings or dwelling houses, or within the curtilage of a dwelling house, in which nets, hunting or fishing apparatus or appliances, wild birds, wild animals or fish may be possessed, kept or carried by the person, and officers may enter on private or public property for such purpose or to patrol, investigate, or examine when there is probable cause that statutes have been or are being violated thereon. Officers shall seize and take possession of nets, hunting or fishing apparatus or other property, wild birds, wild animals, or fish, or parts thereof, which have been caught, taken, killed, shipped, or had in possession or under control contrary to law, and such seizure may be made without warrant. No common carrier shall be held responsible in damages or otherwise to an owner, shipper, or consignee by reason of such seizure. When complaint is made on oath to a magistrate authorized to issue warrants in criminal cases, that wild birds, wild animals, or fish, or parts thereof, or nets, hunting or fishing apparatus or other property, have been or are being killed, taken, caught, possessed, controlled or shipped, contrary to law, and that the complainant believes same to be stored, kept or concealed in a particular house or place, the magistrate, if satisfied that there is probable cause for such belief, shall issue a warrant to search for the property. The warrant shall be directed to the Director or an officer appointed by the Director, or to another peace officer. Wild birds, wild animals, or fish, or nets, or boats, or fishing or hunting appliances, or automobiles, or other property seized by the officers shall be turned over to the Director to be held subject to order of the court (300.12). [For provisions relating to jurisdiction, confiscation, complaints and review, see 300.13 through 300.15.]

The Director and conservation officers: ► are peace officers vested with the powers, privileges, prerogatives, and immunities conferred upon peace officers by general state law; ► have the same power to serve criminal process as sheriffs; ► have the same right as sheriffs to require aid in executing process; ► are entitled to the same fees in performing those duties. The Director may commission state park officers to enforce within state park boundaries Department rules. In performing enforcement activities, commissioned state park officers are vested with the powers, privileges, prerogatives, and immunities conferred upon peace officers under state laws. If a conservation officer or a state park officer arrests a person without warrant for a misdemeanor, committed in the officer's presence, which is punishable by jail up to 90 days, or a fine, or both, instead of immediately bringing the person before the court having jurisdiction, the officer may issue to and serve upon the person an appearance ticket. An appearance pursuant to an appearance ticket may be made in person, by representation, or by mail. The Director, in conjunction with the Michigan State Employees Association, shall study the feasibility of allowing full-time Department employees to perform the duties of conservation officers under certain circumstances. The Director may appoint persons as volunteer conservation officers to assist a conservation officer (300.16 and .16a).

Conservation officers appointed by the Director and trained and certified pursuant to the Michigan Law Enforcement Officers Training Council Act of 1965 are peace officers, and except as provided by law, are vested with the powers, privileges, prerogatives, and immunities conferred upon peace officers by the general laws of this state. Except as provided, conservation officers have the same power to serve criminal process and to require aid in executing criminal process as sheriffs, and are entitled to the same fees as sheriffs in performing those duties (300.21 and .22).

A dog which pursues, kills, or follows upon the track of a deer is a public nuisance and may be killed by a law enforcement or conservation officer without criminal or civil liability (316.803).

Criminal Penalties

A person who obstructs, resists or opposes the Director or an officer appointed by the Director or other peace officer in the performance of duty is guilty of a misdemeanor (300.17).

Violation of Wildlife Conservation Act, a Commission order pursuant to the act, an interim order of the Director, or a condition of a permit issued under the act, except as specified, is a misdemeanor, punishable by jail up to 90 days, a fine of $50-500, or both, and the person shall pay prosecution costs, and the permit shall be revoked, except for violations as follows: ► possession or taking of game, except deer, bear, wild turkey, moose, or elk - misdemeanor, jail up to 90 days, or $100-1,000 fine, or both, and prosecution costs; ► possession or taking of deer, bear, or wild turkey - misdemeanor, jail 5-90 days, $200-1,000 fine, prosecution costs and denial of license to hunt during remainder of the year and the next three years; ► possession or taking of elk - misdemeanor, jail 30-180 days, $500-2,000 fine, or both, prosecution costs and denial of license to hunt during remainder of the year and the next three years; ► possession or taking of moose - misdemeanor, jail 90 days-1 year, $1,000-5,000 fine, prosecution costs and denial of license to hunt during remainder of the year and the next three years; ► taking or possessing of a protected animal, other than an animal listed pursuant to the Endangered Species Act - misdemeanor, jail up to 90 days, $100-1,000 fine, or both, prosecution costs and denial of license to hunt during remainder of the year and the next three years; ► buying or selling game or a protected animal in violation of the Wildlife Conservation Act - misdemeanor, jail up to 90 days, fine up to $1,000, or both, for first offense, and a felony for each subsequent offense and denial of license to hunt during remainder of year and the next three years. When a person so convicted has been convicted two times within the preceding five years, it is a misdemeanor, punishable by jail for 10-180 days, $500-2,000 fine and costs of prosecution (300.267).

A violation of the Sportsmen Fishing Law or rules or orders issued to implement such law, if a penalty is not provided for that violation, is a misdemeanor, punishable by jail up to 90 days, or a fine up to $500, or both. The following specific penalties are provided in these provisions: ► using dynamite, nitroglycerin, lime, electricity, other explosive substance or poison to take or kill fish, or using nets not authorized by law to take game fish, or buying or selling game fish or parts - misdemeanor, jail up to 90 days, $250-1,000 fine, or both; ► taking or possessing sturgeon in violation of these provisions - misdemeanor, jail 30 to 180 days, or $500-2,000 fine, or both, and prosecution costs. If a person convicted of a violation has been convicted three or more times of the violation within the five years immediately preceding, it is a misdemeanor, punishable by jail up to 90 days, or a fine up to $1,000, or both, and prosecution costs, except this does not apply to the following violations: ► failure to possess or display a fishing license and salmon stamp; ► taking or possessing an overlimit of bluegill, sunfish, crappie, perch, or nongame fish; ► taking or possessing not more than five undersized fish; ► fishing with too many lines; ► failing to attach name and address to tip-ups or minnow traps; ► fishing with lines not under immediate control. In addition, when a person is convicted of using illegal methods to take fish, or unlawfully possessing sturgeon, or three or more violations of these provisions, the person's license shall be revoked for the remainder of the year and for the next three years (305.12).

The following penalties are provided in the Sportsmen Fishing Law: ► snagging fish - a misdemeanor, jail up to 90 days, or a $250-500 fine, or both, and prosecution costs; ► second violation of snagging salmon - misdemeanor, jail up to 90 days, or a $500-1,000 fine, or both, prosecution costs, suspension of fishing license for not less than two years, with an order that a fishing license not be issued during that time; ► a third or subsequent violation of snagging fish - a misdemeanor, jail up to 90 days, or a $1,000-2,000 fine, or both, prosecution costs and suspension of fishing license for not less than three years, with an order that a fishing license not be issued during that time; ► selling multipointed hook with a weight permanently attached - a misdemeanor, jail up to 90 days, or a $100-300 fine, or both, and prosecution costs; ► conviction of a second such violation - a misdemeanor, jail up to 90 days, or a $300-500 fine and prosecution costs; ► conviction of a third or subsequent such violation - a misdemeanor, jail up to 90 days, or a $500-1,000 fine, or both and prosecution costs (305.12a).

Violation relating to contamination of waters (307.21 through 307.32) is a misdemeanor, punishable by a fine up to $100, or jail up to 90 days, or both, and violators are liable civilly for damages done (307.31).

It is a misdemeanor to: ► make a false statement as to material facts to obtain a license, or use or attempt to use a license obtained by making a false statement; ► affix to a passbook or a license a date or time other than the date or time issued; ► charge more than the passbook or license fees provided by law; ► hunt, trap, fish, or possess, without a license, a wild animal, wild bird, or fish; ► sell, loan, or permit another person to use the holder's license or use or attempt to use another person's license; ► make falsely, alter, forge, or counterfeit a passbook or hunting, fishing, or trapping license or possess an altered, forged, or counterfeit passbook or hunting, fishing, or trapping license; ► use a tag furnished with a firearm deer, bow and arrow deer, or bear hunting license more than one time, or attach or allow a tag to be attached to a deer or bear other than one lawfully killed by the person. Violation: jail up to 90 days, or a fine of $25-250 and prosecution costs, or both. In addition, the person shall surrender a license and license tag wrongfully obtained. A person licensed to carry a firearm under these provisions, is prohibited from doing so while under the influence of a controlled substance or alcohol or a combination. Violation is a misdemeanor, punishable by a fine of $500 and/or 90 days in jail. A license applicant previously convicted of a violation of state game and fish laws may be required to file an application with the Director together with other information as the Director considers expedient. The license may be issued by the Director (316.701). Violation of statutes or rules under this act for which a penalty is not provided, is a misdemeanor, punishable by jail up to 90 days, or a fine of $25-250 and prosecution costs, or both (316.703).

Violation of the provisions relating to buying, selling or dealing in furs, hides or pelts of fur-bearing animals and the plumage, skin or hides of protected game birds and game animals is a misdemeanor, and the offender shall forfeit to the state all furs, hides and pelts of fur-bearing animals and the plumage, skins, or hides, or parts of protected game birds or game animals illegally bought or held, and reimburse the state for illegal furs or illegal plumage, skins, hides, or parts, of protected game birds and game animals sold. In cases in which a fine with costs is imposed, the court shall sentence the offender to jail until such fine and costs are paid, for a period up to the maximum jail penalty provided for the offense (317.7).

Violation of provisions or rules relating to game breeders and dealers is a misdemeanor, punishable by jail up to 90 days, or a fine up to $100, or both. A second violation is a misdemeanor, punishable by jail up to 90 days, or a fine up to $500, or both (317.84).

Civil Penalties

In addition to penalties provided for violating the Wildlife Conservation Act or an order issued under the act, and the penalty provided in the Endangered Species Act, a person convicted of the illegal killing, possessing, purchasing, or selling, in whole or in part, of game or protected animals shall reimburse the state for value as follows: ▸ bear, elk, hawk, moose, or an animal on a list specified in 299.226, $1,500 per animal; ▸ deer, owl, and wild turkey, $1,000 per animal; ▸ other game, $100-500 per animal; ▸ other protected animals, $100 per animal. Moneys received as forfeiture damages are deposited in the Game and Fish Protection Fund (300.268).

In addition to penalties provided in the Sportsmen Fishing Law, a person convicted of taking game fish during a closed season, taking or possessing game fish in excess of lawful limits, or buying or selling, or taking fish or parts by use of an unlawful device shall forfeit to the state: ▸ for each game fish other than sturgeon weighing 1 pound or more, $10 for each pound or fraction of a pound of fish illegally taken or possessed; ▸ for each game fish other than sturgeon weighing less than 1 pound, $10 for each fish illegally taken or possessed; ▸ for sturgeon, $1,500 for each fish illegally taken or possessed; ▸ for each nongame fish, $5 for each pound or fraction of a pound of fish illegally taken or possessed. Forfeitures collected are credited to the Game and Fish Protection Fund (305.13).

Illegal Taking of Wildlife

It is unlawful to hunt, pursue, worry or kill wild waterfowl or other birds or animals by any means from an aircraft. Violation: misdemeanor (259.179).

License Revocations and Suspensions

If a person is convicted of violating the Hunting and Fishing License Act, or another law relative to hunting, fishing, or trapping which does not otherwise require the revocation of, or prohibit the securing of, a hunting, fishing, or trapping license, the court may order revocation of the license, including a sportsman's license, and by order may provide that the person shall not secure a hunting, fishing, or trapping license during the remainder of the year in which convicted, and during the next succeeding year (316.702). A game breeders or dealers license may be suspended or revoked when the licensee fails to comply with law, or fails to provide accurate reports and records. Whenever a license holder is convicted of a violation of state game laws, the license may be revoked or its renewal denied and the game held under the license may be disposed of only in a manner approved by the Director (317.83).

Reward Payments

★★Except for a license or stamp issued to a senior citizen, in addition to each license and stamp fee, a person shall be charged a $.35 fee to be deposited in the Wildlife Resource Protection Fund. This money is expended by the Director for: ▸ rewards for information leading to the arrest and prosecution of poachers; ▸ hiring conservation officers for the investigation of poaching and tips regarding potential poaching; ▸ a promotional and educational campaign to inform the public on the harm and danger of poaching; ▸ other anti-poaching programs undertaken by the Department. Upon purchasing a license or stamp, the person may make a voluntary contribution to the fund (316.604). ★★

HABITAT PROTECTION

★★The legislature finds that: ‣ the earth's biological diversity is an important natural resource and decreasing biological diversity is a concern; ‣ most losses of biological diversity are unintended consequences of human activity; ‣ humans depend on biological resources; ‣ biological diversity is a valuable source of intellectual and scientific knowledge, recreation and aesthetic pleasure; ‣ conserving biological diversity has economic implications; ‣ reduced biological diversity may have potentially serious consequences for human welfare; ‣ reduced biological diversity may also impact ecosystems and critical ecosystem processes; ‣ reduced biological diversity may diminish the raw materials available for scientific and technical advancement; ‣ maintaining biological diversity through habitat protection and management is often less costly and more effective than efforts to save species once they become endangered; ‣ because biological resources will be most important for future needs, study by the legislature regarding maintaining the diversity of living organisms in their natural habitats and the costs and benefits of doing so is prudent. It is the goal of this state to encourage the lasting conservation of biological diversity (299.233 and .234). [For provisions implementing the Biological Diversity Conservation Act, see 299.221 through 299.237.] ★★

It is the duty of the Commission to prescribe means and to lay down rules and regulations to admit free and uninterrupted passage of fish over or through dams erected over rivers, streams, or creeks, except that the Director is authorized to abrogate these provisions whenever, in the opinion of the Commissioner, the height of the dam or the condition of the river or stream makes the installation of such ladders impracticable or unnecessary. The Director has the duty to draft a general plan that will best permit free passage of large and small fish at the dam. A person owning or using a dam, when so ordered by the Director, within 90 days shall erect and maintain in good repair sufficient and permanent means to allow free and uninterrupted passage of fish over or through such dam. [Details of prosecution and separate offenses provided, in 307.1 through .6.]

It is unlawful for a person, firm or corporation to obstruct the channel or course of a river, stream or creek by placing therein a net, wire screen or other apparatus or material which prevents free passage of fish, except as authorized by law, and an offender is guilty of a violation. The Director may authorize the placing of screens in a river, stream, creek or inlet or outlet of a lake (307.7). It is unlawful to put into such waters sand, coal, cinders, ashes, log slabs, decayed wood, bark, sawdust or filth (307.30).

The Commission is empowered to establish state wildlife sanctuaries and by resolution may accept privately owned lands, when the owners or lessees apply to the Commission to dedicate lands for such purposes. The Commission may accept the dedication only after it determines: ‣ the application is made in good faith; ‣ the lands are suitable for the declared purposes; ‣ the dedication and operation of the proposed wildlife sanctuary will increase the supply of desirable wildlife in the vicinity and will be in the public interest. Applications are not approved for areas of less than 20 acres nor more than 1,500 acres, or for less than five-year periods. Upon application from controlling agencies, lands owned by the state or by the US may be dedicated in the same manner as privately owned lands. Wildlife sanctuaries shall be posted so as to clearly define and mark their boundaries. During the dedication period of lands posted as a state wildlife sanctuary, possession or carrying of firearms, hunting or trapping, or killing or molesting wildlife by a person or by owners or lessees, or their agents is unlawful. The Director may issue permits for taking predatory animals and birds and other birds and animals for control or in connection with experiments in wildlife management or other purposes not inconsistent with the intent of the dedication (317.201 through .204). The Commission has authority to issue and enforce rules and regulations to administer and accomplish these purposes. It is the duty of conservation officers with power to arrest, and of sheriffs and other peace officers, to protect the wildlife on dedicated areas from injury or molestation. Violation of provisions herein is a misdemeanor, punishable by a fine of $25-100, or jail up to 30 days, or both (317.206 through .208). [For specific wildlife sanctuaries and refuges, see 317.221 through 317.252.]

NATIVE AMERICAN WILDLIFE PROVISIONS: None.

MINNESOTA

Sources: Minnesota Statutes Annotated, 1985, Chapters 84, 97A, 97B and 97C; 1993 Cumulative Annual Pocket Part.

STATE WILDLIFE POLICY

It is the policy of the state that fish and wildlife are renewable natural resources to be conserved and enhanced through planned scientific management, protection, and utilization (84.941). The ownership of wild animals of the state is in the state, in its sovereign capacity for the benefit of all its people. A person may not acquire a property right in wild animals, or destroy them, unless authorized under the game and fish laws (97A.025).

RELEVANT WILDLIFE DEFINITIONS: See Definitions section of Appendices.

STATE FISH AND WILDLIFE AGENCIES

Agency Structure

The Department of Conservation is changed to the **Department of Natural Resources (Department)**. The Commissioner of Conservation is changed to the **Commissioner of Natural Resources (Commissioner)**. The Commissioner is appointed by the Governor, and may appoint a Deputy Commissioner (84.01). Subject to the Commissioner's authority to revise, abolish or establish divisions, the Department shall be organized with the following divisions: lands and forestry; waters; soils and minerals; game and fish; parks and recreation; and enforcement and field service. Each division director shall be subject to the supervision of the Commissioner, chosen for knowledge, training, experience and ability in administering the work, and with consideration of applicable professional registration. Each director, with Commissioner approval, may designate a deputy director, with all the powers of the director, subject to the director's control (84.081).

The Commissioner shall be the administrative and executive head of the Department, with charge of state public lands, parks, timber, waters, minerals, and wild animals and of the use, sale, leasing, or other disposition thereof, and of records pertaining to the Commissioner's functions (84.027). [Other extensive powers and duties provided.]

Conservation officers shall have the powers and duties of game wardens and may be assigned to public relations, conservation instructional activities, and law enforcement relating to resources management. The Commissioner shall create a division entitled the Division of Enforcement and Field Service, to be composed of conservation officers and shall appoint a Director (84.028).

Agency Powers and Duties

Each division shall administer the activities indicated by its title and other duties and functions as assigned, subject to Commissioner powers.   ★The **Commissioner** may accept any gift, bequest, devise, or grants or interest in lands, or personal property or money for Department or division purposes. The Commissioner must accept a gift, bequest, devise, or grant of wetlands or public waters wetlands, unless: ▸ the value of the wetland for water quality, floodwater retention, public recreation, wildlife habitat, or other public benefits is minimal; ▸ the wetland has been degraded without a permit by the person offering the wetland; ▸ the wetland has been contaminated; ▸ the wetland is subject to an encumbrance; ▸ access is unobtainable to the wetland (84.085). [84.0887 provides for youth corps programs which may provide services that include wildlife habitat conservation and maintenance, fish culture and fishery assistance.]★

The Commissioner may acquire all dam sites, flowage easements and other interests in land by gift, purchase, condemnation or otherwise for improving habitat for fish, wild fowl and game, wild rice and forestry and fire protection (84.161).   ★★A conservation restriction may be acquired by: the Commissioner, for the state, by gift, purchase or exchange, with funds made available for that purpose; a nonprofit charitable corporation whose purposes include conservation of land or water areas; or a home rule city. A "conservation restriction" is a right, easement, covenant or condition in any instrument to retain areas predominately in their natural, scenic, open or wooded condition, or as habitat for fish and wildlife, to forbid or limit any or all: ▸ construction of buildings, roads, signs, billboards or other advertising, utilities or other structures; ▸ dumping or placing soil or material as landfill, or trash or waste; ▸ destruction of trees or other vegetation; ▸ excavation, removal of loam, peat, gravel, soil, rock or other material; ▸ surface use except purposes permitting the area to remain predominately in its natural condition; ▸ activities detrimental to drainage, flood control, water conservation, erosion control, or soil conservation, or fish and wildlife habitat preservation; ▸ other acts detrimental to retention of land or water areas (84.64). ★★

★The Commissioner shall prepare a comprehensive fish and wildlife management plan to include strategic, long-range and operational plans. The strategic plan must include an analysis of and strategies to address major fish and wildlife management problems and assessment of the need for additional research facilities. The long-range plan must include: ▸ an assessment of historical, present, and projected demand and the capability to meet the demand for fish and wildlife resources; ▸ a database updated and usable as a resource management tool; ▸ major goals, objectives, and policies to address resource management issues. The operational plan must include: ▸ an estimate of expenditures to implement management actions and the sources and amounts of revenue; ▸ a procedure to evaluate the management program; ▸ recommendations for actions to meet fish and wildlife management needs. The Commissioner must coordinate planning efforts with appropriate public agencies and make fish and wildlife management plans available for public input, review, and comment (84.942). ★

A provision of the game and fish laws inconsistent with the code of criminal procedure or penal law is only effective under the game and fish laws. The game and fish laws are subject to, and do not change or modify the authority of the Commissioner to delegate powers, duties, and functions. A provision relating to a wild animal applies in the same manner to its parts (97A.021).

The Commissioner: ▸ shall do all things to preserve, protect, and propagate desirable species of wild animals; ▸ shall insure recreation for anglers and hunters, breed or stock wild animals; ▸ may destroy undesirable or predatory wild animals; ▸ may protect a species by further limiting or closing seasons or areas, or by reducing limits, to prevent depletion or to promote propagation, and may protect a species by emergency rule prohibiting or allowing taking of the animal whether or not protected under game and fish laws or by allowing importation, transportation, or possession of the species or prohibiting except by special permit; ▸ must make findings of the necessity of a rule authorized under this paragraph and may authorize taking by special permit. The Commissioner may regulate the taking, possession, and transportation of wild animals from state and international boundary waters. Rules may include restrictions on limits of fish from international boundary waters by a person with both a Minnesota angling license and one from an adjacent Canadian province. The Commissioner may prescribe the form of permits, licenses, and tags issued. The Commissioner shall encourage the purchase of migratory waterfowl stamps for migratory waterfowl preservation and habitat development, pheasant stamps, and trout and salmon stamps (97A.045).

Agency Regulations

★★After each legislative session, the Commissioner, with the cooperation of the attorney general and the revisor of statutes, shall assemble and index the current laws and permanent rules relating to wild animals. This compilation shall be printed in pamphlet form, and 50 copies distributed to each senator, 25 to each representative, and 10 to each county auditor. Up to 10,000 additional copies may be printed for general distribution. ★★ Rules have the force and effect of law. Violation of a rule has the same penalty as a violation of the law under which the rule was adopted (97A.051).

Agency Funding Sources

★The **Minnesota Critical Habitat Private Sector Matching Account** is established as a separate account in the Reinvest in Minnesota Resources Fund. The account shall consist of contributions from private sources and appropriations. Appropriations transferred to the account may be expended if matched with private contributions or by funds contributed to the **Nongame Wildlife Management Account**. Private contributions may be made in cash, land or interests in land. Appropriations transferred to the account, not matched within three years, shall cancel. Money in the account is appropriated for direct acquisition or improvement of land or interests. The money matched to the account may be used for management of nongame wildlife projects under section 290.431. Acquisition includes purchase by or acceptance of gifts of land or interests in land as program projects (84.943). ★

★A **Reinvest in Minnesota Resources Fund** is a separate fund in the state treasury. Proceeds of state bonds issued for the fund shall be disbursed for costs of acquisition and betterment of public land and easements in land. Money from the fund may be spent only for the following: ▸ development and implementation of the fish and wildlife management plan; ▸ implementation of the conservation reserve program; ▸ soil and water conservation practices; ▸ enhancement of habitat on lakes, streams, wetlands, and public and private forest lands; ▸ acquisition and development of public access sites and recreation easements to lakes, streams, and rivers for fish and wildlife recreation; ▸ matching funds with government agencies, Indian tribes and bands, and the private sector for acquisition and improvement of habitat; ▸ research of species and habitat; ▸ enforcement of laws and rules; ▸ information and education; ▸ aspen recycling under section 88.80 and other forest wildlife management projects; ▸ support services [details of required annual written work plan, public meetings and progress reports provided] (84.95).★

The **Game and Fish Fund** is established. The money in the fund is appropriated for the divisions of fish and wildlife and of enforcement. The fund is credited with all money received under the game and fish laws including receipts from: ▸ licenses; ▸ fines and forfeited bail; ▸ sales of contraband, wild animals, and other division property; ▸ fees from advanced hunter and trapper education courses; ▸ reimbursements of expenditures; and ▸ contributions. Fee adjustments are allowed to reduce yearly fluctuations and provide improved long-range planning (97A.055). The Commissioner shall annually make a payment from the fund to each county having public hunting areas and game refuges [details of distribution allocation between county, town and school districts provided] (97A.061). Money received from the sale of fish and turtles taken under rough fish removal operations is continuously available for rough fish removal. Fines and forfeited bail from violations of the game and fish laws, and any other law relating to wild animals and aquatic vegetation must be paid to the county of prosecution. The county treasurer shall submit half of the receipts to the Commissioner and the balance to the county general revenue fund. If the county submits all fines and forfeited bail to the Commissioner, the Commissioner shall reimburse the county for the cost of keeping prisoners prosecuted under this section (97A.065).

The Commissioner may use the revenue from the fishing license surcharge for: ▸ rehabilitation and improvement of marginal fish producing waters, under cost-sharing agreements; ▸ programs including aeration, stocking of marginal fishing waters in urban areas, shore fishing areas, and fishing piers, with preference to local government and others sharing costs; ▸ upgrading of fish propagation capabilities to improve production, walleye production, introduction of biologically appropriate species, and purchase of fish for stocking; ▸ financing preservation and improvement of fish habitat; ▸ increasing enforcement with covert operations and added surveillance, communication, and navigational equipment; ▸ purchase of the walleye quota of commercial fishing operators. Not more than 10% may be used for administrative and personnel costs. The Commissioner shall prepare an annual work plan and provide copies to the Senate and House committees and to other interested parties. The committees must review issues in the management of fishing resources. Money collected from restitution under section 97A.341 for wild animals illegally killed, injured, or possessed must be used by the Commissioner for replacement, propagation, or protection of wild animals (97A.065).

The **Wildlife Acquisition Account** is established in the Game and Fish Fund. Revenue from the small game surcharge shall be credited to the account and used for this section and acquisition of wildlife lands under section 97A.145. The account may be used for developing, preserving, restoring, and maintaining waterfowl breeding grounds in Canada under agreement with nonprofit organizations The Commissioner may execute agreements to benefit migration of waterfowl into the state. An assessment on lands acquired for wildlife habitat shall be paid from the account (97A.071).

At least $2 from each deer license shall be used for deer habitat improvement. At least $1 from each resident deer and bear license shall be used for deer and bear management programs. The Commissioner may use the revenue from **Minnesota Migratory Waterfowl Stamps** for: ▸ development of wetlands in the state and designated waterfowl management lakes for maximum migratory waterfowl production, including construction of dikes, water control structures and impoundments, nest cover, rough fish barriers, acquisition of sites and facilities for development and management of existing and new migratory waterfowl habitat; ▸ management of migratory waterfowl; ▸ acquisition of and access to structure sites; ▸ administrative costs not to exceed 10% of the annual revenue. The Commissioner may use the revenue from **Trout and Salmon Stamps** for: ▸ development, restoration, maintenance, and preservation of trout streams and lakes; ▸ rearing and stocking of trout and salmon; ▸ administrative costs not to exceed 10% of the annual revenue. The Commissioner may use the revenue from

Pheasant Stamps for: ▸ development, restoration, maintenance, and preservation of suitable habitat for ringnecked pheasants, including nesting cover, winter cover, and reliable food sources; ▸ reimbursement of expenditures to provide pheasant habitat on public and private land; ▸ promotion of pheasant habitat development, maintenance, and preservation; ▸ administrative and personnel costs not to exceed 10% of the annual revenue (97A.075).

PROTECTED SPECIES OF WILDLIFE

An enforcement officer shall enforce a violation of Chapters 84.0895, 84.091, 84.093, 84.152, and 103G.615 in the same manner as a violation of the game and fish laws. A person may not take, import, transport, or sell any portion of an endangered species, or sell or possess with intent to sell an article made with any part of an endangered species except as provided. [Further provisions as to taking of endangered plant species given.] The Commissioner shall designate species of wild animal or plant as: endangered, if the species is threatened with extinction throughout all or a significant portion of its range; threatened, if likely to become endangered within the foreseeable future throughout all or a significant portion of its range; or species of special concern, if although the species is not endangered or threatened, it is extremely uncommon, or has unique or highly specific habitat requirements and deserves careful monitoring. Species on the periphery of their range not listed as threatened may be in this category along with species that were once threatened or endangered but now have increasing or protected, stable populations (84.0894 and .0895).

★The range of the species in this state is a factor in determining status as endangered, threatened, or of special concern. The Secretary of the Interior's designation of threatened or endangered is a prima facie showing. The Commissioner shall reevaluate the designated species list every three years and make appropriate changes. The review must consider further protection of species on the special concern list. Species may be withdrawn from designation in the same manner. The Commissioner may conduct investigations to determine the status and requirements for survival of a resident species, and may undertake management programs, issue orders, and adopt rules to bring a resident species to a point at which it is no longer threatened or endangered. Management programs for endangered or threatened species include research, census, law enforcement, habitat acquisition, habitat maintenance, propagation, live trapping, transplantation, and regulated taking.★ A peace officer or conservation officer may execute a warrant to search for and seize goods, merchandise, plant or animal taken, sold or offered for sale in violation of this section, or items used in connection with a violation. Seized property must be held pending judicial proceedings. Upon conviction, it is forfeited and must be offered to a scientific or educational institution or destroyed (84.0895).

The Commissioner may prescribe conditions for an act otherwise prohibited if: ▸ it is for zoological, educational, or scientific study; ▸ it enhances the propagation or survival of the species; ▸ it prevents injury to persons or property; ▸ the social and economic benefits outweigh the harm caused. An endangered species may not be destroyed until all alternatives, including live trapping and transplantation, have been evaluated and rejected. The Commissioner may prescribe conditions to propagate a species or subspecies. A person may capture or destroy an endangered species, without permit, to avoid an immediate and demonstrable threat to human life or property. The Commissioner must give approval for forest management, including permit, sale, or lease of land for timber harvesting. This section does not apply retroactively or prohibit importation and subsequent possession, transport, and sale of wild animals, wild plants, or parts legally imported into the US or legally acquired and exported from another territory, state, possession, or political subdivision of the US. A violation of this section is a misdemeanor (84.0895).

A person may not take, buy, sell, transport, or possess a protected wild animal unless allowed by the game and fish laws. The ownership of all wild animals is in the state, unless the animal has been lawfully acquired. Ownership of a wild animal reverts to the state if a law relating to sale, transportation, or possession of the wild animal is violated. A person may not take, import, transport, or sell an endangered species, or sell, or possess with intent to sell an article made from its parts, except as provided in section 84.0895 (97A.501).

A person may not possess a wild animal that has been unlawfully taken, bought, sold, or possessed outside the state, or unlawfully shipped into the state. A person that stores protected wild animals for others must plainly mark the package [details provided]. A person may not use a commercial cold storage warehouse for protected wild animals, except lawfully taken fish and furs. Lawfully taken protected wild animals may be transferred by gift and possessed without a license with required written proof. This section does not apply to mounted specimens of wild animals, antlers, tanned hides, and dressed furs lawfully taken (97A.505).

GENERAL EXCEPTIONS TO PROTECTION

Special permits may be issued to municipalities, incorporated natural history societies and high schools, colleges, and universities with a zoological collection, to collect specimens of eggs, nests, and wild animals for scientific or exhibition purposes, or to take, possess, and transport wild animals as pets and for scientific, educational, and exhibition purposes under conditions prescribed by the Commissioner. A special permit may not be issued to take or possess wild or native deer except as pets under established criteria. Special permits may be issued to take a wild animal from game refuges, wildlife management areas, state parks, and other areas opened during a special season, with fees based upon costs, to take protected wild animals damaging property, to take a stated number of beaver, or to take muskrats in danger of freezing or starving in the winter (97A.401).

The Commissioner may take, hire contract persons without competitive bidding, or issue permits to take rough fish, lake whitefish, and rainbow smelt with seines, nets, and other devices, and shall prescribe the manner of taking and disposal. The Commissioner must consider the qualifications of the contractor, including equipment, knowledge of the waters, and ability to perform the work (97C.041).

HUNTING, FISHING, TRAPPING PROVISIONS

General Provisions

Unless expressly allowed, a person may not wantonly waste or destroy a usable part of a protected wild animal (97A.031). A person that transports wild animals in a container must mark or identify the container as prescribed. During the open season a person may transport a protected wild animal both within and outside the state, if the animal may be lawfully sold and is not otherwise prohibited. No one may transport wild animals taken, bought, sold, or possessed in violation of game and fish laws (97A.521).

Anyone with a required license may transport wild animals by common carrier without being in the vehicle if they are shipped to themselves. The wild animals that may be transported by common carrier are deer, bear, elk, and moose, undressed game birds and fish. An employee of a carrier may not transport wild animals as baggage while performing duties. A person that transports protected wild animals by common carrier must attach a statement to each shipment [details provided]. A common carrier may not accept a shipment of game unless shown the license of the shipper. The receipt issued by a common carrier to a shipper must specify the number and species being shipped (97A.525).

A person may ship, with required coupons, wild animals and fish lawfully taken and possessed in Canada that have lawfully entered the state (97A.531). A person may not possess or transport deer, bear, elk, or moose taken in the state unless a tag is attached. The tag must be attached at the site of the kill and must remain so until processed for storage. Deer taken by archery, elk, and moose must be tagged as prescribed, in addition to the tag required above. A person may transport deer, bear, one elk, or moose during the open season and the two days following the season, or as prescribed. A person may transport deer, bear, elk, or moose that the licensee has registered [details provided]. A resident licensed to take deer, bear, elk, or moose may transport the head or hide of the animal within or out of the state for mounting or tanning. ★The hides of deer, bear, elk, and moose, and the claws of bear legally taken and tagged as required, may be bought, sold, and transported at any time (97A.535).★

A nonresident may not possess or transport a raccoon, bobcat, Canada lynx, or fox without a tag as prescribed and attached. A resident may not make more than three shipments, each of the daily limit, during a license year of undressed game birds without being in the vehicle. A nonresident shipping undressed game birds without being in the vehicle must obtain a permit. A person must obtain a permit to ship game birds to another person. The person must have the licenses required to take the game birds. A person may transport into the state undressed game birds that are lawfully taken outside of the state. A resident may ship the undressed game birds within the state or a nonresident may ship them out of the state with each shipment tagged and sealed by a conservation officer (97A.541 and .545). A person may not transport game fish taken outside the state through the state during the closed season or in excess of the limit unless transported by common carrier; or tagged, sealed, or marked [details of number of shipments and permits required provided] (97A.551).

A person may not enter posted land to take a wild animal or after being prohibited by the owner, occupant, or lessee. Private or public land may be prohibited from hunting, trapping, fishing, or trespassing by posting signs [details provided]. A hunter on foot may retrieve wounded game, or may retrieve a dog that has treed or is at bay with a raccoon, bobcat, coyote, or fox, during the open season, from agricultural land that is not posted, without permission of the landowner, and must leave immediately after retrieval. A person may not: ▸ take a wild animal with a firearm within 500 feet of a building occupied by a human or livestock, or of a stockade or corral with livestock, on another person's private agricultural land, without written permission, or on a public right-of-way; ▸ take a wild animal with a firearm on nonagricultural land within 200 feet of an occupied building without permission; ▸ wound or kill another's domestic animal; ▸ destroy, cut, or tear down another's fence, building, grain, crops, live tree, or sign; ▸ pass through another's closed gate without closing it (97B.001).

Licenses and Permits

The Commissioner shall make rules establishing a statewide course in firearm safety and identification of wild mammals and birds. At least one course must be held in each school district. The courses must instruct youths in commonly accepted principles of hunting and firearm safety. The Commissioner shall appoint a person from the enforcement division as Supervisor of Hunting Safety and one or more county directors of hunting safety in each county. The enforcement division may appoint instructors and must supply course materials. A firearms safety certificate shall be issued upon course completion. Except as provided, one born after December 31, 1979, may not obtain a license to take wild animals by firearms except with a firearms safety certificate or equivalent, previous hunting license, or other evidence indicating completion of a hunter safety course recognized under a reciprocity agreement. The Commissioner may establish advanced education courses for hunters and trappers with a fee not to exceed $10 (97B.015, .020 and .025).

Unless allowed under game and fish laws, a person may not take, buy, sell, transport, or possess protected wild animals without a license. The license must be in personal possession while using it and traveling from the activity performed, and exhibited when requested by an authorized officer (97A.405). Stamps issued must be signed by the licensee. The Commissioner may issue a license to take a second deer by archery. Only one trapping and big game license of each kind may be issued in a license year unless authorized. A person may not lend, transfer, borrow, or solicit a license, application for a license, coupon, tag, or seal, or use a license, coupon, tag, or seal not issued to the person. Nonresidents may not obtain a license unless an activity is expressly authorized (97A.411 and .415).

Rules setting dates for a moose season shall set the number of licenses to be issued. Moose license eligibility shall be determined under this section and Commissioner's rule. A person is eligible only if a resident at least age 16 who has not been issued a moose license for any of the last five seasons or after January 1, 1991. The Commissioner may conduct a separate selection for up to 20% of moose licenses issued for an area [details provided regarding landowners]. The Commissioner shall include the number of licenses to be issued in a rule with dates for elk season. A person is eligible for an elk license only if a resident at least age 16 before the season opens and has never been issued an elk license. [Separate selections for landowners described.] The Commissioner by rule shall set dates for turkey season and the number of licenses. A person is eligible for a turkey license only if at least age 16 before the season opens or possesses a firearms safety certificate (97A.431, .433 and .435). [License fee amounts set forth for hunting, fishing, guides, trappers, preserves and commercial licenses] (97A.475).

A person may not take small game without a license, or with traps without a trapping license and a small game license, except as provided. A nonresident may not take raccoon, bobcat, fox, coyote, or Canada lynx without a separate license in addition to a small game license. A person may take small game without a license on land occupied by the person as a principal residence. An owner or occupant may take certain small game causing damage without a small game or trapping license. A person may use dogs to pursue and tree raccoons under section 97B.621 during the closed season without a license. A person may take turkey without a small game license (97B.601).

A person may not take fish: ▸ without an angling license; ▸ by spearing from a dark house without a dark house spearing license and an angling license; ▸ by netting without a license to net fish. An aquatic farm licensee may take aquatic life under that license without additional licenses. Except as provided, a person over age 16 and under

65 required to possess an angling license must have a trout and salmon stamp in possession to take fish by angling in a designated trout stream, a designated trout lake, or Lake Superior. The stamp is not required if the person possesses a license to take fish by angling for 24 hours from the issuance, and is taking fish during that period (97C.301 and .305).

Restrictions on Taking: Hunting and Trapping

A person may not train hunting dogs afield from April 16 to July 14, except by permit or written permission. A person training a dog afield during closed season may possess and use only blank cartridges and shells. The Commissioner may issue special permits to use live ammunition on domesticated or banded game birds from game farms and to possess a raccoon for holding field trials and training retrieving dogs (97B.005). A dog observed killing, wounding, or pursuing so as to endanger, big game, or known to have killed such, may be killed by a peace officer or conservation officer, or, between January 1 and July 14, by any person without liability (97B.011).

[Sections 97B.031 and 97B.035 provide restrictions on types of firearms and archery equipment.] A person may not possess a firearm or ammunition outdoors during the tenth day before the open firearms season and ending the second day after season close where deer may be taken by a firearm, except: ▸ during the open season in a big game area with a big game license in possession; ▸ an unloaded firearm that is in a case or in a closed trunk of a vehicle; ▸ a shotgun and shells with No. 4 buckshot or smaller lead or steel shot; ▸ a handgun or rifle and only .22 caliber cartridges; ▸ handguns possessed by an authorized person; ▸ on a permitted target range (97B.041). A person may not: ▸ transport a firearm in a motor vehicle unless it is unloaded and fully enclosed in a firearm case, unloaded and in the closed trunk of a motor vehicle or an authorized handgun; ▸ transport an archery bow unless the bow is unstrung, completely contained in a case or in the closed trunk of a motor vehicle; ▸ discharge a firearm or an arrow from a bow on, over, or across a public highway or its right-of-way at a big game animal or decoy, the Commissioner being able to extend this ban to migratory waterfowl in designated locations; ▸ take a wild animal with a firearm or by archery from a motor vehicle except as permitted. The Commissioner may issue a permit to take animals for a bounty from an airplane or a snowmobile. If requested by the Commissioner, a report must be submitted stating the number and kind of each animal taken during the preceding license year (97B..045, .051, .055 and 061).

A person may not take protected wild animals, except raccoons and foxes, with a firearm or by archery between established evening and morning times (97B.075). A person may not cast the rays of a spotlight, headlight, or other artificial light to spot, locate, or take a wild animal, except raccoons under section 97B.621, or while tending traps under section 97B.931, while possessing a weapon capable of killing big game. This does not apply to a firearm that is unloaded, in a fully enclosed case and in a closed trunk, and does not apply to an encased or unstrung bow in a closed trunk. If the motor vehicle does not have a trunk, the firearm or bow must be in the rear of the vehicle (97B.081). Without a permit, a person may not use radio equipment to take big game or small game, or unprotected wild animals. This does not prohibit use of a one-way radio between a handler and a dog (97B.085). A person may not use a motor vehicle intentionally to drive, chase, run over, kill, or take a wild animal, or disturb the burrow or den of a wild animal between November 1 and April 1 without a permit, or take a protected wild animal with the aid of a ferret (97B.091, .095 and .101). If two or more persons maintain unaided visual and vocal contact, one person may take and possess more than one limit of small game, but the total number may not exceed the limit of persons in the party. This does not apply to hunting migratory game birds or turkeys (97B.603).

The Commissioner may regulate and designate areas where gray and fox squirrels, cottontail and jack rabbits, snowshoe hares, raccoons, lynx, bobcats, red and gray foxes, fishers, pine martens, opossums, and badgers may be taken and possessed (97B.605). A person may not set fire to a tree or use smoke to take squirrels (97B.611). [Dates for open seasons for gray and fox squirrels, cottontail and jack rabbits, snowshoe hares, and raccoons are set in 97B.611, 97B.615 and 97B.621.] A person may use dogs to pursue and tree raccoons without killing or capturing at specified times in raccoon dog field trials under permit. To take raccoons between sunset and sunrise, a person: ▸ must be on foot; ▸ may use an artificial light only if hunting with dogs; ▸ may not use a rifle other than .22 rimfire ammunition; ▸ may not use shotgun shells larger than No. 4 shot. A person may not take a raccoon: ▸ in a den or hollow tree; ▸ by cutting down a tree; ▸ by setting fire to a tree or using smoke (97B.621). The Commissioner may set the open season for lynx or bobcat, and one may not use a snare to take lynx or bobcat except under permit (97B.625). A person may not remove a fox from a den or trap fox within 300 feet of a den from April 1 to August 31, and may not use a snare except under permit (97B.631). The Commissioner may set the open season for fisher, badger, opossum, and pine marten (97B.635). There is no open season for cougar or wolverine (97B.641). A person may not use a dog or horse to take a timber wolf, and may not use a snare to take a wolf except under permit (97B.645).

Unprotected wild mammals may be taken, except with artificial lights or by using a motor vehicle in violation of section 97B.091. Poison may not be used to take unprotected mammals unless the safety of humans and domestic livestock is ensured. Unprotected mammals may be possessed, bought, sold, or transported in any quantity (97B.651). Protected birds, their nests, and eggs may be taken only as authorized under the game and fish laws. A person may not take protected birds: ▸ with a trap, net, or snare; ▸ using bird lime; ▸ with a swivel or set gun; ▸ dragging a rope, wire, or other device across a field; ▸ using fire (97B.701). Except as provided, a person may not take a bird with a steel jaw leg-hold trap mounted on a pole, post, tree stump, or other perch more than three feet above the ground. A person with a game farm license and a US permit may trap great horned owls from April 1 to October 15. The trap must be a padded jaw trap and mounted so that the trapped owl may rest on the ground. Uninjured birds shall be released alive and injured birds receive appropriate veterinary treatment (97B.705). The Commissioner may prescribe open season in designated areas between September 16 and December 31 for: pheasant; ruffed, sharp tailed and Canada spruce grouse; prairie chicken; gray and chukar partridge; quail; and turkey; and a spring open season for turkey. A person may not take more than five in one day or possess more than 10: pheasant; ruffed and sharp tailed grouse; prairie chicken; gray and chukar partridge. A person may not take more than 10 quail in one day or possess more than 15 bob-white quail. The Commissioner by rule may reduce these limits (97B.711).

Without a pheasant stamp and a small game license in possession, a person may not: ▸ hunt pheasants; ▸ take more than one hen pheasant in one day or possess more than two hen pheasants; ▸ take pheasants between the evening time established and 9:00 a.m. A person may not take turkey without a turkey license (97B.715 and .721). Migratory game birds may be taken and possessed, except in violation of federal law, prescribed seasons and limits in accordance with federal law. Mourning doves may not be taken. The Commissioner shall prescribe a 124-day open season not to be shorter than the maximum season allowed under federal law, and restrictions for taking crows. The remainder of the year crows may be taken as allowed by federal law (97B.731).

A person may not take: ▸ migratory waterfowl without a small game license and a migratory waterfowl stamp in possession, except residents under 18 and over 65, or residents hunting on their own property, the Commissioner to prescribe seasons, limits, and areas for taking migratory waterfowl in accordance with federal law; ▸ migratory waterfowl, coots, or rails in open water unless within a natural growth of vegetation sufficient to partially conceal the person or boat, or unless pursuing or shooting wounded birds; ▸ migratory waterfowl, coots, or rails in public waters from a permanent artificial blind or sink box. Migratory waterfowl may be taken from a propelled watercraft only if it has stopped with the motor off and sails furled. Migratory waterfowl may be taken from a floating watercraft if drifting, beached, moored, resting at anchor, or being propelled by paddle, oars, or pole [details provided on attended boats]. A person may not erect a blind or place decoys more than one hour before the open season for waterfowl, and may not place decoys more than one hour before lawful shooting hours for waterfowl [other restriction on decoys described] (97B.801, .803, .805 and .811).

Deer killed on a public road must be removed by the road authority. Road authorities are provided forms for statistics and tracking (97A.502). There may not be an open season on caribou or antelope (97B.201). A person may not use a dog or horse to take big game (97B.205). A person may not take big game by archery while possessing a firearm [specifications for provided]. A person may not take deer without a license. A person must have a firearms deer license or an archery deer license except as provided. A person may obtain a firearms deer license and an archery deer license in the same year, but may take only one deer. If two or more persons with such licenses are hunting as a party, a member of the party may take more than one deer, but the total number may not exceed the number of persons licensed (97B.211). The Commissioner may allow taking two deer, and shall prescribe the conditions for the second deer including: ▸ taking by firearm or archery; ▸ obtaining an additional license; ▸ payment of a fee not more than a firearms deer license fee; ▸ by a resident family license, with a limit of one per family member not to exceed four deer. The Commissioner may limit the number of persons that may hunt deer to prevent an overharvest or improve the distribution of hunters and may establish a method to select hunters impartially for an area (97B.301 and .305). The Commissioner may prescribe restrictions, designate areas, and prescribe open seasons for deer: ▸ with firearms, other than muzzle-loading firearms; ▸ with muzzle-loading firearms; ▸ by archery). A person may not take deer with the aid of a snare, trap, set gun, or swivel gun (97B.311

and .321). A person may not take deer from a platform or other structure in the right-of-way of a public highway or higher than 16 feet. The height restriction does not apply to a portable stand that is chained, belted, clamped, or tied with rope (97B.325).

A person may not take bear without a bear license, except as provided to protect property (97B.401). The Commissioner may: ‣ limit the number of persons to prevent an overharvest or improve the distribution of hunters; ‣ establish a method to select hunters impartially for an area (97B.405); ‣ prescribe open seasons, areas and restrictions for taking of bear (97B.411). A person may take bear to protect the person's property and must report the bear to a conservation officer within 48 hours and dispose of it as prescribed. A person may not snare a bear except under permit (97B.415 and .421). Notwithstanding section 609.68, a person may place bait to take bear, and must display a tag and register the sites. The Commissioner shall prescribe the method of tagging and registration. A person may not use bait with: ‣ a mammal carcass containing 25% or more of the intact carcass; ‣ mammal meat containing bones; ‣ solid waste containing bottles, cans, plastic, paper, or metal; ‣ nonbiodegradeable materials; ‣ any part of a swine (97B.425). A person may not bait bear or guide hunters for compensation without a bear hunting guide license, but a person is not required to have a hunting license unless attempting to shoot a bear. The Commissioner shall adopt rules for the issuance and administration of the licenses (97B.431).

A person may not take moose without a license. The Commissioner may prescribe the open season, areas and conditions. A person may not take moose from a platform or other structure higher than 9 feet, unless a portable stand is chained, belted, clamped, or tied with rope (97B.501, .505 and .511). A person may not take an elk without an elk license. The Commissioner may prescribe the open season, areas and conditions for taking elk when the precalving population exceeds 20 animals. A person may not take elk from a platform or other structure higher than 9 feet, unless a portable stand is chained, belted, clamped, or tied with rope. The Commissioner must adopt an elk management plan that: ‣ recognizes the value and uniqueness of elk; ‣ provides for integrated management of an elk population in harmony with the environment; ‣ affords optimum recreational opportunities; and restricts elk to nonagricultural land (97B.515 and .516).

Skins of fur-bearing animals and flesh of beaver, muskrat, raccoon, rabbits and hares, legally taken and bearing required seals or tags, may be bought, sold, and transported. The flesh of beaver, raccoon, rabbits, and hare may not be transported out of the state (97A.511). ★★Except as provided, a person may possess, transport, buy, or sell the following inedible portions of lawfully taken or acquired big game animals, fur-bearing animals, and game birds other than migratory waterfowl: bones, including skulls; sinews; hides; hooves; teeth; claws; and antlers. A person may not buy or sell bear paws, unless attached to the hide, or bear gallbladders (97A.512). ★★ The Commissioner may require tagging fur-bearing animals where they are taken, shall prescribe the issuance and type of tag (97B.901), may establish open seasons for muskrat, mink, otter or beaver between October 25 and April 30, with open season for mink and otter not to exceed 90 days, and may prescribe restrictions for taking muskrat and mink. Otter and beaver may be taken only by trapping subject to restrictions (97B.911, .915, .921, and .925). A person may not tend a trap set for wild animals between 7:00 p.m. and 5:00 a.m. A person on foot may use a portable artificial light between 5:00 a.m. and 7:00 p.m. to tend traps, but may not possess or use a firearm other than a handgun of .22 caliber (97B.931). ★Except as the Commissioner may designate in certain counties, a person may not use a snowmobile or all-terrain vehicle during, or for two days after, the open season for beaver or otter, to transport or check beaver or otter traps or to transport such carcasses or pelts (97B.935). ★ No person, except the Commissioner, owner or lessee may remove or tamper with a trap legally set to take fur-bearing or unprotected wild animals. Without a permit, a trap may not be set within 50 feet of water within 30 days before the open season for mink and muskrat (97B.941 and .945).

Restrictions on Taking: Fishing

The Commissioner may designate waters, up to 100 lakes and 25 streams, having free access to the public as experimental waters (lakes and streams where special regulations are used and evaluated to meet a specific fisheries objective). For experimental waters, the Commissioner shall develop an evaluation plan and a termination date, and establish methods and criteria for public initiation and participation of such designation and evaluation. [Details of public meetings and comments provided.] The Commissioner may establish open seasons, limits, methods, and other requirements for taking fish (97C.001). Special management waters are waters having special regulations that have proven effective under an experimental waters designation; or are classified for primary use as trophy lakes, family fishing lakes, designated trout lakes, designated trout streams, special species management lakes, and other designated uses. The Commissioner may designate any waters as special management waters, and shall establish criteria for public participation in the evaluation and designation. [Details of public meetings for designation or change in status of experimental waters to special management waters provided.] The Commissioner may establish requirements for taking fish (97C.005).

A person may take fish only from a designated trout stream during open season. A person may not take fish from or drive motorboats over spawning beds or fish preserves. The Commissioner may establish lakes and rivers containing an unbalanced fish population, or containing species stunted from overpopulation. The list may not include more than 100 lakes and rivers, or more than six in a county. The Commissioner may establish requirements for taking fish to be published in each county with the lake or river (97C.021, .025 and .031).

★★If the Commissioner determines that fish in shallow waters are endangered by lack of oxygen in the winter, or if waters will be restored with the use of piscicides, the Commissioner shall rescue the fish by transferring them to other waters, selling or disposing of them, or allowing the fish to be taken in any quantity in any manner, except by seines, hoop nets, fyke nets, and explosives, and for personal use only. Rough fish may be sold. In an emergency the Commissioner may authorize taking fish without publishing notice if posted conspicuously along the shores (97C.035). The Commissioner shall remove dead fish that are a public nuisance or are detrimental to game fish and that accumulate on the shores of public waters (97C.055).★★ A person may not dispose or allow any substance to enter state waters in quantities that injure or are detrimental to the propagation of wild animals. Each day of violation is a separate offense. An occurring or continuous violation is a public nuisance. An action may be brought by the attorney general to enjoin and abate a nuisance upon the Commissioner's request. This section does not apply to pest control chemicals used for general public welfare (97C.065).

An angler may not use more than one line, except two lines may be used to take fish through ice, and if authorized, two lines in designated Lake Superior areas. An angler may not have more than one hook on a line, except three artificial flies may be on a line to take largemouth and smallmouth bass, trout, crappies, sunfish, and rock bass, and a single artificial bait may contain more than one hook. If two or more persons are angling, the number of fish taken and possessed by the party may not exceed the limit of the party. A person may not take fish with a set or unattended line, except using an unattended line to take fish through the ice if within sight of the line, or a tip-up is attached to the line and the person is within 80 feet, or as provided in 97C.801. Except as authorized, a person may not take fish with explosives, chemicals, drugs, poisons, lime, medicated bait, fish berries, or other similar substances; substances or devices that kill, stun, or affect the nervous system of fish; nets, traps, trot lines, or snares; or spring devices that impale, hook, or capture fish. If a person possesses such a substance or device on waters, shores, or islands, it is presumptive evidence of violation (97C.315, .317, .321 and .325).

A person may not: ▸ take fish with a snagline, snagpole, snaghook, or cluster of fish hooks, designed to be placed in or drawn through the water to hook the body of a fish; ▸ use artificial lights to lure, attract or see fish while spearing; ▸ use live minnows imported, game fish, goldfish, or carp for bait; ▸ take fish with a spear, fish trap, net, dip net, seine, or other device, except as provided, and may not possess those devices on or near waters or in a vehicle, but may possess and use these devices at designated times. This section does not apply to: ▸ nets used to take rainbow smelt during open season; ▸ nets used to land game fish; ▸ seines or traps used for taking minnows for bait; ▸ nets, seines, or traps possessed and used under an aquatic farm license; ▸ angling equipment (97C.331, .335, .341 and .345). A person may not possess a fish net unless specifically authorized or a proper tag is attached. This section does not apply to minnow nets, landing nets, dip nets, and nets in stock for sale by dealers (97C.351). [Detailed provisions are made for licensing and other restrictions on dark houses and fish houses on state waters in 97C.355.]

Only rough fish, catfish, lake whitefish, and northern pike may be taken by spearing. Catfish, lake whitefish, and northern pike may be speared only from dark houses, and not by angling or the use of tip-ups. A resident may: ▸ take rough fish by spearing or archery in the manner prescribed; ▸ use a rubber powered, spring, or compressed air gun to take rough fish by harpooning. [Open season dates to take fish by angling are set forth in detail for various species; for salmon as prescribed.] The Commissioner shall close the season where fish are spawning to protect the resource. For sunfish, white crappie, black crappie, yellow perch, catfish, rock bass, white bass, lake whitefish, and rough fish, the open season is continuous (97C.371, .375, .381 and .395). If the Commissioner closes the open season or puts limits on spearing a game fish species, the Commissioner must do the same the following season for angling for the same species. The Commissioner may not close the open season for taking game fish through ice on more than 50% of the named lakes or streams of a county under section 97A.045 (97C.385). Unless provided, the Commissioner shall prescribe limits on the number of fish taken or possessed in one day (97C.401).

Lake sturgeon, shovelnose sturgeon, and paddlefish may not be taken, bought, sold, transported or possessed except by order of the Commissioner who may allow taking only in waters that the state boundary passes. A person may not take trout, except lake trout between 11:00 p.m. and one hour before sunrise. The Commissioner may prescribe the method of taking and possessing salmon (97C.411 and .415). The Commissioner may establish closed seasons for frogs in specified areas [restrictions on taking, possessing and transporting frogs provided], and shall prescribe rules for buying, selling, possessing, and transporting frogs for other than bait, and may issue permits for importing, raising, and selling frogs for human consumption (97C.601). A person may not take, possess, buy, sell, or transport turtles without an angling license, and may not take, possess, transport, or purchase turtles for sale without a turtle seller's license [details provided]. A person may take turtles, except by use of explosives, drugs, poisons, lime, and other harmful substances; turtle hooks or traps; or nets other than anglers' fish landing nets. A turtle seller licensee may take turtles for sale as prescribed. The Commissioner may issue permits to take turtles with artificial lights in designated waters (97C.605). A person may not possess more than three snapping turtles without a turtle seller's license, and may not take snapping turtles less than ten inches wide (97C.611). Areas may be closed and taking may be prohibited where operations are aiding fish propagation (97C.621).

The Commissioner may prescribe conditions for taking mussels [conditions for taking described]. Mussels and clams may be possessed, bought, sold, and transported during the open season and seven days after (97C.701). The Commissioner may close up to half the mussel-producing waters (97C.705). A person may not take mussels less than 1-3/4" each, and must return others without injury (97C.711). The Commissioner shall prescribe the open season and waters for netting lake whitefish and ciscoes. Specific lakes and waters otherwise closed may be opened if notice is posted. Netting is subject to the restrictions in this subdivision [details provided for meshes, sizes, and locations] (97C.805).

Commercial and Private Enterprise Provisions

A person connected with a commercial enterprise may not possess wildlife in captivity for public exhibition purposes, except under permit. The Commissioner may issue a permit to an applicant qualified in the care and treatment of wildlife. A permit shall allow an enforcement officer to enter and inspect the facilities. An application for a permit must include: ▸ the education or experience in the care and treatment of wildlife of the applicant and each individual employed for that purpose; ▸ a description of the facilities used; ▸ the number of species or subspecies covered and where and from whom the wildlife was acquired; ▸ a signed agreement that the standards will be followed; ▸ other information requested by the Commissioner. The Commissioner shall adopt, under chapter 14, standards for the care and treatment of captive wildlife for public display. If a violation is found notice shall be given to abate. If not abated when the time expires, the Commissioner may request the attorney general to bring an action. This section does not apply to a publicly owned zoo or wildlife exhibit, privately owned traveling zoo or circus, or a pet shop (97A.041).

A person may breed and propagate fur-bearing animals, game birds, bear, moose, elk, caribou, or deer only on privately owned or leased land with a license. Any permitted animals may be sold to other licensed game farms. "Privately owned or leased land" includes non-navigable waters shallow or marshy that are not of substantial beneficial public use. The applicant must confine the animals as approved by the Commissioner. A license may be granted only if the application is found in good faith with intention to conduct the business described and the facilities are adequate. [Details of requirements for transfer of game or fur farm license provided.] Wild animals and their offspring, of the species identified in the license, within the enclosure, are property of the fur farm licensee. A sale of live animals from a licensed farm is not valid unless the animals are delivered to the purchaser or are kept separately. The contract must be in writing. The licensee must notify a purchaser of the death of an animal within 30 days and of the number of increase before July 20 of each year. The Commissioner shall prescribe the manner that pelts and products from fur or game farms may be sold or transported; and the tags or seals to be affixed. Fox and mink may not be bought or sold for breeding or propagating unless pen-bred for at least two generations. Live beaver may not be transported without a permit. A licensee not complying subjects all wild animals on the farm to confiscation (97A.105).

★A landowner may operate a farm for breeding, raising, trapping, and dealing in muskrats. Applicants must file a signed statement describing the land, and where the farm is to be located. The Commissioner shall investigate and issue a license upon determination that the applicant is the owner and establishment of a muskrat farm will conserve natural resources. A licensee is the owner of all muskrats on the farm, and may take and trap muskrats, except by firearm or spear, and may sell and transport them or their pelts from the farm. Muskrats taken for pelts may be trapped only under permit and pelts must be tagged. Within 30 days after issuance, the licensee must post and maintain notices on posts, stakes, or enclosures on the boundary of the farm. An unauthorized person who takes muskrats from a farm is liable to the licensee for $25 and all damages. An action for the trespass and taking must be brought by the licensee. [Details of reporting requirements provided] (97A.111).★

The Commissioner may issue licenses to operate commercial and private shooting preserves if in the public interest and there are no adverse effects on wild game bird populations. Private shooting preserves only may be outside of the pheasant range. The Commissioner may adopt rules to implement this section and section 97A.121. Game released and hunted in a licensed shooting preserve must be specified in the license and is limited to adult pheasant, quail, and chukar partridge for private shooting preserves and adult pheasant, quail, chukar partridge, turkey, mallard duck, black duck, and other species designated. These game birds must be pen hatched and raised. Private shooting preserves must be 40 to 160 contiguous acres and 100 to 1,000 contiguous acres for commercial preserves. The boundaries must be clearly posted. The Commissioner may revoke a license if the licensee or persons authorized to hunt in the preserve have been convicted of a violation under this section or section 97A.121. After revocation, a new license may be issued by the Commissioner (97A.115). A person hunting released birds in a private shooting preserve must have the licenses required. No license is required to hunt authorized game birds on a commercial shooting preserve. The open season in commercial shooting preserves is continuous, and sanctioned registered field trials may be held. The open season for hunting in a private shooting preserve is designated. The Commissioner may restrict the open season after receiving a complaint, holding a public hearing, and finding that the population of wild game birds is in danger. A shooting preserve licensee may determine who is allowed to hunt, the charge for taking game, shooting hours, season, limitations, and restrictions on the age, sex, and numbers that may be taken in the preserve. These provisions may not conflict with this section or section 97A.115 and may not be less restrictive than any rule (97A.121).

Except as provided for pheasants, the Commissioner shall prescribe the minimum number of each authorized species that may be released, the percentage of each that may be taken, and shall prescribe methods for identifying birds to be released. A private shooting preserve licensed to release them may release no more than 300 adult pheasants on the area during season, with no more than 95% harvested. A commercial shooting preserve must release at least 1,000 adult pheasants. Harvested game, except ducks marked in accordance with regulations of the USFW, must be marked by the shooting preserve in a manner prescribed by the Commissioner who may issue tags to remain attached while transported (97A.121).

A preserve licensee must maintain a registration book listing the names, addresses, and hunting license numbers, if applicable, of all hunters, the date they hunted, the amount and species taken, and the tag numbers or other markings affixed to each bird, and must keep records of the number of each species raised, purchased and date and number released. The records must be open to inspection at all reasonable times (97A.121).

A person required to have a license to buy or sell wild animals, to tan or dress raw furs, or to mount specimens of wild animals, must keep records of all transactions and activities covered and submit reports [details of records and reports provided]. The Commissioner may adopt rules governing record keeping, reporting, and marking of specimens by taxidermists (97A.425). A person may not buy or sell raw furs without a fur buying and selling license, except a taxidermist and a fur manufacturer buying raw furs from a person with licenses. An employee, partner, or officer buying or selling only for a licensee may obtain a supplemental license. A nonresident must obtain a license to buy or sell raw furs, except to buy from a person licensed under section 97A.475. Applicants for a raw fur dealer's license must furnish a corporate surety bond for $1,000 payable upon violation of the game and fish laws (97B.905).

A person may not guide turkey hunters for compensation without a turkey hunter guide license. The Commissioner shall prescribe qualifications for the issuance of the licenses (97B.725).

A fish farm license is needed for raising fish for sale to be commercially processed for human consumption. A fish farm licensee may operate a private hatchery without obtaining a private hatchery license. A person operating a fish farm may not obtain fish or fish eggs outside of the state unless approved by the Commissioner, with approval or denial within 30 days after receiving a written request. If approval is denied, a written notice must state the reasons and must designate sources to obtain the fish or eggs or sell the fish or eggs from state hatcheries at market value. The Commissioner shall prescribe rules to allow a person to operate a fish farm and shall prescribe and assess a fee to cover inspection and disease certification (97C.209).

A private fish hatchery license is required for raising fish, including minnows, for sale, stocking waters, angling, or processing. The Commissioner shall prescribe rules that allow a person to operate a private fish hatchery and shall establish and assess a fee to cover inspection and disease certification. A private fish hatchery may not obtain fish outside of the state unless approved by the Commissioner. The Commissioner may apply more stringent requirements to fish or a source from outside the state than within the state, and must either approve or deny the acquisition within 30 days after a written request. Minnows acquired must be processed and not released into public waters, except as provided. If approval is denied, a written notice must state the reasons and designate sources to obtain the fish or eggs or sell the fish or eggs from state fish hatcheries at market value. A person may take fish without a license at a licensed private hatchery or an artificial pool containing fish from a private hatchery, if the operator furnishes each person a certificate prescribed by the Commissioner. The certificate must state the number and species of fish caught and other information prescribed. A person without a fishing license may possess, ship, and transport fish caught in the same manner as fish taken by a resident with a fishing license. A person may not take sucker eggs from waters for a private fish hatchery without a license. The Commissioner may not sell walleye fry for less than fair market value (97C.211).

A person may not buy or sell fish taken from state waters, except: ▸ minnows; ▸ rough fish excluding ciscoes; ▸ fish taken under licensed commercial operations; ▸ fish that are private aquatic life; ▸ fish lawfully taken and subject to sale outside the state. Largemouth bass, smallmouth bass, rock bass, muskellunge, and sunfish may be bought or sold by a private hatchery or aquatic farm, or as prescribed (97C.391).

The following licenses are required to take, buy, sell and/or transport minnows: ▸ a minnow retailer license, except as provided; ▸ a minnow retailer's vehicle license for each vehicle transporting more than 12 dozen minnows to the retailer's business, except if transported by common carrier; ▸ a minnow dealer's license; ▸ a minnow dealer's helper license; ▸ a minnow dealer's vehicle license for each vehicle transporting minnows [details provided]; ▸ exporting minnow dealer and vehicle licenses to transport minnows out of state; ▸ nonresident exporting minnow hauler and vehicle licenses (97C.501). The open season for minnows is continuous, except as provided. The Commissioner may close any state waters for commercially taking minnows to prevent depletion or extinction. A person may not take minnows from one hour after sunset to one hour before sunrise or from designated trout lakes or trout streams without a special permit. A person must use approved equipment to possess or transport minnows for sale. This does not apply to licensed aquatic farms (97C.505). A minnow dealer may take minnows with a seine not longer than 50 feet [other restrictions provided] (97C.511). [Commercial fishing in inland waters, reports, vendors, and packers are covered in 97C.811, 97C.815, 97C.821, 97C.845, 97C.861, and 97C.865.]

Import, Export and Release Provisions

★★The Commissioner may adopt emergency and permanent rules restricting the introduction, propagation, use, possession, and spread of ecologically harmful exotic species (84.9691). "Ecologically harmful exotic species" means nonnative aquatic plants or wild animals that can naturalize, have high propagation potential, are highly competitive for limiting factors, and cause displacement of, or otherwise threaten, native plants or native animals in their natural communities. A long-term statewide ecologically harmful exotic species management plan must be prepared by the Commissioner and address: ▸ detection and prevention of accidental introductions; ▸ dissemination of information about ecologically such species among resource management agencies and organizations; ▸ a coordinated public awareness campaign on ecologically harmful exotic animals and aquatic plants; ▸ a process to designate and classify such species into undesirable wild animals and aquatic exotic plants that must not be sold, propagated, possessed, or transported; ▸ control and eradication of such species on public lands and waters; ▸ development of a list of exotic wild species intended for nonagricultural purposes, or propagation for release by state agencies or the private sector. The plan must include containment strategies that include: ▸ participation by lake associations, local citizen groups, and local government in development and implementation of lake management plans; ▸ an inspection requirement for boats and equipment participating in organized events on state waters; ▸ allowing access points infested with ecologically harmful exotic species to be closed, for not more than seven days during an open water season, for control or eradication, and requiring posting stating the reason for closing; ▸ provisions for reasonable weed-free maintenance of public accesses to infested waters; ▸ notice to travelers of the penalties for violation of laws relating to ecologically harmful exotic species. By January 1 each year, the Commissioner submit a report on ecologically harmful exotic species to the appropriate legislative committees. The report must include: ▸ expenditures for administration, education, eradication, inspections, and research; ▸ an analysis of the effectiveness of management activities, including chemical eradication, harvesting, educational efforts, and inspections; ▸ the participation of other state agencies, local government units, and interest groups in control efforts; ▸ management efforts in other states; ▸ the progress made by species; ▸ an estimate of future management needs; ▸ the financial impact on persons who transport weed harvesters. The Commissioner shall establish a coordinating program to prevent and curb the spread of ecologically harmful exotic animals and aquatic plants. The program may accept gifts, donations, and grants and must seek grants through the federal Nonindigenous Aquatic Nuisance Prevention and Control Act. A portion of these funds shall be used to implement the plan. The governor may cooperate, individually and regionally, with other governors in the midwest for ecologically harmful exotic species management and control (84.967 through .969). ★★

A person may not bring live minnows into the state except as provided in this section. Transporting minnows through the state requires a permit [details provided]. A private fish hatchery licensee may transport minnows from contiguous states, provided they are used for processing or feeding hatchery fish. The Commissioner may require inspection of such minnows. A person may not transport live carp fingerlings (97C.515 and .521). A person may not transport minnows out of the state, except as provided in this section. A resident minnow dealer or a nonresident exporting minnow hauler may transport leeches, suckers, and fathead minnows out of the state. A nonresident exporting minnow hauler must possess a bill of lading issued by a minnow dealer with an exporting minnow dealer's license [details provided]. A minnow retailer transporting minnows from a place of wholesale purchase to the retailer's place of business must use the most reasonably direct route. The exporting minnow hauler must transport the minnows out of the state within 24 hours. A person may not transport minnows in a motor vehicle licensed in another state without an exporting minnow hauler's vehicle license. An exporting minnow dealer may transport minnows by common carrier and must provide on request product, quantity, and destination information (97C.525).

See also STATE FISH AND WILDLIFE AGENCIES and ANIMAL DAMAGE CONTROL.

Interstate Reciprocal Agreements

The Commissioner may enter into an agreement with game and fish licensing authorities in Wisconsin under which Wisconsin residents owning property in Minnesota may purchase annual nonresident game and fish licenses at Minnesota resident fees, provided Minnesota residents owning real property in Wisconsin are allowed to purchase identical licenses. The Commissioners of natural resources in Minnesota and Wisconsin must agree on joint standards for real property ownership, to be presented to the senate and house committees having jurisdiction over environment and natural resources (97A.045). Licenses to take fish or small game in or on boundary waters may be granted to nonresidents upon the same terms and conditions as licenses granted by the adjacent state or province to nonresidents (97A.461). The Commissioner shall not sell or issue a nonresident license outside this state (97A.472). The Commissioner may enter into agreements with North Dakota, South Dakota, Wisconsin, and Iowa, for removal of rough fish in boundary waters, which may include: contracting to remove rough fish; inspection of the work; division of proceeds; and regulating taking (97C.045).

ANIMAL DAMAGE CONTROL

A person may take mink, squirrel, rabbit, hare, raccoon, lynx, bobcat, fox, muskrat, or beaver on land owned or occupied by the person where causing damage. The animal may be taken without a license except by poison, or artificial lights in the closed season. Raccoons may be taken with artificial lights during open season. A person that kills mink, raccoon, lynx, bobcat, fox, muskrat, or beaver must bring the entire animal to a conservation officer or employee of the division within 24 hours. The Commissioner may issue permits to take protected wild animals damaging property (97B.655). The Commissioner may remove beaver from state land if the county board adopts a resolution requesting the removal (97B.661). When a drainage watercourse is impaired by a beaver dam, the Commissioner shall remove the impairment, if: ▸ the county board unanimously consents; ▸ the landowner approves; ▸ the Commissioner agrees; ▸ the action is financially feasible. The Department shall take such action including destruction or alteration of dams and removal of beaver. This does not apply to state parks, state or federal game refuges. If a beaver dam causes a threat to personal safety or property, and consent cannot be obtained, a person may petition the district court for relief, which may order the Commissioner to take action (97B.665).

★If the Commissioner determines that predators are damaging domestic or wild animals and further damage can be prevented, taking of predators shall be authorized. The Commissioner shall define the area for taking, the objectives, payments, methods to be used, and when predator control shall cease, and shall certify a predator controller if the person has not violated this section and meets qualifications of experience, ability, and reliability. The Commissioner shall pay $25 to $60 for each wolf or coyote taken. The Commissioner may require the controller to submit proof and a signed statement (97B.671). The Commissioner may issue a permit to an individual, a group of riparian owners, or a lake improvement association to apply piscicides to restore waters only if all riparian owners have consented in writing, and may set special open seasons, limits, and methods to take fish, and must post the special provisions (97C.051).★

See also Import, Export and Release Provisions under HUNTING, FISHING AND TRAPPING PROVISIONS.

ENFORCEMENT OF WILDLIFE LAWS

Enforcement Powers

The Commissioner shall execute and enforce the laws relating to wild animals, and may delegate execution and enforcement to the Director and enforcement officers. County attorneys and peace officers must enforce the game and fish laws (97A.201). An enforcement officer is authorized to: ▸ execute and serve warrants and processes relating to wild animals, wild rice, public waters, water pollution, conservation, and use of water, in the same manner as a constable or sheriff; ▸ enter land to carry out Division duties and functions; ▸ investigate violations of the game and fish laws; ▸ take an affidavit, if it aids an investigation; ▸ arrest, without a warrant, a person detected in actual violation of the game and fish laws, a provision of chapters 84, 84A, 85, 86A, 88 to 97C, 103E, 103F, 103G, sections 86B.001 to 86B.815, 89.51 to 89.61; or 609.66; and 609.68; ▸ take an arrested person before a court in the county where the offense was committed and make a complaint (97A.205).

When an enforcement officer has probable cause to believe wild animals are possessed or stored in violation of the game and fish laws, the officer may enter and inspect a commercial cold storage warehouse, hotel, restaurant, ice house, locker plant, butcher shop, and other building used to store dressed meat, game, or fish. With probable cause, the officer may enter and inspect any place or vehicle and open and inspect any package or container. An officer may inspect relevant records of any person that the officer has probable cause to believe has violated game and fish laws. An enforcement officer may, at reasonable times enter and inspect the premises of an activity requiring a license and stop and inspect a motor vehicle requiring a game and fish license (97A.215). An enforcement officer may confiscate wild animals, wild rice, and aquatic vegetation taken, bought, sold, transported, or possessed in violation of the game and fish laws or chapter 84; and firearms, bows and arrows, nets, boats, lines, poles, fishing rods and tackle, lights, lanterns, snares, traps, spears, dark houses, fish houses, and wild rice harvesting equipment used with the owner's knowledge unlawfully to take or transport wild animals, wild rice, or other aquatic vegetation. Confiscated property may be disposed of, retained for use by the division, or sold. A whole shipment or parcel and the animals therein are contraband if two or more wild animals are commingled. Confiscation of a shipment includes the entire shipment (97A.221).

★★An enforcement officer must seize all motor vehicles used to: ▸ shine wild animals; ▸ transport big game animals illegally taken or fur-bearing animals illegally purchased; ▸ transport minnows illegally. The enforcement officer must hold the seized property, subject to the order of the court, and upon conviction, the property is confiscated. At any time after seizure, it must be returned to the owner upon execution of a valid bond [details provided]. If the person is acquitted, the court shall order the property returned. Upon conviction, the court shall issue an order directed to any person that may have any right, title, or interest in, or lien upon, the seized property. [Details of court orders and disposition of property provided.] A sale under this section cancels all liens on and security interests in the property sold (97A.225).★★ Upon complaint establishing probable cause to believe that a wild animal taken, bought, sold, transported, or possessed in violation of law, or contraband is concealed or illegally kept a search warrant may be issued. Property seized shall be safely kept for use as evidence in a trial and then disposed of (97A.231).

★★Courts in counties having jurisdiction adjacent to boundary waters and enforcement officers have jurisdiction over the entire boundary waters. The courts and enforcement officers of North Dakota, South Dakota, Iowa, Wisconsin, and Michigan have concurrent jurisdiction over boundary waters (97A.235).★★

★★With approval of the proper authority of another state or the US, the Commissioner may appoint a salaried and bonded officer of that jurisdiction authorized to enforce its wild animal laws, a special conservation officer of this state. Such officer is subject to the supervision and control of and serves at the pleasure of the Commissioner, but may not be compensated and has powers and liabilities of a state conservation officer, except as directed by the Commissioner. An officer of this state may enforce wild animal laws of another state, or the US, under conditions prescribed by the Commissioner. The officer may serve under the laws of another jurisdiction to the extent they are compatible with the officer's duties. This section is effective with respect to another state or the US if there is a similar provision in effect in that jurisdiction (97A.241).★★

A person may not: ► intentionally hinder, resist, or obstruct an enforcement officer or employee of the division in performance of official duties; ► refuse inspection of firearms while in the field, licenses, or wild animals; ► refuse inspection of a motor vehicle, boat, or other conveyance while taking or transporting wild animals. In addition to criminal prosecution, the state may bring a civil action to recover damages and enjoin the violator. The civil actions may be brought by the attorney general on request of the Commissioner (97A.251).

Criminal Penalties

A prosecution under the game and fish laws may not be brought more than three years after commission of the offense. In a prosecution that alleges animals have been taken, bought, sold, transported, or possessed illegally, the burden of establishing that the animals are legal is on the defendant. Each wild animal is a separate offense. If acquitted, a person may not be prosecuted for another animal in the same incident (97A.255). Unless a different penalty is prescribed, it is a misdemeanor if that person: ► takes, buys, sells, transports or possesses a wild animal illegally; ► assists in committing the violation; ► knowingly shares in the proceeds of the violation; ► fails to perform a duty or comply with game and fish laws; ► knowingly makes a false statement related to an affidavit regarding a violation; ► violates or attempts to violate a rule under the game and fish laws. Unless prescribed otherwise, a person convicted of a gross misdemeanor under game and fish laws is subject to a fine of $100-3,000, and jail of 90 days-1 year (97A.301). Purporting to be acting in an official capacity and causing another to be injured or defrauded while falsely impersonating an enforcement or other officer, or falsely claiming to have special authority under game and fish laws, is a gross misdemeanor (97A.305). Altering a license in a material manner; knowingly making a false statement on an application for or on a license or certificate; or a license agent that knowingly issues a license to an ineligible person or predates a license is a misdemeanor (97A.311).

Violation of 97B.001, relating to trespass, is a misdemeanor except: it is a gross misdemeanor if the person: ► knowingly disregards signs prohibiting trespass; ► trespasses after being notified not to do so; ► is convicted of violating this section more than once in three years. If a person is convicted of trespassing while exercising a licensed activity or one requiring snowmobile registration, the license and registration are null and void. A person convicted of a gross misdemeanor may not be issued a license for two years (97A.315). The owner of a dog killing or pursuing a big game animal is guilty of a petty misdemeanor and subject to a civil penalty of up to $500 per violation (97A.321).

★★Buying or selling protected wild animals in violation of the game and fish laws where the sales total $300 or more is a gross misdemeanor and is subject to the penalty in 97A.301, except the fine is $3,000-10,000. Licenses possessed by a person convicted under this subdivision are null and void and they may not take wild animals for three years. Except as provided, the following is a gross misdemeanor: ► illegal buying or selling of deer, bear, moose, elk, or caribou; ► buying or selling small game or game fish where sales total $50 or more; ► buying fur-bearing animals. The following violations are gross misdemeanors: ► hunting under the influence of alcohol or controlled substance; ► use of an artificial light to locate wild animals while in possession of a firearm, bow, or other implement capable of killing big game; knowingly transporting big game illegally; ► taking or illegally possessing big game during the closed season; ► unlawfully taking, transporting, or possessing moose, elk, or caribou, pine marten, otter, fisher, or wolverine; ▸ taking fish with devices, chemicals or substances. Taking or possessing a muskellunge in violation of the game and fish laws is a misdemeanor with a fine of up to $1,000 (97A.325, .331 and .335).★★

Civil Penalties

★★A person who kills, injures, or possesses a wild animal in violation of the game and fish laws is liable for the value of the wild animal as provided in this section. The following groups of species are afforded protection: game fish, game birds, big game, small game, fur-bearing animals, minnows, and threatened and endangered species. Other species may be added after public meetings and notification of appropriate legislative committees. An enforcement officer arresting a person for killing, injuring, or possessing a wild animal illegally must describe the number, species, and restitution value of wild animals on the warrant or the notice. As part of such charge the prosecuting attorney must include a demand that restitution be made to the state for the value. Restitution is in addition to criminal penalties. If a person is convicted of or pleads guilty to killing, injuring, or possessing a wild animal in violation of the game and fish laws, the court must require restitution or state in writing why restitution was not imposed, with a copy to the Commissioner. The court may consider the economic circumstances of the person and, in lieu of monetary restitution, order conservation work representing the amount that will aid the propagation of wild animals. The amount shall be determined by a preponderance of the evidence, with consideration of the value of the wild animal under section 97A.345. The court administrator shall forward the amount to credit the game and fish fund. The Commissioner may prescribe the dollar value of species of wild animals which reflects the value to others to take the wild animal legally, the replacement cost, or the intrinsic value of the wild animals. The Commissioner shall report annually to the legislature the amount of restitution collected and the manner of expenditure (97A.341 and .345).★★

Illegal Taking of Wildlife

License Revocations and Suspensions

The license of a person convicted of a violation of the provisions relating to the license or wild animals covered is void when: ▸ a second conviction occurs within three years under a license to take small game or to take fish by angling or spearing; ▸ a third conviction occurs within one year under a minnow dealer's license; ▸ a second conviction occurs within three years for violations of 97A.425 not involving falsifications or intentional omissions of information, or attempts to conceal unlawful acts; ▸ the conviction occurs under a license not described above or is for a violation of 97A.425 not described in clause (3). Except for big game licenses and as provided, for one year after conviction the person may not obtain the license relating to the violation. A person may not obtain a license to take any wild animal for three years after conviction of buying or selling game fish, big game, or small game, and the sale is $300 or more. A person may not obtain any big game license for three years after conviction of: ▸ a gross misdemeanor relating to big game; ▸ doing an act without a required big game license; ▸ the second violation within three years relating to big game. A person convicted of a violation of provisions relating to hunting while intoxicated or using narcotics may not obtain a hunting license for five years after conviction. If the Commissioner determines that the public welfare will not be injured the Commissioner may reinstate or issue licenses to ineligible persons to: ▸ operate fur or game farms or private fish hatcheries; ▸ take or buy fish commercially [in specific named areas]; ▸ sell live minnows (97A.421).

Reward Payments

The Commissioner may pay up to a $500 reward for information leading to conviction for violation of laws relating to wild animals. A reward for information relating to big game or threatened or endangered species may be up to $1,000. Rewards may be paid only from donated funds and not to salaried conservation or peace officers (97A.245).

Intoxication Testing of Hunters

★★A person may not take wild animals with a firearm or by archery: ▸ when under the influence of alcohol, a controlled substance, a combination of any two or more elements; ▸ when the person's alcohol concentration within two hours of the time of taking is 0.10 or more; or when knowingly under the influence of any chemical compound or combination of chemical compounds that is listed as a hazardous substance and that affects the nervous system, brain, or muscles so as to impair substantially the ability to operate a firearm or bow and arrow. A person having charge or control of a firearm or bow and arrow may not permit another individual to possess it if the person has reason to believe that individual is under the influence of alcohol or a controlled substance. A peace officer may arrest for a violation under the influence without a warrant upon probable cause, whether or not committed in the officer's presence. The officer may require a breath sample for a preliminary screening test, to decide whether to arrest [details of other tests provided]. Violators are subject to the penalties provided in 97A.331. Upon conviction, and in addition to any penalty imposed, the person is subject to the limitations provided in 97A.421. The Commissioner shall notify the convicted person of the period of prohibition from hunting, and shall circulate to law enforcement agencies a list of persons prohibited from hunting. Hunting when prohibited is a misdemeanor. The state or political subdivision employing an officer authorized to arrest for violations is immune from any liability, civil or criminal, for the care or custody of the hunting equipment if the officer acts in good faith and exercises due care. A person who takes wild animals with a bow or firearm in this state or on a boundary water is required to submit to a blood, breath, or urine test for alcohol or a controlled substance. The test shall be administered at the direction of an officer authorized to arrest. The test is mandatory when requested by an officer who has probable cause and one of the following conditions exists: ▸ the person has been lawfully arrested for violating section 97B.065; ▸ the person while hunting has been in an accident resulting in property damage, personal injury, or death; ▸ the person has refused to take the preliminary screening test; ▸ the screening test and indicated alcohol concentration of 0.10 or more. If a person refuses to take a test required, none must be given, but the officer shall report the refusal. On certification by the officer that probable cause existed to believe the person had been hunting while under the influence, and refused to submit to testing, the Commissioner shall impose a civil penalty of $500 and prohibit hunting for one year. Hunting during the prohibited period is a misdemeanor. [Details provided as to informing the person of the law at the time a test is requested.] If there is probable cause to believe there is impairment by a controlled substance not subject to testing by a breath test, a blood or urine test may be required even after a breath test (97B..065 and .066).★★

HABITAT PROTECTION

In determining what critical natural habitat shall be acquired or improved, the Commissioner shall consider: ▸ significance as existing or potential habitat for fish and wildlife and providing fish and wildlife oriented recreation; ▸ significance to maintain or enhance native plant, fish, or wildlife species designated as endangered or threatened; ▸ presence of native ecological communities that are now uncommon or diminishing; ▸ significance to protect or enhance natural features within or contiguous to natural areas including fish spawning areas, wildlife management areas, scientific and natural areas, riparian habitat and fish and wildlife management projects. The Commissioner must prioritize what critical habitat shall be acquired or improved. The critical natural habitat acquired in fee title shall be designated as an outdoor recreation unit, or as provided in 97A.101 (public water reserves and management), 97A.125 (wildlife habitat on private land), 97C.001 (experimental waters) and 97C.011 (Muskellunge lakes). The Commissioner may designate any critical natural habitat acquired in less than fee title (84.944).

★★The Commissioner shall establish a Native Prairie Bank (Bank), determine where native prairie land is located, and prescribe requirements for inclusion in the Bank. "Native prairie" means land that has never been plowed, with less than 10% tree cover and with predominantly native prairie vegetation. The Commissioner may acquire native prairie for conservation by entering into easements. The easements must be conservation easements as defined [details of easement duration provided]. In the easement, the owner must agree: ▸ to place in the program eligible native prairie areas, including prairie covered by a federal or state easement that allows agricultural use and land adjacent to the prairie as determined by the Commissioner; ▸ not to alter the native prairie by plowing, heavy grazing, seeding to nonnative grasses or legumes, spraying with large amounts of herbicides, or otherwise destroying the native prairie character of the easement area, except mowing the native prairie tract for wild hay; ▸ to implement the native prairie conservation and development plan as provided, unless a requirement in the agreement is waived or modified; ▸ to forfeit rights to further payments and to refund payments received if the easement is violated when the owner has control of the land, or if the Commissioner determines that the violation does not warrant termination, the Commissioner may determine refunds or payment adjustments; ▸ not to adopt a practice that would tend to defeat the purposes of the easement; ▸ to additional provisions that the Commissioner determines. [Details of payment terms to owner provided.] To maintain and protect native prairies, the Commissioner may enter into easements that allow selected agricultural practices. [Terms of renewal and termination provided] (84.96). The Commissioner must recognize the value of native prairie land by considering the wildlife, scientific, erosion control, educational, and recreational benefits of native prairie and must plan for management, development, and restoration of prairie land under the Commissioner's jurisdiction and integrated network of protected prairie lands, prairie restoration sites, and private prairie lands. The Commissioner must develop and manage permanent prairie landscape reserves to maintain the native plant and animal populations, landscape features, and habitat types characteristic of intact native prairie ecosystems. The position of Prairie Biologist is established to plan, develop, and manage native prairie reserves and prairie land and the biologist shall be located centrally in the prairie region under the supervision of the scientific and natural areas program (84.961).★★

The Commissioner may post public hunting grounds, food and cover planting areas, game refuges, wildlife lands, and conservation area lands to indicate the management purpose and whether hunting and trapping are allowed (97A.081). The Commissioner shall allow or prohibit hunting and fishing as provided under the game and fish laws, and shall publish information on hunting and fishing on state land, including areas where taking is allowed or prohibited (97A.083). ★★All state parks are designated as game refuges. The Commissioner may designate a contiguous area of at least 640 acres as a game refuge if at least half the area is in public ownership and may designate an area in a landowner's petition as a game refuge. The refuge must be at least 640 acres unless it borders or includes a marsh, body of water, or watercourse suitable for wildlife habitat. The Commissioner may designate as a game refuge an area of at least 640 acres described in a petition by 50 or more residents of the county. The refuge may be designated only if the Commissioner finds that protected wild animals are depleted and in danger of extermination, or that it will best serve the public interest. A public hearing must be held where the majority of the area exists [details of notice provided]. The Commissioner may designate a game refuge for specified species only, and it must be posted. A state game refuge includes all public lands, waters, highways, and railroad rights-of-way within the refuge boundary and may include adjacent public lands and waters. [Details of required posting provided.] A state game refuge may be vacated or modified under the same procedures as for its establishment (97A.085).★★

Except as provided, a person may not take a wild animal, except fish, within a state game refuge, and may not carry a firearm within a refuge unless unloaded and contained in a case or broken down. The Commissioner may allow hunting of a protected wild animal species within a state game refuge during the next regular open season. Hunting in a refuge may be allowed only if the Commissioner, under prescribed rules, finds: ► the population exceeds the refuge's carrying capacity; ► it is causing substantial damage to agricultural or forest crops; ► the species or other protected wild animals are threatened by the species population; ► a harvestable surplus exists. The Commissioner may issue special permits to the owner or lessee of privately owned land within a state game refuge for trap or target shooting. Except as otherwise provided, scientific and natural areas are closed to hunting, trapping, and fishing unless: for scientific and natural areas designated before May 15, 1992, or the Commissioner allows, hunting, trapping, or fishing. The Commissioner shall designate any part of a state game refuge that is primarily a migratory waterfowl refuge, as such with a petition signed by 10 resident licensed hunters. The Commissioner shall post it, and it may not be entered during the open season unless accompanied by a conservation officer or game refuge manager. The Commissioner may designate any part of a lake that is a substantial feeding or resting area for migratory waterfowl as such and post it, with a petition signed by at least 10 local resident licensed hunters, if the Commissioner finds the petition is correct, and that adequate public access to the lake exists. A person may not enter the area during the open season with watercraft or aircraft propelled by a motor, other than an electric motor of 30 pounds thrust, or less if further restricted by the Commissioner (97A.091 through .095).

The Commissioner may designate and reserve public waters to propagate and protect wild animals after published notice and a public hearing in the county where the waters are located. The Commissioner may contract with riparian owners for water projects, and acquire land, accept local funding, and construct, maintain, and operate water level control structures. Seasons or methods of taking fish may not be restricted (97A.101). The Commissioner may acquire property by gift, lease, purchase, or condemnation and may construct, maintain, operate, and alter facilities for game farms and hatcheries (97A.131). The Commissioner may enter into agreements with landowners to develop or improve wildlife habitat on private land and provide financial, technical, and professional assistance and material (97A.125).

The Commissioner or the Commissioner of administration shall acquire and improve land for public hunting, game refuges, and food and cover planting, by gift, lease, easement, purchase, or condemnation. At least 2/3 of the total area acquired in a county must be open to public hunting. The Commissioner may designate such land as a wildlife management area for the outdoor recreation system. The Commissioner shall sell or exchange land, as approved by the executive council, for land of equal value to add to existing public hunting areas. ★On a public hunting, game refuge, or wildlife management area lands, the Commissioner may enter into agreements with nearby farmers on a sharecrop basis, for establishing or maintaining wildlife food or habitat cover. The agreements may provide for bartering for services such as weed control, planting, cultivation, or other wildlife habitat practices.★ Wildlife management areas are open to hunting and trapping unless closed by the Commissioner (97A.135 and .137).

The Commissioner shall acquire access sites adjacent to public waters and rights-of-way to connect to public highways. The land may be acquired by gift, lease, or purchase, or by condemnation with executive council approval. An access site may not exceed seven acres and only acquired where access is inadequate. Access sites may not be acquired adjacent to unmeandered public waters or surrounded by land owned and maintained for educational or religious institutions. If adjacent to public waters containing less than 200 acres within the meander lines they may not be condemned and may be acquired only if the water contains at least 150 acres within the meander lines; or the public waters are to be managed intensively for fishing. The Commissioner shall maintain the sites, easements, and rights-of-way acquired. [Details for joint agreements for maintenance and condemnation provided.] A person may not hunt on water access sites unless allowed (97A.141).

★★The Commissioner or the Commissioner of Administration may acquire wetlands and bordering areas, including marshes, ponds, small lakes, and stream bottoms for water conservation relating to wildlife development. The lands may be developed for wildlife, recreation, and public hunting. The wetlands may be acquired by gift, lease, purchase, exchange of state lands, or tax-forfeited land, and land owned by the state. The wetlands must have public access from a public road. Highest priority wetlands shall be type 3 and 4 wetlands, as defined in USFW Circular No. 39 (1971 edition). Lands purchased or leased may not be used for crops unless needed for wildlife. The Commissioner may designate such land as a wildlife management area for the outdoor recreation system. The Commissioner must notify the county town officers where the land is located. The county board must approve the proposed acquisition within 90 days. [Details on county board approval or disapproval provided] (97A.145).★★

A person may not construct or maintain a dam or other obstruction, except a boat pier, without a permit. The Commissioner may establish permit conditions for construction or modification of a fishway around or over a dam or obstruction. A person may not obstruct fish passage without permission. The person or the owner of the land must immediately remove the obstruction upon order of the Commissioner (97C.071 and .075). If all or a major part of a navigable lake is located within a single county and has been stocked with fish by the US government, the county board may erect and maintain screens at inlets and outlets. If a lake is located in more than one county, the county boards of affected counties may jointly provide for erection and maintenance of screens (97C.077). State agencies may stock fish only where there is public access. The Commissioner shall dispose of game fish eggs and fry to state hatcheries, then to private hatcheries or aquatic farms [details provided]. The Commissioner may issue a special permit to authorized US agents for fish culture operations, rescue work, and related fishery operations (97C.201, .203 and 215).

The Commissioner shall prescribe rules designed to encourage local sporting organizations to propagate game fish in rearing ponds. The rules must prescribe methods to acquire brood stock by seining public waters, by owning and using seines and other equipment and prescribe methods for stocking fish in public waters giving priority to the needs of the community and the organization operating the rearing pond (97C.205).

NATIVE AMERICAN WILDLIFE PROVISIONS

This section is to give recognition and effect to the rights of the Leech Lake Band of Chippewa Indians as preserved by federal treaty relating to hunting, fishing, trapping, and gathering of wild rice on the Leech Lake Indian reservation. These rights have been recognized and given effect by the US District Court. The state desires to settle all outstanding issues and claims relating to the above rights. Notwithstanding other law, the Commissioner shall take actions to carry out duties and obligations arising from the settlement agreement. These actions include but are not limited to: ► the exemption of members of the Minnesota Chippewa tribe from state laws relating to hunting, fishing, trapping, the taking of minnows and other bait, and the gathering of wild rice within the reservation, and from related possession and transportation laws; ► establishment of special licenses and fees for nonmembers of the tribe for hunting, fishing, trapping, or taking minnows and other bait within the reservation. All money collected for special licenses shall be credited to the Leech Lake Band and White Earth Band special license account. To effectuate the terms of the agreement, policies and procedures shall be established for the enforcement of the conservation code adopted by the band by conservation officers and for arbitration of disputes arising under the terms of the agreement. The Commissioner may enter into an agreement with the Leech Lake Band of Chippewa Indians to amend the settlement agreement to provide 5% of the proceeds from all licenses sold in the state for hunting, fishing, trapping, and taking minnows and other bait to be credited to the Leech Lake Band as mutually agreed (97A.151 and .155).

The Commissioner may enter into an agreement with the Leech Lake Indian Reservation to amend the settlement agreement by providing that in lieu of collecting an additional fee for hunting waterfowl on the Reservation, 5% of proceeds from the sale of state migratory waterfowl stamps shall be credited to the Leech Lake Reservation. The Commissioner shall not restrict aquaculture by the Leech Lake Band if it is conducted consistent with state policies, laws, and aquaculture regulations (97A.151 and .155).

This section effectuates resolution of issues between the state and the Grand Portage, Bois Forte, and Fond du Lac Bands of Chippewa Indians that relate to hunting, fishing, trapping, and gathering in the ceded area described in the September 30, 1854, treaty between the Lake Superior Chippewa and the US. [US District Court action settled in 1988 with "Memorandum of Agreement" and described in section.] The Commissioner shall take all actions necessary to carry out the duties and obligations under the Memorandum of Agreement. Powers and duties provided apply only to the extent and amount appropriated by the legislature to carry out the Memorandum of Agreement (97A.157).

The Commissioner may enter into an agreement with the White Earth Band of Chippewa Indians on substantially the same terms as the agreement adopted by section 97A.151 and 97A.155; except that the agreement shall provide that 2-1/2% of the proceeds from licenses sold in the state for hunting, fishing, trapping, and taking of minnows and other bait shall be credited to the White Earth Band as mutually agreed upon. An agreement negotiated under this section shall be for at least four years from execution (97A.161).

Money to make payments to the Leech Lake Band, the 1854 treaty area agreement, and White Earth Band special license account, is annually appropriated in a ratio of 20% from the Game and Fish Fund and 80% from the general fund (97A.165). The pelts, skins, and hides of protected wild animals taken on an Indian reservation, except the Fond du Lac reservation, may be transported, sold, and disposed of as prescribed by the Commissioner (97A.515).

MISSISSIPPI

Sources: Mississippi Code, 1972 Annotated, Title 49; 1992 Cumulative Supplement.

STATE WILDLIFE POLICY

It is declared to be the intent of the legislature to conserve, manage, develop and protect our natural resources and wildlife for the benefit of this and succeeding generations by reorganizing the natural resource and wildlife conservation functions of state government into the Mississippi Department of Natural Resources and the Mississippi Department of Wildlife, Fisheries and Parks (formerly the Mississippi Department of Wildlife Conservation) thereby providing more effective organizations through which the methods of conserving, managing, developing and protecting our natural resources and wildlife can be analyzed, coordinated and implemented (49-4-1). The ownership and title of all mussels found in or upon the fresh water bottoms within the state is declared to be vested in the state (49-9-3).

The legislature finds and declares: it is the policy of the Department to manage certain nongame wildlife for human enjoyment, scientific purposes, and to insure their perpetuation as members of ecosystems; that species or subspecies of wildlife indigenous to this state which may be found to be endangered within the state should be accorded protection in order to maintain and to the extent possible enhance their numbers; that the state should assist in the protection of endangered species or subspecies of wildlife by prohibiting the taking, possession, transportation, exportation, processing, sale or offer of such within this state of species or subspecies of wildlife listed on the US lists of Endangered Fish and Wildlife unless such actions will assist in preserving or propagating the species or subspecies; that funding may be made available to the Department annually by appropriations from the general fund or from other sources separate and apart from the Fisheries and Wildlife Fund for management of nongame and endangered species (49-5-103).

Recognizing the inestimable importance to the state and its citizens of conserving the state's wildlife resources and the desires of many citizens who wish to make a lifetime contribution to preserve our rich legacy of wildlife resources for future generations, it is the intention of the legislature to create a lifetime sportsman license and the Mississippi Wildlife Endowment Fund (49-7-151). (See Agency Funding Sources under STATE FISH AND WILDLIFE AGENCIES.)

★★The legislature finds and declares that there is a need for additional organized, accessible information to identify and make known the types and locations of plant and animal life, geological areas and other natural areas in the state, and that a system of protection and management of these areas should be implemented and maintained through voluntary action by the owners of the property on which these areas are located, and proposes a registration procedure by which owners of natural areas may voluntarily agree to manage and protect the areas according to rules of the Wildlife Commission. The purpose of 49-5-141 through 49-5-157 is also to establish a dedication procedure by which owners of natural areas may voluntarily agree to convey any or all of their right, title and interest in the property to the state to be managed and protected by an appropriate agency designated by the Commission for the people of Mississippi (49-5-143 and -145).★★   (See HABITAT PROTECTION.)

RELEVANT WILDLIFE DEFINITIONS: See Definitions section in Appendices.

STATE FISH AND WILDLIFE AGENCIES

Agency Structure

The former Commission on Wildlife Conservation has become the **Commission on Wildlife, Fisheries and Parks** (Commission), and retains all powers and duties granted to the former agency. The **Executive Director** (Director) of the **Department of Wildlife, Fisheries and Parks** (Department) may assign to the divisions powers and duties to carry out Department duties and expend funds (49-1-3).

The **Commission** is composed of five persons appointed by the Governor, with the consent of the Senate, for a five-year term. One person shall be appointed from each congressional district. The Commission elects from its membership a chairperson and a vice chairperson. The Commission shall be composed of persons with extensive knowledge of or practical experience in at least one of the matters of jurisdiction of the Commission. In addition, one shall be knowledgeable and experienced in marine fisheries management, and at least three in the management of game and freshwater fisheries (49-4-4). The former Wildlife Heritage Committee has become the **Mississippi Commission on Wildlife Conservation** (Commission) and shall exercise the duties granted under 49-5-69 through 49-5-98, and this Commission is the same as the Commission on Wildlife, Fisheries and Parks (49-5-61).

The **Department** is organized into the Office of Wildlife and Fisheries, Office of Parks and Recreation and Office of Support Services. The Department's Executive Director (Director) is appointed by and serves at the pleasure of the Governor. The Commission shall submit to the Governor three nominees for the position, from which the Governor shall appoint the Director with the consent of the Senate. The Director may assign to the offices appropriate powers and duties. The Director appoints heads of offices who serve at the Director's pleasure, and organizes the offices to carry out Department responsibilities (49-4-6). ★The **Head** of the **Office of Wildlife and Fisheries** shall have at least a bachelor's degree in a field related to wildlife conservation or administration, at least six years of experience in a field related to fisheries and wildlife management and be a well-qualified and trained administrator having full knowledge of the laws, rules and regulations pertaining to fisheries and wildlife (49-4-15). ★

★★The **Director** shall have the following minimum qualifications: a master's degree in a field related to wildlife conservation and at least six years of full-time experience in wildlife conservation, including at least three years of management experience; or a bachelor's degree in a field related to wildlife conservation or administration and at least eight years of full-time work in the wildlife conservation field, including four years of management experience; or a bachelor's degree in wildlife, fisheries or parks and recreation and eight years of experience in a management level position with direct personnel supervision responsibilities. A master's degree in wildlife, fisheries or parks and recreation will substitute for two years of experience (49-4-11). ★★

The Director, with the advice and consent of the Commission, shall appoint a **Chief Law Enforcement Officer** who shall: ▸ be qualified and experienced in administrative and law enforcement work; ▸ have been an employee of the Enforcement Division of the Bureau of Fisheries and Wildlife of the Department of Wildlife Conservation for not less than five years; ▸ supervise all **Conservation Officers**; ▸ direct the enforcement of game and fish laws of the state and Commission regulations, including cooperation with the Cattle Theft Bureau of the Department of Public Safety; ▸ instruct Conservation Officers in their duties (49-1-9).

"Conservation Officer" designates the position previously known as "warden" or "game and fish warden," and now refers to Conservation Officers of the Game and Fish Division (49-1-12). ★The Director shall appoint, with Commission approval, Conservation Officers required to enforce the wildlife, theft of cattle, trespass and litter laws, and, as moneys permit, these officers shall be located in different sections of the state where most needed. Conservation Officers shall police the state lands in their respective districts and prohibit the unlawful cutting of timber (49-1-13). Appointments of Conservation Officers shall be under Commission rules, and an appointee must be at least 21, a high school graduate or equivalent, pass the required examination, and be otherwise qualified to perform the duties of the office. The exam shall embrace the applicant's knowledge of the state game and fish, cattle theft and litter laws, and duties and responsibilities of the position. ★ Applicants, prior to performing duties, shall complete an appropriate curriculum in the field of law enforcement at the Mississippi Law Enforcement Officers' Training Academy, and shall periodically complete additional advanced courses in law enforcement (49-1-15).

★★There is a **Conservation Officers' Reserve Unit** (Reserve) to assist Conservation Officers in the performance of their duties, consisting of volunteers approved by the Chief Law Enforcement Officer, and who serve without pay. The maximum number of Reserve officers is limited to the same number as Conservation Officers. Applicants must be 21 years of age, high school graduates, in good physical condition, have a Mississippi driver's license, be in good standing with the community, be available for training and duty, not a member of any police, civil defense or private security agency, have never been convicted of a felony, and have one of the following: honorable military discharge; three years post-high school work experience requiring ability to deal effectively with individuals and groups; completion of 60 semester hours of college work; such qualifications as outlined for Enforcement Officers. Members receive a one-year temporary appointment, and must complete training and qualify on a firearms course [other requirements for training are given, including a reserve training manual and details of assignment of Reserve Officers to Conservation Officers for training and work] (49-1-16).★★

The Director, with consent of the Commission, shall appoint a qualified **Public Relations Officer** who shall make available to the public information concerning Commission rules, regulations and policies, and on game and fish conservation work, and perform other public relations duties as directed (49-1-11).

The **Attorney General** shall be counsel and attorney for the Commission and the Department and shall designate a deputy or assistant to be counsel for the Commission and Department in all actions, proceedings and hearings, and be legal advisor to the Commission and Department (49-4-21).

Agency Powers and Duties

The Commission has the power to: adopt, amend and repeal Department rules and regulations; issue Department licenses and permits; conduct hearings, gather testimony and perform other functions to carry out its powers and duties. Violations of chapter provisions or of Commission regulations are misdemeanors (49-4-35).

The Commission is authorized to publish an official magazine concerning Department activities and other matters of interest to state hunters, fishermen, boaters and other outdoors persons, and to collect a fee (49-1-35). (See also Agency Funding Sources under this section.) The Commission is authorized to acquire interests in real estate and personal property through purchase, donation, bequest or devise in furthering the purposes of 49-5-61 through 49-5-85 and otherwise. ★The Commission is authorized to lease yearly for up to 10 years campsites on its property to persons who hold leases as of June 30, 1986, provided no campsite may be leased after June 30, 2002. Lessees shall pay an annual rent equal to 5% of the fair market value of the leased land, and such lessee shall not sublease, sell, rent or devise the same [other details provided] (49-5-71).★ The Commission may execute deeds or other documents to clear up ambiguities or to make the deed conform to the parties' intent as to the estate, rights or easements (49-1-47). The Commission shall cooperate with other state departments in matters in which the interests of the respective departments overlap (49-1-49). All funds collected by the Commission and Director shall be used by the Commission for carrying out chapter purposes (49-1-51).

★The Commission's **Mississippi Museum of Natural Science** is designated the official state natural science museum within the Game and Fish Commission, and the legislature shall annually appropriate from the general fund a sum to defray not less than 100% of the expenses of the Museum (49-1-55).★

The Department is designated the agency to receive and expend federal funds received or expended by any agency transferred to the Department for matters within the Department's jurisdiction. The Department is responsible for conserving, managing, developing, protecting and coordinating the wildlife and fisheries resources of the state. The Department has the power to: ► conserve, manage, develop and protect state wildlife; ► have full jurisdiction and control over state parks; ► cooperate with other entities and agencies in developing and implementing plans for the conservation, protection, beautification and improvement of the quality of the environment and living natural resources; ► formulate Department policy regarding wildlife and fisheries within Department jurisdiction; ► apply for, receive and expend federal or state funds or contributions, gifts, devises, bequests or funds from any other source; ► conduct studies to determine alternative methods of managing and conserving wildlife and fisheries resources; ► receive the advice and counsel of the advisory committees; ► discharge other duties to implement this chapter's provisions (49-4-7 through -9).

The Director, with Commission approval, has authority to: ► close or shorten the open season in cases of urgent emergency on game birds, game or fur-bearing animals, reptiles, fish or amphibians; ► designate wildlife refuges with the consent of the property owner to secure perpetuation of any species and the maintenance of an adequate supply thereof, and for providing a safe retreat where animals may rest and replenish adjacent hunting, trapping or fishing grounds; ► acquire by purchase, condemnation, lease or agreement, gift or devise, lands or water for fish habitats, game and bird lands or fish habitats, access sites, wildlife refuges or for public shooting, trapping or fishing grounds, 25% of gross proceeds from timber sales on such lands to go into the county general fund; ► extend and consolidate lands or waters by exchange; ► capture, propagate, transport, sell or exchange species of animals for stocking state lands or waters; ► enter into cooperative agreements with persons or government agencies for purposes of this chapter; ► regulate rubbish and marsh burnings to reduce fire danger; ► conduct research in wildlife and fisheries conservation methods, and disseminate information through schools, public media and publications; ► control propagation and distribution of wild birds, animals, reptiles, fish and amphibians, the conduct of hatcheries, biological stations and state game and fur farms, the expenditures for the protection, propagation or preservation of birds and animals of funds acquired from licenses, gifts or otherwise, and of law enforcement; ► grant permits and regulate dog field trials; ► prohibit and regulate the taking of nongame gross fish, except minnows [details given for rough fish removal by the Department in levee districts of the state]; ► enter into agreements with landowners to trap beaver on those lands during open season, with permits, and allowing the landowner and trapper to enter into agreements to sell furs with these permits; ► provide open season on otter in certain counties where the Department determines that otter are depredating and injuring fish life; ► enter into agreements with landowners for trapping quail on a landowner's premises, and the purchase and distribution of quail so trapped; ► operate or lease concessions on Department owned/controlled lakes; ► charge fees, on recommendation of the Beaver Control Advisory Board, to landowners participating in the beaver control program; ► apply for and expend federal, state or local funds or contributions for the purpose of beaver control or eradication (49-1-29).

The Director has the power to: ► supervise and direct Department administrative and technical activities; ► employ, with Commission approval, professional personnel, and technical and clerical staff; ► coordinate studies concerned with the supply, development, use and conservation of wildlife, fisheries and parks; ► prepare and deliver to the legislature and the Governor an annual report, including expenditures and Department recommendations; ► enter into cooperative agreements with a federal or state agency, other public or private institutions, or any person, corporation or association; ► carry out all Commission rules and regulations and enforce licenses and permits (49-4-13).

The Director has general supervision and control of all Conservation Officers and, under the Commission's direction, shall enforce wildlife laws and regulations, and exercise necessary powers not specifically conferred on the Commission. The Director, with Commission approval, shall make an annual report to the Governor and legislature covering Commission operation. It is the duty of all Conservation Officers to enforce, obey and carry out Commission instructions for enforcement of wildlife laws and regulations (49-1-43). (See also ENFORCEMENT OF WILDLIFE LAWS.)

Agency Regulations

Commission rules, regulations and orders shall be published in newspapers of general circulation, if the rule has general application; those of special character having local application, in a newspaper with circulation in that locality. Rules of general or local application shall also be filed with the chancery clerk in each state county affected (49-1-45).

Agency Funding Sources

All moneys collected as fines or penalties for violations of wildlife laws or regulations, except as provided below, shall be paid monthly by the court, justice court judge or other collecting office as follows: 50% of fines shall be paid by the court into the treasury of the county having jurisdiction over the violations; 50% shall go to the Fish and Wildlife Fund, to pay part-time Conservation Officers; 50% of fines collected for illegal taking on a refuge or sanctuary shall go to the informer, or if none, to the officer or person making the arrest, the remainder to the county game and fish fund (49-5-51). The Department is directed to transfer all funds under its control into a special **Fisheries and Wildlife Fund** to be expended as authorized by the legislature for Department purposes. Funds from license sales, fees, fines and other revenues received by the Department shall be deposited in the fund, along with interest. The Department may expend sums authorized by the legislature for salaries, operating and maintaining equipment and for any other authorized purpose. The Department shall submit an annual budget to the legislature. Nothing herein shall be construed as requiring legislative appropriation of such fund, but expenditure shall be under authority of the budget approved and authorized by the legislature (49-5-21).

The Commission is empowered to establish the **Wildlife Heritage Fund** to be deposited in a state depository and expended by appropriation approved by the legislature. Interest earned is to go into the fund. The Commission is authorized to accept gifts or devise, lands, or money to lease or purchase any area for hunting or fishing or for preservation of any species. Such lands and waters shall be under the administration and control of the Commission until a proper plan is developed, after which the land/water shall be transferred to the control of the Department or other agency. The Commission may accept and earmark any gift or devise, lands or money on the donor's terms if not inconsistent with fund purposes (49-5-77). In addition to the hunting/fishing license fees, there shall be collected for specified nonresident licenses a fee of $5 to be used by the Wildlife Heritage Committee to purchase real estate for hunting and/or fishing areas [details given as to purchase procedure] (49-5-78). Each resident taxpayer receiving an income tax refund may designate a contribution to the fund by marking the appropriate box on the tax return. This designated money and interest shall be paid into the fund to be expended for the protection and management of nongame species, threatened or endangered wildlife or plants and unique geological formations, by purchasing, leasing, registering, dedicating and maintaining natural areas (27-7-91 through -93).

The Commission shall establish the **Wildlife Endowment Fund** to be expended by legislative appropriation, which shall consist of proceeds from the sale of lifetime sportsman licenses and interest thereon. No expenditure shall be made from the principal of the fund, which shall be invested, and the income earned from investment shall be spent in furthering the conservation of wildlife resources and Department operations (49-7-155). A resident may purchase a lifetime sportsman license to take fish (including crabs, oysters, shrimp and saltwater fish), game and fowl, except waterfowl, including deer and turkey, and to hunt with primitive weapons and bow and arrow. A lifetime fishing license entitles the holder to fish in state public waters [salt water provisions and fees provided]. A golden lifetime sportsman license shall be issued to any person who donates $1,000 to the fund [other details given as to license categories and qualifications of applicants] (49-7-153).

Assessments collected under 99-19-73 shall be deposited into a special fund designated the **Hunter Education and Training Program Fund** to defray the expenses of the program, the legislature annually appropriating in addition a sum to defray program expenses (49-1-65). The Department is authorized to establish a **MS Outdoors Fund** for proceeds from subscriptions for the Department's official magazine and the interest earned to be used to defray the publishing and related expenses (49-1-35). The Commission shall design and furnish a **State Migratory Waterfowl Stamp** (49-7-163), all revenues to go for protecting and propagating migratory waterfowl and for development, restoration, maintenance or preservation of wetlands; none shall go for administrative salaries. The Commission may enter into contracts with nonprofit organizations for part of such funds outside the US if such contracts are necessary for carrying out stamp purposes, and may enter into reciprocal agreements with other states having a state migratory waterfowl stamp (49-7-163, -167 and -169).

The cost of programs under 49-5-101 through 49-5-119 relating to nongame in need of management and endangered species shall be borne by funds or property donated or granted for such purposes and/or from funds appropriated by the legislature, provided that such donated or granted funds shall be placed in a separate **Endangered Species Protection Fund** to be spent by the Commission in its discretion. ★The Commission may have printed, issue and sell annual editions of Endangered Species Stamps, proceeds to be deposited in the fund (49-5-119).★

Agency Advisory Boards

The Commission shall appoint **Advisory Committees** for the Divisions of Parks and Recreation and of Wildlife and Fisheries to aid the Commission in formulating policies, discussing problems and considering other matters related to these divisions (49-4-7).

There is a **Beaver Control Advisory Board** (Board) composed of the administrative heads of the Department, the State Forestry Commission, Department of Agriculture and Commerce, Highway Department and Mississippi State Cooperative Extension Services. The Board chair shall be the Director of the Department. The Board has the responsibility and duty to: ▸ develop a beaver control program to be administered by the Commission or by a federal agency under an agreement with the Commission; ▸ designate state areas having the greatest need for beaver control or eradication and establish an annual list of priority areas; ▸ recommend to the Commission fees to charge participating landowners; ▸ function in an advisory capacity to the Commission regarding the implementation of the beaver control program (49-7-203).

There is a **Wildlife Heritage Committee** which is the same as the Commission, but with special duties related to the Wildlife Heritage Program. The Committee shall: ▸ utilize inventory data compiled by the program concerning state natural areas; ▸ accept on behalf of the people right, title or interest to any natural area; ▸ establish and maintain a register of natural areas; ▸ select natural areas for placement on the register or for dedication as a natural area preserve, or both; ▸ provide for the management of natural area preserves; ▸ cooperate with any state or federal agency and with private persons to implement the provisions regarding natural areas (49-5-147 and -149). (See HABITAT PROTECTION for details of the natural areas program.)

PROTECTED SPECIES OF WILDLIFE

No wild bird other than a game bird shall be pursued, taken, wounded, killed, captured, possessed or exported, dead or alive. ★★No part of the plumage, skin or body of any bird protected by this section or of any birds coming from without the state, the importation of which is prohibited into the US, shall be sold or possessed for sale in this state.★★ No person shall molest, take or destroy, or attempt to do so, nests or eggs of any wild bird, or have such in possession except under a scientific permit. This section shall not apply to game birds for which an open season is provided, or parts collected or possessed under a scientific permit, or to the house (English) sparrow, crow and starling or their nests, nor shall this section prohibit persons on their own land from killing or destroying any English sparrow, hawk, owl, jay bird, crow, or crow blackbird, or any animal by nature destructive of gardens, crops or property. This section shall not apply to introduced pheasants, which are hereby classified as domestic fowls (49-5-7). No person shall take or destroy any animal, bird, or fish, or bird's nest or egg, or fish eggs or spawn in any refuge, sanctuary, rest ground or other area closed to hunting, trapping or fishing, but an accredited state or federal government employee can take predatory animals or birds on such closed areas (49-5-19).

The Commission shall conduct investigations on nongame wildlife relating to population, distribution, habitat needs, limiting factors and other biological and ecological data to determine management measures necessary for their continued ability to sustain themselves successfully, proposed regulations and management programs. Proposed regulations shall set forth species or subspecies of nongame wildlife in need of management. The Commission shall conduct ongoing investigations of nongame wildlife and may amend regulations by adding or deleting species or subspecies of nongame wildlife. Regulations shall establish proposed limitations relating to taking, possession, transportation, exportation, processing, sale, or offer of such, to manage nongame wildlife, to become effective 60 days after proposal, during which period public comment shall be solicited, the Commission holding a public hearing if appropriate. On the basis of public comments received, the Commission may make changes in the proposed regulations consistent with effective management of nongame wildlife. Except as provided, it is unlawful to take, possess, transport, export, possess, sell, ship, or offer to do so, nongame wildlife in need of management, or for any common carrier knowingly to transport nongame wildlife (49-5-107).

On the basis of investigations on nongame wildlife and available scientific and commercial data, and after consultation with other state and federal wildlife agencies, and interested persons, the Commission shall by regulation propose a list of endangered species and subspecies indigenous to the state. Such regulation becomes effective 60 days after being proposed, during which public comment shall be solicited and a public hearing held if appropriate, after which the Commission may add to or delete from the proposed list. The state list shall be reviewed every two years, and a report submitted to the Governor giving the data used in support of all amendments to the list during the previous two years. It is unlawful to take, possess, transport, export, process, sell, ship, or offer to do so, or for a common carrier to transport or receive for shipment, species or subspecies of wildlife appearing on the list of endangered and indigenous state wildlife and on the US lists of Endangered Native or Foreign Fish and Wildlife, provided wildlife appearing on these lists which enters the state from another state or country for a destination beyond the state may be transported in accordance with any federal permit or permit issued under the laws of another state. ★In the event the US lists are modified by additions or deletions, such modifications whether or not involving species or subspecies indigenous to the state may be accepted as binding if, after the type of scientific determination described above, the Commission by regulation accepts such modification, and such regulation shall be effective upon promulgation (49-5-109).★ (See also HABITAT PROTECTION and ENFORCEMENT OF WILDLIFE LAWS.)

GENERAL EXCEPTIONS TO PROTECTION

The Commission may issue a permit to collect and possess wild animals or wild birds, or bird nests or eggs for scientific purposes, but no permit shall authorize the collection, possession, purchase or sale of migratory birds, or their nests or eggs, included in the terms of the federal Migratory Bird Treaty Act or regulations. Representatives of public educational or scientific institutions or US agencies engaged in scientific study of birds and animals may be granted any permit without enforcement or charge, and no scientific permittee is required to obtain a hunting license. Permits to take, possess, purchase or sell rare or endangered species shall not be issued except at the Commission's discretion to school, college, museum or federal or state agency representatives for scientific or propagation purposes devoted to perpetuating the species. Permits to take game or fur-bearing animals or game birds during the closed season shall not be issued except to accredited representatives or state game commission representatives. A permittee may buy, sell, possess and transport for scientific purposes animals and birds legally taken, and sell them alive for propagation or stocking purposes to another permittee. Such specimens shall be labeled as to contents, species, consignor and consignee. Permittees must file reports within 15 days of a permit expiration date. The Commission shall prescribe regulations covering the possession, sale and transportation of animals and birds for propagation purposes or raised in captivity under this section (49-1-41). A permit is required to take from state fresh waters any kind of mussels for culture or scientific investigation (49-9-5).

The Commission may permit the taking, possession, transportation, exportation or shipment of species on the state or US lists of endangered fish and wildlife for scientific, zoological, or educational purposes, for propagation in captivity, or for other special purposes. Upon good cause shown, and where necessary to alleviate damage to property or to protect human health, endangered species may be removed, captured or destroyed but only pursuant to Commission permit, and where possible, under the supervision of the Commission, provided that endangered species may be removed, captured or destroyed without permit by any person in emergency situations involving an immediate threat to human life. Provisions for removal, capture or destruction of nongame wildlife for these purposes shall be set forth in Commission regulations (49-5-111). (See also ANIMAL DAMAGE CONTROL and PROTECTED SPECIES OF WILDLIFE.)

HUNTING, FISHING TRAPPING PROVISIONS

General Provisions

Mississippi assents to the provisions of the Federal Aid in Wildlife and Fish Restoration Acts for promotion of hunter safety, and the Commission is authorized and directed to establish a course of instruction in hunter safety, principles of conservation and sportsmanship. The Commission shall prepare reports for federal assistance in the program of hunter safety, conservation and sportsmanship (49-1-57 and -59). ★The Department is authorized to purchase liability insurance to cover any officer in charge of an armory used for firearm instruction in the Mississippi Hunter Safety Program, any Mississippi certified hunter and firearm instructor while participating in the program, and any student participating in such courses (49-1-60).★ The Director shall designate a qualified hunter safety officer as administrator of this program who shall outline all phases of instruction, supervise individual programs and distribute information. ★The Commission shall appoint three hunter safety officers, one from each Supreme Court district of Mississippi.★ The Commission may construct, operate and maintain public outdoor and indoor target ranges (49-1-61 through -63). (See also Agency Funding Sources under STATE FISH AND WILDLIFE AGENCIES for the Hunter Education and Training Program Fund.) The Department shall offer a hunter education course whenever six or more residents of the same county have informed a Conservation Officer that they were unable to attend such course within the preceding calendar year, the course to be offered within the general area of their residences at no cost (49-4-27).

There is no open season on pheasant. For deer, the Department is authorized to: ► set and regulate the deer seasons on wildlife management areas; ► permit harvesting of antlerless deer; ► provide a special permit for killing deer depredating and destroying crops, to be supervised by the Department and provision made for the salvaging of the meat; ► designate state areas in which the killing by primitive firearms of any antlerless deer or other deer protected during the regular deer season may be permitted or limited. [Bag limits for deer are set in statute.] The killing of antlerless deer by a nonresident is unlawful except on lands which the nonresident owns or leases. Does and fawns are not to be killed or molested at any season except as provided to thin the existing deer stock. Spotted fawns shall not be taken or molested in any season. Raccoons and bobcats may be run, hunted, chased or pursued throughout the year with dogs by licensed hunters. The Department may establish closed seasons on running, hunting, chasing or pursuing with dogs raccoons, opossums or other wild animals or birds during turkey season in designated areas. When rabbits are depredating or destroying crops, the crop owner may shoot them with guns. There shall be no closed season on predatory animals, except the taking of animals by traps is unlawful except during the open season for taking fur-bearing animals. Beaver and coyote may be taken by trap at any time. It is unlawful to trap fox and coyote after the closed season for trapping other fur-bearing animals, except by a landowner on the landowner's own land. Open seasons, bag limits, methods of taking and hunting zones are set for bobwhite quail, turkey, deer, fur-bearing animals, rabbits, predatory animals, migratory birds, nongame gross fish, fox and coyote. It is the intent of the legislature that the open season for game birds and animals be stabilized for a minimum period of five years beginning July 1, 1990, unless some unforeseen calamity affecting the resource necessitates earlier change (49-7-31). The Commission may set the bag limits for game animals, birds and fish, unless established by the legislature by statute; this section is repealed on July 1, 1995 (49-7-41). The Commission may close all hunting and fishing within lands contracted for with the federal government as necessary, and has authority to prescribe the season for hunting or fishing therein, to issue special licenses therefor and to prescribe bag and size limits and methods for taking game fish and birds. Violation of rules or seasons is a fine of $25-100, or jail for 10 to 30 days for each offense (49-7-43). The Commission may establish closed seasons on the running, hunting, chasing or pursuing with dogs of raccoon, fox or other wild animals or birds during turkey season in designated areas (49-7-32).

Licenses and Permits

A resident between 16 and 65 is entitled to purchase a fishing license. No license is required to fish in totally landlocked private lakes with the permission of the landowner (49-7-9). A resident shall be entitled to receive a hunting license or combination hunting\fishing license. Making a false statement to obtain a resident license is a misdemeanor; fine $500-1,000; or jail three to six months; or both; and such license shall be void. Licensees must carry the license on their person while hunting, trapping or fishing (49-7-3). [A variety of license types and fees are described in 49-7-5.] Residents under 16 and 65 or older, or those with specified disabilities, and landowners hunting, fishing or trapping on their own lands need not purchase a license (49-7-5). No nonresident may hunt, fish, kill, take or trap a game animal, bird or fish without having a license in possession. The Commission shall prescribe the forms and types, determine the number to be issued, establish fees and exercise all incidental powers to develop a nonresident licensing program. Violation: misdemeanor (49-7-8). (See also Agency Funding Sources under STATE FISH AND WILDLIFE AGENCIES.) A nonresident who hunts or fishes without the required licenses is guilty of a misdemeanor and shall be fined $225-500 for the first offense and forfeit all hunting, trapping and fishing privileges for not less than one year. A second or subsequent offense is a fine of $500-1,000, or jail up to 30 days, or both, and loss of license privileges for a minimum of three years (49-7-21).

It is unlawful to take, catch or kill mussels in fresh waters without a license (49-9-5). Funds received shall be credited to the Fisheries and Wildlife Fund and used for law enforcement, propagation and biological investigation (49-9-11). It is unlawful to take mussels by dredges, drags or scoops, other than hand tongs (49-9-5). The license shall state waters closed to the taking of mussels. The Commission shall regulate boats and equipment for mussel taking, may close beds to insure propagation, allowing public notice and hearing. Violation: misdemeanor; fine $100 minimum and not more than the fee for the required license; jail up to three months; or both; and forfeiture of license for not less than one year. Conviction of taking mussels during license revocation is jail for 30 days to 6 months (49-9-9 through -17).

A resident 16 or older is entitled to receive a trapper's license with tag, and such license is required of each helper or assistant 16 or older employed or used by a trapper. No person shall trap or set a trap on lands without a prior agreement with the landowner. Every trap shall be tagged with an identification number and traps must be visited at least every 36 hours. Game Wardens may seize any traps not properly marked. No person shall set a trap within 100 feet of a street or public road. Landowners need no license to trap on their own lands (49-7-13). ★It shall be unlawful for an officer knowingly to issue a license to a person physically or mentally unfit to carry or use firearms (49-7-19).★

Except as provided, it is unlawful for a person born after January 1, 1972 to procure an annual or trip hunting license without a certification of satisfactory completion of an approved hunter education course, nor may license agents issue a license without proof of completion of such course. The Department is authorized to revoke a license and/or hunter education certification if the holder was not entitled to issuance or it was obtained by fraud. ★A resident who has not completed an approved hunter education course may purchase a special three-day hunting permit valid only when hunting in the presence of a licensed hunter over 21 and of good moral character. A person shall not be eligible to purchase more than one such permit during a lifetime. Failure of a permittee to hunt in the presence of a licensed hunter is hunting without a license and punished accordingly (49-7-20).★

The Director may designate constables as deputy conservation officers and they may be permitted to sell hunting and fishing licenses and retain the fee. Hunting, fishing or trapping licenses shall set forth a detailed description of the applicant, and must be sworn to by the applicant. A nonresident who hunts or fishes without the required licenses is guilty of a misdemeanor; fine $225-500 for the first offense; and forfeiture of all hunting, trapping and fishing privileges for a minimum of 12 months. A second or subsequent offense is a fine of $500-1,000; or jail up to 30 days; or both; and forfeiture of license privileges for a minimum of 36 months (49-7-21 and -23). It is unlawful to hunt or take migratory waterfowl without having in possession a state migratory waterfowl stamp (49-7-163). Violation: fine of $25-100 (49-7-173).

The Director shall have authority to: ► close all hunting and fishing within lands contracted for with the federal government pursuant to 49-5-23; ► prescribe the season for hunting or fishing therein; ► fix the amount of fees for special hunting licenses; ► prescribe the number of animals and game, fish and birds that shall be taken therefrom, the size, and the conditions for taking. A person violating such rules, or who shall hunt or fish at a time other than those specified, shall be fined $25-100; jailed 10-30 days for each offense (49-7-43).

Restrictions on Taking: Hunting and Trapping

Except as provided, it is unlawful to hunt, take, kill or wound, or attempt to, any game bird, animal or fish except during open season, or to have them in possession, living or dead, whether taken within or coming from without the state, except that game lawfully taken may be possessed during the open season and 60 days after, or quick frozen within 10 days of the season's close (49-7-57). It is unlawful for any restaurant, hotel, club or public eating place knowingly to have in its possession, or to offer for sale game birds, animals, or fish, whether taken within or without the state, except they may prepare and serve such game to persons who have legally killed or taken it (49-7-55). It is unlawful to buy or sell or offer such, exchange for merchandise or other consideration game birds, animals or fish or parts, whether taken within or without the state, except as permitted, and except that the skins of opossums and raccoons may be bought and sold during open season, and skins of deer may be bought and sold at any time (49-7-51). It is unlawful for any railroad or common carrier knowingly to receive for shipment or to ship any such game animals unless the hunter accompanies the same, or for a person or corporation to ship or carry, or possess with intent to do so, beyond the state limits any game bird, fish or animal except for rabbits and the furs or pelts of beaver, opossum, otter, raccoon or other fur-bearing animals during the open season and 10 days after. The offering or reception by a person within this state of birds, animals or fish for shipment from the state shall be prima facie evidence that such were killed, captured or taken within the state, and each creature transported in violation of this section is a separate offense. Nonresidents may transport lawfully taken game animals, birds and fish when accompanied by sworn affidavits. Violation: Class I violation (49-7-53). It is unlawful to pursue, chase, hunt or kill wild game or waterfowl from an aircraft (61-11-1). ★It is illegal to hunt or discharge a firearm in, on or across any street, public road, public highway, railroad or right-of-way. Violation: misdemeanor; fine $100-500; or jail 60 days to six months; or both. These provisions apply only during the calendar days included in the open seasons on deer and turkey.★ It is the duty of all sheriffs, constables, conservation officers and peace officers to enforce these provisions. It is prima facie evidence that a person is hunting if they possess a loaded firearm on a street, public road, highway or railroad in an area in which wild game is or may be present, whether or not the firearm is within or without a motorized vehicle. These provisions do not apply to a person engaged in a lawful action to protect the person's property or livestock (97-15-13).

It is unlawful to: ► hunt, chase, shoot at, or kill or pursue with this intent any wild animal or bird with firearms or similar devices or through the use of traps, nets, snares or dogs except during the open season, in the number, by the means and in the manner permitted, and then only after securing a license and a tag; ► hunt, take, kill or wound any game animal (except rabbits, opossums, raccoons or deer) or game birds, except by the aid of a dog, decoys and/or with a gun not larger than 10 gauge and fired from the shoulder; ► hunt, take, wound or shoot at game bird from a power boat, sailboat or any boat propelled otherwise than by hand, nor from any sinkbox or battery; ► wound, drown, shoot, capture, take or otherwise kill deer from a boat; ► procure a license under an assumed name or with false statements; ► lend, transfer, borrow or use the license or tag of another while hunting, trapping or fishing; ► aid in securing a license or knowingly issue a license for a person not legally entitled; ► hunt, trap, or fish after the right to do so has been denied by the Commission or the license revoked; ► hunt or trap birds, game or wild animals during the closed season. Violation of taking deer from a boat, procuring a license using false statements or hunting or trapping during the closed season is a Class II offense punishable under 49-7-143, and the Commission may revoke a license for one year for using false statements on a license application (49-7-45). Possessing a trap, fishing tackle or other device used for taking wild animals, birds or fish, or possessing the dead bodies of such, shall be prima facie evidence of hunting, trapping or fishing (49-7-49).

The Commission shall regulate and manage the taking of all alligators and alligator turtles. A combination hunting and fishing license is required to hunt, kill or catch any alligator or alligator turtle for sport, and a special permit is required for commercial purposes. The Commission shall set a fee for an annual special sporting permit, not to exceed $200, and regulate commercial trade in alligators and alligator turtles. Violation: Class I offense (49-7-47).

It is unlawful to hunt game animal or bird during the night from one-half hour after sunset to one-half hour before sunrise, either with or without the use of a light, except opossums, raccoons and fox. Violation: Class II violation. Hunting within one-fourth mile of a church on Sunday while services are being held shall be a fine of $25-100 (49-7-59 and -61). It is unlawful to: ▸ capture wild fowl or game birds by traps, nets or other contrivances except as provided; ▸ hunt, trap, take, kill, wound or capture, or attempt to do so, fur-bearing animals enumerated herein except during the open season, or to possess green pelts except during open season and for 10 days thereafter, except mink may be hunted with dogs during the fur-bearing season with a trapper's license; ▸ sell or buy, or offer to do so, the pelt of any fur-bearing animal knowing it has been unlawfully taken; ▸ use poison, explosives or chemicals in taking or killing fur-bearing animals or fish; ▸ disturb the traps of another or take any fur-bearing animals from them without the owner's permission, the offense being larceny or trespass and punishable as provided by law; ▸ needlessly disturb or destroy the nests of birds or their eggs (Violation: Class II misdemeanor); ▸ set fire to the woods or fields other than on one's own lands to drive out wild animals or birds; ▸ hunt, trap, take, frighten or kill game or fur-bearing animals forced out of their habitat by high water or fire until they have been permitted to return by recession of water or extinguishing of fire, quail being protected from hunting when the ground is covered by snow or when forced from their habitat by high water or fire; ▸ hunt, shoot or trap or trespass after having been warned not to do so, whether in person or by posting of notice (49-7-63 through -79).

See also ENFORCEMENT OF WILDLIFE LAWS.

Restrictions on Taking: Fishing

It is unlawful to take or kill game fish other than by hook and line with one or more hooks, or by use of a trot or troll line. Dip/landing nets may be used when landing a fish caught by hook and line, trot or troll lines. Shad and minnows may be taken as bait with the aid of a dip/landing net by residents for personal use. In private ponds which go dry in summer, dip nets may be used for capturing or rescuing game fish. It is unlawful to kill or take fish by mudding, or by lime, poison, dynamite, India berries, weeds and walnuts, giant powder, gunpowder or other explosive, and no nongame gross fish shall be taken by nets, seines or trap for personal use without a commercial fishing license. It is unlawful to: ▸ place nets or seines in a stream obstructing the passage of fish except as specified; ▸ catch or destroy fish by the use of dynamite, gunpowder or other explosive substance; ▸ use a telephone, battery or other electrically operated device for taking or capturing fish; ▸ use a chemical in a stream or lake where the public fishes for the purpose of killing or taking fish, except for private pond owners in their own ponds; ▸ poison fish by mingling in the water a substance calculated and intended to stupefy or destroy fish. Violation: Class I violation (49-7-81). It is unlawful to fail to return immediately to the water game fish taken by net or seines or other contrivances used for taking of nongame fish (49-7-83). It is unlawful to sell, offer to sell, or exchange game fish enumerated in this chapter, whether taken within or coming from without the state. The Commission may issue a permit to the owner of a private pond to sell fish the owner grows. It is unlawful for a fish dealer to buy, sell, or offer to do so, or knowingly to possess game fish enumerated in this chapter, whether taken within or coming from without the state (49-7-87 and -89). It is illegal to possess illegal nets, wire baskets, slat baskets or fishing equipment for taking fresh water fish, regardless of location, without a permit within 10 days after such equipment is acquired and before use (49-7-99).

★★It is not unlawful to drive, force or dig a fox out of the ground or to scare, knock or shoot one out of a tree or to fell a tree in which there is a fox, provided the owner's consent has been given for felling the tree. It is unlawful to hunt, trap or kill a fox, wild bird or animal with the aid of bait, recordings of bird or animal calls or electrically amplified imitations of calls. Use of liquid scents for any animal or bird and the use of electrically amplified sound devices for hunting coyote and crow shall be permitted. Hunting of coyote is restricted to daylight hours as specified for hunting other game animals and during open seasons for other species, using firearms, ammunition and archery equipment legal during that season, provided that landowners, agricultural leaseholders or their agents may take coyote at any time on lands owned/leased by them. The Commission, upon written petition, may establish a closed season or forbid the killing of fox when the animal may be exterminated in certain areas; unless established, no closed season shall exist. The Commission may relax the restrictions regarding the use of scents, lures or sound devices if a condition arises that may endanger persons or livestock in a certain community, county or area. Persons may at any time shoot, trap or otherwise kill fox or coyote that may be injuring or catching their poultry, lambs, pigs or other domestic animals (49-7-33).★★

★Whenever the beginning of a game season falls on a Sunday, the season shall begin on the preceding Saturday (49-7-35). A resident who is licensed to take any legal game bird or animal with the use of firearms has those same privileges to take by falcons or hawks in compliance with state and federal guidelines, and by bow and arrow or primitive firearms subject to provisions of law. Special bow and arrow hunting seasons are set as specified, and seasons on public hunting areas, game refuges or prescribed areas having surplus deer populations may be extended. Bow and arrow hunters may kill an antlerless deer which shall not be counted against the bag limit otherwise set by law★. A special primitive firearms deer and small game season is set in statute, and the use of such weapons to kill antlerless deer or other deer protected during the regular deer season is prohibited, except in areas the Commission designates. The Commission may make regulations concerning special seasons for the use of falcons, hawks, bow and arrow and primitive firearms. The use of dogs is prohibited for hunting deer during such special hunting seasons. Persons hunting deer with bow and arrow or primitive firearms shall have a special resident archery and/or primitive firearms license in addition to a regular resident hunting license. Violation: Class II violation (49-7-37).

It is lawful with a Commission permit to train bird dogs through the use of release pens and tamed and identified quail. Tamed quail shall be identified with tags or dye, and permits shall be displayed openly upon each release pen. The Commission may set regulations governing the training of bird dogs and the taking of birds, which may be recaptured through the use of release pens (49-7-42).

Commercial and Private Enterprise Provisions

A fur dealer who regularly buys fur-bearing animals from trappers or hunters, shall have a license in possession when engaged in the business of fur dealer. Persons who regularly buy fur-bearing animals from trappers or hunters are authorized to possess inventories of dried or stretched furs and skins. However, dealers or other fur buyers are authorized to buy, transport, sell or offer for sale inventories of fur for only 90 days beyond the close of the trapping season. The Commission may require tagging of furs to account for harvest of a species in a specific location and dealers must maintain records of purchases, such records and fur houses to be open to Conservation Officers for inspection without warrant. Persons acquiring fur for the sole purpose of tanning, dressing, manufacturing or otherwise preparing finished fur products are authorized to buy, sell, possess and transport fur inventories and finished fur products for these and related purposes (49-7-16).

The Department shall license wholesale minnow dealers, but residents growing minnows on their own property shall be exempt. It is unlawful to sell minnows at wholesale within the state without a license, and each sale in violation shall be a Class I violation. Nonresident minnow dealers shall apply for a similar license (49-7-29).

Any person, firm or corporation may engage in propagating pen-raised quail for commercial sale for consumption and may sell either live quail or carcasses within or without this state with a commercial quail breeder's license. Records must be kept and packages labeled for shipment by a public or private carrier. Records shall be open to inspection by any Commission agent or peace officer. Violation: misdemeanor; fine $100-500. Multiple violators shall be assessed fines near the maximum allowable limits and may have their license suspended for one year. "Quail" means all species of native North American quail and coturnix quail. "Pen-raised" quail is one hatched from an egg laid by a quail confined and raised in a pen by a licensed quail breeder (49-13-3 through -23). Nothing herein shall be construed to require a person who raises quail for personal consumption to secure a commercial quail breeder's license, provided the person shall not raise more than 100 quail in a calendar year (49-13-25).

The Commission is authorized to issue licenses or permits to privately owned and operated shooting preserves and to make regulations. Each shooting preserve shall contain a minimum of 100 acres in one tract of leased/owned land and shall not exceed 640 acres. Preserves confined to releasing ducks may operate with a minimum of 50 acres including water area. Exterior boundaries must be clearly posted. Each license shall designate whether the preserve is open to the public on a commercial basis, or is restricted to a membership or limited group. Other licenses may be required as specified. To give a reasonable opportunity for a fair return on a sizeable investment, the shooting preserve season shall be for seven months. Game which may be hunted on shooting preserves shall be artificially propagated pheasants, quail, chukar partridges, mallards and black ducks, and game bird species designated by the Commission. Mallards and black ducks must be marked by a hole punched in the web of the right foot before age six weeks. The license shall entitle holders and guests to recover the total number of each species of game birds released on the premise each year, and licensees may establish their own limits on age, sex and number of species to be taken by each person. Any wild game found on shooting preserves may be harvested in accordance with applicable game and hunting laws pertaining to open seasons, bag and possession limits. Records must be kept by operators, and certificates issued to persons leaving the preserve with quail carcasses, such records to be open for examination by Commission representatives. ★Licensees must consent to the patrolling of shooting preserves by Commission agents without warrant to determine if any game laws are being violated.★ Violation: Class II violation; a multiple violator shall be assessed a fine near the maximum allowable limit, and license may be suspended for one year (49-11-1 through -27).

Import, Export and Release Provisions

It is unlawful for a person to import or cause to be imported a live skunk, or to sell, barter, exchange or otherwise transfer a live skunk, provided that this does not apply to zoos or research institutions, nor does it prohibit the sale of live skunks to persons outside the state by a skunk farmer approved by the USDA. Violation: misdemeanor; fine up to $500; or up to 90 days jail; or both (75-40-1 and -3).

Interstate Reciprocal Agreements

The Commission is authorized to negotiate with Louisiana and Arkansas to effectuate a reciprocity agreement with one or both, providing that the hunting and fishing licenses and regulations shall be acceptable and recognized by the commissions of the participating states when hunters/fishermen hold a license issued by their state of domicile when hunting in the Mississippi River or when hunting waterfowl on the river or adjoining levees. For all counties lying wholly or partially within the Mississippi levee district and bordering upon that river, and having a population over 5,000 persons, the Commission is authorized to effectuate a reciprocity agreement with Arkansas and Louisiana permitting hunting waterfowl and other migratory species, deer, squirrels, turkeys, quail and rabbits in/on the Mississippi River and adjacent lakes and lands and similar arrangements for the Pearl River where it forms a boundary between Louisiana and Mississippi (49-7-133 and -135).

ANIMAL DAMAGE CONTROL

The Department is authorized to cooperate with the US Bureau of Biological Survey in the taking, killing and destruction of predatory animals that are destructive to game birds, animals and livestock. The Department may pay its proportionate share of the expenses/salary of the agents of such survey out of Fisheries and Wildlife Fund moneys (49-5-35). The sum of $25,000, or so much thereof as be necessary, is appropriated out of money in the Commission treasury for eradicating rabies among foxes in any county when the Board of Health or the Commission determines the disease is prevalent (49-5-37). The Commission may issue permits to kill species of animals or birds which may become injurious to agricultural or other interests, but a hawk or owl while committing depredations upon poultry may be killed without a permit, and all species of blackbirds, cowbirds, and grackles may be killed without a permit when such birds are committing or about to commit depredations on shade or ornamental trees or agricultural crops (49-1-39).

There is a beaver control program developed by the Beaver Control Advisory Board and administered by the Commission with the advice of the Board or administered by a federal agency pursuant to Commission agreement. The program is limited to the control or eradication of beavers on private or public lands, excluding federally-owned lands but including lands whereupon easements are granted to a federal entity. State, local or private funds available to fund the program shall be used to match federal funds, and the Commission may execute agreements with any federal agency to obtain such funds. Nonfederal funds may be obtained from legislative appropriations, charges on participating landowners, contributions from participating counties and contributions from other sources. A county desiring to participate in the program shall contribute $2,000. County contributions may be matched by nonfederal funds available to the state for the program (49-7-201). (See Agency Advisory Boards under STATE FISH AND WILDLIFE AGENCIES.)

See also EXCEPTIONS TO PROTECTION.

ENFORCEMENT OF WILDLIFE LAWS

Enforcement Powers

Mississippi is a member of the Gulf States Marine Fisheries Compact.

A violation or attempt to violate provisions of this chapter, or any wildlife law or regulation is a misdemeanor. Sheriffs, deputy sheriffs, constables and peace officers are ex-officio special conservation officers and have the duty to aid in enforcement. It is the duty of the Conservation Officer, sheriff, constable and city, town and village officers within the county to arrest, with or without process, a person whom they know or have good reason to believe is violating game refuge provisions and take them before a justice of the peace. ★Private persons may arrest a person violating the above section in their presence (49-5-43). It is the duty of each district attorney and county prosecuting attorney to prosecute and defend all causes arising under the provisions of this chapter, or any wildlife law or regulation in which the state is a party or has an interest. Circuit judges shall give grand juries the provisions of the wildlife laws and urge strict inquiry into all violations (49-5-45).★ No person called as a witness shall be excused from testifying on the ground that the testimony sought might incriminate the person, but the person shall not be prosecuted for an offense about which called upon to give testimony (45-5-49). (See also Agency Funding Sources under STATE FISH AND WILDLIFE AGENCIES for disposition of fine moneys.) ★In addition to regulations and statutes relating to protection and preservation of wildlife and the environment, Conservation Officers are authorized to assist in the detection and apprehension of violators of state laws which pertain to the theft of cattle, to unauthorized dumping of garbage, obstructing streams and littering, as set forth in the sections specified, in addition to any other powers and duties delegated or assigned (49-1-44). The Department shall distinctively mark all vehicles used by Conservation Officers to enforce game and fish laws, but may use unmarked vehicles when identifying marks would hinder official investigations (49-4-35).★

The Director and each Conservation Officer shall have power to: ► execute all warrants and search warrants for violations of game and fish laws and regulations; ► serve subpoenas issued for the investigation or trial of offenses against wildlife laws or regulations; ► search with probable cause to believe that animals, birds or fish, or parts, or nests or eggs or spawn are possessed in violation of law or regulation; ► examine without warrant the contents of a boat, vehicle, box, locker, creel, game bag or other package on probable cause to ascertain whether wildlife laws or regulations have been violated; ► with a search warrant, search and examine the contents of a dwelling house or other building of a person suspected of violating the provisions of this chapter and to seize all animals, birds, fish, parts and hold subject to Commission order; ► arrest, without warrant, a person committing a violation in the Director or conservation officer's presence; ► arrest a person without warrant for an indictable offense, or a breach of the peace threatened or attempted in their presence, on any state game management area, park land, forest land or any lands/waters owned or managed by the Commission, or when a felony has been committed on such lands and there is reasonable grounds to believe the person committed it, or on a charge made upon reasonable cause of the commission of a felony by the party, and with the Director's or Governor's approval, to aid and assist a peace officer of this state or any other state in the capture of a fugitive from justice who may be found in or on such lands; ► exercise other powers of peace officers in the enforcement of wildlife laws or regulations or of a judgment for violation. In all cases of arrest without warrant, the officer must inform the accused of the object and cause of the arrest, except when the accused is in actual commission of the offense or is arrested on pursuit. ★No Conservation Officer shall compromise or settle out of court any violation of this chapter's provisions or any law or regulation for the protection of wild animals, birds or fish (49-1-43).★

★★Upon notification by a law enforcement officer of a death or injury by a weapon used by a person hunting, a Department Hunter Safety Officer shall immediately initiate an investigation and submit a report to the Director who may submit such report to the Commission. If the Commission determines there is probable cause to believe the accident occurred as a result of culpable negligence, it shall notify the appropriate District Attorney (49-4-31).★★

The edible portions of game or fur-bearing animals, game birds, and fish seized under the wildlife code shall be disposed of to hospitals, charitable institutions and alms houses. Skins or pelts of fur-bearing animals, taken illegally, may be seized and sold by Department order, the funds received to be paid into the Fisheries and Wildlife Fund. Nongame birds or parts and plumes or skins of foreign game birds shall be disposed of by gift to scientific institutions, or kept by the Department for scientific or educational purposes, or may be destroyed. Officers disposing of such animals, birds, fish or parts shall keep receipts, and the Department shall keep a permanent record of such gifts (49-1-37).

Criminal Penalties

Unless a different penalty is specifically prescribed, one who violates a law or regulation for the protection of wildlife, or who fails to perform a duty imposed, or who violates or fails to comply with a lawful order, rule or regulation is guilty of a Class III violation punishable by a fine of $25-100. In addition, such person is liable, at the court's discretion, to an additional penalty of $25 for each animal, bird or fish or part, or each nest or egg of a bird taken, possessed, or transported in violation of law or regulation. Killing a doe deer, a wild turkey hen except as permitted, a turkey out of season or baiting turkeys, unlawfully trapping quail or other game birds is a Class II violation, punishable under 49-7-143. A person transporting, shipping or carrying quail or other game birds within, or to without, this state, without having Director permission, shall, except as provided, be fined not less than $100 (49-7-101).

A person convicted of a Class I violation shall be fined $500-1,000, be jailed for 5 to 15 days, and forfeit all hunting, trapping and fishing privileges for a minimum of 12 months. In addition, a person convicted of violating 49-7-51 or 49-7-53 (unlawful sale/shipment of fish, birds, game and fur-bearing animals), may, at the court's discretion, be fined $100 for each game bird or game fish or part bought, sold, offered for sale, exchanged for consideration, received for shipment, shipped, transported, carried or possessed with the intent to ship, transport or carry (49-7-141). Any person convicted of a Class II violation shall be fined $100-500, jailed for 60 days to six months, or both (49-7-143).

Illegal Taking of Wildlife

Any firearm, equipment, appliance, conveyance or other such property used directly or indirectly in the hunting, capturing or killing of deer at night with a headlight or other lighting device, or in fishing for, killing or capturing fish by using a telephone, magneto, battery or other electrically operated device, including, but not limited to, a truck, automobile, motor vehicle, trailer, jeep, boat, airplane, net light, battery electrical device, or which may be used in the transportation of deer taken, at night with or by means of a headlight or other lighting device, or fish killed, stunned, captured or taken by using electrically operated devices shall be seized by any Department employee or other law officer including a sheriff or deputy sheriff, and proceedings instituted pursuant to 49-7-251 through 49-7-257 (49-7-103). [Extensive details of the forfeiture procedure are given in 49-7-251 through 49-7-257.]

Every violation of hunting on a preserve or sanctuary as specified in 49-5-5 is a fine of $150-300, and jail for 10 to 30 days. ★For every subsequent violation, the fine is $300-500, and jail 10 to 30 days, which sentence shall be served and not suspended, and the person for two years thereafter shall be forbidden to hunt or obtain a license for birds or game in the county of conviction and in the management area within which the refuge was located. No person convicted of a subsequent violation of the above section shall be allowed to hunt or receive a license to hunt for birds or game in the state for two years thereafter.★ Trespassing on a game or fish refuge is a misdemeanor; fine $100-250; jail up to 30 days. Unless a different penalty is prescribed, a person who violates game refuge provisions, or a law or regulation for the protection of wildlife, or who fails to perform a duty imposed by such laws or regulations, or who fails to comply with a Commission order, rule or regulation is guilty of a misdemeanor, and shall be fined $25-100 (49-5-39).

A person who violates provisions of 49-5-107 regarding the illegal taking, shipment or possession of nongame wildlife in need of management or who violates regulations or terms of any permit issued thereunder shall be fined up to $500, or jailed up to six months, or both. A violation of 49-5-109 or 49-5-111 relating to the illegal possession, taking or shipment of endangered species shall be fined $1,000, jailed up to one year, or both. All law enforcement and management officers of the Commission and other law enforcement officers authorized to enforce state laws are authorized to enforce the nongame and endangered wildlife provisions, and may, without warrant, arrest a person who there is probable cause to believe is violating, in the officer's presence or view, such section, regulation or permit, and may search such person or business records at the time of arrest and seize wildlife, records or property taken, or used in connection with such violation. Equipment, merchandise, wildlife or records seized shall be held pending disposition of court proceedings, and thereafter forfeited to the state for destruction or

Mississippi

disposition. Wildlife so seized may be given to a qualified zoological or scientific institution for safekeeping with costs assessable to the defendant (49-5-115).

None of these provisions shall apply retroactively or prohibit importation of wildlife which may be lawfully imported into the US or taken/removed from another state, or prohibit possession, transportation, exportation, processing, sale or shipment of endangered wildlife in this state but not in the state of origin, if the person possessing same can show evidence of lawful taking or possession. This shall not be construed to permit the possession, transportation or sale of wildlife on the US endangered lists except as permitted herein (49-5-117).

A person convicted of killing deer out of season shall be fined not less than $100, and the Commission may revoke the license for one year (49-7-93). ★A person who hunts or takes deer by headlighting or by any lighting device shall be guilty of a Class I violation, shall be punished under 49-7-141, shall forfeit all hunting, trapping and fishing privileges for not less than three consecutive years from the date of conviction and shall attend such courses prescribed by the Commission. This does not apply to deer killed in an accident with a motor vehicle (49-7-95).★ A public officer who wilfully fails to perform a duty imposed by law or by Commission rule or regulation is guilty of a misdemeanor, and shall be fined $100-500, be jailed up to 6 months, or both. A person who swears or affirms to a false statement on a license application for hunting, fishing or trapping is guilty of a misdemeanor and shall be fined $100-500, and such license shall be null and void (49-7-97).

License Revocations and Suspensions

The Commission may revoke a hunting, trapping or fishing license or deny a person the right to such license for one year if the person has been convicted of the violation of a provision of this chapter or any regulation thereunder. Notice and hearing before the Commission must be provided before revocation. A second conviction during any 12 consecutive months for violation of laws with respect to game, fish, nongame fish or animals shall result in forfeiture of a license, which shall not be reissued for one year. Failure to surrender a license upon demand by the Commission shall be a misdemeanor. ★A violator whose license has been revoked and is apprehended within the next 12 months for hunting or fishing without a license shall have a mandatory jail term of 30 days to 6 months (49-7-27). (See also Illegal Taking of Wildlife under this section.)★

HABITAT PROTECTION

★★All state lands whether held in fee or in trust are declared forest reserves and wildlife refuges so long as the state owns them, and no wildlife shall be taken except under Commission regulations. Every public park, golf course and playground up to 50 acres shall constitute a sanctuary or preserve for the protection and propagation of bird and animal life. The State Land Commissioner, with the consent of the Attorney General and the Commission, is authorized to lease for up to 20 years the cut-over, swamp and overflowed lands belonging to the state and unsuitable for cultivation, for establishing game and fish preserves, but the lease of such land for game preserves shall not be applied to less than 1,000 acres of contiguous lands. Such lease shall provide that the lessee of the cut-over or swamp shall not cut timber for commercial purposes or permit waste on the lands and shall not include the right to mine the oil, gas and minerals. As a consideration for the lease, the Land Commissioner shall contract that the lessee shall protect the state's interest in the timber growing. Nothing in this subsection shall prevent the homesteading of any lands so leased (49-5-1). ★★ The Board of Supervisors of any county may add additional territory to any bird and game preserve or sanctuary by an order defining the boundaries, and such additional territory shall be subject to all chapter provisions (49-5-3). It is unlawful to hunt with gun or dog on a sanctuary or preserve, or to rob or destroy the nests of birds, or to catch, snare, trap or net birds within such limits, and a person found with gun or dog on such areas shall be prima facie presumed to be hunting in violation of this section (49-5-5). (See also HUNTING, FISHING, TRAPPING PROVISIONS.)

The Commission may purchase within 10 years land for the construction and maintenance of game and fish management projects or game and fish hunting and fishing refuges (49-5-11). The Commission shall have authority to adopt rules regulating public hunting and fishing in any wildlife conservation management projects or refuges, and may collect fees for hunting and fishing therein [details given as to land acquisition procedure] (49-5-13). The Commission may contract with any county in which such game and fish management project or refuge is located for joint support and maintenance, and may use revenues from timber sales, mineral leases, donations or permit fees for hunting/fishing (49-5-15). ★The Commission may enter into agreements with counties and use federal funds or moneys from other sources for the construction and operation of lodges on Commission lands (49-5-16).★ Bonds may be issued by any town or county to secure funds to purchase lands and to construct game and fish management projects under the Commission's direction (49-5-17). Refuge boundaries shall be posted by the Commission, and orders closing such areas to hunting or fishing must be published (49-5-19). Mississippi consents to the acquisition by the federal government by purchase, lease or gift of lands for the establishment of national migratory bird refuges, and shall retain concurrent jurisdiction with the US in and over such lands (49-5-29). The Federal Migratory Bird Treaty Act and regulations thereunder are made a part of this chapter (49-5-31). The US Commissioner of Fisheries has the right to carry on fish-cultural activities within the state (49-5-33).

Whenever the Commission desires to construct a dam in/across a lake, stream, river or other waters under its control to prevent or control the deterioration or drying up of such waters, and such construction could cause the level of such waters to rise and cause flooding of adjacent properties, the Commission shall have the power to acquire such flooded property from the owner thereof by purchase, grant, donation or by eminent domain (49-1-33). ★★The Commission shall establish programs, including acquisition of land or aquatic habitat, for management of nongame and endangered wildlife and may enter into agreements with federal agencies, political subdivisions or private persons for administration and management of any area established under this section or used for management of such wildlife. The Governor shall review other state programs and to the extent practicable utilize such programs in furtherance of these purposes, and shall encourage other state and federal agencies to do so also (49-5-111).★★

★The owner of any natural area on the Register of Natural Areas established under provisions of the Wildlife Heritage Program may register the natural area by executing a voluntary agreement with the Wildlife Heritage Committee for the owner to manage and protect the area according to Committee rules and to give the Committee first option to purchase (49-5-153). "Natural area" shall mean an area of land, water or air, or combination, which contains an element of the state's natural diversity, including, but not limited to, individual plant or animal life, natural geological areas, habitats of endangered or threatened species, ecosystems or any other area of unique ecological, scientific or educational interest (49-5-147). The registration agreement may be terminated by either party after 30-day written notice (49-5-153). The Committee shall publish and revise at least annually a Register of Natural Areas using the inventory of areas compiled by the Wildlife Heritage Program (49-5-151).★

★★The owner of any natural area may dedicate it as a natural area preserve by executing with the Committee articles of dedication which shall transfer such portion of the owner's estate to the Committee for the people of Mississippi. The Committee shall agree to no articles of dedication which do not provide for the protection, preservation and management of the natural area consistent with the intent and purposes of 49-5-141 to 49-5-157. The articles of dedication shall contain provisions: for the management, custody and use of the natural area preserve; defining the rights and privileges of the owner and the Committee or managing agency; as the owner or Committee deem necessary (49-5-155). A natural area preserve is held in trust by the state for present and future generations and shall be managed and protected according to Committee rules. A natural area preserve is declared to be at the highest, best and most important use for the public. The Committee shall inspect such dedicated areas at least annually to insure that the terms of the articles of dedication are being respected (49-5-157).★★ [Additional definitions and details of the Wildlife Heritage Program are given in 49-4-141 through 49-4-157.] (See also Agency Advisory Boards under STATE FISH AND WILDLIFE AGENCIES.)

NATIVE AMERICAN WILDLIFE PROVISIONS: None.

MISSOURI

Sources: Missouri Constitution; Vernon's Annotated Missouri Statutes, 1990, Chapter 252; 1992 Cumulative Annual Pocket Part.

STATE WILDLIFE POLICY

The ownership of and title to all wildlife of and within the state, whether resident, migratory or imported, dead or alive, are hereby declared to be in the state of Missouri. A person who fails to comply with or who violates this law or rules and regulations shall not acquire or enforce any title, ownership or possessory right in wildlife; and a person who pursues, takes, kills, possesses or disposes of the wildlife, or attempts to do so, shall be deemed to consent that the title of wildlife shall be and remain in the state of Missouri, for the purpose of its control, management, restoration, conservation and regulation (252.030). (See also HABITAT PROTECTION.)

RELEVANT WILDLIFE DEFINITIONS: See Definitions section of Appendices.

STATE FISH AND WILDLIFE AGENCIES

Agency Structure

The control, management, restoration, conservation and regulation of bird, fish, game, forestry and state wildlife resources, including hatcheries, sanctuaries, refuges, reservations and all other property owned, acquired or used for such purposes and the acquisition and establishment thereof, and the administration of all laws pertaining thereto, is vested in a **Conservation Commission** (Commission), consisting of four members appointed by the Governor, with the advice and consent of the Senate, not more than two of whom shall be of the same political party. The members shall have knowledge of and interest in wildlife conservation, and shall hold office for six years. The Commission may acquire by purchase, gift, eminent domain or otherwise, all property necessary, useful or convenient for its purposes. The Commission shall appoint a **Director of Conservation** (Director) who, with its approval, shall appoint assistants and other employees. The Commission shall fix the qualifications and salaries of the Director and all employees (Mo. Const. art. IV, sec. 40, 41 and 42). (See also 252.002 of code.)

Agency Regulations

The rules and regulations of the Commission shall become effective not less than ten days after filing with the Secretary of State and such final rules as are judicial or quasi-judicial in nature shall be subject to judicial review provided in section 22 of article V. The Commission shall supply to all persons on request printed copies of its rules and regulations (Mo. Const. art. IV, sec. 45 and 46).

Agency Funding

★★For the purpose of providing additional moneys to be used by the Commission for the control, management, restoration, conservation and regulation of the bird, fish, game, forestry and wildlife resources of the state, including the purchase or other acquisition of property for said purposes, and for the administration of the laws for those purposes, an additional sales tax of one-eighth of one percent is levied and imposed upon all sellers for the privilege of selling tangible personal property or rendering taxable services at retail in this state upon the sales and services which are listed in and subject to the provisions of and to be collected as provided in the "Sales Tax Law," except as to the amount of the tax. An additional use tax of one-eighth of one percent is levied and imposed for the privilege of storing, using or consuming an article of tangible personal property set forth and collected as provided in the "Compensating Tax Law," except as to the amount of the tax (Mo. Const. art. IV, sec. 43).★★

The moneys arising from the additional sales and use taxes provided for in section 43(a) and all fees, moneys or funds arising from the operation and transactions of the Commission and from the application and administration of the laws and regulations pertaining to the bird, fish, game, forestry and wildlife resources of the state and from the sale of property used for said purposes, shall be expended by the Commission for the control, management, restoration, conservation and regulation of the bird, fish, game, forestry and wildlife resources of the state, including the purchase of property. The moneys shall also be used by the Commission for payment to counties for the unimproved value of land in lieu of real property taxes for privately owned land acquired by the Commission after July 1, 1977 and for land classified as forest cropland in the forest cropland program of the Department (Mo. Const. art. IV, sec. 43). All moneys payable under the provisions of sections 252.010 to 252.240 shall be transmitted to the Department of Revenue, to be credited to the Conservation Commission, the State Treasurer to report monthly to the Commission the exact amount of money in the Commission's funds (252.050).

PROTECTED SPECIES OF WILDLIFE

No wildlife shall be pursued, taken, killed, possessed or disposed of except in the manner, to the extent and at the time permitted by rules and regulations, and pursuit, taking, killing, possession or disposition, except as permitted by rules and regulations, are prohibited. A violation is a misdemeanor, except that violation of rules and regulations pertaining to recordkeeping requirements of licensed fur buyers/fur dealers shall be an infraction and a fine of $10-100 (252.040).

GENERAL EXCEPTIONS TO PROTECTION: None.

HUNTING, FISHING, TRAPPING PROVISIONS

General Provisions

★It is unlawful to cause any deleterious substance to be placed, run or drained into state waters in quantities sufficient to injure, stupefy or kill fish at or below the point where a substance was thrown, run or drained, provided that it shall not be a violation for persons engaged in industry to cause or permit water subject to their control or used in a branch of such industry to be so discharged under such precautionary measures as have been specifically approved by the Commission.★ Violation: misdemeanor (252.210). ★It is unlawful to place an explosive substance or preparation in state waters where fish may be killed, injured or destroyed; and no person by such means shall kill, catch, or take fish from the waters, provided that explosive substances or preparations may be used in the waters with the permission and under the supervision of the Commission.★ Violation: felony; fine $200-1,000; jail up to two years; or both (252.220).

It is unlawful to place or cause to be placed or erected a seine, screen, net, weir, fish dam or other obstruction in or across the waters, rivers, creeks, or other state watercourses in a manner as to obstruct the free passage of fish. Violation: misdemeanor; fine $10-100; and costs of prosecution (252.200). It is the duty of a person owning, operating, or using a dam across any river, stream or creek to erect and maintain a durable and efficient fishway or other such device to enable fish free passage up and down the waters at all times, such fishway to be approved by the Commission. ★Whenever the height or nature of the dam precludes the installation of a fishway, the Commission is authorized to require the establishment and maintenance of a fish hatchery for the purpose of stocking the waters above and below the dam, the plans, adequacy and operation of the hatchery to be subject to Commission approval. The Commission may take fish from the hatchery for distribution to state public waters. A violation or refusal to build a hatchery in lieu of establishing a fishway is a misdemeanor and a fine of $100-300 for each violation.★ The duties and liabilities imposed by this section shall devolve and be imposed upon the president, secretary, or local agent of the corporations involved (252.150).

ANIMAL DAMAGE CONTROL: None.

ENFORCEMENT OF WILDLIFE LAWS

Enforcement Powers

It is the duty of all sheriffs, marshals, constables and their deputies, other peace officers, and prosecuting attorneys and their assistants, within their respective counties, and the city of St. Louis, to aid diligently in enforcing the provisions of the law and all rules and regulations (252.070). An authorized Commission agent shall have the same power to serve criminal process as sheriffs and marshals, in cases which are violations of this law and Commission rules/regulations, and shall have the same right as sheriffs and marshals to require aid in the execution of process.

Agents may arrest, without warrant, a person caught by them whom they have good reason to believe is violating, or has violated, the law or rules/regulations, and take the person before an associate circuit judge or a court having jurisdiction (252.080). Authorized agents of the Commission who are certified as peace officers under chapter 590 are officers of the state and shall be so deemed and taken in all courts having jurisdiction of offenses against state laws. Agents have full power and authority as peace officers when working with and at the special request of the sheriff of a county or the chief of police of a city or the highway patrol superintendent, except that the Commission agent who is working in a county as provided in this section and section 252.225 (telephone network for violation reports) and at the request of an agency other than that of the county sheriff shall notify the sheriff of the county where the request originated. Agents shall have authority to arrest, without warrant or process, a person who they have probable cause to believe has committed or is in the process of committing any violation of the Missouri laws, on lands owned, operated, managed or leased by the Commission, and shall have similar arrest powers for violations of other designated statutory sections, except that no arrest may be made without a warrant for the commission of a misdemeanor committed outside the presence of the agent except upon complaint of the landowner upon whose land the alleged violation occurred (252.085). An authorized Commission agent, sheriff, marshal or deputy may commence proceedings against a person for violation of wildlife laws, rules or regulations. Officers may search, without warrant, any creel, container, gamebag, or boat in which there is reason to believe wildlife is unlawfully possessed or concealed, but must have a warrant to enter and search an occupied dwelling and adjacent outbuildings, motor vehicle, or sealed freight car, and then only in the daytime (252.100).

★Prosecutions for violation of these laws, rules and regulations shall be commenced within one year from the violation, either by indictment, complaint or information (252.120).★ ★Whenever upon conviction the person convicted fails to pay the fine and costs imposed, the person shall be committed to the jail of the county or of the city of St. Louis or to some workhouse and shall be confined one day for each two dollars of the fine, and not more than 20 days for costs adjudged, unless paroled by provisions of law for criminal cases (252.130).★ ★It is the duty of a judge or court clerk before whom a prosecution under sections 252.010 to 252.240 is commenced, within 20 days after the trial or a dismissal, to report in writing the result and fine amount to the Commission (252.140).★

Criminal Penalties

It is the duty of a person holding a license or permit issued pursuant to any rules and regulations to submit it for inspection by an agent of the Commission, or by a sheriff, marshal, constable or deputy; refusal to comply upon proper demand is a misdemeanor (252.060). Violation of the provisions of sections 252.010 to 252.040 wherein other specific punishment is not provided and violation of the rules/regulations relating to wildlife is a misdemeanor with a fine up to $500, or jail up to three months, or both (252.230). It is the duty of a warehouse, merchant or common carrier to permit a Commission agent to examine any package which the agent suspects or believes contains any wildlife not lawfully transported or possessed. Refusal to permit inspection is a misdemeanor and fine of $50-150 (252.090). Obtaining a certificate, license or privilege from the state or from a licensing organization by deceit is a misdemeanor (252.160).

Illegal Taking of Wildlife

★It is unlawful to solicit by correspondence, printed cards, circulars, shipping tags, advertisement or otherwise, illegal shipments, consignments or delivery of wildlife, contrary to state laws and regulations, or to aid or abet a conspiracy to violate the laws, rules and regulations. Violation: misdemeanor; fine $10-100 (252.170). ★ ★A person to whom is consigned wildlife, the taking, transportation, sale or possession of which is prohibited or not permitted by law, rule or regulation, shall upon receipt immediately notify the Commission and safely keep the wildlife in possession or under control subject to Commission order. Violation: misdemeanor; fine $5-50 (252.180).★

Possession or control of wildlife, except in the manner, to the extent and at the times permitted by this chapter and rules and regulations, is a misdemeanor, and any Commission agent, sheriff, or marshal is permitted and authorized to take and confiscate the wildlife (252.190).

The sale of fish or wildlife, or parts, including eggs, which have been taken or possessed illegally is prohibited. A violation of this section is a class A misdemeanor for the first offense if the sale is less than $150. A second or subsequent offense is a class D felony if the sale is less than $150. A violation of the provisions of this section is a class C felony for the first and all subsequent offenses if the sale is more than $150 (252.235). The importation, transportation, or sale of an endangered species of fish or wildlife, or hides or other parts, or the sale or possession with intent to sell an article made in whole or in part from the skin, hide or other parts of an endangered species of fish or wildlife is prohibited. A publicly owned and operated zoo shall be exempt from the provisions of this section, nor shall provisions apply to legally acquired wildlife held under permit or to wildlife legally taken in another state. Violation: class B misdemeanor (252.240).

License Revocations and Suspensions

The Commission may suspend, revoke or deny a hunting permit or privilege for a maximum of five years when a person, while hunting, inflicts injury by firearm or other weapon to another person who is mistaken for game. An opportunity for a hearing before the Commission is afforded. Anyone determined by the Commission to have inflicted injury by firearm or other weapon shall be required to successfully complete a Department-approved hunter safety course before their hunting permit is restored (252.043).

Reward Payments

★The Department may maintain a telephone service operating at all times, capable of receiving and recording reports of violations of sections 252.010 to 252.240 and of rules and regulations. The service shall receive reports over a single, statewide toll-free number. All reports and records made pursuant to this section shall be confidential. Information shall only be made available to: appropriate Department staff; a grand jury, prosecuting attorney or law enforcement officer involved in the investigation of the above sections or rules or regulations or in other court proceedings involving those statutory sections or rules and regulations; a person engaged in research with the Director's permission, provided that no information identifying a person in the report shall be made available to the researcher, or a person who is the subject of a report of a violation under this section. Violation of this section or unauthorized dissemination of information contained in reports or records is a class A misdemeanor. Filing a false report is a class B misdemeanor and a fine of up to $500. All information made available to another person or institution outside the Department shall be disclosed to the subject of the report, except that the Department may obscure/remove the name of the person who made the report (252.225).★

HABITAT PROTECTION

No motor vehicle shall be operated within the boundary of land owned, leased or managed by the Commission except upon roads, thoroughfares or areas specifically designated for travel by the Commission. Unless specifically posted by the Commission, the speed limit within the lands should be 45 miles per hour. Swimming, camping, shooting, fires, use of firearms, digging, tree stands, horses, pets, cave exploring, the operation and parking of motor-driven land conveyances and aircraft are permitted only where, when and in the manner specifically authorized by the Commission on all wildlife refuges, wildlife management areas, state forests, natural areas, lakes, fishing accesses and all land and waters owned, leased or managed by the Commission (252.045).

★It is the intent of sections 252.300 to 252.333, "The Missouri Economic Diversification and Afforestation Act of 1990," to address environmental, economic, and social programs with a long-term, integrated strategy that will result in soil conservation, improved water and air quality, enhanced wildlife habitat, increased job opportunities, and reduced social problems, to the benefit of all citizens of the state of Missouri (252.300). The Department shall develop, in cooperation with various state and federal agencies, agriculture departments, and private industry councils, an agroforestry program. The program is designed to complement a new or extended federal conservation reserve plan which allows and encourages the development of a state program of agroforestry, and shall encourage soil conservation and diversifications of the state's agricultural base through the use of trees planted in lanes with grass strips or row crops or both in between the lanes (252.303). Payments are to be made to landowners who have eligible land, susceptible to soil erosion, which is placed in the federal conservation reserve program to encourage participation in the program and to encourage tree planting to reduce erosion and restore habitats (252.306 and .309).★

NATIVE AMERICAN WILDLIFE PROVISIONS: None.

MONTANA

Sources: Montana Code Annotated, 1979, Title 87; 1991 Replacement Volume.

STATE WILDLIFE POLICY

The Legislature finds and declares: it is the policy of this state to manage certain nongame wildlife for human enjoyment, for scientific purposes, and to insure their perpetuation as members of ecosystems; species or subspecies of wildlife indigenous to this state which may be found to be endangered should be protected in order to maintain and enhance their numbers; the state should assist in the protection of species or subspecies of wildlife which are deemed to be endangered elsewhere by prohibiting their taking, possession, transportation, exportation, processing, sale or offer for sale, or shipment within this state unless such actions will assist in preserving or propagating the species or subspecies (87-5-103). ★It is the policy of this state to protect and preserve game animals primarily for the citizens of this state and to avoid the deliberate waste of wildlife and destruction of property by nonresidents licensed to hunt in this state (87-3-303).★ It is the policy of Montana to protect, conserve, and manage grizzly bear as a rare species of Montana wildlife (87-5-301).

RELEVANT WILDLIFE DEFINITIONS: See Definitions section of Appendices.

STATE FISH AND WILDLIFE AGENCIES

Agency Structure

The **Director of Fish, Wildlife and Parks** (Director) is appointed by the Governor subject to Senate confirmation, and serves at the pleasure of the Governor. The Director is also the Secretary of the **Fish and Wildlife and Parks Commission** (Commission), which consists of five members, one from each district, appointed by the Governor and subject to Senate confirmation. At least one member must be experienced in the breeding and management of domestic livestock (2-15-3401 and 3402).

Agency Powers and Duties

The **Department of Fish, Wildlife, and Parks** (Department) shall: ▸ supervise all game of the state; ▸ possess all powers necessary to fulfill the duties prescribed by law and to bring actions in the proper courts for enforcement of the fish and game laws and rules adopted by the Department; ▸ enforce laws of the state respecting the protection, preservation, and propagation of game; ▸ have the exclusive power to spend for the protection, preservation, and propagation of game all state funds collected or acquired for that purpose. Money from the sale of seized game or hides, from fines or damages collected for violations of the fish and game laws, from appropriations, or received by the Department from any other sources are appropriated to the Department. The Department may: ▸ dispose of all property owned by the state for the protection, preservation, and propagation of game and which is of no further use to the state, the proceeds from the sale to be credited to the fish and game account in the state special revenue fund; ▸ issue permits to carry firearms except to regularly appointed officers or wardens; ▸ promulgate and enforce such rules as will accomplish the purpose of chapter 2; ▸ promulgate rules relative to tagging, possession or transportation of bear within or without the state (87-1-201). ★The Department shall pay bounty claims for predatory wild animals, as approved by the Board of Livestock, out of fish and game funds other than those from license fees, not exceeding $7,500 per calendar year (87-1-206).★ The Department is authorized to establish checking stations to inspect licenses of hunters and fishermen and any game animals, fish or fur-bearing animals in their possession. Failure to stop, report, and allow inspection at a checking station on one's route of travel is a misdemeanor (87-1-207 and -208).

With Commission consent, and with approval of the Board of Land Commissioners in the case of land acquisition of more than 100 acres or $100,000 in value, the Department may acquire land, waters or easements by purchase, lease, agreement, gift or devise and may develop, operate, and maintain the same: ▸ for fish hatcheries, nursery ponds, or game farms; ▸ for game restoration, propagation or protection; ▸ for public hunting, fishing or trapping areas; ▸ to capture, propagate, transport, buy, sell, or exchange game; ▸ for state parks and outdoor recreation; ▸ to extend and consolidate by exchange lands or waters suitable for these purposes. The Department may dispose of these lands and waters after public notice [terms of notice are set forth in detail] (87-1-209). The Department may enter into cooperative agreements with educational institutions and government agencies to: promote wildlife; train persons for wildlife management; develop management and demonstration projects; and may establish an educational and biological program for collection and diffusion of statistics (87-1-210).

The Department may: ▸ acquire by gift, purchase, capture, or otherwise any fish, game, game birds or animals for propagation, experimental or scientific purposes; ▸ provide for the importation of game birds, game and fur-bearing animals, and for the protection, propagation, and distribution of imported or native birds and animals; ▸ use fish and game funds for construction, maintenance, and operation of fish hatcheries, game farms, or other property for the protection and propagation of game; ▸ appropriate moneys for the extermination of predatory animals that destroy game; ▸ spend funds necessary to introduce and propagate wild waterfowl food, securing expert advice as to kinds of waterfowl foods adapted to state climate, soil, and waters (87-1-221).

The Department shall plan, direct and compel construction of fish ladders upon dams and other stream obstructions; may purchase and maintain fish screens, or other devices to prevent fish entering irrigation ditches; may construct and maintain fish nurseries and rearing ponds; may control the waters of any lake, pond, or stream to breed and propagate game fish, after notification to the Department of State Lands (87-1-222 and -223).

★The Legislature finds that management through hunting of wild buffalo (bison) is not appropriate but that significant potential exists for the spread of contagious disease to persons or livestock and damage to persons and property by wild buffalo. Departmental duties, therefore, for management of wild buffalo are: responsibility for developing rules to manage wild buffalo that threaten persons or property other than through contagious disease; development of rules to manage and reduce the number of buffalo that leave Yellowstone National Park. The Department of Livestock shall regulate wild buffalo that pose a threat to persons or livestock through contagious disease. Both departments are strongly urged to enter into an agreement with the National Park Service for long term management of the Yellowstone herd, and to take court action if the agreement does not come about in a timely manner (87-1-215).★

The **Director** shall carry out Commission policies and adopt rules to implement the policies. The Director may appoint a Deputy Director and a sufficient number of wardens for proper enforcement of the fish and game laws and rules. With the Attorney General, the Director shall compile, print and distribute the fish and game laws as soon as practicable after adjournment of the Legislature (87-1-401, -404 and -405).

The **Commission** shall: ▸ set policies for protection, preservation and propagation of the wildlife, fish, game, fur-bearers, waterfowl, nongame species and endangered species of the state and for fulfillment of other Department responsibilities; ▸ establish hunting, fishing and trapping rules; ▸ establish rules governing the use of lands under Department jurisdiction; ▸ establish wildlife refuges and bird and game preserves; ▸ approve all acquisitions or transfers of Department interests in land or water; ▸ review and approve the Department budget and small construction projects; ▸ adopt and revise rules regarding the type of archery equipment for hunting and fishing (87-1-301). The Commission may adopt and enforce rules governing uses of lands acquired or held under easement by the Commission or which it operates under agreement with a federal or state agency or private owner and recreational uses of all public fishing reservoirs, lakes, rivers and streams or those operated under agreement with a state or federal agency or private owner (87-1-303). The Commission may: ▸ fix seasons, bag and possession limits; ▸ open, close, shorten or lengthen seasons on any species of game, bird, fish, or fur-bearing animal; ▸ declare areas open and times for hunting deer, antelope, elk, moose, sheep, and goat by bow and arrow; ▸ declare areas open to deer and\or elk, and limit methods of taking; ▸ declare special seasons and issue special licenses to maintain an adequate supply of game birds, fish or animals, or when such animals are causing damage to property or when written complaint has been made (see also ANIMAL DAMAGE CONTROL); ★▸ adopt rules governing use of livestock and vehicles by archers during special seasons;★ ▸ divide the state into fish and game districts; ▸ declare closed or open seasons in any of those districts to hunting, fishing or trapping; ▸ declare a closed season on any species of game threatened with undue depletion from any cause and later open the area with consent of a majority of property owners affected; ▸ authorize the Director to open or close any special season upon 12 hours notice to the public; ▸ declare certain fishing waters closed to fishing except by persons under 13 years of age (87-1-304).

The Commission may: ▸ establish and close to hunting, trapping, or fishing any game, bird, or fish refuge on public lands, and with the consent of the owner, on private lands; ▸ close streams, lakes or parts to hunting, trapping or fishing; ▸ establish game refuges in which game may breed and replenish, upon petition, notice, public hearing and proper showing that the action is in the best interest of the wildlife within the area; ▸ designate and protect certain areas as havens for resting, feeding and breeding for migratory birds in which hunting and molestation are forbidden (87-1-305). The Commission shall provide open and closed seasons, means of taking, shooting hours, tagging requirements for carcasses, skulls and hides, possession limits, and requirements for transportation, exportation and importation of grizzly bear (87-1-302). The Commission shall review and approve annually the nongame wildlife programs recommended by the Department for funding from the nongame wildlife account, provide for public comment, and adopt rules governing the use of that account (87-5-122).

Agency Regulations

Department orders, rules and regulations shall be published and take effect after publication and posting (87-1-202 and -203).

Agency Funding Sources

★There is a **River Restoration Special Revenue Account** within the state special revenue fund, consisting of all proceeds earmarked for this account and gifts, grants, reimbursements or appropriations from any source intended to be used for this account. Funds may be spent only to carry out the River Restoration Program (87-1-258). [Certain specified amounts from certain licenses are deposited in this account.]★

Except as provided, all money received from sale of hunting and fishing licenses or permits, sale of seized game or hides, damages collected for violations of the fish and game laws, appropriations, or any other state source must be placed in the **State Special Revenue Fund** for the Department. Interest earned must go into the fund to credit the Department's: general license account; license drawing account; and accounts established to administer upland game bird enhancement programs, protection, conservation and development of wetlands and management of mountain sheep and moose, to be spent only by the Department, subject to legislative appropriation. No license fees shall be used or taken for any other purpose than the administration and use of the Department (87-1-601 and -710). Except as provided, all money received from fines and forfeited bonds, except money collected by a justice's court, relating to fish and game violations must be credited to the Department in a state special revenue fund account, minus costs of prosecution which go to the county. Money from the sale or lease of interests in Department lands must go into an account within the nonexpendable trust fund of the state treasury. The interest only may be used for operation, development, and maintenance of Department real property (87-1-601).

★The **Fish and Wildlife Mitigation Trust Fund** is separate and apart from all public money or state funds, administered by the Department and consists of: ▸ money received under Department agreements, contracts, or authorizations for the purpose of fish and wildlife mitigation or enhancement; ▸ any gift, donation, grant, legacy, bequest or devise made for the purpose of fish and wildlife mitigation or enhancement; ▸ any interest, earnings or income of the fund; ▸ property or easements acquired through fund expenditures. Fund money may be spent for fish and wildlife mitigation or enhancement pursuant to written agreement, contract, authorization, or terms of a gift, donation, grant, legacy, bequest, or devise (87-1-611 and -612).★

There is a **Nongame Wildlife Account** in the state special revenue fund. Money collected and interest earned must be used, with Commission approval, for research and education programs on nongame wildlife in Montana and any management programs for nongame wildlife approved by the Legislature, except money cannot be used for purchase of real property or in a way that interferes with production on or management of private property (87-5-121). (See also HABITAT PROTECTION and License and Permits under HUNTING, FISHING, TRAPPING PROVISIONS for big game license auctions.)

Agency Advisory Boards

The **Fish and Wildlife Crimestoppers Board** shall recommend to the Department individuals to be rewarded for providing information used in detecting and combating fish and wildlife-related crimes, the amount of the rewards, and means for promoting the program (87-5-603). (See Reward Payments under ENFORCEMENT OF WILDLIFE LAWS.)

PROTECTED SPECIES OF WILDLIFE

It is a misdemeanor to shoot, trap, kill or capture, or attempt such, any marten, sable, otter, mink, muskrat, beaver, fisher, Canada lynx, or black-footed ferret until an open season is set on any of these animals. The furs and hides of such animals legally taken during the open season may be possessed, bought, and sold at any time, except as provided. Muskrats and beavers may be taken during the closed season by permit if these animals are doing severe injury to an irrigation project or stock water pond, no permit being required from June 1 to August 31 (87-3-501).

The Department shall conduct ongoing investigations on nongame wildlife to develop biological and ecological data to determine management measures so that nongame wildlife will have continued ability to sustain itself successfully. On the basis of these determinations, the Department shall issue management regulations listing species or subspecies in need of management and may amend these regulations, on the approval of the Legislature, by adding or deleting from the list. Regulations shall establish proposed limitations to taking, possessing, transporting, exporting, processing, selling, or shipping of nongame wildlife (87-5-104 and -105).

Based on investigations, data and consultation with agencies and interested others, the Department shall recommend to the Legislature a list of species and subspecies indigenous to the state determined to be endangered within this state. The Department may propose legislation to include specifically any species or subspecies appearing on the US list of endangered native or foreign fish and wildlife. The Department shall review the state list of endangered species every two years and may propose specific legislation to amend the list. Except where provided, it is unlawful to take, possess, transport, export, sell or offer for sale, and for any common or contract carrier knowingly to transport or receive for shipment, any species or subspecies appearing on any of the following lists: list of wildlife indigenous to the state determined to be endangered within the state; any species or subspecies included by the Department and appearing on the US list of endangered native fish and wildlife. Any such species may be transported through the state to a point outside the state in accordance with other state or federal permits. Modification to the US list may be accepted by the Legislature. The Director shall establish programs, including acquisition of land or aquatic habitat, deemed necessary for management of nongame and endangered wildlife, and may enter into agreement to administer such areas (87-5-107 and -108).

Violation: misdemeanor; first conviction, up to $250 fine; second conviction, up to $500 fine; jail up to 30 days, or both; subsequent convictions, $500-1,000 fine; jail up to six months. Wildlife may be seized and transferred to an appropriate institution for safekeeping, and forfeited upon conviction. None of these provisions either apply retroactively; prohibit importation into the state of wildlife which may be lawfully imported into the US or lawfully taken or removed from another state; or prohibit entry or possessing, transporting, exporting, processing, selling or shipping of species or subspecies endangered in this state but not in the state where taken. This section does not permit the possessing, transporting, exporting, processing, selling or shipping within the state of wildlife on the US list of endangered native species (87-5-111 and -112).

See Raptors under HUNTING, FISHING, TRAPPING PROVISIONS.

GENERAL EXCEPTIONS TO PROTECTION

Any bear, wolf, tiger, mountain lion or coyote that is captured alive to be later released or held in captivity for any purpose must be reported to the Department within three days. Failure to report is a misdemeanor. Each animal must be permanently tattooed or identified, and any death, escape, release, transfer or other disposition must be reported. If any such animal causes any damage to the personal property of another person, compensation must be paid by the animal owner. The provisions applying to tattoo and compensation requirements for animals in captivity, which have been captured alive to be later released, do not apply to animals captured and released as part of an ongoing game management or predator control program unless such animals have been involved in livestock killing, or to those captured and released as part of a scientific, educational or research program (87-1-231, -233 and -234).

Under a scientific investigation permit which may set time limits and restrictions on numbers, representatives of accredited institutions of learning or government agencies investigating a scientific subject may take any protected species, and may take protected or unprotected species by any means other than dynamite, taking no more than necessary. Qualifications may be set for applicants and special authorizations and restrictions may be placed on any permit (87-2-806).

The Department may issue avicultural permits for taking, capturing, and possessing migratory game birds for propagation (87-2-807). The Director may permit taking, possessing, transporting, exporting or shipping of species or subspecies on the state list of endangered species and on the US list of endangered native or foreign species for scientific, educational and zoological purposes, for propagation in captivity, or for other special purposes. Upon good cause shown, endangered species may be removed, captured or destroyed pursuant to permit, and when possible, with Director supervision, or without permit in emergency situations involving an immediate threat to human life. The Department shall issue regulations to carry out these sections (87-5-109 and -110).

HUNTING, FISHING, TRAPPING PROVISIONS

General Provisions

Except as provided in regulations, it is unlawful to take, possess, transport, export, sell or offer for sale nongame wildlife deemed by the Department to be in need of management, or for any common or contract carrier knowingly to transport or receive for shipment such nongame wildlife (87-5-106). ★Except as provided, all birds, animals, fish, heads, hides, teeth, or other parts (except grizzly bear) seized or acquired by the Department may be sold at public auction after notice. Grizzly bears parts seized may be donated to museums, educational institutions, government agencies, or scientific studies approved by the Commission. If approved by federal law, parts may be sold at public auction, if after Commission approval, a reasonable attempt has been made to dispose of the parts. Certificates of sale will be issued; only one carcass of deer, elk or moose may be bought; and unsold carcasses may be donated to public or charitable institutions. Resale of heads, hides, pelts or mounts is not prohibited. Money obtained from sale of such property shall be paid to the court before whom the property owner is prosecuted. If convicted, sale money shall be deposited in the fish and game fund; if not convicted, the money will go to the person prosecuted. No officer shall be liable for damages from any search, seizure, examination or sale. If the person or place of taking cannot be ascertained, the money goes to the state treasurer (87-1-511 through -513).★

Licenses and Permits

It is unlawful to: ► take game animals, birds, or any fur-bearing animal; ► take, kill, trap, or fish for any fish; ► have, keep, or possess any game animal, bird, fur-bearing animal, fish or parts, except as provided; ► have, keep, possess, sell, purchase, ship, or reship any imported or other fur-bearing animal or parts without first obtaining a proper license or permit from the Department; ► trap or snare predatory animals or nongame wildlife without a license if a nonresident. It is unlawful to apply for, purchase or possess more than one license of any class or more than one special license for any one species listed in 87-2-701, unless otherwise specified (87-2-103 and -104).

A hunting license may not be issued without presenting a certificate of competency as provided. ★A bow and arrow license may only be issued to those who can present an archery license issued in a prior season or a certificate of completion of a safety course from the national Bowhunter Education Foundation.★   The Department shall provide a course in the safe handling of firearms, may cooperate with a reputable organization which promotes firearm safety, and shall provide for a course from the national Bowhunter Education Foundation (87-2-105).

Except as provided, it is unlawful to purchase any hunting, fishing or trapping license without first obtaining a wildlife conservation license. Hunting, fishing and trapping licenses must be affixed to the conservation license, and it is unlawful to sell hunting, fishing and trapping licenses without presentation of the conservation license. Funds from the license go into the Department special revenue fund. False statements on the license application are unlawful (87-2-201 through -205).

Except as provided, a resident or nonresident age 12 or older may purchase a license to take upland game birds, cranes, rails, snipes, and mourning doves and possess their carcasses as authorized. The Department may issue wild turkey tags to holders of licenses, entitling the holder to hunt and kill one wild turkey and possess the carcass thereof, during open season times and places. Three-day, nonresident shooting preserve licenses are available to hunt or kill game on a shooting preserve (87-2-401 through -404). It is unlawful for any person age 15 or older to take waterfowl without first obtaining a waterfowl stamp. The Department shall contract with an art publisher for selection of a Montana artist's design for the annual waterfowl stamp and arrange for the sale of the art. Funds from sale of stamps and related artwork must be expended only for protection, conservation and development of wetlands in Montana (87-2-411 and -412).

Unless otherwise provided, a resident age 12 or older may purchase an elk, deer, black or brown bear license, entitling the resident to pursue, hunt, shoot, and kill the game animal authorized by the license, and to possess its carcass. [Classes of licenses are set forth.] Subject to certain limitations, one who owns or is purchasing 640 acres or more of contiguous land, at least some of which is used by elk, in a hunting district where certain licenses are awarded shall be issued a license (87-2-501). [Nonresident classes of licenses and big game combination licenses are set forth in 87-2-504 and 87-2-505.] Except as provided, a license may be issued to take mountain lion and possess the carcass under Department rules. The Department may prescribe by rule the number of licenses to be issued, may restrict them to region, district or other area, and may specify species, age, sex and time periods for taking. All licenses shall provide tags, coupons or markers as the Department prescribes, which shall be filled out and attached to the animal taken, so that it can be possessed, used, stored, and transported. It is unlawful to fail to cut, fill out or attach such tags during possession (87-2-506 through -509).

[Classes of] licenses are available for applicants indicating their intent to hunt with a licensed outfitter or resident sponsor on land owned by the sponsor, with a certificate from the outfitter or sponsor that they will: ► direct the hunting and advise applicant of the game and trespass laws; ► submit complete records to the Department; ► accept no consideration for services, except as provided in this title; (if a sponsor) the sponsor is a landowner and the hunting will be within land boundaries (87-2-511). Except as provided, a resident age 13 or older may purchase a license to trap fur-bearing animals and hunt bobcat, wolverine and Canada lynx at times and places and in such manner designated in the license. The same type of licensing is available to a landowner, tenant, or an immediate family member on land owned or leased. A nonresident may purchase a trapper's license to trap and snare predatory animals and nongame wildlife only after October 15. If a nonresident's state does not also sell nonresident trapper's licenses to Montana residents, the nonresident may not get a Montana nonresident trapping license. Licensees must obtain owners' permission to trap on private property (87-2-601 through -604).

Applicants age 12 or older who hold a resident or nonresident wildlife conservation license may apply for a special license for the following animals: moose, mountain goat, mountain sheep, antelope, grizzly bear, black or brown bear. If the licensee kills a grizzly bear, a trophy license shall be purchased within ten days to possess and transport the bear (87-2-701). ★One who has killed any game animal, except a deer or an antelope, during the current license year may not receive a special license to hunt a second animal of the same species; the Commission may require applicants for special permits to obtain a big game license for that species; one may lawfully take only one grizzly bear in a lifetime with a license; a moose, mountain goat, or limited mountain sheep licensee, except an adult ewe licensee, is not eligible for another special license for that species for seven years (87-2-702).★

[The Department may limit special elk permits as to area, provide special permits to hunt antlerless elk, and allow general elk hunting privileges for a certain class of license.] Except as provided, a person who owns 640 acres or more of contiguous land, at least some of which is used by elk, in a district where elk are hunted, shall upon application receive a permit to hunt elk. An immediate family member, or an employee or shareholder of an owning corporation, may receive the permit, and at least 15% of special elk permits must be available to landowners (87-2-704 and -705).

★[Provisions for and classes of special licenses for antelope, special archery seasons, sportsman's licenses, a mountain sheep license, and a male Shiras moose license are contained in 87-2-706 through 87-2-724; moneys from the auction of mountain sheep and Shiras moose licenses must be used for the substantial benefit of that species (87-2-722 and -724).]★

Restrictions on Taking: Hunting and Trapping

Except as provided, it is unlawful to take any game animal or bird: from any self-propelled or drawn vehicle; on, from, or across any public highway; by aid or with the use of any set gun, jacklight or other artificial light, trap, snare, or saltlick, or any other devices to entrap or entice game animals or birds (87-3-101).

★★A person responsible for the death of a black or brown bear or a mountain lion commits the offense of waste of game if the person abandons the head or hide in the field. A person responsible for the death of a grizzly bear commits waste if the person abandons the head or hide or any parts required by Department or Commission regulation for scientific purposes. All such parts must be delivered to an officer or employee of the Department for inspection as soon as possible after removal; bone structures and skulls shall be returned within a year upon request; hides must be returned immediately. A person responsible for the death of any game animal except grizzly, black or brown bear or mountain lion, commits waste if the person: detaches or removes from the carcass only the head, hide, antler, tusks or teeth or any or all of those parts; wastes any part of any game suitable for food by transporting, hanging or storing in a manner rendering it unfit for consumption; abandons in the field the carcass of any game animal or portion suitable for food. A person in possession of a game animal or parts suitable for food commits waste if the person: purposely or knowingly transports, stores, or hangs the animal in a manner rendering it unfit for consumption; disposes or abandons any portion of such animal that is suitable for food. Violation: $50-1,000 fine; jail up to six months; or both (87-3-102).★★ It is a misdemeanor to take more than one game animal of any one species in any one license year unless authorized by Department regulations. It is a misdemeanor to take any species of game animal, bird or fish during the closed season (87-3-103 and -104).

★★When fire danger becomes so extreme that the Governor upon advice of the Department of State Lands closes an area to trespass, the area is automatically also closed to hunting and fishing. A Board of County Commissioners may submit a request for closure to the Department, which may adopt reasonable rules specifying fire prevention and suppression measures that must be taken by the board before a request may be submitted and considered (87-3-106).★★

It is lawful to use a snare trap for snaring any animal or bird under specific conditions: ▸ snare traps must be tagged with a numbered metal device with identification; ▸ landowner's consent is required on private property; ▸ snare traps shall be set in a manner not unduly endangering livestock; ▸ with any injury to livestock, the person must pay damages. Violation: misdemeanor. It is unlawful to use any recorded or electrically amplified bird or animal calls or sounds to assist in taking, except predatory animals and birds not protected by state or federal law (87-3-107 and -108). ★It is unlawful to discharge a firearm or other hunting implement at a simulated wildlife decoy in violation of any statute or rule regulating hunting of the wildlife being simulated when the decoy is being used by a certified peace officer. The penalty for attempting to take a simulated wildlife decoy is the same for unlawful taking of the actual wildlife being simulated (87-3-109).★

A person in lawful possession of a killed grizzly bear or hide, head or mount thereof may sell it if properly registered with the Department. The registration form must specifically describe the bear or part and accompany it on any sale. Bears may be registered within ten days of the kill, and bears killed outside Montana may be registered within three months of kill upon presentation of proof of lawful kill. Registration does not legalize any prior illegal act such as killing or theft (87-3-110).

★★Effective July 1, 1993, it is unlawful to purchase, sell, offer to sell, possess, ship, or transport any protected game fish, animal, bird, migratory game bird, or fur-bearing animal or part, whether of the same or different species native to Montana, except as permitted. This shall not prohibit: possession or transportation within the state of any legally taken such fish, bird or part; sale, purchase, or transportation of hides, heads or mounts of such lawfully killed animals, except sale or purchase of grizzly bears or parts other than as provided; possession, transportation, sale or purchase of naturally shed antlers. Violation: misdemeanor punished according to 87-1-102. ★★ Possession of dead bodies or any part of any game is prima facie evidence that the person in possession has taken the same. Possession of a fishing rod and line, spear, gig, or barbed fork on the banks or shores of a stream or lake is prima facie evidence that the person was using the same to fish. It is unlawful to possess, have, hold, purchase, keep in storage, or possess for any other purpose any game or parts unlawfully taken. No person may unlawfully use any fishing rod and line, fishing lines, spear, gig or barbed fork (87-3-111 and -112).

It is unlawful to possess, ship or take out of the state any illegally taken game, skins or any parts, whether taken within or without the state. All shippers of game, skins, predatory animals or parts are required to label all packages with names and addresses of consignor and consignee and complete contents. No person or agent or employee of any common carrier may transport or receive for transportation, or sell or offer for sale, any game or parts except as specified. All such animals or parts in possession, or which have been shipped, or are being transported in violation of any provision shall be seized, confiscated, and disposed of as provided by law (87-3-113 through -115).

★★The offense of "sale of unlawfully taken wildlife" is purposeful or knowing sale, barter, purchase or exchange for anything of value, or offering to do such. The offense of sale of unlawfully taken wildlife having a value more than $1,000 is purposeful or knowing, actual or constructive possession of, or transport or causing to be transported, such wildlife having a value over $1,000, as determined from the schedule of restitution values in 87-1-111. Violation: felony; fine up to $50,000; state prison up to five years; or both; plus loss of any hunting, fishing and trapping permits and licenses not less than three years, or up to lifetime revocation (87-3-118).★★

★It is unlawful to offer or give any prize, gift or anything of value in connection with or as a bag limit prize for taking any game, fowl, fur-bearing animal or bird or animal now or hereafter protected by the fish and game laws. The Commission shall adopt rules to regulate contests that intend to offer a prize, gift or anything of value for taking protected fish, based on the duty to protect, preserve and propagate fish. This does not prohibit prizes for any one game bird or fur-bearing animal on the basis of size, quality or rarity (87-3-121).★

No person may take into a field or forest or have in possession while hunting any device or mechanism to silence, muffle, or minimize the report of any firearm. Except as provided, no person may chase with dogs any game or fur-bearing animals. Game birds may be taken during open season with the aid of dogs. A person or association for protection of game may run field trials with Director permission. A peace officer, game warden or other authorized person who witnesses a dog attacking or killing hooved animals may destroy the dog without criminal or civil liability. The Department may regulate the use of dogs for hunting mountain lion and bobcat (87-3-123 and -124).

★Motor-driven vehicles may be used only on established roads or trails unless a big game animal has been reduced to possession and cannot be easily retrieved. After retrieval, the vehicle is to be returned to an established road or trail by the shortest possible route. Vehicles may not be used to drive, run, flush or harass any game animal or bird. Only established roads or trails may be used to drive through cropland, brush, slough or timber areas, or open prairie without written permission of the landowner. Except for landowners and their agents engaged in immediate protection of property, it is unlawful to use a self-propelled vehicle intentionally to concentrate, drive, rally, stir up, or harass wildlife, except predators. These restrictions do not apply to federal land unless the federal agency specifically requests or approves state enforcement (87-3-125).★

No game birds or game or fur-bearing animals may be taken or shot at from any aircraft, including helicopters, nor may aircraft be used for concentrating, pursuing, driving, rallying or stirring up any game or migratory birds or game or fur-bearing animals; nor may any powerboat, sailboat or boat under sail or floating device towed by these boats be used for these purposes against upland game birds, game or fur-bearing animals. It is unlawful to spot or locate game or fur-bearing animals from any aircraft and communicate their location to any person on the ground by any communication device. Except as permitted, within a national forest, no aircraft may be used for hunting purposes, including transportation of hunters, wildlife, equipment or supplies. This does not include loading cargo or persons at approved airports, landing fields or heliports, and provisions do not apply in emergencies, search and rescue situations, or predator control as permitted by the Department of Livestock (87-3-126).

★★When it is shown that any violation of this title was for the purpose of preventing great suffering by hunger of any person which could not otherwise be avoided, the provisions of this title shall not apply (87-3-129).★★ A person who takes protected wildlife that is molesting, assaulting, killing or threatening to kill persons or livestock will not be criminally liable but must notify the Department within 72 hours (87-3-130).

It is unlawful to take quail, Chinese or Mongolian pheasant, Hungarian or chukar partridge, sage grouse, sharp-tailed grouse, blue grouse, fool hen, prairie chicken, ruffed grouse, ptarmigan or wild turkey except during open season. Laws relating to migratory birds are prescribed by the rules and regulations of the US Department of Interior and the USFWS, and will be enforced as they apply to Montana (87-3-402 and -403). It is unlawful willfully to destroy, open, leave open or partially destroy a muskrat or beaver house, except when authorized (87-3-503). No person may use a shotgun to hunt, kill, or shoot deer or elk except with weapon type and loads specified by the Department (87-3-301). A landowner's, lessee's or resident's permission is required to hunt big game animals on private property (87-3-304). It is unlawful to: take deer within city or town boundaries; destroy evidence of the sex of a big game animal; ★conduct or sponsor a contest in which a prize is offered to a person who kills a game animal possessing the largest antlers or horns, carrying the greatest weight, having the longest body, or any similar contest based upon the size, weight or part of a game animal, except for the Boone and Crockett Trophy Institute (87-3-305 through -307).★

Rifles may not be used to hunt or shoot upland game birds, except waterfowl from blinds over decoys, unless permitted by the Department. It is unlawful for any person who kills a turkey to fail to attach immediately a tag validated by the holder by complying with tag instructions (87-3-401, -404 and -405).

Properly marked metal tags must be fastened to all traps except those of permitted landowners. Violation of any of the provisions of this part is a misdemeanor. Failing to pick up traps or snares at the end of the trapping season, or attending traps or snares so that fur-bearing animals are wasted is a misdemeanor. Predator control programs are exempt. No person may destroy, disturb, or remove any trap or snare belonging to another or remove wildlife therefrom, without permission of the owner, except from March 1 to October 1 a person may remove any snare from owned or leased land if it would endanger livestock (87-3-504 through -507). It is unlawful to take, purchase, sell, ship, or transport any wild bird, other than a game bird, or any part thereof or to take or destroy the nest or eggs of a wild bird, except under a certificate, falconer's license or permit. Exceptions: hunting, trapping, or killing of house sparrows, crows, starlings, rock doves, blackbirds, magpies, and other birds the Department designates, or taking or destroying their nest and eggs; possession or transportation of parts or plumage of eagles used for religious purposes by a member of an Indian tribe as permitted (87-5-201).

★The Department shall negotiate agreements with owners or lessees of land adjoining any US federal wildlife preserve, including refuges for migratory waterfowl, for the purpose of securing equal hunting and shooting rights for all resident holders of fish and game licenses and for preventing such preserves from being surrounded by lands whereon license holders may not enter. The Department is authorized to negotiate the payment of a reasonable sum to landowners or lessees for the Department's right to create a public shooting area upon their lands (87-1-227).★

A person may not at any time take, purchase, sell or transport a raptor except as provided. The Commission shall adopt rules for: keeping records; trapping, taking and possessing by residents and nonresidents; selling, transferring of possession, or training of raptors used in falconry; and set license qualifications and fees [falconry and captive breeding license provisions detailed]. Predatory hawks and owls destroying livestock or poultry may be killed at any time by the livestock or poultry owners. Eagles may be killed in compliance with federal law and regulation (87-5-203, -204, -207, -208 and -209).

Restrictions on Taking: Fishing

The Director has general supervision over all state fish hatcheries. The Department may prohibit the use of small fish as bait in designated waters, promulgate rules to insure an adequate supply of fish and regulate fishing from boats or other floating devices and the use of fishing lures and baits. No game fish may be caught, or attempts made to do so, by the use of any gun or trap, nor may a gun or trap be set, used or made. Fish may be taken or caught only with a hook and line held in hand or line and hook attached to hand-held rod or pole. No poisonous substance, fish traps, grabhooks, seines, nets, or other similar means may be used. The Department may designate: waters where spears or gigs may be used to take walleyed pike, sauger, northern pike and nongame fish; and seines, nets and spears for swimming sportsmen for taking designated fish species under rules prescribed. Nongame fish taken may be possessed and sold as directed. All fish other than those here designated must be returned uninjured to the water. The Department may designate waters where setlines may be used to fish for certain species of fish and the number and length of lines and hooks. Game fish may only be taken by angling, except: ▸ snagging of paddlefish, silver and sockeye salmon in open seasons; ▸ taking paddlefish, channel catfish and nongame fish with longbow and arrow under Commission rules; ▸ taking walleyed and northern pike, sauger, ling and nongame fish with spear or gig in open season; ▸ using landing nets or gaffs to land fish; ▸ taking minnows other than game fish with a net not over 12 feet by 4 feet in designated waters; ▸ taking game fish through a hole in ice with an unattended line or rod, if the angler is nearby (87-3-201 through -204).

A seine or net found in a vehicle, camp or on the premises of a person is prima facie evidence of unlawful possession. Exceptions exist for private fish ponds or persons having unexpired seine or net licenses in the vicinity of waters designated as waters where traps, seines, or nets may be used for nongame fish and Dolly Varden trout. It is a misdemeanor to use explosives, corrosive or narcotic poisons, or other deleterious substances in taking fish unless authorized by the Department. It is unlawful to place live caged fish in state waters, except as provided by regulation to protect the water from pollution, excessive private use or disease introduction, and to move live or dead salmonid fish or eggs from one in-state location to another when they are known to be infected with fish pathogens specified by the Department as posing a threat to fisheries, without written Department approval (87-3-205 through -209). Paddlefish tags may be issued for fishing with hook and line for paddlefish (87-2-306).

Commercial and Private Enterprise Provisions

Fur dealer's licenses are required to buy, sell or deal in skins or pelts of fur-bearers or predators, and records shall be kept (87-4-301 through 306). ★Game farm licenses are available for game farms that are properly fenced to prevent escape of game farm animals [detailed provisions are made for removal of game animals, inspection, game farm shooting licenses, transportation and sale of game farm animals and quarantines pending inspection and health certification, sale of carcasses and parts, records and reporting, unlawful capture of game animals, escape from game farms, game farm shooting licenses required, taxing, rulemaking, revocation of licenses and penalties, and restrictions on importation of species determined to pose a threat to native wildlife or livestock] (87-4-406 through 424).★ Private shooting preserves of not more than 1,280 acres may be licensed [detailed provisions are made for bird licenses or stamps required, commercial or membership basis of preserve, revocation of license, restrictions on species hunted, amount of game recoverable, shooting restrictions to be established, game tagging, shooter registration, wild game on preserves, and Department inspections] (87-4-501 through -528).

Except as provided, sale of game fish or spawn is unlawful. Owners of private artificial lakes or ponds may obtain a fish pond license and may stock and sell their fish or eggs. Fishing license holders who sell whitefish must report to the Department. Permits are required to take aquatic food organisms for commercial purposes (87-4-601, -603 through -606, -609 and -610).

Merchants, hotel and restaurant keepers are required to keep records and shipping receipts of lawful possession of game, and may not sell any grizzly bear or its parts (87-4-701 through -705). Roadside menageries and zoos require permits, and permits are required to obtain wild animals. Such animals cannot be sold, and any offspring is state property [details are provided for inspections, revocation, enforcement and penalties] (87-4-801 through 808). Game bird farms for rearing, keeping and selling game birds require licenses [details are provided on applications, fees, terms, inspection, birds as private property, transportation, sale, records, reporting, rulemaking, release, field trial permits, tagging, and revocation] (87-4-901 through -916). Fur farm licenses are required for owning, controlling or propogating fur-bearers [details are provided on applications, fees, terms, conditions, revocation] (87-4-1001 through 1005).

Import, Export, and Release Provisions

Except as provided, it is unlawful to import for introduction or to transplant or introduce any wildlife into the state except in accordance with this title (87-3-105). See also Agency Powers and Duties under STATE FISH AND WILDLIFE AGENCIES.

Interstate Reciprocal Agreements

Any person properly licensed to fish in a bordering state and who complies with Montana fish and game laws may fish in any body of water in Montana that lies within ten miles of the boundaries of this state when such water is declared open for fishing by the Department, provided that such bordering states grant the same privileges to holders of Montana fishing licenses and that the state enters into a reciprocal agreement with Montana. ★The Department may enter into reciprocal agreements with corresponding state officials of adjoining states for providing reciprocal fishing privileges, which may include provisions for honoring the license of the other only if the license has a stamp affixed from the other state (87-2-1001).★

ANIMAL DAMAGE CONTROL

Livestock owners or employees of the Department or USFW may use dogs to pursue stock-killing bears, mountain lions and bobcats. Other means of taking may be used, except deadfall. Traps used in capturing bears shall be inspected twice daily with inspections 12 hours apart (87-3-127). ★Whenever beaver dams are obstructing the free flow of a stream flowing through a settled area and into which sewage of a town or city is dumped, the Department of Health and Environmental Science shall immediately investigate. If it finds the work of the beavers endangers public health, it shall report the facts to the Department, which shall immediately issue a permit for the landowner to remove all beaver and beaver dams, the Department furnishing labor and the county furnishing explosives. If the landowner refuses, the Department may do so (87-1-224).★

See also PROTECTED SPECIES OF WILDLIFE and HUNTING, FISHING, TRAPPING PROVISIONS.

ENFORCEMENT OF WILDLIFE LAWS

Enforcement Powers

Wardens must be qualified by experience, training, interest, and skill in protection, conservation, and propagation of wildlife and game. They shall: ► enforce the laws of this state and Department rules with reference to the protection, preservation, and propagation of game and fur-bearing animals, fish and game birds; ► see that persons who hunt, fish, or take such animals, and those who make recreational use of state lands for hunting and fishing, have necessary licenses; ► assist in the protection, conservation and propagation of game and in the planting, distributing, feeding and care of those animals; ► when ordered, shall assist in the destruction of predatory animals, birds, and rodents; ► perform all other duties prescribed by the Department. ★A warden may not compromise or settle violations of fish and game laws out of court.★ A warden has the authority to inspect any and all game at reasonable times and at any location other than a dwelling. Upon request, all persons having in their possession any game shall exhibit it to the warden for inspection (87-1-502). Authorized officers of the Department are granted peace officer status with the powers to: search, seize, and arrest; investigate activities regulated by this title and Department and Commission rules; report violations to the County Attorney where they occur (87-1-502). All sheriffs and their deputies, constables, peace officers, state forest officers, other USFS officers or USFW agents assigned to duty in this state, and Department field personnel as the Director may appoint are ex officio wardens with the same powers to enforce the fish and game, parks and outdoor recreation laws of this state as regularly appointed wardens. It is their duty to assist in enforcing those laws (87-1-503). A warden may: ► serve subpoenas; ► search without a warrant any tent not used as a residence, any boat, vehicle, box, locker, basket, creel, crate, game bag, or package or contents thereof on probable cause to believe that any fish and game law or Department rule for the protection, conservation, or propagation of game has been violated; ► search with a warrant any dwelling house or other building; ► seize game and any parts taken or possessed in violation of law or Department rules; ► seize and hold devices which have been used unlawfully to take game; ► arrest a violator of a fish and game law or rule; ► investigate and make arrests regarding outfitter and guide violations; ► exercise the other powers of peace officers in the enforcement of the fish and game laws, rules and judgments obtained for violation of those laws or rules (87-1-506).

Penalties

★★Purposeful or knowing violation of any provision of this title, any other state law pertaining to fish and game, or the rules of the Commission or Department is a misdemeanor, with a $50-500 fine; jail up to six months, or both, except if a felony and/or unless a different punishment is provided. In addition, upon conviction or forfeiture of bond or bail, persons shall be subject to forfeiture of licenses and privileges to hunt, fish, or trap or to use state lands for recreational purposes for not less than 24 months (87-1-102).★★ A nonresident making a false statement to obtain a resident license shall be fined not less than the greater of $100 or twice the cost of the nonresident license, but not more than $1,000, and/or jailed up to six months. In addition, upon conviction or forfeiture of bond or bail, the person shall forfeit any current licenses and the privilege to hunt, fish and trap for not less than 18 months. It is a misdemeanor purposely or knowingly to assist an unqualified applicant in obtaining a resident license (87-2-106). ★★Any holders of resident or nonresident fishing or hunting licenses or camping permits who are convicted of littering campgrounds, public or private lands, streams, or lakes while hunting, fishing or camping shall forfeit their licenses and privileges to hunt, fish, camp or trap for one year from conviction (87-2-112).★★

Civil Liability

Unlawful taking, killing, possessing, transporting, or wasting of a bighorn sheep, moose, wild bison, caribou, mountain goat, or grizzly bear or any part of these animals is a $500-1,000 fine; jail up to six months, or both. In addition, that person, upon conviction of forfeiture of bond or bail, shall forfeit any current hunting, fishing, recreational use or trapping license and the privilege to hunt, fish or trap for not less than 30 months. Unlawful taking, killing, possessing or transporting a deer, antelope, elk, mountain lion, or black bear or any part, or wasting a deer, antelope, or elk is a $300-1,000 fine; jail up to six months; or both. In addition, that person, upon conviction or forfeiture of bond or bail, shall forfeit any current hunting, fishing or trapping license and the privilege to hunt, fish or trap for not less than 24 months. A person convicted of unlawfully attempting to take a game animal shall be fined $200-600; jailed up to 60 days, or both (87-1-102).

Unlawful taking, killing, possessing, transporting, shipping, labeling, packaging, wasting or taking any game bird, wild turkey or fish or any part, or failure to tag a game animal or bird, is a $50-200 fine; jail up to 30 days; or both. Conviction of purposely or knowingly taking, killing, possessing, transporting, shipping, labeling, or packaging a fur-bearing animal or pelt in violation of any provision of this title is $50-1,000 fine; jail up to six months; or both. In addition, upon conviction or forfeiture of bond or bail, any current license and privilege is forfeited for not less than 24 months and any pelts possessed unlawfully must be confiscated. Conviction of hunting, fishing, or trapping while a license is forfeited or privilege denied is jail from five days to six months, plus a $500-1,000 fine. A person convicted or who has forfeited bond or bail under this section and whose license privileges are forfeited may not purchase, acquire, obtain, possess or apply for a hunting, fishing, or trapping license during the period when license privileges have been forfeited. Violation: $500-1,000 fine; jail up to 60 days; or both. A person convicted or who has forfeited bond or bail under big game provisions, and who has been ordered to pay restitution under the provisions of 87-1-111, may not apply for any special license or enter any drawing for a special license or permit for five years following conviction or restoration of license privileges, whichever is later. Violation: $500-1,000 fine; jail up to 60 days; or both (87-1-102).

★Notwithstanding the above, the penalties of this section shall be in addition to any penalties provided in other sections (87-1-102).★ All fines, bonds, and penalties in this title may be collected by civil action in the name of the state. All fines, bonds, and costs shall be collected without stay of execution (87-1-103). A person who fails to comply with the terms of a court citation or fails to fulfill a sentence resulting in the issuance of a warrant of arrest shall surrender any current hunting, fishing and trapping licenses, and those privileges are suspended until the terms of the court citation or sentence are satisfied. A person who loses privileges under this section must be notified by the Department in person or by mail. A person who hunts, fishes, traps, purchases licenses, or refuses to surrender any current license in violation of this section is guilty of a misdemeanor and subject to the penalties prescribed in 87-1-102 (87-1-108). Any violation of this title is an offense for purposes of the crimes of attempt, solicitation, and conspiracy set out in Title 45, chapter 4 (87-1-109).

In addition to other penalties provided, a person convicted or forfeiting bond or bail upon a charge of illegal killing or possession of a wild bird, mammal or fish listed in this section shall reimburse the state according to the following schedule: ▸ bighorn sheep, grizzly bear, and endangered species, $2,000; ▸ elk, mountain goat, caribou, bald eagle and moose, $1,000; ▸ mountain lion, black bear, lynx, wolverine, buffalo, golden eagle, osprey, falcon, antlered deer and adult buck antelope, $500; ▸ other deer, antelope, and fish, and other raptors, swan, bobcat, and white sturgeon, $300; ▸ paddlefish, grayling and fur-bearing animals not listed above, $100; ▸ game birds (except swan), $25; ▸ game fish, $10. When a court enters an order declaring bond or bail to be forfeited the court may also order that some or all of that money be paid as restitution using the schedule above. A hearing to determine the amount of restitution is not required for an order of restitution (87-1-111, effective July 1, 1993). Before restitution may be ordered, the finder of fact at trial or the court upon entry of a guilty plea must find that such illegal killing or possession was done knowingly or purposely, unless bond or bail was forfeited (87-1-112). For each conviction, the court shall order payment of the sum stated in 87-1-111. Failure to make payment in the time and manner prescribed by the court constitutes civil contempt of court (87-1-113). All money collected by a court pursuant to 87-1-111 through 87-1-113 must be deposited in the State Special Revenue Fund. If restitution is ordered out of a forfeited bond or bail, any balance must be disposed of as provided for use of fish and game money (87-1-114).

Reward Payments

The Department shall: create, maintain and promote a statewide Fish and Wildlife Crimestoppers Program to combat fish and wildlife-related crimes; and consider and take action on the Crimestopper Board's recommendations. The Department may: ▸ advise and assist in the creation and maintenance of local programs; ▸ encourage channeling of information from state and local programs to law enforcement agencies; ▸ foster detection of fish and wildlife crimes by the public; ▸ encourage the public through a reward program to provide information that assists in the prosecution of such crimes; ▸ promote state and local programs through the media; ▸ accept gifts, grants, or donations for furtherance of the program; ▸ adopt rules to administer these provisions (87-5-605). The identities of and information about persons submitting crimestoppers information are confidential (87-5-606).

HABITAT PROTECTION

See also PROTECTED SPECIES OF WILDLIFE.

★Before acquisition of interest in land for wildlife habitat, the Commission shall by rule establish an acquisitions policy which provides for comprehensive analysis of: ▸ wildlife populations and use; ▸ potential value for protection, preservation and propagation of wildlife; ▸ management goals and additional uses such as livestock or timber; ▸ impacts to adjacent private land and plans to address these impacts; ▸ social and economic impacts to local governments and the state. The analysis of a proposed acquisition must be available for review by each owner of land adjacent to the property and to the public. A public hearing must be held in the affected area (87-1-241, temporary - terminates on March 1, 1996).★

The portion of money specified in this section from the sale of each hunting license or permit must be used exclusively by the Commission to secure, develop, and maintain wildlife habitat, subject to appropriation by the Legislature [dollar amounts are set for various licenses] (87-1-242 - temporary, terminates on March 1, 1996). The amount of money specified in this section for the sale of each hunting license listed must be used exclusively to preserve and enhance upland game bird populations in Montana, subject to appropriation by the Legislature [amounts are set for various licenses] (87-1-246). Not more than 10% of the money generated under 87-1-246 may be used to: ▸ prepare and disseminate information to landowners and organizations concerning the Upland Game Bird Enhancement Program; ▸ review potential pheasant release sites; ▸ assist applicants in preparing management plans for project areas; ▸ evaluate the upland game bird enhancement program. The remainder must be used to: share, at $3 a bird, in the cost of releasing pheasants in suitable habitat; and to revert all unexpended funds at the end of each fiscal year to the habitat portion of the program for the development, enhancement and conservation of upland game bird habitat in Montana (87-1-247). [Eligibility is outlined in 87-1-248.]

The Legislature finds that conservation of rivers and their fisheries is of vital social and economic importance. Establishment of a **River Restoration Program**, funded by anglers from across the state and nation, will help ensure that the rivers and fisheries will continue to serve the state and its people. This program, administered by the Department, consists of projects to improve rivers and their associated lands in order to conserve and enhance fish and wildlife habitat. The Department shall work with individuals and organizations and obtain permits and consents to implement programs, but shall not interfere with any water right (87-1-255 and -257).

NATIVE AMERICAN WILDLIFE PROVISIONS

By treaty of July 16, 1855, between the US and the tribes of the Flathead, Kootenai, and Upper Pend Oreille Indians, the tribes have certain rights to fish and hunt; it is the common advantage of the state and Indian tribes to cooperate in hunting and fishing matters. The Department may negotiate and conclude an agreement with the council of the Confederated Salish and Kootenai tribes of the Flathead Indian reservation for the purpose of: ▸ authorizing individuals to serve on a state-tribal cooperative board to develop hunting and fishing regulations; ▸ granting to tribal Indians state permits without charge to hunt and fish off reservation on open and unclaimed lands, or allowing Indians to hunt without licenses, permits or stamps; ▸ issuing jointly with the council licenses, permits and stamps under terms established by mutual agreement and recognized as valid for hunting and fishing throughout the state; ▸ authorizing all revenues collected from sale of joint licenses, permits and stamps to be remitted to the council for a fish and wildlife program; ▸ transferring to the council an amount equal to all fines and restitution collected in state court for fish and wildlife violations within reservation boundaries for use in a fish and wildlife program; ▸ policing Indian and other lands for the protection of fish and game and providing responsibility for redress of violations to state or tribal courts; ▸ carrying out the purposes of this section. Any agreement must satisfy the requirements of Title 18, chapter 11, and prior to concluding any agreement, public meetings shall be held with notice and opportunity for comment (87-1-228). (See also Restrictions on Taking: Hunting and Trapping under HUNTING, FISHING, TRAPPING PROVISIONS.)

NEBRASKA

Sources: Revised Statutes of Nebraska 1943, reissue of 1990, Chapters 37 and 81; 1992 Cumulative Supplement.

STATE WILDLIFE POLICY

The Legislature finds and declares that: ‣ it is the policy of this state to conserve species of wildlife for human enjoyment, for scientific purposes, and to insure their perpetuation as viable components of their ecosystems; ‣ species of wildlife and plants normally occurring within this state found to be threatened or endangered within this state shall be accorded such protection as is necessary to maintain and enhance their numbers; ‣ this state shall assist in the protection of species of wildlife and wild plants which are threatened or endangered elsewhere pursuant to the Endangered Species Act by prohibiting the taking, possession, transportation, or exportation from this state of such endangered species and by carefully regulating such activities with regard to threatened species [exceptions for the purpose of enhancing the conservation of such species may be permitted by law]; ‣ any funding for the conservation of nongame, threatened, and endangered species shall be made available to the Game and Parks Commission from General Fund appropriations, the Nongame and Endangered Species Conservation Fund, or other sources of revenue not deposited in the State Game Fund (37-432). Non-game, threatened, and endangered species have need of special protection, and it is in the public interest to preserve, protect, perpetuate, and enhance such species through preservation of a satisfactory environment and an ecological balance (37-432.01).

The protection of natural diversity promotes the quality of life for Nebraska residents and their descendants and the protection of natural areas maintains species and their genetic diversity for economic development and human benefit. Specific knowledge of the status and location of natural heritage resources, and their recognition can prevent needless conflict with economic development and voluntary cooperation of landowners is an effective and cost-efficient means to protect significant natural resources (37-1401). ★The maintenance of a registered natural area in its natural state is hereby declared to be the highest, best, and most important use of the natural area.★ No local or state government may undertake activities or use a registered natural area in a way that would negatively impact its values without first conducting a public hearing and filing with the Game and Parks Commission Secretary a statement justifying the negative impact of the activities or use (37-1408).

RELEVANT WILDLIFE DEFINITIONS: See Definitions section of Appendices.

STATE FISH AND WILDLIFE AGENCIES

Agency Structure

The **Game and Parks Commission** (Commission) consists of seven members, one from each of seven districts designated by law, appointed to five-year terms by the Governor with the consent of a majority of the Legislature. Members shall be legal residents and citizens of Nebraska, and well informed on wildlife conservation and restoration. At least two members shall be engaged in agricultural pursuits and reside on a farm or ranch, and not more four shall be affiliated with one political party. The members shall meet in January of each year and elect a chairperson from their membership. Regular meetings shall be held quarterly; special meetings may be held upon the chairperson's call, or pursuant to a call by three members (81-801, -802, and -803.01).

The Commission shall appoint a **Secretary** for a six-year term to act as its director and chief conservation officer, who shall have knowledge of, and experience in, the requirements of the protection, propagation, conservation, and restoration of state wildlife resources. Under Commission direction, the Secretary shall have general supervision and control of all activities of the Commission, and enforce provisions of state laws relating to wild animals, birds, fish, parks and recreational areas, and exercise necessary powers not specifically conferred on the Commission (89-807). Under Commission direction, the Secretary is authorized to appoint deputy conservation officers, agents, office employees and other employees to enforce the laws for the protection of wildlife and administration of hatcheries, game preserves, recreational areas and parks. Each conservation officer appointment shall be under civil service

Nebraska

rules, and embrace an investigation of the applicant's character, habits, qualifications, and knowledge of state game and fish laws, and duties and responsibilities (81-809).

Agency Powers and Duties

Whenever the **Commission** acquires title to private lands for wildlife management, it shall annually make the same payments in lieu of taxes as were made by private landowners for the year prior to such acquisitions (37-110).

The Commission shall establish programs, including land or aquatic habitat or interests therein, for conservation of nongame, threatened, or endangered species of wildlife, but this acquisition shall not include the power of eminent domain. The Commission shall consult with other states having a common interest in particular species of nongame, endangered or threatened species and may enter into agreements with federal agencies, other states, state political subdivisions, or private persons with respect to programs designed to conserve such species including agreements for management of an area established for conservation of the species. The Commission shall provide notice and hold a public meeting prior to implementing conservation programs to reestablish threatened, endangered, or extirpated species (37-435).

By regulation, the Commission may authorize the taking of fish by any means and in any number fish management as a result of an emergency created by drying up of waters. Violation: Class V misdemeanor (37-503.06).

Except as otherwise provided, the Commission shall have sole charge of state parks, game and fish, recreation grounds, and all things pertaining thereto. Funds rendered available by law, including funds already collected for said purposes, may be used by the Commission in administering and developing resources. The Commission shall adopt and carry into effect plans to replenish and stock the state with game and fish. It may: ▸ build additions to existing hatcheries and new plants; ▸ purchase, or by gift, devise, or otherwise, acquire title to sites for additional hatcheries, recreation grounds, game farms, game refuges, and public shooting grounds; ▸ take, receive, and hold, exempt from taxation, a grant or devise of lands and a gift or bequest of money or personal property made for the purposes of these provisions. It shall have the funds or property proceeds invested in the State Park and Game Refuge Fund. The Commission may survey lands and areas suitable for state parks, game refuges, or other similar purposes, and designate them and take action to preserve or conserve them (81-805). The Commission may exchange land for other lands if the exchange would provide greater utility or value and materially aid the basic duties and purposes of the Commission (81-805.02). With the consent of the Legislature, the Commission may acquire real estate of scenic, historic, recreational or fish and wildlife management value or unique natural areas or access thereto, by domain (81-815.26). State wildlife management areas shall be administered by the Commission, but not as a part of the state park system nor with park funds (81-815.23).

Agency Regulations

The Commission may publish regulations as to: ▸ open and closed seasons; ▸ bag limits; ▸ methods and specifications of gear used for taking, killing, hunting, harvesting, or pursuing game, game fish, nongame fish, game animals, fur-bearing animals, or game birds; ▸ the age, sex, species, or area in which animals may be taken, hunted, killed, harvested, or pursued; ▸ the taking, killing, hunting, harvesting, or pursuing of particular kinds, species, or sizes of such animals in designated waters or areas after investigation of the distribution, abundance, economic value, breeding habits, migratory habits, and causes of depletion or extermination and of the volume of the hunting, fur-harvesting, and fishing practiced therein and the climatic, seasonal, and other conditions affecting the protection, preservation, and propagation of the same in such waters or areas. The Commission may close or reopen a season set in all or a specific portion of the state in emergency situations in which continuing the open season would result in grave danger to human life or property (37-301). The Commission may adopt and promulgate rules and regulations: ▸ governing administration and use of property under its ownership and control; ▸ permitting hunting, fishing, or public use of firearms, bow and arrow, or other projectile weapons or devices on an area or portion of such under its ownership or control; ▸ permitting trapping and other forms of fur harvesting in the areas (81-805).

Agency Funding Sources

Fees received for lifetime licenses shall be deposited in the **State Game Fund** and shall not be expended but may be invested and income may be expended by the Commission (37-202.03). All money received by county clerks for permits under the Game Law shall be remitted monthly to the Secretary (37-205). The Secretary shall deposit with the state treasurer all tax money and other funds received who shall place such funds in the State Game Fund (37-206). Funds from the sale of permits and publications as provided in the Game Law, the unexpended balance on hand from the sale of hunting, fur-harvesting, and fishing permits, and money required by the Game Law to be paid into the Fund are appropriated to the use of the Commission for the propagation, importation, protection, preservation, and distribution of game and fish and support of boating. Two dollars from each annual resident fishing permit and $2 from each combination hunting and fishing permit shall be used for fish hatcheries and fish distribution (37-212).

The Commission shall issue habitat stamps and trout stamps. The Secretary shall deposit money from the sale of **habitat stamps** with the State Treasurer who shall place such funds in the **Nebraska Habitat Fund**. No expenditure shall be made from this Fund until the Commission has presented a habitat plan to the Committee on Appropriations of the Legislature for its approval. Money received from sale of **trout stamps** shall be placed in the State Game Fund. The Commission shall use the revenue derived from the sale of trout stamps for trout production, distribution and management. Money received from habitat stamp sales shall be administered by the Commission for acquisition on a willing-seller willing-buyer basis only, leasing, taking of easements, development, management, and enhancement of wildlife lands and habitat areas. Such funds may be used in whole or in part to match federal funds. Violation: Class V misdemeanor (37-216.04 through -216.09).

Fees from Commission-authorized put-and-take fishing shall be credited to the State Game Fund, except that fees received from state park rentals or other state park activities shall be credited to the park fund (37-426). There is a **Land and Water Conservation Fund**; its money shall be used by the Commission under the provisions of Public Law 88-578 (37-428). There is a **Nongame and Endangered Species Conservation Fund** which shall be used to assist in carrying out the Nongame and Endangered Species Conservation Act and to pay expenses incurred by the Department of Revenue or other agency in the administration of **Income Tax Designation Program** (37-439).

The Commission may: ▸ collect fees for use of facilities in state wildlife management areas; ▸ grant concessions in such areas for provision of services to the public; ▸ grant permits for certain land or other resource utilization purposes underlying establishment of a state park system; ▸ prescribe and collect fees or rentals therefor. The proceeds of such fees, rentals, and other revenues shall be deposited in the State Game Fund (81-815.32). (See also HABITAT PROTECTION.)

PROTECTED SPECIES OF WILDLIFE

Except for English Sparrows and European Starlings, it is unlawful to shoot, kill, destroy, catch, or possess, living or dead, a song, insectivorous, or nongame bird, or its part, or to attempt such, or to take or needlessly destroy their nests or eggs (37-307).

The Commission shall conduct investigations of nongame wildlife relating to population, distribution, habitat needs, limiting factors, and other biological and ecological data to determine nongame conservation measures. On the basis of such determinations, the Commission shall develop a list of nongame wildlife in need of conservation, issue regulations, and develop conservation programs designed to insure the continued ability of such wildlife to perpetuate itself successfully. The Commission shall conduct continuing investigations of nongame wildlife, and establish limitations on taking, possession, transportation, exportation, processing, sale or offer for sale, or shipment. Except as provided in Commission regulations, it is unlawful to take, transport, export, process, sell or offer for sale, or ship nongame wildlife in need of conservation, or for a person, other than a common or contract motor carrier under the jurisdiction of the Public Service Commission or the Interstate Commerce Commission, knowingly to transport, ship, or receive such for shipment. Violation: Class II misdemeanor (37-433 and -437).

Any endangered or threatened species pursuant to the Endangered Species Act shall be an endangered or threatened species under the provisions of the Nebraska Nongame and Endangered Species Conservation Act. The Commission may determine that a threatened species is an endangered species throughout all or a portion of its range within the state. In addition to endangered or threatened species pursuant to the Endangered Species Act, the Commission shall by regulation determine whether a species normally occurring within the state is endangered or threatened as a result of any of the following factors: ▸ the present or threatened destruction, modification, curtailment of its habitat or range; ▸ overutilization for commercial, sporting, scientific, educational, or other purposes; ▸ disease or predation; ▸ the inadequacy of existing regulatory mechanisms; ▸ or other natural or manmade factors affecting its continued existence within the state. The Commission shall make such determinations on the basis of the best scientific, commercial, and other data available. In determining whether a species is endangered or threatened, the Commission shall take into consideration actions being carried out by the federal government, by other states, or other agencies of this state, or by any other person which may affect the species under consideration (37-434).

The Commission shall issue a list of all endangered or threatened wildlife species normally occurring within the state. Except for wildlife endangered or threatened pursuant to the Endangered Species Act, upon the petition of an interested person, the Commission shall conduct a review of listed or unlisted species proposed to be removed from or added to the lists, but only if the Commission publishes a public notice that such person has presented substantial evidence which warrants such a review. Whenever a species is listed as a threatened species by the Commission, the Commission shall issue regulations to provide for the conservation of such species. Violation of provisions protecting threatened species: Class I misdemeanor. With respect to endangered species, it is unlawful to: ▸ take; ▸ export; ▸ possess, process, sell or offer for sale, deliver, carry, transport, or ship by any means except as a common or contract carrier; ▸ violate a regulation pertaining to the conservation of such species or to a threatened species listed pursuant to the Nongame and Endangered Species Conservation Act. The Commission may permit these prohibited acts for scientific purposes or to enhance the propagation or survival of the affected species. Violation of endangered species provisions: Class I misdemeanor (37-434 and -437).

An endangered species which enters the state from another state, or from a point outside the territorial limits of the US, and being transported to a point within or beyond this state may be so entered and transported without restriction in accordance with the terms of a federal or other state permit. A law, regulation, or ordinance of a state political subdivision which applies to the taking, importation, exportation, possession, sale or offer for sale, processing, delivery, carrying, transportation other than under the jurisdiction of the Public Service Commission, or shipment of endangered or threatened species according to the Nongame and Endangered Species Conservation Act, shall be void to the extent that it shall permit that which is prohibited, or prohibit that which is authorized by the Act (37-434 and -437).

The Commission may take steps necessary to provide for the protection and management of raptors as defined in these provisions. Violation: Class IV misdemeanor (37-720 and -726). (See also Illegal Taking of Wildlife under ENFORCEMENT OF WILDLIFE LAWS.)

GENERAL EXCEPTIONS TO PROTECTION

Permits may be granted by the Commission to take and collect for scientific or educational purposes fauna hereby protected and their nests, eggs and spawn (37-209).

In water where nongame fish abound, the Commission may remove or cause to be removed by written agreement nongame fish for fish management and may sell them, the proceeds to be paid into the State Game Fund. Game fish taken by such methods shall be immediately returned alive to the waters with as little injury as possible (37-504). Nothing shall prevent the Commission from taking or authorizing the taking of fish or spawn belonging to the state for propagation, stocking other waters, or exchanging with the fish Commissioner of other states or of the US. Nothing shall prohibit the purchase, sale, and use of fish or fish eggs for stocking state waters. Sale proceeds of such fish, spawn, or eggs shall be paid to the State Game Fund (37-509).

No person shall keep in captivity wild birds or animals without a permit. Wild birds or animals are: ▸ crows, game animals, fur-bearing animals, game birds, and upland game birds; ▸ nongame wildlife in need of conservation; ▸ wildlife listed as endangered or threatened under the Endangered Species Act. Except as provided, no person shall keep in captivity a wolf, skunk, or a member of the families Felidae and Ursidae (cats and bears); this provision shall not apply to: ▸ domestic cats; ▸ municipal, state, or federal zoo, park, refuge or wildlife areas; ▸ a circus or animal exhibit; ▸ the holder of a commercial game or fur farmer permit who raises Lynx canadensis or Lynx rufus solely for producing furs or breeding stock for sale to fur farmers. The Commission shall adopt regulations governing keeping wild birds or animals in captivity under these provisions. Nothing in the state's game and fur farming and fish culture provisions shall be construed to require a permit by a municipal, state, or federal zoo, park, refuge, or wildlife area or a circus or animal exhibit for keeping in captivity wild birds or animals for selling, trading, or disposing of same (37-713 to 37-718).

See also ANIMAL DAMAGE CONTROL.

HUNTING, FISHING, AND TRAPPING PROVISIONS

General Provisions

Every express company, bus line, or other common carrier, their officers and agents, and every shipper who transfers from one point to another within the state; takes out of state; or receives for transferring from this state, game enumerated in the Game Law, except as permitted by law, is guilty of a Class III misdemeanor. It is lawful for an express company, bus line, railroad, or other common carrier to receive such game for transport, and to transport it from one point to another during the open season if the game is tagged as required, and a statement of the shipper is forwarded to the Commission that the same is not shipped for sale or profit and was not taken contrary to law. Violation: Class III misdemeanor. Except as otherwise provided, it is unlawful to bring into this state fish or game from any state prohibiting the transportation of fish or game from such state. Every express company and common carrier, their officers, and agents, and every other person who transfers from one point to another within the state; takes out of the state; or receives for transferring from this state, raw furs protected, except as otherwise permitted, is guilty of a Class III misdemeanor. It is lawful for an express company, railroad, common carrier, or postmaster to receive raw furs protected by the Game Law for transportation from one point to another by express, baggage, or mail during the open season and ten days thereafter, or such further period as may be specifically granted by the Commission, when tagged. It is lawful for such common carriers to accept and transport to a point within or without the state beaver pelts stamped as required by the Commission (37-506 through -508).

Licenses and Permits

★A mandatory hunter safety training program for persons under age 16 is established to teach safe firearms use, shooting and sighting techniques, hunter ethics, game identification, and conservation management (37-104).★   The Commission shall establish and administer a bow hunter education program consisting of six minimum hours of instruction in the safe and ethical handling of bow hunting equipment. A person born on or after January 1, 1977 may be issued a permit for bow and arrow hunting only after completion of the bow hunter education program and issuance of a certificate of competency. Such permit may be issued to a nonresident who possesses a certificate of competency issued by a state which has an accredited program (37-105).

Every person age 16 or older who hunts for game animals or game birds or takes bullfrogs or other species defined as game or who angles for fish, or who engages in fur harvesting shall obtain a permit [exceptions for landowners outlined]. Violation: Class IV misdemeanor (37-201).

The Commission shall issue permits to hunt for, kill, or take game and fish or to harvest fur-bearers, in lawful season and manner. The Commission may issue to a resident a lifetime hunting, fishing, or combination hunting and fishing license. These lifetime or combination hunting and fishing licenses shall not allow fur harvesting or hunting deer, antelope, turkey, or other hunting or fishing done under a special permit. The holder of a lifetime permit shall be required to purchase a stamp which the holder of a comparable annual license is required to purchase (37-202, -202.01 and -202.02). Except for a US resident who intends to become a state resident and has resided in Nebraska continuously for 90 days before applying for a permit, no person shall be deemed to be a resident or be issued a resident permit. ★The issuance of a hunter's permit to anyone physically or mentally unfit to carry or use firearms is prohibited.★   Nonresident hunters and fur-harvesters regardless of age must obtain a permit. The Commission may limit the number of days for which a permit is issued and the number of fish or game birds taken, and may issue coupons for tagging and identification. Nonresident permits for fur harvesting may be issued only to residents of states which sell similar permits to residents of Nebraska (37-204).

Without a permit it is unlawful for a person age 16 or older to: ► engage in fur harvesting or possess a fur-bearing animal or raw fur, except that after expiration of a permit a person may possess a fur-bearing animal or raw fur for up to ten days; ► hunt, kill, shoot, pursue, take, or possess game birds, animals, or crows; ► hunt or take or attempt to take migratory waterfowl without a federal migratory bird hunting stamp affixed to the permit; ► take, angle for, or attempt to take fish, bullfrog, snapping turtle, tiger salamander, mussel, or minnow from state waters, or possess the same, except owners and their invitees or paraplegic owners of a body of water shall not be required to hold a permit before fishing from or possessing fish or minnows from such water. It is unlawful for a nonresident to hunt, kill, shoot, pursue, take or possess a game bird or animal, mussel, turtle, or amphibian; or to angle for or take fish, or attempt such; or to harvest fur or attempt such with a resident permit illegally obtained. It is unlawful for anyone to attempt any other thing for which a permit is provided in the Game Law without the permit. Except as provided, it is unlawful for a nonresident to trap or harvest fur from a wild mammal or to attempt such. Violation: a Class II misdemeanor; minimum $40 fine. If the offense is failure to hold a permit, the court shall require the offender to purchase the required permit, unless permits are not available (37-213).

Whenever an invitee angles for fish from privately stocked water upon private land, the owner/operator shall give the angler a written statement of the names of the owner and invitee, number of fish taken, and verification that the fish were caught in privately stocked water upon private land. Making or exhibiting to a law enforcement officer a false statement of the facts required by these provisions is a Class V misdemeanor (37-213.01). The landowner/tenant of a farm or ranch may post the property with signs reading "Hunting By Written Permission Only," and may permit or deny hunting, provided that written consent shall be provided for persons other than members of the family. Anyone apprehended by a law enforcement officer for hunting upon another's legally posted private property shall be subject to arrest and prosecution without a signed complaint by the property's operator. Violation: Class III misdemeanor (37-213.03 through -213.06). [Special permits, exemptions from fees, and special licensing provisions exist for persons in the military services; certain students; residents of Civilian Conservation Centers; persons who receive old age assistance; qualified veterans and disabled persons (37-214.01 through 214.03).]

The Commission may issue permits and establish regulations to hunt, kill, transport, and possess deer. Regulations and limitations may include, but not be limited to: ▸ type and caliber of firearms and ammunition and specifications for bows and arrows; ▸ the method of hunting deer; ▸ permits to allow killing deer in the Nebraska National Forest and other game reserves. The Commission shall issue permits first to residents and then to nonresidents. To be issued a permit to kill deer, antelope, or elk, a person must be at least age 14. The Commission may issue permits for hunting and killing antelope and/or elk, and may establish separate and different regulations than for taking deer. Permits to hunt and kill elk issued pursuant to these provisions shall not be issued to nonresidents. A person may obtain only one elk permit in a lifetime, except for farmers and ranchers who may obtain limited permits every five years. The Commission may designate special deer depredation seasons by executive order and issue permits under the order; such a permit shall give the holder the right to take one deer. Hunting during a special depredation season shall be limited to residents and restricted to permissible firearms (37-215).

A farmer or rancher who owns or leases farm or ranch land and resides on the land, or a member of the immediate family residing there, may apply for a limited permit to kill deer, antelope, elk, or wild turkey during the open season. The Commission may issue a limited permit restricted to killing deer, antelope, elk, or wild turkeys only on the lands included in the application. Only one such permit for each species shall be issued annually for each farm or ranch; a limited permit to kill elk shall not be issued more than every five years. No limited permit shall be issued to a nonresident (37-215.03). Except for these limited permits, no resident age 16 or older and no nonresident shall take, hunt, kill, harvest, or possess a game bird, upland game bird, game animal, or fur-bearing animal without possessing a habitat stamp. A habitat stamp shall be validated if the person has signed it prior to taking, hunting, killing, harvesting, or possessing birds or animals (37-216.01).

Except for Commission-operated put-and-take fishing areas or those cases in which a fishing permit is not required, no resident or nonresident age 16 or older shall kill or possess a trout taken in this state without carrying a trout stamp (37-217.01).

Bullfrogs may be taken, possessed, transported, and used under regulations setting forth seasons, bag limits, open areas and manner of taking, by the holder of a fishing permit, and artificial lights may be used (37-226).

The Commission may issue permits to kill wild turkeys and establish regulations to hunt, kill, transport and possess wild turkeys. Permits may allow killing of wild turkeys in the Nebraska National Forest and other game reserves and designated areas. The Commission may issue nonresident permits only after a reasonable time has been provided for issuance of resident permits (37-227). Whenever the number of wild game animals on the State Wild Game Preserve increases beyond the practical carrying capacity of the land, and no disposal of animals to state public parks is practical, the Commission may issue special permits to take surplus animals, and regulate methods and conditions of taking. Special permits shall be distributed by lot (37-401.01).

Restrictions on Taking

During a season which permits taking of deer with rifles using center-fire cartridges, wild animals other than deer may be hunted only with a shotgun, .22 caliber rimfire rifle, or .22 caliber rimfire handgun, except that this provision shall not apply to a holder of a deer permit or a farmer or rancher who owns, leases, or resides upon such land or a member of the immediate family, while hunting on such land (37-213).

It is unlawful to: ▸ shoot birds, fish, or other animals, or attempt such, while in an aircraft; ▸ use aircraft to harass a bird, fish, or other animal; ▸ participate knowingly in using aircraft without a permit to shoot coyotes from aircraft or shoot a coyote under authority of the permit, or attempt to do so, without permission from landowners or tenants. Violation: a Class II misdemeanor (37-232 and -235).

All caught fish which cannot be taken lawfully shall be returned to the water at once with as little injury as possible (37-302). It is unlawful: ▸ for a person in one day to kill, catch, take, or, except as provided, possess a greater number of game birds, animals, or fish than fixed by the Commission; ▸ except as provided, to shoot, harvest, hunt, take, or pursue a species of game birds, animals, or fur-bearing animals, or to angle for or catch protected game fish except during an open season; ▸ except for holders of game farm or fish culture permits, to possess unmounted game, game birds or fish except during open season (37-303, -304 and -304.01).

Except during an open season, a person who unlawfully takes, kills, traps, destroys, or attempts such, or unlawfully possesses buffalo, elk, deer, antelope, swan, whooping crane, wild turkey, quail, pheasant, partridge, Hungarian partridge, wood duck, eiderduck, curlew, grouse, mourning dove, or sandhill crane is guilty of a Class III misdemeanor. A person who unlawfully takes, kills, catches, traps, harvests, destroys, or attempts such, or unlawfully possesses any other game bird, game or fur-bearing animal, or game fish, or unlawfully possesses such animal or raw fur is guilty of a Class V misdemeanor. A person who takes, kills, traps, destroys, or shoots at a mourning dove that is not flying, or attempts such, or possesses a nongame, song or insectivorous bird, or destroys or takes its eggs or nest, is guilty of a Class V misdemeanor. These provisions do not render it unlawful for an operator of a game, fur, or fish farm pursuant to state laws, to kill game or fish raised or lawfully placed there. Holders of special permits for taking or killing game or other birds, or game animals, are not liable while acting under authority of the permits (37-308). A person other than the owner who knowingly shoots, kills, maims, or injures an Antwerp or homing pigeon (Carrier Pigeon), or who entraps, catches, detains, or removes a mark, band or other identification from the pigeon, is guilty of a Class V misdemeanor (37-309).

A person is guilty of a class III misdemeanor who: ▸ takes or attempts to take fish from closed waters; ▸ kills or takes or attempts to take game upon a reserve or sanctuary; ▸ goes there with a gun or dog; ▸ permits a dog to run there; ▸ intentionally disturbs game or birds causing them to depart from the reserve or sanctuary; ▸ goes upon a wild fowl sanctuary to fish during the open season on wild fowl; ▸ violates laws protecting reserves and sanctuaries, closed waters, fishways through dams, game fish in state waters, or meandered lakes, or regulations relating to game preserves or sanctuaries (37-410).

It is unlawful to: ▸ shoot a protected bird or animal from a highway or roadway; ▸ hunt, shoot, or take a bird or animal, except bullfrogs, or attempt such, by spotlight, headlight or artificial light attached to or used from a vehicle or boat in an area inhabited by wild animals or birds while possessing or controlling a firearm or bow and arrow (this does not prohibit hunting raccoons, or hunting, shooting, or taking nonprotected wildlife species in the protection of property by landowners or employees on their land on foot, with a handlight or from a motor vehicle with artificial light); ▸ hunt or kill a protected species, or attempt such, from a boat or watercraft propelled by sail or power, or from an airplane or hydroplane; ▸ use a rifle, pistol, revolver, swivel gun, or shotgun larger than ten gauge in hunting game birds or trap, snare, or net game birds, or attempt such, except game birds obtained from a game farm permit holder or legally obtained, which have been transported, are tagged, and are being used for dog training may be reclaimed by use of recall boxes or pens by a permit holder; ▸ take or needlessly destroy the nests or eggs of game birds; ▸ hunt or kill a game bird, or attempt such, by attracting it to a place where grain or other feed is distributed (baiting); ▸ hunt, kill, take or trap game birds with nets, traps or clubs, except for veterans or disabled persons with special permits, and except as provided; ▸ hunt, drive, or stir up game birds or game animals with or from an aircraft or boat propelled by sail or power; ▸ have or carry, except as permitted by law, a shotgun having shells in either the chamber, receiver, or magazine in or on a vehicle on a highway (37-501).

It is unlawful to take, catch, kill, or destroy a fish, or attempt such, except as provided, by means other than angling with hook and line. While fishing in a lake, pond, or reservoir or in inlets, outlets and canals within one-half mile of a lake, pond or reservoir, it is unlawful to use more than two lines with two hooks on each line; this provision does not apply to ice fishing. It is unlawful to attempt to take or catch fish by snagging it externally by hook and line, except in the Missouri River. While fishing in state waters, it is unlawful to use a line having more than 5 hooks, or lines having more than 15 hooks in the aggregate. All hooks attached as part of an artificial bait or lure count as one hook. Nongame fish may be taken by spearing or by bow and arrow. Game fish may be taken by bow and arrow. The Commission may open specified waters to underwater powered spear fishing (37-502).

It is unlawful to: ▸ catch or take minnows, or attempt to do so, except for bait; ▸ catch or take minnows by use of minnow seines of more than 20 feet in length, or 4 feet in depth; ▸ catch or take minnows with minnow seines or traps, with meshes other than one-quarter inch square; ▸ buy, sell, or barter, or attempt such, or possess minnows except as bait, except for a licensed fish breeder or bait vendor; ▸ keep or retain a game fish taken while netting or taking minnows for bait, game fish to be returned immediately to the water; ▸ take minnows from reservoirs, lakes, or bayous (37-503).

Whenever the possession, use, importation, storage, taxidermy for millinery purposes, sale, or offering for sale of fish, or game, or song, insectivorous, or other bird, is prohibited/restricted, if not specifically stated to be otherwise, prohibition/restriction shall mean any part of the creature. A nonresident person who takes, hunts, kills, or pursues, or attempts such, or possesses a wild mammal, bird, turtle, mussel, or amphibian shall have in possession a nonresident hunt permit, except that a nonresident bait vendor's permit is the only permit required for salamanders (37-507.01).

★It is unlawful to hunt for game, wild animal, or bird or fish upon private lands without the owner's permission. It is unlawful to trap or harvest fur-bearing animals on another's lands without consent. Animals and their pelts taken contrary to these provisions may be replevied by the land owner. "Owner" means the actual owner, tenant or agent in possession or charge for the owner (37-510).★

It is unlawful to: ▸ mutilate or destroy the house or den of a fur-bearing animal except where it obstructs a public or private ditch or watercourse; ▸ cut down or into a tree containing the den or nest of a fur-bearing animal to capture, take, or kill the animal; ▸ use spears or a like device to hunt or take fur-bearing animals; ▸ use explosives, chemicals, or smokers to drive fur-bearing animals out of holes, dens or houses. When a dam, canal, drainage ditch, irrigation ditch, private fish pond, fish hatchery, artificial waterway, railroad embankment, or other property is being damaged or destroyed by muskrats, the Commission may issue a permit to property owners to take or destroy the muskrats, and may make and enforce rules for permit issuance to prevent illegal destruction of muskrats (37-511).

★It is unlawful to: ▸ hunt, kill, take or destroy rabbits, squirrels, or a fur-bearing animal, or attempt such, with or by the aid of a ferret; ▸ place a ferret in a hole or opening in the ground, or in a stone, wall, log or hollow tree where rabbits, squirrels, or fur-bearing animals may be found; ▸ possess or control a ferret in a field or forest, or in a vehicle going to or from hunting territory (37-512).★ It is unlawful to kill or capture game birds or animals while training or running a dog except as provided; except game birds obtained from a game farm permit holder which are being used for training purposes may be pursued and taken on specified land areas or during a sporting dog trial conducted under Commission authority. No dog shall be run upon private property without the permission of the landowner or tenant (37-513).

A person who explodes or aids or abets in the explosion of dynamite, giant powder, bomb, or other explosive in a lake, river, stream, pond, bay, bayou, or other state waters, with the intent to kill, stun, take, or possess fish; or who places or aids or abets in placing a bomb or explosive, or lime or other poisonous/noxious substance, in state waters with that intent, is guilty of a felony and shall be punished by a fine of $200-1,000, and imprisonment for one to three years; provided the Commission may use or authorize use of chemicals and other substances for fish management (37-515).

★★It is unlawful, except as provided, to set or place an explosive trap or device, operated by the use of poison gas or by the explosion of gunpowder or other explosives, to take, stun or destroy wild animals. Violation: Class III misdemeanor (37-523). It is lawful to use a device which: ► is operated by explosion of small amounts of gunpowder or other explosives; ► is designed to discharge poison into the mouth of a wolf, coyote, fox, wildcat or other predatory animal upon grabbing or seizing bait attached to such device; ► does not discharge a ball, slug, shot or other missile; ► does not endanger the life and limb of human being or animal, other than a predatory animal, during the legal trapping season for fur-bearing animals; provided the device may be used by the Commission or the federal government or with Commission permission. The lawful device shall be set not less than 200 hundred yards from a highway and not less than 1,000 yards from a functioning rural school or an inhabited dwelling without written permission of the building's resident; nor may the device be used on the land without the written permission of the owner or operator. It is unlawful to use such devices unless the user posts the land with signs displaying the words "DANGER, CYANIDE GUNS IN USE" (37-524). ★★

A person who intentionally captures, kills, or destroys a fish, game bird or animal and who leaves, abandons or allows the creature, or an edible portion of it, to be wasted wantonly or needlessly, or who fails to dispose of it in a reasonable and sanitary manner is guilty of a Class III misdemeanor (37-525).

It is unlawful to hunt, kill, take, trap, or pursue a wild mammal or bird, or attempt such, within a 200-yard radius of an inhabited dwelling or livestock feedlot, or to trap within a 200-yard radius of a passage used by livestock to pass under a highway, road or bridge; provided that this does not prohibit a land owner, tenant, or operator or their guests from so doing on land under their ownership or control. Violation: Class V misdemeanor (37-526 and -527)).

It is unlawful to: ► use an aircraft, vessel, vehicle, snowmobile, or conveyance of any type to molest, chase, drive, or harass an antelope, deer, game animal, game bird, or waterfowl, or to cause the animal to depart from its habitat areas; ► spot, locate, or place under surveillance an antelope, deer, game animal, game bird, or waterfowl one day before or during the open season, with the aid of an aircraft, vessel, vehicle, snowmobile, or conveyance of any type, and convey information about the animal's location by radio or other electronic device; ► assist or accompany a person who is in violation of these provisions; ► use an aircraft, vessel, vehicle, snowmobile, or other conveyance, firearm, bow and arrow, projectile, device, radio, electronic device, or equipment in the commission of acts prohibited by these provisions. Violation: Class III misdemeanor (37-528 through -533).

It is unlawful to interfere with, injure, destroy or maliciously disturb, to the damage of the owner, a game, fur, or fish farm, or work connected with a game farm, fur farm or private fish pond (37-710). (See also Licenses and Permits under this section.)

Commercial and Private Enterprise Provisions

A person owning, holding, or controlling by lease or otherwise, for five or more years, a contiguous tract of land of 120 to 1,280 acres who desires to establish a game breeding and controlled shooting area to propagate, preserve, and shoot exotic game birds shall apply for a license to the Commission (37-901).

The licensee of a licensed game breeding and controlled shooting area may take, or authorize to be taken, within the season and in numbers as herein provided hand-reared game birds, including pheasants, bobwhite quail, coturnix quail, chukar partridge, Hungarian partridge, mallard ducks, and wild turkey, released on licensed areas during the shooting season as provided. Game birds released for shooting purposes shall be at least 12 weeks of age before liberation and shall be marked by banding, toe clipping, or some other approved method (37-905). No person shall shoot upland game birds or hand-reared mallard ducks upon a breeding and controlled shooting area, except between September 1 and April 1. Taking game birds upon licensed controlled shooting areas requires a hunting license and a habitat stamp (37-907 and -908).

It is unlawful for a person, firm, or corporation dealing in raw furs to conduct business without a fur buyers permit. Violation: Class V misdemeanor, and the court shall require the offender to purchase the required permit (37-211). It is unlawful for a person to perform taxidermy services for other than one's self without a taxidermist permit. A permit authorizes a taxidermist to: ► receive, transport, hold in custody or possession, mount, or prepare game fish, game animals, fur-bearing animals, raptors, and other protected birds and creatures; ► return them to the legal owner; ► sell captive-reared game fish, animals, birds or other birds and mammals which have been lawfully acquired and mounted. Violation: Class III misdemeanor (37-211.01). No fishing permit shall be required for fishing in a licensed commercial put-and-take fishery (37-213).

No protected game or fish may be placed in cold storage in a licensed cold storage plant, butcher shop, ice cream factory, or ice house, except by the lawful owner, and they shall be tagged as required. Game and fish legally taken and tagged in other states may be stored within the state as provided. Every cold storage plant owner in whose plant protected game or fish are held after the prescribed storage season, every person having game or fish in cold storage after such time, and every person who fails to tag game or fish is guilty of a Class III misdemeanor (37-305).

Except as provided, and except for Commission employees and holders of a fur farmer permit, a fur buyer's permit, or a special permit to destroy beaver damaging public waterworks, it is unlawful to possess the raw fur or pelt of a protected fur-bearing animal other than during the open season and 10 days immediately thereafter. A person who by trapping or other lawful means has become the owner of the raw furs or pelts of such fur-bearing animals during the open season and who during the ten days immediately after the season's close has been unable to obtain a satisfactory price for the furs or has been prevented from disposing of them may obtain a permit to retain possession of the furs for additional time. Applications for permits shall be verified under oath and be accompanied by a certificate of a Commission employee or a county sheriff that the applicant has on hand the number and kinds of furs shown. Knowingly making a false certificate is a Class V misdemeanor (37-306).

Operating a recall pen for recapture of banded game birds originating from licensed game farms in conjunction with dog training or dog trials shall be legal when the recall pen owner has paid an annual fee. The Commission may promulgate regulations for the possession, use and licensing of recall pens. Nothing in these provisions shall authorize the use of recall pens for trapping wild game birds (37-501.01).

The Commission may: ► establish, stock, and impose fees for fishing on special public-use areas for put-and-take trout fishing on state-owned land (37-425); ► allow, control, regulate, or prohibit the use of seines, nets, and other devices and methods in taking fish from the Missouri River; ► enact regulations for the taking method, bag limits, size limits, possession, transporting, or selling of fish from the Missouri River. Individuals shall apply for an annual commercial seining vendor permit before taking or selling fish. Individuals over age 16 selling for profit minnows or salamanders as bait must purchase a bait vendor's permit. Residents over age 16 selling crayfish or leopard or striped frogs, must purchase a resident bait vendor permit, provided that permits for minnows or salamanders shall include crayfish and leopard and striped frogs (37-502 and -503).

When authorized by the Commission for fish management, the owner of a privately owned pond may remove fish by methods other than hook and line and in any quantity. The Commission shall adopt regulations which authorize use of commercial seining vendor permits, equipment, and methods authorized by law. Nongame fish and bullheads seined or taken pursuant to this provision may be sold by the permittee. Such sale of bullheads shall not be deemed a violation, except that the owner of a privately owned pond which is privately stocked and which does not connect by inflow or outflow with other water shall be exempt from such regulation or control (37-503.05).

It is unlawful to buy, sell, or barter: ► a game bird or part, except feathers or skins from legally taken upland game birds; ► an antelope, cottontail rabbit, deer, elk, squirrel or bullfrog, except that deer, antelope or elk hides from legally taken animals may be sold; ► a protected game fish except as provided for owners of private fish ponds. Game fish lawfully shipped into Nebraska by residents, or game or fish lawfully acquired from a licensed game farm, from a person having a fish culture permit, or, in the case of bullheads, pursuant to law, may be sold. The burden of proof shall be upon a buyer, seller, or possessor to show that game or game fish possessed or sold was lawfully shipped in from outside the state or was lawfully acquired. Nonresident fish dealer permitees may possess, buy, sell, transport, and ship live bait minnows, live fish, all frogs, and crayfish legally obtained from outside the state or from a licensed fish hatchery (37-505).

A resident who is a commercial fish culturist with a permit may establish and maintain ponds upon private land for culture and propagation of game fish or minnows, subject to Game Law. Permits for game farming, fur farming, and private fish culture may be issued upon written application (37-702 and -703). Game and fish propagated or raised under a permit may be sold or offered for sale and transported, subject to Commission regulations. Before live game raised under authority of a propagation permit is shipped out of state, it shall be offered to the Commission for propagating purposes (37-706). Game birds, animals and fish maintained upon posted land are the private property of the permit holder (37-709). A game fancier or pet permit, may be issued to authorize keeping not more than 50 wild birds and animals acquired lawfully. A commercial game or fur farmer permit may be issued to authorize possession and rearing in captivity of game birds, game animals, Lynx canadenis, Lynx rufus, or fur-bearers which have been or which shall be acquired lawfully (37-714 and -715).

Import, Export and Release Provisions

Upon payment of required permit fees, game animals and game birds, fur-bearing animals, and game fish or minnows, lawfully held in possession in any other state or country may be imported by a breeder's permit holder. The permit shall not confer upon the holder the right to take wild game animals, fur-bearing animals, game birds, or game fish or minnows from Nebraska, or to purchase such animals, birds, or fish from anyone in Nebraska, except from the Commission or persons holding permits for their propagation and disposal (37-705). It is unlawful to import or possess the San Juan rabbit or other species of wild vertebrate declared to constitute a serious threat to economic or ecologic conditions, provided that the Commission may authorize their acquisition and possession for educational or scientific purposes. It is unlawful to release to the wild a nonnative bird, mammal, reptile or amphibian, or to release a nonnative fish to streams and other waters, or to release in public waters fish not taken from there, without Commission authorization. Violation: Class IV misdemeanor (37-719). (See also PROTECTED SPECIES OF WILDLIFE.)

Interstate Reciprocal Agreements

The Commission may enter into agreements with other states bordering on the Missouri River providing for reciprocal recognition of licenses, permits, and laws of the agreeing states (81-805).

ANIMAL DAMAGE CONTROL

A farmer or rancher owning or operating a farm or ranch may destroy a predator, including raccoon and opossum, preying on livestock or poultry or causing other agricultural depredation on those lands without a permit (37-201). On written request of the property owner, the Commission may remove a deer, antelope, or elk causing damage to real or personal property. If for removal it is necessary to kill the animal, its carcass shall be offered first to local hospitals or other local charitable institutions or to the Department of Public Institutions. If they do not desire it, the carcass may be sold or disposed of in any other manner (37-215.01).

To aid in the protection of livestock and other domesticated animals, the Commission shall issue a special permit authorizing the holder to use aircraft to shoot coyotes. The permit shall be issued only after it is shown that the coyote population in an area presents a substantial threat to livestock and other domesticated animals, and property owners will not be detrimentally affected. The permittee shall report to the Commission not later than 15 days after the end of each calendar quarter the number of coyotes taken (37-233 and -234).

It is lawful for an officer or employee of a public power, irrigation, or drainage district to kill or destroy, or to have trapped, a beaver or muskrat found to be damaging dams, ditches, or other works whenever, after written notice that such destruction or damage is being done, the Commission shall fail or refuse to cause the animal to be removed or to take steps to prevent further damage within 30 days after receipt. Before a public power, irrigation or drainage district shall have such animal trapped, it shall submit to the Commission the names of the trappers, and if no written objections are received from the Commission within five days, they shall be approved. No trapper shall be used who the Commission has objected to in writing. Except as describe above, whenever beaver are destroying trees or damaging property the owner may notify the Commission by registered/certified mail. If the Commission does not elect to remove the beaver within 30 days, it shall immediately issue a permit valid for 90 days authorizing the property owner to destroy the beaver or their dens (37-304.02). The Commission may adopt and publish regulations for control of individual nuisance birds or populations of such birds to reduce or avert depredation upon ornamental or shade trees, agricultural crops, livestock, or wildlife or when they constitute a health hazard or other nuisance. Such regulations shall specify the species which may be controlled, the circumstances under which control is to be permitted, and the control methods which may be employed (37-307). (See also Licenses and Permits under HUNTING, FISHING, AND TRAPPING PROVISIONS.)

ENFORCEMENT OF WILDLIFE LAWS

Enforcement Powers

A conservation officer or peace officer in this state or of a municipality or county has authority to conduct searches and to execute a warrant to search and seize equipment (other than equipment owned or operated by a common or contract motor carrier under the jurisdiction of the Public Service Commission or the Interstate Commerce Commission), business records, wildlife, wild plants, or other contraband taken, used, or possessed relevant to the Nongame and Endangered Species Conservation Act. With probable cause, an officer or agent may arrest, without a warrant, a person who is violating in the officer's presence/view provisions of the Act or a regulation or permit provided for in the Act. An officer or agent who has arrested a person for a violation may search the person and business records at the time of arrest, and seize wildlife, wild plants, records, or property taken or used in connection with the violation. Equipment (other than equipment owned or operated by a common or contract motor carrier), wildlife, wild plants, records, or other contraband seized shall be held by a Commission officer/agent pending court proceedings, and thereafter be forfeited to the state for destruction or disposition. Prior to forfeiture, the Commission may direct the transfer of wildlife so seized to a qualified zoological, botanical, educational, or scientific institution for safe-keeping, with costs assessable to the defendant (37-437).

★★It is the duty of county attorneys to prosecute persons charged with offenses against the Game Law (37-601). It is the duty of conservation officers and their deputies, sheriffs and their deputies, and other police officers to investigate promptly and make arrests for Game Law violations observed or reported by a person, and to cause a complaint to be filed before a court having jurisdiction. Full-time conservation officers and deputy conservation officers are state peace officers with the powers of sheriffs. It is their duty to make arrests and/or issue summons, or notify a resident to appear at a place.★★ A resident refusing to give written promise to appear, or a nonresident refusing to give a guaranteed arrest bond or similar written instrument, shall be taken immediately before the nearest magistrate. A person who willfully violates a written promise to appear is guilty of a Class III misdemeanor regardless of the disposition of the charge upon which originally arrested. Conservation officers and deputy conservation officers shall serve writs and processes, civil and criminal, pertaining to enforcement of duties imposed by law on the Commission. It is the duty of an officer, and a county sheriff, to arrest a person whom such officer believes is guilty of a Game Law violation and, with or without warrant, to open, enter, and examine camps, wagons, cars, stages, tents, packs, warehouses, stores, outhouses, stables, barns and other places, boxes, barrels, and packages where the officer believes fish or game, song and insectivorous or other birds, or raw furs, taken or held illegally, are to be found and to seize the same, except that a dwelling house actually occupied can be entered only with a search warrant (37-603).

Game killed, taken, or caught and game and raw furs bought, sold, bartered, shipped, or possessed illegally shall be declared to be contraband and seized and confiscated by a sheriff or Commissioner, conservation officer, deputy conservation officer, or other Commission employee. ★Possession of fish under lawful size is evidence that it is state property and that it was caught, taken, or killed within the state. Possession of the carcass of a game animal or bird which has shot marks upon it is evidence that it was taken in this state, and the burden of proving otherwise is upon the party in whose possession it is found.★ When the contents of a box, barrel, package, or receptacle consist partly of contraband and partly of legal game, or raw furs, the entire contents shall be seized and confiscated. Whenever a person possesses in excess of the number of permitted wild animals or fowls, game birds or fish, game in possession shall be seized and confiscated (37-606 and -607). When a conservation officer, deputy conservation officer, or Commission employee, or sheriff, deputy sheriff, or other police officer has reason to believe that a person, commercial institution, restaurant or cafe keeper, or fish dealer possesses game, fish, raw fur, nets, or devices illegally, the officer may file a sworn complaint before a magistrate and procure and execute a search warrant (37-609). ★Arrest warrants may be served on officers of corporations violating game laws (37-613).★

Contraband game and fish seized and confiscated in accordance with the Game Law or coming into possession of the Commission by other means shall be turned over to the nearest hospital or state institution or disposed of as directed by the Commission, and contraband hides and furs shall be sold and the proceeds paid into the State Game Fund (37-608).

An officer authorized to enforce the Game Law may enter upon a game or fur farm or private hatchery to inspect it or to enforce the Game Law (37-711). ★The Commission may designate an operator of a licensed game breeding and controlled shooting area, or its agents or employees, as a special Commission representative with power to enforce the Game Law, to prevent trespassing, and to hunt and trap rodents and other animals or birds destroying or likely to destroy game birds reared or liberated on the area (37-909).★

Criminal Penalties

Violation of the Game Law, its amendments, or Commission regulations, where a penalty is not otherwise fixed, is a Class III misdemeanor (37-103). Violation of provisions listing offenses relating to game and fish [37-501 through 37-518] where penalties are not otherwise fixed is a Class III misdemeanor and a fine of at least $50 (37-519). It is unlawful to resist or obstruct a Commission officer or employee. Violation: Class V misdemeanor (37-604). Willful violation of state provisions governing game and fur farming and fish culture [37-702 to 37-712] is a Class V misdemeanor (37-712). Violation of provisions governing the keeping of wild birds or animals in captivity [37-713 to 37-718] is a Class IV misdemeanor (37-718).

See also HABITAT PROTECTION.

Civil Penalties

A person who kills, destroys, takes, or possesses illegally an animal, fowl, bird, or fish shall be liable to the state for damages: ▸ $600 for each elk, deer, big horn sheep, antelope, or swan; ▸ $50 for each wild turkey, wild goose, other game bird, game animal, fur-bearing animal or its raw pelt, or nongame wildlife in need of conservation; ▸ $20 for each insectivorous bird or game fish. Damages may be collected by the Commission by civil suit.   ★In every conviction for such offenses, the court or magistrate shall further enter judgment in favor of the state and against the defendant for liquidated damages in the amount set forth in these provisions and collect damages by execution or otherwise. Failure to obtain conviction on a criminal charge shall not bar a separate civil action for liquidated damages.★   Damages collected pursuant to these provisions go to the State Game Fund (37-614).

Illegal Taking of Wildlife

Every device, net and trap and ferret possessed or used by a person in hunting, taking, catching, killing, or destroying game or fish contrary to law is declared to be a public nuisance and subject to seizure and confiscation by a conservation officer, deputy conservation officer, or other enforcement person.   ★Ferrets and every trap, net, and device, the use of which is prohibited, shall be destroyed upon seizure. All guns and nets being used illegally shall be seized upon arrest, but guns, legal fish nets, or other hunting or fishing equipment used illegally seized for evidence shall be returned by the court following disposition of the case.★   The possession of all nets, except minnow nets, shall be construed as illegal possession and they shall be confiscated and destroyed, and a person possessing them shall be guilty of a Class V misdemeanor. Each game animal, bird, and fish killed, captured, caught, taken or destroyed; every such animal, bird, and fish and raw fur shipped, offered or received for shipment, transported, bought, sold, bartered, or possessed illegally; and each seine, net or other device, including ferrets, used illegally, is a separate offense. A person who uses or possesses, or who aids in hunting, taking, or pursuing, a game animal, bird, fish, or raw fur, killed or taken illegally, with sufficient knowledge of the law to charge the person with such knowledge, shall be subject to the same penalties as the violator (37-610 through -612).

License Revocations and Suspensions

★It is unlawful to set carelessly or cause to start a prairie or forest fire, or to willfully injure a person or livestock with firearms, while hunting, fishing, or camping in Nebraska. In addition to any other penalty, a Game Law permit shall be revoked upon conviction of such offense. In addition to losing the permit, a person who is guilty of repetition of such offense or negligent act shall be disqualified to secure a permit for a period of two years. A person who kills another by voluntarily aiming and firing a firearm or other weapon shall be disqualified to secure a hunting permit for a period of ten years. Notice shall be given by either registered or certified mail. On December 31, each year, the Commission shall furnish to each county clerk and others authorized to sell permits a list of persons who are ineligible for permits for the ensuing year. It is unlawful for: ▸ a permit holder to transfer it to another or for a person to borrow/use another's permit; ▸ a person disqualified for a permit to hunt, fish, or harvest fur with or without a permit during a period when such right has been forfeited or revoked; ▸ a nonresident under age 16 to receive a permit to harvest fur from a fur-bearing animal without presenting a request signed by the applicant's parent or guardian. Violation: a Class V misdemeanor, and permits purchased or used in violation shall be confiscated by the court (37-207 and -208).

It is unlawful for a person disqualified from holding a habitat stamp or a trout stamp to kill or possess trout or to hunt game birds, upland game birds, game animals, or fur-bearing animals with or without a stamp during a period when such right has been forfeited or such stamp has been revoked; or for anyone to kill or possess such animals without a permit and the appropriate stamp. Violation: a Class V misdemeanor (37-216.04).

HABITAT PROTECTION

★★The Commission may participate with natural resources districts and other public agencies, pursuant to the Interlocal Cooperation Act, for acquisition on a willing-seller/willing-buyer basis only of leasing, taking easements, development, management, and enhancement of wildlife habitats. The Commission may expend, transfer, or reimburse participants with money received from the sale of hunting and fishing permits and habitat stamps, and it may use money received pursuant to this provision for the matching of federal funds (37-109).★★

★★When a notice is posted on each corner, and on all roads leading into, indicating that the property is a reserve, refuge, or sanctuary, every school section and tract of educational land, and every state-owned lake, pond, or marsh, except lakes and marshes state-owned because meandered, is declared to be a game reserve, bird refuge, and wild fowl sanctuary. Other game reserves, bird refuges, wild fowl sanctuaries, or reservations may be established in a county where necessary to protect and propagate game, or as a refuge or sanctuary for song and insectivorous birds or wild fowl. With the Governor's approval, the Commission may acquire land for such purposes, either by purchase, lease, gift or devise (37-401).★★

★★Owners in freehold of both banks of a state river for a distance of five miles or more along the river may sign a petition requesting that the river along their lands and on lands adjacent to the river and within one-half mile thereof be made a game and wild fowl sanctuary. Upon receiving the owners' written promises to refrain from shooting or molesting game and, to the best of their ability, to prevent others from the same, the Commission may accept the area as a game and wild fowl sanctuary and cause it to be plainly posted and protected from violators. The Commission may expend sums to feed wild fowl upon such sanctuaries. Without Commission consent, a sanctuary so established may not be withdrawn by the owners for five years after establishment, and unless the owners of more than one-half of the river banks on both sides of the river running through the sanctuary sign a petition for vacating it, and file the petition during the first half of the sanctuary's fifth year, or in the first half of the fifth year of an added five-year period, the sanctuary shall continue unless terminated for good cause by the Commission (37-402).★★ The Commission may promulgate regulations to protect game or wild fowl sanctuaries and their game, wild fowl, or song birds, or to regulate in conjunction with other states over the Missouri River to protect its wild fowl and fish (37-404).

★It is the duty of every person who owns or controls a dam or other obstruction across a watercourse, where impounded water is returned to the streambed, to make provision for sufficient water to be returned to the streambed or river below the dam or obstructions to preserve fish life in the stream; these provisions do not apply under conditions of unusual circumstances resulting from natural causes which make the fulfillment impracticable. Every person owning or controlling such dam, shall open and close gates or locks at a rate slow enough to protect the water below from a sudden flushing or sudden decrease in water flow, which would be detrimental to fish and their habitat. The Commission shall supervise enforcement of these provisions and investigate complaints. Violation: a Class V misdemeanor (37-406 through -406.02).★

To protect game fish in state streams, rivers and reservoirs whose waters are used for irrigation, the Commission may provide, and cause to be placed and maintained, a workable woven wire fish screen with mesh no larger than one inch at the mouth of every designated irrigation ditch which opens into such stream or river or reservoir containing trout, bass, crappie and pickerel. Upon ascertaining what ditches are practicable to be screened, the Commission shall give written notice to the owner or controller of those ditches which describes the size of the woven screen to be set in place at ditch mouths to prevent passage of fish. The screens shall be provided by the Commission at cost to the owner or controller of the ditches. For each day's failure to keep such screen in repair, and for each day's neglect after the 20th day to comply with the written notice, the Commission may recover the sum of $5 per day as liquidated damages for loss to the state because of fish lost or destroyed, and the offending party shall be guilty of a Class III misdemeanor (37-407 and -408).

★Meandered lakes, the shore lines of which were meandered by government survey, and their beds, are declared to be state property for the public benefit, and revenue from them and their resources are subject to the statutes and regulations governing game and fish. The Commission shall have authority to improve meandered lakes and to make regulations to make proper use of them (37-411).★

★★The Commission is authorized to create a State Wild Game Preserve, on a 4,000 to 10,000-acre tract of land. After enclosing the wild game preserve with a fence, it is the duty of the Commission to collect, maintain and perpetuate typical specimens of wild game animals and birds indigenous to the state in its pioneer history. Except as provided by law, it is unlawful to carry firearms, hunt or fish within the limits of the wild game preserve (37-415 through -417).★★   To protect birds and to establish breeding and resting places for them, areas are designated and established as state game refuges. It is unlawful to hunt, kill, capture or chase with dogs, game birds, game animals or other birds or animals, or to carry firearms within the refuge limits. This does not prevent: ► carrying firearms or dogs across the preserve; ► taking fur-bearing animals by traps during open seasons; ► the Commission from issuing permits for killing animal or bird predators endangering game birds or animals or domestic property of adjacent landowners; ► issuing permits for taking deer from refuges whenever their number is detrimental to refuge habitat conditions or to adjacent privately owned real or personal property. Violation: a Class III misdemeanor (37-418; -420; -421).

The Commission is authorized and empowered to acquire by gift, devise or purchase real estate bordering on a lake or artificial reservoir constructed for water storage to develop public recreation areas and promote natural resources conservation (37-424). It is unlawful to explode or cause to be exploded a giant powder, dynamite, or other explosive in a lake, river, stream, pond, bay, bayou, or other state waters, without an order from the Commission; provided, this does not apply where immediate use of explosives is necessitated to safeguard public or private property from damage by ice gorges. It is unlawful to: ► dump or drain refuse from a factory, slaughterhouse, gas plant, garage, repair shop, or other place, or refuse, junk, dross, litter, trash, lumber or other leavings into or near state waters or into a bayou, drain, ditch or sewer which discharges the refuse or its parts into state waters; ► place, leave, or permit refuse to escape so that it is carried into state waters through the elements or otherwise. "Refuse" includes oils, tars, creosote, blood, offal, decayed matter, and other substances injurious to aquatic life. Violation: a Class II misdemeanor. It is unlawful to place the carcass of a dead animal, fish or fowl in or near state waters, or leave a carcass where all or part of it may be washed or carried into state waters. Violation is a Class II misdemeanor, and every day that the unlawful act continues constitutes a separate offense (37-515 through -517). It is unlawful to place, run or drain matter harmful to fish into state waters stocked by the Commission. Violation: Class IV misdemeanor (37-520).

★★The Commission shall create and maintain the Nebraska Natural Areas Register, a register of those natural areas which possess significant natural heritage resources. Natural areas include: ► habitats supporting a rare, threatened, or endangered species, a species in need of conservation or other animal or plant species of concern; ► an area with relict flora or fauna persisting from an earlier time; ► an area serving as a seasonal haven for concentrations of birds or other animals (37-1403).★★

★★The Legislature finds that abandoned railroad rights-of-way provide a unique opportunity to develop a statewide system of recreational trails and that the trails may act to preserve wildlife habitats and create conservation corridors. The Legislature further finds that it is in the public's interest to develop abandoned railroad rights-of-way through fostering public and private cooperation. The Trail Development Assistance Fund is created which consists of direct appropriation by the Legislature and funds received as gifts, bequests, or other contributions to the fund from public or private entities. The Commission administers the fund which is to be used to assist in the purchase, development, and maintenance of state recreational trails (37-1502 and -1503).★★

See also STATE WILDLIFE POLICY.

NATIVE AMERICAN WILDLIFE PROVISIONS: None.

NEVADA

Sources: Nevada Revised Statutes Annotated, 1986, Title 45; 1991 Cumulative Supplement.

STATE WILDLIFE POLICY

Wildlife in this state not domesticated and in its natural habitat is part of the natural resources belonging to the people of the State of Nevada. The preservation, protection, management and restoration of wildlife within the state contribute immeasurably to the aesthetic, recreational and economic aspects of these natural resources (501.100). The legislature finds that: the economic growth of Nevada has been attended with some serious and unfortunate consequences. Nevada has experienced the extermination or extirpation of some of her native species of animals, including fish and vertebrate wildlife. Serious losses have occurred and are occurring in other species of native wild animals with important economic, educational, historical, political, recreational, scientific and aesthetic values; the people of Nevada have an obligation to conserve and protect the various species of native fish and wildlife that are threatened with extinction. The purpose of 503.584 through 503.589 is to provide a program for the: conservation, protection, restoration and propagation of selected species of native fish and other vertebrate wildlife, including migratory birds; perpetuation of the populations and habitats of the species (503.584). See also PROTECTED SPECIES OF WILDLIFE.

RELEVANT WILDLIFE DEFINITIONS: See Definitions section of Appendices.

STATE FISH AND WILDLIFE AGENCIES

Agency Structure

The Governor appoints the **Board of Wildlife Commissioners** (Commission), consisting of nine members: one member each shall be actively engaged in wildlife conservation, in farming, and in ranching; four members shall represent sportsmen's interests; two members shall represent the general public's interests. Not more than three members may be from the same county. The Chairman and Vice Chairman are selected from among Commission members (501.167 and .171). The Commission may hold at least nine meetings a year based on need and requests submitted by the County Advisory Boards to Manage Wildlife. (501.177). The **Department of Wildlife** (Department) is created to administer the state wildlife laws and Chapter 488 NRS (501.331). The Governor appoints, from Commission nominees, a **Director** who has an academic degree in wildlife management or a closely related field, substantial experience in wildlife management, and demonstrated experience in public agency administration (501.333).

Agency Powers and Duties

The **Commission** shall establish broad policies for the: ► protection, propagation, restoration, transplanting, introduction and management of state wildlife; ► promotion of vessel safety; ► promotion of uniformity of policy laws. The Commission shall guide the Department in administration and enforcement of title provisions, and establish policies for areas of interest, including: ► management of big and small game mammals, upland and migratory game birds, fur-bearing mammals, game fish and protected and unprotected mammals, birds, fish, reptiles and amphibians; ► control of wildlife depredations; ► acquisition of lands, water rights, easements and other property for the management, propagation, protection and restoration of wildlife; ► entry, access to, occupancy and use of the property, including leases of grazing rights, sales of agricultural products, timber sales; ► control of nonresident hunters; ► introduction, transplanting or exporting of wildlife; ► regulation of the hunting, fishing, trapping period of persons convicted of two violations within five years; ► cooperation with federal, state and local agencies on wildlife and boating programs. The Commission shall establish regulations regarding regular and special seasons for hunting game mammals and birds, for hunting/trapping fur-bearing mammals and for fishing, daily and possession limits, the manner and means of taking wildlife, emergency closing/extension of a season, reducing or increasing bag/possession limits on a species, or the closing of an area to hunting, fishing or trapping. The regulations must be established after consideration of the recommendations of the Department, the County Advisory Boards and others at open meetings. In addition, the Commission shall establish regulations to: ▸ define the manner of using, inspecting, validating or reporting tags; ▸ delineate game management units; ▸ set the number of licenses issued to nonresidents for big game and other game species. The Commission shall adopt regulations: governing the permit to maintain a water reservoir lethal to wildlife under 502.390; and requiring the Department to make public its proposed responses to requests by federal agencies for comment on the environmental effect of proposed actions or regulations affecting public lands (501.181).

★The **Department** is authorized to determine methods of obtaining data from hunters, trappers and fishermen relative to their activities and success, including the return of reports attached to licenses and tags or questionnaires addressed to license holders (501.119).★ The Department may collect and disseminate information to educate and benefit the people regarding wildlife and boating, and Department programs, and may publish and charge for wildlife journals and other official publications, with proceeds to be deposited in the Wildlife Account. No charge may be made for a publication required by regulation (501.343).

The **Director** shall: ▸ carry out Commission policies and regulations; ▸ direct and supervise Department administrative activities and programs; ▸ organize the Department into divisions and alter organization/responsibilities as appropriate; ▸ appoint/remove staff; ▸ train employees as Game Wardens; ▸ submit reports to the Commission as necessary; ▸ approve the biennial Department budget; ▸ administer real property assigned to the Department; ▸ maintain control of state property acquired for the purposes of this title and by Chapter 488; ▸ act as nonvoting secretary to the Commission (501.337). Employees and others designated as Game Wardens shall enforce provisions of this title and Chapter 488, and are peace officers for the purposes of service of legal process, including warrants and subpoenas, and enforcement of state laws while performing their duties (501.349). The Director shall require Department personnel to report a suspicion that a communicable disease may be present in Nevada wildlife, and shall inform the state Department of Agriculture and forward samples collected to the Director of the Division of Animal Husbandry (501.352).

The Director may: ▸ exercise emergency Commission powers with the Governor's approval; ▸ designate employees to act as deputies; ▸ designate persons outside the Department as Game Wardens (501.339). The Director may enter into cooperative/reciprocal agreements with the federal government, adjoining states, agencies, private persons or corporations to carry out Commission policies (501.351).

Agency Regulations

The **Commission** shall establish policies and adopt regulations for the preservation, protection, management and restoration of wildlife and its habitat (501.105).

Agency Funding Sources

Each county has a fund for its Advisory Board, to be kept in the county treasury, and all money received from the Department is placed in this fund (501.310). Each county board prepares and submits an annual budget to the Commission for evaluation and to be funded from the Wildlife Account within the State General Fund (501.320).

The **Wildlife Account** consists of money received by the Department from the sale of licenses, fees pursuant to 488.075 and 488.1795, legislative appropriations, remittances from the state treasurer under 365.535, interest and income earned on Wildlife Account money, and all other sources except money derived from property forfeitures under 501.3857. The Department may use money in the Wildlife Account only to carry out provisions of this title and Chapter 488, and for no other use (501.356). The Department shall receive, deposit and expend all money provided by law for the administration of this title and Chapter 488 and in accordance with Commission policy (501.354). ★The **Wildlife Imprest Account** in the amount of $15,000 is created to pay for postage, travel expenses, and subsistence arising out of official duties, and the account must be replenished periodically from the Wildlife Account upon approval of expenditures (501.359). A **Petty Cash Account** in the amount of $300 for the payment of minor Department expenses is to be kept in a designated employee's custody (501.361). A **Change Account** in the amount of $300 is to be kept in an employee's custody, to be used for making change incidental to the business of the Department (501.363)★.

The **Heil Trust Fund for Wild Horses** is created as a continuing fund without reversion. All money received from the Heil trust, or money received from other sources designated for deposit in the fund, must be deposited in that fund. The Commission for the Preservation of Wild Horses shall administer the fund. The **Fund for the Commission for the Preservation of Wild Horses** is created as a trust fund reversion; all money received for the preservation of wild horses from a source other than the Heil trust must be deposited in the commission fund and used only for the specific purposes for which it was given. Money not given for a specific purpose may be used for any lawful purpose consistent with those provisions. The Commission for the Preservation of Wild Horses shall administer the fund. The money in the funds created by this section must be invested as other money of the state is invested and interest earned must be credited to that particular fund. The principal of the Heil trust fund must not be reduced below $900,000 unless needed for an emergency and approved by the legislature (504.450).

See also ANIMAL DAMAGE CONTROL.

Agency Advisory Boards

★**County Advisory Boards** (Boards) are created to manage wildlife in each of the several counties. Each board consists of three to five members (501.260). The boards of county commissioners shall appoint qualified persons to the Boards who are sportsmen or engaged in ranching or farming in the county, citizens of Nevada, and bonafide residents of the county from which appointed; members serve three years (501.270 and .275). The Boards shall submit recommendations for setting seasons for fishing, hunting and trapping, which must be considered by the Commission in its establishment of regulations covering open or closed seasons, bag limits, hours and other regulations or policies, and (501.290 and .303). The Boards shall solicit and evaluate local opinion and advise the Commission on the management of wildlife within their respective counties (501.297).★

★★There is a five-member **Advisory Board on Guides**, appointed by the governor, the members of which are state residents and licensed guides. Three members are appointed from three designated regions of the state, and two members represent any region of the state. The appointments must be made from a list submitted to the Governor by the Nevada Outfitting and Guide Association. Terms are for two years, and the board advises the Department on matters which affect outfitting and guide services (504.385). Guides must hold a master guide license, be at least 21 years of age, and must have a grazing or special use permit if operating in an area where such is required for the use of pack or riding animals. Guides must keep records of the number of clients served and information the Department requires regarding the number/kind of fish and game taken. The Department may revoke a guide license for up to five years for violations of this title or Commission regulations. "Guide" means to assist another person in hunting wild mammals or wild birds and fishing and includes the transporting of another person or the person's equipment to hunting/fishing locations whether or not the guide determines the destination or course of travel (504.390).★★ A person who acts as a master guide or subguide without a license is guilty of a gross misdemeanor. A vessel, vehicle, aircraft, pack or riding animal or other equipment is subject to forfeiture on the conviction of a gross misdemeanor if that person knew or should have known that it would be used in violation of the license requirements (504.395).

★★The **Commission for the Preservation of Wild Horses** (Commission for Preservation) consists of five members, appointed by the Governor as follows: a representative of an organization whose purpose is to preserve wild horses; an owner of property used for ranching; three members of the general public who are not engaged in ranching or farming and have never been engaged in efforts to protect wild horses. The Commission for Preservation shall meet at least quarterly, and members serve three-year terms (504.440). The duties of the Commission for Preservation are to preserve the herds of wild horses and identify programs to maintain the herds in a thriving natural ecological balance, and the Commission for Preservation shall: ► promote the management and protection of wild horses; ► act as liaison between the state, general public and interested groups on wild horse preservation; ► advise the Governor on the status of wild horses in Nevada and Commission for Preservation activities; ► solicit contributions for the Fund for the Commission for the Preservation of Wild Horses and the Heil Trust Fund for Wild Horses; ► recommend legislation consistent with federal law; ► develop, identify, initiate, manage and coordinate projects to study, preserve and manage wild horses and their habitat; ► monitor activities of state and federal agencies, including the military, which affect wild horses; ► participate in programs to encourage protection and management of wild horses; ► develop a plan to educate and inform the public of the Commission for Preservation activities; ► report biennially to the legislature concerning its programs; ► take action to fulfill the intent of the Heil trust. The Commission for Preservation may: grant an award in an amount it considers appropriate for information leading to the conviction of persons who violate federal or state laws concerning wild horses; ▸ adopt regulations necessary (504.470).★★ The Commission for Preservation may enter into agreements with the federal government to: coordinate research by state and federal agencies concerning wild horses and their habitat; ▸ create a range for wild horses for their study, and to allow the public to view them in their natural habitat; ▸ finance improvements to benefit wild horses on federal lands; ▸ coordinate efforts to apprehend and prosecute violators of federal and state laws concerning wild horses (504.480). The state wildlife agencies which consult with the Secretary of the Interior pursuant to 16 USC section 1333(b)(l) regarding wild horses and burros in the state shall confer with the Commission for Preservation regarding those consultations and allow the Commission for Preservation to participate to the extent possible (504.485). It is a gross misdemeanor for an unauthorized person to: ▸ remove/attempt to remove a wild horse from public lands; ▸ convert a wild horse to private use; ▸ harass/kill a wild horse; ▸ use an aircraft or motor vehicle to hunt a wild horse; ▸ pollute or cause the pollution of a watering hole on public land to trap, wound, kill or maim a wild horse; ▸ make or cause the remains of a wild horse to be made into a commercial product; ▸ sell a wild horse which strays onto private property; ▸ willfully violate a Commission for Preservation regulation for the preservation of wild horses (504.490).

PROTECTED SPECIES OF WILDLIFE

★★For the purposes of this title, wildlife must be classified as follows: ▸ wild mammals, which must be further classified as either game, fur-bearing, protected or unprotected; ▸ wild birds, which must be further classified as either game, protected or unprotected, with game birds being further classified as upland game or migratory; ▸ fish, which must be further classified as either game, protected or unprotected; ▸ reptiles, mollusks and crustaceans, all of which must be further classified as protected or unprotected; ▸ amphibians, which must be classified as either game, protected or unprotected. Protected wildlife may be further classified as either sensitive, threatened or endangered. Each species of wildlife must be placed in a classification by regulation, and species may be moved from one classification to another when in the public interest (501-110).★★

A species/subspecies of native fish, wildlife and other fauna shall be regarded as threatened with extinction when the Commission, after consultation with competent authorities, determines that its existence is endangered and its survival requires assistance because of overexploitation, disease or other factors or its habitat is threatened with destruction, drastic modification or severe curtailment. An animal declared to be threatened with extinction shall be placed on the list of fully protected species, and no member of its kind may be captured, removed or destroyed except under special Department permit (503.585). Where a bird, mammal or other wildlife declared to be in danger of extinction under 503.585 is found to be destructive of domestic animals or fowl or a menace to health, the Department may provide for its destruction or translocating (503.586). The Commission shall manage land for conserving, protecting, restoring and propagating selected species of native fish, wildlife and other vertebrates and their habitats threatened with extinction and destruction (503.587). The Governor shall review the programs which he administers, and to the extent practicable, utilize the programs in furtherance of these provisions, and encourage other state and federal agencies to use their authorities in such a manner (503.588). In carrying out the program authorized by 503.584 through 503.589, the Director may cooperate with other states, counties and legal entities for the management of habitat areas established for the conservation, protection, restoration and propagation of species of native fish, wildlife and other fauna threatened with extinction (503.590).

Except as provided, it is unlawful to kill, destroy, wound, trap, injure, possess dead or alive, or in any other manner to capture or pursue with such intent American eagles or golden eagles, or to take, injure, possess or destroy their nests. The Department may issue permits consistent with federal law to take bald eagles or golden eagles when they have become seriously injurious to wildlife or agricultural or other interests, and the injury is substantial and can be abated only by taking some or all of the offending birds (503.610). Except as provided, it is unlawful to hunt or possess, dead or alive, birds, nests or eggs protected by the Migratory Bird Treaty Act of 1918 as amended, or by Commission regulation (503.620).

GENERAL EXCEPTIONS TO PROTECTION

The Department may take or permit the commercial taking of unprotected wildlife in any manner approved by the Commission, which may fix a price to be paid for wildlife so taken. Unprotected wildlife taken under this authorization may be sold (503.380). ★A person may maintain a private collection of legally obtained live wild animals, wild birds and reptiles if the collection is not maintained for public display nor as part of a commercial establishment. The Commission may regulate the handling, care and safeguarding of animals maintained in a zoo or other collection of wild animals (503.589).★ Nothing in this title prohibits a person, on written Department permit, from taking, killing, possessing or banding any species of wildlife, or collecting its nest or eggs, for scientific or educational purposes, the number and species to be limited by the Department, or prevents shipping wildlife under written permit into any other county or state for scientific or educational purposes (503.650).

See PROTECTED SPECIES OF WILDLIFE; HUNTING, FISHING, TRAPPING PROVISIONS; and ANIMAL DAMAGE CONTROL.

HUNTING, FISHING, TRAPPING PROVISIONS

Licenses and Permits

Hunting or trapping wild birds or mammals or fishing without a license or permit is a misdemeanor. With stated exceptions, no license to hunt or fish is required for residents under age 12 or to fish by nonresidents under age 12. Children under age 14 may not hunt wild birds or mammals with a firearm unless accompanied by a licensed adult. No child under age 12 may hunt big game in Nevada. The Commission may adopt regulations setting forth the species of wild birds or mammals which may be hunted or trapped without a license or permit. This section does not apply to the protection of persons or property from unprotected wild birds or mammals in the immediate vicinity of home or ranch premises (502.010). Licenses, stamps and permits to hunt, fish or trap during the open season must be issued by the Department, upon payment of required fees (502.035). It is a misdemeanor to make a false statement or to furnish false information to obtain a license, tag or permit. It is a gross misdemeanor to make a false statement to obtain a big game tag, permitting the person to hunt a species of prong-horned antelope, bear, deer, mountain goat, mountain lion, bighorn sheep or elk (502.060). Failure to have a license/permit in possession, or failure to exhibit same or a weapon, ammunition, device or apparatus used for hunting, fishing or trapping on the request of an authorized officer is a misdemeanor (502.120). In addition to the regular hunting and trapping licenses, tags are required to hunt deer, elk, antelope, mountain sheep or bear. Tags may be also required by the Commission to hunt, trap or fish for other species of wildlife, and may not be limited in number or to an area, unless a special season has been designated for a management area with limited tags (502.130). Tags may be used by the Commission as a method of enforcing a limit of the number of a species taken by one person in one season or year, and it is unlawful for a person to obtain tags for use in excess of that number (502.140). ★From March 1, 1992, until June 30, 1995, a landowner may apply to the Department for one or more deer and/or antelope tags for resale, the tags to be issued as compensation for damage caused by deer or antelope to the land/improvements thereon. On approval of a landowner's application, the Department shall issue not more than one tag for each 50 animals present on the land. Not more than 200 tags may be issued annually by the Department under these provisions. The landowner may not use the tag himself, but may sell it to a licensed hunter at a mutually agreed upon price. Landowners who receive tags must provide access through their lands to adjacent public lands for hunters holding deer or antelope tags (502.145).★

It is unlawful to have a species in possession without the required tag attached, and possession is prima facie evidence that the game is illegally taken and possessed. Whenever tags are required for a species of fur-bearing mammal, possession of a pelt of that species without an attached tag is prima facie evidence that the pelt is illegally taken/possessed (502.150). Tags must show the name or hunting license number of the hunter, the game for which it may be used, and if necessary, the management area where it may be used (502.160). Tags for nonresident hunters may be limited in number by the Commission in a management area (502.190). A nonresident deer tag may be issued to a nonresident landowner to hunt on personally owned land, if not less than 75% of all land owned by the individual within Nevada is open to public hunting, providing the landowner has a nonresident hunting license (502.230). The Commission may accept sealed bids for and auction two bighorn sheep tags, one antelope tag, one elk tag and two deer tags each year. The money received is to be credited to the Wildlife Account (502.250).

Except for persons under age 12 or over age 65, it is unlawful to hunt a migratory game bird, except jacksnipe, coot, gallinule, western mourning dove, white-winged dove and band-tailed pigeon, without a duck stamp. Money from duck stamp sales goes into the Wildlife Account, and up to 10% may go to reimburse the Department for administering the duck stamp program. Money from duck stamps goes for protection and propagation of migratory game birds, and for the acquisition, development and preservation of wetlands as recommended to the Commission by the Department (502.300, .310 and .322). It is unlawful for a person, except those under age 12, to take/possess trout without a valid state trout stamp. Money from trout stamps is to go into the Wildlife Account, and must be used for the protection, propagation and management of trout (502.326, .327 and .328).

No hunting license may be obtained by a person born after January 1, 1960, unless the person has a Nevada certificate of successful completion of a course in the responsibilities of hunters or an equivalent course provided by another state or Canadian province for the management of wildlife. Persons convicted of violating 503.165 or 503.175 (carrying loaded weapons on/in vehicles on public highways; firing across public highways) may not obtain a hunting license until completion of a course in hunter responsibility (502.330). The Department shall certify instructors and shall regulate fees for the course (502.340 and .350). It is unlawful to obtain a hunting license, unless otherwise excepted, without completing the hunter safety course (502.360).

★★A person who develops an artificial or man-made body of water, other than one maintained for agricultural or recreational purposes, containing chemicals or substances in quantities which, with normal use, causes or will cause the death of wildlife must obtain a Department permit. Denial of a permit may be appealed to the Commission. The permit may be valid for up to five years, and may cost up to $100. A permittee shall also pay an assessment of no more than $10,000 per year per permit, to be determined pursuant to Commission regulations. Failure to obtain the permit, pay the assessment or comply with permit provisions is a misdemeanor for the first offense and a gross misdemeanor for a subsequent offense (502.390).★★

Restrictions on Taking: Hunting and Trapping

It is unlawful to: ▸ kill or attempt to kill birds or animals from an aircraft. except the Commission may authorize by permit the hunting, killing or nonlethal control of coyotes, bobcats or ravens from an aircraft (violation: misdemeanor); ▸ molest, rally, stir up or drive game mammals or birds with an aircraft, helicopter or motor-driven vehicle, including a snowmobile, motorboat or sailboat; ▸ except as provided, shoot at game mammals or birds with a weapon from an aircraft, helicopter or motordriven vehicle, including a snowmobile, except for paraplegics, amputees, or persons otherwise impeded from walking, who may shoot from a stopped motor vehicle which is not parked on the traveled portion of a public highway but may not shoot from, over or across a highway; ▸ spot/locate game mammals or birds with an aircraft or helicopter and communicate this information to a person on the ground for the purpose of hunting or trapping;   ★▸ use a helicopter to transport game, hunters or hunting equipment, except when the cargo or passengers or both are loaded and unloaded at airports, airplane landing fields or heliports, which have been established by an agency of the federal, state, county or municipal government, or when done in the course of an emergency or search and rescue operation.★ "Game bird" does not include a raven under this section even if classified as a game bird under 501.110 (503.005 and .010).

Except as provided, it is unlawful to have in control any wildlife or part, the killing of which is prohibited, during the time when killing is prohibited, and possession is prima facie evidence that it was the property of the state at the time it was caught, taken or killed, when the killing was unlawful. Legally taken wildlife may be stored at the owner's home after the end of the open season, or in a commercial storage facility under Commission rules, but in no case shall more than the legal possession limit be stored. The Commission may make rules requiring evidence of legal taking in this state, or under the laws of another state (503.030). ★It is unlawful to camp within 100 yards of a water hole in such a manner that wildlife or domestic stock will be denied access to the water hole (503.660).★

Meat or game processors may, within 90 days after its receipt, dispose of the game to the Department if the owner of the game has not paid for its storage. The Department shall give the game to public charities (503.035). A commercial preservation facility having in custody game mammals, birds or fish shall maintain accurate records showing their numbers and kinds, and addresses of owners for one year following the open season, and premises must be open to inspection at reasonable hours (503.037). Except as provided, it is unlawful to transport a game mammal, raw furs, wild mammal taken by trapping, game bird or game fish taken within the state. A person legally taking wildlife may use a hunting, trapping or fishing license or tag or stamp as a permit to transport one possession limit to points within or without the state. Persons who legally acquire ownership/custody of a game mammal, raw furs, game bird or fish not taken by them may transport one possession limit of such wildlife without a transportation permit if that wildlife does not require a tag. Others must have a Department transportation permit, and shipments must be labeled according to Commission regulations (503.040).

It is unlawful to cause through carelessness, neglect or otherwise the edible portion of a game bird, mammal, fish or amphibian to go to waste needlessly. It is unlawful to capture or destroy a game mammal, except a carnivore, and detach or remove from the carcass the head, hide, antlers, horns or tusks and leave the carcass to waste. "Game bird" does not include a raven, crow or magpie even if classified as a game bird under 501.110 (503.050). It is unlawful to hunt game mammals or game birds except during the open season. (503.090). Open seasons for game mammals may designate the sex and age class or an obvious physical characteristic for the mammals which may be taken. The Commission may adopt regulations defining "bucks only" and "antlerless" mammals (503.120). It is unlawful for a person subject to the federal migratory bird hunting stamp tax to hunt waterfowl without a federal migratory bird hunting stamp and to hunt game mammals or birds other than at the times set by the Commission, or where not specified, other than between sunrise and sunset (503.135 and .140). Unless otherwise specified, it is unlawful to hunt: ▸ a game bird or mammal with the aid of an artificial light; a big game mammal, except mountain lions, with a dog; ▸ small game mammals with other than a handgun, shotgun, rifle, longbow and arrow or falconry; ▸ game birds with other than a shotgun or longbow and arrow; ▸ big game mammals other than with a rifle or longbow and arrow of specified sizes; ▸ migratory game birds with other than a shotgun. Nothing herein prohibits the use of dogs in the hunting of game birds or small game mammals (503.150). It is unlawful to carry a loaded rifle or shotgun in or on a vehicle which is on or being driven on a public highway, except for certain handicapped persons or officers on duty (503.165). Unless a greater penalty is provided, discharging a firearm from, upon, over or across a federal or state highway or general county road is a misdemeanor (503.175).

Every person involved in a hunting accident resulting in property damage, or the injury or death of another person shall file an accident report with the Department within 30 days. The Department shall revoke the hunting license held by a person convicted of violating 503.165 or 503.175 if the violation results in an injury to or the death of another person, and shall not issue another license for a minimum of two years after the revocation (503.185).

A permit is required for competitive field trials for hunting dogs or competitive field trials for falconry, to be held under Commission rules insofar as the field trials have an effect or bearing on wildlife and state laws regarding closed and open seasons. The Department may authorize the shooting of legally acquired upland game birds during a closed season for permitting field trials. Birds shall be banded and released only in approved areas (503.200). It is unlawful to hunt or trap upon or within an enclosed grounds which are private property and posted without the landowner's permission (503.240). The Commission may limit in any county the number of licenses issued to nonresidents for upland game bird hunting (503.245).

Except as provided in 503.470, it is unlawful to trap or kill fur-bearing mammals other than during a Commission designated open season (503.440). It is unlawful to hunt a fur-bearing mammal other than by trap, gun or bow and arrow (503.450). Each trap, snare or similar device used in taking wild mammals must bear a number registered with the Department or name and address of trapper. ★Registration of traps is permanent, with fee to be paid at time of first registration (503.452).★ Every person who takes fur-bearing mammals by any legal method, or unprotected mammals by trapping, or sells raw furs for profit shall procure a trapping license. It is unlawful to remove or disturb the trap of a trapping license holder while the trap is being legally used by the trapper on public or permitted land (503.454). ★A person taking wild mammals with traps, snares or other devices which do not cause immediate death to the mammals, shall visit the traps at least once each 96 hours during all the time the trap or device is used in the taking of wild mammals. This does not apply to state Department of Agriculture employees or those of the USDA when acting in their official capacities (503.570).★ It is unlawful to set a steel trap for trapping mammals larger than a No. 2 Newhouse trap within 200 feet of a state public road or highway, as defined by statute, unless the trap is placed along or near a fence upon privately owned lands (503.580).

Except as provided in 503.150, it is unlawful for a dog owner to permit a dog to run at large if the dog is actively tracking, pursuing, harassing, attacking or killing a big game mammal, and the dog may be destroyed by a peace officer without liability (503.631). A permit is required to hunt, trap, possess or sell a species, native or otherwise, of owl, hawk or other birds of prey, including all raptors, such trapping, hunting or possession to be governed by Commission regulations (503.582). Persons who practice falconry or train birds of prey must have a license. A licensee, under permit, may obtain from the wild two birds per year only in nonbreeding months of the year. This does not prevent the capture or killing of a hawk or owl by holders of a scientific collecting permit, except that rare and endangered species may not be taken (503.583).

See also ENFORCEMENT OF WILDLIFE LAWS.

Restrictions on Taking: Fishing

It is unlawful to fish in or from state waters except during the designated open season. The Commission may by regulation allow fishing for a species of fish during any hour of the day or night (503.270). Except as provided, it is unlawful to fish in state waters for a species in any manner other than with hook and line attached to a rod or reel closely attended in the manner known as angling. Only one combination of hook, line and rod must be used by one person. The Commission may by regulation authorize other methods for taking fish. Frogs may be taken by spear, bow and arrow, hook and line or by other authorized methods. "Hook" includes not more than three baited hooks, up to three fly hooks, or up to two plugs/lures. No more than two lures may be attached to the line (503.290). The Commission may prescribe the types of bait and methods of use in a designated water, may control the practice known as "chumming," and it is illegal to use bait prohibited by regulation (503.300).

Persons who have erected or who may erect dams, water weirs or other obstructions to fish free passage in state waters shall construct and repair fishways or fish ladders at all such obstructions or dams, so that at all seasons of the year fish may ascend above the dams or obstructions to deposit their spawn. Failure to comply after having been notified by the Department in writing and willfully/knowingly destroying, injuring or obstructing a fishway or fish ladder required by law is a misdemeanor (503.400). It is unlawful to dry up, impede or interfere with the free flow of water through a fish ladder upon a stream when there is sufficient water in the stream, by diverting the same around the fish ladder by means of a ditch, canal or aqueduct and permitting waste, spill or flow back into the stream below the fish ladder by means of a spillway or other device not equipped with an adequate fish ladder. This does not apply to the impairment of a subsisting right to divert water stream for irrigation, domestic or culinary purposes (503.410). The owner of a canal, ditch or artificial watercourse, taking waters from any state waters in which fish have been placed or exist, shall erect and maintain at the intake fish screens to prevent fish from entering the canal. If there is failure to comply, the Commission is authorized to enter upon the lands to install and maintain the grating or fish screens. It is unlawful to remove or tamper with fish screens (503.420). A vacuum, suction dredge, or similar equipment operation in state waters requires a permit after determination that the operation will not be deleterious to fish. A permit shall designate the permitted equipment and areas of operation allowed (503.425).

Except as provided in 445.281, or unless a greater penalty is prescribed by 459.600, placing or allowing to pass, or placing where it can pass or fall, into or upon state waters any lime, gas tar, slag, acids or other chemical, or any sawdust, shavings, slabs, edgings, mill/factory refuse, sewage, garbage or substance deleterious to fish or wildlife is a misdemeanor for the first offense and a gross misdemeanor for a subsequent offense (503.430).

Commercial and Private Enterprise Provisions

It is unlawful to possess, cultivate or propagate live wildlife without a license. The Commission shall adopt regulations for the possession, cultivation and propagation of live wildlife, setting forth allowed species and providing for inspection of facilities. The Department may issue commercial and noncommercial licenses for the possession, cultivation and propagation of live wildlife (504.295).

A person who owns or controls the shooting rights on an enclosed tract of land may establish a commercial or private shooting preserve for the propagation, culture and maintenance of upland game birds under statutory provisions and Commission regulations (504.300). Before shooting on a commercial or private shooting preserve, the licensee must advise the Department in writing of the number of each species of upland game bird reared, purchased or acquired for liberation, and must receive a shooting authorization. Birds must be at least 8 weeks of age, fully winged and in a condition to go wild before liberation, and banded, with season and shooting hours set by the Commission. A licensed private shooting preserve shall not be closed to the general public during the regular open season, but hunters may be charged a fee (504.320, .330 and .340). Detailed invoices for birds taken and other records must be kept by preserve licensees, except that the Commission shall set no daily bag limits (504.350, .360 and .370). Violation of shooting preserve provisions is punishable under 501.385, and the license may be revoked by the Commission or a court for the balance of the license term (504.380).

It is unlawful to engage in the business of buying, selling, trading or dealing in the skins or pelts of a wild animal without obtaining a fur dealer's license pursuant to 502.240. If the dealer resides in or the dealer's principal place of business is within the state, the dealer is a resident fur dealer; all others are nonresident fur dealers. The Department may require the submission of records/reports necessary to carry out these provisions (505.010). A license to practice taxidermy is required to perform taxidermic services for others. The Commission may regulate the receipt, possession, transportation, purchase and sale of wildlife or parts to be processed by a taxidermist and may require record keeping. The Commission may revoke the license of taxidermy violators for up to five years. ★Licensure provisions do not apply to state or US government institutions of learning, or to research activities conducted exclusively for scientific purposes, or for the advancement of agriculture, biology or any of the sciences (502.370).★

Import, Export and Release Provisions

It is unlawful to sell, barter, trade, or purchase wildlife or parts, or attempt such, except as provided in this title or Commission regulation. The importation and sale of game mammals, birds or amphibians or parts is not prohibited if the importation is from a licensed commercial breeder or processor outside of the state (501.379).

The Commission may regulate or prohibit the use of live bait in fishing so that no undesirable species are introduced into the public waters of the state. Persons selling live bait must have a permit, and the Commission may prescribe the species which may be held or sold (503.310).

It is unlawful to: ▸ sell, barter, trade, or purchase game fish or parts, or attempt such, except as provided, it being lawful to import game fish or parts from fish hatcheries outside the state and to import and sell salt water fish (501.381); ▸ fish from a state hatchery or from waters set aside for rearing fish for transplanting (503.360); ▸ receive, bring or have brought or shipped into Nevada, or to remove from one body of water to another, or from one portion of the state to another, or to any other state, any aquatic life, wildlife, spawn, eggs or the young, except with the Department's written consent. The Department shall investigate whether or not the introduction or removal will be detrimental to existing aquatic life, wildlife, eggs or young. The Commission may regulate the inspection of the introduced or removed creatures (503.597).

Interstate Reciprocal Agreements

The Commission may enter into cooperative agreements with adjoining states for the management of interstate wildlife populations and for the establishment of uniform boating regulations (501.182). The Commission may enter into reciprocal hunting and fishing license agreements with corresponding adjoining states for hunting and fishing upon boundary lands and waters between the states, allowing states to honor each other's licenses and tags under specified conditions. It is the purpose of this section to provide a method whereby the fishing opportunities afforded by the Colorado River, Lake Mead, Lake Mohave, Lake Topaz and Lake Tahoe may be mutually enjoyed by Nevada residents and residents of adjoining states; it is not intended to cover rivers which transverse laterally the border of Nevada (502.045).

ANIMAL DAMAGE CONTROL

Fur-bearing mammals injuring property may be taken or killed with a permit. ★When the Department determines from investigations, or upon a petition signed by 25% of the landowners in an irrigation district or area served by a ditch company, alleging that an excessive beaver/otter population exists or that these animals are damaging lands, streams, ditches, roads or water control structures, the Department shall remove the excess or depredating beaver or otter (503.470).★ ★Whenever the Department determines that beaver and otter are doing damage and that it will be necessary to remove them from a person's land to protect the lands of another, the Department is authorized to enter upon such lands and remove beaver/otter for the relief of other landowners and the protection of public welfare (503.540).★ Once landowners or tenants have reported that their land/property is being damaged or destroyed, or is in danger of damage, by wildlife, and after thorough investigation and under Commission regulations, the Department shall take action to prevent/alleviate such damage (503.595).

★★All gifts, grants, fees and appropriations of money received by the Department for the prevention and mitigation of damage caused by elk or game mammals not native to the state, and interest and income earned on the money, must be accounted for separately within the Wildlife Account and may only be disbursed as provided in Commission regulations (504.155). The Commission shall adopt regulations governing the disbursement of money to: prevent/mitigate damage to private property/improvements; compensate persons for grazing reductions and loss of stored/standing crops caused by elk or game mammals not native to Nevada. Regulations must contain: ▸

requirements for eligibility of persons claiming damages, including the requirement that they must enter into a cooperative agreement with the Director for these purposes; ► procedures for the formation of local panels to assess damage caused by elk or nonnative game mammals and to determine the value of a claimed loss if the landowner and Department do not agree on the value of the loss; ► procedures for the use on private property of materials purchased by the state to prevent damage caused by elk or nonnative game mammals; ► other necessary regulations. Money may not be disbursed to a claimant unless they show by a preponderance of the evidence that the damage was caused solely by elk or nonnative game mammals (504.165). ★★ The Director shall submit to the legislature a report summarizing the actions taken to prevent or mitigate damage caused by elk or nonnative game mammals (504.175).

ENFORCEMENT OF WILDLIFE LAWS

Enforcement Powers

★★Nevada is a member of the Wildlife Violator Compact (506.010 through 506.020). ★★ See Model Statute section of Handbook for full provisions of the compact.

Every state Game Warden, sheriff, and other peace officer of this state shall enforce the provisions of this title and seize wildlife taken/held in possession in violation of those provisions. With or without warrant, an officer may conduct a reasonable search of a camp, structure, aircraft, vehicle, box or other package where the officer has reason to believe wildlife taken or held illegally may be found. For search purposes an officer may detain any aircraft, vessel or vehicle, and seize the wildlife and any gun, ammunition, trap, snare, tackle or other device or equipment indicating that a violation has occurred. Except for property described in 501.3857, property seized may be held only for evidence and must be returned. A dwelling house may be searched only pursuant to a warrant (501.375). ★A person halted by a Game Warden for any violation of this title shall either be given a citation, or be taken before the proper magistrate when the person does not furnish satisfactory evidence of identity and the Game Warden has reasonable cause to believe the person will disregard a written promise to appear in court (501.386).★

Civil Penalties

In addition to penalties for violation of title provisions, every person who unlawfully kills/possesses a big game mammal, bobcat, swan or eagle is liable for a penalty of $250-5,000; for unlawful killing of other fish or wildlife, the court may order a civil penalty of $25-1,000; for hunting, fishing or trapping without a license, tag or permit the court may order a penalty of $50-250. Courts shall order a convicted defendant to pay the penalty stated in this section for each mammal, bird or fish unlawfully killed/possessed, with such moneys to be credited to the Wildlife Account (501.3855).

Illegal Taking of Wildlife

Unlawful killing/possession of a bighorn sheep, mountain goat, elk, deer, pronghorn antelope, mountain lion or black bear without a tag is a gross misdemeanor. An animal may be killed to protect the life/property of a person in imminent danger of being attacked by the animal. A tag issued for hunting big game mammals is not valid if used: ► by other than the person specified on the tag; ► outside the specified management area on the tag; ► outside of Commission specified dates or hours for lawful taking of the animal specified on the tag; ► if the tag was obtained by fraud (501.376). It is unlawful to remove, tamper with or alter a tag placed on wildlife or on equipment seized as evidence (501.377).

Punishment provisions for gross misdemeanors are in 193.140. Except as provided by specific statute, a person who performs an unlawful act prohibited by a title provision, fails to perform a required act, obstructs an officer in the performance of his duty, violates a Commission order or regulation, or violates the provisions of a license/permit is guilty of a misdemeanor; fine $50-500; jail up to six months; or both (501.385).

A gun, ammunition, trap, snare, vessel, vehicle, aircraft or other device or equipment used or intended to facilitate the unlawful, intentional killing/possession of a big game animal or used knowingly to transport, sell, acquire or purchase a big game mammal unlawfully killed/possessed is subject to forfeiture (501.3857). Except for property described, equipment seized as evidence and not recovered by the owner within one year from seizure becomes

Department property; the Department must either sell the equipment or retain it for authorized use, the money from the sales to go into the Wildlife Account (501.389).

See also HUNTING, FISHING AND TRAPPING PROVISIONS.

License Revocations and Suspensions

On conviction of a title provision, in addition to the penalty provided, the court may require the surrender of all licenses held by the person. Upon the second such conviction within five years, the court: shall require the surrender of all such licenses held; may recommend to the Commission that no license be issued to the person for a period up to two years. The Commission may refuse to issue a license to a person twice convicted within five years for a period up to two years. The court may cause to be confiscated all wildlife taken/possessed in violation of title provisions (501.387). The Commission may: ▸ revoke a license of a person convicted of a violation of 503.050 (waste of wildlife), in addition to the penalty imposed, and may refuse to issue a new license for a period up to five years; ▸ revoke a license of a person convicted of unlawfully killing/possessing a bighorn sheep, mountain goat, elk, deer, pronghorn antelope, mountain lion or black bear without a tag, in addition to the penalty imposed; ▸ refuse to issue a new license to such person for up to three years; ★ ▸ revoke the person's privilege to apply for a big game tag for a period up to ten years.★ The court shall require the immediate surrender of all such licenses on conviction (501.388).

Reward Payments

A reward of up to $1,000 may be offered by the Department for one or more classes of wildlife for information leading to the arrest and conviction of a person who unlawfully kills/possesses wildlife of the specified class. A reward is to be paid for each person arrested and convicted, and is to be equally distributed among the persons supplying the information. The Commission may adopt regulations to carry out the reward provisions (501.395).

HABITAT PROTECTION

★The Department is authorized, under Commission approval, to enter into agreements with landowners, individually or in groups, to establish wildlife management areas under Commission regulations to provide greater areas for the public to hunt or fish on private lands and to protect the landowner from damage due to trespass or excessive hunting or fishing pressure. Agreements shall provide that the Department shall designate and post certain portions of the area as closed zones for the protection of livestock, buildings, persons and other properties. Agreements may designate the number of hunters/fishermen who may be admitted to the area (504.140).★

To effectuate a balanced program resulting in maximum revival of wildlife and maximum recreational advantages to the people, the Commission maintains state-owned wildlife management areas and cooperative wildlife management areas with the USFW and USDI and other federal agencies. The Commission may permit hunting, fishing or trapping within, access to, and occupancy and use of such areas and may by regulation: ▸ establish, extend, shorten or abolish open/closed seasons; ▸ establish or change bag and creel limits; ▸ prescribe manner and means of taking; ▸ establish, change or abolish restrictions based upon sex, maturity or other physical distinctions within wildlife management areas (504.143). The Department may, if leases or sales do not interfere with the use of real property for wildlife management or for hunting/fishing thereon: ▸ lease for up to five years grazing/pasturage rights in real property assigned to the Department; ▸ sell crops or agricultural products produced on the property; ▸ advertise for bids for lease/sale of the lands (504.147).

NATIVE AMERICAN WILDLIFE PROVISIONS

★All resident Indians of the State of Nevada are exempt from the payment of fees for fishing and hunting licenses. Resident Indians applying for free fishing and hunting licenses shall exhibit written identification stating that the bearer is a resident Indian of the State of Nevada, signed by an officer of the Bureau of Indian Affairs, US Department of the Interior; the chairman of a tribal council or chief of an Indian Tribe; or an officer of a reservation, colony or educational institution. Before hunting for deer or big game off an Indian reservation, all resident Indians shall secure resident deer tags or big game tags and pay the fee provided in 502.250 (502.280).★

NEW HAMPSHIRE

Sources: New Hampshire Revised Statutes Annotated 1955, 1989 Replacement Edition, Title XVIII, Chapters 206 through 214; 1992 Cumulative Supplement.

STATE WILDLIFE POLICY

The Legislature finds: species of wildlife normally occurring within this state found to be in jeopardy should be accorded protection necessary to maintain and enhance their numbers; the state should assist in the protection of species of wildlife determined to be threatened or endangered elsewhere pursuant to the Endangered Species Act by prohibiting the taking, possession, transportation or sale of endangered species and by carefully regulating such activities with regard to threatened species. Exceptions for the purpose of enhancing the conservation of such species may be permitted as set forth in this chapter (212-A:3).

The Legislature finds that New Hampshire's wildlife resources include more than 300 vertebrate species which normally breed in the state, and 120 bird species which occur as transients, migrants, or wintering populations. Of these 420 species, about 60 are considered fur-bearers, game birds or mammals, or sport fish. Native wildlife constitutes an invaluable natural resource with ecological, scientific, educational, historical, recreational, economic and aesthetic values to state citizens. It shall be the policy of the state to maintain and manage this resource for future generations (212-B:2). (See PROTECTED SPECIES OF WILDLIFE.)

The wild black bear has played a vital role in the development and history of the state and is recognized as a valuable game and wildlife resource. It is recognized that bears should be accorded such protection as is necessary to maintain and enhance their numbers (208:24). (See also Agency Funding Sources under STATE FISH AND WILDLIFE AGENCIES; HUNTING, FISHING, TRAPPING PROVISIONS; and ANIMAL DAMAGE CONTROL.)

RELEVANT WILDLIFE DEFINITIONS: See Definitions section of Appendices.

STATE FISH AND WILDLIFE AGENCIES

Agency Structure

There is a **Fish and Game Department** (Department) under a **Fish and Game Commission** (Commission) which consists of 11 members, qualified as provided, appointed by the Governor and Council. The Governor shall publish the names of nominees in a statewide newspaper, and the Council may not approve an appointment sooner than 30 days after the name of the nominee is submitted (206:1 and :2). Each Commission member shall be a resident of a different county except that one shall be a resident of one of the tidewater towns as specified herein, and not more than six shall be members of the same political party. ★★Each member shall: ► be well informed on the subject of fish and wildlife conservation and restoration; ► be dedicated to the conservation and protection of the state's fish and wildlife resources and of an environment conducive to their welfare; ► be committed to a fish and game program providing reasonable balance between research, habitat management and law enforcement; ► be an active outdoorsman holding a resident fishing or hunting license in at least five of the ten years preceding appointment; ► have a personal record free of convictions of violation of fish and game laws and regulations within five years preceding appointment; ► have at least five years experience in one or a combination of the following fields: forestry, agriculture, management of wild lands, soils conservation, conservation of water resources, fish and game management or propagation, conservation engineering, conservation law, wildlife education, active membership in a state conservation or sportsmen's organization; ► if the coastal member, have a general knowledge of crustaceans and bivalves in coastal waters and salt water fishing. Nominees shall file with the Secretary of State an affidavit, setting forth in detail how they comply with the qualifications and affirming their belief in the aims stated herein. Appointments shall not be confirmed by the Council until examined by them and found qualified (206:2-a). ★★ Terms shall be five years, and the Governor may remove a member for inefficiency, neglect of duty or misconduct in office after opportunity for hearing. A majority of members is a quorum. Members shall elect a chairperson and secretary, and meetings shall be held quarterly (206:4 - 206:6).

The Governor and Council shall appoint an **Executive Director** (Director) of the Department from names submitted by the Commission, each with knowledge of, and experience in requirements for the protection, conservation and restoration of state wildlife resources and who shall be a competent administrator. The Director shall hold office for four years and may be removed by the Governor and Council at any time for just cause after opportunity for public hearing. The Director shall have general supervision and control of all activities, functions and employees of the Department, enforce all laws relating to fish, wildlife resources and marine species, exercise all necessary powers, and serve on the Commemorative Rifle or Shotgun Lottery Committee (206:8).

The **Director** shall determine the number of **conservation officers** and **hatchery superintendents**, appoint and remove same, and hire such experts and office assistants as necessary (206:24). The Director may recruit, train and organize a **deputy conservation officer** force to assist conservation officers in the enforcement of fish and game laws, and may appoint deputy officers from retired conservation officers, hatchery personnel, bio-aides, other Department personnel or other persons. Deputy conservation officers shall be under the direction, control, and regulations of the Director (206:27-a). Deputy conservation officers shall be: ‣ citizens; ‣ residents of the state; ‣ free from conviction of a felony in any state; ‣ between the ages of 21 and 55 except for retired Department personnel; ‣ meet any other of the Director's qualifications. They shall have all powers set forth for conservation officers, but only during the period when they are on official active duty under the Director's direction (206:27-b and :27-c). ★Any person recognized by the Director as a **fish and game volunteer** under the supervision of a Department employee and actually performing assigned volunteer duties or search and rescue activities shall be considered a state employee for purposes of defense and indemnification from civil suits unless arising out of a criminal act (206:27-i).★

Agency Powers and Duties

The **Governor** and **Council**, upon the joint recommendation of the Director and the Director of the Division of Forests and Lands, when fire danger in state woodlands during periods of protracted drought requires extraordinary precautions may declare any or all state woodlands closed to hunters, fishermen, trappers and other persons whose presence might create a fire hazard. During periods when woodland is closed, sawmill and other machine operation, except trucks and pleasure motor vehicles, in or near woodland may also be suspended and smoking prohibited. Each day's violation of any such suspension shall be a violation. Proclamations shall be published in two or more state newspapers and posted as the Governor orders. No person shall drop a lighted cigarette, cigar match or other article likely to cause fire, within 200 yards of any woodlands during such closure (207:31, :32, :34 and :35).

The **Director** shall make investigation of the supply of state wildlife, authorize scientific and other studies, and collect and disseminate statistics and information to promote Department objects (206:9). The Director shall submit an annual report to the General Court outlining recommendations for changes in the fee structure for all licenses and permits, considering license fees in contiguous states, inflation rates, previous license fee increases, budget demands, and intensive analysis and justification for any general fund support for the Department (209:9-a). The Director is the chief administrator of the Commission and shall protect, propagate and preserve fish, game and wildlife resources and protect and conserve state nongame birds. The Director has the power to adopt and enforce rules for the management, control, restoration, conservation and regulation of state fish game, bird and wildlife resources, including the rights to open and close the season for taking fish, and to fix the size, number and weight limits for fish and the method and manner of taking same. Such authority shall not extend to setting the seasons for taking game, birds or other wildlife or bag limits of same, except as provided. Resident aliens shall be issued nonresident fishing and hunting licenses, and shall be considered residents when applying for license, permit or stamp (206:10). Once each biennium, the Director shall hold public hearings to hear suggestions from the public on changes in the fishing rules or on any other subject, notice of same to be published as specified. The Commission members shall attend such hearings. The Director may conduct other public or private hearings throughout the year upon petition of interested parties (206:11). The Chief of Game Management and Research may perform the duties conferred upon the Director as an ex officio member of the Pesticide Control Board (206:14-a).

The Director has the authority to close to hunting or fishing, or both, any area in which there is foreseeable harm to property or danger to human life, and may close any season for fishing in any area for up to 60 days for stocking or conservation purposes and 90 days to reclaim ponds for the protection or preservation of the fish. Such orders shall be published to acquaint area residents of provisions (206:15-a). The Director, with Commission consent, may extend any season on fish, game and game birds, including migratory birds and fur-bearing animals, when a season has been closed by a fire ban or other proclamation, not to exceed the total number of days permitted under the regular statutory season (206:15-b). The Director may close the crayfish season for any length of time for the protection of the crayfish population. When seasons are altered, the same penalties shall apply as for regular season violations (206:16 and :17). See also ENFORCEMENT OF WILDLIFE LAWS.

The Director, after consultation with the Commission, may open and close seasons for taking small game and game birds, fix the number and sex limitations for small game, and set conditions governing the methods and manner of taking and reporting, subject to restrictions of statute. Violation of a rule adopted hereunder: deemed a violation if a natural person; misdemeanor if any other person; and also a violation for each game bird or small game animal illegally taken or possessed (207:56).

The Director, not less than 30 days after stocking of fish, shall release information as to the number and size of fish and the name of the stream, pond or lake planted, but in no instance shall any employee disclose this information. The state, the Department and its employees are released from any liability, claims or demands relating to any loss, damage or injury resulting from the stocking (206:18). These provisions do not apply to stocking species for which there is no open season at the time of stocking (206:18-a). Violation: misdemeanor (206:19).

The Director shall file a biennial report with the Governor and Council with recommendations for legislative action. The Director shall enter into cooperation agreements with departments of the federal government and of this and other states for the protection, propagation and preservation of state fish, game, fur-bearing animals and marine species, and shall execute all matters pertaining thereto, including a biological survey of the state, and shall enter into agreements with persons, corporations and partnerships, for implementing fishways or fish ladders and any other matters relative to the protection and preservation of fish, game and fur-bearing animals (206:21, :23 and :23-a).

With **Commission** approval, the USFW may make rules and regulations for protection of game and other animals, birds and fish on federal areas to be designated for propagation, rearing and protection of fish, game and other wildlife. At no time shall such areas exceed 100,000 total acres. USFW regulations shall be posted as specified, and while in effect, state fish and game laws inconsistent therewith shall be suspended. Violation: misdemeanor (206:28 through :32).

★The Director and Commission jointly may, after notice and hearing, issue stamps or permits for taking any species of wildlife. A majority of the Commission and the Director shall agree to such action before it shall be authorized. The purchase of such stamp or permit shall permit the taking of such species. The decision to authorize such stamps or permits shall not be considered a "rule" subject to 541-A, but a fee shall be adopted by rule. By following the identical procedure, the Director and Commission jointly may rescind any such action (214:9-e). ★

Agency Funding Sources

There is a separate nonlapsing account in the Fish and Game Fund, the **Waterfowl Conservation Account**, to which shall be credited all fees collected by the Department from the sale of Migratory Waterfowl Stamps, any donations to the account, and all proceeds derived from the art created for the stamp. Moneys in the account shall be used exclusively for: ▸ development, management, preservation, conservation, restoration, acquisition and maintenance of migratory waterfowl habitat, including development of state wetlands and shores and designated waterfowl management marshes; ▸ protection, conservation and propagation of migratory waterfowl; ▸ up to 25% of the prior year's gross waterfowl receipts, for promotion of the State Migratory Waterfowl Stamp and print. The Director, with Commission approval, shall adopt rules relative to the form, design and manner of issuance of the stamp, and provide for the reproduction, sale, licensing and other disposal of art created for the stamp, proceeds to be added to the Waterfowl Conservation Account. Before the Director and Commission approve any expenditure from the account, the Department shall provide recommendations. ★The Director and Commission shall submit to the General Court at each regular session a detailed financial report of the account and the public benefits derived from disbursements (214:1-d).★

The state treasurer shall establish a separate nonlapsing account to which shall be credited that portion of the $8 collected by the Department from issuance of **super sportsman licenses** and designated for wildlife management, such moneys to be used only for wildlife management projects as determined by the Director with Commission approval. A separate nonlapsing account shall be similarly established with that portion of the $8 designated for fisheries, to be used for fisheries projects only, as determined by the Director and Commission (214;7-c) (See Licenses and Permits under HUNTING, FISHING, TRAPPING PROVISIONS.) Funds from the sale of lifetime licenses shall be placed in a **Prepaid Fish and Game License Fund**. The state treasurer shall annually transfer to the Fish and Game Fund from the Prepaid Fish and Game License Fund an amount equal to the number of lifetime licenses sold in prior years, reduced each year by 3.5% for mortality, times the present cost of annual license and any interest that accrues to the fund in excess of 5%, plus the amount of one annual license fee from the proceeds of each lifetime license sold during the current year, the balance going into the Prepaid Fish and Game License Fund (214:9-c).

There is a separate nonlapsing account within the Fish and Game Fund, the **Nongame Species Account**, to which moneys obtained by the Department shall be applied, including federal moneys which become available under the federal Fish and Wildlife Conservation Act (Nongame Act) of 1980, state funds appropriated, and donations received, such moneys to be used exclusively for development and implementation of a comprehensive nongame species management program. No moneys shall be expended for nongame management except from this dedicated fund. The Department shall issue a certificate of participation to any individual who donates not less than $10 to the Nongame Species Account. The state treasurer shall deposit annually from the general fund into the account an amount equal to the moneys donated during any fiscal year up to $50,000 (212-B:6).

There is a revolving fund known as the **Publications, Specialty Items and Fund Raising Revolving Fund** in the Department to be used to produce, purchase or market publications and specialty items offered to the public, income to be deposited in the fund. ★The Department may promote, market or otherwise engage in fundraising activities for any special account including, but not limited to, the waterfowl conservation program, the endangered and nongame species management programs, and any other program intended to educate, protect, restore, enhance or promote Department responsibilities.★ Proceeds from such activities shall be deposited to the respective special accounts of the programs listed herein, or others established after July, 1992. The amount in the Publications Fund shall not exceed $200,000, any excess to be deposited in the Fish and Game Fund (206:22-a).

The Director shall return monthly to the state treasurer all moneys collected from licenses, permits, fines, forfeitures or whatever source, to a separate account known as the **Fish and Game Fund**. The Fund is annually appropriated for Department use during the fiscal year as herein provided (206:33). Gifts not exceeding $500 in cash or value may be received and expended by the Department with the Commission's consent without the Governor's or Council's approval (206:33-a). The Department may request, with approval of the legislative fiscal committee, that the Governor and Council authorize transfer of additional Fund moneys if expenditures over budget estimates are necessary for functioning of the Department (206:33-b). ★The Director shall recommend a uniform fine schedule for any fish and game law violation, to be submitted to the supreme court for its use.★ Persons charged with violations which are not misdemeanors or felonies may plead guilty or nolo contendere by mail, and shall not be required to appear in court (206:34). Commission, Director, and conservation officers and other Department employees expenses are paid out of the Fund (206:35).

All moneys collected from **Pheasant Stamps** shall be placed in a separate account and used only for purchase or propagation of pheasants as determined by the Director and Commission. A similar account for revenues from **Wild Turkey Stamps** or licenses is to be used only for restoration and management of wild turkeys. ★★The state treasurer shall establish a separate account for moneys collected from **Fish Food Sales** at hatchery vending machines, to be used for acquisition and maintenance of fish hatchery equipment. Any organization holding a **Fishing Derby** on a state-stocked body of water may contribute 20% of net proceeds to the Department to replenish fish taken.★★ A separate account shall be established to which shall be credited federal Wallop-Breaux funds and state matching funds, for land acquisition and construction/maintenance of boat launching sites on state lakes, ponds, streams, Great Bay and the Atlantic Ocean as determined by the Director and Commission (206:35-a through :35-e). The Commission may authorize the Director to print and sell **Wildlife Stamps**, decals, buttons, mementos and other items of various designs and denominations. There is in the Department a **Wildlife Protection Account**, separate from all other moneys, consisting of all revenues received from the sale of wildlife emblems. Disbursements may be made to defray the expenses of producing and selling wildlife emblems, but other disbursements shall be approved by the Commission and the General Court Fiscal Committee and limited to wildlife habitat protection, restoration and enhancement programs (206:41).

The Director, with Commission approval, shall have the exclusive power to expend for the protection, conservation, propagation and restoration of fish, game, fur-bearing animals and marine species, state funds acquired from state appropriations, licenses, gifts or otherwise. The Department is authorized to receive and expend with approval of the Governor and Council any gifts and grants from any source including the US and to hold property, real and personal, acquired thereunder to complete any authorized project (206:39).

The Department shall make available to all license agents for sale tickets for the annual **Commemorative Rifle or Shotgun Lottery.** All revenues generated by the lottery, minus committee administrative expenses, the cost of the rifle or shotgun, and lottery, shall be deposited into the Fish and Game Fund. The Director, in conjunction with the Commissioner of Cultural Affairs, shall adopt rules to carry out lottery provisions (206-A:4, :8 and :9). (See Agency Advisory Boards.)

A separate nonlapsing account in the Fish and Game Fund is the **Moose Management Fund,** consisting of all fees collected from moose licenses and applications to be used exclusively for implementation of a comprehensive moose management program, including education, research, protection and management (208:1-a). (See also PROTECTED SPECIES OF WILDLIFE.) A separate nonlapsing account in the Fish and Game Fund is the **Bear Management Fund,** into which all moneys collected from bear licenses and tags shall be deposited for use exclusively to supplement the research, management and protection of black bears (208:24). A separate nonlapsing account in the Fish and Game Fund is the **Raptor Conservation Account,** to which all fees collected from falconry permits shall be applied, and donations from other sources, to be used exclusively for the implementation of a comprehensive falconry program (209-A:3).

Agency Advisory Boards

★★There is established a **Commemorative Rifle or Shotgun Lottery Committee** composed of the Commissioner of Cultural Affairs, the Director, and two members each, appointed by these two persons. The Committee shall solicit bids to manufacture a commemorative rifle or shotgun annually from firearms manufacturers based in part or in whole in New Hampshire or New England as specified in detail herein (206-A:1, :2, :3 and :7).★★ [Additional details of the selection of the manufacturer and conduct of the lottery are given.] (See Agency Funding Sources under this section and HABITAT PROTECTION for Governor's Fishway Committee.)

PROTECTED SPECIES OF WILDLIFE

No person shall at any time, hunt, take, or possess, any caribou, or elk, or any part of the carcass taken in this state. No person shall hunt, take or possess any moose or any part of the carcass taken in this state without a license. The Director may establish a hunting season for moose in any county, including methods of taking and requirements for reporting, sex limitations, and total take in any one year. This authority shall expire on December 31, 1996. The Director may adopt rules regulating the issuance of licenses or permits for moose. Prior to the establishment of any hunting season for moose, the Director shall implement a comprehensive moose management program to include: ▸ education of the public as to the biological status and management needs; ▸ research to determine the population, distribution, and future trends and needs of the state moose herd; ▸ management measures, which may include hunting as well as habitat enhancement, to promote a healthy moose population. Every two years the Director shall report in writing to the legislature, Governor and Council the status of the moose in the state and the performance of the moose management program (208:1 and :1-a). (See also Agency Funding Sources under STATE FISH AND WILDLIFE AGENCIES.)

No person shall, at any time, shoot, hunt, take or possess any mountain lion or any part of the carcass, except when acting in protection of person or property (208:1-b). The Director may, should mountain lions become a nuisance in any part of the state, authorize measures necessary for control (208:1-c). No person shall, at any time, shoot, hunt, take or possess, any Canadian Lynx or part taken in this state, except when acting in protection of person or property (208:1-d). The Director, after consultation with the Commission, shall open and close seasons for taking wild deer, fix number and sex limitations, and any other conditions governing the methods and manner of taking and reporting deer, subject to other statutory provisions, such authority to be exercised for the state as a whole or for any specified county or part thereof, and shall expire December 31, 1997. The Director shall report annually to the House and Senate committees with jurisdiction over the Department on the condition of the deer herd, the preceding year's harvest and the herd's general status (208:2). (See also Restrictions on Taking: Hunting and Trapping, HUNTING, FISHING, TRAPPING PROVISIONS.)

There shall be no open season for European partridge, spruce grouse, chukar partridge, upland plover, ptarmigan and mourning dove (209:4). No person shall hunt, capture, kill, take, possess, buy or sell any protected bird or part except as otherwise provided. No person shall hunt, capture, kill, take or possess any golden or bald eagle, nor molest or disturb their nests or
young. No person shall take, have in possession or under control, wantonly interfere with or destroy any nest or eggs of any game birds or protected birds (209:8 through :10) (See ANIMAL DAMAGE CONTROL.)

The Director shall conduct investigations on wildlife species to develop information relating to population, distribution, habitat needs, limiting factors and other biological and ecological data to determine conservation measures necessary for their continued ability to sustain themselves successfully, and shall adopt rules and develop conservation programs designed to insure the continued ability of wildlife species deemed in need of conservation to perpetuate themselves successfully, and on the basis of ongoing investigations of endangered and threatened species, from time to time amend such rules. The Director shall establish limitations relating to taking, possession, transportation or sale to conserve threatened or endangered species. Except as otherwise provided, it is unlawful to take, possess, transport or sell wildlife in need of conservation or for any common/contract carrier knowingly to transport same. ★★The Director and the Director of Safety Services may independently or in concert adopt and enforce rules temporarily restricting boat traffic on any state waters as either director deems necessary to protect any threatened or endangered species in the earliest stages of life (212-A:5). ★★

Any species determined to be an endangered or threatened species pursuant to the Endangered Species Act shall be deemed to be an endangered or threatened species under this chapter. The Director may determine whether a threatened species under the Endangered Species Act is endangered throughout all or any portion of its range within this state. ★In addition to species under the Endangered Species Act, the Director may by rule determine whether any species normally occurring within the state is endangered or threatened because of: ▸ present or threatened destruction, modification or curtailment of its habitat or range; ▸ disease or predation; ▸ overutilization for commercial, sporting, scientific, educational purposes; ▸ other natural or man-made factors affecting its continued existence within the state. Within two years the General Court must ratify said action when it pertains to a commercial or sporting species. If ratification does not take place in the first session of the General Court following listing or within two years, whichever comes first, the species shall be removed from the list for two years or until the General Court ratifies the listing. No species shall be determined endangered or threatened based solely on its rarity. ★ Other than species determined to be endangered or threatened under the federal Endangered Species Act, the Director may not add a species to or remove a species from any list published unless the Director first: ▸ notifies the Governor of any state sharing a common border and in which the subject species is known to occur that such action is being proposed, except where an emergency situation exists involving the continued existence of such species as a viable component of the state's wildlife when the Director may temporarily add species to the list after publishing notice of emergency and a summary of facts in support, such addition to be made permanent by rule adoption; ▸ considers the actions being carried out or about to be carried out by the federal government, other states, other state agencies or any other person which may affect the species under consideration, in making the determination whether endangered or threatened. The Director shall adopt rules containing a list of all species normally occurring within this state determined to be endangered or threatened, and shall specify over what portion of its range each species is threatened with extinction. Except for species listed under the Endangered Species Act, the Director shall, upon petition of an interested person who presents substantial evidence that so warrants, review any listed/unlisted species proposed to be removed from or added to the published lists and give public notice of the review (212-A:6).

It is unlawful, with endangered or threatened species, to: ▸ export same from state; ▸ take/kill such species within this state; ▸ possess, process, sell or offer for sale, deliver, carry transport or ship by any means such species; ▸ violate any rule adopted pertaining to the conservation of such species. The Director may permit any act otherwise prohibited for scientific purposes or to enhance the propagation or survival of the affected species (212-A:7). Any law, regulation or ordinance of any state political subdivision which applies with respect to the taking, importation, exportation, possession, sale, processing or transportation of endangered or threatened species is void to the extent that it may effectively: permit what is prohibited herein or by any rule; prohibit what is authorized pursuant to an exemption or permit provided by this chapter or any rule. This chapter shall not be construed to void any law, regulation or ordinance of any state political subdivision which is intended to conserve wildlife or plants (212-A:8). (See also HABITAT PROTECTION.) Violations: deemed violations, except that illegal export, taking, possession, sale, transport or shipping of endangered/threatened species, failure to obtain a scientific permit, or violation of permit terms are misdemeanors (212-A:10). Equipment, merchandise, wildlife or records seized in enforcement of endangered/threatened species provisions shall be held pending case disposition, and if the defendant is found guilty, forfeited to the state for destruction or disposition as the Director provides. Prior to forfeiture, wildlife so seized shall be transferred to a qualified zoological, educational or scientific institution for safekeeping, costs to be assessed to the defendant if convicted (212-A:11). None of these provisions shall apply retroactively or prohibit importation into this state of wildlife which may be lawfully imported into the US, or lawfully taken and removed from one state to another, or prohibit entry into this state or the possession, transportation, exportation, processing or sale of lawfully taken wildlife threatened/endangered in this state but not in the state of origin. This section does not permit the possession, transportation, exportation, sale or shipment within this state of species determined to be endangered/threatened under the Endangered Species Act (212-A:12).

★★No rule promulgated under these provisions shall cause undue interference with normal agriculture or silvacultural practices, nor interfere with the siting or construction of any bulk power or energy supply facility. The Director shall disseminate any scientific data to organizations representing farmers and other landowners whose land includes habitat used by any endangered or threatened species, indicating that action is contemplated to preserve such species, this information to be made available well in advance of any action taken to preserve the endangered/threatened species. On the effective date of this chapter, with the exception of expenditures then authorized from the Fish and Game Fund, no funds used to carry out these provisions shall be derived from license fees of hunters, fishermen, trappers or from taxes on the sale of equipment unless the species for which the funds are expended have been legally hunted, fished or trapped within the previous five-year period (212-A:13 and :15).★★

The Director, with Commission consent, may adopt rules regulating the taking, possession and handling of nongame species, including rules for the enhancement, protection and propagation of nongame species (212-B:4). The Director shall develop and implement a comprehensive nongame species management program that may include, but not be limited to: ▸ education of the public regarding New Hampshire's nongame resources; ▸ research to determine the populations, distribution, future trends and needs of nongame species; ▸ management measures to maintain and promote the health of self-sustaining nongame populations. The Director may establish programs, including acquisition of land or aquatic habitat or interests therein, for the conservation of nongame species, consult with other states having a common interest in particular nongame species and enter into agreements with federal or state agencies, other states, individuals or corporations to conserve nongame species (212-B:5). (See Agency Funding Sources under STATE FISH AND WILDLIFE AGENCIES.)

GENERAL EXCEPTIONS TO PROTECTION

Any person may take protected birds for educational or scientific purposes with a written permit from the Director. Provisions of 214:30 to 214:33 apply to permits granted under these provisions (209:8-a).

The Director may take, remove or transfer fish, game, fur-bearing animals and marine species at times, in such manner and from any places for the protection or propagation thereof (212:21). The Director may sell or exchange fish, including eggs or fry, birds or eggs, game and fur-bearing animals, with, or to, other states or individuals (212:22).

See special licenses (science, ornithology, mamalogy, public museum, ornithology teacher, and taxidermy) under Commercial and Private Enterprise Provisions under HUNTING, FISHING, TRAPPING PROVISIONS.

HUNTING, FISHING, TRAPPING PROVISIONS

General Provisions

No person shall take, buy, sell, or offer to do so, transport or possess, fish, game, fur-bearing animals or protected birds or any part, except as permitted in this title. A person doing anything prohibited or neglecting to do anything required by this title is deemed to have violated this section. A person who counsels, aids or assists in a violation of this title, or knowingly shares in any of the proceeds of a violation shall be fined or imprisoned as provided in this title the same as a person guilty of such violation (207:2).

★No person shall tear down, damage or destroy any fence, wall, boat, dock or leave open any gate or trample any crop on another's land while taking, trapping, hunting or pursuing any fish, game or fur-bearing animal (207:36). No person shall, without the express written permission of the landowner: ► erect, build or use a tree stand or observation blind on another's land that damages or destroys a tree by inserting any metallic, ceramic or other object; ► erect, build or use a pit blind on another's land; ► cut any tree in connection with activities regulated under this section. The permittee shall have the same in possession while in the field and is subject to inspection on demand. Violation: a violation, and liability for the amount of damage caused by the act. The Director shall adopt rules relative to the form, issuance and filing of property owner permits for tree stands, observation blinds and pit blinds (207:36-a).★

★Any person who negligently discharges any firearm while on a hunting trip, in the field or while target practicing, so that the life of any person is endangered or so as to cause damage to the property of another person, is guilty of a misdemeanor, and at the Director's discretion, their hunting license may be revoked for up to 10 years (207:37-a). Any person who, while in woodlands shoots and wounds or kills a human being shall not be issued a license to hunt, or if the person holds same, it shall be revoked and a license shall not be granted for 10 years. The license to hunt may be granted or restored at the Director's and Commission's discretion at any time after 10 years from revocation.★   ★★Persons convicted of negligently shooting and wounding, or killing a human being while hunting in another state shall not be issued a license to hunt for 10 years from the date of conviction in such other state (207:37-b). Any person who has shot and wounded or killed a human being shall render assistance to the injured person and report immediately to the nearest Conservation or Law Enforcement Officer. Violation: Class B felony, and the hunting license shall be revoked for life; this penalty to be in addition to any other penalty imposed by law (207:38).★★   Any person while hunting or in the field who causes any injury by shooting another human being shall report to the nearest officer, giving name, address and hunting license number and other information as required. Violation: a violation (207:38-a).   ★The Director shall publish the two preceding sections in all pamphlet editions of the fish and game laws (207:39).★   ★Any person, while actually engaged in hunting or the pursuit of wild animals or birds, causing death, injury or damage to domestic animals, ducks or fowl shall be liable to the owner, or if caused by discharge of a firearm or bow and arrow, the hunting license shall be revoked for up to five years. This does not apply to a hunter killing or injuring the hunter's own or a borrowed animal or one used by another member of the same hunting party, other than being liable to the owner, nor does it apply to a hunter killing or injuring a domestic animal "gone wild." The Director is empowered to make such license revocation/suspension and determine the term thereof (207:39-a).★

★No foreign corporation, association, club or similar organization shall hold or acquire property in New Hampshire for the purpose of hunting, fishing, sporting or recreation, without first becoming incorporated in this state and obtaining Director approval as to the purposes of such corporation. The superior court shall have power by injunction to restrain any corporation or club and any member thereof from occupying, using or enjoining any property held or acquired in this state in violation of these provisions, except as otherwise provided for the Blue Mountain Forest Association (207:43 through :45).★   The Director, to protect wildlife resources, may initiate an emergency closure for any season on wildlife for which an open season has been declared. Emergency closures shall be publicized in a statewide newspaper for three days. Taking wildlife during an emergency closure is subject to the same penalty which would be imposed for taking the species during a regular closed season (208:4-c).

The dead bodies of birds for which a closed season is provided shall not be sold, offered for sale or possessed for sale within this state except as permitted to authorized game breeders (209:12). A resident may transport, within the state, during the open season, the limit of fish or wildlife, except deer, that may be lawfully taken in two days. If such fish or wildlife is transported by common carrier, the package must be labeled with the kind and number of fish or wildlife, consignor/consignee's names, and destination. A nonresident license holder may transport a two day limit of fish or wildlife, except deer, within or without the state if labeled as specified above, and if the common carrier determines that the license is properly endorsed before accepting for shipment. Any transportation of fish or wildlife, except deer, not provided for above requires a special permit for shipment (207:19 through :21).

Licenses and Permits

No person, except as otherwise provided, shall at any time fish, hunt, trap, shoot, pursue, take or kill freshwater fish, saltwater smelt, shad or salmonoids, wild birds or wild animals in this state without a license, and then only in accordance with the terms of such license and subject to all title provisions. The licensee shall have in possession such license when so engaged, and shall be subject to inspection on demand of any person (214:1). No person shall fish through the ice on Great Bay or its tributaries without a license and in accordance with its terms. No person shall hunt, shoot, pursue, kill or take: pheasants without a pheasant stamp, in addition to a hunting license; wild turkey without a wild turkey permit; migratory waterfowl without a migratory waterfowl stamp, in addition to a hunting license and a federal duck stamp. "Migratory waterfowl" means ducks, mergansers, coots, geese and brant for purposes of this section. Violation of migratory waterfowl stamp provisions is a violation, and a separate offense for each bird taken (214:1-a through :1-d). License and stamp provisions do not apply to resident farmland owners and minor children while upon their own land, to persons fishing in ponds operated by a licensed fish or game breeder and to resident children under age 16 while fishing, hunting or trapping when accompanied by a licensee over age 18. [Other exceptions or special licenses or fees apply to military personnel, disabled veterans, paraplegics, patients at certain state and other institutions, group home patients, residents over age 65, and residents over age 68 as specified (214:3, :6, :7-a, :13, :14 and :14-a through :14-g)]. Minimum residence requirement is two years and a false statement relative to residency is a misdemeanor (214:7-b). The Director shall determine the form of licenses, game tags, permits, stamps and other forms, and the information required (214:8). [A large number of types of licenses and fees are listed in 214:9.] Lifetime resident combination hunting and fishing licenses shall be issued upon payment of the proper fee. (See Agency Funding Sources under STATE FISH AND WILDLIFE AGENCIES.) A bear license and tag may be issued to a lifetime license holder for the current season only at no charge (214:9-c). The Director may issue one-day fishing licenses for state parks (214:14-c).

★No person is authorized to procure a license to hunt or fish without a receipt indicating payment of all resident taxes for the preceding year for which the person is liable, or a certificate indicating they have been lawfully relieved from payment, unless the selectmen or assessors certify that the applicant should be granted such license even though taxes have not been paid. Notwithstanding the above, presentation of a New Hampshire driver's license in lieu of the receipt or certificate is sufficient to permit issuance of the licenses referred to herein. A person no longer a legal state resident, but who retains a driver's license, shall be guilty of a misdemeanor if they try to obtain a resident fishing or hunting license based on this driver's license.★ Filing a false tax receipt is a violation, and the license may be revoked for up to three months. Any other false statement for the purpose of procuring a license is a violation. Fines shall be deposited in the Fish and Game Fund (214:11-a).

★No trapping license shall be issued without a certificate of competency or proof of completion of a trapper education course in any other state, province or country which is equivalent to this state's course, or proof of previously having held a trapping license in this state, another state, province or country. In addition to other penalties, the Director may require a person in violation of this section or the state trapping laws to take the trapper education course as a condition to retain or reinstate a trapping license (214:11-b).★ No hunting license shall be issued unless one of the following is presented: ‣ a certificate of completion; ‣ proof of completion of a hunter education program in this state, another state, province or country which is equivalent to the program provided herein; ‣ proof of previously holding a hunting license in this or another state or country. The Director, after consultation with the Commission, may establish a program for training persons in safe handling of firearms and may cooperate with any public or private association having as one of its objectives the promotion of safety in firearms handling (214:23-a and :23-b).

★The Director and license agents shall refuse to issue any license to hunt if it appears that the applicant is not suitable to carry firearms. Such person has a right of appeal to the Director, whose decision, after hearing, shall be final. Any attempt to secure a license after having been refused and before appeal to the Director, or after being declared nonsuitable, is a violation (214:17).★

★★Any resident who applies for a combination hunting and fishing license, may for an additional fee of $8 obtain a super sportsman license, the additional fee permitting the applicant to designate in which of the following categories they want the additional fee expended: wildlife management; fisheries; a combination of both. The $8 over the basic license fee shall be deposited in the appropriate special fund and used exclusively for that purpose (214:7-c).★★ (See Agency Funding Sources under STATE FISH AND WILDLIFE AGENCIES.)

A resident age 16 or older may be issued an archery license to hunt wildlife with bow and arrow during the open season, and to hunt deer during the special archery season. The licensee may take one deer under the archery license and one additional deer if a regular firearms hunting license is possessed. No person taking deer under these provisions shall take deer with any type of firearm. An archery license is not proof that the licensee has previously had a hunting license in this state or any other state or country (208:5). Otherwise qualified persons over age 16 may be issued a muzzle-loading license to hunt deer (208:5-a).

No person shall take wild black bears without first procuring a bear license and tag in addition to the applicable hunting license. The Director shall determine the form of such license and tag, and the licensee shall tag a taken bear, such tag to remain attached as long as the carcass remains in the state. Only the bear tag issued to the licensee who killed the bear shall be attached to that bear; no person shall attach a tag to a bear the person did not kill, nor possess a tag not issued to the person. A bear license does not constitute proof that the holder thereof previously had a hunting license in this state, another state or country. Violation: misdemeanor (208:24). No person shall hunt, capture, kill, take, possess, buy or sell any migratory game bird or part except as prescribed by Migratory Bird Treaty Act regulations which are hereby made a part of the game law of the state. No person age 16 or older shall take any migratory waterfowl (brant, wild ducks, geese and swans) unless they have on their person an unexpired federal migratory bird stamp (duck stamp), required in addition to a state hunting license. Regulations under the Migratory Bird Hunting Stamp Act are hereby made a part of the state game law (209:6).

Restrictions on Taking: Hunting and Trapping

★Upon application, any person licensed to hunt shall be issued a permit for training bird dogs and trail or tree hounds during the closed season on any wildlife, except deer, moose, caribou, elk, lynx, cougar and turkey. Bear dogs may not be trained between May 1 and June 30, except permittees may train dogs upon land owned/leased by the permittee, or upon land for which they have written permission, in possession while training. Training under this exception is permitted only on wildlife legally possessed by the permittee, and released according to statutory provisions. Any protected species accidentally killed during dog training shall be turned over to the Department intact within 48 hours of taking (207:12-a). (See Interstate Reciprocal Agreements under this section.) A nonresident shall not train or use dogs for hunting any specific wildlife species in this state during the period when residents of New Hampshire are prohibited from training or using dogs for hunting such wildlife species in the nonresident's state, and this shall also apply when the nonresident's state or province of Canada restricts or limits the number of dog training or dog hunting permits issued to New Hampshire citizens. The Director shall determine the states, provinces or territories which prohibit or limit New Hampshire residents from training or use of dogs for hunting, and such determination as to the degree of reciprocity shall be final (207:12-b). Field trials for dogs may be held at times, in such manner, and under such restrictions as the Director prescribes., and a written permit from the landowner is required. The Director shall issue permits for beagle trials to any beagle club recognized by the American Kennel Club. The Director shall issue permits for night hunts to any coon club recognized by the United Kennel Club, which may take place in selected locations except on posted lands, and anyone may participate therein (207:13).★

★Any person, when hunting with dogs is permitted, may post along highways up to two signs reading "Caution Hunting Dogs" of the size prescribed and as specified herein.★ It is unlawful to shoot any wildlife which has been treed or cornered by a dog, unless the owner of the dog, or a hunting party member, is present when the animal is shot. Violation: misdemeanor (207:13-a and :13-b).

Wildlife shall be taken in the daytime between one-half hour before sunrise and one-half hour after sunset with a gun fired at arm's length or bow and arrow, unless otherwise permitted; except that a full automatic rifle shall not be used nor a semi-automatic rifle to which is attached a magazine or clip holding more than five cartridges, nor a full jacketed metal case bullet, either in its original form or any alteration thereof. This does not apply to the use of .22 caliber rimfire rifles, or to the use of pistols or revolvers. A person may take wildlife during the open season with the aid of a dog, unless otherwise prohibited (207:3). These provisions shall not apply to ranch bred mink (207:1-a). It is unlawful to hunt or discharge firearms on another island without permission of the owner, if the person is within 300 feet of a permanently occupied building and on the land of the building's owner. Violation: a violation if a natural person; a misdemeanor if any other person (207:3-a). No person shall discharge a firearm in pursuit of wild birds or wild animals from or across any class I through V public highway including rights of way except as otherwise provided. Violation: a violation (207:3-c). No person shall sell, use, or have in possession any firearm fitted with a silencer. Nothing herein prohibits the use of a muzzle brake, polychoke or compensator. ★No person, while hunting or obviously on the way to or from hunting, shall have a ferret in possession, custody or control. No person shall take game for wages or hire (207:4, :6 and :8).★

★No person shall engage in the practice of baiting for coyote, fur-bearing animals or game animals with the exception of gray squirrel from April 15 to the day before the opening of the season for the taking of wild black bear. No person shall engage in the act of baiting on another's property without a written permit from the owner/occupant, and until a copy has been filed with the conservation office in that district, together with a topographic map showing the specific location of the bait site. Persons with a trapping license who have complied with the landowner permit requirements of 210:11 and 210:17, II(b) may place bait for trapping fur-bearing animals during the open season.★ The Director may grant a special permit for scientific purposes, animal damage control or any other purpose. No person shall place bait less than 300 feet from a dwelling or public roadway, path or trail (207:3-d). ★No person shall use a telemetry receiver to locate trail or tree hounds during nighttime hours while in any motorized vehicle or within 300 feet, as measured from the center of the traveled portion, of any road open to public use. Violation: a violation if a natural person; a misdemeanor for any other person (207:3-e).★

No person shall take wild birds or wild animals from a motor vehicle, OHRV, boat, aircraft or other craft propelled by mechanical power, nor carry in or on such a loaded rifle or shotgun or loaded clip attached to the gun. Disabled persons may obtain a special permit from the director entitling them to hunt while using a motor vehicle, not to include motorized boats or airplanes, following procedures specified. Violation: a violation, plus an additional violation for each wild bird or animal taken/possessed (207:7, :7-a and :7-b). No person shall possess, while hunting or trapping any wild bird or wild animal, including bear, any snare, jack or artificial light, swivel, pivot or set gun, or crossbow except as permitted. Any person convicted of illegal night hunting shall forfeit such firearms, jacks or other equipment. Prohibited devices do not apply to fish and game employees when engaged in removing nuisance animals, birds or fish. No person shall at any time of year affix tags, markers or radio transmitters on any fish, game or fur-bearing animals, or any wild animals or birds without the Director's written permission, and it is unlawful to locate wildlife tagged with the Director's permission with the aid and use of a radio receiver, except by persons authorized (207:10, :10-a amd :10-b).

Wild deer shall not be taken by the use of any firearm, other than a shotgun loaded with a single ball or loose buckshot, muzzle-loading rifle or bow and arrow, in specified counties (208:3). Buckshot is prohibited for listed townships (208:3-a through -c). ★Wild deer shall not be taken by the use of .22 cal. rimfire firearm (208:4). No person shall knowingly take deer with the aid or use of a dog, trap, snare, salt lick, swivel, pivot or set gun, nor drive deer by the use of horns, whistles, or other noise-making devices or by the use of an OHRV, aircraft or other motorized vehicles. It is unlawful for more than six persons to participate in a drive to take deer (208:7).★ It is a misdemeanor knowingly to: take wild birds or animals between one-half hour after sunset and one-half hour before sunrise; use an artificial light during those hours to illuminate, locate or attempt such of wild birds or animals while having in possession or in a motor vehicle, OHRV, boat, aircraft or other mechanically powered craft, a bow and arrow, crossbow and bolt, rifle, pistol, revolver, shotgun or muzzleloading firearm, whether loaded or unloaded. A person convicted of illegal night hunting shall forfeit such firearms, lights or other equipment used. ★The knowledge or belief required for the above is presumed in the case of a person who: uses or is found in possession of a rifle, revolver or pistol larger than .22 caliber long rifle; uses or is found in possession of shotgun shells carrying shot larger than number 4 (208:8).★ Any person who deliberately uses an artificial light during the period from October 1 through December 31 to illuminate, jack, locate or attempt such of wild birds or animals shall be guilty of a violation. The taking of raccoons pursuant to 210:12 shall be an affirmative defense to an alleged violation of this section (208:8-a).

No person shall possess the carcass or any part of a wild deer or moose without the tag attached or by special permission of the Director, nor possess a deer or moose or parts given to the person by another unless each piece or package is clearly labeled with date of receipt and name and address of donor. Violation: a violation for the first offense; a misdemeanor for any subsequent offense (208:9). ★★Any person who shall steal, take and carry away a deer, bear or any part, of another without permission shall be guilty of a misdemeanor if a natural person, or guilty of a felony if any other person (208:9-a). ★★ ★No owner, keeper, or employee of any camp, house or other building used in lumbering operations, shall use, consume, permit to be served as food, store or possess at any time, in, at, or about same any deer or part.★ No person shall buy, sell or offer such of a deer or moose or part except the head, hide or feet. A resident may transport within the state, during the open season and for 10 days thereafter, a legally taken deer, when accompanied by the resident and open to view, if properly tagged and registered, or if shipped by common carrier, properly identified. A nonresident may transport within or without the state a legally taken deer following these provisions. Any transportation of deer not covered herein shall be allowed only under the terms of a special permit signed by the Director. The possession of a deer or any part by a person or common carrier, otherwise than as herein prescribed shall be prima facie evidence of a violation (208:10 through :15). The Director shall establish deer registration stations as necessary, at which legally taken deer shall have a metal seal attached. Any person killing a deer shall present it for registration at the first open deer registration station encountered, and no person shall: ▸ present for registration a deer which the person did not kill; ▸ keep a deer in the home or place of storage for longer than 12 hours unless registered; ▸ leave a deer where it was killed without notifying a conservation officer within 12 hours as to its location and describing the circumstances necessitating leaving it in the woods; ▸ possess at any time any deer or part which has not been legally registered except as otherwise provided (208:15-a through :15-g). The holder of a hunting license shall be provided with a deer tag and shall, upon killing a deer, attach, and leave it attached as long as the deer remains in the state. Only the tag issued to the licensee who killed the deer shall be attached, no person shall possess a deer tag not issued to that person, and no person shall attach a deer tag to a deer the person did not kill (208:16).

The Director, with the Commission's consent, shall adopt rules relative to opening and closing seasons for wild black bear, fixing the number, methods and manner of taking, and reporting. Dog training shall be permitted in accordance with 207:12-a. No bear shall be taken at any time on any island or in any waters, lakes or ponds. Dogs shall not be trained or used for taking bear from baited areas after a date determined by the Director. "Baited area" means an area where meat, carrion, honey or other substance capable of attracting bear has been placed for luring wildlife. Wild black bear may be taken by dogs as permitted by 208:22; by firearms; or by bow and arrow of at least 40 pound pull. No person shall take bear by use of a jack or artificial light, trap, snare, set gun or .22 caliber rimfire firearm unless otherwise provided. Any person who kills a wild bear shall report it in accordance with rules herein. Landowners or their agents may set traps for bear doing damage to property, only after the Director has been notified of damage and has investigated the complaint, and has issued a special permit for the use of traps. Any traps shall be set in accordance with 210:15. ★The carcass of a bear legally taken and reported may be bought and sold. Live bear may not be offered for sale at any time except by a person authorized by the Director.★ ★Violations of provisions involving illegal use of dogs, bows and arrows, illegal devices or lights, illegal setting of traps for bears, illegal buying and selling of bears, alive or dead, or illegal guiding for bear are, for natural persons, a misdemeanor, and for any other person a felony.★ Other violations of these provisions are a violation for a natural person, and for any other person a misdemeanor, except that any person who exceeds the bag limit for bear shall be guilty of a misdemeanor (208:22).

No wild bird for which a closed season is provided shall be trapped or snared or, if so taken, possessed. Any trap, snare, or other device in which any bird may be taken is declared to be a public nuisance, and may be summarily destroyed by any person. These provisions shall not apply to the setting of a trap on a pole for the purpose of taking unprotected birds under a Director permit (209:11). The Director has authority to: ▸ establish seasons, bag limits and registration stations; ▸ issue wild turkey hunting permits; ▸ specify methods for taking and registering wild turkeys; ▸ establish regulations for enhancement, protection, and propagation of wild turkeys. No person shall have in possession any wild turkey or part which has not been registered as required, except for turkeys possessed between the time of killing and the time of presentation to a registration station. Violation: misdemeanor (209:12-a and :13).

It is unlawful for any person to sell, give away, buy, possess, accept as a gift, or transport raw skins or unskinned carcasses of any fur-bearing animal or coyote, except muskrat, skunk or weasel, without an official tag. Nothing prohibits the transportation or possession of raw pelts or unskinned fur-bearing animals or coyotes when accompanied by the hunter/trapper or designee specified in writing. All skins shall be presented to a conservation officer for tagging within 10 days of the close of the season. Any skin that comes into this state from any other state, country or province shall bear an official tag or stamp from that state or country, or if no seal is required, the skins must be tagged within three days of entry into this state, or a bill of sale produced for inspection. ★As a prerequisite of tagging, the Director may require that the skinned carcasses of certain fur-bearing animals or coyotes be turned over for analysis, and notice of this requirement given to hunters/trappers before the opening of the season (210:8).★ No person shall sell, buy, give away or possess any fur seals/tags unless legally affixed to skins or furs, or remove or deface same. Violation: a violation for each offense (210:8-a).

No person shall hunt raccoons at night by the use of a rifle, revolver, or pistol larger than .22 caliber long rifle or shotgun shells larger than number 4. Lights may be used to take raccoons, except for lights from a motor vehicle (210:2). No person shall destroy or injure a muskrat house, den or burrow, or place a trap within 15 feet, nor destroy or injure the house, den or burrow used by any game animal or fur-bearing animal (210:4). During the open season, beaver and otter shall be taken and possessed by resident trappers only, and taken only by traps (210:7). No person shall destroy or interfere with the dams or houses of beaver, without first obtaining a special permit from the Director; however, notwithstanding any other law or rule of the Director or the Water Resources Division of the Department of Environmental Services, a landowner, tenant or agent, or any town, municipal or state official or employee, may destroy beaver and beaver dams on property under their control to protect property, public highways or bridges from damage or submersion, with the permission of the affected landowner if applicable. The Director may require the reporting of beaver so taken. Skins or unskinned carcasses taken shall be sealed as required before they are sold or given away (210:9).

★No person shall set any trap upon land or from the shores of waters of which the person is not the owner/occupant, except such traps as may be placed under water from a boat or canoe or through the ice on any public body of water, until a permit in writing signed by the owner has been secured and the person has filed with the conservation officer in whose district the trapping is to be done a copy and a description of the land on which the trapping is to be done.★ All metal traps shall have the trappers name affixed. Traps shall not be set in a public way, or path commonly used as a passageway by humans or domestic animals. The Director may issue special permits allowing the setting of traps for specified periods and locations under bridges or in ditches within public highway rights-of way to protect the highway (210:11).

It is unlawful to set any conibear traps larger than number 220 except when the trap is: five feet or more above the ground or surface of the snow with the exception of a snowstorm during the previous 24 hours; in water for trapping beaver or otter; set for bear under provisions herein (210:11-a). No person shall set any trap prior to the first day of the open season (210:12). A person shall visit traps at least once a day, during daylight hours, except that a person trapping beaver through the ice shall visit traps once in each 72 hours. Only the trap owner has authority to tend traps, but in emergency may grant written permission to another licensed trapper to tend them (210:13). ★A person who sets a bear trap shall build, a railing or guard not less than three feet high, and shall set at least two painted signs with "bear trap" thereon (210:15).★

No person shall use any device which discharges a firearm (spring gun) for taking game or fur-bearing animals. ★No person shall use a snare or poison, explosives or chemicals or smoke out or dig out any den or house, or cut den trees, for the purpose of taking fur-bearing animals, except that snares set under water or ice are permitted for taking beaver and otter only, during the open season, provided each snare is tagged and that in addition to the landowner permit, the trapper has secured from the landowner a special permit to use snares, and has filed a copy with the conservation officer in whose district the snares will be set. The Director may adopt rules for the use of snares. Any person taking fur-bearing animals or coyotes by the use of snares shall meet all requirements pertaining to traps and trapping.★ Any person causing injury to domestic animals by traps shall be liable to the owner. Violations of provisions relating to unlawful night taking of raccoon or unlawful seal taking, or destruction of muskrat or other game or fur-bearing animal houses: a natural person is guilty of a violation; if any other person, a misdemeanor; and each animal taken or possessed is an additional violation. Violations of provisions for non-posting of bear traps or use of spring guns: a natural person is guilty of a misdemeanor; or a felony if any other person; and such person shall be liable for twice the amount of the damage caused. For each violation involving illegal use of snares, poisons, explosives, or den destruction, a person is guilty of a violation (210:16 through :19).

By April 15, every person licensed to take fur-bearing animals shall file with the Director a report of catch. Failure to report by May 15 is a fine and a violation, and the person shall be refused a license for the next succeeding trapping season, following an appeal procedure (210:21). The Director with the Commission's approval may declare an open or closed season on any fur-bearing animals in any county or town and may make other rules for lengthening or shortening season and bag limits. Notice of season changes shall be published once in a newspaper in the county affected (210:23 and :24). The Director may set a different season for taking of fur-bearing animals for nonresident hunters and trappers (210:24-a). ★There is a program to provide education to citizens on the practice of trapping fur-bearing animals as a recognized conservation and management tool as well as a traditional sport avocation, to be administered by the Director, with Commission approval, and funded from revenues derived from trapping, such funds to be nonlapsing (210:25).★

Restrictions on Taking: Fishing

Fish shall be taken only by angling unless otherwise permitted. Fish unintentionally taken contrary to title provisions shall be immediately returned to the water without unnecessary injury. Tip-ups, set and trap lines, crossbows, spears, grappling hooks, naked hooks, snatch hooks, eel wires, eel pots and nets shall not be used in any state fresh waters to take fish unless specifically permitted (207:9 and :10).

A person who violates any rules promulgated under 206:10 to 206:13 relating to sizes, weights, numbers, seasons and methods of taking fish is guilty of a violation for each fish taken, possessed, bought or sold in violation thereof (211:1). A person who violates any rules of the Director relative to fresh water or salt water fish is guilty of a violation, and an additional violation for each such fish taken, possessed, bought or sold in violation, provided that if all violations are the result of the actions of the person on a single complaint, the maximum total fine shall be $100 plus $10 for each fish taken in violation (211:1-a).

The taking of brook trout, lake trout, lake trout hybrids, aureolus or golden trout and salmon during nighttime hours is prohibited, except that the Director, with Commission consent, may designate certain streams or parts, where brown trout may be taken at night. Violation: a violation, plus a violation for each fish taken, except if all violations are the result of their actions on a single complaint, the maximum total fine shall be $100 plus $10 for each fish taken in violation (211:2-a). No person shall take fish of any species from October 16 to the day prior to the fourth Saturday in April from any lake or pond designated as a trout water by rule. Violation: a violation, plus a violation for each fish taken (211:2-b). No person shall take smelt from state fresh waters by any method other than by angling, unless the Director determines that other methods of taking would not be detrimental to the state smelt resources. The Director may open and close the smelt season, fix the daily bag and possession limits and govern methods and manner of taking and reporting. Violation: a violation (211:2-e). There shall be no weight limit on the taking of black bass during the bass open season (211:6-b).

No person shall take any fish by the use of any poisonous, stupefying or explosive substance. Possession of same by any person on state waters, shores or islands, except for mining or mechanical purposes, is prima facie evidence that it is possessed for use in violation (211:7). No person shall prevent fish passage in any stream or river by any rack, screen, weir or other obstruction except for dams licensed by the Federal Power Commission (211:8 and :8-c). No person shall take fish by shutting or drawing off water. A dip net may be used to assist in taking fish attached to a hook. A circular drop net may be used to take minnows for bait from waters not inhabited by brook trout, and minnow traps may be used in trout waters according to trap size specifications (211:9 and :10). No person shall use, possess, or furnish for another's use for taking fish in state fresh waters, except as otherwise permitted, a net, set line, fishing otter, trawl, grapple, spear, jack, jack light or electrical or other device for killing or stunning fish. A person found on state waters having in possession such devices shall be prima facie guilty of a violation. Such devices are declared to be public nuisances and may be seized and destroyed by any person. These provisions do not apply to the Director or the Director's agents (211:13). No person may use carp or goldfish as live bait when fishing in state waters, and possession of same while fishing shall be prima facie evidence of a violation. No person shall use shad or whitefish for bait for cusk. ★No person shall take or use any species of fish except suckers for fertilizer.★ Unless otherwise provided, violations involving illegal devices, methods or bait are violations (211:15 through :17).

Persons placing a smelt shanty or bob-house on the ice for ice fishing shall label it with the owners name and address. Violation: a violation and hunting and fishing privileges may be suspended for 30 days. Shantys and bob-houses must be removed by April 7, or the Department may claim such property and sell it at a public auction. No person owning a bob-house shall conspire with another to burn same on the ice. Violation: a violation. Fishing holes on Great Bay may not exceed 112 square inches in area unless covered by a bob-house or marked with a stake extending at least 18 inches above the ice. Violation: a violation. Driving OHRV's on the ice on Great Bay is restricted to licensed fishermen, who may not drive closer than 300 feet to any occupied bob-house except their own, nor exceed a speed of 10 miles per hour (211:17-a through :17-c).

Commercial and Private Enterprise Provisions

No person shall promote or operate any commercial fishing contest in state waters without first procuring a special permit from the Director, who may adopt regulations for such contests (211:16-b). No person shall engage in the business of guiding until a guide license is procured. A guide who violates any title provision or regulation or who makes any false statement in the application, or whom the Director deems unsuitable to act as a guide, shall immediately forfeit and surrender the guide license. Guides shall be at least 18 years old, furnish recommendations, be skilled in the use, management and handling of boats or canoes customarily used in fishing and hunting, and be a safe and competent person under all circumstances to be a guide for hunting or fishing parties. Residents over age 65 who have been licensed guides for at least five years may obtain a guide license without fee. Guides shall wear badges furnished by the Director. Violation of any guide provisions is a violation, and license forfeiture at the Director's discretion (215:1 through :9).

"Aquaculture" is the propagation and rearing of aquatic species and marine species and includes the planting, promoting of growth, harvesting and transporting of these species in, on or from the state waters, or the operation of a fishing preserve. The Director shall adopt rules for taking, permitting, inspection, possession, processing, sale, propagation, planting, harvesting and transportation of aquatic or marine species related to aquaculture or fishing preserve operations including, but not limited to: ▸ size, sex, number and quantity that may be taken, processed or imported; ▸ areas to be opened or closed to their taking, rearing, harvesting, planting, and growth promotion; ▸ method and manner of taking; ▸ transportation within or through the state; ▸ sale, inspection, processing and marking; ▸ methods of keeping, recapture, permit fees and definitions. Aquaculture licenses allow release and recapture of domestically reared anadromous fish in state waters. No license shall be issued which interferes with the natural runs of anadromous fish, result in waste or deterioration of fish, or when the proposed operation is on a stream below a state or federal fish hatchery or egg taking station. All fish released into the wild, while in the wild, will lose their status as private property and may be taken by licensed anglers. Any license granted shall contain the following conditions: ▸ domestically reared anadromous fish released into state waters shall be marked if practicable; ▸ if the operation is not in the public interest, the Director may alter the license conditions to mitigate adverse effects or cause an orderly termination of the operation within three years; ▸ if deterioration of the natural anadromous fish runs occurs, the Director shall require the licensee to return the run to the original condition or pay for the costs; prior to release into state waters, all fish to be examined by a qualified pathologist and certified that they are free of disease which could be detrimental to state resources; ▸ provisions for fish recapture after passage through state or federal fish passage facilities shall be followed, and recaptured unmarked fish released as specified (211:62-e). (See also RELEVANT WILDLIFE DEFINITIONS.)

No person shall propagate or sell, dead or alive, wildlife or the eggs or progeny, or operate a hunting preserve, without a permit. The Director may determine the time period and other conditions governing the permit, and may refuse to issue same if it may pose significant disease, genetic, ecological, environmental, health, safety, or welfare risks to persons or wildlife. The Director shall adopt rules relative to the taking, permitting, inspection, possession, processing, sale, rearing, harvesting, identifying, releasing and transportation of wildlife as related to propagation or selling of wildlife, or the operating of a hunting preserve, including: ▸ size, sex, number and quantity possessed, processed or imported; ▸ areas to be opened or closed to their harvesting, rearing, and releasing; ▸ method and manner of harvest; ▸ transportation within/through the state; ▸ sale, inspection, processing and marking; ▸ method of keeping and recapture; ▸ permit fee schedules; ▸ appropriate definitions. Such licenses shall be issued at the Director's discretion, and are subject to revocation and suspension at any time (212:25 and :26). Licensees must submit detailed annual reports. It is a violation to hunt, capture, take or kill any fish, game or fur-bearing animals covered by a license without the permission of the licensee. It is a violation to violate any rule of the Director governing private propagation provisions, plus license forfeiture (212:31 through :33).

No person except as otherwise provided shall at any time engage in the business of buying furs or skins of fur-bearing animals or the hides or skins of deer, without a license. The fur-buyer's license entitles the licensee to buy and sell the furs and skins of deer, coyotes and fur-bearing animals lawfully taken, and to sell and transport them under restrictions in this title. Licensed dealers shall keep records as the Director requires. Every person selling or shipping furs or skins to persons outside the state, not licensed in this state, shall keep the same records and make the same report. ★The Director may grant licenses which may be revoked or suspended at any time to: ▸ a person in the state of known scientific attainment in ornithology or mammalogy; ▸ an agent of any public museum in the state; ▸ a teacher of ornithology in any state school; ▸ a person desiring to practice taxidermy. Such licenses shall state the purpose for which issued and the privileges granted. No license shall be required for the common practice of capturing and banding game and song birds; however, a permit without fee shall be required and issued under the Director's stipulations. This shall not dispense with the necessity of federal permits as required by federal law. Persons desiring a special license shall present a petition, on the Director's forms, accompanied by the written statement of at least two well-known citizens of community where the applicant resides, certifying to the applicant's good character and fitness to be entrusted with the privileges. ★ Upon the Director's request, at the expiration of any special license, the holder shall file a sworn statement, covering all transactions. The licensee shall keep a record of all transactions under the license and such record, together with all plants and premises of the licensee, shall be open to inspection upon demand, and such licensee shall answer any question relative to the ownership of any bird or animal, or part, found in possession or control (214:24 through :32).

No person shall take, sell or offer to sell live fish for bait without a license. Resident and nonresident retail and wholesale licenses are available (214:34). Any person holding a Bait Dealer's license may take smelt, minnows, shiners, suckers, chubs or tommycod by means of a hand-held dip net or other nets or traps as specified, or by minnow seines of detailed sizes (214:34-a). [Details are given as to equipment, ice holes for bait taking, bait houses, molesting the bait-gear of another in 214:34-b and 214:34-c). There shall be no closed season for taking members of the minnow family, including shiners, for bait by methods prescribed in 211:9, except in designated brook trout waters during the closed trout season. The season for taking freshwater smelt for bait is set in statute (214:34-e). ★The Director may adopt and enforce rules for bait dealers dealing in live fish with the exception of daily bag and possession limits which are: a retailer may take 20 quarts per day and hold a maximum of 100 quarts in possession at any one time; a wholesaler may take 100 quarts per day and hold a maximum of 200 quarts. Nothing herein shall affect the sale of garden worms or night crawlers (214:35). ★

See also Import, Export, Release Provisions under this section for wholesale venison and fish licenses and provisions.

Import, Export, Release Provisions

No person shall import, possess, sell, exhibit, or release any live marine species or wildlife, or their eggs or progeny, without a permit. The Director has the authority to determine the time period and other conditions governing the issuance of such permit, and may refuse to issue if issuance may pose significant disease, genetic, ecological, environmental, health, safety or welfare risks to persons, marine species or wildlife. The Director shall adopt rules for importation, possession, exhibition, sale or release of all marine species and wildlife, including, but not limited to: ▸ size, sex, number and quantity; ▸ transportation, within or through the state; ▸ sale, inspection, processing, recordkeeping and marking; ▸ method of keeping, areas of release, method of release, or taking, permit fee schedules and appropriate definitions. The Director may establish a list of marine species or wildlife or eggs or progeny which are exempt from any or all of these provisions. Violation: a violation for each marine species or wildlife illegally possessed (207:14). All fish or fry, living wild birds or eggs, or wild animals imported or released in this state contrary to these provisions shall be seized and forfeited (207:15-a). No person shall buy, sell, offer for sale, carry outside the state, or place in private waters any fish or fry entrusted to the person's care by the Director for distribution in state waters (211:14).

No person shall import any species of wild turkey, hybrid wild turkey, or wild turkey-domestic turkey cross or any egg of same into New Hampshire. Any person in possession of any of these when this section takes effect shall be permitted to keep or propagate them by special permit from the Director. No person not a Department employee, or acting under Department orders shall sell, give away, or release into the wild a live wild turkey, hybrid wild turkey, or wild turkey-domestic turkey cross or any fertile egg (212:25-a).

Freshwater fish raised outside the state may be possessed, bought and sold for food, if labeled as specified. A wholesaler's license is required to sell freshwater fish in the state. Hotels, stores or restaurants wishing to sell freshwater fish raised outside the state shall have bills of sale with information as detailed (212:30-a). Venison, including red deer and elk, but not including Virginia white-tailed deer imported from outside the state may be possessed, bought and sold for use as food in restaurants if accompanied with bills of sale. Residents and nonresidents wishing to sell imported venison of these species shall procure a wholesaler's license and provide bills of sale (212:30-d). Restaurants wishing to sell venison imported from outside the state must obtain a license. Violation of venison provisions is a violation if a natural person and a misdemeanor if any other person (212:30-e).

No fish shall be brought into this state for use as bait without a permit from the Director, valid up to one year. No additional permit is required to import the same species from the same source of supply. Five days' notification of each intent to import shall be filed with the Director (214:34-d).

See PROTECTED SPECIES OF WILDLIFE AND Restrictions on Taking: Hunting and Trapping under this section.

Interstate Reciprocal Agreements

The Director may consult with the Director's counterpart in adjacent states for reciprocal fishing agreements as to licensing requirements and other details for lakes or ponds lying partly in another state, and in order to secure uniformity, may set special rules and regulations as to the whole of such lake or pond, if practicable. Similar arrangements may be worked out with Vermont concerning reciprocal licensing and fishing privileges for the Connecticut River lying between the two states [details as to procedures to be worked out between the states are given] (211:4 and :5). Violation of special rules relating to interstate reciprocity is a violation, and an additional violation for each fish taken or possessed in violation (211:6). ★The Director may issue complimentary lifetime nonresident hunting and fishing licenses to certain disabled or paraplegic or disabled veteran residents from another state if that state provides a reciprocal privilege for New Hampshire residents similarly suffering (214:13-b).★ (See also HABITAT PROTECTION for reciprocal endangered/threatened species provisions.)

ANIMAL DAMAGE CONTROL

★A person who suffers damage to fruit trees from budding by game birds, shall, if damages are claimed therefor, within 10 days from the discovery thereof, and not later than April 15, notify the Director in writing. The Director shall investigate such claim, determine whether such damage was caused by game birds, and appraise the amount to be paid, as soon as practical after the budding ceases in the spring, and shall make a second appraisal just before the fruit crop is harvested. Within 60 days from the second appraisal, the Director shall present a certificate of the amount of appraisal to the Governor who is authorized to draw upon the Fish and Game fund in payment (207:22).★ Any person who posts land shall forfeit the right to collect damages from game or game birds except for persons who post only their land lying within 200 yards of their dwelling or outbuildings, nor shall these provisions apply to persons who post their land for the protection of their crops only during the closed season for the type of game birds or animals for which they seek to collect damages (207:22-a). A person who suffers game damage to annual crops or fruit trees, or well-kept natural stands of blueberries maintained commercially which have been improved shall, if damages are claimed within 10 days of the discovery, notify the Director in writing. The Director shall investigate within 30 days, determine such damage, and appraise the amount to be paid. The appraisal shall be made at time of harvest, and the Director shall present the appraisal to the Governor who shall authorize payment (207:23).

★A person who suffers loss or damage to livestock, bees, orchards or growing crops by bear or mountain lion, shall, if damage is claimed, notify the Director in writing. The Director shall investigate such claim within 30 days, and within one year determine whether such damage was caused by bear or mountain lion and appraise the amount to be paid, and present same to the Governor for payment (207:23-a). Upon receiving a complaint of damages caused by game birds, game animals or mountain lions, the Director may expend funds for materials and other preventive measures to alleviate the damage (207:23-b). If the person sustaining the damage is dissatisfied with the finding of the Director, either as to the cause of damage or the amount thereof, the person may appeal within 30 days, by filing a statement with the Director, and the damages shall be determined as to cause and amount by an impartial board of three persons designated by the Governor (207:24).★

A person may pursue, wound or kill, on land owned or occupied by the person, any wild bird or wild animal found in the act of damage to poultry or the person's property, and may authorize a family member or agent to do so under the written authority from the Director. The person by whom or under whose direction any game or fur-bearing animal is wounded or killed shall, within 12 hours, report all relevant facts to the nearest conservation officer or to the Director. The conservation officer receiving such notice shall immediately investigate and determine whether the game or fur-bearing animal has been wounded or killed as reported. Any game or fur-bearing animal killed or wounded as provided herein shall, at the Director's discretion, be returned to the person who killed it or be given to some charitable institution. This subdivision shall not impair the constitutional rights of persons to protect themselves or their property from injury or destruction by wild birds, game or fur-bearing animals protected by state laws. A depredation permit is required to kill migratory birds for depredation control purposes, and applications shall be submitted to the Director and the appropriate USFW agent (207:26 through :30).

See GENERAL EXCEPTIONS TO PROTECTION and Restrictions on Taking: Hunting and Trapping under HUNTING, FISHING, TRAPPING PROVISIONS for bear damage provisions.

ENFORCEMENT OF WILDLIFE LAWS

Enforcement Powers

New Hampshire is a member of the Atlantic States Marine Fisheries Compact (Chapter 213).

★★New Hampshire is a member of the **Northeast Conservation Law Enforcement Compact**, effective when enacted into law by any two of the states of Connecticut, Delaware, Maine, Massachusetts, New Hampshire, New Jersey, New York, Pennsylvania, Rhode Island, Vermont and West Virginia. The purposes of this compact are to: provide close and effective cooperation and assistance in detecting and apprehending those engaged in illegal fisheries and wildlife and environmental activities; provide mutual aid and assistance and provide for the powers, duties, rights, privileges and immunities of conservation law enforcement personnel when rendering such aid (215:B:1).★★

[New Hampshire has extensive provisions in Chapter 215-A governing Off Highway Recreational Vehicles (215-A:1 through 215-A:40), including intoxication testing, and limitations of travel on ice, snow, and roads, some of which affect wildlife.]

The Director and each conservation officer have the power to: ► enforce all laws, rules and regulations relating to fish, game, fur-bearing animals and marine species, and to go upon any property outside of buildings, posted or otherwise, in the performance of duty; ► execute all warrants and search warrants for the violation of laws and regulations relating to wildlife violations; ► serve subpoenas issued for the trial of all offenses against laws and regulations relating to wildlife; ► carry firearms or other weapons, concealed or otherwise; ► arrest without warrant and on view any person found violating any law or regulation relating to fish and wildlife, take them before a court having jurisdiction for trial, and detain them until trial; ► stop and search without a warrant and examine in the field, on a highway, at an airbase or on a stream, any person, boat, aircraft, vehicle, game bag or other receptacle in the presence of the owner if possible, or any fish house, in the occupant's presence for fish, game or other wildlife when they have reasonable cause to believe that any such wildlife or illegal apparatus subject to forfeiture are concealed therein; ► secure and execute search warrants, and enter any building, enclosure, vehicle and break open any apartment, chest, box, trunk bag or package and examine the contents thereof; ► seize and take possession of fish and wildlife caught, taken, killed or possessed or shipped contrary to state laws and dispose of confiscated wildlife as the Director prescribes; ► seize all fishing tackle, guns, shooting and hunting paraphernalia, licenses, traps, boats, decoys or other appliances used in violation of any wildlife law or regulation when making an arrest, or found in the execution of a search warrant, and hold same at the owner's expense until the fine and costs imposed have been paid; ► caution persons against fire danger and extinguish fires left burning and assume the duties of a fire warden pending the warden's arrival; ► enforce the laws relating to snowmobiles, ATV's, trespass on posted lands, vandalism, dogs at large, use and transportation of firearms for hunting, bob houses, breaking and entering and larceny in remote areas, protection of the environment, littering and dumping; ► conduct search and rescue operations; ► in emergencies upon their requests, cooperate with other law enforcement agencies; ► have and exercise the powers and privileges granted by 594 as to matters within their jurisdiction under this section (206:26). It is unlawful to resist arrest by a conservation officer or to obstruct same in performance of duty. Violation: misdemeanor (206:26-a).

The Director and conservation officers shall be ex officio constables throughout the state and have general power to enforce all criminal laws of the state and to serve criminal processes and make arrests, under proper warrants in all counties. They shall not: serve civil processes; act or be called upon for service within any town in any industrial dispute unless actual violence has occurred, and then only upon the Governor's order; have general power to enforce any provision relative to motor vehicles. When the Director or any Conservation officer shall apprehend any person who has committed or attempted to commit a felony, they shall immediately make a report to the county attorney and sheriff of the county and such cases shall be investigated and prosecuted by said county official. ★These provisions as they pertain to the Director shall not apply to any such Director who has not been certified as a police officer (206:26-b).★

Any game protector, fish and game warden, conservation officer, or other person authorized to make arrests for violation of fish laws of Maine or Massachusetts has power to make arrests of persons fishing, in violation of fish laws of these states, on any part of any waters lying between either of said states and New Hampshire or on the shores thereof, and to take the arrested person for trial to the state in which the violation was committed and prosecute according to such state's laws, if and when such states shall enact a similar law giving similar authority to conservation officers of this state to make arrests on boundary waters between this and those other states (206:27).

Criminal Penalties

Any person who violates the licensing provisions where another specific penalty is not provided shall be guilty of a violation if a natural person, or a misdemeanor if any other person. A person who furnishes to another, or permits another to use a license issued to the person or any other person, or changes or alters such license, or makes a false statement in an application, or knowingly guides a hunter who does not have a license, shall be guilty of a violation. Any person whose license has been revoked and who is convicted of hunting, fishing or trapping after revocation is guilty of a misdemeanor (214:37). Any person who violates a provision of this chapter or any rule of the Director shall be guilty of a violation, except as otherwise provided, and an additional violation for each fish, bird or animal or part bought, sold, offered for sale or transported contrary to the provisions herein. Use of prohibited silencing devices on firearms is a misdemeanor with forfeiture of such firearms and silencing devices. A person convicted of setting or controlling a set gun is guilty of a misdemeanor (207:46). It is a misdemeanor to refuse to stop when so signalled by a uniformed conservation officer, or to refuse to permit such officer to examine a license (207:47). Unless otherwise provided, any person convicted of a violation of any provision of Title XVIII (Fish and Game), or of any rule or regulation made thereunder, is guilty of a violation for the first offense. For any subsequent offense committed during the same calendar year, the person is guilty of a violation if a natural person, or a misdemeanor if any other person (206:19-a). Laws relating to the opening and closing of seasons for taking fish, the size, number and weight limits of fish and other conditions governing the method and manner of taking fish, shall be continued in full force and effect until altered by rule or regulation of the Director (206:20).

Illegal Taking of Wildlife

Possession of fish, protected birds, game and fur-bearing animals during the closed season, except as permitted in this title, shall be prima facie evidence that the same were unlawfully taken. All fish and wildlife protected by this title, found in the possession of any person and not legally taken or possessed, shall be seized and forfeited, and disposed of as the Director specifies. ★The proceeds from the sale of seized and road-killed fur-bearers and coyotes acquired by the Department shall be dedicated to the trapping education program.★ ★Upon conviction of violating any of the provisions of this title, all fishing tackle, guns, shooting or hunting paraphernalia, traps, dogs, boats, decoys, bob houses or other appliances and vehicles except motor vehicles designed for use on the highway and required to be registered under 261 used in such violation may be seized and held until the fine and costs for the violations have been paid in full.★ After one year, if the defendant has not paid the fine and costs imposed in full, or when the property is not claimed, the Director may sell at public auction any of the seized or confiscated property, all proceeds to go to the Fish and Game Fund. If the property has no monetary value and cannot be sold, it may be destroyed (207:16 through :18).

In addition to the penalties provided for violating any of the provisions of Title LXII or XVIII or any rule thereunder, any person convicted of illegal taking or illegal possession of game animals, game birds or fur-bearing animals, resulting in the injury, death or destruction of same, may be sentenced to make restitution to the state for the value of each game animal, game bird or fur-bearing animal illegally taken or possessed as follows: marten, moose and bear, $500; deer, $250; wild rabbit, hare, muskrat and gray squirrel, $10; wild turkey, $200; ruffed grouse, spruce grouse, pheasant, woodcock, ducks or geese, $15; fisher, bobcat, otter, $200; fox, $75; beaver and mink, $20; raccoon, $20. ★In every conviction involving illegal taking or illegal possession of game animals, game birds or fur-bearing animals, the court may order the defendant to reimburse the state in a sum or sums not to exceed these amounts, to be paid directly to the court. If two or more defendants are convicted of illegal taking or illegal possession of animals as specified, the reimbursement shall be declared against them jointly and severally. Moneys collected from such reimbursement damages shall be used for game management activities within the Department and shall be nonlapsing. Any person failing to make a damage assessment payment as ordered by the court shall be guilty of contempt and shall not be eligible to purchase any license until all assessments are paid in full (207:55).★

Illegal taking of a caribou, elk, moose, mountain lion, Canadian Lynx, or taking a deer by use of a dog, trap, snare or other prohibited device, or driving deer by noise, airplane or vehicle, or illegal spotlighting of birds or wild animals or taking with illegal weapons or ammunition is a misdemeanor if a natural person; a felony if any other person. Illegal weapons or ammunition used in taking deer in specified locales, or with a gun during bow and arrow season, or illegal weapon during muzzle-loading season, or illegal hunting in areas reserved for paraplegics, more than six persons in a deer drive, serving deer in lumber camps, or illegal transportation of deer is a violation if a natural person; a misdemeanor if any other person. Illegal selling of deer or moose or parts is a misdemeanor for each deer or moose or part bought or sold if a natural person; a felony for any other person; other illegal taking of deer is a violation, unless the person is guilty of taking deer during the closed season or exceeding the bag limit, which is a misdemeanor (208:21).

See also Restrictions on Taking: Hunting and Trapping under HUNTING, FISHING, TRAPPING PROVISIONS.

License Revocations, Suspensions

★The Director may order the suspension of the license of any person, and without hearing, whenever the Director has reason to believe that the licensee is physically or mentally an improper or incompetent person to carry firearms, or is handling firearms improperly, or so as to endanger human life or property, or for any other sufficient cause; but such suspension shall not be for longer than 30 days unless the Director and Commission, after investigation and hearing, so determine. The Director may order any license revoked after due hearing for any sufficient cause (214:18).★ ★★Any person whose privilege to hunt, trap or guide has been suspended or revoked in any jurisdiction within the US or Canada is prohibited from purchasing a license for such activity in this state during the period of revocation or suspension in the prosecuting jurisdiction provided the offense is contained in Title XVIII, chapters 208, 210 or 215. If such person has previously purchased a license for such activity, it becomes invalid and shall be suspended for the same period as determined in the prosecuting jurisdiction. Such person shall immediately return the license to the Department. No person shall possess a license which has been suspended under this section. Violation: a violation (214:18-b).★★ ★The Director shall revoke the license of any person who has been found guilty in any court of a violation of any provision of this title or any rule or regulation of the Director, or who has been found guilty in a municipal or district court of a violation of 163-B, 236:26, 265:102 or 635:2. Such revocation shall not continue for more than one year, except for a conviction under 208:8 (illegal taking of wild birds or animals by spotlighting), in which case the revocation may be for a period not to exceed 5 years, or except for a conviction under 208:1-a (illegal taking of moose), when the revocation may be for up to two years. The Director shall revoke the license of any person who has been found guilty in a court a second time within five years of a violation of any such laws or regulations, for a period of not less than one nor more than three years (214:19).★ ★★The Director may revoke the hunting license of any person who is convicted of an offense similar to those described in 214:20, 207:37, 207:38 or 208:8 (intoxication while hunting, illegal hunting of wildlife by spotlight, shooting and/or abandoning a person) by a court of any other state (214:20-a). Copies of records of convictions and notices of license revocations kept by the Director of this state and other states and certified by the Director shall be deemed admissible to prove such revocations or convictions in courts (214:20-b).★★

No person shall hunt, fish or trap in this state after suspension or revocation of license until it has been restored by the Director. A person whose license has been revoked indefinitely or for any period of time under any provision herein shall be ineligible to purchase a new license before the expiration of the stated period without written approval of the Director. No person shall be eligible to receive any license issued by the Department if in arrears for any fines or costs for a fish and game law violation (214:21). The Director may declare that a person convicted of fishing, hunting or trapping without a license shall be ineligible to receive any license for up to one year. It is a violation to hold both nonresident hunting and fishing licenses, and also hold a nonresident hunting license, or to hold more than one of either license (214:22-a). No person shall hold at the same time both resident hunting and fishing licenses and a resident hunting license, nor hold at the same time more than one of either of said licenses. Violation: a violation (214:23).

Intoxication Testing of Hunters

Any person convicted of hunting or attempting to hunt and who is in possession of a firearm, while under the influence of intoxicating liquor, or any controlled drug, is guilty of a misdemeanor, the person's license shall be revoked, and another license to hunt shall not be issued for one year. Upon complaint, information, indictment or trial of any person charged with violation of this section, the court may admit evidence of the amount of alcohol in the defendant's blood, as shown by a chemical analysis of breath, urine or other bodily substance. Evidence of an alcohol concentration of 0.05% or less, is prima facie evidence that the defendant was not under the influence of intoxicating liquor; evidence of concentration of 0.05 to 0.10% is relevant evidence but is not to be given prima facie effect in indicating whether the defendant was under the influence, but may be considered with other competent evidence in determining the guilt or innocence of the defendant. Evidence of an alcohol concentration of 0.10% or more is prima facie evidence that the defendant was under the influence. Any person who takes or attempts such of wildlife by use of a firearm shall be deemed to have given consent to a chemical test or tests of any or all or any combination of blood, urine or breath, if arrested for any offense arising out of acts alleged to have been committed while the person was hunting while under the influence, except as otherwise provided [exceptions and procedures for hemophiliacs and diabetics are given and other details of testing requirements and reporting thereof are provided]. If a person under arrest refuses to be tested upon request, none shall be given. Subject to a hearing, the Director shall revoke the license and issue no new license for one year upon receipt of a sworn report from the officer stating that: ▸ the officer had reasonable grounds to believe the arrested person had been hunting while under the influence; ▸ the facts upon which the reasonable grounds to believe such are based; ▸ the person had been arrested; ▸ the person refused to submit to the test; ▸ the person was informed of the right to have a test done by a person of the person's own choosing; ▸ the person was informed that refusal to be tested would result in the revocation of hunting license (214:20). (See License Revocations, Suspensions under this section.)

HABITAT PROTECTION

No person by means of opening gates or dams, other than in the ordinary use of an established water privilege, shall draw down the water in any stream, lake or pond to a degree which will endanger fish life until prior notice in writing has been given to the Director so that the Department may take out the fish in the waters. These provisions do not apply to privately owned lakes or ponds (211:11 and :12).

★★Fish passage facilities shall be constructed and maintained at existing dams or obstructions in accordance with the following procedure: ▸ after determining that a fish passage facility is needed, the Director shall request the Governor to appoint a commission of three disinterested state citizens to review this determination; ▸ the commission shall hold public hearings to determine the desirability of providing fish passage facilities over the dam or obstruction; ▸ the commission shall report its findings to the Governor with recommendations; ▸ the Governor, with the Council's advice shall determine the divisions of costs of construction, the state's share to be a charge on the Fish and Game Fund; ▸ the Director shall determine the actual design and location of the fish passage facility; ▸ the dam owner shall operate the fish passage facility to allow fish passage during normal migration periods; ▸ any party to the proceedings may apply for a rehearing or appeal. The Director or agent may enter and inspect any dam or impoundment to insure adequate installation, maintenance and operation (211:8-a and :8-b).★★

★★Whoever unlawfully discharges contaminants into state inland or coastal waters shall be liable to the state for any damage to the fish, other aquatic life and wildlife or their habitat in said waters caused by such contamination. Upon learning of such damage by contamination, the Director shall investigate and determine the party responsible, and shall compute the damages based on tables for each species of fish as promulgated by the Department and by other reasonable and accurate means. The Director shall calculate the value of fish and other aquatic life or wildlife or their habitat destroyed using standard procedures and other reasonable and accurate means for estimating the value of fish populations and other aquatic life or wildlife or their habitat. The Director shall notify the Water Supply and Pollution Control Commission or any other agency authorized by law to seek injunctive relief against water pollution if the contamination is a continuing offense. When the damage to fish, aquatic life or wildlife or their habitat so warrants, the Director shall request the Attorney General to institute an action at law for damage. Damage moneys received shall be credited to the Fish and Game Fund (211:71 through :74).★★

The Director shall establish programs, including acquisition of land or aquatic habitat or interests therein, for the conservation of endangered/threatened species, and shall utilize all authority vested in the Department for these purposes. The Director shall consult with other states having a common interest in particular threatened/endangered species and may enter into agreements with federal agencies, other states, or private persons to conserve such species. All other state departments and agencies, to the extent possible, shall assist and cooperate with the Director in the furtherance of these purposes for the conservation of endangered/threatened species, and shall insure that actions authorized, funded or carried out by them do not jeopardize the continued existence of such species or result in the destruction or modification of habitat of such species determined by the Director to be critical. These provisions do not apply when a state agency is required by federal law to address the environmental impact on wildlife or wildlife habitat (212-A:9). (See PROTECTED SPECIES OF WILDLIFE for nongame wildlife habitat provisions.)

The state may acquire title to or control of lands or waters, or hunting or fishing or other rights on private lands or waters, suitable for the protection and propagation of fish, game and fur-bearing animals, or for fishing, hunting or administrative purposes, by purchase, lease or gift. Whenever the Governor and Council believe it is expedient for the state to own any lands or water rights needed for protection and propagation of fish and game, and when it is unable to purchase the same for a reasonable price, it may enter upon and take the same by condemnation (212:1 and :2). The Director, with approval of the Governor and Council, may pay a fair price for waters, lands or rights therein required for establishment of fish hatcheries, game farms, game refuges, propagation of fish, game and fur-bearing animals, for fishing or hunting, and may expend during any year only such total sum as may be appropriated and shall report such acquisitions to the Senate President and Speaker of the House. The Director, with the Governor's consent, may authorize the sale or exchange of state lands for privately owned lands of equal or greater value, and suitable for the protection and propagation of fish, game and fur-bearing animals, or for fishing, hunting or administrative purposes. Lands to which title has been acquired by the state, or leased, may be used for creating and maintaining game refuges, or for the propagation of fish, game or fur-bearing animals, or administration thereof. The Director, after consultation with the Director of the Division of Forests and Lands, may cut, remove and sell timber on state lands, or sell buildings or other improvements with the Governor's approval (212:8 through :10).

The Director, in conjunction with the Commissioner of Agriculture, may establish and maintain state fish and game refuges for the protection and propagation of fish, game and fur-bearing animals, wherein such animals shall not be hunted, pursued, taken, disturbed or molested except as provided by the Director by regulation, and may, with consent of the proper authorities, establish such refuges on state forests, national forests or otherwise publicly owned lands or waters. They may establish such refuges on privately owned lands with the consent of the owner and abutters. No such refuge shall exceed one-half of the total area of the state or national forest on which it is located, nor exceed 2,500 acres if not located on a state or national forest. No such refuge exceeding 500 acres in area shall be established within 10 miles of another refuge (212:11 and :15). Each game refuge shall be surrounded by a well defined line, road or cleared strip of land, or fenced, and posted. A person found upon a state game refuge, or upon land established as an area for game propagation, having in possession a loaded firearm is guilty of a misdemeanor. The state may acquire by purchase, lease or gift, hunting and fishing rights to lands or waters and rights of access suitable for public hunting and fishing grounds. The Director may formulate, adopt and post rules for the government of lands and waters under the Director's control, including state game refuges, for the protection and propagation of fish, game, fur-bearing animals and marine species. Violation: a misdemeanor (212:16 through :20).

Any person who violates the provisions of 265:102 which relate to the placing of refuse into or on the ice over any public water, streams or watercourse, approaches thereto or bordering land may, in addition to other penalties, lose a fishing or hunting license for the current year (214:18-a).

NATIVE AMERICAN WILDLIFE PROVISIONS: None

NEW JERSEY

Sources: New Jersey Statutes Annotated, 1937; Titles 13 and 23; 1992 Cumulative Annual Pocket Part.

STATE WILDLIFE POLICY

The legislature finds and declares: The policy of this state is to manage all forms of wildlife to insure their continued participation in the ecosystem; that species or subspecies of wildlife indigenous to the state found to be endangered should be accorded special protection to maintain and if possible enhance their numbers; and the state should protect species or subspecies of wildlife endangered elsewhere by regulating the taking, possession, transportation, exportation, processing, sale or offer for sale or shipment within the state any species or subspecies on any Federal endangered species list (23:2A-2).

RELEVANT WILDLIFE DEFINITIONS: See Definitions section of Appendices.

STATE FISH AND WILDLIFE AGENCIES

Agency Structure

The **Department of Environmental Protection and Energy** (Department) [formerly the Department of Conservation and Economic Development, the Department of Environmental Protection] under the **Commissioner of Environmental Protection and Energy** (Commissioner) [formerly Commissioner of Conservation and Economic Development] is a principal department in the Executive Branch of state government. The **Division of Fish, Game and Wildlife** (Division) [formerly the Division of Fish, Game and Shellfisheries] under a **Director of Fish, Game and Wildlife** (Director) constitutes a Division within the Department. The **Fish and Game Council** (Council) [formerly the Fish and Game Board], together with all its functions, powers and duties is in the Division (13:1D-1, 13:1D-4 and 23:2B-15).

The **Commissioner** shall be qualified by training and experience to perform the duties of office, appointed by the Governor, with the advice and consent of the Senate, and serves at the pleasure of the Governor (13:1B-2). ★There is within the Division a **Fish and Game Council** (Council) consisting of 11 members, each of whom is chosen with knowledge of and interest in the conservation of fish and game. Each member is appointed by the Governor, with the advice and consent of the Senate. Members shall consist of six farmers and six sportsmen, and one shall be the chairman of the committee established pursuant to 23:2A-7 (the Endangered and Nongame Species Conservation Act); and one shall be a person knowledgeable in land use management and soil conservation practices. Each member shall be appointed for a term of four years (13:1B-24).★ The Governor designates one of the members of the Council as chairman (13:1B-26).

The Division is under the immediate supervision of a **Director**, who shall be trained and experienced in wildlife management and qualified to direct the Division. The Director is appointed by the Council, with the Governor's approval. The Director administers the work of the Division under the direction and supervision of the Commissioner (13:1B-27). The Division may appoint fish and game wardens and shall designate one of the wardens as the fish and game protector (protector), who shall have the direction, supervision and control of the other wardens. The compensation shall be amounts fixed by law. Each warden shall be full time and have no other business or occupation (23:2-4).

Agency Powers and Duties

The **Department** has the responsibility of acquiring, maintaining and preserving natural areas within the state as a habitat for rare and vanishing species of plant and animal life (13:1B-15.5). In addition to powers and duties otherwise provided, the **Council**, with the approval of the Commissioner, formulates comprehensive policies for the protection and propagation of fish, birds, and game animals and for the propagation of food fish and their distribution into state waters. The Council consults with and advises the Commissioner and Director on the work of the Division;

holds hearings as necessary; and reports to the Governor and Legislature annually (13:1B-28). The duties of the Council are to: ▸ protect and propagate fish, birds and game animals, enforce the laws relating thereto, and propagate food fish and distribute them into state waters; ▸ close streams or parts of streams for 48 hours immediately following stocking, and may revoke the license of a person who violates the regulation; ▸ permit persons to carry firearms in the woods and fields for the conservation of wildlife; ▸ control state hatching stations; ▸ investigate any complaint, inspect any dam, weir, fish basket, net or other illegal apparatus for taking fish and remove same, and enforce the laws for protection and propagation of fish, birds and game animals by arrest and prosecution of the offender, without complaint or warrant. It reports to the Legislature annually on its operations, including suggestions and recommendations (23:2-2).

The Council may stock fish, birds and game only on state lands and waters open to all anglers and hunters holding a license issued by the Council, or lands designated as public sanctuaries. ★The Council may stock with fish any state water that is controlled and used by organizations such as the Boy Scouts, YMCA, YWCA, or other similar public organizations, but only when such camps are in operation (23:2-3).★ The Council may by regulation determine the fees for hunting, fishing and trapping licenses, permits, tags, certificates and stamps (23:3-1a). ★The Division shall establish and conduct a Remedial Sportsmen Education Program (23:3-22.3).★ The Council may buy land and erect buildings for the propagation game and fish. The Council may sell, exchange or otherwise dispose of any fish or fish eggs from the state hatchery, game birds or game animals, or the eggs of game birds from the state game farm, and any other products of the farms. The proceeds of sales shall be reported by the Council and be paid into the state treasury, subject to the use of the Council (23:8-1; :8-6). The Commissioner has authority to sell, lease or exchange areas of state land and/or water acquired exclusively for public hunting and fishing grounds and game refuges, provided that the Council shall be given an opportunity to review such sale, lease or exchange (23:8A-1). All moneys received from a sale, lease, or exchange shall be placed in the Hunters' and Anglers' License Fund (23:8A-3).

The Council may lease and control by agreement lands suitable for game refuges, and also may acquire title by gift or grant. Game refuges may be fenced by wire on the boundary and one notice reading "State Game Refuge, hunting is unlawful" shall be posted at least every 500 feet of the refuge boundary (23:8-7 and :8-8). Pursuant to law, the Governor shall close or suspend forests, woodlands or open lands to entry, and any open season for taking fish, game birds, game animals or fur-bearing animals. At the end of the period of closure, subject to the Commissioner's approval, the Council may provide for a new or extended open season within the limits of the areas affected, for a period not exceeding the original open season (23:2-2.1).

Agency Regulations

★To provide an adequate and flexible system of protection, propagation, increase, control and conservation of fresh water fish, game birds, game animals, and fur-bearing animals in the state, and for use for public recreation and food supply, the Council is authorized to determine the circumstances under which they may be pursued, taken, killed, or had in possession so as to maintain an adequate and proper supply. After scientific investigation and research, the Council may adopt, amend and repeal such regulations, with penalties as prescribed in Title 23, to preserve, utilize or maintain the best number of any species. The regulations shall be called the State Fish and Game Code (code) (13:1B-30). The Council may adopt regulations to regulate the possession for other than agricultural purposes, and to control, the release, liberation, or distribution of mammals, birds, reptiles, or amphibians into the fields, woodlands or marshes of the state which may menace, damage, or consume agricultural crops or create a hazard to the welfare of the citizens (23:4-63.3).★

Agency Funding Sources

The **Hunters' and Anglers' License Fund** is a fund kept separate and apart from the receipts of the Board and other state moneys, and is disbursed by the state treasurer on vouchers certified by the Board (23:3-12). Fees for licenses and permits received by the Division are placed in the fund, to be used in the best interest of state wildlife resources. ★Not less than 24% of the fund shall be spent annually for law enforcement by the Division (23:3-11).★ Within the Fund is a separate and dedicated account known as the **New Jersey Waterfowl Stamp Account** credited from the sale of New Jersey Waterfowl Stamps. The account is utilized only for funding acquisition, protection, maintenance, improvement and enhancement of waterfowl habitat and associated wetlands and areas (23:3-79).

Moneys recovered for violations of Title 23, or a provision of a supplementary law, or a provision of the fish and game code, except as provided, are paid to the Division (23:10-19).

Agency Advisory Boards

There is in the Division a **New Jersey Migratory Waterfowl Advisory Committee**. The Committee comprises nine members serving terms of three years without compensation. The Committee advises the Division about the creation, design, administration, sale, and distribution of the stamp and makes written recommendations to the Commissioner regarding revenues in the New Jersey Waterfowl Stamp Account, including the advisability of allocating a percentage of the proceeds from qualified nonprofit organizations in North America for utilization in waterfowl habitat programs that provide direct benefits that can be clearly demonstrated to New Jersey's waterfowl preservation and protection efforts (23:3-81).

PROTECTED SPECIES OF WILDLIFE

The Commissioner has the power to adopt, amend and repeal rules and regulations, controlling and prohibiting the taking, possession, transportation, exportation, sale or offer for sale or shipment of any nongame species of wildlife on the endangered species list; and is authorized to conduct periodic inspections to determine compliance with the regulations and to charge and collect fees to cover the costs of inspections. Such fees shall be devoted entirely and exclusively to carrying out the purposes and provisions of the Endangered and Nongame Species Conservation Act (23:2A through 23:2A-13). Except as provided in the act, no person shall take, possess, transport, export, process, sell or offer for sale, or ship, and no common or contract carrier shall knowingly transport or receive for shipment any species or subspecies of wildlife appearing on the lists of: ▸ wildlife determined to be endangered pursuant to the act; ▸ nongame species regulated pursuant to the act; ▸ a federal endangered species list. Wildlife appearing on the foregoing lists which enters and is transported across the state and destined for a point beyond the state may be entered and transported without restriction in accordance with the terms of any permit issued under the laws or regulations of another state or the US (23:2A-5 and :2A-6).

The Commissioner shall conduct wildlife investigations to develop information relating to populations, distribution, habitat needs, limiting factors and data to determine management measures and develop management programs for their continued ability to sustain themselves successfully. On the basis of such investigations and other data the Commissioner by regulation may promulgate a list of endangered species and subspecies indigenous to the state, shall review such list periodically, and by regulation may add or delete species and subspecies (23:2A-4). The Commissioner shall establish programs, including acquisition of land or aquatic habitats, for conservation and management of nongame and endangered species of wildlife, and may enter into agreements for the administration and management of any area utilized for management of nongame or endangered species of wildlife. With the approval of the Governor, the Commissioner may cooperate with and receive money for the "Endangered and Nongame Species Conservation Act" and may establish a separate fund from these contributions for the support of nongame and endangered species programs. The Commissioner may authorize the taking, possession, transportation, exportation or shipment of nongame species and wildlife which appear on the state list of endangered species for scientific, zoological or educational purposes, for propagation in captivity of such wildlife, or for other special purposes. The Commissioner shall appoint a committee of experts to advise and assist in carrying out the intent of the act. Said experts shall include persons actively involved in the conservation of wildlife (23:2A-7).

★★Except as provided by law, rule, or regulation or by the code, no person shall pursue, hunt, take, capture, kill, attempt to take, capture or kill, or have in possession, living or dead, a wild bird. Except pursuant to a Department permit for scientific, zoological, or educational purposes or to a licensed wild bird breeder for obtaining stock to increase genetic variety, no person shall offer for sale, sell, offer to barter, barter, offer to purchase, purchase, deliver for shipment, ship, export, import, transport or cause to be transported, carry or cause to be carried, or receive or cause to be received for shipment, transportation, carriage, or export, living or dead, any wild bird, unless the wild bird was produced from an egg of captive parents and hatched and raised in captivity. A wild bird that is not native to the state is not a defense to a violation. Any wild bird from without the state may be transported across the state with a federal permit or the permit of another state. These provisions do not apply to the cockatiel, budgerigar or common canary. Except as may be provided by law, rule or regulation or by the code, no part of plumage, skin or body of a wild bird shall be sold or possessed for sale. If a person violates any of these provisions, the Department may institute a civil action for injunctive relief to prohibit and prevent such violation. If the violation is of a continuing nature, each day is an additional, separate, and distinct offense. Violation: a penalty of $200-100 for each offense; a penalty of $500 for each bird or part that is subject to the violation; forfeiture of any bird or part that is a subject of the violation. The Department may sell any wild bird or part forfeited pursuant to these provisions and the proceeds of such sale together with any penalties collected shall be deposited in a fund for use by the Department in administering and enforcing these provisions and the Endangered and Nongame Species Conservation Act (23:4-50).★★

A provision to the contrary notwithstanding, no person shall capture, kill, injure or have in possession, living or dead, or attempt to capture, kill or injure, a wild or passenger pigeon. Violation: $250 for each offense (23:4-53). No person shall hunt for, pursue, capture, kill, possess, injure or destroy any female English or ring-necked pheasant under a penalty of $20 for each offense. These provisions do not apply to a licensee operating under the terms of 23:3-28 to 23:3-39 (commercial licenses for propagating game, operating shooting preserves), or to any other person authorized by said licensee to shoot female pheasants (23:4-8).

No person shall sell, trap, take, capture, kill or possess a beaver, possess or sell a raw pelt of a beaver, whether caught within or without the state, unless it has been tagged by the fish and game warden of the county where such pelt is possessed or sale is to be made. No person shall set a trap within 20 feet of any beaver lodge or dam, except persons holding beaver permits, under penalty of $100 for each beaver. The Division may issue such permits to residents to trap beaver and the pelts may be sold if properly tagged under penalty of $100 for each offense. The Division may issue permits to owners or lessees of land, a portion of which is under cultivation, to kill beavers destroying property, but carcasses must be turned over to the Division (23:4-55).

GENERAL EXCEPTIONS TO PROTECTION

As used in Title 23, the terms "waters of this state" means all the fresh waters of this state. All ponds, lakes and waters created by or under the extensive control of individuals or associations, stocked and maintained at their sole expense and not runways for migratory fish shall be considered private waters, and shall be exempt from bag limits, season and size as far as individuals and associations or persons receiving permits (23:1-2). Code provisions do not apply to a public museum or natural history society to prevent the collection of specimens nor to the breeding, raising and producing in captivity, and the marketing of fox, other than red or gray, mink, chinchilla, marten, fisher, caracul or other fur-bearing animals not native to New Jersey (23:1-4). The Division may grant an accredited person a certificate permitting collection of mammals, reptiles, amphibians, fish and birds and their nests or eggs for scientific purposes (23:4-52).

HUNTING, FISHING, TRAPPING PROVISIONS

Licenses and Permits

Without a license, no person shall: ▸ hunt, take or attempt to take, kill or pursue, a wild bird, animal or fowl, or take or attempt to take any skunk, mink, muskrat, or other fur-bearing animal; ▸ shall take or attempt to take fish in the fresh waters of this state by angling with a hand line or rod and line, or with longbow and arrow, if above age 14; ▸ engage in hunting, fishing or trapping unless the license or tag is visibly displayed in a holder in a conspicuous place on the outer clothing. A licensee shall exhibit the license and tag for inspection to any requesting conservation officer, deputy conservation officer, police officer or other person. A person found hunting, fishing or trapping without a license tag shall pay a fine of $10 and costs. Nothing in these provisions prevents a farm occupant without being licensed, who resides thereon, or immediate family members who also reside there, from hunting, taking, killing or pursuing with a gun or firearm, or a longbow and arrow, a wild bird, animal or fowl, from taking any skunk, mink, muskrat, or other fur-bearing animal by means of a trap, or from taking fish on the farm with hand line or rod and line, or a longbow and arrow during the time when it is lawful so to do. This exemption shall not apply to a person residing on the farm who is not a member of the occupant's family. Violation: $25-100 for each offense (23:3-1).

The Division shall issue a special license combining the resident's firearm hunting, bow and arrow, and fishing license (23:3-4) into one license designated as the "All Around Sportsman License." Such license issued to a resident above age 16 shall authorize hunting with a shotgun or bow and arrow and to angle or attempt to take fish in the waters of this state at any time, and in the manner provided by law, except that this license shall not authorize its holder to take trout from the state fresh waters. The fees for this license shall be deposited in the Hunters' and Anglers' License Fund (23:3-1.1).

★No person shall hunt, kill or pursue with a gun or a firearm a woodcock without a special woodcock hunting stamp, in addition to the license required by law.★ Said stamp authorizes its holder to hunt woodcock in the manner provided by law, and shall be valid when permanently attached to the license and when signed in ink. A person who violates these provisions, alters, changes, loans or transfers a stamp issued under these provisions and who takes woodcock during the period prescribed without the required stamp shall be liable for a penalty of $20. A person who kills or has in possession any other bird or animal, the killing of which is prohibited during the prescribed woodcock season, shall be liable for a penalty of $100 for each bird or animal, killed, injured or possessed (23:3-23, :3-24, :3-26 and :3-27). The Division shall issue permits for wild turkeys according to code provisions with fees deposited to the credit of the Hunters' and Anglers' License Fund (23:3-27.1).

No person shall take, or attempt to take, with shirred or purse seines, otter or beam trawls, any fish in state waters without a license (23:3-46). A person intending to take menhaden with purse or shirred nets in state waters shall apply to the Commissioner for a license (23:3-51). The Council may issue a permit with conditions to take carp and suckers by means of a net, with mesh of greater than two and one-half inches. All game and food fish captured is returned uninjured as far as practicable. A person who takes any fish except carp and suckers shall be liable for a penalty of $20 for each fish. The Council may issue permits to catch suckers, catfish, carp and eels by or with the use of a fish basket [details provided]. Every game fish that may come into a basket shall be immediately released. A person who violates the provisions of the permits is liable for a penalty of $50 (23:3-54 through :3-56). No person, between age 14 and 70, shall take or attempt to take trout in state fresh waters without a special trout stamp in addition to the license required. A person who alters, changes, loans, transfers a trout stamp or takes trout without a stamp is liable for $20 for each offense (23:3-57 and :3-60).

When the Council has established a season for deer of either sex and has fixed the number of licenses to be issued, the Division is authorized to charge a fee for each license issued. No fee shall be required of the occupant of a farm, or immediate family members who reside there. This exemption does not apply to a person who is not a member of the occupant's family. A person who hunts, pursues, shoots at, takes, kills or wounds a deer, or attempts to do so, without a deer license is liable for $100-300 for the first offense and $300-500 for the second and subsequent offense (23:3-56.1 and :3-56.2).

No person shall at any time hunt, pursue, kill, take or attempt to take with a firearm or bow and arrow, or possess, any pheasant or quail in wildlife management areas without a special pheasant and quail stamp, in addition to a hunting license. A person who alters, loans or transfers to another such stamp, or who hunts for, pursues, kills, takes or attempts to take with a firearm or a bow and arrow, or possesses a pheasant or quail in a wildlife management area without a proper stamp is liable for a penalty of $25-50 for each offense (23:3-61.1, :3-61.2 and :3-61.4). No person over age 16 shall hunt, pursue, kill, take, possess, or attempt to take ducks, geese, brant, or other waterfowl without possessing for inspection a waterfowl stamp in addition to any other required licenses or permits. A violator is liable for a penalty of $25-1,000 for each offense. Each day is an additional, separate and distinct offense (23:3-76 and :3-80).

Each new applicant for a hunting license, above age 10, shall present a certificate stating the satisfactory completion of a course in gun safety. No hunting license shall be issued to a person above age 10 who has not submitted a hunting license of a previous year or a certificate showing successful completion of a course in gun safety. A person who obtains a hunting license under false information shall be subject to a fine of $20-200 for each offense (23:3-4.2 and :3-4.7). A person possessing a muzzleloader rifle or other rifle while hunting or trapping must have an appropriate rifle permit, in addition to other required licenses. Fees are credited to the Hunters' and Anglers' License Fund (23:3-4.11). A person applying for a bow and arrow license must present either a certificate stating completion of a course in bow and arrow safety and proficiency or a previously issued bow and arrow license. A person who obtains a bow and arrow hunting license under false information shall be subject to a fine of $20 (23:3-7.1 and :3-7.6). Each new applicant for a trapping license, 12 years or older, must present a certificate stating satisfactory completion of a course in trapping methods. A person 12 or older who previously had a trapping license shall submit the license of a previous year or a certification from the Division stating the applicant held such license. A person who obtains a trapping license under false information shall be subject to a penalty of $25-200 for each offense (23:3-7.8 and :3-7.12).

Restrictions on Taking: Hunting and Trapping

No person shall capture, kill, injure, destroy, possess or hunt for, or attempt to capture, kill, injure or destroy any reedbird, wild swans, wood duck, wild geese, brant, wild ducks, rails or marsh hens, gallinules, coot, upland plover, black-bellied plover, golden plover, greater or lesser yellowlegs, willets, sandpipers, dowitchers or robin snipe, brown backs, curlews, turnstones or calico backs, godwits or marlin, tattlers, Wilson snipe or jacksnipe, woodcock or any other birds known as shore birds, surf snipe or bay snipe, unless an open season is prescribed according to USDI regulations relating to migratory birds. No person shall capture, kill, injure, destroy or have in possession any quail, rabbit, hare, gray, black or fox squirrel, raccoon, woodchuck, English or ring-necked pheasant, ruffed grouse, wild turkey, partridge, or any other game bird or game animal, other than those mentioned above, unless prescribed by and according to the code, or, if absent in the code, prescribed by and according to other law. [Details provided for open seasons.] The birds and animals may be possessed during open season and for ten days immediately succeeding the open seasons. Violation of code or other provisions: $20-100 penalty for each game bird or animal or part unlawfully captured, killed, injured, destroyed, possessed, or hunted, hunted for, attempted to be captured, killed, injured or destroyed. A person is liable for $100-300 for each wild turkey, black bear, coyote, bobcat, otter, or part, unlawfully captured, killed, injured, destroyed, possessed, or hunted, hunted for, attempted such (23:4-1).

No person shall capture, kill, injure, destroy or possess in one day more than the number of quail, male English or ring-necked pheasant, partridge, ruffed grouse, gray squirrels or rabbits permitted by the code, or in the absence of such provision, more than ten quail, two male English or ring-necked pheasant, three partridge, three ruffed grouse, six ray squirrels or six rabbits; during the open season more than the number of English or ring-necked pheasants or raccoons permitted by the code, or in the absence of such provision, more than 30 English or ring-necked pheasants or more than 15 raccoons, under penalty of $20 for each bird, squirrel, raccoon, or rabbit captured, killed, injured, destroyed or had in possession in excess of the number permitted. None of these provisions apply to a proprietor of a hotel, restaurant or cafe possessing game raised on licensed game preserves tagged or marked in accordance with law, or to a rabbit during or ten days succeeding the open season (23:4-2). It is unlawful to capture, kill, injure, destroy or possess wild ducks, geese, brant, sora, woodcock, coots, rails (including marsh hens and gallinules), Wilson snipe or jacksnipe, except and in accordance with the bag limits fixed by the regulations of the US Bureau of Biological Survey, relating to migratory birds, under a penalty of $20 for each offense (23:4-3). No person shall shoot into a squirrel's nest at any time of the year, under a penalty of $20 for each offense (23:4-10).

No persons shall capture, kill, injure or destroy or pursue, with the intent, game birds or animals enumerated in Chapter 23 on their own or another's property, except during the seasons, at the times and in the manner provided by the code, or in the absence of such provisions, except during the seasons, at the times and in the manner provided. Violation: liable to the penalties provided in this chapter for the violations thereof. No person shall kill, destroy or injure, pursue with intent to kill or injure, or attempt to take or injure, swans, geese, brant and river and sea ducks; rails, gallinules, coots and mud hens; shore birds, surf snipe or bay snipe, brown backs, curlews, turnstones or calico backs, godwits or marlin, tittlers and woodcocks; wild turkey, grouse, prairie chickens, pheasants, partridge and quails; or any rabbit; gray, black or fox squirrels; or any other game bird or game animal, except in the manner prescribed by the provisions of the code. In the absence of such provisions, one may only hunt with a gun not larger than ten gauge, provided it shall be unlawful while hunting to have both a firearm and a bow and arrow in possession or under control. Violation: $20 for each offense. No person shall use in hunting any firearm except as permitted by the provisions of the code, or in the absence of such provisions, except a shotgun no larger than ten gauge, under penalty of $20 for each offense. The Division may issue rifle permits for woodchucks. No person shall have any missile larger than permitted by the code, or in the absence of such provisions, larger than number four shot in possession in the woods or fields other than during the open season for killing deer. Violation: $100 for each offense. No person shall hunt, kill or destroy, or attempt to hunt, kill or destroy, a hare or rabbit with ferrets, or have a ferret in possession in the woods or fields. Violation: $50 for each offense (23:4-11 through :4-14).

No person shall sow, deposit or place any rye, wheat, oats, corn or other cereal, except wild celery and wild rice, within four hundred feet of a gunning point in state salt or fresh waters, or cause the same to be done, for luring, decoying or baiting a goose, duck, swan, brant or other waterfowl, so that it may be shot at, killed or captured; or shoot at, kill or capture a goose, duck, swan, brant or other waterfowl while feeding or attempting to feed where rye, wheat, oats, corn or other cereal, except wild celery and wild rice, is known to have been sown, deposited or placed in violation of these provisions. Violation: $50 for each offense (23:4-15).

No person shall: ‣ shall hunt, pursue, shoot, shoot at, kill, capture, injure or destroy wildlife while in or on a motor vehicle or vehicle, or by using a light carried on or attached to such ; ‣ use portable lights for hunting wildlife, except raccoon and opossum, or other species provided by the code; ‣ cast an arrow or discharge a firearm from or across a state, county, municipal, or publicly travelled road or highway, to hunt, take or kill wildlife (violation: civil penalty of $100-200 for the first offense, and $200-500 for each subsequent offense); ‣ shall possess a loaded firearm or nocked arrow for hunting, taking or killing wildlife while within 450 feet of an occupied building or a school playground, except the building's owner or lessee and persons possessing written authorization from the owner. "Occupied building" means any building constructed or adapted for use of a person, whether or not a person is actually present. Violation: civil penalty of $100-300 for the first offense, and $300-1,500, and permanent revocation of all license certificates and privileges to take or possess wildlife for each subsequent offense (23:4-16).

No person hunting or gunning after geese, duck, brant or other migratory waterfowl shall place a boat, sinkbox, seaweed, or other vessel or construction to lie in wait to kill the same, at a distance of more than 100 feet from ice, marsh or meadow, bar or bank, not covered with water, or violate regulations under the Act of Congress relating to migratory birds. Violation: $20 for each offense. No person shall pursue any goose, duck, brant or other kind of game bird, or shoot, shoot at, kill or wound the same from a boat or vessel propelled by means, other than by oars or paddles, or from a boat, vessel or other structure anchored or staked upon the waters of any bays, sounds, coves, ponds, rivers, creeks or streams at a greater distance than 100 feet from ice, marsh or meadow, bar or bank, or naturally heaped seaweed not covered with water. Violation: $20 for each offense. While in an airplane, hydroplane or other device propelled through the air, no person shall pursue, shoot, shoot at, kill or injure any of such game birds. Violation: $100 for each offense (23:4-18 and :4-19).

★No person shall possess, sell or offer for sale a game bird or game animal enumerated in Chapter 23, after the same has been caught or trapped by a snare, snood, net, trap or other device, or set a snare, snood, net, trap or other device for catching or trapping the same. Violation: $20 for each bird or animal possessed, sold or exposed for sale, or for any trap or snare so set. The penalties provided shall not apply to a dealer or purchaser of any rabbit or hare upon proof that the rabbit or hare was not trapped in the state (23:4-20). No person shall set or use any snare, snood, net, trap or other device for the catching or trapping of a bird or animal above the level of the surrounding ground and commonly known as "pole traps." These provisions do not prohibit the Council or its employees from trapping on fish hatcheries or game farms. Violation: $20 for each snare, snood, net, trap or device so set or used (23:4-22).★

★★No person shall manufacture, sell, offer for sale, possess, import or transport a steel-jaw leghold type animal trap. No person shall take or attempt to take any animal by this type of trap. Possession of such a trap is prima facie evidence of a violation, except for exhibition by humane or educational institutions, or the possession of such traps by a person of turning in the traps to a law enforcement agency. A study conducted to identify or develop an animal trap which substantially reduces injury and pain to both targeted and nontargeted animals caught in the trap and which could serve as an alternative to the steel-jaw leghold type animal trap shall be published in a report to the Council. If such study identifies or develops a suitable alternative animal trap, the Council shall establish a program for the phased withdrawal of the steel-jaw leghold animal trap from use in the state. A person using a steel-jaw animal trap in violation of any of these provisions or any regulations promulgated pursuant to these provisions, for each illegal trap involved, shall be fined $50-250 for a first offense; $250-500 for a second offense; $500-2,500 for a third or subsequent offense. All equipment used in, or animals and pelts obtained in violation of these provisions shall be confiscated (23:4-22.1 through :4-22.8).★★

No person shall remove the skin or feathers, or mutilate the body of a wild bird or animal killed, caught or taken while hunting, for concealing its identity of sex, under a penalty of $100. Possession of a wild bird or animal or part that has been plucked, skinned or mutilated in the woods, fields, or meadows or on state waters is prima facie evidence of a violation. The removal of the entrails of a deer is not a violation, but the carcass shall not be otherwise mutilated, cut up or divided until the Division has received notification or report from the person who killed it. A person having any part or portion of a deer in possession or control, or in any room, house, tent, camp or building, or in any conveyance while in the woods or fields or on the roads or highways during the open season and during the day following the last day of such open season shall be required to furnish satisfactory proof that the same came from a legally killed deer that has been properly reported. Failing to do so is a penalty of $100 (23:4-23).

No person shall hunt with a hound or with weapons of any kind, or carry a gun in the woods, fields or on the waters on Sunday, under penalty of $20 for each offense; except this provision shall not apply to hunting raccoon between midnight on Saturday and sunrise on Sunday during open season. This provision does not prevent farmers from hunting and destroying at any time and in any manner crows, woodchuck, fox and vermin (23:4-24). (See also ANIMAL DAMAGE CONTROL.)

No person shall have in an automobile or vehicle, a loaded shotgun or rifle for hunting, pursuing, taking or killing a bird or animal, or attempting to do such. Violation: $20-50 for each offense. Whenever a loaded shotgun or rifle is in possession in a vehicle, it shall be conclusive proof that the person was in the act of pursuing or taking birds or animals. No person may transport, possess, or have in control a firearm in a motor vehicle unless unloaded and contained in a closed and securely fastened case, or locked in the trunk of the motor vehicle. Violation: civil penalty of $50-200 (23:4-24.1 and :4-24.1a).

Except under emergency conditions authorized by the Division, no person shall kill, destroy, injure, shoot, shoot at, take, wound, or attempt to take, kill, or wound a game bird or game animal, or have in possession or control any weapon, while elevated in a standing tree, or in a structure of any kind within 300 feet of a baited area under penalty of $50 for each offense. "Baited area" means the presence of placed, exposed, deposited, distributed, or scattered agricultural products, salt, or other edible lure capable of attracting, or enticing such birds or animals. Growing any unharvested crops shall not be considered baiting or feeding game birds or game animals (23:4-24.2 and :4-24.3).

The owner, lessee or custodian of a dog may go into the woods or fields with the dog, without firearms for exercising or training it in daylight, except during open season for deer. On state public shooting and fishing grounds or wildlife management areas exercising or training may be restricted to designated areas. Raccoon dogs may be trained between the hours of sunset and sunrise 4 weeks prior to the last week preceding the opening of raccoon season. Violation: $20 for each offense. A person going into the woods or fields with a firearm, except during the open seasons for those birds and animals, shall be liable for a penalty of $20 for each offense; provided that these provisions shall not apply to the killing of crows, yellow-headed redwinged, bi-colored redwinged, tri-colored redwinged, Rusty and Brewer's blackbirds, cowbirds, grackles, woodchuck and vermin other than birds, which may be taken in any manner and at any time, when in the act of destroying poultry, crops or property (23:4-25). (See also ANIMAL DAMAGE CONTROL.)

★By moonlight or with the aid or by use of a lamp, lantern or artificial light, no person shall shoot or kill with a firearm, a mink, muskrat or otter, or take or attempt to take the same except by means of a trap, or disturb or destroy any muskrat lodge or nesting chamber (23:4-37).★ No conibear or killer type trap shall be used in trapping unless the trap is submerged under water in accordance with regulations. Violation: a fine up to $50 for each offense and forfeiture of the license to trap (23:4-38.2 and :4-38.3). No person shall hunt, pursue, take or trap a mink, otter, or muskrat, at any time, except during such period as provided by the code, or, in the absence of such provisions, from six o'clock p.m., on November 30 to March 15 of the following year. This provision shall not prevent the destruction of muskrats which are damaging dams or canal banks, or the setting of traps after three o'clock p.m. on November 30. Except as otherwise specifically permitted by law, a violator of these provisions shall be guilty of a misdemeanor and shall pay a penalty of $100, and whether or not criminally prosecuted, shall be liable for a penalty of $20 for each offense. No person shall take, carry away or unlawfully appropriate or purloin, with intent to steal, a skunk, mink, muskrat, or other trap, or the contents thereof, the property of another, set along, by or in public or private ditches, streams, ponds or waters (23:4-39 through :4-41).

No person shall hunt, pursue, shoot at take, kill, wound or attempt to take, kill or wound a wild deer or deer prohibited by code provisions, except during the period permitted by the code, or kill in one year more than the number of deer permitted. The owner or lessee of land under cultivation, or their authorized agents having a Division permit countersigned by the owner or lessee, may kill a deer on that land. The deer carcass becomes Division property. Land under cultivation means pasture fields seeded with cultivated grass or land on which planted crops are growing (23:4-42). (See also ANIMAL DAMAGE CONTROL.) Except as provided, no person shall possess a wild deer other than during the open season and it must have been killed as prescribed by the code. A legally killed deer and its parts may be possessed until June 1 following the season; or after June 1 by obtaining Division authorization. No person shall possess a deer, except as provided. Possession of a deer or its parts, except as permitted, is prima facie evidence of unlawful possession. These provisions do not apply to: ▸ a deer killed on a licensed game preserve; ▸ a properly tagged deer coming from another state; ▸ disposal by police officers or authorized personnel of deer found dead on public highways or private property, provided that disposal conforms with prescribed procedures (23:4-43).

No person engaged in hunting for wild deer shall use or carry any firearm or shotgun smaller than 12 gauge, or load such firearm or shotgun with a bullet or other missile larger than buckshot, or have any missile larger than buckshot or number 4 fine shot in possession other than during the open season for killing deer. Nothing in this section prevents deer hunting with a bow and arrow as provided. It is unlawful to possess a firearm while hunting deer with bow and arrow, and no person shall use, possess, or control while hunting any poison arrow, arrow with explosive tips, or any bow drawn, held or released by mechanical means. No person shall hunt, pursue, stalk, shoot at or attempt to take, kill, injure or destroy a wild deer, except by daylight on the days and at the times designated by the code. No person in or on a vehicle shall use a spotlight, flashlight, floodlight or headlight where deer may be found, nor possess or control a weapon capable of killing deer, except a law enforcement officer in the performance of duties. These provisions do not apply to the normal use of headlights. No person shall at any time, or for any reason, hunt, track, search for, seek, capture or kill a wild deer with a dog (23:4-44 through :4-46).

A person who kills a deer during the legal season immediately shall attach the transportation tag and transport the deer to a checking station before 7:00 p.m. on the day the deer was killed, to register the kill and have a legal possession tag affixed, the tag to remain attached until the carcass has been consumed. A person not required to purchase a license under 23:3-1 who kills a deer during the legal season, or a person who has lost the transportation tag, shall make and attach a transportation tag and transport the deer to a checking station. All deer killed during prescribed seasons shall be registered in the hunter's name at the nearest checking station. No person is permitted to register a deer which the person did not kill. A deer shall be transported open to view with a securely attached legal tag. The transporter of a deer other than the licensee must possess written permission signed by the licensee. No person shall possess an unregistered deer, or its parts. The owner of a legally registered deer may give away parts provided each part is labeled with the address and name of the person to whom it was given. A person who fails to tag a deer and transport it to a checking station, or who borrows, loans, transfers, buys, sells or purloins another's deer tag, is liable for a penalty of $100-500 for the first offense and $300-1,000 for the second and each subsequent offense (23:4-47). A person is liable for a penalty of $100-500 for the first offense, and $300-1,000 for the second and each subsequent offense, for: ▸ hunting, pursuing, shooting at, taking, killing, wounding, or possessing a deer or wild deer, or attempting such, other than as permitted by code or law; ▸ killing in one year more than the number of deer permitted; ▸ hunting, pursuing, stalking or shooting at a wild deer, except by daylight on the days designated; ▸ killing a deer and failing to report the same; ▸ killing a deer and failing to properly tag and transport the deer to a checking station; ▸ using or carrying a rifle for hunting deer; ▸ violating other provisions pertaining to the taking of deer (23:4-48).

No person shall hunt foxes with hounds and firearms except during the time prescribed by code. In the absence of such provisions, no person shall hunt foxes with hounds and firearms except in daylight from November 10 to April 30, but foxes shall not be hunted with hounds during the deer season. Violation: $20 (23:4-58.1).

Restrictions on Taking: Fishing

No person shall catch, take, kill or have in possession any black, Oswego, white, rock, calico bass, crappie, pike, perch, or pickerel except during the open season; trout or landlocked salmon except during the prescribed open season and not before 8 a.m. on opening day. Violation: $20 (23:5-1).

No person shall: ▸ take or attempt to take fish from state waters through an opening in the ice, or beneath the ice, prohibited by the code, or in the absence of code provisions, except carp, suckers, pike perch, pike and pickerel may be taken through or under the ice as prescribed (violation: $50 for each fish unlawfully taken or possessed) (23:5-3); ▸ sell or expose for sale perch, pike perch, pike or pickerel caught through the ice, under penalty of $50 for each fish sold (23:5-4); ▸ kill, sell, expose for sale or possess a black, Oswego, white, strawberry or calico bass, crappie, pike perch, pike, pickerel, or trout measuring less than the minimum size set by law (violation: $20 for each fish) (23:5-7); ▸ take, catch or kill in one day more than the number of those species permitted by the code or by law and under no circumstances shall a person take, catch, kill in one day more than the number of fresh water game and food fish, permitted by the code or by law (violation: $20 for each fish in excess of the number permitted) (23:5-10).

New Jersey

Except as provided in provisions relating to fishing through ice, no person shall take or attempt to take fish from state waters by means of any contrivance, except by angling with hand line or with rod and line, except as provided. Violation: $20 for each offense. Eels may be caught at any time by wicker eel baskets. Minnows and other bait fish may be taken as prescribed. All trout, pickerel, bass, pike and pike perch captured immediately shall be released uninjured (23:5-11). No person shall put, place, use or maintain in state waters inhabited by pickerel, pike, pike perch, black bass, Oswego bass, white bass, calico bass, perch or trout, a set line, or use on a line more than nine hooks, or more than three burrs of three hoods attached. No person shall use, possess or offer or expose for sale artificial bait with more than nine hooks or more than three burrs of three hoods attached. Violation: $20 for each offense. No person shall use in state waters the young of carp or tench species for bait, or take the young of any fish species for use as bait or other purposes. Violation: $20 for every fish so used for bait or taken to such waters (23:5-13 through :5-15).

No person shall possess natural bait or lures, other than those specified as legal while angling. Violation: $20 for each offense (23:5-15.1). No person shall take, in any manner, any trout, bass, pike perch, pike or pickerel, between 9:00 p.m. and daylight of the morning following or as prohibited by the code. Violation: $20 for each fish (23:5-17). [Title 23, Chapter 9, 23:9-1 through 23:9-126, enumerates local and special provisions relating to fishing in certain state waters.]

Commercial and Private Enterprise Provisions

The Division may issue: ▸ propagating licenses to propagate game birds or animals, in a wholly enclosed preserve, to ship them alive at any time, and to kill same and sell the carcasses for food; ▸ licenses to propagate pheasant, partridge, or quail in a semiwild state on lands of which the applicant is the owner or lessee; ▸ licenses to keep game birds and animals in captivity; ▸ commercial pheasant, quail and partridge shooting preserve licenses when it appears that an operation shall not conflict with a prior reasonable public interest and evidence is produced that at least 500 such birds on a preserve will be liberated between September 1 and the following March 15 (23:3-29). Game birds or animals bred or raised in a wholly enclosed preserve may be killed in any manner other than shooting, except deer, which may be killed by shooting, and the carcasses sold for food. No game birds or animals shall be sold for food unless the carcass is tagged with a tag or seal supplied by the Board. No pheasants, partridge or quail propagated in a semiwild state shall be sold nor shall such birds be taken, possessed or transported unless in a manner consistent with law and each is tagged with the special tag prescribed by sections 23:3-28 to 23:3-39. Game birds or animals killed in a wholly enclosed preserve and tagged as prescribed may be processed, bought or sold at any time. Tags shall remain affixed until the carcasses are prepared for consumption. Common carriers shall transport game birds and animals so tagged, but to every package shall be affixed a tag or label [details provided]. Nothing in these provisions relating to commercial propagation of game birds or animals shall alter or supersede the laws requiring a license to hunt. No person shall counterfeit a tag or seal. No tag or seal issued by the Board shall be affixed to the dead body of any game bird or animal not propagated in accordance with these provisions. A person violating any of these provisions shall be liable for a penalty of $50-200 for each offense (23:3-31 through :3-34, :3-38 and :3-39).

"Fishing preserve waters" means an artificial or man-made body of water, of 10 acres or less, lying within boundaries of lands owned by one individual, operated to provide fishing facilities to fishermen. Such waters shall not include natural streams, natural ponds or waters impounded by damming natural streams. The water sources for such ponds shall be limited to surface runoff, natural springs or driven wells. An outfall from fishing preserve waters must be constructed to prevent the passage of fish from or to that body of water. The Division may issue to a fishing preserve owner a license to manage such waters and to possess, propagate and rear, and to take or permit others to take fish legally propagated or acquired. A separate license is required for each body of water so defined. The license shall: ▸ contain the town and county in which the waters are located; ▸ specify the fish species authorized to be stocked; ▸ authorize the licensee to stock, propagate, raise and release fish in the licensed waters and to buy, sell, or traffic in fish taken from there; ▸ specify the manner of tagging fish taken; ▸ specify the means of acquisition of fish stocked. The license may authorize the control of undesirable protected fish, wildlife and insects and specify means of control; and specify such other restrictions and controls for the management of fishing preserve waters. A licensee or immediate family members, without license, may take fish according to conditions of the preserve license. A licensee may may grant permission to other persons to take fish without a license. Fish taken from the waters shall be tagged immediately as prescribed in the license or by Division order. The tag shall not be removed until the fish is prepared for consumption. Tagged fish may be possessed, bought, sold and offered for sale, and transported without restriction. Fish raised and possessed under these provisions may be sold for scientific, exhibition, propagation or stocking purposes. The Division, by special permit or authorization contained in the license, may authorize the licensee to use fish toxins in the management of the licensed waters, but only as specifically authorized by permit or license. A violator shall be liable for a penalty of $100-1,000 for each offense (23:3-62 through :3-66, :3-68 and :3-71).

Trout or landlocked salmon which have been artificially propagated may be sold for food, if properly tagged, in accordance with regulations adopted by the Board, or of any duly authorized board, commission or officer of another state in which the trout or landlocked salmon has been propagated. The tag shall be removed only by the consumer (23:5-2). Except for propagating, no person shall purchase, sell or offer, expose or possess for sale in the state, any black or Oswego bass, or export from or import into this state for commercial purposes any black or Oswego bass. Violation: $20 for each fish violation (23:5-25).

Import, Export, and Release Provisions

No person shall sell, offer for sale or possess for sale, whether killed or taken within or without the state, a dead body or part, of any of squirrel, wild rabbit, wild hare, or wild deer, or of a game bird or song bird belonging to a species or subspecies native to this state and protected by law, or belonging to a family, any species or subspecies of which is native to the state and protected by the provisions of the code, under a penalty of $20 for each such squirrel, wild rabbit, wild hare, wild deer or bird so sold, offered or possessed for sale; and $100-300 for each such wild deer sold, offered or possessed for sale. Wild rabbits or wild hares legally killed in another state may be imported for possession, sale and consumption. These provisions do not prohibit sale of commercially raised wild rabbits and wild hares. The carcasses of deer and the unplucked carcasses of mallard, black and wood ducks, Canada geese, ruffed grouse, squirrels, rabbits, hares, quails and pheasants raised on licensed game preserves and properly tagged, and the unplucked carcasses of Scotch grouse, European black grouse, European black plover, redlegged partridge and Egyptian quail coming from a foreign country, which are properly tagged by state authorities, may be sold for food (23:4-27).

When by the laws of any other state or country it is lawful to take out of its confines game, whether fowl or animal, that game may be brought within this state, but not sold or exported for sale. Cottontail rabbits, Belgian hares and jack rabbits legally killed in another state may be brought into the state at any time for possession, sale and consumption. Violation: $20 for each fowl or animal so sold or exposed for sale (23:4-28).

No person shall remove or attempt to remove from this state any protected animal or bird, other than deer. A nonresident holding a hunting license, in any one day may remove from the state the number of animals or birds that may be taken under provisions of the code or laws of the state. During removal, animals or birds shall exposed to open view. Violation: penalty of $20 for each animal or bird removed or sought to be removed. These provisions do not apply to common carriers carrying through the state in unbroken packages any such protected animal or bird, nor shall it apply to English or ring-necked pheasants, mallard, black or wood ducks, Canada geese, ruffed grouse, rabbits, squirrels and quail, properly tagged, raised on licensed game preserves. Except as provided by law, when the possession or sale of fowl or game is prohibited by law or by provisions of the code, prohibitions apply equally to fowl or game coming from without the state and taken within the state (23:4-29 and :4-30).

No person shall: ► liberate a fox within the state (violation: $100 for each offense); ► possess a live fox, except by permission of the Board (violation: $100 for each live fox possessed) (23:4-57 and :4-58); ► liberate a coyote within the state, under penalty of $100 for each offense; ► possess a live coyote, except by permission of the Board, under penalty of $100 for each live coyote; ► possess, release, liberate or distribute a mammal, bird, reptile, or amphibian, nor possess in a manner as may permit the same to be released, liberated or distributed contrary to provisions of law, the code, or regulations (violation: $100-500 for the first offense, and $500-1,000 for any subsequent offense) (23:4-63.1 through :4-63.4).

No person shall place a carp, or its seed, in state waters, under penalty of $200-500, or jail 30 days to 6 months. A person aggrieved or injured by reason of violation of this provision may institute criminal proceedings and civil actions for recovery of damages. These provisions do not apply to owners or lessees of private ponds constructed as to prevent the carp or its seed from escaping into state public or private waters. Without a permit, one shall not place, turn, drain into, or place fish or fish eggs where they can find their way into state fresh waters, under a penalty of $100 for each offense. No permit is required to place fish or fish eggs in an aquarium or waters privately owned, with no inlet or outlet (23:5-30 through :5-33.1). (See also Commercial and Private Enterprise Provisions under this section.)

Interstate Reciprocal Agreements

If and when New York enacts a law for the arrest and punishment of violations of the game or fish laws of this or the state of New York, committed a person fishing in the Hudson river lying between the states, a person of either state who is authorized, shall have power and authority to make arrests on any part of the river between the states or the shores and to take the person so arrested for trial to the state in which the violation was committed (23:9-120).

ANIMAL DAMAGE CONTROL

Nothing contained in Title 23, or in a code provision prevents farmers or fruit growers from shooting, or trapping by means of box traps, gray squirrels, rabbits or hares during the entire year on property owned or leased by the farmer or fruit grower for the raising of fruit, vegetables, trees, shrubbery, nursery stock, or other produce. The person shall make an affidavit that gray squirrels or rabbits have injured the crop on the person's premises and send it immediately to the Division, which may issue a permit to trap or shoot. The person trapping shall keep the gray squirrels or rabbits alive and notify the fish and game warden of the county, who shall liberate them in other parts of the state and the person so shooting shall report the number of gray squirrels or rabbits killed to the game warden of the county, within 48 hours after killing. No person shall barter or sell any gray squirrels or rabbits so trapped or shot (23:4-9).

The English or European house sparrow and the European starling are not protected wild birds. Nothing in the provisions protecting wild birds prescribed by section 23:4-50 makes it unlawful for the owner or occupant of land, the regular employees, or a Department agent to control hawks or owls, when in the act of destroying poultry or livestock, provided that such control activities are conducted in compliance with law and with permits. No permit shall be required to control yellow-headed, red-winged, bi-colored red-winged, tri-colored red-winged, Rusty and Brewer's blackbirds, cowbirds, grackles, and crows when found committing or about to commit depredations upon ornamental or shade trees, crops, livestock, or wildlife or when concentrated in such manner as to constitute a health hazard or other nuisance; provided that none of these birds nor their plumage shall be sold or offered for sale, but may be possessed, transported, and otherwise disposed of and utilized. Nothing in provisions protecting wild birds prohibits control of animals or birds by the Department in instances where there is specific documentation that they are doing damage to wildlife or agricultural crops on state lands (23:4-50).

A provision of law or municipal ordinance to the contrary notwithstanding, any owner of lands used for agriculture pursuant to rules promulgated, with a Division permit, shall have the right to use certain noise making and other mechanical devices intended to scare or repel marauding birds or other wildlife to prevent the damage and destruction of crops and other property. Violation: $20 for each such offense (23:4-63.5 and :4-63.6). (See also Restrictions on Taking: Hunting and Trapping under HUNTING, FISHING AND TRAPPING PROVISIONS.)

ENFORCEMENT OF WILDLIFE LAWS

Enforcement Powers

The Commissioner shall have the power to vest in the conservation officers of the Division, the power to arrest without warrant a person violating any law of this state committed in their presence and bring the offender before any court having jurisdiction. The Department, with the approval of the Attorney General, shall establish and maintain a suitable law enforcement training program for such personnel (13:1A-6.1).

The wardens shall enforce state laws and code provisions for the protection of fish, birds and game animals, and may execute all processes issued for the violation of these laws and the code, and serve subpoenas issued for the examination, investigation or trial of all offenses. Each warden shall keep a daily record of official acts, and report to the Council. The protector shall report to the Council any negligence, dereliction of duty, or incompetency on the part of any wardens, and the operation of the department. Every warden shall seize, remove and destroy as a public nuisance, any net, pound or other device for taking fish found in or upon the waters of this state, or upon the shores or islands of those waters where fishing with nets is prohibited or illegal. No action for damages shall be maintained against a warden for the seizure or destruction. The Council, with the approval of the Governor, may authorize in writing its salaried wardens to possess and carry any weapon or article required in the performance of official duty. The Council may appoint deputy fish and game wardens for the enforcement of the laws regulating the taking of fish, game and birds (13:1B-38, 23:2-6, :2-7 and :2-10).

The Council, the wardens, the deputy wardens and the protector shall have the power of summary arrest in cases of flagrant violation of Title 23, or of the code, and may call in the aid of a constable, sheriff or other peace officer. An officer neglecting or refusing to aid when so required shall forfeit $25 to be recovered in a civil action. Deputy conservation officers shall have the power and authority of conservation officers to enforce Title 23 and the code, and shall be subject to the regulations for enforcement of the title and code, but shall receive no salary or other compensation for the performance of duties of law enforcement (23:2-8 and :2-11).

All provisions contained in Title 23, in any supplementary law and in the code for the protection of fish, game and birds, or in any manner prohibiting or regulating the taking or possession of the same, except as provided, shall be enforced and all penalties shall be recovered in accordance with these provisions. The Superior Court and municipal court, except as provided, shall have jurisdiction to try and punish violations and every penalty prescribed for such violations may be enforced and recovered in a summary proceeding. Proceedings for the recovery of penalties shall be brought in the name of the state, by a duly commissioned warden, deputy warden, police officer, constable or a member of any regularly incorporated fish and game protective association, or the fish and game protector as prosecutor, and no such proceeding shall be instituted by any other person unless authorized. A constable, police officer, fish and game warden, protector, or deputy warden or an officer or member of an incorporated game protective society, for a violation of a provision of Title 23, or a provision of any supplementary law or the code committed within such person's view, may arrest the offender without warrant and carry the offender before a court in the county of the arrest. A person who attempts to deter or prevent a fish and game warden or other person authorized to make arrests from enforcing such provisions, or who resists arrest or the seizure of apparatus illegally used, is subject to a fine of $100 (23:10-1 through :10 -3, and :10-5). The fish and game Protector, fish and game wardens and deputy wardens have the same power as constables and are entitled to the same fees for the service of process as are provided for constables in the court in which the proceedings are had (23:10-17).

A member of the Council and any conservation officer, without a search warrant, may examine any boat, conveyance, vehicle, fish box, fish basket, game bag, game coat or other receptacle for game and fish, when there is reason to believe that a provision of Title 23, or any supplementary law, or the code has been violated, and shall seize and take possession of firearms, bows and arrows, shells or cartridges, fishing rods and reels, fishing lines, knives, lights, slingshots, traps, spears, spear guns or other article or equipment that has been illegally used or any bird, animal or fish unlawfully caught, taken, killed, had in possession or under control, shipped or about to be shipped. A court, upon receiving proof of probable cause for believing in the concealment of a bird, animal, or fish unlawfully taken, or in possession or under control, shipped or about to be shipped, shall issue a search warrant and cause a search to be made in any place, and after demand and refusal, may cause any building, enclosure or car to be entered, and any apartment, chest, box, locker, crate, basket or package to be broken open and its contents examined by a member of the Council or any conservation officer. ★All firearms, bows and arrows, shells or cartridges, fishing rods and reels, fishing lines, knives, lights, slingshots, traps, spears, spear guns or any other article or equipment illegally used and seized shall be returned to the defendant when and if the case has been dismissed, defendant is found not guilty, or if defendant has been convicted and has paid any penalty and costs imposed.★ The Council member or conservation officer shall not be liable for damages by reason of any such search or the seizure of any apparatus in accordance with these provisions (23:10-20).

A person found using a seine, gill, drift, anchor or sink net, fixed net, trap, pot, pound, set line, fyke, weir or other apparatus for the taking of fish, in addition to the penalties prescribed, shall forfeit the same. All constables, sheriffs, fish and game wardens and the fish and game protector shall, and any other person may, seize and secure the same, and shall institute a proceeding for confiscation. The court may proceed in a summary manner and may make the direct confiscation and forfeiture of the same to the Division's use, to dispose of at its discretion. A seine, gill, drift, anchor or sink net, fixed net, trap, pot, pound, set line, fyke, weir or other apparatus for the taking of fish found in state waters, in which the use is in violation of any law, the ownership of which is not known, shall be forfeited and any fish and game warden may seize the same; if claimed within 30 days, the warden shall proceed with forfeiture and if unclaimed within 30 days, the warden shall turn it over to the Division to dispose of at its discretion (23:10-21 and :10-21.1).

Criminal Penalties

If a person fails to pay the penalty or penalties imposed under these provisions, together with the costs of proceedings, the court shall commit the person to the county jail, for up to 90 days, or until the penalty and costs are paid (23:10-14). A person who alters, disfigures or changes, or loans or transfers to another, a license or button or tag issued, gives false information or makes any misrepresentation for a license, or who violates a provision of this article of which a penalty is not otherwise provided, shall be liable for a penalty of $25-50 for each offense, and upon conviction the license and button or tag issued shall be revoked. A person not entitled to a resident's license who procures the same shall be liable for a penalty of $100 (23:3-20 and 3:21).

The Commissioner shall establish a range of costs incurred by the Department for the replacement value of any animal taken or possessed in violation of law. In addition to the civil and other penalties and costs imposed, a court may assess the violator for costs, which sums shall be paid to the Division for deposit in the Hunters' and Anglers' License Fund. The Commissioner shall establish costs within the following range: ▸ an animal for which open or closed seasons or methods of taking have been prescribed in the code, $20-2,000; ▸ a fish for which open or closed seasons or methods of taking have been prescribed, $20-200; ▸ nongame or exotic wildlife as listed in the New Jersey Administrative Code (NJAC), $20-500; ▸ an endangered species as listed in the NJAC, $500-5,000. The Commissioner may adopt rules and regulations to carry out these provisions (23:3-22.2).

Civil Penalties

If a person violates any of the provisions of the Endangered and Nongame Species Conservation Act [through 23:2A-13] or any regulation, the Department may institute a civil action in a court of competent jurisdiction for injunctive relief to prohibit and prevent such violation. The court may proceed in the action in a summary manner. A person who violates the provisions of this act or any regulation promulgated pursuant to the act shall be liable for a penalty of $100 and not more than $3,000 for each offense, to be collected in a civil action by a summary proceeding, or in any case before a court of competent jurisdiction wherein injunctive relief has been requested. Penalties recovered for violations shall be remitted to the Division. The superior Court and municipal court have jurisdiction to enforce the penalty enforcement law. If the violation is of a continuing nature, each day is an additional, separate and distinct offense. The Department is authorized to settle a claim for a penalty under these provisions in an appropriate and equitable amount (23:2A-10).

★★A person who trespasses for hunting, fishing, trapping, or taking wildlife, or attempts to do so, after notice forbidding the trespass has been conspicuously posted, or after having been forbidden to trespass by the owner, occupant or lessee, shall be liable to a civil penalty of $100-200 for the first offense, and $200-500 and the suspension of all license certificates required, and all privileges to take or possess wildlife for five years, in addition to any applicable penalty prescribed by law, for subsequent convictions. A license certificate or privilege suspended pursuant to these provisions shall not be reinstated until the holder has completed the Remedial Sportsmen Education Program. A violator may be arrested without warrant by the owner, occupant, lessee, or any police officer and taken to trial. In a prosecution failure to produce written permission to hunt, fish, trap, or take wildlife on lands on which the defendant is charged with trespassing, signed by the owner, occupant or lessee thereof, is prima facie proof that the defendant was forbidden to trespass (23:7-1 and :7-2).★★

★★While hunting, fishing, trapping or taking wildlife, a person who causes or assists in causing damage or injury to real or personal property of another, including pet animals, shall be liable to a civil penalty up to $2,000, to be paid to the Hunters' and Anglers' License Fund, and for a first offense, suspension of all license certificates and privileges to take or possess wildlife for five years, or for a second offense, permanent revocation of all such license certificates and privileges. A court also may order the violator to pay restitution to the victim for any such damage or injury caused. A suspended license certificate or privilege shall not be reinstated until the holder has first completed the Remedial Sportsmen Education Program (23:7-3).★ A person entering the lands of another for hunting, fishing, trapping, or taking wildlife, or attempting to to do so, who litters, dumps, or discards refuse shall be liable to a civil penalty of $25-500 for each offense (23:7-1.1).

★★A person engaged in hunting, fishing, trapping or taking wildlife, who through the negligent use of a weapon, causes injury or death to another person, is liable to a civil penalty of $500-2,000 and suspension of all license certificates and privileges for five years for a first offense, and $1,000-4,000 and permanent revocation of all license certificates and privileges for each subsequent offense. A suspended license certificate or privilege shall not be reinstated until the holder has completed the Remedial Sportsmen Education Program. A person engaged in hunting, fishing, trapping or taking wildlife who shoots or discharges any weapon in a careless manner or without due caution and circumspection shall be liable to a civil penalty of $100-500 and the suspension of all license certificates and privileges for two years in addition to any suspension required under 23:3-22 relating to subsequent convictions. A suspended license certificate or privilege shall not be reinstated until the holder has completed the Remedial Sportsmen Education Program (23:9A-1 and :9A-2).★★

Illegal Taking of Wildlife

No person shall rob the nests or take or destroy the eggs of a wild bird other than the English sparrow. Violation: $20 for each nest robbed and each egg so removed or destroyed (23:4-51). A fox hunter who kills, injures, destroys or possesses a bird or animal the killing of which is prohibited is liable for a penalty of $100 for each bird or animal (23:4-58.3).

No owner, lessee or tenant of property shall permit the erection, construction or maintenance of contrivances for unlawful taking of fish and game prohibited by law, or permit the unlawful setting of a fyke or other net or the drawing of a net upon such property, under a penalty of $20 for each offense. Such owner, lessee or tenant shall immediately destroy all unlawful contrivances found or placed upon the premises, and no action for damages shall lie or be maintained (23:6-1). (See also HUNTING, FISHING AND TRAPPING PROVISIONS.)

License Revocations and Suspensions

★★Within five years after conviction of a violation of the fish and game laws of this or another state or of a code provision, if a person is again convicted of another violation, any fishing, hunting, or bow and arrow license held is void upon conviction, and it is the duty of such person to surrender the same to the Division for cancellation. A license issued within two years from the date of such second conviction, or of three years from a third or subsequent conviction, shall be void. A person convicted of fishing or hunting under a voided license, or without a license, shall be punished by a penalty of $100 for each offense (23:3-22). A person aggrieved by the voiding of a license held by that person, for a second conviction, or for conviction of negligently causing injury or death to another by gunfire, bow and arrow, or other weapon, may appeal to the Council for an order restoring such license. If the Council determines that the license should be restored, it shall direct the Director to return the license, but only after the person completes the Remedial Sportsmen Education Program. Thereafter the license shall be in full force and effect and licenses may be issued, notwithstanding said hunting accident or second conviction, but the conviction shall be counted as a second conviction in determining a third or subsequent conviction (23:3-22.1).★★ (See also Civil Penalties under this section.)

Intoxication Testing of Hunters

No person shall go into the woods or fields with a gun or firearm when under the influence of a drug or intoxicating liquor, under a penalty of $50 for each offense. Upon conviction for violating these provisions, the license to hunt and fish shall become void, and the court before which the conviction is had shall take the license, mark it "revoked" and send it to the Board. If the conviction is reversed on appeal, the license shall be restored (23:4-36).

HABITAT PROTECTION

★★"Conservation restriction" means an interest in land less than fee simple absolute, stated in the form of a right, restriction, easement, covenant, or condition, in any deed, will or other instrument, other than a lease, executed by or on behalf of the owner of the land, appropriate to retaining land or water areas predominantly in their natural, scenic or open and wooded condition, or for conservation of soil or wildlife, or for outdoor recreation or park, or as a suitable habitat for fish or wildlife, to forbid or limit construction; dumping; removal of vegetation; excavation; surface use except permitting the land or water area to remain predominantly in its natural condition; activities detrimental to fish and wildlife habitat preservation; and other acts or uses detrimental to the retention of land or water areas. A conservation restriction may be acquired by gift, purchase or devise, and in the case of the state or other governmental entity, by condemnation. Such restrictions may be enforced in the same manner as other interests in land (13:8B-2 and :8B-3).★★

★★The Legislature finds and declares that freshwater wetlands provide essential breeding, spawning, nesting and wintering habitats for a major portion of the state's fish and wildlife, including migrating birds, endangered species, and commercially and recreationally important wildlife. The Legislature further finds and declares that the public benefits arising from the natural functions of freshwater wetlands, and the public harm from freshwater wetland losses, are distinct from and may exceed the private value of wetland areas. The Legislature therefore determines that where pressures for commercial and residential development define the pace and pattern of land use, it is in the public interest to establish a systematic review of activities in and around freshwater wetland areas designed to provide predictability in the protection of freshwater wetlands; that it shall be state policy to preserve the purity and integrity of freshwater wetlands from random, unnecessary or undesirable alteration or disturbance and that to achieve these goals it is important that the state assume freshwater wetlands permit jurisdiction (13:9B-2). [For details of the "Freshwater Wetlands Protection Act," see 13:9B-1 through 13:9B-30].★★

★★The Legislature finds and declares that the pinelands area comprises pine-oak forests, cedar swamps, and extensive surface and ground water resources of high quality which provide a unique habitat for a wide diversity of rare, threatened and endangered plant and animal species and that it is necessary to insure implementation of a comprehensive management plan for the pinelands area. The Legislature further finds and declares that the current pace of random and uncoordinated development and construction in the pinelands area poses an immediate threat to the resources, especially to the survival of rare, threatened and endangered plant and animal species and habitat and it is necessary to impose certain limitations upon the approval of applications for development in such areas (13:18A-2). [For details of the "Pinelands Protection Act," see 13:18A-1 through 13:18A-49.]★★

★No person shall put or place any petroleum products, debris, hazardous, deleterious, destructive, or poisonous substances of any kind, where it can find its way into fresh or tidal waters within state jurisdiction; provided that the use of chemicals by a governmental entity for mosquito or other pest control or the use of chemicals by a person on agricultural, horticultural, or forestry crops, or in connection with livestock, or aquatic weed control or structural pest and rodent control, in a manner approved by the Department of Environmental Protection, or discharges from sewage treatment facilities that conform to regulations, is not a violation. Unintentional dropping of scrap steel into state fresh or tidal waters during loading at ports is not a violation if the steel is removed when that area is next dredged. In case of pollution of fresh or tidal waters by any substance injurious to fish, birds or mammals, it shall not be necessary to show that the substances actually have caused the death of these organisms. Violation: a penalty of not more than $6,000 for each offense and each day is an additional, separate, and distinct offense. The Department may institute a civil action for injunctive relief to prohibit and prevent a person from violating these provisions (23:5-28).★

No person shall shut off or draw off the waters of a pond, stream or lake or place a screen in a pond, lake or stream without Council permission. Violation: $100 for each offense. It is unlawful to construct a dam in state water which is a runway for migratory fish without installing a fish ladder or other contrivance to permit the fish to pass over the dam. Violation: $200 (23:5-29 and :5-29.1).

Lands acquired or controlled by the Division are refuges for all birds and animals whose pursuit or taking is regulated or prohibited under the provisions of Title 23. No person shall hunt, pursue, kill or take, or so attempt, within the limits of a game refuge, a bird or animal, the hunting for, kill or taking of which is prohibited by the code or by law. No person shall carry a shotgun or rifle within a game refuge unless authorized. Violation: $50 for each offense (23:8-9 through :8-11).

NATIVE AMERICAN PROVISIONS: None.

NEW MEXICO

Sources: New Mexico Statutes Annotated 1978, Chapter 17; 1988 Replacement Pamphlet; 1992 Cumulative Supplement.

STATE WILDLIFE POLICY

It is the policy of the state to provide a system for the protection of the game and fish of New Mexico and for their use and development for public recreation and food supply, and to provide for their propagation, planting, protection, regulation and conservation to the extent necessary to provide and maintain an adequate supply of game and fish within the state (17-1-1). The state legislature declares that: species and subspecies of wildlife indigenous to the state found to be endangered should be managed and, to the extent possible, enhanced in number within the carrying capacity of the habitat; the state should assist in the management of wildlife deemed to be endangered elsewhere by prohibiting the taking, possession, transportation, exportation, processing, sale or offering for sale or shipment within this state wildlife listed on the US lists of endangered fish and wildlife, unless such actions will assist in preserving or propagating the species or subspecies; adequate funding be made available to the Department of Game and Fish (Department) by annual appropriation from the general fund or from other sources separate and apart from the Game and Fish Protection Fund for management of endangered species (17-2-39). It is the policy of New Mexico to provide an adequate and flexible system for the protection of fur-bearing animals to the end that valuable fur resources shall not be wasted or depleted (17-5-1).

RELEVANT WILDLIFE DEFINITIONS: See Definitions section of Appendices.

STATE FISH AND WILDLIFE AGENCIES

Agency Structure

The **State Game Commission** (Commission) is authorized to carry out the game and fish and wildlife policy of the state. The Commission is composed of seven members, not more than four from the same political party, appointed by the Governor with Senate approval for four-year terms, one member each to be from five specified state districts and two members to be appointed at-large. ★One member shall manage and operate a farm or ranch containing at least two wildlife species which require a license to hunt or fish for on that part which is deeded land, and one member shall have a demonstrated history of involvement in wildlife and habitation protection and whose employment and activities are not in conflict (17-1-2).★ The Commission shall employ a **Director of the Department of Game and Fish** (Director) who shall employ conservation officers and employees necessary to enforce and administer the game and fish laws and regulations (17-1-5). **Reserve Conservation Officers**, under Department and Commission supervision, shall have the authority to enforce laws/regulations and perform wildlife management and education duties. ★Such officers must complete at least 25 hours of training covering wildlife management techniques, law enforcement, public relations and other Department designated topics.★ The position is unsalaried (17-1-7, -8 and -9).

Agency Powers and Duties

The **Commission** is authorized and empowered to: ► define game birds, animals and fish; ► establish open and closed seasons for the taking of game; ► establish bag limits; ► authorize/prohibit the taking of game of any kind or sex; ► prescribe the manner, methods and devices which may be used in hunting, taking or killing game; ► prescribe rules and regulations to prohibit a vehicle used in hunting game from leaving established roadways (17-2-1). The Commission shall have general control over the collection and disbursement of money collected or received under state laws for the protection and propagation of game and fish and the authority to: ► establish and operate fish hatcheries and stock state/private waters; ► declare closed seasons in any locality on a species threatened with undue depletion from any cause; ► establish game refuges; ► purchase lands for game refuges and fish hatcheries; ► receive gifts of land suitable for wildlife; ► designate resting grounds for migratory birds; ► close a lake/stream to prevent fish depletion; ► propagate, capture, purchase, transport or sell a species of game/fish needed for restocking lands/waters of the state; ► suspend/revoke a license or permit up to three years after public hearing; ►

conduct studies of programs for the management of endangered and nongame species of wildlife; ▸ establish, charge and collect fees for licenses, permits and certificates not otherwise provided for by section 17-3-13; ▸ prevent hunting in periods of extreme forest fire danger (17-1-14). The Commission is required to develop a list of indigenous endangered wildlife species (17-2-41).

Agency Regulations

The Commission is authorized to make rules and regulations and establish services necessary to carry out the provisions/purposes of this act, and all other acts relating to game and fish, and in making such rules/regulations to provide when, to what extent, and by what means game animals, birds and fish may be hunted, taken, captured, killed, possessed, sold, purchased and shipped. ★The Commission shall give due regard to the zones of temperatures and to the distribution, abundance, economic value and breeding habits of game animals, birds and fish (17-1-26).★ The Commission is authorized to establish regulations to carry out the provisions and purposes of the **Wildlife Conservation Act** relating to endangered species (17-2-43). ★When 3% of the qualified electors of a county affected by a Commission rule/regulation concerning hunting/fishing within the county shall petition in writing, the Commission shall grant a public hearing after a specified notice period, giving full opportunity for all persons to be heard on the point in controversy (17-1-27).★

Agency Funding Sources

Expenditures by the Commission shall be limited to funds available in the **Game Protection Fund** (17-1-15).

★The purpose of the **Game and Fish Bond Act** is to provide for use of revenues derived from fees from hunting and fishing licenses to issue bonds to provide for fish hatcheries, game and fish habitat acquisition, development and improvement projects and similar capital outlay projects (17-1-16 and -17). The Commission may by majority vote issue and sell bonds not to exceed a total of $2,000,000, the purpose of each bond issue to be approved by the State Board of Finance (17-1-18). Bond proceeds are to be deposited in a special fund and used solely for purposes for which authorized (17-1-21).★ The Commission shall place into the **Game and Fish Bond Retirement Fund** the sum of one dollar from each resident and nonresident fishing, small game, hunting, deer, trapping license; such moneys to be applied to pay the principal and interest on all issued Commission bonds (17-1-22). The **Game and Fish Capital Outlay Fund** consists of excess money from the Game and Fish Bond Retirement Fund, and this excess may be expended by the Department for fish hatcheries and game and fish habitat acquisition projects approved by the Commission and State Board of Finance (17-1-11).

★Money appropriated to the **Shooting Range Fund** or accruing to it from gift, deposit, or other sources shall not be transferred to other funds nor disbursed except for construction or improvement of public shooting ranges (17-7-2). The Commission is to administer the fund and determine eligibility of towns or counties for grants, such county or town to contribute at least 25% of the cost of the shooting range grant proposal. The specifications for shooting ranges are to be set by the Commission (17-7-3).★

PROTECTED SPECIES OF WILDLIFE

The game animals and quadrupeds, game birds and fowl, and game fish as herein defined shall be protected, and hunting, taking, capturing, killing or possession, or attempt to do so, a species named herein shall be regulated by the Commission (17-2-2). Fur-bearing and nongame animals are state property until lawfully taken, killed or trapped during seasons declared by Commission regulation (17-5-2 and -3). ★In making regulations regarding when and by what means fur-bearing animals may be hunted, taken, captured, possessed or killed, the Commission shall give due regard to zones of temperatures and to the distribution, abundance, economic value and breeding habits of such animals (17-5-4).★

★It is unlawful to shoot, injure, ensnare or trap, or injure or destroy a songbird, or insectivorous birds, comprising all the species and varieties of birds represented by the several families of bluebirds, bobolinks, catbirds, chickadees, cuckoos (including the roadrunner), flickers, flycatchers, grosbeaks, hummingbirds, kinglets, martins, meadowlarks, nighthawks or bull bats, nuthatches, orioles, robins, shrikes, swallows, swifts, tanagers, titmice, thrushes, vireos, warblers, waxwings, whippoorwills, woodpeckers, wrens, and all other perching insectivorous birds (17-2-13). Except as provided, it is unlawful to take, attempt to take, possess, trap or ensnare or injure, maim or destroy any of the species of vultures, hawks and owls, and it is unlawful to purchase, sell or trade, or possess parts of these birds (17-2-14).★ Other species protected by statute and regulated by the Commission include: ▸ horned toads may not be killed, sold, nor shipped from state (17-2-15); ▸ bullfrogs require fishing license for taking and may not be sold or bartered (17-2-4 and -16). Minnows and nongame fish may not be taken from state waters for sale as bait without a license (17-3-26). (See also GENERAL EXCEPTIONS TO PROTECTION.)

Endangered and threatened animals are protected under sections 17-2-37 through 17-2-46, **Wildlife Conservation Act**. The Commission shall by regulation develop a list of species and subspecies of indigenous wildlife determined to be endangered, this list to be reviewed by the Director biennially. The Director shall conduct investigations on endangered or threatened wildlife to develop information relating to population, distribution, habitat needs, limiting factors and other biological/ecological data to determine management measures and requirements necessary for their survival (17-2-40). It is unlawful to take, possess, transport, export, process, sell or ship species or subspecies of wildlife on the New Mexico Endangered Species list or the US lists of endangered native and foreign fish and wildlife to the extent that such lists have been adopted by Commission regulation. Transport through the state is allowed under valid federal and state permits (17-2-41). See also RELEVANT WILDLIFE DEFINITIONS, GENERAL EXCEPTIONS TO PROTECTION, and ANIMAL DAMAGE CONTROL.

GENERAL EXCEPTIONS TO PROTECTION

Nongame animals may be taken with a nongame hunting license allowing the hunting or taking of an animal or bird not protected by law (17-3-2). Children under age 12 may fish without a license and may take protected bullfrogs, minnows and nongame fish to sell as bait (17-2-16, 17-3-17 and -26).

★Resident fur dealers who buy/sell less than 50 pelts per year need not purchase a fur dealer license (17-5-6).★ Resident trappers who release all fur-bearing animals trapped during open seasons need not procure trapper's license (17-5-5).

Protected songbirds and insectivorous birds may be taken for scientific purposes under Department permit (17-2-13). The Director may issue permits to take, attempt to take, possess, trap or ensnare, or injure, maim or destroy vultures, hawks and owls, and to purchase, sell, or trade, or possess to sell or trade, parts of these birds for the following: Indian religious purposes; scientific purposes; or falconry purposes. Violation: petty misdemeanor (17-2-14). The Director may issue permits to take, capture, kill game, birds or fish for scientific or propagating purposes (17-3-29). The Director may on another state's request procure and transmit live specimens of game animals, birds and fish to be used for scientific or propagating purposes by that other state (17-3-30). The Director may authorize by permit the taking, possession, transportation, exportation or shipment of species or subspecies endangered or in need of management so long as such use is for scientific, zoological or educational purposes, for propagation in captivity or to protect private property (17-2-42).

HUNTING, FISHING, TRAPPING PROVISIONS

General Provisions

Landowners desiring to protect or propagate game birds, animals or fish within their enclosures shall post their land in English and Spanish and publish notice in newspapers. Thereafter, it is a misdemeanor to enter the posted lands to hunt or fish, or to kill or injure a bird, animal or fish without the owner's permission (17-4-6).

★Where the owner or lessee of deeded property held under a grazing lease agrees to permit hunting of antelope on the property, the Director may issue an antelope license free of charge to such owner/lessee in consideration for permission to hunt on the property (17-3-14). The Director shall issue landowner permits for lawful taking of elk in accordance with Commission regulations (17-3-14). The Commission shall direct the Department to authorize not more than one of the permits available for issuance in the license year for the taking of one bighorn ram to raise funds for programs and projects to benefit bighorn sheep. Permit issuance shall be subject to auction by the Department or by an incorporated nonprofit organization dedicated to conservation of wildlife, and shall be sold to the highest bidder. Money collected from bighorn sheep enhancement permit shall go to the Game Protection Fund to be used exclusively for bighorn sheep preservation, restoration and management (17-3-16).★

Licenses and Permits

Residents over age 12 must have a trapping license to capture, trap or possess a fur-bearing animal. Nonresidents may not capture, trap or possess a fur-bearing animal, skunk or coyote without a nonresident trapping license (17-5-5). A license for fur dealers is required, record keeping is required, and the provisions apply to buying and selling skins of predatory animals as well as to pelts of protected, nonpredatory fur-bearing animals (17-5-6). It is a misdemeanor for a person except children under age 12 to take or attempt to take game fish from a public stream without a license. The presence of a person along a public stream with fishing rod, hook or line without having in possession a proper fishing license is prima facie evidence of violation (17-3-17). A license is required for persons over age 12 to take from public waters minnows and nongame fish for sale as bait (17-3-26).

It is unlawful after April 1, 1972, for persons born after January 1, 1958, to hunt with a firearm unless supervised by parent or guardian, or they have successfully completed the New Mexico hunter training course or that of another state, or are 18 years of age or older. It is unlawful after April 1, 1976, for persons under age 18 to hunt with a firearm unless they have a certificate of completion of the New Mexico hunter training course or an approved course from another state. Violation: petty misdemeanor (17-2-33). The Department shall provide a course of instruction in safe handling of firearms for interested persons, promulgate regulations regarding the **Hunter Training Act**, and prescribe the type of instruction and qualifications of instructors (17-2-34).

Restrictions on Taking

Except as permitted by Commission regulations or statute, it is unlawful to hunt, take, capture, kill, or attempt to, a game animal, bird or fish in the state; or to possess, offer for sale or sell all or part of a game animal, bird or fish (17-2-7). No person shall shoot, hunt, kill, injure or take a game animal, bird or fish without having in possession the proper license (17-3-1). It is unlawful to take a game mammal, bird or fish and fail to transport the edible portions of meat home for human consumption, or to wound a game mammal and fail to make reasonable attempts to track the animal and reduce it to possession (17-2-8). It is unlawful to have in possession or to discharge bows, arrows, crossbows or firearms on game refuges except by the Director's permit (17-2-12). Hunting is prohibited while intoxicated or under the influence of narcotic drugs, or by use of spotlight or artificial light (17-2-29 and -31). ★The **Department** may restrict hunting/trapping of rabbits in an area where rabbits are infected with bubonic plague, such restrictions to be lifted when the danger no longer exists (17-2-32).★

It is a misdemeanor punishable by jail of six months to one year, or a $100-500 fine, to shoot or attempt to shoot from an aircraft to injure, capture, or kill a bird, fish or other animal or to fly aircraft so as to menace a bird, fish or animal (17-3-45). The Director may grant a permit to use aircraft to protect or aid in protection of land, water, wildlife, livestock, human life or crops, the permittee to report to the Director the number of birds, fishes and other animals injured, captured or killed (17-3-47). (See also General Provisions under ENFORCEMENT OF WILDLIFE LAWS.)

Commercial and Private Enterprise Provisions

The Commission may license shooting preserves on private lands and shall regulate size of areas, open and closed seasons, method of hunting and releasing, and possession and use of legally propagated pen-raised game birds thereon. "Game bird" on a shooting preserve shall mean pheasant, quail, chukar and mallards (17-3-36 and -37). Nonresidents must have special shooting preserve license; residents must have appropriate bird or general hunting license (17-3-39 and -40). Game and fish held in a private licensed preserve, park or lake are property of the licensee to the extent that the licensee may lawfully retain, pursue, capture, kill, use, sell or dispose of the game or fish therein, but such numbers of game or fish which existed as state property at the time of licensing shall not be reduced below those numbers unless by permit of Director (17-4-5). Game and fish farms and ponds must be licensed when such game or fish are kept for sale (17-4-8). Unlicensed parks or lakes are public nuisances and shall be abated, and game and fish therein liberated. Each day is a separate offense (17-4-9).

Import, Export, Release Provisions

Licensed fishermen may take minnows and other nongame fish for personal bait use, but it is unlawful to release nongame fish in waters stocked or reserved for game fish by the Commission (17-3-28). A permit from the

Department is required to import live animals, birds or fish into the state except domesticated animals, fowl or fish, in order to protect game animals, birds and fish against the importation of undesirable species and the introduction of infectious/contagious diseases (17-3-32).

ANIMAL DAMAGE CONTROL

The Commission is authorized to spend annually reasonable amounts from its funds not otherwise needed for the eradication of predatory animals (17-1-26). A person engaged in commercial raising of poultry or game birds may take, capture, or kill a hawk, owl or vulture which has killed such poultry or game birds, but must report the action taken to the Department for verification (17-2-14).

The owner of domestic livestock may hunt, take, capture or kill a cougar or bear which has killed domestic livestock, and the taking shall be reported to the Department for verification (17-2-7). Beaver threatening private property may be taken under the Director's permit, and the Director may grant permits to landowners for the capture or destruction of protected game doing damage to their cultivated crops or property, the permit to set the time limits for taking and number of such protected game (17-3-31). The Director may issue permits for the taking of fur-bearing animals doing damage to game, private property or livestock. Livestock producers need no permit to take bobcats doing damage to livestock (17-5-3 and -4). ★Trapping of animals, both fur-bearing and nongame, by residents in order to protect their livestock or domesticated animals or fowl shall not be subject to Commission regulations nor to licensing requirements for trappers (17-5-5).★

Endangered species may be removed, captured or destroyed to alleviate or prevent damage to property or to protect human health under prior authorization by permit from the Director unless otherwise provided by law, provided that endangered species may be removed, captured or destroyed without a permit in an emergency situation involving an immediate threat to human life or private property (17-2-42).

ENFORCEMENT OF WILDLIFE LAWS

Enforcement Powers

The Director, each conservation officer, each sheriff in their respective counties and each member of the New Mexico State Police shall enforce this chapter, shall seize game or fish held in violation, and make arrests, searches and seizures with probable cause. Conservation officers may establish checkpoints for apprehending game and fish law violators, enforce criminal trespass laws, and enforce provisions of the criminal and motor vehicle codes in emergencies (17-2-19). The magistrate court has jurisdiction in all cases arising under this code and Commission regulations (17-2-9). District attorneys are to prosecute and defend for the state in all courts all civil and criminal causes arising under this code (17-2-27). These provisions shall also apply to enforcement of the **Wildlife Conservation Act** relating to endangered species (17-2-46).

Criminal Penalties

A violation of a statute or Commission regulation which relates to the time, extent, means or manner game animals, birds or fish may be hunted, taken, captured, killed, possessed or shipped is a misdemeanor, with jail up to six months and fines as follows: illegal taking, killing, possession of deer, antelope, javelina, bear, or cougar during closed season, $400; illegal taking, killing, possession of elk, bighorn sheep, oryx, ibex or barbary sheep, $1,000; hunting big game without a license, $100; exceeding the bag limit of big game species, $400; attempting to exceed the bag limit by improper tagging of an animal, $200; falsely obtaining a resident license, $400; using another's license, $100; illegal spotlighting, $300; illegal selling or purchasing of big game animal, $1,000. Violation of a statute or regulation not otherwise provided for is a fine of $50-500, jail up to six months, or both (17-2-10 and -20).

Civil Penalties

The Director or an enforcement officer may bring civil action in the name of the state against a person unlawfully wounding, killing or possessing a game quadruped, bird or fish or part, and no verdict or judgment recovered by the state shall be for less than the following sums: each deer or javalina, $50; each elk, mountain sheep, mountain goat or barbary sheep, $200; each antelope or black bear, $100; each cougar, bison, ibex, kudu, or oryx, $300; each bird,

$10; each fish, $1. The action may be joined with an action for possession and recovery had for both possession and damages. The pendency or determination of an action for damages or payment of a judgment or the pendency or determination of a criminal prosecution for the same taking, wounding or possession is not a bar to the other (17-2-26).

Illegal Taking of Wildlife

Hunting, pursuing, capturing or killing of game animals, birds or fish on a game refuge or closed area or during a closed season is a misdemeanor (17-1-14). The following violations shall constitute a misdemeanor: ▸ illegal possession/transportation of big game during closed season; ▸ taking/attempting to take big game during closed season; ▸ taking/attempting to take big game by spotlighting; ▸ selling big game or parts except as permitted by Commission regulation; ▸ exceeding the bag limit on a big game species during open season (17-2-20). Possession of game or fish without a license, game tag or permit is prima facie evidence that the game was taken unlawfully and is a misdemeanor (17-3-33).

Every net, trap, explosive, poisonous or stupefying substance or device used in taking or killing game or fish, and set, kept or found in or upon state streams/waters and every trap, device, blind or deadfall found baited in violation of this chapter is declared to be a public nuisance and may be abated and destroyed by any person, and it is the duty of every officer to seize and destroy them (17-2-20). All firearms and bow and arrows are subject to seizure and forfeiture when used in the illegal possession/transportation of big game during closed season, taking big game during closed season, taking big game by use of spotlight or artificial light, or exceeding the bag limit on a big game species during open season. A motor vehicle shall be subject to seizure and forfeiture when operated in violation of provisions regarding hunting by spotlight or jacklight, or when attempting to take animals by the use of illegal spotlight (17-2-20.1). ★Where game or fish is seized while being transported, the officer may pay reasonable compensation and take possession of and use animals and vehicles used in such transportation for conveying the game or fish seized, and the person arrested, to a place of safekeeping or to a hearing or trial (17-2-24).★

Failure to procure a permit for an endangered species allowing its taking for scientific/educational purposes, propagation, or for the protection of private property, or the failure to abide by the terms of such permit is a misdemeanor with a fine of $50-300, jail up to 90 days, or both. A person who illegally takes, possesses, transports, exports, processes or sells a wildlife specimen on the state or federal endangered species lists shall be fined $1,000 on conviction, jailed for 30 days to one year, or both (17-2-45).

License Revocations and Suspensions

Persistent, flagrant, or knowing violation of the code or regulations shall result in the revocation of a license, permit or certificate by the Commission after notice and hearing (17-3-34). Hunting, fishing or attempting to purchase a license while one's license is revoked or suspended is a misdemeanor (17-3-48). Conviction of hunting or boating while intoxicated or under the influence of narcotic drugs results in the revocation of the hunting/fishing license and all such privileges for a period of 12 months (17-2-30).

HABITAT PROTECTION

The Director shall establish programs, including programs for research and the acquisition of land or aquatic habitat, as authorized by the Commission for the management of endangered species (17-2-42). The Commission may: ▸ acquire land by purchase, gift, bequest or lease; ▸ and develop and improve lands for fish hatcheries, game farms, game refuges, bird refuges, resting and nesting grounds, field stations and trails, for propagation, preservation, protection and management of game, birds, fish and wildlife (17-4-1). The Commission may acquire lands by the power of eminent domain (17-4-2). The Commission may sell or exchange or lease lands or assign an interest in any lands, including timber, oil, gas, or minerals (17-4-3).

Under the **Habitat Protection Act**, 17-6-1 to 17-6-11, the Commission, after public hearings in the affected areas, may close certain areas to vehicles and camping if it is determined that such activities are damaging to wildlife reproduction or habitat. The Commission may recommend that particular areas of land be set aside or made available for recreational vehicles. Camping may be prohibited during certain open hunting seasons, or restricted to designated areas. ★The Commission may enter into agreements with landowners to restrict vehicle use on private lands otherwise open for recreation and hunting, and make agreements with landowners as to enforcement, posting of lands, and cost sharing of performing the functions of this section (17-6-3).★ The Commission shall adopt regulations to carry out the provisions of the Habitat Protection Act, and shall make closed or restricted areas known to the public through public notice and hearings (17-6-4). It is unlawful to drive a vehicle cross-country where such travel is prohibited by regulation (17-6-5). All peace officers of the state, counties and municipalities shall enforce the provisions of this section (17-6-9).

No person owning or controlling a lake or body of water into which public waters flow and which supplies water to a stream containing game fish shall divert or lessen such water flow to an extent detrimental to fish (17-4-14). ★Persons floating logs, timber, or lumber in a stream containing game fish, for each mile of the streams used, shall deposit annually one thousand trout fry or fingerlings at the times and places designated by the Department. Violation is a misdemeanor (17-4-29).★

NATIVE AMERICAN WILDLIFE PROVISIONS

Provisions of this chapter shall apply to all Indians off the reservation within this state or coming into this state from adjoining states, and to all persons hunting on an Indian reservation within this state, provided that no Indian shall be required to have a license to hunt or fish within the limits of the reservation where the Indian resides (17-2-28). (See also GENERAL EXCEPTIONS TO PROTECTION for exception for Indian religious purposes.)

NEW YORK

Sources: McKinney's Consolidated Laws of New York Annotated, 1984, Articles 3, 11 and 71; 1992 Cumulative Annual Pocket Part.

STATE WILDLIFE POLICY

The state owns all fish, game, wildlife, shellfish, crustacea, and protected insects in the state, except those legally acquired and held in private ownership. A person who kills, takes or possesses such animals consents to title remaining in the state for the purpose of regulating and controlling their use and disposition. (11-0105)

RELEVANT WILDLIFE DEFINITIONS: See Definitions section of Appendices.

STATE FISH AND WILDLIFE AGENCIES

Agency Structure

The **Department of Environmental Conservation** has responsibility over all aspects of state environmental policy and protection (3-0101). The head is the **Commissioner of Environmental Conservation** (Commissioner), appointed by the Governor by and with advice of the Senate, who holds office at the pleasure of the Governor (3-0103). The Commissioner has power, among other environmental roles, to promote and coordinate management of water, land, fish, wildlife and air resources, and provide for the propagation, protection and management of fish, wildlife and preservation of endangered species. The **Department of Fish and Wildlife** (Department) has general powers to manage all fish and wildlife resources of the state, including all animal and vegetable life and soil, water and atmospheric environment owned or managed by the state, that constitute fish and wildlife habitat (11-0301 and -0303).

Agency Powers and Duties

★County boards and legislative bodies shall not, except as provided in the Fish and Wildlife Law, provide for protection, preservation, or propagation of fish, game or wildlife in the county, or prescribe or collect penalties (11-0111).★

Powers vested in the **Department** are for efficient management of the state's fish and wildlife resources. Management includes maintenance and improvement of resources, development of measures for accessibility, reciprocal and cooperative agreements with government and private entities, and research and educational programs. The Department shall promote desirable species in ecological balance that leads to sound maintenance with regard to ecological factors, production and harvesting of fish and wildlife compatible with other land uses, public safety, and the need to protect private premises against abuses of access for hunting, fishing or trapping (11-0303).

The Department has the power to: ▸ issue and revoke licenses and permits provided for by law, fix terms and fees; ▸ regulate taking of fish; ▸ increase the mesh size of fish nets; ▸ declare certain waters no longer inhabited by or unsuitable for trout; ▸ manage and control importation, exportation, and handling and shipment of shellfish and crustacea [also leasing of shellfish and oyster beds]; ▸ conduct, manage and control hatching and biological stations, game farms and refuges, rearing stations and public hunting and fishing grounds owned or operated by the state; ▸ enforce all fish and wildlife laws and regulations; ▸ settle or compromise actions to recover penalties; ▸ regulate possession, transportation and sale of Pacific salmon; ▸ designate free fishing days (11-0305); ▸ make regulations for migratory birds, conforming to the Migratory Bird Treaty Act, including creation of stamps and art prints and their sale (11-0307); ▸ extend open seasons after Governor proclamation of emergency closing for fire danger (11-0309); ▸ ★give additional protection to fish or wildlife if ten or more citizens file a petition stating why protection is necessary and a hearing is held (11-0311);★ ▸ close waters when fish are in imminent danger of undue depletion from drought or low water (11-0313); ▸ establish seasons and limits for taking fish in certain border waters and in New York City water supply (11-0317 and -0319); ▸ establish "restricted areas" on private or other property, including landowner obligations to further sound management practices and public access for hunting, fishing and trapping. Restricted areas are to provide safety zones, protect crops, allow research for game management, protect water supplies, or for other purposes (11-0321); ▸ publish the Fish and Wildlife Law each year (11-0323).

The Department shall have power to: ▸ make regulations for use of state-owned boat-launching and access sites and public hunting, trapping and fishing grounds and to prohibit, limit and manage hunting, trapping and fishing on such grounds; ▸ protect any lands or waters, rights or interests owned, leased or otherwise acquired for controlling, managing, propagating or distributing fish or wildlife or for managing hatcheries or biological stations, game farms, rearing stations, refuges, or game management areas; ▸ prohibit taking fish within 50 rods of any fishway or dam erected in public waters; ▸ fix permit terms and regulations permitting taking fish or wildlife on the areas or facilities above; ▸ enter into cooperative agreement with a person for fish and wildlife conservation practices on lands or waters made available as provided in sections 11-0303, 11-0321 or 11-0501; ▸ dispose of pheasant chicks and surplus pheasant eggs of the state's game farms. If removing trees and other products will produce optimum conditions for fish or wildlife, the Department may sell those products in areas held by the Department (11-2101). The Department shall have power to acquire lands or waters, or any right or interest for establishing and maintaining public hunting, trapping and fishing grounds. Lands or waters accepted under this power shall be held for use and improved as the Department deems best and shall not become part of the forest preserve nor be subject to the limitation of section 1 of article XIV of the State Constitution. Moneys received in accordance with the terms of any cooperative agreement for promoting fish and wildlife conservation practices, unless provided, shall be deposited in the Conservation Fund for purposes specified in that section (11-2103 and -2303).

Agency Advisory Boards

★★The **Fish and Wildlife Management Practices Cooperative Program** is authorized to establish, on privately owned or leased state lands and waters, management practices to preserve and develop the resources and improve access for recreation. The Commissioner will establish up to 15 fish and wildlife management regions. Each region's board is three resident members from each county, one from the county board of supervisors or legislative body, one representing landowners, and one representing sportsmen. County members shall be appointed by the chairman of the board of supervisors [alternative appointment methods detailed, as well as extensive details of additional qualifications of regional representatives, terms of office and filling vacancies]. Board chairmen of each soil and water conservation district and regional forest practice board are advisory members. Regional boards elect a state board member to the **State Fish and Wildlife Management Board** and its advisory board to make recommendations to the Commissioner regarding fish and wildlife management, and to advise regional boards. The Commissioner may make cooperative agreements with landowners or lessees within a region to carry out management practices adopted by the regional board. The Commissioner shall provide personnel to assist the boards and cooperators, and provide to cooperators: technical services, trees and shrubs, labor and materials, protection by posting, patrol, inspection stations and other means (11-0501).★★

PROTECTED SPECIES OF WILDLIFE

See RELEVANT WILDLIFE DEFINITIONS for listed protected animals.

No person shall pursue, take, wound or kill, buy, sell, or possess protected fish, game, protected wildlife, shellfish, harbor seals, protected crustacea, or protected insects, except as permitted (11-0107).

Endangered species are those designated by the Department as seriously threatened with extinction, and threatened species are those designated likely to become endangered within the foreseeable future throughout all or a significant portion of their range. Regulations shall include endangered and threatened species designated by the Secretary of the Interior, provided the Commissioner may exclude any species determined to be no longer endangered or threatened. Taking, importation, transportation, possession or sale of endangered or threatened species, or hides or parts, or sale or possession with intent to sell any article made from such species, is prohibited except under permit (11-0535).

★★No part of the skin or body, whether raw or manufactured, or the animal itself, of the following species may be sold or offered for sale by any individual or entity: leopard, snow leopard, clouded leopard, tiger, Asiatic lion, cheetah, alligator, caiman or crocodile of the order Crocodilius, tortoises of the genus Gopherus, marine turtles of the family Cheloniidae and Dermochelidae, vicuna, wolf, red wolf, kangaroo, polar bear, mountain lion, jaguar, ocelot, margay, sumatran rhinoceros or black rhinoceros. The Commissioner may permit under terms and conditions importation and sale of skin, body or parts of alligators, caiman or crocodiles, and importation, transportation, possession and sale of any species listed above for zoological, educational, and scientific purposes, and for propagation in captivity for preservation, unless prohibited by federal law or regulation (11-0536).★★ See ENFORCEMENT OF WILDLIFE LAWS for seizure and forfeiture provisions. It is unlawful knowingly or with wanton disregard for the consequences to take, possess, sell, purchase, barter, offer to sell, purchase or barter, transport, export, or import any bald or golden eagle alive or dead, or any part, nest or egg without a permit (11-0537). No person shall without license or permit, possess, transport or cause to be transported, import or export any live wolf, coyote, coydog, fox, skunk or raccoon, endangered species, restricted species listed in 11-0536 or other species of wildlife or fish where the Department finds that possession would present a danger to the health or welfare of the people or an indigenous fish or wildlife population. Animals possessed without permit shall be seized and disposed of at Department discretion. No person shall possess, sell or breed ferrets, fitch ferrets or fitch except under revocable license (11-0511).

GENERAL EXCEPTIONS TO PROTECTION

The Department may issue a revocable license to collect or possess fish, wildlife, shellfish, aquatic insects, birds, nests or eggs for propagation, banding, scientific or exhibition purposes, licensees to report annually. Licenses may also be issued to possess and sell protected fish, wildlife, shellfish, crustacea or aquatic insects, and to rehabilitate wildlife, with qualifications. Regulations shall govern possession of and protection of such animals from cruelty, disease or undue discomfort and to protect the public from attack or contamination. The Department may take or permit taking wildlife, fish or shellfish for propagation or stocking purposes, or remove fish or shellfish which hinder propagation of foodfish or shellfish or which are in imminent danger of being killed by pollution (11-0515 and -0517). ★★A person discovering protected wildlife in distress, except foxes and skunks, may capture them and render aid. A conservation officer must be notified by telephone and confirm in writing within 24 hours. Within 48 hours the person shall obtain certification from a veterinarian that the wildlife requires continuing aid. If the wildlife is not in distress, it shall be released immediately into suitable wild habitat. If the wildlife is in continuing distress a permit may be issued under 11-0515 (11-0919).★★

HUNTING, FISHING, TRAPPING PROVISIONS

General Provisions

Sections 11-1703, 11-1705 and 11-1707 relating to importation, possession and sale apply to fish, wildlife and game lawfully taken outside the state and transported, except trout raised in a private hatchery, domestic game, fish from a licensed fishing preserve and carcasses of foreign game. These sections do not limit the privileges of a licensee under section 11-0515 to import live fish and wildlife, or privileges with respect to possession, transportation and sale, within the state. The open seasons for fish are specified by order adopted pursuant to section 11-1305; those for game are specified in sections 11-0905, 11-0907 and 11-1103. For the purposes of sections 11-1703, 11-1705 and 11-1707, there is an open season for a species if it is unprotected fish or wildlife, and in any other case, when there is an open season for taking it anywhere in the state. Sale and transportation provisions do not apply to importation, possession, or sale of captive bred and raised North American elk (11-1701).

Except as provided, all species of fish taken outside the state, except trout, black bass, muskellunge and landlocked salmon other than Atlantic salmon, may be imported and transported, and may be possessed, bought and sold without permit or license, during the open season; Atlantic salmon taken outside the state may be imported, transported, bought and sold at any time. Except as provided, a person may, during the closed season, without license or permit, and without limitation by section 11-1707, transport into the state, buy, possess, transport and sell, lake sturgeon, lake trout, whitefish, pickerel, pike, walleye and striped bass taken outside the state, provided a record is kept [details of records and exceptions provided]. The following species taken outside the state shall not be bought or sold or otherwise trafficked in if less than the size limits specified: ► striped bass, fluke or summer flounder, blue porgie, weakfish, mackerel, sea bass, king fish, cod fish, blackfish, winter flounder; ► lake trout, pickerel, Atlantic sturgeon, Atlantic (landlocked) salmon, whitefish, northern pike, all as specified in regulations. Fish named above of less than the size limits, may be imported, transported and possessed as provided in section 11-1707 (11-1703).

Frogs taken outside the state may be imported and transported during the open season. During the closed season a person may transport into the state, possess, buy and sell frogs without a license if a record is kept. ★The carcasses of varying hares and cottontail rabbits may be imported and possessed, transported, bought and sold without license or permit.★ Game for propagation and the plumage or skin of game birds may be imported and transported without license or permit, but shall not be sold or offered for sale or possessed for sale except as permitted (11-1705).

★The head, skin or hide, fur and feet of game and wildlife, except birds, may be bought, sold and imported and transported without license or permit.★ The flesh of game and wildlife, except birds, black, grey or fox squirrels, lynx, bear, deer, moose, elk, caribou and antelope may be bought, sold and imported and transported during the open season, without permit or license, and may be imported during the closed season, as provided. ★The flesh of bear, deer, moose, elk, caribou, and antelope may be imported, transported and possessed as provided. The flesh of such game except bear and white-tail deer may also be imported, transported and possessed pursuant to permit, and if so imported, may be bought and sold only when tagged as provided. Bear flesh may be imported, transported, possessed, bought and sold for food as provided, under permit (11-1705).★ ★Bear possessed under license or possessed outside the state under a license similar in principle, may be killed and imported, transported, bought and sold for food, with a special permit and tagged as provided in section 11-1721 (11-1713).★ See also PROTECTED SPECIES OF WILDLIFE.

The dead bodies of birds of all species or subspecies native to this state, defined as protected, or belonging to any family, species or subspecies native to this state, shall not be sold, offered for sale or possessed for sale for food. They may be imported, transported and possessed, except for sale, as provided in section 11-1707 (11-1705).

Carcasses or parts of trout, black bass, muskellunge and landlocked salmon, other than Atlantic salmon, and fish, the sale of which is prohibited under section 11-1703, and of wildlife (other than migratory game birds), sale of which without license or permit is not authorized by section 11-1705, may be imported during the open and closed season as provided. Carcasses and parts of other fish and wildlife, may be imported during the closed season as provided. Importation of migratory game birds is governed by regulation pursuant to section 11-0307. During the open season, carcasses above may be transported by the taker into the state, without permit or license, except by parcel post, provided that if shipped by carrier, they shall be properly labeled [details provided] (11-1707).

During the closed season, the taker may transport carcasses or parts of any fish or wildlife (other than migratory game birds), into the state, provided the taker accompanies them and has a license permitting such; or may ship by carrier except parcel post with a Department license permitting such transportation [carcass and package labeling, details provided]; or may import and transport carcasses and parts of lawfully taken big game animals without such license, provided the taker accompanies them and they are tagged and identified. From September 1 - February 10 any resident may, with a license permitting it, transport into the state, except by parcel post, carcasses of certain tagged fish and wildlife for which there is no open season at the time. Carcasses of fish and wildlife imported as provided may be possessed and transported within the state (11-1707).

Licenses and Permits

The privileges of license or stamps defined in section 11-0701 (classes of licenses) are only as permitted by Fish and Wildlife Law and regulations. No license or stamp authorizes the holder to trespass upon private lands or waters or interfere with another's property; take fish or wildlife on an Indian reservation; enter upon, or take or disturb fish or wildlife on state lands or waters except with a written permit or order; take fish or wildlife in any closed area. Licenses are not transferable or alterable, and licenses obtained by fraud or improperly detached are void [details of persons eligible for various licenses are provided, as well as restrictions on activity authorized by each class of license]. Holders of licenses, stamps or buttons must carry and exhibit them to conservation officers, and license tags shall be displayed [certain licenses must be displayed on the outer garment]. Failure to do so is presumptive evidence of hunting without a license (11-0703 and -0705). ★License applicants must present evidence of previous licenses or a certificate of qualification in responsible hunting practice, including safety, ethics and landowner relations (11-0713).★

Owners, lessees and their immediate families cultivating farm lands have the right on their land to hunt wildlife except deer and bear; trap bobcat, coyote, fox, mink, muskrat, raccoon, opossum, weasel and skunk and unprotected wildlife; and take fish and frogs except baitfish by net or trap. [Reciprocal fishing rights in certain specified boundary waters of Vermont, Pennsylvania, Connecticut and New Jersey are provided.] Taking destructive or menacing wildlife as authorized, fish farm licensees and family, and fishing preserve licensees and family taking fish are not subject to licensing requirements (11-0707 and -0709). [Procedures for issuing licenses and proof of eligibility are detailed in 11-0713.] Required for various licenses are certifications of qualification in responsible hunting, bowhunting and trapping practices (11-0713).

Restrictions on Taking: Hunting and Trapping

No one shall: ▸ obstruct passage of fish by screen or otherwise; ▸ hold or divert water in any stream supplying a state hatchery or take state hatchery fish; ▸ set bear or deer traps, or place salt licks on lands inhabited by deer or bear; ▸ prevent frogs from access to and from water ▸ rob or willfully destroy nests of protected birds, or disturb a beaver dam or muskrat house or shelter without a permit; ▸ disturb a nest box or structure constructed to harbor wild birds; ▸ kill or capture or attempt to do so, or detain, possess or transport any Antwerp or homing pigeon wearing a ring or seamless leg band with its registered number (11-0505 and -0513).

No person shall: ▸ take wildlife other than migratory birds while in or on a motor vehicle, or use any lights on a vehicle for such purpose; ▸ take wildlife on or from any public highway; ▸ take deer or bear other than by gun or long bow as provided, or while the animals are not on land, with the aid of any artificial light, or with a pre-established bait pile; ▸ take wildlife in a manner prohibited by law [details are provided for various species]; ▸ take wildlife with a prohibited device such as explosive arrows or propelled injections of drugs; ▸ take deer or bear with the aid of a dog or aircraft; ▸ take skunks from holes or dens by digging or with dogs; ▸ take raccoons from dens or houses or by cutting den trees; ▸ take protected wild birds for which no open season is established; ▸ use traps except as permitted in Title 5 or 11; ▸ take wild game except as established by law or regulation; ▸ take upland game birds with bait. Use of artificial lights and possession of a bow or firearm is presumptive evidence of hunting with a light unless the weapon is unloaded, stored, or the person has no ammunition (11-0901).

Open seasons and bag limits for migratory game birds shall conform with the Migratory Bird Treaty Act. Open seasons and bag limits shall be set for the following wild game: Hungarian partridge, black gray and fox squirrels, bobcat, lynx, coyote, fox, European hare, varying hare and cottontail rabbits, pheasants, raccoon, wild turkeys, ruffed grouse [details of permits and restrictions provided]. Special seasons and areas may be set for managing deer or bear (11-0903). [Game are listed by species as to open season and bag limit, usually designated to be set by regulation, in 11-0905.] The Department has authority to establish hunting hours for wild deer and bear, wild upland game birds, and small game other than bobcat, mink, muskrat, raccoon, coyote, fox and skunk, during open seasons (11-0909).

No person shall use in hunting or possess in the fields or forests or on state waters: ▸ silencers; ▸ automatic firearms; ▸ auto-loading firearms that contain more than six shells [exceptions provided]. No firearm except a pistol or revolver shall be carried in or on a motor vehicle unless unloaded, except that a loaded firearm for legally taking migratory game birds may be carried in a motorboat. No person, while in a motor vehicle, shall use a jacklight or other artificial light if in possession or accompanied by one in possession of a longbow, crossbow or firearm except a pistol or revolver, unless the longbow is unstrung or the firearm is fastened in a case or locked in the trunk [definition of motor vehicle provided]. No person shall: ▸ discharge a firearm in a "restricted area" under section 11-0321, contrary to the terms of the restriction; ▸ discharge a firearm or longbow over a public highway; ▸ discharge a firearm or longbow within 500 feet from a dwelling house, farm building or farm structure occupied or used, school building, school playground, or occupied factory or church. These prohibitions shall not apply to: ▸ the owner or lessee of the dwelling house, or immediate family residing therein, employee, or guest acting with consent [500-foot restriction applies]; ▸ public school instruction and training in use of firearms or long bow; ▸ authorized use of a pistol, rifle or target range operated by a police Department, law enforcement agency or duly organized membership corporation; ▸ discharge of a shotgun over water while hunting migratory game birds [500-foot restriction applies including livestock or persons]. In counties where a rifle other than a muzzle loading firearm is not permitted for taking deer, a person afield shall not possess larger than 22 caliber rim-fire rifle during the open deer season. No person while hunting deer or bear pursuant to a bowhunting stamp, and no person accompanying a hunter during a special longbow season, shall possess a firearm [same restrictions as above apply to muzzle-loading firearm and season]. During any open season for deer, a person afield shall not possess shotgun shells loaded with slug or ball without a license or permit to take deer or bear (11-0931).

Except as provided, game and trout required to be tagged, when so tagged may be possessed, bought and sold, and subject to section 11-1725 may be transported. No domestic duck, goose, brant or swan killed shall be bought or sold unless marked by the hind toe of the right foot being removed. No person shall sell or offer for sale game or trout unless tagged. Carriers may receive, and transport carcasses and parts tagged and labeled as provided. When received in this state, or transported within or without the state by a carrier, every shipment of game required to be tagged shall also have attached a label [details of data required provided]. No carrier or employee shall transport, receive or possess any fish or game for shipment unless tagged as required. (11-1723 and -1725).

★It is unlawful for a person engaged in hunting, trapping or fishing without permission upon the lands of another, not to leave immediately when requested to do so by the owner, lessee or lawful occupant. Upon conviction of a violation of this section, all the licenses held by the person shall be revoked and the person shall be ineligible for a license during the ensuing license year, and in the discretion of the court ineligible for up to an additional one year. The punishment shall be in addition to such other fines and penalties as the person may have incurred. No person, while hunting, trapping or fishing, shall without the permission of the owner, lessee or lawful occupant enter upon the land and kill or injure any dog, livestock or domestic fowl, or cut, destroy or damage any bars, gates or fence or part, or deface or damage any vehicle, farm equipment, buildings or appurtenances to the land (11-2115 and -2117).★

[Limitations are set on taking antlerlees deer or deer with antlers less than three inches, as well as bear less than one year old. Regular open seasons are set for deer and big game in named regions and by manner of taking (11-0907).] Bobcat, mink, muskrat, raccoon, coyote, fox and skunk may be taken at any hour. The Department may set uniform hours of hunting in different areas for all other wild deer, bear, upland game birds and small game. A summary shall be published each year. Deer or beer taken shall be tagged immediately as provided and transported with tags attached [complete details of tagging and transport requirements are provided] (11-0909 and -0911). Deer management permits, [which specify areas, seasons, manner of taking and other restrictions] may be issued. The owner of a vehicle in a collision with a deer may possess the deer if it is reported within 24 hours, and the officer investigates, finds damage and issues the permit (11-0913 and -0915).

Wild game, other wildlife and parts, if lawfully taken, may be possessed, transported within the state and out of the state, and bought and sold, as provided. Unprotected wildlife may be possessed, transported, bought and sold except as provided. Game for propagation purposes may be transported except as provided. The plumage, skin or body of any wild bird shall not be sold, possessed or offered for sale except as permitted by section 11-1729 or 11-1731. No live wolf, coyote, coydog, fox, skunk or raccoon shall be possessed or transported, except under a license or permit. Live ferrets, fitch-ferrets and fitch shall not be possessed or sold, except under license as provided in section 11-0511. No wildlife shall be possessed, transported or sold contrary to the terms of any statute, regulation, permit or license pursuant to which it was taken or acquired (11-0917). [Additional provisions are provided in this section for the possession, transportation, buying, selling and storage of specified wildlife and birds, alive or as carcasses.]

★When a wild turkey, deer or bear is taken by a person with a license or permit and it is shown that it was unfit for human consumption at the time it was killed, the taker may surrender the carcass and be issued a permit to take another specimen (11-0921).★

The following provisions apply to dogs: ▸ no owner or trainer shall allow a dog to hunt deer, or to run at large on enclosed lands with wildlife or domestic game or in any state park, reservation, game farm, wildlife refuge or management area or allow it to run at large in fields or woods inhabited by deer outside a city or village, except on lands actually farmed by the owner, trainer or tenant; ▸ dogs shall only be taken afield for training on wild game from August 16 to April 15 or as permitted; ★▸ dogs may be trained on artificially propagated game which is shackled, or confined, or on dummies or other devices, if done to preclude any disturbances injurious to wildlife;★ ▸ during training, a person in the company shall not possess a firearm loaded with ammunition other than blank shells or cartridges, or inflict unlawful injury to animals or game birds; ▸ dogs hunting deer, wildlife or domestic game on enclosed lands, a state game farm, or wildlife refuge or management area, may be killed as provided in section 11-0529; ▸ wildlife, except skunk, deer and bear, may be taken with a dog (11-0923).

Special dog training areas may be established by organizations with 20 or more residents, on land of which the applicant or a member has ownership or control. Areas must be 35 - 300 acres [other details provided]. Licensees shall stock the area with 25 pieces of game per 100 acres per year, under Department supervision. A permit is required for liberation of any wildlife, and may not endanger the health of native wildlife species [details of training allowed and renewal of licenses provided]. Boundaries shall be posted. The landowner may hunt unprotected wildlife, and deer during the open season (11-0925). ★No person shall take part in a field trial except as provided in this section. A field trial may be held on liberated game, liberated artificially propagated game, led or confined game legally possessed, or on wild game on a licensed dog training area without license, if such game is not taken. On areas other than a licensed dog training area, field trials may be held on wild game from August 16 to April 15 without a license.★ A permit is required for liberation of any wildlife [details of taking wild game provided]. Game taken shall be tagged immediately and may be possessed, transported, bought and sold at any time (11-0927). ★The Department may provide certification of leashed tracking dogs and authorize their use to track wounded big game (11-0928).★

Except as provided, no wild bird shall be trapped, netted or snared. Protected wildlife shall not be trapped except in open season with a license or permit with respect to rabies control and predatory, destructive or menacing wildlife, or on a registered muskrat marsh. Protected wildlife trapped shall not be killed or possessed unless a species for which trapping is permitted [special provisions for Southern Zone provided]. On the opening day of a season, no person shall set any trap or deadfall before 7:00 A.M. Except as provided with respect to destructive and menacing wildlife, no person shall use a trap having teeth in the jaws; set a trap so that wildlife when caught is suspended; use, locate or set a noose. No person shall set or use a leg-gripping trap except as provided. No person shall set or use a body gripping type trap except in water during the season for trapping beaver and otter, or according to regulation. ★Leg-gripping traps, as specified, when set on land shall be covered; if needed, the trap shall be re-covered at the time the trap is visited. Coverings shall include soil, sand, leaves, needles, other plant materials, and other substances as permitted, completely cover jaws, and be equipped with a pan tensioning device [detailed description provided]. Except as provided, no person shall take muskrat by box, wire or cage trap, except they may be taken in a trap incapable of taking any species until wildlife previously taken has been released.★ Except as permitted, no person shall set, stake or use a trap within five feet from a muskrat den or house; smoke, chemicals, gas or poison shall not be used on or near any trap used to take beaver, otter, fisher, bobcat, coyote, fox, mink, raccoon, muskrat or skunk. Except as permitted, no person shall: ► trap within 15 feet from a beaver dam, den or house; ► remove any lawfully trapped wildlife or disturb, destroy, take or possess a trap without owner permission; ► set traps on a public highway; ► take beaver, fisher and otter; ► trap wildlife within 100 feet of a dwelling, school building, playground or church without consent of the landowner or lessee (11-1101).

The Department may permit trapping of beaver, fisher, otter, bobcat, coyote, fox, raccoon, opossum, weasel, skunk, muskrat, pine marten and/or mink in specified areas, and may regulate their taking, possession and disposition (11-1103). Traps shall bear the name and address of the operator. They shall be visited each 24 hours, unless otherwise provided, and all wildlife trapped shall be removed immediately. Wildlife lawfully taken alive in traps may be killed unless pursuant to a special license (11-1105). Wildlife taken by trapping may be possessed, transported, bought and sold only as provided in section 11-0917 (11-1107). ★★A registered muskrat marsh must be registered with the Department prior to September 1 previous to the year in which this section is applied. If the Department is satisfied that the marsh is being managed soundly, it shall issue a certificate of registration. The owner of a registered marsh may apply to trap during the closed season for removal of surplus muskrats, except May 1 through October 31. The name and address of every person designated to trap, prior to the trapping, shall be forwarded to the Department. The Department may make regulations governing trapping muskrats on registered marshes, but regulations shall not be more restrictive than provisions of this chapter expressly regulating taking muskrats. Registrants shall furnish reports on the number of muskrats trapped. No person other than the owner or lessee shall trap on a registered marsh without a license (11-1109).★★

Restrictions on Taking: Fishing

Farm fish pond or fishing preserve licensees, their immediate families and others, may take fish thereon without a license (11-0709). Except as provided: ► no fish shall be taken except by angling; ► fish named by regulation pursuant to section 11-1303 shall be taken only during the open seasons within size limits; ► fish named by regulation pursuant to section 11-1303 shall not be taken in excess of daily or seasonal catch limits; ► fish shall not be taken contrary to restrictions closing waters to taking, restricting use of nets or other devices, fixing seasons, size limits or daily or seasonal catch limits, or otherwise restricting taking; ► fish unintentionally taken contrary to any provision or regulation shall be returned to the water without unnecessary injury (11-1301). Notwithstanding any other provision, the Department, until July 1, 1995, may fix by regulation, in state waters, open seasons, size and catch limits and manner of taking of fish, except marine fish (11-1303). The Department may promulgate regulations restricting possession of fish on state waters (except the marine and coastal district and except bait fish named in section 11-1315) that have been cleaned, filleted or skinned so that the species cannot be identified, or the length or numbers taken cannot be ascertained. Regulations shall initially provide that walleye, largemouth and smallmouth bass, brook and lake trout may not be possessed if they have been dismembered, filleted or otherwise prepared for consumption beyond gill and viscera removal and that other species may not be possessed if the skin is removed (11-1305).

The waters impounded by any dam constructed for power on any state stream or waterway, and impressed with a public interest, shall be open to the public to fish, when authorized by applicable provisions, subject to the following limitations: ▸ fishing must be conducted under rules and regulations of the Commissioner in agreement with the person, association or corporation proposing to construct the dam; ▸ rules and regulations must provide that fishing shall be conducted so as not to interfere with the operation and maintenance of the dam or power-generated plant; ▸ damages sustained while fishing shall not constitute a claim either against the state or the person, association or corporation owning the dam; ▸ the Commissioner, after notice and public hearing, shall have power to exempt the waters impounded by any dam hereafter constructed for power purposes; ▸ rules and regulations may vary in different localities; ▸ warning notices shall be posted along the entire boundary of such waters (11-1311).

Except as provided, without the appropriate license, no one shall take for sale as bait, nor sell as bait: ▸ minnows, except carp or goldfish; ▸ top minnows or killifish; ▸ mudminnows; ▸ darters; ▸ sticklebacks; ▸ tadpole stone cats; ▸ smelt or ice fish; ▸ alewives, saw bellies or blueback herring; ▸ suckers. Fish taken pursuant to such license shall be used only for bait in hook and line fishing. All carp, goldfish, and lamprey larvae taken in nets pursuant to such license shall be destroyed immediately. Bait fish named above may be taken for use or sale as bait by angling, nets as permitted, or stunning if tadpole stone cats. Fish named above, taken for personal use and not for sale, may be taken [net restrictions detailed]. Nets for taking bait fish shall not be hauled after sunset or before sunrise, except as permitted. Fish named above, taken for sale as bait under Department license, may be taken by the types of nets specified in such license. Carp, goldfish, and lamprey larvae shall not be used as or sold for bait. Licenses shall be issued only to residents and nonresidents of a state in which residents of this state may be licensed, or are permitted without license, to take such fish for sale as bait (11-1315).

The Department, by regulation, may prohibit the use of minnows or other species as bait in lakes, ponds or tributaries in which trout are the predominant protected species and which are not infested with yellow perch, or if fish have been eradicated by chemical treatment and trout or other game fish have been restocked. No person shall possess any species of fish, dead or alive, in or on waters where the use of fish as bait is prohibited, except species actually present in such waters naturally (11-1316). ★★No aquatic insect or insect that lives in the water during any of its life shall be taken from waters inhabited by trout nor from the banks at any time. No person shall take from state waters or the banks thereof for sale as bait, and no person shall sell as bait, any such insect, without a license. Such licenses shall be issued only to residents and nonresidents of a state in which New York residents may be licensed, or are permitted without license, to take such insects for sale as bait (11-1317).★★

All fish lawfully taken in the state, except as provided, may be possessed, transported, bought and sold only by law and regulations. Such fish shall not be possessed, transported, bought or sold unless lawfully taken, nor transported, bought or sold, unless lawfully possessed. No fish shall be possessed, transported or sold contrary to the terms of any statute, regulation, permit or license pursuant to which it is taken or acquired. Trout, including rainbow trout, Atlantic salmon, black bass, walleye and muskellunge shall not be bought and sold. Bait fish named shall not be sold for bait except as provided. The following fish may be bought and sold at any time: ▸ [marine species and Great Lakes provisions detailed]; ▸ fish not named in section 13-0339, 11-1521 or 13-0347 or in regulation under section 11-1303; ▸ fish for which regulations specify no minimum size limits and the open season is "any time." A person shall not possess fish on state waters or shores in excess of the number which may be legally taken by one person in one day. Carcasses and parts of fish which may be sold may be transported at any time, in any number and in any manner. Carcasses and parts of fish which may not be sold may be transported except no person shall transport in one day more than a two-day catch limit of fish, unless authorized by permit or the fish is frozen or otherwise processed and packaged for storage and is transported from a place of processing or storage, carcasses or parts shall not be shipped by parcel post, and if shipped by carrier, shall be labeled [details provided] (11-1319).

Title 15 and regulations do not apply to: ▸ taking fish by angling as permitted in Title 13; ▸ taking fish or the use of nets in a trout or black bass hatchery, or in a farm fish pond or in a fishing preserve; ▸ the sale or taking for sale of bait fish named in section 11-1315. Title 15 and regulations do not restrict the use of landing nets in completing the catch of fish taken by hook and line, or limit the use of nets and traps for taking bait fish, or of regulations authorizing eel weirs and eel pots. The Department may regulate the use of nets and other devices commonly used to take fish. No person shall use a net or device to take fish without a license. The Department may regulate the manner of taking fish with nets and other devices including but not limited to open seasons, size and catch limits and manner of possession and transportation. A person operating a boat used in taking fish shall permit conservation officers or other Department employees to board it for inspection of its contents and to inspect nets or take fish eggs (11-1501, -1503, -1505 and -1519).

Commercial and Private Enterprise Provisions

The Department may issue to an owner or lessee of wholly enclosed lands or an entire island a shooting preserve license permitting the purchase, possession, rearing and transport, releasing and taking by shooting domestic game birds legally possessed or acquired. No birds may be held for propagation after March 31 without a domestic game bird breeder's license (11-1903). ★The Department may issue a revocable certificate to a domestic game breeder or a person engaged in trout propagation outside the state which allows carcasses and hatchery trout to be possessed, imported and sold for food if tagged as required (11-1715).★

Foreign game means pheasants of all species, Scotch grouse, Norwegian ptarmigan, Norwegian white grouse, European black game, European black plover, European gray-legged partridge, European red-legged partridge, Egyptian quail, tinamou and species or subspecies of birds not native to this state, and European red deer, fallow deer and roebuck. The carcasses or parts of foreign game imported into the US may be bought and sold when tagged as required, subject to dealers' license provisions (11-1717). Except as provided no person shall sell or offer for sale in this state any domestic or foreign game without a dealers' license. The Department may fix terms and conditions and revoke it at its pleasure. A dealer's license is not required for sale: ▸ by a domestic game bird breeder, domestic game animal breeder or shooting preserve licensee, of domestic game killed on the premises; ▸ by the holder of a certificate under section 11-1715, of domestic game raised outside the state on premises operated by the holder; ▸ of live domestic game for scientific, exhibition, breeding or stocking purposes; ▸ of carcasses or parts of domestic or foreign game, by a hotel or restaurant, a retailer in meat, or a club; ▸ of carcasses or parts of processed imported game packed in sealed containers (11-1719).

The provisions of this section apply to carcasses and parts of: ▸ domestic game killed on the premises of a domestic game bird breeder, domestic game animal breeder or shooting preserve; ▸ domestic game raised outside the state on the premises of a holder of a certificate under section 11-1715; ▸ foreign game imported from outside the US; ▸ wild deer (other than white-tailed deer), moose, elk, caribou and antelope imported pursuant to section 11-1711; ▸ bear possessed under license pursuant to section 11-0515 under a similar out of state license and killed, bought and sold for food under permit pursuant to section 11-1713; ▸ trout, black bass, lake trout, landlocked salmon, muskellunge, pike, pickerel and walleye taken from fishing preserve waters. All shall be tagged until finally prepared for consumption. Trout, black bass, lake trout, landlocked salmon, muskellunge, pike, pickerel and walleye taken from fishing preserve waters shall be tagged as prescribed. Domestic game killed in this state shall be tagged as required. Foreign game, domestic and wild game from outside the state shall be tagged before or immediately upon receipt within this state by the consignee. No person shall counterfeit any seal or tag (11-1721). Trout raised in a private hatchery under permit or outside the state under certificate, and carcasses or parts of sealed, labeled processed imported foreign and domestic game may be imported, transported, exported, bought and sold [as described] (11-1727).

★★Except as permitted, no person shall sell live wild birds, unless they were born and raised in captivity. Except as provided, no person shall possess for sale or sell the plumage, skin or body of any wild or unlisted domestic bird [definitions provided for wild bird and other terms]. The possession in a commercial establishment of wild or unlisted domestic bird plumage is presumptive evidence of illegal possession for sale. This section does not apply to: ▸ sale or possession for sale of live game for stocking or field trials; ▸ the unplucked carcasses for sale as food; ▸ fishing flies; ▸ collection, possession or sale of plumage for scientific, exhibition, or educational purposes. This section does not prohibit sale or possession for sale of legally imported plumage, skin or body of birds of the following species for millinery purposes only, or for fish fly purposes licensed under section 11-1731: Lady

Amherst pheasant, golden pheasant, silver pheasant, Reeves pheasant, Swinhoe pheasant, brown-eared pheasant, blue-eared pheasant, and for licensed fishing fly purposes only gray jungle fowl and mandarin duck. Every person who acquires or disposes of plumage of wild or unlisted domestic birds, shall keep written records [details provided]. The Department is authorized to accept, and to deliver or distribute to educational institutions, plumage of wild or unlisted domestic birds but shall not be liable for its destruction or distribution (11-1728 and -1729). No person shall import, export, buy, or acquire, or possess for sale or sell any plumage of wild or unlisted domestic birds for fishing flies without a license and keeping records. This section does not apply to fishing flies. The Department may issue a license for fly tying only, authorizing the holder to import, export, buy or otherwise acquire and possess for sale and sell plumage of wild and unlisted domestic birds as defined in section 11-1729. No person shall engage in the business of preparing, stuffing or mounting skins of fish or wildlife without a license and register [details provided]. Authorized persons shall have access to the register (11-1731 and -1733). ★★

The Department may issue to an owner or lessee of enclosed lands or an island, a domestic game bird breeder's license to possess and propagate such species of domestic game birds as he has facilities for propagating. [Classes of licenses and fees are set forth.] The Department may revoke for two years the license of any licensee convicted of a violation of this section [details of notice and hearing for revocation provided]. On the licensed premises the licensee may kill domestic game birds except by shooting. Nothing prohibits shooting domestic game birds liberated on the licensed premises during the open season or pursuant to a license under section 11-1903. ★Each such domestic duck, goose, brant and swan before attaining the age of four weeks shall have the hind toe of the right foot removed, and may not be possessed or sold without such mark. ★ [Details of recapture upon escape provided.] The licensee shall keep records, make reports [details provided], and on the licensed premises may take any unprotected wild bird or predatory wildlife disturbing domestic game, except that no trap of the leg-gripping type as specified shall be used, nor shall a trap be set to suspend wildlife when caught. Carcasses shall be buried or cremated immediately, except carcasses of other than protected birds, if taken during their open seasons, may be possessed, transported, bought and sold to the extent permitted. The carcass of a domestic game bird shall be tagged and remain until the bird is prepared for consumption. When transporting untagged carcasses for processing, the bearer must have a statement, with tags for each, signed by the licensee stating the number of carcasses and the processor. The licensee shall record the number of tags used [details provided]. Carcasses of domestic game birds, tagged as provided, may be possessed, bought, sold, offered for sale and transported, as permitted by sections 11-1719 and 11-1723 (11-1901).

The Department may issue to an owner or lessee of enclosed lands or an island a shooting preserve license to purchase, possess, rear and transport, release and shoot, domestic game birds legally possessed. No birds may be held for propagation after March 31 without a breeder's license. [Details for leased lands, application forms, classes of license and fees provided.] The Department may revoke for two years the license of any licensee convicted of a violation. [Details of notice and hearing on revocation provided.] The minimum acreage for a shooting preserve is 100 contiguous acres, boundaries to be posted. [Details of initial liberation of pheasants provided.] Domestic game birds must be at least 14 weeks of age before liberation; the licensee must advise the Department of the numbers of each species, and receive a shooting authorization stating numbers of each species that may be taken, not to be less than 80% of the number liberated [details of authorization, contracts and seasons provided]. A licensee shall keep records and make reports [details provided]. The licensee may take any unprotected wild birds or predatory wildlife disturbing domestic game, except with leg-gripping traps, with teeth or a greater spread than six inches, nor shall a trap be set to suspend wildlife [disposal of carcasses provided]. Tags must be affixed to the carcass of a domestic game bird which may be possessed and transported and may be bought, sold and offered for sale as permitted by sections 11-1719 and 11-1723 (11-1903).

The Department may issue to an owner or lessee of enclosed lands or an island a domestic game animal breeder's license to possess and propagate such animals provided they are confined according to regulations [classes of licenses and fees provided]. Licenses may be revoked for two years for violations. The licensee may kill domestic game animals, and with the consent of the licensee, a person may take domestic game by shooting. Licensees shall keep records and make reports (11-1905). [Tagging requirements are similar to above.] ★★Beaver, bobcat, coyote, raccoon, sable or marten, skunk, otter, fisher, nutria and muskrat may be propagated, or held in captivity with a license. Animals propagated or held in captivity pursuant to such license may be disposed of alive for propagation, exhibition, scientific, or educational purposes or killed and pelted. Carcasses and pelts of may be possessed, transported, bought or sold (11-1907). ★★

New York

The Department: ▸ may issue a hatchery permit to propagate, raise and sell trout; ▸ shall establish regulations on the identification of trout raised for sale, sold or transported under such a permit; ▸ may issue a hatchery permit to propagate, raise and sell black bass for propagation or stocking; ▸ shall establish regulations on the transportation of black bass (11-1909).

"Farm fish pond" means water, impounded by a dam, of under 10 acres, lying within privately owned or leased lands. Licenses, with terms, may be issued to manage such for fish production and may include permission to control undesirable fish, aquatic vegetation and insect life interfering with production of fish, and permission to release, stock and propagate fish. The Department may specify methods of control and the manner of taking and type, size and mesh of gear to be used and may for cause, revoke or suspend any license. No person shall release any species into a pond without permission. A licensee, immediate family, and employee may take fish as permitted by the Department. Holders of [various listed fishing and hunting licenses] may take fish from the licensed pond in compliance with open seasons, minimum size and daily and seasonal possession limits. Fish protected by law, except trout, black bass, muskellunge and landlocked salmon, legally taken from a licensed pond, may be possessed, transported, bought and sold during open seasons. Trout, black bass, muskellunge and landlocked salmon, legally taken from a farm fish pond, may be possessed and transported during open seasons and until March 1. Unless taken by an owner or family, are frozen or processed and packaged for storage and being transported for storage or consumption, no person shall transport in one day more than which may be legally taken from that farm fish pond. Protected fish shall not be removed from the premises unless labeled. Unprotected fish may be possessed, transported, bought and sold, except that taking and sale of bait fish shall be permitted only under license (11-1911).

"Fishing preserve waters" means any artificial or manmade water lying wholly within privately owned lands, operated as fishing facilities. Licenses may permit management of such waters and to possess, propagate and rear, and to take or permit others to take, legally propagated or acquired fish. [Details of licenses and restrictions provided.] A licensee or immediate family may take fish as permitted by the license. Any licensee may sell fish taken and may grant permission to take fish and charge a fee, or, if a club, impose dues permitting angling. Persons to whom permission is granted may fish without licenses. The licensee may prescribe restrictions or limitations with respect to the size of fish, limits of catch, open season and manner of taking fish from the licensed waters. Except as noted in the license, Title 13 or 15 shall not apply to fishing in licensed fishing preserve waters. All trout, black bass, lake trout, landlocked salmon, muskellunge, pike, pickerel and walleye taken from those waters shall be tagged immediately. Fish taken and tagged may be possessed, bought, sold and offered for sale, and transported without restriction. Fish raised or possessed under license may be sold for scientific, exhibition, propagation or stocking. Fishing preserve licensees shall keep records as required and make annual reports [details provided]. Farm fish ponds may be licensed as fishing preserves, if not stocked by the Department during five years preceding the application. The Department may authorize the licensee to use fish toxins, and make rules and regulations with respect to management and operation of fishing preserves (11-1913).

Import, Export and Release Provisions

No one shall liberate: ▸ fish or fish eggs without a permit; ▸ European hare, European or San Juan rabbit, Texas or jack rabbit, gray fox, red fox, or nutria, whether taken within or without the state and which may be imported only by permit for scientific, exhibition or breeding purposes; ▸ any wildlife except under permit with terms fixed by the Department; ▸ zebra mussels into waters of the state intentionally, or buying, selling, or offering such except under permit. Zebra mussels may be destroyed at any time (11-0507).

No person shall import, export, own, possess, acquire or dispose of live piranha fish, grass carp or hybrid grass carp within the state without a license or permit for scientific, biological or exhibition purposes. Fish, except those specified above, may be imported and transported for propagation purposes. (11-1703).

★Deer, except white-tail deer, may be imported, possessed, transported bought and sold alive without license or permit. Wild white-tail deer shall not be imported.★ Skunk, bobcat, mink, muskrat, fisher, beaver, otter, marten or sable may be imported alive without license or permit, and may be bought and sold, possessed, and transported alive during open seasons but during closed seasons, only with a Department permit or license (11-1705).

★The Department may establish regulations governing the importation or transportation within the state of any live fish or viable eggs of any species of the family Salmonidae (trout, salmon, whitefish, and grayling) (11-

1709). ★ The flesh of wild moose, elk, caribou and antelope, and of wild deer of all species, except white-tail deer, may be possessed, transported, bought and sold with a permit and tagging, except as provided in 11-1707 (11-1711).

Interstate Reciprocal Agreements

If Vermont, New Jersey, Pennsylvania, Connecticut, or Rhode Island, shall enact a similar law for the arrest and punishment for violations of the conservation law or fish laws of such state or of the provisions listed in section 71-0501 or under Titles 5 through 15 inclusive and Title 33 of this article, committed or attempted by a person fishing in any waters lying between such state and New York, any authorized person, shall have power and authority to make arrests on waters or shores between such state and New York, and to take the arrested person for trial and prosecution to the state in which the violation was committed (71-0913). (See also Licenses and Permits under this section.)

ANIMAL DAMAGE CONTROL

Whenever authorities determine that a disease endangers the health and welfare of fish, wildlife, livestock or human populations, the Department may regulate the taking, transportation, sale or possession of native fish or feral animals to prevent the introduction or spread of such disease and may undertake such control measures to eliminate, reduce or confine the disease (11-0325). The Department may take or issue a permit to take wildlife that becomes a nuisance, destructive of public or private property or a threat to public health or welfare. Landowners or their agents may take beaver under specified permit. Nothing requires issuance of such permits when the nuisance, destruction or threat to public health and welfare will not be effectively abated (11-0521). ★Destructive or menacing wildlife may be taken without a permit as follows: ▸ landowners or those cultivating lands may take unprotected wildlife other than birds, starlings, common crows, subject to section 11-0513, pigeons, when the wildlife is injuring property or becomes a nuisance; ▸ upon finding a bear menacing humans, or killing or worrying livestock, or destroying an apiary, the landowner or agent may kill or take the bear and deliver the carcass to the nearest conservation officer; ▸ red-winged blackbirds, common grackles and cowbirds destroying any crop may be killed from June - October by the owner; ▸ varying hares, cottontail rabbits and European hares injuring property on occupied farms may be taken except with ferrets, fitch-ferrets or fitch; ▸ skunks injuring property or which have become a nuisance may be taken; ▸ raccoons, coyotes or fox injuring property on occupied farms may be taken by trapping or by firearm by the owners or agents; ▸ black, grey and fox squirrels, opossums or weasels injuring property on farms may be taken by the owners or agents; ▸ varying hares, cottontail rabbits, skunks, black, grey and fox squirrels, raccoons, opossums, or weasels taken under this section in the closed season or in a manner not permitted by 11-0901 shall be buried or cremated immediately. No person shall possess or traffic in such skunks, raccoons or their pelts or in such varying hares or cottontail rabbits or their flesh (11-0523). ★ Whenever the disease rabies occurs and infections of wild foxes or other wildlife is certified such that health and welfare of domestic livestock or humans are in danger, the Department can take control measures to reduce or confine the disease (11-0525). It is unlawful for any government agency or subdivision to pay bounties for taking wildlife, except when health or local authorities determine that certain classes or types of animals constitute a health hazard as carriers or potential carriers of disease (11-0531).

★★Persons over age 21 possessing a hunting license may, and conservation officers and peace officers shall, humanely destroy cats found hunting or killing any protected wild bird or with a dead bird of any protected species in its possession.★★ Every environmental conservation officer, forest ranger, state policeman, and a person, may kill any dog or coyote pursuing or killing deer within the Adirondack or Catskill parks and any game or wildlife on a state-owned game farm or wildlife refuge or management area, except dogs legally used to hunt small game or for dog training (11-0529).

ENFORCEMENT OF WILDLIFE LAWS

Enforcement Powers

Unlawfully taken fish, wildlife, shellfish, crustacea or parts, protected insect, or bird plumage seized by or surrendered to enforcement officers, shall be disposed of by the enforcement officer, subject to law and regulations (11-0519). Any officer or agent of the Commissioner may execute warrants to search for and seize goods, merchandise or wildlife sold or offered in violation of 11-0536 (restricted animals) or any property or item used for such violation. Upon conviction or entry of judgement restraining such sale, the seized goods shall be forfeited and offered for science or education, or destroyed (11-0536). A person who counsels or aids in a violation of the Fish and Wildlife Law, regulation or order, or knowingly shares in proceeds by receiving illegally taken fish, game, wildlife, shellfish, crustacea or protected insects is guilty of the violation which the person aided or of sharing the proceeds of illegally taken wildlife (71-0903). ★Provisions of the Fish and Wildlife Law inconsistent with the provisions of any other law shall be effective for the Fish and Wildlife Law only (71-0905).★

All authorized officers shall enforce all laws relating to fish, wildlife, shellfish, crustacea, protected insects and game. Such officers may include conservation officers, regional and assistant regional conservation officers, special game protectors, inspectors of the office of parks and recreation, bay constables, and forest rangers. All police and peace officers, when acting pursuant to their special duties, and all Commissioner designated Department officers and employees, shall enforce the provisions of Article 11 of the Fish and Wildlife Law, and Article 71, except that the Department's enforcement officers are not obligated to prohibit trespass upon private lands, other than licensed game and shooting preserves, unless the trespass consists of hunting, fishing or trapping or disturbing wildlife. Peace officers have the same powers as conservation officers and state police under the Fish and Wildlife Law, except the power to search without warrant. Officers named above shall have power to: ▸ execute all warrants and search warrants issued under the Fish and Wildlife Law and to serve applicable subpoenas; ▸ search without warrant any boat or vehicle, any container and the contents of any building other than a dwelling with cause to believe that any provision of any law for the protection of fish, shellfish, crustacea, wildlife, game or protected insects has been or is being violated and use force as necessary for the search; ▸ search any dwelling and its contents, with a search warrant; ▸ arrest without warrant a person committing a misdemeanor [under various provisions] and to take such person immediately before a magistrate; ▸ seize as evidence without warrant any fish, shellfish, crustacea, wildlife, game, or parts, protected insects or plumage as defined in section 11-1729, with cause to believe it is possessed or transported in violation of law, or with circumstances causing presumptive evidence of illegal taking or bearing evidence of illegal taking; ▸ to seize as evidence without warrant any net, trap or device constituting a nuisance; any net, trap or device other than a boat, a vehicle, or aircraft or a firearm with cause to believe that its possession or use violates the Fish and Wildlife Law or regulation; any firearm, with cause to believe it has been used to take or attempt to take wild deer illegally; and any rakes, tongs, dredges, or device other than a boat or vehicle used, or possessed for illegal taking of shellfish. "Device" includes a bird, dog, or other animal used in taking fish or wildlife, any jack light, spot light or other artificial light, any hunting apparatus and any fishing or netting tackle. This paragraph does not limit seizure pursuant to warrant. Any boat or vehicle may be seized, with probable cause, if a person possesses at the time of use, commercial shellfish harvesting gear. No person shall refuse to comply with any lawful order of any conservation officer or other authorized person (71-0907).

If the defendant is held liable, found guilty or effects a civil settlement for a violation involving the taking deer with the aid of an artificial light all things seized in connection with the violation shall be confiscated by and forfeited to the state. Unless a claim of ownership is made within 30 days and is established by court order, such things shall be disposed of by the Department. If the defendant is held liable or found guilty in any prosecution involving illegal taking, possession, or transportation of any fish, shellfish, crustacea, wildlife, game or protected insects, ownership shall be vested in the state, notwithstanding any claim of the defendant or of a person, unless such claim shall be established or this subdivision shall be stayed by a court. If any such claim is asserted during such prosecution, the court may make such order, or may stay judgment as deemed proper to consider a stay. If the defendant is held liable or found guilty in any prosecution for a violation involving the use of a net or other device, other than a boat, vehicle, aircraft or firearm which is prohibited under any circumstances, or is prohibited except in accordance with a permit; for possession of nets where possession is prohibited; or if the defendant shall effect a civil settlement in favor of the state, the defendant's interest shall be forfeited to the state. Unless a claim of ownership is made by some other person within 30 days, and established by a court or the Department, such device shall be disposed of as the Department directs. If the defendant is held liable or found guilty of illegally taking shellfish or if the defendant shall effect a civil compromise in favor of the state, the defendant's interest in any and all rakes, tongs, dredges or devices other than a boat or vehicle, used for the violation shall be forfeited. Unless a claim of ownership shall be made by some other person within 30 days, and established by a court or the Department, disposal shall be as the Department directs. In addition to any other penalties imposed, illegal taking of shellfish shall be punishable by forfeiture of any boat or vehicle used in the violation (71-0909). (Other claim details are given.) When it appears probable that fish, wildlife or game, shellfish, crustacea, protected insect, or parts illegally taken or possessed, or a net possessed are concealed, any local criminal court having jurisdiction shall issue a search warrant for the discovery thereof (71-0911).

The following are nuisances which may be abated as provided: ▸ any trap, snare or net, set or used without permit for taking a wild bird; ▸ any trap set or used in violation of 11-1101; ▸ any net, bait-line, set line, eel weir or pot, tip-up, baitfish trap, or other device for taking fish or crustacea; ▸ any device for taking insects, set or used in violation of any law or regulation. Where the violation consists only in the fact that the device was set or used without a license, such license is issuable upon application and payment of the applicable fee. Nuisances may be abated by a person or conservation officer, as provided. Upon abatement, the conservation officer shall take into custody the net or device used where the person guilty is not present or cannot be identified. If the net or device is forfeited as provided in 71-0909, or remains unclaimed for thirty days, it shall be disposed of by the Department. Where the person is arrested or served with a summons, the conservation officer may seize the net or other device as evidence. Upon abatement of any nuisance, any fish, crustacea, wildlife or protected insect trapped, confined, hooked or caught shall be released, permitted to escape, or returned to the water or other habitat; or destroyed; or seized as evidence; or taken for future disposition pursuant to 11-0519, as may be appropriate to the circumstances, the animal involved and its condition. Action taken by an enforcement officer as provided in this section and 11-0519 shall not subject the officer or the state to liability, even if it is determined that the trap, net or other device was not in violation, if the officer had reasonable grounds to believe that it constituted a nuisance (71-0915).

Criminal Penalties

Possession of any fish, shell-fish, crustacea or game, protected insects, or parts thereof, when there is no open season for the species, shall be presumptive evidence of an unlawful taking and that it was taken by the possessor. A person who violates the Fish and Wildlife Law or any lawful order, rule or regulation, or terms of any permit, and a person, including a public officer, failing to perform any duty imposed, is guilty of a misdemeanor or violation, punishable as provided. In addition, the person is liable to civil penalties and may be liable to revocation of licenses to hunt, fish or trap, denial of hunting, fishing or trapping privileges, forfeiture and revocation of other licenses, and forfeiture and confiscation of property (71-0917 and -0919).

Any violation of fish and wildlife laws, unless made a misdemeanor by 71-0921 or other provision is a violation, punishable, except as otherwise provided, by jail up to 15 days, or a fine $250, or both. A violation of provisions relating to: ▸ refusal to exhibit a license on demand of any environmental conservation officer or other person, if committed with a special antlerless deer license and consisted of failure to have license in possession (license forfeiture and fine up to $25); ▸ failure to carry or exhibit a license (forfeiture of the applicable license, and of hunting or big game license tag, and fine up to $25); ▸ allowing dogs to run at large (jail up to 10 days, or a fine of not less than $200, or both); ▸ interference with lawful taking of wildlife (jail for up to 10 days, or a fine up to $250, or both); ▸ trapping within 100 feet of a building (jail up to 10 days, or a fine up to $100, or both) (71-0923).

Civil Penalties

The penalties for violation of provisions of the Fish and Wildlife Law, any order, rule or regulation, relating to: ▸ fish, birds or animals or parts, other than shellfish or crustacea, and unless otherwise provided - $60, and an additional $25 for each fish, bird or animal or part, an additional $5 for each bushel of shellfish or each crustacean or part, and an additional $50 for each lobster; ▸ deer, elk (except captive bred and raised North American elk), moose, caribou, antelope, wild turkey, lynx, beaver, or a part thereof - $100, and an additional $200 for each animal or part; ▸ illegal taking of a deer out of season, or taking deer with an artificial light, or illegal taking of a wild deer - $100, an additional $400 for the first deer and an additional $500 for each succeeding deer taken; ▸ fishing, polluting a stream with sewage, or interfering with a state fish hatchery - $500, and an additional $10 for each fish taken, killed or possessed; ▸ polluting a stream with poisons - $500-$1,000 for each offense and an additional $10 for each fish killed; ▸ unlawful taking of wildlife on posted lands or trespass - $25-$100, in addition to actual damages, and costs of suit; ▸ failure by a public officer to perform any duty imposed by the Fish and Wildlife Law or by rule or regulation - $100; ▸ damage of private property or animals - $100, one-half payable to the owner or occupant of the damaged property, in addition to actual damages recoverable by the person sustaining the damage; ▸ illegal taking or possessing of muskrats taken from a registered muskrat marsh, when the violation is committed by the registrant or other person designated to trap - $100-$500; ▸ bird plumage for fish-fly tying - $500; ▸ endangered, threatened, or other protected species - up to $1,000, and an additional penalty of up to $250 for each fish, shellfish, crustacea, wildlife or part; ▸ illegal taking of a moose - $2,000 (71-0925).

Illegal Taking of Wildlife

The following acts are misdemeanors, punishable as provided: ▸ illegal taking of big game out of season, or doe deer or wild deer without antlers or with antlers less than three inches in length, or taking of big game by artificial light, or deer by means not permitted (jail up to one year or a fine up to $2,000, or both); ▸ illegal taking of a bear less than one year old or taking a bear by means not permitted (jail up to one year or fine up to $2,000, or both); ▸ illegal possession, use or discharge of a firearm (jail up to three months or fine up to $200, or both); ▸ making a false statement in applying for a license, stamp, permit, certificate or duplicate big game license tag (jail up to three months, or fine up to $200, or both, or revocation of license, stamp, permit or certificate); ▸ illegal taking of a moose (jail up to one year or fine up to $2,000, or both); ▸ unlawful taking of bald or golden eagles (first violation, class B misdemeanor, fine up to $5,000, jail up to 90 days or both; a second or subsequent violation, class A misdemeanor, fine up to $10,000, or jail up to one year, or both; each prohibited act is a separate violation; one-half of the fine, up to $2,500, shall be paid to the person giving information leading to conviction) (71-0921).

Notwithstanding any other provision, when a violation involves the sale, trade or barter of fish, shellfish, crustaceans, wildlife, or parts, the following additional penalties shall be imposed: ▸ where the value is $250 or less (a fine of $500 and/or up to 15 days in jail); ▸ where the value is $250 - $1,500 (misdemeanor, fine of $5,000, and/or up to 1 year jail); and ▸ where the value exceeds $1,500 (a class E felony). For this section the value of fish, shellfish, crustaceans and wildlife is the fair market value or actual price paid for such resource, whichever is greater (71-0924).

License Revocations, Suspensions

The Department may revoke any or all licenses to hunt, trap or fish, and may also deny the privilege to obtain licenses or stamps for up to five years to a person who is convicted of: ▸ taking deer with an artificial light; ▸ taking deer out of season, illegal taking of a doe deer, moose, or antlerless deer or one having antlers less than 3 inches; ▸ any violation of the Fish and Wildlife Law, or signs an acknowledgement of any violation to effect a settlement, and during the five years preceding has been so convicted or has so signed (11-0719).

★The Department may suspend any license for failure to appear for a violation of a Fish and Wildlife Law. Suspension takes place no less than 30 days from notice being sent. The Department may revoke the hunting, big game, junior archery or trapping license or the hunting and big game hunting portions of the combination license, and deny the privilege of obtaining such licenses when a person while hunting or trapping: ▸ causes death or injury to another by discharging a firearm or longbow; ▸ negligently discharges a firearm or longbow as to endanger the life or safety of another; ▸ negligently and wantonly discharges a firearm or longbow as to destroy or damage property. Revocation or privilege denial shall be after hearing and upon notice. Should a person cause death or injury by firearm or longbow, the Commissioner may suspend hunting rights for up to 60 days pending a hearing, and after a hearing may revoke the license for up to 10 years. In other cases of revocation, licenses may be revoked for up to five years, and in all cases notice shall be sent. The Department may also require a certification in responsible hunting or bowhunting practices (11-0719).★

Intoxication Testing of Hunters

"Intoxicated condition" means the presence of .10 of one per centum or more of alcohol in a person's blood by chemical analyses. An "impaired condition" means a state of impairment of capacity to think or act correctly, or of a loss, even in part of a person's physical or mental faculties. No person shall in hunt while in an intoxicated condition, or if the ability to in hunt without risk of injury or death is impaired by consumption of alcohol or a drug (11-1201 and -1203).

★★Police officers have power to enforce these provisions and take actions, make arrests, and conduct tests. A person hunting is deemed to have given consent to a chemical test of breath, blood, urine, or saliva to determine the alcoholic or drug content of the person's blood, provided the test is at the direction of an authorized officer having reasonable grounds to believe there is a violation, and within two hours after arrest, or within two hours after a breath test indicates alcohol. If such person refuses a chemical test after arrest or a breath test indicates the presence of alcohol, the test is not given, and such refusal shall be reported to the Department within 72 hours. All licenses, stamps, and permits shall be revoked after a hearing upon notice to such person, unless waived. A license, stamp, or permit may be temporarily suspended without notice pending the determination upon any such hearing. No license, stamp, or permit shall be revoked because of a refusal if the person had not been warned that a refusal may result in revocation (11-1205). [Details of chemical analysis techniques provided, and details of evidence of test admitted in court provided in 11-1207.] Whoever hunts while ability is impaired by alcohol is guilty of a violation. Hunting while intoxicated or impaired by a drug is a misdemeanor, punishable by jail up to 1 year, fine up to $500, or both. Notwithstanding any provision, the Department may revoke, for up to two years, any or all licenses, stamps, or permits of a person who hunts while intoxicated. Revocation shall become effective only after a hearing. No person shall hunt or trap while the privilege has been denied [details of notice of revocation and surrender of licenses provided]. Violation of these provisions constitutes grounds for forfeiture (11-1209). ★★

HABITAT PROTECTION

Polluting streams with materials injurious to fish life, protected wildlife or waterfowl inhabiting those waters, or injurious to propagation of those animals, including state fish hatcheries, is prohibited [details provided as to types of substances and sewage from private lands]. Nothing prevents local governments from prohibiting disposal of earth, refuse or other solids in streams, ponds or lakes in their jurisdiction (11-0503).

No person shall take fish by use of explosives or by shutting or drawing off water. Explosives shall not be used or possessed in or on state waters except for mining or mechanical purposes. Possession of explosives in such places is presumptive evidence of violation. Bass, walleye, trout, lake trout and salmon shall not be disturbed on spawning beds in the closed season, nor shall their spawn or milt be taken from spawning beds. ★Any noise or disturbance of waters or banks with intent to drive fish into a net (thumping) is prohibited unless expressly permitted.★ No person owning, leasing, operating or maintaining a dam holding back water who knows or has reason to know is inhabited by fish shall draw off water so as to cause the loss of a substantial number of fish, without written permission of the Department. This does not apply: ▸ to federal, state or local governments or any agency or subdivision; ▸ to any dam or impoundment used in the production of electric power; ▸ in the event of an emergency, such as fire, flood, storm, drought where drawing off water is required for public safety or public health; ▸ to any artificial or man-made water lying wholly within the boundaries of privately owned or leased lands and operated as a farm pond, licensed farm fish pond, licensed fishing preserve water or licensed private trout or bass hatchery. ★No person taking or assisting in taking fish shall discard fish carcass or parts into the waters or upon public or private lands contiguous to and within 100 feet of the waters unless the lands are owned by the person or unless the person enters or remains with the permission of the owner. This section shall not be deemed to prohibit: ▸ the return to the water of live fish; ▸ use of fish or parts as bait; ▸ discarding of fish carcasses or parts not within 100 feet of any shore; ▸ disposal of fish carcasses or parts into suitable garbage or refuse collection systems or by burial; ▸ incidental cleaning of fish for consumption except that no wastes may be disposed of in waters or lands contiguous to and within 100 feet of any public boat launching sites or public docking facilities (11-1321). ★

Any enclosed land or water owned by the state may be set aside as a refuge for protection of fish, wildlife, trees and plants. The consent of the riparian owners shall be obtained before lands under water and the waters shall be set aside. Lands and waters set aside as a game refuge shall remain so until the Department permits taking of fish and wildlife. The Department shall adopt regulations in relation to fish and wildlife on lands of the national wildlife refuge system to conform to the National Wildlife Refuge System Administration Act, and regulations of the Secretary of the Interior. Consent of the state is given to the US to obtain by purchase, gift, devise or lease areas of land or water, in New York, for migratory bird reservations in accordance with the Migratory Bird Conservation Act, reserving to New York full jurisdiction and authority over such areas not incompatible with the administration, maintenance, protection and control by the US (11-2105 through -2107).

★The owner or person having exclusive rights to hunt and fish on private land or water may establish a private park for propagation and protection of fish and wildlife by publishing [details provided] notice stating that it will be used as a private park. Part of a private lake or pond may be a private park, if all riparian owners consent.
An owner or person having exclusive rights to hunt or fish upon enclosed lands or lands used in whole or in part for farming purposes, or lands where foxes are kept in captivity for breeding purposes, or a person having exclusive rights to take fish in private waters, or a game bird breeder's licensee or game animal breeder's licensee may protect such lands or waters, or the licensed premises, by posting or personally serving notices as provided. The limitation against establishment of a private park and the prohibition against posting of private lands and waters stocked by

the state shall not apply to: premises licensed under a game bird breeder's, game animal breeder's, shooting preserve or fishing preserve license, or premises stocked by the state while subject to a cooperative agreement as provided (11-2109).★ Areas protected by the Department and protected private parks and private lands shall be posted [extensive details provided]. All notices on private parks or private lands or on state game refuges shall bear a conspicuous statement [details provided]. A notice in the case of a state game refuge shall also bear a warning against taking or injuring trees or plants [details provided for posting of shooting preserves, fishing preserves and fishways or dams]. Personal service of a notice in writing with a description of the premises and a warning shall be as if the premises described were posted (11-2111).

★No person shall take fish from a stream within 50 rods of a fishway or dam, prohibited in a notice. When other lands or waters are posted, and when written notice is served as provided, no person shall: ► in a state game refuge, take or injure any tree or plant; ► in lands or waters protected by the Department, take or disturb fish or wildlife, or enter the premises, except with written permission or with an order of the Department; ► in a licensed game breeding or shooting preserve, take or disturb wildlife except waterfowl within 25 yards of any shore line without licensee written consent; ► in the case of private parks, a licensed game breeding or shooting preserve, take or disturb fish, wildlife or domestic game or trespass with an implement by which fish or wildlife may be disturbed, taken or killed, without consent of the owner of the preserve or the hunting or fishing rights; ► in other private lands, hunt, trap, fish, or trespass without consent of the owner of the lands or of the hunting or fishing rights; ► in lands where foxes are kept in captivity, approach within 25 yards of their enclosure without consent. When a restricted area is established and notices are erected, no person shall do any act on the restricted area prohibited by the notices or without compliance with directions on the notice. No person shall injure, deface or remove a notice erected and maintained (11-2113).★

See Agency Advisory Boards under STATE FISH AND WILDLIFE AGENCIES for Fish and Wildlife Management Regions Cooperative Program.

NATIVE AMERICAN WILDLIFE PROVISIONS

Enrolled members of an Indian tribe with a reservation in the state may hunt, trap or fish on the reservation without licenses subject to tribal rules, regulations and laws. Before fish and wildlife taken by Indians is transported or possessed off the reservation it shall be tagged as required by the tribal government. Nothing herein limits or impairs existing tribal government powers to regulate and license hunting, fishing and trapping (11-0707). Members of the Shinnecock or Poospatuck tribe or members of the Six Nations, residing in the state, can receive hunting, fishing, trapping or big game licenses, muzzle-loading or bow-hunting stamps free of charge (11-0715).

See also HUNTING, FISHING, TRAPPING PROVISIONS.

NORTH CAROLINA

Sources: General Statutes of North Carolina Annotated, 1990, Chapter 113; 1992 Cumulative Supplement.

STATE WILDLIFE POLICY

The marine, estuarine and wildlife resources of the state belong to the people of the state as a whole. The Department and the Wildlife Resources Commission are charged with stewardship of these resources (113-131).

★The enjoyment of the wildlife resources belongs to all people of the State. The **Wildlife Resources Commission** (Commission) is charged with administering the governing statutes in a manner to serve equitably the various competing interests regarding wildlife resources, considering the interests of those whose livelihood depends upon full and wise use of renewable resources and recreational interests. Thus, except as otherwise provided, all special, local, and private acts and ordinances enacted prior to ratification of this section regulating the conservation of wildlife resources are repealed. This section does not repeal local acts which restrict hunting primarily for protecting highway travelers, landowners, or other persons who may be endangered or affected by hunters' weapons or whose property may be damaged. This section does not repeal statutes or local acts establishing bird sanctuaries, except that local authorities operating same may not regulate the taking of game or otherwise abrogate laws and regulations pertaining to conservation of wildlife resources. Because of strong community interest expressed in their retention, the local acts listed herein are retained to the extent they apply to the county for which listed [a long list of specific laws is appended] (113-133.1).★

The General Assembly finds that recreation and aesthetic needs of the people, the interests of science, the quality of the environment, and the best interests of the state require that endangered and threatened species of wild animals and species of special concern be protected and conserved, and their numbers should be enhanced and that conservation techniques be developed for them; however, nothing in this article shall be construed to limit the rights of a landholder in the management of lands for agriculture, forestry, development or any other lawful purpose without the landholder's consent (113-332). (See RELEVANT WILDLIFE DEFINITIONS, Agency Advisory Boards under STATE FISH AND WILDLIFE AGENCIES, and PROTECTED SPECIES OF WILDLIFE).

RELEVANT WILDLIFE DEFINITIONS: See Definitions section of Appendices.

STATE FISH AND WILDLIFE AGENCIES

Agency Structure

There is a **Department of Environment, Health, and Natural Resources** (Department), and a **Secretary** (113-1). The Department shall investigate state natural resources and take measures to promote their conservation and development (provisions for forest management and recreational areas). The Department has the duty of enforcing laws relating to conservation of marine and estuarine resources, may acquire lands, and publicize knowledge of the state's resources (113-8).

The **Marine Fisheries Commission** has jurisdiction over the conservation of marine and estuarine resources. The **Wildlife Resources Commission** (Commission) has jurisdiction over the conservation of wildlife resources and over all activities connected therewith, unless otherwise provided. To the extent that jurisdiction of the Marine Fisheries Commission and the Commission may overlap, the two commissions are granted concurrent jurisdiction. In cases of conflict between actions taken or regulations promulgated by either agency, the two commissions are empowered to make agreements concerning harmonious settlement in the best interests of the conservation of the state marine, estuarine and wildlife resources. If agreement cannot be reached, the Governor is empowered to resolve the differences. ★Those coastal fishing waters in which are found a significant number of freshwater fish may be denominated joint fishing waters. These waters are deemed coastal fishing waters from the standpoint of Department laws and regulations and are inland fishing waters from the standpoint of Commission laws and regulations. The two commissions may make joint regulations governing agency responsibilities and modifying the applicability of

North Carolina

licensing and other regulatory provisions for rational and compatible management of the marine, estuarine and wildlife resources (113-132).★

There is an **Executive Director** (Director) of the Commission, and a **Fisheries Director** of the Division of Marine Fisheries who shall be qualified for the office by education or experience. **Wildlife Protectors** (Protectors) are Commission employees sworn in as officers and assigned to duties which include the exercise of law enforcement powers (113-128).

Agency Powers and Duties

It is the duty of the **Department**, by investigation, recommendation and publication, to aid: in promoting of the conservation and development of state natural resources; in promoting a more profitable use of lands and forests; in coordinating existing scientific investigations and other related agencies in formulating and promoting sound policies of conservation and development (113-3).

The following powers are granted to the **Department** and the **Commission** and may be delegated to the Fisheries Director and the Executive Director: ▸ comment on and object to permit applications submitted to state agencies which may affect the public trust resources in land and water; ▸ investigate alleged encroachments upon, usurpations of, or other actions in violation of public trust rights; ▸ initiate contested case proceedings under Chapter 150B for review of permit decisions by state agencies which will adversely affect public trust rights, or initiate civil actions to remove or restrain unlawful encroachment upon or any other violation of rights or of access to public trust areas. Whenever there exists reasonable cause to believe that any person has unlawfully encroached upon or otherwise violated the public trust rights or legal rights of access, a civil action may be instituted by the responsible agency for injunctive relief to restrain the violation and for a mandatory preliminary injunction to restore the resources to an undisturbed condition. The Attorney General shall act for the agencies and shall initiate actions at the request of the Department or the Commission (113-131). ★The Department and Commission, in addition to other agencies responsible, may inspect the plans and specifications of all dams proposed to be built in the state or the US which may have an adverse effect upon state fish, and may be heard before the agency approving such plans, and due consideration shall be given to the Department or Commission by the agencies charged with such duty (113-263).★

The Commission may schedule managed hunts for any species of wildlife to be held on game lands. The Commission may cooperate with private landowners in the establishment of public hunting grounds, and may provide for posting of these areas and require that authorized hunters obtain written permission from the owner, and trespass laws and laws concerning damage or injurious activities by hunters and by others carrying weapons on, or discharging weapons across, public hunting grounds or restricted zones (113-264).

★★The Commission must prepare and distribute to license agents informational materials relating to hunting, fishing, trapping and boating laws and regulations. In issuing new licenses and permits by mail, the Commission must generally inform the licensee/permittee of law and regulations applicable, and for renewal licenses/permits by mail, of any substantial changes in the law or regulations which may affect the activities of the licensee/permittee. After adopting regulations which impose new restrictions, the Commission must take steps to publicize the new restrictions. After adopting new restrictions on hunting, fishing, trapping or boating, the Commission must publicize the new restrictions in a manner designed to reach persons affected (113-301.1).★★ In the interests of wildlife resource conservation, the Commission may: ▸ lease or purchase lands, equipment and other property; ▸ accept gifts and grants on the state's behalf; ▸ establish wildlife refuges, management areas, and boating and fishing access areas; ▸ provide matching funds for entering into projects with other agencies or scientific, educational or charitable foundations; ▸ condemn lands; ▸ sell, lease or give away property. The Commission may delegate to the Director all administrative powers. The Commission is authorized to develop policy of wildlife management for all state-owned lands. The Division of State Property and Construction shall determine which lands are suitable for wildlife management purposes. Nothing in the wildlife management plan shall prohibit, restrict, or require the change in use of state property to carry out objectives of the state agency utilizing such land. Each wildlife management plan shall consider the question of public hunting, and whenever and wherever possible, consistent with the primary land use of the controlling agency, public hunting shall be allowed under cooperative agreement with the Commission. Any dispute over the question of public hunting shall be resolved by the Division of State Property and Construction. ★★Subject to Commission policy directives, the Director may institute an action for injunctive relief to prevent irreparable injury to wildlife resources or to prevent or regulate any activity within Commission jurisdiction constituting a public nuisance or presenting a threat to public health or safety (113-306). ★★

Agency Regulations

The Commission may implement statutory provisions with rules that: ▸ regulate license requirements and exemptions applying to wildlife taking on lands/waters lying across county boundaries; ▸ require persons subject to license requirements to carry identification; ▸ require persons aboard vessels or carrying weapons or other taking gear when in an area where wildlife resources may be taken to exhibit identification as required; ▸ implement a system of tagging and reporting fur-bearing animals and big game, and set reasonable fees for tags (113-276.l). Where the Commission is granted authority under any provision of law where there is concurrent federal jurisdiction, the Commission may by reference in its rules adopt relevant federal law and regulations as state rules, to prevent confusion or conflict of jurisdiction or enforcement (113-307) [details of other consent provisions are given].

Agency Funding Sources

One dollar from each nonresident sportsman combination license, nonresident comprehensive hunting license and nonresident six-day hunting license must be set aside by the Commission and contributed to a US agency for expenditure in Canada for the propagation, management and control of migratory waterfowl (113-270.2). A person applying for a hunting license may make a voluntary contribution of fifty cents for funding the Hunter Safety Education Program (113-270.2A). The Commission has exclusive production rights for the voluntary migratory waterfowl conservation print, and shall adopt policy for the annual selection of the print design and the production of the print for sale, arrangements for the reproduction and marketing of prints, and provisions for sharing the revenues. The proceeds from print sales shall be used for the benefit of state migratory waterfowl management (113-270.2B). There is a **Recreation and Natural Heritage Trust Fund** to be used to finance the Recreation and Natural Heritage Trust Program. (See Agency Advisory Boards under this section and HABITAT PROTECTION.) The fund shall be held separate from all other moneys. Investment earnings shall become part of the fund. When the state acquires land pursuant to this article, the Chairperson of the Board of Trustees shall request the State Treasurer to set aside an amount from the fund not to exceed 20% of the land's appraised value, to be placed in a special stewardship account in the fund to be used for the management of the land in the Trust (113-77.7). No wording in any statute shall be construed to abrogate the vested rights of the state to collect fees for licenses for hunting and fishing on any federally owned land or stream including the licenses for county, state or nonresident hunters or fishermen (113-39).

Agency Advisory Boards

The **Nongame Wildlife Advisory Committee** (Committee) is created subject to constitution, organization, and function and shall be comprised of knowledgeable state citizens whose responsibility is to advise the Commission on matters related to conservation of nongame wildlife, including creation of protected animal lists and development of conservation programs for endangered, threatened, and special concern species (113-335). The Committee has the power to: ▸ gather and provide information and data and advise the Commission with respect to all aspects of the biology and ecology of endangered, threatened and special concern species; ▸ investigate and make recommendations as to the status of such species; ▸ ★identify and assemble experts from the disciplines of ornithology, mammalogy, herpetology, ichthyology, taxonomy, ecology and other fields to serve as the **Scientific Council** and to review the scientific evidence, to evaluate the status of candidate species, and to report findings with recommendations; ★ ▸ develop and present to the Commission management and conservation practices for preserving endangered, threatened and special concern species; ▸ recommend critical habitat areas for protection or acquisition; ▸ advise the Commission on matters which involve technical zoological questions or the development of pertinent regulations, and make recommendations (113-336).

There is a nine-member **Recreation and Natural Heritage Trust Fund Board of Trustees** to authorize expenditures from the Natural Heritage Trust Fund. Three members are appointed by the Governor, three by the Lieutenant Governor, and three by the Speaker of the House of Representatives. Members shall be knowledgeable in the acquisition and management of natural areas (113-77.8). (See also Agency Funding Sources under this section and HABITAT PROTECTION.)

PROTECTED SPECIES OF WILDLIFE

All native or resident wild animals on federal lists of endangered or threatened species pursuant to the Endangered Species Act have the same status on the North Carolina protected animals lists. ★The Committee, after considering a report on the status of a candidate species from the Scientific Council, may by resolution propose that a species be added to or removed from a protected animal list. If the Commission finds there is merit in the proposal, it shall examine relevant scientific and economic data and factual information to determine: ▸ whether any other state or federal agency or private entity is taking steps to protect the wild animal; ▸ whether there is present or threatened destruction, modification, or curtailment of its habitat; ▸ if there is over-utilization for commercial, recreational, scientific, or educational purposes; ▸ whether there is critical population depletion from disease, predation or other mortality factors; ▸ whether alternative regulatory mechanisms exist; ▸ the existence of other man-made factors affecting continued viability of the animal in the state. The Commission, with the Committee's advice, shall tentatively determine whether any regulatory action is warranted with regard to the proposal and, if so, the specific action to be proposed.★ Notice of proposed rulemaking shall be published (113-334).

The Commission shall have the power and duty to: ▸ adopt and publish an endangered species list, a threatened species list, and a list of species of special concern, identifying each entry by its scientific and common name; ▸ reconsider and revise the lists in response to public proposals or as the Commission deems necessary; ▸ coordinate development and implementation of conservation programs for endangered and threatened species and for species of special concern; ▸ adopt regulations to implement conservation programs for endangered, threatened and special concern species and to limit, regulate or prevent the taking, collection or sale of protected animals; ▸ conduct investigations to determine whether a wild animal should be on a protected animal list and determine the requirements for survival for resident wild animal species (113-333). (See also STATE WILDLIFE POLICY, RELEVANT WILDLIFE DEFINITIONS and Agency Advisory Boards under STATE FISH AND WILDLIFE AGENCIES.) It is unlawful to take, possess, transport, sell, barter, trade, export or give away any animal on a protected wild animal list, except as authorized by Commission regulations, including those promulgated pursuant to 113-333(1), or to perform any act prohibited by Commission regulations promulgated pursuant to 113-333. Violation: fine of at least $100 for a first conviction; not less than $500 upon any subsequent conviction, in addition to any other penalty prescribed by the court (113-337).

Live wildlife and the nests and eggs of wild birds may be taken, possessed, transported, bought, sold, imported, exported or otherwise acquired or disposed of only as authorized. The Commission may impose reporting, permit and tagging requirements in regulating live wildlife and the nests and eggs of wild birds, and may charge a fee to defray tagging costs (113-291.3).

GENERAL EXCEPTIONS TO PROTECTION

The Commission may provide for licenses to take any wildlife resources under a collection license that may serve in lieu of any other license and which authorizes incidental transportation and possession of wildlife resources. The Commission may impose permit requirements, and may delegate to the Director the authority to impose time limits and restrictions and method of taking and possession. The Commission may regulate tagging, record keeping, limited-purpose permits, cages, and use of assistants by the licensee to take or possess wildlife (113-272.4).

★In the interests of humane treatment of wild animals and wild birds that are crippled, tame or otherwise unfit for immediate release into their natural habitat, the Commission may license individuals to hold particular species in captivity. On refusing to issue the captivity license, the Director may either take possession of the animal or bird or issue a captivity permit for a limited period until proper disposition can be made. ★ The Commission may require standards of caging and care, reports, and supervision by Commission employees to insure humane treatment. The Director may impose restrictions upon the mode of captivity and methods of treatment to enable the wild creature to become self-sufficient and requiring that it be set free when self-sufficient. Any substantial deviation from requirements imposed by rule renders possession of the wild creature unlawful. No captivity license may be issued for any cougar (Felis concolor) except to a zoo, educational or scientific research institution, or a person who lawfully possessed the cougar prior to June, 1977, or where prohibited by municipal ordinance, unless the cougar is held in caging conditions simulating a natural habitat. ★The licensing provisions of this section apply to black bears held in captivity, but where different from this section, Article 2 of Chapter 19A covers keeping black bears in captivity (113-272.5).★

The Department and federal agencies are granted the right to: ► take marine, estuarine and wildlife resources within the state; ► conduct fish cultural operations and scientific investigations; ► survey state fish and wildlife populations; ► conduct investigations to determine the status and requirements for survival of resident species of fish and wildlife; ► propagate animals, birds and fish and erect fish hatcheries without regard to any licensing or permit requirements. ★The Commission may issue permits authorizing persons to take fish or wildlife through the use of drugs, poisons, explosives, electricity or any other generally prohibited manner. Such permits need not be restricted solely to victims of depredations or to scientific or educational institutions, but should be issued only for good cause. No permit to take wildlife other than fish by poison may be issued unless the provisions of Article 22A are met.★ The Department, the Commission and US agencies may take fish and wildlife in a manner generally prohibited by statute or rule (113-261).

HUNTING, FISHING, TRAPPING PROVISIONS

General Provisions

Except as permitted, no person may take, possess, buy, sell or transport any wildlife, dead or alive, in whole or in part, nor take, possess, buy, sell or transport nests or eggs of wild birds. No person may take, possess, buy, sell or transport any wildlife resources in violation of Commission rules (113-291). Lawfully taken dead wildlife may be possessed and transported as provided in 113-291.2, and wildlife possessed under any dealer license may be possessed/transported in accordance with laws and rules. Unless otherwise provided, a person may accept the gift of wildlife lawfully taken if such does not exceed applicable possession limits, and if the person preserves the license information of the donor. A licensed taxidermist or other dealer taking temporary possession of wildlife may possess it under the dealer's license, if the name, address, license information, and dates of receipt of the wildlife are kept. ★The sale of rabbits and squirrels and their edible parts not for resale is permitted. If the Commission finds that game populations would not be endangered, it may authorize the sale of heads, antlers, horns, hides, skins, plumes, feet and claws of game animals or birds, and it may authorize the sale of bobcats, opossums and raccoons and their parts. No part of any bear or wild turkey may be sold under the above provisions, and no part of any fox taken in North Carolina may be sold except as otherwise provided.★ The Commission may impose permit requirements in regulating sales. Lawfully taken fur-bearing animals and parts, including furs and pelts, may, subject to tagging or reporting requirements, be possessed, transported, bought, sold, or given as gifts. The Commission may regulate the importation of wildlife from without the state by fur dealers, the sale of fox fur and other wildlife hides taken within the state, and import, transport, sale and export of furs lawfully taken without the state. ★Nongame animals and birds open to hunting and nongame fish lawfully taken, except as otherwise provided, may be possessed, transported, bought, sold, given or received as gifts, or otherwise disposed of without restriction.★ Accidentally killed animals or those taken to prevent depredations to property are governed by 113-274. Commission rules may govern the marking of packages, crates and other containers in which wildlife may be shipped. ★Any person hiring a hunter or trapper to take game is deemed to be buying game, and any hunter or trapper who may be hired is deemed to be selling game (113-291.3).★

★★Every individual who enters the property of another to hunt or fish without permission from an authorized person is under a duty to look for posted notices. In the apparent absence of such notices, the person is nevertheless under a duty to determine if practicable whether the property is registered under the terms below. No one may hunt or fish, or enter to do so, on the registered and posted property of another without having in possession an entry permit, or do so on the registered property of another without an entry permit if there is reason to know the property is posted. Violation: misdemeanor punishable under 113-135. Unauthorized removal or mutilation of posted notices on registered property is a misdemeanor: fine minimum $50, jail up to 90 days, or both (113-284 through -286). A person who controls the hunting and/or fishing rights to a tract of property and wishes to register it must apply to the Commission providing the following: ► a statement under oath that the person has the right to control hunting and/or fishing on the land to be registered, or is a lessee with such rights; ► three copies of a description of the tract that will allow law enforcement officers to determine in the field, and prove in court, whether an individual is within the boundaries of the tract, in the form of a map, plat or aerial photograph showing boundaries; ► a diagram keyed to known landmarks or similar accurate document. Any boundary amendment of a registered tract must be accomplished by a new registration application meeting these requirements: ► an agreement to post the tract in accordance with requirements herein and maintain same; ► an agreement to issue entry permits to all individuals to whom permission has been given to hunt/fish on the tract; ► a fee to cover administrative registration, consisting of filing the application in a central registry open to the public with an indication whether the property is registered as to hunting, fishing, or both. Tract descriptions must be sent to wildlife protectors and other law enforcement officers for use of sheriffs and county police, and to the appropriate protector stationed in the area of the tract. A registrant must post registered property as soon as practicable after receiving notice of registration acceptance. [Numerous details are given for deletion of registration, failure to post registered land, and changes in property ownership as it affects registration.] Upon registration of property, the Director must furnish the registrant with a reasonable number of standardized permit forms to be carried by persons given permission to hunt and/or fish on registered property. The description filed with the application constitutes prima facie evidence of the registered property's boundaries. If a person hunts or fishes, or enters to do same, on posted registered property, any registrant or agent or enforcement officer or Protector may request that the person produce an entry permit. It is also the duty of sheriffs and their deputies, county police officers, and other law enforcement officers with general enforcement jurisdiction to investigate reported violations and to initiate prosecutions. An entry permit does not substitute for any required hunting or fishing license (113-282, -283 and -287).★★

The flashing or display of any artificial light between a half hour after sunset and a half hour before sunrise in any area frequented or inhabited by wild deer by any person who has accessible a firearm, crossbow, or other bow and arrow constitutes prima facie evidence of taking deer with the aid of an artificial light, except for headlights of vehicles driven normally along a highway or public/private roadway (113-302).

Licenses and Permits

Except as otherwise provided, no one may take wild animals or wild birds without a hunting license (113-270.2). On or after July 1, 1991, a person, may not procure a hunting license or hunt without producing a certificate of competency or a hunting license issued prior to that date, or signing a statement that the person had such a license. The Commission shall institute and coordinate a statewide course of instruction in hunter ethics, wildlife laws and regulations, and competency and safety in firearm handling, and may cooperate with any political subdivision or reputable organization having as one of its objectives the promotion of competency and safety in handling firearms. Commission-designated persons or agencies shall give the courses and shall submit listings of all persons completing the course. Certificates of completion shall be issued and similar certificates issued by other states shall be accepted as complying with these requirements if the privileges are reciprocal for North Carolina residents. Use of fictitious certificates or fraud in obtaining a hunting license shall result in revocation of hunting privileges for up to one year. Persons with lifetime licenses may hunt when accompanied by an adult at least 21 years of age pending completion of a hunter safety course (113-270.1A). [Numerous resident and nonresident license categories are detailed in 113-270.2.]

Except as otherwise provided, no one may take fur-bearing animals by trapping, or by any other authorized method that preserves the pelt from injury, without a trapping license, which, serves in lieu of a hunting license. If fur-bearing animals are taken as game, at the times and by the methods authorized for hunting, hunting license requirements apply (113-270.5).

Except as provided, no one may fish by means of a hook and line in inland waters without a hook-and-line fishing license [a large variety of such licenses are listed]. ★A special guest fishing license may be purchased by a landowner whose property borders inland or joint fishing waters entitling persons to fish from waterfront piers or docks of the landowner only. These provisions shall not apply to residents of the Cherokee Indian Reservation.★ In addition to hook-and-line fishing licenses, no one may fish in public mountain trout waters without a special trout license. ★Public mountain trout waters are those so designated by the Commission which are managed and regulated so as to sustain a mountain trout fishery (113-271 and -272).★ [A variety of licenses for trout, or which include trout fishing privileges are listed.]

★Except as provided, no one may fish in inland fishing waters with any special device without a special device license.★ Special devices are those used in fishing other than hook and line, and authorized by Commission rules for use in specified waters, which may include tagging and periodic catch reports. Unless prohibited, nongame fish taken under this license may be sold. Persons who have a primitive weapons hunting license or other license may take nongame fish from inland fishing waters with a bow and arrow according to Commission rules without a special device license. Any technique of fishing that may be lawfully authorized which employs neither the use of any special device nor hook and line (i.e., "grabbling") must be pursued under the appropriate hook-and-line fishing license. In accordance with established fishing customs, the Commission may by rule provide for use of nets or other special devices as an incident to hook-and-line fishing or for procuring bait fish without requiring a special device license (113-272.2 and -272.3).

In addition to any required hunting, trapping, or fishing license, persons engaging in specially regulated activities must have a special activity license before engaging in the regulated activity, including licenses for resident big game hunting, primitive weapons hunting, game land license (for residents hunting, trapping or fishing on game lands and mountain trout waters designated as managed lands/waters by the Commission), falconry license, and migratory waterfowl hunting license. Persons who kill any species of big game must report the kill to the Commission and tag the carcass as required. Holders of current lifetime, or resident/nonresident sportsman combination or comprehensive fishing licenses may be exempt from certain special licenses (113-270.3).

★★A migrant farm worker who has in possession a temporary certification of status by the rural Employment Service on a Commission form is entitled to resident privileges of the state and county during the term of the certificate for purchasing a resident fishing license and utilizing the natural-bait exemption.★★ A resident fishing with hook and line in the county of residence using natural bait is exempt from the hook-and-line fishing license requirement [extensive details given]. ★The fishing license provisions of this article do not apply upon lands held in trust by the US for the Eastern Band of the Cherokee Indians.★ Food servers may prepare edible wildlife lawfully taken by a patron for serving to the patron and any guest under the Director's rules. A special device license is not required when using a landing net to take nongame fish or to assist in taking other fish in inland waters as long as applicable hook-and-line fishing license requirements are met (113-276).

★A "permit" is a written authorization issued without charge by a Commission agent to a person to conduct some activity over which the Commission has jurisdiction. When sale of wildlife resources is permitted, the Director may require the retention of invoices in lieu of a permit. No one may engage in any activity for which a permit is required without a permit. A depredation permit authorizes the taking, destruction, transfer, transplanting or driving away of undesirable, harmful, predatory, excess or surplus wildlife or wildlife resources and must state the manner of taking and the disposition of same, and the time the permit is valid plus any other restrictions imposed. No depredation permit or license is needed for a landowner to take wildlife committing depredations upon the landowner's property, but the Commission may regulate the manner of taking and the disposition of wildlife so taken, including such killed accidentally by motor vehicle (113.274).★

A captivity permit authorizes possession and retaining of live wildlife. This permit does not substitute for any required collection license or captivity license, but may be temporarily issued for possession of wild animals pending action on such licenses. Animals kept under permit must be humanely treated in accordance with terms of the permit, but the standards of care and caging applicable to species kept under the captivity license do not apply unless specified in the permit [other details given]. A possession permit authorizes the possession of dead wildlife lawfully acquired. The Commission may require the use of transportation permits by persons required to be licensed or by those exempt from license requirements while transporting wildlife resources within the state to encourage orderly transportation within, into, through, and out of the state, and permits may be required for wildlife transported either dead or alive [other details given]. An exportation or importation permit may be required for the importation or exportation of wildlife resources under Commission regulations. A trophy wildlife sale permit authorizes the owner of lawfully taken wildlife specimens that are mounted, stuffed or otherwise preserved to sell individual specimens that may be otherwise lawfully sold. A trout sale permit authorizes sale at wholesale or retail of dead artificially propagated mountain trout for food if lawfully acquired from a Commission approved hatchery and wrapped and identified as required. Persons holding a license otherwise authorizing the sale of trout need no permit. The Commission may issue permits for taking, purchase, or sale of wildlife resources if the activity is lawfully authorized, if there is a need for control of the activity and no other license or permit is applicable, or if closer control is needed than provided by a license (113-274).

It is unlawful to engage in regulated operations and refuse to exhibit any required license, permit, or identification upon the request of any Commission agent or any officer authorized to enforce the provisions of this article. All licenses and permits must be kept ready at hand while engaged in regulated operations. It is illegal to refuse to comply with any provisions herein or rules promulgated hereunder, and a misdemeanor to: ▸ engage in any regulated activity with an improper, false or altered license or permit; ▸ make application for same to which one is not entitled; ▸ make any false fraudulent or misleading statement in applying for a license or permit; ▸ counterfeit, alter or falsify any application, license or permit (113-275).

Restrictions on Taking: Hunting and Trapping

Except as provided by statute or rules permitting use of electricity to take certain fish, it is a misdemeanor and a fine of $100-500, jail up to 90 days, or both, to take any fish or wildlife through the use of poisons, drugs, explosives or electricity, except for persons lawfully using poison or pesticide under the state pesticide acts. Except under a permit, it is unlawful to possess fish or wildlife bearing evidence of having been taken in violation of this section or with knowledge or reason to believe that same was taken in violation (113-262).

Except as provided, game may only be taken between a half hour before sunrise and a half hour after sunset and only by one or a combination of the following methods: ▸ with a rifle, except not for wild turkeys; ▸ with a shotgun not larger than 10 gauge; ▸ with a bow and arrow as specified by the Commission; ▸ with the use of dogs; ▸ by falconry. Fur-bearing animals may be taken at any time during open trapping season with traps, and rabbits may be box-trapped under Commission rules. Nongame animals and birds open to hunting may be taken during the hours authorized by rule during any open season by the methods for taking game. The Commission may prescribe the manner of taking wild animals and wild birds on game lands and public hunting grounds. No wild animals or wild birds may be taken: ★from or with the use of any vehicle, vessel unless manually propelled, airplane or other conveyance, except vessels and vehicles may be used as hunting stands if not in motion, under sail, under power, nor with the engine running or the vehicle passenger area occupied, and same may be used for transportation incidental to the taking;★ with the use or aid of any artificial light, net, trap, snare, electronic or recorded animal or bird call, or fire, provided that crows may be taken with the use of electronic calling devices. No wild birds may be taken with the use of salt, grain, fruit or other bait except as provided. No bear or wild boar may be taken with the use of salt, grain, fruit, honey, animal parts or other bait. Any person who unlawfully takes bear or wild boar with any type of bait is punishable as provided by 113-294(c). It is a misdemeanor punishable at the court's discretion to take wildlife while having in possession any firearm equipped with a silencer or with same readily at hand, or a weapon of mass death and destruction as defined in 14-288.8 (113-291.1).

[Restrictions on dog field trials are provided.] Raccoons and opossum may be taken at night with dogs during seasons set by the Commission, using artificial lights. No conveyance may be used in taking any raccoon or opossum at night, but incidental transportation of hunters and dogs to and from the hunting site is permitted. The Commission may by rule restrict the taking of frogs or other creatures not classified as wildlife which may be found in areas frequented by game, with the use of artificial light, and may regulate the shining of lights at night in areas frequented by deer. ★★After hearing evidence and finding as a fact that an area frequented by deer is subject to substantial unlawful night deer hunting, or that area residents have been greatly inconvenienced by persons shining lights on deer, the Commission may by rule prohibit the intentional sweeping of that area with lights, or the intentional shining of lights on deer during the period either from 11:00 p.m. until one-half hour before sunrise; or from one-half hour after sunset until one-half hour before sunrise. The Commission must propose the rule at a public hearing in the area to be closed and seek the reactions of the local inhabitants. The rule must exempt necessary light-shining by landholders, motorists, and campers legitimately in the area who are not attempting to attract wildlife. The Board of County Commissioners may request extension of the no-shine-light period to all night and the Commission may implement this extension without additional public hearing (113-291.1). ★★

In order to keep North Carolina migratory bird provisions in conformity with federal law and rules, the Commission may by rule expand or modify statutory provisions to achieve such conformity, and in particular may: ▸ prohibit the use of rifles, unplugged shotguns, live decoys, and sinkboxes in the taking of migratory game birds; ▸ vary shooting hours; ▸ adopt specific distances, not less than 300 yards, hunters must maintain from areas that have been baited, and fix the number of days afterwards during which it is still unlawful to take migratory game birds in the baited area; ▸ adopt similar provisions for the use of live decoys. In the absence of Commission regulations to the contrary, the regulations of the USDI prohibiting the use of rifles, unplugged shotguns, toxic shot, and sinkboxes in taking migratory game birds in North Carolina shall apply, and any violation thereof is unlawful (113-291.1).

If a season is open permitting such method of taking for the species in question, a hunter may take rabbits, squirrels, opossum, raccoons, fur-bearing animals and nongame animals and birds open to hunting with a .22 caliber pistol as specified. ★A hunter or trapper lawfully taking a wild animal or wild bird by another lawful method may use a knife, pistol or other swift method of killing the animal or bird taken.★ The Commission may restrict or prohibit the carrying of firearms during special seasons or in special areas reserved for taking wildlife with primitive weapons or other restricted methods. ★The Commission may prescribe the types of handguns and ammunition that may be used in taking big game animals other than wild turkey. During the regular gun seasons for taking bear, deer, and wild boar, these animals may be taken with handguns and handgun ammunition by Commission rule. The Commission shall not provide a special season for the exclusive use of handguns in taking wildlife. The Commission may by rule relax requirements of this section on controlled shooting preserves and in other highly controlled situations.★ The intentional destruction or substantial impairment of wildlife nesting or breeding areas or other purposeful acts to render them unfit is unlawful, including cutting down den trees, shooting into nests of wild animals or birds and despoliation of dens, nests or rookeries. It is unlawful to take deer swimming or in water above its knees (113-291.1).

In accordance with the supply of wildlife and other factors of public importance, the Commission may fix seasons and bag limits upon wild animals and birds for wildlife resource conservation, and it may close seasons completely and fix hours of hunting, and season and possession limits. Different seasons and bag limits may be set in differing areas, early or extended seasons may be set on controlled shooting preserves and public hunting grounds, and special seasons may be set for falconry, primitive weapons or taking wildlife under other special conditions. Unless modified by the Commission, seasons, shooting hours, bag and possession limits fixed by the USDI for migratory game birds must be followed. When federal rules require that the state limit participation in seasons or bag limits, the Commission may schedule managed hunts for migratory game birds. Where there is a muzzle-loading firearm season for deer, with a bag limit of five or more, one antlerless deer may be taken. Dogs may not be used for hunting deer during such season. Any hunter or trapper who has wounded or disabled a wild animal or bird must make a reasonable effort to capture and kill same, and count in applicable bag limits. Lawfully taken game may be possessed and personally transported as specified for a person's own use by virtue of a hunting license without any additional permit, subject to tagging and reporting requirements set by the Commission. [Details are given as to length of storage time and possession limits.] The Commission may impose reporting, permit and tagging requirements for: ▸ possessing wildlife taken in open season after season's close; ▸ transporting dead wildlife from an area having an open season to an area with a closed season; ▸ transporting wildlife lawfully taken in another state into this state; ▸ possessing dead wildlife after such transportation (113-291.2).

★★Upon application of any landholder and required fee, the Director may require a survey of the deer population on the land of such landholder. If it is determined that there is an overpopulation of deer in relation to carrying capacity of the land, that the herd is dependent on such land for food and cover, and that such imbalance is not readily correctable by an either-sex deer season of reasonable length, the Director may issue to the landholder a number of special antlerless deer tags sufficient to correct the population imbalance. Subject to applicable hunting license requirements and bag, possession and season limits, the special deer tags may be used by any person(s) selected by the landowner to take antlerless deer, including male deer with "buttons" not readily visible, on the land concerned during such time as prescribed by the Director. A special antlerless deer tag shall be affixed in addition to the required big game tag, and such kill shall be reported immediately in the wildlife cooperator tagging book supplied with the special tags. Such book and unused tags shall be returned to the Commission within 15 days of the close of the season, and such deer shall count as part of the daily bag, possession and season limits of the hunter (113-291.2).★★

★★All regulatory powers of the Commission with respect to game, wild animals and wildlife apply to foxes unless there are specific overriding restrictions herein. Except for any closed season, foxes may be taken with dogs both night and day on a year round basis. Foxes may not be taken with firearms except: ▸ as otherwise provided herein; ▸ as an incidental method of humanely killing them following any lawful method of taking that does not result in death; ▸ when they are lawfully shot under laws and rules pertaining to destruction of animals committing depredations to property. Foxes may not be taken with the aid of any electronic calling device. The Commission is directed to improve its capabilities for studying fox and fur-bearer populations generally, and to implement management methods and impose controls designed to produce optimum fox and fur-bearer populations. If the Commission determines the fox population in an area is fully adequate to support harvesting, it may, upon passage of local legislation, open a season for taking foxes by trapping, and foxes may also be taken by use of methods lawful for taking game. Any bag, possession or season limits imposed on foxes from that area will apply in the aggregate to all foxes killed without regard to method of taking. Open seasons for taking foxes with weapons and trapping may be continued from year to year so long as fox populations remain adequate to support such harvest in counties as specified herein. The Commission may provide for the sale of foxes lawfully taken in open season areas under a system providing strict controls. The Commission must implement a system of tagging foxes and fox furs with a special fox tag. The number of tags issued to a person may be limited as to area and number in accordance with bag and other limits that may be imposed. No person may continue to hunt or trap foxes without having at least one valid unused fox tag lawful for use in the area in question. Persons hunting foxes with dogs not intending to kill them need not have a fox tag, but accidentally killed foxes must be disposed of without sale as provided by the Commission, and untagged foxes may not be sold. The Commission may impose strict controls on disposition of foxes taken under depredation rules. In any area where the Commission determines that fox hunting with dogs is harmful to turkey restoration projects, it may declare a closed season upon taking with dogs of all species of wild animals and birds. This does not prohibit lawful field trials or dog training. Upon notification by the State Health Director of contagious animal disease in a local fox population, the Commission may establish population control measures until the problem has passed. There is an open season for taking foxes with firearms in areas of the state as specified. The selling, buying, or possessing for sale of any fox or fox part taken in this season is prohibited. The Commission shall set bag and season limits for foxes and make rules governing the possession of foxes killed by vehicles or accident (113-291.4 and -291.4A). ★★

The Commission may regulate the use of dogs taking wildlife with respect to seasons, times and places of use as specified. On game lands, wildlife refuges and public hunting grounds, the Commission may regulate the possession and use of dogs and may impound dogs found running at large without supervision or identification. ★★The Commission may not by its rules restrict the number of dogs used in hunting or require that any particular breed of dog be used in hunting. It is unlawful to allow dogs not under the owner's control to run or chase deer during the closed season. Nothing herein is intended to require the leashing or confining of pet dogs (113-291.5). ★★

No one may take wild animals by trapping on another's land without possessing written permission issued and dated within the previous year by the owner/agent. This does not apply to public lands on which trapping is not specifically prohibited. No one may take wild animals by trapping with any steel-jaw, leghold or connibear trap unless it has a permanent identification tag attached, is smooth edged without teeth or spikes, and meets other criteria as specified. No person may set a trap so that animals or birds when caught will be suspended. No hook of any type may be used to take wild animals or wild birds by trapping. Connibear traps may be set only in water in areas where beaver and otter may be lawfully trapped where water is deep enough to quickly drown the animal. It is unlawful to disturb lawfully placed traps of another or to remove any fur-bearing animal from the trap except for law enforcement officers performing their duties. Steel or metal-jaw traps may be used by state public health officials to control the spread of disease. ★The Commission must include the trapping requirements of this section in its annual digest of hunting and trapping rules provided to each person buying a license (113-291.6). ★ The Commission shall by rule supersede local acts closing the season on bears, by either opening a season in the county affected or carrying forward the closed-season provision after 1981 (113-291.7). In specified counties, beavers may be taken by firearm, connibear traps as specified, and snares as specified (113-291.9).

★No one may take any animal or bird with the use of poison or pesticide except as provided. Taking fish by the use of poison is governed by 113-261 and 113-262, and the prohibitions of those sections against the taking of wildlife by poison apply unless specifically permitted. Otherwise, the Commission may, by rules consistent with the North Carolina Pesticide Laws, regulate, prohibit, or restrict the use of poisons or pesticides upon or severely affecting wildlife resources (113-300.1). ★ (See also ANIMAL DAMAGE CONTROL.)

Restrictions on Taking: Fishing

The Commission is authorized to license, regulate, prohibit, prescribe or restrict all fishing in inland fishing waters, and the taking of inland game fish in coastal fishing waters, with respect to: ▸ time, place, type or dimensions of any methods or equipment; ▸ seasons for taking fish; ▸ size limits and maximum quantities of fish that may be taken, possessed, bailed to another, transported, bought, sold or given away. The Commission is authorized to license, regulate, prohibit or restrict the opening and closing of inland fishing waters entirely or only to the taking of particular classes of fish, use of particular equipment or other activities within its jurisdiction and the possession, cultivation, transportation, importation, exportation, sale, purchase, acquisition and disposition of all inland fisheries resources and all related equipment, implements, and vessels. The Commission shall make rules pertaining to the acquisition, transportation and possession of fish in connection with private ponds, and issue proclamations suspending or extending the hook-and-line season for striped bass in the inland and joint waters of coastal rivers and tributaries. The Director shall make reasonable effort to give notice of the terms of such proclamations, including press releases and posting of notices where affected persons may gather. It is unlawful for any person in inland fishing waters to: ▸ set a net across the main channel of a river or creek; ▸ erect a dam or weir that extends more than three-fourths of the distance across a river or creek; ‣ erect a dam or other obstruction required to be left open for fish passage and to fail to keep same open. These provisions may not be construed to conflict with the laws and rules of any other agency with jurisdiction over the activity in question (113-292 and -293).

Commercial and Private Enterprise Provisions

No one may serve for hire as a hunting or fishing guide without a hunting and fishing guide license for an individual who meets the criteria set by the Commission. The guide must meet other applicable license requirements. A nonresident may be licensed only upon the same terms that a North Carolina resident may be licensed in the nonresident's state. The Commission may enter into reciprocal agreements with other states as necessary and may provide for the qualifications and duties of all hunting and fishing guides, and provisions for revocation of hunting and fishing guide licenses must be set out in the rules of the Commission (113-270.4).

No person, except as otherwise provided, may engage in an activity for which a dealer license is provided without a license. The Commission may by rule govern every aspect of the licensee's dealing with wildlife resources including requiring the licensee to: ‣ implement a system of tagging or otherwise identifying species regulated under the license and pay a fee for such tags; ‣ keep records and statistics; ‣ be subject to inspection at reasonable hours and audit of records; ‣ make periodic reports; ‣ post performance bonds payable to the Commission; ‣ otherwise comply with rules and requirements imposed. A commercial trout pond license is required for artificial impoundments of three acres or less on private land stocked exclusively with hatchery-reared mountain trout obtained from approved hatcheries. The Commission may regulate qualifications of operators, standards of operation, and conditions under which trout may be taken, transported, possessed, bought and sold. A fish propagation license is required to operate hatcheries for fish found in inland fishing waters, and the Commission may prescribe standards of operation, operator qualifications, and conditions under which fish may be taken, transported, possessed, bought and sold, or propagated. Any person who deals in furs must obtain a fur-dealer license to engage in buying or selling fur-bearing animals or other wild animals that may lawfully be sold, the raw furs, pelts or skins thereof, or the furs, pelts or skins of animals which may not themselves be sold, but whose pelts may be sold. A hunter or trapper who has lawfully taken wild animals and sells the pelts is not a fur dealer if the hunter sells to licensed fur dealers. Fur processors must have a fur-dealer station license. Records as to purchase, sale, importation, exportation and other dealings in furs must be kept. The Commission shall set standards for and issue controlled hunting preserve operator licenses of two types: an area marked with boundary signs on which only domestically raised game birds other than wild turkeys are taken; ★an area enclosed with a dog-proof fence on which foxes may be hunted with dogs only, and such controlled fox hunting preserve operated for private use may be of any size. A commercial controlled fox hunting preserve shall be not less than 500 acres or as set by the Commission, taking into account differences in terrain and topography, as well as fox welfare. Operators of fox hunting preserves may purchase live foxes from licensed trappers who live-trap foxes during the open trapping fox season, and may at any time take live foxes from their preserves for sale to other licensed operators (113-273).★

A game bird propagation license is required to propagate game birds in captivity. The Commission may prescribe the activities to be covered by the license, species to be propagated, and the manner of keeping and raising the birds for wildlife conservation. Except as limited otherwise, propagated game birds may be raised and sold for propagation, stocking, food, or taking in connection with dog training. Migratory game bird operations must also comply with any applicable provisions of federal law and rules. The Commission may impose requirements as to shipping, marking, banding, tagging propagated birds and others designed to reduce the chance of illicit game birds being disposed of under cover of licensed operations. The Game Bird Propagation License authorizes propagation and selling of designated game birds except: wild turkey and ruffed grouse may not be sold for food; production and sale of pen-raised quail for food is under Department of Agriculture control, but the Commission may regulate the possession, propagation and transportation of live pen-raised quail. Wild turkey raised under this license shall be confined in a cage, shall not be released for any purpose or allowed to range free. It is a misdemeanor and a fine of not less than $100 in addition to other court-imposed punishment to sell wild turkey or ruffed grouse for food, to sell quail other than lawfully acquired pen-raised quail, or to release or allow a wild turkey to range free (113-273).

A fur-bearer propagation license is required to raise or sell animals or their pelts, including bobcats, opossums and raccoons, or red and silver fixes, for use as fur. The Commission may regulate activities covered by the license including the manner of keeping, raising, and killing the animals prior to sale in accordance with objectives of conservation of resources and humane treatment of wild animals in captivity, and may require tagging of pelts or carcasses. It is unlawful to sell any pelt or carcass of any fur-bearing animal or fox to a person not authorized to buy and possess same, or to sell or deliver a live specimen of any such animal to one not authorized to buy, receive, or hold the animal in captivity. An individual who engages in taxidermy involving wildlife for any compensation, including cost of materials reimbursement, must have a taxidermy license, and must keep records as to the origin and owner of the wildlife. No taxidermist may sell any game or game fish except by possessory lien as otherwise provided. Wildlife acquired by a taxidermist is deemed personal property (113-273).

Import, Export and Release Provisions

The Commission is authorized to license, regulate, prohibit, prescribe or restrict acquisition, importation, possession, transportation, disposition or release into public or private waters or the environment of exotic zoological or botanical species or specimens that may create a danger to or an imbalance in the environment. It is unlawful to: ▸ release exotic species of wild animals or wild birds in an area for stocking for hunting or trapping; ▸ release species of wild animals or wild birds not indigenous to that area in an area for stocking for hunting or trapping; ▸ take by hunting or trapping any animal or bird released or placed in an area in contravention of these provisions except under a permit issued by the Commission for eradicating or controlling the population of any species of wildlife that has been released (113-292). (See Licenses and Permits under HUNTING, FISHING, TRAPPING PROVISIONS.)

Interstate Reciprocal Agreements

The Commission is authorized to make agreements with other jurisdictions as to reciprocal honoring of licenses in the best interests of the conservation of wildlife resources. If the Commission finds that a state has a nonresident license fee related to wildlife that exceeds the fee for a comparable nonresident license in this state, it may by resolution in official session increase the nonresident license fee applicable to citizens of that state to an amount equal to the fee a North Carolina resident is required to pay in that state (113-275). (See Licenses and Permits under this section and Enforcement Powers under ENFORCEMENT OF WILDLIFE LAWS.)

ANIMAL DAMAGE CONTROL

When there is factual basis for the declaration, any wild animal or bird may be declared a pest by the Commissioner of Agriculture in accordance with restrictions imposed by the Structural Pest Control Committee or the Pesticide Board under the Pest and Pesticide acts. When a wild animal or bird is declared a pest, the Commission shall be notified in writing of the action taken, areas in which the declaration is effective, and the type, amount and mode of application of any poison or pesticide proposed for use against the pest. The Commission may then hold a public hearing as to whether it should concur in the declaration of the wild animal or bird as a pest and should be open to taking with poison or pesticide as specified in the notice. The Commission must decide within 60 days whether it concurs or refuses to concur in the pest declaration. If the Commission takes no action, the concurrence will occur automatically. Upon concurrence of the Commission, the wild animal or bird may be taken with poison or pesticide as specified in the notice. ★★If the Wildlife Resources Commission refuses to concur, no poison or pesticide may be used to take the wild animal or bird. After public hearing, the Commission may rescind its concurrence or grant previously withheld, or may grant a qualified concurrence to a declaration, imposing further restrictions as to the use of poison or pesticide in that instance (113-300.2). ★★ Each day in which poisons or pesticides are used unlawfully in taking wild animals or birds is a separate offense, and willful taking in violation of the restrictions or approvals is punishable under 113-262(a). Taking a wild animal or bird declared a pest with the use of poison or pesticide while neglecting applicable restrictions is a misdemeanor; fine up to $100; jail up to 30 days; or both (113-300.3). (See Restrictions on Taking and Licenses and Permits under HUNTING, FISHING, TRAPPING PROVISIONS.)

ENFORCEMENT OF WILDLIFE LAWS

Enforcement Powers

North Carolina is a member of the Atlantic States Marine Fisheries Compact and Commission (113-251 *et seq.*).

Wildlife protectors are authorized to enter and make a reasonable inspection at an appropriate time of day of any premises in which a person subject to administrative control conducts operations to determine whether wildlife is possessed in accordance with law and rule, required records are kept, and other legal requirements are observed. Protectors who believe that wildlife may be on the premises of any public refrigeration storage plant, meat shop, hotel or other public food-storage or eating place may request permission to enter the nonpublic areas of the premises to make a reasonable inspection to see if wildlife thereon is possessed legally. If permission is refused, the protector may procure and execute an administrative search warrant. Nothing herein is intended to prevent a lawful search of premises, with or without a search warrant, when circumstances so justify (113-302.1). The Commission is empowered to make reciprocal agreements with other jurisdictions respecting matters governed in this subchapter, and may by rule modify provisions of this subchapter in order to effectuate the purposes of such agreements in the interests of wildlife resource conservation (113-304). The Commission is empowered to enter into cooperative agreements with public and private agencies and individuals respecting matters governed herein, and may expend funds, assign employees to additional duties within or without the state, and take other actions required by virtue of such agreements (113-305).

Inspectors and wildlife protectors are granted the powers of peace officers anywhere in this state, and beyond its boundaries to the extent provided by law, in enforcing all matters within their jurisdiction as set out herein. The jurisdiction of inspectors extends to matters within Department jurisdiction as specified in the general statutes. Inspectors also have jurisdiction over all offenses involving property of, leased to, or managed by the Department in connection with the conservation of marine and estuarine resources. The jurisdiction of protectors extends to all matters within the Commission jurisdiction. The Commission is specifically granted jurisdiction over all aspects of: ▸ boating and water safety; ▸ hunting and trapping; ▸ fishing, exclusive of that under jurisdiction of the Marine Fisheries Commission; ▸ activities in woodlands and on inland waters governed by 112-60.1 and 112-60.3. Protectors also have jurisdiction over all offenses involving property of the Commission or occurring on wildlife refuges, game lands or boating/fishing access areas. ★Inspectors and protectors are additionally authorized to arrest without warrant under 15A-401(b) for felonies, breaches of the peace, assaults upon them or in their presence, and for other offenses evincing a flouting of their authority as enforcement officers or constituting a threat to public peace and order.★ They are authorized, subject to the direction of administrative superiors, to arrest for violations of 14-223, 14-225, 14-269, and 14-277. A protector has the authority to enforce criminal laws under the following circumstances, in addition to law enforcement authority granted elsewhere: when the protector has probable cause to believe a person committed a criminal offense in the protector's presence and at the time of the violation the protector is engaged in enforcement of laws otherwise within the protector's jurisdiction; the protector is asked to provide temporary assistance by the head of a state or local law enforcement agency and the request is within the scope of the agency's subject matter jurisdiction. When acting pursuant to this subsection, a protector shall have the same powers invested in law enforcement officers by statute or common law, but when acting pursuant to request of another agency a protector shall not be considered an officer, employee or agent for that state or local law enforcement agency. Nothing herein shall be construed to expand the authority of protectors to initiate or conduct an independent investigation into violations of criminal laws outside the scope of their subject matter or territorial jurisdiction (113-136). Inspectors and protectors: ▸may serve arrest warrants, search warrants, and other process connected with any cases within their jurisdiction, and are subject to provisions relating to police officers set out in Chapters 15, 15A, and elsewhere; ▸ are authorized to stop temporarily any persons reasonably believed to be engaging in activity regulated by their respective agencies to determine if such activity is being conducted lawfully, including license requirements. If the person is in a motor vehicle being driven at the time, and the inspector or protector is also in a motor vehicle, a siren or light must be activated before the stop. Protectors may not temporarily stop or inspect vehicles proceeding along primary state highways without clear evidence that someone within the vehicle is, or has recently been engaged in, a Commission-regulated activity. Refusal of any person to stop in obedience is unlawful and a fine of $50-$200, jail up to 30 days, or both. It is unlawful to refuse to exhibit upon request by a law enforcement officer any license, permit, or identification, or to refuse to allow inspection of weapons, equipment, fish or wildlife that the officer reasonably believes to be possessed incident to a regulated activity. Nothing herein authorizes searches within the curtilage of a dwelling or a vessel's living quarters in contravention of constitutional prohibitions (113-136).

Every inspector or protector who arrests a person for an offense is authorized to search the person arrested and the surrounding area for weapons and for fruits, instrumentalities and evidence of any crime. If a citation is issued instead of arrest, where arrest is authorized, the inspector or protector may seize all lawfully discovered evidence, fruits and instrumentalities of any crime as to which they have arrest jurisdiction and probable cause. When live fish are returned to public fishing waters, the citation shall state the quantity returned. Every inspector or protector who has probable cause for believing a violation has occurred may seize any fish, wildlife, weapons, equipment, vessels or other evidence of the crime notwithstanding the absence of any person in the immediate area subject to arrest or the inability of the inspector to capture the person guilty of the violation. Such seized property shall be returned to the owner who satisfies the Director that there was no knowledge or culpability.   ★The Commission may provide by rule for summary disposition of live or perishable fish or wildlife seized, including transport of live fish the distance necessary to effect placement in waters.★   Where the seizure consists of edible fish or wildlife which is not alive, may not live, or may not otherwise benefit conservation objectives if again released on lands or waters, the property must be disposed of in a charitable or noncommercial manner as the Commission regulates [extensive details of property seizure and confiscation and disposal or sale procedures are given]. Upon conviction of any defendant for a violation of laws or Commission rules, the court may order the confiscation of all weapons, equipment, vessels, conveyances, fish, wildlife and other evidence and fruits of the offense, to be sold or disposed of as authorized herein (113-137).

★The Commission by rule may confer law enforcement powers over wildlife matters within its jurisdiction upon USFW employees who: ▸ possess special law enforcement jurisdiction that would not otherwise extend to the subject matter herein; ▸ are assigned during the duration of such appointment to duty stations within North Carolina; ▸ take the oath required of public officers. Exercise of this authority shall be limited to situations when: the best interests of the conservation of wildlife resources managed by the respective state and federal agencies are being adversely affected by restrictions upon jurisdictional subject matter that limit law-enforcement authority; the best interest of the conservation of wildlife resources will benefit by conferring law enforcement authority on the USFW. The enabling rule shall specify the particular officers or class of officers upon whom the law enforcement powers are conferred and the geographic areas within which they can exercise such powers over matters within the Commission's jurisdiction, such powers to be used only during the scope of employment of the special conservation officers. Such special enforcement officers shall have the same jurisdiction and powers and the same rights, privileges and immunities as state officers, in addition to those the federal officer normally possesses (113-138).★   ★In enforcing the laws and rules within their jurisdiction, wildlife protectors may, under this section's criteria, issue warning tickets instead of initiating criminal prosecutions. A protector may issue a warning ticket only if all the following conditions are met: ▸ the protector is convinced that the offense was not intentional; ▸ the offense is not of a kind or committed in a manner as to which warning tickets have been prohibited; ▸ the offender's conduct was not calculated to result in any significant destruction of wildlife; ▸ the offender's conduct did not constitute a hazard to the public. A warning ticket may not be issued if the offender has previously been charged with or issued a warning ticket for a similar offense. The Director must institute a procedure to ensure an accurate accounting for, and recording of, all warning tickets issued before any are issued. This section does not entitle any person who has committed an offense with the right to be issued a warning ticket, nor restrict in any manner the powers of a wildlife protector in dealing with hunters or fishermen. Issuance of a warning ticket does not constitute evidence of the commission of an offense, but may be used to prevent issuance of a subsequent warning ticket for a similar offense (113-140).★

Criminal Penalties

It is unlawful, while hunting, to discharge a firearm carelessly and heedlessly in wanton disregard for the safety of others, or without due caution, and in a manner so as to endanger any person or property and resulting in property or bodily injury. Violation is a misdemeanor punishable as follows: if property damage only, a fine of $250-1,000, jail up to 60 days, or both, and the court shall order the payment of restitution to the property owner; if bodily injury not leading to disfigurement or total or partial permanent disability of another, fine of $500-2,000, jail up to two years, or both, and property restitution payment; if bodily injury leading to disfigurement or total/partial permanent disability results, a fine of $750-2,000, jail 15 days to two years, and property damage restitution; if death results, a fine of $1,000-2,000, jail 30 days to two years and property damage restitution.   ★The fact that a person was impaired at the time of a violation shall be an aggravating factor and the court shall impose an additional fine and/or imprisonment in accordance with the above. "Impaired" means being under the influence of an impairing substance or having consumed sufficient alcohol to test at .10. In addition, the Commission shall suspend all hunting privileges for one to five years as specified, depending on severity of the violation.★   A person convicted of hunting or taking wildlife while the person's hunting license is suspended shall be fined $500-2,000, jailed up to two years, or both, shall have all hunting privileges suspended for an additional five years, and shall be issued no new license until satisfactory completion of the hunter safety course. This article shall be enforced by law enforcement officers of the Commission, by sheriffs, deputy sheriffs, and peace officers with general subject matter jurisdiction. A violation resulting in the death of another person constitutes a separate and distinct offense from, and is not a lesser included offense of, the crime of involuntary manslaughter (113-290 and 290.1).

Any person who violates any provision of this Subchapter (Conservation of Marine and Estuarine and Wildlife Resources), or any rule adopted by the Commission, is guilty of a misdemeanor except that punishment for violation of Commission rules is limited under 113-135.1. Unless a different level of punishment is set out, anyone convicted of a misdemeanor under this section is punishable as follows: first conviction, fine of $25-100, or jail up to 30 days. For a second or subsequent conviction within one year, a fine of $100-500, jail up to 90 days, or both. ★★In interpreting this section, provisions in this Subchapter making an offense a misdemeanor "punishable in the discretion of the court" are considered to set a different level of punishment, to be interpreted under 14-3 or its equivalent statute. Noncriminal sanctions, however, such as license revocation or suspension, and exercise of powers auxiliary to criminal prosecution, such as seizure of property involved in the commission of an offense, do not constitute different levels of punishment. Any previous conviction under this Subchapter or rules serves to increase the punishment under the above, even though for a different offense than the second or subsequent one (113-135).★★ ★To prevent unsuspecting members of the public from being subject to harsh criminal penalties for offenses created by Commission rules, the penalty for a violation of Commission rules is limited to a fine of $10, except that offenses set out below are punished as set forth in 113-135 or other sections, and the limitation upon penalty does not apply to rule violations: ► punishable under 113-294 or otherwise involving aggravating elements which result in a greater punishment; ► which involve a defendant subject to the collection-license provisions of 113-272.4 or who is a dealer under 113-273; ► relating to seasons, bag limits, creel limits, taking fish other than with hook and line, buying or selling wildlife, possessing or transporting live wildlife, taking wildlife at night or with the aid of a conveyance, or falconry (113-135.1).★

It is unlawful to take or destroy fish or aquatic species being cultivated from an aquaculture facility without the owner's permission, or knowingly to possess same which have been stolen from such facility. Violation for fish or aquatic species valued at $400 or more is punishable under 14-72. Violation for fish valued at $400 or less is a misdemeanor; minimum fine of $500, jail up to one year, or both. Destruction of an aquaculture facility or the aquatic species therein is a misdemeanor; minimum fine of $1,000, jail a minimum of one year, or both. ★The sentencing judge, in deciding to impose any sentence other than an active prison sentence, shall consider and may require restitution to the victim for the amount of damage to the facility or aquatic species or for the value of the stolen fish or aquatic species (113-269).★

Civil Penalties

★To provide information to the courts and other officials taking action under statutes as specified, the Commission and the Marine Fisheries Commission are authorized to adopt rules setting forth the factors that should be considered in determining the replacement costs of fish and wildlife and other marine, estuarine and wildlife resources that have been taken, injured, removed, damaged or destroyed, and may make similar rules respecting costs of investigations required by statute or which are made pursuant to a court order. For common offenses resulting in the destruction of wildlife resources, the commissions may adopt schedules of costs which state the likely replacement costs and investigative costs, and such rules must be treated as prima facie evidence of the actual costs, but do not prevent a court or jury from examining the reasonableness of the regulations or from assessing the special factors in a case which may make the true costs either higher or lower than the amount stated in the rules. "Replacement costs" must be broadly construed to include indirect costs of replacement through habitat improvement or restoration, establishment of sanctuaries and other recognized conservation techniques when direct stocking or replacement is not feasible (113-267).★

Illegal Taking of Wildlife

The following violations are misdemeanors, to be punished as specified herein unless a greater penalty is prescribed: ► unlawful selling, possession for sale, buying of any wildlife - fine $50-500, jail up to 90 days, or both; ► unlawful sale, possession for sale, or buying any deer or wild turkey - minimum fine $250; ► unlawful taking, possession or transport of a wild turkey - minimum fine $250; ► unlawful taking, possession, transport, sale or purchase of any bear or bear part - minimum fine $2,000, jail up to two years, or both, and each act is a separate offense; ► unlawful taking, possession, transportation, sale or purchase of any cougar - minimum fine of $10,000, jail up to two years, or both; ► unlawful taking, possession or transport of a deer - minimum fine $100; ► unlawful taking of deer by spotlighting - minimum fine of $250; ▸ unlawful taking, possession, sale or transport of any beaver or violation of any Commission rule adopted to protect beavers - fine of $50-200, jail up to 90 days, or both; ▸ unlawful taking of wild animals or birds from a motorized vessel - $50-500 fine, jail up to 90 days, or both; ▸ wilfully making false statements to secure any license, permit, privilege or exemption - punishment at the court's discretion; ▸ violation of trap or trapping provisions under 113-291.6 - $50-200 fine, jail up to 90 days, or both; ▸ unlawful taking of a fox by trapping or with an electronic calling device - $50-200 fine, jail up to 90 days, or both; ▸ a subsequent offense relating to unlawful taking of foxes, including unlawful selling, possessing for sale, buying a fox, taking a fox by unlawful trapping or use of an electronic calling device to take a fox - minimum fine of $250; ▸ unlawful taking, possession, sale or transport of any bald eagle or golden eagle, alive or dead, or any part, nest or egg - fine up to $1,000, jail up to one year, or both; ▸ unlawful taking of a migratory game bird with a rifle, unlawful taking with the use of live decoys or bait, or taking during the closed season or during prohibited shooting hours or exceeding the bag or possession limits applicable to any migratory game bird - minimum fine of $150 in addition to any other penalty prescribed (113-294).

License Revocations, Suspensions

Upon conviction of any licensee or permittee for a violation of any law or Commission rule, the court in its discretion may order surrender of that license or permit plus any others issued by the Commission. The court may order suspension of any license/permit for some stipulated period or may order revocation of the remainder of any license or permit. Suspension may extend past the expiration date of the license, but no suspension longer than two years may be imposed. During suspension or revocation, the licensee/permittee is not entitled to purchase or apply for any replacement, renewal, or additional license/permit regulating the same activity. Upon conviction of any person not a licensee/permittee, the court may suspend the entitlement to possess or procure any specified licenses issued by the Commission for up to two years. It is a misdemeanor punishable at the court's discretion for any person during suspension or revocation to: ▸ engage in any activity licensed without the proper license or permit; ▸ apply for a license/permit to which they are not entitled; ▸ make any false or misleading statement in applying for a license/permit; ▸ counterfeit or falsify any application or license or permit; ▸ retain and use any license/permit which has been ordered revoked or suspended; ▸ circumvent the terms of suspension or revocation in any manner whatsoever (113-277).

★★Before issuing any license or permit to persons subject to administrative control as specified below, the Director must be satisfied that the person meets the qualifications set by statute, rule or administrative guidelines. The following provisions apply to: persons, other than individual hunters/fishermen taking wildlife as sportsmen, holding permits under this article; persons holding special device licenses, collection licenses, captivity licenses or dealer licenses. Before reissuing any license or permit to any person specified below, the Director must review all available information and apply the same standards that governed initial issuance. Upon refusing to issue/reissue a license/permit, the Director must notify the person in writing of the reasons and of the procedure for appeal. The Director shall revoke a license/permit if a person does not meet the qualifications required, has committed a substantial criminal violation of a statute or rule, or has seriously or persistently failed to comply with the terms and conditions upon which the license/permit was issued. Before revocation, the Director shall notify the licensee of intention by personal service, and of the person's right to commence a contested case. Upon revocation of a license or permit, the Director must request return of the license/permit and all associated paperwork and other Commission property required to be kept. In securing such property or closing out the affairs conducted under the license/permit, Commission agents may enter any premises at reasonable hours where wildlife resources or property pertaining to the license are kept, to inspect, audit, inventory, remove or take other action, and any wildlife resources in the person's possession which may no longer be possessed must be disposed of in accordance with 113-137. Failure to permit entry or surrender wildlife resources or other obstruction of a Commission agent is a misdemeanor and fine of $50-500, jail up to 90 days or both, and each day's violation is a separate offense. No person refused or revoked a license or permit is eligible to apply again for that or any similar license/permit for two years. The Director is required to make investigations and cause disclosure of information by all persons subject to administrative control in this category, to determine that the real party in interest is seeking or has been issued the license or permit. Any attempt to circumvent these provisions is a misdemeanor punishable at the court's discretion. If effective conservation of wildlife resources would be seriously impaired by continued unfettered operations or by continued possession of property by the persons covered herein, the Director may apply for a court order: ▸ imposing special reporting and inspections on the person; ▸ impounding records or other property associated with the license or permit; ▸ limiting the scope of operations thereunder; ▸ suspending the operations of the person if there is clear evidence of a serious threat to the conservation of wildlife resources; ▸ placing other appropriate restrictions upon the person (113-276.2). ★★

★★Any violation of laws or regulations relating to the conservation of wildlife resources which is subject to a penalty greater than the one provided in 113-135(a)(1) (misdemeanor: fine $10-50, or jail up to 30 days) is a suspension offense and results in a suspension for a period of one year. A conviction of any of the following suspension offenses results in a two-year suspension: ▸ unlawful sale, possession for sale or purchase of any deer or wild turkey; ▸ unlawful taking, possession or transportation of a wild turkey; ▸ unlawful night taking of deer by spotlighting; ▸ unlawful selling, possessing for sale or buying a fox, taking a fox by unlawful trapping, taking a fox with the aid of an electronic calling device. Unless otherwise provided, any action by a court under 113-277 to suspend or revoke a license or permit supersedes any suspension mandated by this section. If the judgment after a conviction for a suspension offense does not include any suspension or revocation action, this section applies. The presiding judge may order surrender of all applicable licenses and permits to a Commission agent, but if the judge fails to do so, or if there is for any other reason a failure by the defendant to surrender all applicable licenses/permits, a Commission agent must demand surrender. Each day's failure or refusal to surrender a license or permit upon demand, is a separate offense, and the court may institute contempt proceedings if a failure or refusal to surrender a license/permit also violates a court order. Agents accepting surrender of licenses/permits in the courtroom or subsequently must transmit them to the Director with a written notation of the date of surrender and other information the Director requires. The Director must institute a procedure for the systematic reporting by authorized Commission agents of all convictions of suspension offenses, and must determine if all appropriate licenses and permits have been surrendered; if not, the Director must notify the Commission agent to demand surrender or renew a demand for surrender. Upon satisfying himself that all licenses and permits have been received for which surrender may feasibly be obtained, the Director must mail the defendant a notice of the suspension of defendant's entitlement to possess or procure any license/permit (113-276.3). ★★ (See also Licenses and Permits and Restrictions on Taking under HUNTING, FISHING, TRAPPING PROVISIONS.)

HABITAT PROTECTION

At least once each year, the Secretary, the Chairperson of the Commission, and the Commissioner of Agriculture shall propose to the Recreation and Natural Heritage Trust Fund Board of Trustees lands to be acquired from the National Heritage Trust Fund (see also Agency Funding Sources and Agency Advisory Boards under STATE FISH AND WILDLIFE AGENCIES). For each tract or interest proposed, they shall provide the Trustees with the following information: ▸ value of the land for recreation, forestry, fish and wildlife habitat, and wilderness purposes and its consistency with the plan developed under the State Parks Act; ▸ any rare or endangered species on or near the land; ▸ whether the land contains a relatively undisturbed and outstanding example of a native ecological community that is now uncommon in the state; ▸ whether the land contains other river, landscape, geologic, wetland or other land features as specified, or has historic significance; ▸ other sources of funds available to assist in acquiring the land; ▸ the state agency that will manage the land; ▸ what assurances exist that the land will not be used for purposes other than those for which it is being acquired. The Trustees may authorize expenditures to acquire land that represents the ecological diversity of the state, including natural features and areas to ensure their preservation and conservation, and as additions to the system of parks, state trails, forests, fish and wildlife management areas, wild and scenic rivers and natural areas for public use [other details of land acquisition procedure are provided]. ★No provision of this article shall be construed to eliminate hunting and fishing, as regulated, upon properties purchased pursuant to this article (113-77.9). ★

★No person may obstruct, pollute or diminish the natural flow of water into or through any fish hatchery in violation of Environmental Management Commission requirements. It is unlawful to throw into the channel of any navigable waters fish offal likely to hinder the passage of fish. The Commission may impose further restrictions upon the throwing of fish offal in any inland fishing waters (113-265). ★1

NATIVE AMERICAN WILDLIFE PROVISIONS

See Licenses and Permits under HUNTING, FISHING, TRAPPING PROVISIONS.

NORTH DAKOTA

Sources: North Dakota Century Code, 1991, Title 20.1; 1992 Special Supplement.

STATE WILDLIFE POLICY

The ownership of and title to all wildlife within this state is in the state for the purpose of regulating the enjoyment, use, possession, disposition, and conservation thereof, and for maintaining action for damages as herein provided. Any person catching, killing, taking, trapping, or possessing any wildlife protected by law at any time or in any manner is deemed to have consented that the title thereto remains in this state for the purpose of regulating the taking, use, possession, and disposition thereof (20.1-01-03).

RELEVANT WILDLIFE DEFINITIONS: See Definitions section of Appendices.

STATE FISH AND WILDLIFE AGENCIES

Agency Structure

The Governor appoints the **Director of the Game and Fish Department** (Director) for a term of four years. The Director is subject to removal by the Governor for cause only and must be bonded by $10,000 (20.1-02-01 and -02). The Director shall appoint a **Deputy Director** who is under the Director's control and supervision (20.1-02-06). The Director, with the Governor's approval, may appoint: a **Chief Game Warden** who shall enforce all state game and fish laws and supervise all **Deputy Game Wardens; District Deputy Game Wardens** to enforce all state game and fish laws within specific appropriation limitations; biologists and technicians with specialized training and experience (20.1-02-07). The Director may appoint one or more **Special Deputy Game Wardens** in each county who serve without compensation but are entitled to a reward pursuant to section 20.1-02-16 (20.1-02-10). ★No person owning land in this state under lease or contract for hunting purposes, nor the person's employees or agents, may be appointed as chief, district or special deputy game wardens (20.1-02-13).★

Agency Powers and Duties

The **Director** shall: ▸ enforce state laws involving wildlife; ▸ collect and distribute statistics and information germane to this title and publish a monthly bulletin for the education of the public in conservation matters; ▸ examine all state waters and arrange to plant, stock or deposit available fish, spawn or fry in suitable waters; ▸ remove from public waters any surplus of fish for stocking other public waters, propagation purposes, or exchange with other states; ▸ control and construct state fish hatcheries, state game farms, game refuges and game reserves owned, leased or controlled for the propagation and protection of game birds, game animals and fish; ▸ assist clubs and individuals in fish stocking endeavors; ▸ supervise the breeding, propagation, capture, distribution and preservation of game birds, game animals and fish; ▸ adopt rules for carrying out section 20.1-10-01, which have the force of law after one publication in daily state newspapers; ▸ keep records of all permits issued for propagation and domestication of game birds or protected animals; ▸ provide and distribute license forms; ▸ cooperate with USFW to apply for fish, spawn and fry for stocking state waters (20.1-02-04).

The Director may: ▸ gather or purchase fish, spawn or fry for distribution in state waters; ▸ take alive birds or animals for propagation or for exchange with other states and foreign countries for game birds and animals of other species; ▸ order additional protection for any fish with an open season when the Director finds danger of extinction, undue depletion in any waters, or to aid in the propagation and protection of immature fish, by prescribing how, how many, when and where the fish may be taken, such orders to have the force of law; ▸ take at any time from state waters any suckers, carp or pickerel; ▸ purchase, lease, condemn or sell lands; ▸ conduct lease agreements for land improvements for recreation purposes; ▸ secure specimens of game birds, animals and fish for breeding by purchase or otherwise and by exchange with other states; ▸ issue special permits to handicapped persons to shoot from stationary vehicles or to use a crossbow for hunting game; ▸ adopt rules and issue permits for the transporting or introducing of fish, fish eggs, small game, big game or fur-bearers after inspection for disease and determining that the transplanting or introduction will be in compliance with state law; ▸ cooperate with the Commissioner of Agriculture and USWF in the destruction of predatory animals, destructive birds and injurious field rodents; ▸ adopt rules in accordance with plans of the Department of the Interior for the destruction of these birds and animals, including issuance of permits, and rules and regulations for the use of private aircraft to assist in this destruction and to aid in the administration or protection of land, water, wildlife, livestock, domesticated animals, human life or crops; ▸ establish programs and administer state and federal funds for preservation and management of resident species threatened or endangered in compliance with the Endangered Species Act of 1973; ▸ provide for the funding of a private land habitat improvement program with moneys derived from the interest earned on the Game and Fish Fund; ★▸ carry out a private land habitat improvement program by entering into cost-sharing agreements with landowners to help defray all or a portion of their share of federally sponsored conservation practices considered beneficial to fish and wildlife, annual leasing of fish and wildlife habitat or sport fishing areas on private lands and carrying out practices that will alleviate depredations caused by predatory animals and big game animals; ★ ▸ lease and exchange lands for improved management of wildlife resources; ▸ adopt rules and issue permits for fishing contests; ★▸ issue up to 50 complimentary fishing licenses per year to nonresident visiting dignitaries to promote economic development; ★ ▸ carry out a coyote depredation prevention program by conducting practices that will alleviate depredations caused by coyotes; ▸ establish noncriminal penalties for any rules adopted by the Director, the maximum penalty to be a fine of $250, other nondesignated rule violations to be considered criminal violations (20.1-02-05).

★The **Chief Game Warden** shall keep a complete record of transactions and of the name of each person violating the game and fish laws, the date of that person's arrest and the name of the judge before whom that person appeared, such record book to be open to inspection by the public (20.1-02-09).★

Orders and Proclamations of the Governor

The Governor may by order: ▸ vary statutory open and closed seasons whenever a species of wildlife for which an open season is provided is in danger of depletion or extinction, or for protection during the propagation period; ▸ declare an open season on a wildlife species which has become sufficient in numbers to warrant such; ▸ declare an open season or extend the season on fur-bearing animals which have become sufficient in numbers to warrant an open season or have become a menace to other species of wildlife; ▸ close, postpone or reopen any hunting seasons due to climatic conditions upon reasonable notice through the media. Any order or proclamation issued by the Governor pursuant to this chapter has the force of law. Violation for which a noncriminal penalty is not provided: class B misdemeanor (20.1-08-01 and -.02). ★The Governor may not establish bag limits on upland game birds which exceed 15 birds in the aggregate. A gubanatorial order under this chapter must prescribe, for each wildlife species named therein, the manner, numbers, places, and times at which they may be taken and possessed. The Governor may determine the: ▸ number of resident and nonresident big game licenses to be issued for the taking of each species, age or sex; ▸ manner of license issuance; ▸ issuance of special permits to hunt big game in certain restricted areas designating species to be hunted and boundaries of the restricted area; ▸ number of permits to be issued, procedure of selecting successful permit applicants, manner and times in which the big game may be taken (20.1-08-03 and -04).★

★The Governor by proclamation may provide for a bighorn sheep season and determine the manner, number, places and times for taking, licenses to be issued by lottery to residents only or auctioned to the highest bidder, resident or nonresident.★ Bighorn sheep licensees are not eligible to apply for another such license. The Governor by proclamation may also: ▸ provide for a similar season for residents to hunt moose, such licensees being not eligible to apply for another such license; ▸ regulate the use of fishhouses, darkhouses, underwater spearfishing and set areas and seasons for each (20.1-08-04.1 and -04.2). The Governor shall by proclamation provide for a one-week muzzleloading deer season following the regular firearms deer season with a maximum of 700 licenses to be issued by the Director by lottery (20.1-08-04.5). The Governor may also by proclamation provide for an elk season regulating the manner, number, places and times for hunting, such licenses to be issued by lottery for residents only, and ★may make available to the Rocky Mountain Elk Foundation a resident license to hunt elk, the license to be raffled, with only 10% of the gross proceeds to be used for promotion and all net proceeds to be used for elk management and related projects. A person may only receive one license to hunt elk issued by lottery and one Rocky Mountain Elk Foundation raffle license in a lifetime (20.1-08-04.6).★

Notwithstanding any other provision, the Governor by proclamation may provide for the taking of any wildlife, protected or unprotected, determined to be a harmful predator, in a manner and number, at any place, and during any time, including after dark (20.1-08-04.7). A summary of each order or proclamation issued by the Governor must be published once in the official newspaper of each affected county, including species that may be harvested, season dates, bag and possession limits, and changes from the previous year or hunting units. No order becomes effective until a copy is distributed to each county auditor affected (20.1-08-05).

Agency Funding Sources

All income of the Game and Fish Department must be credited to the **State Game and Fish Fund**, to be used only by the Department. There is a **Nongame Wildlife Fund** to be expended subject to appropriation by the Legislative Assembly, to be used by the Department for preservation, inventory, perpetuation, and conservation of nongame wildlife, natural areas, and nature preserves (20.1-02-16.1 and -16.2). (See RELEVANT WILDLIFE DEFINITIONS.) ★★There is a **Small and Big Game Habitat Restoration Trust Fund** to further farmer-sportsmen relations and enhance small and big game habitat by providing funds for the leasing of private land to establish or preserve small and big game habitat and food plot development, and to carry out a private land habitat improvement program by entering into cost-sharing agreements with landowners or agencies working on private land to help defray portions of their share of costs of federally sponsored conservation practices considered especially beneficial to small and big game.★★ No more than 40 acres per owner may be leased. No land may be purchased with trust fund moneys under this program, nor funds used for administrative purposes. The amount of $100,000 must be transferred annually from the State Game and Fish Fund to the Small and Big Game Habitat Restoration Trust Fund. A **Clam Harvesting Privilege Fee** of ten percent of the market value of clam shells harvested in the state is imposed, for deposit in the State Game and Fish Fund, and to be regulated by rules adopted by the Director (20.1-02-16.3 and -16.4). (See also Other License Provisions under HUNTER, FISHING, TRAPPING PROVISIONS.)

Agency Advisory Boards

★The **Private Land Habitat Improvement Program Advisory Committee** shall advise the Director concerning expenditures from the Small and Big Game Habitat Restoration Trust Fund. Members of the advisory committee must be state residents and serve without pay (20.1-02-16.3).★ ★The **Wetlands Mediation Advisory Board** consists of the Governor as chairman; the Director; the Commissioner of Agriculture; the presidents of the North Dakota Farmers Union, the North Dakota Farm Bureau, and the North Dakota National Farmers Organization; the state engineer of the Water Commission; the USFW Regional Director; the executive director of the State Association of Counties; and the executive vice president of the State Association of Soil Conservation Districts. Persons aggrieved by a decision of the USFW pertaining to wetlands may petition the Governor for aid after all administrative remedies have been exhausted.★ The Wetlands Mediation Advisory Board shall mediate the dispute or conflict and may hold hearings to receive evidence from all interested parties upon not less than ten days written notice. The Board shall make a recommendation to the Governor and the Regional Director of the USFW within 30 days of submission of the dispute; such recommendation is not subject to judicial review (20.1-02-18.4 and -18.6).

★★The **Game and Fish Advisory Board** consists of eight members, one from each of eight designated districts within the state, appointed by the Governor, and four members, each of which must be farmers/ranchers and sportspeople. Each farmer or rancher appointment must be made from a list of three names submitted by agricultural organizations as requested by the Governor and each sportsperson appointment must be made from a list of three names submitted by outdoor, sportspersons, wildlife and conservation organizations requested by the Governor to submit the list. Terms are for four years. Each Board member shall hold a public meeting at least twice a year in their district to determine the needs and opinions of their constituents. The Board has the authority to advise the Director regarding any policy of hunting, fishing, and trapping regulations and may make general recommendations concerning the operation of the Department and its programs. The Board shall forward its recommendations to the Governor, but this shall not restrict the Governor in the issuance of orders and proclamations as provided in 20.1-08 (20.1-02-23 and -25).★★

PROTECTED SPECIES OF WILDLIFE

No person without a permit shall kill, catch, take, ship, purchase or possess, any harmless wild bird, or part, whether it was captured or killed in or out of this state. Imported songbirds used as domestic pets may be bought, sold, shipped, ir possessed. No person, without a permit from the Director, may take, possess, break up or destroy, or interfere with the nest or eggs of any bird, the killing of which is prohibited. No person may take, kill, hunt, possess, sell, purchase, pursue, shoot at, disturb, capture or destroy any golden eagle, bald eagle, or any nest or egg thereof, within North Dakota (20.1-04-03 through -05). (See also RELEVANT WILDLIFE DEFINITIONS.)

GENERAL EXCEPTIONS TO PROTECTION

See Orders and Proclamations of the Governor under STATE FISH AND WILDLIFE AGENCIES.

HUNTING, FISHING, TRAPPING PROVISIONS

Licenses and Permits

No person born after December 31, 1961, may be issued any hunting license without a certificate of completion of a hunter safety course containing instruction on firearm and bow safety and hunter responsibility, or a certificate issued by any other state or province of Canada. Violation: class 2 noncriminal offense (20.1-03-01.1 through -01.3). A general game license plus a specific license is required for any resident or nonresident to hunt, catch, take or kill any small game or big game animal. A resident small game or resident fur-bearer license or fishing license or big game license is required to hunt, catch, take or kill small game, fish, big game or fur-bearer by state residents. Each violation of this section is a distinct and separate offense. Residents and family members residing with them may hunt small game, fish or trap during the open season on their own lands (20.1-03-02 through -04). No resident frog license is required for: ▸ persons taking frogs during open season on their own agricultural lands; ▸ residents under age 15, a maximum of 24 frogs each for resident fishing license holders; ▸ licensed bait vendors who take, buy, or ship frogs within the state for angling (20.1-03-04.1). Residents having a hunting, fishing or fur-bearer license and lawfully possessing big game, small game, fur-bearer or fish may ship or carry such game or fish to their residential address (20.1-03-24). Properly tagged and identified big game, small game, fur-bearers or fish may be carried or shipped by nonresidents who have licenses and are lawfully in possession of such game or fish (20.1-03-25).

No person shall hunt, kill, take or attempt to take big game without a big game hunting license and a locking seal/tag corresponding to the number of the big game hunting license or stamp. Big game hunting licenses may not be issued to persons under age 14 except for bow and arrow. Each violation is a separate offense. ★The number of licenses issued shall not exceed the number of licenses authorized by the Governor's proclamation.★ Persons who lease or own land for agricultural purposes of at least 1/4 section in acreage, within a district open to hunting of deer, elk or antelope may be issued without charge a license for these animals to be hunted only upon the described lands. Persons who are permanently unable to walk and who have a license to take deer may take any sex or species of deer in their assigned hunting areas. [Other restrictions apply regarding lotteries, land areas to be open, and number of available licenses (20.1-03-11).] ★Special white-tailed deer licenses may be available to guides or outfitters which may be sold to nonresidents along with outfitting services with specified restrictions (20.1-03-11.2).★ An applicant for a license/permit to hunt elk, moose, bighorn sheep, or antelope must be assessed a nonrefundable application fee for each license/permit in addition to license/permit issuance fee (20.1-03-12.2). (See Orders and Proclamations of the Governor under STATE FISH AND WILDLIFE AGENCIES.)

★A habitat restoration stamp is required for every resident and nonresident general game license, in addition to the annual general game license fee. No land may be purchased with habitat restoration stamp moneys. All money from the habitat restoration stamp program goes into a special fund to lease privately owned lands for wildlife habitat, and not more than 10% of the fund may be used for administrative purposes. Any land needed for reestablishing the wildlife population and habitat may be leased for up to 6 years, but no more than 40 acres in any section of land may be leased for these purposes. Hunting may not be prohibited on these lands. In those districts encompassing the historically prime pheasant range, as determined by the Director, 50% of the expenditures must be for pheasant restoration and enhancement (20.1-03-12.1).★ (See also Agency Funding Sources under STATE FISH AND WILDLIFE AGENCIES.)

Restrictions on Taking: Hunting and Trapping

Except as otherwise provided, no person, for the purpose of catching, taking, killing, or raising any game birds or game animals may: ▸ set, lay or prepare any trap, snare, artificial light, net, birdlime, or swivel gun, except that the use of snares for taking coyotes is allowed under 20.1-07-03.1; ▸ drag any wire, rope or other contrivance; ▸ use, except for transportation, any floating device operated by electricity, steam or gasoline or any other floating vessel (20.1-01-05). No person may be afield with a firearm or a bow and arrow while intoxicated or under the influence of alcoholic beverages or drugs. Violation: voiding of hunting license. Game wardens, including special wardens, have the authority of a general peace officer in the enforcement of this section. A person convicted of a subsequent offense is ineligible for a hunting license for two years (20.1-01-06). Except for handicapped hunters with permits, no person, while hunting big or small game, other than waterfowl or cranes, may: ▸ use a motor-driven vehicle on land other than an established road or trail unless retrieving a big game animal reduced to possession; ▸ drive, run, molest, flush or harass such game with the use or aid of a motor vehicle; ▸ drive through retired cropland, brush area, slough area, timber area, open prairie, or unharvested or harvested cropland, except upon an established road or trail (20.1-01-07).

It is unlawful to pursue, shoot, kill or take wildlife between sunset and sunrise with the aid of a spotlight or other artificial light, except it is lawful to use a lantern, spotlight or other artificial light in pursuing on one's own premises any coyote, fox, skunk, mink, raccoon, weasel, owl, rabbit or other predatory animal or bird, attacking or destroying poultry, livestock or other property, and it is lawful to use a two cell, four volt light while hunting afoot for raccoon during the open season, such light to have a red or amber filter, except when taking a raccoon treed or at bay (20.1-01-08). In taking raccoon with use of such a flashlight, it is illegal to use a rifle or handgun larger than .22 caliber long rifle or four-ten gauge. Violation: class 1 noncriminal offense (20.1-01-09). No person operating an aircraft or motor vehicle or a snowmobile may intentionally kill, chase or harass any wild animal or wild bird, protected or unprotected, except for the protection of life or property (20.1-01-11).

Landowners may post their land against hunting with signs showing their name, placed no more than 880 yards apart, or at all gates on enclosed lands (20.1-01-17). No person may hunt or pursue game, or trap, or enter for those purposes, upon legally posted land without the landowner's written permission (20.1-01-18). Proof that persons having firearms or other legal weapons in their possession entered upon legally posted premises of another without permission is prima facie evidence they entered to hunt or pursue game (20.1-01-20). No person may hunt or pursue game upon the premises of another within 440 yards of any occupied building without occupant's consent (20.1-01-21). ★It is unlawful to hunt or pursue game in unharvested cereal crops without the owner's permission, including crops of alfalfa, clover and other seed grasses (20.1-01-22). No person may hunt birds resting on utility lines or fixtures adjacent to such lines (20.1-01-22.1). It is illegal to open gates or bars in a fence enclosing farm premises without closing them. Violation: class B misdemeanor and hunting license forfeiture for the remainder of the hunting season. A summary of these provisions must be printed on each general game and fur-bearer license (20.1-01-23).★ No person may destroy, molest, disturb, or tamper willfully with a net, trap, crib, or other contrivance being used by the Department for catching or holding wildlife, nor remove any wildlife from such net, trap or contrivance (20.1-01-25.1).

Nothing in this title prohibits the use of any part of a legally taken game bird for decorative purposes or in the making of art works for private use or sale, except that any part of a legally taken migratory bird may not be sold except as provided under federal regulations (20.1-04-02.1). No person may possess, control, ship, can, or otherwise preserve more than the number authorized in the Governor's proclamation of any species of game bird, but properly tagged game birds legally taken out of state may be possessed, transported or shipped in state (20.1-04-06). The Governor may provide for a permit season to take wild turkeys in the manner, number, places and times deemed in state's best interest (20.1-04-07). Wild ducks and geese may be taken: ▸ in the open or from a stationary natural or artificial blind on land or water except a sinkbox; ▸ from a floating craft if it is beached or tied to a fixed hunting blind or resting at anchor if authorized by governor's proclamation (excluding sinkboxes); ▸ with the aid of artificial decoys. The use of live duck or goose decoys is not permitted (20.1-04-11). Violation of falconry provisions: class B misdemeanor (20.1-14-01). The Department shall make rules and regulations governing the issuance and use of falconry licenses and in compliance with federal regulations. The Department may revoke a falconry license and seize the raptors pursuant thereto if the licensee fails to provide proper raptor care; allows raptors to become a public nuisance; violates rules, regulations or statutes relating to falconry; fails to abide with statutes and rules applicable to the hunting of the game taken (20.1-14-03).

No person may hunt, harass, chase, pursue, take, possess, ship, sell or exchange any big game animal except as provided in this title (20.1-05-02). Violation of big game provisions or regulations: class A misdemeanor (20.1-05-01). A district game warden may kill an unattended dog harassing or killing big game (20.1-05-02.1). A big game license allows a person to take, kill and transport, during the open season, one big game animal in the state. Transportation, shipment and possession within the state of big game legally taken in other states is allowed if properly tagged (20.1-05-03). In taking big game animals, it is unlawful to: ‣ use any animal except horses or mules; ‣ use any artificial light, including spotlights and automobile and motorcycle headlights; ‣ engage in shining for deer. A person who shines an area commonly frequented by big game animals with an artificial light is in violation. Proof that a person was found between sunset and sunrise possessing a firearm, trap, snare, or artificial light useful in the taking of big game animals in territory where big game animals are frequently found is prima facie evidence of hunting illegally (20.1-05-05). A person who is totally or partially blind and who holds a valid big game hunting license may be accompanied by and have a person designated on the license who is otherwise qualified to hunt big game for that individual (20.1-05-08).

Persons or firms raising and owning any protected fur-bearing animal, or in the possession of the pelt of any wild animal lawfully obtained, have the same property rights therein as enjoyed by owners of domestic animals, subject to rules of the Director regarding the introduction and release into the state of the animals (20.1-07-02). No person may hunt, shoot, trap or take in this state any fur-bearer, except during the open or lawful season (20.1-07-03). Violation for which a penalty is not specifically provided: class B misdemeanor (20.1-07-01). It is unlawful to molest or destroy the natural burrow, den, or retreat of any protected fur-bearer, or to damage or injure the property of another while taking a fur-bearer. The Governor, on the Director's advice, may by proclamation determine the manner in which fur-bearing animals may be taken. Violation: class 2 noncriminal offense (20.1-07-05). No person may unlawfully kill, take, possess, buy, sell or dispose of a fur-bearing animal or part, take a fur-bearer outside a regularly prescribed season or without a license. Each violation is a distinct and separate offense (20.1-07-06).

★The Governor shall establish by proclamation an upland snaring season for the taking of coyotes. No person may set a snare for coyotes without the written permission of the landowner. Snares must have owner identification attached by a tag. The Director shall establish and publish in pamphlet form safety standards for snares used in taking coyotes which will prevent the accidental holding of deer and other animals, these standards to be followed by a person using a coyote snare (20.1-07-03.1).★

Restrictions on Taking: Fishing

No person may take, catch, kill or destroy any species of fish in this state except as provided in this title. ★A person who takes into possession and kills or destroys any paddlefish or pallid sturgeon in violation of this title is guilty of a class C felony.★ It is unlawful to take, catch, kill or possess any fish smaller than that prescribed by the Governor's proclamation. No person except as elsewhere provided may set, use, or have in possession any setnets, seines, setlines or fishtraps, which are considered to be public nuisances, and any peace officer or warden shall, without warrant or process, seize and hold them subject to court order. No person may lay, set or use any drug, poison, lime, medicated bait, fishberries, dynamite or other injurious substance whatever; or lay, stretch, or place any tip-up snare, trap, set or trotline, wire string, rope, or cable of any sort in state waters for catching, killing, or taking fish. License holders may use a minnow net or trap for personal bait use, and dip nets may be used to land legally taken fish. Ice fishhouses must be licensed and tagged with owners name. Violation: class 2 noncriminal offense. Spearfishing is allowed from licensed darkhouses through the ice. It is illegal to deposit any refuse or other matter which may prove harmful to fish or fish eggs in waters where the state or federal government has deposited or may deposit fish, fish eggs, or fry, or in which fish naturally abound, except as municipalities are authorized to dispose of sewage. Fish abounding in state waters, and legally caught out of state, may be possessed, transported or shipped in state with evidence that they were legally caught. Violation where a penalty is not specifically provided: class B misdemeanor (20.1-06-01 through -11).

Commercial and Private Enterprises

A person operating a private fish hatchery is not subject to fishing seasons, limits, legal size restrictions or other methods of taking fish, except as the Governor shall set operating regulations. No license is required to take fish by angling at a licensed private fish hatchery. A private hatchery license may be suspended for noncompliance with the Director's regulations. A person, firm, or corporation raising and owning lawfully possessed fish, wild by nature,

North Dakota

has the same property rights therein as enjoyed by owners of domestic fish, but are subject to rules adopted by the Director regarding the introduction and release into the state, as provided in 20.1-02-05(14) (20.1-06-12 and -13).

Permits to propagate, domesticate or possess protected birds or animals may be issued by the Director to any resident. One permit may cover several species of birds or animals, but a single permit may not cover both birds and animals. No person may possess a live protected animal or bird without a permit. Permits must specify premises where animals will be kept, number and kind of birds or animals in possession at the time of application, whether they are wild or domesticated and any other information the Director requires. Annual reports to the Director are required of permittees. Protected birds or animals held for propagation and domestication under a permit may be sold or transported live for propagation. Their eggs may be collected, sold, or transported during prescribed seasons. Collections, sales and shipments must be with the Director's written permission. Protected birds or animals raised in North Dakota under a propagation permit may be disposed of or used as food when tagged properly or under the written permission and conditions the Director prescribes (20.1-09-02 through -05).

Commercial taking of turtles by trapping or hooking requires a Director's permit which shall state valid waters and other restrictions. The taking of frogs for sale for human consumption or scientific purposes requires a frog license. It is unlawful to take frogs on private land without written permission of the owner (20.1-06-16 and -17).

A person who desires to establish a shooting preserve may apply to the Director for a permit. The acreage amounts must include lands used for hatching, game production areas or headquarters areas. [Details of stock provided.] All game birds released must be marked, and mallard ducks must have right hind toenails clipped before release. The season for shooting preserves may be all or part of the seven-month period from September to the end of March. Boundaries of preserves must be posted. Preserve operators may set restrictions on the age, sex and number of game birds to be taken by each guest, fees to be paid, and hours of hunting subject to gubanatorial proclamation. Permittees must agree to reasonable inspections by law enforcement or game and fish personnel. Birds taken on the preserve must be tagged before removal from premises, and must be distinguishable from wild birds (20.1-12-02 through -06). Twenty percent of the game birds released on any preserve must remain unharvested, and the operation of the preserve must cease after 80% of the birds released have been harvested until more birds have been released (20.1-12-06.1). Violation of shooting preserve provisions for which another penalty is not specifically provided: class B misdemeanor (20.1-12-01).

Import, Export and Release Provisions

No person may transplant or introduce fish or fish eggs into state public waters, or transplant or introduce any species of small game, big game or fur-bearers into this state without a permit (20.1-02-05). (See also Commercial and Private Enterprise Provisions under HUNTING, FISHING, TRAPPING PROVISIONS, STATE FISH AND WILDLIFE AGENCIES, and PROTECTED SPECIES OF WILDLIFE.)

ANIMAL DAMAGE CONTROL

A person may kill any harmful wild bird during daylight hours. A propane exploder or similar noisemaking device designed to ward off blackbirds which is located within 160 rods (804.67 meters) of an inhabited dwelling may be used only during daylight hours. Violation: class 2 noncriminal offense (20.1-04-13 and -14). The Director or a designee may kill or take fish from state waters in any manner prescribed by the Director when in the best interest of public fishing, all such fish to be disposed of at the Director's discretion, and moneys to go to the Game and Fish Fund (20.1-06-05). The Director has authority to contract with a person to remove turtles from state waters or areas, moneys to go to the Game and Fish Fund (20.1-06-16). A landowner, tenant or agent may catch or kill any wild fur-bearing animal that is committing depredations upon that person's poultry, domestic animals, or crops, but the person shall notify and obtain the approval of the Commissioner before catching or killing a mountain lion or black bear. Except as provided in this section, a landowner may not commercialize in, sell or ship an animal or pelt or any part of an animal caught or killed under this section during the closed season. The landowner may possess a mountain lion or black bear killed under this section (20.1-07-04). The Director, with the consent of the refuge owner or lessee, may designate a game warden or other person to destroy, subject to regulations, predatory birds or animals within a state game refuge (20.1-11-08). (See also Orders and Proclamations of the Governor and Agency Powers and Duties under STATE FISH AND WILDLIFE AGENCIES; HUNTING, FISHING, TRAPPING PROVISIONS; and HABITAT PROTECTION.)

ENFORCEMENT OF WILDLIFE LAWS

Enforcement Powers

The Director, Deputy Director and any bonded appointees of the Director have the powers of peace officers for enforcing this title and other state wildlife laws or rules; to make arrests upon view and without warrant for any violation, committed in that person's presence, of this title and other state wildlife laws or rules; to regulate dealers in green furs, propagation or possession of live protected wildlife, taxidermists, shooting preserves, guides, commercial fishing, private fish hatcheries and commercial bait vendors (20.1-02-15). The Director, Deputy Director, Chief Game Wardens or District Game Wardens have the powers of peace officers to enforce state laws and rules on any game refuge, game management area or other land or water owned or managed by the Department; to respond to requests from other law enforcement agencies for aid and assistance in the case of particular violations (20.1-02-15.1).

Civil Penalties

The office of the attorney general may institute and maintain any action for damages against any person who unlawfully causes the death, destruction or injury of wildlife, except as authorized by law. The state has a property interest in all protected wildlife. This interest supports a civil action for damages for the unlawful destruction of wildlife by willful or grossly negligent act or omission. The Director shall adopt by rule a schedule of monetary values of various species of wildlife to represent the replacement costs and the value lost to the state due to the destruction or injury of the species, together with other material elements of value. The schedule constitutes the measure of recovery for wildlife killed or destroyed in any action brought under this section. Funds recovered go into the general fund to be devoted to the propagation and protection of desirable species of wildlife (20.1-01-03).

Penalties

The fees required for a noncriminal disposition pursuant to sections 20.1-01-28 and 20.1-01-29 are: a class 1 noncriminal offense, $50; class 2 noncriminal offense, $25; violation of a rule of the Director or of an order or proclamation issued by the Governor, the amount set in the rule or order, up to a maximum of $250 (20.1-01-30). Violation of rules governing endangered and threatened species: class B misdemeanor (20.1-02-05). Violation of license and permit provisions for which another penalty is not specifically provided: class B misdemeanor (20.1-03-01). A person who has been cited for a violation that is designated as a noncriminal offense in this title or in related rules/proclamations may appear before a court and pay the statutory fee at or prior to the time scheduled for a hearing, or may forfeit any posted bond, which must be identical to the statutory fee established by section 20.1-01-30. A person appearing at a scheduled hearing may explain, and the judge may waive, reduce or suspend the statutory fee or bond, or both (20.1-01-28).

Illegal Taking of Wildlife

Possession or control by a person of wildlife, or any part, the killing, taking, or possessing of which is unlawful, is prima facie evidence the wildlife was caught, taken or killed in violation of this title. No person may knowingly aid in the concealment of game that has been unlawfully taken or possessed. No person may hire another person to hunt small or big game for him, nor may a person hunt small game or big game for another for remuneration (20.1-01-12 through -14). No transportation company or common carrier may receive for transportation protected game birds, animals, or fish except during the open season on such birds, animals or fish (20.1-01-16). ★Any person who brings into this state any mounted trophy head or horns, has any trophy head or horns mounted in this state, or comes into possession of any horns of dall sheep, stone sheep, desert bighorn sheep, or rocky mountain bighorn sheep shall have the trophy head or horns plugged or tagged by the Department. Trophy heads plugged in Canada or Mexico where the sheep were taken satisfy the requirements of this section (20.1-02-26).★

The Director, Deputy Director, or any bonded game warden shall seize all wild birds, wild animals or fish or any part thereof, taken, killed, or possessed or transported contrary to law, and shall seize all dogs, guns, seines, nets, boats, lights, vehicles, and devices unlawfully used or held with intent to be used in pursuing, taking, or attempting to take, concealing or disposing of wild birds, wild animals or fish, or any part thereof. Property used or held with the intent to be used unlawfully in pursuing, taking, concealing wild birds, wild animals or fish may not be confiscated when the violation is a noncriminal offense. Property seized must be held subject to court order. Wildlife packed or commingled with contraband wildlife must be confiscated along with the contraband wildlife or parts. Courts may order the disposition of all birds, animals or fish or parts, or other property that has been confiscated after notice and hearing and a finding by the court that the property was taken, killed, possessed or transported contrary to law; was being used in violation of this title at the time it was seized; had been used in violation of this title within six months previous to the time it was seized (20.1-10-01 through -03).

Confiscated property that a court has ordered to be disposed of by the Director must be turned over to the North Dakota Wildlife Federation to be sold for the highest price obtainable. Sale proceeds are to be remitted to the North Dakota Wildlife Federation Report All Poachers Fund. Perishable property confiscated may be sold without a court order by the officer making the seizure for the highest price obtainable, with proceeds deposited in court to await case disposition. A person may make a complaint to a judge having authority to issue warrants in criminal cases that they know or have good reason to believe that wildlife or parts taken, killed or possessed contrary to this title are concealed in a particular house or place, and the judge may issue a search warrant on reasonable cause to search the premises and to seize wildlife and bring it and the accused person before a judge (20.1-10-04 through -06).

License Revocations and Suspensions

In addition to the penalty provided upon conviction under this title, the court may suspend the defendant's hunting, trapping or fishing privileges for up to three years. The court may not suspend the defendant's privileges for a noncriminal violation if the defendant has not been convicted for a violation of this title in the last three years. Upon a conviction for a violation of section 20.1-01-18 (hunting on posted lands; trapping on private land without permission), the court shall suspend the defendant's hunting, fishing and trapping privileges for at least one year, two years for a second conviction, and three years for the third or subsequent conviction. At the time of the suspension, the court shall determine whether the defendant must successfully complete an approved hunter education course before being allowed to purchase a new license. The court is to forward any suspended license to the Director with a certified copy of the suspension order. The Director is to reinstate the violator's license at the expiration of the suspension. "Conviction" includes an admission or adjudication of a noncriminal violation. No person may directly or indirectly hunt, trap, or fish or assist in these activities while privileges have been suspended by a court. Violation: class A misdemeanor (20.1-01-26 and -26.1).

Reward Payments

The Director, out of legislative reward appropriation, may pay complainants, upon the arrest and conviction of any person violating this title, a reward not to exceed: $100 for a violation relating to big game; $50 for a violation relating to game birds, fish, fur-bearers, or other protected animals (20.1-02-16).

Intoxication Testing of Hunters

★★A person who is afield with a firearm or a bow and arrow is deemed to have given consent, and shall consent, to a chemical test of the blood, breath, saliva or urine to determine the alcoholic, other drug, or combination thereof, content of the blood. The chemical test must be administered at the direction of a game warden only after a person has been placed under arrest and informed that the person is or will be charged with the offense of being afield with a weapon while under the influence of liquor, drugs or a combination. Taking a minor into custody satisfies the arrest requirement. Neither the game warden or law enforcement officer's efforts to contact, nor any consultation with, the parent or legal guardian may be permitted to interfere with the administration of chemical testing requirements under this chapter. The warden also shall inform the person charged that refusal to submit to the test will result in a revocation for up to four years of the person's hunting privileges. When a hunter is involved in an accident resulting in the death or serious bodily injury of another person and there is probable cause to believe intoxication, the hunter may be compelled by a game warden or a police officer to submit to a chemical test. A person who is dead, unconscious or otherwise in a condition rendering that person incapable of refusal is deemed not to have withdrawn the consent provided above, and the chemical test may be given. If a test shows that a person has an alcohol, drug or combination concentration of at least ten one-hundredths of one percent by weight at the time of the test and within two hours after being afield with a gun or bow and arrow, the game warden immediately shall issue a statement of intent to revoke, suspend or deny hunting privileges and take possession of the person's license. This statement shall serve as the Director's official notification of intent to suspend, revoke or deny hunting privileges (20.1-15-05). Failure to submit to testing results in the license being taken by the arresting warden and submitted to the Director (20.1-15-01 through -06).★★

HABITAT PROTECTION

A person owning, erecting or controlling a dam on any river, creek or stream within or forming the boundary of the state, shall construct and keep in good repair, a durable and efficient fishway in the manner, shape and size as the Director may direct. After ten days notice to comply, the Director may construct or repair the fishway and recover the costs from the violator who owns the dam (20.1-06-15).

Game Refuges and Game Management Areas

★A person owning or having control by lease or otherwise, for the required time, of any lands within this state may establish a state game refuge thereon by filing with the Director a written application, giving: ► name, written consent, time for which refuge is to be established which must be a minimum of five years from date of application and which may be renewable by mutual consent; ► the extent and legal description of the lands involved which must be a minimum of ten acres but cannot exceed six sections in any one township; ► a brief dedication of the lands to the state for a game refuge; ► a waiver by the owner of all rights of that person and family to hunt, shoot, trap or kill any game bird or protected animal during the life of the dedication of the lands as a state game refuge. After filing with the Director, and acceptance, the lands described in the application become a state game refuge for the stated time (20.1-11-02).★   ★The owner, lessee of land surrounding or adjoining any lake within this state, pursuant to section 20.1-11-02, may dedicate the lake to the state for a breeding, resting and refuge place for migratory waterfowl (20.1-11-03).★   The owner or lessee of lands or water set aside as a state game refuge may not hunt or carry firearms thereon, nor permit family or other persons to do so. However, with the Director's permission, carnivorous birds or animals within the refuge may be hunted, trapped and killed if preying upon protected game birds or animals within the refuge (20.1-11-08). The Director shall mark/post all game farms, state game refuges, game or fish management areas, breeding grounds and resting places under the Director's protection, and destruction or mutilation of signs or marks is illegal (20.1-11-10). Department posting of private land as a waterfowl rest area requires the permission or consent of landowner (20.1-11-11).

The Director may establish game or fish management areas upon any state-owned lands for the use and benefit of the Department, or upon any publicly or privately owned land leased or given by license to the Department for hunting and fishing purposes. These management areas may be opened for hunting, fishing and trapping purposes as provided by statute and regulations adopted by the Director.   ★The Director may establish state game refuges on any unsold public lands of this state. The refuge continues to exist until canceled by the Director or until the land is sold to a private person.★   The Director shall keep a record of all state game refuges established on privately owned or leased lands or on public lands, listing each by county and showing name of the dedicator, period of dedication, and legal description of the land, such record to be open to public inspection. Each such area is to be posted by the Director (20.1-11-04 through -07).   ★The **Board of University and School Lands**, for wildlife restoration projects, may transfer and convey to the Department any state school land not exceeding 640 acres for any one project, such transfer to be made in exchange for other land of equal value owned by the state for the use of the Department or acquired by the Department for exchange purposes (20.1-11-12).★

Except as otherwise provided, no person may: ► hunt, shoot, trap, kill, wound, take or capture any game bird or protected animal within any state or federal game refuge or state game management area; ► drive any game bird or protected animal out of such refuge to kill or capture it; ► or be found within the boundaries of such refuge in possession of a firearm (20.1-11-13). Violation relating to game refuges or management areas for which a penalty is not specifically provided: class B misdemeanor (20.1-11-01).)See also Agency Powers and Duties, under STATE FISH AND WILDLIFE AGENCIES, and License Provisions under HUNTING, FISHING, TRAPPING PROVISIONS.)

NATIVE AMERICAN WILDLIFE PROVISIONS: None.

OHIO

Page's Revised Code Annotated, 1986 Replacement Volume, Title 15; 1992 Supplement.

STATE WILDLIFE POLICY

The ownership of and the title to all wild animals in the state, not legally confined or held by private ownership legally acquired, is in the state, which holds such title in trust for the benefit of all the people. Individual possession shall be obtained only in accordance with the code or Division of Wildlife orders. No persons shall at any time take in any manner or possess any number or quantity of wild animals, except as the code or Division orders permit to be taken, hunted, killed or possessed, and only at such time and place, and in such manner as prescribed. No person shall buy, sell, or offer any part of wild animals for sale, or transport any part of wild animals, except as provided. No person shall possess or transport a wild animal taken unlawfully outside the state. A person doing anything prohibited or neglecting to do anything required by this chapter or Chapter 1533, or contrary to a Division order violates this section. A person who counsels, aids, shields or harbors an offender, or who knowingly shares in the proceeds of such violation, or receives or possesses a wild animal in violation of code or order violates this section. No person shall hunt a wild bird or wild quadruped, except coyotes, fox, groundhogs or migratory waterfowl as defined by federal statute on Sunday or use a rifle, at any time, in taking migratory game birds (1531.02).

RELEVANT WILDLIFE DEFINITIONS: See Definitions section of Appendices.

[Note: every provision relating to a wild animal protected by the code also applies to any part thereof.]

STATE FISH AND WILDLIFE AGENCIES

Agency Structure

There is within the **Department of Natural Resources** (Department) a **Division of Wildlife** (Division), with a **Chief** of the Division (Chief), and a **Wildlife Council** (Council). There is a **Director of Natural Resources** (Director). The **Council** has eight members, not more than four of whom may be of the same political party, appointed by the Governor with the advice and consent of the Senate, for four-year terms, and who shall be interested in conservation of state natural resources. At least two members shall be engaged in farming as their principal means of support. The Council holds at least four meetings each year, and special meetings may be held at the behest of the chairman or a majority of the members. The Governor may remove a member for misfeasance, nonfeasance or malfeasance in office. The Division shall cooperate with the other Department divisions and with all agencies of state and federal government for promotion of a general conservation program. Division orders relating to establishment of seasons, bag limits, size, species, methods of taking and possession shall be adopted only upon approval of the Council, which shall not approve or disapprove such orders prior to 15 days following a public hearing (1531.03).

Division law enforcement officers are known as **game protectors**. The Chief, game protectors, other designated Division employees, and officers who are given like authority, shall enforce all laws pertaining to taking, possession, protection, preservation, management and propagation of wild animals and all Division orders or rules (1531.13). (See also ENFORCEMENT OF WILDLIFE LAWS.)

Agency Powers and Duties

The **Council** shall: ▸ be represented by at least three members at all public hearings held pursuant to Chapter 119 for establishing seasons, bag limits, size, species, methods of taking and possession; ▸ advise on Division policies and its planning, development and institution of programs; ▸ investigate, consider and make recommendations in matters pertaining to protection, preservation, propagation, possession and management of wild animals as provided in Chapters 1531 and 1533; ▸ report to the Governor the results of its investigations concerning state wildlife resources, with recommendations to conserve or develop such resources and preserve them (1531.03).

The **Division**, at the direction of the Chief, shall: ▸ plan, develop, and institute programs and policies approved by the Director; ▸ have general care, protection and supervision of wildlife in state parks and lands owned by the state or in which it is interested or may acquire, except lands and lakes vested in some other officer, body, board or organization; ▸ enforce by legal action or proceeding state laws and orders for protection, preservation, propagation and management of wild animals, and sanctuaries and refuges for propagation; ▸ adopt measures to perform its duties (1531.04).

The **Chief**, with the Director's approval, may: ▸ acquire by gift, lease, purchase or otherwise lands or surface rights upon lands and waters for wild animals, fish or game management, preservation, propagation, protection, outdoor and nature activities, public fishing and hunting grounds and flora and fauna preservation; ▸ receive by grant, devise, bequest, donation or assignment evidences of indebtedness, proceeds to be used for purchase of lands or waters or surface rights; ▸ acquire land for establishing state fish hatcheries and game farms; ▸ establish user fees for public facilities or participation in special activities on lands and waters administered by the Division, including hunting or fishing on lands and waters intensively managed or stocked with artificially propagated game birds or fish, and field trial facilities, wildlife nature centers, firearm ranges, boat moorings, and camping sites; ▸ enter into lease agreements for rental of concessions or other special projects on state-owned/leased lands or waters and set and collect fees; ▸ regulate through contracts between the Division and concessionaires the sale of tangible objects; ▸ keep records of fee payments to be paid into a Department fund for the purposes of 1533.15; ▸ sell conservation promotion items, including pins, books, maps, and educational articles relating to wildlife; ▸ sell confiscated or forfeited items, surplus structures, equipment and timber or crops from Division owned or controlled lands. Fees set by the Chief shall be approved by the Council. Lakes, reservoirs and state lands dedicated to public use for park and pleasure resorts are under the supervision of the Chief to enforce wildlife laws. Laws for protection of fish in inland rivers and streams and for protection of birds, fish, game and fur-bearing animals shall apply to state reservoirs and lakes. No person shall disturb, injure or destroy plants or disturb a waterfowl, water animal, bird, game or fur-bearing animal, kept as a semidomestic pet upon an island or waters as defined herein, or on territory under state jurisdiction, nor disturb fish in a lagoon or other waters set aside for fish propagation (1531.06 and .07).

★There is a "special hunting area" established on Department lands and waters, the Magee Marsh State Public Hunting Area. The Chief may provide a special daily hunting permit for $5 for hunting on this area, moneys to go into the Wildlife Fund as provided in 1533.15. A hunting and trapping license is required thereon (1533.06).★

Agency Regulations

The **Chief** has authority and control in all matters pertaining to the protection, preservation, propagation, possession and management of wild animals and may issue temporary written orders for their management. Each year there shall be a public fish hearing and a public game hearing. The results of the investigation and public hearing shall be filed in the Chief's office and open for public inspection. Modifying or rescinding orders does not require a public hearing. The Chief may establish, modify, rescind and enforce orders throughout the state, to be filed in proposed form and available at wildlife offices at least 30 days prior to the hearing date required by code. ★Orders shall be based upon a public hearing and investigation including: ▸ distribution, abundance, breeding conditions, food, cover, life history and economic importance of the wild animals involved; ▸ influence of topography, soil, weather and other nonliving or living things on these animals; ▸ whether or not such animals are materially destroying property or are otherwise becoming a nuisance; ▸ the sexes are not properly balanced or the natural food supply is insufficient; ▸ whether additional numbers may be taken without depleting the brood stock. Orders shall describe the waters, areas or parts affected and whether applicable to all wild animals or only to certain species, and the length of time each order shall remain in effect. The Chief may regulate: ▸ taking and possessing wild animals; ▸ transportation of animals or any part; ▸ buying, selling, or offering such of an animal or part; ▸ taking, possession, transportation, buying, selling and offering such of commercial fish or any part.★ ★If during the effective dates of an order, not to exceed five years, an investigation shows that the order should be modified for any cause not known, fully understood or present at the time such order was made, the Chief may modify any part. Such modified order shall not be effective longer than the dates of the original order. For similar cause, the Chief may rescind an order or modifying order, except that if the order required Council approval for adoption, it may be modified or rescinded only upon Council approval.★ Orders shall be filed with the Secretary of State and with the clerk of the court of each county affected and shall be advertised to the public. A copy of an order, rule or regulation shall be printed in compilations of the Division lawbook (1531.08 through .10). The Chief is not authorized to provide or change a penalty prescribed by law for a violation of its provisions, or to change the amount of any license fee, unless otherwise permitted by code (1532.12).

The Chief shall make rules, in accordance with Chapter 119, for protection of state-owned or leased lands, waters and properties against wrongful use or occupancy to protect them from depredations and to preserve them from molestation, spoilation and destruction, and shall make rules with respect to recreational activities, management and use. The Chief may issue orders benefiting wild animals, fish or game management, preservation, propagation and protection, outdoor and nature activities, public hunting and fishing grounds, flora and fauna preservation, and regulate the taking and possession of wild animals on Division lands or waters, and may for a specified period of years prohibit or recall the taking and possession of a wild animal on such lands or waters. The Division shall define and mark the boundaries of Division lands and waters upon which the taking of a wild animal is prohibited (1531.06).

Agency Funding Sources

Moneys from fees for licenses and permits are paid into the state treasury to the credit of the **Wildlife Fund**, exclusively for Department use for: ▸ education of hunters and trappers; ▸ purchase, management, preservation, propagation, protection and stocking of wild birds and quadrupeds; ▸ establishing and acquiring title to lands for game preservation, propagation and protection; ▸ public hunting grounds under the Chief's rules. On such lands, the Chief may employ game management agents and game protectors for improving habitat for wild birds and quadrupeds and for game management, propagation and protection, including: ▸ biological investigations; ▸ printing summarized game laws and the Division lawbook; ▸ printing educational leaflets, pamphlets and books; ▸ promoting educational survey and research pertaining to management, preservation, propagation and protection of wild animals as approved by the Chief and code. The Department shall not spend more than 35% of this fund for administration and enforcement. No moneys derived from hunting licenses, deer, turkey or trapping permits shall be spent for other than hunting and trapping purposes. The Wildlife Fund shall be reimbursed for the cost of hunting and fishing licenses, permits and stamps issued free of charge under 1533.12, and the Chief shall compile the amount of fees that would otherwise have been collected for them. Beginning with fiscal year 1992, the Director of Budget and Management shall transfer the lesser of one million dollars per year or the amount so certified from the General Revenue Fund to the Wildlife Fund (1533.15).

Moneys derived from fishing licenses are appropriated exclusively to the Department for: ▸ purchase, protection, propagation, preservation and stocking of fish; ▸ construction of fish chutes and dams; ▸ securing of more public fishing waters, including leasing, purchasing or otherwise acquiring stream banks, lakes, ponds gravel pits and quarries and other suitable grounds; ▸ improvement of streams, lakes and ponds, including food, cover, breeding conditions, erosion and reforestation; ▸ cooperation with other agencies to assist in stabilizing water levels and controlling ditching, dredging, debrushing, aquatic vegetation removal and control of stream, lake and pond turbidities; ▸ other practical fish management work, including biological investigations and printing the summarized fishing laws, the fish and game lawbook, conservation bulletins, and fish management leaflets; ▸ promoting educational and research activities, methods of fish propagation and fish culture, and other conservation activities; ▸ use as provided in the sections specified herein. No funds derived from fishing licenses shall be spent for other than fishing purposes as defined. Not more than 25% of such moneys shall be used for administration or overhead of the Division and Council; the remaining 75% shall be used exclusively for the purchase, protection, propagation, preservation, and stocking of fish and for the purposes detailed herein (1533.33). All fines, penalties, and forfeitures arising from prosecutions, convictions, confiscations or otherwise under this chapter, and Chapters 1517 and 1533, shall be credited to the Wildlife Fund. License fees on nets in the Lake Erie fishing district shall be credited to the Wildlife Fund for use only in the betterment and propagation of fish therein. All investment earnings of the fund go into the fund (1531.17).

The **Nongame and Endangered Wildlife Fund** consists of moneys paid into it by the tax commissioner as provided and contributions made directly to it. A person may contribute directly to the fund in addition to, or independently of, the income tax refund contribution system established in 5747.113. Moneys in the fund shall be expended by the Division solely for: ▸ purchase, management, preservation, propagation, protection and stocking of wild animals not commonly taken for sport or commercial purposes; ▸ establishing, purchasing or otherwise acquiring title to lands for the preservation, propagation and protection of wild animals; ▸ management, propagation and protection of wild animals, including biological investigations, law enforcement and printing of educational materials; ▸

promoting educational, survey and research activities pertaining to the management, propagation and protection of wild animals and for carrying out endangered species provisions under 1531.25. Investment earnings are credited to the fund. Subject to the Director's approval, the Chief may enter into agreements to obtain additional moneys for the protection of nongame native wildlife under the federal Endangered Species Act. Moneys appropriated from the fund are not intended to replace other moneys appropriated for these purposes (1531.26).

The **Cooperative Management Fund** in the state treasury consists of all revenue generated on land owned by the US Army Corps of Engineers and is managed by the Division pursuant to an agreement with the Corps, to be spent for fish and wildlife management purposes and for management of the lands, including investment earnings (1531.30). ★There is in the state treasury the **Ohio River Management Fund**, consisting of moneys received by the Division pursuant to negotiated mitigation settlements and investment earnings from persons who have adversely affected the fish and wildlife of the Ohio River or their habitats and of gifts and contributions made to it, to be used for the preservation, development and management of the Ohio river through the acquisition of critical habitat areas, monitoring of fish and wildlife populations, production and stocking of game fish, and research for improving public access to the Ohio River (1531.31).★

The **Wildlife Habitat Trust Fund** facilitates the acquisition and development of lands for the preservation, propagation and protection of wild animals, and consists of money from gifts, donations, bequests and other moneys contributed to the Division for these purposes, and investment earnings until transferred to the Wildlife Habitat Fund. The principal shall not be spent (1531.32). The **Wildlife Habitat Fund** consists of the investment earnings of the Wildlife Habitat Trust Fund, and is used by the Division to acquire and develop lands for the preservation, propagation and protection of wild animals. All expenditures must be approved by the Director (1531.33).

The **Wildlife Refunds Fund** consists of money received from application fees for special deer permits that are not issued which shall be used to make refunds of such application fees (1533.11).

The **Wetlands Habitat Fund** consists of moneys received from sale of the **Wetlands Habitat Stamp** required under 1533.11.2. Moneys and investment earnings shall be expended on the Director's orders only as follows: 60% for projects the Division approves for the acquisition, development, management or preservation of waterfowl areas in the state; 40% for contribution by the Division to an appropriate nonprofit organization for acquisition, development, management or preservation of lands and waters within Canada that provide habitat for waterfowl with migration routes that cross this state. The Chief shall establish a procedure to obtain subject matter to be printed on the wetlands habitat stamp, and shall use, dispose of or distribute such, and shall make orders to administer the stamp provisions (1533.11.2). ★★The Chief, with the Director's approval, is authorized to print and issue stamps portraying state wild animals, a **Wildlife Conservation Stamp**, the fee for which shall be $5. The purchase of such stamp shall provide no privileges but recognizes the purchaser as voluntarily contributing to the management, protection and perpetuation of state wildlife resources. Stamp sales moneys go to the credit of the Wildlife Fund to be used exclusively for purposes outlined in 1533.15 and for management of all forms of wildlife for its ecological and nonconsumptive recreational value (1533.15.1).★★

PROTECTED SPECIES OF WILDLIFE

The Chief, with Council approval, shall adopt and may modify and repeal rules, in accordance with Chapter 119, restricting the taking or possession of native wildlife, eggs or offspring thereof threatened with statewide extinction. The rules shall identify the common and scientific names of each endangered species and shall be modified from time to time to include all species listed on the US list of native endangered fish and wildlife native to this state, or that migrate or are otherwise likely to occur within the state. The rules shall provide for the taking of species threatened with statewide extinction, for zoological, educational and scientific purposes, and for propagation in captivity to preserve the species, under written permits from the Chief. The rules shall in no way restrict the taking or possession of species listed on the US list for zoological, educational, or scientific purposes, or for propagation in captivity to preserve the species, under a permit or license from the US or an instrumentality thereof. No person shall violate a rule adopted pursuant to this section (1531.25).

No person shall catch, kill, injure, pursue, or possess, either dead or alive, or purchase, expose for sale, transport or ship within or without the state, or receive or deliver for transportation a bird other than a game bird, or possess part of the plumage, skin, or body, except as permitted by code, nor disturb or destroy the eggs, nest or young of such bird. This does not prohibit the lawful taking, killing, pursuing or possession of a game bird during the open season. Hawks or owls causing damage to domestic animals or fowl may be killed by the animal owner while such damage is occurring. Bald or golden eagles and ospreys shall not be killed or possessed, except for educational purposes by governmental or municipal zoological parks, museums, and scientific or educational institutions. European starlings, English sparrows, common pigeons, other than homing pigeons, and crows may be killed at any time, except Sunday, and their nests or eggs may be destroyed at any time. Blackbirds may be killed at any time, except Sunday, when doing damage to grain or other property or when they become a nuisance. Each bird or part taken or possessed contrary to this section is a separate offense (1533.07). (See also GENERAL EXCEPTIONS TO PROTECTION and HUNTING, FISHING, TRAPPING PROVISIONS.)

GENERAL EXCEPTIONS TO PROTECTION

A person desiring to collect wild animals protected by law and their nests or eggs for scientific study, school instruction or other educational uses shall apply to the Chief for a scientific collecting permit, with written recommendations of two well-known scientific persons or science teachers, certifying to the good character and fitness of the applicant. The Chief shall issue to approved applicants a permit to take, possess and transport at any time and in any manner specimens of wild animals, nests and eggs protected by law for such purposes under Council regulations. Permittees shall carry their permits and exhibit them upon demand to a game protector or other officer, or the owner of the land upon which they are collecting, or to a person. Failure to do so is an offense. Permittees shall keep daily records of all specimens collected and disposition of same for Division inspection upon demand. Permit fees go into the Wildlife Fund. Permittees shall submit written reports annually of their operations and disposition of collected specimens on Division forms. Failure to file results in permit forfeiture. No permittee shall take, possess or transport wild animals for a purpose not specified in the permit. Violation of a permit regulation or law concerning wild animals results in revocation and forfeiture of the permit for one year (1533.08 and .09). The Division may take fish at any time or place, in any manner, for cultivation of fish in hatcheries, or for stocking ponds, lakes or rivers, or for exterminating rough fish, and may set aside waters for propagation of fish or waterfowl (1531.15). (See also PROTECTED SPECIES OF WILDLIFE and HUNTING, FISHING, TRAPPING PROVISIONS.)

HUNTING, FISHING, TRAPPING PROVISIONS

General Provisions

No person shall take, kill, possess, transport, buy or sell wild animals contrary to a Division order or rule (1531.11). On lands acquired and set aside for wild animal management, preservation, propagation and protection or public hunting grounds with plainly marked boundaries, or with knowledge that such lands are so acquired and set aside, no person shall take, hunt or trap, kill or pursue a wild animal, except as provided by law or Division order, nor enter upon lands held by the state for reforestation with intent to cut growing timber or otherwise commit waste. Hunting may be engaged in on lands set aside for reforestation as provided by Division order and the Division of Forestry (1533.15).

Fish and fur-bearers in the inland and Lake Erie fishing and trapping districts, and game birds and game quadrupeds throughout the state may be taken and possessed only in open season, in compliance with law or Division order, stipulating the length of fish and the number of fish, game birds, game quadrupeds and fur-bearing animals [waters and lands constituting the "districts" are detailed]. Minimum legal lengths, bag and possession limits, and seasons for listed species of game fish are set in statute, or otherwise provided by Division order. Open seasons for game birds, certain game quadrupeds and fur-bearers are set herein, as are bag and possession limits according to district. There is no open season on sharp-tailed or pinnated grouse, black-breasted or golden plover, greater and lesser yellowlegs, red or pine squirrel, deer, bear or beaver. There is no closed season on ground hog or woodchuck, weasel, muskellunge, yellow pike-perch, bluegill, rock bass, yellow perch, white bass, crappie, sunfish or catfish. The season for taking fox does not prohibit chasing of foxes by dogs or on horseback when such does not result in killing the fox. The owner/operator of a farm used to breed and raise raccoon, skunk, mink, muskrat or opossum may take or possess at any time such animals, although the farm is also used during the open season for hunting other game (1533.02).

No person shall buy, sell, offer for sale or possess any fish or part mentioned in this section, whether taken within or without the state, except such fish as are protected and taken by licensed commercial fishermen as provided by law. No person shall buy, sell, offer for sale or possess for such purpose a game bird or game quadruped or part, whether taken within or without the state. Each such fish, game bird, game quadruped or part bought, sold, offered for sale or possessed for such purposes contrary to this section or Division order is a separate offense (1533.02).

No person shall receive for transportation, transport or cause same of a box, package or other receptacle containing fish, game birds or wild quadrupeds, or parts, unless labeled as required. No person shall receive for transportation or possess with intent to transport, or secure transportation of, beyond the state limits a game bird or quadruped mentioned in Chapters 1531 and 1533 and killed in this state. The reception and acceptance by a person within this state of such game bird or game quadruped for shipment outside the state is prima facie evidence that it was killed within the state for conveyance beyond the limits thereof. Legally taken game possessed by a nonresident may be transported if the person accompanies it and is licensed. Game taken outside of Ohio by a resident may be transported into the state by the resident with proper documentation thereof as specified herein. Each game bird or game quadruped killed, taken, possessed, transported, or received for same contrary to this section is a separate offense [additional common carrier and other details given] (1533.30). [Extensive details of transporting fish which are for sale, sold or purchased, permits, permit exceptions, required labeling of trucks and containers, inspections, records, violations and penalties are given in 1533.30.1, which appear to relate to commercial fish transport.] (See also Import, Export and Release provisions under this section.)

Licenses and Permits

Except as provided, no person shall hunt a wild bird or wild quadruped without a hunting license. Each day a person hunts within the state without a license is a separate offense. Every resident over age 16 shall procure a resident hunting license. Landowners, their children, and tenants may hunt on their own lands without a hunting license. Nonresidents shall procure a nonresident hunting license unless their state of residence has a reciprocal agreement with Ohio under 1533.91. No person shall procure a hunting license by fraud, deceit, misrepresentation or false statement. In addition to a hunting license, a special deer or wild turkey permit is required to take those animals, and the taking of ducks, geese or brant requires a wetlands habitat stamp, and trapping fur-bearing animals requires an additional trapping permit. No hunting license shall be issued unless the applicant has previously held a hunting license or has a certificate of competency from a hunter safety and conservation course approved by the Chief, or has equivalent training in content and manner approved by the Chief. Issuance of a hunting license in violation of these requirements is an offense by both the purchaser of the illegal license and its issuer, and is void. ★★The Chief, with Council approval, shall by rule prescribe a hunter safety and conservation course for first-time hunting license buyers and for volunteer instructors, consisting of: ▸ hunter safety and health; ▸ use of hunting implements; ▸ hunting tradition and ethics; ▸ the hunter and conservation; ▸ law relating to hunting. Courses shall be conducted with such frequency and at such locations throughout the state as reasonably to meet the needs of license applicants. The Chief shall issue a certificate of competency to persons completing the course and who pass an examination (1533.10)★★. [License and permit exceptions for hunting, fishing and trapping are detailed in 1533.12 for certain armed forces personnel, residents with specified disabilities, residents over age 66, residents of specified state or county institutions, former prisoners of war, and certain categories of physically handicapped persons.]

Except as provided, no person shall trap fur-bearing animals on another's land without an annual trapping permit concurrent with the hunting license. Moneys received go into the Wildlife Fund. After 1979, no trapping permit shall be issued unless the applicant presents a previously held trapping license or permit or evidence of having held same in content and manner approved by the Chief, a certificate of competency issued upon completion of a trapper education course, or evidence of equivalent training, approved by the Chief. A trapping permit issued without such proof is void. The Chief, with Council approval, shall prescribe a trapper education course for first-time trapping permit buyers and for volunteer instructors, consisting of subjects including: ▸ trapping techniques; ▸ animal habits and identification; ▸ trapping tradition and ethics; ▸ the trapper and conservation; ▸ law relating to trapping. Other provisions of the course, examination, and certificate of completion are similar to the hunter education course described above. Persons must carry their trapping permit while trapping. Landowners, their children and tenants need no trapping permit to trap fur-bearing animals on their own lands (1533.11.1). Except as provided, no person shall hunt ducks, geese or brant on another's lands without an annual wetlands habitat stamp, moneys to go into the Wetlands Habitat Fund. Every person hunting ducks, geese or brant shall personally carry such stamp while hunting and exhibit it to a law enforcement officer on request (1533.11.2). (See also Agency Funding Sources under STATE FISH AND WILDLIFE AGENCIES.)

Except as provided, no person shall hunt deer or turkey on another's lands without an annual special deer and/or wild turkey permit concurrent with the hunting license. Money from permit fees goes into the Wildlife Fund exclusively for Division use in acquisition and development of land for deer or wild turkey management, investigating deer or wild turkey problems, and stocking, management and protection of deer or wild turkey. Permits must be carried while hunting deer or turkey on another's lands and exhibited to an enforcement officer on request; failure to do so is an offense. Landowners, children and tenants may hunt deer or wild turkey on lands where they reside without such permit. Deer or wild turkey permits are not transferable. No person shall carry a permit issued in the name of another person (1533.11).

A person who kills a deer by striking it on a highway with a vehicle may take possession of the deer, but within 24 hours must report the accident to a game protector or other law enforcement officer who shall investigate the incident, and issue a certificate entitling the driver to the carcass for consumption, or to give it to a charitable institution (1533.12.1).

No hunting license is transferable, and no hunter shall carry a license issued in the name of another. Every person hunting or trapping on another's lands shall carry the hunting license and exhibit it to a game protector or other law enforcement officer or the owner or person in lawful control of the land, or to a person. Failure to so do is an offense. ★★Every person hunting or trapping on another's lands shall wear on the back of the outer garment a tag bearing the person's hunting license number in figures easily visible and legible at least one inch in height, such tag to be furnished to every licensee. Failure to wear the tag as specified is an offense. Chapters 1531 and 1533 do not allow hunting or trapping on land without written consent of the owner★★. A hunting license entitles a nonresident to take from this state game birds or game quadrupeds killed and possessed as provided by law or Division order. Every applicant for such license or permit shall make and subscribe an affidavit setting forth name, occupation, residence, citizenship and other information as required and records of licenses and permits kept by the clerk shall be uniform throughout the state and open to inspection at reasonable hours (1533.13 and .14).

Except as provided, no person without a license shall: ▸ take or catch fish by angling in state waters; ▸ engage in fishing; ▸ take or catch frogs or turtles, or mussels for bait. Persons fishing in privately owned ponds, lakes or reservoirs open to public fishing through an agreement or lease with the Division shall comply with the license requirements set forth. No person shall alter a fishing license or possess one that has been altered, nor attempt to procure a license by fraud, deceit or a false statement. Owners of land over, through, upon or along which water flows or stands, except where such land is in or borders on state parks or state-owned lakes, and immediate family members, and tenants residing thereon, may take frogs, turtles, mussels for bait, and may catch fish of permitted kinds without a fishing license. Licenses must be carried on one's person while fishing or taking frogs, turtles or mussels, and exhibited to a person; failure is an offense (1533.32). No fishing license issued under 1533.32 is transferable and no fisherman shall carry a license issued in the name of another (1533.36). No person shall take or sell mussels, except for bait purposes as provided in 1533.32, without an annual mussel taking permit from the Chief [additional details regarding commercial mussel taking, buying, and selling are given] (1533.32.4). No person, firm or corporation shall use or operate for taking fish a boat, net or device other than a minnow net or hook and line with bait or lure, in state waters wherein fishing with nets is licensed by law, without a license for such gear from the Chief [additional commercial net applications are given] (1533.34). [Details of the quota management system for taking fish in the Lake Erie fishery resource district, the Commercial fishery quota advisory committee, Lake Erie sport and commercial fishing and guide licenses are given in 1533.34.1 through 1533.36; Lake Erie fishing seasons, reporting requirements and net restrictions in 1533.41 through 1533.50.]

Restrictions on Taking: Hunting and Trapping

★No person shall take a hare or rabbit using a ferret, or place a ferret in a hole in the ground, stone wall, log or elsewhere outside a building, in which a hare or rabbit might be confined, or posses or control a ferret while hunting or returning from hunting. Each hare or rabbit caught, killed or possessed in violation is a separate offense. The owner, tenant, or employee of a fruit orchard or nursery may possess or use a ferret to take or kill rabbits or hares substantially damaging fruit trees or nursery stock.★ No person shall take a wild bird or wild quadruped from its nest, house, den or burrow, or destroy same, or with a spear hunt, pursue, injure or kill a wild bird or quadruped, except as provided in 1531.01 through 1531.26, or by Division order. Each wild bird or quadruped, or each hide, skin or pelt of such animal or bird, or part, taken or possessed in violation is a separate offense. The possession of the hide, skin or pelt of a wild bird or quadruped during closed seasons is prima facie evidence of illegal taking, unless an original invoice signed by a shipper shows proof of legal taking (1533.02).

Game birds and wild quadrupeds shall be taken only by hunting with a gun, gun and dog, bow and arrow, or bow and arrow and dog, unless otherwise provided. Fur-bearing animals may be taken by trapping according to code or Division order. No gun larger than 10 gauge shall be used in taking game birds or wild quadrupeds. No person shall throw or cast the rays of a spotlight or other artificial light from a vehicle into a field, woodland, or forest while possessing a hunting device, or do the same for the purpose of locating a wild animal, except for law enforcement officers or landowners having a reason to use a light while engaged in surveillance or protection of property. An officer whose duty is to enforce Division orders or code provisions may arrest a person when there is reasonable grounds to believe there is violation of this section, search the person's vehicle for firearms or other hunting implements, and seize them. No person shall hunt or trap upon another's land, pond, lake or private water, except water claimed by riparian right of ownership in adjacent lands, or shoot, catch, kill, injure or pursue a wild bird, wild waterfowl or wild animal thereon without written permission from the owner or authorized agent. A person who in the act of hunting, pursuing, taking or killing game or birds acts in a negligent, careless or reckless manner so as to injure persons or property is guilty of a misdemeanor (1533.16, .17 and .17.1).

Game birds, game quadrupeds and fur-bearing animals raised in a wholly enclosed preserve, under a commercial propagating license, may be killed in any manner but shooting, except during the open season. No game birds, game quadrupeds or fur-bearing animals shall be sold for food unless the carcasses are tagged with a Division seal, and then they may be possessed, bought or sold, and transported by common carriers if packages are tagged as required. Game sold for consumption must be tagged with Division tags, to remain affixed until prepared for consumption. The sale of a portion of a game bird, game quadruped or fur-bearing animal without tag affixed is a violation. Hotels, restaurants or retail meat dealers may sell portions of such animals so tagged to a guest, customer or club member for consumption (1533.74 and .75). Provisions pertaining to hunting on a licensed shooting preserve do not alter or supersede laws requiring a resident license to hunt. A nonresident must have a nonresident hunting license, or a special nonresident licensed shooting preserve license (1533.80).

[Details of organized dog field trials provided, in 1533.19.1] Dog training grounds shall not be used to conduct shooting trials, except as provided (1533.19.1). ★★The Division may acquire lands for conducting field trials for dogs. In each conservation district the Division shall set aside field trial areas on available state-owned or controlled land where field trials for dogs may be conducted, and shall stock such areas with wild game. Such areas may be used by the Division for propagation of wildlife and for experimental purposes, provided such experiments do not interfere with their use for field trials. Clubs and individuals may be permitted to stock the areas with wild game and provide food and shelter for game.★★ Clubs or groups may acquire areas of land for at least 12 months and apply to have such areas designated as field trial areas during that period. No person shall hunt or trap within a field trial area except as provided (1533.20 through .22). A nonresident shall not exercise, train or work a dog when this state's residents are prohibited from doing so in the nonresident's state, except as provided by Division order. A nonresident may enter field trials (1533.22.1).

Restrictions on Taking: Fishing

Fish shall be taken only by angling, unless otherwise provided by code or Division order. If a fish is unintentionally taken contrary to code or order, it shall be returned immediately to the water without injury (1533.37). No person shall draw, set, place, locate or possess a pound net, crib net, trammel net, fyke net, set net, seine, bar net fish trap or any part thereof, or throw or hand line, with more than three hooks, or other device for catching fish, except a line with not more than three hooks attached, or lure with not more than three sets of three hooks each, in the inland fishing district except for taking carp, mullet, sheepshead and grass pike as provided by code or Division order. No person shall catch or kill a fish in the inland fishing district with bob lines, trotlines, float lines, or by grabbing with the hands, or by spearing, shooting, or with any device other than by angling. In inland fishing waters, except those controlled by the state, a trotline may be used with not more than 50 hooks and no two hooks less than three feet apart by the landowner or person having the owner's consent in that part of the stream bordering on or running through the owner's lands (1533.54). In the inland fishing district, seining for minnows is regulated by season in certain waters, and no person shall: ► take minnows except with a minnow seine up to four feet in depth and eight feet in length; ► possess more than 100 minnows, alive or dead, except for persons or firms buying, selling or dealing in bait who are licensed; ► take, catch, buy or sell minnows, except for bait, and the taking, transporting or shipping of minnows out of state is prohibited (1533.57). ★Fish may be taken in the ponds or lagoons formed by the receding waters of a river when such are no longer connected with stream channels.★ Prohibitions regarding nets, traps or other devices for catching fish do not apply to devices possessed by the owner of a private artificial fish pond or lake when used in such waters only, or as otherwise provided for Lake Erie, or for a holder of a scientific collecting permit who is taking fish with a gill net (1533.60 and .61). [Provisions and locations for taking carp, buffalo, mullet and other designated species in bays, marshes and inlets bordering Lake Erie are detailed in 1533.62.]

Minimum taking and possession lengths for whitefish, sturgeon, catfish, yellow perch, white bass, bullhead, cisco, buffalo fish, suckers and coho are detailed by statute. All such fish caught or taken of a weight or length less than that prescribed shall be released immediately with as little injury as possible. No person shall release undersized fish or protected species into a privately owned pond, lake or other enclosure. Commercial fishermen may not take game species as specified herein [extensive details for violations and penalties therefor by commercial licensees are given] (1533.63). Each fish caught, killed, taken or possessed contrary to an order of the Division or Chapter 1531 or 1533 is a separate offense (1533.65).

No person shall: ► trespass upon another's lands, lying in or bordering upon a natural or artificial pond or brook less than ten miles in length into which have been introduced brook, speckled, and brown trout, or land lock salmon, California salmon or other fish artificially propagated or imported for fishing, catching or killing; ► catch or kill fish in such pond or brook or buy, receive or possess fish caught therein; ► place willfully poison or other substance injurious to the health of such fish in a such pond or brook for capturing or harming the fish; ► drain the water out of such pond or brook with intent to take or injure fish. Prosecutions for violations shall be instituted upon the complaint of the person upon whose lands or waters the trespass has been committed (1533.66).

Commercial and Private Enterprise Provisions

No person shall deal in or buy green or dried furs, skins or parts, taken from fur-bearing animals except domesticated rabbits without a fur dealer's permit from the Division. Every fur dealer shall operate under regulations as provided by the Chief. Licenses fees go into the Wildlife Fund for Division use for purchase, preservation, protection and stocking of fur-bearing animals. Fur dealers shall keep records of purchases and sales of furs, skins or parts made during the year, including number and kinds bought and sold, dates of each purchase, and origin of furs and other information the Division requires, with records open to inspection at reasonable times. No common carrier knowlingly shall ship, transport or receive green or dried furs, skins or parts unless there is plainly written thereon the name of the shipper and the fur dealer or hunting license number (1533.23 and .24).

The Chief may issue permits to regulate the possession, propagation, use, protection, transportation and sale of live fish and fish food under Division control for propagation and stocking of waters only, under the Chief's regulations, for private ponds. Each license shall regulate the species of fish and fish food as prescribed, and may be issued based on the suitability of a person's private hatchery ponds and equipment for breeding, hatching, raising, and wintering of live fish and fish food. The brood stock of live fish shall be procured only by angling or under the Chief's regulations. Commercial species of fish of legal size and suitable for propagation may be purchased from licensed commercial fishermen. Fish and fish food, their eggs or young, shall not be sold except alive and in proper condition for propagation and stocking purposes. Each person, firm, or corporation which buys, sells or deals in minnows, crayfish or hellgrammites for sale shall obtain a permit from the Chief and operate under Division rules. Nonresidents who collect, seine or pick minnows, crayfish or hellgrammites for bait shall have a nonresident fishing license (1533.39 and .40).

Raising and selling game birds, game quadrupeds or fur-bearing animals in a wholly enclosed private preserve, or having such animals in captivity, requires a license. After investigation and approval, the Division shall issue one of the following licenses: ► commercial propagating license, which allows propagation of game birds, game quadrupeds or fur-bearing animals in the enclosed preserve, sale and shipment of live animals, killing of same, and sale of carcasses for food, subject to code provisions; ► non-commercial propagating license, which allows propagation of game birds, game quadrupeds or fur-bearing animals and holding them in captivity for the licensee's own use, such animals not to be sold; ★ ▸ a free raise-to-release license for clubs or individuals raising game birds, game quadrupeds or fur-bearing animals for release only, and not for sale or personal use. ★ Except as provided by law, no person shall possess game birds, game quadrupeds or fur-bearing animals during closed season, except municipal or governmental zoological parks. License moneys go to Division use for the purchase, preservation and protection of wild animals (1533.71).

A shooting preserve on private lands may be licensed by the Division subject to the following conditions: ▸ the operation of the shooting preserve does not conflict with a prior reasonable public interest; ▸ ★ the applicant shall deliver to the Division each year, for distribution on lands other than private hunting preserves, 12 male pheasants for each 100 acres of land within the preserve, or with the Chief's approval, a like number of quail if the principal shooting preserve use is for quail; ▸ the applicant shall produce evidence that at least 500 pheasants will be raised or purchased for liberation and will liberated on the shooting preserve during the period specified herein, or a like number of quail, with the Chief's approval. Failure to deliver the required number of birds to the Division, or to release the required number of birds during the season, is a violation. ★ Under a shooting preserve license, pheasants, quail and other game birds on which there is an open season and exotic birds which the Chief may approve, and which are legally acquired, may be taken on the preserve without regard to sex and daily bag limit, and on Sundays, by licensed hunters authorized by the licensee during the season. ★The licensee is liable for damage to or destruction of growing crops adjacent to the preserve caused by pheasants raised on such preserve. ★

Not more than four licensed shooting preserves may be established in a county, and preserves must be from 80 to 640 acres in area, and in one continuous block of land except as intersected by roads. No preserve shall be located within 1,500 feet of another preserve. A person may not own/operate more than one preserve in one county. Licensed preserves operated by a municipal corporation are exempt from these provisions. Mallard or black ducks, and game birds which have an open season in Ohio, and any approved exotic birds legally acquired or propagated under a propagating license and marked and banded as provided may be released and shot within a licensed shooting preserve only during the season for shooting pheasants in 1533.72. Birds liberated on a preserve shall be banded, and no birds shall be possessed or transported outside the licensed area unless tagged as required. ★If a bird without a band is shot within a licensed shooting preserve, the licensee shall immediately replace each such bird with a like live banded bird to be released outside the preserve under Division supervision (1533.72 and .73). No licensee shall ship live pheasants propagated under provisions of 1533.70 to 1533.80 from the state until they are first offered to the Division at a price which shall not exceed the price they are offered for sale outside the state. ★ Each propagating license holder shall display the license at the place of business and keep records as specified, such records to be open for inspection by Division personnel at reasonable times. A propagation licensee or employees may take a predatory bird or animal in the act of destroying propagated game birds, game quadrupeds or fur-bearing animals on the land described in the license. The Chief may promulgate regulations to control or eradicate parasites and diseases of domesticated or semi-wild game birds, game quadrupeds or fur-bearing animals on propagation-licensed lands (1533.76 through .79).

Every person who owns, or controls land or water, within a state or federal waterfowl management area, shall obtain a permit from the Chief prior to permitting taking waterfowl on that land or water. The permit entitles the permittee to possess or control blinds, pits, or similar concealment devices on the lands and waters described in the waterfowl hunting area permit. The Chief, with the Director's approval, shall set qualifications and fees for the permit, and permittees shall operate in conformance with Chapter 1531 and rules as the Chief prescribes. No person shall hunt waterfowl on land or water for which a waterfowl hunting area permit has been issued without the landowner/permittee's permission. The landowner, children of the owner, and persons residing within a waterfowl management area are not required to secure the permit while hunting on those lands. Permittees shall keep daily records of hunters and the number and kinds of waterfowl taken on the area, such records to be available for Division inspection at reasonable times. Falsifying records or failure to submit same constitutes grounds for the Chief to deny future permits (1533.81).

★The Chief, with the Director's approval, may issue a permit for the operation of a tag fishing tournament on state-administered and other public waters, and shall adopt, and may amend or rescind rules relating to their operation [details regarding rules provided] (1533.92 and .93). No person who has been convicted of or pleaded guilty to a theft or fraud offense, or a gambling offense in this or another state, or the US, shall be eligible to apply for a tag fishing tournament permit (1533.96). ★ Nothing shall prohibit a fishing tournament in which a prize is awarded for quantity, size or weight of fish and not for catching specifically marked fish. No person shall operate a tag fishing tournament contrary to special conditions of the permit, or in violation of the Chief's rules, nor charge an entry fee in excess of 10% of the permit fee established by the Chief if less than $200. Each violation of a rule is a separate violation (1533.97 and .98). [Additional details are given regarding Department immunity from liability and rules and special conditions for permits in 1533.97.]

Import, Export and Release Provisions

The Chief may permit or forbid or otherwise regulate the receiving of a species of live wild animals within the state and shipping such wild animals to any point within or without the state. The Chief may seize, impound, destroy or otherwise dispose of such wild animals when received, shipped or transported in violation. This doesn not authorize action to prevent transport of wild animals in interstate commerce shipped by common carrier, providing neither the point of sending nor the point of receiving is within the state (1533.31).

Interstate Reciprocal Agreements

★★A person duly licensed by a state, district, country or sovereignty other than this state to take or catch fish by angling shall be exempt from fishing license provisions in 1533.32 and 1533.99 if such person has complied with fishing by angling law in the state or other entity where licensed and complies with such law while fishing by angling in this state. Such exemption shall be operative only if the law of such other state, country or sovereignty makes substantially like and equal exemptions to persons duly licensed by this state to take fish by angling, and according to reciprocal agreements made between this and any other state or sovereignty (1533.32.2). The Attorney General, the Chief and the Director may enter into reciprocal contracts and agreements with authorities of other states to regulate fishing by angling in state waters and game hunting by licensed residents of such other states. Said officials may also confer and advise with officers and legislative bodies of this and other states and the District of Columbia for promoting reciprocal agreements under which hunting and fishing licenses issued to residents of this state shall be recognized by other states and federal districts (1533.32.3)★★.

The Chief, upon approval of the Council and the Attorney General, may enter into agreements with the appropriate officials of one or more states, whereby the Chief will issue nonresident fishing licenses, hunting licenses, and hunting and trapping permits to residents of other states for the fees charged Ohio residents, and Ohio residents may obtain nonresident licenses in other party states for the fees charged residents thereof (1533.91).

ANIMAL DAMAGE CONTROL

See PROTECTED SPECIES OF WILDLIFE and HUNTING, FISHING, TRAPPING PROVISIONS.

ENFORCEMENT OF WILDLIFE LAWS

Enforcement Powers

The Chief, game protectors, and other Division employees as specified may serve and execute warrants and other processes of law issued in the enforcement of 2923.12 and 2923.16 and in the enforcement of a law or Division order for taking, possession, protection, preservation or propagation of wild animals, or for protection against wrongful use or occupancy of state-owned or leased lands and waters, and property under Division control, or in the enforcement of 3767.31 and 3767.32, or other code sections prohibiting the dumping of refuse into or along waters, or in the enforcement of a criminal law when violation involves equipment or property owned, leased or controlled by the Division, in the same manner as a sheriff or constable may serve or execute a process, and may arrest on sight and without a warrant a person found violating any such law or order. The Chief or game protector have the same authority as sheriffs to require aid in executing a process or making an arrest. They may seize without process each part of a wild animal in the possession of a person violating a law or Division order governing the taking, possession, protection, preservation or propagation of wild animals, together with a boat, gun, net, seine, trap, ferret or device with which such animals were taken or killed or which was used in taking them, and a firearm, deadly weapon, or dangerous ordnance as defined in 2923.11, used or possessed contrary to 2923.11 and 2923.16, and forthwith convey the person before a county or municipal court judge having jurisdiction. No person shall interfere with, threaten, abuse, assault, resist, deter or attempt such of a game protector from carrying into effect a law or order for: ▸ taking, possession, protection, preservation or propagation of wild animals; ▸ protection against wrongful use/occupancy of state-controlled lands and waters and Division property; ▸ wearing of a license or permit required by Chapter 1531 or 1533; ▸ regulating hunting and trapping on the lands of another. No person shall interfere with or resist in any manner or deter a game protector or officer from enforcing or serving or executing a warrant or other process issued in the enforcement of 3767.31, 3767.32 or other code section prohibiting dumping of refuse into or along waters, or a criminal law when violation involves Division-owned or controlled property, or provisions of 2923.12 or 2923.16 regulating use of firearms and deadly weapons (1533.67).

Game protectors and other officers: ▸ shall enforce all laws against hunting without permission of the owner/agent of the land on which hunting is done; ▸ may arrest on view and without issuance of a warrant; ▸ may inspect a container or package at any time except when within a building and the owner objects. Such inspection shall be only for bag limits of wild animals taken in open season or for those taken during the closed season, or for any kind or species thereof. The Chief may assist game protectors and other employees in duty discharge. Landowners are not liable to game protectors for injuries suffered while carrying out their duties unless caused by willful or wanton misconduct of the owners or tenants. Game protectors may enter private lands or waters if they have good cause to believe a law is being violated. A game protector, Sheriff, Deputy Sheriff, Constable or officer with similar authority may search a place which there is cause to believe contains a wild animal or part contrary to law or Division order, or a boat, gun, net, trap, ferret, or device used in a violation, and seize any they find so taken or possessed. If the owner refuses a search, the game protector may obtain a search warrant and may forcibly search the place described, and if a wild animal, part, boat, gun, trap, ferret, or device is found in the owner's possession, seize same and arrest the person, such wild animal, boat, gun, net or ferret to escheat to the state. The Chief and game protectors are vested with the authority of police officers under 2935.03 of the code for the purpose of enforcing state criminal laws on property owned or controlled by the Department, and may throughout the state enforce 2923.12 and 2923.16 of the code and may arrest without warrant a person who, in the presence of the Chief or any game protector, is engaged in the violation of any of those laws (1531.13). A game protector shall enforce 3767.32 of the code and other laws prohibiting dumping of refuse into or along waters, Department rules and regulations adopted under 1517, and the Director's rules and regulations adopted under 1519, and shall make arrests for their violation. Such jurisdiction shall be concurrent with that of the peace officers of the county, township or municipal corporation in which the violation occurs (1531.13.1). Division employees conducting research, restocking game or fish, or other work incident to game or fish restoration projects or in enforcing laws or orders of the Division relating to game or fish or dumping of refuse along streams, or watercraft laws, while in the normal, lawful and peaceful pursuit of such investigation or enforcement may enter and remain upon privately owned lands and shall not be subject to arrest for trespass while so engaged, but shall identify themselves to the owner/tenant with badge or card certifying Division employment (1531.14).

Sheriffs, Deputy Sheriffs, Constables and other police officers shall enforce the laws and orders of the Division for the taking, possession, protection, preservation and propagation of wild animals, and for this purpose have the power conferred upon game protectors. Prosecution for offenses not committed in the officer's presence shall be instituted only upon the approval of the county prosecuting attorney where the offense is committed or as otherwise specified (1531.16). [Details of service of summons on corporations are given in 1531.19.]

A motor vehicle, all-terrain vehicle, boat, net, seine, trap, ferret, gun or other device used in the unlawful taking of wild animals is a public nuisance. Each game protector or other officer with like authority shall seize and keep such property and the illegal results of the use thereof, and unless otherwise ordered by the Chief, shall institute within five days proceedings in a proper court for its forfeiture. A writ of replevin shall not lie to take such property from the officer's or court's custody, nor shall such proceeding affect a criminal prosecution for the unlawful use or possession of such property [details given as to forfeiture action procedure, notice, and disposal of forfeited property] (1531.20). ★If the defendant in a prosecution or condemnation proceeding under a Division order or code provision is convicted, judgment shall be rendered for costs in addition to the fine imposed or forfeiture declared. The judgment shall be the first lien upon the property and no exemption shall be claimed or allowed against such lien. Failure to pay the fine and costs imposed shall result in commitment to the county jail or workhouse for one day for such amount of fine, determined as provided in 2747. The defendant shall not be discharged or paroled by a board or officer except upon payment of the fine remaining unpaid or upon the Chief's order (1531.23)★. [Details for prosecutions for violations of Division orders are in 1533.69.]

Criminal Penalties

Violation of 1531.02 relating to taking wild animals contrary to law and rule, or sale or transport thereof, or of a rule or order is a misdemeanor of the fourth degree. Violation of 1531.02 concerning taking or possession of deer illegally, polluting state land or water under 1531.29 or disturbing plants or animals on state lands under 1531.07 as specified is a misdemeanor of the third degree, and a subsequent offense is a misdemeanor of the first degree. Violation under 1531.25 involving illegal taking of endangered or threatened species is a misdemeanor of the first degree. Violation of 1533.17 (hunting or trapping on another's lands without written permission) is a minor misdemeanor. If the offender persists in the offense after reasonable warning or request to desist, it is a misdemeanor of the fourth degree. Violation of a section of this chapter for which no penalty is otherwise provided is a misdemeanor of the fourth degree. Violation of 1533.97(D) relating to fishing tag tournament fees is a misdemeanor of the fourth degree, and the court shall require a refund to fishing tournament participants of entry fees paid. Violations of code sections herein relating to illegal spotlighting, fur dealing, fish transport, minnow sales, poisons, explosives or other deleterious materials in waters, trespass on trout waters, tag tournament rules, and licensed shooting preserves and game farms, as well as certain commercial fishing and net provisions, are misdemeanors of the third degree. Violation of listed statutes and provisions relating to hunter harassment, injury to persons or property while hunting, illegal taking of nongame birds, lengths and weights of specified fish, failure to have a fishing tag tournament permit, certain commercial fishing provisions, resisting an officer, and hunting/fishing on a revoked or suspended license are misdemeanors of the first degree. ★A court that imposes sentence for a violation of a section of this chapter governing the holding, taking, or possession of wild animals, including, without limitation, section 1531.11 relating to taking, killing, possessing, transporting, buying or selling wild animals contrary to a Division order or rule, in addition to a fine, jail term, seizure and forfeiture imposed, shall require restitution for the minimum value of the wild animal illegally held, taken or possessed as established under 1531.20.1 of the code. An officer who collects moneys paid as restitution shall pay those moneys to the state treasury to the credit of the Wildlife Fund established under 1531.17 (1533.99).★

Civil Penalties

The Chief or the Chief's representative may bring a civil action to recover possession of or the value of a wild animal held, taken or possessed in violation of this chapter or Chapter 1533 or Division order against a person who held, took, possessed or exercised control over the wild animal. Except as otherwise provided by Division order, the following are presumed to be the minimum value to the state of each wild animal illegally held, taken or possessed: ‣ whitetail deer, $400; ‣ fur-bearing animal, game bird or game quadruped, $50; ‣ nongame bird, $25; ‣ eagle, $1,000; ‣ osprey, $750; ‣ hawk or owl, $100; ‣ fish, $10; ‣ wild turkey, $300; ‣ endangered or threatened species, $750; ‣ each other wild animal, $75. Nothing in this section affects the right of seizure under any other code section (1531.20.1).

Illegal Taking of Wildlife

Finding a gun, net, seine, boat, trap, or other device which is set, maintained, used or possessed in violation of the code or Division order is prima facie evidence of guilt. Finding a wild animal or part, unlawfully in possession is prima-facie evidence of the possessor's guilt (1533.29). (See also HUNTING, FISHING, TRAPPING PROVISIONS; and Civil Penalties and Criminal Penalties under this section.

License Revocations and Suspensions

★★The court before whom a violator of laws or Division orders for the protection of wild animals is tried, as a part of the punishment, shall revoke the license or permit of a person convicted, and the license or permit fee shall be forfeited to the state, and such person shall not procure or use any other license or permit or engage in hunting wild animals or trapping fur-bearing animals during the period of revocation ordered by the court (1533.13). If a person is convicted of a violation of a law relative to taking, possession, protection, preservation or propagation of wild animals, or a violation of 2909.08 while hunting, or is convicted of an order of the Division, the court or magistrate as an additional part of the penalty in each case shall suspend or revoke each license or permit issued pertaining to hunting, fishing, trapping, breeding and sale of wild animals or the sale of their hides, skins or pelts, and fees paid for such license or permit shall be forfeited to the state. No person with a suspended or revoked license or permit as provided herein, in the event of a hunting or trapping violation, shall engage in hunting or trapping; in a violation of 2909.08 while hunting, engage in hunting; or if a fishing violation, engage in fishing, or purchase, apply for, or receive a license or permit for: ▸ three years after conviction, if convicted of taking or possessing a deer in violation of 1531.02; ▸ not more than three years after conviction, if convicted of taking or possessing any other wild animal in violation of 1531.02, or if convicted of a misdemeanor violation of 2909.08 while hunting; ▸ not more than five years after conviction, if convicted of violating 1533.17.1 (negligent injury of persons or property while hunting), or of taking or possessing an eagle or osprey in violation of 1533.07, or convicted of a felony violation of 2909.08(C) while hunting. All licenses and permits suspended or revoked shall be taken by the magistrate, sent to the Department to be filed with a record of the arrest until the convicted person is lawfully entitled to obtain a license or permit (1533.68). ★★

HABITAT PROTECTION

The US Commissioner of Fisheries may establish, operate and maintain fish hatcheries in Ohio, and may acquire by lease, gift or purchase lands and equipment necessary for same, and may conduct in any manner at any time investigations and fish cultural operations (1531.24).

The Chief shall pay to county treasurers where state-owned lands are located 1% annually of the total value of such lands exclusive of improvements from funds from the sale of hunting or fishing licenses and federal wildlife restoration funds, their allocation to be determined by the Director. Such payments to the counties shall be credited to the fund for school purposes within school districts. The Division, in the management of lands it administers, shall have authority to contract with private persons for the creation or improvement of wildlife habitat thereon, such contracts to be paid for in money or in goods produced incidentally to such contract (1531.27 and .28).

★★No person shall place or dispose of garbage, waste, vegetable peelings, fruits, rubbish, ashes, cans, bottles, wire, paper, boxes, automobile parts, furniture, glass, oil or anything else of an unsightly or unsanitary nature on state-controlled land or in a ditch, stream, river, lake or pond, except those which do not effect a junction with natural surface or underground waters, or upon the bank thereof, where same is liable to be washed into the water by flow or flood, except by permit or exemption issued under 6111.04 (1531.29). ★★ No person shall take, catch, injure or kill wild animals, or destroy their habitats, in state waters by means of quicklime, electricity or explosive or poisonous substances, or place same in such waters, except for engineering purposes and with the written permission of the Chief. Each wild animal taken, killed or possessed in violation of this section is a separate offense. No person shall locate, place or maintain in state waters an obstruction to the natural transit of fish. The Chief or a game protector may take up, remove or clear away such obstructions, except milldams, and if such obstruction is a net or other device used for leading or catching fish, it may be seized and condemned as provided in 1531.20 (1533.58 and .59).

See Agency Funding Sources under STATE FISH AND WILDLIFE AGENCIES.

NATIVE AMERICAN WILDLIFE PROVISIONS: None.

Ohio

OKLAHOMA

Sources: Oklahoma Statutes Annotated, 1991, Title 29; 1992 Cumulative Annual Pocket Part.

STATE WILDLIFE POLICY

All wildlife found in this state is the property of the state (7-204).

RELEVANT WILDLIFE DEFINITIONS: See Definitions section in Appendices.

STATE FISH AND WILDLIFE AGENCIES

Agency Structure

The **Wildlife Conservation Commission** (Commission) prescribes rules, regulations and policies. The **Department of Wildlife Conservation** (Department) is governed by the **State Wildlife Conservation Director** (Director). The Commission shall consist of one member from each of eight districts composed of designated counties, appointed by the Governor with consent of the Senate for eight-year terms. The Director is appointed by a majority vote of the Commission (3-101, -102, and -104).

Agency Powers and Duties

The **Commission** shall constitute an advisory, administrative and policy making board with which the Director shall consult and to which shall submit required reports. The Commission shall: ▸ institute an affirmative action plan with a goal of hiring women and minorities throughout the agency; ▸ elect officers; ▸ appoint a Director and determine the Director's qualifications; ▸ prescribe rules, regulations and policies for control of the Department; ▸ acquire by purchase, lease, gift or devise waters, real and personal property; ▸ acquire real property through condemnation with the Attorney General's approval; ▸ supervise establishment, extension, improvement and operation of wildlife refuges, propagation areas, public hunting and fishing areas, game management areas and fish hatcheries; ▸ prescribe the manner of cooperation with Tourism, state universities, state agencies and federal agencies in conservation and propagation of wildlife and development of educational materials, recreational facilities, hunting and fishing facilities; ▸ prescribe rules and regulations for regular or special licenses; ▸ publicize the conservation and appreciation of wildlife and other natural resources; ▸ regulate seasons and harvest of wildlife; ▸ annually report activities of the Department to the Governor; ▸ provide the Governor an annual inventory of all property and equipment (3-103). The Commission may lease state owned lands for grazing or agricultural purposes when not inconsistent with state or federal laws, for oil, gas and other mineral rights for five years or so long as production is in paying quantities. Mineral, oil and gas leases shall reserve to the state a royalty of not less than one-eighth part of such minerals, oil and gas produced. Profits from bonuses, rents and royalties shall go to the Wildlife Conservation Fund (3-304).

The Commission is authorized to: ▸ declare an open season on game mammals and birds in counties where game exists in sufficient quantity to warrant open season, and the season shall be announced ten days prior to opening; ▸ prescribe rules and regulations for the conduct and policing of open seasons, the amount and kind of game that may be taken and the dates and time limits of seasons, the quail season being in statute; ▸ require persons participating in open seasons in certain areas to procure special permits or licenses and to put part of this fee into compensation for landowners who participate in the Acres for Wildlife program, no exceptions being permitted. Open seasons, closed seasons, bag limits, possession limits and territorial limits set forth in the statutes pertaining to wildlife of every sort are to be based on the existence of a normal population of species of wildlife, compatible with and not damaging to the proper agricultural use of state lands. Seasons shall prevail for each species of wildlife so long as the numbers of wildlife remain normal or are not damaging crops. The Commission, after ten days notice of a public meeting, shall determine if there does or does not exist a normal population of the wildlife species under consideration, which does or does not endanger the crops of the state or local area. If the species population is determined to be not normal at public meetings in areas affected, the Commission shall make necessary changes in season by extending, shortening, opening or closing seasons or changing bag limits, and methods of taking. Administrative order shall take effect after publication in at least one paper of general state circulation (5-401). The Commission may close waters of the state to fishing as necessary, and it is illegal to fish in closed waters until reopened by the Commission (6-502).

The **Director** is to ▸ manage the Department under Commission regulations; ▸ manage all wildlife refuges and Department properties; ▸ appoint and employ rangers and other employees; ▸ promote and manage wildlife propagation by raising and distributing wildlife over the state at the Commission's direction; ▸ capture, propagate, transport, buy, sell, or exchange species of fish, game, fur-bearing animals and protected birds needed for stocking, and care for and feed the same; ▸ cause proceedings to be commenced against violators of wildlife laws (3-105).

Game Wardens shall have the full powers of state peace officers in the enforcement of the wildlife code, and authority to enforce state laws on Department-owned/managed lands, and shall enforce other state laws when ordered by the Governor. Game Wardens are vested with the authority and power of sheriffs in making arrests for wildlife conservation violations and nonconservation-related crimes in cooperation with other state law enforcement officers. Game Wardens may take into possession protected wildlife which has been killed, taken, shipped or possessed illegally; cause proceedings to be commenced against violators of any wildlife law; be authorized agents of the Commission or Department; assist in fire law enforcement. ★A Game Warden who accepts a bribe is guilty of a felony and on conviction shall be sentenced to two to seven years in prison and removed from office (3-201).★

★A city council or board of town trustees in a city or incorporated town owning/operating a lake may establish a **Wildlife Conservation Commission** of three or more members to be appointed by the city mayor or board's president, such commission to have exclusive control and jurisdiction of fishing/hunting in the town's lake, but may not pass a regulation contrary to the state Wildlife Commission laws/regulations (6-503).★

Agency Funding Sources

No person may hunt or take waterfowl during the open season on waterfowl unless they have obtained an **Oklahoma Waterfowl Hunting Stamp**. The license fee is to go into the Wildlife Conservation Fund to be used exclusively for developing, managing, preserving, restoring and maintaining wetland habitats and for the conservation and management of waterfowl and ecologically related species (4-131). ★The Department is to issue a **Wildlife Habitat Stamp** on the voluntary payment of $5 by a person.★ Moneys are to be deposited in the **Wildlife Land Acquisition Fund**. The moneys in the fund are to be used by the Commission for acquisition on willing-seller basis only, leasing, taking of easements, development, management, and enhancement of lands for the following purposes: management of game animals, protected animals and birds, fur-bearing animals, game birds, fish and their restoration, propagation and protection; and creation and management of public hunting, fishing and trapping areas. The Commission may accept private contributions, grants, donations to funds, and lands, which if not needed, may be sold and moneys put into the fund (4-132).

★After January 1, 1987, no person born after January 1, 1923, who is exempt from licensing requirements of 4-110 or 4-112 shall fish, hunt, pursue, trap, harass, catch, kill, or take wildlife without a senior citizen lifetime hunting or fishing or combination license, the funds from license sales to go into the **Wildlife Heritage Fund** (4-133).★

★All moneys received from fines and forfeitures for violations of the wildlife conservation laws shall be deposited as follows: 50% with the County Treasurer to be credited to the general fund of the county; 50% to the state Wildlife Conservation Fund (3-301).★

The **Wildlife Conservation Fund** consists of all moneys appropriated to, on deposit in, or credited to the **State Game and Fish Fund**, and all license fees, penalties, fines or forfeitures collected, all donations and other moneys received by the Department. Expenditures of the fund shall be under Commission control. ★A reserve fund of not less than $100,000 is to be maintained for emergencies on approval of the Governor, and $200,000 is to be maintained for liquidation of unsold licenses.★ All moneys or funds arising from Commission operation and transactions, from the application and administration of wildlife laws and regulations, and from the sale of property used for said purposes shall be expended by the Commission for the control, management, restoration, conservation and regulation of state wildlife resources, including the purchase of property and for laws administration pertaining to wildlife resources and for no other purposes (3-302).

PROTECTED SPECIES OF WILDLIFE

It is unlawful to take willfully or destroy the nest or eggs of a game bird, except as specifically permitted by law. Violation: $10-100 fine; jail up to 30 days, or both (5-207). Taking, killing, or capturing of more than 15 bullfrogs in one day during open season, or selling or shipping bullfrogs out of state is prohibited except by commercial enterprise (5-403). No person may take otter (5-405). Killing of squirrels is prohibited except from May 15 to January 1, and bag limits are set by the Commission (5-409). No person may knowingly and willfully, by means of a device, molest, injure or kill a species of hawk, falcon, owl or eagle, their nests, eggs or young except as permitted by federal law for licensed falconers (5-410).

No person may hunt, chase, harass, capture, shoot at, wound or kill, take, trap an endangered or threatened species or subspecies without specific written permission of the Director, such permission not to conflict with federal law. Violation: $100-1,000 fine; jail up to 30 days; or both (5-412). ★The Department shall print a list of endangered or threatened species or subspecies as part of the published general hunting regulations booklet (5-412.1).★

See also RELEVANT WILDLIFE DEFINITIONS, ANIMAL DAMAGE CONTROL and HUNTING, FISHING, TRAPPING PROVISIONS.

GENERAL EXCEPTIONS TO PROTECTION

No person may kill or capture wildlife or take their nests or eggs for scientific purposes without a license from the Director. Licensee must be age 16 or older, have testimonial from one well-known scientist or institution, and the application lists species sought, means to be used to take, and reason for collection. The license is to list permitted species and valid taking period. A final report is required from licensee detailing number and species taken (4-118). The running, chasing of fox, bobcat and raccoon with dogs for sport only is permitted (5-405).

See also HUNTING, FISHING, TRAPPING PROVISIONS and ANIMAL DAMAGE CONTROL.

HUNTING, FISHING, TRAPPING PROVISIONS

General Provisions

It is illegal to hunt on another's lands without consent unless the lands are not occupied by a resident and are not posted and to operate a motor vehicle on lands which are posted, fenced or in cultivation without the owner's permission. Violation: $40-100 fine; up to 30 days jail; or both (5-202). No hunting, pursuing game or use of firearms is allowed within 440 yards of a church, school or other public place. No person may shoot at wildlife from or across a public road or highway or railroad right-of-way. Violation: $10-100 fine; 30 days jail; or both (5-204).

Licenses and Permits

An upland game license shall be required for legally acquired captive raised pheasants, all species of quail, Indian chukars, water fowl, and other suitable gallinaceous birds, and shall include turkey if no other big game species are listed on the license application (4-106).

A commercial hunting area wherein wildlife or domesticated animals are propagated or held in captivity for commercial hunting requires a license and proof that stock will be acquired from a source other than state wildlife. Violation: $500-1,500 fine; jail up to 60 days; or both. A big game license shall be required for legally acquired exotic ungulates and domesticated animals as designated by the Commission, and legally acquired whitetail and mule deer, turkey and other species of big game lawfully taken under 5-411 and 5-401. Wildlife crossbred with exotic wildlife shall be considered native and not exotic unless documentation shows otherwise (4-106). The commercial breeding, or raising of wildlife requires a commercial wildlife breeder license. Violation: $100-200 fine, and possible license revocation for rest of license term (4-107). A fur dealer license is required, and advance notice must be given to the Director of where business transactions are to take place before buying, bartering or dealing in furs or pelts. Violation: $250-500 fine; jail up to 30 days; or both (4-111).

Except as otherwise provided for in this code, no person may hunt, pursue, trap, harass, catch, kill, take or attempt to take, use, have in possession, sell or transport a portion of wildlife except fish without having procured a license for such. ★A person arrested for hunting game other than deer, antelope, elk or turkey without a license may purchase a temporary 30-day license from the arresting game warden in lieu of posting bond. Proof of hunter safety certification will not be required for such temporary substitute licenses.★ Fees from hunting licenses will go into the Wildlife Conservation Fund to be used exclusively for developing, managing, preserving and protecting wildlife and wildlife habitat. Unless a substitute license is purchased on arrest, violation for residents: $25-100 fine; jail up to 30 days; or both. Violation for nonresidents: $200-500 file; jail up to 6 months; or both (4-112).

A hunting license and a license for a falconer to use hawks, owls or eagles to hunt, chase or take game is required. Violation: $25-200 fine. ★The Department is to issue rules regarding discretionary bonding for falconers to allow them to post bond in lieu of confiscation of their raptors (4-108).★ Falconry is a legal method for hunting and taking resident game. Exotic species of hawk, falcon, owl or eagle and a native species as provided by code may be used for such sport. Such birds may not be sold, traded or bartered and may be possessed, trained and used only by licensed falconers. Birds bred in captivity may be sold. Violation: $25-200 fine (5-206).

A trapping license is required to trap fur-bearers. Violation: $10-1,000 fine, depending on license class and residency (4-119). No person may hunt, kill, capture or otherwise take or destroy a fur-bearer except from December 1 to January 31. Pelts taken shall be sold or disposed of within ten working days after close of the season (5-405). Trapping on the land of another without written permission from the landowner is prohibited. Violation: $25-200 fine (5-501).

Except as otherwise provided, no person shall fish, pursue, harass, catch, kill, take, use, have in possession, sell or transport fish without having a license in possession. Fishing license moneys are to go into the Wildlife Conservation Fund (4-110). No person may transport or ship minnows for sale into or out of the state without a minnow dealer's interstate license except for persons leaving the state with three dozen or fewer minnows (4-115). A person in possession of more than 20 mussels or parts shall have a mussel harvesting license (4-129). Mussels or shells collected outside the state shall not be sold in Oklahoma. No person may harvest, sell, buy or export mussels from state waters without a proper license. A person may take six or fewer mussels per day of any size for noncommercial personal use (4-129). A trout license is required to fish in designated trout waters as determined by Commission. Violators may purchase a temporary 30-day license from the arresting warden in lieu of posting bond. Violation: $10-100 fine; jail up to 30 days; or both for residents/nonresidents, if the temporary license is not purchased (4-120). Aquatic culture of catfish, minnows, fingerlings, fish, frogs or other water species requires a license. Violation: $25-100 fine; up to ten days jail; or both (4-102). No person may seine, trap, transport or sell minnows within the state without a valid minnow dealer's license, and without observing statutory requirements as to net sizes, use of helpers, landowner permission, and vehicle transport aeration regulations. Violation: $100-$200 fine; jail up to 30 days; or both (6-401).

Restrictions on Taking: Hunting and Trapping

During field trials, no person may take legally-acquired domestically-reared pheasant, coturnix quail, bobwhite quail, Indian Chukars or similar birds without a hunting license and a field trial license. Violation: $25-100 fine (4-109). Except as otherwise provided, no person may utilize the following means to kill or capture a game mammal, game bird or nongame bird: ▸ a trap, net, snare, cage, pitfall, baited hook or similar device; ▸ a drug, poison, narcotic, explosive or similar substance; ▸ a swivel or punt gun greater than ten caliber; ▸ a device which generates electricity. Violation: $100-500 fine (5-201). Spotlighting is prohibited in killing or attempts to kill deer or other wildlife except fish and frogs. It is permitted to use a .22 caliber firearm and a carried light to pursue fur-bearers with hounds during legal, open fur-bearers season while possessing a hunting license. It is illegal to hunt from a boat with a firearm from sunset until one-half hour before sunrise. No harassing, hunting, taking, capturing of wildlife with the aid of a motor-driven land, air or water conveyance is allowed except for nonambulatory persons with the Director's written permission. Motor driven conveyances may be used to follow dogs in the act of hunting on public roads or waterways. Violation: $250 minimum fine for first offense and $500 minimum for second offense; or jail from ten days to one year; or confiscation of conveyances, firearms or other items used as an aid in a second or subsequent violation of sections 411 and 412 of this title; or by fine, imprisonment and confiscation. A bird-hunting dog may be used in the legal hunting of quail, dove, prairie chickens, pheasant and waterfowl. Dog trainers may carry firearms on otherwise closed public or private property if they notify the warden in their region, have a dog training shoot-to-kill license, and use pen-raised, tagged birds. Violation: $100-500 fine; jail 10 days to 1 year; or both (5-203).

No person may hunt, capture, or kill migratory birds including, but not limited to, ducks, brant and geese, except as provided by federal law and Commission regulation (5-406). Quail may be killed only by a shotgun, longbow or falconry, between sunrise and sunset. At no time shall a quail or covey be shot while resting on the ground ("pot shooting"). The quail bag limit is ten per day; possession limit is two days' bag limit (5-407).

The use of a trap, snare, deadfall or other device for catching wildlife, except fish and frogs, is prohibited, except for the use of box traps; smooth-jawed single spring or double spring offset, leg-hold steel traps with a jaw spread of no more than eight inches for land sets or water sets; no trap may be set in the open or in paths, roadways commonly used by persons, domestic animals, or dogs. Traps set for the purpose of catching wildlife shall be tended once during each 24-hour period and must bear owner's name, except for traps on one's own property. Violators are subject to civil liability for damages in addition to criminal penalty for violations. Lands where smooth-jawed double spring offset traps are used must be posted as mandated by the Commission. Violation: $25-200 fine (5-502).

Restrictions on Taking: Fishing

Except as specifically provided, no person may use a trotline or throwline unless labeled and used in lakes of over 100 surface acres or in navigable rivers to catch fish. No more than three such lines may be used at one time; no more than 100 hooks may be used, at least 24 inches apart; each line must be inspected every 24 hours; and the main line must be constructed of nonmetallic material. Limblines or juglines are prohibited except where tagged with name and address of owner and in lakes of over 100 surface acres in size, and line is attended every 24 hours. Violation: $25-100 fine. Scientific license holders are exempt from these prohibitions (6-301).

No person may use in state waters for taking, catching, capturing or killing game or nongame fish: rotenone or other poison; dynamite or other explosive; an electrical device used to shock. Possession of these shall be prima facie evidence of a violation. A device or explosive or equipment, boat, or motor vehicle used in violation is subject to immediate seizure and forfeiture. No person may manufacture, sell or buy an electrical device designed to shock fish. Violation: $500-1,000 fine; jail up to 30 days; or both. A second conviction within two years is the same fine, jail up to 90 days or both, and revocation of license for one year (6-301).

No person may take, catch or kill from state water stocked by state or federal fish, or from state stocked private waters any game fish except by hook and line attached to a pole or rod, throwline, trotline or with speargun by underwater divers, nor may a person sell or offer to sell game fish. Game species open to taking by speargun include all except black bass, striped bass, walleye, northern pike and trout. The Commission shall set bag limits, length limits and methods of taking of game fish. Violation: $25-100 fine. A person convicted of netting, snaglining or selling game fish shall be fined $100-500; jailed up to 30 days; or both. A second conviction within two years is a fine of $500-1,000; jail up to 90 days; or both; and all fishing licenses and privileges shall be revoked for one year (6-302).

No person may take, kill or catch nongame fish from state waters except as follows: by all legal hook and line methods in state waters legally open to these methods; by nets or seines used to take nongame fish only in waters declared open to such nets or seines by the Commission. Such nets are to be hoop nets, tagged with identification of the owner and must be attended once every 24 hours. No fish taken pursuant to this noncommercial netting provision may be sold or transported from the state. Noncommercial netting is prohibited statewide during April and May. Fish may be taken by arrows, gigs, ropes, grab hooks, spears and spearguns, by noodling, by cast nets, handnets and trawl nets used to take nongame fish for bait. The Commission is to designate state waters to be open to taking of nongame fish by the above methods. Violation: $25-100 fine. Violation of netting, snaglining or selling nongame fish is a minimum fine of $100; jail up to 30 days; or both. A second violation within two years is a fine of $500-1,000; jail up to 90 days; or both; and revocation of license for one year (6-303).

No person may fish upon land of another without owner's consent unless the land is not occupied, unless posted by the owner, or it is non-leased state land occupied by a resident. Trespassing on lands which are fenced and exhibit posted signs at all entrances is prohibited. Violation: $10-100 fine; jail up to 30 days; or both (6-304). The

Department may stock fish in privately owned ponds only so long as no fish are illegally taken therefrom or marketed by the owner. Violation: $25-100 fine (6-305).

A boat or vessel, boat trailer, motor, fishing device, vehicle or equipment used or operated in violation of the provisions of sections 4-129, 6-301 or 6-302 of this title (relating to means of taking game or nongame fish and harvesting of mussels) shall be subject to immediate seizure by a peace officer or warden and on conviction, any of the above may be forfeited (6-306).

Except as provided, no person may deposit, place, or throw lime, dynamite or other explosive, poison, drug, sawdust, salt water, crude oil or other deleterious, noxious or toxic substance into a state stream, lake or pond or in a place where such substances may run or be washed into waters. Violation by persons, firms, corporations is a fine of not less than $100-500, and each day or part of a day is a separate offense. Contamination by salt water or crude oil resulting from drilling of the petroleum industry shall be reported to the Oklahoma Corporation Commission for corrective action or criminal proceedings (7-401). ★It shall be the duty of the Commission to initiate appropriate legal action in federal court, or through cooperation with other state wildlife commissions or the federal government, in all cases where actions of individuals, firms or corporations in other states are injurious to wildlife of this state (7-402).★

The placing of a stationary dam, net, trap or obstacle for the purpose of blocking minnow or fish movement up or down a waterway is prohibited. Such devices shall be removed and are subject to seizure and forfeiture. Violation: fine up to $1,000; jail from ten days to one year; or both. ★On forfeiture, 25% of moneys are to go to the Wildlife Conservation Department and 75% to the district court where the proceeding was brought (6-501).★

When fishing in state waters with a device that automatically recoils (yo-yo), the device may not be left unattended for longer than four hours; must be labeled with the owner's name and address; may not be strung from a horizontal line or wire across a channel or navigable water; and no more than ten devices may be attached from one line or support. Violation: $10-100 fine; devices used shall be confiscated (1001).

Commercial and Private Enterprise Provisions

Commercial propagators, subject to neither season nor bag limit, may permit under their own conditions within their commercial hunting area hunting with or without dogs, and may allow hunters to shoot, kill, use, sell, or give away dead or live propagated wildlife or domesticated animals hunted for sport provided that the hunter has a regular hunting license (5-101). Wildlife removed or shipped from commercial hunting areas must be tagged with tags furnished by the Commission (5-102). All wildlife or domesticated animals hunted for sport which are commercially propagated or transported into the state may be liberated into the wild subject to Commission regulations (5-103). An owner of a private park, preserve, club or resort shall have authority to make and enforce additional rules/regulations not inconsistent with the wildlife conservation laws (7-303).

Noncommercial wildlife breeders licensees may breed and raise wildlife for: breeding for a hobby; educational and scientific purposes; personal consumption; release on private property (except a bear or cat that will grow to exceed 50 pounds); care and rehabilitation of sick or injured wildlife. Wildlife held under this license may not be sold. Violation: $10-200 fine; possible license revocation for remaining term of license (4-122 and -123). Licensed wildlife breeders may sell and transport live wildlife for propagation purposes, or minnows, and may sell/transport live or dead wildlife for food in compliance with tagging and reporting provisions. All fur-bearers except mink, game mammals, game birds, game fish and minnows raised under the provisions of this code must be confined to the lands or waters described in the license application to prevent wildlife belonging to the state from becoming part of the enterprise (5-601 and -602).

Catfish, minnows, fingerlings, fish, frogs and other water species commercially produced shall be confined to waters controlled by the propagator so as to prohibit wild fish or other species from becoming a part of the enterprise. There are no restrictions as to the manner in which propagators may gather or impound the species raised within the impoundments of their operations. Selling game fish from public waters which are commingled with privately produced fish is prohibited. Violation: $50-200 fine (6-102 and -105).

Import, Export, and Release Provisions

No person may ship a live or dead cottontail or swamp rabbit from the state (5-404). Fish shall not be released, deposited, placed or permitted to be released in public streams, lakes or ponds whose stocking is controlled by the Commission without the consent of the Director. Violation: $25-100 fine; up to 30 days jail; or both (6-504). The Commission is authorized to regulate the importation of exotic wildlife, and no exotic wildlife may be released into the wilds of Oklahoma without a written permit from the Director. A bear or cat that will grow to an excess of 50 pounds held in violation may be confiscated and disposed of by the Department after notice and hearing (7-801).

ANIMAL DAMAGE CONTROL

★No person may set or use cyanide coyote getter using cyanide gas or other poisonous gas for killing predators except as follows: ▸ signs must be posted as specified on all lands where coyote getters are used; ▸ devices shall not be set from April 1 to September 30; ▸ required signs shall be in place 24 hours before devices are set; ▸ a permit from game warden must be obtained prior to setting such devices; ▸ in applying for a permit, a landowner shall state the number of devices to be set and locations to nearest 40 acres; ▸ a permit shall not exceed six months, but may be renewed; ▸ no predator control devices are to be placed on a property without the owner's written permission. Predator control conducted by the state Department of Agriculture or Department are exempt from this section. Violation: $50-100 fine; jail up to 30 days; or both (5-301).★ Nothing shall prevent the killing of fur-bearers actually found destroying livestock or poultry (5-405). A species of hawk or owl in the act of destroying domestic birds or fowl may be destroyed (5-410).

ENFORCEMENT OF WILDLIFE LAWS

Enforcement Powers

It shall be a misdemeanor to violate a Commission rule or regulation under this code. Violation: $10-100 fine; jail up to 30 days; or both (8-104). A person convicted of violating any section of this code, for which there is otherwise no penalty, shall be fined $10-100; jailed 10 to 30 days; or both (7-201). Attempts to violate any provision shall be punished in the same manner as if the act was completed (7-202). Aiding and abetting in a violation shall be punished by the same manner as if the violator was a principal offender (7-203). ★The jurisdiction for the commission of an offense of the Oklahoma Wildlife Conservation Code shall be in the county in which the offense occurred, unless it occurred within 500 yards of the county boundary, then it shall be in either county (3-205.2). Game wardens may arrest without warrant a person for a wildlife violation of which the warden has visual or electronic perception, including perception by aircraft, radio or electronically enhanced night vision equipment (3-205.3).★

Violation of a provision of 5-203 and 5-401 through 5-410 of this title (relating to seasons, bag limits, big game, fur-bearers, headlighting, dog training and vehicle use) is a fine of $25-100. Violation of a provision of 5-411 and 5-412 (relating to big game poaching and endangered/threatened species illegal taking) is a fine of $500-1,000; or jail for 10 to 30 days; or by both. The state is authorized to institute legal action against the owner or operator of an air, land or water conveyances, firearms or other items or equipment so used, if such owner or operator is found guilty of a second or subsequent violation of 5-203.1 (relating to illegal spotlighting or vehicle use) in cases of deer, turkey, antelope and elk or when violations involve possession of a legal deer rifle or shotgun with slug or buckshot; or a violation of 5-411 or 5-412 (relating to illegal taking of big game or endangered/threatened animals). All of the above-mentioned items are subject to seizure and forfeiture proceedings pursuant to 7-206, if it is found that such items were used as an aid in violation (5-402).

★Persons who have been convicted of or have pleaded guilty to two wildlife violations in a two-year period shall be known as Habitual Wildlife Violators, and their hunting and fishing licenses may be canceled and denied for a minimum of one year. No habitual wildlife violators shall fish or hunt while their license is suspended or canceled. Violation: minimum fine of $500; jail for 15 to 90 days; or both (1002).★

Illegal Taking of Wildlife

★No person may capture, kill, mutilate or destroy wildlife protected by law and remove the head, claws, teeth, hide, antlers, horns or parts with the intent to abandon the body, nor may a person capture or mutilate living wildlife protected by law by removing claws, teeth, hide, antlers or body parts. No person may kill wildlife protected by law and abandon the body without disposing of the body in the most appropriate manner. Violation: $500-1,000 fine; jail for six months to one year; or both (7-205). When a habitual wildlife violator, as defined by section 1002, is convicted of a wildlife offense which involves the unlawful possession, taking or killing of deer, turkey, elk or antelope from an unlawful hunt, chase, trap, capture, shooting, killing or slaughter, netting, shocking, or poisoning, the court, in addition to the execution of sentence in whole or in part, shall order payment of restitution to the Department. The amount of restitution shall include, but not be limited to, replacement costs established by professional recommendation and approved by the Commission on an estimated average of the most recent values compiled from various surrounding states. Of the restitution amount, 100% shall be forfeited to the Department in the event of a guilty plea or conviction (7-207).★

No person, including, but not limited to, persons licensed for commercial hunting or wildlife breeders, may hunt, chase, capture, shoot, wound, kill or slaughter an antelope, moose, whitetail or mule deer, bear, elk, mountain lion, rocky mountain bighorn sheep, wild turkey or subspecies except in open season under 5-401 of this title (relating to seasons and bag limits), nor sell or offer to sell or buy these animals or parts except as provided by law or Commission regulation. This provision does not apply to a hide from a legally taken deer which is to be sold or traded. It is unlawful to have in possession meat, head, hide or part of the carcass of wildlife not legally taken, and meat, head, hide or carcass part shall be subject to immediate seizure by a game warden. This provision does not apply to privately owned, domesticated animals as designated by the Commission (5-411).

★Mounted specimens of deer and turkey shall be considered as the type of wildlife they represent for purposes of enforcement of sections 5-202, 5-401, 5-411 or 8-104 (relating to trespassing, taking big game out of season, and violating Commission regulations). Such mounted specimens shall not be placed alongside state or interstate highways for the purpose of enforcing Title 29 of the statutes.★ ★An item, equipment, vehicle or other property used or operated in violation of sections 5-401, 5-411 or 8-104 of Title 29 shall not be subject to seizure and forfeiture unless a person so convicted is a habitual wildlife violator (5-413).★

No person may possess, except as provided, wildlife or parts during the closed season or an endangered or rare species or parts. Exceptions are: ▸ legal storage of wildlife in freezers; ▸ possessing hides, heads or horns as trophies; ▸ possessing wild waterfowl taken under provisions of federal laws; possessing legally obtained wildlife as pets or for purpose of training hunting dogs. Propagators must have wildlife breeders license. Possession of game during closed season is prima facie evidence of taking in closed season. Violation: $100-500 fine; or jail up to 30 days; or both (7-502). Except as otherwise provided, no person may buy, barter, trade, sell any part of a fish or wildlife or the nest or eggs of a protected bird. Persons licensed to propagate or sell fish or wildlife and those with documentation of legally purchased fish or wildlife are exempt. Wildlife seized and determined to be unfit for release shall be sold and proceeds go to the Wildlife Conservation Fund. No person shall buy, barter, sell fur-bearing animal, game animal or game fish or part acquired from a source within or outside of the state without an invoice showing from whom the seller purchased said wildlife and which shows the source, species and quantity. Violation: $100-500 fine; jail for 10-30 days; or both. Subsequent violation: fine of not less than $1,000; or jail for 10-60 days, or both (7-503).

★No person may import, sell or possess for sale aigrettes, egret plumes and the feathers, quills, heads, wings, tails, skins or parts of skins of wild birds, either raw or manufactured or an endangered or rare species. Exemptions are importations, sales or possession for sale for scientific or educational purposes; feathers or plumes of domestic fowl. Violation: $100-1,000 fine; or jail up to 30 days; or both (7-504).★ No person may ship into or out of, transport into or out of or have in possession with intent, or cause to be removed from this state: wildlife or parts, nests, eggs or their young; an endangered or rare species. Exceptions are game legally possessed by licensed hunters or fishermen which may be shipped. Deer legally killed, or transported from another state, may be shipped if properly tagged; rough fish products processed into food may be exported; rough fish caught by fishermen under special permit may be shipped; minnows, fish, game and other wildlife lawfully bred or propagated may be sold, shipped within or without the state. Violation: $50-200 fine; jail for 10-60 days; or both (7-602).

Reward Payments

The Department may offer and pay a standing reward in an amount not to exceed the sum of $500 for the capture and conviction, or for evidence leading thereto, of a person violating the wildlife conservation laws (3-308).

HABITAT PROTECTION

See Wildlife Land Acquisition Fund and Wildlife Conservation Fund under Agency Funding Sources, STATE FISH AND WILDLIFE AGENCIES.

A person who catches fish from the waters of this state and the fish are dead when taken or die as result of such act shall remove those fish from waters and shall bury or burn them, except noncommercial fishermen may return fish remains to the lakes and reservoirs of the state. Dead fish must be buried or burned where they are not liable to become exposed through erosion or where land is subject to overflow. Violation: $100-1,000 fine; or jail for up to one year; or both; and violators shall reimburse a state agency for costs of clearing waters or land of those dead fish (7-403).

No person may enter upon a state or federal wildlife refuge or management area with dog or gun, except for Commission approved dog field trials, or when such hunting, killing or trapping of wildlife is specifically permitted by Commission resolution. Violation: $25-100 fine; jail for 10 to 30 days; or both (7-304). No person may cut down or remove a tree being used as a den or nest by raccoons or squirrels without specific permission of the landowner (5-408 and -409).

★It is unlawful to import into, transport into, place or cause to be placed in the waters of, or cultivate or cause to propagate in state waters any noxious aquatic plant or seed or reproductive part, as declared to be injurious to the environment of the state and declared to be noxious by Commission regulation. Violation: $10-100 fine; jail up to 30 days; or both. Commission may enforce this provision by injunctive action, and may grant individual and conditional exceptions (6-601).★

NATIVE AMERICAN WILDLIFE PROVISIONS: None.

OREGON

Sources: Oregon Revised Statutes Annotated, 1953, Chapters 496, 497, 498 and 501; 1992 Supplement Part 9.

STATE WILDLIFE POLICY

It is the policy of the state that wildlife shall be managed to provide optimum recreational and aesthetic benefits for present and future generations of citizens. In furtherance of this policy, the goals of wildlife management are to: ▸ maintain all species of wildlife at optimum levels and prevent the serious depletion of indigenous species; ▸ develop and manage the lands and waters of this state in a manner that will enhance the production and public enjoyment of wildlife; ▸ permit orderly and equitable utilization of available wildlife; ▸ develop and maintain public access to state lands and waters and wildlife resources; ▸ regulate wildlife populations and the public enjoyment of wildlife in a manner compatible with primary uses of state lands and waters and providing optimum public recreational benefits (496.012). Consistent with other provisions of law, it is declared to be a goal of the state to restore native stocks of salmon and trout to their historic levels of abundance by engaging in a program to rehabilitate and improve natural habitat and native stocks, and insuring that harvest level does not exceed capacity of stocks to reproduce (496.435).

★★The Legislative Assembly finds it imperative that the wildlife resources of the state be augmented to a level sufficient to provide Oregonians the recreational benefits of hunting and angling, an abundance of wildlife, and the reasonable expectation that their efforts will result in the taking of game or fish. The intent of this legislation is to provide adequate revenue to the Commission whereby game mammal herds and game fish populations may be increased for the benefit of Oregon hunters and anglers. Concomitant with the purposes for which the Legislative Assembly approves this legislation, the Commission is directed to expend the revenues created by this section and 497.102 to 497.134 in achieving wildlife management objectives including, but not limited to: ▸ habitat management; ▸ predator control; ▸ replenishing fish and game populations; ▸ reducing the anadromous bag limit; ▸ adjusting seasons to protect returning anadromous adults; ▸ supplemental wildlife feeding; ▸ protecting game mammals and birds with characteristics of high reproductive potential; ▸ enforcing closings necessitated by herd or population depletion; ▸ Expanding the road and access closure program when necessary to reduce hunting pressure in specific areas (497.071).★★

RELEVANT WILDLIFE DEFINITIONS: See Definitions section of Appendices.

STATE FISH AND WILDLIFE AGENCIES

Agency Structure

The **Department of Fish and Wildlife** (Department) consists of the **Fish and Wildlife Commission** (Commission), the **Fish and Wildlife Director** (Director), and other personnel necessary for efficient performance of the functions of the Department (496.080). The Commission consists of seven members appointed by the Governor for four-year terms, subject to Senate confirmation. One member shall be appointed from each congressional district, and one each from those portions of the state lying west and east of the Cascade Mountains. No member of the Commission may hold office in sports or commercial fishing organization or have ownership or direct interest in a commercial fish processing business. Failure to maintain compliance shall vacate membership. Members of the Commission may otherwise be removed only for cause (496.090).

The **Commission** shall select a chairman and vice chairman, for such terms and with duties and powers as the Commission determines. A majority constitutes a quorum. The Commission shall meet at least quarterly at times and places specified by the chairman or a membership majority. The Commission may meet jointly with authorities of other states or the US to consider problems of mutual interest (496.108). The Commission shall appoint a **Director** for a four year term, and may delegate administrative authority, powers and duties granted to or imposed upon it by law (496.112).

Oregon

Agency Powers and Duties

The Director is the executive head of the Department and shall: ► be responsible to the Commission for administration and enforcement of wildlife laws; ► appoint and supervise Commission employees; ► be responsible for all Commission functions and activities; ► establish sections and divisions to carry out the work of the Commission; ► be responsible for the collection, application and dissemination of information for the management, regulation and uses of wildlife resources; ► coordinate Department activities related to a watershed enhancement project approved by the Governor's Watershed Enhancement Board under 541.375 with other cooperating state and federal agencies; ► in emergency, exercise full Commission powers until the emergency ends or the Commission meets in formal session (496.118).

In addition to divisions established by the Director, there are established within the Department a Fish Division and a Wildlife Division (Division), responsible for the management of wildlife, except fish and other marine life, over which the Commission has regulatory jurisdiction (496.124).

The Commission shall report biennially to the Governor and the Legislative Assembly, and shall additionally report as they may direct (496.128). Before submitting budget requests or information to the Governor, the Commission shall hold a public hearing on planned expenditures and enhancement packages (496.132).

The Commission may formulate and implement state policies and programs to manage wildlife, perform acts to administer wildlife law provisions, and promulgate rules to carry out the wildlife laws (496.138).

The Commission may: ► accept and use appropriations, gifts or grants of money or other property for wildlife management; ► sell or exchange state property used for wildlife management; ► acquire, introduce, propagate and stock wildlife species to carry out wildlife policy and management programs; ► by rule authorize issuance of licenses, tags and permits for angling, hunting and trapping and prescribe tagging and sealing procedures; ► may issue special hunting permits to hunt on land owned by that person where permits for deer or elk are limited by quota; ► by rule prescribe procedures requiring license, tag or permit holders to keep records and make reports concerning the time, manner and place of taking wildlife, quantities taken and other information; ► establish special hunting and angling areas or seasons in which only persons less than 18 or over 65 are permitted to hunt or angle; ► acquire by purchase, lease, agreement or gift real property for wildlife management and recreation purposes; ► acquire by purchase, lease, agreement, gift, or exercise of eminent domain real property and establish, operate and maintain thereon public hunting areas; ► establish and develop wildlife refuge and management areas and prescribe rules governing their use; ► by rule prescribe fees for wildlife licenses, tags, permits and applications, and user charges for angling, hunting or other recreational uses of Commission lands; ► enter into contracts with a person or governmental agency to develop and encourage wildlife research, management programs and projects; ► perform acts to implement cooperative wildlife management programs with federal agencies; ► offer and pay rewards for arrest and conviction of a person who has violated wildlife laws (496.146).

The Commission shall not commence an eminent domain proceeding to acquire real property that was devoted to farm use on January 1, 1974, unless it first obtains approval from the Joint Committee on Ways and Means, or from the Emergency Board. Upon a change in the use of land from farm use, the Commission may acquire property by eminent domain without first obtaining legislative approval. The Commission shall not commence such proceeding unless it has obtained approval of its intended use of such property from the local governmental agencies having land use planning authority (496.154).

In carrying out duties and powers for propagation of anadromous fish prescribed in the wildlife and commercial fishing laws, the Commission shall give high priority to propagation assistance for transportation of upstream and downstream migrants in areas where dams and other obstacles present a passage problem to juvenile or adult salmon, (496.156).

After investigation of the supply and condition of wildlife, the Commission annually shall prescribe: ► the times, places, number of, and manner in which wildlife may be taken by angling, hunting or trapping; ► other restrictions or procedures regarding the angling, hunting, trapping or possessing of wildlife; ► the amount of each wildlife species that may be taken and possessed in terms of sex, size and other physical characteristics; ► regular and special time periods and areas closed to angling, hunting and trapping of wildlife species to protect the supply of wildlife;

► regular and special time periods and areas open to angling, hunting and trapping of wildlife species, and establish procedures for regulating the number of eligible participants, maintain the supply of wildlife, alleviate damage to other resources, or provide a safe and orderly recreational opportunity. Except as otherwise provided or during times and at places prescribed by the Commission for elk hunting it shall not prescribe limitations on the times, places or amounts for taking predatory animals. Before prescribing the numbers of deer and elk to be taken, the Commission shall consider the: ► supply and condition of deer and elk herds; ► availability of forage for deer, elk and domestic livestock on public and private range and forest lands; ► recreational opportunities from deer and elk populations; ► effects of deer and elk herds on public and private range and forest lands (496.162).

★★To benefit all users of these state resources, a Salmon and Trout Enhancement Program shall be conducted by the Commission to provide the greatest possible opportunity for citizen volunteer participation (496.440). In carrying out the salmon and trout enhancement program, the Commission shall: ► provide Department personnel as community advisors to develop enhancement projects with citizen volunteers and evaluate these projects with the citizens responsible for implementation; ► provide technical assistance to citizens responsible for implementation of such projects; ► coordinate such projects with the activities of Department staff and other agencies; ► provide educational and informational materials to promote public awareness and involvement in the enhancement program; ► supervise the activities of citizens developing local brood stocks; ► grant funds to citizens for the implementation of projects from available Commission moneys (496.445).★★

A citizen or group may submit to the Commission a proposal for a project to be implemented under the Salmon and Trout Enhancement Program or a request for advice and assistance in developing such a project. An enhancement project may include, but is not limited to, habitat improvement, installation and operation of streamside incubators, brood stock development, fish stocking and spawning ground surveys and data collection. The Commission shall approve only enhancement projects based on sound biological principles and shall use fish stocks most adapted to the locale. A project must maximize survival, adult returns and genetic diversity while minimizing disease. Conditions for approval include but are not limited to satisfactory provisions for inspection and evaluation of the project, and controlling the expenditure of and accounting for funds granted (496.450).

Agency Funding Sources

The **State Wildlife Fund** is established distinct from the General Fund. Except as otherwise provided, moneys received by the Commission pursuant to the wildlife laws, except as required for payroll and emergency expenses, shall be credited to the fund. Except as otherwise provided, fund moneys are appropriated continuously to the Commission to carry out the wildlife laws. Interest earned shall be retained in the fund. All moneys received from migratory waterfowl stamp sales go to the fund. Moneys from sales of art work and prints related to the migratory waterfowl stamps go to a separate subaccount in the fund to be expended only for activities that promote the propagation, conservation and recreational uses of migratory waterfowl and for activities related to the design, production, issuance and arrangements for migratory waterfowl stamp and print sales. Subaccount moneys may be expended as the Commission determines, on such terms and conditions as will benefit most directly state migratory waterfowl resources. The Commission shall keep a record of all moneys deposited in the fund, indicating by separate accounts the sources and the activity/program against which each withdrawal is charged. The **Fish Screening Subaccount**, established in the State Wildlife Fund, consists of: ► penalties recovered under 536.900 to 536.920; ► moneys received pursuant to section 2, chapter 858; ► gifts, grants and moneys from whatever source that may be used to carry out the provisions of 498.248, 509.615 and section 2, chapter 858. Moneys in the subaccount are appropriated continuously to the Department to carry out provisions of 498.248, 509.615, 509.620 and section 2, chapter 858. The **Fish Screening Administration Subaccount**, established in the State Wildlife Fund, consists of moneys received from the surcharge on angling licenses imposed by section 15, chapter 858. Moneys in the subaccount are appropriated continuously to the Department to carry out provisions of 316.139, 317.145, 496.300, 498.252 and 498.276 (496.300). [Statute notes state that under 858.013 the subaccount is abolished July 1, 1995, and the administration subaccount is abolished January 1, 1996.]

The **Fish Endowment Account** is established in the Treasury, separate and distinct from the General Fund, consisting of transfers of moneys authorized by the Legislative Assembly from the State Wildlife Fund and gifts and grants of moneys for maintaining fish hatcheries operated by the Department. Interest earnings, but no portion of the principal, may be transferred to the State Wildlife Fund to be expended for maintenance of Department fish hatcheries (496.300). [The statute note states under 749.008, that until June 30, 1995, one-half of all investment and interest earnings on moneys in the State Wildlife Fund shall be transferred to the Fish Endowment Account.]

The **Halibut Research Account** is a subaccount in the State Wildlife Fund. Moneys received from issuance of halibut tags pursuant to 497.121 shall be credited to the account, and may be expended only for halibut population studies and other research (496.300).

[Statute notes state that under 406.007 and 406.008 moneys received by the Commission from the sale of upland bird stamps and related art works and prints shall be deposited in a separate subaccount in the State Wildlife Fund, to be expended only for promoting propagation and conservation of upland birds and the acquisition, development, management, enhancement, sale or exchange of upland bird habitat, and for activities related to design, production, issuance and arrangements for sale of upland bird stamps and related art works and prints, as determined by the Commission.]

Individual taxpayers receiving an Oregon income tax refund may designate a contribution to the **Nongame Wildlife Fund** by marking the appropriate box printed on their return (496.380). The Nongame Wildlife Fund in the State Treasury consists of: ‣ a credit to the fund under 305.835 (tax return designations), to be transferred by the Department of Revenue to the fund; ‣ gifts, grants and donations which the State Treasurer may solicit and accept from private and public sources; ‣ interest or other earnings. Fund moneys are continuously appropriated for Department use only to protect and preserve nongame wildlife and their habitat (496.385 and .390).

The Commission shall arrange to select the annual Migratory Waterfowl Stamp design and to produce and sell the stamps, and may make stamps available for migratory waterfowl art prints and related art works and arrange for their sales (496.550).

[Statute notes state that under 406.001, 406.002, 406.006 and 406.008, the Commission is authorized until January 1, 1994, to issue to hunters an upland bird stamp for a specified fee; establish a fund to be financed by sale of upland bird stamps and related art works and prints for promoting the propagation and conservation of upland birds and acquiring, developing, managing, enhancing, purchasing or acquiring through lands exchange upland bird habitat; and providing the Commission with improved data on the location and number of upland bird hunters. The Commission may arrange for design selection, production and sale of the annual stamp.]

The Commission is authorized to issue each year one special mountain sheep tag to hunt mountain sheep, to be auctioned to the highest bidder as prescribed by the Commission (497.112).

Agency Advisory Boards

[Statute notes state that under 512.011 and 512.012 there is established within the Department the **Restoration and Enhancement Board** (Board), consisting of seven members appointed by the Commission. Three shall represent the ocean and inland recreational fisheries. Three members shall represent the commercial troll and gillnet fisheries and the fish processing industry. One member shall represent the public. In making appointments, the Commission shall consider recommendations from the Director. The Department and the Board jointly shall submit biennially to the Legislative Assembly a report on expenditures and the status of various projects. In recommending fish restoration and enhancement programs, the Board shall: ‣ recommend a mix of projects balancing restoration and enhancement benefits; ‣ recommend projects that are to be implemented by the salmon and trout enhancement program and nonprofit organizations; ‣ encourage projects which result in obtaining matching funds from other sources. Moneys made available for the fish restoration and enhancement program from surcharges and from gifts and grants made may be expended only if recommended by the Board and approved by the Commission. Such amounts may be expended on programs benefiting the commercial fishing industry, and on programs benefiting recreational angling. The Board may accept from whatever source, gifts or grants. Unless otherwise required by their terms, gifts or grants shall be expended as provided in this section. Individuals who reside in the various regions established for administration of the salmon and trout enhancement program may form advisory councils to discuss and consider fish restoration and enhancement programs and projects and shall make recommendations to the Board. When the Board considers proposals affecting a region, the Board shall consult with the advisory council for that region if one exists. Department employees who are residents of the various regions may act in an advisory capacity to the various councils (496.265).]

The **Salmon and Trout Enhancement Program Advisory Committee** (Committee) is an advisory committee to the Commission, which shall be of the size and geographical representation the Commission deems appropriate. Members are appointed by the Governor. The Committee shall review Department policies and make recommendations to the Commission and Department concerning implementation of salmon and trout enhancement projects (496.460).

PROTECTED SPECIES OF WILDLIFE

In carrying out provisions for management of threatened or endangered species, the Commission shall: ► conduct investigations of native wildlife species and determine whether threatened or endangered; ► by rule establish, publish, and periodically revise a list of threatened or endangered species; ► by rule establish programs for protection and conservation of threatened or endangered species, "conservation" is using procedures to bring a species to the point at which the measures under 496.172 to 496.182 are no longer necessary, including but not limited to scientific resources management such as research, census, law enforcement, habitat acquisition and maintenance, propagation and transplantation; ► by rule, establish a system of permits for scientific taking of threatened and endangered species which will minimize impact on the species; ► cooperate with the State Department of Agriculture in carrying out applicable provisions; ► adopt administrative rules to carry out statutory provisions; ► set priorities for establishing programs under this section. In proposing and implementing programs for those species that are secure outside this state, the Commission shall give preference to cooperative agreements, acquisitions and similar methods (496.172).

Lists of threatened or endangered species shall include those listed as of May 15, 1987 pursuant to the federal Endangered Species Act; and those species determined as of May 15, 1987 by the Commission to be threatened or endangered. The Commission by rule, may add, remove or change the status of a species on either list (496.176).

★★A determination that a species is threatened or endangered shall be based on documented and verifiable scientific information. To list a species, the Commission shall determine that the natural reproductive potential of the species is in danger of failure due to limited population numbers, disease, predation or other natural or man-made factors affecting its continued existence. In addition, the Commission shall determine that one or more of the following factors exists: ► most populations are undergoing imminent or active deterioration of their range or primary habitat; ► overutilization for commercial, recreational, scientific or educational purposes is occurring or is likely to occur; ► existing state or federal programs or regulations are inadequate to protect the species or its habitat. Determinations shall be based on the best available scientific and other data after consultation with federal agencies, interested state agencies, the Natural Heritage Advisory Council, other states having a common interest in the species and interested persons and organizations (496.176).★★

A person may petition the Commission to add, remove or change the status of a species on the list. A petition shall clearly indicate the action sought and include documented scientific information about the species' biological status. Within 90 days of receipt, the Commission shall write to the petitioner indicating whether the petition presents substantial scientific information to warrant the action requested. If so, the Commission shall commence rulemaking. A final determination shall be provided within one year. If denied, the petitioner may seek judicial review. Notwithstanding other provisions herein, the Commission shall take emergency action to add a species to the threatened or endangered list if there is a significant threat to its continued existence within the state. The Commission shall publish notice of such addition in the Secretary of State's bulletin and shall mail notice to affected or interested persons. Such emergency addition shall take effect immediately upon publication in the bulletin and shall be valid no longer than one year, unless during that period the Commission completes rulemaking procedures as provided (496.176).

The Commission shall periodically review the status of all threatened and endangered species. Each species shall be reviewed at least once every five years to determine whether substantial, documented scientific information exists to justify its reclassification or removal from the list, according to the criteria listed herein. If a species is to be reclassified, or removed from the list, the Commission within 90 days shall commence rulemaking to change its status. ★Notwithstanding this section, the Commission may decide not to list a species that otherwise qualifies as threatened or endangered within this state if it determines that the species is secure outside this state and is not of cultural, scientific or commercial significance to the people of this state (496.176).★

★★In developing protection and conservation programs pursuant to 496.172, the Commission shall consult with other states having a common interest in particular threatened or endangered species and with other affected state agencies. In furtherance of programs to conserve or protect such species, state agencies shall consult and cooperate with the Department. Before an agency takes, authorizes or provides financial assistance for action on state owned/leased land, or for which the state holds a recorded easement, in consultation with the Department, the agency shall: ▸ determine that the action is consistent with established Commission programs pursuant to 496.172; ▸ if no program has been established for a threatened or endangered species, determine whether such action has the potential to reduce appreciably the likelihood of the survival or recovery of such species. If an agency determines that the proposed action has the potential to reduce appreciably the likelihood of the survival or recovery of such species, it shall notify the Department. Within 90 days of notice, the Department shall recommend alternatives to the proposed action consistent with conserving and protecting the affected species. ★If an agency fails to adopt the recommendations, after consultation with the Department, it shall demonstrate that: ▸ potential public benefits of the proposed action outweigh the potential harm from failure to adopt the recommendations; ▸ mitigation and enhancement measures shall be taken, to the extent practicable, to minimize the adverse impact of the action on the affected species.★ When an action under this section is initiated by a person other than a state agency, the agency shall provide final approval or denial within 120 days of receipt of written request. These provisions do not apply to lands acquired through loan foreclosures under the Department of Veterans' Affairs (496.182).★★

★Nothing herein is intended to require an owner of a commercial forest land or private land to take action to protect a threatened or endangered species, or to impose additional requirements or restrictions on the use of private land. Notwithstanding the above, other statutes may authorize administrative rules or programs to protect wildlife, including threatened or endangered species, and nothing in the statutes as specified shall diminish the force or effect of such rules or programs (496.192).★

Live wildlife shall not be removed from its natural habitat or acquired and held in captivity illegally. The Commission may promulgate rules that include but are not limited to: ▸ providing for wildlife permits for holding or removal from habitat; ▸ prescribing species for which holding or habitat removal permits are required; ▸ prescribing terms and conditions of holding and removing wildlife from habitat to insure its humane care and treatment. No permittee shall violate permit terms or conditions (497.308).

Commission rules that authorize the acquisition and holding in captivity of a coyote must require: ▸ the permittee to obtain rabies inoculations; ▸ the animal to wear at all times a Commission issued identification tag; ▸ notification to the Commission upon the death, sale, transfer, removal from the state, or other disposition of the animal; ▸ the permittee not to abandon the animal; ▸ the permittee to neuter the animal. A permittee is subject to the same liability and other statute requirements for dogs, and shall at all times be able to demonstrate physical custody of the animal or evidence of its death or other disposition in compliance with statutory provisions. Nothing in this section authorizes acquisition and holding in captivity of a coyote not held at the State Fish and Wildlife Facility at Pendleton before September 10, 1976, or pursuant to a scientific taking permit (497.312).

The Commission may revoke a scientific taking or wildlife holding and habitat removal permit upon violation of its terms or conditions. Permit revocation is in addition to and not in lieu of any other penalty provided by law for the violation (497.318).

No person shall remove the eggs from green or white sturgeon, for artificial propagation, nor operate a fish hatchery for same, without a permit. Permit activities must be for educational and scientific purposes, and are subject to Commission terms and conditions to protect, perpetuate and enhance the sturgeon population of the Columbia River and other state waters. All permits issued prior to October 3, 1989, for sturgeon hatchery operation or egg propagation under which no activity has taken place prior to that date are cancelled. Existing permits may be continued under existing conditions (497.325 and .330).

Wildlife is the property of the state. No person shall angle for, hunt, trap or possess, or assist another in such activities in violation of the wildlife laws or rules (498.002). Except as the Commission by rule may provide, no person shall chase, harass, molest, worry or disturb wildlife except while engaged in lawfully angling for, hunting or trapping (498.006). Except as provided, no person shall purchase, sell or exchange, or offer to so, or its parts (498.022). Except as otherwise provided, no person shall take, import, export, transport, purchase or sell, or attempt to, a threatened or endangered species, or the skin, hides, parts, or an article made from them, and acquired after

1973 by the seller (498.026). No person shall offer for sale, trade, barter or exchange as a household pet a fox, skunk or raccoon; such an animal may be offered for sale, trade, barter or exchange to a public park, zoo, museum or educational institution for educational, medical, scientific or exhibition purposes under a Commission permit. The Commission may refuse to issue a permit if the organization does not have physical facilities adequate to maintain the animal in health and safety and to prevent its escape (498.029).

GENERAL EXCEPTIONS TO PROTECTION

Taking wildlife for scientific purposes requires a scientific taking permit. The Commission by rule shall prescribe a procedure for application, and terms and conditions of taking wildlife to insure that it will be used only for scientific purposes (497.298).

HUNTING, FISHING AND TRAPPING PROVISIONS

Licenses and Permits

The holder of a license, tag or permit to angle, hunt or trap must consent to inspection of these and wildlife taken by a Commission employee, person authorized to enforce wildlife laws, or the owner/agent of land upon which the license holder is angling, hunting or trapping (497.036).

Except as otherwise provided, no person shall angle for, hunt or trap wildlife, or assist another without having in possession required licenses, tags and permits. An angling license is not required: ► of a person younger than 14; ► of a resident and immediate family members, to angle on land they own and reside upon; ► to angle for or otherwise take smelt. An angler for salmon or steelhead trout must have in possession a salmon-steelhead tag, and an angler for sturgeon must have in possession a valid sturgeon tag. A hunting license is not required: ► of a person younger than 14 to hunt wildlife, except those species for which a tag or permit is required; ► of a resident and immediate family members to hunt wildlife on land they own and reside upon; ► of a holder of a trapping license to take fur-bearing mammals or predators by a weapon during open seasons; ► to take wildlife pursuant to 498.012, notwithstanding any other provision of this subsection. A trapping license is not required: ► of a resident and immediate family members to trap fur-bearing mammals or predators, except those species for which a tag or permit is required, on land they own and reside upon; ► of a person younger than 14 to trap fur-bearing mammals or predators, except those species for which a tag or permit is required; ► to trap wildlife that is not protected by state or US laws (497.075). [Categories of licenses, tags, and fees are listed in 497.102, .112, and .121.]

At the time of issue, the Commission may designate upon game tags whether an animal is to be taken with bow and arrow or with firearms. Rules may prescribe that the tag holder is not authorized to take the game animal by any other means. A person is not eligible to obtain, in a lifetime, more than one mountain sheep tag and one mountain goat tag. The number of nonresident mountain goat and mountain sheep tags shall be decided by the Commission, but not less than 5% nor more than 10% issued shall be nonresident tags. The Commission shall decide the number of nonresident tags to be: ► issued by drawing for deer, elk, bear, cougar and antelope, but not more than 3% of all tags of each class shall be issued for a particular area, except one nonresident tag may be issued for each hunt when authorized tags are less than 35; ► issued under this section for the general hunting season, but not more than 3% of all tags issued the previous year for a particular area (497.112).

Salmon-steelhead, sturgeon and halibut tags are in addition to and not in lieu of angling licenses, however, such tags are not required of holders of one-day angling licenses. Each salmon-steelhead tag authorizes the holder to take 10 fish. No person shall apply for or obtain more than four salmon-steelhead tags in one year, but all four tags may be issued at the same time (497.121).

The Commission may provide a means for voluntary contributions to be used for special fish and wildlife management programs, including programs to improve access for recreational angling, and may seek contributions in conjunction with sale of hunting and angling licenses and tags or by other means. If the Commission implements an electronic licensing system, it shall provide a means for voluntary contributions in conjunction with the sale of licenses and tags. All such voluntary contributions may be expended only for projects for which applications are made pursuant to 496.450 (497.134).

The Commission is authorized to issue to persons desiring to hunt migratory waterfowl an annual migratory waterfowl stamp. The stamp is in addition to and not in lieu of hunting licenses required (497.151).

No one younger than 18 shall hunt wildlife, except on the person's own land or land owned by the parent or legal guardian, without a certificate of satisfactory completion of a Commission prescribed course in safe handling of hunting weapons. The Commission by rule shall prescribe and administer a hunter safety training program in the handling of hunting weapons, which may include instruction on wildlife and natural resource conservation, first aid and survival and other subjects to promote good outdoor conduct and respect for the rights and property of others. The Commission may enter into agreements with other public or private agencies and individuals; the Departments of State Police and Education are directed to cooperate with the Commission to carry out these provisions (497.360).

No person shall: ► apply for, obtain or possess for personal use or another's use more licenses, tags or permits than are authorized during the current year; ► alter, borrow, loan or transfer to another a license, tag or permit; ► knowingly make a false statement on an application; ► possess any license, tag or permit that has been altered, borrowed, loaned or transferred or for which false statements were knowingly made; ► ★ apply for or obtain a license, tag or permit when civil damages due pursuant to 496.705 or when moneys due the Department from court ordered restitutions have not been paid (497.400).★

Restrictions on Taking: Hunting and Trapping

The Commission is authorized to issue licenses and tags for taking fur-bearing mammals [classes and fees set forth] (497.142). The Commission shall prescribe and administer a trapper education program for proper use of trapping equipment. The program may also include instruction on wildlife and natural resource conservation, firearms safety, first aid and survival and other subjects to promote good outdoor conduct and respect for the rights and property of others. Except as provided in this section, no person shall trap mammals with commercial fur value unless the person has in possession a certificate of satisfactory completion of a course in trapper education. The certificate is not required of a person and immediate family members to trap mammals with commercial fur value on land they own or lease. Nothing is intended to prevent a person or the person's agent from taking mammals with commercial fur value that are damaging livestock or agricultural crops on lands the person owns or leases. As used in this section, "mammals with commercial fur value" are badger, beaver, bobcat, coyote, red fox, gray fox, marten, mink, muskrat, nutria, opossums, raccoon, river otter, striped skunk, spotted skunk and weasel (497.146).

No person shall: ► angle for or hunt, or offer to for compensation wildlife in violation of provision of the wildlife laws or rules (498.032); ► except as otherwise provided, possess in the field or forest, or in transit, the carcass of wildlife that has been skinned, plucked or mutilated so that the sex, size or species cannot be determined (498.036); ► remove from the carcass of a game mammal or bird the head, antlers, horns, hide or plumage, and utilize only those parts, except when engaged in lawful trapping or when utilizing game mammals or birds the Commission declares to be inedible; ► waste the edible portion of a game mammal, bird or fish or the pelt of a fur-bearing mammal (498.042); ► place a toxic substance where it is accessible to wildlife unless the substance used and the method of application is approved (498.046).

A dog not wearing a collar with a license found unlawfully hunting, running or tracking a game mammal or bird may be killed by a person authorized to enforce the wildlife laws. If the dog is wearing a collar with a license number, the owner shall be notified, and if the person disclaims ownership, the dog may be killed. If the owner has been notified that the dog has been found unlawfully hunting, running or tracking game mammals or birds and thereafter fails to prevent it, the dog may be killed by an officer. No dog owner shall permit the dog to hunt, run or track unlawfully a game mammal or bird. Field trials for hunting dogs may be held as the Commission may prescribe. No person shall use live birds as targets for competitive shooting (498.102, .106 and .112).

★No person shall hunt upon the cultivated or enclosed land of another without permission. Boundaries of "enclosed" land may be indicated by wire, ditch, hedge, fence, water or by visible or distinctive lines, and includes established and posted boundaries of Indian reservations (498.120).★

No person shall hunt game mammals or game birds from or with the aid of aircraft, or transmit from an aircraft information regarding the location of game mammals or birds, or otherwise use aircraft to assist in hunting/locating game mammals or birds.   ★★No person shall hunt game mammal within eight hours after having been transported by aircraft to or from a place other than an airport licensed as a public use airport, registered as a personal use airport or specifically exempted from licensing or registration. Every pilot shall maintain a log book with names and addresses of persons transported, points of departure and destination, time, and date of each flight made in an aircraft within this state to transport a person to or from a place to hunt. The log book may be inspected by a person authorized to enforce the wildlife laws (498.126).★★

Except as provided, no person shall hunt wildlife from a motor-propelled vehicle (498.136).

Except under Commission rules for taking raccoon, opossum or bobcat or to alleviate damage by wildlife to other resources, no person shall hunt wildlife with the aid of an artificial light. No person shall cast from a motor vehicle or from within 500 feet of a motor vehicle an artificial light upon a game mammal, predatory animal or livestock while in possession or in the immediate physical presence of a weapon. This does not apply to a person who casts artificial light upon a game mammal, predatory animal or livestock: ▸ from the headlights of a motor vehicle that is being operated on a road in the usual manner, if no attempt is made to kill the game mammal or livestock; ▸ when the weapon is disassembled or stored, or in the trunk or storage compartment; ▸ on land owned or lawfully occupied by that person; ▸ on publicly owned land when that person has an agreement with the public body to use that property (498.142 and .146).

The Commission may enter into agreements with land owners to restrict the operation or parking of motor-propelled vehicles when damaging wildlife or wildlife habitat. The Commission shall post notice of restrictions, including effective date, on the main traveled roads entering the restricted area (498.152). Operating or parking a motor-propelled vehicle in violation of posted restrictions is an offense punishable as provided in 496.992. The owner of an unattended motor-propelled vehicle parked in violation of restrictions is guilty of a violation punishable as in 161.635 without regard to culpable mental state. It is a defense to prosecution that use of the vehicle was not authorized by the owner, either expressly or by implication (498.153). [Additional details as to notice adequate to charge defendant; delivery or posting; and jurisdiction are in 498.154.] If a cited vehicle owner fails to appear or to forfeit bail on or before the date and time stated on the citation, the court and the Motor Vehicles Division may take actions authorized under the Oregon Vehicle Code, except no arrest warrant may be issued nor criminal prosecution be commenced unless more than 10 days prior a letter has been sent to the registered owner advising of the charge (498.155).

★Except as provided, no person shall hunt or trap wildlife within the boundaries of a city, public park, cemetery or on school lands, unless the governing body, after notice and hearing, authorizes hunting or trapping by ordinance or resolution; and the Commission determines it would not adversely affect public safety or unreasonably interfere with other authorized uses of such lands (498.158).★

Except as provided in 498.412, no person shall operate an outdoor club without a license, if the outdoor club activities are to be conducted on land that is leased from the owners, if the members of the club are not parties to the lease, and if the members do not have financial or proprietary interest in the club. No person required to obtain a license to operate an outdoor club shall engage in promotional activities for sale of membership without a license (498.406). This section does not apply to a landowner offering to sell recreational access to private property (498.412). [Details of application and investigations of outdoor clubs, and license revocations, are provided in 498.418 through 498.452. Provisions for expiration and renewal of license is made in 498.458. Provision for restraining actions which threaten wildlife resources are in 498.464.] Violation of provisions for outdoor clubs is punishable by a fine not to exceed $1,000; or in the case of a person other than an individual, by a fine not to exceed $10,000 (498.993).

The Governor by proclamation may suspend a hunting season when hunting may result in extreme fire danger. The suspension may be applicable in all or a portion of this state, and shall be for a specified or indeterminate period. No person shall hunt during a period in an area where the appropriate season has been suspended pursuant to this section (501.005).

Restrictions on Taking: Fishing

Nothing in the wildlife laws is intended to affect the provisions of the commercial fishing laws. However, nothing in the commercial fishing laws is intended to authorize taking game fish in any manner prohibited by the wildlife laws (496.016).

Except as provided in 498.279, no person shall conduct, sponsor or participate in a competition or contest in which a prize value of more than $50 is offered for amount, quality, size, weight or other characteristic of game fish taken (498.202).

Except as the Commission by rule may provide, in a body of water no person shall: ▸ use an electric current; ▸ place a foreign substance such as blood or fish offal or a gas, chemical, drug or powder that may attract, frighten, retard, stun, kill or obstruct the movement of game fish; ▸ use an explosive device for taking game fish. No person shall possess game fish that the person has reason to know was taken illegally (498.208). ★Except as otherwise provided, no person shall trespass upon or angle from a fishway or angle within a boundary line extending across the 200 feet above the upper end and 200 feet below the lower end of a fishway (498.216).★

A person who diverts water in which game fish exist shall install, operate and maintain, at the expense of the person, fish screening or by-pass devices to prevent fish from leaving the water and entering the diversion. Upon failure to install, operate and maintain fish screening or by-pass devices, the Department may install, operate and maintain, at the expense of the responsible person, fish screening or by-pass devices. The Department shall have the right of ingress and egress to and from those places, doing no unnecessary injury to the property, for the purpose of installing, maintaining and replacing such devices, or to determine if such fish screening or by-pass devices meet Department requirements. The Department may order the repair or replace fish screening or by-pass devices, at the expense of the responsible person. If the Department considers the installation, operation, maintenance, repair or replacement of fish screening or by-pass devices necessary, it shall so notify the person of the action required. The person may request a hearing before the Commission. No person shall interfere with, tamper with, damage, destroy or remove fish screening or a by-pass device. The Department may maintain an action to recover costs the Department incurs in installing, maintaining or replacing fish screening or by-pass devices on behalf of a person responsible under this section (498.248). [Statute notes also refer to chapter 858 for further requirements for fish screening, including a Fish Screening Subaccount and Task Force.]

The Department shall establish guidelines to determine the need for and location of potential fish screening and by-pass projects. The guidelines shall include a plan for determining priorities for and expected costs of installing and maintaining the fish screening and by-pass devices. Nothing is intended to prevent the Department from expending federal or other funds if available for the installation and maintenance of fish screening and by-pass projects (498.256). Section 498.248 does not require installation of fish screening or by-pass devices in those water diversions for which the Commission, by contract or other agreement, has made other provisions for protection of the game fish (498.262).

Except as otherwise provided, no person shall construct, operate or maintain a dam or artificial obstruction across water in which game fish exist without providing a fishway for upstream and downstream passage for fish. If the Commission determines a fishway does not provide adequate passage, it shall notify the responsible person, and require appropriate alterations within a reasonable time. A person required to alter a fishway may file with the Water Resources Commission a protest against the alteration requirements. [Terms of protest, hearing and determination set forth.] If the person fails to make alterations in the manner and within the time required, the Commission may remove the dam or obstruction, or parts. No person who has constructed or operates or maintains a dam or artificial obstruction for which a fishway is required shall fail to keep the fishway free from obstruction. Every day of violation after the Commission has given written notice constitutes a separate offense (498.268). The Commission may maintain a suit to enjoin a person, including state agencies and political subdivisions, from violating the provisions of 498.248 or 498.268 (498.274).

In a competition or contest in which prizes are offered for the amount, quality, size, weight or other physical characteristics of black bass, the same fish may be used in different categories of competition if the prize awarding system is such that the value of prizes awarded to a participant does not exceed two times the individual prize value limitation (498.279). [Provision is made for requirements of contest, reports, and limitations. Similar provisions for walleye contests are noted in chapter 373.]

Commercial and Private Enterprise Provisions

No person shall engage in the business of buying skins or pelts of a fur-bearing mammal without a fur dealer license. Every fur dealer shall maintain a record of transactions involving skins or pelts which contains information regarding date, type and number of skins or pelts received and the name and address of the person with whom such transaction was made (497.218). No person shall engage in the business of propagating game birds or mammals for sale without a wildlife propagation license. The Commission may refuse to issue a license if it finds the business would harm existing wildlife populations. The Commission by rule may prescribe requirements for the care, inspection, transportation and sale, taking or other disposition of game birds or mammals and for record keeping and reporting procedures to insure that the propagation activities will not harm existing wildlife populations (497.228). No person shall engage in the taxidermy business without a taxidermist license and maintaining the prescribed record (497.238).

No person shall operate a private hunting preserve for hunting privately owned/propagated game birds without a private hunting preserve license. The Commission shall issue such a license to an applicant if: ▶ the preserve contains not more than 640 acres and is on one continuous tract of land owned or leased by the applicant for at least five years; ▶ the preserve is located at least three miles from other licensed private hunting preserve; ▶ no portion of the preserve is located closer than one-half mile to a park, wilderness area, refuge or wildlife management area operated by a government agency; ▶ preserve exterior boundaries are clearly marked; ▶ there are facilities to propagate or hold not less than 500 of each wildlife species to be released for hunting; ▶ the applicant will not prevent public hunting on adjacent lands. The Commission by rule shall prescribe the time, manner and place of hunting on private preserves, species to be hunted, requirements for care and marking of wildlife raised on the preserve, release of wildlife received from another state, procedures for marking indigenous wildlife incidentally taken on the preserve and fees, record keeping and reporting. No person shall hunt on a private hunting preserve without a hunting license or a private hunting preserve permit (497.248).

Except as provided, no person shall engage in the business of propagating game fish or food fish for sale without a propagation license. The Commission may refuse to issue a license if it finds the business would harm existing game fish or food fish populations. The Commission may prescribe requirements for the care, inspection, transportation and sale, taking or other disposition of fish, and for record keeping and reporting to insure the propagation activities will not harm existing game/food fish populations. Propagators of the following food fish under this license are exempt from the licensing provisions of 508.025 and 508.035: ▶ fish raised entirely in, then harvested from facilities which are enclosed or designed to prevent escape and from which the fish are not released for natural rearing; ▶ fish harvested from the wild under licenses prescribed in 508.025 and 508.035 and on which the appropriate fee has been paid at the time holding or rearing commences in the licensed facility (497.252). A licensee shall consent to license and records inspection by a person authorized to enforce the wildlife laws (497.268).

Import, Export and Release Provisions

No person shall release within this state domestically raised wildlife or wildlife brought to this state without a permit from the Commission (498.052).

No person shall transport live fish, or release or attempt to release into water a live fish that was not taken from that water, without a permit from the Commission. The Commission may refuse to issue the permit if such a release would adversely affect existing fish populations. This section does not apply to live fish for aquaria use (498.222). Except as provided, no person shall possess or import a game fish from Pacific Ocean waters without the required angling licenses, tags and permits, nor possess or import from any waters beyond the state boundaries game fish in excess of the amount prescribed. This section does not apply to possession or importation of fish taken pursuant to commercial fishing laws; or possession or importation of fish taken in the waters of another state, a US territory or a foreign country pursuant to those laws (498.228). The Commission by rule shall establish a program to protect all finfish and shellfish in state waters, both public and private, from infection by the introduction of detrimental fish diseases. Such rules shall not apply to live aquaria species imported or transported for aquaria use unless reared in facilities from which effluent directly enters state waters. These requirements are in addition to other requirement regarding importation of live game fish or eggs (498.234).

Except as otherwise provided, no person shall possess live walking catfish, or caribe or piranha. A public park, zoo, museum or educational institution may possess those fish for educational, medical, scientific or exhibition purposes if the organization first obtains a permit. The Commission may refuse to issue the permit if the organization has physical facilities that are inadequate to prevent their escape (498.242).

Interstate Reciprocal Agreements

Angling, hunting or trapping in the Snake River or on its islands, on the boundary line between Oregon and Idaho, by a holder of either an Oregon or Idaho license is lawful. Nothing in this section is intended to authorize Oregon or Idaho license holders to angle, hunt or trap on the shoreline, sloughs or tributaries of the state for which they are not licensed (497.012).

ANIMAL DAMAGE CONTROL

Nothing in the wildlife laws is intended to prevent a person from taking wildlife that is damaging land the person owns or lawfully occupies or is damaging livestock or agricultural or forest crops on such land. However, when prohibited by the Commission, no person shall take a game mammal or bird, fur-bearing mammal or nongame wildlife species without a permit. No permit is needed to take cougar, bobcat, red fox or bear causing damage, but a person who takes such an animal must possess written authority from the landowner or lawful occupant. The Commission is not required to issue a permit for taking wildlife species for which a USFW permit is required pursuant to the Migratory Bird Treaty Act. A person who takes a cougar, bobcat, red fox, bear, game mammal, game bird, fur-bearing mammal or wildlife species whose survival is endangered shall immediately report to a person authorized to enforce the wildlife laws, and dispose of the wildlife as the Commission directs. Written authority from the landowner or lawful occupant must set forth: ▸ authorization issuance date; ▸ name, address, telephone number and signature of the authorizer; ▸ name, address and telephone number of the grantee; ▸ wildlife damage control activities to be conducted, and on what species; ▸ authorization expiration, not later than one year from issuance (498.012).

★★Nothing in the wildlife laws prohibits killing a crippled or helpless wildlife when done for a humane purpose. A person so killing wildlife shall immediately report to a person authorized to enforce the wildlife laws, and shall dispose of the wildlife as the Commission directs (498.016).★★

ENFORCEMENT OF WILDLIFE LAWS

★★Oregon is a member of the Wildlife Violator Compact (496.750).★★ [See Model Statute section of Handbook for full provisions of the compact.]

Enforcement Powers

The Director and deputies, and all other peace officers of this state or a political subdivision, have jurisdiction of and may enforce wildlife law provisions (496.605).

★The Department of State Police shall employ a sufficient number of state police to enforce the wildlife laws, their services and expenses to be paid from the State Wildlife Fund. The Police Superintendent may appoint special enforcement officers who must be special agents of USFW or the National Marine Fishery Service, who shall serve without additional compensation. Each officer shall have all powers and authority of a peace officer in serving warrants, subpoenas and other legal process in wildlife law enforcement (496.610). With approval of the Governor and State Police Superintendent, the Commission may employ persons to enforce the wildlife laws, their services and expenses to be payable from the State Wildlife Fund. It is the intention of this section and 496.610 that the Commission employ only persons agreed upon between the Commission, the Governor and the State Police Superintendent, and that the duties of wildlife law enforcement be performed by the Department of State Police (496.615).★

No person authorized to enforce the wildlife laws shall suffer a civil liability for the enforcement or exercise of the duties or privileges granted to or imposed upon the Commission or such person (496.620). Upon information or complaint of the Commission, of a person authorized to enforce the wildlife laws or of a private person as provided in 153.710, district attorneys shall prosecute every criminal case in which it appears that there has been a violation of the wildlife laws or rules (496.630).

A person authorized to enforce the wildlife laws has all powers and rights of a peace officer in serving warrants, subpoenas or other legal process in wildlife law enforcement, and may without warrant arrest a person violating wildlife laws. The court shall without delay hear, try and determine the matter and enter judgment (496.640 and .645). Should an officer making an arrest for violation of the wildlife laws desire not to take the person into immediate custody, the officer may issue a citation to the person arrested (496.650).

A court having jurisdiction of the offense, upon receiving proof or probable cause for believing in the concealment of wildlife taken, killed or possessed, under control, or shipped contrary to the wildlife laws, shall issue a search warrant and cause a search to be made, and cause any building, enclosure, car, automobile, boat, apartment, chest, box, parcel, crate or basket to be opened and examined. All wildlife or parts discovered shall be held as evidence, and upon conviction, the wildlife, or parts, shall be disposed of by the Commission. Funds from disposal go to the State Wildlife Fund (496.655).

Authorized persons may at any time, without warrant, seize and take possession of wildlife caught, taken or killed, possessed, or shipped contrary to the wildlife laws, and of guns, boats, fishing or other apparatus used for hunting or fishing (496.675). All wildlife taken by, or in the possession of a person in violation of wildlife laws, and all guns, boats, traps, fishing apparatus and implements used in angling, hunting or trapping or taking may be seized by an authorized person and may be forfeited, to be turned over to the Commission by court order at the time of sentencing or for forfeiture of bail. The Commission may dispose of the property, but proceeds derived from sale of seized guns, boats, traps, fishing apparatus or implements go to the Common School Fund. Wildlife illegally taken may be disposed of or used for food to prevent spoilage (496.680).

Possession of wildlife or parts when it is illegal to take or have same is prima facie evidence that such wildlife was killed illegally (496.690). A person who counsels, aids or assists in a violation of the wildlife laws, or shares in the proceeds by receiving or possessing wildlife, shall incur the penalties provided for the person guilty of such violation (496.695). ★Upon being furnished information of a wildlife law violation, the Commission may proceed to the place where the offense was committed and summon and examine under oath witnesses to ascertain facts and avoid useless and frivolous indictments or prosecutions. Witnesses shall be paid by the Commission from the State Wildlife Fund at the rate of $5 per day and mileage from their residence at eight cents per mile. No witness summoned shall refuse to attend or testify under this section (496.700).★

Illegal Taking of Wildlife

The Commission may institute suit for recovery of damages for unlawful taking or killing of specified wildlife as follows per each: ► game mammal other than mountain sheep, mountain goat, elk or silver gray squirrel, $400; ► mountain sheep or mountain goat, $3,500; ► elk, $750; ► silver gray squirrel, $10; ► game bird other than wild turkey, $10; ► wild turkey, $50; ► game fish other than salmon or steelhead trout, $5; ► salmon or steelhead trout, $125; ► fur-bearing mammal other than bobcat or fisher, $50; ► bobcat or fisher, $350; ► wildlife species specified by the state or US laws as threatened or endangered, $500; ► wildlife species otherwise protected by state or US laws, but not otherwise referred to in this subsection, $25. In such an action, the court shall award reasonable attorney fees to the prevailing party, and costs and disbursements. Civil damages shall be in addition to other penalties prescribed by the wildlife laws for unlawful taking or killing of wildlife (496.705). (See also License Revocations and Suspensions in this section.)

In an action or proceeding for enforcement of a wildlife law, or in an investigation before a grand jury, district attorney or other officer, or a criminal proceeding, no person shall be excused from testifying concerning an offense committed by another or by the person on the ground that the testimony may incriminate the person. However, the testimony shall not be used against the person in prosecution for a crime or misdemeanor under state laws, nor the person be subject to a criminal prosecution or a penalty or forfeiture for a matter concerning which the person has been compelled to testify or to produce evidence (496.710).

★One-half of all wildlife fines imposed in justice courts shall be credited within 20 days to the general fund of the county, and one-half credited to the state. Fines imposed and collected in district courts shall be credited to the state (496.715).★

License Revocations and Suspensions

Upon a conviction of illegally taking a game mammal out of season, the court shall order the Commission to revoke all hunting licenses, tags and permits. Revocation is in addition to and not in lieu of other penalties, and no such person shall apply for, obtain or possess a hunting license, tag or permit for 24 months after conviction (497.435).

Except as provided in 497.435, when a person is convicted of a violation, forfeits bail or otherwise fails to comply with the requirements of a citation, the court may order the Commission to revoke licenses, tags and permits as the court considers appropriate. Revocation is in addition to and not in lieu of other penalties. Revocation provisions apply when a person forfeits bail or otherwise fails to comply with the requirements of a citation when bail has been set at $50 or more and the person is convicted of: ► a violation of the wildlife laws or rules; ► a violation of 164.245, 164.255, 164.265, 164.345, 164.354 or 164.365 committed while angling, hunting or trapping; ► a violation of 166.630 or 166.638 while hunting. When a court orders revocation of a license, tag or permit pursuant to this section or 497.435, it shall take the licenses, tags and permits and forward them, with a copy of the revocation order, to the Commission (497.415).

For purposes of the Wildlife Violator Compact, the Commission shall: ► suspend a violator's license for failure to comply with the terms of a citation from a party state, a copy of a report of failure to comply from the issuing state being conclusive evidence; ► revoke a violator's license for a conviction in a party state, a report of conviction from the issuing state being conclusive evidence. No person who has had a license, tag or permit revoked pursuant to this section for the first time shall apply for or obtain another for 24 months; for a second time, no person shall apply for or obtain another for three years; for a third or subsequent time, no person shall apply for or obtain another for five years. If a person convicted does not possess the licenses, tags and permits at the time of conviction, the court shall specify the licenses, tags and permits that would have been revoked and forward a copy of the order to the Commission. No person who is the subject of such a court order shall apply for, possess or obtain another license for 24 months; for a second time, no person shall apply for or obtain another for three years; for a third or subsequent time, no person shall apply for or obtain another for five years (497.415).

HABITAT PROTECTION

A person may apply to the Department for preliminary certification of a fish habitat improvement project. The Department shall develop rules and procedures for administering its responsibilities and others to clarify the criteria for such projects. Applications for preliminary certification shall be on a Department form and contain: ► a detailed description of the proposed project and a statement of expected benefits; ► blueprints/drawings of the project; ► a detailed estimate of project costs; ► other required information. The Department shall act on all applications for preliminary certification before 120 days after receipt. At any time during that period the Department may request clarification, additional detail or modification. If the Department rejects an application, it shall give written notice, with a statement of findings and the reasons. Preliminary certification of a fish habitat improvement project by the Department shall not qualify the applicant for a tax credit nor exempt the project from state or federal law, or local ordinance. Upon completion, construction or installation of a fish habitat improvement project preliminarily certified, a person may apply for final certification. The application shall be made on Department forms and shall include a detailed statement of project costs. Upon application for final project certification, the Department shall inspect to determine the project will result in the improvement of riparian or in-stream habitat. If the Department determines that the project conforms to the approved plans, the Department shall provide written notice of final certification (496.260). Notwithstanding provisions to the contrary, the Department shall not preliminarily certify, in one calendar year, as eligible for tax credit, fish habitat improvement project costs over $100,000. The Department shall not grant preliminary certification for a fish habitat improvement project unless application is filed on or before January 1, 1998 (496.265).

Except for activities or projects authorized by municipal, state or federal government, no person shall disturb, damage, destroy or interfere with operation of a salmon and trout enhancement project (496.465).

Except as provided, no person shall hunt or trap wildlife on a wildlife refuge (501.015). Notwithstanding restrictions to the contrary regarding uses of wildlife refuge, the Commission may authorize hunting or trapping wildlife on the refuge to manage the supply or condition of the wildlife (501.025). When a wildlife refuge is created, the Commission shall post signs around the boundary giving notice of restrictions on hunting or trapping and on other specified uses (501.035).

The Commission may enter into contracts with landowners for establishing a wildlife refuge on the land. The contract shall be for the period and contain the terms, conditions and restrictions regarding hunting and trapping and other uses of the land as the Commission considers appropriate to manage the supply and condition of wildlife on the land (501.045).

NATIVE AMERICAN WILDLIFE PROVISIONS

Through the Department, the state shall provide surplus salmon to: the Confederated Coos, Lower Umpqua and Siuslaw Indian tribes for their historical, traditional and cultural salmon ceremony in August; the Cow Creek Band of the Umpqua Indians for their historical, traditional and cultural salmon ceremony in July. The salmon shall meet the expressed needs of the Confederated Coos, Lower Umpqua and Siuslaw tribes and the Cow Creek Band of Umpqua Indians up to 300 pounds total; it may be either surplus whole fish or carcasses, and be from hatcheries under either the complete or joint control of the state (496.201).

The Indian tribes are required to set forth, in writing, their request for salmon, to be submitted no later than 40 days prior to the ceremony and shall include the: ▸ poundage required; ▸ ceremony date; ▸ contact person. Prior to an action, the written request must be received by the Department, the Attorney General, and the USDI. The salmon shall be provided to the Indian tribes no later than 30 days after receiving a proper written request (496.206). The state shall be limited to a once a year provision of salmon, and if the tribes use state provided salmon for this purpose in any manner other than that described, they shall pay to the Department the prevailing wholesale rate per pound of the entire amount of salmon supplied to the tribe(s) for that year (496.211). Salmon remaining after the ceremony may be distributed to tribal members without charge for their subsistence consumption only and not for sale, barter or gift to others, or may be donated to a nonprofit institution or agency (496.216). Nothing in 496.201 to 496.221 is intended to extend legal or political recognition to Indians described in 496.201 for a purpose other than provided in these sections (496.221).

The Commission shall furnish a permanent hunting and angling license, without fee, to all Columbia River Indians who are eligible to hunt and angle under the terms of the Treaty of 1855. The chief authority of the Columbia River Indians shall furnish periodically to the Commission a list of all Indians who have become eligible, and shall certify under oath that Indians named are included in the terms of the treaty (497.170).

PENNSYLVANIA

Sources: Purdon's Pennsylvania Consolidated Statutes Annotated, 1958, Titles 30, 32 and 34; 1992 Cumulative Annual Pocket Part.

STATE WILDLIFE POLICY

The Commonwealth has sufficient interest in fish, game and wildlife to give it standing, through its authorized agencies, to recover damages against a person who kills fish, game or wildlife, or who pollutes streams, or damages habitat. The proprietary ownership, jurisdiction and control of fish, game or wildlife are vested in the Commonwealth by the expenditure of funds and efforts to protect, perpetuate, propagate and maintain the fish population and protect, propagate, manage and preserve the game or wildlife population as a natural resource (30-2506 and 34-2161).

It is declared that: ▸ numerous flora and fauna, including those rare or endangered, are not commonly pursued, killed or consumed for sport or profit; ▸ such species need more active management; ▸ it is in the public interest to preserve and enhance such species for the benefit of all. It is the purpose of the Wild Resource Conservation Act to: ▸ provide for such species to enhance the constitutional rights guaranteed in section 27, Article 1 of the Constitution of Pennsylvania; ▸ provide support for the management of wild resources by establishing a contribution system on state income tax forms; ▸ promote the cooperation of the Department of Environmental Resources, Fish and Boat Commission (Fish Commission) and Game Commission in the management of wild resources; ▸ establish an interagency Wild Resources Conservation Board to channel cooperation, promote the voluntary contribution system and administer the program; ▸ establish and promote a cooperative statewide system of private wild plant sanctuaries; ▸ conserve and protect wild plant species (32-5302).

RELEVANT WILDLIFE DEFINITIONS: See Definitions section of Appendices.

STATE FISH AND WILDLIFE AGENCIES

Agency Structure

The **Pennsylvania Fish and Boat Commission** (Fish Commission) is an independent commission consisting of 10 citizens, appointed by the Governor with Senate approval, for eight-year terms. Two members serve at large and are experienced in boating and water safety education and registered boat owners; eight bipartisan members informed on conservation, restoration, fish and fishing, boats and boating, from various geographic districts. Except for powers relating to acknowledgment of guilt and receipts for payment [detailed in 30-925], members may exercise powers conferred on waterways patrolmen. With the Governor's approval, the Fish Commission appoints an Executive Director (Director) in charge of activities under the jurisdiction of the Fish Commission. The Director is the chief waterways patrolman and has charge of all waterways patrolmen, and Fish Commission employees. With Fish Commission approval, the Director may: ▸ appoint two assistant directors, one in charge of watercraft safety and one in charge of fisheries and engineering; ▸ appoints waterways patrolmen and other employees. New deputy patrolmen shall be trained. Except as provided, and acknowledgment of guilt and receipts for payment, deputy waterways patrolmen have the same powers as waterways patrolmen. Waterways patrolmen are designated as waterways conservation officers (30-301 through -307).

The ownership, jurisdiction over and control of game or wildlife is vested in the **Game Commission** as an independent agency, to be controlled, regulated and disposed of in accordance with the Game and Wildlife Code. ★The Game Commission shall utilize hunting and trapping as methods of effecting management of game, fur-bearer and wildlife populations (34-103).★ The Game Commission consists of eight citizens, appointed by the Governor for 8 year terms from various geographical locations, with Senate approval, and informed about wildlife conservation and restoration. The Game Commission selects the **Director**. The Director is in charge of all activities under the jurisdiction Game Commission and the code. The Director is the chief Game Commission officer and supervises all employees, represents the Game Commission in land purchase contracts, leases and other agreements (34-301 and -302). The Director selects Game Commission officers, and others to fulfill the code, and may appoint

Deputy Game Commission officers who, except as otherwise provided, possess the rights and powers of Game Commission officers (34-303 and -304).

Agency Powers and Duties

The **Fish Commission** enforces the Fish and Boat Code and laws relating to the encouragement, promotion and development of fishery interests; protection, propagation and distribution of fish; management and operation of boats; and development of recreational boating (30-321). The Fish Commission may enter into agreements with government agencies, and private or commercial interests for impounding, managing, using, maintaining and operating waters for public fishing, may expend moneys from the Fish Fund for their cost, acquisition, construction, operation and maintenance (30-521). The Fish Commission may acquire title to, or control of, lands, waters and buildings, fishing rights, easements, rights-of-way or other interests in land and waters for: ▸ protection, propagation and management of fish life; ▸ public fishing and boating; ▸ administrative purposes; ▸ other uses as provided. The Fish Commission may purchase tax delinquent lands and waters and may purchase, construct, repair and maintain buildings and other improvements thereon for fish experimental activities or other purpose, and may lease or otherwise secure rights-of-way on and across public or private lands or other rights required to conduct its functions. The title to lands or waters acquired is taken in the name of the Commonwealth for the use of the Fish Commission. Such lands, waters or buildings are exempt from taxes except fixed charges imposed upon Commonwealth forests. The entire control of all lands or waters owned, leased or otherwise controlled is under direction of the Fish Commission which may promulgate regulations for its use and protection. Violation of such regulations is a second degree summary offense, but violation of a regulation governing parking of vehicles on Fish Commission property is a fourth degree summary offense (30-721 through -723, -726, -728 and -741).

Lands and waters acquired by the Fish Commission may be used to maintain fish cultural stations, fish propagation areas, public fishing grounds, fish propagation experiments or special preserves. The Fish Commission may: ▸ permit its employees to reside on these lands; ▸ authorize the exchange or sale of lands, waters or buildings in return for fair market value or privately-owned lands, waters or buildings with equal or greater value; ▸ exchange timber cut from lands for lands having an equal or greater value; ▸ dispose of timber, minerals, oil and gas on its lands; ▸ charge for and grant rights-of-way or licenses for roads, for pipe, electric and other utility lines and water rights or rights to maintain airway signals or forest fire observation towers when they will not adversely affect fish protection and propagation. With Fish Commission approval, the Director may lease land for a term up to 25 years when it will promote public fishing, boating or access to waters, or will otherwise further Fish Commission interests (30-742 through -746).

The **Game Commission** may by purchase, gift, lease, eminent domain or otherwise, acquire title to or control of lands, waters, buildings, oil, gas and minerals, hunting or trapping rights, easements, rights-of-way or other interests for the protection, propagation and management of game or wildlife, public hunting or trapping or access, administrative purposes, or other uses as provided in the code. The Game Commission may purchase tax delinquent lands, waters, oil, gas and minerals from counties as provided by law. The title to lands or waters acquired is taken in the name of the Commonwealth solely for the use of the Game Commission. The Game Commission may: ▸ purchase, construct and maintain improvements on lands acquired for protection, development, administration, and propagation of game or wildlife, experimental or research activities, or other purposes incident to game or wildlife, hunting, or fur-taking; ▸ lease or otherwise secure rights-of-way on and across public or private lands and waters to implement the code (34-701 through -703, and -706). Administration of lands or waters owned or controlled by the Game Commission is under sole control of the Director. Acquisition, use and management of such lands or waters, including timber cutting and crop cultivation, is not subject to regulation by counties or municipalities. Except as provided, such lands may be used only to create and maintain public hunting and fur-taking, game or wildlife areas, farms or facilities for propagation of game or wildlife, special preserves, or other uses incidental to hunting, fur-taking and game or wildlife resource management. ★The Game Commission may issue permits and licenses and enter into leases for uses of its lands, except it shall not issue permits or licenses or enter into a lease which would permit use of the land for disposal of hazardous, toxic or radioactive waste, or permit the mining of uranium or other radioactive minerals.★ The Game Commission may: ▸ authorize the exchange of lands, waters or buildings in return for equal or greater value; ▸ exchange timber, minerals, oil or gas for lands having an equal or greater value; ▸ sell lands to the Department of Environmental Resources for state forests or to the federal government for national forests or national wildlife refuges; ▸ dispose of timber, buildings, minerals, oil and gas, or rights therein, or other product on or under its lands. On Game Commission lands, the Director, for a fee, may grant: ‣ rights-of-way or licenses for purposes not inconsistent with the purpose of these lands; ‣ water rights or other rights when these will not adversely affect the game or wildlife resource or their use; ‣ rights to erect antennas, towers, stations, cables and other devices for radio or television broadcasting; ‣ rights to establish roadside rests and highway maintenance facilities; ‣ rights to a federal or state agency or political subdivision to construct, maintain and operate water impoundments for flood control or recreational use. The Director may approve the granting, lease or exchange of an easement, right-of-way or license for use of Game Commission property, and, with Game Commission approval, may lease land up to 25 years to promote public hunting or fur-taking, benefit the game or wildlife resource, or otherwise further Game Commission interests (34-721 through -726).

The Game Commission may set aside areas for the protection and propagation of game or wildlife where they shall not be hunted, pursued, disturbed, molested, killed or taken except as authorized, and may cooperate with private landowners and others who desire to aid in the conservation of game or wildlife by creating and maintaining public access projects, the hunting rights to be made available to the Game Commission by written agreement. The Game Commission may authorize the Director to execute agreements and shall promulgate regulations to govern these projects (34-728 and -729). The Game Commission has authority to administer and enforce the code and laws of the Commonwealth relating to the encouragement, promotion and development of game or wildlife conservation interests and the protection, propagation, distribution and control over game or wildlife, and concurrent authority to enforce the Dam Safety and Encroachments Act and its regulations, with respect to encroachments and water obstructions only if the violation would negatively impact upon a swamp, marsh or wetland (34-2101 and -2161).

Agency Regulations

The Fish Commission may promulgate fishing regulations for: ‣ protection, preservation and management of fish and fish habitat; ‣ permitting and prohibiting fishing; ‣ the ways, manner, methods and means of fishing; ‣ the health and safety of persons who fish. Violation of regulations for the protection of fish, fish habitat, or for the health and safety of persons who fish is a second degree summary offense. Violation of any other regulation is a third degree summary offense. Regulations may establish seasons, sizes and possession limits for fish and fishing, regulate the possession of species, the number and types of devices and tackle allowed, the identification of such devices and their use and possession. Violation: summary offense of the third degree. Regulations may concern transportation, introduction of, or importation into or within the Commonwealth or exporting of fish, the selling, offering for sale or purchase of fish or the disturbing of fish in their natural habitat. Violation: second degree summary offense. Regulations may stipulate the size of traps, seines, nets and other devices, along with mesh sizes of the devices, the manner and location where they may be used, the species they may be used for, and the season for use. Violation: first degree summary offense (30-2102). The Fish Commission may promulgate regulations: ‣ specifying the procedures for revoking or suspending fishing licenses, special licenses and permits and privileges (30-928); ‣ for licensing and operation of regulated fishing lakes (30-3101); ‣ applicable to boundary lakes for fisheries protection and management; ‣ for ways, methods and means of fishing and the health and safety of persons and property. Regulations may prohibit fishing for species in boundary lakes and may limit the number or types of licenses and permits issued for fishing therein (30-2903). The Fish Commission shall promulgate regulations to protect and manage fish within one mile of a chute, fishway, gate, dam, or similar device. Violation: a second degree summary offense (30-3507). The Fish Commission administers and enforces laws of the Commonwealth relating to the encouragement, promotion and development of fishery interests, and the protection, propagation and distribution of fish, and determines policy pertaining to propagation and distribution of the fish produced at hatcheries or otherwise acquired, and may make comprehensive studies of the migratory habits of fish, may cooperate with the Joint State Government Commission and accept from the federal government cooperation and financial aid in connection with such studies. The Commission may designate waters for specific purposes and promulgate regulations to protect and manage the fishing therein; violation is a third degree summary offense (30-2101, -2301, -2304 and -2307).

The Game Commission shall promulgate regulations for the use and protection of lands or waters it owns, leases or controls. Violation: fifth degree summary offense (34-721). The Game Commission may promulgate regulations to: ‣ govern conduct within propagation areas with the approval of authorities or persons owning or controlling same (34-728); ‣ protect users, improvements, lands and buildings under its control, and cover removal of material and damage to protect and preserve lands for their intended use (34-741); ‣ specify procedures for revoking hunting and fur-taking privileges, licenses, permits and registrations (34-929). The Game Commission promulgates regulations concerning game or wildlife and hunting or fur-taking, including: ‣ protection, preservation and management of game or wildlife and its habitat; ▸ permitting or prohibiting hunting or fur-taking; ▸ methods and means of hunting or fur-taking; ▸ the health and safety of persons who hunt or take game or wildlife; ▸ seasons and bag limits for hunting or fur-taking; ▸ possession of certain species or parts; ▸ the number and types of devices and equipment allowed; ▸ identification of devices and their use and possession. If the Game Commission fails to establish seasons, bag limits or other regulations, the seasons and bag limits, Sundays excepted, unless otherwise provided, shall be the same as set for the previous license year. The Game Commission shall promulgate regulations concerning the transportation, introduction into the wild, importation, exportation, sale, offering for sale or purchase of game or wildlife or the disturbing of game or wildlife in their natural habitat, and regulations stipulating the size and type of traps, the type of firearms and ammunition and other devices, the manner in which and the location where the devices may be used, the species the devices may be used for and the season when the devices may be used (34-2102).

The Game Commission shall protect, propagate, manage and preserve the game and wildlife of the Commonwealth and enforce the laws relating thereto. The Game Commission has the power and duty to take actions for the administration and enforcement of the code and shall (34-2102): ▸ fix seasons, daily shooting or taking hours, and daily, season and possession limits for game or wildlife; ▸ remove protection, open or close seasons; ▸ increase or reduce bag or possession limits; ▸ define geographic limitations; ▸ fix the type and number of devices to take game or wildlife; ▸ limit the number of hunters or fur-takers in an area and prescribe methods of hunting or taking fur-bearers; ▸ govern the use of recorded or amplified calls or sounds for taking or hunting game or wildlife; ▸ add to or change the classification of a wild bird or wild animal; ▸ prohibit the possession, importation, exportation or release of birds or animals considered dangerous or injurious to the general public or wildlife; ▸ manage and develop lands and waters under agreement with the owners to insure proper use; ▸ collect, classify and preserve statistics and information to promote code objectives and keep reports, books, papers and documents which come into its possession or control; ▸ take action to accomplish the purposes of the code. The Game Commission may enter into cooperative agreements with any government agency, individual, corporation or educational or research institution to further its programs (34-322 and -323).

Agency Funding Sources

Except as otherwise provided, all fees, royalties, fines, penalties and other moneys paid, received and collected under provisions shall be placed in the **Fish Fund** and used for: ▸ processing, issuing or supervising the issuance of fishing licenses, special licenses and permits; ▸ salaries, wages, and other expenses of Fish Commission employees; ▸ support of the work of Fish Commission employees; ▸ propagation, protection, management and distribution of fish and stocking of waters; ▸ support of fish cultural stations; ▸ field work, gathering spawn and transferring fish; ▸ purchase or lease of lands and waters and impounding of waters for use by state citizens (30-521). The Fish Commission may accept donations of money or securities, to be placed in the Fish Fund, or real or personal property, to be utilized or disposed of as provided. Net proceeds from the sale of lands, waters, timber, oil, gas or other minerals, leases of Fish Commission lands, waters, interests or rights from the production or sale of minerals and from licenses are deposited in the Fish Fund. Fines received for violation of the Fish and Boat Code are paid into the State Treasury for the use of the Fish Fund or Boat Fund (30-701, -747, and -926).

Except as provided, fees, royalties, fines, penalties and other moneys paid, received, recovered and collected under the code are placed in the **Game Fund** and used for expenses in carrying on the work of the Game Commission, including, but not limited to: ▸ the purchase of land; ▸ the costs of promotion of public interest in recreational hunting and fur-taking; ▸ nongame species, endangered or threatened species and all other game or wildlife. The Game Commission may accept donations of money or securities to be placed in the Game Fund and used for Code purposes, or of real or personal property to be utilized or disposed of as provided. Sale proceeds from waters, timber, buildings, oil, gas or minerals, leases of commission lands, waters or interests, rights from the production or sale of minerals, oil or gas, and licenses are deposited in the Game Fund. Fines recovered from Code violations are deposited in the Game Fund (34-521, -523, -727, and -927).

In order to carry out the purposes of the Wild Resources Conservation Act, there is created, the **Wild Resource Conservation Fund**, the moneys of which are continuously appropriated to the Wild Resource Conservation Board by a contribution system. The Department of Revenue provides a space on the Pennsylvania individual income tax return form whereby an individual may voluntarily designate a contribution to the Wild Resource Conservation Fund (32-5304 and -5305).

Agency Advisory Boards

The **Wild Resources Conservation Board**, consists of the Secretary of the Department of Environmental Resources, the Directors of the Fish and Game Commissions, the majority and minority chairpersons of the House Conservation Committee and the Senate Environmental Resources Committee. The board meets annually to: ▸ determine and prioritize the management objectives to preserve and enhance wild resources; ▸ establish management projects or programs to preserve and enhance wild resources and allocate moneys; ▸ administer the Wild Resource Conservation Fund; ▸ develop a comprehensive management plan (32-5306).

PROTECTED SPECIES OF WILDLIFE

The Director of the Fish Commission shall establish Pennsylvania Threatened and Endangered Species Lists. The lists and revision are published in the Pennsylvania Bulletin. The Fish Commission may promulgate rules and regulations governing the catching, taking, killing, importation, introduction, transportation, removal, possession, selling, offering for sale or purchasing of threatened and endangered fish species and, may issue permits for catching, taking or possessing those species. Violation: third degree misdemeanor. Each fish caught, taken, killed, imported, transported, removed, introduced, possessed, sold, offered for sale or purchased in violation of a regulation pertaining to threatened or endangered species is a separate offense. Catching a threatened or endangered species is not a violation if it is immediately released where captured in the condition in which it was captured (30-2305).

Except as provided, it is unlawful to kill or attempt or conspire to kill or take or attempt, assist, aid or abet in the taking of protected birds or possess protected birds, or parts. It is lawful for protected hawks, falcons or owls to be taken and possessed for use in falconry, but they shall not be bought, sold or bartered for, or held in possession for falconry. Except under a Game Commission permit, no protected bird or part shall be mounted or retained in possession. Violation: fifth degree summary offense for each protected bird or part. Violation relating to birds listed as threatened or endangered is, in addition to other penalties, a third degree misdemeanor. Game, wildlife or eggs possessed in violation is contraband. ★Except as provided, it is unlawful to take or possess or control either the active nest or egg of a game bird or protected bird or to interfere with or destroy the active nest or egg. Violation: fifth degree summary offense for each active nest or egg possessed or interfered with. Violation relating to birds listed as threatened or endangered is, in addition to other penalties, a third degree misdemeanor for each nest or egg possessed. An active nest or egg possessed in violation is contraband. Except as provided, it is unlawful to have a protected bird or a bird belonging to the same family as those protected birds found in a wild state in the Commonwealth or is similar in appearance to a native protected bird, the eggs or a part, in possession or under control for sale or barter, or to offer or expose theme for sale or barter, or to transport, ship or remove, or attempt to transport, ship or remove from the Commonwealth such bird, living or dead, or the eggs or part. Violation: fourth degree summary offense for each bird or part. Violation relating to birds which are listed as threatened or endangered is, in addition to other penalties, a third degree misdemeanor for each bird or part. A protected bird or an egg or part possessed in violation is contraband.★ Except as provided, it is unlawful to bring into or remove from the Commonwealth, or to possess, transport, capture or kill, or attempt, aid, abet, or conspire such of a wild bird or wild animal, or part, or the eggs of an endangered or threatened species. It is the duty of every officer having authority to enforce the code to seize all wild birds or wild animals, or parts, or the eggs, declared endangered or threatened. Violation: third degree misdemeanor. All wild birds or wild animals, or parts, or the eggs seized which are found to be in violation are contraband. The Game Commission by regulation may add or remove a native wild bird or wild animal to or from the state native list of endangered or threatened species (34-2164 through -2167).

The Game Commission may issue permits for the importation, exportation, sale, exchange, taking or possession of birds or animals classified as endangered or threatened, living or dead, or parts, including eggs, and permits for native birds or animals taken from the wild and which are classified as endangered or threatened in Title 58 (Oil and Gas). The Game Commission may join with federal agencies in issuing joint permits for birds or animals not native which are classified as endangered or threatened in the Code of Federal Regulations. It is unlawful for a person to import, export, transport, sell, resell, exchange, take birds or animals of an endangered species, living or dead, or parts, including eggs, or to possess or conspire, aid, abet, assist or attempt to do so, or to violate regulations pertaining to such wildlife. A permit violation is a first degree summary offense. The penalty for a violation of other provisions relating to endangered or threatened species is a misdemeanor of the second or third degree. A person who proves possession of a species prohibited by these provisions on or before March 28, 1974, is exempt from the penalties and forfeitures for mere possession (34-2924).

GENERAL EXCEPTIONS TO PROTECTION

The Director of the Fish Commission or agent may catch, take, kill or possess fish in any season and with any kind of net or device (30-302). Restrictions on fishing imposed by the code do not apply to a resident farm owner or lessee, family and employees, who permanently reside on the farm, while fishing in an artificial pond the water source for which is wholly within the farm limits. A person may possess and transport fish lawfully taken from a farm pond during the closed season accompanied by a signed written statement from the owner/lessee showing the: ▸ date, place, and by whom taken; ▸ number and species; ▸ name and address of the person transporting the fish; ▸ date they are being transported. Nothing authorizes a person to transport, introduce or import fish, bait fish or fish bait, the transportation, introduction or importation of which is prohibited by law, rule or regulation. Violation: third degree summary offense (30-2105 and -2108). With Fish Commission approval, the Director may grant permits to catch fish in waters within or bordering the Commonwealth at any season, with nets or devices, without regard to size or possession limits, to a person who possesses a fishing license and is engaged in scientific or educational research or other approved collecting activities. Permittees shall make a report in writing to the Director within 30 days after the expiration of the permit or conclusion of collecting. With Fish Commission approval, the Director may grant permits for use of explosives in waters for engineering purposes. A person using explosives under the permit shall make restitution for all fish destroyed (30-2905 and -2906). Fish may be taken from a regulated fishing lake without limitation on size, season or possession limit (30-3103).

★★It is unlawful to kill game or wildlife for protection unless it is clearly evident that a human is endangered to a degree that the immediate destruction of the game or wildlife is necessary. A person so killing game or wildlife to protect a person shall report the event to an officer within 24 hours, provide for safekeeping of the animal where it was killed and be available for interview by the officer. The person shall answer questions of the investigating officer. At the conclusion of the investigation, the officer may exonerate the person for the otherwise unlawful killing. In all cases the officer shall seize and dispose of the game or wildlife as required by the Code or upon instructions of the Director. If the officer is dissatisfied with the explanation, or if the physical facts of the killing do not support the facts alleged, the officer shall proceed with prosecution as though the game or wildlife was unlawfully killed. Violation: ▸ threatened or endangered species, third degree misdemeanor; ▸ elk or bear, first degree summary offense; ▸ deer, second degree summary offense; ▸ bobcat or otter, third degree summary offense; ▸ wild turkey or beaver, fourth degree summary offense; ▸ other game or wildlife, fifth degree summary offense (34-2141).★★

★Unless provided, persons wishing to band birds under authority of a federal bird banding permit shall pay a fee, have the federal permit validated by the Game Commission Director, and submit project outlines, reports or other information. It is unlawful to trap or band protected birds without permits or to violate other provisions relating to special licenses and permits. Except for endangered or threatened species, a violation is a fifth degree summary offense. Each bird captured, banded or held is a separate offense. Permits authorizing collection of protected birds, their nests and eggs, and animals, for exhibition in public museums, scientific study or school instruction may be issued to persons with ornithology or mammalogy credentials, or to agents of public museums or institutions of learning for exhibition. Applicants shall include an outline of the project, including benefits for game or wildlife or useable scientific information they expect to generate and the minimum number of specimens of each species needed. The application and project outline is reviewed by the Director who may approve, reject or modify the project. The permit shall specify the number of specimens to be taken and the method of taking. It is unlawful to: ▸ take more than the number of specimens shown on the permit; ▸ sell or offer for sale or barter a specimen obtained; ▸ transfer control of a specimen to another person without written permission from the Director; ▸ violate other provisions. Except for endangered or threatened species, a violation is a fifth degree summary offense (34-2921 and -2922).★ (See Licenses and Permits under HUNTING, FISHING AND TRAPPING PROVISIONS.)

HUNTING, FISHING, TRAPPING PROVISIONS

General Provisions

Under the Game and Wildlife Code, any of the following constitutes prima facie evidence of hunting: ▸ possession of a firearm, bow and arrow, raptor, trap or other device usable for hunting or taking game or wildlife; ▸ possession of the carcass or part of game or wildlife; ▸ pursuing game or wildlife in a prohibited manner. ★Notwithstanding any other provision, a person who lawfully has taken the bag or season limit for a species of game or wildlife may aid, assist, abet or cooperate in any manner specified by regulation with another person who is engaged in a lawful activity (34-2301).★ It is unlawful to aid, abet, attempt or conspire to hunt for or take or possess, use, transport or conceal game or wildlife or parts unlawfully taken or not properly marked, or to hunt for, trap, take, kill, transport, conceal, possess or use game or wildlife contrary to code provisions. Except as fixed by regulation, game or wildlife lawfully taken during the open season may be retained by residents until the end of the license year. Nothing prohibits possession of wild birds or wild animals lawfully taken outside the Commonwealth which are tagged in accordance with the laws of the state or nation where taken. It is unlawful to transport or possess wild birds or wild animals from another state or nation which have been unlawfully taken, killed or exported. A violation relating to: ▸ threatened or endangered species is a third degree misdemeanor; ▸ elk or bear is a first degree summary offense; ▸ deer is a second degree summary offense; ▸ bobcat or otter is a third degree summary offense; ▸ wild turkey or beaver is a fourth degree summary offense; ▸ other game or wildlife is a fifth degree summary offense (34-2307).

It is unlawful to cast or to assist another in casting the rays of a spotlight, vehicle headlight or other artificial light from a vehicle, watercraft, airborne craft or an attachment to search for or locate game or wildlife, other than as specified, between the hours of 11 p.m. and sunrise on the following day. Violation: fifth degree summary offense. It is unlawful to search for or locate game or wildlife at any time during the antlered and antlerless deer rifle seasons. Violation: third degree summary offense. These provisions do not apply if it is proven that the headlights of a vehicle or conveyance were being used while traveling on a roadway in the usual way (34-2311).

Licenses and Permits

Persons age 16 to 64 are entitled to resident fishing licenses, and persons age 65 years are entitled to senior resident fishing licenses (30-2701). No person shall fish in state or boundary waters without a license, to be kept on the person while fishing and shown upon request of a waterways patrolman or other officer. The Fish Commission may promulgate regulations for displaying identification, license certificates, license buttons or other devices. Violation relating to license display is a fourth degree summary offense. Violation of any other regulation is a third degree summary offense. No person shall alter, borrow, lend or transfer a license, or give false or misleading information in an application. Violation: second degree summary offense (30-2703 and -2705). [Special license provisions exist for disabled veterans, and other disabled persons, residents of Commonwealth institutions, blind and handicapped persons (30-2707, -2708, -2709; 34-2706 and -2923.) These provisions do not prevent the owner, or family members, of land who actually resided thereon throughout the year from fishing without a license in waters wholly within the land. This exemption does not apply to a person temporarily residing on the land, a tenant who is not a family member, nor to a servant or employee (30-2709). Provisions relating to fishing licenses do not apply to holders of licenses issued by New York, New Jersey, Ohio or Maryland when fishing in common boundary waters within the jurisdiction of the Commonwealth if holders of Pennsylvania fishing licenses fishing in boundary waters within the jurisdiction of the sister state are not required to have such state's license (30-2712).

With a special license issued by the Fish Commission, a person may use an eel chute to catch eels in designated waters. The Fish Commission may issue permits for a fee to make, sell or possess nets larger than four feet square or in diameter, or other seine, trawl or gill net. The permits shall specify when and where the nets shall be used (30-2901 and -2902). With Fish Commission approval, the Director may require permits for taking, catching, killing, possession, introduction, removal, importing, transporting, exporting or disturbing fish when permits are needed to insure proper protection and management of a species. The Fish Commission may establish permit fees for permits and promulgate regulations concerning permit provisions which may be revoked at any time, and the Commission shall not establish a fee in excess of $5 per permit for taking, catching, killing, possession, introduction, removal, importing, exporting or disturbing trout and salmon, nor issue such permits for game fish other than trout or salmon. These provisions do not affect the issuance of permits for tagged fish contests in boundary lakes. The Fish

Commission issues permits for tagged fish contests on boundary lakes where the other state which bounds the lake permits such contests, unless the Commission finds that the proposed contest threatens the fisheries resources of the Pennsylvania portion of the boundary lake (30-2904 and -2907.1).

Except in defense of person or property or pursuant to authorized exemptions, prior to engaging in the privileges granted by the code, every person shall obtain the applicable license. Only one full-term or distinct hunting license and fur-taking license shall be valid during a full-term license year (34-2701). Persons meeting code requirements who are age 12 or older, whose hunting and fur-taking privileges are valid, who meet the application requirements and pay the license costs are eligible to obtain the applicable hunting or fur-taking license. ★Persons who have not held a hunting license from the Commonwealth or another state or nation or have not hunted under the exceptions relating to resident license and fee exemptions or do not possess a certificate of training approved by the Director prior to the enactment of the code are required to attain accreditation in a hunter education program approved by the Director before a hunting license is issued (34-2706). These provisions do not apply to a person who presents evidence of honorable separation from the armed forces within six months of the date of application or evidence of current service in the armed forces.★ No resident or nonresident fur-taker's license shall be issued unless the applicant presents evidence of having held a trapping or fur-taker's license issued by another state or nation, or a certificate of training issued under these provisions, or a signed certification on the fur-taker's license application that the applicant completed a voluntary Game Commission sponsored trapping course or has hunted or trapped fur-bearers within the last five years. These provisions do not apply to persons under age 12 who trap under the direct supervision of an adult licensed fur-taker over age 18. The Game Commission shall provide a course of instruction in the safe and ethical utilization of firearms, traps and other devices used to take fur-bearers and may designate a competent person to give instruction in the handling of firearms, traps or other devices, who shall issue certificates of training to persons successfully completing the training. No charge is made for the course of instruction, except for materials or ammunition. Persons under age 12 who trap under the direct supervision of an adult licensed fur-taker over age 18 are not required to have completed the fur-taker's training course. ★Subject to Game Commission approval, the Director may combine the courses of instruction in hunter education and fur-taker's training into one comprehensive course (34-2704).★ [A variety of adult and junior resident, and nonresident license types are detailed in 34-2705.]

★Unless the privilege to hunt or take fur-bearers has been denied, a resident over age 12 who is eligible for a license and, as a primary means of gaining a livelihood, is engaged in cultivating the soil for general farm crop purposes, or commercial truck growing, orchards or nurseries, as either the owner, lessee, tenant, or family member, is eligible to hunt and take fur-bearers on these lands without a hunter's or fur-taker's license. These persons may hunt or take fur-bearers on detached land operated under lease as a part of the same farm and within 10 air miles of the home farm. A person eligible to hunt or take fur-bearers on these lands without the required license may also, with written consent of the owner or lessee thereof, hunt or take game or wildlife upon lands which lie immediately adjacent to and are connected with the lands upon which these persons may lawfully hunt or take game or wildlife without a license.★ Eligible owners of 50 or more contiguous acres of land within a county who desire to hunt antlerless deer are entitled to obtain one antlerless deer license for that county, issued only to the person whose name appears on the deed. These antlerless deer licenses are allocated to landowners in advance of their availability to the general public if: ► the 50 or more contiguous acres are owned by a natural person individually or as tenants by the entirety, or by a corporation of four or fewer shareholders, or by tenants in common of four or fewer natural persons; ► the lands are open to public hunting and trapping and remain open during the antlerless deer license year; ► the applicant furnishes proof of ownership of 50 or more contiguous acres to the county treasurer. ★A resident landowner with more than 80 contiguous acres farmed under a conservation plan who permits public hunting shall be entitled to purchase a landowners hunting license (34-2706).★

Except as provided, it is unlawful to: ► hunt or take game or wildlife without displaying the required license; ► make a false or misleading statement in securing a license; ► lend or transfer a license or tag to another; ► aid in procuring for another a license for which that person is not legally entitled; ► possess while hunting or taking game or wildlife a report card, license tag, license stamp or kill tag belonging to another; ► receive a hunting or fur-taking license if under age 12; ► use firearms or a bow and arrow to hunt game or wildlife or attempt to do so if under age 12, or when hunting or trapping game or wildlife or attempting such if between age 12 and 14, unless accompanied by a person age 18 or older serving in loco parentis or as guardian, or when hunting if between age 14 and 16, unless accompanied by a person age 18 or older; ► remove a hunting or fur-taking license from the place where it is required to be displayed to conceal the identity of that person; ► hunt or take, or aide, assist or attempt such of fur-bearers or take game or wildlife anywhere, either with or without a license, or make application, receive or attempt to conspire to receive a license, during a period that these privileges have been denied or withdrawn; ▸ conspire to or duplicate, reproduce, alter, forge or counterfeit a permit, license, tag or stamp; ▸ refuse or fail to provide positive identification to a landowner upon whose land a person may be exercising license privileges or to an officer whose duty it is to enforce the code; ▸ violate regulations relating to hunting and fur-taking licenses. Violation relating to: ▸ hunting by a nonresident without a license is a fourth degree summary offense; ▸ fur-taking by a nonresident without a license is a second degree summary offense; ▸ hunting or fur-taking by a resident without a license is a fifth degree summary offense; ▸ failure to sign or display a license is an eighth degree summary offense; ▸ making misleading statements in securing a license, lending a license to another, possessing a license, permit or tag of another while hunting or fur-taking, or removing a license to conceal identity is fifth degree summary offense; ▸ age requirements for license eligibility and hunting or fur-taking is a seventh degree summary offense; ▸ conspiring to or duplicating, altering or forging a license is a third degree summary offense. A convicted violator, in addition to the imposition of a penalty, shall incur a mandatory revocation of the privilege to hunt or trap. Violation relating to other provisions concerning hunting and fur-taking licenses is fifth degree summary offense. Each day of violation or each illegal act is a separate offense (34-2711).

The Game Commission may issue special permits as specified (34-2901 through 34-2965). Except as provided, the permits are issued only to residents age 18 years of age or older. Federal permits when countersigned by the Director are valid. The Director may issue permits relating to Game Commission lands and other permits to control taking of game or wildlife for scientific study or other purpose consistent with the code. The Director may require reports from a permit holder, except with respect to species of fox not indigenous to the Commonwealth. It is unlawful to: ▸ exercise privileges granted by permit without the permit; ▸ fail to carry, show or display the permit; ▸ aid, assist or conspire contrary to these provisions; ▸ make a false or misleading statement on an application or required report; ▸ fail to submit reports when required; ▸ violate provisions relating to special permits. Except for endangered and threatened species, violation is a fifth degree summary offense (34-2901, -2902, -2907 and -2908). Unless provided by Game Commission regulations, a permit allows the holder to have a protected specimen mounted for personal use. This permit shall be issued by the Director for specimen not protected by federal laws or regulations. The applicant shall not be involved with the killing of the protected specimen. It is unlawful: ▸ to possess a protected specimen without a permit; ▸ for a taxidermist or other person to mount a protected specimen unless the owner has presented a copy of a permit issued by the Game Commission. Violation: fourth degree summary offense (34-2927).

Restrictions on Taking: Hunting and Trapping

Except as provided, it is unlawful to hunt for a fur-bearer or game on Sunday, except for fox hunting. This does not prohibit training dogs, participation in dog trails, or removal of lawfully taken game or wildlife from traps or resetting traps on Sunday. Violation: a fifth degree summary offense. ★The carcass of game or wildlife lawfully taken is the property of the person who inflicts a mortal wound which enables the person to take possession of the carcass. No officer whose duty it is to enforce the code shall be called upon to arbitrate a dispute concerning the ownership of game or wildlife or to testify concerning such dispute (34-2303 and -2304).★

Except as provided, it is unlawful to hunt or aid, abet, assist or conspire to hunt game or wildlife through the use of: ▸ an automatic firearm or similar device; ▸ a semiautomatic rifle or pistol; ▸ a crossbow; ▸ a semiautomatic shotgun or magazine shotgun for hunting or taking small game, fur-bearers, turkey or unprotected birds unless it is plugged to a two-shell capacity in the magazine; ▸ a device operated by air, chemical or gas cylinder by which a projectile can be discharged or propelled; ▸ a recorded call or sound or recorded or electronically amplified imitation of a call or sound or imitations thereof prohibited by regulation [the Game Commission may regulate the limited use of recorded calls or sounds or electronically amplified imitations to protect the public health and safety or to preserve that species or any other endangered by it]; ▸ a vehicle or conveyance of any kind or attachment propelled by other than manpower, except for a motorboat or sailboat if the motor has been shut off or sail furled, and its progress ceased; ▸ artificial or natural bait, hay, grain, fruit, nut, salt, chemical, mineral or other food to entice game or wildlife, or to take advantage of such an area or food or bait prior to 30 days after its removal, except for normal farming, habitat management practices, oil and gas drilling, mining, forest management activities or other legitimate commercial or industrial practices. Upon discovery of baited areas, whether prosecution is contemplated or not, the Game Commission may cause an area surrounding the enticement to be posted against hunting or taking game or wildlife, for 30 days after complete removal of the bait; ▸ a shotgun, net, bird lime, deer lick, pit or pit fall, turkey blind or turkey pen or explosive, poison or chemical; ▸ a device which permits the release of two or more arrows simultaneously on a single full draw of a bow; ▸ any other device or method prohibited by the code. ★These provisions do not apply to an archery sight or firearm's scope which contains and uses a mechanical, photoelectric, ultraviolet or solar-powered device to solely illuminate the sight or crosshairs within the scope. No archery sight or firearm scope shall use a device, no matter how powered, to project or transmit a light beam, infra-red beam, ultraviolet light beam, radio beam, thermal beam, ultrasonic beam, particle beam or other beam outside the sight or scope onto the target.★ Violation: fifth degree summary offense. Violation of provisions relating to motor vehicles or conveyances: third degree summary offense. Violation of other provisions: fourth degree summary offense. It is unlawful to cut a dead or living tree, use smoke or other method to take game or wildlife or to dig game or wildlife out of its place of refuge. Woodchucks may be dug out of their dens in cultivated fields by a person who, if not the owner, lessee or occupant, family member, or hired help, shall secure permission of the person in charge and, immediately after the removal of the woodchuck, replace the earth and level the area dug out. Violation: fifth degree summary offense. Each violation is a separate offense (34-2308 and -2309).

It is unlawful to: ▸ cast the rays of an artificial light on game or wildlife, or in an attempt to locate same, while on foot, in a vehicle or watercraft or airborne craft while in possession of a firearm, a bow and arrow, or an implement with which game or wildlife could be killed or taken even though it is not shot at, injured or killed; ▸ aid, assist or conspire in killing or taking or in an attempt to kill, take, possess, transport or conceal game or wildlife or part which has been killed or taken by use of artificial light; ▸ operate, allow or permit a vehicle, watercraft or airborne craft to be used for killing or taking or attempting such of game or wildlife by using the rays of an artificial light. A person on foot may use an artificial light normally carried on the person to take raccoons, skunks, opossum or foxes. A craft or vehicle, artificial lights, a firearm or paraphernalia being unlawfully used, and game or wildlife unlawfully taken, killed or possessed are contraband. Violation: fifth degree summary offense (34-2310). Except as provided, it is unlawful to: ▸ kill or take or attempt or conspire to kill or take more than the lawful number of big game animals allowed in a license year; ▸ possess or transport a big game which was killed or taken unlawfully; ▸ assist, aid or abet a person in a violation, or conspire to do so. This does not prohibit transportation of one or more big game animals lawfully killed and tagged. Unless the head is attached in a natural manner, the possession, transportation or control of big game or parts is prima facie evidence that it was killed unlawfully, and the person possessing, transporting or controlling the big game shall produce the head or the name and address of the person killing the big game or other satisfactory evidence that the carcass is part of a lawfully taken animal. Violation relating to: ▸ bear or elk is a first degree summary offense; ▸ deer is a second degree summary offense; ▸ wild turkey is a fourth degree summary offense. Each bird or animal or part is a separate offense. Except as provided, no person shall hunt, kill or take big game, or attempt, aid, abet, assist or conspire in such, except wild turkey: ▸ with a device other than a centerfire or muzzle-loading firearm or bow and arrow; ▸ with an automatic or semiautomatic firearm; ▸ with a firearm propelling more than one projectile per discharge; ▸ with a projectile which is not all lead or which is not designed to expand on contact; ▸ when big game is swimming. Big game killed contrary to these provisions is contraband. Violation: fifth degree summary offense (34-2321 and -2322).

Each licensed person who kills big game immediately shall complete the game kill tag and attach it to the big game to remain until processed for consumption or prepared for mounting. In a year in which the Game Commission establishes check stations, each person within 24 hours after killing big game shall present it for examination and tagging. Within 10 days of the kill, the person shall fill in the report card supplied with the hunting license for reporting big game killed and mail it to the Game Commission. A person not required to secure a license who lawfully kills big game shall make and attach a tag to it containing in English the person's name, address, date, township and county where it was killed. Within five days following the kill, the person shall mail to the Game Commission a statement setting forth information required on the tag and the sex of the big game. It is unlawful to: ▸ use a duplicated game tag or to use a game kill tag to mark a second big game animal or to remove a tag from big game in violation; ▸ possess a big game kill tag, after killing the legal limit of big game, while in the fields, forests or on the waters or highways within or bordering the Commonwealth. Failure to return the report card supplied with the hunting license within 10 days of the kill is an eighth degree summary offense. Violation of any other provision is a fifth degree summary offense. Except as provided in 34-2301(b) (relating to lawful cooperation or assistance), it is unlawful for a person who has lawfully killed big game to hunt for or cooperate with another person hunting for big game of the same species while carrying a loaded firearm, a bow and nocked arrow or other device capable of killing big game. With a proper license, nothing prohibits a person from carrying a loaded handgun in the field. Violation: fourth degree summary offense. ★It is unlawful for a body of persons hunting in unison, or cooperating with each other while hunting, to kill or possess more than the lawful number of big game, and such persons shall be individually liable for the penalty imposed for big game killed in excess of the number set by regulation. In circumstances where more than the lawful number of big game is killed by a hunting party, any excess shall be turned over to the nearest officer of the Game Commission within 12 hours after the killing.★ Big game killed contrary to these provisions is contraband. Violation relating to bear or elk: second degree summary offense. Violation relating to other big game: fourth degree summary offense. ★The Game Commission may establish roster requirements and limitations applicable to groups or parties of persons hunting together or in unison or in any other manner cooperating with others while hunting for big game. Each roster shall be open to inspection. Violation: seventh degree summary offense (34-2323 through -2326).★

★A person who legally kills big game and discovers that its flesh was unfit for human consumption at the time of killing shall deliver within 12 hours the entire carcass, less entrails, but including the head and hide, to a Game Commission officer who, being satisfied that the big game was indeed unfit shall issue a written authorization to kill a second animal or bird of the same species during the unexpired portion of the season.★ Unless tagged as specified, it is unlawful to ship or transport the carcass of big game. A person may transport an unmarked part of a big game carcass that has been legally taken and cut up, but upon request shall furnish the name, address and license number of the person killing it and other required information to establish legal possession. It is unlawful to furnish false or misleading information concerning the carcass or parts. Violation: fifth degree summary offense (34-2327 and -2328). Except as provided, it is unlawful to transport small game in excess of the daily possession limits unless it is accompanied by the owner or is carried upon the conveyance with the owner. Properly tagged small game unaccompanied by the owner may be transported if a hand-made tag is attached containing information as specified. Small game shall be carried to permit easy inspection. Small game transported in violation of these provisions is contraband, and a seventh degree summary offense (34-2341).

Except as provided, it is unlawful to: ▸ take, kill, wound, capture, possess or attempt, aid, abet, assist or conspire to take, kill, wound or capture, fur-bearers except during the open fur-taking season and in such numbers or by such methods as fixed by the Game Commission or the code; ▸ possess the green pelt, or part, of a fur-bearer taken except during the open season, and for 10 days thereafter without a permit; ▸ stake out or set traps for fur-bearers prior to the date and hour fixed as the open season; ▸ stake out, set or tend, traps in an attempt to take, kill or capture fur-bearers without displaying licenses or permits required; ▸ buy or sell, or offer such, or export a fur-bearer, or part, which has been taken, possessed, killed, transported, imported, or exported unlawfully or improperly tagged regardless of where taken; ▸ possess live fur-bearers taken from the wild without a permit; ▸ set traps closer than five feet from a hole or den except for underwater sets; ▸ use a pole trap, deadfall, poison, explosive, chemical, leghold trap with teeth or with a jaw spread exceeding six and one-half inches, or a device prohibited by regulation; ▸ smoke out or dig out a den or house or cut den trees; ▸ use a trap unless visiting and removing/releasing animals and birds at least once every 36 hours; ▸ use or set a body-gripping trap outside an established watercourse, waterway, marsh, pond or dam; ▸ set a trap not marked with an identification tag as specified; ▸ bait a trap with meat or animal products if the bait is visible from the air; ▸ leave traps set after the close of the fur-taking season; ▸ remove wildlife from the trap of another without permission to do so; ▸ set or place a cage or box trap in water; ▸ use a cage or box trap not approved; ▸ destroy, disturb or interfere with the dams or houses of beavers without permission of a Game Commission officer. It is unlawful to disturb the traps of another, except when traps are set on private property without permission, the landowner, lessees or employees may remove the traps and notify an officer of the Game Commission within 48 hours, who shall notify the trapper within 10 days to claim the traps. If the traps are not claimed within 30 days following notification or the trapper cannot be located, the traps shall be forfeited to the Game Commission. Nothing herein prevents: ▸ possession of imported green pelts lawfully taken and exported from another state or nation with attached proof of origin and tagged in accordance with the requirements of that state or nation; ▸ killing of lawfully taken fur-bearers with a firearm as prescribed by regulation; ▸ lawful taking of fur-bearers by a resident age 12 or older with a fur-taking license; ▸ sale of pelts or carcasses of lawfully taken fur-bearers. Except for provisions relating to the fur-taker's certificate of training, these provisions shall not prevent persons under age 12 from trapping fur-bearers, but they shall not use a firearm other than a .22 caliber rimfire rifle or sidearm and must be accompanied by an adult. A violation of fur-taking regulations relating to bobcat or otter is a fourth degree summary offense. Except for threatened or endangered species, any other violation of fur-taking regulations is a fifth degree summary offense (34-2361 through -2364).

★Except as provided, it is unlawful to permit a dog to chase, pursue, follow upon the track of, injure or kill game or wildlife. It is lawful to train a dog as specified. Persons who are training dogs and who comply with these provisions are not required to have hunting or fur-taking licenses. The Game Commission, by regulation, may restrict or relax training periods for specific dog breeds. A dog being trained shall be accompanied by and under the control of the owner or handler, and such person shall not carry a bow and arrow or a firearm while training a dog. No dog shall be permitted to kill or inflict injury upon the pursued game or wildlife. It is lawful to train dogs on raccoons and foxes during any hour of the day. It is unlawful to train dogs on privately owned property on Sunday, except on national or state forest land, state game lands, or privately owned property when the consent of the person in charge is obtained. Violation relating to training dogs on small game is a fourth degree summary offense, and the violator is also liable for the replacement costs of the game or wildlife killed or injured (34-2381, -2382 and 2386). ★ It is unlawful to use a dog to hunt or take big game or to permit a dog to pursue, harass, chase, scatter, injure or kill big game. A dog pursuing or following upon the track of a big game animal in such close pursuit as to endanger it or in the act of attacking a big game animal is declared to be a public nuisance and may be destroyed. Violation: third degree summary offense, and the violator is liable for the replacement costs of the game or wildlife killed or injured (34-2383, -2384 and -2386).

It is unlawful to shoot at game or wildlife while it is on a public highway or to shoot across a public highway open to use by the public unless the line of fire is high enough above the elevation of the highway to preclude danger to the users of the highway. ★It is unlawful for a person, after alighting from a motor vehicle being driven on or stopped on a public highway, to shoot at a wild bird or wild animal while within 25 yards of the traveled portion of the public highway or road open to public travel. Violation: fourth degree summary offense. ★ ★Except as provided, it is unlawful for other than the lawful occupant, while hunting game or wildlife, taking fur-bearers, or pursuing a privilege granted by the code, to hunt for, take, trap, pursue, disturb or otherwise chase game or wildlife or to discharge a firearm, arrow or other deadly weapon within or through a safety zone, or to shoot at game or wildlife while it is within the safety zone without advance permission of the lawful occupant. "Safety zone" means the area within 150 yards around and that area which is below the highest point of an occupied dwelling house, residence, or other building or camp occupied by humans, or a barn, stable, or other building used in connection therewith or an attached or detached playground of a school, nursery school or day-care center. Violation: fourth degree summary offense. It is unlawful to hunt, take or trap game or wildlife or to discharge a firearm or other deadly weapon into or within, or to dress out game or wildlife within a cemetery or other burial grounds. Violation: fourth degree summary offense (34-2504 through -2506). ★

★It is unlawful during the open season for taking of big game other than turkey to: ▸ shoot at a mark or target other than legal game or wildlife with a firearm or a bow and arrow; ▸ discharge a firearm or release an arrow at random in the general direction of game or wildlife not plainly visible for routing or frightening them; ▸ discharge a firearm or release an arrow at random or in a manner contrary to these provisions. ★ This does not apply to the discharge of a firearm to signal for assistance while in distress; ▸ the use of rifle, pistol or archery ranges; ▸ the discharge of a muzzle-loading firearm at a target for safe transportation of the muzzle-loaded firearm; ▸ shooting at a target or mark or a dead tree protected by a natural or artificial barrier, except target shooting is lawful only when done upon property owned by the shooter or by a guest or within 200 yards of the camp or headquarters where the person shooting is quartered or is an invited guest or visitor. Violation: fourth degree summary offense. It is unlawful to hunt for or take a game or wildlife or to discharge a firearm or bow into or upon: ▸ lands, waters or premises of a hospital or sanatorium or health care facility; ▸ a park or resort set aside for public use where people may congregate in the open for health, recreation or pleasure; ▸ a publicly owned institution where people are hospitalized, quartered or incarcerated at public expense. These provisions do not apply to designated shooting ranges or to a part of the lands of a hospital, sanatorium, park, resort or institution which lies outside the posted areas and is open to the public for hunting. The boundaries of such lands, waters or premises shall be posted with markers prohibiting hunting. No privileges shall be granted by those owning or operating the posted lands or waters to another person to hunt for game or wildlife upon the property; nor shall the person or persons owning or in charge of the lands be eligible to hunt for game or wildlife on the lands or waters. Violation: fourth degree summary offense (34-2507 and -2508).

It is unlawful while hunting game or wildlife or taking fur-bearers to: ▸ cause damage or injury to real or personal property; ▸ leave gates or bars open; ▸ damage fences; ▸ tear down or scatter rail, post, wood or stone piles; ▸ harass, injure or kill livestock; ▸ hunt or trap in unharvested buckwheat, corn, sorghum or soybean fields without the permission of the owner. These provisions shall not be construed to prevent the removal of mortally wounded game or wildlife from its place of refuge in a rail, post, wood or stone pile or fence if permission has been obtained from the owner and the property is restored to the condition in which it was found. It is unlawful to hunt foxes by means of horses and hounds on another person's lands. Violation: fifth degree summary offense, and a violator is liable for the cost of damages to real or personal property. ★★While hunting or fur-taking, or while on lands or waters open to same, it is unlawful to litter, drive a motor vehicle on a cleared field except with permission, or park a motor vehicle so as to block the means of ingress or egress to a person's property, cattleways or fields. Littering is a third degree summary offense. A person convicted of a second or subsequent violation for littering shall pay twice the fine imposed for the first offense. A conviction for a violation shall not bar a civil action by the property owner. Any other violation is a seventh degree summary offense. In addition to the fine, an additional fine of $10 may be imposed for each item of litter thrown, discarded, left, emitted or deposited in violation of these provisions.★★ ★★While hunting or preparing to hunt for game or wildlife, it is unlawful to cause damage to a tree located upon public or privately owned lands or to use or occupy a tree stand, platform or other man-made support which, when constructed, damages a tree, except for landowners upon their lands or persons with a landowner's written permission. Violation: fifth degree summary offense. The defendant shall be sentenced to remove the man-made device. In addition to any other penalty imposed, the defendant shall be liable to pay to the one in control of the tree the amount of damage done (34-2509 through -2511).★★

★On Game Commission lands or waters, without consent or a permit, it is unlawful to: ▸ go upon lands or waters posted against entry; ▸ cut down or otherwise destroy trees, shrubs or other flora; ▸ do or cause to be done an act to the detriment of such lands, structures, roads, trails, trees, shrubs or flora thereon; ▸ remove organic or inorganic material; ▸ destroy, mutilate or remove a sign or placard; ▸ fish, swim or boat on posted waters; ▸ post Game Commission signs or placards, or similar signs, on lands not owned or controlled by it; ▸ violate regulations for use and protection of such lands or waters or its users. Violation: fifth degree summary offense. Upon conviction, the defendant shall pay for all damages done or materials removed. In addition to any other penalty imposed, where the damages or materials removed are extreme or an agreeable arrangement cannot be reached between the concerned parties, the case shall be heard by the district justice who may appoint an independent person to appraise the damage to be paid to the Game Commission, costs for the appraiser to be added to costs of prosecution (34-2512).★

Every person who causes or is involved in an accident in which a human is injured by a firearm or bow and arrow while hunting or taking game, wildlife or fur-bearers or incurs a self-inflicted injury shall render a report to the Game Commission, or a Game Commission officer, within 72 hours after the injury. Each 24-hour period thereafter is a separate offense. If the person is physically incapable of making the report, it is the duty of the persons involved in the accident to designate an agent to file the report. Violation involving a nonfatal accident: fifth degree summary offense. Violation involving a fatal accident: fourth degree summary offense. It is unlawful for a person while hunting or fur-taking, through carelessness or negligence, to shoot at, injure or kill a human through the use of a firearm, bow and arrow or other deadly weapon. The penalty for a violation is determined as follows: ▸ to shoot at but not hit or injure a human is a first degree summary offense; ▸ to injure a human is a third degree misdemeanor; to kill a human is a second degree misdemeanor. A person who shoots at, injures or kills a human shall be denied the privilege to hunt or take game or wildlife anywhere in the Commonwealth, with or without a license, for the following periods: ▸ for shooting at but not hitting or injuring a human, two years; ▸ for injuring a human, two years to five years; ▸ for killing a human, 10 years. A person who fails to pay the fine imposed within 180 days shall be jailed up to one year or until the fine is paid in full. It is unlawful to hunt or take game or wildlife or attempt such, with or without a license, contrary to a sentence imposed by these provisions. Violation: jail three to six months. Nothing herein bars recovery of damages in a civil action by an aggrieved party. Upon inflicting injury, or witnessing same, to a human with a firearm or bow and arrow, while hunting or fur-taking, it is unlawful to flee or to fail or refuse to render immediate assistance to the person injured. A violation where a human is injured is a second degree misdemeanor, and the defendant forfeits the privilege to hunt or take wildlife anywhere in the Commonwealth, with or without a license, for 10 years. Violation by the person inflicting an injury to a human is a first degree misdemeanor. In addition to the fine, the defendant forfeits the privilege to hunt or take wildlife for a period of 15 years. Violation by a witness of an injury to a human is a third degree summary offense. Violation by a witness of an injury where the human is killed is a first degree summary offense. A second or subsequent violation is a fine twice the amount of the penalty imposed by these provisions, and forfeiture of privilege to hunt or take wildlife for an additional period of 10 years (34-2521 through -2523). (See also Illegal Taking of Wildlife under ENFORCEMENT OF WILDLIFE LAWS.)

Restrictions on Taking: Fishing

Commonwealth waters stocked with fish by the Fish and Boat Commission are open to the public for free lawful fishing. This does not exempt a person trespassing on another's lands of liability for damages to those lands or improvements, crops, livestock or poultry thereon. ★No person shall fish on Sunday on privately owned land without the consent of the owner or lessee of the land abutting on a stream or body of water and the bed. Consent shall be implied unless the landowner takes reasonable action to negate consent to Sunday fishing. Violation: third degree summary offense (30-2103 and -2104).★

Commercial and Private Enterprise Provisions

Upon application accompanied by a license fee, the Fish Commission shall issue an annual regulated fishing lake license to an applicant who meets the eligibility criteria. Each application for a license or renewal shall be signed by the owner/operator of the regulated fishing lake and shall state the approximate total area of fishing water on the premises to be licensed and whether the area consists of one or more bodies of water, and other required information (30-3101).

No person required by law to procure a license to propagate fish for sale is required to secure a fishing license in order to exercise the rights conferred by the license (30-2709). The Fish Commission may issue an artificial propagation license for any fish species. A separate propagation license is required for each separate propagation facility even though owned and operated by the same person. The license authorizes the licensee to: ► carry on the business of propagation and sale of the species of fish or eggs specified in the license; ► catch and kill the fish specified in the license except by explosives or poisonous substances; ► sell or dispose of the game fish or eggs specified in the license, at any time of the year the license authorizes public transportation companies to receive and transport the fish or eggs. The license does not authorize the catching of fish out of a stream flowing over the property of the licensee or other state waters. Licensees shall not stock or maintain establishments with fish species, or eggs thereof, taken from state waters not occupied, owned or controlled by them and covered by their licenses, except licensees may exchange fish eggs or fry with the Fish Commission (30-3301, -3303, -3304 and -3307).

The Fish Commission may issue: ► a live bait fish license, a live fish bait dealer's license, or a live fish dealer's license to buy and sell certain approved species of fish; ► a license to persons who do not propagate fish but who buy and sell live bait fish, live fish bait and live fish. Resident live bait fish, live fish bait and live fish dealers who purchase their fish from legal sources outside the state shall obtain a transportation license. Nonresidents who bring live bait fish, live fish bait and live fish into the state shall secure a nonresident dealer's license. No licensee shall distribute a species not on a Fish Commission list of approved live bait fish, live fish bait or live fish in the state without having it inspected and approved for desirability of species. No person shall sell or offer for sale bait fish or fish bait taken from state waters which were not artificially propagated and sold under an artificial propagation license, except under a license specified bait fish species may be netted from Lake Erie for sale purposes. No person shall purchase, sell or offer for sale a species of fish taken from state waters or illegally taken from waters outside the state and received in interstate commerce, except those species which the Fish Commission approves for sale. Violation by selling, offering for sale or purchasing fish with a market value or sale price of $50 or more is a third degree misdemeanor. Violation where the market value or sale price is not shown or is less than $50 is a first degree summary offense (30-3309, -3310, -3311 and -3313).

Except as provided, it is unlawful to buy, sell, barter or exchange, possess, offer such or to aid, abet or conspire in the possession, sale, barter, or exchange, or to give away endangered or threatened species or subspecies of wild birds or animals, or parts. It is the duty of every enforcement officer to seize all endangered or threatened wild birds or animals, or parts. Violation is a second degree misdemeanor. All wild birds or animals, or parts, found in violation are contraband. ★These provisions shall not be construed to permit an individual or agency other than the Game Commission to sell the skins or parts of game or wildlife or the plumage or parts of birds killed as protection to crops or accidentally killed upon the highways or seized as contraband (34-2167).★

Unless provided, it is unlawful to buy, sell or barter, or aid, abet, assist or conspire or offer to do such, or possess for sale or barter, any game or edible parts, protected bird, or animal or parts. It is unlawful to sell or barter, or offer for sale or barter, game or wildlife protected by this title imported, dead or alive, from another state or nation unless there is attached a tag identifying the game or wildlife in English and giving the state or nation from which originally shipped. This does not prevent the purchase or sale of game raised under authority of a propagating permit in the Commonwealth or the capture and sale of game or wildlife after securing a permit, or the purchase or sale of the tanned, cured or mounted heads or skins, or parts, of game or wildlife not killed in a wild state in the Commonwealth, or the sale or purchase of any inedible part thereof from game or wildlife lawfully killed, if such parts are disposed of by the original owner within 90 days after the close of the season in which the game or wildlife was taken. Prior to selling parts of game or wildlife under these provisions, all edible parts shall be removed. No person or agency other than the Game Commission may sell the skins or parts of game or wildlife killed as a protection to crops, or accidentally killed upon the highways, or seized as contraband. Violation relating to: ► elk or bear is a first degree summary offense and forfeiture of hunting and fur-taking privileges for five years; ► deer is a second degree summary offense and forfeiture of hunting and fur-taking privileges for three years; ► bobcat or otter is a third degree summary offense and forfeiture of hunting and fur-taking privileges for three years; ► wild turkey or beaver is a fourth degree summary offense and forfeiture of hunting and fur-taking privileges for two years; ► each other wild bird or wild animal is a fifth degree summary offense and forfeiture of hunting and fur-taking privilege for one year (34-2312).

★Unless provided by regulations, a person now holding a taxidermy permit shall be eligible for renewal. The Game Commission shall set up a system of examinations to determine the fitness of all future applicants for the permits.★ Nothing shall preclude the requirements of any other state or federal law. Resident permits authorize the holder, unless otherwise restricted, to receive from a person a bird or animal that has been legally or accidentally killed, keep the specimen or any part in possession indefinitely and mount the specimen or part; sell or dispose of an unclaimed specimen; mount and sell a bird or animal which is lawfully disposed of under authority of the code and the state or nation where killed or taken. ★It is unlawful for a taxidermist to mount a bird or animal, or part, protected by the code, which was not lawfully killed or raised, until the owner presents a Game Commission permit and, in the case of migratory birds, the required federal permit.★ It is unlawful to do taxidermy work for another without a permit, except for taxidermy employees. Violation: fourth degree summary offense (34-2926).

Regulated hunting grounds require a minimum of 100 acres of land, or land and water combined, on which the permittee must release one of the following species of domestically produced game birds: ringneck pheasants, bobwhite quail or mallard ducks. Any of the species and chukar partridges may be released only if they are listed on the permit application and propagated by the permittee or received from a legal source. At least 100 of each species listed on the permit shall be released. Classes of permits are: ► commercial, open to the public for a fee or other charge; ► noncommercial, used by permittee only or guests with no fee for use of the area or the birds. The boundaries of regulated hunting grounds shall be marked to warn an intruder of the area's purpose, and it is unlawful to enter the area without permission. Permittees and their guests may shoot birds released by them during the regulated hunting grounds season as set each year by the Game Commission without regard to the general statewide season. Persons hunting or taking game birds on regulated hunting grounds are not required to have hunting licenses, but the methods of hunting and taking these game birds shall be in compliance with code provisions. All species of game, other than those specified, found on the premises covered by the permits may be taken only by persons possessing hunting or fur-taker licenses and only in accordance with general code provisions and regulations governing seasons and bag limits. The permittee shall attach a tag to each bird killed, to remain attached to each bird until prepared for consumption. Dogs may be trained or field trials held at any time of year upon the regulated hunting grounds. It is unlawful to: ► remove from or consume on the premises of a regulated hunting grounds untagged pheasants, bobwhite quail or mallard ducks; ► violate provisions regarding marking and tagging of birds; ► use methods to hunt or kill birds not permitted by code; ► trap game birds or have a trap set capable of taking game birds alive on regulated hunting grounds unless authorized by code; ► hunt for or take game on a three-day license except as permitted by these provisions. Violation: fifth degree summary offense. Each animal or bird involved in a violation is a separate offense (34-2928).

Holders of resident fur dealer permits shall establish a regular place of business where they receive or buy furs for resale. The permittee may also receive or buy furs for resale anywhere within the state. Unless further restricted by regulation, a permit issued to a nonresident or nonresident firm or corporation shall authorize the nonresident to receive, buy or sell raw furs reselling. The permit must be carried when such person is engaged in buying furs. It is unlawful to: ► obtain furs by purchase or barter for reselling without a permit; ► purchase furs without being shown the seller's fur-taking license; ► sell raw furs without a nonresident fur dealer permit. Violation is a third degree summary offense if the violator is a resident; a first degree summary offense if a nonresident (34-2929).

No person may propagate a game bird, wild bird, game animal or wild animal presently found in a wild state within the Commonwealth for sale, barter, gift or other transfer of possession, or offer to sell or barter, unless they obtain a Game Commission permit naming the species covered. The Commission shall adopt regulations concerning the type and size of pens, shelters and enclosures used for propagating a species of game or wildlife, to provide for the health and comfort of the animals and designed to protect the public and exclude a species of game or wildlife present in the wild. No person shall transfer possession of a bird or animal held under a propagating permit unless it is marked by one of the following methods: ▸ a toe is clipped; ▸ a marker furnished by the Game Commission is attached; ▸ a receipt, detailed invoice or consignment document accompanies the live bird or animal; ▸ a label is attached to a package or container containing a dead bird or animal or parts or the bird or animal itself; ▸ any reasonable method approved by the Director. Where game or wildlife is raised or eggs produced under a propagating permit, disposal of same must comply with Code provisions. Each shipment of eggs, pelts, birds or animals, living or dead, or parts, raised or held under a propagating permit shall be accompanied by a receipt. It is unlawful to have game or wildlife in possession without the required permit receipt, detailed invoice or consignment document or to violate any of these provisions. Violation: fifth degree summary offense. These provisions do not apply to a public zoological garden which receives government grants or appropriations or private zoological park open to the public and accredited by the American Association of Zoological Parks and Aquariums or a nationally recognized circus (34-2930 and -2965),

The Game Commission may issue permits for establishment and operation of menageries. Prior to issuance, it shall adopt regulations for the housing, care, treatment, feeding, sanitation, purchase and disposal of wild birds and animals kept in menageries and for the protection of the public. It is unlawful to: ▸ keep a wild bird or animal in captivity for public exhibition, or to have it in custody or control for this purpose, without a permit; ▸ release a bird or animal into the wild; ▸ fail to exercise due care in safeguarding the public from attack by exotic wildlife; ▸ engage recklessly in conduct which places another person in danger of attack by exotic wildlife. Violation relating to permits or regulations is a second degree summary offense. Any other violation is a seventh degree summary offense. Each day of violation is a separate offense, but, under no circumstances, shall the accumulated penalty for purposes of a field receipt exceed $300. There is no limit on an accumulated penalty a court may assess. In addition, for a violation the Director may revoke or suspend a permit and order the disposal of wildlife held in the menagerie. These provisions do not apply to a public zoological garden which receives government grants or appropriations or private zoological park open to the public and accredited by the American Association of Zoological Parks and Aquariums or a nationally recognized circus (34-2964 and -2965).

Import, Export and Release Provisions

Nothing in the Fish and Boat Code relating to regulated fishing lakes authorizes a person to transport, import or introduce a species of fish, bait fish or fish bait into the Commonwealth if such activity is prohibited by other laws or regulations (30-3107). It is unlawful to bring or have transported into the state a living game or wildlife or bird eggs, the importation of which is prohibited by the Game Commission or federal law, or to release game or wildlife reared in captivity or domesticated, the importation of which is prohibited. It is unlawful to bring into, sell or possess game or wildlife or bird eggs or to release imported game or wildlife or game or wildlife reared in captivity or domesticated in the state contrary to any regulations the Game Commission promulgates to safeguard native game or wildlife. Except for endangered or threatened species, a person importing, selling, releasing or possessing game or wildlife or bird eggs contrary to these provisions, or causing them to be released or imported, commits a fifth degree summary offense. Each bird, egg or animal is a separate offense. Violation relating to an endangered or threatened species is a third degree misdemeanor. Each bird, egg or game or wildlife is a separate offense. Any game or wildlife or egg possessed by a person contrary to these provisions is contraband (34-2163).

The Game Commission may issue a permit to act as an exotic wildlife dealer authorizing the holder to import, possess, buy, sell, locate or find for a fee, barter, donate, give away or otherwise dispose of exotic wildlife. A dealer or third person who arranges trades, sales or purchase for any type of fee or commission is required to have an exotic wildlife dealer permit. No permit shall be granted by the Game Commission until it is satisfied that the provisions for housing and caring for the exotic wildlife and protection for the public are adequate. It is unlawful to: ▸ import, possess, buy, sell, locate or find for a fee, barter, donate, give away or otherwise dispose of in a calendar year more than one bird or one animal classified as exotic wildlife without an exotic wildlife dealer permit; ▸ release exotic wildlife into the wild; ▸ fail to exercise due care in safeguarding the public from attack by exotic wildlife; ▸ engage recklessly in conduct which places another person in danger of attack by exotic wildlife. Violation of provisions relating to permits or regulations is a first degree summary offense. Any other violation is a sixth degree summary offense. Each day of violation is a separate offense, but under no circumstances shall the accumulated penalty for purposes of a field receipt exceed $500. There is no limit on an accumulated penalty a court may assess. In addition, for a violation, the Director may revoke or suspend a permit and order the disposal of an exotic wildlife held. These provisions do not apply to a public zoological garden which receives government grants or appropriations or private zoological park or garden open to the public and accredited by the American Association of Zoological Parks and Aquariums or a nationally recognized circus, nor to a holder of a menagerie permit providing the purchase or sale of exotic wildlife is conducted for the sole purpose of maintaining stock for the menagerie. The Game Commission may issue permits to possess exotic wildlife which authorize the holder to purchase, receive or possess exotic wildlife from a lawful source. No permit shall be granted until the provisions for housing and caring for such exotic wildlife and for protecting the public are adequate. It is unlawful to: ▸ possess, purchase or receive exotic wildlife without an exotic wildlife possession permit; ▸ release exotic wildlife into the wild; ▸ fail to exercise due care in safeguarding the public from attack; ▸ engage recklessly in conduct which places another person in danger of attack by exotic wildlife. Violation relating to permits is a third degree summary offense. Any other violation is a fifth degree summary offense. Each day of violation is a separate offense, but under no circumstances shall the accumulated penalty for purposes of a field receipt exceed $300. There is no limit on an accumulated penalty a court may assess. In addition, for a violation, the Director may revoke or suspend a permit and order disposal of exotic wildlife held. These provisions shall not apply to a public zoological garden which receives government grants or appropriations or private zoological park or garden open to the public and accredited by the American Association of Zoological Parks and Aquariums or a nationally recognized circus (34-2961 through -2965).

See Agency Regulations under STATE FISH AND WILDLIFE AGENCIES, PROTECTED SPECIES OF WILDLIFE, GENERAL EXCEPTIONS TO PROTECTION and Commercial and Private Enterprise Provisions under this section.

Interstate Reciprocal Agreements

★So long as the State of New York or the State of New Jersey, has in effect an analogous statutory provision, a person authorized to enforce the Fish and Boat Code or a reciprocating state may enforce the Fish and Boat Code on any part of the Delaware River between those states or on the shores of that river (30-905).★ The Game Commission may enter into cooperative agreements with government agencies and interstate compact agencies for impounding, managing, using, maintaining and operating lands and waters for game or wildlife management, public hunting and fur-taking and may expend monies from the Game Fund for those costs, and may enter into similar agreements with private or commercial interests (34-709). So long as the State of New York or the State of New Jersey has in effect a statutory provision analogous to this provision, a person who is authorized to enforce the Game and Wildlife Code or an officer of a reciprocating state may enforce this code on any part of the Delaware River between those states or on the shores of that river (34-908).

ANIMAL DAMAGE CONTROL

★A license issued by the Fish Commission for the commercial propagation and sale of fish authorizes the licensee or agent to: ▸ kill, in compliance with law, wild birds or animals destructive to fish life whenever found on waters or lands controlled, used or occupied for the propagation of fish; ▸ kill and dispose of, on the premises, amphibians and reptiles found on such waters or lands to protect the fish propagation plant against depredation, except these amphibians and reptiles may not be sold without a propagation license. These provisions do not authorize the destroying and disposing of threatened or endangered fish or other animals (30-3308).★

★In areas where deer and elk are present on lands open to public hunting and are injuring or destroying farm crops, fruit orchards, commercial tree nurseries or commercial forest lands, the owners or lessees may apply to the Game Commission for assistance in erection of a deterrent fence. Except where produce is raised on a commercial basis, this provision does not apply to gardens or truck patches. Where bears are present on lands open to public hunting and are damaging or destroying beehives where 10 or more hives are placed in one location or imminent danger exists of such damage or destruction, the owner may make application to the Director of the Game Commission for assistance in the erection of a deterrent fence (34-541).★ Except as provided, the Game Commission may pay for damage done to livestock, poultry, bees, or bee-keeping equipment by bears on lands open to public hunting and lands within safety zones if damages are reported to the Game Commission within 10 days. No claim for damage to bees, their hives or bee-keeping equipment shall be paid if: ▸ the bear is killed; ▸ the affected hives are located more than 300 yards from the domicile of the owner or employee in charge; ▸ the claim is a second or subsequent claim filed by the claimant who has not erected, maintained and operated an approved bear deterrent fence. Payments for bear damages are restricted to persons domiciled in the Commonwealth (34-551). A person who collects or attempts to collect a fraudulent claim for damage by bears contrary to provisions of the code commits a first degree summary offense. Any other violation of these provisions is a fifth degree summary offense (34-556).

★★Nothing in the Game and Wildlife Code shall be construed to prohibit a person from killing game or wildlife which the person may witness destroying cultivated crops, fruit trees, vegetables, livestock, poultry or beehives, anywhere on the person's property, including detached lands being cultivated, immediately following such destruction; or where the presence of the game or wildlife on cultivated lands or fruit orchards is just cause for reasonable apprehension of additional imminent destruction. Lands divided by a public highway shall not be construed as detached lands. A person who wounds game or wildlife shall immediately make a reasonable effort to find and kill it. Every person shall comply with all regulations relating to destruction of game or wildlife for agricultural protection pertaining to method and manner of killing, reporting the killing and the disposition of game or wildlife and their skins and carcasses. Before game or wildlife, designated by regulation of the Game Commission, or a bird or animal classified as threatened or endangered may be killed, every reasonable effort shall be made to live trap and transfer such game or wildlife, to be done in cooperation with a representative of the Game Commission. The word "person" is limited to one cultivating, as a primary means of livelihood, lands for general or specialized crop purposes, truck farming or a fruit orchard or nursery being regularly maintained, as either owner, lessee or family member assisting with the cultivation of the land, or a domiciled member of the owner's household or employee, regularly and continuously assisting in the cultivation of the land. A person who kills game or wildlife, other than raccoons, under these provisions, within 24 hours shall report the killing to a Game Commission officer. Except as provided, the carcass of one deer, bear or elk killed to protect property may be retained for food. All portions of the carcass generally considered edible shall be consumed only within the household of a person having authority to kill and possess the game or wildlife. No additional animals may be retained for food until the entire carcass of the animal previously retained has been entirely consumed. The head and hide of each deer, bear or elk killed and retained for food shall be salted, placed in safekeeping and turned over to a Game Commission officer. No carcass, or parts, of a deer, bear or elk shall be retained for food if the animal was killed upon land located within a wildlife deterrent fence provided by the Game Commission or upon land on which access for hunting is denied at any time. Unless otherwise directed by a Game Commission officer, the entire carcass intact, less entrails, of each edible bird or animal killed shall be held in a place of safekeeping pending final disposition pursuant to the code. Except as provided by an officer, the entire carcass, including the head and hide, of all big game animals and the entire carcass of any other game or wildlife, other than raccoons, shall be made available, intact, less entrails, to a Game Commission officer calling for them (34-2121 through -2125).★★

While killing game or wildlife to protect property, it is unlawful to: ▸ place salt, bait or food or use an artificial means for attracting or luring game or wildlife upon such lands; ▸ use any method not approved by the Game Commission, except that traps may be used to take fur-bearers and groundhogs; ▸ use a firearm except a center fire propelling a single all-lead, lead alloy or expanding bullet or ball to kill or attempt to kill a big game animal; ▸ fail to report killing game or wildlife other than raccoons; ▸ fail to care for a game or wildlife carcass, or part thereof, other than a raccoon; ▸ refuse to answer upon request of a Game Commission representative, a question pertaining to the killing or wounding of game or wildlife, or the disposition of the carcass or part; ▸ fail to produce satisfactory evidence that material damage was done within the preceding 15 days and that there was just cause for reasonable apprehension of additional imminent destruction; ▸ fail to relinquish to an officer the entire carcass, less the entrails, of game or wildlife killed to which the person is not legally entitled, other than raccoons; ▸ fail to comply with other related provisions. Violation pertaining to big game: a fourth degree summary offense. Violation pertaining to other game or wildlife, other than raccoon: seventh degree summary offense. Each bird or animal involved in a violation is a separate offense (34-2126).

ENFORCEMENT OF WILDLIFE LAWS

Enforcement Powers

Every waterways patrolman has the power and duty to: ▸ enforce all laws of the Commonwealth relating to fish and watercraft and arrest with or without warrant a person violating the Fish and Boat Code; ▸ execute warrants and search warrants for violations of the code; ▸ serve subpoenas issued for the investigation and trial of offenses under the code; ▸ carry firearms or other weapons in performance of their duties; ▸ stop vehicles or boats and search or inspect, where probable cause exists that a violation has occurred, a boat, basket, conveyance, vehicle, fish-box, bag, coat, or other receptacle, while enforcing this code; ▸ seize and take possession of fish which may have been caught, taken or killed, or possessed or under control, or shipped or about to be shipped contrary to the law and fish seized shall be disposed of at the Director's discretion; ► enter upon land or water in performance of duties; ► demand and secure proper assistance in case of emergency; ► purchase fish to secure evidence; ► stop and board a boat to inspect for compliance with laws and regulations; ► seize rods, reels, nets or other fishing devices, fishing or boating paraphernalia, bait, boats or unlawful devices, in violation, when making an arrest or when found in the execution of a search warrant; ► pursue, apprehend or arrest an individual suspected of violating a provision of the law relating to crimes and offenses (Title 18) or other misdemeanor or felony offenses or to serve and execute warrants for such offenses; ► arrange for administration of chemical tests of breath, blood or urine to persons operating or in actual physical control of a watercraft to determine the alcoholic content of the blood or the presence of a controlled substance. Except for the power to pursue, apprehend or arrent an individual suspected of violating a provision of the law relating to crimes and offenses or other misdemeanor or felony offenses or to serve and execute warrants for such offenses, deputy waterways patrolmen may exercise all the powers and perform all the duties of waterways patrolmen. All waterways patrolmen and deputies are authorized to enforce Commonwealth laws, and rules and regulations promulgated, relating to game, parks and forestry, under the direction of the Game Commission and the Department of Environmental Resources, respectively. A person employed or elected by the Commonwealth or by a municipality, whose duty it is to preserve the peace or to make arrests or to enforce Commonwealth laws, may be designated and empowered by the Executive Director of the Fish and Boat Commission, with the approval of the Commission, to enforce the provisions of the Fish and Boat Code (30-901 through -903).

None of the provisions of the Game and Wildlife Code apply to a member of the Game Commission or its lawfully qualified representatives or duly appointed officers or other person charged with the enforcement of the code, when acting for the Game Commission. This code shall not impose liability upon a person while acting in a lawful manner and within the limitations of the code or performing a lawful duty or function imposed or authorized by the code. Every officer, employee or representative of the Game Commission in the exercise of their powers and duties has the authority to enter property outside of buildings (34-104 and -303).

An officer whose duty it is to enforce or to investigate a violation of the Game and Wildlife Code has the power and duty to: ► enforce all laws of the Commonwealth relating to game or wildlife and arrest a person who has violated provisions of the code while in pursuit of that person immediately following the violation; ► go upon land or water outside of buildings in performance of the officer's duty; ► serve subpoenas issued under provisions of the code; ► carry firearms or other weapons in performance of duty; ► purchase and resell game or wildlife, or part, to secure evidence; ► stop, inspect or search, without warrant, any means of transportation, provided that the officer is in uniform, presents official identification and states the purpose of the inspection or search; ► inspect, examine or search a person or means of transportation or its attachment or occupants, or clothing worn or a bag, clothing or container when the officer presents official identification and states the purpose of the search; ► inspect, examine or search, without warrant, a camp, tent, cabin, trailer or means of transportation or its attachments when the officer presents official identification and states the purpose of the search; ► secure and execute all warrants and search warrants for code violations, with proper consent, search or enter a building dwelling, house, hotel, enclosure, vehicle, craft or attachments thereto, and open a door, compartment, chest, locker, box, trunk, bag, basket, package or container, examine its contents and seize evidence or contraband found; ► seize and take possession, when making an arrest or an investigation or when found in the execution of a search warrant, all game or wildlife or parts, which have been taken, caught, killed, or held in possession, and seize all firearms, shooting or hunting paraphernalia, vehicles, boats, conveyances, traps, dogs, decoys, automotive equipment, records, papers, permits, licenses and all contraband or an unlawful device, used in violation of game or wildlife laws; ► administer oaths required by the code or relative to a violation of a game or wildlife law and, where game or wildlife is found in a camp, in possession or control of an individual or hunting party, question the persons under oath relative to the taking, ownership or possession; ► demand and secure assistance and/or identification from a person; ► enforce laws and regulations relating to fish, boats, parks and forestry and other environmental matters, under the direction of agencies charged with administering those laws; ► pursue, apprehend or arrest, when acting within the scope of employment, an individual suspected of violating a provision of the criminal code or other misdemeanor or felony offense, to serve and execute warrants for such offenses, and to serve subpoenas issued for examination. Deputy Game Commission officers, unless restricted by law or Director decree, shall exercise the powers and perform the duties conferred by the code on Game Commission officers. A person elected or employed by the state or by a municipality, whose duty it is to preserve the peace or to make arrests or to enforce the laws, may be designated and empowered by the Director, with the approval of the Game Commission, to enforce code provisions under the Director's policies (34-901 through -903).

In cases of violation of code provisions, the possession of game or wildlife or parts or the possession or operation of equipment or other devices unlawfully used or prohibited is prima facie evidence of the violation. A person who causes an unlawful act to be done by another person which, if directly performed by the person causing the unlawful act would be in violation of the code, is punishable as a principal. Notwithstanding provisions relating to the judiciary and judicial procedure (Title 42), District Justices have jurisdiction for all violations of the Game and Wildlife Code classified as summary offenses or misdemeanors (34-923 through -925). The operator of a vehicle or craft transporting game or wildlife shall answer any question posed by a Game Commission officer. An officer making an inquiry who is not satisfied as to the legal possession or ownership of the game or wildlife may seize and take possession of it pending further investigation. If satisfied that the game or wildlife was lawfully taken, possessed and transported, the officer shall return it. Game or wildlife transported in violation of these provisions is contraband. Violation: fifth degree summary offense (34-2313).

Except as provided, it is unlawful to have a firearm in, on or against a conveyance propelled by mechanical power whether or not it is in motion unless the firearm is unloaded. This does not apply to: ▸ police or Game Commission officers engaged in the performance of duty; ▸ a person carrying a loaded pistol or revolver when in possession of a firearms license; ▸ persons killing game or wildlife to protect property on lands they control; ▸ a motorboat or other craft or sailboat if the motor has been shut off or the sail furled and its progress has ceased. These exceptions do not apply when attempting to locate game or wildlife with an artificial light or when exercising privileges granted by the code which may be exercised only when not in the possession of a firearm. Violation: fourth degree summary offense if the vehicle is in motion, otherwise a fifth degree summary offense (34-2503).

Criminal Penalties

A person who by force, menace, threat or in any manner resists inspection or arrest for violation of Fish and Boat Code provisions or who refuses to go with a waterways patrolman after an arrest has been made, or interferes with an officer in the performance of duty under the code, commits a first degree summary offense. A person who attempts or causes bodily harm to an officer performing the officer's duties commits a third degree misdemeanor (30-904). A person who has been given a visual or audible signal to stop by an officer and who willfully fails or refuses to stop or flees or attempts to elude a pursuing officer or enforcement vehicle or boat commits a first degree summary offense (30-906). In cases of violation of code provisions, possession of fish, nets, equipment or devices prohibited is prima facie evidence of the violation (30-922).

The following penalties shall be imposed for Fish and Boat Code violations: ▸ first degree summary offense, $100 fine, or jail up to 90 days; ▸ second degree summary offense, $50 fine, or jail up to 20 days; ▸ third degree summary offense, $25 fine; ▸ fourth degree summary offense, $10; ▸ third degree misdemeanor degree, $250-5,000 fine, or jail up to 90 days, or both; ▸ first degree misdemeanor, $2,500-10,000 fine, or jail up to five years, or both; ▸ third degree felony, $2,500-15,000 fine, or jail up to seven years, or both. In addition, a person convicted of fishing without a license or operating an unregistered boat shall pay an additional penalty equal to two times the cost of the annual license, permit or registration the person was required to possess. A person convicted of a second or subsequent violation of the code or regulations within 12 months of a prior offense shall pay an additional fine of two times the maximum fine. A person convicted of a summary offense, in addition to the fine imposed, shall be sentenced to pay costs. ★A person charged with violating a code provision which is a summary offense may sign, within five days of the commission, an acknowledgment of the offense committed and pay to a waterways patrolman the penalty in full as fixed by the code. Before a person signs such acknowledgment, the person will be advised of the right to a hearing in a judicial proceeding. A person who makes payment to the Fish and Boat Commission by personal check and who stops payment on the check commits a second degree summary offense (30-923 through -925).★ A person convicted of an offense under the code forfeits fish seized by waterways patrolmen and any device confiscated and such property shall be sold or disposed of by the Executive Director (30-927). Fishing privileges are suspended automatically until assessed penalties are paid in full (30-929).

A person who by false representation receives or stocks fish from the Fish and Boat Commission or induces the Commission to stock fish in waters where the public is not allowed to fish without charge commits a first degree summary offense, is civilly liable to the Commission for the value of the fish falsely procured and is not eligible in the future to receive fish from the Commission (30-2301). A person who engages in any activity for which a special permit or license is required without a license or who violates a provision or regulation governing special permits commits a third degree summary offense. A person engaged in an activity for which a special commercial permit or license is required without a license commits a third degree misdemeanor (30-2908). A regulated fishing lake owner/operator who operates without a license, who makes a false statement knowingly in an application for a license, or who violates regulated fishing lakes provisions, commits a first degree summary offense. No person shall fish, or trespass with such intent, in the waters of a licensed regulated fishing lake without paying the fee fixed by, or obtaining permission from, the owner/operator, nor destroy willfully or maliciously or damage a lake, property or appliances used in connection with the operation of a licensed regulated fishing lake. Violation: first degree summary offense (30-3108 and -3109). Unless otherwise specified, violation of commercial propagation and sale of fish provisions is a first degree summary offense (30-3313).

Hunting, taking, killing or disturbing game or wildlife in a propagation area established by law, or violating a regulation governing conduct in such area, is a fifth degree summary offense. Entering a propagation area is a seventh degree summary offense (34-728). Violation of regulations promulgated by the Game Commission to protect its property is a fifth degree summary offense (34-741). When an officer is in the performance of duty, it is unlawful to resist or interfere or to refuse to produce identification upon request. Violation: first degree summary offense. Attempting to cause bodily injury to an officer making an arrest or investigation for a violation, or performing duties, is a second degree misdemeanor. Making a false or fraudulent statement on a report or application required by the code, or to a Game Commission representative, is a fourth degree summary offense. ★Operating a motor vehicle or craft, without lights, or turning off lights, or failing or refusing to stop, to avoid identification or inspection of its attachments, contents or passengers, upon request or signal of a uniformed officer with official identification, is a fourth degree summary offense (34-904 through -907).★

In addition to other permits, the following fines shall be imposed for violation of the Game and Wildlife Code: ▸ first degree misdemeanor, $2,000-10,000; ▸ second degree misdemeanor, $1,000-5,000; ▸ third degree misdemeanor, $500-2,500; ▸ first degree summary offense, $800; ▸ second degree summary offense, $500; ▸ third degree summary offense, $300; ▸ fourth degree summary offense, $200; ▸ fifth degree summary offense, $100; ▸ sixth degree summary offense, $75; ▸ seventh degree summary offense, $50; ▸ eighth degree summary offense, $25. In addition to these fines, costs of prosecution shall be assessed. Violation of code provisions for which a particular penalty is not applicable is a third degree misdemeanor if the violation involves an endangered or threatened species and no more severe penalty is fixed; a fifth degree summary offense for any other violation. ★Where game or wildlife is taken, killed, wounded, possessed, transported, purchased, concealed or sold and the offense is a second or subsequent offense in a two-year period, one and one-half times the amount of fine shall be imposed. Unless provided, a person who fails to pay the fine imposed, after hearing before a district justice, may be imprisoned until the fine is paid in full, but no such jail term shall exceed 90 days. Where game or wildlife is unlawfully taken, killed, wounded, possessed, transported, purchased, concealed or sold, each bird or animal or part involved in the violation is a separate offense (34-925).★

A person charged with violating a code provision which is a summary offense may sign an acknowledgment of the offense committed and pay to an officer the penalty in full, as fixed in the code, plus costs of prosecution. Such acknowledgment and payment shall not limit the Game Commission from further revoking hunting and fur-taking privileges. A person who makes payment by personal check and who stops payment on the check or issues a nonnegotiable check or instrument commits a seventh degree summary offense. A person failing to forward fines for violations commits a third degree misdemeanor. All guns, traps, dogs, boats, vehicles or conveyances, or any device, implement or appliance, and other shooting, hunting trapping or fur-taking paraphernalia seized, where the owner thereof escapes arrest and refuses to make claim to the property, shall be held for a period of not less than 30 days and then forwarded to the Game Commission for disposal at the Director's discretion, sale proceeds to be applied to costs of prosecution and the remainder deposited in the Game Fund (34-926 through -928). [Nonresident and other citation provisions are given in 34-926, 34-932, 34-2307.] Unless provided, any other violation of a Game Commission regulation is a fifth degree summary offense (34-2102). A violation relating to dogs pursuing game or wildlife is a fifth degree summary offense unless otherwise provided (34-2386).

Civil Penalties

In addition to criminal penalties provided by the Fish and Boat Code, the Fish Commission may bring civil suits in trespass on behalf of the Commonwealth for the value of fish killed or a stream or stream bed destroyed or injured in violation of law relating to protection of property and waters (Title 30, Chapter 25). In determining the value of fish killed, the Fish Commission may consider the commercial resale value, the replacement costs or the recreational value of angling for the fish killed. In addition, it may recover the costs of gathering the evidence, including expert testimony, in a civil suit brought under this provision where the defendant is found otherwise liable for damages (30-2506). When a person causes damage to Game Commission-controlled lands or buildings and a satisfactory settlement in the form of a donation to the Game Fund cannot be reached, the Game Commission, may bring civil actions for the value of damage done or materials removed from its lands and buildings, and may recover the costs of gathering the evidence, including testimony, in a civil action so brought where the defendant is found liable for damages (34-741).

★In addition to fines and costs imposed for violations of the Game and Wildlife Code, the costs incurred by the Game Commission for the replacement of the species involved in the violation shall be assessed by the District Justice in such amount as is fixed by regulation of the Game Commission. Replacement costs shall only be assessed for violations relating to threatened or endangered species of North American game or wildlife and such other species of state game or wildlife designated by the Game Commission (34-925).★ ★★In addition to the penalties provided in the code, the Game Commission may bring civil actions for compensatory and punitive damages for game or wildlife killed or habitat injured or destroyed. In determining the value of those, the Commission may consider all factors that give value to the game or wildlife or habitat, including the commercial resale value, the replacement costs or the recreational value of observing, hunting or fur-taking. In addition, it may recover the costs of gathering evidence, including expert testimony, in a civil action so brought where the defendant is found liable for damages (34-2161).★★

★★A person who, while hunting or trapping game or wildlife which may be lawfully taken, by accident or mistake kills or attempts to kill game or wildlife other than bears, elk or threatened or endangered species, contrary to Game and Wildlife Code provisions, shall pay restitution to a Game Commission officer. The person immediately shall remove the entrails of edible game or wildlife and deliver the carcass to a Game Commission officer in the county where killed for disposition, and make a written sworn statement explaining when, where and how the accident or mistake occurred. Restitution for killing or attempted killing by accident or mistake for each animal taken is: ▸ deer, $25; ▸ turkey, $20; ▸ other wild bird or animal, other than a bear, elk or an endangered or threatened species, $15. After investigation, if the officer is not satisfied the killing or attempted killing was an accident or a mistake but was caused by negligence or carelessness, or if the person fails to pay the prescribed restitution within 10 days, the officer shall cause the person to be prosecuted for the unlawful killing or attempted killing of game or wildlife, and if convicted, any amount paid shall be applied to the payment of the penalty and costs (34-2306).★★

Illegal Taking of Wildlife

No person shall fish, or trespass with such intent, in hatchery waters or waters designated by the Fish and Boat Commission as nursery waters, upon the bank of such waters or upon hatchery lands controlled, owned, or occupied by the Fish and Boat Commission, federal government, or cooperative nursery approved by the Commission. Violation: fishing or trespassing in hatchery or nursery waters: first degree summary offense. Violation: taking fish from hatchery or nursery waters: first degree summary offense if the market value of the fish taken from the hatchery or nursery waters is less than $50 or a third degree misdemeanor if the market value of the fish taken is $50 or more. A person shall not sell, offer for sale or knowingly purchase fish taken from hatchery waters in violation of law. Violation: first degree summary offense if the market value of the fish sold, offered for sale or purchased is not shown or is less than $50; a third degree misdemeanor if the market value or price of the fish sold, offered for sale or purchased is $50 or more (30-2106 and -2107). ★★It is unlawful for a person who kills fish while engaged in activities permitted by the Fish and Boat Code to refuse or neglect to make a reasonable effort to dispose lawfully of such fish. Violation: third degree summary offense (30-2108).★★

It is unlawful to drive or disturb game or wildlife except while engaged in lawful activities set in the Game and Wildlife Code. This provision does not apply to a landowner, a member of the Game Commission, the Director, a Game Commission representative or other law enforcement officer engaged in an otherwise lawful action. Violation: first degree summary offense (34-2162). ★★Any attempt made to take game or wildlife, or possession of a firearm or implement capable of killing or wounding wildlife, while unlawfully using lights while hunting, is a fifth degree summary offense and a sentence of additional penalties for each: ▸ endangered or threatened species, a fine of $1,000 and forfeiture of hunting and fur-taking privileges for 10 years; ▸ elk or bear, a fine of $800 and forfeiture of hunting and fur-taking privileges for 5 years; ▸ deer, a fine of $500 and forfeiture of hunting and fur-taking privileges for 3 years; ► bobcat or otter, a fine of $300 and forfeiture of hunting and fur-taking privileges for 3 years; ► turkey or beaver, a fine of $200 and forfeiture of hunting and fur-taking privileges for 2 years; ► other bird or animal, a fine of $100 and forfeiture of hunting and fur-taking privileges for 1 year (34-2310). ★★

License Revocations and Suspensions

A fishing license, special license, permit or privilege granted under authority of the Fish and Boat Code may be revoked by the Fish Commission when the holder is convicted of an offense and the Commission may refuse to grant a new fishing license, special license, permit or privilege for up to two years. It is a first degree summary offense to perform an act for which a fishing license, special license or permit is required or exercise a privilege while the license, permit or privilege is suspended or revoked. It is a third degree misdemeanor to commit a second or subsequent violation of a suspension or revocation during its term. Except as provided, a hunting or fur-taking license, special license, permit or registration may be revoked by the Game Commission when the holder is convicted of an offense or has acted contrary to the intent of the license, special license, registration or permit, with each offense a separate violation subject to separate revocation. The Game Commission may refuse to grant a new license, special license, permit or registration for up to five years unless otherwise provided. ★Privileges granted by the Game and Wildlife Code are suspended automatically if a defendant fails to respond to a citation or summons within 60 days or fails to pay all penalties in full within 180 days following a conviction (34-929 and -930). ★

★In addition to a penalty imposed by the Game and Wildlife Code, the Game Commission may revoke a hunting or fur-taking license and deny a person the privilege to secure a license or to hunt or take fur-bearers if the person has been convicted of violating code provisions for such periods as specified in laws relating to license revocations; or has been accused of having violated code provisions relating to the protection of property and persons even though such person has not been convicted of a violation of those provisions as prescribed. ★ A district court having jurisdiction may revoke a hunting or fur-taking license and deny the privilege to secure a license or to hunt or take fur-bearers. Except as provided, for the first offense a person convicted or having signed an acknowledgment of guilt may be denied the privilege to hunt or take wildlife for up to three years; on a second or subsequent offense, the person may be denied the privilege to hunt or take game or wildlife for such period as the Game Commission determines (34-2741 and -2742). (See also Licenses and Permits and Restrictions on Taking: Hunting and Trapping under HUNTING, FISHING AND TRAPPING PROVISIONS.)

Intoxication Testing of Hunters

It is unlawful to hunt or take game, fur-bearers or wildlife or aid, abet, assist or conspire to hunt or take same while in possession of a firearm or a bow and arrow while under the influence of alcohol or a controlled substance, or both. Violation is a third degree summary offense, and the violator shall be denied the right to hunt or trap for one year (34-2501). ★★A hunting and fur-taking license shall be refused a person who has been denied the privilege to secure that license by the Game and Wildlife Code or has been certified to the Game Commission by a licensed medical authority or by a court having jurisdiction to be mentally or physically unfit or addicted to alcohol or controlled substances to the degree that the person is unfit to exercise the privileges of the Game and Wildlife Code (34-2741). ★★ (See also Enforcement Powers under this section.)

HABITAT PROTECTION

The Fish and Boat Commission may set aside refuge areas in which fishing or entry shall be prohibited for periods as it prescribes. Notices of closings shall be posted at refuge areas. Violation by fishing in a refuge area: first degree summary offense. Violation by entering a refuge area: third degree summary offense (30-2306). No person shall alter or disturb a stream, stream bed, fish habitat, water or watershed in a manner that might cause damage or loss of fish without permits. Violation: third degree misdemeanor (30-2502). No person, regardless of intent, shall: put or place in waters within or on state boundaries any electricity, explosives or poisonous substances, except for research and fish management, agents authorized by the Fish Commission Director may use any method to collect, eradicate or control fish; or allow any substance, deleterious, destructive or poisonous to fish, to be turned into or allowed to run, flow, wash or be emptied into waters within or bordering the Commonwealth. ★In criminal prosecutions for water pollution known to be injurious to fish, it is not necessary to prove that the violation has actually caused the death of, or damage to, a particular fish. ★ This provision does not supersede "The Clean Streams Law." Violation: third degree misdemeanor (30-2504).

No dams, ponds, or other devices which prevent free migration of fish shall be erected or placed by a person licensed to propagate and sell fish in a stream flowing over the person's property. No person shall use the ponds so licensed for other than commercial propagation and rearing of fish (30-3302). A person erecting or maintaining a dam in state waters, immediately on a written order from the Fish and Boat Commission, shall erect chutes, slopes, fishways, gates or other devices to enable the fish to ascend and descend the waters at all seasons of the year. ★In lieu of requiring the erection of such devices at a dam where they are not practicable or advisable, the Commission may enter into an agreement with the owner, lessee or operator of the dam to pay to the Commission a sum to be expended for: ▸ stocking with fish of the dammed waters; ▸ the propagation, rearing and distribution of fish placed in the waters and the acquisition of the facilities therefor; ▸ carrying out other fish managing practices in the waters for the improvement of public fishing opportunities.★ Money received by the Commission under such an agreement shall be paid into the Fish Fund. When funds are available, the Commission shall conduct and encourage surveys and experimentation to develop chutes, slopes, fishways, gates or other devices to pass migratory fish over the dams. Every chute, slope, fishway, gate or other device shall be operated in a manner prescribed by the Commission and shall remain open and be maintained in good repair by the person owning or maintaining the dam. A person failing to comply with these provisions within three calendar months of the date of notice shall forfeit and pay a civil penalty of $100 for every day of failure to comply. The penalty shall be recovered in civil suit or process. If the person owning, leasing or maintaining a dam fails to erect or to maintain a chute, slope, fishway, gate or other device after the lapse of three calendar months from the date of notice, the Commission may enter upon the dam and erect such device or make repairs, and the cost shall be charged to the person owning or maintaining the dam and may be recovered by civil suit or process (30-3501, -3502, 3504 and -3505).

No person shall draw off dam waters inhabited by fish without written permission from the Fish and Boat Commission, nor obstruct the flow of water through a dam without allowing a minimum flow of water to enable fish to live. Dams, deflectors, retards or similar devices placed across or in waters inhabited by fish, with permission of the owners of the land adjacent thereto or through which those waters flow, shall not be destroyed, removed, breached or disturbed, except by written permission from the Commission. Violation: first degree summary offense (30-3506).

★A person owning, leasing or maintaining a raceway, flume or inlet pipe leading to a water wheel, turbine pump or canal shall immediately upon receipt of a written order from the Fish and Boat Commission place and maintain a bar rack as specified, in or near that raceway, flume or inlet pipe to prevent fish from entering it. If one month after notice of violation there is no compliance, the Commission may enter upon the raceway, flume or inlet pipe and place such a bar rack. The cost shall be charged against the owner, lessor or operator and may be recovered by civil suit or process. A person failing to comply within one calendar month shall forfeit and pay a civil penalty of $100 for every day of violation (30-3508).★

★No person shall place a device or object in state waters in a manner that obstructs the migration or passage of fish or obstructs a fishway, but the Fish and Boat Commission may authorize the erection and prescribe conditions for the operation and maintenance of such devices for a fee. After giving written notice to the Commission, an organization or club that has been in existence for one year or more may obstruct the passage of fish for up to 48 hours for conducting fish rodeos to encourage fishing by children. Such obstructions shall not be erected more than twice in one year within a distance of one mile from a similar obstruction on the same stream. The obstruction shall be at least one-half mile from other obstructions and erected and designed in such manner that fish will not normally be injured. Violation: first degree summary offense (30-3509).★

NATIVE AMERICAN WILDLIFE PROVISIONS: None.

RHODE ISLAND

Sources: General Laws of Rhode Island, 1956, Title 19; Reenactment of 1989; 1992 Cumulative Pocket Supplement.

STATE WILDLIFE POLICY

The General Assembly finds that the animal life inhabiting the lands of the state, its lakes, ponds, streams, and rivers, and the marine waters within its territorial jurisdiction, are a precious, renewable, natural resource which, through application of enlightened management techniques, can be developed, preserved, and maintained for the beauty and mystery that wild animals bring to our environment. The General Assembly further finds that management of fish and wildlife through establishment of hunting and fishing seasons, setting of size, catch, possession, and bag limits, regulation of the manner of hunting and fishing, and establishment of conservation policies should be pursued utilizing modern scientific techniques, having regard for the fluctuations of species populations, the effect of management practices on fish and wildlife, and the conservation and perpetuation of all species of fish and wildlife (20-1-1).

The State of Rhode Island and Providence Plantations recognizes that a diversified, stable, clean, and aesthetically satisfying natural environment is essential to the health, safety and welfare of the people of Rhode Island; such an environment contributes significantly to economic and social development and progress and is also of high value for educational, scientific, recreational and other purposes; it is further recognized that the continued existence of such a natural environment within Rhode Island is dependent upon maintenaning a high order of diversity of life forms and is equally dependent upon the maintenance of sufficient and suitable natural habitat in which such a diverse fauna and flora can reproduce, find food, shelter, and clean soil, water, and otherwise to sustain their existences; it is recognized that in addition to appropriate habitat, diversity and numbers of species and individuals in native faunal and floral populations is the key to maintaining a healthy, stable, and productive natural environment within which the citizens of Rhode Island can function, it is acknowledged that Rhode Island has a distinctive natural community of living things worthy of protecting for its own sake and for the use and benefits of its people; it is further recognized that the existence of many individual species of animals and plants within Rhode Island has been and may continue to be threatened by intentional and unintentional activities of humans. It is declared to be the intent of the state, to provide a means by which "nongame wildlife" research and management may be financed through a voluntary check-off of a portion of an income tax refund owed to a taxpayer by the state. It is also intended that funds generated by the check-off be supplemental to funds which would otherwise be available for the above purposes, and that the funds be used only for "nongame wildlife" research and management (20-18.1-1). (See also RELEVANT WILDLIFE DEFINITIONS and Agency Funding Sources under STATE FISH AND WILDLIFE AGENCIES.)

It is the policy of this state to contribute to the maintenance of a high quality environment for the safety, health and welfare of its citizens by forbidding the importation, sale, offering for sale, transportation, storage, traffic, ownership, or other possession or use of a dead or live animal or plant or part, or body, whether raw, manufactured, processed, or preserved, of any species of animal or plant under the provisions of the Federal Endangered Species Acts of 1969 and 1973 (20-37-1). (See also RELEVANT WILDLIFE DEFINITIONS and PROTECTED SPECIES OF WILDLIFE.)

RELEVANT WILDLIFE DEFINITIONS: See Definitions section of Appendices.

STATE FISH AND WILDLIFE AGENCIES

Agency Structure

The General Assembly vests in the **Director** of the **Department of Environmental Management** (Department) authority and responsibility over the state's fish and wildlife, and with the **Marine Fisheries Council**, over the fish, lobsters, shellfish, and other biological resources of state marine waters (20-1-2).

Agency Powers and Duties

The **Director** is authorized to promulgate, adopt and enforce rules and regulations necessary to carry out duties and responsibilities under this title (20-1-4). The Director and his agents, employees and designees shall protect the wild birds, animals, fisheries and shell fisheries throughout the state and shall administer and enforce the provisions of this title and the rules/regulations adopted pursuant thereto and shall prosecute violations of these laws and rules and regulations (20-1-5). The Director shall appoint **Conservation Officers** for detection and prosecution of violations of the laws enumerated in 20-1-8, and may delegate powers and duties to the officers who shall serve at his/her pleasure (20-1-6). The Director may appoint **Deputy Wardens** as necessary, who may not carry firearms, but shall be authorized to detect violators of laws enumerated in 20-1-8, to be reported to the Director who may prosecute (20-1-7).

The Director and Conservation Officers have the power to enforce state laws, rules and regulations pertaining to: ▸ fish, wildlife and all vertebrates, invertebrates, plants; ▸ fresh water wetlands, dams and resources; ▸ areas and activities subject to the jurisdiction of the Coastal Resources Management Council; ▸ state parks, reservations, management areas, hatcheries and game preserves and state laws within the areas; ▸ solid and hazardous waste transportation, storage and disposal; ▸ boating safety and water safety; ▸ water and air pollution and open burning; ▸ firearms; ▸ littering; ▸ trees and forests, forestry and fire hazard protection; ▸ agriculture, farmland and pest control (20-1-8).

They also have the power to: ▸ issue summonses and execute warrants and search warrants for violations of laws and regulations; ▸ serve subpoenas issued for trial or hearing of all offenses; ▸ arrest without warrant a person found violating a law or regulation; ▸ seize and take possession of all fish, shellfish, crustaceans, marine mammals, amphibians, reptiles, birds and mammals in possession/control of any person or which have been shipped illegally; ▸ seize all fishing tackle, firearms, shooting and hunting paraphernalia, licenses, traps, decoys, or other devices used in violation of a wildlife law or regulation, or equipment, materials or implements used in the violation of any other law; ▸ board vessels engaged in fishing and examine any license and vessel for compliance with laws concerning the taking of any wildlife; ▸ carry firearms in the course of duty performance; ▸ arrest without a warrant any person for the criminal offenses of assault, assault with a dangerous weapon, larceny, vandalism, or obstruction of an officer while executing his duty. It is a misdemeanor and fine up to $500, and/or jail up to 30 days to refuse to stop on the oral command of a Conservation Officer (20-1-8).

The Director or his/her agents may enter upon and pass over private property without liability for trespass in the discharge of their duties (20-1-15). The Director may require that reports detailing hunt, catch, effort and other data be provided by a person who hunts or fishes in the state, such reports to remain confidential, and disseminated to the public only in a statistical format (20-1-20).

The Director shall adopt and be responsible for the design, production, procurement, distribution, and sale of all Trout Conservation Stamps and marketable by-products such as posters and calendars (20-2-41). The Director shall establish uniform sale prices for all categories of by-products (20-2-42).

The **Department** is empowered to introduce, protect and cultivate fish in the inland waters and to construct and operate breeding facilities and undertake fish cultivation projects. The Director may take fish from state fisheries for fish culture or for scientific observation (20-12-1). For protecting and propagating fish and providing fishing preserves, the Director may acquire by gift, lease or purchase, land, freshwater streams, lakes or ponds or rights and interests therein (20-12-2). The Department shall establish and maintain freshwater hatcheries for providing freshwater and anadromous game fish for stocking the state's ponds and streams. Surplus hatchery output shall be sold at fair market price for cash only, with money to go to the general treasury for state use (20-12-3).

Agency Regulations

The Director is authorized to adopt regulations fixing seasons, bag limits, size limits, possession limits and methods of taking on any species of fish, game, bird or other wild animal occurring within the state, other than marine species regulated by the Marine Fisheries Council. Regulations may prohibit the taking, holding or possession of a species, prohibit the taking, molestation or disturbance of nesting, breeding or feeding sites of a species, and prohibit or regulate commercial use, importation or exportation of a species. Regulations may be of statewide applicability or for a specified locality. Regulations shall be adopted only after a public hearing (20-1-12). Notice of intent to adopt regulations and a public hearing shall be published in a newspaper of statewide circulation not less than 20 days prior to the hearing. Such regulations shall remain in effect not longer than one year following the date of their effectiveness (20-1-13).

Agency Funding Sources

All monies derived from freshwater fishing, hunting and combination licenses and permits shall be deposited with the General Treasurer and appropriated to the Department for protection and propagation of fish and game. Two dollars from each license and permit shall be placed in a special fund to acquire and develop fish and wildlife lands (20-2-6). Monies from licenses and permits are to be used only for: ▸ lease and purchase of land and rights-of-way to streams and ponds to be stocked by the Department and opened for public fishing; ▸ stream improvement; ▸ enforcement of fish and game laws; ▸ protection and propagation of fish and game; ▸ leasing and purchase of land or conservation easements for creating wildlife reservations and protecting wildlife habitats (20-2-7). A minimum of $40,000 shall be allocated for establishing a **Shellfish Transplant Program** from revenues derived from licenses and fees during the 1992-1993 fiscal year (20-2-7.1)

Monies from marine and commercial licenses (20-2-20 through -28.1) over and above $200,000 in any fiscal year shall be appropriated to the Department of Environmental Management and used only for: ▸ propagation of marine fish, lobsters and shellfish; ▸ transplanting shellfish from closed areas; ▸ fishing port development; ▸ Marine Fisheries Council staff expenses; ▸ lease and purchase of land or acquisition of conservation easements (20-2-28.2).

All **Trout Conservation Stamp** receipts and all receipts from the sale of stamp by-products shall be deposited in a special **Trout Conservation Fund**, and the receipts used for operations, trout habitat including acquisition, improvement research and culture projects (20-2-43).

All **Waterfowl Stamp** receipts and those from the sale of stamp by-products shall be deposited in a special **Waterfowl Fund** and used for waterfowl habitat, acquisition, improvement, and research projects (20-2-38).

There is a separate **Nongame Wildlife Fund** within the General Fund consisting of sums collected as a result of the taxpayer check-off provided for in 44-30-2.2. The Director is authorized to accept any grant, devise, bequest, donation, gift or assignment of money, bonds or other valuable securities for deposit in and credit to the Nongame Wildlife Fund. The monies shall be made available immediately and are appropriated specifically to the Director to be used solely to research, manage, protect, inventory, and establish a body of ecological information pertaining to nongame wildlife species. These uses may include habitat acquisition, educational programs, personnel needs, enforcement of laws pertaining specifically to nongame wildlife, planning, writing and implementation of management programs, utilization of funds from other sources and cooperation with other public and private programs with similar or parallel objectives. The monies shall not be used for animal control programs, nor for any program or activity related directly to game or domestic animals (20-18.1-3).

Agency Advisory Boards

The **Marine Fisheries Council** is created with jurisdiction over all marine animal species within the state (20-3-2).

PROTECTED SPECIES OF WILDLIFE

No person shall buy, sell, offer for sale, store, transport, import, export, or otherwise traffic in an animal or part, living, dead, processed, manufactured, preserved, or raw if the animal has been declared to be an endangered species by either the US Secretaries of the Interior or Commerce or by the Director. The only exception shall be for scientific research or educational displays either of which must be done by or under the formal supervision of a legitimate college or university, with a special permit for each individual excepted species, to be issued by the Director. The permit will be denied if issuance would not be entirely justified or in the best interests of preservation and protecting of the species. ★Under no circumstances will a permit be granted if commercial considerations are involved (20-37-3).★

The Director and all enforcement personnel, all members of the state police force and all authorized city and town law enforcement authorities shall have the power to enforce this law. They shall have authority under warrant to search for and seize goods, merchandise or animal sold or offered for sale or otherwise used or possessed illegally, or property or item used in connection with a violation of this section; the seized goods, wildlife or property shall be held pending proceedings in a court of jurisdiction. Upon conviction, the seized goods, merchandise or animals shall be forfeited, and either offered to a university for scientific or educational purposes, or destroyed. ★The possessor of an animal included under this chapter shall have the burden of proof that the animal or parts is not held in violation. Individuals in possession of skins of endangered species must show that the skins were purchased or obtained prior to January 1, 1974 (20-37-4). Violation: $500-5,000 fine; and/or jail up to one year (20-37-5).★ (See also STATE WILDLIFE POLICY for Endangered Species Provisions.)

No person shall hunt, pursue, shoot or trap defined fur-bearing mammals except in accordance with the Director's regulations (20-16-1). No person shall hunt, trap, take, or kill an otter in this state. Violation: $100 fine for each offense (20-16-17).

See also STATE WILDLIFE POLICY for statement on nongame wildlife.

GENERAL EXCEPTIONS TO PROTECTION

Killing or destruction of nests or eggs of English or European house sparrows or European starlings is not prohibited (20-14-3).

The Director may issue special permits for the taking, handling and/or possession of a species of wild animal, of any size, age and numbers appropriate for carrying out scientific experiments and cultivation projects under the Director's regulations. The Director may require information to ascertain that the person is involved in a bona fide experiment. Failure to abide by permit restrictions or failure to report information required by the Director shall be cause for suspension/revocation of the permit (20-1-18).

HUNTING, FISHING, TRAPPING PROVISIONS

Rhode Island is a member of the Atlantic States Marine Fisheries Compact (20-8-1 through -12).

Licenses and Permits

The Director may issue such licenses as are required under this title for hunting, fishing, and the taking of fish, game, birds, shellfish, lobsters or other wild animals within the state and its territorial waters, pursuant to regulations, and may appoint responsible citizens to act as license issuing agents (20-2-1). A license application form shall bear the name, age, occupation, place of residence, signature and identifying description of the applicant (20-2-2). Falsification of license information is punishable by a fine up to $50, the license shall be void, and no new license can be obtained for one year (20-2-8). Licensees must have the license in possession at all times while engaged in the licensed activity and shall present same for inspection on demand by an authorized person (20-2-9). Exceptions to the license requirement to hunt and fish may be made under statutory provisions for the blind, disabled veterans and other citizens, persons over age 65, certain armed forces or merchant marine members, and on free fishing days designated by the Director (20-2-31).

No hunting license shall be granted to or possessed by: ▸ a person under age 15, except a junior hunting license is available for ages 12-14, with a hunter's safety certificate and hunting only with an adult; ★★ ▸ a person who has been convicted of a crime of violence or who is a fugitive from justice under the Firearms Act; ▸ a person under guardianship, treatment, or confinement by virtue of being a mental incompetent, drug addict or who has been adjudicated or is under treatment as a drug addict or a habitual drunkard. Such persons, other than those who have been pronounced criminally insane, after five years from being pronounced cured by a competent medical authority, may obtain a license on presentation of an affidavit from such authority to the effect that the person is mentally stable and a proper person to possess a hunting license.★★ Every hunting license shall bear the name, age, occupation, place of residence and an identifying description of the licensee (20-13-5). A non-resident license shall enable the licensee to carry from the state up to two day's bag limit of native game birds or animals or the limit of migratory game birds set by federal regulations, if carried open to view for inspection (20-13-6).

★All persons granted a license are deemed to have consented to the reasonable inspection of a boat, vessel, net, dredge, trap, vehicle, structure or other contrivance used regularly for the keeping or storage of fish or shellfish, or a game bag, firearms, creel, box, blind, or hunting or fishing paraphernalia used in connection with the licensed activity by the Director's agents (20-2-32).★

The Department shall formulate courses of instruction in safe hunting practices and the handling and use of firearms and/or bow and arrow for persons applying for a license for the first time, and shall designate competent persons or organizations to give that instruction and issue certificates of competency. The Department may designate the police authorities of the several cities and towns to give safety instruction. No civil liability nor cause of action shall arise against the Department or its agents under this section (20-13-2). Safety instruction shall be made available on a continuing basis throughout the year at sites convenient to the public and shall be offered at least once a month (20-13-2.1). Persons refused a competency certificate may appeal to the Director who shall make the final determination of competency of the applicant (20-13-3). No hunting license shall be issued unless the person has held a hunting license in a prior year, or the person presents a certificate of competency in hunter safety from an approved program from this or another state, or the license is marked "archery only." ★Any person serving in or honorably discharged from the armed services or women's auxiliary branch is not be required to obtain a certificate of competency (20-13-4).★

No person over age 15 shall take trout without a regular fishing license and a **Rhode Island Trout Conservation Stamp**, available for issue at all fishing license outlets (20-2-40). No person over age 16 shall take migratory waterfowl without a regular hunting license which includes a **Migratory Waterfowl Stamp** (20-2-35).

Restrictions on Taking: Hunting and Trapping

No person shall hunt, pursue, take or kill a wild bird or mammal or a vertebrate, or attempt such, without a license; provided that a resident and immediate family members may hunt without a license on land leased by the resident on which the family is domiciled, and which is used exclusively for agricultural purposes, and not for club shooting purposes (20-13-1).

It is unlawful while hunting to discharge a firearm or other deadly weapon within 500 feet of an occupied dwelling house or a barn, stable, or other building used in connection therewith without the owner's permission (20-13-7). It is unlawful to: ► have more than five persons hunting in unison or cooperating with each other to hunt for wild birds or animals; ► hunt anywhere or to enter fields, woods or water within or bordering the state while possessing a firearm or other weapon for hunting when intoxicated or under the influence of intoxicating/controlled substances; ► hunt or shoot at a bird or animal along, upon or across a public highway; ► have in possession a loaded firearm in or on a vehicle or conveyance while upon or along a public highway, road, lane or trail (20-13-8 through -11).

★Every person causing injury to his or herself or another human by gunfire while hunting or trapping shall report to the Department within 72 hours of the injury unless physically incapable, in which event it is that person's duty to designate another to make the report within the specified time (20-13-12). A person who causes an injury to another person by firearm or arrow while hunting who fails to render assistance, in addition to other penalties, shall be fined up to $1,000, jailed up to one year, or both (20-13-15).★

★Whoever uses or possesses while hunting a rifle other than a 22 caliber rim fire or muzzle loading rifle, or shotgun and shells loaded with ball, bullets, slug or shot larger than no. 2 shot, shall be fined up to $500, or jailed for up to 30 days, or both, provided that from April 1 to September 30, no center fire rifles larger than .229 caliber may be used during daylight hours; persons hunting waterfowl in a blind or over decoys may use steel shot of size no. 1 or BB (20-13-13).★

It is unlawful to sell or offer for sale a wild bird, mammal, vertebrate, or parts, except as provided; this does not prohibit sale of inedible parts of game such as antlers, hides, feet or tails (20-13-14).

No person shall hunt, pursue or have in possession a wild bird except during the open season; possession of a bird during closed season shall be evidence that the bird was taken in violation, and each bird so possessed shall constitute a separate offense (20-14-1). No person shall willfully disturb or destroy the nest or eggs of a wild bird, except under the Director's authorization (20-14-2). (See also GENERAL EXCEPTIONS TO PROTECTION.) The open season for hunting and bag limits for migratory game birds shall be no less restrictive than those under federal provisions for migratory birds (20-14-4). During the open season, taking of more than the permitted bag limit for game birds in one day is illegal. Possession of game birds in the field in excess of the numbers allowed shall be evidence of the illegal taking or killing of them. Violation: up to $50 for each bird in excess of the bag limit (20-14-5).

No person shall: ▸ take upland or migratory game birds over baited areas where salt, corn or other grains have been scattered to lure such birds to, on, or over where hunters are attempting to hunt them (but not over areas where grains are scattered as the result of normal agricultural operations); ★ ▸ hunt or take migratory game birds by the use of live birds as decoys; ★ ▸ hunt or take wild birds by use of electronically amplified bird call recordings (except for crows); ▸ take or destroy a wild bird by means of a trap, snare, net, spring, crossbow, rifle, pistol, fishhook, poison, drug, explosive or stupefying substance; ▸ shoot migratory game birds by means of a shotgun other than 10 gauge or smaller or a longbow and arrow (20-14-7). No person shall carry or send outside the state more than a two-day bag limit of game birds (20-14-6). Migratory game birds may not be taken from a motorized boat unless such motor is shut off and/or sail furled or the boat is used solely to pick up dead or injured birds, nor shall such birds be taken with aid of a motor driven land, water or air conveyance used to concentrate, drive, rally or stir up waterfowl (20-14-9).

No person shall hunt, pursue or shoot deer except as provided under seasons, times, manner of taking and bag limits in the Director's regulations. The following restrictions shall always apply to deer hunting: ▸ No hunting within 500 feet of a building or dwelling house in use without the owner's specific written permission; ▸ hunting is allowed only from ½ hour before sunrise to ½ hour after sunset; ▸ no dog shall be employed in deer hunting activities; ▸ no hunting on private land without the owner's written permission; ★ ▸ only a shotgun, muzzle loading rifle, or longbow and arrow may be used in deer hunting; ★ ▸ no person shall make, set or use a trap, snare, salt lick or other device for the purpose of ensnaring, enticing, taking or killing a deer; ▸ no person shall individually, or in conjunction with others, use an artificial light to locate or show up wild birds, mammals or other vertebrates when the person has in actual possession, or in a vehicle (unless locked in a case) a crossbow, longbow, rifle, gun or pistol. Upon conviction of a provision of this section or regulations, in addition to the penalties in 20-1-16, any weapons, guns, lights or other equipment used in killing a deer shall be forfeited to the state (20-15-1). Deer must be properly tagged and conveyed within 24 hours of taking to a deer check point or Conservation Officer for checking (20-15-2). [Sizes of archery equipment to be used in deer hunting are prescribed in statute 20-15-4.] No person shall use or have in possession while hunting for deer pistols, guns or other firearms, spear guns, crossbows, explosive points, poisonous or barbed points or other projectile capable of injecting an incapacitating drug or chemical; a licensed person may hunt for deer by shotgun, muzzle loading rifle or longbow. Possession of a deer showing evidence of taking with a prohibited device is a violation, and on conviction, any weapons, guns or ammunition shall be forfeited to the state (20-15-5). A city or town council may prohibit hunting, possession or taking deer within the city/town boundaries by ordinance (20-15-6). Wounding or killing of a deer by vehicle shall be reported within 24 hours to a Conservation Officer who may allow the person ownership of the carcass and consumption of same by his family (20-15-7).

It is unlawful to have in possession a deer or part unless it has been taken legally under this chapter's provisions or has been imported legally from another state or country. It is unlawful to sell or offer for sale a deer or part except non-edible parts such as heads, hides or skins, except as elsewhere provided. Each possession of deer or part in violation is a separate and distinct offense (20-15-9).

No person shall set, maintain, or tend a trap for taking, killing or destroying a fur-bearing animal without obtaining a trapping license from the Department; provided that a resident may set traps on his own land where he is actually domiciled. Traps must be marked with the owner's name or license number as the Director designates. ★No trapping license shall be issued to a non-resident from a state which does not afford to Rhode Island residents trapping privileges (20-16-7). ★ No person shall use a steel jawed leghold trap to capture a fur-bearing mammal or other animal; provided that the Director may issue special permits to use such traps to abate animal nuisances which the Director determines cannot reasonably be abated by other means. Such permit shall not exceed 90 days. Violation: up to $500 fine; and/or jail up to one year, and revocation of trapping license for one year (20-16-8).

No trap shall be set on the enclosed land of another without the landowner's written permission. Every trap shall be placed in a hole, brush pile, or stone wall, so as to be inaccessible to a domestic animal. Traps shall be visited at least once daily. No traps shall be set where animals may be taken before or after the closing day of the season (20-16-9). The possession of a green pelt except during the open season and for ten days thereafter, shall be prima facie evidence that the pelt or part was unlawfully taken/possessed (20-16-10). No person shall disturb the trap of another or take an animal from the trap unless authorized by the owner (20-16-11). Every holder of a trapping license shall make a report of the number and species of fur-bearing animals taken to the Department within 30 days of the close of the trapping season. No license renewal shall be granted unless such report has been made (20-16-12). A person convicted a second time of a violation of a trapping provision, in addition to the penalties elsewhere prescribed, shall be deprived of the privilege of trapping fur-bearing animals for three years thereafter under a penalty of 30 days jail for each offense (20-16-13). No person shall own or have in possession in this state a European ferret, except by permit of the Director, nor shall a person use ferrets in hunting game. Violation, in addition to other penalties, is forfeiture of the ferret (20-16-3).

Raccoons may be taken and possessed with a gun when the taker is accompanied by a dog. No person shall hunt raccoons at night using a rifle larger than 22 caliber rim fire long rifle or by use of shotgun shells with shot larger than no. 4 or by use of a light other than a kerosene lantern exclusive of the pressure type or a flashlight with more than six cells. No person shall take raccoons by use of a light from a motor vehicle (20-16-4). Persons with a permit may keep a live raccoon(s) for breeding or other purposes (20-16-5).

No person shall erect, set or tend a snare, or spread poison for catching or killing an animal, except within buildings located on land personally occupied or as allowed by regulation (20-16-6). No person shall remove or attempt to remove a live muskrat, raccoon, mink, otter, skunk, or fox from a hole in the ground, from a stone wall, from within a ledge or from under a stone, from a den or house or from a hole in a log or tree by digging or smoking, or by probing with a wooden, metal or other device. No person shall set a trap within eight feet from a muskrat house. The Director may waive these provisions on application by a landowner seeking to protect personal property from nuisance fur-bearers (20-16-16).

It is unlawful to have in possession a fur-bearer, or part, unless it has been legally taken under the provisions of this chapter or chapter 17, or shall have been legally imported from another state or country. It is unlawful to sell or offer for sale a cottontail rabbit, varying hare, or gray squirrel, or part, except inedible parts such as heads, feet, hides, skins or tails (20-16-18).

Restrictions on Taking: Fishing

No person over age 15 shall catch or take fish in a state freshwater stream or pond without a license; provided that no license is required for a resident and immediate family members to fish in a brook or pond running through or bordering upon land owned/leased by the resident and on which the resident is domiciled (20-11-1). No person shall catch fish in a pond or stream stocked by the Department with trout except during open seasons and subject to the catch, size, and method of taking regulations established by the Director (20-11-2).

Unless otherwise specified by regulations, only a rod and reel or other device held in and operated by hand shall be used to catch fish in state fresh waters, except that suckers, fall fish and carp may be taken by snares, spears or bow and arrow, and minnows may be taken as provided. No person may use more than two devices for taking fish, and no more than three hooks may be attached to each device; provided that for ice fishing, a person may place and superintend five lines with a single hook each, if properly licensed (20-11-3). Fish artificially cultivated in private ponds may be taken, if the body of water is completely in the ownership of one taxpayer (20-11-4). No person shall sell or offer for sale within the state trout, black bass, pickerel, northern pike, Atlantic salmon, American shad or yellow perch taken from state freshwaters, except those artificially cultivated in private ponds as authorized by law (20-11-5). No person shall stock a state freshwater stream or pond with fish or place or liberate fish in those waters without a Department permit. No person shall place or operate a device intended for taking fish in private waters used for fish breeding without the owner's consent (20-11-6).

Freshwater minnows, not including the young of game fish, may be lawfully taken for bait with minnow traps, dip nets and seines of specified size in any waters (20-11-8). Larger minnow seines may be used by licensed persons in waters specified by the Director, and for payment of additional fees according to minnow seine sizes used (20-11-9).

No person shall place, deposit, or explode a substance injurious to the health or life of fish in a stream or freshwater pond; provided the Director may issue a permit to use certain chemicals for the eradication of vegetation and control of fish populations under regulations (20-11-10). The Department is authorized to construct fishways around or through existing dams to provide passage for anadromous fish species to their traditional spawning grounds, and dam owners shall cooperate with the Department and shall not be liable for damage as the result of construction of the fishways (20-12-4).

No person shall catch fish or use a seine in waters acquired by the Director for fish cultivation projects without a permit. The Director may seize and remove all obstructions erected to obstruct or impede the growth and culture of fish, and persons who rebuild the same after removal and notice from the Director shall be fined not less than $500 for each offense (20-12-6). No person shall take fish or fish spawn or a device used in hatching or protecting fish, from a waters stocked with or set apart by the Director, town council or private party without consent, nor shall a person violate any rule adopted regarding fish cultivation projects (20-12-7). The General Assembly shall annually appropriate such necessary sum to effectuate these provisions (20-12-8).

[Extensive sections of the Code deal with the licensing and regulation of the taking of shellfish, lobsters and other crustaceans, with the regulation of shellfish grounds and taking shellfish from polluted areas, enforcement, penalties for violations, and issues of aquaculture in coastal waters (Chapters 6, 7, 8.1, and 10). Because of the marine nature of these provisions, they are excluded.]

Private Shooting Preserves

Shooting Preserves must be licensed (20-2-16.1).

Commercial and Private Enterprise Provisions

A Commercial Minnow License is available (20-2-19). Other categories of commercial licenses include: raising game for liberation; sale of domestic game bird carcasses; fur trapper; fur buyer (20-2-29 and -30).

It is unlawful to sell or engage in the business of taking/catching for the purpose of sale live freshwater minnows for bait, or to possess more than 100 live freshwater minnows without first obtaining a Commercial Minnow License from the Department. Minnows are defined to include all minnows and the young of all species of freshwater fish except the game species: trout, northern pike, pickerel, largemouth bass, smallmouth bass, shad, Atlantic salmon, and alewives (20-11-7).

No person, firm or corporation shall purchase raw furs without a valid Fur Buyer's License issued by the Department (20-16-14). All licensed fur buyers shall keep records of fur purchases within the state which are open to Department inspection at all times, under penalty of license forfeiture (20-16-15).

A person holding a Game Propagation Permit may rear within an enclosure wild birds, game quadrupeds, or domestic game, to be disposed of for purposes of propagation under the Director's regulations, or in the case of domestic game, for liberation at field trials or upon game preserves. Such artificially propagated domestic game shall be tagged before being disposed of. Game so tagged may be possessed, transported, bought and sold (20-17-1).

No person shall engage in commercial raising/selling of wild birds, game quadrupeds, or domestic game birds without a Commercial Game Propagation License. Game raised under the license may be bought, sold and possessed live for propagation. Carcasses may be sold only by a person who holds both a Commercial Game Propagation License and a license issued by the Department authorizing sale of game carcasses. All game carcasses sold under the license must be tagged, and records must be kept by the licensee (20-17-2 and -3).

Common carriers may transport carcasses of domestic game birds and animals properly tagged, but packages must be labeled with the name of the licensee, and number and species of carcasses contained in the package (20-17-5). Without additional licenses, hotels and retail meat dealers may sell domestic game birds and animals to patrons for actual consumption (20-17-6). Frozen game may not be imported into the state without a license from the Director. Frozen game taken in another state by a Rhode Island resident may be imported if properly labeled without additional permits (20-17-7). Violations may be cause for revocation of a license and no similar license shall be issued by the Director for three years (20-17-8).

No person shall conduct a field trial at which domestic game birds may be taken by shooting without a license from the Director. Domestic game birds may be taken by shooting at field trials between September 1 and April 15 only (20-19-1). No person shall operate a shooting preserve without a license from the Director. The shooting area shall be a single body of land not less than 120 acres in size. The licensee shall keep an accurate record of all domestic game held; how, when and where acquired; how many released and when released; how many taken on the area, by whom and when, and shall provide the information to the Department if required. Domestic game birds killed on the preserve shall be banded and may be possessed and transported in any number, but only when bearing the band. Persons hunting or taking domestic game birds on a shooting preserve shall have a valid hunting license or special shooting preserve license (20-19-2). Only domestic game birds may be utilized by persons conducting a field trial or operating a shooting preserve (20-19-3).

Import, Export and Release Provisions

By regulation the Director may prohibit or regulate importation of live fish, birds or animals from another state or foreign country which is not regulated by the Department of Health under chapter 18 of Title 4 (20-17-9).

See also Restrictions on Taking: Fishing under HUNTING, FISHING, TRAPPING PROVISIONS, STATE WILDLIFE POLICY and PROTECTED SPECIES OF WILDLIFE.

Interstate Reciprocal Agreements

The Director may cooperate with the fish and wildlife commissioners or agencies of other states in carrying out the purpose of this title (20-1-17). If and when New York, Connecticut and Massachusetts, or any of them, shall enact similar laws for the arrest and punishment for violations of the conservation or fish laws of this state or the state enacting the similar law, committed by persons fishing in waters between the states, any Wildlife Protector, Fish Warden or other person authorized to make arrests for fish and game law violations of that state, shall have power to make arrest on any part of the waters between the states/shores and to take an arrested person for trial to the state in which the violation was committed for prosecution (20-1-19).

ANIMAL DAMAGE CONTROL

A person owning/occupying property and the person's employees, while on the premises may kill a deer destroying crops, vegetables or fruit trees, or otherwise damaging the property; provided that no person shall shoot a deer without a permit from the Director. ★No permit shall be issued until the Director has investigated to determine that actual damage has been done to crops, vegetables or fruit trees by the deer, and that no practical alternative to shooting the deer is available.★ Any taking/wounding of deer under the permit shall be reported to a Conservation Officer within 24 hours (20-15-3).

A landowner or employee on his/her own premises may kill and take a fur-bearer which is worrying, wounding or killing domestic animals or livestock on the property, or destroying or mutilating agricultural crops or fruit trees; provided that, except for rabbits, the carcass of the fur-bearer shall be presented to the Department within 24 hours. Such animal may then be possessed for the immediate family's use, and shall not be sold except by permission of the Director (20-16-2).

See also RELEVANT WILDLIFE DEFINITIONS, HUNTING, FISHING, TRAPPING PROVISIONS and HABITAT PROTECTION.

ENFORCEMENT OF WILDLIFE LAWS

Enforcement Powers

It shall be the duty of the Attorney General to prosecute all court proceedings brought by or requested by the Director (20-1-11).

A vessel, fishing tackle, gun, shooting and hunting equipment, trap, decoy or other device used illegally, which by this title's provisions is subject to forfeiture to the state shall be seized pursuant to 20-1-8(f) and forfeited. The Attorney General shall show cause why such equipment used in the knowing and willful violation of any wildlife law, rule or regulation is subject to forfeiture with proof that such devices were used in the violation. The Department may retain the property for official use or sell forfeited property not required by this title to be destroyed, with proceeds paid to the General Treasurer for state use (20-1-8.1).

All wild birds and wild animals seized under this title which were taken, possessed, or kept in violation of the law, shall be forfeited to the state and disposed of at the Director's discretion (20-17-11).

Unless otherwise specifically provided, the violation of any law or rule or regulation relating to wild animals, wild birds, lobsters and fish, marine, freshwater and anadromous fisheries and shellfisheries shall be a misdemeanor, punishable by a fine of not more than $500, and/or jail up to 90 days (20-1-16).

License Revocations and Suspensions

The Director may suspend or revoke the license of a person who has violated the provisions of this title or its rules and regulations for such period as the Director shall determine by regulation. Aggrieved persons may appeal an order of suspension or revocation in accordance with provisions of the Administrative Procedures Act, Chapter 35 of Title 42 (20-2-13).

HABITAT PROTECTION

For state use, and subject to State Properties Committee approval, the Director may acquire by gift, lease, purchase or easement, state land for protecting, conserving, cultivation, or propagating a wildlife species, and with the owner's consent, control land suitable for the same purposes. Land so acquired shall be posted and designated as a state park or management area (20-18-1). It is unlawful to hunt, trap, pursue, take or kill, or molest or destroy a wild bird or the nest or eggs, or a wild animal, on land leased or controlled by the Department except the Director may authorize in writing a deputy and/or landowner, to hunt, take or kill a wild bird or animal detrimental to its species or other species, to agriculture or other plant life, or to man (20-18-2).

It is unlawful to hunt, trap, take or kill, or molest or destroy wild birds, or their nests or eggs, or a wild animal within the boundaries of a state management area, park, or land held in trust for public use, except, with advisable limitations, and consistent with state laws and rules relating to seasons, bag and size limits and manner of taking, the authorities controlling such lands may authorize persons by written permit to hunt, take or kill within the boundaries unprotected wild birds or animals (20-18-3).

NATIVE AMERICAN WILDLIFE PROVISIONS: None.

SOUTH CAROLINA

Sources: Code of Laws of South Carolina, 1976, Title 50; 1992 Replacement Volume.

STATE WILDLIFE POLICY

All wild birds, wild game, and fish, except fish in strictly private ponds and lakes and lakes entirely segregated from other waters or held and grown in aquaculture operations, are state property (50-1-10).

RELEVANT WILDLIFE DEFINITIONS: See Definitions section of Appendices.

STATE FISH AND WILDLIFE AGENCIES

Agency Structure

The head and governing board of the **Wildlife and Marine Resources Department** (Department) is the **Wildlife and Marine Resources Commission** (Commission), composed of seven members, one from each congressional district and one at large, appointed by the Governor with Senate advice and consent (50-3-10). Members serve six-year terms, and the Governor designates one member as chairperson (50-3-20 and -30). The Commission may create as many divisions within the Department as it deems advisable, and Commission powers and duties shall be discharged by such divisions. The Commission shall appoint an executive officer to serve as the Department head, who shall appoint division heads and assign duties with Commission advice and consent (50-3-50).

The Commission shall appoint **conservation officers** (game wardens), and may remove them on proof that they are not fit for the position (50-3-310). ★The Commission shall use criteria required by the Division of Human Resources and the Commission, including a written examination, physical examination and interview in hiring the officers, who must perform at minimum required levels. When employing the officers within a county, otherwise qualified county residents have priority (50-3-316). ★ The Commission may appoint volunteer **deputy conservation officers** for two-year terms, with jurisdiction. Deputies have authority to enforce fish and game, trespass and litter laws within that assigned jurisdiction. The powers and duties of deputies shall be established by Commission regulations. All wardens must take an oath and execute a bond. Game wardens acting in their official capacity have state-wide authority to enforce fish and game laws (50-3-315, -330 and -340). ★A majority of a county legislative delegation, with the senator, from Game Zone No. 2 may authorize employment of additional deputy game wardens for up to three months during the hunting season, to be compensated from Game Fund moneys on hand (50-3-360). ★

The state is divided into 11 game zones by designated counties (50-1-60). State laws affecting game shall apply, unless changed, to all state zones except where otherwise specified (50-1-70).

Agency Powers and Duties

The **Department** continuously shall investigate state game and fish conditions and laws, and shall report annually to the General Assembly and recommend legislation conducive to the conservation of wildlife. Department agents may conduct game and fish cultural operations and scientific investigations at the request of the Directors of the Game or Commercial Fisheries Divisions. No such operations shall be made on private lands/waters except at the request of the landowner (50-3-80 and -90).

The Department may acquire, own, sell, lease or rent real property, alone or in cooperation with the federal government, for providing game reserves, fish ponds, game farms, public hunting and fishing grounds and for proper management, protection or propagation of fish and game and furnishing hunting and fishing facilities. Only Department funds not essential to its normal operation may be so used (50-3-100).

The **Commission** shall have charge of the warden force and supervise enforcement of state laws, regulatory, tax, license or otherwise, in reference to birds, nonmigratory fish, game fish, shellfish, shrimp, oysters, oyster leases and fisheries (50-3-110). All Department law-enforcement personnel are designated conservation officers with the power and authority of game wardens and inspectors as provided in this title (50-3-120). Conservation officers shall wear distinctive uniforms and use distinctive vehicle emblems which may not be confused with other law enforcement agencies (50-3-130). ★The Commission shall file a quarterly report to each member of the General Assembly explaining the status of each county fish and game fund, and watercraft fund, including total funds for each county and an itemized list of expenditures (50-3-170).★ The Commission may contract for selective cutting and sale of timber on lands held by the Department on behalf of its Game Division. No such contract shall be entered into nor timber sold unless it is in the best interests of and will improve its lands by reason of timber thinning, harvesting over-age trees, and improving general forestry conditions (50-3-510).

Game wardens shall: ▸ obtain information on all violations of the bird, nonmigratory fish, and game laws, and check all bag limits, size and species; ▸ see that bird, nonmigratory fish and game laws are enforced and prosecute persons illegally possessing birds, nonmigratory fish or game; ▸ procure search warrants on probable cause that birds, fish or game are held/possessed illegally, and search cars, warehouses, and any place where it is believed such animals are held in violation and may seize same; ▸ possess and exercise all powers and authority held and exercised by the constable at common law and under state statutes, and have the authority of inspector under Chapter 5 of this title. Game wardens may: ▸ issue warning tickets for misdemeanor violations; ▸ cite violators for littering (50-3-370 through -400).

Agency Funding Sources

There is a **Wildlife Endowment Fund**, whose income and principal must be used only to support wildlife conservation programs (50-3-710). Fund assets include proceeds of gifts, grants and contributions designated for inclusion; proceeds from sales of lifetime combination and lifetime hunting/fishing licenses; any amount in excess of the statutory fee for a particular lifetime license which qualifies as a tax-exempt donation; other sources specified by law (50-3-730). The fund is a special trust derived from a contractual relationship between the state and the public whose investments contribute to the fund. Any limitations specified by donors are respected, but are not binding; no expenditure may be made from the principal except as provided by law; the income from investments must be spent only in furthering wildlife resources conservation and efficient operation of the Commission in accomplishing agency purposes. The Board must approve expenditures, and fund moneys do not take the place of state appropriations to the Department [additional fund restrictions and provisions are given] (50-3-740 through -770).

★Except as otherwise provided, revenues from fines and forfeitures of any game, nongame or fish law shall be paid by the counties to the credit of the **Game Protection Fund** and be expended for fish and game propagation in the counties where they are collected.★ Remittances shall include information as to all persons fined, amounts of fines, and court where collected. License fees go to the credit of the Game Protection Fund of the state treasury. One dollar of each nonresident hunter's license fee and 50 cents of each temporary nonresident license shall be used by the Department for propagation, management and control of ducks and geese, and a like portion of license fees shall be contributed by the Department to proper agencies in Canada for propagation, management and control of ducks and geese (50-1-150 and -160).

Costs of endangered and nongame wildlife programs shall be borne by the General Fund, except that the Department shall issue permits for $35 each for the sale of alligator products, and collect permit and sale proceeds to administer the Alligator Control Management Program, such funds to go to the Game Protection Fund (50-15-60).

There is an Operation Game Thief Program to be funded by: moneys authorized from the County Game Fund of the state treasury, not to exceed $30,000 annually; moneys from donations to be used for general program purposes (a donor may not specify donation use); moneys appropriated by the General Assembly for the purposes provided by statute (50-11-2300). (See also Reward Payments under ENFORCEMENT OF WILDLIFE LAWS.)

Agency Advisory Boards

There is a **Migratory Waterfowl Stamp Committee** of nine members. The Ducks Unlimited Regional Director for South Carolina and the immediate past and present chairpersons of Ducks Unlimited shall serve ex officio. Two members are appointed by the Governor, two by the Chair of the Agriculture and Natural Resources Committee, and two by the Chair of the Fish, Game and Forestry Committee; appointees must be cognizant of waterfowl. The committee is responsible for the creation of the annual migratory waterfowl stamp and the creation and distribution of related artwork. After expenses, 50% of the stamp and print sales shall go to the Commission for its projects, and the remainder must be disbursed to a nonprofit organization to develop Canadian waterfowl propagation projects which specifically produce waterfowl for the Atlantic Flyway (50-11-20).

There is a **Board of Trustees of the Wildlife Endowment Fund** of the Commission, whose chair and members are the chair and members of the Commission (50-3-720).

PROTECTED SPECIES OF WILDLIFE

Game bird species for which no specific open season has been provided are protected and may not be shot, trapped, destroyed nor may such be attempted at any time. The Department may prescribe an open season for the taking of exotic game birds, and prescribe areas, sex of birds and taking methods for any zone in which these species become numerous enough to be harvested. Areas not specifically open to hunting are closed. Taking or possessing exotic game birds illegally or taking in any way not prescribed by the Department is a misdemeanor, with a $50-100 fine, or jail for 15-30 days. These provisions apply to ruffed grouse (50-11-810).

It is unlawful to: ‣ kill, catch, possess or sell a resident or migratory wild bird other than a game bird except as otherwise permitted; ‣ sell or possess for sale the plumage, skin or body of a protected bird whether caught within or without the state; ‣ take, destroy or possess the nest or eggs of a wild bird except for scientific purposes; ‣ ship, carry or transport a resident or migratory wild nongame bird; ‣ shoot, kill or maim an Antwerp or homing pigeon (misdemeanor; up to $10 fine; or jail up to 10 days); ‣ molest or kill a bird of prey, including hawks, eagles, falcons, kites, vultures, owls and ospreys (misdemeanor; $25-100 fine; or jail up to 30 days); ‣ catch, capture or kill a banded homing, racing or carrier pigeon (misdemeanor; up to $200 fine; or jail up to 30 days) (50-11-820 through -853).

The Commission shall conduct investigations on nongame wildlife to develop information about population, distribution, habitat, needs, limiting factors, and other biological and ecological data to determine management measures necessary for their continued ability to sustain themselves successfully, and shall develop such management programs. Regulations shall name the species or subspecies of nongame wildlife in need of management. Ongoing investigations shall be conducted to amend such regulations periodically to add or delete species of nongame wildlife. The Commission by regulation shall establish proposed limitations on taking, possession, processing, sale or shipment necessary to manage nongame wildlife, to become effective 60 days after public hearing and comment opportunities are afforded. It is unlawful to take, possess, transport, export, process, sell or ship wildlife in need of management except as otherwise provided, or for common carriers knowingly to accept such nongame wildlife for shipment (50-15-30).

The Commission shall by regulation propose a list of indigenous species determined to be endangered within the state, allow public comment on the proposed list, and may add to or delete species from the list after review at least every two years. It is unlawful, except as otherwise provided, to take, possess, transport, export, sell or ship, or for a common carrier to do so, any species or subspecies of wildlife on the state indigenous endangered species list, or the US lists of native or foreign endangered species as modified, except that listed wildlife which are transported through may enter and exit the state under the terms/permits of federal or other state regulations. The Commission may accept modifications to the federal lists as binding by regulation after scientific determination of their endangered status (50-15-40).

Violation of endangered species provisions is a misdemeanor, with a fine up to $500 and/or jail up to six months. Illegal taking, possession, transport, export or shipment of endangered species contrary to 50-15-40(c), or permits issued under 50-15-50(d) and 50-15-50(e), or regulations promulgated is a misdemeanor, with a $1,000 fine and/or jail up to one year. Wardens or state police officers shall have authority to conduct searches and execute warrants to search for and seize equipment, records or wildlife taken, used or possessed in violation of an endangered species provisions, and may arrest without warrant a person they have probable cause to believe is violating such provision or regulation or permit. Seized equipment, merchandise or wildlife shall be confiscated and destroyed or disposed of on conviction, with seized wildlife transferred to a zoological, educational or scientific institution. Violators of regulations pertaining to illegal possession, transport or sale of parts or products of an alligator must be fined not less than $1,000-5,000, or jailed up to one year. Wildlife legally taken in another state may be possessed, transported, or sold, but unless otherwise provided, no wildlife on the US list of endangered native fish and wildlife may be possessed, transported, exported, processed, sold or shipped (50-15-80 and -90).

The Commission shall establish programs, including acquisition of land or aquatic habitat, for management of nongame and endangered wildlife, and may enter into agreements with federal or state agencies or private persons for the administration and management of areas so established. The Governor shall encourage state and federal agencies to utilize their authorities in furtherance of these purposes (50-15-50). (See also GENERAL EXCEPTIONS TO PROTECTION and ANIMAL DAMAGE CONTROL.)

GENERAL EXCEPTIONS TO PROTECTION

The USFW may allow the hunting of antlered and antlerless deer by licensed hunters on a sea island within a federally owned game reserve, national park or game refuge during the state's open season for deer hunting, when the island's deer population exceeds that which can properly maintain itself. The USFW shall notify the Department 10 days prior to the hunt, and advertise in a newspaper at least one week before the hunt in the applicable coastal area (50-11-1140).

Permits may be granted by the Department to accredited persons for collecting protected wildlife for scientific or propagating purposes only. No permit is required for collecting or taking nonprotected wildlife. The Director shall investigate the applicant and the project, and may issue a permit renewable for one year. All collecting or taking must be conducted according to recognized scientific methods, and where practicable, data, results, and specimens must be made available to the public on request. The permittee shall submit a report as required. Collecting permits for endangered species may be issued only in accordance with 50-15-50, and the provisions of 50-17-70 are not superseded by this section. Violation: misdemeanor; $25-100 fine; or jail up to 30 days; and revocation of permit (50-11-1180). Under terms and regulations, the Commission may permit the taking, possession, transportation, exportation or shipment of species or subspecies of wildlife on the state or federal endangered species lists for scientific, zoological or educational purposes, for propagation in captivity, or for other special purposes (50-15-50). It is lawful to trap or kill a coyote at any time, but a permit must be obtained from the Department before trapping coyotes outside the trap distance limits as prescribed (50-11-1760).

★Most trapping prohibitions do not apply to a person owning a foxhunting-enclosed preserve or pup training facility where live foxes obtained from a licensed commercial trapper are not retained or marketed for fur utilization. The Department shall issue permits for the foxes at no cost to the preserve owner and shall require reports and records of their sale or transfer (50-11-2580).★ (See also HUNTING, FISHING, TRAPPING PROVISIONS.)

HUNTING, FISHING, TRAPPING PROVISIONS

General Provisions

It is unlawful to fish or hunt from the banks of a navigable stream without the landowner's written permission if the owner is not within one mile of where the person is fishing/hunting (50-1-100).

It is lawful to sell and ship live foxes within the state (50-11-1770). It is unlawful to buy or sell or possess for sale a willet or dove (50-11-1930). Sale of venison in eating establishments is a misdemeanor, except for private functions, and is punished the same as illegal sale of deer parts. (See ENFORCEMENT OF WILDLIFE LAWS.) It is unlawful to buy or barter for sale wild quail within the state. Violation: $25 fine; or up to 30 days jail per bird (50-11-1940). It is lawful to own, possess, sell or otherwise dispose of pheasant eggs, or sell them beyond the state borders under Department regulations (50-11-1950). The Department shall promulgate regulations to permit and regulate field trials during the year, including the closed season. Violation: misdemeanor; up to $200 fine; or jail up to 30 days for each offense (50-11-2100).

It is unlawful to keep birds or animals forbidden to be sold under 50-11-1910 or 50-11-1940 in cold storage, except in a private dwelling, unless they are labeled with the hunting license number, and name and address of the owner. Violation: $50-100 fine; or jail one day for each dollar fined or unpaid; either or both (50-11-1700). It is unlawful for common carriers to receive for shipment packages of game birds or animals unless they are labeled showing consignor or consignee and number and kind of animals (50-11-1710). During two days during any one week, it is lawful to ship within the state up to the bag limit of domestic game birds or animals with a Department permit/label if the shipment is for personal use and not for sale (50-11-1740 and -1750). During any one week, it is lawful for a landowner or licensee to ship or carry beyond state limits up to the bag limit of game birds or animals as provided by law and regulations and with a Department permit. Violation: $50-100 fine; or jail for 30 days for each offense. No person shall knowingly receive for transport or transport beyond state borders any partridge, grouse, wild turkey, snipe, woodcock or other game bird or game animal except as otherwise permitted, and receipt, transport or possession, or causing same, of each bird or game animal is a separate offense. This does not apply to common carriers who are in the process of transporting birds or game which are in transit through the state. ★Nothing herein prohibits persons from possessing birds or animals for domestication and propagation (50-11-1720 and -1730).★

Licenses and Permits

No child under age 16 is required to have a hunting or fishing license or other permit or license required for hunting or fishing unless they engage in the taking of game or fish for commercial purposes (50-9-860). Residents over age 65 may obtain a hunting/fishing license without cost (50-9-260 and -840). Alteration of a license/permit is a misdemeanor; $50-200 fine; or jail up to 30 days (50-9-170). Licensees must carry licenses/permits on their person while engaging in the permitted activity and must show these to any conservation officer on demand (50-9-190 and -510). Lending a license to another results in forfeiture of the license for the remainder of the season, and hunting while license is revoked is a fine of $50-100, or jail 10-30 days (50-9-220 and -540). With permission resident employees may fish without a fishing license on their employer's lands (50-9-440). [Other penalties for license/permit infractions are detailed in 50-9-240, -250, -460, -480, -550, and -560.]

Except as otherwise provided, it is unlawful to fish in state waters by use of manufactured tackle, equipment or artificial bait, other than hook and line without a fishing license (50-9-410). It is unlawful except as otherwise provided, to fish in fresh water by use of a fly rod, casting rod, artificial bait or any manufactured tackle or equipment, other than ordinary hook and line, without an angler's license. A license is not required for a landowner and family to fish on their own lands (50-9-420). No fishing license is required to fish in private ponds with the written permission of the landowner. This does not apply to commercial ponds (50-9-430).

Except for those exempt, it is unlawful to hunt migratory waterfowl without a state migratory waterfowl stamp. Violation: misdemeanor; $50-200 fine; or jail up to 30 days (50-9-155).

Restrictions on Taking: Hunting

[Seasons, bag limits, certain landowner options, and certain ammunition or weapon restrictions for small game animals (including rabbit, squirrel, fox, raccoon, opossum, quail, turkey) and big game animals are set in statute according to game zones or other specified locations or designated by counties, as are penalties for buying, selling or displaying carcasses for sale in certain designated zones. These restrictions vary by zone (50-11-120 and -150).]

During any period in which raccoons and opossums are allowed to be hunted without firearms, it is unlawful to hunt them when carrying a firearm, saw, ax, artificial calling device, or tree-climbing device. Mouth-operated calling devices may be used in field trials as provided by the Department (50-11-140). It is unlawful to trap rabbits, except that a landowner/tenant may use up to five rabbit boxes on landowner's lands during the open season (50-11-160). Trapping or snaring of quail is prohibited except as provided for scientific or propagation purposes (50-11-180).

★It is unlawful to discharge a weapon within 300 yards of a poultry layer or broiler house containing live poultry without the owner's permission,★ or to hunt deer within 300 yards of a residence without permission of the owner/occupant. Knowing violation: misdemeanor; up to $200 fine; or jail up to 30 days (50-11-355 and -356). It is unlawful to use bait to concentrate the bear population in an area, or to lure them to give a hunter an unnatural advantage (50-11-440). It is unlawful to hunt, catch, take or kill a game bird or game animal by the use of recorded calls or sounds or electronically amplified calls or sounds. Violation: misdemeanor; $50-100 fine (50-11-40).

It is unlawful to hunt or kill deer from a motorboat, raft or other water conveyance or to molest deer while any part of the deer is in the water. Violation: misdemeanor; mandatory jail at least 30 to 90 days; or $100-500 fine. "Hunting" includes the transportation of a hunter, or carcass or part of a deer which has been unlawfully hunted/killed. Every boat, raft, vehicle, animal, firearm or other device used in violation must be confiscated according to procedures in 50-11-740. A conviction for unlawfully hunting deer from boats is conclusive as against a convicted owner of the above-mentioned property (50-11-730).

Every vehicle, boat, animal, and firearm used in hunting deer or bear at night is forfeited to the state and must be confiscated by a peace officer. "Hunting" includes any transportation of a hunter to/from the place of hunting, or the carcass or any part of a deer or bear which has been unlawfully killed at night. A conviction for unlawfully hunting deer or bear at night is conclusive as against a convicted owner of the above-mentioned property. In all other instances, forfeiture must be accomplished by an action in the circuit court of the county where seizure occurred giving opportunity to the owner/lien holder to show why the property should not be seized, and according to other procedures as detailed. Confiscated property shall be sold for cash to the highest bidder after 10 days notice of sale, and according to stated procedures. When the device has value greater than $1,000, the owner may redeem it before sale by paying $1,000 to the Director; if of lesser value, the retail market value. Moneys received go into the Game Protection Fund (50-11-740).

It is unlawful to feed or entice an American alligator, except those in protective captivity under a Department permit, for education, scientific, commercial purposes, or as otherwise provided. Violation: misdemeanor; up to $200 fine; or jail up to 30 days (50-11-750). No dog is required to be leashed when it is actually hunting game under supervision, and the owner is in the vicinity or in the process of trying to retrieve the dog (50-11-780). It is a misdemeanor to hunt on lands of another, or enter thereon for hunting, fishing or trapping purposes without the consent of the landowner. First offense, up to $200 fine, or up to 30 days jail; second offense, $100-200 fine, or jail up to 30 days; third or subsequent offense, $500-1,000 fine, or jail up to six months, or both; and convictions must be reported to the Law Enforcement Division for record keeping and investigation as to prior records within the past 10 years (50-11-770).

★The Department may declare a closed season up to 10 days in an area when it appears from abnormal conditions that deer or other game cannot protect themselves, after publishing such closed season lengths in newspapers as specified. Anyone found hunting with a game-taking device or dog within the restricted area during the closed season is guilty whether game is taken or not. Violation: $100-200 fine; or jail for not less than 30 days (50-11-1105). When in any county abnormal conditions exist which affect the game supply, on written request of a majority of the legislative delegation, and the senator, the Director may shorten/close the hunting season after giving notice as specified. Violation: $25-100 fine; jail for not less than 30 days (50-11-1110).★

Using artificial lights from a vehicle or water conveyance for observing or harassing wildlife is unlawful after 11:00 p.m. Violation: misdemeanor; up to $100 fine; or jail up to 30 days (50-11-700). [Artificial light prohibitions are given for particular game zones (50-11-703 through -706).] Night hunting is unlawful except that raccoons, opossums, foxes, mink, and skunks may be hunted at night; however, they may not be hunted with artificial lights except when treed or cornered with dogs, or with specified weapon and ammunition sizes. Violation: first offense, up to $1,000 fine, jail up to one year, or both; second offense within two years, minimum of $400-2,000 fine, or jail for 90 days to one year, or both; third or subsequent offense within two years, $500-3,000 fine, jail 120 days to one year, or both, and mandatory suspension of hunting privileges for two years. The penalty for hunting with a suspended license is mandatory jail for 90 days to one year. Persons convicted after more than two years since the last conviction must be sentenced as for a first offense. These provisions do not prevent landowners from protecting their property from destruction by wild game as provided by law. It is unlawful to use artificial lights at night, except vehicle headlights while traveling normally, while in possession of weapons or ammunition of a type prohibited for use at night as provided by law, and violation is punishable under 50-11-720 (50-11-710). (See Illegal Taking Provisions under ENFORCEMENT OF WILDLIFE LAWS.)

The federal migratory bird treaty regulations of the US are state law and violation is a fine of not less than $25-100 or 30 days jail. A person must be fined $100-200 or jailed up to 30 days who: ► trespasses to hunt waterfowl; ► hunts or shoots waterfowl over bait; ► hunts waterfowl more than 15 minutes before or after designated hunting hours; ► possesses more than one waterfowl over the legal limit; ► hunts waterfowl out of season (50-11-10).

It is unlawful to: ▸ rob a wild turkey nest or possess, sell or dispose of wild turkey eggs except by permit; ▸ trap or snare wild turkey or hunt a wild turkey from any natural or artificial blind when the turkey is lured by bait except for Department approved mechanical feeder programs; ▸ hunt or possess female wild turkeys unlawfully killed unless the Commission sets special open seasons; ▸ buy, sell or possess for sale wild turkeys; ▸ release to the wild pen-raised wild turkeys except by permit and under Department supervision, and such released turkeys are certified disease free within 30 days of release; ▸ buy, sell or possess for sale pen-raised turkeys, wild or domestic, for purposes of release in the wild except by Department permit on licensed private shooting preserves and such are certified disease free; ▸ sell or give away pen-raised wild turkeys authorized for release on licensed shooting preserves without written Department consent; ▸ shoot a wild turkey on its roost during specified nighttime hours; ▸ possess pen-raised wild turkeys without a Department possession permit; ▸ take a wild turkey from a vehicle on a public road; ▸ take a wild turkey with a rifle; ▸ hunt wild turkey without wild turkey transportation tags and fail to have bagged wild turkeys checked at a designated check station; ▸ exceed the daily bag limit of two, or five total during one license year. Violation: misdemeanor; $200 fine; or jail up to 30 days. Illegal sale/possession of a wild turkey or wild turkey eggs is a $25 fine for each turkey or egg possessed or sold; each day's violation is a separate offense (50-11-500). It is unlawful to hunt wild turkey by means of bait or on a baited area as defined by statute; an area is deemed baited for 10 days following complete removal of all bait (50-11-510). The Department may make special studies in game zones restocked with wild turkeys, and may declare open or closed seasons (50-11-520). The Commission may prescribe methods and areas of taking wild turkey in each zone and may designate sex and other restrictions (50-11-530). Illegal taking/possessing of wild turkeys is a misdemeanor; $50-100 fine; or jail up to 30 days. Every vehicle, boat, animal, firearm or other equipment used in a violation, or in possession at the time of same, is forfeited and may be confiscated by a peace officer according to statutory provisions (50-11-540).

It is unlawful to hunt deer on a wildlife management area within 300 yards of a residence. Violation: misdemeanor; up to $200 fine; or jail up to 30 days (50-11-2200). ★The abuse of wildlife management area land and improvements is unlawful, including littering; damage to vegetation, fences, buildings; or illegal fire-building. Violation: misdemeanor; $200 fine; and mandatory restitution to the landowner by court decree to repair, rebuild, restore or clean up the property to its condition before the abuse occurred. Failure to make restitution within the court's time limit is a mandatory 10-day jail sentence which may not be suspended. These provisions are in addition to other criminal penalties (50-11-2210).★ A convicted violator shall lose privileges of entry into wildlife management areas for one year. ★In addition to the penalties listed above, a person with a second conviction within three years of management land abuse, or of unlawful commercial hunting or fishing on such lands is forever barred from obtaining a wildlife management area permit and shall lose the right to hunt and fish within the state for one year, in addition to other criminal penalties (50-11-2220).★

Restrictions on Taking: Trapping

It is unlawful to sell, make or use a foot-hold trap or like device, except for certain sizes and specified exceptions for protecting a landowner's property within specified distances of a residence or poultry house. Body-gripping Conibear traps may be used without bait or scents for vertical water and slide sets only. Foot-hold traps of specified sizes may be used in certain game zones, with approval of a majority of the legislative delegation (50-11-2410). It is lawful to use rubber padded steel foot-hold traps for the capture of live foxes in designated zones (50-11-2415). Trappers shall have proof that they are property owners of the land, or have in possession a landowner's written permission (50-11-2430). A trapper shall visit traps daily, but may not visit traps at night, and may not set traps "in the open" or in paths, roadways or runways commonly used by persons or domestic animals (50-11-2440). It is a misdemeanor to remove lawfully trapped wildlife from a legally set trap not one's own. Violation: misdemeanor; $50-200 fine; or jail up to 30 days (50-11-2445). In addition to a hunting license, a commercial fur license is required to sell, or to take by any means except trapping, fur-bearing animals for commercial purposes, and for all persons who trap or who attempt to trap fur-bearing animals. A person possessing more than five fur-bearing animals or pelts shall have a valid commercial fur license, except for processors, manufacturers or retailers (50-11-2420). Commercial licensees shall report annually the number and type of fur-bearing animals taken, sold or shipped; on a second offense they shall be denied a license for the following year (50-11-2450). [Lawful trap types are specified by statute.] Other traps, including "deadfall" traps, are illegal unless permitted by Department regulation (50-11-2460).

A licensed person who takes a fur-bearing animal must tag the fur or animal with a Department tag at the time the fur is removed or the carcass is stored, or before it is sold. [Tag fees are listed in the statutes.] The Department may limit the number of tags issued for each species and the area in which they may be used. Fur-bearing animals taken to be sold as live animals are not required to be tagged. Tags are not transferrable (50-11-2510). Except as permitted, it is unlawful to possess, transfer or acquire an untagged fur, pelt, hide or whole animal. Violations are punished according to 50-11-2560, are misdemeanors, and each fur, hide, pelt or animal found untagged is a separate offense (50-11-2515). The Department may confiscate all traps, devices, furs, pelts or whole animals which are illegally tagged, possessed or used, sell them at reasonable price and hold the proceeds pending case outcome. On conviction, devices or pelts may be disposed of by the Department, and proceeds used for the propagation and protection of game (50-11-2530). Penalties are specified by statute number, are all misdemeanors, and range from $50-1,000 fines, or jail up to 60 days plus license revocation, depending on the statutory violation (50-11-2560 and -2565). A permit is required to ship/transport untanned furs, pelts, hides or whole fur-bearing animals out of the state, such permit to be issued by a conservation officer after shipment inspection (50-11-2550).

Restrictions on Taking: Fishing

Catching of game fish in all state waters shall be only with hook and line, fly rod, casting rod, pole and line and hand line, no more than two of which devices may be used by one individual while fishing (50-13-10). Persons fishing in a boat may use an unlimited number of lawful fishing devices if all boat occupants have valid fishing licenses (50-13-11). The Director shall declare a closed season for up to 60 days on fish in a state stream on the written recommendation of the senator and at least one half of the representatives from a county in which the stream is situated, and the Director shall give notice of such closed season as specified by statute. Fishing during closed season is a $50-100 fine, or a minimum jail term of 30 days (50-13-60 and -70). [Provisions are given for particular game zones as to fishing methods, closed seasons, night fishing, salt/freshwater dividing lines and other restrictions.] A person found fishing with hook and line or in any other manner within a restricted territory during closed season shall be prima facie guilty of violation whether or not fish have been caught (50-13-80).

There is a closed season on trout on state streams from October to March. "Trout" means rainbow, brook, brown or other species of cold-water trout and not fresh-water bass. Possession of trout during closed season is unlawful and there is a presumption of taking from state streams. There shall be no size limit on fresh-water game fish caught in the state, nor on any species of trout (50-13-90 through -120). It is unlawful to catch more than 40 game fish in one day, of which not more than 10 may be striped bass or hybrid bass; not more than 10 may be black bass of all types; not more than 10 may be trout; not more than 8 may be sauger or walleye; not more than 30 of the total may be any game fish not specified (50-13-210). [Different creel limits, fishing methods, prohibited devices, and penalties for violations are specified for certain waters, game zones, and for different species in sections throughout the statutes.] Whenever creel limits are in conflict with a reciprocal agreement with another state, such limits shall not apply (50-13-240). Game wardens may lawfully search creel (50-13-260). Creel limits do not apply in private ponds entirely segregated from other waters if the pond owner has permission to exceed statutory limits (50-13-270). It is unlawful to possess in one day more than the creel limit, but one may travel in a vehicle with two days possession limit or store same in one's refrigerator (50-13-280). Violation of creel/possession limits is for first offense a $30-200 fine, or jail up to 30 days; subsequent offense within two years, $300-500 fine, or jail up to 60 days, or both (50-13-285).

It is unlawful to throw, run, drain or deposit dyestuffs, coal tar, oil, sawdust, poison or other deleterious substance in fresh or salt waters frequented by game fish within the jurisdiction of the state in quantities sufficient to injure, stupefy or kill fish/shellfish or their spawn. Violation: $300-1,000 fine; jail three months to one year, or both. The Commission shall see that this section is enforced (50-13-1410). Should a person cause to flow into or be cast into inland waters impurities that are poisonous to fish or destructive to their spawn, they shall be fined not less than $500 or jailed not less than six months (50-13-1430). It is unlawful to poison state waters for taking fish or to introduce, produce or set up electrical currents or physical shocks, pressures or disturbances for taking fish. Muddying streams or ponds or introducing any substance to sicken fish so that they may be caught is "poisoning." No sawdust, acid or other injurious substance shall be discharged into state streams where fish breed or abound. Violation: $25-300 fine; or jail for 1-30 days (50-13-1420). It is unlawful to use dynamite, gun powder, lime or other explosive in state waters to take fish, or to cause or procure the same to be done, to aid, assist or abet anyone so doing, or to have in possession dynamite or other explosive in a paddling boat, sailboat, motorboat, raft or barge commonly used for fresh-water fishing. ★Using explosives or having them in possession on state waters is a misdemeanor and the violator shall be sentenced to serve a term at hard labor on the Penitentiary chain gang or to pay a fine as follows: first offense, jail up to three months, or up to $500 fine; second offense, jail one year, or $1,000 fine; third offense, jail two years, or $2,500 fine (50-13-1440).★ A person convicted under this section shall be prohibited from hunting or fishing for five years, and any hunting or fishing license shall be immediately revoked; a person found hunting/fishing while their license is revoked shall be guilty of a misdemeanor and fined or jailed at the court's discretion (50-13-1460). Picking up fish within two hours after they have been killed, stunned or disabled by an explosive shall be deemed prima facie of having used explosives to take fish from such waters (50-13-1450). One who witnesses but fails to report a use of explosives violation to a game warden within two weeks is guilty of a misdemeanor, and shall be fined or jailed at the court's discretion (50-13-1470). A person who testifies as a witness against anyone for violating 50-13-1440 shall not be subject to prosecution for slander or malicious prosecution, nor be subject to a civil action in connection with such use of explosives (50-13-1480).

It is unlawful at any time to sell, barter, or purchase game fish so classified under 50-1-30, except trout as provided below, regardless of where caught. Violation: misdemeanor; first offense $100-300 fine; second offense within five years, $200-500 fine; third or subsequent offense within five years, $500-1,000 fine and jail up to 30 days (50-13-1610). A violation as to freshwater trout is a misdemeanor, with a $50-100 fine, or jail for 15-30 days. Each such violation is a separate offense (50-13-1620).

It is unlawful to fish or trespass in private artificial ponds used to breed fish or oysters which the owner has posted, and such person is guilty of trespass and a misdemeanor if they fish therein or use any means to destroy or injure the fish or oysters therein, or break a dam and allow the fish or oysters to escape. Violation: $20-100 fine; or jail at the court's discretion. Fine money shall go one-half to the informer and one-half to the pond owner. This does not apply to ponds used as water power for manufacturing purposes (50-13-350). Shooting fish in waters of designated counties is prohibited (50-13-360). Persons owning private ponds may catch fish therein with traps or nets for propagation purposes with a permit from the Director and under restrictions the Director imposes. Such permits must be endorsed in writing by the game warden in the county (50-13-510). ★There shall be a closed time of fishing in all muddy streams from sunset each Saturday until sunrise each Wednesday during which all seines, nets or other devices for the collecting of shad and herring shall be removed from such waters (50-13-530).★ Game fish taken by net or other nongame fishing device while fishing for nongame fish must be immediately returned to the water. Violation: misdemeanor; $50-200 fine; or jail up to 30 days, plus forfeiture of devices used (50-13-580). A person having in possession on state waters, or going to or coming from such waters, any fish in excess of statutory limits shall be presumed to have killed/caught such fish (50-13-980). Fishing restrictions shall not apply to persons fishing on the bottom with ordinary fishing poles, fly rods or rods and reels or hand lines in their possession (50-13-1010). Violations of fishing restriction provisions unless otherwise provided are misdemeanors. First offense, $25-100 fine, or jail up to 30 days; second offense, $50-100 fine, or jail up to 30 days; third offense, a minimum $100 fine, or jail up to 60 days; each subsequent offense is a doubling of the fine or jail for the previous offense. Each violation is a separate offense (50-13-1020). Under supervision and in the presence of a Division of Game representative, private pond owners may draw down their pond and dispose of the fish caught by sale or otherwise at the pond site (50-13-1640).

Nongame fish, except shad and herring, are protected in state freshwaters and coastal rivers by restrictions on fishing devices (50-13-1110). The following devices may be used for taking nongame fish where authorized: trotlines, set hooks, jug fishing devices, traps, eel pots, gill nets, hoop nets, skimbow nets, bows and arrows, gigs, spears, tires, minnow seines, cast nets, seines, pump nets. Possession or use on state freshwaters of devices not authorized by this article is unlawful. Nongame fish may be taken with lawful game fishing devices (50-13-1115). Permitted devices must be labeled and/or have a floating marker attached (50-13-1116). [Designated devices are defined and size and other specifications are set in statute 50-13-1120.] A commercial or noncommercial fishing license is required for taking nongame fish in state freshwaters by the use of certain of the above specified devices as detailed by statute (50-13-1135). No license is required to fish for nongame fish with not more than two set hooks or jugs, except in lakes and reservoirs where a permit is required (50-13-1140). Exclusive of private ponds, no person shall fish with more than 50 jugs, 1 skimbow net, 50 set hooks, 50 hoop nets, 50 traps or 2,000 trot line hooks (50-13-1145). The use of certain specified devices requires an additional tag for each device, in addition to any fishing license (50-13-1155). The use of "yoyos" (spring-loaded set hook devices) is unlawful (50-13-1190). [Baits, trap and net sizes, permitted fishing hours and other details are specified in 50-13-1165 through -1188.] It is unlawful to have in possession game fish or tackle when fishing for nongame fish, or to use, disturb or take fish from the nongame fishing devices of another (50-13-1189 and -1191). Violation: misdemeanor; for tampering with a device,

$100-200 fine, or jail up to 30 days; for stealing a device or fish, $500-1,000 fine, jail up to six months, or both (50-13-1197).

The Division may adopt regulations for the management, control and enforcement of nongame fishing in state waters. Violating a law or rule relating to nongame fish is a misdemeanor with a $50-200 fine, or jail up to 30 days. In addition, any fish or fishing device shall be confiscated and, on conviction, forfeited and sold at public auction, the money to go to the Game Protection Fund. The boat, motor and fishing gear of a person unlawfully using or possessing a gill or hoop net shall be confiscated and sold at auction (50-13-1194 through -1196).

Other than a dam for manufacturing purposes, no permanent obstruction shall be placed in inland waters so as to obstruct free migration of fish. Violation: misdemeanor; $200 fine; or jail three to six months; or both. Wardens may destroy such obstructions (50-13-1210). Navigable streams obstructed by dams must have a fishway. Violation is $25 fine each day after notification of violation (50-13-1220). Unless excused by the county, dams across state waters must provide fishways for migratory fish. Failure to comply within 30 days is a $5,000 fine recoverable by the county (50-13-1230). Counties shall designate fish sluices on rivers, and blockage is a public nuisance and may be abated (50-13-1240).

It is unlawful to deliver, receive for transport or transport beyond state limits, game fish caught in the state, except that a licensed nonresident may carry from the state up to 50 lawfully taken game fish during one week. Violation: misdemeanor; $100 fine for each offense. A second conviction within three years is a $200 fine and 30 days jail for each offense (50-13-1650). Any game warden or other law enforcement officer may search, on reasonable information, any package of fish and seize and hold such as evidence; such are forfeited on conviction and can be sold at auction (50-13-1660).

It is illegal to sell white perch caught in this state. Only fish with proper invoices imported from another state may be sold, and other specified conditions must be met (50-13-1760).

Commercial and Private Enterprise Provisions

The Department may grant operating licenses for privately owned shooting preserves which are not established for extending hunting seasons for native species. ★No new preserve may be licensed without approval of the majority of the legislative delegation of the county where it is to be located.★ The operator must own/lease 100 to 1,500 contiguous acres. Shooting preserves for pen-raised turkey may not be smaller than 10,000 contiguous acres. Nonresident big game permits are not required on specially licensed shooting preserves. Boundaries must be clearly marked or fenced as specified. Regular hunting licenses or permits are required, except as otherwise provided (50-11-1200 through 50-11-1260).

Legal species for shooting preserves are: pen-raised bobwhite quail, pheasants, chukars and other Department designated species, and pen-raised mallards conforming to USFW regulations. There is no bag limit on shooting preserve species; there is a specified six-month season. All harvested game must be tagged until it is prepared for consumption. The Department shall furnish no game for stocking a shooting preserve. A preserve operator may apply for a quail call pen trap to recover quail that are not killed. Sanctioned bird dog field trials may apply for special permits allowing the release and shooting during the field trial only of designated species outside of the normal preserve season. ★All animals held in captivity at a shooting preserve must be confined in cages constructed as specified in statutes, and must receive proper care, proper food and water, parasite and disease control, cover and bedding, and fresh air while being transported in vehicles.★ The operator must keep records including hunters, dates, and amounts of game released, taken, and otherwise disposed of (50-11-1270 through -1390). The licensee is responsible for a violation of these provisions. Violation: misdemeanor; $100-200 fine; or jail for 15-30 days; and license revocation at the Department's discretion. Operating a shooting preserve without a license is a misdemeanor, with a $200-500 fine, or jail 30 days to six months (50-11-1400 and -1410).

With Department approval, a person may propagate pen-raised quail for commercial purposes after obtaining a commercial quail breeder's license. Licensees may sell live pen-raised quail for propagating purposes, or for food. Hotel or restaurant keepers may sell such quail for food on their premises without a license. The Department may revoke a license for noncompliance and refuse to issue required tags and seals. The Department is to receive a copy of an invoice of pen-raised quail sold or shipped in state. Pen-raised quail must be killed otherwise than by shooting. It is unlawful to trap wild quail to obtain birds to be pen-raised or to obtain wild quail eggs to be hatched and pen-raised. Violation of provisions is a misdemeanor; $200 fine; or jail 30 days for each offense; and license/tag forfeiture (50-11-1420 through -1530).

Artificially reared trout, properly tagged or marked, and produced in a private hatchery may be sold; such trout must be tagged, marked or stamped showing where produced and species. Restaurants or retail markets must specify that trout are imported or artificially reared, and retail establishments are responsible for violations on their premises. Violation: misdemeanor; $50-100 fine; or jail 15-30 days; each violation a separate offense (50-13-1680 through -1740).

A person may sell, barter and transport game fish for strictly stocking purposes if they obtain a game fish breeder license from the Director and keep required records. Violation: misdemeanor; $100 minimum fine; and license suspension/revocation for three years (50-13-1750).

Except for a retailer of finished fur or hide products, a fur buyer's license is required to buy furs, pelts, hides, whole fur-bearing animals or parts (50-11-2470). A fur processor's license is required to process hides. A taxidermist who possesses a fur, pelt, hide or whole fur-bearing animal legally owned by another, which is being temporarily held for processing, is not required to obtain this license. Fur processors must keep records as specified by the Department (50-11-2475). Persons who acquire not more than five furs, pelts, hides or whole animals for their personal use and not for sale, and fur processors, taxidermists, or persons acquiring carcasses without hides, need not acquire a fur dealer license (50-11-2480). Daily records must be kept by all fur dealers, buyers and processors, and submitted monthly to the Department, and untagged furs may be declared contraband and seized (50-11-2490). Commercial fur trapping season is set in statute, and it is lawful to take fur-bearing animals by other lawful means during the general open hunting seasons (50-11-2540). (See also Restrictions on Taking: Hunting and Trapping under this section and GENERAL EXCEPTIONS TO PROTECTION for foxhunting-enclosed preserves.)

Import, Export and Release Provisions

No person may possess, sell, import, or release into state waters any of the following fish: ▸ carnero or candiru catfish; ▸ freshwater electric eel; ▸ white amur or grass carp; ▸ walking catfish or any member of the Clariidae family; ▸ piranha; ▸ stickleback; ▸ Mexican banded tetra; ▸ sea lamprey. The Department may issue special import permits to qualified persons for research purposes only, and also for stocking nonreproducing white amur or grass carp hybrids. It is unlawful to take grass carp from waters stocked as permitted by this section and such grass carp must be returned to the water immediately. The Department shall prescribe the methods, controls and restrictions for special permits, and shall promulgate regulations to prohibit the importation of additional species of fish when they are potentially dangerous (50-13-1630).

It is unlawful to import, possess or transport for release, or introduce or bring into the state live wildlife of the following types without a Department permit: ▸ a fur-bearer, including any red or gray fox, raccoon, opossum, muskrat, mink, skunk, otter, bobcat, weasel, and beaver; ▸ a member of the family Cervidae (elk, deer); ▸ a non-domestic member of the families Suidae (pigs), Tayassuidae (peccaries), Bovidae (bison, mountain goat, mountain sheep); ▸ coyote, bear, or turkey; ▸ a species of marine or estuarine fish, crustacean, mollusk, or other marine invertebrate not already found in the wild, or not native to this state. A permit may be granted only after investigations and inspections of the wildlife have been made and possession or importation is approved. The Department may not issue a permit unless: ▸ the wildlife was taken lawfully in the jurisdiction in which it originated; ▸ the importation, release or possession of the wildlife is not reasonably expected to impact adversely the natural resources of the state or its wildlife populations (50-16-20). It is unlawful to possess, transport or bring into the state, or release or introduce diseased wildlife or other animal that reasonably might be expected to pose a public health or safety hazard as determined by the Department of Health and Environmental Control after consultation with the Department (50-16-30). Wildlife imported for exhibition purposes only by state wildlife departments, zoos or parks, or public scientific/educational institutions operated not for profit, and transient circuses do not need a permit. Nothing herein prevents the Department from possessing, importing or releasing wildlife (50-16-40). The Department may promulgate regulations to effectuate wildlife importation provisions (50-16-50). The importation of wildlife for sale in the pet trade does not require a permit [list includes tropical birds, fishes, rats and mice, rabbits, reptiles, hamsters, guinea pigs and amphibians], but this section does not privilege the import/possession of a species otherwise protected or regulated by other provisions of this title (50-16-60). Violation of importation provisions is a misdemeanor; up to $1,000 fine; jail up to six months, or both (50-16-70). It is lawful to ship live fish and eggs for breeding or stocking purposes in interstate commerce when such shipment originates and terminates outside the state (50-13-1670).

It is unlawful to bring a coyote into the state, except those in captivity for exhibition purposes, or to release a coyote. Violation: up to $500 fine; or jail up to one year (50-11-1760). It is unlawful to sell live wolves or coyotes within the state or import live wolves or coyotes except for exhibition or scientific purposes under Department approval and regulations. A person may not have a live wolf or coyote in possession without a Department permit (50-11-1765).

ANIMAL DAMAGE CONTROL

Where wildlife is destroying property the Department may issue a permit authorizing the landowner, under Department supervision, to take action necessary to remove the destructive wildlife (50-11-1050). Bobcats may be killed by officers and by landowners on their holdings without license at any time (50-11-1070). ★A persons desiring to put out poison on their lands for poisoning predatory animals shall obtain a Department permit, publish the dates the poison will be put out, and describe the areas where it will be placed by one notice in a county newspaper. Violation: misdemeanor; $25-100 fine; or jail 10-30 days (50-11-1060).★ Whenever coyotes or foxes are destroying birds, poultry, pigs, lambs or other property in any county, or there is an apparent rabies epidemic, upon the written request of a majority of the county's legislative delegation, the Director shall declare an open season on coyotes and foxes with the use of firearms in the county suffering the destruction and for such time as the delegation considers desirable (50-11-1080 and -1120). The Department may permit the taking of game animals, and prescribe the methods for taking, when they become so numerous that they cause excessive damage to crops and property. An animal so taken is under the Department's supervision, and deer must be given to eleemosynary institutions (50-11-1090). Raccoons and squirrels may be killed by landowners from July 15 to the regular open season if they are destroying crops (50-11-1130).

The Department may trap with steel or other traps any fox, wildcat, bobcat, wolf, coyote, skunk, raccoon or other predatory animal on state lands and on cooperative wildlife management areas within USFS lands. USFW employees and employees of a national park or game refuge may trap predatory animals within the confines of such national park, reserve or refuge. The Department of Game shall cooperate with US employees and agencies in trapping programs and may accept their aid and advice to control predators more effectively (50-11-1150 through -1170).

The Department may issue special permits for the taking, capturing or transportation of fur-bearing or other game animal which is destroying or damaging private or public property, timber, or growing crops, or for scientific or research purposes, and may issue special depredation permits at no cost to allow the use of snares for beavers in water-sets (50-11-2570 and -2575).

Upon good cause shown, and where necessary to alleviate damage to property or to protect human health, endangered species may be removed, captured or destroyed pursuant to a Commission permit, and where possible, under the supervision of a Department agent; endangered species may be removed, captured or destroyed without permit in emergency situations involving an immediate threat to human life. Commission regulations shall provide for the removal, capture or destruction of nongame wildlife for these purposes (50-15-50).

ENFORCEMENT OF WILDLIFE LAWS

Enforcement Powers

It is the duty of all sheriffs, deputy sheriffs, constables, rural policemen and special officers to cooperate with the Department, Division and game wardens to enforce state fish and game laws (50-1-80). Officers are immune from prosecution for failure to comply with wildlife, motor vehicle or boat laws, or for entering private property, when acting within their official capacity within their territorial jurisdiction to enforce those laws (50-3-420).

It is unlawful to attempt such or to catch, kill, possess, or transport an alligator, bird or animal or part in violation of any provisions of the fish and game laws (50-1-120). Wildlife unlawfully taken, shipped or found in the possession of a person or wildlife legally taken which comes into the possession of the Department may be disposed of at its discretion (50-1-110).

Criminal Penalties

Unless otherwise specified, a violation of this title is a misdemeanor; $25-200 fine; or jail 10-30 days (50-1-130).

The entry of a plea of guilty, or forfeiture of a posted bail for a fish and game law violation has the same effect as a conviction. In any case where bail is posted, forfeiture is not effective for 10 days following arrest (50-1-135). Conspiring to violate a game and fish law is a misdemeanor, and subject to a penalty not greater than that provided by law for the violation. Conspiring to violate two or more provisions of law is a misdemeanor; up to $2,000 fine; or jail up to one year, or both; and revocation of any hunting or fishing license for one year (50-1-136).

While preparing for, engaging in, or returning from hunting, it is unlawful to use a firearm or archery tackle in a criminally negligent manner in reckless disregard for the safety of others. Violation: misdemeanor; if no personal/property damage, fine of up to $200, or jail up to 30 days; if property damage only, $500-1,000 fine, or jail up to six months, and the court must order restitution to the property owner; if bodily injury, fine of $500-2,500, or jail up to two years. If disfigurement, or permanent disability results, mandatory jail 60 days to two years; in case of death, mandatory jail for three months to three years. No part of the minimum fines/penalties may be suspended by a state court. The Department also must seize and revoke the license of the convicted person for one to five years, as specified for severity of the crime. Hunting while a license is suspended under this section is a fine of $500-2,500, or jail up to two years, and additional license suspension of five years. The person must also complete a hunter safety program. Monetary penalties shall go to the Victim's Compensation Fund (50-1-85).

Hunting, fishing or trapping on the lands of another without the owner's consent is a misdemeanor; first offense, up to $200 fine, or jail up to 30 days; second offense, $100-200 fine, or jail up to 30 days; third/subsequent offense, $500-1,000 fine, or jail up to six months, or both. Records of convictions shall be maintained so that any law enforcement agency can determine prior offenses within the past 10 years (50-1-90).

Illegal Taking of Wildlife:

Hunting deer during the closed season is a minimum fine of $100-200, or jail up to 30 days. None of the fine may be suspended (50-11-340). Taking, attempting to take, or possessing deer illegally; taking deer by prohibited methods in designated game zones or in wildlife management area lands; or possessing deer with the head detached when in transit from woods, swamps or fields is a misdemeanor; up to $200 fine; or jail up to 30 days (50-11-350, -400 and -410). It is a misdemeanor to have in possession recently killed venison or fresh deerskin during the closed season; $50-100 fine, or jail up to 30 days (50-11-420).

It is unlawful to: ▸ hunt, take, or attempt to take a bear except during the open season; ▸ buy sell, barter or exchange a bear or bear part; ▸ possess or transport a freshly killed bear or bear part except during the open season for hunting/taking bears. Each act constituting a violation is a separate offense and a misdemeanor; up to $2,500 fine; or jail up to two years, or both; plus mandatory suspension of hunting and fishing privileges for three years. Equipment used in violation is forfeited to the Department. The court may order that restitution be paid to the Department of not less than $1,500 for each bear or bear part which is the subject of a violation (50-11-430).

Notwithstanding other provisions, a person convicted of night hunting for deer or bear must either be jailed as provided in 50-11-710, or be fined: ▸ up to $2,500 for a first offense; ▸ $500-2,500 for a second offense within two years; ▸ $600-3,000 for a third or subsequent offense within two years following a second offense (50-11-720). (See also Restrictions on Taking: Hunting and Trapping under HUNTING, FISHING, TRAPPING PROVISIONS.)

Illegally buying, selling or trafficking in wildlife is punished as follows: ▸ first offense, if value exchanged for the wildlife is $200 or less, up to $200 fine, or jail up to 30 days; ▸ first offense, if consideration exchanged for the wildlife is more than $200, $500-5,000 fine, or jail 30 days to one year, or both, plus loss of hunting and fishing privileges for one year; ▸ second offense within three years, $1,000-5,000 fine, or jail 30 days to one year; ▸ third offense within three years of last conviction, $5,000 fine, which may not be suspended, or jail for one year, or both, plus loss of hunting and fishing privileges for three years (50-1-125).

It is unlawful to buy or sell, barter, or possess for sale, or offer such, a deer or part of a deer, except the hide of legally taken deer may be bought, sold or bartered during certain open seasons or periods as specified in statutes. Violation: first offense, minimum $100-300 fine, or jail up to 30 days; second offense within three years, $300-500 fine, or jail up to 30 days; third offense within three years, $1,000 mandatory fine, or jail up to 60 days (50-11-1910).

License Revocations and Suspensions

★★There is a point system to be used by the Department in suspending hunting and fishing privileges. Each time a person is convicted of a violation, the number of points assigned to the violation shall be charged against such person. For each calendar year thereafter in which the person received no points, one-half of the accumulated points shall be deducted if the total number is greater than three. If a person has three or fewer points at the end of the year in which no points were received, points revert to zero. Points range from a low of four for using an unplugged gun to 18 for night hunting of deer or bear (50-9-1020 and -1030). The Department shall suspend for one year the hunting and fishing privileges of a person who has 18 or more points, after notice in writing and opportunity for hearing/review or appeal (50-9-1040 through -1060). The points and penalties assessed shall be in addition to and not in lieu of other civil remedies or criminal penalties which may be assessed (50-9-1110). Hunting/fishing while under suspension is a misdemeanor; $250-500 fine, or jail up to one year, or both, and additional revocation of any hunting/fishing privileges for three years (50-9-1100). After the expiration of the suspension period, the record shall be cleared (50-9-1070). ★★   (See also HUNTING, FISHING, TRAPPING PROVISIONS for wildlife management area permit revocations.)

Reward Payments

Funds from the Operation Game Thief Program may be expended only for: ▸ financing of reward payments to persons other than law enforcement or Department personnel for information leading to the arrest of persons unlawfully taking, wounding or killing, possessing, transporting or selling wildlife, and attendant acts of vandalism; ▸ financing a statewide telephone reporting system under the name of "Operation Game Thief"; ▸ promoting public recognition and awareness of the program. The Law Enforcement and Boating Division's director and Advisory Board shall establish the schedule of rewards to be paid. (50-11-2310). Moneys appropriated by the General Assembly or received from donations must be used before County Game Fund moneys are used, and balances shall not lapse (50-11-2320). (See also Agency Funding Sources under STATE FISH AND WILDLIFE AGENCIES.)

HABITAT PROTECTION

The Department may enter into a cooperative agreement with the US for the protection and management of the wildlife resources of the national forest lands within the state and for restocking them with desirable species of game, birds, other animals and fish (50-1-190). The Director may close hunting and fishing on national forest lands for such time periods as are necessary, prescribe hunting and fishing seasons, set fees for special national forest licenses, and set numbers and sizes of animals that may be taken (50-1-200). Violators shall be fined up to $200; or jailed up to 30 days for each offense (50-1-210). These provisions apply to other properties acquired from the US by the state, or to other US properties within the state. Hunting and fishing shall not be allowed on lands controlled by the State Commission of Forestry except by written agreement. Nothing herein shall interfere with the use and management of lands by state agencies in charge of such lands (50-1-220).

Residents and nonresidents must have a big game permit to hunt deer, bear or turkey, in addition to the required hunting license (50-9-135). The Department may distribute and regulate the issuance of special, nonresident shooting preserve licenses (50-9-140). A permit is required to hunt on wildlife management areas, the funds so derived to be used exclusively for procurement of such areas by rent, lease or exchange, and for their management. The Department may not lease, and may not pay more than fair market value for, any land for the Wildlife Management Area Program which during the preceding two years has been held under a private hunting lease by a club or individual unless the former lessee executes a voluntary consent or other conditions are met. The Department may not have under lease at one time more than 1,600,000 acres in the program. The Department may establish open and closed seasons, bag limits and methods for taking game on all wildlife management areas (50-9-150).

Without cost to the state, the Department shall designate and establish sanctuaries where game, birds and animals may breed unmolested, if a landowner enters into an agreement with the Director to set aside and turn over a certain number of acres of land for that purpose. There may be no hunting or trespassing for five years upon lands so designated, and the Director may post those lands and prosecute violators. The Department or landowner may terminate such agreement at any time (50-11-860). [Numerous bird, bird and squirrel, nongame bird, duck and geese, wildlife and environmental sanctuaries are listed in 50-11-870 through 50-11-980, wherein it is unlawful to use shotguns, rifles, pellet guns and BB guns, or to kill wildlife. Each of these sections has its own restrictions, prohibitions and penalties for violation.] Anyone hunting or trespassing upon land designated as a sanctuary must be fined for each offense not less than $100-200, or jailed up to 30 days (50-11-990).

Before a person may lease property to the Wildlife Management Area Program, there must be either public or private access for individuals hunting on the property under the program during the term of the lease (50-11-2230). (See also HUNTING, FISHING, TRAPPING PROVISIONS.)

The Commission may acquire a sufficient number of acres in close proximity to a dam or other water for establishing fish hatcheries, and may exercise the power of eminent domain if necessary (50-13-1920). It may also lease or purchase land for the USFW to establish fish hatcheries, the expense to come from the Game Protection Fund (50-13-1930). The Department shall charge fees for stocking fish in private waters sufficient to cover all costs of operating the Cheraw Fish Hatchery Private Pond Fish Stocking Programs (50-13-1935).

★★The Director may select any place on a state river or stream as a fish sanctuary after approval of the county's legislative delegation. No such sanctuary shall exceed two miles in length, and boundaries shall be marked (50-13-1960). Sanctuaries may be established on lakes and ponds on agreement with landowners to turn them over to the state for such purpose (50-13-1970). Such sanctuary continues until it is directed to be closed by the landowner or the county's legislative delegation; there may be no fishing or trespassing upon sanctuary waters (50-13-1980). Violation: misdemeanor; up to $200 fine; or jail up to 30 days (50-13-1990). The Department manages the lakes and ponds which it owns/leases and may establish terms for fishing, boating and other activities, after Commission approval and the majority of the county's legislative delegation wherein such waters are located (50-13-2020).★★

NATIVE AMERICAN WILDLIFE PROVISIONS: None.

SOUTH DAKOTA

Sources: South Dakota Codified Laws, 1991, Title 41; 1992 Pocket Supplement.

STATE WILDLIFE POLICY

No person shall at any time or in any manner acquire any property in, or subject to his dominion or control, any game bird, game animal, or game fish or any part thereof, but they shall always and under all circumstances be and remain the property of the state unless taken in the manner provided by law or regulations prescribed by the **Game, Fish and Parks Commission** (Commission) and for the purposes authorized by law, and during permitted periods of killing, when the same may be used by any person during the time, in the manner and for the purposes expressly authorized by law (41-1-2 and -3). All wild birds or animals as defined in 41-1-1, both resident and migratory, in the state are the property of the state (41-11-1).

RELEVANT WILDLIFE DEFINITIONS: See Definitions section of Appendices.

STATE FISH AND WILDLIFE AGENCIES

Agency Structure

There is a **Department of Game, Fish and Parks** (Department), and a **Commission** comprised of eight members, appointed by the Governor, subject to confirmation by the Senate (41-2-1). ★No more than four members of the Commission shall be members of the same political party, and at the time of their appointment, not less than four shall be farmers actually residing on a farm, engaged in agriculture and interested in wildlife conservation, and not less than three shall reside west of the Missouri river and not less than five shall reside east thereof (41-2-2).★ The term of office of the Commissioners shall be four years, and the Governor shall preserve a rotation of terms between the republican and democratic parties (41-2-3). The Commission shall be administered under the supervision of the Department and the Secretary of the Department (Secretary), but shall retain the quasi-judicial, quasi-legislative, advisory, and budgetary functions otherwise vested in it and shall exercise those functions independently of the Secretary (41-2-1.2).

Agency Powers and Duties

The **Department** has the authority to employ an adequate force of **Conservation Officers** to enforce the provisions of this title who shall meet requirements as to education and training of law enforcement officers provided pursuant to chapter 23-3. Conservation Officers shall: be familiar with the provisions of this title; be of good moral character; be employed regardless of party affiliations; and perform such duties as may be assigned by the Department (41-2-12). Rangers and park managers employed by the Department shall be Conservation Officers without additional compensation. In emergency, the Department may appoint additional Conservation Officers who shall serve without additional compensation (41-2-1a through -13).

The Department: ▸ has the power to acquire public or private property by gift, grant, devise, purchase, lease or condemnation, and to manage and improve the same for the purposes granted in this title (41-2-19); ▸ may acquire by any means or methods a public or private real property especially desirable for public shooting areas or for water conservation or recreation, and develop and improve the same (41-2-21); ▸ ★has the same responsibility for a railroad right-of-way that it acquires as a hiking or biking recreation trail as it has for public shooting area land, but such property may not be taxed by a local district (41-2-21.1);★ ▸ may establish and operate controlled hunting areas when in the best interest of the people (41-2-22); ▸ has the duty, when directed by the Commission, to expend funds for the improvement of wildlife habitat, access to hunting, fishing or recreation areas on state land, public or private, provided that land so improved shall be open to reasonable public use (41-2-23); ▸ has the power to grant easements, leases or permits on property which it owns or controls for public utilities, agricultural purposes, electrical power or telephone lines, radio and TV towers, cabin sites and concessions, for the management of facilities to service public needs (41-2-26); ▸ ★has the power and duty to publicize the game and fish, scenic, and recreational resources of the state to attract immigrants, tourists and others (41-2-27);★ ▸ ★may authorize sales of forest products on Department lands, such proceeds to become part of Department funds (41-2-29);★ ▸ may sell its lands which are no longer needed for game, fish or parks (41-2-29.1); ▸ has the power and duty to engage in predatory animal control activities and to cooperate with the US or an agency thereof, with other states, or with other state departments in the execution of this duty (41-2-30).

The Department shall: ▸ have charge of the propagation and preservation of such varieties of game and fish deemed to be of public value (41-3-1); ▸ have charge of the collection and diffusion of conservation statistics and information (41-3-2); ▸ cooperate with federal agencies in the propagation, preservation and protection of game and fish (41-3-3). Wildlife mitigation condemnations of land by the federal government shall be restricted to lands owned by direct beneficiaries of the project of which the wildlife mitigation is the part (41-3-4.l). The Department: ▸ may secure by purchase or otherwise, game animals, birds, fish and fur-bearing animals, and exchange specimens of the same with the game commissions of other states for breeding and not otherwise (41-3-7); ▸ shall have charge of the construction and management of all fish hatcheries, including the control of grounds owned or leased for such purposes (41-3-10); ▸ shall have charge of receiving from the USFW and gathering, purchasing and distributing fish, spawn and fry to state waters, the taking of fish from state waters for propagation, and transferring of game animals or birds within the state for stocking purposes (41-3-12 and -13); ▸ shall have authority to acquire or condemn private property where necessary to carry out the purposes and intent of this title through proceedings by the attorney general (41-4-1). Notice and hearing must be provided to adjacent landowner(s) before purchase of land by the Department (41-4-1.1). Funds for condemnation proceedings and lands so acquired shall come from the Department of Game, Fish and Parks Fund (41-4-2). The **Commission** may establish a season on fowl specified in 41-11-4 (see PROTECTED SPECIES OF WILDLIFE) throughout all or a portion of the state and provide the extent of the season by rule, and may close or curtail open seasons (41-11-5).

Agency Regulations

The Commission may adopt rules to implement the provisions of chapters 41-1 to 41-15, regulating the: ▸ hunting, taking, sale, and transport of all wild birds, animals and fish; ▸ conservation, protection, importation and propagation of wild animals and fish; ▸ management of nongame, endangered and threatened wildlife to ensure their perpetuation; ▸ gathering, purchasing, and distributing wild animals and fish for population management, stocking and scientific studies; ▸ form of tags and permits for transportation of wild game; ▸ sale, breeding, transportation and domestication of wild animals except for domesticated big game animals as defined in 38-1-41; ▸ form and content of license applications; ▸ devices, weapons, ammunition, traps, tackle, bait which may be used to hunt, kill, capture a wild animal or fish; ▸ hunting, fishing and trapping in boundary waters; ▸ release, hunting and taking of animals and birds on private shooting preserves; ▸ opening, closing and changing seasons for hunting, fishing and trapping; ▸ setting of special license fees not set by statute to manage specific and limited wildlife populations; ▸ number of persons who may act as a group when hunting game birds or animals; ▸ use of raptors; ▸ release of fish from private fish hatcheries; ▸ operation of controlled hunting areas. Violation of any rule is a class 2 misdemeanor. If the same incident is a violation of a statute and of the rules, only the statutory penalty may be imposed (41-2-18). ★The Commission may adopt reasonable rules to specify eligibility criteria, application procedures and standards for distribution of the grant funds for the Pheasants-for-Everyone Program (41-2-18.1).★

Agency Funding Sources

★Moneys collected under state game and fish laws, including license fees, bonds or contracts, and money due from any other sources connected with game and fish laws, except fines, shall be credited to the **Department of Game, Fish and Parks Fund** (Fund). Excepting receipts from sales of timber on school lands, all sums received from rentals, contracts, licenses, sales of personal property or any source, except sums derived from the operation of the Division of Forestry and Parks and Custer State Park, shall be credited to the Fund (41-2-34).★ Revenue from sale of the **Wildlife Habitat Stamp** provided for in 41-6-16 and 41-6-17 shall be deposited in the Fund and shall be used to restore the state pheasant and wildlife population. Land purchased with funds collected pursuant to this section shall be identified as game production areas, and must be from a willing seller and approved by the Governor. No land acquisition made pursuant to this section may be accomplished through eminent domain (41-2-34.1). All moneys in the Fund are hereby annually appropriated to pay the expenses of effectuating this title (41-2-35). Three dollars from the sale of each nonresident small game license shall go into the **Land Acquisition and Development Fund,** to be used to acquire by purchase or lease real property to be used primarily for game production, such property to remain open for public hunting; for improving and maintaining game production areas; for the payment of taxes on public shooting areas, but no more than 25% of the fund, after the payment of taxes, shall be used for fund administration or for game production area improvements (41-4-3). State shooting area lands and state game production lands or controlled hunting area lands are subject to taxation by local school districts within which such lands are located (41-4-8).

PROTECTED SPECIES OF WILDLIFE

No person may hunt, kill, or capture black bears, mountain lions and wolves in South Dakota except pursuant to 41-6-29 (41-8-2.1). Except as otherwise expressly provided, no person may hunt, pursue, take, possess or capture a big game animal within the state, violations to be punished pursuant to 41-8-18 (41-8-2). Except as permitted, no person may kill, catch, or have in possession, living or dead, a wild bird other than small game, or ship within or without the state, or sell, a wild bird or small game after it has been killed or caught (41-11-2). Except as provided, no person may hunt, kill, take or have in possession or control a snipe, prairie chicken or pinnated grouse, white breasted or sharp-tailed grouse, partridge, or ruffed grouse, sage grouse, Hungarian partridge, chukar partridge, Chinese ringnecked or English pheasant, wild turkey, upland plover, golden plover, crow, mourning dove, quail, wild duck of any variety, wild geese of any variety, brant or any variety of aquatic fowl or part thereof (41-11-4). Except as permitted by statute, no person may take or have in possession or break or destroy a nest of the eggs of the above birds (41-11-7). No part of the plumage, skin or body of a protected bird may be sold or had in possession for sale, irrespective of whether such bird was captured or killed within or without the state, except that the plumage or skin of the Chinese pheasant, sharptail grouse, Hungarian partridge and prairie chicken legally taken may be sold or had in possession for sale (41-11-8). A Department raptor license is required in order to possess or capture a raptor (41-11-11). Violations of all of the above are class 2 misdemeaners.

The Department and the Department of Agriculture may participate in programs to reintroduce the black-footed ferret under the following conditions: areas containing prairie dogs but without the potential to support black-footed ferrets shall be identified, evaluated and declared ferret-free; existing USFS prairie dog management plans shall be strictly adhered to, and if future increases in acres are needed, a funding mechanism shall be established to compensate landowners suffering lost income; no additional land may be acquired for ferrets through condemnation, and the USFS multiple use concept shall be continued; initial ferret reintroduction efforts shall be concentrated within Badlands National Park, and after techniques are refined, the Buffalo Gap management plan is functioning, and there is citizen input, reintroduction efforts may be expanded to the grasslands; the USFW shall provide for continued meetings of personnel from USFS, Pine Ridge Indian reservation, US Park Service, USFW, affected state agencies, private organizations and local landowners during and after reintroduction of the ferret (41-11-15).

See also RELEVANT WILDLIFE DEFINITIONS; HUNTING, FISHING, TRAPPING PROVISIONS; ANIMAL DAMAGE CONTROL; and ENFORCEMENT OF WILDLIFE LAWS.

GENERAL EXCEPTIONS TO PROTECTION

The Commission may grant permission to an accredited representative of an incorporated society of natural history to collect for scientific purposes only, nests, eggs, birds, animals, or fish protected by this title, such specimens not to be sold or transferred (41-3-9). Persons who possess and who are acting within the scope of a scientific collector's license are exempt from the other criminal sanctions in this title. The Secretary may issue the license authorizing the licensee to take, possess, exchange, transport and collect birds, nests, eggs or wild animals in such manner as the Secretary may prescribe. A scientific collector's license must be approved by the Commission (41-6-32). The English or European house sparrow and European starling are not included among the birds protected by this chapter. Purple grackle, crow, magpie, red-winged blackbird, Brewers blackbird, rusty blackbird, and the bronzed grackle may be taken when committing or about to commit depredation upon ornamental or shade trees, agricultural crops, livestock or wildlife, or when concentrated in such numbers and manner as to constitute a health hazard or other nuisance (41-11-10). The Commission may permit seining of scavenger or nonprotected fish from rivers, lakes or boundary waters (41-12-17). The Department may remove and dispose of or contract for the removal and disposal of rough fish and bullheads from public waters by the use of seines, nets, chemicals or by other means when necessary (41-13-5 and -7). The Commission may by rule declare one or more species of game fish to be considered and treated as rough fish in particular waters when necessary to maintain a desirable fish population (41-

13-6). Game fish inadvertently taken in rough fish removal operations are to be sold as rough fish, with proceeds to go to the Department of Game, Fish and Parks Fund (41-13-9 through -11).

See also HUNTING, FISHING, TRAPPING PROVISIONS.

HUNTING, FISHING, TRAPPING PROVISIONS

General Provisions

Except as otherwise expressly provided, it is a class 2 misdemeanor to hunt, pursue, take, possess, shoot at, kill or capture a big game animal within the state (41-8-2). Wanton waste or destruction of protected birds, animals and fish is a class 2 misdemeanor (41-1-4). The Commission may open, close, or modify a big game, small game and migratory waterfowl season in emergencies, and evidence of imminent peril to the public health, safety or welfare need not be provided (41-8-1). ★The Commission shall reimburse annually the various counties for services rendered in connection with the sale of licenses in the amount of 10% of all license fees for licenses sold by the county treasurer, and also 10% of the east and west river prairie firearm deer license and antelope licenses sold by the Department. The county monies go into a special highway fund of each county (41-6-70).★

Licenses and Permits

Only residents may get a basic game and fish license. No one under age 12 may be granted a hunting license (41-6-12). Persons under age 16 must have a parental application for a license. Such parent or guardian must have been a resident for at least 90 days preceding such application. Children under age 16 must be accompanied by a parent, guardian or responsible adult when hunting; violation is a class 2 misdemeanor (41-6-13). It is a class 2 misdemeanor to obtain special licenses or permits without also having a resident basic game and fish license (41-6-11). It is a class 1 misdemeanor to make false statements to secure a license/tag or to lend the same to another not legally entitled to it (41-6-73). Only one license of one type, except a visitor fishing license, nonresident small game license and nonresident waterfowl license may be obtained under 41-6-16 through 41-6-45.1 by one person. The Commission may promulgate rules to define license types (41-6-55).

It is a class 2 misdemeanor for: ▸ an unlicensed person to enter upon or into a boundary river or stream on the South Dakota side of the waters to hunt, fish or take protected game, fish or wild fowl therefrom without a state hunting or fishing license (41-6-7); ▸ a nonresident to take, shoot or kill protected game, fish or wildfowl on any boundary water or river or to transport from those waters onto the South Dakota side any small game, big game, wild turkey, waterfowl or fish without a license (41-6-8); ▸ a resident to hunt small game without a resident small game license and a habitat stamp or to hunt waterfowl without a waterfowl restoration stamp (except for landowners on own lands and residents under age 16) (41-6-16); ▸ a nonresident to hunt small game, other than waterfowl, without a nonresident small game license (entitles holder to two hunting periods of five consecutive days and for each such license sold, an amount equal to the cost of a habitat stamp shall be placed into the Department of Game, Fish and Parks Fund to restore the state pheasant and wildlife populations) (41-6-17).

A nonresident fishing license entitles the licensee to all the privileges of a resident fishing license (41-6-36), as does a temporary fishing license (41-6-37). It is a class 2 misdemeanor for a person to take fish from state public waters by the use of a hoop net, trap, setline or similar device without a special hoop net license permitting the licensee to take rough fish from the public waters, such nets to be tagged with the licensee's name (41-6-38).

The hunting of mourning doves by a minor is a class 2 misdemeanor unless the minor is accompanied by a parent, guardian or responsible adult (41-6-16.l). It is a class 2 misdemeanor for nonresidents to hunt waterfowl without a special nonresident waterfowl license and a federal migratory bird stamp, allowing hunting for 10 consecutive days, $4 of each such license to go into the Land Acquisition and Development Fund, an equal amount to the cost of a habitat stamp to go into the Department of Game, Fish and Parks Fund for pheasant and wildlife restoration, and an amount equal to the cost of the waterfowl restoration stamp will go into the Resident Waterfowl Restoration Fund. The Commission may issue no more than 4,000 nonresident licenses in a calendar year, and a lottery selection may be used to limit the number of nonresident waterfowl licenses sold in any season (41-6-18.1 and -18.2). It is a class 1 misdemeanor for a resident or nonresident to take a big game animal, except wild turkey, without a big game license, or for a resident to take an elk without a resident elk license (41-6-19, -19.1 and -20). Ranchers and farmers (and immediate family members) living on their own land may apply for a permit to take one deer on that land if they did not lottery in to the main season lottery for deer permits (41-6-19.3 and -19.4). There is a nonrefundable application fee for resident bighorn sheep, mountain goat or elk licenses, such licensees to be selected by drawing, and proceeds from the application fees to go for big game research and management as the Commission dictates (41-6-19.6). It is a class 2 misdemeanor for residents or nonresidents to hunt, take or kill wild turkeys without the proper license or in violation of Commission rules (41-6-27 and -28).

Children between the ages of 11 and 16 shall take a firearms safety course before being granted a free resident basic game and fish license (41-6-14). No hunting license shall be issued to persons under age 16 unless they present a certificate of competency in firearms safety instruction or a hunting license from another state (41-7-1). The Department shall provide the firearms safety course and cooperate with the public school system and school superintendents where training shall be held at least three times a year, the cost of such instruction not to exceed $5,000 during any fiscal year (41-7-2 through -5).

Resident or nonresident, temporary, or nursing home licenses are required for catching, killing or possessing fish, frogs or turtles (41-6-35, -76 and -77). No license is required for residents: ▸ to hunt in a lawful manner game birds or fish during the open season on land or waters occupied by them; ▸ to hunt fur-bearing animals on their own lands during open season; ▸ under age 16 to hunt fur-bearing animals; ▸ who are landowners to kill raccoons, skunks, fox and badger doing damage on their lands; ▸ under age 16 to fish (41-6-2 through -6); ▸ to hunt raccoon, skunk, badger, jackrabbit, fox and coyote with firearms, nor for residents to trap raccoon, skunk, badger, jackrabbit, fox and coyote between April 1 and August 31 (41-6-23).

Restrictions on Taking: Hunting and Trapping

The Department shall not authorize the taking of more than 40 mountain goats within one year (41-8-5). No taking of big game is allowed except with a big game license (41-8-6). Each violation of big game hunting restrictions is a separate offense, as without a big game license, and every act of pursuing, hunting or killing of a big game animal during the closed season shall be a distinct and separate offense (41-8-7). It is illegal to: ▸ use a dog in hunting; ▸ use any salt or salt lick or construct, occupy or use a screen, blind or scaffold or other device near a salt lick to bait or entice animals to the same to hunt or kill them (41-8-15 and -16); ▸ use a spotlight or headlight on a highway, field, pasture, woodland, forest or prairie to spot, locate, or take an animal while having in possession a firearm, bow or other implement by which game could be killed, except for taking raccoons treed by dogs, a landowner and one guest using artificial light on the landowner's land in taking rabbits, hares, coyotes, foxes, raccoons, opossums, badgers, skunks or rodents, or Department personnel taking nuisance animals with landowner's permission (41-8-17).

It is a class 2 misdemeanor to hunt, catch, take, attempt to take or kill any small game or game animal in any other manner than by shooting with a firearm except: game birds and animals may be taken by falconry or by bow and arrow; disabled hunters with permit may use a crossbow; licensed blind hunters may use a designated hunter to take game birds and animals (41-8-31). It is illegal to: ▸ use rifles and handguns in hunting game birds with certain muzzleloading exceptions for wild turkeys (41-8-32); ▸ hunt mourning doves on or within 50 yards of a public road or highway (41-8-32.1); ▸ set a trap or snare, or use artificial light, net, bird line, swivel gun, set gun or a contrivance to catch, take, or kill game animals or birds (except decoys and stationary blinds for migratory game birds) (41-8-33); ▸ use a floating battery, sink box or similar device when hunting, or shooting from a motorboat except if at rest (41-8-35 and -36).

It is a class 2 misdemeanor to: ▸ take game with or discharge a firearm at wild animals, except for coyotes, rabbits, hares, rodents and foxes, while in or on a motor vehicle or a conveyance attached to a motor vehicle which is on a public highway or in a field of unharvested grain; ▸ discharge a firearm or other implement with which a big game animal could be killed from a motor vehicle or other means of transportation during a time and in a place that big game hunting is permitted except for hunters with a disabled hunter permit (41-8-37); ▸ chase, drive, harass or hunt a game animal or game bird with or from a motorcycle (41-8-37.1); ▸ intentionally kill a wild bird or animal from an aircraft while in flight, or use an aircraft to hunt, take, concentrate, drive, rally, stir up, locate or spot game birds or animals (41-8-39).

It is a class 2 misdemeanor to fish, hunt or trap on private land without permission of the landowner (41-9-1). ★This does not apply to fishing, trapping or hunting on highways or other public rights-of-way within the state except for controlled access facilities, unimproved section lines not commonly used as public rights-of-way or highways within parks or recreation areas or within or adjoining public shooting areas or game refuges. No person, except the adjoining landowner or one with the landowner's permission, may use the highways or rights-of-way for hunting or trapping purposes within 660 feet of an occupied dwelling, church, school or livestock (41-9-1.1). Posting private lands against hunting without the permission of the landowner is prohibited. Violation: class 1 misdemeanor (41-9-4).★   No person may discharge a rifle or bow and arrow at a big game animal from within the right-of-way of an improved public highway maintained by the state, county or township, except for disabled hunters with a permit who may hunt on public rights-of-way adjoining public hunting areas or adjoining private lands with the owner's permission, and lawfully taken big game is permitted on all public rights-of-way. Violation: class 2 misdemeanor (41-9-1.2). Persons who knowingly enter or remain on private property to hunt, fish or trap in violation of 41-9-1 or 41-9-2 shall have their hunting, fishing or trapping privileges revoked for one year. Retrieval, unarmed, of lawfully taken small game from Department land or private land is not a crime or offense, provided that such retrieval does not involve the use of a motor vehicle, but this does not limit the civil remedies available to landowners (41-9-8).

Except as otherwise authorized by chapter 41-6, it is a class 2 misdemeanor to trap, catch, take, kill a fur-bearing animal (41-8-19). It is a class 2 misdemeanor for a resident to hunt, take, kill or trap fur-bearing animals without a license or in violation of license conditions or Commission rules. It is a class 1 misdemeanor for a person to apply for a fur-bearing animal license unless the person has been a state resident for at least 90 days (41-6-24). A fur-bearing license entitles the resident licensee to set or operate a trap or traps, hunt, catch, take, trap or kill fur-bearing animals, except the blackfooted ferret, to the extent and in the manner provided in 41-8-20 through 41-8-26 (41-6-3). (See also Exceptions to License Requirements under this section.) Fur-bearing animals may be hunted, taken, trapped, or killed by a trapping license holder during seasons prescribed by the Commission. The season on fox and coyote shall be open year round west of the Missouri River, and open year round on coyote only east of the Missouri River (41-8-20). Nonresident predator licensees may not take, trap or kill a fur-bearing animal, except that fox, coyote and skunk may be taken by shooting (41-8-22). It is unlawful to: ► hunt a mink or muskrat with the aid of a dog, or to dig, disturb or molest a mink den or beaver house to capture these animals, or use poison, gas or smokers to kill, take or capture these animals, or shoot or spear muskrats except under permit under 41-8-23 (41-8-24);   ★ ► molest, injure or destroy a muskrat house, except in the open season for the taking, catching or killing thereof, providing that muskrat houses, for the purpose of placing traps therein, may be opened so as to not destroy, damage or injure them as a place of habitation for muskrats (41-8-25);★   ► purchase the skins of fur-bearing animals, including jackrabbits, without a fur dealer's license or in violation of Commission rules (41-6-25). Raw furs may be had in possession after the close of the season if they have been checked with a Conservation Officer within ten days after the close of the season (41-8-21). It is a class 1 misdemeanor and mandatory loss of trapping license for two years to steal, damage or destroy a trap of another, or to steal, damage, or destroy animals, carcasses, or pelts held fast by such traps (41-8-28 and -29). Violation of any of the above is a class 2 misdemeanor (41-8-21).

Restrictions on Taking: Fishing

Residents with fishing license may take suckers, red horse, buffalo, carp, eel, eel pout and catfish (except bullheads) from the Missouri River as prescribed by 41-12-5 to 41-12-8 and 41-12-12 (41-12-16). It is a class 2 misdemeanor to: ► catch, kill, take fish in any manner from private water used for fish propagation except by consent of the owner; ► use methods other than hook and line to take fish except as otherwise provided in state waters opened for fishing by the Commission; ► fish with an excess number of lines as established by the Commission or leave lines unattended outside the unaided observation of the legal user; ► use carp, goldfish or game fish (except the cleanings thereof) for bait; ► erect or use an ice house unless labeled with owner's name (41-12-2 through -8).

It is a class 1 misdemeanor to have in possession or place in state public waters a trammel or gill net, seine or other similar device for capturing fish, or to take fish by the erection of a weir, dam or artificial obstruction or by the use of a trammel or gill net, trap or similar device. The Department may authorize private landowners to use specified devices to take minnows or control undesirable or over-populated species of fish in their private waters (41-12-9). The following are subject to forfeiture: a trammel or gill net or similar device used illegally to capture fish in state public waters; a conveyance, including aircraft, vehicle or vessel, used to transport, possess or conceal a trammel or gill net, seine or similar device used illegally to capture fish in state public waters (41-12-9.1).

It is a class 2 misdemeanor to use spears, spear guns, bows and arrows, snaghooks, setlines, hoop nets, traps, artificial lights and other devices except hook and line for fishing except as expressly provided by the Commission's rules. Landing nets, gaffs and similar devices may be used to land legally taken fish (41-12-12). It is a class 2 misdemeanor to explode giant powder, giant caps, dynamite, lime or other explosive in public waters, or to kill or take fish in waters by use of an explosive or electrical device, or a poisonous, deleterious, or stupefying drug, unless authorization is given by the Department (41-12-13). The taking of fish with a net or seine in a river, lake or waters forming a boundary line between this and any other state in any manner or at any time prohibited by the laws of the adjoining state is a class 2 misdemeanor, except as provided by 41-12-16 to 41-12-19 (41-12-15). Rough fish, legally taken, may be sold and transported within or without the state if done in conformity with state Department of Agriculture rules (41-14-29). It is a class 1 misdemeanor to take, barter, trade, sell or export baitfish without a baitfish license, except that licensed sport fishermen may trap, seine and possess up to 12 dozen baitfish for personal use (41-14-34 and -35).

Commercial and Private Enterprise Provisions

A private "shooting preserve" is an acreage privately owned or leased on which hatchery raised game is released for hunting for a fee over an extended season (41-10-1). The acreage shall not exceed more than 1,280 acres, a permit is required, and extensive requirements must be met (41-10-3 and -7). Game which may be hunted on shooting preserves is mallard ducks, pheasants, quail, partridges, turkey and other Commission designated species. The Commission may exclude mallard ducks to protect the species (41-10-9). All released game must be marked as prescribed by the Commission, tagged, and within limits set by the Commission; the operator may set bag limits and restrictions on age, sex and number of each species that may be taken, fees, and rules for shooting. A resident basic game and fish license or nonresident general hunting license is required, or a resident/nonresident small game license and a habitat stamp is required for issuance of a shooting preserve license (41-10-10 through -16). It is a class 1 misdemeanor to operate a shooting preserve without a license, or to violate other rules relating to such preserves, or to fail to keep required records of hunters, tag numbers, and number and kind of species taken (41-10-17 and -18).

It is a class 2 misdemeanor to breed or domesticate, or to ship or sell domesticated antelope, deer, moose, elk, caribou or game birds without a license for breeding and domesticating animals and birds or in violation of the license conditions or Commission rules (41-6-31). It is a class 2 misdemeanor for a person to preserve or mount birds, animals or fish that the person does not own without a taxidermist's license, or in violation of the license conditions or Commission rules (41-6-33).

It is a class 2 misdemeanor for a person to maintain, operate or sell fish from a fish hatchery without a private fish hatchery license and written permission to sell fish (41-6-39). Licensees may allow fish purchasers to fish for the same in hatchery pools and transport fish so caught under Commission rules and with the Secretary's permission (41-6-40). No fishing license is required to fish in a private hatchery (41-6-41). Illegal transportation of hatchery fish is a class 2 misdemeanor (41-6-42).

★It is a class 2 misdemeanor for a resident to sell to a retail, wholesale or export bait dealer or to possess or transport bait or other wild animals commonly used as fish bait or biological specimens or to transport or sell bait and specimens to retail outlets, public fish hatcheries, aquariums or biological supply companies without a resident wholesale bait dealer's license. Persons over age 16 may be issued such license by the Department, permitting the licensee to raise, trap, seine, buy, sell to a retail, wholesale or export bait dealer, possess and transport bait and other wild animals commonly used as fish bait or biological specimens within the state and to transport and sell bait and specimens to retail outlets, public fish hatcheries, aquariums and biological supply companies for forage or study purposes in an adjoining state under Commission rules to protect and perpetuate the bait and biological specimen animal resources of the state (41-6-44). It is a class 2 misdemeanor for a nonresident to transport bait and biological specimens into the state, possess the same within the state or sell the same within the state without a nonresident wholesale bait dealer license, which may be issued by the Department if the nonresident home state provides a like opportunity for South Dakota residents to be licensed in that state and under the same restrictions as apply to resident wholesale bait dealer licensees (41-6-44.1). The Department may issue a resident or nonresident (with other state reciprocity) retail bait dealer license, permitting the licensee to raise, trap, seine, buy, sell, possess and transport bait and biological specimen animals, but the licensee may not sell to wholesale bait dealers licensed under this chapter (41-6-45).★

Import, Export and Release Provisions

It is a class 2 misdemeanor to: ▸ transplant or introduce fish or fish eggs into state public waters without Department authorization; ▸ import live fishes or viable eggs of the family salmonidae unless such importation complies with Department rules; ▸ empty the contents of a minnow bucket containing bait into state public waters (41-13-3, -3.1 and -4); ▸ transport bait or biological specimen animals from the state for resale without an export bait dealer license which allows the licensee to buy and possess bait and biological specimen animals within the state and to export/transport same without the state for resale (41-6-45.1).

Interstate Reciprocal Agreements

Taking of game, including any game bird or animal, in a river, lake or waters forming the boundary line between this and any other state at any time or in any manner prohibited by the laws of the adjoining state is a class 2 misdemeanor. The Department may enter into agreements with bordering states to provide for reciprocal recognition of licenses and permits and reciprocal enforcement of hunting, fishing, trapping and boating regulations (41-8-40).

ANIMAL DAMAGE CONTROL

The Department shall have the power and duty to engage in predatory animal control activities and to cooperate with federal agencies, other states and other state agencies or public corporations of this state in the execution of such control activities (41-2-30). Landowners or lessees, who represent to the Department that threatened or actual loss of domestic animals or livestock has occurred, may receive an aerial permit or contract with another to kill coyotes or foxes from their aircraft on their own land and up to two miles onto the land of their immediate adjoining neighbor with permission, or as otherwise authorized by a Department official (41-8-39.1). The Department is authorized to contract with aerial hunters to control foxes and coyotes when requested by landowners (41-8-39.2). Landowners need no license to kill raccoons, skunks, fox and badger doing damage on their lands (41-6-5). (See also Agency Powers and Duties under STATE FISH AND WILDLIFE AGENCIES and GENERAL EXCEPTIONS TO PROTECTION.) Whenever game animals, game birds, black bears, mountain lions or wolves are a threat to the public's health, safety and welfare, or doing damage to property, the Secretary may by written permit authorize a conservation officer or the landowner to take or kill such animals under permit restrictions. The Commission by resolution may authorize the Secretary to issue a specific number of depredation permits to respond to property damage by game animals which cannot be resolved by any other method, authorizing the permittee to kill game animals identified by the Department as causing property damage. The Secretary shall establish when and where each permit is valid and the number of game animals that may be killed under each permit. A permit violation is a class 1 misdemeanor (41-6-29).

It is a class 2 misdemeanor for a nonresident to hunt, take or kill jackrabbits, prairie dogs, gophers, ground squirrels, coyotes, red fox, grey fox, skunk, crow, porcupine or marmot without a nonresident predator license or in violation of license conditions or rules. No nonresident predator license is required to take the above listed animals if the person possesses a nonresident small game or big game license (41-6-30). It is a class 2 misdemeanor for a nonresident predator licensee to take, trap or kill a fur-bearing animal, except fox, coyote and skunk may be taken by shooting (41-8-22). Mink may be killed when doing damage around buildings, but all animals killed shall be state property if taken during the closed season. When muskrat or beaver are injuring irrigation ditches, dams, or public highways, the Director may issue a permit to trap or kill such animals. The Commission may authorize the killing or trapping of beaver upon public lands and game preserves (41-8-23).

ENFORCEMENT OF WILDLIFE LAWS

Enforcement Powers

The Department shall enforce the laws of this state involving the protection and propagation of all game animals, game birds, fish and harmless birds and animals (41-3-8 and 41-15-1). The courts and Conservation Officers shall have jurisdiction over the entire state boundary waters to the farthest shoreline, and concurrent jurisdiction with the courts and administrative officers of the adjoining states of Minnesota, North Dakota, Montana, Wyoming, and Nebraska over all boundary waters between such states is hereby recognized (41-15-2). It is the duty of the state's attorney, sheriff, constables and other peace officers to enforce state game and fish laws (41-15-3). Conservation

Officers have full power and authority to serve and execute all warrants regarding game and fish laws as any constable or sheriff may serve and execute same, or arrest, without warrant, a person detected in the act of violating game laws. Conservation Officers may call to their aid a peace officer or other persons (41-15-10). A properly certified Conservation Officer shall enforce every state statute which: is a crime under Title 22; pertains to game, fish, parks, forestry or boating; pertains to driving while intoxicated, reckless driving or eluding an officer. While performing their duties, Conservation Officers are law enforcement officers with the same authority as other law enforcement officers (41-15-10.1).

Persons possessing a game bird, animal or fish shall permit the inspection and count of same upon the request of an enforcement officer, and a motor vehicle may be stopped for such inspection and count by a uniformed law enforcement officer. Refusal to submit to inspection is a class 2 misdemeanor (41-15-6 and -7). The Department shall have charge of the seizure of and disposition of all game birds and animals taken or possessed contrary to law, and of all dogs, guns, seines, nets, boats, lights or other instrumentalities unlawfully used or held with intent to use in pursuing, taking, concealing or disposing of game. All law enforcement officers are authorized to seize and hold for evidence at trial any hunting and fishing equipment used in violation of the game and fish laws, to be returned after case disposition, or regarded as abandoned if not claimed within one year. A certified law enforcement officer may without warrant or process take, seize and destroy a net, seine, snare, device or contrivance used or maintained for illegally catching, taking, killing, attracting or deceiving a wild animal or fish. On complaint showing probable cause for believing that a bird, animal, fish or skin of fur-bearing animals or part thereof, caught, killed, possessed, shipped or transported contrary to law or concealed in a building, motor vehicle, or receptacle, any court may issue a search warrant therefor and cause such to be searched. A bird, animal, fish or skin illegally held shall be contraband and the Secretary, conservation officers, sheriffs, deputy sheriffs, constables and peace officers shall seize the same pending court action. Officers seizing/taking contraband shall without delay report all facts attending such seizure to the Secretary (41-15-14 through -19). Guns, implements or vehicles unlawfully used in the killing, taking or transporting of elk or buffalo one hour after sunset to one hour before sunrise during open season or closed season shall be deemed contraband and officers shall seize the same pending case determination (41-15-18.1). The Secretary shall sell contraband at the highest market price obtainable therefor for furs, fish, game animals, game birds, hunting and fishing equipment and other materials, such proceeds to go into the Department of Department of Game, Fish and Parks Fund (41-15-20).

Criminal Penalties

See HUNTING, FISHING and TRAPPING PROVISIONS; PROTECTED SPECIES OF WILDLIFE; Illegal Taking of Wildlife and License Revocations and Suspensions under this section.

Civil Liability

A person other than a minor under age 16 who willfully and unlawfully kills, takes, possesses an animal hereafter designated is liable to the state for the following damages: $5,000 for each elk or buffalo; $10,000 for each mountain goat or mountain sheep; $1,000 for each deer, antelope or bobcat. The return of the animal uninjured to the place where it was captured is discharge of such damages. These provisions do not apply to persons who, after giving two days written notice to the Department, take reasonable actions to protect their land or crops from serious and extraordinary damages caused by deer or antelope. Conviction of a criminal offense for the same incident leading to the charges in 41-1-5.1 and 41-1-5.3 through 41-1-5.5 shall be prima facie evidence of the defendant's civil liability. Failure to obtain criminal conviction is not a bar to a separate civil action for such liquidated damages. Fees to agents authorized to collect on a judgment under this section may not exceed 50% of the total amount collected. Damages to the state for unlawfully killing, taking or possessing a small game bird or wild turkey during a closed season or without a license is $100 for each small game bird or $200 for each turkey taken. Unlawful possession of five or more small game birds or two or more turkeys in excess of the legal limit is $100 for each game bird and $200 for each turkey taken in excess of the legal limit. Possession of five or more fish in excess of the daily/possession limit for a species with a daily limit less than ten fish is $50 civil liability damages to the state for each fish held in excess of the legal limit (41-1-5.1 through -5.5). ★A statement of liability provisions of the above sections shall be printed on the reverse side of citations given by arresting officers and a special receipt form is to be used to draw attention to these civil penalties (41-1-5.6).★

Illegal Taking of Wildlife

The unlawful taking, shipment, or possession of a game bird, animal or fish results in the forfeiture of the right of possession of such animal and the state shall be entitled to the sole possession thereof (41-1-5). Illegal taking of black bears, mountain lions, wolves, big game animals, illegal use of dogs in big game hunting, or illegal spotlighting of big game animals is a class 1 misdemeanor for each prohibited act or each big game animal or part thereof taken, killed, sold or in possession, or transported or offered for sale in violation of law. Upon conviction of a person for hunting or taking big game, except wild turkey, during the nighttime, during a closed season or without a license, the court shall revoke the person's hunting privileges for one year and shall impose a fine of not less than $250 for each animal involved and a minimum jail term of three days. A second or subsequent conviction is a class 6 felony, and the court shall revoke hunting privileges for five years (41-8-18).

It is a class 2 misdemeanor to have in possession or control a bird, animal or fish or part thereof which has been unlawfully taken, caught, or killed in this or any other state or foreign country or which has been unlawfully transported into this state. It is a class 1 misdemeanor to have in possession or control a big game animal or part thereof which has been unlawful taken, caught or killed in any other state or foreign country, or which has been unlawfully transported into this state (41-14-1). It is a class 1 misdemeanor to transport within the jurisdiction of the state a big game animal lawfully taken outside of South Dakota or upon tribal or trust land of an Indian reservation unless such animal is properly tagged or other lawful taking proof is provided by the license issuing government (41-14-33). It is a class 1 misdemeanor to transport any part of a big game animal without a transportation permit or in violation of permit conditions or Commission regulations; such permit allows transportation by common carrier, within or without the state of a part of any big game animal lawfully taken within the state (41-6-22). Possession or control by a person of a bird, animal or fish or part, the killing of which is prohibited, is prima facie evidence that it was state property when it was caught, taken or killed, and that it was caught, taken or killed in this state (41-14-2). Possession or control when the killing, taking, or possession thereof is by law declared to be unlawful, is prima facie evidence that the taking or killing occurred during the closed season. The person in possession must show that at the time the animal was taken it was taken lawfully either within or without the state and lawfully possesseed (41-14-3). Possession of the carcasses, skins, heads or antlers of more than one big game animal is prima facie evidence of violation of big game license provisions except by licensed taxidermists (41-14-11).

It is a class 2 misdemeanor for a public eating house to serve a guest any game, the taking or killing of which is prohibited by law, during the periods when the taking is prohibited except for introduced Chinese ringneck or English pheasant produced by a licensed breeder or game birds taken under chapter 41-10 (41-14-5 and -6). It is a class 1 misdemeanor to purchase, barter or sell the meat of a big game animal except that meat of elk sold by the Department may be resold. The skins, heads and antlers of a big game animal lawfully caught, taken, killed or possessed may be sold. It is unlawful to buy or sell antlers in the velvet state unless they are tagged according to Commission regulations. Violation: class 1 misdemeanor. Transportation of big game animals requires proper tagging and locking seal. It is a class 2 misdemeanor to have in possession or to buy, sell or ship the raw skins of protected fur-bearing animals taken within or without the state except as specifically provided. The possession/control of a raw skin of a protected fur-bearer or part thereof, shall be prima facie evidence that it was state property when taken, and that it was taken in this state. Possession/control of the raw skin of a protected fur-bearer during closed season for such animal is prima facie evidence that the taking occurred during the closed season, and the person in possession must show that it was lawfully taken and that he or she is in lawful possession thereof (41-14-12 through -20). Except as provided in this chapter, it is a class 2 misdemeanor for a common carrier to ship or transport within or without the state a protected fur-bearing animal or migratory bird (41-14-7 and -21). It is a class 2 misdemeanor to unlawfully take, possess, catch, kill, possess, ship or sell game birds, animals other than big game animals, or fish or part thereof in violation of a state law or Department rule, and each animal, bird, fish, or part thereof illegally held or shipped is a separate violation. For big game, each animal or part is a separate violation, which is a class 1 misdemeanor. The total imprisonment for violations of this section which occur at the same time may not exceed one year (41-14-32).

License Revocations and Suspensions

In any case of a game and fish law conviction of a felony or class 1 misdemeanor or a violation of 41-12-12 or 41-12-13 or a violation of any other law or regulation pertaining to fishing or hunting or possessing game without a license or during closed season, the court shall revoke the person's hunting, trapping or fishing privilege for one year and surrender of the license to the Department. It is a class 2 misdemeanor to fish, hunt or trap or attempt to purchase a license while under license revocation (41-6-74 and -75).

Reward Payments

The Department has authority to pay to any person furnishing information which shall cause the arrest and conviction of a person violating the game and fish laws relating to: ▸ deer and antelope or the killing of fish by explosives, $50; ▸ a game bird or fish or other protected animal, $10; ▸ American bison and elk belonging to the state, $150 (41-15-4). The Department can pay to any person for information leading to the location and seizure of any hoop net illegally used in state waters a sum not to exceed $2.50 for each such hoop net so located and seized (41-15-5).

HABITAT PROTECTION

★The Department may acquire by gift or lease from willing landowners the right to maintain unused, terminated or abandoned section-line rights-of-way for game production areas, excluding section lines where roads have never been developed. The roadways may be reopened for public travel. Every state political subdivision east of the Missouri River having highways or roadways under its jurisdiction which are undeveloped or not maintained as public highways may notify the Department of these, and shall cooperate with the Department in acquiring and maintaining such rights-of-way for use as game production areas. The sand and gravel islands formed in the Missouri River can be administered by the Secretary primarily for wildlife habitat or public recreation, or both, and the Secretary may also lease out contracts for sand and gravel taking.★ It is a class 2 misdemeanor to hunt within the limits of the boundaries of the "state game preserve" and game and bird refuges which may be hereafter established, or to carry a rifle, shotgun or other hunting firearm across such refuges unless enclosed in a case, and residents within refuges may carry firearms for killing nongame and predatory wildlife on their own premises within the refuge. It is the duty of Conservation Officers and state Forest Service members to enforce refuge provisions (41-5-7 through -11).

It is a class 2 misdemeanor to place chemicals to control plants in state public waters which contain game fish without explicit authority to do so from the Department, which may prescribe such rules as necessary to safeguard game fish and other animals (41-13-2). ★It is a class 1 misdemeanor to empty, place sawdust, manure, refuse matter, sedimentary materials, pollutants or chemicals in state waters containing fish and wildlife, or to deposit the same within such distance that it may be carried into such waters by natural causes except as expressly provided in this chapter. Persons who knowingly or willfully empty, place, discharge pollutants or chemicals into state waters are liable to the Department for an amount, to be deposited in the Department of Game, Fish and Parks Fund, which will compensate the state for restoration of fish and game losses (41-13-1). Agricultural producers are not liable for the result of normal farming practices if fish or wildlife kills occur (41-13-1.1).★

NATIVE AMERICAN WILDLIFE PROVISIONS

A special Pine Ridge Indian Reservation big game license is required for reservation hunting, and game taken must be properly tagged for transport (41-6-10 and 41-14-33).

TENNESSEE

Sources: Tennessee Code Annotated, 1987 Replacement Volume, Title 70; 1992 Cumulative Supplement.

STATE WILDLIFE POLICY

The ownership of and title to all forms of wildlife within the state, that are not lawful individual property, is declared to be in the state. A person taking wildlife shall consent that title shall be in the state for possession, use and transportation after such taking. The taking of any and all forms of wildlife at any time, in any manner, and by a person, shall be deemed a consent that the title to such wildlife shall be in the state for regulating its possession, use and transportation for the public welfare (70-4-101). (See also STATE FISH AND WILDLIFE AGENCIES.)

RELEVANT WILDLIFE DEFINITIONS: See Definitions section of Appendices.

STATE FISH AND WILDLIFE AGENCIES

Agency Structure

The **Wildlife Resources Commission** (Commission), an independent administrative board of conservation for game, fish and wildlife, consists of the Commissioners of Environment and Conservation and Agriculture, and nine state citizens appointed by the Governor who are well-informed on the conservation of state game animals, birds and fish. ★The Governor shall strive to ensure that at least one person serving on the Commission is at least 60 years old and that at least one person is a member of a racial minority. Members must be confirmed by the House Conservation and Environment Committee and the Senate Energy and Natural Resources Committee and by joint resolution of the General Assembly prior to taking office.★ Three of the members shall be appointed from each grand division of the state. Members serve six-year terms. Not more than one member shall be appointed from any one county. The Governor serves as an ex officio member of the Commission. All appointments shall be made from persons having the qualifications specified by 70-1-201, as determined by consultation with recognized conservation leaders in Tennessee. Commissioners are not eligible for consecutive reappointment (70-1-201, -203 and -204).

The **Wildlife Resources Agency** (Agency) has exclusive jurisdiction of the duties and functions relating to wildlife formerly held by the Game and Fish Commission or of any other law relating to management, protection, propagation and conservation, including hunting and fishing, except those duties conferred upon the Commission by this title. The state policy is that the Agency shall: ▸ be nonpartisan; ▸ place first and foremost the welfare of wildlife and its environment in its planning and decisions; ▸ encourage full development of the state's natural resources to the benefit of all Tennessee citizens; ▸ create a comprehensive long-range management plan to integrate the Agency's efforts and implement full utilization of Tennessee's wildlife resources consistent with realistic conservation principles (70-1-301). ★The **Executive Director of the Agency** (Director) is appointed by the Commission, with preference given to candidates with a bachelor of science degree in wildlife management practices and the administration of wildlife programs (70-1-303).★

Agency Powers and Duties

The **Commission** is authorized to: ▸ appoint and dismiss the **Executive Director** (Director); ▸ approve the budget; ▸ promulgate rules, regulations and proclamations as required; ▸ establish policy objectives enabling the Wildlife Resources Agency to develop, manage and maintain sound programs of hunting, fishing, trapping and other wildlife related outdoor recreation activities; ▸ promulgate regulations for the administration of the Reelfoot Lake Natural Area; ▸ become knowledgeable in the special needs of handicapped and disabled veterans (70-1-206.).

The **Agency** is authorized to make expenditures from the Wildlife Resources Fund under Title 9, and to protect, propagate, increase, preserve and conserve state wildlife and enforce existing laws. The Agency may acquire by purchase, condemnation, lease, gift or devise, lands or waters for: ▸ fish hatcheries and nursery ponds; ▸ game, bird, fish, or fur-bearing animal restoration, and propagation, protection, and management; ▸ access for public hunting, fishing or trapping areas; ▸ protection, preservation and enhancement of Reelfoot Lake. The Agency may: ▸ extend and consolidate by exchange lands or waters suitable for the above purposes; ▸ capture, propagate, transport, buy, sell or exchange a species of game, fish, bird, fur-bearing animal or other wildlife and exercise control measures for undesirable species; ▸ enter into cooperative arrangements with landowners for utilization of their lands for protecting, propagating, conserving, restoring, taking or capturing state wildlife under Agency regulations; ▸ enter into cooperative agreements with state, federal and educational institutions to promote wildlife management and conservation. The Agency may enter into cooperative agreements with the USTVA, USFW, NPS, USFS or with any state to regulate fishing, hunting or trapping in areas under jurisdiction of federal agencies or the state or in interstate waters. The Agency may require creel census reports and reports of mussels and fish taken under commercial licenses (70-1-302).

The **Director** shall: ▸ be head of the Agency under the direction and supervision of the Commission; ▸ serve as Commission recording secretary; ▸ publish wildlife resources laws in pamphlet form for distribution and information; ▸ perform duties as prescribed by the Commission, but without authority to make rules or regulations other than those relating to employee conduct (70-1-304). The Director has the power to: ▸ enforce wildlife laws and go upon property, outside of buildings, posted or otherwise, in the performance of duties; ▸ execute all warrants, search warrants and subpoenas issued for the violation of wildlife laws; ▸ arrest without warrant a person found in the act of violating wildlife provisions of this title; ▸ enforce any other law as directed by the legislature; ▸ designate Agency employees and officers of another state or the federal government who are full-time wildlife enforcement personnel to perform duties and have powers prescribed herein; ▸ arrest without warrant a person observed dumping or throwing litter or debris in the lakes, waters or on public property; ▸accept gifts of personal property on behalf of the Agency; ▸ arrest without warrant a person violating the prohibited uses of waters posted pursuant to 69-3-107. ★In view of the vast expanse of isolated wildlife habitat extant throughout the state, and to facilitate the effective protection of public and private rights and property, particularly in, but not limited to, these isolated areas, the Director shall be vested with the authority to arrest without warrant or process a person committing or attempting to commit a criminal offense in violation of state laws if the offense is committed on public lands, rights-of-way or waters under the Agency's management or control through lease, cooperative agreement or otherwise (70-1-305).★ The Director must prepare for the Governor and each member of the Commission an annual report showing Agency expenditures, moneys received and sources (70-1-307).

Agency Funding Sources

The expenses incurred by the Agency shall be limited to the amount of money in the **Wildlife Resources Fund** (Fund), and in no event shall the state pay such expenses or be liable in any manner, except to the extent of the Fund. Purchases of real property shall be made in the name of the state. The Commission shall approve the budget for each fiscal year. The Agency shall not contract indebtedness beyond the funds available to its use, which shall be drawn by the Director by warrant upon the Department of Finance and Administration (70-1-306). Moneys sent to the state treasury in payment of licenses, contraband, fines, penalties and forfeitures arising from state wildlife resources laws shall constitute the Fund, to be used for: ▸ payment of the Agency's expenses; ▸ payment of personnel salaries and expenses; ▸ purchasing lands for wildlife resources farms; reservations; management, fishing and access areas; fish hatcheries and rearing ponds; ▸ constructing buildings, ponds, and propagation pens and purchasing and propagating wildlife and essentials to restock or maintain wildlife resources farms and other facilities; ▸ promotion, advancement and efficient management of wildlife, including educational activities. No funds realized from the sale of licenses, contraband, fines, penalties, forfeitures or from privilege taxes levied under this title shall be used for other purposes than those set out nor diverted to the general fund. Interest accruing on Fund investments and deposits shall be returned to the Fund (70-1-401).

★★Persons, firms and corporations engaged in the business of buying, selling, distributing, storing, receiving, having in possession or using shotgun shells or metallic cartridges, shall pay a special privilege tax in addition to other taxes in an amount equal to ten cents per individual container upon all center-fire ammunition, shotgun shells, and rim-fire ammunition, to be applied to the Wildlife Resources Fund (70-3-101).★★ The tax shall be paid and the stamps affixed by the entity first having possession and ownership of the ammunition. The Agency may employ bonded agents to sell stamps for a 2% commission or may sell the stamps directly. Dealers in ammunition and common carriers delivering ammunition in the state must keep detailed records of transactions and permit inspection of ammunition, stamps or records by the Director (70-3-102 through -105). It is unlawful to sell or display for sale, or to possess for sale or gift, ammunition which does not have the required stamp properly affixed. The Commission may make rules allowing ammunition to remain unstamped when it is to be sold out of state. It is the legislative intent not to cause manufacturers, jobbers and wholesalers manufacturing ammunition unnecessary inconvenience in affixing stamps to boxes of ammunition, and the Commission may make reasonable regulations concerning the time, method and place the stamps shall be affixed. It is unlawful for a dealer to sell ammunition at a greater price than the retail price noted on the affixed stamp, such stamps to be printed and distributed by the Agency. Counterfeiting, forging, or altering ammunition stamps, or unlawful use is a misdemeanor. Ammunition held, owned or possessed in avoidance, evasion or violation of the tax provisions are declared to be contraband goods and the title forfeited to the state, and it is the duty of the Director or deputies to seize the same, and the ammunition shall be sold to the highest bidder with proceeds to go to the Wildlife Resources Fund. Agency officers, sheriffs, and other peace officers charged with enforcement of state laws are required to enforce the provisions of the Ammunition Tax chapter. The Director shall administer the tax provisions, the costs of stamps and other expenses to be paid from the funds collected (70-3-107 through -113).

Agency Advisory Boards

To enhance and protect the state's mussel industry, the governor is authorized to appoint a five-member group of mussel industry representatives to advise the Commission and state agencies on policy development and enforcement matters, their terms to run concurrently with that of the Governor (70-2-223). (See also Commercial and Private Enterprise Provisions under HUNTING, FISHING, TRAPPING PROVISIONS.)

PROTECTED SPECIES OF WILDLIFE

★★Live wildlife, kept and maintained for any purpose, shall be classified into five classes with included species specified by statute: ▸ Class I - species inherently dangerous to humans, which only may be possessed by zoos, circuses and commercial propagators except as otherwise provided; ▸ Class II - all native species except those listed in other classes; Class III - all species not listed in other classes, subject to additions or deletions by the Commission; ▸ Class IV - native species that may be possessed only by zoos and temporary exhibitors, provided that rehabilitation facilities may possess Class IV wildlife as provided by Commission rules and as authorized by the Director; ▸ Class V - species that the Commission in conjunction with the Commissioner of Agriculture may designate as injurious to the environment and which may be only held in zoos under conditions preventing escape (70-4-403).★★

The Agency shall issue permits for possessing live wildlife, and the Commission shall adopt rules for the permits and for establishing conditions to insure the health, welfare and safety of animals and the public. The Director may authorize possession of a class of wildlife for research studies or for temporary holding of animals in the interest of public safety. ★Details of the classes of permits and qualifications of applicants to possess live wildlife are in the statutes, including the requirement of a written examination covering basic knowledge of habits and requirements in regard to proper diet, health care, exercise and housing of species to be covered by the permit (70-4-404).★ [Housing and transportation of wildlife requirements, liability for escape, transfer to new owners/facilities, and keeping of records are detailed in the statutes 70-4-405 through 70-4-409.] Owners of unpermitted wildlife who do not qualify for a permit shall dispose of it to an approved recipient on 30 days notice by the Agency. Each day of possession after this period is a separate violation (70-4-408). A violation of a provision or Commission rule regarding captive wildlife is a Class A misdemeanor; in the court's discretion in lieu of, or in addition to, a fine or jail sentence, or both, the permit may be revoked and no new permit issued for up to three years. Wildlife held illegally or in unsafe or inhumane conditions may be seized and sold at public sale or retained by the Agency for educational purposes after final case disposition (70-4-415).

It is unlawful to operate without a permit a private wildlife preserve for propagating and/or hunting any class of wildlife reared in captivity. It is lawful to hunt approved species of pen-reared and farm-reared animals on such a preserve without a hunting license (70-4-413).

The Legislature declares that: ▸ it is the state policy to manage certain nongame wildlife to insure their perpetuation as members of ecosystems, for scientific purposes, and for human enjoyment; ▸ species or subspecies of the state's indigenous wildlife found to be endangered or threatened within the state should be accorded protection in order to maintain and to the extent possible enhance their numbers; ▸ the state should assist in the protection of species or subspecies of wildlife which are endangered or threatened elsewhere by prohibiting the taking, possession, transportation, exportation, processing, sale or offer for sale or shipment within this state of species or subspecies of wildlife listed on the US List of Endangered Fish and Wildlife unless such actions will assist in preserving or propagating the species or subspecies; ★▸ adequate funding shall be made available to the Agency annually by appropriations from the general fund or from other sources for management of nongame and endangered species (70-8-102).★

The Director shall conduct investigations on nongame wildlife to develop information about population, distribution, habitat, needs, limiting factors, and biological and ecological data to determine management measures to sustain them and to develop programs designed to insure the continued ability of nongame, endangered or threatened wildlife to perpetuate themselves. Proposed regulations shall set forth species or subspecies of nongame wildlife in need of management, giving common and scientific names by species or subspecies. The Director may recommend amendments to such regulations by adding or deleting species or subspecies of nongame wildlife. The Commission by regulation shall establish limitations relating to habitat, alteration, taking, possession, transportation, exportation, processing, sale or shipment necessary to manage nongame wildlife. Except as provided in Commission regulations, it is unlawful to take, possess, transport, export, process, sell or ship nongame wildlife, or for a common or contract carrier knowingly to transport or receive such for shipment (70-8-104). Violation of these provisions or regulations issued under 70-8-104, or failure to procure or violation of permit terms is a Class B misdemeanor (70-8-108).

The Director shall establish programs, including acquisition of land or aquatic habitat, to manage nongame and endangered or threatened wildlife, including entering into agreements with federal agencies, private persons or state political subdivisions for administration and management of an area established or used for wildlife management, and shall encourage other state agencies in their furtherance of these provisions. The Director may permit the taking, possession, exportation or shipment of endangered or threatened species for scientific, zoological, or educational purposes or for propagation in captivity. Upon good cause and where necessary to alleviate damage to property or to protect human health and safety, endangered or threatened species may be removed, captured or destroyed but only pursuant to a permit issued by the Director and under Agency supervision. Endangered or threatened species may be removed, captured or destroyed without permit in emergency situations involving an immediate threat to human life. The Director shall issue regulations for removal, capture or destruction of nongame wildlife (70-8-106). A violation of the provisions of 70-8-106 relating to permits to take endangered or threatened species for scientific, zoological or educational purposes, for captive propagation or other specific purposes, is a Class A misdemeanor. An officer authorized by the Director or a state peace officer may conduct warrantless searches as provided by law, and execute a warrant to search for and seize equipment, business records or wildlife taken, used or possessed illegally. The officer may arrest without a warrant a person who the officer has probable cause to believe is violating, in the officer's presence, a law, regulation or permit relating to nongame and endangered species, and may search and seize wildlife, records or property used in connection with the violation, such wildlife to be transferred to a zoological, educational or scientific institution for safekeeping, costs assessable to the defendant (70-8-108).

GENERAL EXCEPTIONS TO PROTECTION

It is lawful for the USFW Director and agents to take from state public waters all fish required for operation of state and federal hatcheries, and the USFW shall be exempt from state game law provisions, and may conduct fish hatching and fish culture operations in any manner at any time (70-4-121). The Director may permit a reliable person to take, capture and transport wild birds, nests and eggs, and wild animals and fishes, to be used for purely scientific purposes. Permits shall specify the number of a species to be taken. Permittees must report the number and disposition of the collections. Violation: $25-100 fine; and voiding of permit (70-2-213). (See also Agency Powers and Duties under STATE FISH AND WILDLIFE AGENCIES; HUNTING, FISHING, TRAPPING PROVISIONS; and PROTECTED SPECIES OF WILDLIFE.)

HUNTING, FISHING, TRAPPING PROVISIONS

General Provisions

It is unlawful to hunt, kill, trap, ensnare, or destroy, or possess wildlife, or attempt such, except subject to the restrictions, means, devices and time prescribed by this title. Violations of Commission rules and regulations are punishable as provided in this title, and the illegal taking or possession of each bird, animal or fish shall constitute a separate offense. Violation: misdemeanor; fine $25-50 (70-4-102). Wild animals, birds, or wild fowl lawfully taken may be possessed or in storage by legal license holders during an open season, but never more than the possession limit prescribed by the Commission. Violation: misdemeanor; fine $25-50 (70-4-105).

It is unlawful to hunt, kill, or trap a wild animal, bird, fowl or fish upon the land of another without the owner's permission. Violation: Class C misdemeanor; court may revoke license. It is unlawful to hunt game upon lands posted "Hunting By Written Permission Only" without having written permission on one's person or unless accompanied by the landowner. Violation: Class C misdemeanor; court may revoke license. Provisions are to be enforced by Agency officers, sheriffs and other state peace officers (70-4-106).

★★There is a closed season for hunting and fishing upon wildlife protected by state laws. When the supply of game and/or fish existing in any area, lake or stream is adequate to allow taking without material danger of extinction or undue depletion of the game or fish, it is lawful to hunt and/or fish in the area within the creel, size and bag limits, and in the manner and by the means prescribed by the Commission. The adequacy of the supply of game and/or fish for taking without danger of extinction or undue depletion shall be determined by the Commission, after a complete survey of the area. When sufficient supplies exist, the Commission shall announce by proclamation the species of game and/or fish which may be taken, and the dates/hours they may be taken. Upon such announcement, it is lawful within the designated area to take designated game or fish. Proclamations become effective 30 days after filing with the Secretary of State. During emergency conditions, seasons may be closed, reopened or extended summarily. The Commission shall publish annually a list of destructive and/or unprotected wildlife. During an open season the provisions of general game and fish laws shall remain in force. The open season on private lakes may be set by the owner, but creel limits on fish caught from such lakes shall not exceed that for public waters. The Commission may establish open seasons, bag and creel limits for the taking of game and fish on state lands, including lands leased by the state for wildlife management, and may make regulations to enforce these provisions. Violation: Class B misdemeanor (70-4-107).★★

Licenses and Permits

It is unlawful to hunt wildlife in the open season without the license prescribed. A federal migratory waterfowl stamp is required for a person over age 16. Violation: misdemeanor; fine $10-25. Before hunting, fishing or trapping every person shall possess a license in accordance with the schedules in this title, except as otherwise provided. Violation: Class C misdemeanor (70-2-102).

Every person born on or after January 1, 1969, shall possess proof of completion of an Agency approved hunter education course, except persons under age 10 who are accompanied by an adult at least age 21, or persons hunting on their own land. "Accompanied" means being able to take immediate control of the hunting device. Violation is suspension of hunting privileges and loss of license until proof of satisfactory completion of an approved hunter education course. ★The State Board of Education is encouraged to develop a section related to hunter education as a part of its safety education curriculum (70-2-108).★

Residents need no fishing license to fish in their county of legal residence, if they use only hook and line, or a single trotline with up to 50 hooks, and natural or cut bait. A license is required to fish: ► outside one's county of legal residence, if minnows or artificial lures are used; ► in a state lake or state-owned wildlife management area; ► for lake trout. Violation: Class C misdemeanor. Owners and tenants of farm lands actually residing on such lands, and their dependent children, may hunt and fish subject to state wildlife laws during lawful seasons without a hunting and sport fishing license. Violation: Class C misdemeanor (70-2-203 and -204).

★In a premiere tourist resort city, a special permit for trout fishing is required in addition to a state license. A "premiere tourist resort city" is one having a population of 2,500 or more based on latest census, in which at least 40% of the assessed tax valuation consists of hotels, motels, tourist courts, tourist shops and restaurants. The Commission may pay to the premiere tourist resort city an amount not to exceed the permit fees collected (less the state license fee) for the cost incurred by the city for the stocking of trout (70-2-219).★

Restrictions on Taking: Hunting and Trapping

It is unlawful to use a pitfall, deadfall, cage, snare, trap, net, baited hook, poison, chemical, explosive, set gun, spotlight, electric light or torch, bait (including grain), or other device for killing or capturing protected birds or animals, except as otherwise expressly provided. Violation: Class C misdemeanor. Spot, electric or torch lights may be used in the hunting and taking raccoons, opossums and frogs, and box traps may be used to take rabbits during the open season. (See also ANIMAL DAMAGE CONTROL.) It is unlawful to: ▸ disturb, mutilate, or destroy the home, nest or den of a protected wild animal or bird; ▸ use a spear or like device in hunting or taking protected wild animals; ▸ blind with lights, except as provided in 70-4-113; ▸ use explosives, chemicals, or mechanical devices or smokers to drive protected wild animals out of their dens, holes or houses. Violation: Class C misdemeanor (70-4-114). It is unlawful to be in possession of firearms, bow and arrow, shotgun or rifle, while traversing a refuge, public hunting area or wildlife management area inhabited by big game except during lawful open seasons. A violator is deemed guilty of hunting big game. Violation: Class B misdemeanor. ★It is mandatory for the court to impose the prison sentence for a second/subsequent offense, and the sentence shall not be suspended. For first or subsequent offenders, the court shall revoke license for one year (70-4-117).★

Foxes may be chased with dogs the entire year, except for periods which the Commission fixes for the protection of the species. Illegal taking of a fox is a Class C misdemeanor (70-4-103). It is lawful to chase raccoons with dogs but no raccoon shall be killed or taken except during the open season. No raccoon shall be shot from a boat or motor vehicle. The Commission shall establish a minimum six-month training season for "coon" dogs within certain counties, and shall establish a minimum raccoon hunting season of six weeks each year, and may extend either the training season or hunting season based on the raccoon population of an area. Violation is a Class C misdemeanor and prohibition from hunting, chasing or trapping for one year (70-4-112). No person knowingly shall hunt deer being chased by dogs, nor permit a dog to hunt/chase deer. Agency officers may capture a dog known to have hunted deer and give notice to, or advertise for, the owner who may reclaim the dog within 10 days; if not claimed, the dog is deemed a public nuisance and ownerless and shall be destroyed. Violation: Class B misdemeanor; court is mandated to impose the prison sentence, and the minimum time shall not be subject to suspension, but may be served on such days as judge designates (70-4-118). It is lawful to train bird dogs through the use of release pens and tamed and identified quail under Commission regulations (70-4-120).

It is unlawful and a Class C misdemeanor to: ▸ hunt big game with a bow and arrow while in possession of firearms or to be accompanied by a person possessing firearms during the archery-only deer season (70-4-123); ▸ deposit or place out of doors on the property of another a poisonous substance or any matter rendered poisonous which is capable of causing death or injury to wildlife, hunting dogs, or domestic animals, except for rabies control activities of public health officials; ▸ use an electronic or battery operated device for luring or killing a fox, or attempting such, except for rabies control activities of public health officials (70-4-125 and -126); ▸ bait a field or other area by the intentional placement of grain or other mixture for killing, injuring, or capturing doves. Baiting does not include sowing of grain in normal agricultural practice, the placement of salt for livestock, or leaving standing crops in the field. Baiting the fields of another is criminal trespass and a Class C misdemeanor. Agency officers who suspect that a field has been baited shall post the field prohibiting hunting. If the officer discovers baiting but fails to post the field, no person shall be subject to prosecution for hunting on the field. Agency officials are exempt from civil liability in the enforcement of this section (70-4-127 and -128).

It is unlawful and a Class C misdemeanor to: ▸ hunt, chase or catch wild animals, birds or fowl from a public right of way, or to shoot firearms across or on a public road, or within 100 yards of a visible dwelling house, whether on public or private lands, without the owners permission; ▸ chase or hunt wild birds, animals or fowl from a craft propelled by electric, gasoline, steam or sail power, an airplane or hydroplane or an automobile or motor vehicle. Persons confined to wheelchairs may hunt or kill wildlife from a stationary automobile or motor vehicle during the lawful hunting season, but may not shoot across a road, and must be accompanied by another person who shall retrieve all game taken. It is unlawful to throw or cast willfully the rays of a spotlight, headlight, or other artificial light from a motor vehicle or vessel on a highway or in a field, woodland, or forest or state waters in an attempt to locate deer. Violation: Class B misdemeanor; the court shall prohibit first or subsequent offenders from hunting, fishing or trapping for one year (70-4-108 through -110).

It is unlawful to set or bait a trap or snare upon the lands or waters of a person to catch or kill a wild animal, except during open season, and then only with written consent of the landowner, provided that nets, spring poles and deadfalls are prohibited. Steel traps placed about a hole, cave or den or hollow log shall be placed 12 inches or more within the entrance. It is unlawful to place steel traps in the open except for water sets. Cushion-hold traps may be placed in the open with the written permission of the landowner. All traps shall be inspected and animals removed within each 36-hour period. Trappers shall make the landowner a written report at once of livestock, fowls or dogs caught in traps, and shall be liable for all damages done by traps. Traps must be labeled with the trapper's name; unlabeled traps are to be confiscated. Trapping and cable snare traps of any diameter are banned in certain counties. Violation: Class C misdemeanor, and prohibition from trapping or fur selling/buying for a minimum of one year (70-4-120). A permit is required to take, transport, import or possess raptors for falconry in accordance with Commission regulations, such permit to be supplemental to other hunting permits and licenses. A written examination is required (70-4-414).

Restrictions on Taking: Fishing

Taking fish, mussels, turtles and other aquatic animal life, other than game fish species, from state waters is prohibited, except that: ▸ all varieties of fish, mussels, turtles and other aquatic animal life may be sold commercially subject to Commission regulations; ▸ the Commission shall designate waters, types of gear, and regulations for commercial taking of fish and other aquatic life; ▸ possession of unauthorized or unlicensed gear is forbidden; ▸ wildlife accidentally taken by a commercial operation shall be released with the least possible injury; ▸ commercial gear must be tagged with Agency tags; ▸ the Commission may make regulations as to the use of slat baskets by sport fishing license holders. Violation is a Class B misdemeanor and prohibition from engaging in sport or commercial fishing for one year minimum. It is unlawful to use or possess dynamite, electrical devices, explosives, chemicals, lime or poison to kill or stun fish, or attempt to do so. A violation is a Class B misdemeanor and each fish killed and each stick of dynamite or dynamite cap used is a separate offense (70-4-119).

Fish may be taken with rod and reel, by hook and line held in the hand, by not more than three poles constantly attended or by one or more trotlines not having a combination of more than 100 hooks, and must be attended once each day. Use or possession of any other instrument for killing, catching, or taking fish or other aquatic life is forbidden except as provided in this title or by Commission regulation (70-4-104). It is unlawful to use nets, seines, snag or drag lines, grab hooks, baskets or other fishing equipment, or other obstruction to the free passage of fish within 100 yards of the mouth of a river, creek, slough, inlet or outlet, except bait or casting plugs with not more than three treble hooks, and ordinary fly fishing equipment or pole and line with not more than three single hooks attached. The "mouth of a stream" is defined by statute. Violation: Class C misdemeanor (70-4-211).

Commercial and Private Enterprise Provisions

A person, firm or corporation engaged in commercial fishing, a musseler, commercial helper, wholesale fish dealer, boat dock operator, fur dealer, professional dog trainer and taxidermist must be licensed to conduct operations and must submit required reports and permit inspections by Commission authorities. Violation of fur dealer provisions: Class C misdemeanor; conviction of a second or subsequent offense within one year is license revocation for one year and sentence to the county jail/workhouse. The sentence may be suspended if violator purchases the required license(s). Violation of taxidermy provisions: misdemeanor; fine $10-25. (70-2-205, -206, -208, and -215). It is unlawful to purchase, receive for sale or have in possession for commercial purposes green hides, raw furs or pelts of wild animals without a license. Violation: misdemeanor; fine $25-50 (70-2-209). Hunting dog trainers must have a hunting license except when competing in recognized field trials. Field trials for raccoon dogs, rabbit dogs, foxhounds and bird dogs are permitted only under Commission regulations. Violation: misdemeanor; fine $25-50 (70-2-214).

A fish dealer license is required for bait dealers (persons who capture legal species of fish or other aquatic life for sale as bait); fish farming (the business of rearing for sale legal species of fish and other aquatic life); and catch-out operations (making legal species of fish placed in a pond or tank available to persons wishing to buy them; fish must be reared fish or wild commercial fish obtained legally and approved by the Agency). These businesses must report to the Commission which may seize and destroy diseased fish or minnows, and must operate according to Commission regulations. Violation: misdemeanor; fine $25-50 (70-2-221). ★Persons who buy or obtain freshwater mussels for export from Tennessee shall pay to the Agency the amount equal to $.0145 per pound of shells or $0.0124 per pound of mussels (shells with meat). Revenues shall be used for mussel management, research and up to 25% maximum for enforcement. Violation: Class A misdemeanor (70-2-222).★ ★Pearl culturing in public waters requires a license, and no nonresident shall be granted a license if the nonresident's state or country prohibits Tennessee residents from engaging in the business of culturing pearls. The Director shall select five people for a committee that will include the Director, the Director's representative, the Chief of Fisheries, a fisheries biologist and two industry representatives to assist in the initial drafting of rules and regulations (70-2-220).★ (See also PROTECTED SPECIES OF WILDLIFE.)

Import, Export and Release Provisions

Persons desiring to stock wildlife shall obtain a permit from the Director. Approved USFW applications for fish are sufficient permits. The Agency may inspect all live fish entering the state and destroy any diseased shipment (70-2-212). It is unlawful to import, possess, or cause to be imported a live skunk, or to sell, barter, exchange or otherwise transfer a live skunk; provisions do not apply to zoological parks and research institutions. Violation: Class C misdemeanor (70-4-208). It is unlawful to buy or sell green hides, raw furs or pelts of a red fox, except as provided and/or in counties open to the lawful taking of red fox. Violation: Class C misdemeanor. ★When a red fox is legally killed, it is lawful to buy or sell its green hide, raw fur or pelt in counties with certain specified population, according to the most recent census (70-4-209).★

It is lawful to buy, sell, store, or ship for sale the hides of deer and the pelts and tails of grey and fox squirrels taken during the open season (70-4-210). It is unlawful to possess, transport, import, export, buy, sell, barter, propagate or transfer any wildlife, except as provided by law and Commission regulations. No person shall possess Class I (wildlife inherently dangerous to humans) or Class II (native species) wildlife without documents showing the supplier's name, address and date of acquisition (70-4-401). It is unlawful to release any class of wildlife except in accordance with Commission rules. The importation of Class I and II wildlife requires a permit and Agency notification within five days of importation. An importation permit is required for all interstate movement of live wildlife except Class III (other species); no permit is required for zoos or temporary exhibitors (70-4-411 and -412). (See also PROTECTED SPECIES OF WILDLIFE for animal classifications.

Interstate Reciprocal Agreements

See Agency Powers and Duties under STATE FISH AND WILDLIFE AGENCIES.

ANIMAL DAMAGE CONTROL

The Director and agents may use any chemical, biological substance, poison or device under controlled conditions to capture or kill a bird or animal for scientific, propagating, enforcement, humane or rescue purposes or to reduce or control a species that may be detrimental to human safety, health or property. The Director shall take no action to control rabies or other diseases spread from wildlife to human beings without: ▸ approval by the county board of health in the affected county; ▸ establishment of an official quarantine on all dogs, cats and pets in the county; ▸ an official request for help from the county board to bring the disease under control (70-4-113). Landowners may destroy wild animals, birds, or fowl that are are destroying their property. A landowner must have an Agency permit to destroy big game. Destroyed big game, or a wild bird or animal killed accidentally or illegally, is state property and may be disposed of by the Agency by gift to a worthy recipient. Big game killed by motor vehicles may be possessed only by Agency permit. Violation: Class C misdemeanor (70-4-115). The Director and agents may use any substance or chemical or device to stun or kill fish for scientific, propagating, enforcement or rescue purposes, and may use poison in certain state waters or lakes when necessary to remove/eradicate undesirable species of fish (70-4-119). (See also Agency Powers and Duties under STATE FISH AND WILDLIFE AGENCIES; HABITAT PROTECTION; PROTECTED SPECIES OF WILDLIFE; EXCEPTIONS TO PROTECTION.)

ENFORCEMENT OF WILDLIFE LAW

Enforcement Powers

[The misdemeanor provisions in this title may have been affected by the Criminal Sentencing Reform Act of 1989. See sections 39-11-114, 40-35-110, 40-35-111 for details of penalties.]

The Director or Agency officers, or officers of another state or the federal government, who are designated wildlife enforcement personnel, shall enforce all laws enacted for propagation and preservation of state wildlife, and shall prosecute violators. The officers shall seize wild animals, fowls, and birds, and fish, frogs and other aquatic animal life, or parts, that have been killed or taken, possessed, shipped, or transported from another state illegally. It is the duty of every person taking or possessing wildlife to permit Agency officers to ascertain whether title and license requirements are being complied with. Obstruction of an officer in such an inspection or count is a misdemeanor; fine $25-50. Search of a person's dwelling or place of business requires a search warrant. The Commission is to provide by regulation a system for issuing warning citations (70-6-101). (See also Agency Powers and Duties under STATE FISH AND WILDLIFE AGENCIES.)

Each wild animal, wild bird, wild fowl or fish caught, killed, shipped, transported, possessed or sold, and each trap, snare, net or other device used illegally constitutes a separate offense, and unless otherwise provided shall be punishable by a $25-50 fine. Violation of provisions of this title for which a penalty has not been expressly provided shall be a Class C misdemeanor; in a corporation, every participating officer and/or agent shall be guilty and punished as stated. Whoever aids, abets, counsels, commands, induces or procures the commission of a violation of this title or regulations is punishable as a principal (70-1-102 through -104). ★In a prosecution for title violations, it shall not be a defense that the person killing, taking, selling, shipping or storing animals, fish or birds was mistaken as to its variety, sex, age or size, it being one of the purposes of this section to penalize recklessness resulting in the violation of its provisions (70-6-105).★

Magistrates or court clerks shall report all fines and forfeitures collected on a monthly basis, shall retain 10% of those funds, and shall pay one-half of the balance to Wildlife Resources Fund and one-half to the county in which the fine/forfeiture was collected (70-6-106). ★The grand juries of the several counties shall inquire into to offenses which are punishable by a fine of more than $50 or by imprisonment (70-6-107). ★

Agency officers, sheriffs and deputies shall seize all furs, fish, wild animals, wild birds, guns, rods, reels, nets, creels, boats or other instruments, tackle or devices which have been used, transported or possessed illegally and take them before the court trying the arrested person. Courts may issue a search warrant on probable cause that protected wild animals, birds or fish are being illegally kept in a building, car or receptacle and cause such to be searched. Contraband animals or devices shall be advertised and sold by the Director at the courthouse of the county where the offense was committed upon final case disposition, except that prohibited devices shall be destroyed. Sale proceeds go into the Wildlife Resources Fund (70-6-201). ★A firearm, equipment, appliance, or conveyance used in violation of 70-4-116 through 70-4-118, including a truck, automobile, boat, airplane or other vehicle in which a deer, bear or wild boar is located, or which is used to transport the animals illegally, is declared contraband and shall be confiscated and forfeited to the state. A motor vehicle seized as contraband and forfeited to the state shall be sold at public sale. When a verdict of not guilty is rendered the Director shall have the right to appeal to the county circuit court where the verdict was rendered for a hearing de novo (a new hearing) solely on the question of the propriety of the property seizure (70-6-202).★

Illegal Taking of Wildlife

Types of ammunition and firearms are designated for the taking of deer, bear or wild boar. ★It is unlawful to hunt, transport or store a deer, wild turkey, bear or wild boar other than as designated. This does not apply when when proof is presented to the Director or to the court that such game has been killed outside state boundaries. Possession of such game in a closed season or boundary area except as provided by statute is prima facie evidence of guilt. These designated animals must be properly tagged immediately after taking. Violation: Class B misdemeanor. It is mandatory for the court to impose the prison sentence on conviction for a second or subsequent offense; the sentence may not be suspended, and the court shall prohibit either first or subsequent offenders from hunting, fishing or trapping for one year.★ The Commission may issue special quota tags for certain species or sexes requiring limited harvest, and may grant landowners special consideration in the issuance of tags. Violation: Class C misdemeanor. When a person illegally or improperly kills or possesses a dead deer, bear, wild turkey or wild hog, the Agency may also seek civil damages which are payable to the Agency and shall not be less than $200 for each deer, bear, wild turkey or wild hog so killed or possessed (70-4-116). It is a Class B misdemeanor to hunt or kill big game during the closed season (70-4-111).

It is unlawful for a person, firm, restaurant, club or hotel to barter, sell, transfer or offer to purchase wildlife, except as provided in this title or in regulations. Each wild animal, bird, or fowl, or game fish, or part sold, offered for sale, transferred or unlawfully possessed, constitutes a separate offense. A person who hires another to kill wild birds or animals and then receives them shall be subject to the penalties of this title. ★Agency officers or persons specially employed by the Director or by the USFW may buy, sell, or offer wild birds or wild animals or parts for the sole purpose of obtaining evidence of violation of this title.★   The carcasses of a lawful possession limit of opossum, raccoon, or beaver may be bought, sold or shipped for sale during the open hunting/trapping season. Violation: Class A misdemeanor. A person who makes use of or has in possession wild animals or their green hides, wild birds, wild fowl or fish, or parts, which have been caught, taken, killed or destroyed illegally shall be equally liable under these provisions for the penalties imposed against the person who caught, took, or destroyed such wild animals, hides, birds or fish (70-4-201 and -202).

Persons may take protected game or fish out of the state if they: ► possess at the time of transporting a hunting or fishing license; ► take from the state no more than two days' bag or creel limit on ducks or other migratory birds or protected game or fish; ► file with a common carrier a statement giving name, address, license number, and number of game/fish to be transported, and that such were legally killed by the person and are not for sale. Agency officers have the right to inspect licenses and a refusal to comply is a misdemeanor. It is unlawful for a person or common carrier to ship/transport birds, game or fish without ascertaining that the shipper has a hunting/fishing license. Violation: Class C misdemeanor. No person shall place in cold storage at one time more than two days' bag or creel limit of wild animals, birds, fowl or game fish, nor place such in storage without filing an affidavit stating that they have been killed lawfully and are stored for the person's own use and are not for sale; no cold storage operation shall receive wild animals, birds or game fish without such affidavit being posted in a book open to examination by Agency officers. Violation: Class C misdemeanor (70-4-203 and -204).

License Revocations and Suspensions

On conviction of an offense under this title or any Commission regulation, the court may revoke the license and/or suspend the fishing, hunting or trapping privileges of the licensee for not less than one year.   ★A violation of a revocation order is a minimum $25 fine, and jail or workhouse 10 days to 11 months and 29 days; it is mandatory for the court to impose the prison sentence, and the minimum time may not be subject to suspension (70-2-101).★   (See also HUNTING, FISHING, TRAPPING PROVISIONS.)

Reward Payments

The Director shall offer rewards or payments for information which may aid in the conviction of an offender violating any section of this title or other wildlife law (69-3-107).

HABITAT PROTECTION

Where a state agency owns in fee simple or controls by lease water areas or lands bordering such waters, it is illegal to place houses, docks, or floats, or to use as a landing area for boats, state owned lands or waters unless such rights are held by a signed written agreement, for which a fee may be charged. Each 24-hour period or violation is a separate offense. Violation: Class C misdemeanor (70-4-205).

No pollution, including, but not limited to, dye waste, petroleum products, brine waste, or refuse from a mine, sawmill or construction activity, or industrial or domestic sewage, or any deleterious or poisonous substance or activity shall be thrown or allowed to run into, wash into or take place in public or private waters in quantities injurious to fish life or other aquatic organisms, or which could be injurious to the propagation of fish, or which results in the destruction of habitat for fish and aquatic life. Violation: Class A misdemeanor; each day's violation is a separate offense, and each five day's continuous violation constitutes a public nuisance, subject to abatement by permanent injunction (70-4-206). Defacing or destroying Commission notices is a Class C misdemeanor, and the violator must pay for replacement of signs (70-4-207).

The Agency may establish, with the property owner's consent, public hunting areas, refuges, or wildlife management areas for the protection, propagation and/or management of wildlife. It is unlawful to hunt or molest wildlife within such areas or to trespass there, except as provided by regulation. Such areas shall be posted. The Director may issue permits for the destruction of predatory wildlife within such areas. The Agency may acquire by purchase, gift, lease or otherwise, and hold title thereto in the name of the state, lands and waters to be known as state wildlife preserves, and pay out of the Wildlife Resources Fund any taxes due.   ★The Agency shall not construct dams or dikes on preserve property in such a way as to cause flooding on adjacent private lands, and private landowners may seek injunctive relief for lands so harmed.★   The Agency may acquire delinquent tax lands for wildlife preserves in cooperation with the county and Governor (70-5-101 through -103). The Governor may designate and set apart lands and waters which revert to the state due to delinquent taxes, or are given to the state by donation, and shall by public proclamation dedicate such lands and waters for wildlife preserves and fix their limits (70-5-105).

The Commission may set aside waters within the state's jurisdiction as fish preserves in which it is unlawful to take or kill fish after public notice is given and the areas are posted. The Commission may close or open such waters for fishing when sufficient time for restocking has occurred. Violation: Class C misdemeanor (70-5-106). The Director may acquire by gift, devise or otherwise the exclusive game and fish rights on privately owned lands or waters in the state, including the right to manage, administer, protect, stock and propagate wild birds, animals and fish upon these areas, and the right to permit hunting and fishing upon them in accordance with Commission rules. Violation: Class C misdemeanor (70-5-108).

NATIVE AMERICAN WILDLIFE PROVISIONS: None.

TEXAS

Sources: Vernon's Texas Codes Annotated, 1991, Titles 1, 2 and 5; 1993 Cumulative Annual Pocket Part.

STATE WILDLIFE POLICY

All wild animals, fur-bearing animals, wild birds, wild fowl, fish and other aquatic animal life contained in the freshwater rivers, creeks, and streams and in lakes or sloughs subject to overflow from rivers within state borders are the property of the people of the state. All the beds, bottoms, products thereof, of the public rivers, bayous, lagoons, creeks, lakes, bays and inlets in the state and in the Gulf of Mexico within the state's jurisdiction are state property. The state may permit the use of the waters and bottoms and the taking of products therefrom. The Parks and Wildlife Department shall regulate the taking and conservation of fish, oysters, shrimp, crabs, turtles, terrapins, mussels, lobsters, and all other kinds of marine life, or sand, gravel, mud shell or marl (1.1.011). The purpose of the Wildlife Conservation Act of 1983 is to provide a comprehensive method for the conservation of an ample supply of state wildlife resources to insure reasonable and equitable enjoyment of the privileges of ownership and pursuit of same, and to provide a flexible law to enable the Commission to deal effectively with changing conditions to prevent depletion and waste of wildlife resources (5.61.002).

RELEVANT WILDLIFE DEFINITIONS: See Definitions section of Appendices.

STATE FISH AND WILDLIFE AGENCIES

Agency Structure

The **Parks and Wildlife Department** (Department) is under the policy direction of the **Parks and Wildlife Commission** (Commission) (2.11.011). The Commission consists of nine members appointed by the Governor with the advice and consent of two-thirds of the senate, and members must be from the general public (2.11.012). ★Members (or spouses) may not be employed by a business entity regulated by the Department or receiving funds therefrom, may not own or control more than a 10% interest in such business entity, or use/receive a substantial amount of tangible goods, services or funds from the Department, and may not be registered lobbyists on behalf of a profession related to the operation of the Commission, nor be employees or paid consultants of a statewide association in the field of conservation or outdoor recreation (2.11.0121 through 2.11.0123).★ Removal may be made by the Governor for specified reasons (2.11.0125). The Governor designates a chairman for two years, and members have six-year terms. At least quarterly meetings shall be held. One meeting annually shall be public, to receive comments concerning any issue relating to the Commission's regulatory powers and duties, and the Commission shall develop policies that will allow the public reasonable opportunity to appear before it on any issue under its jurisdiction (2.11.013 through 2.11.016). The Commission shall make available information of public interest describing its functions and procedures for filing complaints (2.11.0161). The Commission appoints an **Executive Director** (Director) who is the chief executive officer of the Department, and who serves at the Commission's will (2.11.017). The Director appoints division heads, law enforcement officers and other employees, who serve at the Director's will (2.11.018). The Director may commission unsalaried **Deputy Game Wardens** for up to four years. The Commission shall regulate the qualifications, conduct and duties and implement an education course in Game Warden duties. Deputy Game Wardens may enforce state laws relating to hunting, fishing, preservation and conservation of wildlife and marine animals. The Department shall prescribe the geographical area in which a deputy may operate, but they may not operate on coastal waters, bays or estuaries. Deputies must be uniformed, carry identification which must be presented before making an arrest, and wear a badge (2.11.020).

Agency Powers and Duties

The **Department** shall administer the laws relating to game, fish, oysters and marine life and may: ▸ collect and enforce payment of all taxes, licenses, fines and forfeitures due to the Department; ▸ inspect all taxable products relating to game, fish, oysters and marine life and verify weights and measures thereof; ▸ examine on request all streams, lakes and ponds for fish stocking purposes; ▸ manage the propagation and distribution of fish, birds and game in state hatcheries and reservations (2.12.001). The Department is responsible for protecting the state's fish and wildlife resources by: ‣ investigating fish kills and pollution that may cause loss of fish or wildlife resources, identifying the cause and party responsible, estimating the monetary value of lost resources, and seeking restoration through court action; ‣ providing recommendations to protect fish and wildlife resources to local, state and federal agencies that approve, license or construct developmental projects; ‣ providing information on fish and wildlife resources to any government agencies or private groups that make decisions affecting those resources; ‣ providing recommendations to the Texas Department of Water Resources on scheduling of in-stream flows and freshwater inflows to estuaries for the management of wildlife resources (2.12.0011). The Department: shall keep records as specified concerning the condition of the fish and oyster industry, including number of licenses issued, fees collected, fish stock furnished to whom and where by number of species, reporting annually to the Governor; shall maintain a complete list of all license fees and fines collected as a public record; may provide or sell information including books, prints and bulletins to the public about wildlife values and management, and may receive royalties on Department-owned materials (2.12.002 through .006); may use the services of volunteers to help carry out the duties of the Department, such volunteers not being used to enforce code provisions or working on private property without the owner's consent (2.11.028).

The Department may lease grazing or farming rights on its lands as game preserves, sanctuaries and management areas, and may harvest, sell or sell in place any timber, hay or other product grown on the land in excess of wildlife management needs, the proceeds to go to the Game, Fish and Water Safety Fund (2.12.008). The Department shall notify the Governor of extreme fire hazards in designated areas, so that the Governor may declare a temporary closed hunting season (2.12.012). The Department shall keep records of complaints filed relating to a licensee or entity regulated by it, shall keep the parties to a complaint informed of its status quarterly, and shall keep copies of all permit applications to store, take or divert water, so as to make recommendations to the Department of Water Resources concerning impacts on wildlife and mitigation (2.12.022 through .024).

The **Commission** by proclamation shall define as "game fish" those species having sporting value, define as "rough fish" those bony or rough-fleshed fish having no sporting value, and define as "bait fish" those species that may be taken or used as bait (5.66.114). The Commission may contract with a person for designing and producing wildlife art prints, decals and stamps, and may authorize an agent to sell and make them widely available to the public at a cost of $5.00 for decals or stamps, and shall establish a reasonable price and royalty for wildlife art prints (2.11.055 and .056). The Commission may regulate the use of Department lands for oil, gas and other mineral recovery as it considers necessary to protect the surface estate of such lands including state parks, wildlife management areas and natural areas (2.11.071). (See also HUNTING, FISHING, TRAPPING PROVISIONS.)

Agency Regulations

The Department shall provide the open season, means and methods for taking/possession of migratory game birds. An open season may be provided only for the length of time justified by the supply of the species of migratory game bird affected. The Department shall conduct investigations before issuing of regulations on an open season. The Commission may adopt an emergency regulation governing the taking of migratory game birds if it finds that emergency conditions affecting the supply or condition of such birds exists. ★A party dissatisfied with a regulation may file suit against the Department to test the validity of the regulation in a Travis County court.★ No person may hunt or possess a migratory game bird by any method or device except as provided by regulation. Violation of law or regulation: Class C misdemeanor (5.64.022 through .027). (See HUNTING, FISHING, TRAPPING PROVISIONS for Commission proclamations regulating taking of wildlife resources in designated counties or other areas of the state.)

Agency Funding Sources

(See also Licenses and Permits under HUNTING, FISHING, TRAPPING PROVISIONS for certain stamp/permit fees and permitted uses of those funds.)

The Department shall deposit to the credit of the **Game, Fish and Water Safety Fund** all revenues from: ‣ all types of fishing, hunting, shrimping, and trapping licenses, stamps, and permits; ‣ sale of marl, sand, gravel, shell; ‣ sale of property less advertising costs; ‣ fines and penalties collected for violations of laws pertaining to the protection and conservation of wild birds, wild fowl, wild animals, fish, shrimp, oysters, game birds and animals, fur-bearing animals, alligators, and any other state wildlife resources; ▸ sale of rough fish by the Department; ▸ fees for importation permits; ▸ fees for stocking waters on private property; ▸ sale of seized pelts; ▸ sale/lease of grazing rights to and products from game preserves, sanctuaries and management areas; ▸ contracts for removal of fur-bearing animals and reptiles from wildlife management areas; ▸ motorboat registration fees; ▸ fines from violations of water safety laws; ▸ alligator hunter's license or buyer's license; ▸ sale of alligators or parts by the Department; ▸ fees and revenue collected under 2.11.027 that are associated with the conservation of fish and wildlife; ▸ any other source provided by law (2.11.032). This fund may be used only for: ▸ enforcement of fish, shrimp, oyster, game, sand, shell, gravel laws; ▸dissemination of information on marine life, wild animal life, wildlife values, wildlife management; ▸ establishment of fish hatcheries, wildlife management areas, public hunting grounds and tidal water fish passes; ▸ propagation and distribution of marine life, game animals, and wild birds; ▸ protection of wild birds, fish, game; ▸ research, management and protection of the fish and wildlife resources of the state, including alligators and fur-bearing animals; ▸ salaries and Department expenses; ▸ expansion and development of additional opportunities of hunting and fishing in state lands/waters; ▸ removing rough fish from public water; ▸ enforcement of water safety laws; ▸ purchase and maintenance of boat ramps on public waters; ▸ resource protection activities; ▸ any other use provided by law (2.11.033). All expenditures from the Game, Fish and Water Safety Fund must be approved by the Director (2.11.034).

The Department may accept gifts of property or money in support of any purpose authorized by code (2.11.026). ★The Commission shall establish fees for the administration of Department programs, but may not maintain unnecessary fund balances, and by rule may establish a fee to cover costs associated with the review of a permit application. The Department may sell any item in which the state has title, or acquire and resell items if a profit can be made, to provide funding for Department programs. The Department may accept funds raised by a volunteer group to promote its work, and use such funds for the specific project for which the funds are intended, and the Director may expend funds from dedicated funding sources to establish an insurance program for volunteers while on duty and for recognition of volunteer group services (2.11.027 and .028).★ The **Parks and Wildlife Operating Fund** consists of appropriated funds for travel, supplies and capital outlay (2.11.038). The Department may accept a gift or donation for funding any program relating to wildlife conservation, and those gifts other than money may be auctioned off or used as a prize in conjunction with a fund-raising event (2.12.018).

The Department shall deposit into the **Special Nongame and Endangered Species Conservation Fund** all money from: private donations and grants to the fund; net proceeds from wildlife art, prints, decals and stamps; interest from investments; income from entrance fees, easements, mineral leases, grazing leases and sale of products from lands purchased with funds from this Fund (2.11.053). The Nongame Fund may be used only for: ▸ disseminating information on nongame and endangered species conservation, management and values; ▸ scientific investigation and survey of those species for better protection and conservation; ▸ propagation, distribution, protection and restoration of such species; ▸ research and management of such species; ▸ development and acquisition of habitats for such species; ▸ matching of federal funds for projects for such species. Appropriations from the Nongame Fund are supplemental, and other funds may be appropriated for fund purposes (2.11.054).

The **Lifetime License Endowment Fund** consists of all money from: lifetime hunting, fishing or combination licenses; private contributions and grants for these purposes; interest income; any other source provided by law. The interest earned may be used only to acquire, develop, manage and repair public hunting and fishing areas (2.11.062 and .063). The Department may deposit in an **Operation Game Thief Fund**, outside the state treasury, donations from any person made for reward purposes (2.12.201). (See also Agency Advisory Boards under this section and ENFORCEMENT OF WILDLIFE LAWS.) Receipts from the **Turkey Stamp** and **Waterfowl Stamp** shall go only for research, management and protection of turkeys and waterfowl and for acquisition, lease or development of turkey and waterfowl habitats (5.43.254 and .305). The Department may use the net receipts from the sale of **Conservation Permits** for the sole purpose of acquiring, leasing, or developing state lands or operating land or facilities under the Department's control, and as otherwise designated by statute (5.43.524).

Agency Advisory Boards

The **Aquaculture Executive Committee** consists of the Chairman of the Parks and Wildlife Commission and the Commissioners of Agriculture and the General Land Office. Each shall designate a person to review biennially each state agency's rules regarding aquaculture to determine if changes in the rules are necessary due to new technology, so as to benefit the industry to the greatest possible extent. These members shall form an **Advisory Committee** to study the environmental and economic impact of the aquaculture industry. The Executive Committee may accept grants and gifts from public and private sources for state coordination of the aquaculture industry (1.1.201 through .206). The Director shall appoint a nine member **Operation Game Thief Committee** to administer the Operation Game Thief Fund. Members shall have a demonstrated interest in game and fish conservation, and the Director may consider the nominations of any club or association in making appointments. Members may not be Department employees, serve for six years, must meet at least twice a year, and five must be present for approval of reward disbursements (2.12.202).

PROTECTED SPECIES OF WILDLIFE

The Department shall develop and administer management programs to insure the continued ability of nongame species of fish and wildlife to perpetuate themselves successfully. Regarding nongame species, the Department may: ▸ disseminate information pertaining to conservation, management and values; ▸ conduct scientific investigations for better protection and conservation; ▸ propagate, distribute, protect and restore nongame species; ▸ research and manage nongame species; ▸ develop and acquire habitats (5.67.002). The Department shall conduct ongoing investigations of nongame fish and wildlife to develop information on populations, distribution, habitat needs, limiting factors and other biological or ecological data to determine appropriate management and regulatory information. The Department shall conduct a public hearing on all proposed regulations and publish notice in at least three major newspapers at least one week before the hearing. On the basis of the information received, the Department may modify a proposed regulation. Regulations become effective 60 days after date of proposal unless withdrawn by the Department (5.67.003 and .004). Violation: Class C misdemeanor; a subsequent offense is a Class B misdemeanor; two or more subsequent violations after previous convictions under this chapter is a Class A misdemeanor (5.67.005). (See also GENERAL EXCEPTIONS TO PROTECTION.)

Species of fish or wildlife indigenous to Texas are endangered if listed on the US list of endangered native fish and wildlife, or the list of fish or wildlife threatened with statewide extinction as filed by the Director. The Director shall file with the Secretary of State a list of fish or wildlife threatened with statewide extinction, so classified if the Department finds that the continued existence of the fish or wildlife is endangered due to destruction, modification or curtailment of its habitat, overutilization for commercial or sporting purposes, disease or predation, or other natural or man-made factors (5.68.002 and .003). ★If the list is modified, the Director shall file an order with the Secretary of State accepting the modification effective immediately. The Director may amend the list by similar filing, effective immediately, but shall give notice at least 60 days before the order is filed, showing the contents of the proposed order, allowing a reclassification petition to be filed during this period. Three or more persons may petition the Department to add or delete species from list, and must present substantial evidence for addition or deletion. If fewer than 50 people join in the petition, the Department may refuse to review the classification list, but if more than 50, the Department shall conduct a review hearing, open to the public, with notice by publication as specified. Based on findings at the hearing, the Department may file an order with the Secretary of State altering the statewide extinction list which becomes effective on filing (5.68.004 and.005).★ It is a violation to possess, take or transport endangered fish or wildlife for zoological gardens or scientific purposes or to take or transport them from their natural habitat for propagation for commercial purposes without a permit. A commercial propagation permit is required to possess endangered species for the purpose of propagation for sale (5.68.006 and .007). [Details for obtaining an endangered species propagation permit, renewal of permit, reporting requirements, provisions for permit refusal or cancellation, required veterinarian inspections, appeal procedure, and provisions for disposal of endangered wildlife after permit cancellation or expiration are given in 5.68.008 through .013.]

The Department shall make regulations necessary to administer endangered species provisions governing permit application, hearings, identifying endangered fish and wildlife or goods made from them which may be possessed, propagated or sold, and publication and distribution of endangered species lists to the public (5.68.014.) No person may: possess, sell or distribute, or offer such, endangered fish and wildlife unless lawfully raised in captivity for commercial purpose; possess, sell or distribute any goods made from endangered fish or wildlife unless made from legally held captive species, or from fish or wildlife lawfully taken in another state, accompanied by proper documentation; sell, advertise or offer for sale any species of fish or wildlife not classified as endangered under the name of any endangered fish or wildlife. Any goods sold made from endangered fish or wildlife must be properly tagged as specified (5.68.015 and .016).

Peace officers may seize endangered fish or wildlife or goods made from them which were taken, possessed or made in violation of endangered species provisions and hold them pending case disposition, and may dispose of them if the court determines that the property was used in violation. All revenue received under endangered species provisions shall go into the Nongame and Endangered Species Conservation Fund (5.68.017 and .018). Violations of endangered species provisions are for first offense, Class C misdemeanors; second offense, Class B misdemeanors; two or more prior convictions, Class A misdemeanors (5.68.021). If the Commission finds that there is an immediate danger to a species regulated by the Department, it may adopt emergency rules (2.12.027).

★No person may capture or transport any game mammal or game bird captured from the wild that is indigenous to Texas without a Department permit, issued as a means of better wildlife management.★ This does not apply to game animals or game birds privately owned or raised. Violation: Class B misdemeanor (5.43.061 and .062). Except as otherwise provided, no person may: catch, kill injure or possess, dead or alive, or purchase, sell or transport a bird that is not a game bird; possess any part of the plumage, skin or body of a bird not a game bird; disturb or destroy the eggs, nest or young of a bird not a game bird. Canaries, parrots and other exotic nongame birds may be sold, bought and kept as pets. No person may take or destroy the nest, eggs or young of any wild game bird, wild bird or wild fowl protected by this code except as provided by permit. Violation: class C misdemeanor. No person may hunt, trap, or kill a golden eagle or Mexican brown eagle without a permit under Chapter 43 (5.64.002, .003, .005 and .011).

The Commission may regulate the taking, possession, propagation, exportation, importation and sale of alligators or parts to manage this species, including: ▸ permit forms, fees and procedures; ▸ hearing procedures; ▸ times when lawful to take, possess, sell alligators, hides, or parts; ▸ limits, size, means, methods, manner and places to take or possess alligators, hides or parts (5.65.003). The Department shall conduct scientific studies to develop information on populations, distributions, habitat needs, limiting factors and other biological/ecological data or to determine management for public safety. No person may take, sell, purchase or possess an alligator, its egg or part except as permitted by Commission regulations, except for manufactured goods from alligators taken lawfully. No person may take, possess or accompany another attempting to take an alligator during the open season without an alligator hunter's license, nor purchase from such hunter any alligator, hide or part without an alligator buyer's license. Violation of any provisions relating to alligators are Class C misdemeanors; if a prior offense exists, a Class B misdemeanor; if two or more previous violations, a Class A misdemeanor (5.65.004 through .008). (See also ENFORCEMENT OF WILDLIFE LAWS.)

GENERAL EXCEPTIONS TO PROTECTION

A person may collect and hold protected species for scientific, zoological and propagation purposes with a Department permit (5.49.002). The Department may issue a permit to take protected wildlife for propagation, zoological gardens, aquariums, rehabilitation and scientific purposes. Applications must be made under oath, state the protected species to be taken and the purpose of collection, and be endorsed by two recognized specialists in the relevant biological field; except endorsement is not required for a permit application to take alligators or marine life for an aquarium, but these persons must be qualified to capture in a scientific manner without cruelty. Possession of such permit is a complete defense to prosecution of unlawful taking if the conduct was authorized under permit terms. ★No permit may be issued to take or transport endangered fish or wildlife, the possession, taking or transportation of which is prohibited by federal law. The Department may refuse to grant a permit for taking/transporting endangered fish or wildlife from their natural habitat for commercial propagation if they may be legally obtained from a source in Texas other than from such habitat.★ A permit for taking migratory birds is not valid unless the applicant has a federal permit. No permit may be issued for the taking or possession of alligators unless it is a public hunt or commercial enterprise (Alligator Farmer's License) (5.43.022 through .025). The Department may assess and collect a fee to cover costs of scientific review, facility inspection or background investigation of an applicant's qualifications. A federal or state regulatory agency is exempt from the fee if they have concurrent jurisdiction for wildlife management with the Department, have statewide authority to regulate environmental contaminants or public health, or are an accredited educational institution (5.43.0281). The Department shall specify permit conditions, including the number and species of wildlife that may be taken and contents of required reports (5.43.026 through .029). Violation of permit conditions or report filing is a Class C misdemeanor (5.43.030).

The Department may take, transport, release and manage any of the wildlife and fish in the state for investigation, propagation, distribution or scientific purposes (2.12.013). The Department may take brood fish from public water at any time in any manner to supply state and federal fish hatcheries (5.66.112). European starlings, English sparrows, grackles, ravens, red-winged blackbirds, cowbirds, feral rock doves, and crows may be killed at any time and their nests or eggs destroyed (5.64.002). A person must have a permit to possess a restricted wild animal for breeding, exhibition, or personal use, and the Commission shall prescribe requirements for safe possession, except for persons licensed under other state or federal laws to breed or exhibit a wild animal. The Department may revoke such permit for noncompliance, removing the animal and disposing of it in a manner determined to be in the animal's best interest. ★Local governments may also regulate wild animal possession.★ Violation: Class C misdemeanor. "Wild animal" for purposes of this subsection means lions, tigers, ocelots, cougars, leopards, cheetahs, jaguars, hyenas, bears, lesser pandas, binturongs, wolves, apes, elephants and rhinoceroses (2.12.601 through .607). The Department may issue permits for the taking, possession, transportation, sale or exportation of a nongame species of fish or wildlife for proper management, and charge a fee for a commercial activity permit (5.67.0041). Endangered species provisions in chapter 68 do not apply to coyotes, cougars, bobcats, prairie dogs, or red foxes, nor to the possession of mounted or preserved endangered fish or wildlife acquired before 1973 which is documented as to time of acquisition (5.68.020).

The Department may contract for the removal of fur-bearing animals and reptiles in wildlife management areas according to sound biological management practices and state law regarding sale of state property, except that the Department shall determine the means, methods and quantities of fur-bearing animals and reptiles to be taken, and it may accept or reject any bid received by the State Purchasing and General Services Commission. Fur-bearing animals may be removed only during the open season. Reptiles may be removed at any time unless there is an open season for a specific species (5.81.404). The Department may take, possess, hold, transport or propagate any game animal of this state for public purposes (5.44.015).

HUNTING, FISHING, TRAPPING PROVISIONS

General Provisions

★Under chapter 61, the Commission may make proclamations relating to wildlife resources in a particular county or place. [Section 101.001, *et seq.*, prescribes the counties, places and wildlife resources affected, unless otherwise stated by Commission proclamation (5.61.003 and .004).] In counties or locations so designated, no person may hunt, catch or possess a game bird, game animal, fish, marine animal or other aquatic life except as permitted by proclamation, nor without the landowner's consent (5.61.021 and .022). The Department shall conduct scientific studies of all species of wildlife resources to determine: supply; economic value; environments; breeding habits; sex ratios; effects of hunting, trapping, fishing, disease, infestation, predation, agricultural pressure and overpopulation; any other factors causing increases/decreases in supply. The Commission shall make findings of fact based on these studies. The Commission shall regulate open seasons, means, methods, manners and places in which it is lawful to take/possess wildlife resources in designated counties or locations. Open seasons shall be declared if studies reveal that they may be safely provided or if the threat of waste requires it to conserve wildlife resources. The Commission shall make proclamations regulating the possession or taking of wildlife resources in these designated locations specifying: the species, quantity, age or size and if possible the sex to be taken; the methods and manner that may be used; the region, county, area or portion of a county where wildlife resources may be taken. If the Commission finds that there is danger of depletion or waste, it shall amend/revoke proclamations (5.61.051 through .055).★

★Before a Commission proclamation is adopted, the Department shall hold public hearings in the affected county if the Director receives a petition signed by at least 25 county residents, and in at least five locations to ensure public participation. Notice of hearings must be published in the county at least 10 days prior to the hearing, or in an adjacent county with wide circulation. Proclamations must be adopted by a quorum of the Commission, and any person interested is entitled to be heard at the meeting and may introduce evidence on the imminence of depletion or waste. A quorum for this purpose is five members.★ Copies of proclamations shall be filed with each county affected, and the venue for any suit challenging the validity of a proclamation is in Travis County, with the burden of proof on the complaining party to show invalidity (5.61.101 through .106). Violations of proclamation provisions are Class C misdemeanors. Conviction for violation of 5.62.003 or .004 (hunting from vehicles or at night) is a Class B misdemeanor (5.61.901). [Other penalties are designated for marine violations.]

No person may take, sell, purchase or possess a fur-bearing animal, pelt or carcass except as provided by Commission proclamation. This does not prohibit a landowner from taking a fur-bearing animal causing depredation on that person's land, but no person may possess a fur-bearing animal taken for depredation purposes except as authorized by the Commission. No person may take a fur-bearing animal on private land or water unless the landowner consents. The Commission may regulate the taking, possession, propagation, transportation, exportation, importation, sale and offering of such of fur-bearing animals, pelts, and carcasses necessary to manage fur-bearing animals or to protect human health or property. Commission proclamation may provide for: ▸ permit application fees, forms and reports; ▸ hearing procedures; ▸ time periods when it is lawful to take, possess, sell, purchase or transport; ▸ catch and possession limits; ▸ lawful means, methods, manner and places. The Department shall conduct scientific studies of fur-bearing animals on populations, distribution, habitat needs and limiting factors to determine appropriate management policies for public safety (5.71.002 through .004).

Licenses and Permits

★★The Department may require one person in each vehicle using land under Department control that is open to the public to possess a conservation passport permit. Use of land includes consumptive or nonconsumptive purposes. The Department may require each person to possess a conservation permit to participate in certain activities and to enter certain facilities designated as wildlife management areas, state natural areas, or lands that have not been fully developed. A conservation permit is not required for hunting if the person possesses a current Type II hunting permit (5.43.521). Possession of a conservation permit does not relieve the holder of the requirement for other permits or paying other fees for entrance/use of land. It is a Class C misdemeanor to use land under Department control and to fail or refuse to show a conservation permit to a Game Warden on request, unless such person entered the area in the vehicle of a permit holder, or is a member of a group that the Department has exempted (5.43.522 through .525).★★ (See also Agency Funding Sources under STATE FISH AND WILDLIFE AGENCIES.)

Except as otherwise provided for certain age groups, no person may fish in state public waters without a fishing license, nor hunt any bird or animal without possessing a hunting license. A resident alligator hunter's license, trapper's license or fur-bearing animal propagation permit needs no additional license to take or possess the relevant species (5.46.001 and 42.002). No nonresident may hunt a mule deer, white-tailed deer, turkey, pronghorn antelope or desert bighorn sheep within the state, or aoudad sheep or elk in designated counties without a general nonresident hunting license. No nonresident may hunt any bird or animal without a general nonresident hunting license, a special nonresident license or a five-day special license (5.42.005). A nonresident may acquire a banded bird hunting license for taking pen-reared banded birds from licensed private bird hunting areas only (5.42.0142).

No person may hunt wild deer or turkey during an open archery only season unless they have an archery hunting stamp, as well as a regular hunting license. Violation, including refusal to exhibit an archery hunting stamp on request: Class C misdemeanor (5.43.201, .203 and .205). No person may hunt turkeys without a turkey stamp and a hunting license (5.43.251 and .253). Violation, or refusal to exhibit a stamp at request is a Class C misdemeanor (5.43.255 and .256). No person may hunt waterfowl without a Department waterfowl stamp in addition to a hunting license (5.43.302 and .304). Refusal to show one's waterfowl stamp or other offense is a Class C misdemeanor (5.43.307 and .309).

No person may hunt white-winged dove without a white-winged dove stamp in addition to a hunting license, and refusal to exhibit it on demand is a Class C misdemeanor. Stamp sales receipts may be used only for research and management for the protection of white-winged dove and for acquisition, lease or development of dove habitat. Not more than 50% may be spent on research and management (5.43.012 through .016). The Department shall prescribe the form of and issue licenses and tags for animals or birds allowed to be killed. A person commits an offense by not properly filling out a license or tag when purchased (5.42.010).

No person may take trout from public waters without possessing a freshwater trout stamp in addition to a fishing license. Violation of stamp provisions or failure to show a stamp on demand is a Class C misdemeanor (5.43.502, .504, .506 and .507). No person may fish in state public water without a fishing license, except persons under 17 or over 65 if the person is a resident or, if a nonresident, if the person's state of residence grants a similar exemption to Texas residents (5.46.001 and .002). Violation of license provisions or refusal to produce a license on request is a Class C misdemeanor (5.46.015).

Texas

No person may take, capture, possess or attempt to take any native raptors without a Department permit (5.49.002). (See also PROTECTED SPECIES OF WILDLIFE.) The Department may prescribe rules for taking and possessing raptors, time and area from which they may be taken, and provide standards for housing, reporting, and raptor permit eligibility. The holder of a raptor permit and a hunting license may hunt native species of wild birds, wild animals and migratory game birds during the open season and may hunt unprotected species of wildlife. All raptors captured, taken or held in the state remain state property except as otherwise provided (5.49.010, .012 and .014). [Provisions for falconer and joint federal-state permits are given, and provisions regulating sale, transportation, and limits on the number of raptors taken or possessed are also given under chapter 49.] Violation of raptor/falconry provisions is a Class C misdemeanor (5.49.017). (See also Agency Advisory Boards under STATE FISH AND WILDLIFE AGENCIES.)

★The Department shall issue permits for trapping, transporting and transplanting of wild white-tailed deer upon satisfactory showing of an overpopulation of deer in an area where harvest provisions are inadequate and that they will be transplanted to an area of suitable habitat for appropriate harvest at no cost to the state. No person may hunt such transplanted deer except as allowed by law for hunting native white-tailed deer in the county to which the deer are transplanted. Permits issued under this section do not entitle a person to take, trap or possess wild white-tailed deer on any private land without the landowner's written permission (5.63.007).★

The Department may establish and administer a statewide hunter education program which must include instruction concerning: ▸ safe handling and use of firearms and archery equipment; ▸ wildlife conservation and management; ▸ hunting laws and applicable rules and regulations; ▸ hunting safety and ethics, including landowner rights. ★If the funds are available, the Commission may establish a mandatory hunter education program to be completed successfully before hunting alone with firearms or archery equipment, may establish a minimum age for the program, and may provide that comparable courses or certificates from another state be accepted. Persons age 17 or older on September 1, 1988, or on the date on which a mandatory hunter education course is implemented, whichever is later, are exempt from course requirements. The Department shall offer mandatory hunter education courses in each county when a substantial number of residents request a class, or at least once a year. The Commission may utilize volunteer instructors and may cooperate with any groups interested in hunter education, and shall adopt rules to implement the course. Violation of any provision is a Class C misdemeanor, but if the person fails to possess the required certificate, the person may, within 10 days, request to take such course, and be given 90 days to complete it, after which charges will be dismissed (5.62.014).★

No person may take a fur-bearing animal or pelt without a trapping license, nor purchase a pelt or carcass without a retail fur-buyer's license, nor possess a live fur-bearing animal for propagation or sale without a fur-bearing animal propagation license, all issued by the Department. No retail fur buyer may purchase a pelt or carcass except from a licensed trapper. No wholesale fur dealer may purchase a pelt or carcass except from a licensed trapper, retail fur buyer, a fur-bearing animal propagator, or another licensed wholesale fur dealer (5.71.005 through .008). All licensees shall carry their license, or display it at their place of business, and shall display it on request. Places of business and vehicles of any fur-bearing animal propagator, wholesale fur dealer, or retail fur buyer are subject to inspection without a warrant by a Game Warden or other peace officer at any time. Dealers shall submit any required Department reports. Violation of any fur-bearing animal provisions is a Class C misdemeanor on first offense; Class B misdemeanor on second offense within 36 months; Class A misdemeanor for two or more convictions within preceding 60 months (5.71.011, .012, .014 and .015).

Restrictions on Taking: Hunting and Trapping

★A Commission regulation authorizing the taking of antlerless deer or antelope or of elk in designated areas is not effective for a specific tract of land unless the landowner agrees in writing to the number of animals to be removed (5.61.056).★ Unless the Commission makes exceptions for certain locations, no person may hunt an antlerless deer or antelope (or elk in designated counties) without an antlerless deer, antelope or elk permit issued by the Department, and such permit may not be sold or traded for anything of value (5.61.057).

The Department may enter into cooperative agreements with landowners for restoring, protecting and managing bighorn sheep, and such agreement may provide that bighorn sheep hunting permittees may hunt on that owner's land. A permit holder may hunt only on the lands designated. A limited number of permits shall be distributed to parties to a cooperative agreement and the general public. Bighorn sheep permits may not be traded or sold for anything of value. A person may not possess a mounted or unmounted Bighorn sheep head unless proper tags are attached (5.61.204 through .206).

No person may possess the carcass of a wild deer or wild turkey without properly tagging the carcass (5.42.018 and .0185). Nonresidents must also have a spring turkey hunting license (5.42.005). No person may possess the carcass of a wild deer with the head removed unless the carcass has been finally processed and delivered to the final destination. No person other than the taker may receive or possess any part of a deer without a legible hunter's document attached to the carcass which is signed and completed. No person may purchase or use more bird or animal tags during a license year than authorized by the Commission; use the same tag on more than one bird or animal; use another's tag; use the wrong tag on an animal; kill an animal/bird and fail to attach a tag immediately; hunt a bird or animal requiring a tag and fail to possess such tag while hunting (5.42.019 and .020). ★Use of tags does not authorize exceeding any bag limit or hunting deer or turkey during closed season, and attachment of such tags is not prima facie evidence that the deer or turkey was lawfully killed (5.42.021).★ Any violations of general hunting license provisions in Chapter 42, or failure to exhibit a license on request, are Class C misdemeanors (5.42.024 and .025). No person may set a trap, net or other device for taking game birds or snare a game bird without a Department permit (5.64.004).

★No person may hunt any wild bird or animal from any type of aircraft, motor vehicle, powerboat, sailboat, or other floating device, except animals and birds not classified as migratory may be hunted from a motor vehicle, powerboat, sailboat, or floating device within private property boundaries by one legally on the property for hunting, if no attempt is made to hunt on any part of the state road system.★ It is illegal to hunt at night at any season during the hours specified, or to hunt any protected bird or animal with aid of a headlight, hunting lamp or other artificial light including those attached to a vehicle; possession of such light during nighttime hours where deer are known to range is prima facie evidence of violation. No person may employ another or be so employed for compensation to hunt any protected bird, wild fowl or game animal. Authorized Department employees may search game bags, automobiles or receptacles if there is reason to believe that they contain game unlawfully taken; refusal to allow a search is an offense. Unless otherwise provided, possession of a wild game bird, animal or other protected wildlife, dead or alive, during a time hunting is prohibited is prima facie evidence of guilt. ★A person who, for the purpose of establishing testimony, purchases a game bird or animal whose sale is prohibited, is immune from prosecution for the purchase, and a conviction for the unlawful sale of game may be sustained on the uncorroborated testimony of the purchaser.★ No person may: kill/take more than the daily, weekly or seasonal bag limits for game birds or animals; hunt any game bird or animal other than during the open season; kill, take, wound, or capture any game bird or animal for which no open season is set out by this code; possess an illegally killed game bird or animal. It is an offense if a person: lawfully hunting kills or wounds a game bird or game animal and intentionally or knowingly fails to make a reasonable effort to retrieve the animal or bird and include it in the bag limit and if a person intentionally takes a game bird, game animal or fish and intentionally or recklessly, or with criminal negligence, fails to keep the edible portions of the bird, animal or fish in an edible condition (5.62.003 through .011). Violations: Class C misdemeanors, except for spotlighting, which is a Class B misdemeanor; if there are prior convictions for spotlighting, a Class A misdemeanor. Subsequent violations of hunting at night or from a vehicle within a five-year period are Class B misdemeanors (5.62.013). [There are provisions, including certain prohibitions, for hunting in state parks, forts and historic sites, and on lands of the Lower Colorado River Authority, including fees, weapons, and license requirements in 5.62.061, *et seq*.]

★In counties with a population of 2,000,000 or more, no person possessing a firearm may hunt a wild animal or wild bird, or engage in target shooting on another's land without that owner's written permission; such permit must contain the name, address and phone number of the permitted hunter, identify the land and be signed by the landowner or agent. Persons hunting accompanied by the landowner need no permit (5.62.012).★ No person may hunt an exotic animal on a public road or its right-of-way, hunt an exotic animal on another's land without the owner's consent or possess the carcass of an exotic animal, except for its owner, a person who holds a permit to control depredating animals from an aircraft, a public health or law enforcement officer or veterinarian. Violation: misdemeanor; fine up to $1,500; jail up to 6 months; or both (5.62.015).

No person may sell, offer for sale, buy or possess after purchase a protected wild bird, wild game bird, or wild game animal, dead or alive, or part thereof, regardless of whether the bird or animal is taken or killed in this state, except for deer hides. The Commission by proclamation shall authorize and regulate the sale, purchase and possession of deer antlers (5.62.021). A person may transport or ship to a taxidermist or tannery for mounting or preserving a specimen or part of a wild bird or wild animal if lawfully taken, if specimen is not for sale, and the person has executed a transportation affidavit. It is an offense to ship game from any place in the state, for an agent to receive or ship game, or for railroad personnel to permit a person to carry game without an attached transportation affidavit (5.62.0265 through .028). Owners of public cold storage plants shall maintain detailed records to be available for Department inspection at any time. A person may place in cold storage lawfully taken or killed animals not in excess of the number permitted by law. Department employees may enter and inspect a cold storage plant, taxidermist shop or tannery where protected wildlife are stored during normal operating hours. Violation: Class C misdemeanor, but if prior conviction within five years, a Class B misdemeanor (5.62.029 through .032).

No person may take, injure or kill any fish kept in state hatcheries or any bird or animal kept on state reservation grounds for propagation or exhibition purposes, nor may any person enter such grounds without Department permission. No person may fish or attempt to take fish from a fish sanctuary, nor attempt to or take or possess any wildlife or fish from a wildlife management area except as permitted by the Department. Violation: Class C misdemeanor (5.81.001 through .007).

Restrictions on Taking: Fishing

[Saltwater sport fishing and commercial fishing are not covered. See 5.66.201 through .219 and 47.001, *et seq.*]

No person may catch fish by net, seine, explosive, poison, pollution, muddying, ditching or draining in any privately owned lake or pond without the owner's consent, nor place in state waters an explosive, poison or other substance deleterious to fish except for construction purposes as authorized in writing by a county judge. No person may catch fish by the use of, manufacture or sell, or possess an electricity-producing device commonly used to shock, stun, kill or disorient fish, and possession in a boat or within one-half mile of any state waters is a violation. Such device is a nuisance, and an officer with probable cause to believe such device is possessed or used in violation may search a boat, vehicle, campsite or person and seize the device and hold it as evidence. On conviction, such device shall be destroyed or used for research. No person may possess a device designed to catch fish or other aquatic wildlife in or on state public waters where the device is not permitted by the code or Commission regulation except as provided (5.66.002 through .006).

No person may fish from the road surface of any bridge or causeway on a road maintained by the State Highway Department, nor leave any dead fish or bait on such road. No person may use a seine, net, trotline or other device, except hook and line, to catch fish in a channel, turning basin or other water of a navigation district, and possession of such illegal device is prima facie evidence of violation.   ★It is an offense to leave edible fish or bait fish taken from state public waters to die without intent to retain them for food or bait.★   [Except as otherwise provided, violations are Class C misdemeanors, but range from Class A to Class C misdemeanors, as detailed, and depending on prior convictions.] Vehicles transporting uncooked, fresh or frozen aquatic animal life for commercial purposes must be clearly identified; violation is a class C misdemeanor (5.66.008 through .014).   ★It is a class A misdemeanor to commit fraud in freshwater fishing tournaments, with the intent to affect the outcome of the contest, by providing, selling or accepting a fish, or representing a fish was caught by a participant when in fact it was bought from or provided by another person. It is an offense for a contest sponsor to fail to notify law enforcement officers if fraud is discovered. If the offense occurred during a tournament in which any prize or combination of prizes exceeds $10,000, the offense is a 3rd degree felony (5.66.119).★

It is unlawful to buy, sell, possess for sale, transport or ship bass, blue marlin, cobia, crappie, flathead catfish, jewfish, king mackerel, longbill spearfish, muskellunge, northern pike, red drum, sailfish, sauger, snook, Spanish mackerel, spotted sea trout, striped bass, tarpon, wahoo, walleye, white bass, white marlin, yellow bass, or hybrids of any of these, regardless of where the fish was taken, caught or raised, except for fish in transit by common carrier through the state or fish raised by a licensed fish farmer in a state private pond, and lawful importation of those species by a holder of a Texas finfish import license. [Details as to fish importation, tagging, documentation and other requirements for finfish import license holders are specified.]   ★It is an offense to possess fish described above without required documentation, or to fail to present same to a Game Warden on request, and culpable mental state (intent) is not required for such offense. A Department agent may, for the purpose of establishing testimony, buy or sell any aquatic life which is otherwise illegal with immunity from prosecution. A conviction for unlawful purchase or sale of any aquatic animal may be sustained on the uncorroborated testimony of the agent.★   It is unlawful to buy, sell, transport, ship, or possess for sale trout of the family Salmonidae taken from state waters

(5.66.020 through .023). [Sale, purchase, transport of certain fish species taken from numerous designated state waters is prohibited as specified (5.66.024).] No person may buy, sell, transport or ship for sale freshwater crappie, bass, striped bass or hybrids, white bass, walleye, sauger, northern pike, muskellunge, trout, flathead catfish or other fish taken from state fresh waters except for nongame fish, fish other than bass raised in private waters, fish legally possessed outside the state and transported into the state, Micropterus bass raised under a fish farmer's license, channel and blue catfish of certain sizes from certain waters, and minnows as specified by county. Fish shipped into the state must have a bill of lading containing information as specified, such records to be kept for one year by the receiver of the shipment (5.66.111).

Commercial and Private Enterprise Provisions

No person may place in captivity or engage in the business of propagating any game animal unless they have a game breeder's license. The Department shall issue a serial number on permanent metal tags to be attached to the ear of each antelope held in captivity or sold by the game breeder. A licensed game breeder may: ▸ engage in game breeding in the immediate locality for which the license was issued; ▸ sell or hold in captivity for propagation or sale antelope, collared peccary and wild squirrels; ▸ sell or hold in captivity elk in any county in which elk is a game animal. Records must be kept, a single enclosure for any game animal may not contain more than 320 acres, and Department employees may inspect at any time without warrant any game pen, coop or enclosure. A common carrier may not accept nor ship a live game animal except as specified, and a breeder must have a Department transportation permit to ship the same. Only healthy game animals may be sold, bartered or exchanged by a game breeder, and such animals must be tagged. No game breeder may sell or ship within the state any antelope or collared peccary during the open season or 10 days before or after the season (5.44.002 through .012). It is an offense for a breeder: ▸ to take, trap or capture game animals from the wild; ▸ to allow hunting/killing of game animals held in captivity; ▸ fail to furnish to a Game Warden information as to the source of animals held in captivity (5.44.0125). The above listed game animals may be purchased or received in this state only for liberation for stocking purposes or holding for propagation. In order that native game species may be preserved, game animals held under a breeder's license are subject to all laws and regulations pertaining to wild game animals except as specifically provided. Violation: Class C misdemeanor (5.44.013, .014 and .016).

A person engaged in the business of propagating game birds must have a game bird breeder's license; a person may possess not more than 12 game birds for personal use without a license if the person can show documentation of lawful purchase (5.45.001). No licensee may retain migratory birds in an enclosure larger than 320 acres, nor other game birds in an enclosure larger than 40 acres, nor sell a live game bird without documents showing origin. Pen-raised game birds offered for sale must be killed other than by shooting, birds must be healthy, carcasses must be stamped and labeled, sources of game birds held by nonbreeders revealed to the Department upon request and detailed records kept. ★Persons may purchase live pheasant from a game bird breeder for any purpose, a breeder may slaughter game birds for personal consumption at any time, and restaurants, clubs and other food sale businesses may sell game birds for consumption on the premises of the business.★ Department employees may inspect game bird breeder premises without warrant during normal business hours. Applicable federal bird permits must also be held. Violation of game bird breeder provisions: Class C misdemeanor (5.45.004 through .012).

★The Department shall issue a scientific breeder's permit to qualified persons to possess white-tailed deer and mule deer for propagation, management and scientific purposes under conditions determined by the Commission, including number of deer and providing for an endorsement by a certified wildlife biologist. Application must be made under oath and must state the purpose of possession or transportation of deer (5.43.352 through .355).★ The Department shall issue a serial number on a permanent metal tag to be placed in the ear of each white-tailed or mule deer held in captivity or sold. A scientific breeder may engage in the business of breeding white-tailed or mule deer in the locality for which the license is issued, and sell or hold them in captivity for propagation or sale under Commission regulations. The Department may inspect at any time without warrant any pen or enclosure, and a single enclosure for deer may not contain more than 320 acres. Reports must be filed with the Department. [Other provisions regarding shipment, sale during open season, purchase, use, and prohibited acts are generally the same for white-tailed and mule deer as for the game breeder's license discussed above, and are covered in sections 5.43.361 through .365.] White-tailed and mule deer held under this permit are subject to state laws and regulations pertaining to deer, except that this subchapter may not be construed to restrict or prohibit the use of high fences. Violation of a statute, permit conditions or a Commission regulation is a Class C misdemeanor (5.43.356 through .367).

No person may release banded pen-reared birds or have paying guests to hunt, unless they have a private bird hunting area license, fees to be charged according to hunting area size from 2,000 to 8,000 contiguous acres. Such area may not contain more than 8,000 contiguous acres. The area shall be clearly distinguished from any other club, hunting lease or other leased premises for hunting purposes by clearly marking its boundaries with signs. A licensee or guest may take banded pen-reared birds on such area during the private bird hunting area season. Pen-raised birds may be held in captivity on the area only for release to provide hunting, and all such birds shall be banded. If birds are propagated, a commercial game bird breeder license is also required. The Department shall require records as specified and may adopt regulations to manage and protect game birds occurring naturally in the wild, and shall prescribe the license application form. Licensees may also apply for dog field trial permits. Violation of any provisions regarding private bird hunting areas is a Class C misdemeanor. Except for field trial participants, hunting pen-raised birds on licensed private bird hunting areas requires a state hunting license (5.43.0721 through .078).

[There are additional commercial license provisions for commercial fishermen, commercial oyster fishermen, wholesale fish dealers, shrimp house operators, wholesale truck dealer's fish license, retail fish dealers, bait dealers, seine/net license, menhaden fish plant license, and details of fish transportation, aquatic product size and shipment, fish sizes, net/seine restrictions covered in chapter 47 of the statutes.]

The Department may issue a permit to a licensed fish farmer authorizing the taking of a specified quantity of fish brood stock from specified public water under Commission rules. The permit may allow the taking of fish brood stock reasonably necessary for the operation of the fish farm, but quantities limited as necessary to protect the availability of fish in public water, under Commission guidelines (5.43.551 through .553).

★The owner of a hunting lease may not receive hunting guests for pay or other consideration unless the landowner has a hunting lease license. [See 5.43.041 for definitions of "hunting cooperative," "hunting lease" (replaces "shooting preserve"), "guest," and related terms.] Applications shall include the name, signature, address and number of acres for each participating landowner included in a hunting cooperative permit that is part of a hunting lease. Fees for hunting lease licenses and hunting cooperative licenses are determined by the size of the hunting lease area, from 500 to 50,000 or more acres (5.43.042, .0431 and .044).★ Licensees shall certify that they will: not violate any hunting lease provisions; endeavor to prevent any guest from violating any such provisions; not receive guests who do not have valid hunting licenses. Records of activities on the hunting lease shall be kept as the Department directs, shall be submitted annually and may be inspected by Game Wardens at any time. Violation of any hunting lease provisions: Class C misdemeanor (5.43.048, .0485 and .055).

Import, Export and Release Provisions

The Department shall regulate the introduction and stocking of fish, shellfish, and aquatic plants into state public waters. The Commission may charge a reasonable fee for each species of fish placed in lakes or other bodies of water located solely on private property (2.12.014 and .015). No person may import, possess, sell or place into state waters exotic harmful or potentially harmful fish, shellfish or aquatic plants except as authorized by Department permit. The Department shall publish a list of exotic fish, shellfish and aquatic plants for which a permit is required and make rules as needed. A fish farmer may import, possess or sell harmful exotic fish species as provided by 134.020, Agricultural Code, but may not import, possess, propagate or transport exotic shellfish unless shown to be free from disease. "Exotic" means a nonindigenous fish, shellfish or aquatic plant not normally found in state public waters (5.66.007). No person may place any species of fish, shellfish or aquatic plant into any state public water without a Department permit and under its rules. This does not apply to native, nongame fish as defined by the Commission. It is a violation if such fish, shellfish or aquatic plants are placed in nonpublic water and escape into public water if the person does not hold a permit (5.66.015).

★No person may possess, transport, receive or release a live wolf in the state except for state/county officials or licensed operators of circuses, zoos or menageries for exhibition or scientific purposes. Offense is a felony.★ No person may sell or possess for sale a living armadillo except for operations related to zoos, educational, medical or research institutions as authorized by permit, or sales to commercial dealers. A peace officer with probable cause to believe that an animal is held in violation shall seize it, hold it for observation of rabies or other disease, and release or destroy the animal if found to be dangerous or otherwise harmful or diseased. Offense is a class B misdemeanor plus all costs (5.63.102 through .104). Except for agricultural purposes or as otherwise provided, no turkeys may be propagated, purchased, sold, transported or released for the purpose of establishing a free-ranging wild turkey population. The Department may release turkeys, or contract to do so, to maintain a wild turkey population, and may regulate turkey release by other persons (64.006).

★No person may bring into the state a protected bird or animal for sale, barter, exchange or shipment for sale during the open season, except that it is lawful to ship or bring any wild game birds, wild game animals or other protected species from Mexico into the state with proper US Customs documents and according to Department regulations and quotas. No person may bring into the state any protected animal or bird during the closed season for the same except as provided (5.62.024 through .026).★

Interstate Reciprocal Agreements

The Department may negotiate reciprocal agreements with neighboring states for waterfowl hunting if that state has a similar stamp requirement and fee (43.308). Nonresidents between the ages of 17 and 66 may hunt and fish without a Texas license if they have a valid license from a state that allows hunting and fishing by licensed Texas residents. Reciprocal agreements may be made with any other state to license sport hunting and fishing by residents of the other state at the same fee as Texas residents. The Director shall negotiate reciprocal agreements for fishing and migratory waterfowl hunting on rivers and lakes on common boundaries between Texas and adjoining states. [Provisions are given for approving, proclaiming, terminating, and regulating such reciprocal agreements in 5.41.004 through 41.006.] Violation of reciprocal provisions is a Class C misdemeanor (5.41.001, .003., .007 and .008).

ANIMAL DAMAGE CONTROL

No person may bring into or keep any cat, dog or other predacious animal on a fish hatchery or reservation for the propagation or exhibition of birds or animals. Any predacious animal found on such grounds is a nuisance and any Department employee shall destroy the animal with immunity from prosecution (5.81.002).

★Under 16 USC 742j-1, the Department may issue permits for the control of depredating animals or wildlife management by use of aircraft. Such permit may be issued if the Department finds that control of depredating animals by use of aircraft is necessary to protect or to aid in the protection of land, water, wildlife, livestock, domesticated animals, human life or crops, or aid in management of wildlife if such use will not have a deleterious effect on indigenous species (5.43.102 and .104). Each permit shall have the landowner's authorization stating the kind and number of depredating animals to be controlled, and applicants must meet other Department criteria, including submitting detailed reports as to dates of flights, animals taken, and areas covered (5.43.105 and .107). The Commission may regulate control of depredating animals and management of wildlife by aircraft by proclamations which: ▸ prescribe procedures for permit applications; ▸ establish procedures for controlling depredating animals by use of aircraft; ▸ limit the time and place for which a permit is valid; ▸ prohibit acts and limit or prohibit any activity as deemed necessary (5.43.109). It is an offense to: ▸ hunt or kill, or attempt such, from an aircraft any animal or bird that is not specifically authorized by a permit; ▸ possesses a firearm or other device capable of killing or wounding an animal or bird other than a device specifically authorized by the permit; ▸ use an aircraft to hunt, kill, or manage depredating animals without a permit; ▸ use an aircraft to harass wildlife or any other animal or bird. It is a defense to harassment of wildlife if the person is engaged in counting, photographing, relocating or capturing wildlife under a permit to manage wildlife by use of aircraft. A person may not conduct activities under a depredating animal control permit and a wildlife management permit simultaneously (5.43.1095). Violation is a Class A misdemeanor. If at trial it is shown that the defendant has a prior conviction under this chapter within the prior 10 years, the violation is a felony (5.43.111).★

A Game Warden may seize and hold as evidence an aircraft, vehicle, gun or other device used if the person is charged with a violation of hunting from aircraft provisions or the person used the aircraft, vehicle or gun in committing that violation. The Department may sell the aircraft, vehicle, gun or other seized device to the highest bidder if the owner is convicted, the Department receives at least three written bids, and the highest bid is not less than the appraised value of the property. If the Department is not authorized to sell or required to release the property, it may keep and use the aircraft, vehicle or gun to protect wildlife resources. Money received from forfeiture sales shall be deposited in the Game, Fish and Water Safety Fund for the enforcement of fish, shrimp, oyster, game, and sand, shell and gravel laws (5.43.112).

★★A person who has evidence clearly showing that protected wildlife is causing serious damage to agricultural, horticultural or aquicultural interests or other property, or is a threat to public safety, and who desires to kill the protected wildlife shall give written notice of the facts to the appropriate county judge. The county judge shall cause the notice to be posted in the courthouse and notify the Department of the property location where damage is occurring, the nature of the damage or threat, and the name of the applicant. The Department shall investigate and make recommendations for controlling the damage. An application for a damage/depredation permit must: ▸ be in writing and sworn; ▸ contain a statement of facts as to the damage/threat; ▸ contain an agreement to comply with specified provisions relating to the disposition of the protected wildlife; ▸ be signed by a Department employee testifying that inspection was made and control measures recommended; ▸ contain a statement that all recommended measures for damage prevention have been taken; ▸ contain a certification by the county judge (5.43.151 through .153).★★ The Department may issue such permit without regard to the closed season, bag limit or means and methods, and shall deliver the permit to the county judge. The permit must specify the time of validity; the area in which it applies; the kind of wildlife authorized to be killed; the persons permitted to kill the noxious wildlife. ★No permit for killing migratory game birds may be issued unless the applicant has received a permit from USFW, and no permit may be issued for taking of endangered species under chapter 68.★ The permittee shall give the location of wildlife killed under the permit to a local Game Warden who shall dispose of the carcass by donation to a charitable institution or other recipient or as the court directs. No permittee may fail to notify a Game Warden of the killing of wildlife, nor dispose of wildlife carcasses themselves, nor violate a term or condition of the permit. Violation: Class B misdemeanor (5.43.154, .155 and .157). (See also HUNTING, FISHING, TRAPPING PROVISIONS.)

ENFORCEMENT OF WILDLIFE LAWS

Enforcement Powers

Texas is a member of the Gulf States Compact, and of the Gulf States Marine Fisheries Commission, provisions of which are detailed in Chapter 91 of the statutes.

The Director may commission as peace officers any of the employees provided for in the general appropriations act. Law enforcement officers have the same powers, privileges and immunities as peace officers and have the same authority as a sheriff to arrest, serve criminal or civil process, require aid in so doing, and may arrest without a warrant any person found in the act of violating any law (2.11.019). Law enforcement officers commissioned by the Director and any other peace officers have authority to enforce all provisions of this code (2.11.0191). A Department employee who violates any code provision relating to game, fish and oysters which the employee is authorized to enforce commits a Class C misdemeanor (2.12.111).

To enforce fish and game laws and to conduct research, Department employees may enter on any land or water with immunity where wild game or fish are known to range or stray. A Game Warden may search a game bag, vehicle or other container with reasonable cause to believe that it contains unlawfully taken wildlife, and may inspect wildlife or parts discovered during such search. The Department may file complaints in the name of the state to recover fines and penalties for violations of game laws without the approval of any county attorney. Any peace officer or Department employee who arrests a violator may give a written notice to appear before the justice court within 15 days; failure to appear is a Class C misdemeanor, and an arrest warrant may be issued. Fines collected by any court for game law violations shall be remitted to the Department within 10 days, with a statement as to name of violator, amount of fine, and section of law violated. The county courts remit 80% and justice courts 85% of the fines collected (2.12.103 through .107).

When Game Wardens believe a person has unlawful possession of any fish, oysters, shrimp or other aquatic life, they shall seize and sell such to the highest of three bidders, the proceeds to be held until the outcome of the case. When possible, such confiscated game animals, birds or fish shall be given to a charitable institution and expenses of cold storage charged to the violator (2.12.109 and .110). A Game Warden may seize the pelt of any fur-bearing animal taken in violation of law or regulation, and hold same as evidence; on conviction, the pelts may be sold to the highest of three written bids. Game Wardens/peace officers shall seize without warrant any seines, nets, trawls, traps or other devices on the public water in violation of law or regulation, and upon conviction of the owner, or if the owner is not known, destroy the devices or give them to a university for teaching or research. Unregistered vessels belonging to persons convicted of committing violations may be seized and sold to the highest bidder, proceeds to go to the Game, Fish and Water Safety Fund (2.12.1101, .1105 and .1106).

A Game Warden or peace officer may seize an alligator, hide or any part with probable cause to believe it was taken, possessed, sold or purchased in violation of law or regulation, and if the person is charged with a violation, shall hold the alligator, hide or part as evidence. On conviction, the alligator, hide or part shall be sold by the Department to the highest bidder after taking a minimum of three written bids (5.65.009).

★Persons age 17 or older who have a license or permit issued under this code must carry on their person a driver's license or personal identification certificate while engaging in the licensed activity, and must display it to any peace officer on request. Violation: Class C misdemeanor. If a person is convicted in justice court for a violation that provides enhanced penalties for subsequent convictions, the court on request shall submit to the Department an affidavit certifying the conviction, including the driver's license number of the violator, and such affidavit, if admissible under the Texas Rules of Evidence, is available in subsequent prosecutions for violations of the same law or regulation. The court shall also compile and send to the Department copies of any photograph, description or measurement of the defendant made by any law enforcement agency in connection with the offense [other details are given] (2.12.114 through .117).★

Criminal Penalties

Persons adjudged guilty of an offense shall be punished in accordance with provisions herein and the Code of Criminal Procedure. Offenses are designated as Parks and Wildlife Code misdemeanors or felonies as follows: Class A misdemeanor, $500-2,000 fine, jail up to one year, or both; Class B misdemeanor, $200-1,000 fine, jail up to 6 months, or both; Class C misdemeanor, $25-500 fine. A Parks and Wildlife Code felony shall be punished by imprisonment in the Texas Department of Corrections for two to ten years, and in addition, may be fined $2,000 to $5,000. The use of a conviction for enhancement purposes does not preclude the subsequent use of a conviction for enhancement purposes. Each fish, bird, animal, reptile, or amphibian or part taken, possessed, killed, left to die, imported, offered for sale, sold, bought or retained in violation of any code provision or regulation is a separate offense (2.12.401 through .409).

★★If a corporation or association is adjudged guilty of an offense that provides a fine only, a court may fix the fine, not to exceed the amount provided by the offense. If guilty of an offense that provides a penalty including imprisonment or that provides no specific penalty, a court may sentence the corporation to pay a fine not to exceed $20,000 for a felony; or $10,000 for a Class A or B misdemeanor (2.12.410).★★

Violation of 2.12.015, 2.12.017 or 2.12.504 or a regulation thereunder (illegal introduction of fish, destruction of water buoys, violation of license revocation) is a Class C misdemeanor. A second violation of 12.017 within five years is a Class B misdemeanor. Engaging in an activity while a license is suspended or revoked is a Class A misdemeanor (2.12.019). Violation of provisions relating to fish ladders, fish screens, illegal sale of game fish (5.66.109, .110 and .117) is a class C misdemeanor (5.66.121).

See also HUNTING, FISHING, TRAPPING PROVISIONS and PROTECTED SPECIES OF WILDLIFE for other penalties.

Civil Penalties

Wildlife Code provisions do not deprive a court of other authority to forfeit property, suspend or cancel a license or permit, cite for contempt, or impose any other civil penalty, which penalty may be included in the sentence (2.12.402).

A person who kills, possesses or injures any fish, shellfish, reptile, amphibian, bird or animal in violation of law or regulation is liable to the state for the value of each such animal caught, taken, possessed or injured. The Commission shall adopt rules for determining the value of such injured or destroyed animals. The attorney general or county attorney may bring a civil suit in the name of the state to recover the value of each animal. Multiple defendants are jointly and severally liable for the judgment. The recovery amounts are in addition to any fine, forfeiture, penalty or costs imposed under another law. The pendency or determination of a suit brought hereunder, or of a criminal prosecution for the same killing or possession does not bar the other action. Damages recovered shall be deposited into the Game, Fish, and Water Safety Fund, except that 50% of any damages recovered in a suit brought by a county attorney shall be deposited in the general fund of the county (2.12.301 through .307).

License Revocations and Suspensions

The Director may suspend or revoke a license or permit if it is found, after notice and hearing, that the permittee or licensee: ▸ has been convicted of a violation relating to the permit/license to be revoked; ▸ violated a provision of law or rule relating to the permit/license to be revoked; ▸ made a false statement in the license application or related documents; ▸ is indebted to the state for taxes, fees or payment of penalties imposed by law or rule relating to the permit/license to be revoked. The Department must provide opportunity for a hearing concerning the suspension/revocation. Notice of suspension or revocation must be given personally or by registered/certified mail. A license/permitee may not be suspended for more than 60 days after it takes effect, and the holder may not apply for another license of the same type during the period of suspension. A person whose license has been revoked may not apply for another of the same kind for one year from the date of revocation. Violation of suspension or revocation is an offense. An appeal may be had in a district court of Travis County. ★★In lieu of suspending a license, the Department may give the person an opportunity to pay a civil penalty, after consideration of economic impact a suspension would have on the licensee/permittee engaging in a commercial activity and the amount reasonably necessary to deter further violations. The amount of the civil penalty may not be less than $150 for each day the license/permit was to have been suspended, and if not paid before the sixth day after notification of the amount due, the opportunity to pay it is lost and the Department may impose the suspension. Civil penalties received shall go into the Game, Fish and Water Safety Fund (2.12.501 through .507).★★

Reward Payments

A person who furnishes information leading to arrest and conviction for a flagrant violation of fish and game laws or regulations that apply to the taking, possession or sale of an animal, bird, reptile or fish may apply to the Operation Game Thief Committee for a reward to be paid from the Operation Game Thief Fund. "Flagrant violation" means a violation so extreme, conspicuous or outstandingly bad as to be impossible not to notice. A violation of license provisions in chapter 42 or 46 is not a flagrant violation. No amount in excess of the amount in the Game Thief Fund is payable as a reward, and no reward may be granted to a Department employee, family member, peace officer or member of the judiciary. The Department may provide a toll-free telephone number for reporting game and fish law violations 24 hours a day, and may establish procedures for donations to the fund (2.12.203 through .205).

HABITAT PROTECTION

[Numerous statutory sanctuaries and preserves are listed by name, including boundaries, unlawful acts, penalties and other information in chapter 82.]

The Department may provide technical guidance to landowners who request information concerning fish, wildlife, nongame, and habitat management, and shall support landowner education programs. Land purchased primarily for a purpose authorized by this code may be used for any authorized function if the Commission determines that multiple use is the best utilization of the land's resources (2.12.025 and .026). The Commissioners Court of each county may require the owner of a public or private dam on a regularly flowing stream to construct or repair fishways or fish ladders sufficient to allow fish in all seasons to ascend the dam. Failure to comply after 90 days notice is an offense, and each week of violation thereafter is a separate offense. The Department may direct persons taking state fresh water to use screens on intake canals or pipes to protect fish. No person may fail to comply with a written order of the Department regarding fish screens, and each day's failure to comply is a separate offense (5.66.109 and .110).

★★The Department may establish a state system of scientific areas for education, scientific research and preservation of flora and fauna of scientific or educational value, and to carry out these purposes may: ▸ determine proposed scientific areas; ▸ make and publish regulations for the management and protection of scientific areas; ▸ cooperate and contract with agencies, groups or individuals; ▸ accept gifts, grants, bequests of money or property to be used in accordance with the tenor of such gift, grant or bequest; ▸ formulate policies for the selection, acquisition, management and protection of scientific areas and negotiate for and approve the dedication of such areas; ▸ advocate research, interpretive programs, and publication of information pertaining to scientific areas; ▸ acquire interests in real property by purchase; ▸ hold and manage lands within the system. All public entities and agencies are authorized and urged to acquire, administer and dedicate land as state scientific areas. The Commission may use only funds appropriated for the acquisition of scientific areas (5.81.501, .502, .503 and .506).★★ The Department may: acquire, develop, maintain and operate wildlife management areas; manage wildlife and fish on such lands; prohibit hunting and fishing, or may open seasons for hunting or fishing on such areas and prescribe the number, kind, sex and size of game or fish that may be taken, and the means, methods and conditions for such taking. The Department may issue special permits for hunting wildlife in compliance with hunting license laws on game management areas, using a fair method of distribution of such permits (5.81.401 through .403). (See also EXCEPTIONS TO PROTECTION.)

★★The Department, with approval of the Commissioners Court of the affected county, shall set aside and reserve portions of each public freshwater stream or other body of water as fish sanctuaries in the county for the propagation of freshwater fish in their natural state. The Department shall use fish sanctuaries to increase and preserve the supply of freshwater fish in all fresh water where the fish supply has been reduced from any cause below the maximum number of fish in their natural state that the water will support, and when such depleted water areas are found, the Department shall set aside one or more portions of the water as a sanctuary without delay. Sanctuaries so designated may be used as such up to five years. No more than 50% of the public fresh water in any county may be so set aside and designated. The sanctuary designation proclamation must state the area to be included, reason for creation, date of effect, duration of the proclamation, and statutory citation. The Department shall give notice by all of the following: posting copies of the proclamation on the county courthouse door; publication in a county newspaper; posting with at least six signs around the sanctuary boundaries (5.81.201 through .207).★★

The Commission may purchase land for construction and operation of freshwater fish hatcheries, and may condemn land, easements and property in the state for constructing fish hatcheries or maintaining tidewater passages under the provisions allowed for condemnation proceedings by railroads (5.81.102 through .104). The Department may make grants to appropriate international nonprofit organizations for acquiring, developing and maintaining waterfowl propagation areas within Canada that provide waterfowl for the Central Flyway, but may not condition a grant on approval by the Department of improvements or construction performed in Canada (5.43.306).

★★The Department and the Land Office shall develop and adopt a State Wetlands Conservation Plan for state-owned coastal wetlands. The Texas Water Commission and other state agencies and local governments shall assist in developing and implementing this plan (2.14.002). [The details and provisions of this excellent plan are worthy of review by those interested in wetlands conservation.]★★

NATIVE AMERICAN WILDLIFE PROVISIONS: None.

UTAH

Sources: Utah Code Annotated, 1984, Title 23; 1992 Cumulative Supplement.

STATE WILDLIFE POLICY

All wildlife existing within this state, not held by private ownership and legally acquired, is the property of the state (23-13-3). All wildlife within this state, including but not limited to wildlife on public or private land or in public or private waters, shall fall within the jurisdiction of the Division of Wildlife Resources (23-15-2).

RELEVANT WILDLIFE DEFINITIONS: See Definitions section of Appendices.

STATE FISH AND WILDLIFE AGENCIES

Agency Structure

The **Division of Wildlife Resources** (Division) within the **Department of Natural Resources** (Department) is under the administration of the Executive Director (Director) of the Department. The Division is the wildlife authority for Utah and is vested with the functions, powers, duties, rights and responsibilities provided in this title and other law (23-14-1).

The **Wildlife Board** (Board) consists of five members from five designated groups of counties comprising Wildlife Districts. Members are appointed by the Governor with advice and consent of the senate, and must be well informed about wildlife conservation and restoration. No more than three members may be from the same political party. Each member shall be a citizen of the US and of the state and a resident of the district from which appointed, and the term of office is four years (23-14-2).

The **Board of Big Game Control** (BBGC) consists of the Director as chairman and four other members appointed by the Governor with advice and consent of the senate for four-year terms each, as follows: one member each from the Utah Cattlemen's Association, the Utah Woolgrowers Association and the Utah Wildlife and Outdoor Recreation Federation; and a representative of the US Forest Service regional office in Utah (23-14-5).

Agency Powers and Duties

Subject to the broad policy making authority of the Board and the BBGC, the **Division** is charged with the duty to protect, propagate, manage, conserve and distribute protected wildlife throughout the state. The Division is appointed the trustee and custodian of protected wildlife and may initiate civil and criminal proceedings to recover damages; compel performance; compel substitution; restrain or enjoin; initiate other appropriate action; seek appropriate remedies. State law shall prevail over ordinances or regulations concerning hunting, fishing, trapping adopted by political subdivisions. Communities may close areas to hunting for safety reasons on Board confirmation (23-14-1).

The Division may determine the facts relative to the wildlife resources of the state. Upon a determination of these facts, the **Board** shall establish policies designed to accomplish the purposes and fulfill the intent of wildlife laws and the preservation, protection, conservation, perpetuation, introduction and management of wildlife. No authority given the Board shall supersede the administrative authority of the Director of the Division or divest the rights, authority or powers of the BBGC as prescribed in this title. The Board elects one member as chairman and the Director shall act as secretary of the Board. The Division is empowered to investigate and determine facts relative to state big game resources. The **BBGC** shall have full authority to establish hunting seasons for big game animals and establish Division policy relating to the harvest of big game animals. The BBGC shall hold at least one public meeting in each wildlife district before establishing big game hunting seasons (23-14-3, -4, and -6).

The Division shall have the power to enter into cooperative agreements and programs with other states, federal agencies, educational institutions, cities, counties, landowners, and individuals for wildlife conservation, subject to approval of the Director and Board review (23-22-1). The Board is authorized to enter into reciprocal agreements with other states for licensing and regulating fishing, hunting and related activities, and promoting wildlife management programs, such agreements to be approved by the Director (23-22-3). The **Director** is executive and administrative head of the Division and shall be experienced in administration and requirements for protection, conservation, restoration and management of state wildlife resources. The Director carries out policies of the Board and the BBGC in accordance with state laws, has authority over personnel matters, and has full control of all property acquired and held for this title's purposes. The Director may declare emergency open or closed seasons in the interest of state wildlife resources (23-14-7 and -8).

To provide an adequate and flexible system of protection, propagation, introduction, increase, control, harvest, management and conservation of protected wildlife for development for public recreation and food supply, the BBGC (for big game mammals) and the Board (in all other matters covered by this code) are authorized to: ▸ determine under what circumstances, when and in what localities, by what means and in what amounts and numbers wildlife may be taken or killed to maintain an adequate supply, and, except as fixed by code, shall fix seasons and shorten, extend or close seasons on protected wildlife; ▸ close or open areas to fishing, trapping or hunting; ▸ establish refuges and preserves; ▸ regulate and prescribe means by which protected wildlife may be taken; ▸ regulate transportation and storage of protected wildlife or parts; ▸ establish or change bag and possession limits; ▸ prescribe safety measures and establish other regulations for wildlife conservation and the safety and welfare of hunters, trappers, fishermen, landowners and the public; ▸ establish the use, forms and fees of permits, tags and certificates of registration; ▸ prescribe rules to control the use and harvest of protected wildlife by private associations, clubs or corporations provided the regulations do not preclude landowners from personally controlling trespass upon their property nor from charging a fee to trespass for hunting or fishing, except on posted pheasant hunting units. The Board and the BBGC shall exercise their powers by orders, rules and regulations promulgated pursuant to this code (23-14-18 and -19).

Agency Funding Sources

The **Wildlife Resources Account** consists of: ▸ money collected from the sale of licenses, permits, tags, certificates of registration, fines and forfeitures; ▸ revenue from the sale, lease, rental or other granting of rights to real or personal property; ▸ interest, dividends or other income earned on account moneys; ▸ funds appropriated from the General Fund by the Legislature and other moneys received under a provision of this title. Moneys in the Wildlife Resources Account shall be used for the administration of this title. The Division is authorized to accept grants or gifts of money, property, water rights or other endowments that will benefit state wildlife resources, and which will go into a special account to be used for specific use as indicated by grantor (23-14-13 and -14). The **Wildlife Resources Trust Account** contains fees received from the sale of lifetime licenses and interest thereon. Money in this account is subject to restriction of 23-22-2 that no money from hunting and fishing license fees shall be diverted for any other purpose than the enhancement of wildlife by the Division (23-19-17). There shall be an annual appropriation from the General Fund deposited to the Wildlife Resources Restricted Account. The amount of this deposit shall be equal to the total of the fees, as determined by the previous year's license sales, that would have otherwise been collected for fishing licenses had full fees been paid by those over age 65, blind, paraplegic or otherwise disabled or mentally retarded (23-19-39).

Within the General Fund is a restricted **Upland Game Account**, consisting of moneys from the upland game habitat stamp sales and accrued interest. Moneys in the account shall be used for: ▸ control of predators; ▸ development, improvement, restoration or maintenance of critical habitat through the establishment of landowner incentives, cooperative programs or other means; ▸ the acquisition or preservation of critical habitat; ▸ the production, sale, distribution costs of the stamp and related artwork; ▸ landowner habitat education and assistance programs; ▸ public access to private lands; ▸ upland game transplant and re-introduction programs; ▸ payments in lieu of property taxes for lands purchased with stamp revenues. Moneys in the account may not be used for acquisition, development, improvement, restoration or maintenance of habitat within commercial hunting areas. No more than 5% of the net annual revenues may be used for landowner habitat education programs. Approximately 75% of the account moneys shall be allocated to programs relating to pheasant; the remaining moneys to be allocated to programs and activities relating to other upland game species based generally on the proportion of average annual hunter participation for each species. Projects for which free public access is assured receive first priority for funding (23-17-11).

PROTECTED SPECIES OF WILDLIFE

See RELEVANT WILDLIFE DEFINITIONS for listed animals.

It is unlawful: ▸ to hold in captivity protected wildlife except as provided by code or regulations of the Board; ▸ for persons to take, or to permit their dog to take, protected wildlife, except as provided by code or regulations of the Board or BBGC (23-13-3 and -4); ▸ to take protected aquatic wildlife or eggs of same in state waters except as provided by code or Board regulation; ▸ to seine for protected aquatic wildlife in state waters or to sell or transport protected wildlife except as prescribed by the Board; ★to pollute waters deemed necessary by the Board for wildlife purposes or waters containing protected aquatic wildlife and stoneflies, mayflies, dragonflies and damsel flies, water bugs, caddis flies, spongilla flies and crustaceans, each day of pollution constituting a separate offense (23-15-6 through -8).★

★The Legislature recognizes that the number of breeding sites of the American White Pelican has been reduced as a result of the removal of water barriers around breeding sites, loss of food supply and human disturbance of nesting colonies. The Legislature further recognizes that Gunnison Island in the Great Salt Lake, one of the seven remaining pelican rookeries in North America, produces over 20% of the world's population of the American White Pelican and is the only remaining major pelican rookery that does not have refuge status. It is declared to be the policy of the state that areas that will support certain threatened life forms shall be preserved for their benefit and for the benefit and enjoyment of present and future generations of people. The state shall initiate condemnation and purchase of the 163-acre Gunnison Island and 22-acre Hat (Bird) Island in the Great Salt Lake to be designated as wildlife management areas under the jurisdiction of the Division to be administered for the protection and perpetuation of the American White Pelican (23-21a-2 and -3).★

GENERAL EXCEPTIONS TO PROTECTION

The coyote, fieldmouse, gopher, ground squirrel, jackrabbit, muskrat and raccoon are not classified as protected wildlife. It is lawful for the Division to take wildlife in the interest of wildlife conservation. Division employees and federal game agents charged with managing wildlife may without permit use fireworks and explosives to rally, drive, or otherwise disperse concentrations of wildlife to protect property or wildlife resources (23-13-2, -6 and -7).

HUNTING, FISHING, TRAPPING PROVISIONS

Licenses and Permits

No person may hunt, trap, fish or seine protected wildlife, nor engage in sale, trade of protected wildlife or parts, without having in possession the necessary licenses, certificates of registration, permits and tags. The Board shall prescribe the forms of licenses, tags and permits. Alien residents may purchase licenses upon the same terms as a resident citizen. Fraud, deceit or misrepresentation in obtaining a license is a class B misdemeanor. Counterfeiting a license, permit or tag is a class A misdemeanor (23-19-1 through -6).

No hunting license shall be issued to a person born after December 31, 1965, without proof of completion of an approved Division hunter education course, or completion of an approved hunter education course in another state, including applicants for nonresident licenses. The Division is to provide course of instruction in safe handling of firearms, hunting ethics, conservation and related topics for instructors (23-19-11 and -12).

Persons over age 16 must have a waterfowl stamp in possession. A Waterfowl Stamp Committee is established to supervise rules for creation of artwork for stamp design, and to advise the Board on production and sale of stamp. Waterfowl stamp revenues shall only be used for developing, restoration and preservation of wetlands that will be beneficial to waterfowl. Up to 20% may be allocated by Legislature for use by a nonprofit conservation organization for wetland development projects in the Pacific flyway to benefit waterfowl resources of Utah. Persons over age 16 must have an **upland game habitat stamp** before hunting game birds and animals, except when hunting in a commercial hunting area or in possession of a lifetime hunting or fishing license. Revenue from the sale of upland game stamps and related artwork shall go into the Upland Game Account (23-17-10 and -11).

Persons holding a fur-bearer license may take fur-bearers in accordance with Board regulations. The Board shall govern all trapping on lands controlled by the Division. Fur dealers must have certificate of registration to sell and buy furs. No certificate is required for licensed trappers or fur farmers to sell skins or pelts which have been lawfully taken or raised, nor for persons who buy furs or pelts for their own use (23-18-2, -3, -5).

★It is unlawful to take more than one of a big game species during a license year, regardless of how many licenses or permits purchased, except as otherwise provided by code or proclamations of BBGC (23-16-5).★

The Board may authorize the practice of falconry and capturing and keeping in possession of birds under rules and regulations specified by it (23-17-7).

Restrictions on Taking

It is unlawful to: ▸ possess or use weapons in the pursuit of wildlife while under the influence of alcohol or illegal drugs; ▸ take wildlife from an airplane or other airborne vehicle or device or a motorized terrestrial or aquatic vehicle, including snowmobiles and other recreational vehicles, except as provided by code or Board regulation, except for paraplegics with special Board permit who may be authorized to hunt from a vehicle (23-20-11 and -12).

Private landowners may post their lands against hunting by the use of designated signs at all corners, fishing streams, roads, gates and rights of way entering the property. While taking wildlife or engaging in related activities, a person may not enter posted lands of another without permission, refuse to leave, or obstruct entrances. Hunting by permission cards will be provided to landowners by the Division on request. Persons may not post lands they do not own or legally control (23-20-14).

Persons under age 14 must be accompanied by a parent or other responsible person over age 21 at a distance within which visual and verbal communication is maintained while hunting with a weapon. Persons between age 14 and 16 must be accompanied by parent or other responsible person over age 21 while hunting big game with a weapon, and must be accompanied by a person age 21 or older while hunting wildlife, other than big game, with a weapon. A person under age 12 is not permitted to hunt for protected wildlife except as provided by Board rules (23-20-20).

Commercial and Private Enterprise Provisions

A person may establish and maintain private wildlife farms for propagating, rearing, and keeping fur-bearers or birds classified as protected wildlife and may sell or dispose of wildlife reared on such farms, but may not release such animals to the wild without written authorization from the Division. Escaped wildlife becomes the property of the state. Provisions do not apply to domesticated mink or chinchilla farms, nor for propagating, rearing or keeping protected wildlife other than those specified in this section (23-13-8).

Operation of a private fish installation requires a certificate of registration from the Division and operation under Board regulations. Such installations may not be developed on natural lakes or streams. Sale of protected aquatic wildlife taken from private fish installations requires certification of registration under Board conditions (23-15-10 and -11).

Commercial hunting areas for release and shooting of pen-raised birds require a certificate of registration under Board regulations concerning species of birds and number of such areas per county. Persons hunting on commercial hunting areas must have a combination license, small game license or commercial hunting area license (23-17-6).

Import, Export and Release Provisions

It is unlawful for a person to import or export species of live native or exotic wildlife or to possess or release from captivity such imported live wildlife except as provided in this code or the rules and regulations of the Board, without written permission from the Division (23-13-5). It is unlawful to release terrestrial or aquatic wildlife into the wild except as provided in this title. Violation: class A misdemeanor (23-13-14).

ANIMAL DAMAGE CONTROL

★When livestock are damaged by a bear or mountain lion, the owner may receive compensation for 50% of the fair market value of the damage by notifying the Division of the damage no later than four days after damage is discovered. Such notice is required each time damage is discovered.★ Proof of loss forms shall be filed no later than 30 days after the original notification to the Division. The Division, with the assistance of the Department of Agriculture, shall either accept or deny the claim for damages within 30 days after proof of loss form is filed. The Division shall pay all accepted claims to the extent of money appropriated by the Legislature for this purpose. The Division shall not pay mountain lion and bear damage claims to livestock owners who have failed to file with the Commissioner of Agriculture their completed livestock form and fee for the preceding and current year. Claimants may appeal the Division decision to a panel of three persons (one each selected by claimant and Division, and a third selected by the first two panel members), who shall decide if Division should pay all or part of the claim. The Board may make and enforce rules to administer and enforce this section (23-24-1).

★When pheasants damage cultivated crops, the owner shall immediately notify the Division orally and in writing, upon which the Division shall, as far as possible, control such damage (23-17-4). The Division may pay the crop owner for pheasant damage an amount not to exceed $200 yearly if the owner notifies the Division of damage within 48 hours after damage is discovered.★ Damage appraisal is to be made by the crop owner and the Division, who shall call upon a third party if agreement of damage amount cannot be reached (23-17-5). When beavers are doing damage to, or are a menace to, private property, a landowner may request authorization to kill or trap the beavers and the Board is empowered to grant authorization under conditions it prescribes (23-18-4).

ENFORCEMENT OF WILDLIFE LAWS

Enforcement Powers

★★Utah is a member of the Wildlife Violators Compact (23-25-1 through -13).★★ See Model Statute Section of Handbook for full provisions of the compact.

Division conservation officers shall enforce title provisions with the same authority and following the same procedures as other peace officers. They may search vehicles, camps or other places where wildlife may be possessed or stored with probable cause that illegally taken wildlife may be found, except that a dwelling place may not be searched without a search warrant. Conservation officers shall seize protected wildlife illegally taken and upon conviction, the wildlife shall be confiscated by the court and sold or disposed of by the Division, proceeds to be deposited in the Wildlife Resources Account. Migratory waterfowl may not be sold, but must be given to charitable institutions. Materials and devices used for unlawful taking/possessing of protected wildlife shall be seized, confiscated upon conviction, and sold, proceeds to go into the Wildlife Resources Account. Conservation officers may seize and impound a vehicle used for unlawful taking/possessing protected wildlife to: ▸ provide for safekeeping of the vehicle if the owner is arrested; ▸ search the vehicle; ▸ inspect the vehicle for evidence that wildlife was unlawfully taken or possessed. The vehicle shall be released to the owner no later than 30 days after the date the vehicle was seized, unless the vehicle was used for the unlawful taking of wildlife by a person who is charged with committing a felony under this title. On conviction of a felony under this title, the vehicle may be confiscated by the court and sold, proceeds to go into the Wildlife Resources Account. The owner of the vehicle is liable for impound fees if the charges are dropped involving the use of the vehicle for the unlawful taking/possessing of wildlife, or if the person is found not guilty. The Director may appoint temporary special deputies with authority to enforce code provisions and regulations promulgated under the code (23-20-1 and -2).

Criminal Penalties

Unless otherwise provided, a violation of a provision of this title or a rule, proclamation or order issued by the Board or BBGC is a class B misdemeanor (23-13-11). Refusal to stop on order of a conservation officer or an attempt to flee or elude an officer is a class A misdemeanor, with a fine of not less than $250 and a jail term not less than 60 days. Failure to exhibit one's license, permit, or tag on request of a conservation or other peace officer is a misdemeanor. The penalty for aiding or assisting another person to violate a provision of the wildlife code or regulation is the same as for the provision or regulation for which aid or assistance is given. Assault on a conservation officer is a class A misdemeanor. Altering a license with intent to defraud is a misdemeanor (23-20-3 through -27).

Civil Penalties

When a person is guilty of illegal taking, illegal possession, or wanton destruction of wildlife, the court may order the defendant to pay restitution as set forth herein, or a greater or lesser amount, for the value of each animal taken, possessed, or destroyed, unless the court finds that restitution is inappropriate. Suggested minimum restitution values for protected wildlife per each animal are: ► $1,000 for each bison, bighorn sheep, rocky mountain goat, moose, bear, cougar or endangered species; ► $750 for each elk or threatened species; ► $500 for each golden eagle or river otter; ► $400 for each pronghorn antelope or deer; ► $350 for each bobcat; ► $100 for each swan, sandhill crane, turkey, pelican, loon, egret, heron or raptor, except those that are threatened or endangered; ► $35 for each fur-bearer, except bobcat, river otter and threatened or endangered species; ► $15 for each game bird, except turkey, swan, and sandhill crane; ► $10 per each fame fish; ► $8 per pound dry weight of processed brine shrimp including eggs; ► $5 per animal for protected wildlife not listed. ★If the court finds that restitution is inappropriate or if the value imposed is less than the suggested minimum value provided, the court shall make the reasons for the decision part of the record.★ ★★Any restitution shall be deposited in the Wildlife Resources Account, and such moneys shall be used by the Division for activities and programs to help stop poaching, including: educational programs on wildlife crime prevention; acquisition and development of wildlife crime detection equipment; operation and maintenance of anti-poaching projects; wildlife law enforcement training.★★ Restitution shall be in addition to any other fine or penalty imposed for a violation of this title. A judgment imposed under this section constitutes a lien when recorded and shall have the same effect and is subject to the same rules as a judgment for money in a civil action (23-20-4.5)

It is unlawful to waste or permit to be wasted or spoiled protected wildlife or their parts (23-20-8). Gifts of protected wildlife or their parts from one person to another require a donation slip showing the donor's name and license number. It is unlawful for a butcher or locker plant operator to process or store protected wildlife carcass unless it has a proper tag or required donation slip attached (23-20-9 and -10).

Illegal Taking of Wildlife

Except as provided in this title or rule of the Board or the BBGC, a person may not: take or permit his dog to take protected wildlife or their parts, an occupied nest or an egg of protected wildlife; transport, ship or cause to be shipped protected wildlife or their parts; sell or purchase protected wildlife or their parts; possess protected wildlife or their parts unaccompanied by a license, permit, tag, certificate of registration, bill of sale or invoice. Possession of protected wildlife without a license, permit or other documentation is prima facie evidence that the protected wildlife was illegally taken and is illegally held in possession. A person is guilty of a class B misdemeanor if the person violates any of these provisions and does so with criminal negligence as defined in 76-2-103(4) (23-20-3).

★★A person is guilty of wanton destruction of protected wildlife if the person: ► violates 23-13-4, 23-13-5, or 23-13-13, 23-15-6 through 23-15-9, 23-16-5 or 23-20-3; ► captures, injures or destroys protected wildlife; does so with intentional knowing or reckless conduct as defined in 76-2-103; ► intentionally abandons protected wildlife or a carcass; ► commits the offense at night with the use of a weapon; ► is under a court or Wildlife Board revocation of a license, tag, permit, or certificate of registration; ► or acts for pecuniary gain. This does not apply to actions taken in accordance with Title 4, Chapter 23, Agriculture and Wildlife Damage Prevention Act; section 23-16-3; or Title 4, Chapter 14, Utah Pesticide Control Act. Wanton destruction of wildlife is punishable as: ► a third degree felony if the aggregate value of the protected wildlife as determined by the values in 23-20-4(4) is more than $500; ► a class A misdemeanor if such aggregate value is $250-500; ► a class B misdemeanor if the aggregate value of the protected wildlife is under $250. Regardless of the restitution amounts imposed under 23-20-4.5, the following values shall be assigned to protected wildlife per each animal for determining the offense for wanton destruction: ► $1,000 for each bison, bighorn sheep, rocky mountain goat, moose, bear, cougar or endangered species; ► $750 for each elk or threatened species; ► $500 for each golden eagle or river otter; ► $400 for each pronghorn antelope or deer; ► $350 for each bobcat; ► $100 for each swan, sandhill crane, turkey, pelican, loon, egret, heron or raptor, except those that are threatened orendangered; ► $35 for each fur-bearer, except bobcat, river otter and threatened or endangered species; ► $15 for each game bird, except turkey, swan, and sandhill crane; ► $10 per each fame fish; ► $8 per pound dry weight of processed brine shrimp including eggs; ► $5 per animal for protected wildlife not listed. For purposes of sentencing for a wildlife violation, a person who has been convicted of a third degree felony under subsection (3)(a) is not subject to the mandatory sentencing requirements prescribed in 76-3-203(4) (taking animal valued at $1,000) (23-20-4). ★★

License Revocations and Suspensions

A license, permit, tag or certificate of registration shall be revoked by the Board when a person flagrantly and knowingly violates or countenances the violation of a provision of this title or rule/regulation of the Board or BBGC, or upon receiving notice from another state's wildlife agency that a person has: failed to comply with the terms of a wildlife citation; or been convicted of a violation that would warrant such action within the state of Utah. The Board may not revoke a license, etc., if a person was found not guilty of the violation in a court of law, or if the charges are removed. Prior to revocation, a person must be given notice and an opportunity for hearing. The Board may prohibit the person from obtaining a new license, permit, tag or certificate for up to five years. The Board may construe a subsequent conviction during the revocation period as a flagrant violation and may prohibit the person from obtaining a new license, etc., for up to an additional five years. The Board may reinstate a license, etc. upon receiving a report that the person has complied with the citation (23-19-9). No license, etc., may be purchased by a person who has a Utah warrant outstanding for failure to appear in answer to a summons for a violation of the Wildlife Code or regulation. or if the person has failed to comply with a wildlife citation in a state which is a party to the Wildlife Violator Compact set forth in Title 23, Chapter 25. The Division may allow a person to purchase a license, etc. if satisfactory proof is given that the warrant is no longer outstanding or that the person has complied with the wildlife citation (23-19-9.5).

A person convicted of trespassing on lands posted by the owner against hunting may have any license, tag, or permit relating to the activity revoked by the Board. The Board may construe a subsequent conviction within five years as a flagrant violation and may prohibit the person from obtaining a new license, tag or permit for a period up to five years. ★The Division shall provide information regarding owner rights and sportsmen's duties to anyone licensed to take wildlife, by using the public media and other sources. Restrictions relating to trespassing in this section shall be stated in all hunting and fishing proclamations issued by the Board and the BBGC (23-20-14). ★

★Whenever the Division receives notice from a court that a person has failed to appear to answer charges for a wildlife violation after having been issued a citation to appear, the Board may revoke the license, permit, tags or certificates of registration for a period of at least one year and up to three years (23-20-17). ★

HABITAT PROTECTION

See Pelican Management Act under PROTECTED SPECIES OF WILDLIFE.

Except in anticipation of and to provide for safe disposal of natural storm and flood waters, no person may without existing rights divert so much water from a natural stream, lake, pond or natural lake or pond which has increased storage due to construction of a dam that the diversion unduly endangers protected aquatic wildlife (23-15-3) It is unlawful to take water from the state streams, lakes or reservoirs for power purposes or for waterworks without furnishing and maintaining suitable screens to prevent fish from entering such power plants, millraces or waterworks. Such screens are to be built and maintained under the direction of the Board, and failure to comply after 30 days notice in writing from the Board is a misdemeanor (23-15-4). A person desiring to drain an irrigation canal, ditch, reservoir or other waterway containing protected aquatic wildlife, or who intends to divert waters so as to endanger the protected aquatic wildlife therein, shall give five days written notice to the Division prior to the diversion, or reasonable notice in case of emergency (25-15-5).

The Division shall have the power to acquire lands, waters and rights-of-way by purchase, lease, agreement, gift, exchange or other lawful means for authorized activities (23-21-1). The Division may not acquire title to real property held in private ownership without the Governor's approval. The Governor shall submit notification of the proposed acquisition to the county commission of the county in which the property is located and invite comments, after consideration of which the Governor may approve the acquisition in whole or in part, or disapprove the acquisition (23-21-1.5). The Division will reimburse each county for the amount of property taxes, or for the amount of fine moneys, the county would have received on the land. The amount of this reimbursement will not exceed what the regularly assessed real property taxes would be if the land had remained in private ownership (23-21-2).

There is reserved to the public the right of access to all lands owned by the state, including those lands lying below the official government meander line or high water line of navigable rivers for the purpose of hunting, trapping and fishing (23-21-4). The Board is authorized to use unsurveyed state-owned lands below the 1855 meander line of the Great Salt Lake for the creation, operation, maintenance and management of wildlife management areas, fishing waters and other recreational activities (23-21-5). Consent is given for the acquisition by the US for land or water areas in the state for refuges for migratory birds with certain reservations and conditions (23-21-6).

★Posted Hunting Units are established to: ▸ provide income to landowners; ▸ create satisfying hunting opportunities; ▸ increase wildlife resources; ▸ protect landowners who open their lands for hunting. The Board is authorized to make and enforce rules for posted hunting units (23-23-3). Posted Hunting Units are to be operated by landowner associations (associations) (23-23-4). The Board may grant variances from general statewide permit fees and season lengths for posted hunting units (23-23-6). Associations must obtain a certificate of registration from the Board before operating a posted hunting unit (23-23-5). The Division shall provide permits for the unit free of charge. At least 50% of the permits shall be offered to the general public, and at least 75% of the acreage within the boundaries of each Posted Hunting Unit shall be open to hunting by holders of permits. The associations shall clearly post the boundaries of the Posted Hunting Unit (23-23-7). Landowners who incur damages caused by a hunter on their land within the unit may submit claims and receive compensation from permit fee funds collected by the associations (23-23-8). The associations may appoint agents to protect private property on the unit, and such agents may refuse entry to persons without permit or who have damaged property within the area (23-23-9). Hunters must have a Posted Hunting Unit permit and the necessary hunting licenses, permits, tags and stamps, and may hunt only on the unit specified on their permit (23-23-10). Violation: class B misdemeanor (23-23-13).★

The Division shall prepare a management plan for each deer and elk herd unit in the state, and submit the plans to the BBGC for approval. The herd unit shall be managed in accordance with the approved plan. In preparing a plan, the Division shall confer with federal and state land managers, private landowners, sportsmen and ranchers. Each plan shall establish target herd size objectives, considering available information on each unit's range carrying capacity and ownership, and seek to balance relevant multiple uses for the range. Until a management plan for a herd unit is prepared and approved, the herd unit shall be manageed to maintain the herd size as range conditions and available data dictate. Management plans shall be prepared and approved by May 1994 for elk; May 1996 for deer. An annual progress report on the plans shall be made to the Energy, Natural Resources and Agriculture Interim Committee until plans are completed. The management plans may be revised as the Division or BBGC determine necessary, following these provisions (23-16-7).

See also Agency Funding Sources under STATE WILDLIFE AGENCIES.

NATIVE AMERICAN WILDLIFE PROVISIONS

The provisions and penalties of this code shall apply to all persons, including Indians when off an Indian reservation (23-23-12).

VERMONT

Sources: Vermont Statutes Annotated, 1981 Replacement Edition, Title 10; 1992 Cumulative Pocket Supplement.

STATE WILDLIFE POLICY

It is the policy of the state that the protection, propagation control, management and conservation of fish, wildlife and fur-bearing animals in this state is in the interest of the public welfare, and that safeguarding of this valuable resource for the people of the state requires a constant and continual vigilance. The Fish and Wildlife Board is the state agency charged with carrying out these purposes. An abundant, healthy deer herd is a primary goal of fish and game management. It is also acknowledged that although a statewide open season on antlerless deer is not recognized as desirable or necessary to achieve this goal, a limited antlerless season on a deer management unit basis could be an effective tool for harvesting an overpopulation of the deer herd [details of establishing antlerless deer hunting season provided] (10-4081).

RELEVANT WILDLIFE DEFINITIONS: See Definitions section of Appendices.

STATE FISH AND WILDLIFE AGENCIES

Agency Structure

There is hereby established a **Fish and Wildlife Department** (Department) which shall be administered by the Commissioner. The Commissioner shall be appointed pursuant to the provisions of 10-2851, and shall also be Executive Secretary of the **Fish and Wildlife Board** (Board), which shall consist of seven members appointed by the Governor with the advice and consent of the senate, for a term of six years, and during their terms they shall reside in the county from which they are appointed. In the event a member no longer resides in that county, the Governor shall appoint a member from that county for the unexpired portion of the term. The Governor shall biennially designate a chairman (10-4041 and -4042).

The Commissioner, with the approval of the Governor, may appoint and employ a Chief game warden and State game wardens for enforcement of state fish and wildlife laws, who shall be sworn to the faithful performance of their duties. With approval of the Board, the Commissioner may appoint and employ for a limited time as many Deputy game wardens as deemed necessary. The number of game wardens shall be determined by the Board with the approval of the Governor (10-4191).

Agency Powers and Duties

The Board, with approval of the Governor, may: ▸ acquire by gift, purchase or lease in the name of the state, lands, ponds or streams, and hunting and fishing rights and privileges in state lands or waters, with rights of ingress or egress; ▸ with the approval of the Board, may regulate the taking of wild animals on the lands and close or open these lands or any part to the taking of wild animals, such regulations to be posted; ▸ regulate the use by the public of access areas, landing areas, parking areas or of other lands or waters acquired or maintained pursuant to 10-4144, such regulations to be posted; ▸ with the approval of the Governor, ▸ exchange, sell or lease lands under its jurisdiction when it is advantageous to the state for development of lands and management of game. A person shall not trespass, in violation of regulations, upon property under the jurisdiction of the Board (10-4144, -4145, -4147 and -4148).

The **Commissioner:** ▸ shall have charge of the enforcement of the provisions of this part; ▸ may publish information and instruction bulletins concerning Department work; ▸ shall keep an account of the Department business and proceedings of the Department; ▸ may confer with the fish and game Directors or Commissioners of other states and Canada; ▸ shall pay into the state treasury to be deposited to the Fish and Wildlife Fund all moneys received; ▸ shall issue proper documentation to the Commissioner of Finance and Management for disbursement of funds from the state treasury (10-4132 and -4135).

The Commissioner shall have charge, under the direction of the Board, of the propagation and distribution of fish and wild animals, and shall provide for construction, maintenance and operation of game farms, rearing stations, hatcheries, fishways, screens and weirs. With Board approval, the Commissioner may: introduce fish into closed waters and into such waters not private preserves; ► take and transport fish and wild animals for artificial propagation, scientific purposes, and management of lands controlled by the Department; ► sell, exchange or dispose of fish and wild animals for the best interest of the state (10-4136).

The Commissioner, subject to Board approval, may: ► take, permit or cause to be taken fish which hinder or prevent the propagation of game or food fish; ► take, permit or cause to be taken wild animals doing damage; ► take necessary measures to control, in public waters, aquatic vegetation, insects or aquatic life, for improving such waters as a habitat, any measures involving temporary pollution of waters to be carried out in accordance with the provisions of chapter 47; ► sell fish fry, fingerlings and adult trout to residents for stocking state waters in the state and sell to residents fish reared by the state. A person shall not make other use of such fish fry or fingerlings than is represented in the application therefor or is prescribed by the Commissioner, or make a false statement in such application (10-4138 and -4143).

The Commissioner, with approval of the Board, may: ► establish public shooting grounds on land acquired or controlled by and under the jurisdiction of the Department; ► prohibit or regulate the taking of wild animals in accordance with law on any part of such lands; ► make regulations for the protection and management of such lands. At least 30 days before such a prohibition or regulation takes effect, the Commissioner shall file a copy in the office of the town clerk, and shall publish it three times. Part(s) of such shooting grounds closed against the taking of game shall be surrounded by at least one wire and suitable notices shall be placed along such boundaries (10-4146).

The Commissioner shall be State Ornithologist and: ► may employ, subject to the approval of the Governor, one or more assistants; ► shall investigate the distribution, food and unity of state birds, study their relations to insects and other pests and disseminate the information; ► may prepare bulletins regarding state birds, means of protecting them, methods of protecting crops from birds and other economic matters relating to birds; ► may deliver public lectures and addresses provided that expenses incident thereto are met by those requesting such services (10-4149 through -4151).

★★The Commissioner is authorized to hold an annual drawing for a permanent fishing license or, if the applicant is eligible, a combination fishing and hunting license. Fees collected shall be deposited into the Fish and Wildlife Fund (10-4153).★★

When conditions exist which constitute an emergency calling for protection measures for fish or game additional to those provided by existing law, the Secretary, through the Commissioner, shall certify its opinion to the Governor and attach a statement of the measures it recommends. The Governor by proclamation may suspend or close the open season in whole or in part for a species of fish, game or fur-bearing animal in any localities or may impose additional restrictions upon the number of a species to be taken. A proclamation issued under 10-4402 shall continue in force until the date specified or until the Governor shall recall it or until, but in no instance beyond, the convening of the next regular session of the general assembly. When the fishing or hunting season is wholly or partly closed by such proclamation, the Commissioner shall report to the Governor upon the effect of such action and the Governor may reopen or extend the season by proclamation for a period not to exceed the closed period (10-4402 through -4404).

Proclamations made under 10-4401 or 10-4402 shall be published in state newspapers and posted in such places and in such manner as the Governor may order. A copy of such publication and order, attested by the Secretary of Civil and Military Affairs, shall be filed with the Secretary of State and a copy shall be furnished to the Secretary who shall attend to publication and posting. During the time made a closed season as provided in 10-4401 or 10-4402, the provisions of law relating to closed seasons shall be in force and persons violating a provision thereof shall be subjected to the penalty provided for taking fish and wild animals in closed season (10-4405 and -4406).

Orders and Proclamations of the Governor

During an open season for the taking of game or fish, when it appears that by reason of drought, hunting, fishing and trapping is likely to cause forest fires, the Governor may by proclamation suspend hunting, fishing and trapping and make it a closed season for a designated time. In such proclamation, localities not affected by drought and certain game birds, animals and fish may be excepted. When it appears to the Governor that the necessity therefor has ceased to exist, the Governor shall remove the suspension, except that in case the period of suspension includes the open season for taking deer, the open season shall not be reopened, but the Governor by proclamation shall fix some period of equal number of days in the same year as the open season for the taking of deer (10-4401).

Agency Regulations

The Board may adopt rules, under chapter 25 of Title 3, to be known as the "Vermont Fish and Wildlife Regulations" for regulation of fish and wild game except as otherwise specifically provided by law. The rules shall be designed to maintain the best health, population and utilization levels of the regulated species and of other necessary or desirable species which are ecologically related to the regulated species. The rules shall be supported by investigation and research conducted by the Department on behalf of the Board. The Board may annually adopt temporary rules relating to the management of migrating game birds. For each such rule, the Board shall conduct a hearing but, when necessary, may schedule the hearing for a day before the terms of the rule are expected to be determined (10-4082).

Any regulation which relates to species or varieties of fish may apply to all or a portion of the state and may: ► establish, extend, shorten or abolish open and closed seasons; ► establish, change or abolish daily, season, possession and size limits; ► establish and change territorial limits for the pursuit, taking, or killing of species or varieties, and close or open lakes, streams or parts thereof; ► prescribe the manner and means of pursuing, taking or killing a species or variety, including, but not limited to, the prescribing of type or kinds of bait, lures, tackle, equipment, traps or other means or devices for taking such fish; ► prescribe rules relating to transportation and exportation of fish (10-4083).

Rules concerning wild game may: ► establish open seasons, the open season for deer, however, to be as established under chapter 113 of this title; ► establish daily, season and possession limits; ► establish territorial limits for any rule under this subchapter; ► prescribe the manner and means of taking any species or variety, and including reporting and tagging of game; ► establish restrictions on taking based upon sex, maturity or other physical distinction of the species or variety pursued; ► designate management districts for various species or varieties. On or before July 1 of each year, the Commissioner shall publish a report showing all the management districts and proposed deer seasons including supporting data. Each January the Commissioner shall publish an annual report showing the specific Department programs, plans and operational goals and include a progress report of each deer management district. After management districts have been established by the Board, the districts shall not thereafter be altered without approval of the general assembly; however, the Board shall have authority to subdivide established districts (10-4084).

Agency Funding Sources

The receipts of the Department shall not become a part of the general fund but shall be used solely for the Department. A **Nongame Wildlife Account** is created and shall consist of: funds appropriated by the general assembly; funds from public and private sources which the Commissioner accepts and funds from federal government aid for state activities in nongame conservation. Amounts in the account shall not lapse (10-4047 and -4048). All waterfowl stamp receipts and receipts from the sale of stamp by-products shall be deposited in the **Fish and Wildlife Fund**, and shall be expended by appropriation for waterfowl acquisition and improvement projects (10-4277).

Agency Advisory Boards

There is a committee on endangered species, the **Endangered Species Committee** consisting of nine members, including the Commissioners of Agriculture, Food and Markets, Fish and Wildlife, Forests, Parks, and Recreation, and six members appointed by the Governor from the public. Of the six public members, two shall be actively engaged in agricultural activities, two shall be knowledgeable concerning flora, and two shall be knowledgeable concerning fauna. The chairman shall be elected from among and by members each year. Members shall serve terms of three years. The Committee shall advise the Secretary on all matters relating to endangered and threatened species, including whether to alter the lists of endangered and threatened species and how to protect those species (10-5404). (See PROTECTED SPECIES OF WILDLIFE.)

There is a **Migratory Waterfowl Advisory Committee** consisting of five persons appointed by and serving at the pleasure of the Commissioner. The Commissioner shall designate a chairperson. The committee shall be consulted with and may make recommendations to the Commissioner on projects and activities supported with waterfowl stamp related funds. The Commissioner shall make an annual financial and progress report to the committee (10-4277).

PROTECTED SPECIES OF WILDLIFE

The Commissioner shall adopt a rule establishing a plan for nongame wildlife. The rule may be amended from time to time, and shall be reviewed, after public hearings, at least every five years. The plan shall contain: ► strategies to manage, inventory, preserve, protect, perpetuate and enhance all nongame wildlife in the state, including identification of wildlife species in need of protection and information on their population distributions, habitat requirements, limiting factors and other pertinent biological and ecological data on nongame wildlife species in need of protection; ► estimates of resources available for these strategies; ► plans for research and education in nongame wildlife. In accordance with the plan, the Commissioner may make expenditures from the Nongame Wildlife Account. Expenditures shall be restricted to programs specified in the adopted plan, may be made under the terms of contracts with private organizations and groups, consistent with the purposes of the plan, and shall not exceed the moneys available in the account. The Commissioner may take appropriate actions to encourage taxpayers to make designations to the account, including explaining the purposes of the fund and the uses to which the account has been or will be applied (10-4048). (See Agency Funding Sources under STATE FISH AND WILDLIFE AGENCIES.)

The Secretary shall adopt by rule a state endangered species list and a state threatened species list. The listing for a species may apply to the whole or to a part of the state. The Secretary shall determine a species to be endangered if it normally occurs in the state and its continued existence as wildlife or a wild plant in the state is in jeopardy, and shall determine a species to be threatened if its numbers are significantly declining because of loss of habitat or human disturbance and unless protected will become endangered. In determining whether a species is endangered or threatened, the Secretary shall consider: ► the present or threatened destruction, modification or curtailment of the range or habitat of the species; ► over-utilization of the species for commercial, sporting, scientific, educational or other purposes; ► disease or predation affecting the species; ► the adequacy of existing regulation; ► actions relating to the species carried out or about to be carried out by a governmental agency or other person who may affect the species; ► other natural or man-made factors affecting the continued existence of the species. In determining whether a species is endangered or threatened, the Secretary shall: ► use the best scientific, commercial and other data available; ► consult with interested state or federal agencies, other states having a common interest in the species, and interested persons; ► notify the Governor of any state contiguous to Vermont in which the species affected is known to occur (10-5402).

Except as authorized under this chapter, a person shall not take, possess or transport wildlife or plants that are endangered or threatened. The Secretary, with advice of the endangered species committee, may adopt rules for protection and conservation of endangered and threatened species. Violation: fine up to $500. Violation for an endangered species: fine up to $1,000 on first offense; subsequent conviction, fine of $500 to $1,000. Violation for a threatened species: fine up to $500 on first offense; a subsequent conviction, fine of $250 to $500. ★★A person who knowingly injures a threatened or endangered species may be required by the court to pay restitution of no more than $500 for veterinarian costs and related expenses incurred in treating and caring for the injured bird or animal (10-5403).★★

The Secretary, with the advice of the Endangered Species Committee, may establish conservation programs for threatened or endangered species of wildlife or plants, including the purchase of land or aquatic habitat and the formation of contracts for management of wildlife or wild plant refuge areas or for other purposes. All state agencies shall review programs administered by them which may relate to this chapter and in consultation with the Secretary shall utilize their authorities only in a manner which does not jeopardize conservation programs established by this chapter or by the Secretary. In addition to other methods of enforcement authorized by law, the Secretary may direct under this section that wildlife or wild plants seized because of violation of this chapter be transferred to a zoological, botanical, educational or scientific institution, and that the costs of the transfer may be charged to the violator. The Secretary, with the advice of the Endangered Species Committee, may adopt rules for the implementation of this section (10-5405 through -5407).

After obtaining the advice of the Endangered Species Committee, the Secretary may permit, under such terms and conditions as the Secretary may prescribe by rule any act otherwise prohibited if done for the following purposes: ▸ scientific purposes; ▸ to enhance the propagation or survival of a species; ▸ economic hardship; ▸ zoological exhibition; ▸ educational purposes; ▸ special purposes consistent with the purposes of the federal Endangered Species Act. Nothing in this chapter shall prevent a person who holds a proper permit from the federal government or any other state from transporting an endangered or threatened species from a point outside this state within or without this state. Nothing in this chapter shall prevent a person from possessing in this state wildlife or wild plants which are not determined to be "endangered" or "threatened" under the federal Endangered Species Act where the possessor is able to produce substantial evidence that they were first taken or obtained in a place without violating the law of that place. No rule adopted under this chapter shall cause undue interference with normal agricultural or silvicultural practices. This section shall not be construed to exempt a person from the provisions of the federal Endangered Species Act. Nothing in this section permits a person to violate a provision of federal law concerning federally protected endangered species (10-5408).

GENERAL EXCEPTIONS TO PROTECTION

The Commissioner may issue permits authorizing collection of birds, their nests and eggs, and fish and wild animals or parts, for public scientific research or educational purposes, or for subjects of art and photography (10-4152).

HUNTING, FISHING, TRAPPING PROVISIONS

General Provisions

A person without a firearm may train a hunting dog to hunt and pursue: ▸ bear from June 1 to September 15 and only from sunrise to sunset; ▸ rabbits and game birds from June 1 to the last Saturday in September and only from sunrise to sunset; ▸ raccoon from June 1 to the last Saturday in September at any time; ▸ bobcat and fox from June 1 to March 15, except during regular deer season as prescribed in 10-4741. The Commissioner may permit a person without a gun to train and condition a hunting dog between the second Monday in March and June 1, and the Board may adopt rules to control the training and conditioning (10-5001).

The Commissioner may issue permits to organized groups to hold field trials for hunting dogs. The Commissioner may issue a license to a responsible person or field trial group to hold a field trial for retrieving dogs, or bird dogs, with game birds which have been propagated or legally acquired and released on the day of the trial on premises owned or controlled by the individual or group conducting the same, and shot during daylight hours. Trials shall be supervised by the Department. A person who participates in a trial shall not be required to have a hunting license. No person shall pursue black bear with the aid of dogs, either for training or taking, without a permit. A nonresident may train dogs to hunt bear only while training season is in effect in the nonresident's home state and subject to the laws and regulations of this state (10-5002, -5003, -5006 and -5007).

A person shall not: ▸ transport fish or game taken by another except in the presence of the person who took that fish or game; ▸ transport fish or game during the closed season; ▸ transport in one day more than the limit of fish or game which may legally be taken in a day. However, a person travelling on land between a temporary abode and the person's domicile may transport in one day the limit of fish and game which may legally be taken in two days. While on the state waters, a person in no case may transport more than the limit of fish which may be taken in one day unless the fish is frozen, processed and packaged for storage. Quadrupeds lawfully taken in the protection of property may be transported at any time subject to the provisions of this chapter. Deer and bear may be transported during the first 20 days following the open season, subject to the provisions of this chapter. Fish which have been sold at wholesale or retail may be transported at any time by a person (10-5101).

A common carrier shall not transport as owner fish or game, or receive for transportation or transport fish or game protected by law unless accompanied by the owner and tagged or marked as provided by law, except as otherwise provided. Fish, game and fur-bearing animals, or a package containing the same, if placed in the custody of a common carrier, shall have affixed thereto a required tag. The carcass of a deer taken by a resident or by a person as provided in 10-5201 through 10-5203, when open to view, may be transported during the time specified in 10-5101 by a common carrier without being tagged when accompanied by the owner thereof, or, if tagged, may be transported unaccompanied. Fish and game imported from without the US, or raised on propagation farms, when tagged, may be transported unaccompanied by the owner in any number and quantity. Fish and game for propagation purposes, and the head, hide, feet and fur of quadrupeds and the plumage and skins of game birds legally taken and possessed may be transported without being tagged when accompanied by the owner (10-5102 through -5104).

A person required to have a license, as provided in 10-4251, who takes fish or wild animals shall exhibit the license to a common carrier when placing the fish or wild animals in the carrier's custody [types of licenses detailed]. A common carrier receiving fish or wild animals for shipment, shall indorse in ink on the back of the license, the name of the station from which the shipment is made, the destination and the number of each kind of wild animal or the weight of each kind of fish. Such fish and wild animals shall have affixed thereto a tag plainly marked (10-5105 and -5106).

Licenses and Permits

Except as otherwise provided, a person shall not take wild animals or fish without a license. Subject to provisions of this part and regulations of the Board: ► a fishing license shall entitle the holder to take fish; ► a hunting license shall entitle the holder to take wild animals, except those that require a separate big game license, and to shoot pickerel; ► a trappers' license shall entitle the holder to take animals with the use of traps; ► a combination fishing and hunting license shall entitle the holder to take fish and wild animals, except those that require a separate big game license, and to shoot pickerel; ► an archery license shall entitle the holder to take deer by bow and arrow; ► a muzzle loader license shall entitle the holder to take deer with a muzzle loading firearm; ► a turkey license shall entitle the holder to take wild turkey; ► a small game license shall entitle the holder to take small game by a lawful means other than a trap; ► a second muzzle loader license to allow taking one wild deer in addition to the number allowed under a muzzle loading license; ► a second archery license, to allow taking one wild deer in addition to the number allowed under an archery license (10-4251 and -4252).

A resident owner of lands and immediate family may take, without a license, fish from the waters, shoot pickerel, and take wild animals or wild birds therein. A nonresident may do likewise, unless the lands are posted under provisions other than 10-4710. A fishing license may be issued to a person age 15 or older. A resident or nonresident hunting license or combination fishing and hunting license may be issued to a person, provided that the applicant prior to issue first presents: ► a certificate of satisfactory completion of a Vermont hunter safety course or an equivalent approved by the Commissioner; ► or a certificate of satisfactory completion of a hunter safety course in another state or a province of Canada which is approved by the Commissioner; ► or a hunting license, or a combination hunting and fishing license, issued for this state or another state or a Canadian province and valid for any license year; ► or other satisfactory proof that the applicant has previously held a hunting, or combination hunting and fishing license (10-4253 and -4254).

The Commissioner shall provide for a course of basic instruction in safe handling of firearms, survival training and first aid training, and may cooperate with a reputable association, organization or agency, and may designate a competent person to give such instruction. A person satisfactorily completing the course of instruction shall receive a certificate, and no fee shall be charged (10-4254).

A person who is required to have a license shall not take fish or wild animals, or transport fish, game or fur-bearing animals unless in possession of the license. On demand of a game warden or other officer authorized to make arrests, or of the owner of the land on which the person is fishing or hunting, the licensee shall exhibit the license. No person shall make a false statement in an application for a license, change or alter a license or coupon, furnish to another or permit another to have or use such license or coupon, use such license or coupon issued to another, or knowingly guide a hunter or angler without a license (10-4266 and 4267).

Restrictions on Taking: Hunting and Trapping

A person: ► shall not take game except with a gun fired at arm's length or with a bow and arrow, unless otherwise provided; ► shall not take game between sunset and sunrise unless otherwise provided; ► may take game and fur-bearing animals during the open season, with the aid of a dog, unless otherwise prohibited; ► shall not throw or cast the rays of a spotlight, jack, or other artificial light on a highway, field, woodland, or forest, for spotting, locating or taking a wild animal, but a light may be used to take skunks and raccoons in accordance with Board regulations; ► shall not at any time set or use a device, the object of which is to discharge a firearm for taking a wild animal, a violator being liable for twice the amount of damage caused by the act, to be recovered by a person damaged thereby, in a civil action on this section; ▸ when hunting wild animals shall not use, carry or have in possession a machine gun of any kind or an autoloading rifle with a magazine capacity of over six cartridges, except a .22 caliber rifle using rim fire cartridges (10-4701 through 4704).

A person shall not: ▸ take, or attempt to take, a wild animal by shooting from a motor vehicle, motorboat, airplane, snowmobile, or other motor propelled craft or a vehicle drawn by a motor propelled vehicle except as otherwise permitted; ▸ carry or possess while in or on a vehicle propelled by mechanical power or drawn by a vehicle within the right of way of a public highway a rifle or shotgun containing a loaded cartridge or shell, except as otherwise permitted, and a person shall upon demand exhibit a possessed firearm for examination; ▸ take or attempt to take a wild animal by shooting with a firearm or bow and arrow, while on the travelled portion of a public highway. This section shall not restrict the possession or use of a loaded firearm by an enforcement officer in performance of duty. Violation: fine of $25-50. A person shall not take an animal by snaring nor possess a snare with intent to use the same (10-4705 and -4706).

A person may on land owned or occupied by the person and within 500 feet of an occupied dwelling house, residence or other building or camp, or a barn, stable, or other building used in connection therewith, maintain posters furnished by the Department containing the words "safety zone, shooting prohibited." An area bounded by such posters shall be considered enclosed land for the purpose of this section and is hereby defined as a "safety zone." Without advance permission of the owner or occupant, a person shall not discharge a firearm or take a wild animal within a "safety zone." Violation: fine of $50 (10-4710).

For the 16 days commencing 12 days prior to Thanksgiving, a person may take one wild deer, with antlers not less than three inches long, and additional deer as prescribed by the regulations (10-4741). For the nine consecutive calendar days commencing on the first Saturday after the completion of the regular deer hunting season, a person may take one wild deer by muzzle loading firearm, provided that only deer with antlers of three inches or greater length and additional deer as prescribed by rule may be taken. Persons wishing to hunt with a muzzle loading firearm under this section shall obtain a license. Persons licensed pursuant to this section shall not carry while hunting during the special season any firearms other than one single barreled muzzle loading firearm. Persons violating this section shall be subject to the penalties set forth in 10-4518. A muzzle loading firearm defined under 10-4001 or used pursuant to fish and wildlife regulations shall be considered loaded when it has been charged with powder and projectile and is primed or capped (10-4743).

For the 23 calendar days commencing on the first Saturday in October, and the 9 days commencing on the first Saturday after the completion of the regular deer hunting season, a person may take by bow and arrow one wild deer anywhere in the state. During the period allowed after the end of the regular deer hunting season, only deer with antlers of three inches or more may be taken [details provided for second license]. Hunting with a bow and arrow requires a bow and arrow license. No person taking deer may carry a firearm and no deer may be taken by firearms during the season except as provided. Crossbows shall not be used or be carried by a person taking deer except under the provisions of this section (10-4744).

A person shall not: ▸ take a wild deer except specified wild deer during the seasons provided, and then only between one-half hour before sunrise and one-half hour after sunset, this not being construed to prohibit taking deer under 10-4826; ▸ take or possess big game by the aid of a snare, trap, salt lick, jack or other light or use these devices to entrap or ensnare big game; ▸ use a dog for hunting big game except black bear and wild turkey as provided, nor harbor or possess a dog for this purpose (10-4745 and -4747).

A dog that has been found to hunt or pursue deer and whose owner or keeper has had notice to that effect shall not run at large unaccompanied by the owner or keeper. A state game warden, deputy warden, sheriff, deputy sheriff, constable, police officer or state police may kill dogs by shooting, whether licensed or unlicensed, when in such close pursuit as to endanger the life of a deer or found in the act of wounding, maiming or killing deer. This section shall be subject to limitations set forth in 10-4710. A warden or other person authorized under this subsection who does not kill a dog shall issue a warning that the dog was in violation of this section and each future violation shall result in the owner or keeper being fined not more than $200 nor less than $50. When a licensed dog is killed, the game warden, deputy game warden, sheriff, deputy sheriff, constable, police officer or state police forthwith shall report the same to the owner. No person shall have a cause of action against a designated warden, sheriff, deputy sheriff, constable, police officer or state police exercising the authority herein granted (10-4748).

A game warden, deputy game warden, sheriff, deputy sheriff, constable, police officer, state police or selectman may kill a deer which has been so injured that its chance for recovery is remote. The official by whom such a deer is killed shall forthwith report the same to the Commissioner or a game warden and such deer shall be disposed of as provided in 10-4513 (10-4749). A person shall not take a deer which is swimming in a lake, pond, river or other body of water (10-4751). A person shall not take more than three deer in a calendar year (10-4753).

A resident or nonresident trapping license may be issued to a person, provided that the applicant presents: ▸ a certificate of completion of an approved trapper education course or its equivalent; ▸ a certificate of completion of an approved trapper education course in another state or a province of Canada; ▸ a trapping license issued for this state or another state or Canadian province and valid for any license year; ▸ other satisfactory proof that the applicant has previously held a valid trapping license. The Commissioner shall provide a course of basic instruction in trapper education, and may cooperate with a reputable association, organization or agency and may designate a person competent to give such instruction (10-4254a). A person who intends to set a trap on the property of another shall notify the owner of the intention and of the prospective location of the trap. The owner may refuse to grant or revoke the permission (10-4707). The Commissioner may fix a fee not to exceed $1.00 to be paid by the trapper to the game warden for each skin required to be tagged and marked by regulations (10-4863).

Restrictions on Taking: Fishing

The Commissioner, by agreement with the owners of lands through which private waters flow or in which private waters lie, not being boatable waters, may close such waters, or parts thereof, against fishing. In the name of the state, the Commissioner may receive from the owners of such lands such deeds or writings as are necessary. During the term for which they are closed, such waters shall not be included in private preserves or propagation farms. Notice shall be posted conspicuously. Not less than 10 days prior to and continuing 10 days after the usual spawning periods of a species of game or food fish, the Commissioner may close portions of waters where such species congregate preparatory to or during the spawning season. Waters stocked by the Commissioner, shall be treated as public waters, but the Commissioner may prohibit fishing therein for not more than five years and notice shall be given. A person who would make a private preserve or propagation farm may do so at the expiration of five years from filing with the Commissioner a written notice of such intent. Such notice shall contain a description of the waters intended to be made a private preserve or propagation farm and shall be kept on file (10-4139 through -4141).

The Commissioner may designate as test waters streams and ponds to secure fish propagation data, cause notice of such a designation to be published in a newspaper in the vicinity and post notice. Fishing in such test waters shall be in accordance with regulations of the Commissioner. A person fishing in test waters shall report each day's catch as required on forms supplied in convenient locations on or near such test waters (10-4142).

A person shall not take fish, except in accordance with this part and regulations, or possess a fish taken in violation. When a fish is unintentionally taken contrary to a provision of this part or of regulations, it shall be immediately returned to the water, without unnecessary injury. The person so returning shall not be subject to penalty. When it is unlawful to take more than a specified number of pounds of any fish in one day, taking additional fish by a person having less than the number of pounds specified shall not be regarded as violating the limit. A person who holds a fishing license and a person who is allowed to take fish without a license shall not take fish through the ice except in accordance with regulations (10-4601 through -4604).

A person shall not: ▸ take fish by explosives, or use or possess explosives upon waters, shores or islands, except for mining or mechanical purposes; ▸ place in waters lime, creosote, coculus inducus or other drug or poison destructive to fish; ▸ take or kill fish by shutting or drawing off water; ▸ except as provided, use or possess for use or furnish for another's use, for taking fish, a pound net, trap net, seine, snare, gill net, set net, fyke net, set line, fishing otter, trawl or grapple or similar device for killing fish or possess such device on waters, shores or islands. Such devices may be summarily seized and destroyed by a game warden. Except as authorized and utilized by the Department, electrofishing is prohibited in all waters (10-4606).

A person shall not, unless authorized by the Commissioner, prevent the passing of fish in a stream or the outlet or inlet of a natural or artificial pond on a public stream, by means of a rack, screen, weir or other obstruction, and shall comply with the terms of the notice provided below. The Commissioner may order such an obstruction removed by the person erecting the same or by the owner of the land on which it is located, by serving on such person or owner a written notice requiring the removal of such obstruction within ten days. When such person fails to remove such an obstruction within the time required, the Commissioner may remove the same and recover the expense thereof in a civil action (10-4607).

The owner of a fishing house shall not place the fishing house or cause the same to be placed on the ice earlier than November 20, and then only if the owner's name and address are affixed. The owner shall remove the fishing house, together with its contents and surrounding debris, before the ice loses its ability to support the fishing house, or on or before the last Sunday in March, whichever occurs first. Under no circumstances shall a fishing house be allowed in the waters of this state (10-4612).

A person owning a natural pond of not more than twenty acres or an artificial pond entirely upon the persons's premises, stocked at the person's expense with fish artificially hatched or reared, may take fish from such pond at any time for propagation or consumption, provided that the sources of water supply for such pond are entirely upon the person's premises, or that fish do not have access to such pond from waters not under the person's control or from waters stocked at state expense (10-5210).

Big Game Provisions

A person shall not possess big game except during the open season and for a reasonable time thereafter unless otherwise provided, nor possess big game taken by illegal devices, nor big game taken in closed season. A part of the carcass of big game legally taken may be possessed at any time in cans or in a cold storage locker or home freezer. A person shall not buy or sell big game or the meat of big game within the state except during the open season and for 20 days thereafter. A person may buy or sell at any time: ▸ the head, hide and hoofs of deer or moose legally taken; ▸ the head, hide, paws and internal organs of a black bear, legally taken. Neither anadromous Atlantic salmon taken in the Connecticut River Basin nor wild turkey shall be bought or sold at any time. The meat of big game animals shall not be bought or sold to be transported out of the state (10-4781 through -4783).

A person shall not transport big game taken by illegal devices, or in closed season. A person shall not transport a wild deer with antlers less than three inches in length except under the provisions of this title. Game suppers may be held at any time by a church, volunteer fire department, rod and game club, or other nonprofit organization under permit. Wild animals and fish legally taken in this state, or another state or country, may be transported and sold as part of a game supper authorized by permit. Big game provided by the Department may also be sold at such suppers. Migratory waterfowl and anadromous salmon shall not be sold (10-4784 and -4786).

Bird, Waterfowl Provisions

No person 16 or older shall attempt or take migratory waterfowl in this state without a state migratory waterfowl stamp in addition to a regular hunting license. Stamps shall be validated by the signature of the licensee and shall not be transferable. The Commissioner shall be responsible for the design, production, procurement, distribution and sale of all stamps and by-products such as posters, artwork, calendars and other items (10-4277).

Wild birds, other than pigeons shall not be taken, possessed, bought or sold, at any time, except as provided by this part, rules of the Board or order of the Commission. Birds coming from without the state belonging to the same family as those protected by this subchapter shall not be bought or sold. A person shall not take a bird with the aid of a jack or other light. A person shall not take a wild bird by trapping, netting or snaring, or possess such a bird, or set, place or use, where birds may be taken, a net, trap or snare for taking birds. Such device is declared to be a public nuisance and may be summarily abated and destroyed by person, and game wardens shall seize and destroy such devices. The Commissioner may authorize the taking of birds by nets or traps or other devices, under regulations. A person shall not take or wilfully destroy the nest or eggs of wild birds, other than pigeons, the English sparrow, starling, or purple grackle, except when necessary to protect buildings or when taken as provided in 10-4152 (10-4902, -4904 and -4905).

A person shall not place a waterfowl blind or cause the same to be placed on or in state waters earlier than the first Saturday of September, and then only if the name and address are affixed. A waterfowl blind, together with its contents and surrounding debris, located on or in state waters, except Lake Champlain, shall be removed on or before May 15. "Waterfowl blind" means any manufactured place of concealment or a boat, raft or similar structure which has been designed partially or completely to conceal a person taking ducks or geese (10-4907).

Fur-bearing Animals

Fur-bearing animals shall not be taken except in accordance with the provisions of this part, and rules of the Board. The fur or skins of fur-bearing animals may be possessed at any time unless otherwise provided by this part or by rules of the Board or orders of the Commission. A person may take muskrat by shooting from March 20 to April 19, inclusive (10-4861 and -4865).

Commercial and Private Enterprise Provisions

A person who, without the written consent of the owner or person having the exclusive right to take fish or wild animals, takes fish, game, or other animals or carries or possesses a firearm, bow and arrow, or wild animal trap in private preserves as posted under 10-5201, or mutilates or defaces the notice shall be fined not less than $25 nor more than $100. The owner or person in control of such private preserve may recover actual damages in a civil action on this statute. A person shall not damage or remove a notice maintained under 10-5201. A person shall not maintain a notice prohibiting fishing for more than one year after such waters were last stocked (10-5204 through -5206).

The Commissioner may issue a license to propagate fish and wild animals and shall make and publish regulations governing such industry. The application for a breeder's license and shall describe the land or waters owned or leased by such breeder to be used for such purpose and shall contain other facts required by the Commissioner. The Commissioner may issue such a license, which shall continue in force for one year. A breeder may sell and transport fish and wild animals at all times, alive for propagation, and for food during such season as the Commissioner may prescribe. Such fish and wild animals shall be identified either by marking the packages or by individual tagging. A breeder selling game procured from lands other than lands covered by a license under 10-5207, or who violates a provision of this part or a regulation issued under the provisions of 10-5207 and 10-5208 shall be fined not more than $100, and in addition shall be punished as provided for such particular violation (10-5207 through -5209).

A person shall not, without permission, enter upon the premises of a propagation farm and take fish, or wild animals, or upon a pond as defined in 10-5210 and take fish, or foul the waters of such farm or pond with a substance injurious to the life or growth of fish or break or destroy a dam, reservoir or embankment, or divert the water, or wilfully damage such farm or pond. Such person shall be liable to the owner for damages in a civil action. An owner who gratuitously gives another permission, either actual or implied, to enter upon the owner's land for recreational purposes, shall owe the invitee no greater duty except as to acts of active negligence than is owed a trespasser (10-5211 and -5212).

The Commissioner may issue a shooting grounds permit to operate a shooting ground upon which to propagate and release game birds, including, but not limited to, pheasants, bobwhite quail and chukar partridges, under Commissioner regulations and upon which to release game birds when regularly propagated or purchased for shooting and other purposes. The boundary of the licensed premises shall be posted with printed notices not more than one hundred yards apart, and containing such words as the Commissioner may prescribe. Such permit shall entitle the holders, and their guests, to kill or take, by shooting only, the pheasants, bobwhite quail, and chukar partridges and other game birds propagated or purchased and released on the premises. All birds released on the regulated shooting grounds shall be fully winged and fully able to care for themselves in a wild state. The propagated or released birds may be taken without regard to sex, age or bag limits. The period for taking such game birds on such regulated shooting grounds shall be fixed by the Commissioner. All species of game, other than those specified or approved by the Commissioner for propagation and release found on the premises, may be taken only under the general provisions of the law governing the taking and possession of the same. Every person hunting on such regulated shooting grounds shall be the holder of a resident or nonresident hunter's license year, or be the holder of a one-day shooting ground license issued by the owner of the shooting ground. Such shooting ground license shall be valid only on the shooting ground where issued and only for taking the game birds designated by the Commissioner in the permit. At the end of each calendar quarter, the owner of a shooting ground shall forward to the Commissioner all revenues from one-day license sales and records of sales required (10-5217 through -5223).

The owner or operator of a shooting range and a person lawfully using the range shall not be subject to civil liability for damages resulting from noise or noise pollution, provided the range is in existence on or before July 1, 1991 and has not expanded subsequent to that date (10-5227).

The furs and skins of fur-bearing animals and skins of deer, legally taken, may be bought and sold at any time, subject to the provisions of this title, provided that a person wishing to engage in the business of buying the furs or skins of fur-bearing animals or skins of deer shall first secure a license. The Commissioner may issue a license which shall authorize a person to engage in the business of buying furs or skins throughout the state. Licensed dealers shall keep records as the Commissioner may require. Such records shall be open to inspection by the Commissioner, and such dealer shall within 30 days after license expiration, and upon request of the Commissioner, file a sworn statement of such record. Such licenses shall be effective July 1 through June 30. A person while engaged in the business of buying furs and skins shall have in possession a license as provided in 10-4268 and on demand shall exhibit such license (10-4268 through -4271).

A licensed dealer who has lost the license issued under 10-4269 may demand and shall receive from the Commissioner a certificate, stating the name and residence of such dealer, the fact that a license was issued to the dealer, the date thereof and the fee paid therefor. A certificate so issued shall have the same force and effect as the original license and the holder shall be subject to all the provisions applicable to such license. No person shall make a false statement in an application for a fur buyer's license or change or alter such a license nor permit another to have or use such license (10-4272 and -4273).

A person shall not buy or sell a salmon, trout, lake trout, walleye, northern pike, muskellunge or black bass taken in this state, or imported from another state or country where sale of such fish is prohibited, except such fish reared in licensed propagation farms within the state (10-4611).

Import, Export and Release Provisions

A person shall not introduce or attempt to introduce pickerel or great northern pike into waters, or fish, except trout or salmon, into public waters frequented by trout or salmon. A person shall not bring into the state for planting or introducing into inland or outlying state waters a live fish or spawn without a permit. The Commissioner shall investigate and inspect the fish as necessary and the importation permit may be granted pursuant to Board regulations. The Department may dispose of unlawfully imported fish and the state may collect damages from a violator for all expenses incurred. Nothing in this section shall prohibit the Board, the Commissioner or their agents from bringing into the state for planting, introducing or stocking, or from planting, introducing or stocking fish (10-4605).

A person shall not bring into the state a live wild bird or animal without a permit. The importation permit may be granted under Board regulations and only after the Commissioner has made investigation and inspection of the birds or animals. The Department may dispose of unlawfully imported wildlife, and the state may collect treble damages from the violator of this subsection for all expenses incurred. Nothing in this section shall prohibit the Commissioner or duly authorized agents from bringing into the state for the purpose of planning, introducing or stocking, or from planting, introducing or stocking in the state, a wild bird or animal (10-4709).

Beaver skins that come into this state in the raw state from another state or country shall have the official stamp, tag or seal of the state or country in which such skins were taken. All beaver skins not tagged and marked shall be seized and confiscated (10-4864).

Interstate Reciprocal Agreements

While the state of New York shall have in effect a law similar to this subsection for the arrest and punishment of violations of the conservation or fish laws of this state or New York, committed or attempted to be committed by a person fishing in that portion of Lake Champlain lying between such states, a game protector, game warden, sheriff, deputy sheriff or other person of either state, who is authorized to make arrests for violations of the conservation or fish laws, shall have power and authority to make arrest on any part of such lake between such states or the shores thereof and to take the person so arrested for trial to the state in which the violation was committed and prosecute according to the laws of such state (10-4193).

Persons holding a New Hampshire fishing license may take fish from the Connecticut River, provided New Hampshire grants the same right to persons holding a Vermont fishing license. Such taking shall be only in accordance with rules and regulations adopted by New Hampshire relative to open and closed seasons, limits of catch, minimum sizes of fish caught and methods of fishing and upon agreement with the Director of Fish and Game of New Hampshire. Whereupon, the laws of this state covering such matters shall be suspended as to the waters above described. A violation of said provisions shall be punished as provided in 10-4515 (10-4609).

ANIMAL DAMAGE CONTROL

A person, including a member of the person's family or an employee, may take, on land owned or occupied by the person, a deer doing damage to the following: ▸ a tree being grown in a plantation or cultivated for an annual or perennial crop or to produce a marketable item; ▸ a crop bearing plant; ▸ a crop, except grass. A person by whom, or under whose direction, the deer is wounded or killed, shall report in writing within 12 hours all facts to a game warden. A person who kills the deer shall immediately dress the carcass and care for the meat. The game warden shall immediately investigate and if satisfied that the deer was taken lawfully, give the person a certificate entitling the person to the ownership of the carcass, but the person shall not sell or give away the carcass. A carcass not needed for home consumption in the household of the certificate holder shall be turned over to a game warden. When a game warden finds that a deer has been wounded or killed contrary to the provisions of this section, the game warden shall dispose of the deer under the direction of the Commissioner and any moneys received shall be paid to the Commissioner (10-4826).

A person may take black bear at any time in defense of the person's property. The provisions of law or regulations of the Board relating to the taking of raccoon, rabbits or other fur-bearing animals shall not apply to an owner, the owner's employee, tenant, or caretaker or to the selectmen of a town protecting public highways or bridges from such damage or submersion with the permission of the owner of lands affected, except that an owner, employee, tenant or caretaker, or the selectmen, who desire to possess during the closed season the skins of fur-bearing animals taken in defense of property, highways, or bridges shall notify the Commissioner within 84 hours after taking, and with the exception of raccoon, shall hold such pelts for inspection. Before disposing of such pelts, except raccoon, the property owner, employee, tenant, caretaker or selectmen shall secure from the Commissioner a certificate describing the pelts, and showing that the pelts were legally taken during a closed season and in defense of property, highways or bridges. In the event of storage, sale or transfer, such certificates shall accompany the pelts (10-4827 and-4828).

A person who suffers damage by deer to crops, fruit trees, crop-bearing plants or shrubbery on land not posted against hunting deer, or a person who suffers damage by black bear to cattle, sheep, swine, poultry or bees or bee hives on land not posted against hunting or trapping of black bear is entitled to reimbursement for the damage, and may apply to the Department within 72 hours of the occurrence for reimbursement. The Board shall adopt rules and regulations relating to application for reimbursement, examination by fish and game wardens of damage and reimbursement. A person who is denied reimbursement or who is dissatisfied with the amount granted may appeal to the superior court of the county in which the person resides (10-4829 through -4832).

The Commissioner shall develop a coyote control program for implementation in areas where predation by coyotes is posing a threat to domesticated animals, deer and other wildlife. In no event shall the program use poison (10-4833 and -4903).

ENFORCEMENT OF WILDLIFE LAWS

Enforcement Powers

Deputy Game Wardens shall have authority to enforce all provisions of this part and orders and rules thereunder. They shall also have authority to enforce provisions of chapter 47 of this title and [selected other provisions from other chapters] (10-4192).

The game warden shall seize fish, or wild animals taken or held in violation of a provision of this part or regulations or orders authorized under this part. They may arrest, without warrant and on view, in any part of the state, a person violating a provision of this part or regulations or orders authorized under this part and take such person before a magistrate and detain such person until opportunity is had to notify a prosecuting officer, who shall forthwith prosecute (10-4192).

While in and about the woods, the game wardens shall caution persons as to the danger of fires and shall extinguish a fire left burning. When a fire is threatening to extend beyond the warden's control, the warden shall notify all parties interested and the forest firewarden of the town in which such fire occurs. Until the arrival of such firewarden, the game warden shall have all the powers of such firewarden (10-4195).

Upon certification by the Executive Director of the criminal justice training council of the successful completion of the training program for law enforcement officers as established in section 2358 of Title 20, state game wardens shall have the same duties and powers as state police, sheriffs, constables and municipal police; and shall have all immunities and defenses now or hereafter available to state police, sheriffs, constables and municipal police in a suit brought against them in consequence of acts done in the course of their employment. State game wardens shall receive their regular compensation during the time they are enrolled in the training program (10-4198).

Criminal Penalties

A person who counsels or aids in a violation, or who knowingly shares in the proceeds of such a violation by receiving or possessing fish or wild animals, shall be punished as a principal (10-4501).

Violators of 10-4251, 10-4268 or 10-4608 relating to hunting or fishing without license, shall be fined not more than $100 nor less than $25. Whoever wilfully or carelessly damages, injures, interferes with or destroys property, real or personal, belonging to or controlled by the state for fish, game or wildlife purposes shall be fined not more than $2,500. Whoever violates a provision of this part or orders or rules of the Board relating to taking, possessing, transporting, buying or selling of big game shall be fined not more than $500, nor less than $200 or imprisoned for not more than 60 days, or both. Upon a second and all subsequent convictions, the violator shall be fined not more than $1,000 nor less than $500 or imprisoned for not more than 60 days, or both (10-4516 through -4518).

A violation of a provision, or rule of this part, other than a violation for which a term of imprisonment may be imposed, shall be known as a fish and game violation (10-4551).

Illegal Taking of Wildlife

A person convicted of violating 10-4747 or 10-4606 relating to taking big game by illegal means, shall forfeit to the state the firearms, jacks, artificial lights, motor vehicle or other device used in taking or transporting big game. Forfeiture of a motor vehicle shall not apply to the illegal taking or transporting of wild turkey or anadromous Atlantic salmon. When firearms, jacks, artificial lights, motor vehicles and other devices used in the taking or transportation of big game are seized or taken by a game warden or other officer, with or without a warrant, the officer shall forthwith give notice to a grand juror of the town in which the seizure is made or to the state's attorney of the county. The game warden or other officer shall retain possession of firearms, jacks, lights, motor vehicles and devices taken until final disposition of the charge against the owner, possessor or person using the same in violation of 10-4747 or 10-4606. Upon conviction, the court shall cause the owner, if known, and possessor and all persons having custody of or exercising control over devices seized, either as principal, clerk, servant, or agent and the respondent to appear and show cause, if any, why a forfeiture or condemnation order should not issue. If upon hearing, it appears that such device was used or intended to be used contrary to law, it shall be forfeited and condemned, and turned over to the game warden or other officer for the benefit of the state as the court shall direct. If the device is illegal, such officer shall destroy the same upon court order (10-4503 through -4506).

Upon condemnation of such device, any and all persons shall be liable to pay the costs of the condemnation proceedings, if, in the judgment of such court, any of them by themselves, clerks, servants or agents, shall have engaged in, aided in, assisted in or abetted in the unlawful use of such device, or have been privy thereto, or have knowingly permitted the use of the same by them. Upon seizure of such firearm, jack, light, vehicle or device without a warrant, a game warden or other officer shall forthwith make complaint to a court or magistrate having jurisdiction of offenses. In the event such device is ordered forfeited and is a device not illegal in itself, shall be sold at public auction (10-4507 and -4508). [Details of disposition of proceeds after liens to the Department are provided in 10-4509.] Fish, wild animals and illegal devices for taking fish or wild animals found in the possession of a person in violation of a provision of this part, shall be seized and confiscated and the Commissioner may sell or otherwise dispose of the same in the best interests of the state and for that purpose may order its transportation at any time (10-4513).

When legally taken, the flesh of a fish or wild animal may be possessed for food for a reasonable time thereafter and may be transported and stored in a public cold storage plant. Nothing shall authorize possession of game birds or carcasses or parts contrary to regulations pursuant to the Migratory Bird Treaty Act. A person convicted of illegally taking, destroying or possessing wild animals, in addition to other penalties provided, shall pay into the fish and wildlife fund for each animal taken, destroyed, or possessed, no more than the following amounts: ▸ big game, $1,000 each; ▸ endangered or threatened species, $1,000 each; ▸ small game, $250 each; ▸ fish, $25 each. Whoever violates or attempts to violate a provision of this part or an order or regulation of the Board or of the Commissioner for which no other penalty is provided shall be fined not more than $1,000 (10-4514 and -4515).

License Revocations and Suspensions

A uniform point system which assigns points to those convicted of a violation of a provision of this part is established. The conviction report from the court shall be prima facie evidence of the points assessed. In addition to other penalties assessed for violation of fish and wildlife statutes, the Commissioner shall suspend licenses issued under this part which are held by a person who has accumulated ten or more points (10-4502).

A person violating provisions of statutes or rules shall receive 5 points for convictions, except the following will be assessed 10 points: ▸ trespass on state property (10-4148); ▸ fur buyer's records (10-4270); ▸ destruction of state property (10-4517); ▸ placing fish in waters (10-4605); ▸ obstructing streams (10-4607); ▸ sale of game fish (10-4611); ▸ use of machine guns and autoloading rifles (10-4704); ▸ shooting from motor vehicles or aircraft (10-4705); ▸ snaring animals (10-4706); ▸ traps (10-4707); ▸ interference with hunting, fishing or trapping (10-4708); ▸ importation, stocking of wild animals (10-4709); ▸ safety zone (10-4710); ▸ dogs pursuing deer (10-4748); ▸ deer, annual limit (10-4753); ▸ transporting beaver skins (10-4864); ▸ fish and game, restrictions on transportation (10-5101); ▸ poaching, private preserves (10-5204); ▸ injuring notice of posted land (10-5205); ▸ special penalty, breeders (10-5209); ▸ poaching, propagation farms (10-5211); ▸ Mansfield State Forest Game Refuge (10-5213); ▸ birds released (10-5220); ▸ Bomoseen State Game Refuge (10-5226); ▸ reporting of deer, bear (Appendix 2); ▸ big game tags (Appendix 2a); ▸ rabbit, squirrel, sale (Appendix 3); ▸ bobcat (Appendix 8); ▸ turkey reporting (Appendix 22e); ▸ waterfowl hunting methods (Appendix 23d); ▸ waterfowl, wanton waste (Appendix 23h); ▸ method of taking (trapping) (Appendix 43); ▸ trapping (Appendix 44). Twenty points shall be assessed for: ▸ general powers and duties, failure to obey warden (10-4192); ▸ falconry license (10-4278); ▸ eel fishing (Subchapter 2 of Chapter 105); ▸ taking fish by unlawful means (10-4606); ▸ use of light (firearm or bow involved) (10-4702); ▸ use of set guns (10-4703); ▸ muzzle loader deer season (10-4743(c)); ▸ bow and arrow deer season (10-4744a,b); ▸ taking deer out of season prohibited (10-4745); ▸ taking big game by illegal means (10-4747); ▸ big game possession (10-4781); ▸ purchase and sale of big game (10-4783); ▸ transportation of big game (10-4784); ▸ taking, possession or transport of endangered or threatened species (10-5403); ▸ bear, taking with aid of dogs (Appendix 7); ▸ turkey season (Appendix 22); ▸ migratory birds (Appendix 23); ▸ seasons, bag limits for bear, caribou, elk and moose (Appendix 31); ▸ Atlantic salmon in the Connecticut River (Appendix 116) (10-4502).

In addition to other points assessed under this subsection, a person shall be assessed one point for each fish, bird, animal or pelt possessed, taken, transported, bought or sold in excess of the limits established in statutes or rules adopted under this part. Licenses shall be suspended as follows: ▸ for 10 to 14 points accumulated in five years, a one-year suspension; ▸ for 15 to 19 points accumulated in five years, a two-year suspension; ▸ for 20 or more points accumulated in five years, a three-year suspension (10-4502).

The Commissioner shall establish a centralized registry of licensees and shall track all convictions and point accumulations, against licensees. The Commissioner shall provide adequate notice to licensees of their point accumulations, and suspensions. The Commissioner shall revoke a hunting license issued under this part when the holder has been convicted of a violation of subdivision 1023(a)(2) of Title 13 or has been convicted of manslaughter by the careless and negligent use of firearms, and another license shall not be issued to such person within five years from the date of such revocation or within five years from the date of such conviction if such person had no license. The court before which such person is convicted shall certify such conviction to the Commissioner. A revocation shall be deemed effective when notice is given in person, or three days after the deposit of such notice in the US mails, if made in writing (10-4502).

HABITAT PROTECTION

A landowner, or a person having the exclusive right to take fish or wild animals upon land or waters thereon, who desires to protect such land or waters, may maintain notices stating that shooting and trapping are prohibited, or, that fishing is prohibited, or, that fishing, hunting and trapping are prohibited. Notices prohibiting the taking of wild animals shall be erected upon or near the boundaries of lands at each corner. Notices prohibiting the taking of fish shall show the date that the waters were last stocked and shall be maintained upon or near the shores of the waters. Legible signs must be maintained at all times and shall be dated each year. Signs shall be of a standard size and design as the Commissioner shall specify. The owner or person posting the lands shall record this posting annually in the town clerk's office. The town clerk shall file the record and it shall be open to public inspection. Land posted as provided shall be enclosed land (10-5201).

To post a stream as a private preserve under 10-5201, a person annually shall: ▸ stock the waters of each half mile of stream with at least 1,000 fry, 600 advanced fry, 300 fingerlings or 150 fish, each not less than 6 inches in length, and ▸ file with the Commissioner and the town clerk of the town in which the waters lie, immediately after stocking the waters, a sworn affidavit declaring that the provisions of this section have been complied with. The affidavit shall identify the number and kind of fish placed in the waters, the date they were purchased, and the person from whom they were purchased. When land or waters are stocked by the state with fish, wild animals or game, with the knowledge and consent of the owner, the owner may not prohibit the taking of fish, wild animals or game under 10-5201. However, the Commissioner may stock a private fishing preserve which allows some charitable or nonprofit organizations to use the area at no charge. In that case, the owner may prohibit the taking of fish or game by the general public (10-5202).

Permits for the control and destruction of vermin upon a game refuge may be granted by the Commissioner to such person and at such times as advisable (10-5214).

For a specified period of years, the Commissioner may prohibit or regulate the taking of wild animals upon public lands set aside with the approval of the Governor or upon private lands set aside, with the consent of the owner, for game refuges. At least thirty days before such a prohibition or regulation takes effect, the Commissioner shall file a copy of the same in the office of the town clerk of the town in which such lands lie. Notices reading "State Game Refuge; hunting is unlawful" shall be placed at conspicuous places on the boundaries of refuges. The Commissioner may issue a permit to a person, organization or group for rehabilitating sick or injured wild animals to a sufficient state of health so that may be returned to the wild. The Commissioner shall promulgate rules to implement this subsection (10-5215).

Consent of the state is given to the acquisition by the U.S. by purchase, gift, devise, or lease of such land or water, or of land and water in Vermont, as the U.S. may deem necessary for the establishment of migratory bird reservations in accordance with the act of Congress, approved February 18, 1929, entitled, "Act to more effectively meet the obligations of the United States under the migratory bird treaty with Great Britain (10-5216).

NATIVE AMERICAN WILDLIFE PROVISIONS: None.

VIRGINIA

Sources: Code of Virginia, 1950, Title 29; 1992 Replacement Volume.

STATE WILDLIFE POLICY

Wild birds, wild animals and fish are property of the Commonwealth and may be reduced to personal possession only in accordance with law. Any wild bird, wild animal or fish which is illegally taken, possessed, sold, purchased, transported or imported shall be forfeited to the Commonwealth (29.1-557).

RELEVANT WILDLIFE DEFINITIONS: See Definitions section of Appendices.

STATE FISH AND WILDLIFE AGENCIES

Agency Structure

The Commission of Game and Inland Fisheries is continued and shall be known as the **Board of Game and Inland Fisheries** (Board), consisting of not more than one member from each congressional district. Members are appointed by the Governor, confirmed by the General Assembly for terms of one to four years, and may be removed by the Governor. The Board elects the chairperson and meets a minimum of four times a year (29.1-102).

The **Department of Game and Inland Fisheries** (Department) shall provide public, educational and informational services and serves as the agency responsible for administration and enforcement of all Board rules, statutory provisions and legislative acts. The Board shall appoint a **Director** to head the Department and to act as principal administrative officer (29.1-109).

The Director shall appoint regular and special **Game Wardens** to enforce game and inland fish laws (29.1-200). Game Wardens shall post a $1,000 bond on condition that they will: account for and legally apply all money received in their official capacity; pay all judgments rendered against them for malicious prosecution or unlawful search, arrest or imprisonment; faithfully perform all duties enjoined by law (29.1-201). All sheriffs, police officers or other peace officers shall be ex officio Game Wardens (29.1-202). Game Wardens prosecuted on criminal charges arising out of official duties may be defended by special counsel employed by the Director and approved by the Governor (29.1-218).

On request of an employer owning more than 1,000 acres in the Commonwealth, the Director may appoint as **Special Game Wardens** persons employed by the owner, such persons receiving no state compensation. The powers and authority of Special Game Wardens shall not extend beyond the employer's lands. The Director may require Special Game Wardens to perform duties on such lands as required for enforcement of this chapter (29.1-217).

Agency Powers and Duties

In addition to other powers, the **Director** has the power to: ► enforce all laws for protection, propagation and preservation of game birds, game animals and fish in inland waters; ► initiate prosecution of persons who violate such laws, and seize and confiscate wild birds, wild animals and fish illegally killed, caught, transported or shipped; ► employ persons necessary for administrative requirements of the Board; ► perform acts necessary to conduct and establish cooperative fish and wildlife projects with the federal government; ► enter into contracts for performance of the Director's duties including with local, state and federal agencies (29.1-109).

The **Board** is responsible for carrying out the purposes and provisions of this title and is authorized to: ► appoint the Director of the Department; ► acquire, by purchase, lease, gift or otherwise, lands and waters and establish buildings, dams, lakes and ponds; ► conduct operations for preservation and propagation of game birds, game animals, fish and other wildlife to increase, replenish and restock the lands and inland waters; ► purchase, lease lands and waters for game and fish refuges, preserves or public shooting and fishing and establish such lands and waters under regulations; ► acquire by purchase or lease lands and structures for public landings or docks, and control regulation; ► acquire and introduce a new species of game birds, animals or fish; ► restock, replenish and increase a depleted native species of game birds, animals or fish; ► publish and distribute educational matter pertaining to wildlife; ► hold exhibits to educate school children, agriculturists and others in preservation and propagation of wildlife; ► control in designated lands any drilling, dredging or other operation designed to recover shells, minerals or other substances to prevent practices and operations harmful for fish and wildlife; ► exercise powers for conserving, protecting, replenishing, propagating and increasing the supply of game birds, animals, fish and other wildlife; ► adopt regulations giving the Director all powers and duties as the Board deems necessary to carry out this title's purpose; ► administer and manage the Virginia Fish Passage Grant and Revolving Loan Fund (29.1-103). The Board may receive gifts, grants, bequests and devises of property and of money which shall be held for uses prescribed by the donor and in accord with this title's purposes, and shall manage such properties or money so as to maximize their value to Virginia citizens (29.1-104).

After careful study of each species of wild bird, animal and fish within the Board's jurisdiction, the Board has the power to prescribe seasons and bag limits for hunting, fishing, trapping or taking by regulation. ★The Board may close or shorten open seasons in a county or city: ► when extreme weather threatens the welfare of birds, animals or fish; ► whenever such birds, animals or fish have been seriously affected by adverse weather conditions; ► when Board investigation shows that there is an unusual scarcity of a species; ► when there is substantial demand from a county or city.★ The Board shall give notice immediately of a closing or shortening of a season by publication. The Board may adopt rules to prescribe and enforce seasons, bag limits and methods of taking fish and game on lands it owns or controls (29.1-506 through -508). The Director is authorized to manage and harvest timber on Board-owned lands in accordance with the best timber and game management practices and to sell timber (29.1-111).

Game Wardens shall have jurisdiction throughout the state to enforce the hunting, trapping and inland fish laws and may serve process in all matters arising from violations (29.1-203). Game Wardens shall assist the Director in discharging official duties, and each shall be under the supervision of certain Game Wardens specified by the Director (29.1-204). (See also ENFORCEMENT OF WILDLIFE LAWS.)

Agency Regulations

The Board may promulgate regulations pertaining to hunting, taking, capturing, killing, possessing, selling, purchasing and transporting of a wild bird, wild animal or inland water fish. Any proposed regulation or change shall be published 15 to 30 days before it may be acted upon, stating the time and place of a public hearing. Publication of proposed regulations or changes shall be made. The Board may adopt regulations and amendments upon completion of hearing and notice requirements. All laws relating to hunting, fishing and trapping, together with Board regulations of both general and local application, shall be published annually by the Department. Violation of any regulation is a Class 3 misdemeanor (29.1-501 through -505). All rules, resolutions, regulations and policies adopted by the Board shall be reduced to writing for the Director, shall be public documents and available to the public on request (29.1-107).

Agency Funding Sources

Money from sale of hunting, fishing and trapping licenses and other items shall constitute the **Game Protection Fund**, the income and principal of which shall be a separate fund in the state treasury and used only for salaries, wages, and expenses for carrying out the hunting, trapping and inland fish laws except as otherwise provided (29.1-101 and -332).

There is a special fund in the state treasury, the **Lifetime Hunting and Fishing Endowment Fund**, consisting of proceeds from sale of lifetime hunting and fishing licenses and gifts, grants and contributions specifically designated for inclusion in the Fund. The income and principal shall be used only to administer the lifetime license program and for supporting wildlife conservation programs. The Board shall serve as trustee of the Fund, and shall authorize withdrawal and expenditure of fund moneys (29.1-101.1).

The **Virginia Fish Passage Grant and Revolving Loan Fund** is a permanent fund comprised of general fund moneys, receipts from loans made by it, income from investments, and other sums designated for deposit from a public or private source. The Fund shall be used solely for administration of the fund and the Fish Passage Program

(29.1-101.2). The Department, after consultation with the Commissioner of the Virginia Marine Resources Commission, may offer to finance construction of fishways for a local government which owns a dam, paying 75% of the cost of the fishway and lending the balance to the local government to be repaid over 10 years at no interest, or 20 years at two percentage points below the current municipal bond rate. The Department shall approve the design of the fishway prior to granting a loan (29.1-101.5). The Department may make similar loans to construct fishways to non-government owners for 20 years at the prime rate, or as otherwise designated by statute (29.1-101.6). The owner of every dam or other artificial impediment to the migration of anadromous fish in a Chesapeake Bay tributary is responsible to provide appropriate fishways as soon as reasonably possible after being offered financing from the fund. Failure may result in an injunction to compel compliance (29.1-101.9)

The Department has exclusive productions rights for a **Virginia Voluntary Migratory Waterfowl Conservation Stamp**, to be sold for $10, and for the sale of related artwork. Proceeds shall be used to benefit migratory waterfowl management (29.1-339.1).

★★There is a **Damage Stamp Program** to provide for funds to compensate damage to crops, fruit trees, commercially grown Christmas trees, nursery stock, livestock or farm equipment caused by deer, bear or big game hunters. It is the intent of the General Assembly that persons suffering loss or damage as the result of these activities should be realistically compensated for damages which occurred to their property. A local governing body shall encourage utilization of the Damage Stamp Fund for payment of claims (29.1-352). A local governing body may adopt an ordinance consistent with these provisions to establish a Damage Stamp Program (29.1-353). Moneys from stamp sales shall be paid into the local treasury to the credit of a Special Damage Stamp Fund and used for: ▸ payment of damages to crops, trees, livestock or farm equipment by deer, bear, or big game hunters during hunting season; ▸ payment of program costs, stamp printing and claims investigations; ▸ in the discretion of the local governing body, payment of the costs of law enforcement directly related to carrying out these provisions and general game laws; ▸ fire fighting on big game hunting lands open to the public (29.1-355). Landowners suffering damage shall report to a locally designated official who shall investigate and make payment arrangements if the official and landowner are in agreement as to the amount of damage. No damages shall be paid to persons who do not permit hunting big game by licensed hunters on their property, but they may reasonably restrict the number of hunters. If agreement is not reached, the claimant may initiate an action in district court (29.1-356). Where damage is by a hunter whose whereabouts are known, the claimant shall first proceed against that hunter in a civil action before payment is made under the Damage Stamp Program (29.1-357). Localities shall report claims paid and investigated to the Department annually (29.1-358).★★ (See also Licenses and Permits under HUNTING, FISHING, TRAPPING PROVISIONS for other Damage Stamp details and for the National Forest Permit provisions.)

The disbursements of the Department and Board shall be limited to the amount appropriated by the General Assembly from the Game Protection Fund and to expenditures from the Lifetime Hunting and Fishing Endowment Fund (29.1-110).

PROTECTED SPECIES OF WILDLIFE

The taking, transporting, processing, selling or offering for sale of fish or wildlife appearing on a list of threatened or endangered species published by the US Secretary of the Interior is prohibited except as otherwise provided (29.1-564). The Board is authorized to: ▸ adopt the federal list and modifications thereto by regulations; ▸ declare by regulation, after recommendations from the Director of the Department of Conservation and Historic Resources and other reliable data sources, that species not appearing on the federal lists are endangered or threatened in Virginia; ▸ prohibit by regulation the taking, transporting, processing, selling or offering for sale within the state of threatened or endangered species (29.1-566). Violation of endangered species provisions is a Class 1 misdemeanor, and an officer authorized to issue criminal warrants has the authority to issue warrants for search and seizure of goods, business records, merchandise or fish or wildlife taken or used in violation of a provision of this article, such items to be forfeited at the direction of the court. The Director may direct fish or wildlife seized to go to a qualified zoological, educational or scientific institution for safekeeping, with costs assessed to the defendant (29.1-567). (See also GENERAL EXCEPTIONS TO PROTECTION and RELEVANT WILDLIFE DEFINITIONS for nuisance species.)

GENERAL EXCEPTIONS TO PROTECTION

There is a continuous open season for trapping nuisance species as defined in 29.1-100, and a continuous closed trapping season on all wild birds and wild animals which are not so defined, except as provided by regulations. A landowner may trap and dispose of, except by sale, squirrels creating a nuisance on the landowner's property at any time in an area where the use of firearms for such purpose is prohibited by law or local ordinance. A landowner may trap fur-bearing animals, except beaver, muskrat and raccoons, upon the landowner's land during closed season (29.1-511, -512 and -530). A landowner may shoot fur-bearing animals except beaver, muskrats or raccoons, upon the landowner's land during closed season (29.1-517). The Board may permit the taking, exporting, transporting or possessing of fish or wildlife listed as endangered for zoological, educational or scientific purposes and for propagation in captivity for preservation purposes (29.1-568). (See also PROTECTED SPECIES OF WILDLIFE.) A permit to collect specimens of fish, wild birds, wild animals and amphibians in limited quantity, for scientific or museum purpose, may be issued by the Board or Director to collect a certain number of specimens of one or more designated species when the collection is an essential part of a specific research project (29.1-418).

HUNTING, FISHING, TRAPPING PROVISIONS

General Provisions

It is unlawful and a Class 3 misdemeanor to: ▸ violate a regulation of the Board concerning refuges, sanctuaries and public shooting or fishing preserves in impounded waters or in forest and watershed areas owned by the US government; ▸ damage boundary enclosures or enter a game refuge owned by the Board for the purpose of molesting a bird or animal, or permit a dog or livestock to go thereon; ▸ fish or trespass on waters or lands being utilized for fish propagation, or damage a pond, dam, or device being used by the Board; ▸ interfere with, obstruct, pollute or diminish the natural flow of water into a fish hatchery (29.1-554).

When taken in accordance with this title, each species of wild bird, wild animal or fish may be possessed at any time (29.1-537). When taken in accordance with law or regulation, bear, muskrat, opossum, rabbits, raccoon and squirrels may be bought and sold during open hunting season only, but hides, furs, pelts or carcasses of fur-bearing animals legally taken and possessed may be sold in accordance with 29.1-400 through 29.1-407 (29.1-536). Deer or bear killed by motor vehicles may be kept for the person's own use after notice to the Game Warden and inspection of the carcass and obtaining a certificate that the animal was killed by the vehicle (29.1-539). A licensee of a shooting preserve may dress, pack and sell bobwhite quail raised for use as food under Board regulations (29.1-544).

When lawfully taken, wild birds, animals or fish may be transported by properly licensed persons: during open season, for lawful use within or without the state; via freight, express or airplane mail, as a gift and not for market or sale, and so marked on proper tags, during open season. Such properly tagged animals in transit during the open season may continue in transit for five days to reach their destination (29.1-540). It is unlawful to store wild birds, animals, or fish if selling them is prohibited by law, except they may be stored in a bona fide domicile or a licensed cold storage facility, which shall tag each lot of game with information as the Board requires. Cold storage facilities must keep required records as to species, dates received, and from whom and to whom delivered. Violation: Class 2 misdemeanor (29.1-541).

Licenses and Permits

It is unlawful to hunt, trap or fish in or on the lands or inland waters of the state without a license, except as otherwise provided (29.1-300). Violation: Class 3 misdemeanor, plus an amount to purchase the required license. Purchase of a license after arrest for hunting, fishing or trapping without a license shall not relieve the person from the specified penalties (29.1-335). Failure to carry a license while engaging in the licensed activity is a Class 4 misdemeanor (29.1-336). Refusal to display one's license upon the demand of a Game Warden or other officer is a Class 3 misdemeanor, and licenses must also be shown upon demand of an owner/lessee upon whose lands or waters the person may be hunting, fishing or trapping (29.1-337). Falsification of a license application or license is a Class 2 misdemeanor (29.1-337.1).

Persons who have never obtained a hunting license, or those under age 16, must have a certificate of completion in hunter education issued or authorized by the Board before obtaining a hunting license. This does not apply to persons on horseback hunting foxes with hounds but no firearms (29.1-300.1). The Department shall provide a course in hunter safety, principles of conservation and sportsmanship and may cooperate with an association promoting these goals. The Board shall establish six full-time hunter education coordinator positions, each assigned to a Game Warden district. The Board shall designate competent instructors (29.1-300.2).

Residents/nonresidents may obtain Lifetime Hunting and Fishing Licenses, funds to go into the Lifetime Hunting and Fishing Endowment Fund (29.1-302.1). An owner/lessee of land bordering waters adjacent to North Carolina may obtain a Special Guest Fishing License to fish from the property and private dock except for trout (29.1-302.3). Nonresidents must have a special license to hunt within shooting preserves (29.1-304). There are special licenses required to hunt bear, deer and turkey, for bonus deer, for archery and for muzzle-loading firearm seasons (29.1-305 through -307). ★Licenses are available to hunt only in the county or city of residence (29.1-303).★ The Board may charge use fees and issue permits to fish in specially stocked trout waters as designated by the Board. Proceeds from fees are exclusively for stocking and management of the streams (29.1-318).

★No person shall hunt, fish or trap on national forest lands in the state without first obtaining, in addition to the regular resident/nonresident license, a special permit to hunt, fish or trap in the national forests as the Board and Forest Service may agree upon, except for persons under age 16 to fish or trap, residents over age 65 to fish, and other specified exceptions (29.1-408). Funds from these special permits shall be used by the Director for game and fish management within national forests in the state, or, at the Board's discretion, paid into the US treasury as a cooperative deposit for use of the USFWS for game and fish management in Virginia national forests (29.1-410). The Board shall enter a cooperative agreement with the USFWS defining means and methods to be taken to improve the fish and game resources of the national forests and shall program expenditure of all funds from the special permit (29.1-411).★

It is unlawful to hunt bear or deer in a locality adopting a Damage Stamp ordinance with the Commonwealth without first obtaining the special stamp. Violation: Class 3 misdemeanor (29.1-354).

★Except for waters as defined by statute, floating and stationary blinds for hunting waterfowl must be licensed as provided (29.1-340). Owners of riparian rights have the exclusive privilege of licensing and erecting blinds on their shorelines, or in the public waters offshore, and rights may be renewed annually (29.1-344). No person shall hunt migratory waterfowl or shoot in the public waters from a boat, float, raft within 500 yards of a legally licensed erected stationary blind of another without permission. Violations of article provisions are Class 2 misdemeanors (29.1-349 and -351.1). [Extensive details are given for distances between blinds, license renewals, exempted shores, waters and riparian owners, tagging of blinds, and construction specifications.]★

Restrictions on Taking: Hunting and Trapping

For the purpose of hunting and trapping laws, big game shall include bear and deer, and small game shall include other game animals and all game birds (29.1-510). It is lawful to hunt wild birds and wild animals specified in this article within applicable daily and season bag limits during open seasons as provided by Board regulations (29.1-513).

The following nonmigratory game birds may be hunted during prescribed open seasons: birds introduced by the Board; bobwhite quail; grouse; pheasants; turkey. The Board may issue a permit to raise or purchase pheasants entitling the permittee to release and hunt pheasants on the permittee's land under Board regulations. The Board may open the season on pen-raised game birds on controlled shooting areas under regulations (29.1-514). Migratory game birds may be hunted in accordance with Board regulations which shall conform to US government regulations for open seasons and bag limits (29.1-515).

It is unlawful to: ► ★hunt or kill a wild bird or animal, including nuisance species, with a gun, firearm or other weapon on Sunday, which is declared a rest day for all species of wild bird and animal life, except raccoons, which may be hunted until 2:00 a.m. on Sunday mornings;★ ► destroy or molest the nest, eggs, dens or young of a wild bird or animal, except nuisance species, at any time without a permit as required by law; ► hunt or attempt to kill or trap a species of wild bird or animal after having obtained the daily bag or season limit; ► occupy a baited blind or other baited place for taking a wild bird or animal or to put out bait or salt to take/kill them, except for baiting nuisance species of animals and birds or baiting traps for taking fur-bearing animals that may be lawfully trapped;

▸ ★kill or capture a wild bird or animal adjacent to an area while a field or forest fire is in progress; ★ ▸ shoot or attempt to take a wild bird or wild animal from an automobile or other vehicle; ▸ set a trap on lands or waters of another without attaching the trapper's name and address; ▸ fail to visit all traps once each day and remove all animals caught and immediately report to the landowner stock, dogs or fowl which are caught and the date; ▸ hunt, trap, take, capture, kill, sell, purchase, transport or attempt any of these at any time or in any manner, except as specifically permitted by law and only by the manner or means and within the numbers stated. ★These provisions shall not be construed to prohibit use or transportation of legally taken turkey carcasses or portions for the purposes of making/selling turkey callers.★ Violation: Class 3 misdemeanor (29.1-521).

Unless the Board declares otherwise, it is unlawful to kill male deer in a county or city unless it has antlers visible above the hair (29.1-522). It is unlawful to kill or attempt to kill a deer in the water of a stream, lake or pond, or to hunt deer with dogs in counties west of the Blue Ridge Mountains. There shall be a continuous open season for hunting fox with dogs only. It is unlawful to kill rabbits and squirrels during the closed season except for landowners, family members or tenants with the landowner's permission, or resident members of hunt clubs who own the land in fee (29.1-516). Killing or attempting to kill a bear in violation of any provision of this article or regulation is a Class 1 misdemeanor (29.1-530.2). Nonmigratory game birds and animals may be hunted from one-half hour before sunrise to one-half hour after sunset. Fur-bearing and nuisance species may be hunted by day or night, except that muskrats may be hunted by day only. Violation: Class 3 misdemeanor (29.1-520).

Shotguns, rifles, bows and arrows, pistols, and muzzle-loading pistols may be used to hunt all wild birds and wild animals, unless expressly prohibited. [There are detailed statutory requirements as to ammunition size, caliber, cartridge foot pounds of energy, type of animal and time of day for use of certain weapons. Provisions for weapon and ammunition sizes are also detailed for counties east or west of the Blue Ridge Mountains.] Hunting wild birds or animals with weapons other than those authorized is a Class 3 misdemeanor (29.1-519).

Killing or attempting to kill a deer during specified nighttime hours by use of a light attached to a vehicle, spotlight or flashlight is a Class 2 misdemeanor. The flashing of a light or spotlight from a vehicle at night by a person in possession of a firearm, bow and arrow or speargun, without good cause, raises a presumption of an attempt to kill deer in violation of this section, and every person in or on such vehicle, or a person who aids and abets or acts in concert with a violator shall be deemed a principal in the first degree. In addition to the prescribed penalty, the court shall revoke the current hunting license of the violator, prohibit the issuance of a hunting license for the next license year, and shall forward notice of such revocation/prohibition to the Department (29.1-523).

A city or county government may by ordinance prohibit hunting with a firearm within 100 yards of a primary and secondary highway or trapping a game animal or fur-bearer within 50 feet of the shoulder of such highway and make either offense a Class 3 misdemeanor. This does not prevent trapping where permission of the landowner is obtained. The governing body must notify the Director no later than May 1 of the year the ordinance is to take effect, or it shall be unenforceable (29.1-526). Similar ordinances may be passed by cities or counties prohibiting shooting or hunting with a firearm within 100 yards of a public school or city, county or town park, and make a violation a Class 4 misdemeanor. Such ordinances may not be enforced within national or state parks or forests, or wildlife management areas (29.1-527). Governing bodies may also by ordinance prescribe ammunition sizes and permitted firearm types during certain hunting seasons (29.1-528).

Trappers shall be responsible for all damage done by an illegally set trap, and a person finding an illegally set trap may report it to the landowner or to a Game Warden who may destroy or disable the trap. Licensed trappers may shoot wild animals caught in traps during the open hunting season if they have a hunting license. It is lawful to trap wild animals within daily bag and season limits during the open season provided by Board regulations (29.1-530).

Restrictions on Taking: Fishing

It is unlawful to use an explosive for destruction of fish, or knowingly to cast a noxious substance into a watercourse where fish or spawn may be destroyed, or to place or allow to pass into the waters any sawdust, ashes, lime, gas, tar or refuse of gas works injurious to fish. Violation: Class 3 misdemeanor, except conviction for use of explosives is a Class 1 misdemeanor. The owner of a property on which fish are destroyed by explosives shall be entitled to recover liquidated damages in an amount determined by the court from a person convicted of destroying fish by such means (29.1-533).

Unless otherwise provided by regulation, it is unlawful to take fish in inland waters other than shad, herring or mullet, except by fishing with a hook and line or rod and reel, held in the hand. It is unlawful to catch, trap, take, capture, kill, sell, purchase, transport export or import at any time or in any manner, or attempt such, a species of game fish, carcass or part, except as specifically permitted by this article. In waters specified by statute, certain types of traps, fish pots or haul seines and nets may be used, but game fish caught must be returned to its waters. The Board may close streams or rivers in localities when the waters are stocked by the Department. It is lawful to sell for food trout lawfully acquired, provided they have been propagated and raised in a hatchery or by other artificial means, and the Board shall by regulation establish a practical system of identification of trout offered for sale for table use. Violation of any of these provisions is a Class 2 misdemeanor (29.1-531).

A dam or other object which obstructs navigation or passage of fish, shall be deemed a nuisance, unless it is used to work a mill, factory or other machine useful to the public and is allowed by law or court order. Persons owning such dams shall provide fishways unless excepted by the Board, and shall keep them in good repair, or shall remove dams not authorized by law at their expense when the Board determines that they interfere with anadromous fish passage. The courts may order compliance with construction provisions, to be completed within three years. Penalties for non-compliance shall go to the Department as detailed by statute (29.1-532).

Commercial and Private Enterprise Provisions

It is unlawful to buy, sell, barter, or trade in hides, furs or pelts of wild animals or otherwise deal in fur as a business without a permit, except for hunters and trappers disposing of hides, furs or pelts from animals legally taken, or persons lawfully engaging in fur farming (29.1-400 and -402). Permittees may be required to submit reports annually (29.1-405). Violations: Class 3 misdemeanor and the court shall revoke the permit for the current and following seasons (29.1-406). Furs possessed in violation shall be forfeited to the state (29.1-407).

Special permits, issued at the Board's discretion, are required: ▸ to engage in the business of taxidermy; ▸ to net fish in inland waters for private table use or for sale where permitted; ▸ to take, hold, trap or carry live falcons, hawks and owls for falconry purposes; ▸ to collect specimens for scientific purposes; ▸ to hold and dispose of game animals, game birds including bobwhite quail, game fish and game fur-bearers for an authorized purpose including use as food; ▸ for bona fide field trial clubs to hold dog field trials (29.1-412 through -422). [Details as to fees, restrictions and other provisions are given for each type of permit.] (See also Restrictions on Taking: Hunting and Trapping under this section for pen-raised pheasant and other game bird provisions.)

The Director may issue licenses for shooting preserves when operations will result in an increase in hunting opportunities and will otherwise be in the public interest. The applicant must own or lease the land, must clearly post boundaries as the Board prescribes, and shall develop the lands to meet Board requirements. Until these requirements have been met, it is unlawful to shoot or take game of the species specified on the license (29.1-600 through -603). Once all requirements are satisfied, the licensee and other persons designated by payment of fees or otherwise may hunt and shoot, possess, transport and dispose of by gift game birds or animals of the species licensed. Game birds and animals not covered by the license may be taken and possessed by the licensee/guests as otherwise provided. Game shot on the preserve shall be tagged before removal. The Board shall set the hunting season and bag limit on such preserves, and may make other rules. The Director may revoke the license of a shooting preserve operator not in compliance with law or rules. Violation: Class 2 misdemeanor (29.1-604 through -611). Nothing in this title shall be construed as permitting a person to hunt, trap or fish in or on the lands or waters of a public or private club or preserve as a landowner or in another capacity without a proper license (29.1-612).

Import, Export and Release Provisions

Live wolves or coyotes, or birds and animals otherwise classed as predatory or undesirable, may not be imported into the Commonwealth nor liberated or possessed therein, except under a special Board permit. Nonpredatory birds, animals or fish may be imported, but shall be subject to laws governing the possession of such birds, animals and fish. A person may bring into the state, either in personal possession or as baggage on the same conveyance and properly labeled or tagged, game and fish legally taken in another state or country, but in no greater quantity than could be legally possessed in that other state or country (29.1-542). It is unlawful for a person to possess, sell, or liberate live nutria (29.1-545). It is unlawful for the owner of an exotic reptile or non-native reptile, including the

American alligator, to keep the reptile in any manner that will permit its escape or knowingly to permit it to run at large. Violation: Class 4 misdemeanor (29.1-569).

Interstate Reciprocal Agreements

A Virginia resident and resident of an adjoining jurisdiction which has inland water lying adjacent to Virginia land or water may take fish with hook and line after complying with their state's provisions for taking fish in such interjurisdictional waters, including the District of Columbia (29.1-534). The Board may enter into reciprocal agreements with adjoining jurisdictions for reciprocal honoring of fishing licenses used in either inland waters of Virginia or the other jurisdiction, or bordering each, according to conditions specified by statute. Violation of creel limits, open seasons or other provisions of the agreement is a Class 2 misdemeanor (29.1-535).

ANIMAL DAMAGE CONTROL

When beaver, muskrats or raccoons are substantially damaging crops or lands, the landowner or tenant may kill the animals or have them killed, under permit obtained from the Game Warden (29.1-517 and -518). A black bear may be killed when it is inflicting or attempting to inflict injury to a person, or when a person is in pursuit of the bear commenced immediately after the commission of such offense. Killing a bear under this provision shall immediately be reported to a Game Warden. Foxes may be killed at any time by a landowner/tenant when doing damage to domestic stock or fowl. When rabbits and squirrels are committing substantial damage to fruit trees, gardens, crops or other property, the landowner may kill them or have them killed under a Game Warden permit (29.1-516).

Whenever deer or bear are damaging fruit trees, crops, livestock or personal property, the landowner shall immediately report the damage to the local Game Warden for investigation. If it is found that deer or bear are responsible for the damage, the warden shall authorize in writing the landowner/lessee or other designated person to kill such deer or bear when they are found upon that land. The Game Warden may specify in writing the time period for which the permit is effective. During certain months, they may specify in writing the sex of deer which may be killed. ★Whenever deer are creating a hazard to the operation of an aircraft or to connected facilities, persons responsible for aircraft operations shall report such fact to the local Game Warden for investigation. If deer are found to be creating a hazard, the Game Warden shall authorize such person to kill the deer when they are found to be creating a hazard.★ The carcass of every deer or bear so killed may be awarded to the landowner by the Game Warden, with a certificate to that effect. The carcass may then be used as if taken during the hunting season for deer or bear (29.1-529). (See also GENERAL EXCEPTIONS TO PROTECTION.)

ENFORCEMENT OF WILDLIFE LAWS

Enforcement Powers

Game Wardens have authority to issue a summons or to arrest a person found violating any provisions of the hunting, trapping, inland fish and boating laws. Regular Game Wardens are vested with the same authority as sheriffs and other law enforcement officers to enforce all of the criminal laws of the state. A special game warden has general police power while performing duties on Board controlled/owned properties. ★A commissioned warrant or petty officers of the US Coast Guard and US Coast Guard Reserve, while on active duty, and US Customs Officers, in uniform in conduct of official duties, have the same power to make arrests under Chapter 7 of Title 29.1 as Game Wardens (29.1-205).★ A person who, by threats or force, attempts to intimidate or impede a law enforcement officer enforcing game, inland fish and boating laws shall be guilty of a Class 2 misdemeanor (29.1-207).

All Game Wardens have the authority to search a person arrested and any box, package or other container, hunting bag, trunk or fish basket in possession and the authority immediately after arrest to enter and search a refrigerator, building, vehicle or other place in which the officer has reasonable cause to believe the person has concealed a wild bird, animal or fish which will furnish evidence of a violation of the laws. Such search may be made without a warrant except for a dwelling. The Game Warden shall seize and hold as evidence the container, together with a wild bird, animal or fish and an unlawful gun, net or other device which has been illegally taken, possessed, sold, purchased or transported and found as a result of such search (29.1-208). Game Wardens have the power to inspect game, fur-bearing animals and fish taken by a person found hunting, trapping or fishing to see that bag/creel limits are being observed (29.1-209). Persons arrested for a violation of the game and fish laws may be committed to jail pending trial, admitted to bail or released on recognizance as provided by general law, or issued a summons to appear for trial at a time and place designated. Violation of a written promise to appear before the court is a Class 2 misdemeanor (29.1-210).

★Upon request by a member of the governing body of a county, city or town, Game Wardens shall take samples of water from a stream when there is reason to believe that the water may be polluted, and send the sample to the State Water Control Board as specified in this section (29.1-213).★ Game Wardens shall caution persons of fire danger, and if possible, extinguish all fires left burning, or notify proper fire officials (29.1-212).

Criminal Penalties

Conviction of violation of any of the provisions of this title is a Class 2 misdemeanor, unless otherwise specified (29.1-546). Conviction of trapping, selling, buying or attempting such of a migratory game bird as defined in statute or conviction of possessing a migratory game bird taken by means of a trap is a Class 1 misdemeanor (29.1-547).

Killing deer in violation of regulations, exceeding the bag limit, or taking a deer during closed season is a Class 2 misdemeanor. Killing a deer illegally during the open season is a Class 3 misdemeanor, if the person immediately delivers the complete carcass in good condition to the Game Warden, who shall confiscate and dispose of it as otherwise provided. Such person shall be exempt from replacement cost of the deer as provided in 29.1-551. It is a Class 4 misdemeanor to kill a deer from a boat or other watercraft. Every boat, watercraft, motor, rifle, shotgun, crossbow, bow and arrow or speargun used with the knowledge and consent of the owner, in killing a deer in violation of this section shall be forfeited to the state as provided by law (29.1-548 and -549).

It is unlawful and a Class 2 misdemeanor to: take a wild bird, animal or fish during the closed season; exceed the bag or creel limit; possess over the daily bag or creel limit a wild bird, animal or fish while in the forests, fields or waters of the Commonwealth (29.1-550).

A person who offers for sale, sells, offers to buy or does buy a wild bird, animal or part, or a freshwater fish, except as provided by law, is guilty of a Class 1 misdemeanor. However, when the aggregate of such sales or purchases or combination thereof totals $200 or more during a 90-day period, it is a Class 6 felony. This does not affect prosecutions for illegal purchase or sale of migratory game birds (29.1-553).

No person shall be excused from testifying for the Commonwealth as to an offense committed by another under the game and fish laws because the testimony may tend to incriminate the testifier, but testimony given by a person on behalf of the state when called as witness shall in no case be used against the person, nor shall the person be prosecuted as to the offense to which testified (29.1-561).

A person conspiring with another to commit an offense defined in this title or in a Board regulation shall be guilty of conspiracy and subject to the same punishment prescribed for the offense which was the object of the conspiracy (29.1-505.1).

[Provisions are given for operating boats, water skis, or spearfishing while intoxicated, including implied consent provisions (29.1-738 and -739)]

Civil Penalties

★★It is unlawful knowingly to release into the atmosphere within a one-hour period fifty or more balloons which are made of a nonbiodegradable or nonphotodegradable material or any material which requires more than five minutes of contact with air or water to degrade and which are inflated with a substance lighter than air. A violator is subject to a civil penalty not to exceed $5 per balloon released above the allowable limit, to be paid into the Lifetime Hunting and Fishing Endowment Fund. These provisions do not apply to balloons released from Commonwealth agencies, or the US or any other state, territory or government for scientific or meteorological purposes, or to hot air balloons recovered after launch (29.1-556.1).★★

Illegal Taking of Wildlife

The judge, upon convicting a person for violation of 29.1-548, 29.1-550 or 29.1-552 (illegal taking of deer or turkey or other game) shall, in addition to imposition of the punishment prescribed in those sections, ascertain the approximate replacement value of animals, birds or fish taken in violation and shall assess the value against the person convicted. The assessment shall be paid within the time prescribed in the judgment, not exceeding 60 days. Such payments go into the Game Protection Fund (29.1-551).

Illegal Taking of Wildlife

Every vehicle, rifle, shotgun, pistol, crossbow, bow and arrow, or speargun used with the knowledge or consent of the owner/lienholder thereof, in killing or attempting to kill deer during nighttime hours as specified by statute in violation of 29.1-523 (spotlighting) and every vehicle used in transportation of the carcass or part of a deer so killed shall be forfeited to the Commonwealth as provided in chapter 22, Title 19.2 (19.2-329, *et seq.*) and the proceeds of sale disposed of according to law (19.1-524). A person in a vehicle and in possession of a firearm or other weapon who employs a light attached to the vehicle, spotlight or flashlight to cast a light beyond the water or roadway surface to a place used by deer shall be guilty of a Class 2 misdemeanor, and each person in the vehicle shall be deemed prima facie a principal in the second degree with the same punishment as a principal in the first degree. It is a Class 4 misdemeanor deliberately to employ a light on a vehicle or a spotlight/flashlight to cast a light beyond the surface of the roadway upon a place used by deer except on one's own land, or with the landowner's permission, and every person in the vehicle shall be deemed a principal in the second degree and subject to the same punishment as a principal in the first degree. In addition to the penalties prescribed herein, the court shall revoke the current hunting license and forbid the issuance of a hunting license for one year (29.1-525). (See also Restrictions on Taking: Hunting and Trapping under HUNTING, FISHING, TRAPPING PROVISIONS.)

Killing a wild turkey during the closed season or a beardless turkey during an open season for bearded turkeys is a Class 2 misdemeanor for each turkey killed. If the person immediately delivers the complete carcass in good condition to the local Game Warden for confiscation and disposal, the person shall be exempt from replacement cost provided in 29.1-551 (29.1-552).

A firearm, trap, net or other device of any kind for taking wild birds, animals, or fish, except as specifically permitted by law, shall be considered unlawful. Violation: Class 3 misdemeanor, and the device shall be forfeited to the state. ★Nets, traps or other such devices, excluding firearms, shall be destroyed by the Game Warden if the owner cannot be located within 30 days. Unlawful fixed devices may be destroyed by the Game Warden at the place where found (29.1-556).★

License Revocations, Suspensions

If a person is found guilty of violating hunting, trapping or inland fish laws or provisions of 18.2-131 through 18.2-135 and 18.2-285 through 18.2-287.1, or regulations pursuant thereto, a second time within three years of a previous conviction on any provisions governing dumping refuse, trash or other litter while hunting, trapping or fishing, the license issued to such person shall be revoked by the court and the person shall not apply for a new license for one year. The court may also prohibit obtaining a license to hunt, fish or trap for one to five years. Hunting, fishing or trapping during the prohibited period is a Class 2 misdemeanor (29.1-338).

See also HUNTING, FISHING, TRAPPING PROVISIONS for deer spotlighting provisions.

HABITAT PROTECTION

There is nothing specific pertaining to habitat protection in Title 29.

NATIVE AMERICAN WILDLIFE PROVISIONS

No license to hunt, trap or fish shall be required of an Indian who habitually resides on an Indian reservation and who carries an identification card signed by the chief of the Indian's reservation, setting forth that the person is an actual resident, which may be rebutted by proof of actual residence elsewhere (29.1-301).

WASHINGTON

Sources: Revised Code of Washington, Annotated, 1962, Titles 75 and 77; 1992 Cumulative Pocket Part.

STATE WILDLIFE POLICY

Wildlife is the property of the state. The Department shall preserve, protect, and perpetuate wildlife. Game animals, birds and fish may be taken only at times, places, or in manners or quantities as in the Commission's judgment maximizes public recreational opportunities without impairing the supply of wildlife. The Commission shall attempt to maximize recreational fishing opportunities of all citizens, particularly juvenile, handicapped and senior citizens. Nothing herein shall be construed to infringe on the right of private property owners to control their own property (77.12.010).

The Legislature declares that the public and private propagation, production, protection and enhancement of fish is in the public interest (77.18.005). (See HABITAT PROTECTION.)

Currently, many of Washington's salmon stocks are critically reduced from their sustainable level. The best interests of all fishing groups and citizens are served by a stable and productive salmon resource. Immediate action is needed to reverse the severe decline of the resource and to insure its very survival. The Legislature finds a state of emergency exists and that immediate action is necessary to restore the fishery. Disagreement and strife have dominated the salmon fisheries for many years. Conflicts among fishing interests have only served to erode the resource. It is time for the state to make a major commitment to increasing productivity of the resource and to move forward with an effective rehabilitation and enhancement program. The Department of Fisheries is directed to dedicate its efforts to make increasing the productivity of the salmon resource a first priority and to seek resolution to the many conflicts that involve the resource. Success of the enhancement program can only occur if projects efficiently produce salmon or restore habitat. The expectation of the program is to optimize the efficient use of funding on projects that will increase artificially and naturally produced salmon, restore and improve habitat, or identify ways to increase the survival of salmon. The full utilization of state resources and cooperative efforts with interested groups are essential to success of the program (75.50.010).

★The fish and game resources of the state benefit by the contribution of volunteer recreational and commercial fishing organizations, schools, and other volunteer groups in cooperative projects with the Department of Fisheries or the Department of Wildlife. These projects provide educational opportunities, improve the communication between the natural resources agencies and the public, and increase the fish and game resources. In an effort to increase these benefits and realize the full potential of cooperative projects, the Departments of Fisheries and Wildlife each shall administer a cooperative fish and wildlife enhancement program and enter into agreements with volunteer groups relating to the operation of cooperative projects (75.52.010). ★ [Details are under HABITAT PROTECTION. Details of the "Salmon Enhancement Program," including the formulation of long-term regional policy statements, the formation of "Regional Fisheries Enhancement Groups" and projects are in Chapter 75.50 but not discussed here.]

The people declare that an emergency exists in the management of salmon and steelhead trout resources such that both are in great peril. An immediate resolution of this crisis is essential to perpetuating and enhancing these resources (75.56.010). The people of the state petition the US Congress immediately to make the steelhead trout a national game fish protected under the Black Bass Act (75.56.020).

The people of the state declare that conservation, enhancement, and proper utilization of the state's natural resources, including lands, waters, timber, fish and game are responsibilities of the state and shall remain within the express domain of the state. While fully respecting private property rights, all resources in the state's domain shall be managed by the state alone such that conservation, enhancement and proper utilization are primary considerations. No citizen shall be denied equal access to and use of any resource on the basis of race, sex, origin, cultural heritage, or by and through any treaty based upon the same (75.56.030).

RELEVANT WILDLIFE DEFINITIONS: See Definitions section of Appendices.

STATE FISH AND WILDLIFE AGENCIES

Agency Structure

The **Department of Wildlife** (Department) consists of the **State Wildlife Commission** (Commission) and the **Director of Wildlife** (Director). The Director is responsible for the administration and operation of the Department, subject to title provisions. The Commission may delegate to the Director additional duties and powers necessary to carry out this title. The Director shall perform the duties prescribed by law and carry out the basic goals and objectives under 77.04.055 (77.04.020).

The **Department of Fisheries** shall preserve, protect, perpetuate and manage the food fish and shellfish in state and offshore waters and conserve the same as not to impair the resource; and shall promote orderly fisheries and enhance and improve recreational and commercial fishing (75.08.012). The **Director of Fisheries** shall supervise administration of the Department of Fisheries, have general knowledge of fisheries resources and commercial and recreational fishing industry, investigate the habits, supply and economic use of food fish and shellfish in the state and offshore waters, and report as required (75.08.014 and .020). The Directors of Fisheries and of Wildlife with Commission concurrence may enter into agreements and receive US funds for construction and operation of fish cultural stations and devices in the Columbia River basin to improve feeding and spawning conditions for fish, for protection of migratory fish from irrigation projects and for facilitating free migration of fish over obstructions (75.08.055). [Numerous other provisions deal with the Director of Fisheries duties relating to food fish or shellfish. Duties relating to nontidal, inshore waters are similar to those of the Director of Wildlife.]

The **Commission** consists of six registered voters appointed by the Governor with advice and consent of the Senate. Persons eligible for appointment to the Commission shall have general knowledge of the habits and distribution of wildlife and shall not hold other office. The Governor shall seek to maintain a balance reflecting all aspects of wildlife in making Commission appointments. The Commission in odd-numbered years shall elect one member as chairperson and another as vice chair, for two-year terms. At least four meetings per year must be held, and special meetings when called by the Chairperson or by four members (77.04.030, .040 and .060).

Persons eligible for appointment by the Governor as **Director** shall have practical knowledge of the habits and distribution of wildlife. The Governor shall seek recommendations from the Commission on the qualifications, skills and experience necessary for the position. The Director is ex officio secretary of the Commission, shall attend its meetings, may appoint necessary Department personnel, and shall provide staff for the Commission (77.04.080).

Agency Powers and Duties

The Commission shall establish and review with the Governor and Legislature the Department's basic goals to preserve, protect and perpetuate wildlife and wildlife habitat, maximize hunting and fishing recreational opportunities, establish hunting, trapping and fishing seasons and prescribe the time, place, manner and methods for harvesting wildlife (77.04.055).

In cooperation with the Director of Fisheries, the Director shall develop proposals to reinstate the natural salmon and steelhead trout fish runs in the Tilton and Cowlitz rivers (77.04.100). The Director shall report annually to the Governor, agencies, and legislative committees on: revenues generated; program costs; capital expenditures; personnel; department projects and research; environmental controls; intergovernmental agreements; ongoing litigation; concluded litigation and any major issues with the potential for state liability, including the status of the resource and its recreational and tribal utilization. The Commission shall report on recreational hunting and fishing opportunities, wildlife and wildlife resources in the state, and the Department's progress towards meeting Commission goals, and solicit public input in preparing this annual analysis (77.04.111). The Commission may make agreements with persons, state political subdivisions, the US or its agencies regarding wildlife-oriented recreation and the propagation, protection, conservation and control of wildlife. The Director may make agreements with landowners to use the property for wildlife-oriented recreation, make rules governing persons on such property, and accept compensation for wildlife losses or gifts of land or personal property for Department use (77.12.320). The Commission may cooperate with the Oregon Fish and Wildlife Commission to adopt rules that assure an annual yield of wildlife on the Columbia river and prevent taking of wildlife at places or times that might endanger wildlife (77.12.325). The Commission may establish by rule exclusive fishing waters for minors (77.12.330). The

Commission may authorize the Director to acquire by gift, purchase, lease or condemnation lands, buildings, waters for purposes consistent with this title. Condemnation powers may be exercised only when an appropriation has been made by the Legislature for acquisition of a specific property (77.12.200).

The Director shall maintain real or personal property owned, leased or held by the Department, control the construction of improvements and adopt rules for property operation. The Commission may authorize the Director to sell timber, gravel, sand and other materials from Department property and to sell or lease such property or grant concessions or rights of way for roads or utilities. ★Oil and gas resources lying below such lands shall be offered for lease by the Commissioner of Public Lands, with proceeds to go to the State Wildlife Fund, provided that leases shall be conditioned at Department request to protect wildlife and its habitat.★ Property not needed for Department uses may be sold or returned to the donor/grantor, with notice of public auction of lands and proceeds to be deposited in the State Wildlife Fund (77.12.210). The Commission may make agreements to obtain real or personal property or to transfer state property to the US, political subdivisions of the state, public service companies or other persons, if in the public interest (77.12.220). [Details are given for withdrawal from lease of state-owned lands in conformity to the state outdoor recreation plan, approvals of counties, and provisions for such transfers and public hearings (77.12.360 through .390).]

The Director may authorize removal, relocation, reconstruction or other modification of an inadequate fishway or fish protective device without cost to the owner. Modifications may not materially alter the flow of water. The fishway shall be maintained at the expense of the owner (77.12.425). The Director may spend moneys to improve natural growing conditions for fish by constructing fishways, installing screens and removing obstructions to migratory fish. The eradication of undesirable fish shall be authorized by the Commission, and the Director may enter into cooperative agreements with government agencies and with private persons for these purposes (77.12.420). **Wildlife agents** and **ex officio wildlife agents** shall enforce the law and rules adopted pursuant to this title within their respective jurisdictions (77.12.070).

Agency Regulations

The Commission shall adopt rules, amendments and repeals by approval of four members by resolution, recorded in Commission minutes, and adopt emergency rules by approval of four members in conformance with 34.05. Judicial notice shall be taken of rules filed and published (77.04.090). The Commission shall adopt, amend, or repeal and enforce reasonable rules prohibiting or governing the time, place, and manner of taking or possessing game animals, birds or fish and may specify taking quantities, species, sex and size, and regulate the taking, sale, possession and distribution of wildlife and deleterious exotic wildlife. The Director may adopt emergency rules to close or shorten a season for game and shall advise the Commission of the adoption of emergency rules. If the Director finds that game animals have increased in an area so that they are damaging public or private property or over-utilizing their habitat, the Commission may establish a special hunting season, designating the number, sex, area and manner of taking for the area. The Director shall randomly select hunters for special hunts in those areas (77.12.150). The Commission may establish by rule game reserves and closed areas or waters where hunting or fishing for game fish may be prohibited (77.12.040).

Agency Funding Sources

There is established in the state treasury the **State Wildlife Fund** consisting of moneys from: ► rentals or Department concessions; ► sale of real/personal Department property; ► sale of licenses, permits, tags, stamps and punch cards required by this title; ► fees for informational materials published by the Department; ★fees for personalized vehicle license plates;★ ► articles or wildlife sold by the Director; ► compensation for wildlife losses or gifts or grants received under 77.12.320; ► excise tax on anadromous game fish; ► sale of personal property seized by the Department for wildlife violations (77.12.170). Moneys in the State Wildlife Fund may be used only for the purposes of this title, including the payment of principal and interest on bonds issued for capital projects (77.12.190). There is within the State Wildlife Fund a special **Wildlife Account**. Moneys received as compensation for wildlife losses shall be credited to this account, with any surplus invested and income placed in the account (77.12.323).

The **State Wildlife Conservation Reward Fund** is established in the custody of the state treasurer. The Director shall deposit in the fund all moneys designated by rule. Moneys in the fund shall be spent to provide rewards to persons informing the Department about violations of this title or rules, to be paid on Director authorization (77.21.080).

The **Migratory Waterfowl Stamp** shall use the design provided by the Migratory Waterfowl Art Committee. All revenue derived stamp sales shall go into the State Wildlife Fund to be used only for stamp production costs and for migratory waterfowl projects for acquisition and development of migratory waterfowl habitat and for their enhancement, protection and propagation. Gifts of real estate, any interests or the rental, lease or purchase of real estate may be accepted. If the Department acquires any fee interest, leasehold, or rental interest in real property, it shall allow the general public reasonable access to that property and shall insure such access, if possible in the form of a covenant running with the land. The landowner shall retain the right of granting access to the lands by written permission. Excess numbers of stamps may be produced and sold to the public (77.12.670).

★★The Commission and Director may authorize hunting of post-mature male trophy-quality animals from herds in areas not normally open to general public hunting, under the **Washington Trophy Hunt**. The Department may contract with an organization to sponsor the hunt. Any permits or tags required for the hunt shall be sold at public auction to raise funds for the Department and the organization for wildlife conservation purposes. Department representatives may participate in the hunt to insure that animals are properly identified. A wildlife conservation organization may petition the Commission to authorize a special trophy hunt. Participants must have the hunt permit fee and any required licenses, permits or tags (77.12.700). ★★

There is a **Firearms Range Account** in the state general fund. Moneys in the account shall be subject to legislative appropriation and shall be used to purchase and develop land, construct range facilities, safety improvements, noise abatement and liability protection for public and nonprofit firearm range training and practice facilities. Grant funds shall not be used for expendable shooting supplies or normal operating expenses, nor supplant funds for other organization programs. The funds will be available to nonprofit shooting organizations, school districts and state, county or local governments on a match basis. Ranges receiving matching funds must be open on a regular basis and usable by law enforcement personnel or the general public who possess concealed carry permits or hunting licenses. Grant applicants must open their range facility on a regular basis for hunter safety education training [details as to grant payback, application procedures and other range rules are given] (77.12.720).

Proceeds from the following are deposited in the state general fund: ▸ sale of licenses relating to fisheries; ▸ sale of property seized or confiscatedl; ▸ fines and forfeitures; ▸ sale of real or personal property; ▸ moneys received for damages to food fish, shellfish or department property; ▸ proceeds from food fish or shellfish taken in test fishing; ▸ proceeds from the sale of salmon and salmon eggs by the Department (75.08.230). The Fisheries Department may supply at reasonable charge surplus salmon eggs for use in salmon cultivation, but shall not intentionally create a surplus of salmon to provide eggs for sale. The Department shall only sell salmon eggs from stocks not suitable for salmon population rehabilitation or enhancement in state waters, and shall assess suitability and productivity of each watershed for receiving eggs before their sale (75.08.245).

Agency Advisory Boards

The **Migratory Waterfowl Art Committee** consists of nine members appointed by: the Governor (1); the Director (6); the Chairman of the State Arts Commission (1); and the Department of Agriculture (1), such members to represent state-wide interests and be knowledgeable in farming, fine art reproduction, waterfowl and waterfowl management. Members appointed by the Director shall represent eastern and western Washington sports groups, a waterfowl conservation group, a state-wide conservation organization, a state-wide sports hunting group, and the general public. The Committee shall review the Director's expenditures of the previous year of stamp money, prints and related artwork money (77.12.680). The Committee selects the annual Migratory Waterfowl Stamp design and creates collector art prints and related artwork for sale and distribution. Net funds shall be used to contract with one or more individuals or nonprofit organizations which provide waterfowl for the Pacific flyway, except those organizations that obtain compensation for allowing waterfowl hunting (77.12.690). The Committee and its powers and duties shall terminate June 30, 1994 (77.12.900).

There is a ten-member **Firearms Range Advisory Committee** to provide advice and counsel to the Interagency Committee for Outdoor Recreation, which Director shall appoint members from the following groups: law enforcement; Washington military department; black powder shooting sports; pistol shooting sports; shotgun shooting sports; archery shooting sports; hunter education; hunters; and the general public. With the Interagency Committee, the Committee shall develop an application process and audit programs, screen, prioritize and approve grant applications, and monitor compliance by grant recipients. Various state agencies are encouraged to provide land, facilitate land exchanges, and support development of shooting range facilities (77.12.730). The Interagency Committee may accept gifts/grants under Committee terms, for deposit in the Firearms Range Account (77.12.740).

PROTECTED SPECIES OF WILDLIFE

The Director shall investigate the habits and distribution of wildlife species native to or adaptable to state habitats. The Commission shall determine whether a species should be managed by the Department, and may classify wild animals as game animals, game animals as fur-bearing animals, and wild birds as game birds or predatory birds. All wild birds not otherwise classified are protected wildlife. In addition to species listed in 77.08.020, the Commission may classify game fish except those classified as food fish by the Director of Fisheries. The Director may recommend to the Commission that a species of wildlife should not be hunted or fished and may designate species of wildlife as protected. If a species is seriously threatened with extinction in the state, the Director may request its designation as an endangered species by the Commission. ★If the Director determines that a non-native species is dangerous to the environment or wildlife of the state, the Director may request its designation as deleterious exotic wildlife by the Commission (77.12.020).★ If the Director determines that a severe problem exists in an area because deer and elk are being pursued, harassed, attacked or killed by dogs, an emergency may be declared and the area specified where wildlife agents may take into custody or destroy the dogs if necessary with immunity from civil or criminal liability (77.12.315). Except as authorized by Commission rule, it is unlawful to hunt, fish, possess or control protected wildlife or endangered species or to destroy or possess the nests or eggs of game birds or protected wildlife (77.16.120). Except as authorized by law or rule, it is unlawful to hunt, offer for sale, sell, possess, exchange, buy, transport or ship an albino wild animal (77.16.320).

The Department shall cooperate with government agencies to protect bald eagles and their essential habitats through existing governmental programs, including: the Natural Heritage Program managed by the Department of Natural Resources; the Natural Area Preserve Program; and the Shoreline Management Master Programs adopted by local governments and approved by the Department of Ecology (77.12.650). ★The Department shall adopt and enforce rules defining the extent and boundaries of habitat buffer zones for bald eagles. Rules shall take into account the need for variation of the extent of the zone from case to case, and the need for protection of bald eagles, and shall establish guidelines and priorities for purchase or trade and establishment of conservation easements/leases to protect such designated properties. Department rules shall provide adequate notice to property owners of their options under these provisions (77.12.655).★

See also Restrictions on Taking under HUNTING, FISHING, TRAPPING PROVISIONS.

GENERAL EXCEPTIONS TO PROTECTION

The Director may obtain by purchase, gift, or exchange and may sell or transfer wildlife and their eggs for stocking, research or propagation (77.12.140). A scientific permit allows the holder to collect for research or display wildlife, nests and eggs as required under the Director's conditions. Applicants shall demonstrate their qualifications and establish the need for the permit. The Director may require a bond of up to $1,000 to insure permit compliance. Permit holders may exchange specimens with the Director's approval. Violators of this section shall forfeit the permit and bond and shall not receive a similar permit for one year (77.32.240). A permit is required from the Director of Fisheries to take food fish or shellfish for propagation or scientific purposes within state waters (75.08.274).

See also Agency Powers and Duties under STATE FISH AND WILDLIFE AGENCIES.

HUNTING, FISHING, TRAPPING PROVISIONS

General Provisions

Washington is a member, with Oregon, of the **Columbia River Compact** (concurrent jurisdiction to regulate, protect, preserve fish in the Columbia river and its tributaries), and a member of the **Pacific Marine Fisheries Compact** with

Alaska, California, Idaho and Oregon (75.40.010 through .040). The Director may adopt and enforce the US/Canada treaty concerning Pacific salmon and the regulations adopted under its authority (75.40.060). [Each of these provisions is also covered in Title 75, Food Fish and Shellfish.]

[There are extensive provisions in Chapter 75 relating to salmon, salmon fisheries enhancement, sale, purchase and transport of salmon smolts and eggs, and other provisions relating to the salmon fishery resource. Although some of these provisions relate to inland, freshwater salmon fishing, most relate to salmon as a saltwater and commercial resource, and are only summarized if expressly related to inland water sport fishing.]

It is unlawful for any hunter or fisherman to fail to stop and report at a check station or produce licenses/permits when directed to do so by a uniformed wildlife agent (77.16.610). The Director shall administer Commission rules governing the time, place and manner of holding hunting and fishing contests and competitive field trials for hunting dogs, and shall prohibit contests/field trials that are not in the best interests of wildlife (77.12.530). The Department may file with the Commissioner of Public Lands to withdraw from sale or lease lands to be used as public shooting grounds (77.12.540). Tidelands granted to the Department for public shooting grounds shall revert to the state if used for another purpose (77.12.550). The Commission may adopt rules governing tidelands as shooting grounds (77.12.560).

Licenses and Permits

Applicants for a license, permit, tag, stamp or punchcard shall furnish the information required by the Director who may adopt rules requiring licensees/permittees to keep records and make reports concerning the taking of wildlife (77.32.070). The Director may adopt rules pertaining to the form, period of validity, use, possession, and display of licenses, permits, tags, stamps and punchcards (77.32.090).

A license is required to hunt for wild animals or wild birds or to fish for game fish (77.32.010). Persons under age 18 must complete a course of instruction of at least six hours in the safe handling of firearms, safety, conservation and sportsmanship when applying for a hunting license. The Director may establish a training program in the safe handling of firearms, conservation and sportsmanship and may cooperate with the National Rifle Association, organized sportsmen's groups or other public or private groups. The Director shall prescribe the type of instruction and instructors' qualifications. Certificates of completion of similar courses from other states may be accepted (77.32.155).

★A trapping license allows the holder to trap fur-bearing animals throughout the state; a trapper may not place traps on private property without permission of the landowner/tenant where the land is improved and apparently used, fenced or enclosed in a manner designed to exclude intruders, a property boundary line is indicated, or notice is posted. All trappers must have licenses (77.32.191). Persons purchasing a trapping license for the first time shall present certification of completion of a course of instruction in safe, humane and proper trapping techniques or pass an examination to establish that the applicant has the requisite knowledge. The Director shall establish a training program in trapping techniques and responsibilities, including the use of trapping devices designed to painlessly capture or instantly kill. The Director shall cooperate with national and state animal, humane, hunter education and trapping organizations in the development of a curriculum. A trapper's training certificate is evidence of compliance with this section (77.32.197).★

In addition to a basic hunting license, a separate transport tag is required to hunt deer, elk, bear, cougar, sheep, mountain goat, moose or wild turkey. Tags must have a valid hunting license number affixed. Persons who kill the above species must immediately attach such tag to the carcass (77.32.320). ★In addition to a basic hunting license, a supplemental license, permit or stamp is required to hunt for quail, partridge, pheasant or migratory waterfowl, to hunt with a raptor, or to hunt with a dog.★ A hound permit is required to hunt wild animals, except rabbits and hares, with a dog. An eastern or western Washington upland game bird permit is required to hunt for quail, partridge and pheasant. Permit season options are: early season, late season, juvenile full season or two-day. A falconry license is required to possess or hunt with a raptor (77.32.350). A Migratory Waterfowl Stamp affixed to a basic hunting license is required to hunt migratory waterfowl as required by 77.32.350 (77.16.330). A steelhead catch record card is required to fish for steelhead trout. Persons returning a steelhead catch record card by June 1 following the season shall be given a $5 credit towards that day's purchase of any license, permit, transport tag, catch record card or stamp required by this chapter (77.32.360). A special hunting season permit is required to hunt in each special season established under chapter 77.12 (77.32.370). A "special hunting season" is established by Commission rule for taking specified wildlife under a special hunting permit (77.32.007). ★★Persons over age 16 who use clearly identified Department lands and access facilities must possess a conservation license or a hunting, fishing, trapping or free license while using the facilities.★★ A spouse and children, guests under age 18, and youth groups accompanying a conservation license holder may use such lands and facilities. The conservation license is not transferrable and on request shall be exhibited by a person using Department lands (77.32.380).

It is unlawful to promote, conduct or sponsor a contest for hunting or fishing of wildlife, or a dog trial involving live wildlife, without a hunting or fishing contest permit, and such contest/trial must be held in accordance with Department rules (77.16.010). No hunting shall be permitted from a motor vehicle parked on or beside the maintained portion of a public road. A disabled hunter with a permit may be accompanied by one nondisabled licensed hunter who may assist by killing game wounded by the disabled hunter and by tagging and retrieving such game, but the nondisabled hunter may not shoot from a motor vehicle nor possess a loaded gun in such vehicle (77.32.238).

The following recreational fishing licenses are administered and issued by the Department of Fisheries Director authority: Hood Canal shrimp license; razor clam license; personal use fishing license; salmon and sturgeon licenses (75.25.005). No personal use license is required to take as food fish carp, sturgeon in certain waters, smelt or albacore. A salmon license in addition to a personal use license is required to fish for salmon taken for personal use from state waters or offshore waters. Reciprocity with Oregon is provided for certain licenses in certain defined waters (75.25.090, .100 and .120).

See also Commercial and Private Enterprise Provisions under this section.

Restrictions on Taking

It is unlawful to: ▸ hunt, fish, possess or control a species of game bird, game animal or game fish during the closed season for that species except as provided; ▸ kill, take, catch those species in excess of the lawful bag limit; ▸ hunt within a game reserve or fish for game fish within closed waters; ▸ hunt wild birds or wild animals within a closed area except as authorized by Commission rule; ▸ hunt or fish for wildlife, practice taxidermy for profit, deal in raw furs for profit, act as a fishing guide, operate a game farm, stock game fish or collect wildlife for research or display without having in possession the license, permit, tag, stamp or punchcard required for these activities (77.16.020).

It is unlawful to bring into the state, offer for sale, sell, possess, buy, transport or ship wildlife or articles made from an endangered species, or for a common carrier knowingly to ship wildlife or articles made from an endangered species (77.16.040). It is unlawful to hunt big game with a spotlight or other artificial light. It is prima facie evidence of violation to be found with such light and with a firearm, bow and arrow or crossbow after sunset in a place where big game may reasonably be expected (77.16.050). It is unlawful to lay, set or use a net to take game fish in state waters unless authorized by the Commission. Game fish taken incidental to a lawful season shall be returned immediately to the water. Landing nets may be used to land fish otherwise legally hooked (77.16.060). It is unlawful to: ▸hunt while under the influence of intoxicating liquor or drugs; ▸ lay, set or use a drug, explosive, poison or other deleterious substance that may endanger, injure or kill wildlife except as authorized by law; ▸ take or possess game animals, game birds or game fish and allow them to needlessly go to waste; mutilate wildlife so that the size, species or sex cannot be determined visually in the field or while being transported. The Director may prescribe specific criteria for field identification (77.16.070 through .095). It is unlawful to allow a dog to pursue or injure deer or elk or to accompany a person who is hunting deer or elk. During the closed season, a dog found pursuing a game species, molesting its young, or destroying a game bird nest may be declared a public nuisance. It is unlawful to carry firearms, other hunting weapons or traps or to allow a dog upon a game reserve, except on public highways or as authorized by Director rule (77.16.100 and .110).

It is unlawful to take a wild animal from another person's trap without permission, or to damage or destroy the trap, except for a landowner on his own land who may remove such traps. Trappers shall tag their traps with a Department wildlife identification number or with their name as specified. ★A person may request a trapper's identification by presenting the identification tag number to the Department, which shall provide that information after obtaining the inquirer's name and address, such information to be given to the trapper whose name and address was disclosed (77.16.170).★

It is unlawful to: ▸ damage or interfere with a fish ladder, screen or trap operated by the Department; ▸ remove, possess or damage Department signs; ▸ wilfully post signs, warn against or otherwise prevent hunting or fishing on lands not one's own (77.16.160 through .190). Persons or agencies managing, controlling or owning a dam or other obstruction across a river or stream shall construct, maintain and repair durable fishways and fish protective devices that allow the free passage of game fish, and shall provide sufficient water to insure such free passage (77.16.210). It is unlawful to divert water from a lake, river or stream containing game fish unless intakes are equipped with fish screens. Plans for such fish guards, screens and bypasses shall be approved by the Director before construction and/or water diversion. The Director may close a water diversion device operated in violation of this section until compliance is achieved (77.16.220).

Except as otherwise provided, it is unlawful to: ▸ carry, possess or control in or on a motor vehicle a shotgun or rifle with shells/cartridges in the magazine, or a loaded muzzle-loading firearm; ▸ shoot a firearm from, across, or along the maintained portion of a public highway; ▸ purchase, possess or attempt to purchase a license using false information or while one's license is revoked, or in excess of the one license, permit, tag, or stamp permitted by the Commission (77.16.250 through .310).

Commercial and Private Enterprise Provisions

Except as otherwise provided, a license issued by the Director is required to: ▸ practice taxidermy for profit; ▸ deal in raw furs for profit; ▸ act as a fishing guide; ▸ operate a game farm; ▸ purchase or sell anadromous game fish; ▸ use Department-managed lands or facilities. A Director's permit is required to: ▸ conduct, hold, or sponsor hunting or fishing contests or competitive trials using live wildlife; ▸ collect wild animals, wild birds, game fish or protected wildlife for research or display; ▸ stock game fish. Aquaculture is exempt from these requirements, except public waters are stocked under Department contract (77.32.010). Licensed taxidermists, fur dealers, anadromous game fish buyers, fishing guides, game farmers, and persons stocking game fish or conducting a hunting, fishing, or field trial contest shall report as required (77.32.220). A professional salmon guide license is required to offer or perform the services of a professional salmon guide in the taking of salmon for personal use in freshwater rivers and streams (75.28.710). The Commission shall establish the qualifications and conditions for issuing a game farm license, and the Director shall adopt rules governing their operation. Private cultured aquatic products under 15.85.020 are exempt from this section (77.12.570). A licensed game farmer may purchase, sell, give away or dispose of the eggs of game birds or game fish lawfully possessed as provided by rule (77.12.580). Wildlife given away, sold or transferred by a licensed game farmer shall be tagged or invoiced as required by rule (77.12.590). A common carrier may transport wildlife shipped by a licensed game farmer if properly tagged (77.12.600).

See also Import, Export and Release Provisions under this section.

Import, Export and Release Provisions

Except as authorized by the Director, it is unlawful to release wildlife or to plant aquatic plants/seeds within the state (77.16.150). Except by Director of Fisheries' permit, it is unlawful to release, plant or place food fish or shellfish in state waters (75.08.295). The Director may prohibit the introduction, transportation or transplanting of food fish, shellfish, organisms, material or other equipment which may transmit any disease or pests affecting food fish or shellfish (75.08.285). Except for the US, a recognized Indian tribe, the state, subdivisions or municipal corporations, it is unlawful for any person to release salmon or steelhead trout into the public waters and subsequently to recapture and commercially harvest them. This does not prohibit rearing salmon or steelhead trout in pens where they are confined and never permitted to swim freely in open water. Violation: gross misdemeanor (75.08.300). The Director of Fisheries and the Director of Agriculture shall jointly develop a program of disease inspection and control for aquatic farmers to protect the aquaculture industry and wildstock fisheries from a loss of productivity due to aquatic diseases and/or infestations of parasites or pests [details of quarantine, preventative control, disease inspections are specified] (75.58.010).

Interstate Reciprocal Agreements

The Commission may cooperate with the Idaho Fish and Game Commission to adopt and enforce rules regarding wildlife on that portion of the Snake River forming the boundary between the two states. Courts, wildlife agents and ex officio wildlife agents have jurisdiction over the boundary waters to the furthermost shoreline, concurrent with reciprocal powers in Idaho. The taking of wildlife from the boundary waters or islands of the Snake river shall be in accordance with the wildlife laws of the respective states and officers shall honor the license of either state and the right of the holder to take wildlife from the boundary waters in accordance with the laws of the state issuing the license (77.12.450 through .480).

ANIMAL DAMAGE CONTROL

The Director may authorize the removal or killing of wildlife that is destroying or injuring property, or when necessary for wildlife management or research. The Director or employees shall dispose of wildlife taken by them in the manner determined to be in the state's best interest, with sales proceeds to be credited to the State Wildlife Fund (77.12.240). The Director may make written agreements to prevent damage to private property by wildlife, and may furnish money, material or labor under such agreements (77.12.260).

Landowners/tenants may trap or kill on their property wild animals or wild birds, other than endangered species, that are damaging crops, domestic animals, fowl or other property. Except in emergencies, deer, elk, and protected wildlife shall not be killed without a permit issued by the Director. "Emergency" means an unforeseen circumstance beyond the control of the landowner that presents a real and immediate threat to crops, domestic animals, fowl or other property. When sufficient time for permit issuance is not available, verbal permission may be given by a Department Regional Administrator to landowners to trap or kill any deer, elk, or protected wildlife which is doing damage, and may delegate, in writing, a staff member to give the required permission in emergency situations. ★★Nothing in this section authorizes in any situation the trapping, hunting, or killing of an endangered species. Wildlife trapped or killed under this section remains the property of the state and the person shall notify the Department immediately. The Director shall dispose of wildlife so taken within three working days of receiving such notification. If the Department receives recurring complaints regarding property being damaged from one landowner, or from several such owners in a locale, the Commission shall consider a special hunt to reduce damage potential. "Crop" means an agricultural/horticultural product growing or harvested including wild shrubs and range land vegetation on private cattle ranching lands. On such lands, the owner may declare an emergency when the Department has not responded within 48 hours after having been contacted regarding the crop damage by wild animals or wild birds. However, the Department shall not allow claims for damage to wild shrubs or range land vegetation on such lands. Under this section, deer and elk shall not be killed on privately owned cattle ranching lands that were closed to public hunting during the previous season, except for closures which are coordinated with the Department to protect property and livestock. The Department shall work closely with landowners/tenants suffering game damage problems to control damage without killing the animals when practical, to increase the harvest of damage-causing animals in hunting seasons, or to kill the animals when no other practical means of damage control is feasible (77.12.265).★★

The Director may compromise, adjust, settle and pay claims for deer/elk damage in accordance with statutory provisions. Payments for claims shall not exceed $2,000, and payment constitutes full and final payment for the claim, and the Director shall advise the Commission quarterly of all damage claims paid (77.12.270). Claims under this section may be filed under 4.92.040(5) if within one year of filing with the Director the claim is not settled and paid. The Risk Management Office shall recommend to the Legislature whether the claim should be approved, and if so, the Department shall pay it from moneys appropriated for that purpose. If a claim has been refused or has not been settled and paid by the Director within 120 days, either the claimant or the Director may serve a notice of intent to arbitrate [details of the arbitration process and selection of arbitrators are given]. The arbitrators give an advisory award (77.12.280). ★Claims for damages under 77.12.270 shall be filed with the Department within 90 days following the discovery of the claimed damage; failure to timely file is a bar to damage payment. Payments shall not be made for damages occurring on lands leased from a public agency (77.12.290).★ The Director may adopt rules prescribing the form of proof of claims and other details, and may refuse to consider/pay claims of persons who have posted the property on which the damage occurred against hunting during the prior season (77.12.300).

ENFORCEMENT OF WILDLIFE LAWS

Enforcement Powers

Jurisdiction and authority granted under 77.12.060 through 77.12.080 to the Director, wildlife agents and ex officio agents is limited to laws and rules adopted under this title regarding wildlife, the management, operation, maintenance, use of, or conduct on real property used, owned, or controlled by the Department and other statutes as prescribed by the Legislature. However, when acting within the scope of these duties and when an offense occurs in the presence of the wildlife agent who is not an ex officio agent, the wildlife agent may enforce all state criminal laws. Wildlife agents must successfully complete the basic law enforcement academy course of the Criminal Justice Training Commission or approved supplemental course prior to enforcing criminal laws. Wildlife agents are peace officers, and liability claims arising out of their exercise of authority rests with the Department unless otherwise specified. The Director, wildlife agents, and ex officio agents may serve and execute warrants and processes issued by the courts, and may call to their aid any ex officio agent or citizen to render aid (77.12.055 and .060). [Similar qualifications and powers/duties pertain to Fisheries Patrol Officers. Chapter 75 should be consulted for particulars relating to searches and seizures on vessels, boating and water safety, commercial salmon licenses and other provisions.]

Wildlife agents and ex officio agents may: ► arrest without warrant persons found violating the law or rules under this title; ► without warrant make a reasonable search for wildlife of conveyances, vehicles, other receptacles, tents, camps or similar places which they have reason to believe contain evidence of a violation of law or rules; ► inspect without warrant at reasonable times the premises, wildlife and records of any commercial enterprise operating under a license/permit issued by the Department or any commercial business that sells, stores, transports or possesses wildlife (77.12.080 through .095).

Wildlife agents may seize without a warrant wildlife they have probable cause to believe has been taken, killed, transported or possessed in violation of this title or rule. Agents may seize without warrant boats, vehicles, airplanes, gear, appliances or articles they have probable cause to believe are held with intent to violate or were used in violation of this title or regulations when the species is listed in 77.21.070 (specified big game animals and endangered species) or any game fish under 77.16.060. Items may not be seized, except as evidence, if it is reasonable to conclude that the violation was inadvertent. Seized articles shall be forfeited to the state upon conviction, guilty plea or bail forfeiture, but may be recovered by their owner by depositing a cash bond with the court which is subject to forfeiture in lieu of the seized articles. [Details of forfeiture procedure and right to hearing are given.] No conveyance, including vessels, vehicles or aircraft is subject to forfeiture when a violation was committed without the owner's knowledge or consent. Forfeited property may be retained by the Department for official use, unless required to be destroyed, or may be sold and proceeds deposit in the Wildlife Fund (77.12.101). ★Authorized state, county or municipal officers may be subject to civil liability for willful misconduct or gross negligence in the performance of their duties or in the seizure and forfeiture of personal property involved with wildlife offenses (77.12.103).★

Except as otherwise provided, a person who has lawfully acquired possession of wildlife and who desires to retain or transfer it may do so in accordance with adopted rules. Upon complaint showing probable cause that wildlife unlawfully caught, taken, possessed or transported is concealed in any receptacle, business place, or vehicle, the court shall issue a search warrant. Articles or devices unlawfully used, possessed or maintained for catching, taking, killing, or decoying wildlife are public nuisances, subject to destruction by wildlife agents without warrant or process (77.12.105 through .130).

To facilitate the Department's gathering of biological data for managing wildlife resources and to protect wildlife resources, wildlife check stations are established. The Department may require hunters and fishermen occupying a motor vehicle approaching or entering a check station to stop and produce for inspection: any wildlife in their possession; licenses, permits, tags or stamps. The Department may also operate wildlife information stations at which persons are not required to stop and report (77.12.610 through .630).

Criminal Penalties

A violation of provisions involving license fraud, traffic in endangered or other wildlife species, spotlighting, use of unlawful devices or poisons, illegal fishway use, commercial license violations, closed seasons violations, hunter harassment, illegal taking of protected wildlife and eggs, or a violation provisions involving big game or an endangered species is a gross misdemeanor: $250-1,000 fine; jail 30 days to one year; or both. Each subsequent violation within a five year period involving big game or an endangered species is a class C felony. With felony prosecutions, the Director shall provide the court with an inventory of all articles/devices seized or disposed of in connection with the violation. Placing traps on private property without the landowner's permission when land is improved, fenced or posted is a misdemeanor of trespass: fine $250 or more for each offense. Violation of any law or rule for which no penalty is otherwise provided is a misdemeanor; $500 fine for each offense; jail up to 90 days; or both. The Commission may provide that violation of a specific rule is an "infraction" under chapter 7.84. Persons convicted of a violation shall pay prosecution costs and penalty assessment in addition to the fine or imprisonment. The unlawful killing, taking or possession of each wildlife member is a separate offense. District courts have jurisdiction concurrent with superior courts of misdemeanors and gross misdemeanors; superior courts have jurisdiction over felonies in violation of this title (77.21.010).

Persons who fish for food fish or shellfish for personal use and violate Title 75 shall be subject to penalties as follows: ► failure to record salmon or sturgeon on a catch record card, the use of barbed hooks in a barbless hook-only fishery, and other personal use violations specified under 75.10.110 are "infractions"; ► retention of undersized food fish or shellfish, excess bag limit, and intentional waste of recreationally caught food fish or shellfish, illegal setting of shrimp pots at night in Hood Canal are misdemeanors, snagging of food fish, fishing in closed areas or during closed seasons, commingling personal food with commercial food fish catches; ► retention of more than three times the allowed personal use limit of fish/shellfish, and selling such fish/shellfish with a wholesale value less than $250 are gross misdemeanors. The sale, barter, trade of food fish/shellfish with a wholesale value of over $250 caught with personal gear is a Class C felony (75.10.180). Violations of hydraulic permits or fish screen provisions mandated by the Department of Fisheries are gross misdemeanors. It is a Class C felony to: ► discharge explosives in waters containing adult salmon or sturgeon (except lawful discharge of devices to frighten or kill marine mammals or for the lawful removal of snags are exempt); ► knowingly purchase food fish or shellfish with a wholesale value greater than $250 taken by methods or during times not authorized, by an unlicensed person or with personal use gear (75.10.200).

Illegal Taking of Wildlife

Wildlife unlawfully taken or possessed remains the property of the state. The Director may sell at public auction articles or devices seized and forfeited. Notice shall be given to the public of such auctions and proceeds shall be credited to the State Wildlife Fund (77.21.040).

★★If a person is convicted of illegal killing or possession of wildlife listed below, the court shall order reimbursement to the state in the following amounts for each animal killed/possessed: ► moose, antelope, mountain sheep, mountain goat, and all endangered wildlife species, $2,000; ► elk, deer, black bear and cougar, $1,000; ► mountain caribou and grizzly bear, $5,000. For this section, "convicted" includes a plea of guilty, a finding of guilt regardless of whether the imposition of the sentence is deferred or suspended, and the payment of a fine. No court may establish a bail amount for illegal possession of wildlife listed herein less than the bail established for hunting during the closed season, plus the value of wildlife listed above. If two or more persons are convicted of illegal possession of wildlife, reimbursement shall be imposed jointly and separately. The reimbursement amounts provided are imposed in addition to and regardless of any penalty, including fines or costs for violating any provision of Title 77. Reimbursement under this section shall be included by the court in any sentence and may not be suspended, waived, modified or deferred in any respect. Nothing herein may be abridged or alter other rights of action or remedies criminal or civil. A defaulted reimbursement or installment payment may be collected by authorized means for enforcement of court orders or collection of fines or costs, including vacating deferrals or sentence suspensions (77.21.070).

Washington

License Revocations, Suspensions

It is unlawful to resist or obstruct wildlife agents or ex officio wildlife agents in the lawful discharge of their duties. The Director shall revoke all licenses and privileges under Title 77 of a person convicted of assault on a wildlife agent or other law enforcement officer if the agent or officer was on duty at the time of the assault and was enforcing the provisions of Title 77 [statutory definitions and citations for "assault" and "conviction" are listed]. ★No license shall be reissued to a person violating this section for a minimum of ten years, at which time a person may petition the Director for reinstatement of the license. The ten-year period shall be tolled during incarceration, community supervision or home detention for an offense under this section. Upon review, if all provisions of the court have been completed, the Director may reinstate in whole or in part the licenses and privileges (77.16.130 and .135).★

The Director shall revoke the hunting license of a person who shoots another person or domestic livestock while hunting. A hunting license shall not be issued unless the Director so authorizes, and damages caused by the wrongful shooting have been paid (77.21.030). In addition to other penalties, the Director shall revoke the hunting license of a person convicted of a violation involving big game hunting in closed season or spotlighting big game. Forfeiture of bail twice during a five-year period for these violations constitutes the basis for a revocation. No new license shall be issued for two years [an appeal procedure is provided under 34.05] (77.21.020). Upon conviction of a violation of this title or rules, the court may forfeit a license, in addition to other penalties. ★Upon subsequent conviction, license forfeiture is mandatory. The Director may prohibit issuance of a license to a person convicted two or more times or prescribe conditions for subsequent issuance.★ It is unlawful to conduct an activity requiring a wildlife license, permit, tag or stamp for which they have had a license forfeiture or for which the Director has prohibited the issuance of a license (77.21.060). The Commission may revoke the trapper's license of a person placing unauthorized traps on private property and may remove those traps (77.32.199).

★Persons who repeatedly demonstrate indifference and disrespect for the fisheries laws of the state shall be considered a threat to the fisheries resource and these habitual offenders shall be denied the privilege of harvesting food fish or shellfish. The Director of Fisheries may revoke or prescribe conditions for issuing the personal use license of persons who have four or more gross misdemeanor or class C felony convictions within 12 years, and all fishing privileges shall be suspended during license revocation periods. A revoked license shall not be reissued for at least two years from revocation (75.10.210).★

Reward Payments

See Agency Funding Sources under STATE FISH AND WILDLIFE AGENCIES for information on the Wildlife Conservation Reward Fund.

HABITAT PROTECTION

★★The Legislature directs the Department to determine the feasibility and cost of doubling the state-wide game fish production by the year 2000. The Department shall seek to equalize the effort and investment expended on anadromous and resident game fish programs, and provide a specific plan for that purpose for legislative approval. The plan shall contain specific provisions to increase both hatchery and naturally spawning game fish to a level that will support that production goal consistent with wildlife commission policies. Steelhead trout, searun cutthroat trout, resident trout and warm water fish producing areas of the state shall be included in the plan. The plan shall be presented to designated legislative committees by December 31, 1990, and shall include the following elements and/or methods to: ▸ determine current catch and production and that of the year 2000; ▸ involve fishing groups, including Indian tribes, in a cooperative manner; ▸ use low capital cost projects to produce game fish as inexpensively as possible; ▸ renovate all existing hatcheries to maximize production capability; ▸ increase the productivity of natural spawning game fish; ▸ apply new technology to increase hatchery and natural productivity; ▸ analyze the potential for private contractors to produce game fish for public fisheries; ▸ optimize public volunteer efforts for maximum efficiency; ▸ develop trophy game fish fisheries; ▸ coordinate with Pacific Northwest Power Council programs to ensure maximum Columbia river benefits; ▸ determine the role to be played by private consulting companies in implementing the plan; ▸ coordinate with federal fish and wildlife agencies, Indian tribes, and Department of Fisheries fish production programs; ▸ determine future needs for game fish predatory control measures; ▸ develop disease control measures; ▸ obtain access to waters currently not available to anglers; ▸

develop research programs to support game fish management and enhancement programs. The Department and the Department of Revenue, shall assess various funding mechanisms and make recommendations to the Legislature. The Department and the Department of Trade and Economic Development shall prepare an analysis of the economic benefits to the state when the game fish production is increased by 100% by the year 2000 (77.12.710).★★

If the Department requires that resident hatchery game fish be stocked by the permittee or licensee for mitigation of environmental damage, the Department shall specify the pounds or numbers, species, stock, and/or race of resident game fish that are to be provided. The Department shall offer the licensee the option of purchasing under contract from Washington aquatic farmers those game fish, unless the fish specified by the Department are not available from Washington growers (77.18.020). Any government agency, private or public utility company, corporation or sports group, or any purchaser of fish may purchase resident game fish from an aquatic farmer for stocking purposes if permit requirements have been met (77.18.030).

★★Under the **Volunteer Cooperative Fish and Wildlife Enhancement Program**, the Departments of Fisheries and Wildlife shall encourage cooperative projects of the following types: ▸ food fish and game fish rearing projects, including egg planting, egg boxes, juvenile planting, pen rearing, raceway rearing and egg taking; ▸ fish habitat improvement projects, including fish migration improvement, spawning bed rehabilitation, habitat restoration, reef construction, lake fertilization, pond construction, pollution abatement, and endangered stock protection; ▸ fish or game research projects of a research nature with results made available to the public; ▸ game bird and game animal projects including habitat improvement, replanting, transplanting, nest box installation, pen rearing, game protecting and supplemental feeding; ▸ cooperative nongame projects including habitat improvement, nest box installation, establishment of wildlife interpretive areas, pollution abatement, and endangered species preservation and enhancement; ▸ cooperative education projects including landowner relations, outdoor ethics, natural history of Washington's fish, shellfish and wildlife, and outdoor survival (75.52.030).★★ (See also STATE WILDLIFE POLICY.)

The Department of Fisheries may authorize the sale of surplus salmon and eggs by cooperative projects (75.52.035). ★★The Department shall: ▸ encourage and support cooperative agreements for the development and operation of cooperative food fish, shellfish, game fish, game bird, game animal and nongame wildlife projects, and projects which provide an opportunity for volunteer groups to become involved in resource and habitat-oriented activities; ▸ identify regions, species or activities particularly suitable for projects; ▸ determine availability of rearing space, net pens, egg boxes, incubators and other needed facilities and allocate them fairly to volunteer groups; ▸ publicize the programs; ▸ exempt volunteer groups from fee payments for project related activities; ▸ not approve projects that are incompatible with legally existing land, water or property rights; ▸ provide professional expertise and help volunteer groups to evaluate their progress. [Extensive details are provided concerning Department rules, duration of volunteer agreements (up to five years), duties of volunteer groups, and establishment of the Cedar river spawning channel by Department and volunteer cooperation.] (75.52.040)★★

See also PROTECTED SPECIES OF WILDLIFE.

NATIVE AMERICAN WILDLIFE PROVISIONS

The Director of Fisheries may issue permits to members of the Wanapum band of Indians to take salmon for ceremonial and subsistence purposes, and shall establish the areas in which the permits are valid, regulate the times for, and manner of taking. This section does not create a right to fish commercially (75.08.265). [Additional provisions concerning Indian fisheries are given in 75.12.320 relating to the taking of food fish or shellfish in treaty Indian fisheries, family participation, and vessel use.]

★The people of the state of Washington declare that under the Indians Citizens Act of 1924, all Indians became citizens of the US and subject to the laws and Constitution of the US and state in which they reside. The people further declare that any special off-reservation legal rights or privileges of Indians established through treaties that are denied to other citizens were terminated by that 1924 enactment, and any denial of rights to any citizen based upon race, sex, origin, cultural heritage, or by and through any treaty based upon the same is unconstitutional. No rights, privileges, or immunities shall be denied to any citizen upon the basis of race, sex, origin, cultural heritage, or by and through any treaty based upon the same (75.56.040).★

WEST VIRGINIA

Sources: West Virginia Code Annotated, 1989 Replacement Volume, Chapter 20; 1992 Cumulative Supplement.

STATE WILDLIFE POLICY

This chapter is enacted to provide a comprehensive program for the exploration, conservation, development, protection, enjoyment and use of the natural resources of West Virginia and may be cited as the State Natural Resources Law (20-1-1).

★★The Legislature finds that acquisition of land to construct new or expand existing state recreational facilities is becoming more costly, as is the construction of recreational facilities. After facilities are constructed, they must be maintained indefinitely and, often, personnel must be employed to operate them, with a continuing burden on state revenues. Furthermore, these costs are continually increasing. The Legislature declares that there is an ultimate limit to how many recreational facilities this state, with its size, population and financial resources can or should support. Further, the Legislature declares that it must establish, provide for, and maintain limits on state recreational facilities. After July 1, 1977, neither the Director, nor any other Department officer, employee, or agent may, without express authorization of the Legislature: acquire land for a new state park, forest, public fishing and hunting area or other recreational facility; or construct a new facility or building in a state park, forest, public hunting and fishing area. Prior appropriations and approved projects may be completed (20-1-20).★★

It is declared to be the public policy of West Virginia that state wildlife resources shall be protected for the use and enjoyment of all the citizens of this state. All species of wildlife shall be maintained for values which may be either intrinsic or ecological or of benefit to man. Such benefits shall include: hunting, fishing and other diversified recreational uses; economic contributions in the best interests of the people of this state; and scientific and educational uses (20-2-1). The ownership of and title to all wild animals, wild birds, both migratory and resident, and all fish, amphibians, and aquatic life in West Virginia is declared to be in the state, as trustee for the people. No wildlife shall be taken or hunted in any manner, or at any time, unless the person so taking or hunting consents that the title thereto shall be and remain in the state for the purpose of regulating the taking, hunting, using and disposing of the same. Taking or hunting of wildlife at any time or in any manner shall be deemed such consent, except, that fish, frogs and other aquatic life in privately owned ponds are, and shall remain, the private property of the pond owner(s) and may be caught, taken or killed by such owner(s) (20-2-3).

RELEVANT WILDLIFE DEFINITIONS: See Definitions section of Appendices.

STATE FISH AND WILDLIFE AGENCIES

Agency Structure

There is a **Department of Natural Resources** (Department), a **Director** of the Department, and a **Natural Resources Commission** (Commission) (20-1-3). The **Director** is appointed by the Governor and organizes the Department into offices, divisions and agencies for Department administration. The Director shall be at least age 30 and selected with reference to and consideration of the applicant's training, experience, capacity and interest in the natural resources program (20-1-4). **Divisions of Game and Fish, Forestry, Water Resources, Law Enforcement, and Reclamation** are established within the Department, and the Director selects a qualifed person to be **Chief** of each division and allocates functions/services to its sections, offices and activities (20-1-14).

The **Commission** is composed of seven members, one from each congressional district and the remainder from the state at large, appointed by the Governor with the advice and consent of the Senate, for seven years. Commissioners shall be state residents, selected with special reference to their training and experience in relation to required Commission activities and to their ability and fitness to perform their duties. The Commission advises the Director and the Department (20-1-16). The Director is an ex officio member of the Commission and its presiding officer;

a Commission majority constitutes a quorum. Four regular meetings are held each year, with special meetings convened as needed (20-1-17).

Agency Powers and Duties

In addition to other powers and duties granted, the **Director** is authorized to: ▸ prepare and administer, with the Commission's advice, through the divisions created by this chapter, a long-range comprehensive program for the conservation of state natural resources; ▸ execute contracts and agreements with the federal government, state agencies, corporations, or individuals; ▸ conduct research in improved conservation methods and disseminate information to citizens; ▸ conduct a continuous study of the habits of wildlife, and for purposes of control and protection to classify by regulation the various species into necessary categories; ▸ prescribe the locality in which and the manner and method by which wildlife species may be taken or chased; ▸ hold at least six meetings each year at places within the state to give interested persons an opportunity to be heard concerning open seasons for their respective areas before season and bag limits are fixed by the Commission; ▸ suspend open hunting season with the Governor's approval in case of emergency such as drought, forest fire hazard or epizootic disease; ▸ designate localities for the perpetuation of wildlife species; ▸ enter private lands to make surveys for conservation purposes, investigate for violations, serve and execute warrants and make arrests; ▸ acquire lands, gifts, or bequests of money, security or property by purchase, condemnation, lease or gift deemed desirable for public hunting, trapping or fishing grounds, for fish hatcheries, game farms, wildlife research areas, feeding stations, or other Department purposes; ▸ conduct education programs; ▸ promulgate rules and regulations to make effective the powers and duties vested in the Director by this chapter's provisions in accordance with Chapter 29A-1-1 et seq.; ▸ capture, propagate, transport, sell or exchange any species of wildlife; ▸ sell timber with the Governor's approval on lands under the Department's control; ▸ sell or lease coal, oil, gas, sand, gravel and other minerals on Department lands with the Governor's approval except state park lands; ▸ require necessary reports from persons issued a license or permit; ▸ conduct and encourage research to further new and more extensive uses of natural resources, and publicize the findings; ▸ encourage and cooperate with public and private organizations in efforts to publicize state attractions (20-1-7). The Director shall designate a qualified person to be Chief Conservation Officer, who shall be responsible for enforcement of chapter provisions and for selection and training of conservation officers (20-1-13).

The Director is authorized to advance the state's interests under provisions of Congress providing for cooperation between the governments of the US and of the several states in the exploration, development, conservation, use and enjoyment of natural resources, including land acquisition by purchase or lease for parks, wildlife and water areas, and the development of such properties. ★All projects shall be in the interest of and for the benefit of the state and may be geared and timed to relieve economic hardship and unemployment.★ The Director shall study the state land and water boundary areas, and where practicable, cooperate with adjacent states in programs for development, conservation and use of waters, forests, minerals, wildlife and other natural resources (20-1-18).

★★To further an appreciation and understanding of the outdoors by state youth, the Director is authorized to enter into long-term agreements, with the Governor's approval, leasing to the County Board of Education where there are Department lands, for nominal consideration, one parcel of rural land not exceeding one acre for each 500 students registered in the county public schools at the time of the lease. The land shall be used by the County Board of Education exclusively to establish an outdoor education program. Counties containing no Department lands may join with other counties to establish joint programs, the combined enrollments of students to determine the maximum acreage that may be leased by the Department. If the Department finds that the leased lands have ceased to be used for these purposes for a period of three consecutive years, the lease shall become null and void and control shall revert to the Department unless a County Board of Education appeals for review (20-1-10a).★★

The Department shall collect, organize and distribute to the public interesting facts, information and data concerning the state's natural resources and Department functions and services. The Director shall designate a public relations officer and may organize and promote lectures, demonstrations and other educational programs relating to the state's natural resources, including motion pictures, slides and films which may be provided for instruction and use by schools, government agencies and civil organizations (20-1-11).

The **Commission** shall serve as a body advisory to the Director and shall have the duty to: ▸ consider and study the entire field of legislation and administrative methods concerning forest management and fish and game protection; ▸ advise the Director concerning conservation problems of particular localities of the state; ▸ recommend policies and practices to the Director relative to the Director's duties; ▸ investigate the work of the Director and have access to all official books, papers and records; ▸ advise or make recommendations to the Governor relative to natural resources (20-1-17). The Commissioner of the Department of Commerce shall establish an "adopt a state park or forest program" to encourage and coordinate the efforts of volunteers to help maintain and improve state parks, forests, or other public lands within the state (20-1A-7).

Agency Regulations

The Commission has the power to fix by regulation, in accordance with the provisions of chapter 29A, wildlife open seasons and bag, creel, size, age, weight and sex limits (20-1-17).

Agency Funding Sources

Subject to Department of Finance regulations, the Director shall establish in the Department an adequate budget, finance and accounting system to accurately reflect the fiscal operations of the Department at all times, and shall appoint a fiscal department officer. Mneys received by the Department shall be paid as special revenue to the Department, except in cases where certain receipts are to be paid into a special fund by specific chapter provisions (20-1-9).

There is an appropriated, interest-bearing special revenue account, designated as the **Whitewater Study and Improvement Fund**. All proceeds from this fund shall be used exclusively for administration, regulation, promotion and study of the whitewater industry. The Special Study and Assessment Fee collected by the Commission under 20-2-23a shall be deposited into this fund (20-2-23b). There is an appropriated, interest-bearing special revenue account designated as the **Whitewater Advertising and Promotion Fund**. Each whitewater license holder may contribute any sum desired to this fund which shall be used for advertising and promoting whitewater in West Virginia (20-2-23c).

Funds from licenses and permits shall be paid into the state treasury and credited to the Department, and further credited to and kept in a separate fund designated **"License Fund-Wildlife Resources"** to be used solely for law enforcement and purposes directly relating to the conservation, protection, propagation and distribution of wildlife. ★No funds from the "License Fund-Wildlife Resources" shall be expended for recreational facilities or activities that are used by or for the benefit of the general public rather than purchasers of hunting and fishing licenses.★ Of the annual license fund income, the Director shall retain 10% for capital improvements and land purchases benefiting wildlife, 40% shall be budgeted to the wildlife resources division, 40% to law enforcement and 10% apportioned by the Director within provisions of this section. All interest from game and fish license fees after 1991 shall be used by the Director in the same manner as provided for the use of license fees (20-2-34). A hunter licensed to hunt bear shall in addition to a hunting license must have a **Bear Damage Stamp** issued by the Department, proceeds of which shall be paid into the **Bear Damage Fund** maintained by the Department for paying claims of property owners for damages to real and personal property caused by bear and to cover the expense of hunting, capturing and removing offending bear to remote areas (20-2-44b).

Except as provided, no person may hunt or take any migratory waterfowl without a **Migratory Waterfowl Conservation Stamp**. Persons under age 16 or who are otherwise exempt from payment for a hunting license are also exempt from this stamp. Fees from sale of the waterfowl stamp shall be appropriated to the department as follows: 50% for Department projects to attract waterfowl and to improve public migratory waterfowl areas within the state, but not for administrative purposes; 50% for the development of waterfowl propagation areas within the Dominion of Canada which specifically provide waterfowl for the Atlantic flyway. Projects must be approved by the appropriate Canadian governmental agencies. The Department may enter into agreements with nonprofit organizations to carry out these provisions. The Department has exclusive production rights for the waterfowl conservation stamp and the marketing of prints of the stamp design, revenues of which shall be credited to the Department and used for conservation of migratory waterfowl and other wildlife, except that no such moneys shall be used for purposes for condemnation of any state land (20-2-63).

It is in the public interest to preserve, protect and perpetuate all species of wildlife for the use and benefit of the citizens of West Virginia. The **Voluntary Wildlife Check-Off Program** is to provide additional funding for wildlife programs, to be primarily used to enhance nongame wildlife programs and for the management, preservation, protection and perpetuation of nongame species. Funds will be derived from a voluntary check-off and contribution designation on state personal income tax return forms of a portion or all of a taxpayer's refund. This funding shall be supplemental to existing revenues (20-2A-1). Recognizing the inestimable importance to the state and its people of conserving the wildlife resources of West Virginia, and for the purpose of providing the opportunity for citizens and residents to invest in the future of its wildlife resources, there is a **Wildlife Endowment Fund**, the interest and principal of which shall be used only for supporting wildlife conservation programs of the state (20-2B-1). Fund assets shall come from the sale of lifetime hunting and fishing licenses under 20-2B-7 and from any gifts, grants, contributions or other moneys accruing to the state specifically designated for inclusion in the fund (20-2B-3). The Wildlife Endowment Fund is a special fund within the Department, to be expended only after legislative approval and according to the following limitations: ▸ income received and accruing from investments of the fund shall be spent only in furthering the conservation and management of wildlife resources; ▸ such income and investments shall be distributed among divisions within the Department and according to certain license types as designated in 20-2B-6 of this article; ▸ expenditures from the principal of the fund are regulated by statute; ▸ any expenditure must result in benefits to the Department and must be spent only for conservation and management of wildlife resources (20-2B-4). The Board of Trustees of the Wildlife Endowment Fund directs expenditures from the income of the fund under statutory limitations and restrictions (20-2B-5). This fund and its income shall not take the place of other appropriations accruing to the Department, but any portion of the fund's income shall be used to supplement other income and appropriations to the Department to improve and increase its services. No modification of this section shall alter the fundamental purposes to which the Wildlife Endowment Fund may be applied and no future dissolution of the Department shall invalidate any lifetime license issued (20-2B-5). Income from the investment from the sale of lifetime trout licenses shall go for trout hatchery production as provided for in 20-2-46c for the regular annual trout license. Income from the investment of any portion of the principal of the fund which is specifically designated for the activities of a particular division within the Department, shall accrue solely to that division (20-2B-6). (See also Agency Advisory Boards under STATE FISH AND WILDLIFE AGENCIES.)

There is a **Conservation Stamp** which must be purchased in addition to a hunting, fishing, or trapping license. The revenue from the sale of conservation stamps shall be credited to the Department and used for capital improvements and land purchases or leases benefiting wildlife, except that at the Director's discretion, a maximum of 20% of the revenue may be used for operation and maintenance of capital improvements and lands. ★None of this revenue shall be used to purchase wetlands, or for land to be flooded so as to create wetlands, to attract migratory waterfowl within 60 air miles of any established poultry industry. None of this revenue shall be used for recreational facilities or activities that are used by or for the benefit of the general public rather than by or for purchasers of hunting, fishing or trapping licenses (20-2B-9).★

Agency Advisory Boards

★There is a **Whitewater Commission** consisting of the Director, the Director of Parks and Tourism and the representatives of private river users who have no affiliation with any commercial river enterprise, and four persons representing four different licensed commercial whitewater outfitters to be appointed by the Governor. No more than one representative of the private river users may be from each whitewater zone. The Superintendent of New River Gorge National Park shall be a nonvoting member of the commission. All commission members must be state residents. The Director shall serve as chair. The commission has the duty to investigate and study commercial whitewater rafting, outfitting and activities [other duties defined] (20-2-23a).★ (See also Agency Funding Sources under STATE FISH AND WILDLIFE AGENCIES for information on Whitewater Study and Improvement Fund).

The **Board of Trustees** of the **Wildlife Endowment Fund** (Board) has authority over administration of this fund. The Chairperson is the Director, and members are the Executive Secretary of the Department, the Departmental Fiscal Officer, the Chief of the Wildlife Resources Division, the Chief of the Law Enforcement Division, and two citizen members to be appointed by the Governor (20-2B-2). The Board may accumulate investment income of the fund until the Board believes the fund can provide a significant supplement to the budget of the Department, after which it may direct expenditures from the income of the fund (20-2B-5).

PROTECTED SPECIES OF WILDLIFE

See RELEVANT WILDLIFE DEFINITIONS and HUNTING, FISHING, TRAPPING PROVISIONS.

GENERAL EXCEPTIONS TO PROTECTION

The Director may issue a permit to hunt, kill, take, capture or maintain in captivity wildlife or reptiles exclusively for scientific or propagation purposes, but not for commercial purposes. The permit must set the minimum number/kind of wildlife or reptiles to be taken, the purpose and manner of taking and the applicant's name, residence and profession. No permit may be issued to kill deer or bear (20-2-50). ★The Director may issue a permit to keep in captivity as a pet, a wild animal or bird acquired from a commercial dealer or during the open season (20-2-51). The Director may issue a permit for keeping and maintaining in captivity wild animals, wild birds, amphibians or reptiles as a roadside menagerie, such animals to have been purchased from a licensed commercial dealer within or without the state, or have been taken legally, and the Director must be satisfied that housing, care, and public safety provisions are adequate (20-2-52).★ (See also RELEVANT WILDLIFE DEFINITIONS and HUNTING, FISHING, TRAPPING PROVISIONS.)

HUNTING, FISHING, TRAPPING PROVISIONS

General Provisions

Except as provided, no person shall have in possession any wildlife during closed seasons. Lawfully taken wildlife may be in possession during the open season, and for 60 days thereafter, and for additional time by permission of the Director.   ★★Wildlife lawfully taken outside of this state shall be subject to the same laws and rules as that taken within this state.★★ Migratory wild birds shall be possessed only in accordance with the "Migratory Bird Treaty Act" and its regulations. The Director and authorized agents may take or maintain in captivity any wildlife for the purpose of carrying out this chapter's provisions (20-2-4).

Licenses and Permits

Except as provided, no resident between the ages of 15 and 65, and no nonresident, shall take, hunt, trap, kill or chase any wild animals or wild birds, or fish for, take, or catch any fish, amphibians or aquatic life of any kind without a license/permit, and then only during the respective open seasons, except that nonresidents under age 15 may fish for, take or catch any fish, amphibians or aquatic life without a license/permit. No person under age 15 shall hunt any wild animals or wild birds upon lands of another unless accompanied by a licensed adult. A resident or nonresident member of any club, or persons owning or leasing a game or fish preserve or pond shall not hunt or fish therein without a license/permit, except that resident landowners and children may hunt and fish on their own land during open seasons according to law without a license/permit (20-2-27). Hunting or fishing while one's license is revoked is a misdemeanor, and for each offense, a fine of $100-500, or jail 10 to 100 days, or both (20-2-36a).

After 1990, no hunting license may be issued without completion of a certificate of training in firearm/bow and arrow safety from a course approved by the Hunter Education Association, or a certificate from another state or Canadian province, or an affidavit stating that the person has held a prior hunting license issued by this or another state or Canadian province. The Director shall establish a course in the safe handling of firearms/bows and arrows to be offered at least once a year in each county. Proof of course completion shall be required to consider reinstatement of a hunting license which has been revoked due to a conviction for negligent shooting of a human being or of livestock, or for reduction in license revocation time for other offenses, but the revocation time may not be reduced to less than one year. School districts are not responsible for implementing hunter safety education programs (20-3-30).

Pursuant to establishment of the Wildlife Endowment Fund, several categories of lifetime hunting, fishing and trapping licenses are created, which, for the lifetime of the licensee, shall serve in lieu of the equivalent annual license (20-2B-7). A Conservation Stamp and Migratory Bird Stamp must be purchased in addition to certain hunting, fishing or trapping licenses (20-2B-9). (See also Agency Funding Sources under STATE FISH AND WILDLIFE AGENCIES.)

Restrictions on Taking

Except as authorized by the Director, it is unlawful to: ★▸ shoot at any wild bird or animal unless it is plainly visible;★ ▸ dig out, cut out or smoke out, or in any manner take any live wild animal or wild bird out of its den or place of refuge except as authorized by law or regulation; ► make use of or take advantage of any artificial light in hunting, locating, attracting, taking, trapping or killing any wild bird or wild animal while having in possession any firearm, bow, arrow or other implement suitable for taking, killing or trapping a wild bird or animal, except it is lawful to hunt raccoon, opossum or skunk by the use of artificial light. It is not a violation to look for, look at, attract a wild bird/animal with the use of artificial light unless one possesses at such time a firearm or other implement for taking, or unless such artificial light is attached to or used from within or upon an automobile or other land conveyance (except headlights). Violation: misdemeanor; fine $100-500; jail 10-100 days. It is unlawful to: ► hunt for wild animals or wild birds from an airplane, automobile or motor driven water conveyance except by regulation; ► take any beaver or muskrat by any means other than by trap; ► catch, capture or kill by seine, net, bait, trap or snare, or like device of any kind, any wild turkey, ruffed grouse, pheasant or quail; ► destroy needlessly/willfully the nest or eggs of any wild bird or possess any such nest or eggs except under regulation or Director's permit; ► carry an uncased or loaded gun in state woods except during open firearms hunting season for wild animals and nonmigratory wild birds within any county, except this does not prohibit hunting unprotected species of wild animals and wild birds and migratory wild birds, during the open season, in open fields, open water and open marshes. It is unlawful to carry a loaded gun: ► after 5 a.m. on Sunday in any woods or on any highway, railroad right-of-way, public road, field or stream except at a regularly used target/skeet range; ► in or on any vehicle or conveyance or its attachments except as provided; ► between 5 p.m. and 7 a.m. of the following day unless firearm is taken apart and securely wrapped. It is unlawful to: ► hunt, catch, kill or pursue with firearms or other implement by which wildlife may be taken after 5 a.m. on Sunday any wild animals or wild birds except for traps legally set, and trapper may carry a .22 caliber firearm for dispatching trapped animals; ► hunt with firearms or long bow while under the influence of intoxicating liquor; ► hunt, catch or pursue a wild animal or bird with the use of a ferret; ► buy raw furs or skins of fur-bearing animals without a license (20-2-5).

It is unlawful to: ► have in possession, without written permission of the Director, any hunting/fishing devices which cannot be used lawfully in the state, and conservation officers shall remove and destroy such devices whenever found; ► catch or kill fish by means other than by rod, line and hooks with natural or artificial lures, except that it is lawful to snare any species of suckers, carp, fallfish and creek chubs; ► employ or hire, induce or persuade by money or other things of value, or by any means, any person to hunt or kill any wild animal or wild bird except species on which there is no closed season, or to fish for any fish, amphibian or aquatic life protected by law or regulation, or the sale of which is prohibited (20-2-5). It is unlawful to hunt, kill, transport or possess any migratory game or nongame birds except during the time and in the manner and numbers prescribed by the Federal Migratory Bird Treaty Acts of 1916 and 1936, or to kill, take, catch or possess, living or dead, any wild bird other than a game bird; or to sell or transport within or without the state any such bird except by law. No part of the plumage, skin or body of any protected bird shall be sold or possessed for sale except mounted or stuffed plumage, skins, bodies or heads of legally taken and mounted birds, whether captured within or without the state, except the English or European sparrow, starling, crow and cowbird are not protected and killing is lawful (20-2-5). It is unlawful to use dynamite or any like explosive or poisonous mixture placed in any state waters for the purpose of taking or killing fish. Violation: felony; fine up to $500; or jail 6 months to three years; or both. It is unlawful to: ► have a bow and gun or arrows in the fields or woods at the same time; ► have a crossbow in the woods or fields or use a crossbow to hunt any wildlife; ► take turkey, bear, elk or deer with any arrow unless the point has two sharp edges and is at least 3/4 inch wide; ► shoot an arrow across any public highway or from an aircraft, motordriven watercraft, motor vehicle or other land conveyance (20-2-5).

No person may permit a dog to chase any wild animal or wild bird, either day or night, between May 1 and August 15, except that dogs may be trained on wild animals and wild birds (except deer and turkey), and field trials may be held on private lands on written permission of the owner or on public lands. Certain dog restrictions apply to nonresidents and during bear season in designated counties. Except as provided, it is unlawful to hunt, catch, take or kill any wild animal, wild bird or wild fowl except during the open season established by regulation of the Director (20-2-5). No person shall permit the person's dog to hunt/chase deer. Conservation officers shall seize dogs known to have chased deer, advertise for the owner, and destroy unclaimed dogs (20-2-16).

No person shall hunt, capture, trap or kill fur-bearing animals except as authorized by the Director's regulations, nor have in possession the fresh skin of any fur-bearing animal, except beaver, after 10 days after the close of the open season. No person shall disturb properly marked traps of another person or remove animals from such traps (20-2-17). The Director shall regulate the number, kind and type of traps to be used in taking game or fur-bearing animals, and all traps must be tagged with the owner's name (20-2-18 and -19). On Sunday, a person checking traps may carry only a 22 caliber firearm for dispatching trapped animals (20-2-19a). When trapping beaver, it is illegal to set more than the legal limit of traps, to set traps within fifteen feet of the waterline on a beaver house, to have in possession untagged beaver hides after 30 days after the season closes, or to destroy or disturb dams, houses or burrows of beavers (20-2-20). Licensed trappers must present pelts to a game checking station for tagging within 30 days of the season's close (20-2-21). Deer and wild turkey must be tagged immediately after taking, and the carcasses/skins inspected at an official checking station before transport out of the county adjacent to where the kill was made (20-2-22).

No person shall hunt, capture or kill any bear, or possess any bear or part, including fresh pelts, except during the hunting season for bear. Within 24 hours of taking, the bear or fresh skin must be inspected and tagged at an official checking station before the bear can be transported more than 75 miles from the point of the kill. It is unlawful to: ▸ hunt bear without a bear damage stamp and proper hunting license; ▸ hunt a bear with a shotgun with more than one solid ball, a rifle of less than 25 caliber, or a crossbow; ▸ kill a bear using poison, explosives, snares, steel traps or deadfalls other than as authorized; ▸ shoot or kill a bear cub weighing less than 100 pounds or kill a bear accompanied by such cub; ▸ possess any part of a bear not properly tagged; ▸ enter a state game refuge with firearms for the purpose of pursuing or killing a bear; ▸ hunt bear with dogs during seasons other than those designated, or, after a bear is spotted, to pursue the bear with other than the pack of dogs used at the beginning of the hunt; ▸ train hunting dogs on bear or cause dogs to chase bear at other than designated seasons; ▸ organize for commercial purposes or professionally outfit a bear hunt, or give or receive any consideration in money, goods or services in connection with a bear hunt; ▸ for nonresidents to hunt bear with dogs (20-2-22a).

It is lawful for resident landowners and their families to carry uncased guns, with or without being accompanied by a dog, in looking after livestock or poultry on their lands (20-2-6). It is unlawful to hunt, fish or trap on the fenced, enclosed or posted lands of another person without written permission of the landowner. A person who trespasses for purposes of hunting, trapping or fishing and kills or injures any domestic animal or fowl, cuts trees, or damages any gates or fence is guilty of a misdemeanor and is liable to the owner for all costs and damages. ★It is lawful for the landowner to arrest any trespasser and take the trespasser before a justice of the peace for trial, and such landowner is vested with all the powers and rights of a game protector for such purposes.★ Law enforcement officers shall enforce these provisions only if requested to do so by a landowner (20-2-7). Landowners may post unenclosed lands against hunting, fishing or trapping (20-2-8). ★It is unlawful and a misdemeanor to post lands not lawfully owned for the purpose of preventing hunting or fishing (20-2-9).★

Only licensed private game preserve/propagation farm operators and those legally licensed to propagate and sell fish, amphibians and other aquatic life, shall purchase, sell or possess for sale any wildlife or part which has been designated as game animal, fur-bearing animal, game bird, game fish or amphibian, or any of the song or insectivorous birds, or other species which the Director designates, ★except that pelts of game or fur-bearing animals taken during the legal season may be sold and the hide, head, antlers and feet of legally killed deer, and the hide, head, skull, organs and feet of a legally killed black bear may be sold.★ No person, including a common carrier, shall transport any wildlife, the sale of which is prohibited, if the person knows or has reason to believe that the wildlife has been or is to be sold illegally. The illegal selling, possessing for sale, transporting or carrying shall each constitute a separate misdemeanor offense. Game birds and game bird meats sold by licensed retailers may be served at a licensed eating place. The Director may promulgate regulations regarding the sale of wildlife and the skins thereof (20-2-11). ★Under the Director's regulations, heads, hides, antlers and feet of deer and the hide, head, skull, organs and feet of legally killed black bears may be transported outside the state. Residents and nonresidents may transport legally taken wildlife outside the state.★ Illegal transportation of deer or wild boar outside the state is a separate offense for each animal so possessed or transported, and is a misdemeanor; fine $20-300; and jail 10-60 days (20-2-12).

It is unlawful, while engaged in hunting or pursuing wild animals, wild birds or wild fowl, carelessly or negligently to shoot, wound or kill any human being or livestock, or to destroy or injure any other chattels or property. Violators shall file with the Director a full description of the accident/casualty within 72 hours following such incident. Violation: misdemeanor; fine $1,000-10,000; or jail up to one year; or both. Restitution for the livestock or property injured or destroyed is required (20-2-57). It is unlawful to shoot or discharge any firearm across or in any public road, or within 400 feet of any schoolhouse or church, or within 500 feet of any dwelling house. Violation: misdemeanor. Certain licensed persons operating a gun repair shop may be exempt (20-2-58).

Commercial and Private Enterprise Provisions

No person shall propagate wildlife for commercial purposes except when licensed (20-2-14). The Director may issue a license to operate a private game preserve for propagation of wild animals and wild birds for commercial purposes and authorizing the holder to breed or raise animals and birds as specified by the license, to sell the same dead or alive, or to sell bird eggs in accordance with regulations. The Director shall determine that the game farm property shall be properly enclosed, that housing and sanitation conditions are proper, and that public safety is ensured (20-2-47). The Director may issue a license for the operation of a private plant, pond or business for the propagation, sale or purchase of fish, frogs, turtles and other aquatic life for commercial purposes, authorizing the holder to breed/raise the designated species and to buy and sell the same dead or alive or the eggs thereof in accordance with regulations. The Director shall determine that the pond will not interfere with free fish passage, that riparian rights of adjacent landowners are not violated, and that the pond will not interfere with public stocking/propagation of fish (20-2-48). The Director may issue licenses for buying or dealing in raw furs, pelts or skins of fur-bearing animals, including: resident county license; resident statewide license; nonresident statewide license; and agent license (20-2-49).

Outfitters, Guides and **Commercial Whitewater Outfitters** may be licensed under the Director's regulations (20-2-23). Whitewater outfitter licensees must be bonded in the amount of $1,000. The Whitewater Commission may revoke the license for failure to pay the bond or for violation of any license provisions, on conviction of the licensee of a crime, or for other cause after notice and hearing. Violation of whitewater license provisions or regulations of the Director is a misdemeanor; fine per violation $500-7,500; jail up to six months; or both (20-2-23d). Licensed outfitters and guides shall be financially responsible citizens and shall possess proper equipment to provide hunters, fishermen and others the advertised services. The Director shall investigate all outfitter and guide applicants and determine their qualifications prior to license issuance (20-2-24). Applications must be approved and signed by three resident real property owners residing in the applicant's county. Approval from National Forest supervisors is required before guides and outfitters operate in such forests (20-2-25). Operating without a guides/outfitter license or proper bond is a misdemeanor; fine up to $100; or jail up to 90 days; or both (20-2-26).

The Director may issue a license for operation of a private pond to be used as a commercial fishing preserve if such impoundments meet the requirements of 20-2-27. The licensee shall have authority to establish the fishing seasons, size and creel limits for such licensed ponds, and persons fishing there need no license (20-2-53). A private commercial shooting preserve license may be issued to applicants who own a minimum of 300 acres in one tract of land/water and no more than 3,000 contiguous acres. Duck-release preserves may operate with a minimum of 50 contiguous acres. The boundaries of each commercial shooting preserve shall be clearly defined and posted and the Director shall designate the game which may be hunted, and may allow a more liberal season. No more than 80% of each species of released game bird may be recovered by the owners or guests, except for mallard, black duck, ringnecked pheasant, chukar partridge and other nonnative game species upon which 100% recovery is allowed. Shooting preserve operators may establish their own age, sex, and number of birds per person restrictions. The operator must maintain records of the number of birds released, raised, purchased and taken, and names, addresses and license numbers of all shooters. Wild game on such preserves may be harvested in accordance with applicable game and hunting laws regarding open seasons and bag limits. State hunting licenses are required of all persons except nonresidents on such preserves (20-2-54). Minnow and bait fish operations must be licensed by the Director, including the catching of minnows (20-2-55). The Director may issue permits for field trials, shoot-to-retrieve field trials, water races or wild hunts to individuals, clubs or organizations. No state hunting license is required for participation in such trials (20-2-56).

Import, Export and Release Provisions

No person shall transport into or have in possession any live wildlife or viable eggs thereof from outside the state except as authorized by Director permit. The Director may not issue a permit to import coyotes into the state. Salmonidae fish or viable eggs or wildlife species require disease free certification before importation to protect native populations of fish and wildlife. All imported wildlife is subject to inspection by Department agents. Illegal importation of coyotes is a misdemeanor; fine $100-300 for each offense; or jail 10-100 days; or both (20-2-13).

Interstate Reciprocal Agreements

Certain reciprocal agreements exist for residents of Maryland and Ohio to hunt or fish in waters between the respective states, if the adjoining state provides reciprocity (20-2-28). The Director may issue a license to any resident of West Virginia or Ohio to take fish or mussels for commercial purposes from the Ohio River (20-2-59).

ANIMAL DAMAGE CONTROL

Whenever deer or other wildlife are causing damage to cultivated crops, fruit trees or commercial nurseries, the owner may report to the conservation officer or biologist of the county or to the Director who shall investigate the reported damage, and if found substantial, shall issue a permit to the landowner to kill one or more deer or other wildlife in the manner prescribed by the Director. The Director shall establish procedures for the issuance of permits necessary to control deer or other wildlife causing property damage. Persons taking deer/wildlife under these provisions are subject to the same minimum caliber and other firearm or bow poundage restrictions as apply when hunting the same species during the regular hunting season (20-2-15).

Property owners suffering damage to real or personal property including livestock loss caused by a bear may complain to a conservation officer who shall immediately investigate, and if found to be justified, may, together with the landowner, hunt and destroy or capture the bear, provided that only the conservation officer or designated wildlife biologist shall determine whether the bear shall be destroyed or captured. If the complaint is justified, the officer may summon/use dogs to effectuate the hunting, destruction or capture of such bear. If nonresident dogs are used, their owners are the only nonresidents permitted to participate in hunting the bear. When a property owner has suffered damage as the result of a bear, such owner shall file a report with the Director stating whether or not such bear was hunted and destroyed and if so, the sex, weight and estimated age of the bear, and also submit an appraisal of the property damage signed by three competent appraisers. ★A commission, composed of the complaining property owner, a Department officer, and a third person to be selected by these shall examine the damage appraisal report and rule upon the claim according to Department regulations. Approved claims shall be paid from the Bear Damage Fund (20-2-44b), and if insufficient, from the Special Revenue Account of the Department. Where the complaint is the killing of livestock, the value will be the fair market value of the livestock at the date of death plus any unborn issue.★ Killing a bear in violation of this section is a misdemeanor; fine $500-1,000; or jail 30-100 days; or both; and suspension of hunting and fishing licenses for one year (20-2-22a).

ENFORCEMENT OF WILDLIFE LAWS

★★West Virginia is a member of the Interstate Wildlife Violator Compact (20-2C-1 through 20-2C-3).★★ See Model Statute Section of Handbook for full provisions of the compact.

Criminal Penalties

When no specific punishment or penalty is otherwise provided for violations of the provisions of this article, violations of any provision hereof is a misdemeanor, and, upon conviction, is subject to the punishment and penalties prescribed in 20-7-9 (20-2-2). (See HUNTING, FISHING AND TRAPPING PROVISIONS.)

Exceeding the creel limit on trout or otherwise violating trout fishing rules and laws is a misdemeanor; fine $50-300; jail 10-100 days; or both (20-2-5b).

Illegal Taking of Wildlife

A person convicted of violating any criminal law and the violation causes/results in the injury, death or destruction of game or a protected species of animal, in addition to any other penalty, shall forfeit the cost of replacing such game or protected species of animal to the state. Replacement values for game and protected species of animals are: ▸ for each game fish or protected species fish taken illegally other than by pollution kill, $5 for each pound and any fraction thereof; ▸ for each bear, elk or eagle, $500; ▸ for each deer or raven, $200; ▸ for each wild turkey, hawk or owl, $100; ▸ for each beaver, otter or mink, $25; ▸ for each muskrat, raccoon, skunk or fox, $15; ▸ for each rabbit, squirrel, opossum, duck, quail, woodcock, grouse or pheasant, $10; ▸ for each wild boar, $200; ▸ for any other game or protected species of animal, $10 each. Upon conviction, the court shall order the violator to forfeit the proper amount based on the values set forth herein. Two or more defendants are liable jointly and equally. The forfeiture shall be paid by the person within the time prescribed by the court, not exceeding 60 days. The court shall pay such moneys to the state treasury where it shall be credited to the Department to be used only for the replacement, habitat management or enforcement programs for injured, killed or destroyed game or protected species of animal (20-2-5a).

License Revocations and Suspensions

The Director may, for cause, refuse a license/permit to any person or revoke a license/permit which had been granted. The violation of any provision of this chapter by one holding a license shall be sufficient cause to refuse or revoke a license. On notification to a licensing agent that the Director desires to refuse a license to a person, the agent shall report to the Director any application made by the person. The hunting license of one convicted under 20-2-57 of negligent shooting, wounding or killing of a human being or livestock while hunting shall be revoked and no new license issued for a period of five years, unless the shooting was not a negligent shooting of a human being, in which case the person may petition the Director for reinstatement of all hunting license privileges after two years, and the Director may reinstate the license privileges according to circumstances of the case (20-2-38). The Director shall suspend the license/permit of any person upon notice from a court that such person has defaulted on the payment of costs, fines, forfeitures or penalties imposed for any hunting or fishing violation, after 90 days following such conviction. Any reinstatement of a license or permit shall be subject to a reinstatement fee to be deposited into the law-enforcement division account (20-2-38a).

Reward Payments

The Director is authorized to offer and pay rewards for information regarding violation of any of the provisions of this section or for the apprehension and conviction of any violators (20-1-7).

HABITAT PROTECTION

The Division of Forestry, within the Department, has under its supervision the state forests, other forests and woodland areas, the protection of forests from fire, disease and insects, and the administration and enforcement of all laws relating to the conservation, development and protection, use and enjoyment of all state forest lands (20-3-1). The Director, with the Governor's consent, may purchase lands suitable for forest culture, state forests or wildlife refuges, public hunting areas, public fishing areas, public access sites, and dams for fish refuges. The Director may also receive gifts of lands by deed or bequest. The Director shall protect, preserve and maintain lands so acquired as forest culture areas, state forests, wildlife areas, public hunting or fishing areas and other such lands for the propagation and distribution of forest trees and for the protection, management, propagation and distribution of the fish, wild animals and birds thereon. The Director may prescribe and enforce rules prohibiting all hunting and fishing, pursuing, catching, trapping or killing of fish, wild animals and birds upon such areas for any length of time deemed proper, and may provide special regulations and open seasons for taking animals, birds or fish upon such lands (20-3-2).

The Director shall establish and maintain wildlife areas on lands purchased, leased or given for this purpose, upon which the Director shall regulate public hunting, chasing for sport, shooting, and limit the number of wildlife which may be taken from areas open to public shooting in any year. It is unlawful to hunt, pursue or molest any animals, birds or fowls on any section of a wildlife area designated as a wildlife refuge, except for the killing of predatory animals or birds by persons designated by the Director. Such wildlife refuge areas shall be posted as closed to hunting, or, if a public shooting ground, posted as to when hunting is legal on such land. The Director may lease lands for wildlife refuge purposes for not less than 10-year periods. The Director may, with the owner's consent, set aside any tract of land in the state as a wildlife area. Such lands shall be managed in the same manner and for the same purpose as wildlife areas owned by the state. At the expiration of the agreement, the lands shall be reorganized as wildlife areas or be discontinued (20-3-3). See also Agency Powers and Duties and Agency Funding Sources under STATE WILDLIFE AGENCIES.

NATIVE AMERICAN WILDLIFE PROVISIONS: None.

WISCONSIN

Sources: Wisconsin Statutes Annotated, 1989, Chapters 15, 23, 25, 29 and 71; 1992 Cumulative Annual Pocket Part 1992.

STATE WILDLIFE POLICY

The legal title to, and custody and protection of, all wild animals is vested in the state for regulating enjoyment, use, disposition, and conservation. The legal title to any wild animal, carcass or part, taken or possessed in violation of this chapter, remains in the state; and the title to any wild animal, or carcass or part, lawfully acquired, upon violation in possession, use, giving, sale, barter or transportation shall revert to the state. In either case, any such wild animal, carcass or part may be seized by the Department of Natural Resources or its wardens. This does not permit seizure of nor prohibit possession or sale of lawfully obtained wild birds and animals which are mounted for a private collection, nor permit seizure, or prohibit the possession or sale, of commercially raised deer. Department agents, after making reasonable efforts to notify the owner or occupant, may enter private lands to retrieve, diagnose or determine if there are dead or diseased wild animals upon such lands, and take actions to prevent the spread of contagious disease (29.02).

See PROTECTED SPECIES OF WILDLIFE.

RELEVANT WILDLIFE DEFINITIONS: See Definitions section of Appendices.

STATE FISH AND WILDLIFE AGENCIES

Agency Structure

The **Department of Natural Resources** (Department) is in charge of providing an adequate and flexible system for protection, development and use of forests, fish and game, lakes, streams, plant life and other outdoor resources (23.09). The Department is under the direction and supervision of the **Natural Resources Board** (Board), which consists of seven members appointed for staggered six-year terms, three from the territory north, and three from the territory south, of a specified line through the state. No person may be appointed, or remain a member, who receives a significant portion of income directly or indirectly from permit holders or applicants of permits issued by the Department (15.34).

The Department shall secure enforcement of all laws which it is required to administer. The persons appointed by the Department to exercise and perform these powers and duties conferred upon deputy fish and game wardens, shall be known as **conservation wardens** and shall be subject to Chapter 230. ★Whenever the county board by resolution authorizes the appointment of **county conservation wardens**, the chairperson of the county board, district attorney and county clerk, shall select them and certify their names to the Department which, if it approves, shall issue commissions. Such wardens have, within their county, all the powers and duties of conservation wardens. The Department shall furnish each with identification and wardens shall make full reports as required by the Department and shall at all times be subject to its direction and control in the performance of their duties (23.10).★

Agency Powers and Duties

The **Department:** ► may promulgate rules, inaugurate studies, investigations and surveys, and establish services to carry out conservation provisions; ► shall establish long-range plans, projects and priorities for conservation; ► may designate localities as fish, game or bird refuges for providing safe retreats in which game or birds may rest and replenish adjacent hunting grounds; ► may acquire by purchase, lease or agreement, gift or devise, lands or waters for state forests, parks, public shooting, trapping or fishing grounds, or areas to hunt, trap or fish, for fish hatcheries and game farms, for forest nurseries, for preservation of species defined under 29.415, for state recreation and natural areas; ► may capture, propagate, transport, sell or exchange species of game or fish for stocking or restocking state lands or waters; ► may conduct research to improve management of natural resources and disseminate information; ► may enter into cooperative agreements consistent with the purposes herein; ► may receive funds for research; ‣ may acquire easements in furtherance of public rights including rights of access and use of lands and waters for hunting and fishing (23.09). [Numerous forest and recreation-related powers are detailed.] The Department may establish zones within state recreation areas for recreational uses, including hunting and fishing, consistent with the master plan for the area (23.091).

The Department shall have general care, protection and supervision of all state parks, fish hatcheries, state forests and state lands in which it has interests, except those vested in another officer, body or board, and is granted powers to enable it to exercise duties required, but it may not perform an act upon state lands held for sale that will diminish their value. The Department shall have police supervision over state-owned lands and property under its supervision, management and control, and its agents may arrest, with or without warrant a person committing an offense against state laws or in violation of a Department rule, and deliver the person to the county court where the offense was committed. The District Attorney of that county shall prosecute those actions. The Department may require an applicant for a permit or statutory approval to submit an environmental impact report if the area affected exceeds 40 acres or the estimated cost exceeds $25,000 (23.11). Prior to acquisition of lands after 1977 for a new facility or project, the proposal shall be submitted to the Governor for approval, including state parks, state forests, public shooting, trapping or fishing grounds, fish hatcheries, game farms, endangered species preservation areas, natural areas, wild rivers, and others (23.14).

★The County Board of a county may by resolution indicate its desire to plan and carry out a program of coordinated fish and/or game management projects and make application to the Department for funds. Such projects include but are not limited to: game food seeding, browse improvement cutting, prescribed burning for game habitat improvement, creating game cover brush piles, creation of impoundments, game and fish habitat creation, lake and stream rehabilitation, construction of fish shelters, stream side fencing, rough fish control and other approved fish and game management projects. County boards may apply for funds appropriated for improvement of habitat and environment for game and nongame species on such county lands. The annual appropriation for each county shall not exceed five cents per acre. Projects shall be limited to ones designed to benefit both game and nongame species and the natural environment (23.09).★

The Department shall design and produce waterfowl hunting stamps, wild turkey hunting stamps, pheasant hunting stamps, inland waters trout stamps and Great lakes trout and salmon stamps, and may select artwork for stamps through a contest or otherwise (29.09).

The Department shall have charge of: ‣ propagation and breeding of fish; ‣ collection and diffusion of information about the propagation and conservation of fish; ‣ control, supply and repair of state fish hatcheries, ponds, and other property for propagation of fish; ‣ land acquisition, and purchase and construction of new hatcheries; ‣ receiving all spawn, fry or fish donated to the state or purchased, and by exchange or otherwise to procure, distribute and dispose of spawn and fish to promote the abundant supply of food fishes in state waters; ‣ keeping an inventory of hatchery property, expenses and fish distribution. The Department for any time period may erect and maintain fish screens in navigable streams for preventing the invasion of rough fish (29.51).

See also Agency Regulations under this section; Licenses and Permits under HUNTING, FISHING, TRAPPING PROVISIONS; and HABITAT PROTECTION.

Agency Regulations

★★The Department shall establish and maintain open and closed seasons for fish and game and bag limits, size limits, rest days and conditions as will conserve the fish and game supply and ensure state citizens continued opportunities for good fishing, hunting and trapping. All fishing seasons on inland waters shall open on a Saturday. The Department may: ‣ regulate the number of hunters and the harvest of Canada geese by requiring hunters to tag each goose killed, requiring registration of each farm on which goose hunting is allowed and each goose killed at the farm, or prohibit goose hunting without Department permit; ‣ limit the number of trappers and the harvest of wild fisher, otters and beaver; ‣ limit the number of hunters or trappers and the harvest of bobcats; ‣ impose a system for permits; ‣ promulgate rules, conducting public hearings after publication of notice, and after sending written notice to the Wisconsin Conservation Congress delegates affected. The Department shall make investigations as necessary, and may organize advisory committees on a matter under consideration. Emergency rules may be made by the Secretary. Present statutes regulating open and closed seasons, bag limits, size limits, rest days and other conditions shall continue in full force until modified by Department rules or legislative action. Nothing herein confers upon the Department the power to alter statutory provisions relating to forfeitures, penalties, license fees or bounties. In even-numbered years, the Department shall submit to the legislature, the Governor and the Wisconsin Conservation Congress a report identifying accomplishments and use and expenditure of all fishing, hunting and trapping approval fees collected during the previous biennium. No funds accruing to the state from fishing and hunting license fees shall be diverted for any purpose than those provided by the Department. The Department shall establish the open season for hunting raccoon two weeks earlier for residents than for nonresident licensees (29.174).★★

See HUNTING, FISHING, TRAPPING PROVISIONS.

Agency Funding Sources

The **Endangered Resources Program** means purchasing or improving land or habitats for native Wisconsin endangered or threatened species as defined in 29.415 for nongame species as defined in 29.01, conducting wildlife and resource research and surveys and providing wildlife management services and damage control, the payment of claims for damage associated with endangered or threatened species, and other purposes as specified. The program is funded by a voluntary designation on an individual's state income tax return of a refund due that individual [other details of the tax return provisions and procedures are given] (71.10).

★★There is a separate nonlapsible trust fund, the **Conservation Fund** to consist of: all moneys accruing to the state for or in behalf of the Department under Chapters 26 through 29 and 350, and parts of Chapters 77, 23, 30, 70 and 71 as specified herein, including grants received from a federal agency except as otherwise provided; one percent of all sales and use taxes under 77.61 on all-terrain vehicles, boats and snowmobiles; an amount equal to the estimated motorboat gas tax payment; license fees and other state moneys collected by field employees of the Department; funds accruing to the Conservation Fund from license fees paid by hunters and from sport and recreation fishing license fees, which shall not be diverted for any purpose other than those provided by the Department or as specified herein; gifts or bequests in accordance with the directions of the donor; all moneys received from the US for fire prevention, forest planting, and for wildlife restoration projects and as provided in 29.174, for the purposes for which these moneys are received; other tax proceeds as specified herein for forest development and emergency fire warden compensation (25.29).★★

See Agency Regulations; HUNTING, FISHING, TRAPPING PROVISIONS

Agency Advisory Boards

Under the Board are a number of special commissions, boards and councils which have duties and powers that relate to fish and wildlife in addition to other responsibilities. Some of these are the **Wisconsin Waterways Commission**, the **Lake Superior and Lake Michigan Commercial Fishing Boards**, the **Fox River Management Commission**, the **Great Lakes Fish and Water Resources Council**, the **Natural Areas Preservation Council**, and the **Inland Lakes Protection and Rehabilitation Council** (15.347). [Details of the membership of these groups and citations to their duties are given in detail.]

PROTECTED SPECIES OF WILDLIFE

The Department may conduct investigations of nongame species to develop scientific information for population, distribution, habitat needs and other biological data to determine conservation measures. On the basis of these determinations, the Department may promulgate rules and develop conservation programs to ensure the ability of nongame species to perpetuate themselves. The rules may require harvest information and establish limitations for taking, possession, transportation, processing and sale or offer for sale, to conserve nongame species. ★No rules promulgated or programs developed may impede, hinder or prohibit the utilization of lands for construction, operation or maintenance of authorized or permitted utility facilities (29.175).★

A person who takes, catches, kills or impedes the progress of a homing pigeon shall forfeit not more than $50 (29.256). No person may possess or control a game bird, animal or carcass without a hunting, sports, conservation, taxidermist or scientific collector permit or license and carrying it. No person may take, destroy or possess the nest or eggs of a wild bird for which a closed season is prescribed without a scientific collector permit. This does not prohibit possession or sale of lawfully obtained wild birds and animals mounted or being mounted for a private collection, nor prohibit possession or sale of commercially raised deer under 92.25 kept in compliance with this chapter (29.42).

★★The legislature finds that certain wild animals and plants are endangered or threatened and are entitled to preservation and protection. The Federal Endangered Species Act and the Lacey Act together provide for protection of wild animals and plants threatened with worldwide extinction by prohibiting their importation and by restricting and regulating interstate and foreign commerce in wild animals and plants taken in violation of state, federal and foreign laws. The states must also assume responsibility for conserving these wild animals and plants and restricting the taking, possession, transportation, processing or sale of endangered or threatened wild animals and plants within their jurisdictions to assure their continued survival and propagation for the aesthetic, recreational and scientific purposes of future generations. The legislature finds that by eliminating taking, possession or marketing of endangered species and by establishing a program for conservation and restoration of these endangered or threatened species, their potential for continued existence will be strengthened, and further finds that activities of both persons and governmental agencies are tending to destroy the few remaining whole plant-animal communities in this state. Since these communities represent the only standard against which the effects of change can be measured, their preservation is of highest importance, and the legislature urges all persons and agencies to consider fully all decisions in this light (29.415).★★

The Department shall by rule establish an endangered and threatened species list consisting of wild animals and plants on the US list of endangered and threatened foreign species, native species and a list of Wisconsin endangered species. Wisconsin endangered species shall be compiled by issuing a proposed list of species approaching state-wide extirpation; that of threatened species by issuing a proposed list of species which appear likely, within the foreseeable future, to become endangered. Issuance of the proposed lists shall be followed by solicitation of comments and public hearing. Wild animals and plants shall be deemed approaching state-wide extirpation if the Department determines, based upon the best scientific and commercial data available to it, after consultation with other state game directors, federal agencies and interested persons and organizations, that the continued existence of such wild animals and plants is in jeopardy. The Department shall periodically review and after public hearing, may revise its lists, maintaining a summary report of the scientific data used to support all amendments to the lists. Upon the petition of three persons, the Department may review a listed or unlisted wild animal or plant if the persons present scientific evidence to warrant such review, after which it may by hearing and rule amend the state-wide list (29.415).

Except as otherwise permitted, no person may take, transport, possess, process or sell within this state a wild animal on the Department's endangered and threatened species list (plant prohibitions are not included here). Violation: $500-2,000 fine, and the court shall order revocation of all hunting approvals for one year. Intentional violation: $2,000-5,000 fine, or jail up to 9 months, or both, and the court shall order the revocation of all hunting licenses for three years. A Department officer or police officer shall have authority to execute a warrant to search for and seize goods, records, merchandise or wild animal taken, used or possessed in violation and may arrest a person with probable cause. An officer or agent who has arrested a person in connection with a violation may search the person or business records at the time of arrest and seize wild animals or property taken, used or employed in connection with a violation. Goods, merchandise, wild animals or records seized shall be held pending disposition of court proceedings and then forfeited for destruction or disposition. The Department may direct the transfer of wild animals seized to a qualified zoological or scientific institution or qualified private propagator for safekeeping, with costs assessable to the defendant (29.415).

The Department shall permit the taking, exportation, transportation or possession of a wild animal on the endangered/threatened lists for zoological, educational or scientific purposes, for propagation in captivity or for preservation purposes, unless prohibited by a federal law or other state law. An endangered species which enters the state from another state or country to be transported within or beyond the state may enter without restriction in accordance with a federal or state permit. ★Possession, sale or transportation within this state of any endangered species on the US list of endangered and threatened foreign species shall not require a state permit.★ The Department shall conduct research and shall implement programs directed at conserving, protecting, restoring and propagating selected state-endangered and threatened species to the maximum extent practicable, and may enter into agreements with federal and other state agencies or private persons with respect to programs designed to conserve such species. ★Agreements with private persons may include providing for the movement of an endangered or threatened species to another appropriate habitat, preferably to one on state-controlled land. ★ These provisions do not apply to zoological societies, municipal zoos or their employees (29.415).

No person may possess live game or a fur-bearing animal unless authorized for game farms, deer farms, parks, fur farms or other excepted activities as specified [definitions of "control," "removal," "restraint," "possession" are given]. ★The governing body of a county, city or town may by ordinance prohibit a person from possessing or selling live game animal or a fur-bearing animal. ★ No person may sell live game animal or a fur-bearing animal unless authorized under listed provisions and unless the purchaser is authorized and presents evidence to the seller. A person who sells live game animal or a fur-bearing animal shall keep a record of each sale, to be open to Department inspection. ★A person who hunts or traps a game animal or a fur-bearing animal shall kill the animal when it is taken and make it part of the daily bag limit or shall release the animal unless licensed for a commercial operation. Violation: fine of $100-1,000 (29.425). (See also Import, Export, and Release Provisions and Commercial and Private Enterprise Provisions under HUNTING, FISHING, TRAPPING PROVISIONS.)

See RELEVANT WILDLIFE DEFINITIONS and NATIVE AMERICAN WILDLIFE PROVISIONS.

GENERAL EXCEPTIONS TO PROTECTION

The Department may issue a scientific collector permit authorizing collection or salvage for scientific purposes only, the eggs, nests and wild animals specified in the permit subject to permit and Department conditions and rules. The Department shall investigate and if satisfied that the applicant is engaged in a program leading to increased, useful scientific knowledge, it may issue a scientific collector permit stating the type, species and number of specimens to be collected, the area and period of time for collection, the place specimens shall be kept and other limitations. The permit may authorize the use of net guns and tranquilizer guns. Violation of permit conditions or Department rules results in revocation for one year in addition to other penalties (29.17). On application of a park board, the Department may grant permits to take, have, sell, barter or transport live wild animals for park purposes or grant a permit to take and transport wild animals for propagation within the state under the supervision of the Department or wardens. A public zoo may have, purchase, barter or sell a live animal, domestic or foreign, to or with another public zoo, licensed deer farm or reputable animal dealer, within or without this state (29.55).

The owner or occupant of any land and family members may hunt or trap beaver, foxes, raccoons, woodchucks, rabbits and squirrels on the land without a license at any time, except during the 24-hour period prior to opening of deer season. ★Landowners and families may take beavers, rabbits, raccoons and squirrels on the land at any time with box traps in cities or villages or other areas where the discharge of a firearm is unlawful (29.24). ★The Department may regulate training hunting dogs and dog trials to encourage the use of hunting dogs and to safeguard wildlife, but rules shall not be promulgated for general hunting with dogs of small game during general hunting season (29.255).

The Department may give, present, or turn over alive, for educational purposes, to a public zoo any predatory animal, which shall not be sold, bartered or given away, except that it may be returned to the Department (29.605). The Department may take rough fish by seines, nets or other devices or cause them to be taken from state waters, to be disposed of (29.62). When the Department finds that any species of fish is detrimental to state waters, it may by rule, designate the species and specify the waters in which the fish are found to be detrimental, and may then remove or cause them to be removed (29.623). Permission may be granted by the Department upon its terms and conditions to take carp and other undesirable rough fish, which are detrimental to game fish, in waters as designated. A person with a contract may be authorized to erect a temporary pond under Department supervision in navigable water pending sale of such fish (29.625). The Department may take or cause taking of fish from state waters for stocking other waters or for securing eggs for artificial propagation. Such fish or eggs may be taken only under a special permit and only in the presence of the Department or wardens. The permittee shall pay for services of the person approved by the Department to spawn the fish and fertilize the eggs (29.51).

Nothing in the provisions herein concerning protection of wild animals shall affect the: ► operation of state hatcheries; ► removal of fish which die from natural causes or removal of deleterious fish by the Department; ► propagation or transportation, collecting and transplanting of fish or fry by state authority; ► transportation of fish into or through the state by the fisheries commissioners of other states or of the US; ► operation of private fish hatcheries or propagation of fish in private waters or sale of fish therefrom. The Department shall not furnish fish or fry from state hatcheries to private ponds, clubs or preserves and shall not plant them in waters where the general public is not allowed (29.50).

See Commercial and Private Enterprise Provisions under HUNTING, FISHING, TRAPPING PROVISIONS.

HUNTING, FISHING, TRAPPING PROVISIONS

General Provisions

The following are declared public nuisances: ► an unlicensed net, or other unlicensed device, trap or contrivance for fishing, or a licensed net or device for fishing set, placed or found in waters where prohibited, or use in a prohibited manner; ► an unlicensed setline, cable, rope or line with more than one fish line attached thereto, or the same found in prohibited waters or set in a prohibited manner, or a fish line left in the water unattended; ► a screen set in public waters to prevent free passage of fish, or set in a stream stocked by state authorities unless authorized by the Department; ► a building, shelter or structure placed, occupied or used on ice in violation of this chapter; ► an unlicensed trap, snare, spring gun, set gun, net or other device, or any trap without a metal tag attached as required; ► a boat, with its machinery, sails, tackle and equipment, or a lamp, light, gun, pivot gun, swivel gun or firearm used in violation, or a boat, floating raft, box or blind set in open water and used in hunting game birds; ► decoys left unattended in the water; ► a dog found running deer, or used in violation of this chapter; ★► a ferret, rat, weasel or guinea pig in possession or used while hunting;★ ► any blind used in hunting waterfowl in violation of 29.27 (29.03). (See also Agency Regulations under STATE FISH AND WILDLIFE AGENCIES.)

Except as otherwise provided, no person may possess, control, or have in storage, game or other wild animal or the carcass or part during the period from July 1 to the last day of the closed season in each year, or in excess of the bag or possession limit or below the minimum size for game, game fish or other wild animal at any time. The seasons, bag, possession and size limits of the state or country in which taken shall apply to wild animals lawfully killed outside the state (29.39). It is unlawful to possess at any time the carcass or part or skin of a protected wild animal showing that it was taken during the closed season (29.395).

★★The Department shall establish and supervise administration of a state-wide trapper education program and shall enter into an agreement with a state-wide organization with demonstrated ability and experience in the trapper education field to assist. The program shall provide classroom and correspondence instruction and shall include: ► principles of wildlife management; ► responsibilities of trappers to landowners; ► interrelationships between trapping activities and conservation of natural resources; ► techniques for fur-bearer trapping. The program shall use certified instructors when providing instruction on techniques of trapping, and the Department shall establish criteria and standards for instructors. [Extensive administrative and program details are provided.] The Department shall issue a certificate for completing the course, which may be used by a resident in place of a trapping license for the period specified in 29.093. Except as otherwise provided, or those who have a certificate from an approved trapper education course with substantially the same content from another state, no person may be issued an approval authorizing trapping without a certificate of accomplishment (29.224).★★

★★The Department shall establish by rule a state-wide hunter education and firearm safety program providing for a course in each school district or county, and shall conduct such course in cooperation with qualified individuals and organizations and federal, state and local governmental entities. The course shall provide instruction in principles of: ► safety in handling hunting firearms and equipment; ► responsibilities of hunters to wildlife, environment, landowners and others; ► recognizing threatened and endangered species which cannot be hunted; ► principles of wildlife management and conservation. The Department Law Enforcement Administrator shall administer, supervise and enforce the program, and the Department shall appoint a qualified law enforcement person as the Hunter Education Administrator and prescribe duties, and shall appoint county directors, master hunter education instructors and regular instructors. Fees from the course shall go 50% to defray expenses and 50% into the Conservation Fund. The Department shall issue a certificate for completing the course, which may be used in place of a small game hunting license (29.225). Except for persons with an approved hunter education certificate from another state recognized under a reciprocal agreement, or a person who has completed armed forces basic training, no person born after January 1, 1973, may obtain approval authorizing hunting unless issued a certificate (29.226). ★★

Except as otherwise provided, it is unlawful to transport, cause, or deliver or receive for transportation, game or game fish or carcass or part other than during open season and three days thereafter. Whenever game or game fish or part is offered to a person for transportation at any other time, the person shall notify the Department or wardens giving full particulars of the offer and by whom made. No person shall transport or deliver or receive for transportation into or through this state game or game fish or carcass or part from another state in violation of the laws of such state; nor have same in possession during the closed season or in excess of bag limits without a license issued by the state in which taken, but a person who has lawfully killed a deer in this state, on the person's license only, may take the deer into an adjoining state as permitted. No common carrier may receive for transportation a deer or carcass unless tagged and registered and during the open season for deer and three days after, for delivery only within the state, or if a nonresident licensee, only in that state of residence. No common carrier shall receive for transportation a game bird, carcass or part except as provided. Licensed residents may transport in personal possession the legal daily bag or possession limit of game birds for which there is an open season, within the state. No person may transport a migratory game bird for which there is a season unless the head or one fully feathered wing remains attached during transport. No person shall transport, deliver or receive game fish taken from inland waters other than as specified. All fish subject to a minimum size limit taken by hook and line may be transported with the head or tail, or both removed and may be filleted before transport, but only if the dressed fish continues to meet the minimum size limit and remains in one piece with skin and scales intact (29.43 through .47). [Extensive additional transportation details are given in these sections.]

Except as otherwise provided, no person may sell, buy, barter or trade or offer to do so, or possess for such, any: deer, bear, squirrel, game bird, game fish or carcass at any time; other wild animal or carcass during the closed season, whether lawfully or unlawfully taken within or without the state. Commercially raised deer and fish species authorized for sale by permit are exempt. Eggs from trout and salmon lawfully taken and possessed, when removed from the fish, are exempted if the whole fish is taken to the egg buyer, the eggs removed in the buyer's presence and the fish carcass legally disposed of. The tails and skin of squirrels lawfully killed, when severed from the carcass are exempt. ★The hide of a bear lawfully killed is exempt if the hide includes the claws, head and teeth of the bear. No person may sell, buy, barter, trade or possess for sale bear claws or teeth which are not part of a bear hide.★ Except as provided in 29.52 and 29.581, no innkeeper or manager of a restaurant, club, logging camp or mining camp may sell, barter or serve, or cause such, to guests or boarders: meat of deer, bear, squirrel, game bird or game fish taken from inland waters at any time; meat of any other game or other wild animal or carcass or part during the closed season, whether of animals lawfully or unlawfully taken within or without the state. The Department may issue permits authorizing the serving of lawfully taken wild animals at any time. ★The giving, offering or affording opportunity to take free lunch in any of the places named above shall be embraced within the prohibitions (29.48 and .49).★

Licenses and Permits

Except as provided otherwise, no person may hunt a wild animal or trap game or fish in state waters unless approval is issued, and carried at all times while hunting, trapping or fishing, and exhibited on demand. Definite proof of identity and residence must be presented to obtain a license, and licenses may not be used by another person nor obtained by persons who are prohibited from obtaining the particular type of license. Wild turkey hunting stamps must be signed. The Department shall keep a complete record of all licenses (approvals) issued, and specify procedures for license issuances. [Wisconsin has very detailed provisions relating to licenses for both permanently and temporarily disabled persons shooting from stationary vehicles, use of trolling motors, or use of crossbows. Included are sufferers of lung disease, cardiovascular disease, and the visually handicapped, as well as those with specified ambulatory disabilities. A review procedure is required for these permits, and other applicable licenses must also be held. Assistants may be authorized to field dress, tag and retrieve game for the permit holder. An appeal process using licensed physicians is available.] If the Department issues approvals for any of the following, a nonrefundable processing fee, in addition to the license fee, shall be collected: hunter's choice deer permit; bobcat hunting and trapping permit; otter and fisher trapping permits; Canada goose or wild turkey hunting permit (29.09). [License fees for numerous resident and nonresident license types and stamps are given in 29.092. Unusual license categories include those for husband and wife, family, hunter education course fee, and sturgeon spearing, and various combination license categories.] A fishing license applicant, in addition to the license fee, may make a voluntary $1 contribution to be used for lake research. A senior citizen recreation card and a conservation patron license are available. In addition to the fees for licenses, an applicant for a resident small game, deer, bear, archer or nonresident annual small game, five-day small game, deer, bear, fur-bearing animal, archer or resident sports license shall pay a wildlife damage surcharge of $1. The surcharge shall be collected as are other approval fees and deposited in the Conservation Fund to be used for the Wildlife Damage Abatement Program, the Wildlife Damage Claim Program and for removal activities of the Department under 29.59 (29.092). [Effective periods of licenses, permits, stamps and certificates and certain restrictions on license issuance are given in 29.093.]

No one may hunt waterfowl without a conservation patron license or a waterfowl hunting stamp unless exempt from license requirements. The Department shall expend 67% of the waterfowl hunting stamp revenues for developing, managing, preserving, restoring and maintaining wetland habitat and for producing waterfowl and ecologically related species of wildlife. The remaining 33% shall go for the development of waterfowl propagation areas within Canada which will provide waterfowl for this state and the Mississippi flyway, and be provided to nonprofit organizations with approved projects (29.102). A pheasant hunting stamp is required under similar restrictions, the fees to be deposited in the Conservation Fund (29.1025). A wild turkey hunting stamp and a turkey hunting license are required, unless specifically exempt, and in addition a turkey hunting permit for certain wild turkey hunting zones. Up to 30% of such licenses may be allocated to landowners through the landowner preference system if they own at least 50 acres in the turkey zone and allow others to hunt wild turkeys with permission [additional details of preference system are given] (29.103). Special deer hunting and other permit/license types are available for persons with disabilities. Landowner preference is available for deer hunting permits in deer management areas under a system similar to that for wild turkey permits (29.107). No person may shoot, kill, take or possess a bear without a bear harvest permit and bear hunting license issued under a preference system, fees from which shall be paid into the conservation fund for administering the licenses and for bear management activities (29.1085). [Numerous license and permit types are discussed in detail in the statutes.] Each person to whom a hunting or trapping license has been issued, when requested to do so by the Department, shall report the number and kind of each animal taken and other required information (19.125).

A trapping license authorizes trapping fur-bearing animals and is required if engaged in trapping or employed by a trapper. Traps must be tagged, or they shall be seized and confiscated, and trappers must report annually the number and value of each variety of animals taken during the year. All shipments of hides must be marked as to number and type, and show the shipper's license number. No person may molest or take a trap or animal from a lawfully placed trap belonging to another. Violation: fine of $300 to $1,000, or jail up to 90 days, or both, and the court shall revoke all licenses issued for five years (29.13).

Nonresident and resident two-day sportsfishing license fees shall be deposited in the Conservation Fund for use as specified. Nonresidents must have a fishing license (29.14). [Numerous nonresident fishing license categories are given.] Except for residents under 16 years of age, certain senior citizens and certain physically and mentally handicapped persons, no resident may fish in state waters without a fishing license (29.145). Husband and wife resident fishing licenses, sports combination licenses, and conservation patron licenses are available to residents subject to age and tag purchase requirements (29.146, 29.147 and 29.1475). A sturgeon spearing license is available to applicants at least 14 years of age or holders of a conservation patron license, allowing to spear rock or lake sturgeon during the open season. A tag, issued with the license, must be attached. No person may fish in inland waters for trout without an inland waters trout stamp or unless otherwise excepted. Moneys from trout stamp sales shall be spent on improving and maintaining trout habitat in inland trout waters (29.148 and .149). No person may fish in outlying waters as defined for trout or salmon (coho and chinook) without a trout/salmon stamp except as otherwise specified, and funds from such stamp shall be expended to enhance the existing trout and salmon rearing and stocking program for outlying waters. The Department may set certain days for fishing events which require no license (29.15 and .155).

Restrictions on Taking: Hunting and Trapping

A person casting the rays of light on a field, forest or other area which is frequented by wild animals is presumed to be shining wild animals. "Shining" means casting rays of a light on a field or forest for the purpose of illuminating, locating or attempting such of wild animals. No person may use or possess with intent to use a light for shining deer or bear or wild animals while hunting, or in possession of a firearm, bow and arrow or crossbow, except for Department or police officials or persons conducting a game census. A person may use a flashlight while hunting on foot raccoons, foxes or other unprotected animals during the open season. No person may use a light for shining wild animals between 10 p.m. and 7 a.m., September 15 to December 31, except the above excepted persons or a person who uses a flashlight while on foot and training a dog to track or hunt raccoons, foxes or other unprotected animals. A county may restrict the use of lights for shining wild animals, but the ordinance may not be less restrictive than the provisions herein. A county may provide up to a $1,000 fine for violation of a shining ordinance. Statutory violation for shining deer or bear: fine of $1,000-2,000, or jail up to 6 months, or both, and in addition the court shall order revocation of all licenses issued for three years. Violation of other shining provisions: fine up to $1,000 (29.245).

No person shall hunt or trap within a game or wildlife refuge nor possess or control a gun or rifle unless unloaded and enclosed within a carrying case. Taking predatory game animals and birds shall be done as the Department directs. All state game or wildlife refuge boundary lines shall be posted as specified (29.56). No person shall hunt with the aid of an airplane, to spot, rally or drive animals for hunters on the ground. No person shall hunt within 1,700 feet of a hospital, school grounds or sanatorium. The Department may furnish signs designating the restricted area and no conviction shall be had unless the restricted area is designated by signs. ★★No person may hunt deer unless there is attached to the center of the person's coat or shirt where it can clearly be seen the back tag issued authorizing the hunting of deer (29.23 and .22).★★

A person who, while hunting, discharges a firearm or arrow, and thereby injures or kills another, shall give his or her name to the injured person and render assistance, obtain immediate medical aid and immediately report the injury or death to the sheriff or police of the accident locality. Intentional violation: fine up to $5,000, or jail up to one year, or both; negligent violation: fine up to $5,000, or jail up to 9 months, or both. Every person who shall have caused or been involved in such accident, or who shall have inflicted an injury upon themselves with firearm or bow and arrow while hunting or trapping, shall report to the Department within 10 days after the injury or designate an agent to do so. Violation: fine up to $50, and the court may revoke a license for a period deemed just (29.221 and .222).

A person who kills a deer shall immediately attach a current validated deer carcass tag. No person may possess, store or transport a deer carcass unless so tagged, the tag to remain attached until butchering and retained until the meat is consumed. Deer meat may be given by a person who retains a tag to another. The head and skin of a deer lawfully killed, when severed from the carcass, are not subject to these provisions, but no person shall possess the green head or skin of a deer for 30 days after the close of the open season and opening of the next season, or at any time a deer head in the velvet, or a deer skin in the red, blue or spotted coat (fawn). ★A deer taken during an open season for hunting antlered deer only or for hunting antlerless deer only from which the antlers have been removed, broken, shed or altered so as to make determination of the deer's legality impossible is an illegal deer.★ Deer killed accidentally by motor vehicles may be retained once tagged by a conservation warden (29.40). ★★Two or more hunters hunting in a group, all using firearms, and each of whom holds an individual deer license may as individuals kill a deer for another group member if the following conditions are met: at the time and place of the kill, the person who kills the deer is in visual or voice contact (without mechanical/electronic aid) with the person for whom the deer is killed; the person for whom the deer is killed possesses a current unused deer carcass tag authorized for that type of deer. A person who kills a deer hereunder shall ensure that a member of the party attaches a current deer tag, and the person who kills the deer may not leave it unattended until after it is tagged (29.405).★★

No person may: possess the skin of a mink, muskrat, fisher, pine marten or otter showing that the animal was shot; possess the green skin of a fur-bearing animal, except beaver, from the 5th day after the season close until the end of that season; possess the raw skin of a muskrat, mink, otter, fisher or pine marten at any time without a scientific collector permit, fur dealer license, trapping license or conservation patron license. No license is required for breeding domestic fur-bearing animals in captivity under 29.579 or for a person authorized to take muskrats on a cranberry marsh under Department permit (29.41).

Except as otherwise provided, it is unlawful to use baits containing poison in forests, fields or other places where it might destroy wild animals or birds, and possession of such poison or baits in a hunting or trapping camp or on a person while hunting or trapping shall be prima facie evidence of a violation. No person may take, capture or kill, or attempt to do so, a wild animal with the aid of an explosive or poison gas or set same near or on beaver or muskrat houses, except that a landowner or government highway maintenance agency with property subject to beaver damage may possess explosives near beaver houses for destroying beaver dams within beaver damage control areas as otherwise provided. Possession of an explosive or a poison gas in these places is prima facie evidence of intent to violate this provision. Violation: fine of $300, or jail up to 30 days, or both. It is unlawful to take, capture or kill, or attempt to do so, a bird by setting or operating a trap designed, built or used to capture birds on a pole, post, tree stump or other elevated perch more than three feet above the ground. This does not prevent the Department from using dynamite near beaver houses for their removal when damage is being caused to property owners (29.60).

The Department shall regulate waterfowl blinds and fishing shanties on ice, and such structures may be declared nuisances and seized and destroyed if they do not comply with rules as to labeling and removal by certain dates. Failure to remove or erect a waterfowl blind at the proper time on state property is a fine of $10-200. Owners are liable for the cost of removal of fishing shanties declared to be public nuisances (29.27 and .283).

Restrictions on Taking: Fishing

No person shall possess or control a trammel, gill, or hoop net, or other kind of net or fish trap in designated counties, except minnow nets and traps, whitefish and cisco nets, dip nets, crab traps and turtle traps as provided by law or rule, except for Department employees or contract fishers under Department supervision (29.286). A person owning all land bordering on a navigable lake that is completely landlocked may apply for a permit to remove, destroy or introduce fish. The Department shall hold a public hearing in the lake's vicinity, and may issue a permit authorizing such, subject to Department conditions. All work done shall be under Department supervision, and agents shall be afforded free access to the lake at all times, expenses paid by the permittee, and all fish removed turned over to the Department (29.513).

No person may take, capture or kill fish or game of any variety in state waters by dynamite or other explosives or poisonous or stupefying substances or devices; or place in state waters explosives which might cause destruction of fish or game except for raising dead bodies as ordered by public authorities, or for clearing a channel or breaking a log or ice jam; or have in possession or control, upon inland waters, any dynamite, explosive or poisonous or stupefying substances for taking, catching or killing fish or game. Violation; fine up to $500, jail up to 90 days, or both. No person shall use, set, or lay in state waters lime, poison, fish berries or other substance deleterious to fish life. No person may throw or deposit, or permit same, into state waters lime, oil, tar, garbage, refuse, tanbark, ship ballast, stone, sane, slabs, sawdust, planing mill shavings or waste material, or acids, chemicals or waste arising from manufacturing or other substance deleterious to game or fish life other than authorized drainage and sewage from municipalities and industrial or other wastes discharged from mines or ore or commercial or industrial processing plants or operations through treatment and disposal facilities installed and operated under plans approved by the Department under Chapter 1244. Violation: fine up to $200, and each day of continuing violation is a separate offense. Intentional violation is fine up to $200, jail up to 90 days, or both. The Department, after public hearing, may promulgate rules governing any pesticide which it finds is a serious hazard to wild animals other than those it is intended to control. The Department shall consider the need for pesticides to protect the well-being of the general public. It shall obtain the recommendation of the Pesticide Review Board and such rules, other than rules to protect groundwater, are not effective until approved by that board (29.29).

Nets and setlines may be used for taking fish, subject to statutory restrictions, but no person shall set, place or use in state waters a net, trap, snare, set hook, or setline intended to take or kill fish, other than a landing net, dip net, or minnow dip net, without a license. Rough fish caught in nets shall not be returned to waters, but buried, sold or otherwise lawfully disposed of. No fish shall be taken or retained in a net other than those authorized to be taken in such nets, and other fish taken shall be immediately returned with as little injury as possible (29.30). [Extensive details are given in related sections concerning net use in various state waters, including virtually unique definitions of types of nets and their uses in 29.336. It is presumed that this information relates to commercial fishing. Material on clamming and license types appears in 29.38.]

★★A person fishing in state waters shall deliver on demand, to the Department, agents or wardens, all kinds of fish, during the spawning season, for stripping of their eggs and milt, and the fish shall be returned to the owner after stripping. A person shall permit the Department, wardens, or agents to enter boats, grounds or other places where such fish may be, for stripping while alive, and shall render assistance to expedite mixing the eggs and milt.★★   No Department employee while catching wild fish from public waters for artificial propagation shall take or possess fish other than those directed to take. No person shall remove fish eggs or live fish from the state without a permit, except as authorized (29.51). It is unlawful to enter the grounds of a state hatchery to kill or take fish, or to kill, take or catch fish from grounds or waters which the person knew or should have known belong to a state hatchery, or intentionally or negligently injure fish or interfere with ponds, streams or state fish hatchery property (29.515).

Commercial and Private Enterprise Provisions

Licenses and/or permits, with or without fee, are required for guides and sport trolling, trapping, fur dealing and taxidermy, commercial fishing and clamming and wholesale fish dealers, bait dealers, and fish hatcheries, bird and game farms, and for captive wildlife and scientific collectors. There are separate licenses or permits for deer farms, venison serving and retailers, and wildlife exhibitors (29.092).

No person shall engage in the business of buying, bartering, bargaining, trading or otherwise obtaining raw furs without a fur dealer license. Fur auctioneers must be licensed. All licensees must keep detailed records, and all shipments of furs must be labeled as required. All beaver and otter skins shipped into the state from Canada or elsewhere must be shown to the Department or wardens and be stamped or tagged as required. Persons may buy raw or dressed furs for personal garment manufacture with a permit. Violation: fine up to $1000, jail up to nine months, or both. Wholesale fish dealers must be licensed and must comply with [extensive] provisions as to record keeping, tagging and labeling, and inspections. Such licensees may not sell, buy, barter, possess or transport rock or lake sturgeon. Persons mounting or preserving wild animal carcasses for consideration must have a taxidermy permit and a seller's permit to possess and transport wild animals and carcasses regardless of bag limits, rest days, and closed seasons, granting the same privileges as a Class A fur dealer's license. Commingling of carcasses is not allowed, and records must be kept as required and inspections of premises allowed. ★★The Department shall issue a taxidermy school permit to persons who hold a taxidermy permit and who wish to operate a school, authorizing the holder to purchase muskellunge, bass, bluegill, sunfish, crappie, rock bass or northern pike, or their carcasses, from persons who caught the fish and to resell the fish only to students enrolled in a taxidermy course at the taxidermy school. The permit shall limit the number of each species of fish that the school operator may possess on any given date to the number needed for its two-year course, beginning on that date. Tagging and inspection requirements must be complied with. Violation: first conviction, fine up to $25; second or subsequent conviction within three years, fine of $25-500 (29.134 through .136).★★

A bait dealer license may be issued to residents who have complied with Department rules governing taking, handling and storage of bait, equipment, and reports. No person shall engage in the business of bait dealer without a license [exceptions for children provided]. The Department may issue permits for taking bait from specified waters and restrict the number of permits for a body of water, except for bait produced in a private fish hatchery. One who molests, damages, or takes the bait traps of another shall be fined up to $100 (29.137).

No person may engage or be employed for compensation or reward to guide, direct or assist in hunting, fishing or trapping without a guide license. No guide license may be issued to nonresidents nor to persons under age 18. Violation: fine up to $100 and revocation of license for one year. A sport trolling license for trout or salmon on outlying waters of the Great Lakes is required for guides, and records must be kept as specified (29.165 and .166).

The Department may issue pheasant and quail farm licenses for shooting preserves and the releasing, shooting, possession and use of pheasants and quail on the farms if the operations will result in a net increase in the supply of such birds in the state and will be in the public interest. Applicants must own or lease the area and must post the boundaries. The Department shall determine the minimum number of pheasants and quail to be released for shooting and fix time limits during which birds may be hunted. Small game licensees and their designates may hunt, possess and dispose of as gifts such pheasants or quail. Persons hunting on a licensed shooting preserve do not need a hunting license for species for which the preserve has been licensed. Records must be kept, birds tagged before removal, and only birds killed by shooting may be removed. Violation: fine of up to $300. Unauthorized hunters are liable for damages to the preserve or birds, but actions for trespass shall be brought by the licensee (29.573).

The owner of lands suitable for breeding and propagating of game, birds or animals as may be approved by the Department shall have the right to establish, operate and maintain a game bird and animal farm for breeding, propagating, killing and selling game birds and animals, the acreage to be determined by the Department. All waterfowl bred or held shall be held in a covered enclosure throughout the waterfowl open hunting season as required. The applicant shall file with the Department a verified declaration, describing the lands and other details as required, and must purchase all wild game within the boundaries of the proposed farm of the species designated in the license, and the Department shall appoint one member, the applicant one member and these two shall select a third member to act as a board to go upon the lands and determine the number of wild birds and animals of the desired species at the time of license granting. The licensee shall pay the Department a specified sum for those species desired for propagation, after which the licensee shall become the owner of the wild game birds or animals and their offspring produced on the farm and remaining thereon, subject to the jurisdiction of the Department over game. Game birds and animals, except waterfowl, upon game farms may be taken at any time in any manner by persons qualified to hunt thereon, without a license, as specified. Waterfowl may be taken according to Department rules. Live birds and animals may be sold or transported. [Extensive details of bird tagging, records, and sale and transport provisions are given.] Unauthorized hunting on such farm is a fine of $100, in addition to damages to the farm or to birds, animals or property, action to be brought by the licensee. The owner/lessee of lands suitable for breeding and propagation of fur animals may by following a similar procedure to that above, apply for a license for a fur animal farm for one or more of the following animals: beaver; muskrat; mink, except domestic mink; otter; raccoon; and skunk. A similar "board" shall assess the number of wild fur animals on the property [fees for each detailed]. The licensee has the right to manage and control the lands and the licensed fur animals, to take same at any time or in any manner to the best advantage of the business, and to sell and transport at any time such animals or their pelts (29.574 and .575). [Penalties, required records, and investigation of the proposed fur farm lands for licensing are similar to those for those for game bird and animal farms.]

★★A similar application procedure allows a landowner to establish, operate and maintain a deer farm for breeding, killing, propagating and selling deer, to be completely enclosed by a fence as prescribed by the Department. The licensee shall pay the Department $25 for each wild deer found on the land, and then becomes the owner of the deer and of their offspring, and may sell and kill them. Deer on a deer farm shall be killed only by the licensee or employees, or as authorized, without a hunting license, and must be tagged. The licensee must notify the Department in advance of taking of deer, and shall pay $1 for each deer killed. Only the entire carcass shall be sold or transported. In case of revocation of the deer farm license for failure to comply with these or Department provisions or other cause, the court shall provide that title to all deer on the farm and their progeny be forfeited to the state and that the land shall not be used for a deer farm for five years, and that until relicensed, the fences shall be opened for free egress of the animals, and the lands shall be a sanctuary and no hunting or trapping practiced thereon. A venison serving permit is required to serve venison from a licensed deer farm, under Department regulations, and the Department may issue a special retail deer sale permit authorizing to retail venison in the carcass from a deer lawfully killed under this section to a retailer of meats. The Department may sell to deer farm licensees for propagating fawns and deer at a price to be fixed, not to exceed $25 each, and the Department shall make orders and promulgate necessary rules to carry out deer farm provisions to the end that the industry may be encouraged (29.578). [Extensive details relating to unauthorized hunting on deer farms, compliance with license provisions, reporting requirements, deer transportation and tagging, posting of boundaries, and other details are given.]★★

★[There is also provision for commercial deer farm licensing, with a similar application procedure.] Such commercial farms must be completely fenced according to Department specifications and all white-tailed deer within the boundaries of the commercial deer farm must be driven outside the farm's boundaries. Records must be kept [details provided]. The Department may inspect deer, records, vehicles, equipment and buildings related to the farm during business hours, and the licensee may not prohibit such inspection (29.58).★ ★★No person may sell to consumers venison from a commercial deer farm without a venison retailer permit, nor purchase, possess, transport such venison for sale. A person over age 18 is eligible for such permit. The Department shall have similar inspection privileges for licensees of records, vehicles, equipment, buildings and structures as are required for commercial deer farms, and no consent is necessary for an inspection warrant to be issued.★★ The Department may seize and dispose of or authorize the disposal of a deer that has escaped from regular or commercial deer farms if the licensee has not had the deer returned within 72 hours of discovery, and may dispose of the deer immediately if it poses a risk to public safety or to the health of other domestic or wild animals. (29.583).

The Department may grant licenses for wildlife exhibits. "Wild animal" as used herein means any mammal, fish or bird of a wild nature as distinguished from domestic animals under the common law or state statutes, whether or not bred or reared in captivity. These provisions do not include exhibition of wild animals by public zoos, parks, state agencies, educational institutions or circuses or exhibitions sponsored by organizations with Department approval. The Department shall promulgate and enforce rules and regulations for housing, care, treatment, feeding and sanitation of wild animals kept in exhibits and for protection of the public from injury. No person may keep a live wild animal in captivity for exhibition or advertising, or have a wild animal in custody or control for such purpose without a license, in addition to a game bird and animal farm, deer farm license, or fur farm license required for the possession, breeding, propagating or dealing in these wild animals if these farms are wildlife exhibits. Reports are required. The Department has authority to examine all lands and buildings licensed as game, fur or deer farms to determine that wild animals held in captivity are treated in a humane manner and confined under sanitary conditions with proper housing, care and food, and may order a licensee to comply with prescribed standards as contained in an official order. Failure to comply within 10 days subjects the licensee to a fine up to $100 (29.585 and .586).

The breeding, raising and producing in captivity, and marketing by the producer, of foxes, fitch, nutria, marten, fisher, mink, chinchilla, rabbit or caracul, as live animals, or as animal pelts or carcasses is an agricultural pursuit, and animals so raised deemed domestic animals, subject to state laws governing domestic animal activities, and persons raising same are farmers for statutory purposes (29.579).

Private fish hatcheries may be licensed by the Department if the land and water areas to be included are approved and meet Department specifications. Waters must be artificially constructed unless excepted by the Department and screened as required. Several private fish hatchery license types are available, according to the size of the lands and the type of activities. Private hatcheries may not be stocked with fish or fry obtained from a state-owned hatchery or from state waters unless taken lawfully, nor may they stock unlicensed lakes or streams with live fish other than trout without a permit for planting or stocking. Trespassing on a private hatchery is a fine of $200 if boundaries are posted (29.52). [Extensive details are given for each license type and as to license application procedure.]

Import, Export and Release Provisions

No person may bring into the state for stocking or introducing any fish or spawn or any wild bird or animal without a Department permit. Permits to import fish or spawn of the family salmonidae, including trout, char or salmon, may be issued only if the source is certified free of diseases. Imported fish or spawn under a permit are subject to inspection and removal of specimens for biological examination, and the Department may seize and destroy fish or spawn infected with designated disease organisms. This does not prohibit the Department or its agents from importing for planting, or stocking any fish, bird or animal, nor does it apply to civic organizations, news media, television stations or promoters of sport shows in connection with demonstrations of trout for periods of up to 10 days. Brook, brown or rainbow trout used for such purposes shall be obtained only from private fish hatchery operators and records kept (29.535). The Department may take or purchase wild mammals and birds and eggs for propagation. Distribution shall be made throughout the state under the Department's supervision and rules. No person shall take, remove, sell or transport from state waters to any place outside the state any duck potato, wild celery or other plant except wild rice native in such waters and commonly known to furnish food for game birds (29.54). [Wild rice and Ginseng, licensing, harvest and conservation provisions are provided.] No live rough fish except goldfish, dace and suckers shall be transported into or within the state without a permit, except a person holding a state contract to remove rough fish may transport rough fish under that contract's authority, and licensed taxidermists may transport fish in connection with their business (29.47).

No person may possess a live wild skunk unless authorized under 29.55, except temporarily to control the skunk for removal, transportation, game censuses or other Department purposes. No person may possess a live domestic skunk raised on a licensed fur animal farm unless authorized, except temporarily to control the skunk. The governing body of a county or town may prohibit a person from possessing or selling live wild or domestic skunk. No person may sell live wild skunk except as permitted, and records must be kept. ★★A person who sells live skunk shall inform the purchaser that the release of a skunk is illegal and that the seller will accept the return of the skunk. No person may operate on a live wild skunk to remove its scent glands unless authorized under 29.55, and a veterinarian to whom a person brings a wild skunk for such operation shall notify that person that possession of a live skunk is illegal and shall notify the Department. No person may release a domestic skunk into the environment.★★ A person may kill a wild skunk which is a nuisance to activities pertaining to game, deer, fur or other game farms as specified. ★A person who kills an adult wild skunk with young shall attempt to kill the young skunks.★ Violation: fine of $100-1,000 (29.427).

Interstate Reciprocal Agreements

★★Whenever any other state confers upon the officers of this state reciprocal powers, an officer of the other state authorized to enforce laws relating to wild animal protection is an agent of that state within this state. It shall be lawful for the officer to follow a wild animal, carcass or part unlawfully shipped or taken from the officer's state into this state, seize and convey it back to the officer's state; and so far as concerns any such wild animal, carcass or part, the laws of the state from which the it was brought into this state are adopted as the laws of this state. Transportation companies shall deliver to such officer any wild animal, carcass or part so demanded or seized by the officer, who may dispose of it within this state in accordance with the laws of the state from which it was taken or shipped, under supervision of the Department or wardens. Expenses for such assistance shall be a lien upon the wild animal, carcass or part, or the proceeds thereof. Except as provided, the Department or wardens shall seize, hold and dispose of a wild animal, carcass or part brought or shipped into or through this state in violation of the laws of any other state. The state game warden of every other state, and deputies and all other officers charged with enforcement of wildlife laws are designated agents of this state for taking possession, seizing, holding and disposing, within such state, of a wild animal, carcass or part, protected by state laws. Whenever and so long as any other state confers upon the officers of this state reciprocal powers, the Department may appoint persons who have been appointed game wardens or deputy game wardens of such other state to act as and have all the powers of wardens of this state, but without compensation (29.08). The Department may regulate hunting and fishing on and in all interstate boundary waters, and outlying waters as specified, and any Department act shall be valid, all other provisions of the statutes notwithstanding, provided powers are exercised pursuant to 23.09 and 29.174 (29.085). ★★

Whenever and so long as the states of Michigan, Minnesota or Iowa confer reciprocal rights, privileges and immunities to Wisconsin licensees, a hook and line or other fishing license issued by the other state shall entitle the licensee to such rights and privileges in and upon the boundary waters between that state and Wisconsin as enjoyed by Wisconsin licensees, subject to the duties, responsibilities and liabilities imposed on its own licensees by the laws of this state (29.16).

ANIMAL DAMAGE CONTROL

★★"Damage" herein means harm to forest products, streams, roads, dams, buildings, orchards, apiaries, livestock and commercial agricultural crops, including Christmas trees and nursery stock [other definitions provided]. The Department may remove or authorize removal of: a wild animal causing damage or a nuisance; a structure of a wild animal causing damage or a nuisance. Within 48 hours after receipt of a written complaint from a person who owns, leases or occupies property on which a wild animal or its structure is allegedly causing damage, the Department shall investigate the complaint and may remove or authorize removal of the animal or structure if it finds that it is causing property damage. A person who owns or leases property outside an incorporated municipality on which a wild animal or its structure is allegedly causing damage and who has made a complaint may remove the animal or structure during daylight hours if all of these conditions apply: the Department has failed, within 48 hours after receipt of the complaint, to investigate and determine whether to authorize removal or not; the Department has not refused to investigate as permitted; the wild animal is not endangered or threatened and is not a migratory bird. A person who owns, leases or occupies property located within an incorporated municipality on which a wild animal or its structure is causing damage may capture; and relocate the wild animal or structure if a complaint has been made and the above conditions are met. Upon receipt of a complaint, the Department may investigate and may remove or authorize removal of animal or structure if it finds that a nuisance is being caused, whereupon the landowner shall open the property to others for hunting and trapping for one year from when the removal activity started unless hunting is prohibited under law or rule or city ordinance. The Department may refuse to investigate complaints if the person refuses to participate in any available wildlife damage abatement program or to follow reasonable abatement measures recommended by the Department (29.59). ★★

★★A person who owns, leases or occupies property on which a beaver or structure is causing damage and who fails or refuses to give consent to the Department to remove it is liable for damage caused by the beaver or structure to public property or the property of others. The landowner owes no duty to keep the property safe for removal activities and no duty to inspect the property nor warn those entering the property to engage in a removal activity. Such landowner is immune from liability as specified herein; nor is the landowner liable for injuries to, nor caused by, persons engaging in removal activities; nor does the common law attractive nuisance doctrine create any duty of care or ground of liability toward a person using the private property for removal activities unless malicious failure to warn exists as specified herein (29.59). ★★ [Other details are given.]

★★As used in Wildlife Damage Abatement Program provisions, "wildlife damage" means damage caused by wild deer, bear or geese to commercial seedings or crops on agricultural land, orchard trees or nursery stock or to apiaries or livestock. The Department shall assist counties in developing and administering the Wildlife Damage Abatement and Wildlife Damage Claim programs, and shall provide technical aid, program guidance, research, demonstrations, funding, plan review, audit and evaluation services. The Department shall provide guidelines to counties applying for participation in the programs, and review each plan submitted and approved. The Department shall provide funding to each county participating in either or both programs for administration of these programs. Eligibility for the programs requires participation of the county in the administration of the programs. Counties seeking to participate shall apply on Department forms by November 1, and shall include a plan of administration, including: ▸ an agreement that the county shall make all records relating to programs, including access of hunters to lands for which damage claims are filed, available to the Department for audit; ▸ a description of authorized wildlife damage abatement measures; ▸ a summary of billing and accounting procedures; ▸ a commitment that the county agrees to administer programs so that participants are encouraged to pursue sound conservation as well as normal agricultural practices; ▸ a summary of agency organization for administration; ▸ an estimate of anticipated administrative, abatement costs, and damage claim payments; ▸ other information the Department requires. In order to be eligible for damage abatement assistance, the land must be in a participant county, proper forms must be filed and other eligibility requirements met. The county shall review each application for damage abatement assistance to determine if wildlife damage is occurring or likely to occur, and may provide reimbursement of costs associated with abatement measures, or for a woven wire deer fence as specified. The Department may pay participating counties up to 50% of the actual cost of assistance. In order to be eligible for wildlife damage claim payments, the land must be in a participating county, the claim for damages made within 14 days after damage first occurs, the person seeking damages shall comply with damage abatement measures recommended by the county; hunting must be allowed by the landowner and on contiguous land under the same ownership and control. If hunting is not permitted, the damage claim payments shall be reduced as provided. The land must be open to hunting by the public or at least two persons per 40 acres suitable for hunting must be permitted to hunt each day during the open season, and the land must either not be posted against hunting or be posted for hunting by permission only. A participating county shall investigate each claim and determine the amount of the wildlife damage. No person may receive a damage claim payment unless approved by the county; nor receive a payment in excess of the actual amount of the damage or $5,000, whichever is less; nor receive payment for the first $250 of each claim for wildlife damage; nor receive payment for damages to seedings or crops not managed or harvested in accordance with normal agricultural practices; the payment shall be reduced by an amount equal to payments received from persons hunting on the land. The Department shall pay participating counties from appropriations as specified herein. A participating county shall obtain from a person who is required to permit hunting an affidavit so stating. Nothing herein prohibits a person who owns, leases or occupies land on which wildlife damage occurs, and who does not have authority to control entry on the land for hunting from seeking wildlife damage abatement assistance or wildlife damage claim payments (29.59).★★

The Department may enter into contracts with public or private agencies for accelerated research and development of a specific toxic material for control and eradication of carp in state waters (23.093).

See Import, Export, Release Provisions under HUNTING, FISHING, TRAPPING PROVISIONS.

ENFORCEMENT OF WILDLIFE LAWS

Enforcement Powers

The Department and wardens may execute and serve warrants and processes issued under a law enumerated herein in the same manner as a constable may serve and execute the process, and may arrest, with or without warrant, a person detected in the actual violation, or whom the officer has probable cause to believe has violated any laws cited herein, whether the violation is punishable by criminal penalties or civil forfeiture, and may take the person before a court in the county where the offense was committed and make complaint. Officers may stop and board any boat and stop an automobile, snowmobile or other vehicle to enforce laws cited herein, and if the officer reasonably suspects there is a violation of those sections. [Additional provisions for warrants and arrests involving field archaeology, racial harassment are given.] In addition to these arrest powers, a conservation warden who has completed training approved by the law enforcement standards board and has been certified as qualified to be a law enforcement officer while on duty and in uniform, or on duty and upon display of credentials, may assist another law enforcement agency, including arresting at the request of the agency, may arrest pursuant to an arrest warrant concerning a felony or may arrest one who has committed a crime in the warden's presence. If such arrest is made without the presence of another law enforcement agency, the warden shall take the person to the chief of police or sheriff in the arresting jurisdiction. The conservation warden shall be available as a witness for the state, but may not conduct investigations for violations of state law except as authorized herein and in 23.11(4). A conservation warden acting under this authority is considered a Department employee and subject to its direction, benefits and legal protection. This does not apply to county conservation wardens or special conservation wardens. Department agents, after reasonable efforts to notify the owner/occupant, may enter upon private lands to retrieve, diagnose or otherwise determine if there are dead or diseased wild animals, and take actions necessary to prevent the spread of contagious disease. Upon receiving notice or information of violations, conservation officers shall make a thorough investigation as soon as possible and cause proceedings to be instituted (29.05).

★In the performance of duty, wardens may operate Department vehicles on highways as designated without lighted headlamps or tail lamps, to aid in a lawful arrest or in ascertaining whether a violation of this chapter or rules has been or is about to be committed.★ The Department and wardens may examine and open a package in the possession of a common carrier when there is probable cause to believe contraband wild animals, carcasses or parts are contained therein. Cold storage warehouse owners shall permit wardens to enter and examine the premises, and the owner or employee shall deliver a wild animal, carcass or part possessed during the closed season, taken within or without the state. wardens shall seize and confiscate a wild animal, carcass or part caught, killed, taken, possessed, sold or transported in violation of this chapter, and with or without warrant, may open, enter and examine all buildings, camps, boats, or vehicles where there is probable cause to believe that wild animals taken or held in violation, are to be found. wardens shall seize and hold subject to court order in the county in which the alleged offense was committed any apparatus, appliance, vehicle or device, declared by this chapter to be a public nuisance, when there is probable cause to believe it is used in violation. ★If it is proven that within six months before seizure, the device or vehicle was used in violation, it shall be confiscated if the court so directs.★ Perishable property seized may be sold at the highest available price, and proceeds turned into the court to await case disposition. A conservation warden or other officer may kill a dog found running, injuring, or killing a deer, or destroying game birds, eggs or nests, if immediate action is necessary to protect them from injury or death. Members of the Natural Resources Board and wardens shall be exempt from liability for acts done or property destroyed by law, in the performance of their duties, and shall be represented by the district attorney of the county in which the action is commenced. No taxable costs or attorney fees shall be allowed to either party (29.05).

All confiscated wild animals, carcasses or parts and apparatus or devices, if not destroyed as authorized, shall be sold at the highest obtainable price, and the net proceeds remitted to the Department with documentation. Of such proceeds, 18% shall be paid into the Conservation Fund to reimburse it for expenses incurred in seizure and sale, and the remaining 82% shall be paid into the common school fund. Confiscated motor vehicles shall be sold within 20 days after judgment of confiscation. Confiscated fish or game sold to restaurants or clubs may be served to the guests, if the certificate of purchase is publicly displayed (29.06). All sheriffs, deputy sheriffs, coroners and other police officers are deputy conservation wardens, and shall assist the Department and its wardens in the enforcement of this chapter whenever notice of a violation is given to any of them (29.07). (See also Interstate Reciprocal Agreements under HUNTING, FISHING, TRAPPING PROVISIONS.)

[Details of procedures in forfeiture actions, complaints, citations, natural resources assessments and restitutions, arrests with and without warrant, searches of various types, and court proceedings which are relevant for all violations of natural resources provisions, including game and fish violations, are given in sections 23.50 through 23.99 under Chapter 23, Conservation.]

Criminal Penalties

A person, or agent, servant or employee, who violates this chapter shall be punished as follows: ▸ violation relating to fishing, fish dealing or rules therefor, fine up to $1,000 except as otherwise provided; ▸ illegal possession of fish valued under 29.65 from $300-1,000, a fine up to $5,000, jail up to 30 days or both; ▸ illegal possession of fish valued over $1,000, fine up to $10,000 or jail up to two years, or both (salmon, trout and noncommercial game fish shall be valued per fish according to the dollar amounts under 29.65 [listed under Civil Penalties], and other species of commercial fish shall be valued per fish according to current average wholesale value, the average price received by producers on the date of violation), and failure to hold a license is an additional natural resources restitution payment equal to the license fee; ▸ hunting or trapping without a license, fine of up to $100 and payment of a natural resources restitution payment equal to the license fee; ▸ violation of a law or rule relating to hunting, taking, transportation or possession of game or game birds of all kinds, fine up to $100; ▸ unlawfully hunting a moose, fine of $1,000-2,000 and mandatory revocation of all licenses held, and no new licenses issued for the time specified by the court, which must be not less than three nor more than five years; ▸ a violation of a law or rule for which no other penalty is prescribed, a fine of not less than $100 (29.99).

Additional penalties are: ▸ for illegal sale of game or birds or parts under 29.48, a fine of $1,000-2,000, jail up to 6 months, or both, and the court shall order the revocation of all hunting and fishing licenses and prohibit issuance of same for five years; ▸ violation of 29.49 (illegal sale or serving of game as specified), fine up to $500, jail up to 90 days, or both, and the court shall order revocation of all hunting and fishing licenses for three years; ▸ ★violation of a law or rule relating to staking of lake sturgeon, a fine of $1,500, jail up to 90 days, or both, for each lake sturgeon illegally taken or possessed, and mandatory three-year revocation of all licenses;★ ▸ violation of bag or possession limits under 29.39 for inland waters brook, rainbow, brown or lake trout, or inland water muskellunge, fine of $100-200 per fish in excess of the bag/possession limit, jail up to 30 days, or both; ▸ violation of 29.23 relating to hunting from an airplane or using same to spot, rally or drive animals for hunting, fine up to $1,000 for first violation, and not more than $2,000 for subsequent violations, jail up to 90 days, or both, and mandatory three-year revocation of all hunting, fishing and trapping licenses, and an airplane so used is declared a public nuisance; ▸ violation relating to the registration of a wild animal, fine up to $100; ▸ improper validation of a carcass tag, fine up to $500; ▸ hunting deer without a license, during the closed season, by spotlighting or with the aid of an aircraft, snaring deer, or illegal possession of a deer carcass under 29.39 or 29.40, fine of $1,000-2,000, jail up to 6 months, or both, and the court shall order revocation of all licenses issued under this chapter, and not reissue same for three years; ▸ failure to reimburse the Department for removal of hunting blinds or ice shanties, fine up to $100. "Person" includes natural persons, firms, associations and corporations. ★No penalty prescribed in this chapter shall be diminished because the violation for which it is prescribed falls also within a more general prohibition.★ In a prosecution under this section it is not necessary for the state to allege or prove that the animals were not commercially raised deer or domesticated animals, that they were not taken for scientific purposes, or that they were taken or in possession or under control without a required approval, but the person or defendant claiming innocence has the burden of proof (29.99).

★★Penalties relating to bears are: shooting, killing, taking, catching or possessing a bear without a valid bear harvest permit, or possessing an untagged bear carcass, possessing a bear during closed season, a fine of $1,000 -2,000, jail up to 6 months, or both for the first violation and a fine up to $5,000, jail up to one year, or both for a subsequent violation, and the court shall revoke all hunting licenses for three years; entering the den of a hibernating black bear and harming the bear, a fine up to $10,000, jail up to one year or both, unless such activity was approved by the Department and was necessary to conduct research. For other violations relating to bear hunting or bear tag validation or registration of a bear, a fine up to $1,000 (29.99).★★

★In an action against a person for damages from trespassing on lands bordering streams stocked by the consent of the landowner, with fish received from a state hatchery, where damage shall exceed $2, the trespasser shall be liable for double the amount of such damage and the taxable costs; and where the damage is $2 or less, the trespasser shall be liable for the amount of such damage and costs not to exceed the amount of the damage (29.626).★

A person who assaults or otherwise resists or obstructs a conservation warden in the performance of duty shall be fined up to $500, jailed up to 9 months, or both (29.64). A person who falsely represents to be a conservation warden or who assumes to act as such without due appointment shall be fined up to $100, jailed up to 90 days, or both. A person who provides incorrect information for obtaining a license issued to which the person is not entitled, or who alters the correct date of license issuance shall be fined up to $200, jailed up to 90 days, or both, and shall pay a natural resources restitution payment equal to the statutory fee for the approval (license) which should have been obtained. A person who obtains a license during the time when that license is revoked shall be fined up to $200, jailed up to 90 days, or both. A person who breaks, removes or interferes with a seal or tag attached to an animal, carcass, article or other item by the Department, or who interferes with such, or who counterfeits a seal or tag shall be fined up to $500, or jailed up to 90 days, or both. No person, without the owner's permission, shall molest, disturb or appropriate a wild animal, carcass or part which has been lawfully reduced to possession by another (29.64 through .645).

★★If a person is convicted of a violation of this chapter or of a Department order, and it is alleged in the indictment, information or complaint, and proved or admitted on trial or ascertained by the court after conviction that the person was previously convicted within five years for a chapter violation or Department rule by a state court, the person shall be fined up to $100, jailed up to six months, or both, and all hunting, fishing and trapping licenses shall be revoked and no new approvals issued for one year. If the person is shown to have been convicted three times within three years for violations of this chapter or Department order regarding illegal use of explosives, sale of wildlife, illegal fur dealing, or for violation of a statute or rule regulating taking or possession of a wild animal or carcass during the closed season or any combination of such violations by a state court, such person shall be fined up to $2,000, jailed up to 9 months or both. No penalty for such violation may be reduced or diminished by reason of this section.★★ Whoever is a principal in the commission of a chapter violation or Department order for which a fine is imposed may be charged with and convicted of the violation although not directly committing it, and although the person who directly committed it has not been convicted. A person is concerned in the violation if the person: directly commits the violation; aids and abets the commission of it; is a party to a conspiracy with another to commit it or advises, hires or counsels or otherwise procures another to commit it (29.995 and .996).

Civil Penalties

★The Department may bring a civil action in the name of the state for damages against a person unlawfully killing, wounding, catching, taking trapping or unlawfully possessing any of the following protected wild animals, birds, or fish, or part, and the sum assessed for damages for each wild animal, bird or fish shall not be less than the amount stated herein: ▸ an endangered species protected under 29.415, $875; ▸ moose, elk, fisher, prairie chicken or sand hill crane, $262.50; ▸ deer, bear, wild turkey or wild swan, $175; ▸ bobcat, fox, beaver or otter, $87.50; ▸ coyote, raccoon or mink, $43.75; ▸ sharptail grouse, ruffed grouse, spruce hen, wild duck, coot, wild goose or brant, $26.25; ▸ pheasant, Hungarian partridge, quail, rail, Wilson's snipe, woodcock or shore bird, or protected song bird or harmless bird, $17.50; ▸ muskrat, rabbit, squirrel, $8.75; ▸ muskellunge or rock or lake sturgeon, $43.75; ▸ largemouth or smallmouth bass, $26.75; ▸ brook, rainbow, brown or steelhead trout, $26.25; ▸ walleye pike, northern pike, or other game fish not mentioned herein, $8.75. Damages recovered shall be paid into the State Conservation Fund and disbursed by the Department. A civil action shall be a bar to a criminal prosecution for the same offense and a criminal prosecution for an offense under this section shall be a bar to a civil action (29.65).★

Illegal Taking of Wildlife

★★If a court imposes a fine for a violation of a provision of this chapter or rule for unlawful killing, wounding, catching, taking, trapping or possession of a wild animal as specified, or part, the court may impose a wild animal protection assessment that equals the amount specified for a wild animal as follows: ▸ any endangered species under 29.415, $875; ▸ moose, elk, fisher, prairie chicken or sand hill crane, $262.50; ▸ bear, wild turkey, wild swan, $175; ▸ wildcat, fox, beaver, otter, $87.50; ▸ deer, coyote, raccoon, mink, $43.75; ▸ sharptail grouse, ruffed grouse, spruce hen, wild duck, coot, wild goose or brant, $26.25; ▸ pheasant, Hungarian partridge, quail, rail, Wilson's snipe, woodcock or shore bird, or protected song bird or harmless bird, $17.50; ▸ muskrat, rabbit or squirrel, $8.75; ▸ muskellunge, rock sturgeon or lake sturgeon, $43.75; ▸ largemouth or smallmouth bass, $26.25; ▸ brook, rainbow, brown or steelhead trout, 26.25; ▸ walleye pike, northern pike, any other game fish not mentioned above, $8.75; ▸ a game or fur-bearing animal or bird not mentioned above, $17.50. If a fine or forfeiture is suspended in whole or in part, the wild animal protection assessment shall be reduced in proportion to the suspension. If a deposit is made for an offense to which this section applies, the person shall also deposit a sufficient amount to include the wild animal protection assessment. If the deposit is forfeited, the amount of the assessment shall be transmitted to the state treasurer, for deposit into the Conservation Fund (29.9965).★★ If a court imposes a fine relating to ice fishing shanties, it shall impose a fishing shelter removal assessment equal to the costs that should have been reimbursed [additional details are given] (29.9967). ★If a court imposes a fine for a chapter or rule violation where payment of a natural resources restitution is required, the court shall impose a fine equal to the amount of the fee for the license or approval which was required and should have been obtained. [Details of collection, deposit, and reduction of natural resources restitution payment are given.] All moneys collected shall be deposited in the Conservation Fund and appropriated for use under 20.370(3) (29.998).★

See HUNTING, FISHING, TRAPPING PROVISIONS and Civil Penalties under this section.

License Revocations and Suspensions

Upon a second conviction within a three-year period for illegal possession of fish, fishing with illegal gear, fishing in closed areas or refuges, fishing during a closed season, violation of quota fisheries or false reporting, a person licensed under this chapter shall have all fishing and fish dealing licenses revoked and not reissued for at least one year after conviction. During the period of revocation for two convictions of illegal fish possession valued at over $300, the person may not fish in any manner, operate or assist in operation of fishing gear or engage in sale or transportation of fish. The revoked license may not be issued to another during the period of revocation. In addition to any other penalty for violation of this chapter or rule, the court may revoke or suspend any or all privileges and licenses for up to three years. If a person is convicted of reckless or highly negligent conduct in handling a firearm or bow and arrow in violation of 940.08 or 941.20 and either death or bodily harm to another results, the court shall revoke every approval issued and shall provide a fixed period during which no new approval may be issued. If no death or bodily harm results from the violation, the court may revoke a license and may provide a fixed period during which no new license may be issued (29.99).

See HUNTING, TRAPPING, FISHING PROVISIONS and Criminal Penalties under this section.

Reward Payments

★★The Department shall maintain a toll free telephone number at Department headquarters during normal business hours to receive reports of violations of this chapter, and shall relay same to the appropriate warden for investigation and enforcement, such number to be publicized as widely as possible in the state. The Department shall maintain records which permit release of informant information while protecting the identity of the informant, and shall retain same for confidential Department use, unless expressly released by the informant (29.055).★★

See PROTECTED SPECIES OF WILDLIFE and HUNTING, FISHING, TRAPPING PROVISIONS.

HABITAT PROTECTION

★★The owner(s) of any tract, or contiguous tracts, of land not less than 160 acres located outside the limits of a city or village, may apply to the Department for its establishment as a wildlife refuge. If, upon investigation or hearing it appears to the Department that the establishment of such lands as a wildlife refuge will promote the conservation of one or more useful species or varieties native within the state, it may by order designate the lands as a wildlife refuge, and see that the landowners post same. After 30 days notice, the order becomes effective, and thereafter such lands shall be a wildlife refuge and shall so remain for not less than five years. Except as provided in 29.56, no owner of lands embraced within the wildlife refuge, and no other person may hunt or trap within its boundaries or possess or control a gun or rifle unless unloaded and cased as specified, but deer may be hunted in those state parks or portions as designated by the Department. Nothing herein shall prevent or interfere with the Department, wardens or agents in the destruction of injurious animals. The Department may place within any such wildlife refuge, for propagation, wild animals of any species or variety (29.57).★★

The Department may acquire, lease, develop and maintain public hunting and fishing grounds and may agree to pay damages arising from their operation (29.555). A city, town or village, upon direction and supervision of the Department, may appropriate money for and acquire, lease or contract for a land, pond, lake or slough for a fish hatchery, and erect a fish hatchery for hatching, propagating and fishing for game fish. Application procedures must be followed and the Department shall regulate stocking, maintaining and fishing (29.536). Except as provided, no person may hunt or trap on land located in state parks or state fish hatcheries, nor possess a firearm on such lands unless unloaded and in a carrying case. A person may hunt deer or wild turkeys in a state park designated by rule for that type of hunting with the proper licenses (29.557).

★★The Department shall establish an animal wildlife exhibit where wild animals, allowed to roam at will, may be viewed by the public without charge on state owned lands over which the Department has jurisdiction, or upon lands donated to the state for the purpose. The boundary of the area shall be marked at intervals of not over 500 feet, with the words "Wisconsin Wildlife Exhibit Area." The Department shall provide for housing the caretaker and the sheltering, nursing and caring for orphaned wild animals, and may accept private donations of animals, which shall be sheltered and cared for until old enough to release, but by providing food and shelter, efforts shall be made to induce the animals to return to the area year after year. The Department shall employ a caretaker with long experience with wild animals, preferably a retired game warden, to manage the exhibit. No person at any time or in any manner shall hunt or trap within the boundaries, nor possess any gun or rifle unless unloaded and enclosed in a carrying case. The Department may promulgate rules for effective accomplishment of these purposes including the exhibition season (29.565).★★

See Agency Powers and Duties under STATE FISH AND WILDLIFE PROVISIONS and HUNTING, FISHING, TRAPPING PROVISIONS.

NATIVE AMERICAN WILDLIFE PROVISIONS

American Indians hunting, trapping or fishing off Indian reservation lands are subject to the provisions of Chapter 29 (29.025). If a federally recognized American Indian tribe or band consents to the enforcement of its conservation code by the Department or if a federal court order authorizes/directs such enforcement, the Department and its wardens may execute and serve warrants and processes for violations of the tribe's or band's conservation code that occur outside the boundaries of reservations; and may arrest a person, with or without a warrant, detected committing such a violation, or whom the warden has probable cause to believe is guilty of such violation, and take the person before the tribal court of appropriate jurisdiction and make proper complaint, and may stop and board any boat, stop any vehicle or snowmobile or other vehicle, if violation of the conservation code is reasonably suspected (29.05).

Enrolled members of the Winnebago Indian tribe and state residents who practice the traditional Winnebago religion may hunt deer during daylight hours for members' use in religious ceremonies without obtaining licenses under this chapter. Each hunting party shall be designated by the respective clan. Each clan leader shall obtain permission for deer hunting from the Department not less than 24 hours prior to each hunt. The Department shall make rules to control the conditions and location for hunting, and may deny permission for hunting to manage the deer population. The number of deer taken by all of the Winnebago clans for religious purposes during any calendar year shall be established by Department rule when necessary to manage the deer population. Hunting privileges under this section may not be exercised during the regular open season for deer. Nothing herein may be construed to eliminate a requirement that a landowner's permission must be obtained prior to hunting on private land (29.106). No person shall remove or take from an Indian reservation the carcass of a protected wild animal, bird or fish or part, including fur, during the closed season for such animal, without a permit (29.475).

In order to be eligible for reimbursement from the Department for costs incurred after August 1, 1987, by law enforcement agencies in response to members of federally recognized American Indian tribes exercising or attempting to exercises their right to engage in spearfishing, a county or municipality must do all of the following: maintain daily records of costs for additional law enforcement services that are directly related to spearfishing and make same available to the Department for inspection; file an application for aid with the Department by July 1, specifying names and salaries of officials who provided additional services during the spearfishing season [details provided]. "Additional law enforcement services" means an extraordinary type or level of service which is not normally provided or budgeted for by a law enforcement agency. "Spearfishing" means a method of taking fish authorized by an agreement between the state and federally recognized American Indian tribes or bands domiciled in Wisconsin relating to the tribes' or bands' treaty-based, off-reservation rights to hunt, fish and gather. Except as provided, the Department may pay each participating county or town up to 100% of their actual costs that are directly attributable to providing additional law enforcement services during the spearfishing season. Payments must be approved by the Secretary of Administration (29.599).

WYOMING

Sources: Wyoming Revised Statutes Annotated 1989, Title 23; 1992 Cumulative Supplement.

STATE WILDLIFE POLICY

For the purpose of this act, all wildlife in Wyoming is the property of the state. It is the purpose of this act and the policy of the state to provide an adequate and flexible system for control, propagation, management, protection and regulation of all Wyoming wildlife. There shall be no private ownership of live animals classified in this act as big or trophy game animals (23-1-103).

RELEVANT WILDLIFE DEFINITIONS: See Definitions section of Appendices.

STATE FISH AND WILDLIFE AGENCIES

Agency Structure

The **Wyoming Game and Fish Commission** (Commission) is composed of eight members including the Governor as an ex officio member. Not more than four of the seven appointed commissioners shall be of the same political party, and all shall have a general knowledge of wildlife and wildlife propagation, management and control. Terms are for six years, and a commissioner shall be appointed from each appointment district (23-1-201). A majority of commissioners is a quorum, and officers are elected for one-year terms (23-1-301).

The **Wyoming Game and Fish Department** (Department) is under the supervision of the Commission and consists of the **Director** and such divisions as the Commission may create (23-1-401). The Director is appointed by the Governor and holds office at the Governor's pleasure. The Director supervises all activities, functions and employees of the Department, under direction and supervision of the Commission (23-1-402). The Director, with the Commission's consent, shall appoint a **Chief Game Warden**, a **Chief Fish Warden** and necessary division chiefs. These shall be persons of knowledge and experience in the fields administered by their respective divisions, and shall supervise all activities and personnel of their divisions. All appointments of Game Wardens shall be based on competitive examinations and applicants shall be knowledgeable about wildlife and the duties and responsibilities of Game Wardens. The Commission shall provide for the investigation of the qualifications of each applicant (23-1-405).

Agency Powers and Duties

The **Commission** is directed and empowered to: ▸ fix season and bag limits; ▸ open, shorten or close seasons on a species/sex of wildlife for any type of legal weapon, except on predatory animals, predacious birds, or protected animals/birds, in any specified locality of Wyoming; ★ ▸ establish zones/areas in which trophy game animals may be taken as game animals with a license or in the same manner as predatory animals without a license, giving regard to the livestock and game industries in those areas; ★ ▸ acquire lands and waters by purchase, lease or otherwise, not including powers of eminent domain, and to develop, improve, operate the same for fish hatcheries, rearing ponds, game farms, bird farms, management of game and protected animals, birds and fur-bearers and their restoration, propagation or protection, public hunting, fishing or trapping areas; ▸ acquire easements for access roads; ▸ sell/exchange lands no longer needed; ▸ capture, propagate, transport, buy or exchange a species of game animal, bird, fish, fish eggs or fur-bearing animal needed for propagation/stocking, and exercise control over undesirable species and protected species; ▸ direct the capture of wildlife where abundant and transport and distribute them in the best interests of Wyoming; ▸ make provisions for feeding game animals, birds and fish; ▸ enter into cooperative agreements with educational institutions to promote wildlife research and with federal agencies, corporations, individuals and landowners for developing state control of wildlife management and demonstration projects; ▸ supervise the protection, management and propagation of fish and hatcheries; ▸ grant licenses for scientific or educational purposes to capture or ship the wildlife, nests or eggs of nonpredacious birds, establishing appropriate compensation therefor and limiting the number of species so taken; ▸ prescribe the form for and issuance of licenses and tags; ▸ require record keeping/reports from authorized commercial operations; ▸ provide for enforcement; ▸ open game preserves for hunting when overstocked and a serious shortage of feed exists; ▸ designate as protected, game, or predatory, a species not designated in 23-1-101 and establish rules for control of those species; ▸ authorize the collection and dissemination of statistics and information; ▸ establish check stations and establish kill/catch reports; ▸ promulgate orders to carry out the act's intent; ▸ regulate the use of power vehicles on Commission lands; ▸ regulate or prohibit importation of exotic species, small game animals, fur-bearing animals, protected animals, game birds, migratory birds, protected birds and fish into Wyoming, and regulate and permit importation of big or trophy game animals into Wyoming only for exhibition or for zoos; ★ ▸ designate individual bison or identifiable herds of bison as wildlife when approved by the Wyoming Livestock Board (23-1-302).★

★The Commission shall not ban the use of lead shot except in areas where shotgun shell pellets will exceed 20,000 per acre as determined by sampling methods approved by the Commission. Banned lead shot areas shall not exceed areas reasonably necessary for practical enforcement of the ban. This does not apply if federal regulations are adopted forcing designation of additional areas as nontoxic shot zones. The Commission shall negotiate with the USFW to minimize the extent to which lead shot is banned (23-1-302).★ To promote the maintenance of wildlife habitat and management goals, the Commission shall promulgate regulations governing the issuance of elk, deer, antelope and turkey hunting licenses to Wyoming landowners without subjection to prescribed means of competitive public issuance, the license fees to be the same as for regular resident licenses (23-1-302).

Agency Regulations

Commission orders shall be written and the original signed by the presiding Commission officer. License vendors shall, upon request, deliver a copy of the order to each purchaser of a license or tag. When a Commission order closes an area of land, lake or stream from hunting or fishing, a description of the area shall be posted in the manner and place determined by the Commission to be adequate notice of the closure. Commission regulations shall be promulgated in accordance with the Wyoming Administrative Procedure Act, 16-3-101 to 16-3-115 (23-1-303).

Agency Funding Sources

All income received by the Commission or Department shall be credited to the Wyoming **Game and Fish Fund**, to be expended as the Commission directs to carry out the purposes of this act and for no other purpose. The Commission shall not contract debt in excess of 20% of its anticipated revenue for the ensuing year according to its budget approved by the Governor. The Commission shall submit an annual report of its transactions and the conditions of Wyoming wildlife (23-1-501 through -503). Hunting and fishing license fees may only be used for administration, and for protection, propagation, preservation, and investigation of fish and game (23-1-601 and -602). With designated exceptions, sportspersons obtaining fishing, hunting or wild bison licenses under 23-2-101, 23-2-107 or 23-2-201 shall purchase a single conservation stamp for $5 which is valid for one year. A person may contribute to the enhancement of fish and wildlife habitat by purchasing a fish and wildlife habitat card showing the name of the purchaser and the amount of the contribution by a letter designation, ranging from $5 to $50 or more. Proceeds from voluntary purchases of the cards shall be transferred to the Game and Fish Fund (23-2-306).

Agency Advisory Boards

★The **Wyoming State Board of Outfitters and Professional Guides** (Board) is established under the Department of Commerce and consists of seven members as follows: two appointed by the Governor from the public-at-large who are not employed by, and do not receive a income from, outfitters or professional guides; four members representing a variety of types and sizes of outfitters appointed by the Governor from a list of nominations submitted by licensed outfitters. Nominees shall be licensed outfitters or professional guides with not less than five years experience in outfitting or professional guiding in Wyoming. Two nominees shall be submitted for each Board vacancy and appointments shall rotate among Commission appointment districts within the state. Terms are for three years, not more than four appointees shall be of the same political party, and appointments shall be made with the advice and consent of the Senate. The Board selects a chairperson and vice-chairperson for one year terms; four members is a quorum. The Board may request legal opinions from the state Attorney General, or may employ an attorney to represent the Board (23-2-408).★

The Board shall: ▸ adopt rules and regulations to carry out this act including requirements for training, experience and knowledge of relevant law and regulations as may be imposed upon outfitters and professional guides, and the content and requirements for examination of license applicants and other necessary rules; ▸ report to the governor as required; ▸ license and regulate outfitters and professional guides; ▸ examine applicants for licensure; ▸ deny or approve applications for licensure; ▸ conduct hearings upon complaints received relative to licensees; ▸ impose reasonable restrictions upon licensees; ▸ designate areas as recommended by the Commission for game management in which a licensee may conduct outfitting or professional guiding; ▸ specify whether the license is a big game/trophy game license or a deer-antelope outfitter's license (23-2-410). (See also Licenses and Permits under HUNTING, FISHING TRAPPING PROVISIONS).

PROTECTED SPECIES OF WILDLIFE

A person who takes an eagle is guilty of a 2nd degree misdemeanor. Taking a bighorn sheep, mountain goat, mountain lion or grizzly bear without a license is a 4th degree misdemeanor. Taking an elk or moose without a license is a 6th degree misdemeanor. Taking big or trophy game animals not otherwise specified without a license is an 8th degree misdemeanor. Taking a fur-bearing animal or game bird without a license, except as otherwise provided, is a 9th degree misdemeanor (23-3-101 through -103). No person shall take or intentionally destroy the nest or eggs of a nonpredacious bird. Violation is an 11th degree misdemeanor. The nest or eggs of predacious birds may be taken/destroyed. Violation in regard to eagle nests or eggs is a 2nd degree misdemeanor (23-3-108).

See also "protected bird" and "protected animal" under RELEVANT WILDLIFE DEFINITIONS.

GENERAL EXCEPTIONS TO PROTECTION

See "predacious bird" and "predatory animal" under RELEVANT WILDLIFE DEFINITIONS.

HUNTING, FISHING, TRAPPING PROVISIONS

General Provisions

★★When a big game animal, trophy game animal or turkey is killed under a license, the licensee shall detach, sign and date the proper coupon and attach same to the carcass before leaving the kill site, the coupon to remain on the animal at all times until the meat is processed, or reaches the hunter's home or taxidermist. Antelope, deer and elk licenses shall have two coupons, one designated "antelope, deer or elk coupon" and one designated "landowner's coupon." The landowner's coupon shall promptly be detached, dated, signed and delivered to the landowner, who shall deliver to the Department the coupon and an affidavit that the antelope, deer or elk was killed on the landowner's land. Upon receipt of the coupon and affidavit, the Department shall pay the landowner nine dollars for each coupon from the license. Landowner's coupons are not transferrable and unauthorized use is a 2nd degree misdemeanor. When antelope, deer or elk are killed on federal or state land, the licensee shall detach, date, and sign the landowner's coupon and deliver it to the Cheyenne office of the Department (23-3-104 and -105).★★

Licenses and Permits

A qualified person may purchase a hunting license from the Department to take an animal, bird or fish as provided by law and Commission regulation. The Commission may issue deer or antelope licenses at a lower fee in areas in which all licenses initially authorized were not purchased or in which additional harvest is desired for management. Nonresidents shall pay a $5 application fee for certain licenses (deer, elk, bighorn sheep, mountain goat, moose, black bear) in addition to the license fee, 25% of which shall go to establish a working balance of $500,000 to compensate owners or lessees for property damaged by game animals and birds. Forty percent of available nonresident elk licenses, 20% of nonresident deer licenses and 30% of nonresident antelope licenses shall be offered to nonresidents on receipt of the application fee. Seventy-five of the nonresident deer licenses set aside shall be used for a national bow hunt for deer. Licenses for nonresidents shall be offered by drawing. Nonresident applicants for elk, deer or antelope licenses must pay a $100 to $200 fee, the nonresident license fee for each species, and the $5 application fee (23-2-101).

Persons born after 1966 may not obtain a hunting license nor take wildlife using firearms except on their own land without completing a firearms competency and safety course and a certificate of competency. The Department shall institute and coordinate a statewide course of instruction and safety in firearm handling and may cooperate with local government agencies or private organizations in providing hunter safety courses (23-2-106).

Wild bison licenses are available to persons over age 14 by drawing and payment of a $5 nonrefundable entry fee. Illegal taking of a bison is a 1st degree misdemeanor (23-2-107). The Commission may limit the number of resident or nonresident big or trophy game animal licenses to be sold in a calendar year. No person may apply for/receive more than one moose, one grizzly bear, one mountain goat, or one bighorn sheep license in a five-year period. The Commission shall reserve 80% of the moose and 75% of the bighorn sheep, mountain goat, and grizzly bear licenses to be issued in any one year for resident hunters (23-1-703). ★Bow and arrow or crossbow is permissible equipment to take game animals, nongame animals, game birds and nongame fish. No license is required to take nongame animals and nongame fish with bow and arrow or crossbow.★ The Commission may establish special hunting seasons for taking big game or trophy game animals by bow and arrow or crossbow in designated areas. ★★No person shall hunt big game or trophy game with bow and arrow/crossbow without an archery license and the appropriate hunting license. [Minimum draw weights of longbows and crossbows for taking big game are specified] (23-2-104).★★ No nonresident shall hunt big or trophy game animals on a designated wilderness area, as defined by federal or state law, unless accompanied by a licensed professional guide or a resident guide. At least one licensed professional guide or resident guide shall accompany each two nonresident hunters. The Commission may specify other state areas, or specific big or trophy game species, for which a licensed professional or resident guide is required for nonresidents, for proper game management, protection of hunter welfare and safety, or enforcement of game and fish laws. The Commission may allow licensed guides to accompany more than two but no more than six hunters in specific areas (23-2-401).

Restrictions on Taking: Hunting and Trapping

No person shall use a dog to hunt, run, or harass a big or trophy game animal, protected animal, or fur-bearing animal. Dogs may be used to pursue and take mountain lions during the mountain lion hunting season with a Game Warden's permission, and to pursue and take trophy game animals under statute sections relating to animal damage control. Game Wardens may kill dogs in cases where big game animals have been injured or are being threatened with immediate injury (23-3-109). Firearm and ammunition sizes for hunting various types of game birds and big game or trophy game animals are specified by statute. No person shall take into the game fields or forests fully automatic weapon or device designed to silence the report of a firearm. Violation: 1st degree misdemeanor (23-3-111 and -112). Persons wishing to acquire game birds from a private source shall obtain a Department permit prior to acquiring, possessing or transporting game birds. The permittee shall notify the Department to establish proof of ownership and allow the game birds to be banded. Birds purchased outside the state must be certified disease free. The permittee is then entitled to take the permittee's privately owned game birds without a game bird or turkey license (23-3-116). No person shall sell, barter or dispose of for pecuniary consideration, or obtain by sale or barter an edible portion of a game animal, game bird or game fish except as permitted by this act (23-3-302).

No person shall take and leave, abandon or allow a game bird, fish or animal except trophy game animal, or edible portion intentionally or needlessly to go to waste. Failure to dress properly and care for a big game animal within 48 hours or to transport it to one's camp is prima facie evidence of violation. No person shall abandon meat from a big game animal or game bird at a meat processing plant; leaving meat in excess of 90 days is prima facie evidence of violation. It is a 3rd degree misdemeanor to: ▸ take/wound a game animal, game bird or game fish by use of a pit, pitfall, net, trap, deadfall, poison; ▸ use parts of a game animal, game bird or game fish for bait to trap or poison wildlife. It is illegal to: ▸ hunt, shoot or kill wildlife from a public road or highway; ▸ enter on private property to hunt, fish or trap without the landowner's permission; ▸ fire a firearm from or across a public road or highway; ▸ fire a rifle from enclosed lands of one person onto the enclosed lands of another without the permission of both landowners; ▸ hunt at night; ▸ hunt at night on private lands without permission. It is a 4th degree misdemeanor to: ▸ harass, pursue, hunt or kill Wyoming wildlife except predatory animals with, from or by use of a flying machine, automotive vehicle, or snowmobile; ▸ take wildlife with artificial lights except that predators may be taken with the aid of artificial light by predator control officials and landowners. Raccoons may be hunted with the aid of a handlight if the hunter is with a dog, on private lands, and has the landowner's permission. It is a 10th degree misdemeanor to carry a firearm or to take wildlife while intoxicated or under the influence of a controlled substance. Hunters and fishermen entering or leaving check station areas shall stop and report at the stations. Violation: 11th degree misdemeanor (23-3-303 through -308).

Restrictions on Taking: Fishing

No person shall take or destroy fish by using a poison or deleterious drug, electrical device, chemical, explosive or similar substance/device, nor allow refuse to pass into public water which is injurious to fish or wildlife or which obstructs the natural flow of the stream. Violation: 1st degree misdemeanor. No person shall erect or place a net, trotline or similar obstruction across a river or lake so as to prevent free passage of fish. The Commission may erect or require the erection of fishways on dams. Violation: 10th degree misdemeanor. The Commission may designate specified waters in which live fish or corn may be used as bait and may designate the types of and origin of live fish which may be used as bait. It is an 11th degree misdemeanor to use or possess live fish or bait corn while fishing in nondesignated areas, or to release live baitfish without authorization. It is a 10th degree misdemeanor to take or wound a game fish with a firearm. Fish may only be taken with a single rod or pole, with line and hook attached, and with the user in attendance, with specified numbers of hooks or flies attached unless otherwise specified by the Commission in designating areas open to set lines or other types of tackle or bait. Violation is a 10th degree misdemeanor. Shipment of game fish is restricted to one bag limit in a single container no more than once a week if a Wyoming interstate game tag is affixed to the container. Violation: 11th degree misdemeanor (23-3-201 through -205).

A qualified person may purchase a fishing license to take fish as provided by law and Commission regulation. Persons over age 14 must have a fishing license except on licensed preserves or hatchery catch-out ponds, except that nonresidents under age 14 may fish with a licensed adult as part of the adult's bag limit (23-2-201 and -202). At the Governor's request, the Commission shall annually issue up to 20 complimentary hunting and 20 complimentary fishing licenses. No complimentary licenses may be issued at the request of the appointed Commissioners, and records shall be submitted to the Secretary of State as public record of the names of licensees and type of license issued. The Commission may issue up to 80 licenses each year for the exclusive use of not more than a single one-shot antelope hunt, and may issue up to 25 licenses each year for the exclusive use of gunpowder and buckskin hunts. Free lifetime bird, small game and fish licenses are available to residents over age 65, and reduced fee licenses for deer, antelope, and elk to residents at least 70 years of age, residing in Wyoming for at least 40 years, and physically able to hunt and pursue their own game (23-1-705). A person with the approval of the Game Warden in the person's district may, at the Department's discretion, obtain a license to trap a fur-bearing animal. Nonresidents may be issued trapping licenses only if there is trapping permission reciprocity between the states in question for the same species. The Department shall determine the area where the trapper may take fur-bearing animals and the allowable harvests for that area. Steel leg hold traps must be labeled with the owner's name, and traps shall be checked at least once during each 72-hour period, excluding traps set underwater. Violation: 11th degree misdemeanor. Unlabeled traps are to be confiscated (23-2-303).

A person holding a license for game birds or small game animals may purchase a falconry license entitling the licensee to take game birds and small game animals with falcons or hawks. The Commission may regulate and grant licenses for taking falcons or hawks for lawful falconry purposes, and shall regulate or prohibit the exportation of hawks or falcons from the state. Special seasons for falconry may be set by the Commission (23-2-105).

Commercial and Private Enterprise Provisions

No person shall engage in a commercial operation or business authorized under this act without a license (23-3-401). No person shall deliver to a tannery, nor shall a tannery receive a game specimen unless tagged with a Wyoming game tag. Violation: 11th degree misdemeanor (23-3-404). Taxidermists must be licensed, post a cash bond, and shall keep required records. No person shall deliver to, nor shall a taxidermist receive, any game specimen unless tagged with a Wyoming game tag. Taxidermists, with proper records, may receive, purchase, handle, ship, sell and deliver any hide from cloven hoof big game animals, within or without Wyoming, without tagging the hide with a Wyoming game tag. Persons engaging in the business of buying, collecting, selling or shipping raw furs other than hides from cloven hoof big game animals shall obtain a resident/nonresident fur dealer license. Fur dealers may receive, store, ship and deliver hides from cloven hoof big game animals within or without the state without tagging the hides if required records are kept. Residents desiring to capture fur-bearing animals for domestication or propagation shall obtain a license under Department conditions and restrictions (23-2-302, -304, -305).

A person who owns/operates a fish hatchery, artificial lake or pond for raising fish for resale, may stock the fish hatchery or pond with eggs or fish procured from a lawful source, but sources other than the Department or federal government shall be inspected by the Department before planting. The owner may take fish from the hatchery or pond in any manner, except by poison, explosives or fishing except as otherwise provided, and may sell and dispose of fish subject to certain restrictions. The owner shall procure a license, and his artificial lake cannot exceed 100 acres in size and must be wholly artificial in nature, except that a catchout pond of 10 acres or less where fish may be caught can be operated. Records must be kept of disposal of fish or eggs by the owner or by a hotel or business serving fish purchased from the private hatchery. Every parcel of fish or eggs transported by a common carrier shall have a Wyoming game tag attached and the owner shall keep a strict record of all tags used. The Department may license persons to seine or trap fish at times, places and in a manner the Commission regulates, and may issue live bait licenses to qualified applicants, the Commission to determine the type of live bait which may be sold and its sources (23-4-102 and -103).

Once properly licensed, landowners holding or leasing lands for a minimum of five years may establish, operate and maintain game bird farms to breed, propagate, kill, hunt and sell game birds. Licensing requires a legal description of the tract of land and proposed methods of breeding, hunting and sale of game birds. The licensee shall purchase or replace to the state all game birds within the boundaries of the proposed farm; to effect this, the Department and landowner shall each appoint one person, these two will appoint a third, and these three will act as a board to determine the number of wild game birds occupying the proposed tract. After all investigations of the applicant and the proposed game farm lands have been completed, the licensee becomes the owner of all offspring of the game birds on the land or thereafter produced. No person shall entice game birds into the licensed premises by baiting or other means. All game birds must be tagged, and the licensee must release a minimum of 100 game birds each year on the premises. The licensee has the exclusive right during the license term to breed, propagate, hunt and sell the licensed game birds, but shall not kill over 96% of the birds reared/released. No person shall take game birds except during the established season for game bird farms and must have in possession a game bird/special bird license, and birds taken or removed from the premises must have a receipt stating sex and species of the birds removed. Special three-day bird licenses may be issued by the licensee to be used only on the game farm premises. The licensee may sell live or dressed game birds to restaurant operators if the birds are properly receipted. Game bird farms shall have a consecutive 183-day season between August and February, the exact season to be approved by the Commission (23-5-101 through 110).

Fishing preserve waters, artificial or manmade bodies of water not to exceed 100 surface acres, lying wholly within the boundaries of privately owned lands may be licensed to permit the owner to provide fishing facilities for fishermen and permitting the acquisition, possession and rearing of fish therein. The fishing preserves are not to include natural ponds or streams with a stream flow of over five second feet. The water sources for fishing preserves are limited to surface runoff, natural springs, wells, natural waters lawfully diverted or dammed natural streams with a normal stream flow under five second feet. A separate license is required for each fishing preserve water as defined by statute. The license shall specify the species of fish to be stocked, the approved source of fish, and the means to be used to trap the fish below the licensed waters. A licensee may permit other persons to take fish from the licensed fishing preserve waters and may charge a fee for fishing. No license is required to fish in these waters, but fish removed must have a receipt (23-5-201 through -204).

A resident with a resident big or trophy game animal license may receive a resident guide license without charge upon receipt by the Commission or Game Warden of an affidavit from the resident stating the names and addresses of the nonresident hunters to be guided, the game to be hunted, the area to be hunted and that the resident has not received nor will accept directly or indirectly compensation for guide services. A resident landowner may guide hunters on the landowner's own land without a guide license, or may authorize nonresidents to hunt without a guide on those lands by signing on the nonresident's license (23-2-401). No person shall engage in the business of or act in the capacity of an outfitter or engage in the occupation of a professional guide as an independent contractor, unless licensed as an outfitter or professional guide, nor may the person maintain an action for compensation of outfitting or guiding services provided to another person unless licensed at the time of providing services (23-2-407). ★★An applicant for an outfitter's license shall, in addition to other Board criteria, be at least 19 years old, have had experience as a licensed professional guide for at least one year, possess or lease equipment and facilities necessary to the type of services offered, be free of conviction and bond forfeiture of an amount exceeding $100 for a violation of federal or state wildlife law within the past two years prior to the application, and have no criminal record equal to a felony conviction and no conviction for a violation of federal/state law relating to criminal fraud. Persons holding an outfitter's license may operate as professional guides without holding a separate professional guide license (23-2-411).★★

★★Applicants for a professional guide's license shall be at least 18 years of age, employed by a licensed outfitter, free of conviction and bond forfeiture of a bond amount exceeding $100 for a violation of federal/state law relating to wildlife, game and fish within five years prior to filing application, and free of any criminal record equal to a felony conviction. A professional guide's license is valid only while the licensee is employed by a licensed outfitter (23-2-412).★★ Each applicant for an outfitter's or professional guide license shall submit to examination by the Board. The examination is to: ▸ be standardized for each type of license; ▸ require sufficient knowledge of the services to be provided under the license; ▸ test the ability of the applicant to perform services in a safe manner; ▸ require special knowledge applicable to the particular type of license. In addition to examination, the Board may investigate the qualifications of applicants. The Board shall require applicants to post and maintain a liability insurance policy to protect clients and property owners against injury or damage as a result of negligence of outfitters or their employees, the coverage to be not less than $25,000 for property damage, and not less than $100,000 for injury or death to one person and not less than $300,000 for all injuries/death arising out of one occurrence (23-2-413). An outfitter or professional guide licensed under this act shall promptly report a violation of federal or state law or regulation governing wildlife, game and fish personally observed to a Game Warden or to the Board (23-2-415). Violation: misdemeanor; with fine up to $750; and/or jail up to 6 months (23-2-417). The Board may require payment of damages by the licensee including payment to the client of a court ordered damages and fees paid by the client to the outfitter or guide, travel/lodging expenses and other expenses incurred by the client in attempting to use the outfitter's or guide's services, if a client is injured by the following causes: ▸ fraud or substantial misrepresentation in obtaining a license; ▸ fraudulent advertising; ▸ conviction of a felony; ▸ violation of a significant federal or state wildlife law; ▸ unethical or dishonorable conduct; ▸ substantial breach of contract with a client; ▸ willful violation of the terms and conditions of the license; ▸ inhumane treatment; ▸ violation of this act or a Board regulation (23-2-416).

Import, Export and Release Provisions

No person shall import a living antelope, bear, deer, elk, moose, mountain goat, mountain lion, bighorn sheep, wolf, nor living wildlife except as otherwise permitted by this act. No person shall sell a living antelope, bear, deer, elk, moose, mountain goat, mountain lion, bighorn sheep, wolf or falcon except as permitted by the Commission (23-3-301). No person shall plant or release fish or fish eggs in public waters of Wyoming without Department consent and supervision (23-4-101).

Interstate Reciprocal Agreements

In order to provide a method whereby residents of Wyoming and adjoining states may enjoy fishing opportunities in boundary lakes and reservoirs, the Commission is authorized to enter into reciprocal agreements with adjoining states for fishing licenses for Wyoming residents and for fishing on artificial water impoundments forming state boundary waters. The agreements may include provisions for a stamp to be purchased by residents of either state fishing in the boundary waters and for the use of fishing devices in such waters which are otherwise prohibited by Wyoming law (23-1-801 through -804).

ANIMAL DAMAGE CONTROL

★★A landowner whose property is being damaged by big game or trophy game animals or game birds shall report the damage to a Game Warden or the Commission within 15 days of discovering the damage. A landowner claiming damages from the state for injury or destruction of property by big or trophy game animals or game birds shall present a verified claim for damages to the Department within 60 days of discovery of the damage, specifying the damage and the amount claimed. The Department shall consider the claims based upon a description of the livestock damaged/killed by a trophy game animal, the damaged land, growing cultivated crops, stored crops, seed crops, improvements and extraordinary damage to grass. The Department shall reject or allow claims within 90 days and pay the amount determined. If the Department fails to act within 90 days, the claim, including interest, shall be deemed to have been allowed. No award shall be allowed to a landowner who has not permitted hunting on his property during authorized hunting seasons. A claimant aggrieved by the Department's decision may appeal to the Commission within 30 days of the decision. The Commission is to review the appeal at its next meeting, and may approve, modify or reverse the Department's decision. Within 90 days of receiving the Commission's decision, the claimant may ask for arbitration in writing to the Department. The claimant and Department shall each appoint a disinterested arbitrator residing in the county where the damage occurred, the arbitrators to appoint a third arbitrator within 20 days after their appointment. Further appeal of the decision may be made by either party to the arbitration board or to the District Court. If further appeal is not made, the Commission shall promptly pay the amount, including interest, awarded by the arbitration board (23-1-901). ★★

Predatory animals and predacious birds may be taken without a license except as otherwise provided. The Department shall report annually to the Wyoming Department of Agriculture the number of predatory animals and predacious birds taken by the Department's animal damage control agents, including the area where taken and the control method used. ★In areas designated by the Commission under 23-1-302, specified trophy game animals may be taken in the same manner as predatory animals without a license (23-3-103). ★ A landowner or lessee of state lands may take beaver which are flooding meadows, damming irrigation systems or constructing dams/ponds which would be dangerous to livestock on private or state lands. A bear, mountain lion, bobcat, weasel, gray, red, and fox squirrel or muskrat damaging private property may be immediately taken/killed by the landowner. The landowner shall immediately notify the nearest Game Warden of the killing of a bear, bobcat or mountain lion, and shall save the skin and procure a game tag for the skin of black bear. Grizzly bear or mountain lion skins shall be given to the Department for disposition. If a bobcat hide has monetary value, it shall be given to the Department and if sold, the Department shall rebate 50% of the proceeds to the landowner (23-3-114 and -115).

ENFORCEMENT OF WILDLIFE LAWS

Enforcement Powers

A Game Warden, Commissioner or other designated Department employee and any Wyoming law enforcement officer may arrest without warrant a person violating a provision of this act, the arrested person to be taken before the nearest court of jurisdiction unless the officer accepts a written promise to appear at a later time or a bond (23-6-101). Failure to obey a citation written promise to appear is a 9th degree misdemeanor (23-6-103). ★Every person issuing a game and fish citation shall deposit one copy with the court, after which the citation may be disposed of only by trial in that court, or other official action of that court, including bail forfeiture. No person shall dispose of a citation or the record of the citation issuance other than as provided in this act. A copy of every citation is to be returned to the Director, who shall also maintain a record of the disposition of the charge by the court (23-6-106). ★ ★★Every justice of the peace or judge of a court shall keep a record of every game and fish complaint, citation or other legal form of game and fish charge presented to the court, and shall keep a record of every official action by the court, including a record of every conviction, acquittal, and the amount of fine or forfeiture. Within 30 days of disposition of the case, every justice of the peace or judge or court clerk in which the conviction was had shall forward to the department a certified abstract of the court record. The abstract shall be upon a Departmental form and shall include the name and address of the violator, the game or fish license number, the nature of the offense, the date of hearing, the plea, the judgment or whether bail was forfeited, and the amount of fine, forfeiture or penalty imposed (23-6-108). ★★ A person authorized to enforce this act may seize and take into custody wildlife which has been unlawfully taken or which is in possession, such wildlife to be sold and funds credited to the Wyoming Game and Fish Fund. Authorized persons may search without warrant a camp, pack, pack animal, boat or motor vehicle with probable cause to believe that unlawfully taken wildlife is hidden therein (23-6-109). Owners of commercial operations permitted under this act shall allow inspection of the records required to be maintained, and of the premises during reasonable business hours (23-6-111).

Criminal Penalties

For the purposes of this act, misdemeanors are classified 1st degree through 11th degree. When no separate penalty is provided, the offense is a 9th degree misdemeanor. A person who has been convicted of, or pleaded guilty to, a misdemeanor offense under this act may be fined, sentenced to the county jail, or both, as follows: 1st degree-up to $2,000 plus up to one year jail; 2nd degree-up to $1,000 plus up to one year jail; 3rd degree-up to $600 plus up to one year jail; 4th degree-not less than $200 nor more than $750 plus up to six months jail; 5th degree-up to $750 plus up to six months jail; 6th degree-not less than $150 nor more than $600 plus up to six months jail; 7th degree-up to $600 plus up to six months jail; 8th degree-not less than $50 nor more than $400 plus up to six months jail;

9th degree-up to $400 plus up to six months jail; 10th degree-up to $200 plus up to six months jail; 11th degree-up to $200 (23-6-201 through -203).

Civil Liability

In addition to the penalties imposed under this section, a person illegally taking big game animals may be required to make restitution to the state for the value of the wildlife taken in an amount determined by the court based upon the recommendation of the Commission, the amounts to be paid to the state general fund (23-6-204).

Illegal Taking of Wildlife

No person shall ship, transport or receive for shipment a game animal, bird, or any part, unless tagged with a Wyoming game tag or Wyoming interstate game tag unless the transportation is by a person accompanying the carcass of a big or trophy game animal with the proper coupon, or by a licensed bird or small game hunter accompanying not more than his daily bag/possession limit of game. No big or trophy game animal, or any part, shall be shipped/transported from the state unless accompanied by the licensee who harvested the animal unless: ▸ the amount does not exceed 25 pounds and is properly tagged; ▸ only 25 pounds of any one big/trophy game animal may be exported from the state; ▸ the part to be exported is of a nonedible trophy or hidelike nature and properly tagged with an interstate tag; ▸ the big/trophy game animal was legally harvested by a nonresident and is tagged with an interstate tag. Tag selling agents may tag meat from any number of big game animals if the person lawfully accompanying the animals signs an affidavit that each animal was lawfully taken (23-3-106). It is a 5th degree misdemeanor illegally to take bighorn sheep, mountain goat, mountain lion, or grizzly bear, where no separate penalty is provided. It is a 7th degree misdemeanor to illegally take elk or moose. Illegal taking of remaining wildlife where there is no separate penalty is a 9th degree misdemeanor (23-6-204).

License Revocations and Suspensions

The court may revoke for the remainder of the year a license issued under this act to a person convicted of a violation, and except for conviction of a 10th or 11th degree misdemeanor, may suspend the person's privilege to purchase another license for: ▸ up to six years for conviction of a 1st through 6th degree misdemeanor; ▸ up to three years for conviction of a 7th through 9th degree misdemeanor. It is illegal to purchase another license while one's license is forfeited or suspended. Violation is suspension for another year and a 9th degree misdemeanor. The Commission may revoke the license of a commercial operation or business for a violation of a Commission order, and may refuse to issue another license for a period of time it deems desirable (23-6-206 and -207).

Reward Payments

No person shall wantonly take or destroy a big or trophy game animal. The Director may offer a standing reward not exceeding $500 to be paid from the Game and Fish Fund for evidence leading to the arrest and conviction of a person violating this section, the purpose of which is to protect big game or trophy game animals from wanton, ruthless or needless destruction. Violation is a 1st degree misdemeanor (23-3-107).

NATIVE AMERICAN WILDLIFE PROVISIONS: None.

PART III

WERNEKE ©1991

STATE LAWS COMPARED

Chapter 5

Tables Comparing State Wildlife Laws

Comparison of various state wildlife law provisions are made in the tables. Provisions were listed for each state with as much accuracy as possible; however, please refer to actual state law sections.

Introduction
Tables 1-3. Director, Commissioner and Commission:
Appointments and Qualifications

There is considerable variation in how the fish and wildlife director, commission, commissioners, and various agency advisory board members are chosen. We recommend that qualification requirements such as various types of examinations, qualifications by experience or training, representation from various state interest groups (sportsmen, farmers, ranchers, commercial fishermen, conservation groups, geographic location, etc.), and mixing members by age, sex, and ethnicity in commission and advisory board composition be imposed by all states, limitations on the number of members allowed to be from the same political party may be desirable. Ideally, appointments would not be tied to one political party by Governor appointments. Criteria such as written exams, physical exams and interviews for hiring department leaders and conservation officers are a good idea (see New Mexico, South Carolina and others).

Some states provide that although the Governor appoints Commission members, they must be selected from a list of eligible candidates, so that at least some expertise can be guaranteed in those who are appointed. Other states expressly set up commissions and advisory boards to allow input from competing interests, and thus are able to mediate and discuss the concerns of such interests. Examples include Colorado's Habitat Partnership Council which consists of representatives of agriculture, wildlife and rangeland management interests, designed to resolve rangeland forage issues; the Hawaii Natural Area Reserves System Commission, whose members have academic degrees in wildlife or marine biology, botany, forestry, ecology, resource management, biogeography, zoology, or geology; the Indiana Heritage Trust Program committees, whose membership include various organized hunting and fishing, environmental and other groups; and the New Mexico Fish and Game Commission, which must have one farmer/rancher member whose land contains at least two species for which the state requires a license to hunt or fish, and one member with demonstrated involvement in wildlife and habitat protection.

Every state has experts in many relevant areas, and such expertise should be utilized to the benefit of fish and wildlife agencies. There are many excellent examples in the state summaries of required qualifications, representation of different state interests, and inclusion of persons with widely differing backgrounds. Maine mandates that the Commissioner shall review other states' provisions for developing good relationships between hunters and landowners and implement similar programs with emphasis on courtesy and responsibility for private lands.

Tables 1-3 give a rough outline of appointment qualifications of the director, commissioner and commission members. In states with no director, but rather a "secretary" of a natural resources department, such secretary was treated as a director for purposes of this table.

Table 1. Director of Agency: Appointment and Qualifications

State	Governor Appointed	Appointed by Commission or Other	Submitted from List	Legislative Approval	Gubernatorial Approval	Serves at Pleasure of Commission	Academic/ Experience Qualification	Knowledge/ Interest Qualification	Other Qualification
AK	Not applicable								
AL		♦			♦				
AR	No statute information								
AZ		♦					♦		
CA	♦				♦				
CO		♦							♦[1]
CT	Not applicable								
DE		♦							
FL		♦							
GA	Not applicable								
HI		♦							
IA	♦			♦			♦	♦	
ID							♦	♦	
IL	Not applicable								
IN		♦		♦					
KS	Not applicable			♦			♦		♦[2]
KY	♦								♦[3]
LA	♦				♦				
MA		♦				♦	♦	♦	
MD	Not applicable						♦	♦	
ME	Not applicable								
MI		♦							
MN	Not applicable								
MO		♦							
MS	♦		♦	♦			♦		
MT	♦			♦					

[1] Commission establishes qualifications.

[2] Director serves at the pleasure of the governor.

[3] Director shall be appointed as provided by law.

Table 1. Director of Agency: Appointment and Qualifications (continued)

State	Governor Appointed	Appointed by Commission or Other	Submitted from List	Legislative Approval	Gubernatorial Approval	Serves at Pleasure of Commission	Academic/ Experience Qualification	Knowledge/ Interest Qualification	Other Qualification
NC							●		
ND	●				●				●
NE	Not applicable								
NH	● [4]						●	●	
NJ	●				●		●		
NM	No statute information								
NV	●		●				●	●	
NY	Not applicable								
OH	No statute information								
OK		●							
OR		●							
PA		●							
RI				●					
SC		●							
SD	Not applicable						●		
TN		●	●						
TX		●				●			
UT	Not applicable								
VA	Not applicable	●							
VT	Not applicable								
WA	●						●	●	● [5]
WI	Not applicable						●	●	
WV	●				●				● [6]
WY	●								

[4] Governor and Council jointly appoint Director.

[5] Governor shall seek recommendations from the Commission on the qualifications, skills and experience necessary for the position.

[6] Must be at least age 30.

Table 2. Commissioner: Appointments and Qualifications

State	Governor Appointed	Legislative Approval	Appointed from Within Commission	Serves at Pleasure of the Governor	Academic or Experience Qualification	Knowledge or Interest Qualification	Other Qualification
AK						♦	
AL	♦						
AR	Not applicable						
AZ	Not applicable						
CA							♦[1]
CO	Not applicable						
CT	♦	♦			♦		
DE	♦[2]						
FL	♦	♦	♦				
GA	Not applicable						
HI	Not applicable						
IA	♦	♦			♦	♦	
ID	♦		♦			♦	
IL	Not applicable						
IN	♦						
KS	♦	♦		♦	♦		
KY					♦	♦	♦[3]
LA	Not applicable						
MA	No statute information						
MD	♦	♦		♦	♦		
ME	♦	♦			♦		
MI	Not applicable						
MN	♦						
MO	Not applicable						
MS	♦		♦		♦		

[1] The president of the Commission may be a member ex-officio of the Migratory Bird Conservation created by the federal Migratory Bird Conservation Act.

[2] Secretary appointed, but Governor approved.

[3] Commission appoints Commissioner.

Table 2. Commissioner: Appointments and Qualifications (continued)

State	Governor Appointed	Legislative Approval	Appointed from Within Commission	Serves at Pleasure of the Governor	Academic or Experience Qualification	Knowledge or Interest Qualification	Other Qualification
MT	Not applicable						
NC	◆				◆		
ND	Not applicable						
NE	◆		◆		◆	◆	
NH	Not applicable						
NJ	◆	◆		◆	◆		
NM	Not applicable						
NV	◆		◆		◆		
NY	◆	◆	◆	◆			
OH	No statute information						
OK	Not applicable						◆[4]
OR	◆		◆				
PA	Not applicable						
RI	Not applicable						
SC	◆	◆					
SD	Not applicable						
TN	Not applicable						
TX	◆	◆					
UT	Not applicable						
VA	Not applicable						
VT	[5]						
WA	Not applicable						
WI	Not applicable						
WV	Not applicable						
WY	Not applicable						

[4] May not hold office in sports or commercial fishing organization or have ownership or direct interest in a commercial fishing business.

[5] Appointed pursuant to the provisions of 10-2851.

Table 3. Commission Members: Appointments and Qualifications

State	Governor Appointed	Geographic Selection	Legislative Approval	Must be Mixed Party	Academic or Experience Qualification	Knowledge or Interest Qualification	Other Qualification
AK	Not applicable						
AL	Not applicable						
AR	No statute information						
AZ	◆	◆		◆	◆		
CA	Not applicable						
CO	◆	◆		◆			
CT	Not applicable						
DE	Not applicable						
FL	◆		◆				
GA	◆	◆	◆				
HI	◆		◆				
IA	◆	◆		◆		◆	◆ [1]
ID	◆	◆		◆		◆	
IL	Not applicable						
IN	◆ [2]				◆		
KS	◆	◆		◆	◆		
KY	◆	◆		◆		◆	◆ [3]
LA	◆	◆	◆				
MA	◆	◆					◆ [4]
MD	Not applicable						
ME	Not applicable						
MI	◆	◆	◆		◆		
MN							
MO	◆		◆	◆		◆	

[1] Cannot hold any other state of federal office.

[2] Governor appoints 5 of 12 positions.

[3] Vacancies are filled by appointment by the Governor from a list of five names submitted by the sportsmen of each wildlife district.

[4] The Governor appoints one member from 3 candidates submitted by the Massachusettes Audubon Society, Sierra Club, Appalachian Mountain Club and Trustees of Reservations.

729

Table 3. Commission Members: Appointments and Qualifications (continued)

State	Governor Appointed	Geographic Selection	Legislative Approval	Must be Mixed Party	Academic or Experience Qualification	Knowledge or Interest Qualification	Other Qualification
MS	●	●			●		
MT	●	●	●				●[5]
NC	Not applicable						
ND	Not applicable						
NE	●	●		●	●	●	
NH	●[6]	●		●	●	●	
NJ	●		●			●	●[7]
NM	●	●	●	●	●		
NV	●	●			●		
NY	Not applicable						
OH	●		●	●		●	●[8]
OK	●	●	●				
OR	●	●	●				●[9]
PA	●	●	●				
RI	Not applicable						
SC	●		●				
SD	●	●	●	●	●		
TN	●	●	●			●	●[10]
TX	●		●			●	●[11]
UT	●	●	●	●			

[5] At least one member must be experienced in the breeding and management of domestic livestock.

[6] Appointed and approved by the Governor and Council.

[7] Six farmers and six sportsmen, one of whom serves as Chairman.

[8] At least two shall be engaged in farming as their principal means of support.

[9] May not hold office in sports or commercial fishing organization or have ownership or direct interest in a commercial fish processing business.

[10] Includes Commissioners of Environment and Conservation and Agriculture; strives to have one person at least 60 years old and at least one person of a racial minority.

[11] All nine members must be from the general public; members or spouses may not be employed by a business entity regulated by the Department or received funds therefrom, may not own or control more than a 10% interest in such business entity, or use/receive a substantial amount of tangible goods, services or funds from the Department, and may not be registered lobbyists on behalf of a profession related to the operation of the Commission, nor be employees or paid consultants of a statewide association in the field of conservation or outdoor recreation.

Table 3. Commission Members: Appointments and Qualifications (continued)

State	Governor Appointed	Geographic Selection	Legislative Approval	Must be Mixed Party	Academic or Experience Qualification	Knowledge or Interest Qualification	Other Qualification
VA	◆	◆	◆				
VT	◆	◆	◆				
WA	◆		◆			◆	◆ [12]
WI		◆ [13]					
WV	◆	◆	◆		◆		
WY		◆		◆		◆	

[12] Shall not hold other office; must represent a balance reflecting all aspects of wildlife management.

[13] No person may be appointed, or remain a member, who receives a significant portion of income directly or indirectly from permit holders or applicant of permits issued by the Department.

731

Table 4. Agency Funding Sources

The California Legislature aptly stated: "Revenues have been declining while the [Fish and Game] Department's responsibilities have been expanding into numerous new areas. Limitations on Department revenues have resulted in its inability to effectively provide all the programs and activities required under this code and to manage the wildlife resources held in trust. (Ca. Fish & Game Code Section 710.5). Virtually all state fish and wildlife agencies spend valuable time and energy seeking funding. Most continue to be under-funded, especially for management of nongame wildlife. Agency funding sources are listed in Table 4, and these present a wide array of possibilities for funding for departments in addition to fees from hunting, fishing and trapping licenses. These additional sources range from voluntary income tax refund contributions to a commemorative shotgun and rifle lottery. And Arizona's Game and Fish Commission Heritage Fund receives ten million dollars from the state lottery.

We suggest that all departments be more innovative in creating funding ideas, and that public input be solicited when possible. More use should be made of the concept of "Conservation Passports" (Texas) which require persons using department lands to have one permit per vehicle, whether using the land for consumptive or nonconsumptive purposes. Public lands "users fees" of some sort will enable persons besides hunters and fishermen to use lands and support wildlife. West Virginia provides that license moneys go into the License Fund-Wildlife Resources Fund to be used solely for law enforcement and purposes directly relating to the conservation, protection propagation and distribution of wildlife, with no funds to be used for recreation facilities or activities that are used by or for the benefit of the general public rather than purchasers of hunting and fishing licenses. Several states, such as Indiana, explicitly state that programs for endangered species shall not be funded by moneys dedicated to fish and game purposes. More use should be made of lotteries or auctions of certain big game licenses, hunting equipment, gun lotteries, guided trips, or other incentives and prizes to raise money (see North Dakota, Montana, Connecticut and other states), and of the ammuntition tax and Missouri's constitutional sales tax provision which provides funding for the fish and game department. Other easily implemented fundraising ideas include: sale of excess Department equipment (Texas); marketing and fundraising activities for special endangered, waterfowl or other accounts (New Hampshire); more use of bond issuance to raise money for fish hatcheries and habitat acquisition (New Mexico's Game and Fish Bond Act) ; sales of certain products on Department lands (South Dakota, Washington and others); building of lodges and other facilities in certain locales (Mississippi); more revenues from fines and forfeitures to go to the arresting county to encourage enforcement and prosecution (South Carolina); special fees to hunt on designated hunting areas (Ohio); fees from license plate sales for wildlife fund (Washington).States should explicitly state what revenues shall be spent for, and exactly how money from pheasant, waterfowl, fur-bearer, trout and other stamps shall be spent (Illinois and Indiana are examples).

The sources for program funding are myriad, yet this table is only a cursory overview of state funding sources and is not as definitive as the complete "Agency Funding Sources" sections in the state summaries. Some states' general funds were excluded from the table because they had no particular title or clear definition. Also excluded were nonspecific or undefined sources of funding, in order to maintain the clarity and brevity of this table. The reader is urgered to carefully examine the" Agency Funding Sources" section of the state summaries for details on well-conceived and valuable ideas for obtaining and using funds for fish and wildlife management and protection.

Alabama
- Game and Fish Fund: charges, fines and privilege taxes.
- Game and Fish Endowment Fund: lifetime licenses and gifts.
- Nongame Wildlife Endowment Account: print/stamp sales and gifts.

Alaska
- Fish and Game Fund: licenses, sales of predator hunter specimens, settlement money from resource damage, donations, federal money and raffle of one bison permit.

Arizona
- Game and Fish Fund: licenses and appropriations.
- Game and Fish Federal Reclamation Trust Fund: irrigation assessments.
- Land and Water Conservation and Recreation Development Fund: matching funds for federal restoration acts.
- Game, Nongame, Fish and Endangered Species Fund: appropriation and interest earned.
- Game and Fish Publications Revolving Fund: appropriations and publication sales.
- Wildlife Endowment Fund: appropriation, lifetime licenses, gifts and interest.

Table 4. Agency Funding Sources (continued)

- Conservation Development Fund: issuance of bonds.
- Arizona Game and Fish Commission Heritage Fund: state lottery fund pursuant to §5-552 and interest.

Arkansas
- Game Protection Fund: interest on the average daily balance of funds administered by the Commission.
- Nongame Preservation Program: money and interest from the income tax check-off system.

California
- Native Species Conservation and Enhancement Account: donations, sale of native species stamps, sale of annual wildlife area passes and nature and nature study aids.
- Endangered and Rare Fish, Wildlife, and Plant Species Conservation and Enhancement Account: money from the income tax check-off system.
- Animal Trust Fund: appropriations and donations.
- Fish and Wildlife Habitat Enhancement Fund: issuance of bonds.
- Wildlife and Natural Areas Conservation Fund: appropriations.
- Fisheries Restoration Account: appropriations.
- Cigarette and Tobacco Products Surtax
- Habitat Conservation Fund: appropriations.
- Fish and Game Preservation Fund: sale of upland game bird and state duck stamps.
- California Waterfowl Habitat Preservation Account: investments earned from Fish and Game Preservation Fund money.
- Fish and Wildlife Pollution Cleanup and Abatement Account: settlement money from damages and civil penalties.

Colorado
- Wildlife Cash Fund: money and interest from licenses.
- Wildlife for Future Generations Trust Fund: donations and interest earned from these donations.
- Habitat Partnership Cash Fund: appropriations, gifts, reimbursements, and interest earned.
- Search and Rescue Fund: costs incurred for search and rescue of licensees.

Connecticut
- General Funding: licenses, appropriations, sale stamps, artwork, and publications.

Delaware
- Nongame Fish and Wildlife, Nongame Habitat and Natural Area Preservation Fund: voluntary tax contributions and license fees to match federal funds.
- State Duck Stamp Account: sale of duck stamps.
- Delaware Trout Fishing Stamp: sale of trout stamps.
- Wildlife Theft Prevention Special Fund: penalties, donations, and appropriations.

Florida
- Endangered and Threatened Species Reward Trust Fund: penalties, donations, and appropriations.
- State Game Trust Fund: funds specially provided.
- Florida Waterfowl Stamp, Turkey Stamp, & Management Area Stamp: revenues from the sale of each respective stamp.
- Florida Panther Research and Management Trust Fund: donations.
- Wildlife Law Enforcement Trust Fund: appropriations and donations.
- Nongame Wildlife Trust Fund: appropriations and donations.
- Internal Improvement Trust Fund: lands acquired through voluntary negotiations, donations, mitigation contributions, and appropriations.
- Lifetime Fish and Wildlife Trust Fund: gifts, lifetime licenses, and investments.
- Dedicated License Trust Fund: five-year licenses.

Georgia
- Nongame Wildlife Conservation and Wildlife Habitat Acquisition Fund: money from the income tax check-off system, fund raising or promotional programs, and contributions.
- Waterfowl Stamp Fund: sale of stamps and interest.

Table 4. Agency Funding Sources (continued)

Hawaii
- Wildlife Revolving Fund: all licenses, attendance fees for hunter education programs. fees for public target ranges, and penalties.
- Natural Area Reserve Fund: public sources and donations.

Idaho
- Fish and Game Account: licenses, sale of predatory animal furs, and interest.
- Fish and Game Expendable Trust Account: donations of real or personal property and money from their sales.
- Fish and Game Federal Account: federal money, appropriations, and investment earnings.
- Fish and Game Set-Aside Account: licenses, sale of migratory waterfowl stamps and artwork and money from the income tax check-off system.
- Animal Damage Control Account: appropriations.
- Wildlife Restoration Project Section & Fish Restoration and Management Project: match federal grants.

Illinois
- Wildlife and Fish Fund: fees and penalties.
- Salmon Fund, State Migratory Waterfowl Stamp Fund, State Fur-Bearer Stamp Fund, & State Pheasant Stamp Fund: sales of stamps and artwork for each respective fund and donations to each respective fund.

Indiana
- Fish and Wildlife Fund: sale of items and rights to market items made by Department employees, gifts, sale of nonmonetary gifts, penalties, and donations in excess of license fees for distinctive licenses.
- Migratory Waterfowl Stamp, Game Bird Habitat Restoration Stamp, & Lifetime Hunting and Fishing License Trust Fund: sales of respective stamps and licenses.
- Nongame Fund: appropriations and entrance fees to fish and wildlife areas.
- Deer Research and Management Fund: nonresident deer licenses.

Iowa
- Fish and Game Protection Fund: licenses and money from income tax check-off system.

Kansas
- Wild Trust Program: donations.
- Wildlife Fee Fund or Park Fee Fund: proceeds from mineral leases and production.
- Funds from the operation or leasing of public facilities.
- Wildlife Fee Fund: licenses, lifetime licenses, and privilege taxes.
- Migratory Waterfowl Propagation and Protection Fund: sale of stamps.
- Wildlife and Parks Private Gifts and Donation Fund: donations.
- Nongame Wildlife Improvement Fund: money from income tax check-off system.

Kentucky
- Game and Fish Fund: licenses and penalties.
- Nongame Fish and Wildlife Fund: appropriations, donations, federal funds, and interest earned.
- Kentucky Nature Preserves Fund: money from the income tax check-off system.

Louisiana
- Bond Security and Redemption Fund: funds collected by Commission and alligator licenses.
- Wildlife Stamp Research Fund, Duck Stamp Fund, Louisiana Alligator Resource Fund, & Wildlife and Fisheries Conservation Fund: remaining money from Bond Security and Redemption Fund.
- Louisiana Help Our Wildlife Fund: appropriations, penalties, and federal anti-poaching money.
- Wildlife Stamp Research Program & Louisiana Duck Stamp Program: public sources, donations, sale of respective stamps and prints, and appropriations.

Maine
- General Fund: licenses and any unencumbered balances in the state treasury as undedicated revenue.
- Maine Endangered and Nongame Wildlife Fund: money from the income tax check-off system.

Maryland
- State Wildlife Management and Protection Fund: licenses.
- State Fisheries Management and Protection Fund: fish licenses.
- Fisheries Research and Development Fund: commercial licenses, taxes, royalties from oysters and clams removed from tidal waters, and penalties.
- Birdwatchers' Fund: sales of stamps, decals and donations.

Table 4. Agency Funding Sources (continued)

- State Chesapeake Bay and Endangered Species Fund: money from the income tax check-off system and other donations.
- Bow and Arrow Stamps, Black Powder Deer Stamps, & State Migratory Wild Waterfowl Stamps: sales of respective stamps.

Massachusetts
- Inland Fisheries and Game Fund: licenses, authorized sales, reimbursements from federal government, grants in aid, and penalties.
- Wildlands Acquisition Account: $1 from each license, sales of wildland conservation stamps, appropriations, and donations.

Michigan
- Nongame Fish and Wildlife Trust Fund: appropriations, donations, and sales of stamps and artwork.
- Game and Fish Protection Fund: penalties, gifts, appropriations, certain royalties from the Kammer Recreational Land Trust Fund Act, mineral revenues, other state land revenues, license and stamp revenues, and interest earned.
- Wildlife Resource Protection Fund: sales of passbooks and license revenues.
- Game and Fish Lifetime License Trust Fund: sales of lifetime licenses.

Minnesota
- Minnesota Critical Habitat Private Sector Matching Account: appropriations and donations.
- Nongame Wildlife Management Account: donations and appropriations.
- Reinvest in Minnesota Resources Fund: issuance of bonds.
- Game and Fish Fund: appropriations, license revenues, penalties, sale of property under Division control, education fees, reimbursements, and donations.
- Wildlife Acquisition Account: revenue from the small game surcharge.
- Minnesota Migratory Waterfowl Stamps, Trout and Salmon Stamps, & Pheasant Stamps: sales of respective stamps.

Mississippi
- Fisheries and Wildlife Fund: penalties, licenses, and interest.
- Wildlife Heritage Fund: appropriations, gifts, nonresident licenses, money from the income tax check-off system, and interest.
- Wildlife Endowment Fund: lifetime licenses, "golden" lifetime licenses, and interest.
- MS Outdoor Fund: proceeds and interest earned from magazine subscriptions.
- State Migratory Waterfowl Stamp: stamp sales.
- Endangered Species Protection Fund: appropriations and donations.

Missouri
- Special Taxes provided for in State Constitution.

Montana
- State Special Revenue Fund: licenses, sales of seized game or hides, penalties, appropriations, sale or lease of interests in Department land, and interest earned.
- Fish and Wildlife Mitigation Trust Fund: contracts or authorizations for wildlife mitigation or enhancement, donations, property or easements acquired through fund expenditures, and interest earned.

Nebraska
- State Game Fund: licenses, publications, money from income tax check-off system, and $2 from each annual resident fishing permit.
- Nebraska Habitat Fund: sales of habitat stamps.
- Money from the use of state facilities, resources, and concessions.

Nevada
- Wildlife Account: licenses, appropriations, and interest.
- Heil Trust Fund for Wild Horses: private fund.

New Hampshire
- Waterfowl Conservation Account: donations and sale of stamps and artwork.
- Prepaid Fish and Game License Fund: lifetime licenses.
- Nongame Species Account: federal money under the Nongame Act of 1980, appropriations, and donations.

Table 4. Agency Funding Sources (continued)

- Fish and Game Fund: licenses, penalties, appropriations, gifts, and revenues from the Commemorative Rifle or Shotgun Lottery.
- Pheasant Stamps, Wild Turkey Stamps, & Wildlife Stamps: sale of respective stamps, licenses, and various mementos.
- Wildlife Protection Account: sale of wildlife emblems.
- Moose Management Fund, Bear Management Fund, & Raptor Conservation Account: respective licenses, permits, and donations.

New Jersey
- Hunters' and Anglers' License Fund: licenses.
- New Jersey Waterfowl Stamp Account: sale of stamps.

New Mexico
- Game and Fish Bond Act: licenses, issuance of bonds, and $1 from each resident and nonresident license to the Game and Fish Bond Retirement Fund.
- Game and Fish Capital Outlay Fund: excess money from the Retirement Fund.
- Shooting Range Fund: gifts, deposit, and other sources.

New York
- None statutorily enacted.

North Carolina
- Recreation and Natural Heritage Trust Fund: money from specialized license plates, taxes on real property transactions, and investments.

North Dakota
- Nongame Wildlife Fund: appropriations.
- State Game and Fish Fund: income of the Department and a percentage of the market value of clam shells harvested.
- Small and Big Game Habitat Restoration Trust Fund: money transferred from State Game and Fish Fund and interest earned.

Ohio
- Wildlife Fund: licenses, penalties, and investment earnings.
- Nongame and Endangered Wildlife Fund: money from the income tax check-off system and federal money under the Endangered Species Act.
- Cooperative Management Fund: revenue generated on land owned by the US Army Corp of Engineers and managed by the Division.
- Ohio River Management Fund: mitigation settlements, gifts, and investment earnings.
- Wildlife Habitat Trust Fund: gifts.
- Wildlife Habitat Fund: investment earnings from the Wildlife Habitat Trust Fund.
- Wildlife Refunds Fund: special deer permits.
- Wetlands Habitat Fund: sales of stamps and investments earned.
- Wildlife Conservation Stamp: $5 contribution for recognition stamp.

Oklahoma
- Wildlife Conservation Fund: sales of Oklahoma Waterfowl Hunting Stamp, penalties, and licenses.
- Wildlife Land Acquisition Fund: voluntary $5 payment for Wildlife Habitat Stamp, private donations, and donated lands which may be sold.
- Wildlife Heritage Fund: senior citizen lifetime licenses.

Oregon
- State Wildlife Fund: money received pursuant to wildlife laws, sales of migratory waterfowl stamps, and interest earned.
- Fish Endowment Account: appropriations and gifts.
- Halibut Research Account: halibut tags.
- Nongame Wildlife Fund: money from the income tax check-off system, gifts, and interest earned.

Pennsylvania
- Fish Fund: fees, royalties, mineral leases, donations, and penalties.
- Game Fund: fees, royalties, mineral leases, donations, and penalties.

Table 4. Agency Funding Sources (continued)

- Wildlife Resource Conservation Fund: money from the income tax check-off system.

Rhode Island
- Shellfish Transplant Program: license revenues and fees during the 1992-1993 fiscal year.
- Trout Conservation Fund & Waterfowl Fund: sales of respective stamps.
- Nongame Wildlife Fund: money from the income tax check-off system and grants.

South Carolina
- Wildlife Endowment Fund: gifts, lifetime licenses, and tax-exempt donations.
- Game Protection Fund: penalties, $1 from nonresident licenses, and $.50 from temporary nonresident licenses.
- Operation Game Thief Program: money from the county game fund of the state treasury, donations, and appropriations.

South Dakota
- Department of Game, Fish, and Parks Fund: licenses, bonds or contracts, rentals, sales of personal property, and sales of Wildlife Habitat Stamp.
- Land Acquisition and Development Fund: $3 from nonresident small game licenses.

Tennessee
- Wildlife Resources Fund: licenses, contraband, penalties, ammunition tax, and interest earned.

Texas
- Game, Fish, and Water Safety Fund: all types of fishing, hunting, shrimping, and trapping licenses, stamps, and permits, (including alligator hunter's and buyer's licenses), sales of marl sand, gravel, and shell, sale of property, wildlife penalties, sale of rough fish by the Department, fees for importation permits, fees for stocking water on private property, sale of seized pelts, sale/lease of grazing rights to and products from management areas, contracts for removal of fur-bearing animals and reptiles from management areas, motorboat registration fees, water safety penalties, sale of alligators or parts by the Department, and conservation law revenues.
- Parks and Wildlife Operating Fund: gifts, sales of state items, and private and state fund-raising events.
- Special Nongame and Endangered Species Conservation Fund: donations, sales of stamp and artwork, entrance fees, easements, mineral leases, grazing leases, sales of products from lands purchased from this fund, and investment earnings.
- Lifetime License Endowment Fund: lifetime licenses, donations, and interest earned.
- Operation Game Thief Fund: donations.

Utah
- Wildlife Resources Account: licenses, penalties, revenues from real or personal property, appropriations, gifts, interest, and dividends.
- Wildlife Resources Trust Account: lifetime licenses and interest earned.
- Upland Game Account: upland game habitat stamp sales and interest earned.

Vermont
- Nongame Wildlife Account: appropriations, donations, and federal aid.
- Fish and Wildlife Fund: sales of waterfowl stamps and artwork.

Virginia
- Game Protection Fund: licenses.
- Lifetime Hunting and Fishing Endowment Fund: lifetime licenses and donations.
- Virginia Fish Passage Grant and Revolving Loan Fund: general fund money, receipts from loans made by it, investment income, and donations.
- Damage Stamp Program: stamp sales.

Washington
- State Wildlife Fund: rentals or Department concessions, sale of real/personal Department property, licenses, fees for informational material, fees for personalized license plates, articles or wildlife sold by Director, gifts, excise tax on anadromous game fish, waterfowl stamp sales, and sale of seized property.
- Wildlife Account: compensation for wildlife losses.
- State Wildlife Conservation Reward Fund: money designated by Director.
- Firearms Range Account: appropriations.

Table 4. Agency Funding Sources (continued)

- State General Fund: licenses relating to fisheries, sale of seized property, penalties, sale of real/personal property, money received for damages to food fish, shellfish or Department property, and sale of salmon and salmon eggs.

West Virginia
- Whitewater Study and Improvement Fund: whitewater license holders' contributions.
- License Fund-Wildlife Resources: licenses.
- Bear Damage Fund: bear hunter must also have a Bear Damage Stamp.
- Wildlife Endowment Fund: money from income tax check-off system, lifetime licenses, gifts, and interest earned.
- Conservation Stamp: must be purchased in addition to hunting, fishing, and trapping licenses.

Wisconsin
- Endangered Resources Program: money from the income tax check-off system.
- Conservation Fund: federal grants, privilege taxes, money collected by field employees, licenses, and gifts.

Wyoming
- Game and Fish Fund: licenses, income received by Commissioner or Department, and contributions.

Table 5. State Advisory Boards

Advisory boards and councils are viable, but significantly untapped, human resources available to fish and wildlife managers. Unlike other natural resources, the potential members for these councils are abundant. In reviewing this table and the statutory summaries, it is apparent that knowledgeable experts or well-learned and concerned citizens comprise most advisory boards and councils.

This table presents a summary of the councils and advisory boards of the various states that study or make recommendations regarding fish and wildlife issues. The councils range from stamp committees, which select the art of the stamps and oversee expenditures from these funds, to boards of outfitters and guides, which maintain the standards for quality and integrity of guides. Such groups can offer fresh and innovative insight into each state's economic, fish, wildlife, and resources concerns.

Qualifications for Advisory Board members are quite varied among boards and among states, depending on the goals and purpose of the board. A vast majority of states seek specific geographic representation from within the state, most often based on county or legislative districting. While many qualifications match those required for state wildlife commissions, often specific attributes are also sought. These include interest in commercial hunting, guiding, fishing ranching, and agriculture; academic or scientific experience; representatives from certain state universities; administrators from state or federal wildlife and fish management agencies; state game wardens; and expertise in environmental education and conservation.

We suggest that agency advisory boards be reviewed for each state, with attention given to the composition of the board memberships, the interests served, and the duties undertaken. There is an amazing variety of board types, ranging from county advisory boards, to local guide advisory boards, to importation of exotic species boards. It is suggested that as many opportunities as possible be taken by agencies to include a wide variety of citizen interests in wildlife concerns by having more, not fewer boards, and that more ordinary citizens of varied backgrounds be encouraged to participate. Several states are putting great reliance on volunteer boards and community organizations, such as California, Washington and Oregon which are trying to replenish the salmon supply in those states. Many persons would welcome chances to become trained wildlife rehabilitators, or would gladly serve as game thief hotline operators, poaching spotters in the field, operate game tagging stations, or engage in other activities if the opportunity were afforded and widely advertised. Increased volunteer participation in a variety of endeavors can free the salaried department employees for other duties, as well as gaining support for department programs by more citizens of the state (see Florida for establishment of "citizen support organizations" to provide assistance, funding and promotional support for commission programs and fund raising. For further insight into the composition, workings, and complete duties of these councils, the reader should consult the Agency Advisory Boards section of a state statutory summary.

Alabama
Advisory Board of Conservation and Resources:
Assist in formulating Department policies; examine rules and regulations promulgated by the Commissioner and make recommendations; assist in giving wildlife and Debarment publicity; the Board's rules and regulations have the force and effect of law.
Alaska
Board of Fisheries:
Conserve and develop fishery resources.
Board of Game:
Conserve and develop game resources.
Advisory Committee on Hunting and Firearm Safety:
Advise in fulfilling responsibilities related to hunting and firearm safety.
Arkansas
Appraisal Board:
Investigate and determine amounts to be paid to those who suffer crop damage by wildlife on or near game reservations.
Nongame Preservation Committee:
Concerned with preservation of nongame.

Table 5. State Advisory Boards (continued)

California

Striped Bass Stamp Advisory Committee:
  Allocates funds from striped bass stamps.
Wildlife Conservation Board:
  Determine areas most essential and suitable for wildlife preservation, production, and recreation.
Aquaculture Industry Advisory Committee:
  Assist in developing and implementing a state aquaculture plan.
Interagency Committee for Aquaculture Development:
  Advise on all matters pertaining to aquaculture and act in a coordinating role among agencies.
Wildlife Habitat Enhancement Program Finance Committee:
  Authorize the issuance of bonds for wildlife habitat.
Advisory Committee on Salmon and Steelhead Trout:
  Advise on preservation of salmon and steelhead trout.

Colorado

Habitat Partnership Council:
  Advise local committees and monitor program effectiveness amongst other duties.
Habitat Partnership Committee:
  Director appoints Committee when conflicts arise between wildlife and rangeland managers. Committee has other duties.
Fish Health Board:
  Review or initiate and consider every proposed rule relating to fish health.

Connecticut

Citizens' Advisory Board for Nonharvested Wildlife:
  Advise the Commissioner on program for species not traditionally harvested.
Natural Area Preserve Advisory Committee:
  Advise the Commissioner relative to the establishment of natural area preserves.

Florida

Waterfowl Advisory Council:
  Advise regarding revenues generated by sale of Florida Waterfowl Stamp.
Florida Panther Technical Advisory Council:
  Advise on specific technical matters concerning the panther recovery program.
Nongame Wildlife Advisory Council:
  Recommend policies, objectives, and specific actions for nongame wildlife research and management.

Hawaii

Natural Area Reserves System Commission:
  Among other duties pertaining to reserves, establish criteria to determine reserve inclusion.
Animal Species Advisory Commission:
  Advise on proposals for the deliberate introduction of aquatic life and wildlife into a habitat.
Aquatic Life and Wildlife Advisory Committee:
  Recommend and make findings on matters affecting taking and conservation of aquatic life and wildlife.

Idaho

Fish and Game Advisory Committee:
  Act as liaison between Commission and public and private groups and organizations. Give independent advice on animal damage compensation.

Illinois

State Duck Stamp Committee:
  Review and recommend projects and expenditures.
State Pheasant Stamp Committee:
  Review and recommend stamp allocations.
State Fur-Bearer Stamp Committee:
  Review and recommend projects and expenditures.

Table 5. State Advisory Boards (continued)

Endangered Species Protection Board:
  Among other duties, review status of species.

Indiana

Indiana Heritage Trust Program:
  Acquire historically, geologically, and archaeologically significant sites.

Program Committee:
  Propose projects under the Indiana Heritage Trust Program, provide technical assistance, propose budgets, and promote broad public participation.

Trust Committee:
  Determine whether proposed projects should be approved.

Iowa

Farmer Advisory Committee:
  Provide information regarding crop and tree damage caused by predators.

State Advisory Board for State Preserves:
  Oversee preservation of natural lands, waters, and historic sites.

County Conservation Board:
  Among other duties, has custody and control of property acquired by counties for conservation and recreation.

Louisiana

Wildlife Stamp Research Program Advisory Council:
  Assist in administering wildlife stamp research program.

Louisiana Fur and Alligator Advisory Council:
  Approve programs for the Fur and Alligator Public Education and Marketing Fund and the Alligator Resource Fund.

Maine

Atlantic Sea Run Salmon Commission:
  Undertake projects in research, planning, management, restoration, and propagation of the Atlantic Sea Run Salmon.

Inland Fisheries and Wildlife Advisory Council:
  Among other duties, provide information and advice to the Commissioner concerning the Department.

Maryland

Wildlife Advisory Commission:
  In addition to numerous other commissions, promote the future of hunting and the preservation of wildlife.

Sports Fisheries Advisory Commission:
  Provide advice on recreational fisheries.

Captive Wildlife Advisory Committee:
  Review proposed regulations and give recommendations to the Director and advise on captive wildlife.

Massachusetts

Nongame Advisory Committee:
  Advise the Director regarding nongame wildlife and wild plants.

Michigan

Hunting Area Control Committee:
  Empowered to regulate and prohibit hunting.

Mississippi

Beaver Control Advisory Board:
  Develop a beaver control program, designate area having control needs, recommend fees, and advise on program implementation.

Wildlife Heritage Committee:
  Utilize inventory data of natural areas, accept right, title, or interest to any natural area, select natural areas for placement on the register or dedication as a natural preserve, provide for management of these areas, and cooperate with agencies or private persons to implement provisions regarding natural areas.

Table 5. State Advisory Boards (continued)

Advisory Committees:
  Aid Commission in formulating policies, discussing problems, and other considerations.

Montana

Fish and Wildlife Crimestoppers Board:
  Recommend individuals and amounts to be rewarded under the program and promote the program.

Nevada

County Advisory Boards:
  Manage wildlife in each of several counties. Boards recommend seasons, bag limits, and other regulations and policies, and solicit and evaluate local opinions.

Advisory Board on Guides:
  Advise the Department on matters which affect outfitting and guide services.

Commission for the Preservation of Horses:
  Preserve herds of wild horses, identify programs to maintain herds in a thriving natural ecological balance, and other duties.

New Hampshire

Commemorative Rifle or Shotgun Lottery:
  Solicit bids to manufacture a commemorative rifle or shotgun for lottery.

New Jersey

New Jersey Migratory Waterfowl Advisory Committee:
  Advise concerning creation and sale of waterfowl stamp and recommend regarding stamp revenues.

New York

Fish and Wildlife Management Practices Cooperative Program:
  Preserve and develop fish and wildlife resources and improve access to recreation.

State Fish and Wildlife Management Board:
  Recommend fish and wildlife management practices and advise regional boards.

North Carolina

Nongame Wildlife Advisory Committee:
  Citizens advise the Commission regarding conservation of nongame wildlife, including creation of protected animal lists and development of conservation programs.

Scientific Council:
  Among other duties, review scientific evidence to evaluate the status of candidate species.

Recreation and Natural Heritage Trust Fund Board of Trustees:
  Authorize expenditures from this fund.

North Dakota

Private Land Habitat Improvement Advisory Committee:
  Advise concerning expenditures from the Small and Big Game Habitat Restoration Trust Fund.

Wetlands Mediation Advisory Board:
  Mediate and hold hearings concerning persons aggrieved by a decision of the USFW pertaining to wetlands and make recommendations not subject to judicial review.

Game and Fish Advisory Board:
  Each Board member holds a public meeting to determine needs and opinions of their constituents. Board advises the Director concerning hunting, fishing, and trapping regulations, and makes general recommendations concerning operation of the Department and its programs.

Oregon

Restoration and Enhancement Board:
  Recommend fish restoration and enhancement programs. Individuals in regions affected may form advisory councils and make recommendations to the Board, as may Department employees in various regions.

Salmon and Trout Enhancement:
  Review policies and make recommendations concerning implementation of enhancement projects.

Table 5. State Advisory Boards (continued)

Pennsylvania
Wild Resources Conservation Board
  Develop a comprehensive management plan and administer the Wild Resources Conservation Fund.
Rhode Island
Marine Fisheries Council:
  After public meeting, promulgate regulations concerning limits, seasons, and manner of taking all marine species.
South Carolina
Migratory Waterfowl Stamp Committee:
  Responsible for the creation of the annual stamp and creation and distribution of related artwork.
Board of Trustees of the Wildlife Endowment Fund:
  Administer the Wildlife Endowment Fund.
Tennessee
Mussel Industry Representatives:
  Enhance and protect the state's mussel industry.
Texas
Aquaculture Executive Committee:
  Biennial review of aquaculture rules in light of new technology to benefit the industry.
Operation Game Thief Committee:
  Administer the Operation Game Thief Fund.
Vermont
Endangered Species Committee:
  Advise the Secretary on all matters relating to endangered species, including list alteration and how to protect listed species.
Migratory Waterfowl Advisory Committee:
  Recommend and consult concerning related fund activities.
Washington
Migratory Waterfowl Art Committee:
  Review and select Director's choice of artwork and review subsequent expenditures.
Firearms Range Advisory Committee:
  Provide advice and counsel to the Interagency Committee for Outdoor Recreation.
West Virginia
Whitewater Commission:
  Study the use and misuse of state white waters.
Board of Trustees of the Wildlife Endowment Fund:
  Accumulate investment income of the Wildlife Endowment Fund until Fund can provide a significant supplement to the Department budget, after which it may direct expenditures from Fund income.
Wisconsin
Natural Areas Preservation Council
Inland Lakes Protection and Rehabilitation Council
Wisconsin Waterways Commission
Lake Superior and Lake Michigan Commercial Fishing Boards
Fox River Management Commission
Great Lakes Fish and Waters Resources Council
Milwaukee River Revitalization Council
Aquatic Nuisance Control Council
Wyoming
Wyoming State Board of Outfitters and Professional Guides:
  Police the profession and set standards.

Introduction
Table 6. Hunter Education Courses
and Table 7. Trapper Education Courses

Hunter Education courses play a vital role in promoting hunting and trapping safety. By far the majority of the states, 43 of 50, provide for hunter education in statute. All of these courses provide instruction in safety; some states include training in archery equipment and trapping methods. The majority of states now require a hunter education course for first-time license recipients, or proof of completion of a similar course from another state. A few states require a "remedial course," for persons convicted of certain wildlife law violations. States should require a mandatory course for all new hunters; however, this is an area in which national standards and guidelines for course content could be widely beneficial, and such a course, or separate courses for firearms, archery equipment, and trapping methods, could result in a national certification of competency, valid in all states. It can be seen in the tables that there is disparity among topics covered in state hunting and trapping education courses, although some states may include additional requirements in their regulations. Relatively few states have trapper education courses specifically mandating training in hunter ethics, survival skills, wildlife identification, responsibility to landowners or wildlife laws.

Trapper education is important to the conservation and humane treatment of fur-bearing animals, the safety of people enjoying the outdoors and the safety of those animals not being trapped. A majority of states do not have trapper education courses of any kind. Of the states that do have trapper education, very few cover topics such as ethics, conservation, or the humane treatment of animals. Trapping law is only listed in Indiana and Ohio as being part of their trapper education program. Only New York, Oregon and Wisconsin include landowner relations as part of their trapper education programs. Wildlife identification was included only in Ohio's program. Minnesota law provides that an advance trapper education program may be established, but does not list course content. Oregon includes survival techniques as part of its trapper education program. Vermont has a trapper education program, but the content is not listed in the statute. Trapper education should be mandatory for all persons wishing to obtain a trapping license. Courses should include topics such as ethics, conservation, responsibility to landowners, and the humane treatment of animals. Trappers should be required to pass some type of proficiency exam in trapping skills before they are granted a license to trap.

It is recommended that states make an effort to establish national standards for hunter education courses, or that all state courses include at a minimum: firearm, bow and arrow, or trapping equipment safety; wildlife identification (Idaho, Minnesota, and Nebraska); target identification; survival skills (Idaho, Oregon and Virginia); humane dispatching of animals wounded by shooting or trapping; wildlife management and conservation; hunter ethics and responsibilities towards landowners and their property, domestic animals and livestock (Idaho, New York, Oregon, Tennessee and Wisconsin); the federal and state Endangered Species Acts; the necessity for, and details of, state and federal wildlife laws (New York, Ohio, Texas and Wisconsin); and practical tests of competency. Cooperation of hunting organizations, hunting-related magazines, and national firearms interest groups should be sought in developing additional course criteria. It is in the interest of all hunters and trappers that hunters are educated to behave in an ethical, sportsmanlike manner and cooperate with landowners so that more lands remain available for hunting; that wildlife laws be enforced so that all hunters and trappers have equal opportunities to take game; and that new hunters have adequate training.

Table 6. Hunter Education Courses

State	Statute Present	Archery	Shooting Safety	Ethics, Conservation or Sportsmanship	Use of Equipment	Responsibility to Landowners	Hunting Law	Other Details in Statute	Statute Does Not List Course Content
AK									
AL									
AR	◆		◆		◆				
AZ	◆								
CA	◆		◆						
CO									
CT	◆	◆	◆	◆					
DE	◆		◆	◆	◆				
FL	◆	◆	◆	◆					
GA	◆		◆		◆				
HI	◆		◆	◆					
IA	◆		◆	◆					
ID	◆	◆	◆	◆		◆			
IL	◆		◆						
IN	◆		◆	◆					
KS	◆								◆
KY									
LA	◆								◆
MA									
MD	◆		◆	◆					
ME	◆	◆	◆						◆
MI	◆		◆						
MO									
MN	◆		◆						
MS	◆		◆						
MT	◆	◆	◆						
NC	◆		◆	◆	◆		◆		
ND	◆	◆	◆						
NE	◆	◆	◆	◆	◆				

745

Table 6. Hunter Education Courses (continued)

State	Statute Present	Archery	Shooting Safety	Ethics, Conservation or Sportsmanship	Use of Equipment	Responsibility to Landowners	Hunting Law	Other Details in Statute	Statute Does Not List Course Content
NH	◆		◆						
NJ	◆	◆	◆						
NM	◆		◆						
NV	◆		◆						
NY	◆	◆	◆	◆		◆		◆	
OH	◆		◆	◆	◆		◆		
OK	◆		◆						
OR	◆		◆	◆	◆	◆		◆	
PA	◆		◆	◆					
RI	◆	◆	◆		◆				
SC	◆		◆						
SD	◆		◆						
TN	◆		◆						
TX	◆	◆	◆	◆	◆	◆	◆		
UT	◆		◆	◆					
VA	◆		◆	◆					
VT	◆		◆		◆				
WA	◆		◆	◆	◆	◆	◆	◆	
WI	◆		◆	◆	◆			◆	
WV	◆	◆	◆						
WY	◆		◆		◆				

Table 7. Trapper Education Courses

Fifteen states provides courses in trapping education. In addition to the topics listed below, two states, Kansas and Ohio, include trapping law in the course; New York and Wisconsin include landowner relations; and Nebraska and Vermont do not list full course content in their statutes.

State	Statute Present	Trapping Techniques	Ethics or Conservation	Other Details in Statute
AZ	◆	◆	◆	
CT	◆		◆	
IL	◆	◆	◆	
IN	◆	◆	◆	
KS	◆	◆	◆	◆
ME	◆			
NH	◆	◆	◆	
NJ	◆			

State	Statute Present	Trapping Techniques	Ethics or Conservation	Other Details in Statute
NY	◆	◆	◆	◆
OH	◆	◆	◆	
OR	◆	◆	◆	◆
PA	◆	◆	◆	
VT	◆			
WA	◆	◆	◆	
WI	◆	◆	◆	
WY				

747

Table 8. Restitution, Spotlighting and Waste Statutes

Restitution

Civil Penalties and other forms of restitution are now required by most states for illegal taking of certain species of wildlife or big game animals. Several states, of which Colorado is a good example, provide for setting rules for replacement costs of fish and wildlife, costs of investigations, and setting schedules of replacement or restitution costs for court use, but usually do not prevent a court or jury from examining the reasonableness of the regulations or from assessing the special factors in a case which may make the true costs higher or lower than the amount stated in the rules. Colorado provides that "replacement costs" must be broadly construed to include habitat improvement or restoration where direct stocking is not feasible". There are many good examples of restitution provisions among the states, and schedules of specific animals and their "values" given (see Pennsylvania, Wisconsin, Louisiana, Minnesota and others for examples). Valuable restitution provisions should be mandatory and the amounts or values set for each species should be adequate to effect deterrence and to pay to restock the animal or otherwise compensate for its loss, and collection should be made for each animal, bird or fish as a separate offense. Most states do stipulate that restitution shall be required and collected. Colorado provides that the amounts collected for each animal "may not be for less than the sum stated by statute, but may be for such greater amount as the evidence may show the value of the wildlife to have been when living and uninjured". Wisconsin also provides that "no penalty prescribed in this chapter shall be diminished because the violation for which it is prescribed falls also within a more general prohibition," and that the burden is on the defendant to show that animals were commercially raised, taken for scientific purposes, or otherwise innocently and legally taken.   Nearly all states provide that the civil or restitution penalties are in addition to any criminal penalties imposed. Pennsylvania, however, only assesses replacement costs for violations involving threatened or endangered species, or others designated by the Commission, but provides that additional compensatory and punitive damages for game or wildlife killed or habitat injured or destroyed may be sought by civil action, including costs of gathering evidence, expert testimony and other costs. Wisconsin, however, notes that a civil action shall be a bar to a criminal prosecution for the same offense and vice-versa. Amounts shall not be less than those stated in the statutes, and shall be for each protected animal, bird, fish or part taken. In Colorado, the division may bring a civil action against an owner whose dog inflicts death or injury to any big game other than bear or mountain lion, and to small game, birds and mammals according to established restitution values.

Spotlighting

Please refer to discussion in Chapter 3, "Wildlife Poaching in the U.S."

Waste

Please refer to discussion in Chapter 3. All states should have a "waste" provision and should clearly define what is "edible meat." Alaska and some other Western states are good examples; also Oklahoma and a few others include waste of aquatic resources, salmon or other wildlife, and more states should do so. Oklahoma is the only state to mention that "no person may capture, kill, mutilate or destroy wildlife protected by law and remove the head, claws, teeth, hide, antlers, horns or parts with intent to abandon the body, nor capture or mutilate a *living* wild animal protected by law by removing claws, teeth, hide, antlers or body parts, with such "waste" fines being up to $1,000. It is disturbing to realize that live animals may be mutilated for valuable parts, but since some wildlife parts are worth more per ounce than cocaine, the lengths to which commerical poachers and others will go are not surprising.

Table 8. Restitution, Spotlighting and Waste Statutes

State	Restitution Statute Present	Spotlighting Statute Present	Waste Statute Present	State	Restitution Statute Present	Spotlighting Statute Present	Waste Statute Present
AK			♦	MT	♦	♦	♦
AL		♦		NC	♦	♦	
AR			♦	ND	♦	♦	
AZ	♦	♦	♦	NE	♦	♦	♦
CA	♦	♦	♦	NH	♦	♦	
CO	♦	♦	♦	NJ	♦	♦	
CT		♦		NM	♦	♦	♦
DE		♦		NV	♦	♦	♦
FL		♦		NY	♦	♦	
GA		♦	♦	OH	♦	♦	
HI				OK	♦	♦	♦
IA	♦	♦		OR	♦	♦	♦
ID	♦	♦	♦	PA	♦	♦	
IL	♦	♦	♦	RI		♦	
IN	♦	♦		SC	♦	♦	
KS	♦	♦		SD	♦	♦	♦
KY	♦	♦		TN	♦	♦	
LA	♦	♦		TX	♦	♦	♦
MA	♦	♦		UT	♦		♦
MD	♦	♦		VA	♦	♦	
ME		♦		VT	♦	♦	
MI	♦			WA	♦	♦	♦
MN	♦	♦	♦	WI	♦	♦	
MO				WV	♦	♦	
MS		♦		WY	♦	♦	♦

Introduction
Table 9. Permission to Hunt on Private Land
and Table 10. Permission to Trap on Private Land

Nearly all states have some statutory requirement that hunters and/or trappers obtain permission from the landowner, agent, tenant or employee to hunt or trap (and sometimes to fish) on private lands. Violation of these requirements can lead to prosecution for unlawful trespass on private property. Fewer than half of the states specifically require written permission of the landowner, and in many states the statutory language is not clear as to what kind of permission is required. Hunting and trapping on private lands pose certain dangers to humans, domestic animals and livestock, and these activities, if not permitted by the landowner, can lead to injuries, damage and misunderstandings.

A few states condition obtaining permission on whether or not the land is obviously "private" (Washington: "no trapping without permission where land is improved, apparently used, fenced or enclosed in a manner designed to exclude intruders, a property boundary line is indicated or notice is posted"; Oregon: "no person shall hunt upon cultivated or enclosed land of another without permission as indicated by wire, ditch, hedge, fence, water or by visible or distinctive lines, including posted boundaries of Indian reservations"). Other states (Kansas, North Dakota) provide for posting to specify hunting, trapping, or fishing is by written permission only. In Maryland, in specified counties, written landowner permission is required. Texas states that in counties with a population of over two million, no person may hunt or target shoot without written permission including the hunter's name, address and phone number, signed by the landowner, and further, a Commission regulation authorizing taking of antelope, antlerless deer, or elk in designated areas is not effective for a specific tract of land unless the landowner agrees in writing to the number of animals to be taken.

In several states (see Maryland and Illinois), conservation officers cannot enforce trespass laws against persons hunting/trapping unless the officer has notice or request from the landowner. Other states allow the landowner to arrest the trespasser. North Dakota states that hunting game in unharvested cereal crops without permission is a misdemeanor resulting in license forfeiture for the season, such provisions to be printed on each general game and fur-bearer license. New Hampshire has detailed provisions requiring that trappers have a signed permit from the landowner, and that the owner has filed with the local conservation officer a description of the land on which trapping is to be done; written permission is also required to snare coyotes, beaver or otter (see also North Dakota). Nebraska prohibits trapping on another's land without permission, and the owner may replevy any animals or pelts taken. In Washington, a landowner may request the trapper's identification by presenting the ID tag from the trap to the Department which shall provide such information to the landowner, who may remove illegal traps. This provision allows landowners some recourse as to who has been, or is, trapping on their land.

A number of states have detailed provisions making it illegal to damage or destroy fences, boats, docks, leave gates open, trample crops, build or use tree-stands or observation blinds that damage or destroy trees, build pit blinds, or cut trees without the landowner's permission, or otherwise damage structures, flora, remove minerals or inorganic materials, or commit other damage on another's property. Alabama provides double damage liability for killing a horse, mare or other domestic animal, the landowner to bring the suit, and has strict liability for civil damages for causing injury to a person or domestic animal with a trap used to take fur-bearers. Delaware has gun forfeiture up to 30 days, or until the fine for trespassing is paid, and if not paid, the gun is publicly sold. Massachusetts holds violators liable in tort to the owner for using a firearm, bow and arrow or other article in a careless or negligent manner causing damage to another's property or livestock while hunting, fishing, trapping or target shooting.

It is recommended that statutes be specific as to whether lands must be posted against hunting, fishing or trapping and provide exact details about posting. Uniform "landowner permission forms" issued by the Department (already in use by some states), and required to be signed by the landowner would clarify whether permission had actually been granted. Permission should be carried by the hunter or trapper at all times and requiring that hunters wear "back-tags" with their license number visible would aid landowners. All states should adopt severe penalties, including license revocations, for damages to private lands, domestic animals, crops, and other property. Landowners should be able to restrict the number of hunters or trappers and should be able to specify where traps may not be set.

Table 9. Permission to Hunt on Private Land

State	Statute Present	Simple Permission	Written Permission	Must be Carried	Posted (Notice)	See Statute for Other Details
AK						
AL	♦		♦			♦
AR	♦				♦	
AZ	♦	♦				♦
CA	♦		♦		♦	
CO	♦	♦				
CT	♦			♦		
DE	♦	♦				
FL	♦					♦
GA	♦	♦				
HI	♦	♦				
IA	♦	♦				♦
ID	♦	♦				
IL	♦	♦				♦
IN	♦	♦				
KS	♦		♦	♦	♦	
KY	♦	♦	♦			♦
LA	♦	♦				
MA	♦	♦			♦	♦
MD	♦	♦	♦			♦
ME	♦	♦				
MI	♦		♦		♦	
MO						
MN	♦				♦	♦
MS	♦	♦			♦	
MT	♦	♦				
NC	♦		♦	♦	♦	
ND	♦		♦		♦	♦
NE	♦		♦			
NH	♦	♦				♦
NJ	♦	♦			♦	♦
NM	♦	♦			♦	
NV	♦	♦			♦	
NY	♦	♦				
OH	♦		♦			
OK	♦	♦				
OR	♦	♦				
PA	♦					♦
RI	♦	♦				♦
SC	♦		♦			
SD	♦	♦				

Table 9. Permission to Hunt on Private Land

State	Statute Present	Simple Permission	Written Permission	Must be Carried	Posted (Notice)	See Statute for Other Details
TN	♦	♦	♦			♦
TX	♦	♦	♦			♦
UT	♦		♦		♦	♦
VA						
VT	♦	♦			♦	
WA						
WI						
WV	♦		♦		♦	
WY	♦	♦				

Tables Comparing State Wildlife Laws

Table 10. Permission to Trap on Private Land

State	Statute Present	Simple Permission	Written Permission	Posted (Notice)	Enclosed Lands	See Statute for Other Details
AK						
AL	♦		♦			
AR	♦					♦
AZ						
CA	♦		♦			
CO	♦		♦			
CT	♦		♦			
DE	♦	♦				♦
FL						
GA	♦		♦			♦
HI	♦	♦				
IA						
ID	♦	♦		♦	♦	
IL	♦	♦				
IN	♦	♦				
KS	♦		♦	♦		♦
KY	♦		♦			
LA	♦	♦				♦
MA	♦	♦		♦		
MD	♦	♦				♦
ME	♦	♦				
MI	♦		♦			♦
MO						
MN	♦	♦		♦		♦
MS	♦		♦			
MT	♦	♦				
NC	♦		♦			
ND	♦		♦	♦		
NE	♦	♦				
NH	♦		♦			♦
NJ	♦		♦	♦		
NM	♦	♦		♦		
NV	♦	♦		♦	♦	
NY	♦	♦				
OH	♦		♦			
OK	♦		♦			
OR						
PA	♦	♦				
RI	♦		♦		♦	
SC	♦		♦			
SD	♦	♦				

Tables Comparing State Wildlife Laws

Table 10. Permission to Trap on Private Land (continued)

State	Statute Present	Simple Permission	Written Permission	Posted (Notice)	Enclosed Lands	See Statute for Other Details
TN	♦		♦			
TX	♦	♦				♦
UT	♦	♦		♦		
VA	♦	♦				
VT	♦	♦				
WA	♦	♦		♦	♦	
WI						
WV	♦		♦	♦	♦	
WY	♦	♦				

Introduction
Table 11. Statutory Regulation of Selected Hunting Businesses

Maine, Wyoming, Nevada and Idaho have outstanding guide/outfitter statutes. We recommend that many of those states' ideas be adopted by other states, including: establishment of guide/outfitter advisory boards; ► written examinations for guides covering safety, a working knowledge of state game and fish laws and US Forest Service regulations; ► humane treatment of animals,; ► unethical conduct or breach of contract with clients; ► watercraft certification where needed; ► a course of instruction should be prepared for guide applicants; ► the commission or department should set ethical and safety standards for guides; ► penalties for violations should be misdemeanors and include reexamination or loss of license. In certain situations, such as trophy hunting, guides for nonresidents should be required for proper game management, hunter welfare and safety or enforcement of game and fish laws.

Taxidermy licensing provisions generally specify what records must be kept of specimens to assure that they were legally taken, and regulate shipping and other transport of specimens.

Wisconsin provides for a "taxidermy school permit" for persons wishing to teach taxidermy, and authorizing the purchase of certain otherwise restricted species of fish for instruction purposes. Maine has an advisory board for licensing taxidermists, and a few states require submission of samples of taxidermy work before licensing an applicant. Fur-dealer and related statutes which apply to hide-tanners, fur-auctioneers, and others generally govern the records which must be kept, and regulate possession and shipment and labeling of carcasses, hides, pelts, furs, or other parts, green or processed. We suggest that examinations be required for taxidermists, that some schooling or formal training be required, that premises of taxidermy or fur-dealing operations be subject to frequent inspection by fish and wildlife departments to insure compliance with regulations, and that penalties include loss of license.

Tables Comparing State Wildlife Laws

Table 11. Statutory Regulation of Selected Hunting Businesses

State	Guide/Outfitter Provisions	Taxidermy Provisions	Fur-dealer Provisions	State	Guide/Outfitter Provisions	Taxidermy Provisions	Fur-dealer Provisions
AK	♦	♦	♦	MT	♦		♦
AL			♦	NC	♦	♦	♦
AR	♦		♦	ND	♦	♦	♦
AZ	♦	♦	♦	NE		♦	♦
CA	♦	♦	♦	NH	♦	♦	♦
CO				NJ			
CT		♦	♦	NM			♦
DE			♦	NV	♦	♦	♦
FL			♦	NY	♦	♦	♦
GA		♦	♦	OH			♦
HI				OK			♦
IA		♦	♦	OR		♦	♦
ID	♦	♦	♦	PA		♦	♦
IL		♦	♦	RI			♦
IN		♦	♦	SC			♦
KS	♦		♦	SD		♦	♦
KY	♦	♦	♦	TN		♦	♦
LA			♦	TX		♦	♦
MA		♦	♦	UT			♦
MD	♦	♦	♦	VA		♦	♦
ME	♦	♦	♦	VT			♦
MI	♦	♦	♦	WA	♦	♦	♦
MN	♦	♦	♦	WI	♦	♦	♦
MO			♦	WV	♦		♦
MS			♦	WY	♦	♦	♦

Introduction
Table 12. Animal Damage Control

Animal damage control programs and issues reflect the competing interests of wildlife management, human health and safety, and agricultural, rangeland and economic segments. The best damage control programs are those that encourage cooperation between interests. State aid in building deterrent fences to keep predators out of crops, orchards, pens, corrals, and hives is an example of such a program. These programs mitigate damages for both concerns and encourage cooperation. At the other extreme are programs that award bounties for the heads and paws of depredating wildlife. These programs are near-sighted and outdated.

Many forms of animal damage control too numerous to list reside between these two extremes. This graph is a sampling of states' fish and wildlife agency efforts to mitigate and control damages. The graph contains examples of some efforts that are worthwhile and productive and some that may be counterproductive or overly vague. It should be noted that each state has its own particular demographic and other concerns for animal damage control. These particular concerns and methods are not individually listed.

Most of the concerns addressed in damage control programs are not contained in the state's fish and wildlife codes, but rather in the agriculture codes. The nine categories of this graph are a small sampling of the many possible fish and wildlife agency animal damage control efforts. We urge the reader to consult the "Animal Damage Control" section within the state statutory summaries, and the section on "Animal Damage Control" in Chapter 6.

Table 12. Animal Damage Control

State	Department Investigates & Issues Permits Pre-ADC	Official Bounties	Certain Animals Taken at Anytime	Must Mitigate Damages to Receive Compensation	May Control with Otherwise Illegal Means	Department Furnishes Material Support	No Compensation for Posted Land	State May Control Carcass or Parts	Broad or Vague Statutes
AK	♦								
AL	♦	♦							♦
AR		♦							♦
AZ	♦					♦		♦	
CA	♦					♦		♦	
CO	♦					♦		♦	
CT	♦				♦	♦		♦	
DE									♦
FL	♦								♦
GA	♦								♦
HI	♦					♦			♦
IA	♦								♦
ID	♦			♦		♦	♦		
IL	♦							♦	♦
IN	♦								
KS	♦		♦		♦				
KY									♦
LA	♦					♦			
MA						♦	♦	♦	
MD	♦		♦		♦	♦			
ME	♦		♦			♦			
MI	♦								♦
MN	♦	♦			♦				
MO									
MS						♦			♦
MT		♦							♦
NC	♦								
ND	♦					♦			

758

Table 12. Animal Damage Control (continued)

State	Department Investigates & Issues Permits Pre-ADC	Official Bounties	Certain Animals Taken at Anytime	Must Mitigate Damages to Receive Compensation	May Control with Otherwise Illegal Means	Department Furnishes Material Support	No Compensation for Posted Land	State May Control Carcass or Parts	Broad or Vague Statutes
NE	♦				♦	♦		♦	
NH	♦					♦		♦	
NJ	♦		♦				♦		
NM	♦				♦	♦			
NV	♦					♦			
NY	♦	♦				♦			
OH	♦		♦						
OK					♦				♦
OR									♦
PA				♦		♦			
RI	♦							♦	
SC	♦		♦		♦	♦			
SD	♦				♦	♦		♦	
TN	♦				♦	♦		♦	
TX	♦				♦			♦	
UT	♦								
VA	♦							♦	
VT							♦	♦	
WA	♦					♦	♦	♦	
WI	♦			♦		♦			
WV	♦						♦	♦	
WY									

759

Introduction
Table 13. License Revocation and Suspension

Although most states provide for mandatory hunting, fishing, trapping, commercial or other license revocations for certain egregious offenses, the suspension or revocation is usually discretionary, and even if imposed, is easily appealed, and often reinstated after an informal hearing. The mandatory/discretionary, or "may-shall" provisions in most state statutes is confusing and frustrating. Often excellent language exists, with good enforcement provisions, but either the penalty or the license revocation/suspension is discretionary.   Often states have a mandatory revocation of license provision for illegal taking of certain specified animals, for spotlighting, shooting at people, or trespassing on posted lands (see Idaho, New Hampshire, Washington, Iowa, Mississippi, Louisiana, Wisconsin for examples. Mississippi is one of the few that also requires that a spotlighting violator attend such courses as the Commission prescribes before license reinstatement. Other states "may revoke" for failure to appear regarding a citation, illegal taking of big game, using illegal traps, number of violation points accumulated or convictions for violations in other states, or for being accused of violations relating to protection of persons and property (Colorado, Delaware, Nevada, New Hampshire, North Carolina and Pennsylvania). See also the discussion on this topic in Chapter 3, "Wildlife Poaching in the U.S."

We suggest that more penalties and license suspensions and revocations be mandatory, and so stated in the statutes, and that periods of revocation be stated in specific terms and not in a range of "one to three years" or some such, and that the suspension/revocation period be long enough to be a deterrent. The privilege of having a license is not and should not be considered sacrosanct, and such revocations and suspensions, if enforced, could have a much needed deterrent effect. Permanent license revocation should be mandatory for major or repeated wildlife offenses.

Table 13. License Revocation and Suspension

State	Mandatory Revocation	Discretionary Revocation	Mandatory Suspension	Discretionary Suspension	No Reissue for Prescribed Period	Revocation Discretionary First Mandatory Subsequent	Forfeiture or Confiscation	Permanent Revocation
AK					●	●	●	
AL						●	●	
AR						●		●
AZ		●		●				
CA	●	●	●	●	●			●
CO		●		●				
CT	●	●		●	●			
DE		●					●	
FL	●	●		●	●	●	●	●
GA	●	●	●	●		●		
HI	●	●			●			
IA	●	●		●	●			
ID	●	●			●			●
IL		●		●	●		●	
IN	●	●		●	●			
KS		●			●	●	●	
KY	●				●		●	
LA	●	●		●	●		●	
MA		●	●		●	●	●	
MD		●		●	●		●	
ME	●	●			●			
MI	●	●	●	●	●		●	
MN		●			●			
MO		●		●	●			
MS	●		●	●	●	●	●	
MT					●		●	
NC		●		●			●	
ND			●	●				
NE	●				●		●	

Table 13. License Revocations and Suspensions (continued)

State	Mandatory Revocation	Discretionary Revocation	Mandatory Suspension	Discretionary Suspension	No Reissue for Prescribed Period	Revocation Discretionary First Mandatory Subsequent	Forfeiture or Confiscation	Permanent Revocation
NH	●	●		●	●		●	
NJ			●		●	●		●
NM	●				●			
NV	●	●			●	●	●	
NY	●	●					●	
OH	●	●	●		●		●	
OK	●				●			
OR	●	●	●		●			
PA	●	●	●		●		●	
RI	●	●		●	●		●	
SC			●		●			
SD	●				●		●	
TN	●	●			●			
TX		●		●	●			
UT	●	●			●			
VA	●				●			
VT	●	●	●		●			
WA					●			
WI								
WV	●	●	●	●	●			
WY		●						

762

Table 14. States with Criminal Felony Provisions for Various Violations

Felony Provision Present

Arizona	Idaho	Missouri	North Dakota	Texas
Arkansas	Illinois	Montana	Ohio	Utah
California	Indiana	Nebraska	Oklahoma	Virginia
Colorado	Kansas	New Hampshire	Oregon	Washington
Florida	Michigan	New York	South Dakota	West Virginia

Although only twenty-four states provide for felony provisions for various wildlife violations, virtually every state provides for misdemeanor violations. Examples of the types of violations that constitute felonies in various states are listed below.

Categories for profit or commercial gain include:
*   knowingly capturing, killing, possessings, exporting, importing, or receiving an endangered species for profit or commercial enterprise;
*   buying or selling game or protected animals for profit;
*   game wardens accepting bribes;
*   commercialization in general (aggregate value varies);
*   combined sales greater than $200 within a 90-day period by someone not possessing a commercial license;
*   sale of fish with a value greater than $250 caught with personal fishing gear; and
*   wanton destruction of wildlife whose value is greater than $500.

Examples of specific animals include:
*   killing a raptor;
*   releasing a live wolf;
*   taking big game during closed seasons;
*   destroying paddlefish or pallid sturgeon;
*   killing a panther;
*   using bull, bear, dog or other animal for fighting, baiting or as a target;
*   killing an endangered species or destroying its nest or eggs; and
*   illegally shipping a protected animal.

Examples of previous violations include:
*   subsequent misdemeanor violations;
*   subsequent violation of illegally taking fish or eggs;
*   subsequent violations within 5 years involving big game or endangered species; and
*   multiple convictions of using aircraft to harass wildlife.

Other examples include:
*   resisting an enforcement officer;
*   using an explosive substance to kill or catch a fish;
*   abandoning, or not rendering assistance to someone hunter shot and/or not reporting it immediately;
*   buying, selling, or using illegal devives for bear, deer or moose parts, bear traps, and spotlighting if not a natural person of that state; and
*   having knowledge that fraud was committed in a tournament having a prize greater than $10,000 and not notifying law enforcement.

Table 15. Statutory Prohibitions Against Hunting While Intoxicated

Intoxication while hunting poses a dangerous threat to hunters and to all those who enjoy the outdoors. The states are fairly evenly split between those states that have intoxication statutes and those that do not, but few have detailed testing systems. Hunting usually takes place in remote forested areas which makes enforcement of intoxication laws very difficult. As hunting or trapping while intxocated may also involve traveling to and from the hunting area while intoxicated, this should be be regarded as an area of concern by states. The establishment of a national maximum blood alcohol level standard and uniform testing methods may serve to reduce the amount of alcohol related hunting accidents. State wildlife officers should also be equipped with field kits for testing hunters suspected of being under the influence of alcohol.

It is interesting that not more states specifically address the issue of intoxication or being under the influence of alcohol or a controlled substance in their fish and wildlife laws, and when they do, the penalties are relatively inconsequential. For example, the violation in Pennsylvania is a third degree summary offense (not even a misdemeanor), and the violator is denied the right to hunt or trap for one year. In North Carolina, the fact that a person was "impaired at the time of a violation shall be an aggravating factor and the court shall impose an additional fine and/or jail in accordance with the penalty schedule for reckless use of firearms, with license suspension for one to five years depending on the severity of violation". A few states (see Pennsylvania) provide that a hunting or trapping license shall be refused a person who is certified to the Commission by a licensed medical authority or a court to be mentally or physically unfit or addicted to alcohol or controlled substances "to the degree that the person is unfit to exercise the privileges of the Game and Wildlife Code."

Minnesota has one of the more comprehensive intoxication statutes with copious details on testing hunters for intoxication. A hunter must submit to a mandatory blood, breath, or urine test when: a wildlife officer has arrested the individual for hunting under the influence of alcohol; the person has been involved in an accident while hunting, resulting in property damage, personal injury,or death; the person has refused to take the preliminary screening test; or the screening test indicated an alcohol concentration of 0.10 or more. On certification by the officer that probable cause existed to believe the person had been hunting under the influence, and refused to submit to testing, the commissioner shall impose a civil penalty of $500 and prohibit hunting for one year. In New York refusal to submit to a test for intoxication results in a report of refusal being forwarded to the department of Environmental Conservation within 72 hours and all licenses, stamps, or permits to hunt shall be revoked after a hearing held by the department upon notice to such person, unless such hearing is waived. In North Dakota refusal to submit to an intoxication test that is deemed appropriate will result in a revocation for up to four years of the person's hunting privileges.

Stricter enforcement of hunting intoxication laws will help reduce the number of hunting accidents that occur each year, but enforcement should be accompanied by better and more prompt testing methods. Hunter education courses should provide information on the illegality and danger of hunting while intoxicated. Finally, states should impose stringent penalties on those hunters found guilty of hunting while intoxicated.

Intoxication Statute Present			Testing System Present
Arizona	Massachusetts	North Dakota	Maine
California	Minnesota	Rhode Island	Minnesota
Colorado	New Hampshire	Utah	New Hampshire
Delaware	New Jersey	Washington	New York
Georgia	New Mexico	West Virginia	North Dakota
Maine	New York	Wyoming	
Maryland	North Carolina		

Table 16. Rewards for Assisting with Enforcement Against Violators

A viable reward system for citizen assistance with law enforcement can play a crucial role in the enforcement of state wildlife laws. Of the states that have reward systems, only a few have statutory provisions for a toll-free reporting system or a special reward fund. Missouri, New Mexico and Wisconsin have toll-free hot lines, but no rewards are provided for in the statutes. However, every state in the nation now has a hotline for reporting fish and wildlife violations, albeit most programs are not set forth in statutory provisions. A national toll-free hotline is now available (1-800-800-WARD). Operation Game Thief out of New Mexico has become a model program and many states have adopted it in one from or another. If a state such as New Mexico does not provide for a reward system in the statutes, reward systems and toll-free numbers may have been established under regulations promulgated by the responsible state agency.

Reward systems for successful criminal conviction have been proven to work as both an enforcement tool and a deterrent against violation of state wildlife laws. Therefore, it is recommended that reward systems be established in states where they now do not currently exist, and they could be modeled after current successful systems. Reward programs cannot exist without funding. Therefore, it is critical that states find sources to fund their programs. Those states that provide for special reward funds within their statutes are listed on the chart. Potential funding sources include: a specified percentage of hunting license fees to go toward funding rewards; money collected from fines or from forfeiture and sale of equipment used in the illegal taking of wildlife; and donations from private individuals and wildlife conservation organizations.

State	Statute Present	Special Fund	Toll-free Line
Arizona	◆	◆	◆
Arkansas	◆		
California	◆		
Delaware	◆	◆	◆
Florida	◆	◆	
Hawaii	◆		
Indiana	◆		◆
Louisiana	◆	◆	◆
Minnesota	◆		
Missouri			◆
Montana	◆		
Nevada	◆		
North Dakota	◆		
Oklahoma	◆		
South Carolina	◆	◆	◆
South Dakota	◆		
Tennessee	◆		
Texas	◆	◆	◆
Washington	◆		
West Virginia	◆		
Wisconsin			◆
Wyoming	◆		

Introduction
Table 17. Status of Hunter Harassment Statutes

Hunter harassment statutes exist in 47 states. Most make illegal intentional interference with lawful hunting activities. The language of each state's hunter harassment law is slightly different from all others. Laws against harassing hunters have been motivated by the appearance of animal rights activists onto hunting grounds to protest hunting. Often activists obtain hunting licenses to gain access to hunting areas. Hunter harassment statutes have gained media attention when animal rights activists have appealed their convictions on freedom of speech grounds.

Courts have found that some protest activities on hunting grounds are considered protected speech under the U.S. Constitution's First Amendment. However, states can restrict even protected speech if the restriction is incidental to achieving a compelling governmental interest such as public safety, if the restriction is not overbroad or vague, and if the restriction leaves open alternate avenues of speech. Courts are divided as to whether individual state hunter harassment statutes unconstitutionally restrict free speech. For instance, a Connecticut statute was held to be unconstitutionally overbroad because it contained such sweeping and all-inclusive language that it targeted protected as well as unprotected speech. See *Dorman v. Satti*, 678 F. Supp. 375 (D. Conn.), *aff'd*, 862 F.2d 432 (2d Cir. 1988), *cert. den.*, 109 S. Ct. 2450 (1989). On the other hand, a Maryland circuit court upheld its statute as constitutional, although the language in the Maryland law varied only slightly from that of Connecticut. See *State of Maryland v. Amini*, Crim. Nos. 57440-43, 57480, 57495 (1990).

The vast majority of hunter harassment statutes contain a general prohibition against intentionally interfering with lawful hunting. About three-quarter also contain at least one exemption. Commonly, landowners engaging in their normal activities and law enforcement personnel are exempted. The penalty for violating a hunter harassment statute usually is a criminal misdemeanor conviction. The punishment varies widely from state to state, from a $50 fine up to a $1000 fine and/or a prison term from a few days up to one year. In addition, approximately one-third of the states allow hunters and/or the state to seek damages or injunctive relief from the convicted criminal. Finally, about 20% of the states with hunter harassment statutes authorize the state to revoke or suspend the violator's hunting license upon conviction.

Table 17. Status of Hunter Harassment Statutes

State	Hunter Harassment Statute	Intentional Interference Provision	Intentional Disturbance of Wildlife	Entering Hunting Lands Provision	Common Additional Provision(s)	Exemption: Incidental Interference	Exemption: Law Enforcement	Exemption: Landowner Activities	No Exemptions
AK	◆	◆							
AL									
AR	◆	◆					◆	◆	
AZ	◆	◆	◆	◆		◆	◆		
CA	◆	◆	◆			◆	◆	◆	
CO	◆	◆	◆	◆	◆[1]		◆	◆	
CT	◆	◆	◆	◆	◆[1]				◆
DE	◆	◆	◆			◆	◆		
FL	◆	◆	◆						◆
GA	◆	◆	◆				◆		
HI									
IA	◆	◆						◆	
ID	◆	◆	◆	◆		◆		◆	◆
IL	◆	◆	◆	◆	◆[2]				◆
IN	◆	◆	◆	◆				◆	
KS	◆	◆					◆		
KY	◆	◆				◆		◆	
LA	◆	◆	◆	◆	◆[2]			◆	◆
MA	◆	◆		◆	◆[1]			◆	
MD	◆	◆	◆			◆			
ME	◆	◆	◆					◆	
MI	◆	◆	◆	◆	◆[1]		◆	◆	
MN	◆	◆	◆	◆				◆	
MO	◆	◆	◆	◆				◆	
MS	◆	◆	◆						◆
MT	◆	◆	◆		◆[2]			◆	

[1] Prohibitions include: using "natural or artificial visual, aural, olfactory or physical stimuli to affect wildlife behavior in order to hinder or prevent the lawful taking of wildlife"; "plac[ing] an object or substance that will tend to disturb or otherwise affect the behavior of" wildlife; erecting barriers; throwing oneself into the line of fire; disturbing a hunting blind; or miscellaneous other conduct intended to disrupt lawful hunting.

[2] It is illegal to disturb a lawful hunter, with intent to "dissuade" the hunter from taking wildlife.

Table 17. Status of Hunter Harassment Statutes (continued)

State	Hunter Harassment Statute	Intentional Interference Provision	Intentional Disturbance of Wildlife	Entering Hunting Lands Provision	Common Additional Provision(s)	Exemption: Incidental Interference	Exemption: Law Enforcement	Exemption: Landowner Activities	No Exemptions
NC	♦	♦	♦		♦[1]	♦		♦	
ND	♦	♦	♦			♦		♦	
NE									
NH	♦	♦		♦		♦	♦	♦	
NJ	♦	♦		♦	♦[1]		♦		
NM	♦	♦			♦[1]			♦	
NV	♦	♦				♦			
NY	♦	♦							♦
OH	♦	♦			♦[1]		♦	♦	
OK	♦	♦					♦	♦	
OR	♦	♦							♦
PA	♦	♦[3]	♦	♦				♦	
RI	♦	♦	♦			♦		♦	
SC	♦	♦	♦						♦
SD	♦	♦	♦					♦	
TN	♦	♦	♦	♦				♦	
TX	♦	♦	♦	♦			♦		
UT	♦	♦	♦			♦			
VA	♦	♦	♦						♦
VT	♦	♦	♦			♦			
WA	♦	♦[3]	♦				♦		
WI	♦	♦	♦		♦[1]				
WV	♦	♦	♦						♦
WY	♦	♦	♦					♦	

[3] Interference does not have to be intentional or knowing.

768

Table 18. Native American Provisions

Most provisions exempt Native American hunting on reservation land from licensing requirements; some allow for animal parts to be used for religious ceremonies (See Native American section in Chapter 6, "Discussion and Recommendations." Others refer to provisions not necessarily listed the state summaries. Three states, Maine, Maryland and Virgina, have provisions for Native Americans, but do not have substantial Native American populations.

State	Substantial Native American Populations [1]	Native American Statute Present	State	Substantial Native American Populations [1]	Native American Statute Present
AK	♦	♦	ND	♦	
AZ	♦		NM	♦	♦
CA	♦	♦	NV	♦	♦
CO	♦		NY	♦	♦
FL	♦	♦	OH	♦	
ID	♦	♦	OK	♦	
KS	♦	♦	OR	♦	♦
LA	♦		SD	♦	♦
ME	[2]	♦	TX	♦	
MD	[2]	♦	UT	♦	♦
MI	♦		VA	[2]	♦
MN	♦	♦	WA	♦	♦
MO	♦		WI	♦	♦
MT	♦	♦	WY	♦	
NC	♦	♦			

[1] "Substantial" is defined as those states whose Native American populations exceed a percentage of state or national population. States included in this column have Native American populations greater than or equal to 1% of total state population or Native American populations greater than or equal to 1% of the national population. Information is derived from 1990 US Census data.

[2] These states have Native American populations less than 1% of their state population or of the national population.

WERNEKE © 1991

Chapter 6

DISCUSSION
AND RECOMMENDATIONS

INTRODUCTION

After reviewing the fish and wildlife laws of all of the fifty states, we found that it is difficult to make across-the-board recommendations for all states to take action on a certain issue in a particular fashion. What we did find was that the wildlife issues and the conservation, preservation and management needs of the states appear to vary according to their geography, climate zones, human population, and types of wildlife that inhabit that region. As a result, our discussion and recommendations have focused on examples of what certain states have already done that is recommended for adoption or consideration by other states. As we reviewed states, we were taken with the sheer number of excellent provisions and the wealth of ideas for every conceivable wildlife area of interest. Chapter 3, "Poaching in the U.S.," contains numerous policy recommendations, especially regarding enforcement of wildlife laws, that can be applied to legislative or regulatory action on those issues. Recommendations in this chapter are organized under the ten major headings followed in the state summaries of Part II, and specific recommendations for legislative action are highlighted in bold.

Failure to mention a state in examples of certain topics does not mean that the state does not already contain good or adequate provisions; only that space for review is limited and possibly that other states were more detailed, unique or useful for generation of ideas for other states. Every state has at least one or more excellent examples of statutory provisions.

The initial recommendation to readers is to review every other state's provisions regarding a particular topic of interest, for creative programs, cooperative endeavors, appropriate language, and ways to save money. As always, although a provision may look terrific in print, its effectiveness or success in actual practice may depend upon adequate funding, degree to which it is enforced, and consistency of application. State agencies should be contacted regarding their first-hand experience as to a program or provision's effectiveness.

STATE WILDLIFE POLICY

Policy statements in the fish and wildlife statutes usually begin with "The legislature declares that...," or "It is the policy of this state that...," or a similar declaration. Such policy statements set the foundation and philosophy for the legislation that follows and they range from no easily discernable overall statement (Massachusetts) to statements limited to expressing that "the title and ownership to all fish and wildlife is in the state, the management and regulation of which shall be delegated to the department...." This is sometimes combined with illegal taking restrictions or penalties (examples are Alabama, Arizona, Iowa, Indiana, Louisiana, Missouri, North Dakota, Oklahoma, South Carolina, South Dakota, Tennessee, Utah, Virginia, Wisconsin, and Wyoming). Some states combine a title and ownership declaration with a statement that "it is the policy of the state to conserve and manage wildlife..." (Kansas, Maine, and Minnesota). A number of states incorporate "endangered and threatened wildlife" statements, including the value of diversity of native plants and nongame animals, the importance of habitat conservation and restoration for these species, and plans for funding these endeavors through tax return writeoffs or other methods (Arkansas, Delaware, Georgia, Illinois, Maryland, Montana, Nebraska, and New Jersey). A few states mention the historic or economic value of particular game animals and the need for their protection and management, including grizzly bear, black bear and deer (Montana, New Hampshire and Vermont).

In contrast to general statements concerning state values and policy regarding wildlife, and of the "state duty to preserve for future generations...," a number of states have more explicit policy statements. Some are exemplary in their focus on conservation and economic management issues, pressures from the federal government, and solutions the state declares it intends to pursue, including public education, augmented funding sources, animal damage control, increased cooperation with volunteers and landowners, enhanced resource inventory, environmental impact monitoring, and increased efforts at managing and restoring wildlife habitats.

We suggest that setting forth problems, goals and philosophy in a policy statement is a worthwhile legislative effort in itself, in that it focuses the attention of the legislature, fish and wildlife agency and the public on the issues, the particular conditions the state faces, and allows a recognition of conditions, limitations, and approaches for finding solutions. For example, when Washington states, "The people declare that an emergency exists in the management of salmon and steelhead trout resources such that both are in great peril, and the people appeal to the US Congress to make the steelhead trout a national game fish...," one perceives that more than a general platitude has been stated. The statement continues "... conflicts have eroded the resource, and that it is time for the state to make a major commitment to increasing salmon productivity and to move forward with an effective rehabilitation program..." which is exemplary in stating the problem and an approach to the solution. Washington also notes that no citizen shall be denied equal access to state resources on the basis of race, sex, origin, cultural heritage, or by treaty agreement. Similarly, Oregon clearly sets forth its problems, and the approach to augment game mammal herds and fish for the benefit of hunters, fishers and others and describes steps to be taken and encourages participation of citizen volunteers.

The majority of states have policy statements that define their particular conditions. North Carolina recognizes the conflict between various competing interests regarding wildlife resources and the livelihoods dependent on such resources. Alaska is concerned with land settlement, development of resources, balancing beneficial uses, and sustainable yields. Colorado's emphasis is on preservation of water rights, beneficial use of state waters, and hunting, fishing and trapping as primary methods of effecting necessary wildlife harvests. Connecticut recognizes that extinction and reduction in numbers of numerous species is significant and the conservation and protection of remaining species and habitats is of concern. New Hampshire cites the number of bird and vertebrate species in the state, emphasizing that the majority are nongame species with ecological, historical and aesthetic values to current and future generations. Florida notes that it has more endangered and threatened species than any other state, and that its intent is to preserve them by increasing public awareness of all wildlife species. Florida also expresses concern for sustaining commercial and recreational fishing operations and limiting zoning restrictions that tend to eliminate or have such operations declared nuisances. Texas policy is directed toward insuring an adequate supply of wildlife, preventing depletion and waste, and providing flexibility with changing conditions in a large and diverse state. Idaho also recognizes the need for flexibility in managing wildlife management due to changing conditions and encourages county commissioners to raise money through taxes to support game fish propagation and plating. Hawaii recognizes the contribution of human activities to the extinction and endangerment of numerous species on the islands and the need for immediate action to preserve the economic and aesthetic values of wildlife, aquatic life, and plants and to lessen the impact on native habitats and ecosystems.

Nevada notes the obligation to conserve native fish and wildlife and recognizes that economic growth has led to serious losses in fish and vertebrates with economic, historical, scientific and aesthetic values. Montana expresses a policy to protect and preserve game animals for its citizens, to avoid deliberate waste of wildlife and property destruction by nonresidents, to preserve the grizzly bear and to manage wild buffalo, including encouraging agencies to reach agreement with federal officials on migrating buffalo. Illinois and Rhode Island have interesting policy statements on the need for supplemental funding for nongame wildlife and its value to the state.

The value of natural and genetic diversity and the protection of natural areas is emphasized by Nebraska, which states that knowledge of the status and location of natural heritage resources can prevent needless conflict with economic development and that voluntary cooperation of landowners is an effective and cost efficient means to protect those resources. Maintenance of a registered natural area is declared to be its highest, best and most important use. Mississippi and other states also emphasize landowner cooperation, registration and management of vital critical habitat areas.

STATE FISH AND WILDLIFE AGENCIES

Agency Names

Fish and wildlife departments have in the past often carried the title "Game and Fish Department". **There appears to be a trend toward, and we recommend, changing department titles to "Fish and Wildlife Department" or "Wildlife Department." Such titles better reflect the roles and duties of such a department, which include increased responsibilities for stewardship and protection of nongame or otherwise unprotected wildlife and habitat.**

Agency Structure

State fish and wildlife agencies generally are similar in duties and organization. The basic structure of Fish and Wildlife or Fish and Game Departments, with Directors, Commissions and Commissioners, and Conservation Officers or Game Wardens, with some variations, is universal among the states. Some states are tending toward reorganizing state government agencies into larger, all-encompassing units under a Department of Natural Resources or Department of Environment, Health and Natural Resources, with a Secretary, under which may be a wide variety of agencies, including those for mining, oil and gas, solid waste disposal, forests and parks, fish and wildlife, marine fisheries, reclamation and law enforcement. However, the possibility for conflicts of interest appears to exist between agencies under the umbrella type structures where the secretary, for example, must mediate between interests such as mining, fish and wildlife, the state clean air act, the pesticide boards, the wetland development council and the electric power agency. **Free standing agencies appear to have more autonomy and funding independence.**

Agency Regulations

We recommend that state statutes explicitly state what is to be regulated, how and what factors are to be considered in promulgating regulations, and that provisions be made for citizen participation in the regulatory process. (In New Mexico, 3% of a county's electors may petition in writing for a public hearing; in Texas, aggrieved persons may file suit against the department to test the validity of the regulation.) Several states have regulation content provisions, including Ohio (orders are to be based on distribution, abundance, breeding conditions, food, cover, life history, economic conditions, topography, soil, weather, living or nonliving influences, nuisance factors, imbalance of sexes, and specify areas or waters affected); New Mexico (consideration is given to temperature zones and distribution, abundance, economic value and breeding habits of game animals, birds and fish); Idaho (an animal classification is required for all animals except predators, which must include game, threatened, endangered, protected, protected nongame, and unprotected categories); and Connecticut (regulations are based upon accepted standards of wildlife conservation, scientific and biologic findings, availability of species, unusual weather conditions and special hazards, available food supply and natural cover, general condition of woods and streams, control of a species, number of permits issued, area available, rights and privileges of sportspersons, landowners and the general public, and a sound program of wildlife management and recreation).

Agency Powers and Duties

A sampling of provisions regarding miscellaneous agency powers and duties that are recommended as useful include the following: ► counties are encouraged to acquire and develop lands for parks, preserves, and conservation areas, and to have their own conservation boards (Iowa); ► endangered species stamps should be sold to raise money for the Endangered Species Fund (Connecticut); ► departments should compile reports from hunters as part of the licensing requirement (Nevada); ► a "scientific council" should be established to evaluate the status of candidate endangered or threatened species and advise the commission (North Carolina); ► the department should print a list of endangered or threatened species in the hunting regulations booklet (Oklahoma); ► use of voluntary wildlife habitat or related stamps to raise money (Oklahoma and Massachusetts); ► Commission can appoint qualified persons to be deputy wardens with enforcement powers to serve without state compensation on private game preserves, thus allowing enforcement of state laws paid for by private persons (Alabama); ► appointment of state mammologists, ornithologists, ecologists and other experts to advise the Commission or Director on wildlife issues; ► provisions for counties or cities to receive funds to carry out projects including creating game cover, seeding, controlled burning and cutting for habitat improvement, creation of ponds and fish habitats, fencing, rough fish control, lake and stream rehabilitation, managing fishing lakes and other projects (Oklahoma and Wisconsin); ►

Discussion and Recommendations

prohibition of leasing lands for disposal of hazardous, toxic or radioactive waste, or permitting any mining of uranium or other radioactive materials, or usage resulting in irreparable damage to habitat or wildlife, and adopting regulations for leased lands to minimize damage to fish and wildlife habitat (Louisiana and Pennsylvania); ► keeping a complete list of game law violation prosecutions, including fine, court, forfeitures, restitution assessments, and other information concerning the disposition of the case (North Dakota and others); ► increased use of county conservation wardens with full enforcement powers under the supervision of the department (Wisconsin); ► game wardens should be vested with powers of arrest without warrant of persons committing criminal offenses if committed on public lands, waters or right-of-way (Tennessee); ► preparation of long-range, comprehensive fish and wildlife management plans with specific details, open for public inspection, comment, review and input, and including procedures to evaluate the management program and make modifications as needed (Minnesota).

Agency Advisory Boards. (Please refer to discussions and recommendations preceding tables in Chapter 5 on "Agency Advisory Boards.")

Agency Funding Sources. (Please refer to discussions and recommendations preceding tables in Chapter 5 on "Agency Funding Sources.")

PROTECTED SPECIES OF WILDLIFE

The original intent of the "protected species of wildlife" section in the state summaries was to list for each state the animals given protection. It soon became apparent that states vary as to the meaning of "protected" and "unprotected," and rarely is the term defined or applied to particular species (an exception is Georgia which states that "protected species" means species declared by the department to be subject to the protection of the endangered species act). A few states (Connecticut, Idaho, Kentucky, Nebraska) clearly announce that particular species (most often sparrows, starlings, and "predacious birds") are not "protected species."

There is a lack of uniformity among the states in defining "protection," with definitions running the gamut from "everything is protected unless it is not," to "nothing is protected unless the commission or department says it is." **It is recommended that states clearly define what "protection" means, and that species that are "protected" be enumerated; or that the state designate everything as "protected" unless specifically exempted by statute.**

Specific Protected Species

Some states single out particular species as either "protected" or deserving of "special protection," other than, or in addition to, endangered species. Examples are Alabama: flattened musk turtle; Colorado: protection of female black bears nursing cubs and "fair chase" provisions prohibiting bait or dogs in taking bears; Connecticut: eagle and swan; Delaware: eagle, terrapin; Florida: Florida panther; New Hampshire: caribou, elk, mountain lion, Canadian lynx, golden and bald eagle, black bear; New Mexico: horned toad, bullfrog, minnow, nongame fish; Rhode Island: otter; Michigan: snowy heron and American egret; South Dakota: black bear, mountain lion, wolf, listed game birds and black-footed ferret; Utah: American White Pelican; Washington: bald eagle; Wyoming: eagle. New York lists specific exotic species, parts or products that are prohibited from being sold or offered for sale, such as the leopard, tiger, rhino, marine turtle and polar bear.

Nevada and a small number of other states require that all animals be classified into categories including predators, game, fur-bearing, upland game birds, migratory game birds, game fish, nongame fish, reptiles, mollusks, and crustaceans, all of which must be further classified as "protected" or "unprotected" (Tennessee requires detailed classification of all live captive wildlife). In contrast, Washington requires classification of all native wildlife species into game birds, predatory birds, game animals and fur-bearing game animals; all wild birds not otherwise classified are "protected," and the director may designate wildlife species as "protected." Unfortunately, since these classifications are done by regulation, it is impossible to tell from the statutes themselves exactly what species are protected or unprotected.

Some states define protected wildlife in groups (see Appendices). Examples are: Delaware: protected wildlife is all forms of game and wildlife except those not protected. Kentucky: protected wildlife is wildlife for which an open or closed season for taking has been designated. Maryland: unprotected mammals are only nutria or woodchuck. Wyoming: protected animals are black-footed ferret, fisher, lynx, otter, pika or wolverine; protected birds are federally designated migratory birds; predacious birds are English sparrow and starling; predatory animals are coyote, jackrabbit, porcupine, raccoon, red fox, wolf, skunk, stray cat. See also Minnesota, New Hampshire, New

York, North Carolina, North Dakota, South Carolina and Texas (anything regulated as to taking is protected) and West Virginia. Nuisance species or predators, which are presumably not protected, also may be defined and specific species listed (see California, Hawaii definitions in Definitions Appendix).

Nearly all states mention protection for song, insectivorous, and non-predacious birds, nests and eggs, and homing pigeons. New Mexico has the most complete list of protected song and insectivorous bird families. New York and Utah are two of the few states which appear to provide protection from pollution or taking for protected aquatic wildlife and stoneflies, mayflies, water bugs, damsel flies and crustaceans. Arkansas designates the entire state as a sanctuary for wild fowl of all species except blackbirds, crows, starlings, pigeons and sparrows, however, only game bird nests and eggs are protected from collection except by permit.

Finally, a few states appear to say that "everything is protected unless it is not." For example, Maine states that there is a perpetual closed season on hunting or trapping any wild bird or animal, except as otherwise provided by wildlife laws or regulations (see also Missouri).

Endangered, Threatened and Other Species

All states have some provisions for "endangered," "threatened," "candidate species," "species of special concern," or "species in need of management," (although the specifics may be in regulations and not in fish and game laws). Provisions are usually made for how such species shall be determined and listed, for modifications of the list including input from the public through petitions, hearings or otherwise, and specifics of how, when, where, and in what manner and for what purposes such species may be taken, possessed, held in captivity, shipped, bought, sold and transported. Endangered species provisions are fairly consistent among states with regard to protection and designation of endangered, threatened, and special concern species. **California's statute is exemplary in its level of detail, public participation requirements, lead agency consultation with the department when actions may impact endangered species, and in its similarity to the federal Endangered Species Act.**

It is suggested that states give particular consideration to the preservation of entire ecosystems and significant habitats (see Massachusetts for excellent provisions) rather than to the protection of isolated, threatened or endangered species. Michigan has a policy statement that it is the goal of the state to encourage the lasting conservation of biological diversity and gives reasons why diversity is desirable. Wisconsin makes the laudable statement that: "The legislature finds that activities of both persons and governmental agencies are tending to destroy the few remaining whole plant-animal communities in the state...since these communities represent the only standard against which the effects of change can be measured, their preservation is of the highest importance, and the legislature urges all persons and agencies to consider fully all decisions in this light."

We encourage states to utilize the abilities of the best scientific minds on their technical or endangered advisory committees, and to seek representation from a broad cross section of state and community interest groups. Although private landowners and certain commercial interests and public utility concerns cannot be required to affirmatively protect endangered species, efforts should be made to enlist their support in preserving critical habitats on their lands (see Oregon; significant habitat provisions in Massachusetts). **There needs to be more cooperation between bordering states to insure that migrating species are afforded similar protections in all of the states concerned. Citizen petition procedures should be designed so that public input in decision making and listing species (or removing them from the lists) allows relatively small groups of citizens to have input (see Texas).**

Provisions like California's and Maine's should be adopted: that except for certain variances, a state **agency or municipality shall not permit, license or fund projects that will significantly alter endangered species' identified habitat, jeopardize the species, or violate Commission protection guidelines. Fish and wildlife agencies should more actively publicize the state's endangered lists, and solicit public support and funding for these programs, or adequate funding should be made available by legislative appropriation or other sources (see Tennessee).** States with good provisions include, but are not limited to, Alaska, Connecticut, Hawaii, Illinois, Maryland, Massachusetts, Minnesota, New Hampshire, Rhode Island, South Carolina, Tennessee, Texas, and Wisconsin. **Efforts should be made to cooperate with landowners to move endangered species when necessary from private lands to other appropriate habitats on state-controlled lands (see Wisconsin). Any collecting or scientific permits for endangered species should be strictly monitored so that none are issued under any circumstances if commercial considerations are involved (see Rhode Island).**

GENERAL EXCEPTIONS TO PROTECTION

Unprotected Species

Certain species considered to be pests such as the sparrow and starling are almost universally given no protection by states. Other specific animals with no protection include woodchuck or groundhog (Indiana and Delaware), crows, which may be taken according to federal regulations, moles and gophers (Kansas), coyotes (South Carolina), grackles, ravens, red-winged blackbirds, cowbirds, feral rock doves and crows and nests and eggs (Texas), coyote, fieldmouse, gopher, ground squirrel, jackrabbit, muskrat and raccoon (Utah). Idaho requires tattooing and registration of any captured wolves or wolf/dog hybrids. Nebraska clearly defines "wild birds and game" which cannot be kept in captivity without a permit, including crows, game birds, game animals, fur-bearers, and nongame and endangered species. A number of states have provisions for taking undesirable or inedible fish or turtles by any means, including chemical, electrical or mechanical (see Arkansas, Connecticut, Illinois, Minnesota, Nebraska, Pennsylvania, South Dakota, Wisconsin).

New Mexico is one of the few states that has a "nongame hunting license," allowing taking of birds or animals not protected, and is one of the few states to permit taking for Indian religious purposes of vultures, hawks and owls. The department in Nevada may permit the commercial taking of unprotected wildlife approved by the Commission, which may charge a price for the wildlife taken, and such wildlife may be sold, or maintained in a private collection. Oklahoma allows the running or chasing of fox, bobcat and raccoon with dogs for sport. A few states, such as North Dakota and Missouri, have no provisions at all relating to these topics, other than taking of predators or nuisance animals. **It is recommended that contracts or permits for taking rough fish be monitored carefully to assure that game fish are not being taken.**

Wildlife in Captivity

States have a variety of provisions for keeping wildlife in captivity. A few states allow possession of birds or animals for domestication and/or propagation (South Carolina), and private collections of legally obtained live wild animals, birds and reptiles if not for public display (Nevada). Idaho allows animals other than big game, threatened or endangered species to be held in captivity if legally obtained. West Virginia permits wild animals or birds acquired from commercial dealers or during open season as pets and allows menageries to take animals from the wild. Some states regulate keeping wild animals for display by traveling menageries. Oregon allows keeping certain species for humane care. Other states require a license for wildlife rehabilitation (examples are Iowa, Maryland "wildlife cooperator" permit) and keeping tame animals. Illinois and Iowa permit crippled protected species to be "salvaged" for donation to scientific, educational or zoological entities, or rehabilitation. Tennessee requires basic knowledge of the habits and diet, health, exercise and housing of the particular species in captivity before permits may be issued. Alabama requires five experts to set standards for care and treatment of captive wildlife.

A few states, such as Florida and Georgia, classify wildlife according to its degree of danger to humans or the habitat, and prohibit certain classes as pets, allowing keeping of other classes by permit with stringent requirements. Maine allows wildlife to be kept in captivity for exhibition and allows a licensee to purchase, take, import, breed or sell live moose, caribou or bear under compliance with housing and care standards. Massachusetts does not allow zoos, natural history associations or museums to transfer protected fish, spawn, birds, nests, eggs or mammals without a permit. Texas requires a permit for the breeding, exhibition, or personal use of a wild animal on its restricted list. Local governments may also regulate wild animal possession, including wolves, bears, exotic cats and other exotics. West Virginia issues permits to keep in captivity wildlife or reptiles for science or propagation and allows keeping wild animals or birds acquired from a commercial dealer or from the wild as pets and issues permits. **We recommend that: ▸ training, licensing and assistance with housing and care requirements be afforded to rehabilitation groups or individuals; ▸ traveling zoos, menageries or animal exhibits be discouraged when possible, and otherwise strictly regulated because of myriad opportunities for abuses in care and housing of animals; ▸ any keeping of wildlife as "pets" should be prohibited or carefully regulated.**

Perhaps the worst "keeping in captivity" provision is Alabama's "coon on the log" contest, which allows a sportsmen association with 25 members or more to trap and cage up to 10 raccoons for use in "demonstrating the abilities" of a raccoon to resist being retrieved by dogs from on a log in a lake. The "coon on the log" contest is allied closely to bear baiting, cock fights and dog fights and conjures up unsavory images of "sportsmen" that fish and wildlife agencies could well do without. **We recommend removing old or antiquated provisions for keeping wildlife in captivity. "Coon on the log" type events should not be encouraged by statutory sanction.**

Discussion and Recommendations   776

Scientific, Educational and Other Taking

Nearly every state provides for taking, under strictly regulated conditions and procedures, endangered or threatened species for scientific, zoological or educational purposes, for propagation in captivity, or allows taking when public health or welfare is involved. States with good scientific taking permit provisions include Ohio, Oklahoma, Pennsylvania, South Carolina, South Dakota, Texas, Washington and Wisconsin. (Texas is the only state to declare that no permit may be issued to take or transport endangered fish or wildlife for commercial propagation if they may be legally obtained from a source other than the wild.) All states allow taking exceptions for virtually any species by fish and wildlife agency personnel and USFW personnel, for control, stocking, breeding or exchange with other states. **It is recommended that: ▸ a collecting plan showing clear need for specimens be submitted and approved by a recognized scientific or educational institution; ▸ scientific, educational and other permits be strictly monitored, with the specific number and species of animals to be collected and method of taking stated, area and time limits of collection, the place of keeping specimens and final disposition; ▸ a final report of the collecting activity and results be filed and open to the public; ▸ the scientific or educational need of the project be evaluated before permit issuance; ▸ collectors be certified and have letters of recommendation from recognized authorities before permit issuance; ▸ collectors be under active supervision of accredited mammologists, zoologists, ornithologists, or other trained persons; ▸ approved projects have clear benefits for wildlife, and duplication be minimized; ▸ a scientifically valid report should be the end product; ▸ collected specimens should not be traded, sold or exchanged without approval; ▸ departments should check permittees' daily records and perform inspections to insure compliance. There should be some limits on the numbers of nongame animals of any species which may be taken, not just limits on "nongame in need of protection" or "species of special concern."**

HUNTING, FISHING, TRAPPING PROVISIONS

Licenses, Permits and Stamps

State wildlife laws involving hunting/fishing/trapping licenses, permits and stamps are extremely diverse, and it is only possible to list some innovative or unusual provisions that might be worth using by other states. Only Maryland clearly states a rationale for issuing hunting licenses ("to provide a fund to pay the expense of protecting and managing wildlife and preventing unauthorized persons from hunting"), and only North Carolina clearly differentiates between "permit" and "license," and may provide both for the same activity, but with different privileges. For an example of the wide variety of license types which may be issued under the wildlife laws of a state, see Massachusetts, which includes some unusual licensed activities.

The following are miscellaneous useful license and permit ideas: ▸ several Eastern states provide that no license is needed to fish in the county or city of residence, or that hunting licenses are available for use only in the city or county of residence at a lower fee than the statewide license (Virginia); ▸ licenses are required for floating and stationary waterfowl hunting blinds (Virginia); ▸ wearing of back-tags with visible license numbers are required for deer hunting (Wisconsin); ▸ Conservation or Habitat Restoration Stamps are required in addition to game licenses to lease private lands for hunting or to improve habitats and for other projects (North Dakota, West Virginia); ▸ "Use" stamps are required for all persons entering public lands for hunting, fishing, trapping or any recreation purpose (Texas); ▸ restrictions are put on the number of license types one may hold in a lifetime, for example only one grizzly bear license in a lifetime, only one moose, mountain sheep or mountain goat every seven years (Montana); ▸ it is unlawful to take more than one big game species in a license year regardless of how many licenses purchased (North Carolina); ▸ a "depredation permit" is required to take excess predators (North Carolina); ▸ special "guest" and "special device" fishing licenses are required (North Carolina); ▸ a "noise-making" permit is required for animal damage control purposes (Connecticut); ▸ National Forest permits are required for hunting (Virginia); ▸ special "premiere tourist resort city" trout license required in addition to state license in cities of specified size with significant tourist income (Tennessee).

Maryland allows persons arrested for no license on their person to present same to the court within five days, and the fine will be reduced by half. Oklahoma allows persons arrested for hunting game other than deer, antelope or elk without a license to purchase a temporary 30-day license in lieu of posting bond, and no hunter education certificate is required for such substitute temporary license. Several states require special licenses for "hound hunters," other dog hunting, field trial, falconry and raptor permits (see Arkansas, Idaho, New Hampshire, Oklahoma and Washington), and Connecticut and Delaware require that dog club training areas be licensed. Arkansas requires hunting dogs to be specially licensed, and it is felony theft to try to steal a licensed dog.

It is recommended that states use a screening process to deny licenses to persons deemed unfit to hunt/ fish/ trap using various provisions. Some states refuse to issue licenses to persons "deemed not suitable" (New Hampshire); persons convicted twice of certain violations or who are habitual drunkards, or have been convicted of grand larceny (Arkansas); declared physically or mentally unfit (Nebraska); persons convicted of burglary or criminal trespass, theft of trapping, hunting or fishing equipment, theft of another's game (Maine); persons who have not paid all resident taxes for the preceding year (New Hampshire); persons convicted of theft, fraud or a gambling offense are ineligible for a tag fishing tournament permit (Ohio). A hearing or appeal shall be provided, with the director's decision final.

Hunter, Trapper, Archery Education. (Please refer to discussion and recommendations preceding tables on "Hunter Education Programs" and Trapper Education Programs" in Chapter 5.)

Restrictions on Taking

We recommend the following general restrictions on taking practices and provisions: ▸ Nevada and Arizona make it unlawful to camp within certain distances of waterholes or stock tanks such that access is denied wildlife or domestic stock to the only reasonably available water; ▸ New Mexico may restrict rabbit hunting during times of bubonic plague infection; ▸ use of live waterfowl as decoys should be prohibited (Rhode Island prohibits such use; Delaware allows it); ▸ many states prohibit the use of ferrets, with exceptions for orchard growers and others (see Nebraska, New Hampshire, Ohio and others); ▸ Maine and West Virginia prohibit shooting at any wild bird or animal unless plainly visible, and Pennsylvania makes it unlawful to discharge a firearm or arrow at random in the "general direction of game or wildlife not plainly visible for routing or frightening them"; ▸ North Carolina is alone in providing for humane dispatch of wounded animals by knife, pistol or other swift method of killing; ▸ New Hampshire penalizes negligent firearm use while hunting or target practicing resulting in injury or death by mandatory 10 year license revocation; ▸ use of radio transmitters, electronic tracking devices on boats or airplanes to track, locate or determine direction of game, bur-bearing animals or fish is prohibited (see Iowa, Louisiana, Maryland, New Hampshire and others); ▸ it is unlawful to use helicopters in taking game, or loading hunters and gear except at recognized airports (Idaho, Maine, Nevada); ▸ hunting game from planes is outlawed, as is using vehicles or planes to rally or drive animals (Colorado, Montana, New Hampshire, Texas); ▸ prohibition of archery or firearm scopes which use infra-red light, radio beams, thermal beams, or ultrasonic or other beam (Pennsylvania); use of ATVs, ORVs and other cross-country vehicles to hunt, chase, rally game is prohibited (Arizona, New Hampshire); ▸ details of permitted traps and methods must be included in hunting and trapping rules provided to each licensee (North Carolina); ▸ traps must be visited at a minimum every 36 hours, 96 hours is too long (Nevada); ▸ a permanent trap number registry should be established so trap ownership can be identified (Nevada); ▸ it is illegal to take game for hire, or aid and abet others in illegal taking (New Hampshire, Pennsylvania and others).

New Hampshire prohibits more than six persons participating to take deer. Pennsylvania makes it unlawful for a body of persons hunting in cooperation to kill or possess excess number of big game, with each person liable for any penalty. The Commission may establish roster requirements and limitations applicable to groups of persons hunting big game. **Group hunting should be strictly regulated to prevent abuses.**

Discharge of weapons from in, on and across streets, roads and highways should be prohibited, and "safety zone" provisions enforced. Pennsylvania makes shooting at wildlife on or across a public highway unlawful only if the line of fire is not high enough above the highway to preclude danger to highway users. Some Western states appear to allow limited shooting from highways.

It is also recommended that, particularly with regard to fishing, there be a clear delineation in the statutes as to permitted commercial taking methods as opposed to sports angling taking methods, and that the licensing requirements for each be clarified.

Montana is exemplary in its prohibition against conducting or sponsoring contests in which a prize is offered for the largest antlers, horns, weight, longest body or other "trophy" attributes. If trophy hunts are to be encouraged, conducting hunts using tranquilizer guns should be more widely adopted, as the animal goes free to propagate or to be "taken" again. Montana also makes it unlawful to give prizes for taking any game, fowl, fur-bearer or protected bird or animal, and any such permitted contests shall be strictly regulated. Texas has severe penalties, up to $10,000 and a 3rd degree felony, for fraud in freshwater fishing contests.

Lead shot should be phased out over five years because of adverse impacts, such as lead accumulation in wetlands with subsequent ingestion by waterfowl. Several states have strong policy statements restricting the use of lead shot for waterfowl hunting. However, Maryland states that the secretary and department may not adopt regulations banning use of lead shot while hunting waterfowl, and any such regulation is null, void and of no effect;

nor may the state or any agency request the federal government enforce any federal regulation regarding a ban or limit on the use of lead shot except in nontoxic shot zones as classified by the USFW (see also Illinois). In Wyoming, the Commission shall not ban the use of lead shot except where shotgun shell pellets will exceed 20,000 per acre as determined by approved sampling methods; and banned lead shot areas shall not exceed those reasonably necessary for practical enforcement of the ban, unless adoption of federal regulations forces designation of additional areas as nontoxic shot zones, and the Commission shall cooperate with the USFW to minimize the extent to which lead shot is banned.

We suggest that states move in the direction of confining dog-related hunting events to controlled field trials on shooting preserves or private dog club facilities, and that chasing of bears, rabbits, raccoons and foxes, despite years of tradition, are activities that should gradually be eliminated in favor of events requiring more skill and training of the dogs. Despite this caveat, a number of states have good dog hunting provisions (see Pennsylvania).

Restrictions on Taking During Exceptional Conditions, and on Sundays

We recommend that states adopt provisions prohibiting taking of wildlife during periods of exceptional weather, or situations involving fire and flood. Examples include Delaware (muskrats cannot be taken during floods when they are out of their usual places of hiding and shelter; no hunting allowed of any protected bird or animal except muskrats, minks and otters in the snow, nor on Sunday, except for foxes with dogs); South Carolina (a closed time for fishing in all muddy streams from sunset Saturday until sunrise Wednesday); Maine (commissioner shall establish criteria for identification of deer wintering areas and notify towns and property owners and provide information); South Carolina (department may close seasons up to 10 days in areas when deer or other game cannot protect themselves because of abnormal conditions, and anyone found with a game-taking device or dog within such restricted areas is guilty whether game is taken or not). **In order to prevent waste, states should allow taking by any means of fish which have been stranded in small ephemeral ponds by receding flood waters (see Ohio).**

Prohibitions on Sunday hunting appear frequently in the Eastern states. Examples are Pennsylvania and Virginia where Sunday is declared a rest day for all species except raccoons, which may be hunted until 2:00 a.m. The "day of rest" perhaps should be more widely adopted as beneficial to humans and wildlife alike.

Benefits for Landowners Who Allow Access to Their Lands

Many states issue free licenses for taking big game animals to landowners. Kansas provides that 50% of the big game permits authorized for a management unit shall be issued to landowners. North Dakota issues to landowners deer, elk or antelope licenses for use on their own lands. New Mexico makes antelope and elk permits available to landowners in consideration for letting hunters hunt on the property. Pennsylvania makes antlerless deer licenses available to landowners ahead of the general public subject to certain restrictions. Nevada will make available deer or antelope tags for landowners to sell to hunters as compensation for damage caused by such animals to the land or improvements. The landowner does not use the tag but sells it at any price the landowner and buyer agree on, and the landowner must provide access to adjacent public lands for hunters holding deer or antelope tags. Montana may pay landowners a reasonable sum for the department's right to create public shooting areas and to secure hunting and shooting rights on lands adjoining federal wildlife preserves to prevent them from becoming "landlocked." **It is suggested that landowner benefits be provided by states to encourage landowners to open their lands for hunting, to recompense them for animal damage losses to forage, and to create better relationships and cooperation between fish and wildlife agencies, hunters/trappers and landowners.**

Permission to Hunt/Trap on Private Lands. (Please refer to discussion and recommendations preceding tables on this subject in Chapter 5.)

Reciprocal Agreements between States

Many states have statutes providing for reciprocal licensing agreements between that state and usually neighboring states which will allow nonresidents to fish in boundary waters without licenses, if the other state reciprocates in the same manner. Often the other state must respond exactly in the same way for reciprocity to exist (see Arkansas, Illinois, Indiana, Iowa, Pennsylvania, Rhode Island and others). Some reciprocal agreements involve government agencies and interstate compact agencies for impounding waters, for managing game on boundary lands and waters, and for regulating hunting and fishing (Pennsylvania). Kansas allows reciprocity with non-boundary states, such as Texas. New Hampshire has reciprocal lifetime licenses for hunting and fishing for certain disabled veterans, if the other state reciprocates. Several states have reciprocal wildlife law enforcement provisions, allowing pursuit across state lines or across boundary waters (see Wisconsin). Montana has good reciprocal fishing provisions, including not only boundary waters, but up to 10 miles into the adjoining state. Ohio has one of the most open reciprocal arrangements in that persons licensed by any other state for fishing may be exempt from Ohio license provisions if they comply with the angling laws of their state while fishing in Ohio, and if the other state has similar exemptions. Reciprocal hunting privileges are also available. **We recommend that open reciprocal fishing agreements be developed where possible between states, both within boundary waters and in other state waters. In states where big game herds migrate across state boundaries, there should be some reciprocal licensing arrangement. The problem of boundary lakes is sometimes solved by a special lake license, but it is easier to allow residents of adjoining states to use their respective state license.**

Possession, Sale, Transport, Purchase of Animal/Bird Carcasses or Parts:

There is reason for increasing concern with possession, sale, transport and purchase provisions for carcasses, internal organs, hides, horns, skins and other parts of wildlife, particularly big game animals, because of increases in lucrative poaching in the US, in part due to the increasing traffic and market in illegally taken animal parts, such as bear gall bladders. At present, there is a lack of consistency between the states, which encourages abuses in interstate trafficking in wildlife parts. This issue is addressed in greater detail in Chapter 3 in this text. Only a few states address the problem of "corporate" taking and illegal transport (taking by groups for commercial profit). **The situation involving bear organs and paws has reached the point that all transport, possession, sale, or other dealing in these parts should be prohibited; the same is recommended for any animal or animal part which becomes very valuable on the world market.**

Examples of statutes include: ‣ California (illegal to sell the meat, skin, hide, teeth, claws or other parts of any bear, and possession of more than one bear gall bladder is prima facie evidence of possession for sale); ‣ New Hampshire (bear carcasses legally taken may be bought and sold, but not live bear; illegal buying and selling of bears alive or dead is a misdemeanor for natural persons; a felony for others); ‣ Maine (head, teeth, gallbladder, claws and hide of any bear may be sold, parts transported by common carriers in or out of state with a bear transport tag); ‣ Minnesota (a person may not buy or sell bear gallbladders or bear paws unless attached to the hide; inedible portions of lawfully taken big game animals, fur-bearers and birds other than migratory birds including bones, skulls, sinews, hides, hooves, teeth, claws and antlers may be possessed, transported and sold); ‣ North Carolina (no part of any bear, wild turkey, or fox may be sold except as provided); ‣ West Virginia (under regulations, heads, hides, antlers and feet of deer and hide, head, skull, organs and feet of legally killed black bears may be sold or transported); ‣ Wisconsin (hide of a bear may be sold, transported if it includes the claws, head and teeth, but no person may sell, barter, trade or possess for sale bear claws or teeth which are not part of the hide); ‣ Maryland (secretary may prohibit any taking, transporting, sale, possession of black bears). Several states provide provisions for preserving evidence of sex and species in birds and big game animals, particularly deer, until the meat is prepared for consumption or examined at a department check station, and deer from which the antlers or sex organs have been removed are illegal (see Colorado, Maryland and Wisconsin); in Tennessee, legally killed red fox hides, fur, or pelt may be sold in counties with a certain specified population, according to the most recent census. Virtually all states have a statutory provision prohibiting the sale, purchase, possession or exchange of endangered or threatened species or their parts (Pennsylvania is an example).

Import, Export, Release Provisions

Regulation of import, export and release of nonnative or exotic plants, birds, animals or other wildlife is becoming increasingly important. In some states these matters are regulated by the state department of agriculture or other entity, and thus do not appear in wildlife statutes. Other states have detailed and explicit lists, either in wildlife statutes or regulations, of "prohibited" species, or species which may be imported only under certain conditions. **We suggest that states list in statutes those species for which import, export, release or possession is forbidden, and that states in the same geographic region attempt to reach some uniformity in what is prohibited.** It is evident that some near disasters from imported and inadvertently released species continue to be a problem in the Great Lakes (lampreys, zebra mollusks), in the South (various plants, fish and animals), and in the West (contagious diseases of imported ungulates which affect domestic stock and native wildlife). If one state prohibits minnow-dumping in its state waters, but its neighbor does not, undesirable species may soon inhabit the waters of both states.

Discussion and Recommendations   780

Among the more common prohibitions are those against propagating, selling, buying, or importing skunks, raccoons, nutria, carp and other fish, wolves and coyotes (see Connecticut, Texas, Wisconsin and others). Alaska is one of the few states that restricts import of live venomous insects or reptiles and their eggs. Several Western states mandate testing of all ungulate wildlife for diseases that could be transmitted to livestock, and attempt to immunize wildlife against domestic diseases (Arizona, Idaho). Most states involved in salmonid propagation require testing of eggs, fry or adult salmon before import, or require that they come from certified disease-free sources. Many states restrict the release of wild turkeys or turkey hybrids into the wild. These provisions are in addition to restrictions on importation, care, and accidental release of more exotic zoo animals, tropical fish and pet birds, which may be covered by wildlife provisions, or by other statutory sections. California has particularly detailed provisions for regulating the importation of nonnative species, with extensive inspection, quarantine and testing provisions.

Commercial and Private Enterprise Provisions

In addition to the businesses of taxidermy, fur-dealing, and guide/outfitting which are common to many states (see table in Chapter 5, "Statutory Regulation of Selected Hunting Businesses"), there is a variety of other commercial and private wildlife concerns which should be licensed or issued permits for their operation. Among these are: ▸ muskrat breeding farms (Minnesota); ▸ wildlife exhibitors (Maine and others); ▸ various types of bird and game shooting preserves, both private and commercial and game farms (Mississippi, Montana, New Hampshire, Ohio, South Carolina and almost every other state); ▸ various types of fishing concerns (Connecticut); ▸ commercial deer and elk breeding farms (Louisiana, Texas, Wisconsin); ▸ controlled fox-hunting preserves (North Carolina, South Carolina); ▸ "hunting leases" and "hunting cooperatives" on small to enormous acreages (Texas); ▸ nongame quadruped breeder and exhibitor, including imported or native mink, raccoon, opossum, skunk, muskrat, otter, nutria, bobcat, coyote, beaver, fox and alligator (Louisiana); ▸ "propagator" or "dealer" license for any undomesticated fish, birds, mammals, reptiles or amphibians (Massachusetts); ▸ commercial waterfowl shooting areas (Illinois). **With respect to taxidermy, fur-dealing, hide dealing, fur auction and similar licenses, we recommend that regulation of these businesses be rigorous and continuous, that records be required, that penalties be severe for violations and licenses or permits revoked permanently, and that for taxidermy, recent work samples be required and an examination given before licensing (see Maryland).**

Most states have some provisions for acquiring animals from commercial farms or from the state, or by taking from the wild with a permit (Louisiana). Usually fencing and other confinement provisions are specified, especially for big game farms. Usually there are regulations providing for recovery of escaped animals and for damages to adjacent landowners by pheasants or other game birds raised on preserves (Ohio). Louisiana, Montana and Wisconsin are among the states with extensive details concerning game farms and shooting preserves.

Although virtually every state has some sort of game or bird shooting or breeding preserves, relatively few mention the care the animals should receive, and we suggest that care provisions be specified in statutes, as well as what general enforcement shall take place on preserves. Shooting preserves should be subject to frequent inspection to insure they do not become preserves for "sitting duck" hunts, whether birds or game animals are involved. South Carolina provides that animals in captivity at a shooting preserve must be confined in cages constructed as specified and must receive proper care, food, water, parasite and disease control, cover and bedding, and fresh air while being transported in vehicles. North Carolina requires that fox welfare be considered on controlled fox hunting preserves. Mississippi states that game and shooting preserve operators must consent to patrolling by commission agents without warrant to determine if game laws are being violated, and other states provide enforcement personnel at the operator's cost.

Allowing wildlife exhibitors to take wild animals from the state for exhibition purposes, even by permit, should be discouraged (see Maine, which allows wildlife exhibitors to take live moose and caribou by permit from the wild, breed and sell them, and to display, breed and sell bears and their offspring). Any type of permitted "travelling wildlife exhibit" should be closely monitored and should conform to department standards of sanitation, care, housing, and disease prevention, and the department should make frequent inspections of these.

ANIMAL DAMAGE CONTROL

Animal damage control issues and problems receive frequent and widespread media coverage, and are the focus of highly charged debates. Complicating factors include the involvement of ranchers, environmentalists, federal and state departments of agriculture and other federal and state agencies. State and federal public health officials often become involved when there are rabies or plague outbreaks. The issue of too much control or not enough can arise unexpectedly, such as concerning the recent "hantavirus" outbreak in the Southwest. Since the virus is suspected to be carried by deer mice, which have had an unusually high population in recent years, the question has been raised that perhaps if eradication of predators like coyotes had not been undertaken, the deer mice would not pose a threat to humans. Similarly, questions have been raised about attempts to eradicate predators such as wolves to provide more game animals to hunt, and thus more hunter-related income for a state's economy. The table "Animal Damage Control" in Chapter 5 illustrates some approaches and issues from wildlife statutes concerning animal damage control. It appears that many states are moving in the direction of more landowner cooperation, relocating of animals and department aid and material support for mitigation of damage by wildlife.

Methods of Taking

When poisons, piscicides, herbicides, are used for animal damage control, or other methods of taking are allowed which are otherwise illegal, such as use of airplanes, it should only be by permit, strictly regulated and controlled by the department. Most states which address the use of rodenticides, poisons and cyanide "coyote getters" require permits for their use (see Maine, Massachusetts, Minnesota, North Carolina, Oklahoma and South Carolina). **When states allow the hiring of commercial predator controllers or "bounty hunters," there should be strict requirements as to qualifications, and controls to prevent abuse and profiteering from carcass sales, with strict penalties for violations. Carcasses should remain the property of the state and should be disposed of other than by selling.** Texas has detailed provisions regarding controller airplane use for predator control, but landowner permission is required, and a second offense by a controller within 10 years is a felony. Minnesota lists qualifications controllers must meet, and has standards of proof that they must satisfy to be paid.

Beavers

Beaver dams on public and private lands are a concern for many states, and many allow landowners to do as they wish with beavers on their own lands. Other states require a permit to destroy beavers, or require that beaver control be done by the department. Montana and Nevada allow the department to enter private lands and control beavers for the relief of other landowners if the involved landowner refuses to do so, and Nevada provides that adjacent landowners may petition for department control of beavers. Wisconsin states that if a landowner refuses to give consent to the department to remove beavers causing damage, the landowner is liable for damage caused by the beaver dam to public and private property. **When possible, beavers or other animals causing damage should be transferred to another area or state. This is an area where more interstate cooperation is needed. Provisions should be made to allow for controlled restoration of riparian areas by beavers and beaver dams.**

Birds

Nearly all states provide that starlings, sparrows, and sometimes crows, blackbirds, cow birds and others are unprotected and may be taken at any time, and a few mention the problem of birds gathering in such numbers as to become a nuisance. Only Arkansas states that if starlings or similar birds are a problem, officials must meet with representatives of the Audubon Society, other bird clubs, garden clubs, humane societies, or with several of these, to discuss possible solutions to the problem. If no solution is found, the birds may be destroyed under state police supervision. **When large numbers of birds must be destroyed, local conservation groups should be involved and other alternatives considered such as noise-makers and fireworks.** Some states include game bird crop damage in their provisions for mitigation efforts or compensation for landowners if the department cannot control the damage (New Hampshire, North Carolina). **We recommend that provisions include monetary compensation for damages by birds to landowners, after department investigation and mitigation efforts by both landowner and department, and that, as in New Hampshire, damage be reevaluated at the time of harvest before final damage appraisals are made. Destruction of birds by landowners should be allowed only by permit specifying the number and type of birds which may be trapped, poisoned, or otherwise taken.**

Discussion and Recommendations   782

Ecologically Harmful Species

A detailed treatment of the problem of introduction, propagation, and spread of ecologically harmful exotic species is in Minnesota, which has adopted a long-term, statewide ecologically harmful exotic species management plan to address public awareness, classification of species and control and eradication measures. Grants are available to states through the federal Nonindigenous Aquatic Nuisance Prevention and Control Act, and from other sources. **We recommend that: ▸ governors and wildlife agencies in affected states cooperate to control ecologically harmful exotic plants, animals and aquatic wildlife; ▸ states specifically state which species shall not be imported into the state; ▸ stringent disease and parasite inspection provisions be instituted for any allowed imported species; ▸ public awareness campaigns be undertaken utilizing state agency resources.** (See also "Import, Export and Release Provisions in this chapter.)

Landowner Compensation and Mitigation

Landowner compensation for wildlife damage and requirements for mitigation are recommended. In Idaho, despite other animal damage control measures, bears and mountain lions may be destroyed without permit "to protect livestock," but in Idaho landowners have an obligation to take steps to prevent property loss by wildlife and to mitigate damages. In North Carolina, when livestock is damaged by bear or mountain lion, the owner may get 50% of the fair market value of the livestock if the department is notified within four days. In Pennsylvania, landowners or beehive owners may apply to the department for assistance in erecting a bear-deterrent fence. No claim for damages shall be paid for hive damage if the bear is killed, or if the claim is a second/subsequent one filed by a person who has not erected and maintained an approved fence. New Hampshire also provides for mitigation measures such as fences, and uses an impartial board to assess damages. In West Virginia, a bear may be destroyed, and then reported to the department, along with a damage claim, and the owner may recover the fair market value of livestock and unborn issue. Damage by elk, deer and moose trampling or browsing crops, produce or trees can likewise be mitigated by fences and deer repellents with department assistance, and most states require some mitigation and that the department investigate and corroborate the damage and issue a permit before deer are killed (see "Animal Damage Control" table).

We recommend that: ▸ whenever possible, landowners be required to mitigate damage; ▸ the department attempt to aid materially in providing fencing materials or similar mitigating materials rather than paying for damage claims; ▸ damage claim payments are preferable to killing the predator; ▸ the department be notified of damage before killing the wildlife whenever possible; ▸ efforts be made to trap and move offending wildlife to more remote areas instead of killing; ▸ when animals are killed, the department retain the meat or donate it to charity; ▸ comprehensive control plans be put into place clearly specifying the duties of the landowner and department in effecting control, compensating the landowner for damages and for engaging in mitigation before the fact; ▸ an independent appraisal board be utilized to assess damages; ▸ the department not award damages to landowners who refuse to participate in available wildlife damage abatement programs or to follow reasonable abatement procedures the department recommends; ▸ damage awards be reduced, but not eliminated, for landowners who do not open their lands for hunting, and that payments be reduced proportionally if the landowner charges a fee to hunt on the land (see Wisconsin). In particular, see the programs of Arkansas, Colorado, Idaho, Maine, Massachusetts, Minnesota, Pennsylvania, Washington, Wisconsin and Wyoming.

ENFORCEMENT OF WILDLIFE LAWS

In summarizing each state's statutes, the topic of enforcement on the one hand has abundant model statutes and ideas worthy of emulation by other states, and on the other hand is fraught with antiquated language, redundancies, obvious loopholes, and inconsistencies from state to state. Enforcement issues and policy recommendations are discussed in detail in Chapter 3, "Poaching in the U.S."

Assistance to Enforcement Officers

A major problem facing fish and wildlife agencies is acquiring adequate funding to place enough enforcement personnel in the field properly to enforce the fish and wildlife statutes. Several states have partially solved this problem by using volunteer, auxiliary, or other personnel who either have the same enforcement powers as regular officers, or who take over other duties in conservation management or education to free commissioned officers for actual enforcement activities, particularly in Western states where adequate enforcement involves coverage of hundreds of square miles. The Arizona Reserve is one of several good examples, and Arizona also provides for contracting with the State Department of Corrections to use inmate labor, including juveniles, in constructing, operating or maintaining game and fish facilities. If actual arrest powers cannot be conferred on volunteers, the mere presence of uniformed personnel can act as a deterrent to fish and wildlife violations. Some states (Connecticut) allow towns and villages to appoint their own constables for fish and game protection who enforce local laws and Commission regulations. Usually these volunteer deputy wardens receive some training, are covered by state insurance while on duty, and serve a specified number of hours a week with no compensation.

Another solution is utilizing other officers in certain situations (besides the common "shared enforcement powers" of sheriffs, constables, state police and other non-fish and wildlife officers). The North Carolina Commission may confer law enforcement powers onto USFW employees under specified conditions. Oregon may, with state police and Governor approval, employ persons, in addition to authorizing state police, to enforce wildlife laws. Minnesota, with approval of another state or the US government, may appoint any salaried, bonded officer of that jurisdiction authorized to enforce wildlife laws to be a special conservation officer, and may enforce wildlife laws of the US or another state if a reciprocal arrangement exists. Several states provide by statute that pursuit across boundary waters and into adjacent states for enforcement of wildlife laws is allowed (Maryland), or provide that county courts and enforcement officers have jurisdiction over boundary waters in a reciprocal arrangement with bordering states (Minnesota).

Related to these efforts to maximize enforcement assistance for officers are the various reward and "hotline" programs in many states. All states now have a hotline, and there is a national game thief hotline number (1-800-800-WARD). Mississippi has detailed hotline and violator reporting provisions that specify to whom the information may be released, and provides punishment for filing a false violation report. See table in Chapter 5 regarding states' reward programs (covering statutory provisions only). **Other solutions to the adequate personnel problem are: ▸ private citizens may arrest violators of game laws (Mississippi); ▸ licensed game farm and other restricted preserve operators may be designated as special representatives to enforce game laws, prevent trespass, and to hunt or trap animals destroying game birds reared or liberated on the area (Delaware, Illinois and Nebraska); ▸ any person may refer charges against a specific hunting license in writing, and on hearing of and finding violation, the director must revoke the license for up to five years on first offense (Idaho); ▸ a landowner is vested with the powers and rights of a game protector to arrest any trespasser for trial before a justice of the peace (West Virginia).**

Officer Failure to Enforce or Other Misconduct

Few states have statutory provisions to punish officers who accept bribes, or who fail to enforce the wildlife laws. **We suggest that failure to arrest, reluctance of prosecution, or failure fully to investigate wildlife violations be dealt with promptly and severely in the statutes.** This is an area where it is very important to avoid the appearance of impropriety. Unfortunately, there exists a certain amount of public suspicion that officers and judges may be reluctant to arrest and prosecute persons hunting for subsistence or who are friends or acquaintances, especially in small communities.

A game warden who accepts a bribe in Oklahoma is guilty of a felony, and shall serve two to seven years in prison. Mississippi and Montana provide that no conservation officer shall compromise or settle out of court any violation of wildlife laws. Other states (Arkansas, Nebraska, Oregon, Tennessee and Washington) place an affirmative duty on grand juries to investigate certain classes of offenses, to serve arrest warrants on officers of corporations who violate game laws, or award prosecutors or counties a percentage of the fine to encourage prosecution. Washington subjects officers and state officials to civil liability for willful misconduct or gross negligence in performance of duty, and for either failure to seize and confiscate property used in violation of wildlife laws, or for negligently seizing that which should not have been held in violation of a wildlife provision. Delaware provides that no penalties under wildlife laws shall be suspended and failure of an officer to do his assigned duty is punishable.

Records of Offenses

We recommend that all states require courts to keep records of the disposition of all wildlife violation prosecutions and that details of case disposition be reported to departments (Delaware, Louisiana Mississippi and others); that records of all citations be kept; and that citations be disposed of only by trial or other court action (Wyoming). Further, if a court finds restitution inappropriate, or imposes a lesser value than the

minimum value recommended, the court should make its reasoning part of the record filed with the department (North Carolina), and such records should be public so that the efficiency, frequency and uniformity of prosecutions and convictions can be ascertained.

Penalties

The treatment of "penalties" varies widely among states, in amount of discretion given to the courts, explicitness of the statutes, level of punishment, and assessment of additional penalties such as restitution for illegal taking, requirements for habitat restoration, court costs, and mandatory or discretionary license revocations or suspensions. **Most states need clarification of penalties in their statutes. Few states provide in the statutes how penalties shall be set, and more should do so.** In Alaska, the Supreme Court shall: specify those misdemeanors appropriate for disposition without court appearance; establish bail amounts and consult with an advisory committee composed of fish and wildlife protectors, department representatives, two district court judges and chairs of the house and senate judiciary committees of the legislature to establish the misdemeanor schedule. Many states provide the penalty in every statute or refer to the criminal statutory provision.

We recommend that: ▸ penalties be clarified and classified into a limited number of categories; ▸ fines and jail term lengths be standardized into a manageable number of categories; ▸ more penalties be mandatory; ▸ mandatory license revocations and suspensions be assessed; ▸ the courts be directed not to suspend or reduce a penalty; ▸ violations of license revocation orders or failure to pay fines result in mandatory jail sentences (see Mississippi, Ohio and Tennessee); ▸ for certain offenses involving illegal taking or egregious habitat destruction (as by explosives in state waters) penalties be felonies, or at least mandatory jail terms (see South Carolina - mandatory term at hard labor or hefty fine for explosives, and New Hampshire - taking paddlefish or pallid sturgeon is a Class C felony). If all offenses are classified as "misdemeanors" of one class or another, the penalty for each should be clearly stated (see Pennsylvania, where each such penalty is stated in one section). Several states assess penalties or classify offenses according to the aggregate market value of illegally taken animals (Indiana, Pennsylvania and others). The low fines and/or penalty suspensions by courts in some states for certain violations bring into question their deterrent value, if any.

A few states specifically provide penalties for mistaken or accidental taking of the wrong species while otherwise taking, and if not paid, prosecution results. "It is not a defense in a prosecution that the person taking wildlife was mistaken as to species, sex, age, size or other fact or that the person lacked criminal intent, as it is one of the purposes of the wildlife laws to penalize recklessness" (Georgia and Tennessee). **We also suggest that those engaging in an activity requiring a license who have not procured such license be required as part of the penalty to pay the license fee (Wisconsin). Due to the problem of poaching, illegal taking of fish or wildlife for profit should receive felony penalties (see Illinois for example). Imposition of higher fines is also a chance to fund certain department programs that could not otherwise be undertaken, such as Idaho's $7.50 fine added to each civil penalty which funds the Search and Rescue Program.**

Restitution. Please refer to discussion and recommendations in Chapter 5 table, "Restitution, Waste and Spotlighting."

Alternatives to Penalties

Some states provide alternatives to criminal penalties. Georgia provides that as an alternative to criminal enforcement, the department may employ: civil liability with a penalty up to $1,000 for each violation; or an administrative proceeding for certain violations regarding fish health, spread of aquatic diseases, or importation or distribution of exotic aquatic species, and amounts cited are less than the fines for misdemeanors. Minnesota provides that instead of imposing restitution in addition to criminal penalties for illegal taking, the court may consider economic circumstances of the person and, in lieu of restitution, order conservation work representing the amount that will aid the propagation of wild animals, to be determined by consideration of the value of the wild animal (including intrinsic value, replacement cost, value to others to legally take the animal). **Sometimes it is not so much the amount of the fine or length of jail term specified that is of vital importance, but that some fine or sentence or license revocation be imposed. Community service for some offenders would be a greater deterrent than a fine or jail term. As much publicity as possible should be given to the state's enforcement program, with emphasis on the loss of opportunities for law-abiding hunters if illegal taking is unabated. If a violation is to be classed as a felony, or if vehicles or drivers' licenses are to be automatically confiscated**

for spotlighting, media publicity should be sought, and arrests and trials, especially of groups of hunters in violation, should be given wide publicity.

License Revocation or Suspension. Please refer to discussion and recommendations in Chapter 5 table, "License Revocation and Suspension."

Subsequent Offenders

Among the more remarkable omissions among the states is the lack of attention given to subsequent offenses and/or habitual offenders. Only a couple of states (Oklahoma and Washington) actually use the term "habitual offender," and even in these, one must commit quite a few violations to be so classified. This seeming reluctance among states to deal severely with habitual offenders is surprising. Washington requires four or more gross misdemeanors or class C felony convictions within 12 years before being considered "a threat to the fisheries resource" and denied the privilege of harvesting food fish or shellfish; Oklahoma requires two wildlife convictions in a two-year period before revoking a license for a minimum of one year. Several states provide enhanced penalties or mandatory prison sentences for subsequent convictions for illegal taking of certain animals or use of illegal fishing equipment (example, Wisconsin: three pervious convictions within three years for violations involving illegal use of explosives, sale of wildlife, fur dealing, or taking during closed season is a mandatory $100 fine, jail up to 6 months and revocation of all licenses for one year; see also Massachusetts, Tennessee, Texas and others). Texas provides that courts shall submit to the department an affidavit certifying previous convictions, to be available in subsequent prosecutions for violations of the same law or regulation. **It is recommended that more states adopt "habitual violator" provisions, and that consideration be given to implementing mandatory long term (up to 10 years) or lifetime license revocations for illegal and commercial trafficking in wildlife and other violations including hunting while intoxicated and shooting human beings.**

Intoxication Prohibitions. Please refer to Chapter 5 table, "Statutory Prohibitions Against Hunting While Intoxicated."

Forfeiture of Equipment, Vehicles

All states appear to have some provision for confiscation, seizure and forfeiture of illegal devices or devices used illegally to take fish or wildlife, and most of these statutes are quite similar. States do differ in whether or not vehicles, guns, airplanes, boats and "major economic impact" devices are allowed to be seized or confiscated and forfeited to the state. Examples of these differences include: ▸ Virginia (nets, traps or other devices, excluding firearms, shall be destroyed); ▸ New Hampshire (on conviction of violating any title provisions, all fishing tackle, guns, shooting paraphernalia, traps, dogs, boats and vehicles, except vehicles designed for use on the highway and required to be registered, used in the violation may be seized and held until fine and costs are paid in full, and then auctioned after one year); ▸ Louisiana (an officer shall seize vessels, airplanes, vehicles and equipment used illegally, and if license has been obtained by fraud, the vessels and the equipment shall be disposed of); ▸ Tennessee (a firearm, equipment, appliance or conveyance used in violation of specified statutes, including truck, auto, boat, airplane or other vehicle in which a deer, bear or wild boar is located or used to transport same, is declared contraband and shall be confiscated and forfeited to the state, and motor vehicles shall be sold at public sale); ▸ Alaska (confiscated aircraft may be disposed of to the Alaska civil air patrol); ▸ Minnesota (an enforcement officer must seize all motor vehicles used to shine wild animals, transport big game animals illegally taken or transport minnows illegally).

It is recommended that vehicle, boat, and firearm seizure, confiscation, and forfeiture provisions be adopted. It is apparent that loss of a firearm, vehicle, plane or boat is a strong incentive to obey the fish and wildlife laws. It may be worthwhile to chance a $500 fine for illegally taking a deer; it is another matter entirely to face losing one's $20,000 new truck. Especially in the large Western states where enforcement over large areas is difficult and staffing effective checkpoints is impossible, stringent consequences are needed to deter violators.

Protection for Landowners

States should have strong penalties for trespass, damage to a landowner's property, littering, cutting trees and otherwise destroying habitat, especially where landowners have opened lands to hunting and fishing. As available lands for hunting, fishing, trapping and other recreation dwindle, it behooves sportsmen to treat kindly lands that are available, whether public or private. A few states have a "Damage Stamp" which is mandatory along with a license, the proceeds to go to repair damage to private lands. North Carolina and a few other states provide information regarding landowner rights and sportsmen's duties by use of public media and putting trespassing restrictions and penalties on licenses and hunting and fishing proclamations.

Interstate Enforcement Compacts

We recommend that the excellent enforcement provisions in the Wildlife Violators Compact and the Northeast Conservation Law Enforcement Compact be examined (see Chapter 7, Sample Statutes, for full text of Violators Compact); that states join such a compact; and that efforts be made to computerize records of violations so that violators cannot move from state to state. Please see additional ideas under Chapter 3, Wildlife Poaching in the U.S.

HABITAT PROTECTION

The area of habitat protection contains some of the most innovative and unusual ideas in state fish and wildlife laws. States are making efforts to preserve natural areas, reestablish or preserve relict prairie lands, obtain new lands by purchase, lease, donation or other methods, and cooperate with landowners to restore habitat and open more lands for hunting, fishing and other recreation. There are numerous ideas covered in the "Habitat Protection" and "State Fish and Wildlife" sections for each of the states. An interesting example: Connecticut, Florida and Virginia prohibit release of helium filled balloons made of nonphotodegradable materials or tied with strings, since wildlife can get tangled in or ingest them. For those interested in pursuing similar ideas or programs, we recommend that the state's fish and wildlife agency be contacted for further details, an assessment of the success of their programs, enforcement details and other information. California's programs are particularly excellent: the California Riparian Habitat Conservation Program, Inland Wetlands Conservation Program, Significant Natural Areas Program, and the Private Wildlife Habitat Enhancement and Management Program. With continual loss of lands to farming and commercial and private development, additional efforts will be needed in the future to insure that adequate lands remain available for public hunting, fishing, trapping, other recreation, and for wildlife habitat. It is essential that many avenues be explored to insure that public and private entities can cooperate to avert losses of game, other wildlife, habitats and lands open to use by the public, and to avoid excess hunting, fishing, trapping and recreational pressures.

Polluting Aquatic Habitat

Virtually every state has some provision for prohibiting the placing of debris, refuse and pollutants in state waters. Most states specify injunctive relief for continuous violations and each day of violation is a separate offense. A few states, such as North Carolina, specify that it is illegal to pollute waters deemed necessary for wildlife or waters containing protected aquatic wildlife and various fish-food insects including stoneflies, mayflies, dragonflies, damsel flies, and water bugs (the benefits and value of protecting insect life for fish is rarely mentioned by states). Indiana and Oklahoma prohibit allowing accrual of fish offal from fish cleaning operations in or near waters, and mandate that such offal shall be burned, buried or otherwise disposed of in a sanitary manner. Although this would seem to be a priority, few states mention it. Oklahoma also prohibits placing any noxious aquatic plants, seeds or reproductive parts declared injurious by the Commission in state waters. **It is recommended that statutes be as specific as possible regarding what materials and devices are prohibited and that specific penalties be mandatory for violations.**

There may be loopholes in water pollution provisions which allow industries, with Commission approval, to discharge pollutants, allow runoff into waters, or use explosives, as in Mississippi. Most states exempt agricultural producers engaged in "normal farming practices" from liability for the fish and wildlife kills which occur, notably from pesticide runoff. Ohio prohibits disposal of garbage, furniture, wire, automobile parts, glass and other listed items except by permit or exemption, and there are other exemptions for explosive uses for engineering purposes. Only Virginia provides that a city or county governing body can request game wardens to take water samples for analysis where water pollution is suspected. **It is suggested that more states follow South Dakota's example, and make those who place illegal sawdust, manure, refuse and other pollutants in state waters liable to the department to compensate the state for restoration of fish and game losses, and that exemptions for industries, businesses or practices seeking exemption from pollution requirements be kept to an absolute minimum.**

A related problem of contamination of artificial or man-made bodies of water, other than those maintained for agricultural or recreational purposes, has been addressed by Nevada, which requires that polluters contaminating waters with substances which will cause the death of wildlife must obtain a department permit and pay an assessment of up to $10,000 per year to compensate for loss of wildlife. Some efforts have been made in some states to cover contaminated water, to which wildlife are attracted, with netting or screens.

Fishways and Screens

Related stream habitat issues involve maintaining adequate stream flowage below dams, providing fishways and fishladders, protecting stream banks and beds, and drawing off waters for irrigation and other purposes. Virtually all states deal with these issues with variations in specificity, definition of violations and penalties, and better or more varied alternatives for protecting stream habitats. Nearly all states provide that placing temporary dams, nets, traps or obstacles which block fish passage are illegal, and that such devices may be seized and confiscated. Oklahoma encourages such seizure by giving 75% of the forfeiture proceeds from illegal devices to the district court where the proceeding was brought. Connecticut allows private landowner petitions to force the construction of fishways on dams, and has strict provisions allowing the Commission to regulate minimum flow standards for all streams in the state, consistent with public needs. Most states require that raceways, flumes or inlet pipes be screened to prevent fish entry, and may, as does Pennsylvania, allow the Commission to construct such screens and charge the cost against the owner. Maryland mandates that electric power dam operators and the secretary shall cooperate to assure release of adequate waters for aquatic habitat maintenance, and states such as Alaska, Mississippi, and Pennsylvania provide that where fish ladders are impractical, the dam owners pay the state to build fish hatcheries, or in some other way provide for fish replacement, and Alaska provides severe penalties for violations. Nebraska makes it the duty of dam operators to provide for sufficient water to be returned to the streambed to preserve fish life, and prevent sudden flushing or decreases in flow which would be detrimental to habitat or aquatic life. North Carolina prohibits restricting water flow through fish hatcheries and blocking navigable waters with fish offal. In Pennsylvania and some other states, it is not necessary to prove that fish were actually killed, but only that harmful substances entered the water, to obtain restitution for damages. Tennessee provides that the agency shall not construct dams or dikes on game preserve property in such a way as to cause flooding on adjacent private lands, and private landowners may seek injunctive relief.

Streambed Diversions

Alaska, California and Colorado have excellent provisions for controlling hydraulic projects that involve dredging and changing stream beds, and may require submission of plans to the Commissioner for approval or modification, and provide that violators must restore the stream to its initial condition. In Colorado, the final decision on the plans is arbitrated by the Governor, whose decision is final. **It is suggested that: ▸ strict compliance be required for fishway, fish screen, and stream bed diversion requirements; ▸ state agency inspections be frequent and continuing; ▸ penalties for violations be mandatory and of a reasonable monetary amount to compensate the state for aquatic life losses, or that restitution be adequate to raise and stock additional fish in hatcheries; ▸ continuous offenses be halted by injunction or additional penalties; ▸ each day of violation be a separate offense; ▸ streamside and bank damage by livestock be controlled and alleviated; ▸ agricultural, industrial, or engineering/construction related exceptions be subject to careful and detailed review before approval. Where possible, sources of contamination or damage should be addressed before the damage to wildlife occurs, by requiring permits, damage assessments, or other mitigation efforts by the offending party. The statutes should clearly set forth the standard of compliance: procedures, including petitions, public hearings and input from other agencies and others, to be followed; how violations will be punished; the mode of appeal, review, or arbitration, and other details.**

Off-Road Traffic

An increasing problem, particularly in Western states with fragile desert or dryland habitats, is uncontrolled cross-country all-terrain vehicle (ATV) or other vehicle use, and even damage caused by pack animals and foot traffic. Such damage can lead to gullying and erosion, and may take years for vegetation to cover scars. Passage by one vehicle in some locales can leave tire track scars for years. A few states such as Arizona and New Mexico are addressing this issue by entering into agreements with landowners to restrict vehicle use on private lands otherwise open for recreation and hunting, and to aid in enforcement, posting, and cost-sharing. They may also, after public hearing, close certain areas to motor vehicle operation for periods, while setting aside other areas for use by ATVs and other recreational vehicles, and may include mandatory penalties for violations.

Landowner Cooperation

Most states encourage landowners to cooperate in developing, maintaining, or improving fish and wildlife habitat. "Incentives to Landowners" programs among the states are varied and imaginative, and include such ideas as: ▶ stocking fish, birds and game on private lands; ▶ donating fish foods, chemicals, lake and pond bottom contour maps and other commodities for fish management; ▶ aiding in posting lands and restricting areas from hunting or fishing; ▶ furnishing trees, seeds, other materials and labor to aid the landowner in habitat development; ▶ planting hedgerows and trees, grass strips or row crops for windbreaks, wildlife cover, and habitat development; ▶ limiting the number of hunters, trappers, and fishers allowed on private lands during a season; ▶ providing services such as weed control, planting and cultivation assistance; ▶ entering into agreements with farmers on a sharecrop basis to establish or maintain wildlife food or habitat cover; ▶ aiding in predator, noxious weed and fish control; ▶ special game animal licenses for landowners to use or sell to hunters they allow on their lands; ▶ regulating waterfowl feeding stations; ▶ providing technical assistance and advice to allow landowners to maintain lands as refuges; ▶ providing supervisory officers and check-in stations to monitor hunters on private lands; ▶ allowing landowners to charge hunting fees; ▶ providing enforcement monitoring of private lands to prevent trespass and excessive hunting or fishing pressure or damage to lands or livestock; ▶ prompt prosecution of violations (see state summaries for Connecticut, Illinois, Louisiana, Maine, Maryland, Massachusetts, Minnesota, Mississippi, Nebraska, Nevada, North Carolina and others for examples). Some of these provisions apply to private lands open to public hunting, fishing and other activities; others apply when the private lands are set aside in some manner as wildlife refuges. Louisiana's "Acres for Wildlife" voluntary program encourages private landowners to maintain food, water and cover for wildlife, and provides assistance to qualified landowners, including seeds, plants, instructions, wildlife habitat evaluation surveys, and materials to guarantee that certain lands be used for wildlife habitat.

A number of states provide excellent plans for private landowners to set aside lands as refuges, and may, upon petition of landowners, set aside large contiguous tracts of lands as such. Owners of lakes or contiguous landowners along rivers may similarly apply to set aside waters and lands for fish and waterfowl refuges. A number of states have "Natural Area Preserve Systems," "Heritage Trust Areas," "Posted Hunting Units," "Wildlife Management Cooperative Areas," "Acres for Wildlife," or systems for registering or dedicating private lands as refuges for specified periods of time, often as part of a state Heritage Lands Program involving lands with critical habitats, geologic or historic features. Mississippi declares that such preserves are the highest public use for the lands. In exchange for registering or dedicating the land to the state, the state aids in managing, protecting and developing private land for wildlife (see Alabama, Hawaii, Illinois, Louisiana, Massachusetts, Minnesota, Mississippi, Nebraska, North Carolina and Wisconsin).

Habitat Acquisition

Ideas for acquiring protected lands for both public hunting, fishing and trapping and for wildlife refuges, parks and sanctuaries are equally varied. Louisiana provides that parishes may have their own game and fish commissions, establish their own preserves, and that levee boards and school boards owning certain lands may sell the lands to establish preserves. An outstanding conservation easements program is Minnesota's "Native Prairie Bank" for land that has never been plowed, through cooperation with and payments to landowners, and preservation is regulated by monitoring herbicide use, grazing, and seeding of non-native grasses. Other states declare that all state lands are forest and wildlife reserves and refuges, including public parks, playgrounds and school lands (see Mississippi). Nebraska makes use of abandoned railroad rights-of-way for state trails and wildlife habitat, has a Natural Areas Register program for landowners to preserve endangered or relic species and other resources, has provisions for river waterfowl sanctuaries by landowner petition, and provides that every school section and state-owned lake or pond is a game and bird refuge. Rhode Island has similar provisions for landowner-permitted river or stream fish sanctuaries. Washington has extensive programs for department, landowner, and volunteer cooperation to enhance fish and wildlife habitat, production and protection, including monetary, equipment and technical assistance.

Additional methods of acquiring lands include: ▶ obtaining tax-delinquent lands desirable for game and fish refuges which are not suitable for agricultural or industrial uses (Arkansas); ▶ designating all state parks as game refuges (Minnesota); ▶ acquiring lease rights from landowners of abandoned section-line rights of way for game production areas and utilizing other abandoned state road rights-of-way (South Dakota); ▶ declaring special areas as nature preserves to be maintained in original condition or restored to such (Massachusetts, Nebraska); ▶ using any unsold public lands as refuges until sold to a private person (North Dakota); ▶ using state school lands for projects in exchange for other lands (North Dakota); ▶ investigating all possible areas of cooperation with the US and the state in exploring and developing areas for state use, including development opportunities to relieve economic hardship and unemployment (West Virginia).

Several states (Minnesota and Montana are examples) state criteria for acquiring certain kinds of habitats, critical or otherwise, including wildlife current populations, management goals, livestock uses, impacts to adjacent private lands, potential value for preservation and propagation of wildlife, degree of restoration needed, potential for fish and wildlife-oriented recreation, potential for achieving related objectives, and other factors. Clearly defining objectives is recommended because a plan for management naturally results. Many states have nature preserve, critical habitat, or other types of advisory councils with interesting and diverse memberships representing a variety of interests, to aid in formulating land use and habitat preservation, development and protection policy. **States should take advantage of the expertise of citizens and varied interests in the state through boards or councils to enhance public and private cooperation for protecting habitats, aiding wildlife propagation, and ensuring opportunities for recreation, hunting and fishing.**

Nebraska and Wisconsin each have interesting provisions for specific wildlife preserves. Nebraska provides for a State Wild Game Preserve of 4,000 to 10,000 acres to be stocked with indigenous and historic wildlife, and which will maintain or restore native vegetation. The Wisconsin department has a mandate to establish an animal wildlife exhibit where wild animals, allowed to roam at will, may be viewed by the public without charge on state-owned lands, with a caretaker and rehabilitation provided for wild animals.

Endangered Species Habitat

With regard to critical habitats or endangered species habitats, Massachusetts has unusually comprehensive provisions regarding "significant habitats" and any alterations to them. Maryland mandates that the "Governor shall review other state's programs for habitat protection for nongame and endangered wildlife...and all state agencies shall utilize their authorities in furtherance of these purposes for the conservation of endangered species...." Similarly, Massachusetts, Minnesota and Texas have very good provisions regarding protection for wetlands, which provide habitat for many endangered species. **States should become involved in identifying and acquiring lands for "natural preserve areas" should include areas which are essential habitats of endangered and threatened species.** California has priorities for acquiring parcels of land containing endangered species and their habitats, with funding to acquire lands on which only a certain number of species occur. California states that its policy to fund endangered habitats is in the public interest without regard to economic value.

Prohibiting Activities on Refuges

Although all states have some provision for penalizing trespass and prohibited hunting on refuge lands, it is urged that, as with other areas of enforcement, penalties be mandatory, and that license revocations be a part of the penalty, at least for subsequent offenses. South Carolina provides a good example, where abuse of a wildlife management area, including littering, damage to vegetation, fences, or buildings, or illegal fires, is punished by mandatory restitution to the landowner for repairs or clean-up to restore the property to its original condition. Failure to do so is a mandatory 10-day jail sentence which may not be suspended, in addition to other penalties. A second conviction within three years, or unlawful commercial hunting or fishing on such lands results in the violator being forever barred from obtaining a wildlife management area permit, and loss of hunting and fishing privileges elsewhere in the state for one year, plus other criminal penalties. In New Jersey, it is the duty of conservation officers with power to arrest and of sheriffs and other peace officers to protect wildlife on sanctuaries.

NATIVE AMERICAN WILDLIFE PROVISIONS

It is difficult to make recommendations regarding Native American provisions, because the treaty rights of the different tribes may vary according to the terms of each tribe's treaty. Nineteen of the fifty states have some sort of provision regarding Native Americans in their fish and wildlife laws (see Chapter 5 table, "Native American Provisions"). For a number of states, the provision simply states that Native Americans are subject to the state's wildlife code provisions when off their reservation, but that state wildlife code hunting, fishing and trapping licenses are not required, (although big game tags or certain stamps may be required) subject to certain conditions.

Conditions usually include that members of Native American tribes carry an identification card showing membership on tribal rolls and authenticated as specified in statute by a Bureau of Indian Affairs officer, tribal council chairman, or other designated official, when off reservation and engaging in code-regulated activities (examples are Kansas, Maine, Nevada, New York, Utah and Virginia). California, New York and North Carolina have code provisions stating that state wildlife laws do not apply on Native American reservation lands, but that tribal rules apply. Other states require that code provisions apply to all Indians off the reservation within the state, or coming into the state from adjoining states, and to persons hunting on an Indian reservation within the state, but that Indians shall not be required to have a license to hunt or fish within reservation limits where they actually reside (New Mexico). South Dakota requires a special Pine Ridge Reservation big game license for reservation hunting. Oregon provides free hunting and fishing licenses to Columbia River Indians, and provides surplus salmon to designated tribes for traditional salmon ceremonies following procedures set by statute. Montana has a state tribal board to develop regulations with certain tribes to monitor hunting and fishing rights, allows state tribal permits to hunt and fish without charge off reservation on unclaimed lands, and has other cooperative agreements with certain tribes. Wisconsin, among other provisions, allows Winnebago Indian tribe members to hunt deer under department regulations licenses for ceremonial purposes, and provides for extra law enforcement personnel for counties and towns who request such aid, during the off-reservation seasons and times for spearfishing by tribal members.

Washington may issue permits to certain tribal members to take salmon for ceremony and subsistence, but the state regulates the areas, methods and manner of taking, and no right is created to fish commercially. California allows subsistence fishing, without regard to seasons, for Yurok tribal members, as provided by statute and permit restrictions. Idaho provides for Indian taking of steelhead trout according to treaty provisions, and allows purchase of same for personal consumption from Indians without a license. Alaska has extensive and detailed "subsistence" and "personal use" wildlife taking provisions, which of course apply to Native Americans, but these provisions are also available to non-Indians. **It is recommended that states review Native American provisions where applicable and consult with Native American leaders throughout the state to review religious, cultural, and treaty concerns regarding wildlife issues, and address these concerns in the fish and wildlife code through the legislative or regulatory process.**

WERNEKE © 1991

Chapter 7

SAMPLE STATUTES

In this chapter we list, in order of states, wildlife statutes that we think are unusually clear treatments of a wildlife topic, innovative approaches to problems, and various unique and unusual provisions. These include, for the most part, provisions that are double-starred (★★) in the individual state statute summaries. It should be noted that in the state summaries, many of the single-starred (★) statutory provisions are exemplary in some way as well, and could have been included in this list. We suggest that readers pay attention to both single and double starred entries in the state summaries when looking for different treatments of wildlife topics by the states. There are also excellent statutes that were not marked with single or double stars in the summaries and which are not in this list. Initially, we had hoped to print the full text of many model statutes, but soon found that this was impossible because of page limitations. However, we have printed the full text of the Wildlife Violator Compact, because we think that it, and similar compacts for wildlife law enforcement, are the wave of the future in interstate cooperation, and we strongly recommend that states join such a compact.

The model statutes are organized under our major outline headings as used in the statute summary for each state, but are not further subdivided. The statutory citation and the state name abbreviation follow each entry. The entries are a brief summary of the statute's contents. More detailed treatment is given for each entry under the summary for that state in Part II.

STATE WILDLIFE POLICY

Policy statements regarding habitat protection (2780; 2781).(CA)
Policy statement and prohibition on materials of, tying of and release of helium-filled balloons (372.995).(FL)
Policy statement on landowner registration and dedication of lands with the state for preservation of natural areas for wildlife and other purposes (49-5-143 and -145).(MS)
Policy statement concerning augmentation of wildlife resources and providing adequate revenues therefor, and objectives to be achieved (497.071).(OR)
State policy statement limiting the construction of new or unlimited numbers of recreation facilities, and legislature to limit Department land acquisitions for parks, hunting and fishing and other areas after 1977 (20-1-20).(WV)

STATE FISH AND WILDLIFE AGENCIES

Provisions and qualifications for Deputy Game and Fish Wardens to enforce wildlife laws on privately owned game preserves and refuges, to serve without state compensation, but exams and references required (9-11-17).(AL)
Provisions for subsistence taking and resource allocation (16.05.258).(AK)
Use of wildlife management consultants by Department and their fees is a proper expenditure (1017).(CA)
Considerations to be used by Commission in setting regulations (203.1).(CA)
Funding necessity policy statement (710.5).(CA)
Mandatory budget inclusions for nongame programs; details (713).(CA)
Preference for projects to acquire habitat as corridors to link habitats (2789).(CA)

Wildlife Future Generations Trust Fund, grants and donations (33-1-112).(CO)

Search and Rescue Fund, from surcharge on licenses (33-1-112.5).(CO)

Habitat Partnership Council, for cooperation between livestock, agriculture, state wildlife interests, sportsmen, and provisions therefor (33-1-110).(CO)

Habitat Partnership Council, agriculture, wildlife, rangeland managers, to resolve rangeland forage issues, and resolve issues between local habitat partnership committees (33-1-110).(CO)

Community Volunteer Assistants appointed by Commissioner, with same authority as other Department members except for enforcement or arrest powers (16-7).(CT)

Protection measures for landowners' lands to prevent abuses by hunters (26-66).(CT)

Statement on Commission regulations based on accepted standards of wildlife conservation and considerations to be used in issuing same (26-67).(CT)

Regulations to protect landowners from abuses and damages by fishermen (26-112).(CT)

Endangered and Threatened Species Reward Trust Fund provisions (372.073).(FL)

State natural resources conservation camps funded with grants and donations (27-1-13 and -14).(GA)

Animal Species Advisory Commission for deliberate introduction of aquatic and wildlife species into the state (12-197-2).(HI)

Aquatic Life and Wildlife Advisory Committee provisions (12-197-4).(HI)

Fish and Game funding for the Caine Veterinary Teaching and Research Center for disease research on interaction between wildlife and domestic livestock (36-107).(ID)

Conservation training schools for employees and other groups ([56]1-155) and [61]1.11).(IL)

Indiana Heritage Trust Program, Trust Committee, Program Committee and membership composition, operation, duties, and the Indiana Natural Resources Foundation (Chapter 20; 14-3-20-1 through -30; Chapter 17 and 14-3-17-1 through 15).(IN)

Eminent domain statement of policy (32-840, -850, -852).(KS)

Department erection and operation of cabins, hotels, restaurants for the public on lands under its control, and provisions for rental incomes from its lands (32-860).(KS)

Details of Auxiliary Agents/Wildlife Volunteers, qualifications and training (56.69.5).(LA)

Details of Help our Wildlife Fund to aid in reporting wildlife law violators (56:70.3; 70.4).(LA)

Louisiana Fur and Alligator Public Education and Marketing Fund for economic development (56:266).(LA)

Louisiana Fur and Alligator Advisory Council; composition of council and duties (56:266).(LA)

Louisiana Alligator Resource Fund expenditures and purposes (56:279).(LA)

Commissioner shall review other states' provisions for developing good relationships between hunters and landowners and implement similar programs with emphasis on courtesy and responsibility for private lands (12-7035).(ME)

Birdwatcher's Fund for nongame wildlife and uses thereof (10-2A-06.1).(MD)

Chesapeake Bay and Endangered Species Fund and Chesapeake Bay Trust and details of programs and funds' uses (1-701 through -706).(MD)

Captive Wildlife Advisory Committee, membership details and duties (10-910).(MD)

In all prosecutions of wildlife law violations, the court shall assess as costs the sum of $10 to go to the credit of the Game and Fish Protection Fund (300.18). (MI)

Department may sell its license application lists or information filed with the department and may establish price for the lists, information and publications, proceeds to go to Game and Fish Protection Fund (316.606).(MI)

Hunting Area Control Committee to regulate shooting in dangerous areas (317.332; .336).(MI)

Conservation restriction provisions for retaining natural area habitat (84.64). (MN)

Qualifications of Director of Department of Wildlife, Fisheries and Parks (49-4-11).(MS)

Qualifications and provisions, duties for Conservation Officers' Reserve Unit (49-1-16).(MS)

Missouri State Constitution provisions for sales taxes to be levied to support the conservation, regulation and restoration of state wildlife and forestry resources (Mo. Const. art. IV, sec. 43).(MO)

Advisory Board on Guides, membership, duties, and provisions for licensing guides (504.385).(NV)

Commission for the Preservation of Wild Horses, membership and duties in administering the Heil Trust Fund for Wild Horses (504.470).(NV)

Fish and Game Commission membership education, experience and other requirements (206:2-a).(NH)

Fish food sales in vending machines at fish hatcheries and fishing derby monies as fund raisers (206:41).(NH)

Commemorative Rifle or Shotgun Lottery Committee and duties and details of lottery as fund raiser (206-A:1, :2, :3 and :7).(NH)

Composition of Commission membership (17-1-2).(NM)

Reserve Conservation Officers qualifications, duties (17-1-7 through -9).(NM)

Fish and Wildlife Management Practices Cooperative Program, establishment of management regions, composition of boards for each region, materials and aid furnished landowners (11-0501).(NY)

Duty of Commission to inform licensees of changes in laws and regulations by publication or in a manner to reach those persons affected (113-301.1).(NC)

Director may seek injunctive relief to prevent irreparable injury to wildlife resources or stop public nuisances (113-306).(NC)

Small and Big Game Habitat Restoration Trust Fund to further farmer-sportsmen relations and provide funds for leasing private lands to preserve habitats, and cost-sharing provisions for conservation practices (20.1-02-16.3 and 16.4).(ND)

Composition and membership requirements of Game and Fish Advisory Board (20.1-02-23 and -25).(ND)

Conservation Stamp provisions for management of wildlife for ecological and nonconsumptive recreational value (1533.15.1).(OH)

Felony and two to seven years in prison for game warden receiving a bribe (3-201).(OK)

Endangered/threatened species list to be printed in hunting regulations (5-412.1).(OK)

Salmon and Trout Enhancement Program using citizen volunteer participation and Department community advisors, and provisions of program (496.445).(OR)

Conservation officer; deputy conservation officer qualifications, duties (50-3-310; -316; -315; -330; -340).(SC)

Fines and forfeitures from wildlife law violations is expended for fish and game propagation in the counties where collected (50-1-150; -160).(SC)

Counties to receive some of license fee revenues and return of l0% on deer and antelope licenses for highway funds (4l-6-70).(SD)

Ammunition special privilege tax of 10 cents on every box of shotgun shells or metallic cartridges, and provisions of program, ammunition dealer records, violations and enforcement of program (70-3-101 through-113).(TN)

Annual drawing for permanent fishing license or fishing and hunting license as fund raiser (10-4153).(VT)

Damage Stamp Program to fund damages caused by hunters of deer, big game or bear; details of program; requirements for landowners to participate and be compensated for damages (29.1-352 through -358).(VA)

Washington Trophy Hunt of post-mature male trophy-quality animals from special herds as a fund raiser by tag and permit auction; program details (77.12-700).(WA)

Youth education program involving the lease of Department lands, one acre per 500 students, for outdoor education, and program details and restrictions (20-1-10a).(WV)

Provisions regarding what the Department may regulate; investigations; other details (29.174).(WI)

Sales and use taxes on ATVs, boats and snowmobiles, motorboat gas taxes, license fees go into Conservation Fund; other provisions; uses of fund (25.29).(WI)

PROTECTED SPECIES OF WILDLIFE

Commissioner shall appoint a committee of recognized experts in exhibition, conservation, preservation and humane care of public wildlife to recommend standards for care and treatment of captive wildlife (9-11-322).(AL)

Policy statement on cooperation of landowners in preservation of endangered species (2056).(CA)

Female bear protection and fair chase provisions regarding bait and dogs (33-4-101.3).(CO)

State agency duties to protect habitats for endangered and threatened species, and mitigation and other measures required (26-310).(CT)

Commission may withhold from disclosure maps and records of essential habitat locations for endangered and threatened species for their protection (26-311 through -313).(CT)

Wolf/dog hybrids and policy on wolf recovery issues (36-715).(ID)

Program for conservation of endangered species and state agencies' responsibilities and public policy statement therefore ([520]10.11).(IL)

Endangered fish annual status report details and requirements, including effects of acid rain (4-2A-04 and 10-2A-04).(MD)

Details and provisions of "significant habitats" program and requirements for landowners regarding endangered species (131A-4).(MA)

No part of the plumage, skin or body of any protected bird, or birds from without the state, the importation of which is prohibited into the US shall be sold or possessed for sale (49-5-7).(MS)

Mandatory classification system of all wildlife into a number of categories and subdivisions, including protected/unprotected and sensitive, threatened or endangered (501-110).(NV)

Director and Director of Safety Services may temporarily restrict boat traffic on state waters to protect any threatened or endangered species in earliest stages of life (212-A:5).(NH)

Restrictions on habitat protection measures due to agriculture, silvaculture, other economic considerations, warnings to farmers of contemplated endangered species actions, restrictions on use of license fees for endangered species (212-A:13 and :15).(NH)

Restrictions on taking, shipping, selling wild birds; licensed wild bird breeder provisions; injunctions and civil restitution (23:4-50).(NJ)

Prohibitions on sale of skin, body, manufactured articles of designated endangered species; exceptions (11-0536).(NY)

Rescue of animals in distress provisions, reporting same, veterinary aid required (11-0519).(NY)

Statement of how threatened or endangered species shall be determined, and procedures therefor (496.176).(OR)

Procedures for conservation of endangered and threatened species and habitats, required consultation with other states, required cooperation of other Oregon agencies, and requirements and mitigation and other procedures to be followed by state agencies, and approval of plans by the Department (496.182).(OR)

Live wildlife, kept for any purpose, must be classified into five classes and regulated according thereto (70-4-403).(TN)

A person who knowingly injures a threatened or endangered species may be required by court to pay restitution for veterinary and related care costs for the animal (10-5403).(VT)

Endangered species policy statement and provisions (29.415).(WI)

GENERAL EXCEPTIONS TO PROTECTION

Conservation officers may use ferrets to take rabbits for restocking (26-87).(CT)

"Emergency taking" to save human life provisions; investigation; penalties by species type (34-2141).(PA)

HUNTING, FISHING, TRAPPING PROVISIONS

Strict liability for civil damages for injury to person or domestic animal when using trap to take fur-bearing animals, and landowner need not prove negligence (9-11-264).(AL)

No licenses or permits issued if right is suspended/revoked in another state(16.05.330).(AK)

Waste provisions and definition of "edible meat" (16.30.017).(AK)

Trapping education course is unusually good in its provisions (17-333.02).(AZ)

Policy statement and provisions of Hunter Ed. program, though safety only (15-43-238).(AR)

Prima facie evidence of bear gall bladder possession as evidence of illegal taking; restrictions on sale, possession, transportation, purchase of bear parts (4758)(4760).(CA)

Injured and killed birds on shooting preserves shall be recovered and not released again (3307).(CA)

Live elk mutilation restrictions; other elk importation provisions (2118.3).(CA)

Committee for humane care and treatment of wildlife; provisions; duties (2150.3).(CA)

Soliciting another to take wildlife with intent to abandon; severe fines; policy statement on intent to protect wildlife from wanton and wasteful mutilation for heads, hides and internal organs, and felony provisions (33-6-117).(CO)

Illegal contests to kill, compare wildlife specimens or parts (33-6-118).(CO)

Posting provisions for inland and marine district waters for regulation (26-111).(CT)

Permit and provisions for taking and raising red fox whelps by dog pack owners (7-793 through -795A).(DE)

Restrictions on use and disposal of certain fishing net types in state waters (12-188-29.1; -30;-30.5).(HI)

Policy, provisions and restrictions for deliberate introduction of wildlife and aquatic life into the state, and considerations required therefore (12-197-3).(HI)

Bighorn sheep tag lottery and auction; uses of moneys therefrom (36-408).(ID)

Intent of Outfitters and Guides act to promote tourism and regulate guides (36-2101).(ID)

Reciprocal agreements with other states to manage and regulate hunting of big game herds that migrate across state boundaries (36-1006).(ID)

Trapper education program provisions (14-2-10-2).(IN)

No hunting from aircraft or snowmobiles (109.120).(IA)

Restrictions on traps; must be designed to take wildlife alive or unhurt or to kill instantly; snares, deadfalls, wire cages or box traps may be used but not for deer, elk, bear (150.410).(KY).

Restrictions on seines, gill nets, and use of airplanes in taking finfish (56:320; .321).(LA)

Policy on program for hunters to properly identify targets before shooting (12-7406-A).(ME)

Guide licensing provisions, examinations and safety standards (12-7314).(ME)

The Department shall furnish every licensee with list of hospitals with emergency care (10-301).(MD)

Illegal to possess game except during open season whether hunted in this or another state (10-403 through 10-408).(MD)

Cats found hunting game or protected birds or mammals may be destroyed by officer or any person (10-413).(MD)

Nighttime wild waterfowl hunting and light use provisions (10-602).(MD)

Waterfowl processing operation licenses and provisions (10-425).(MD)

Negligent shooting of persons, property, livestock with firearms or bow and arrow and liability (131-61).(MA)

Restrictions on use of steel leghold traps in general and for animal damage control (131-80A).(MA)

Provisions for licenses for propagation, cultivation, dealing in fish, birds, mammals, reptiles or amphibians and standards of care, protections for native wildlife, and other restrictions (131-23).(MA)

Transport in or out of state of lawfully taken wildlife; restrictions thereon (131-85).(MA)

No licensing of persons whose privilege to hunt, trap or fish has been suspended or revoked in any US jurisdiction or Canada; procedures therefore (131-90A).(MA)

A person who owns, keeps or uses a bull, bear, dog or other animal for the purpose of fighting or baiting, or as a target to be shot at as a test of skill, or who is a party to or causes fighting, baiting, or shooting of a bull, bear, dog or other animal is guilty of a felony and jail up to five years, fine up to $5,000, or both (750.49).(MI)

Unlawful for private game preserves or farms to exceed 15,000 acres in size or be closer than two miles from another such facility (317.263).(MI)

Restrictions on transport, sale, purchase of specified big game parts; prohibition on sale of bear gall bladders (97A.512). (MN)

Provisions for foxes, coyotes, uses of lures and scents to take same (49-7-33).(MS)

Waste provisions for big game and other animals and penalties (87-3-102).(MT)

Fire danger closure provisions for fishing and hunting (87-3-106).(MT)

Felony provisions and penalties for the offense of "sale of unlawfully taken wildlife", including possible lifetime license revocation (87-3-118).(MT)

Provisions for preventing great suffering by hunger by taking of otherwise illegal wildlife (87-3-129).(MT)

Penalties for knowing or purposeful violations of fish and game laws and mandatory license revocations (87-1-102).(MT)

Unlawful to purchase, sell, ship or transport any protected game or fish, whether native to Montana or not, except as permitted, effective July, 1993 (87-3-111; -112).(MT)

Provisions for use of poison gas and other devices for taking predators, and posting requirements (37-524).(NE)

Penalties for negligent shooting, wounding, killing humans while hunting, felony provisions and 10 year to life license revocations (207:38).(NH)

Super Sportsman License which allows licensee to designate area of wildlife or fisheries management they wish the extra fee to go for (214:7-c).(NH)

Theft of a deer or bear or part from another can be up to a felony (208:9-a).(NH)

Steel-jaw traps; restrictions on; plan to phase out; violations and penalties (23:4-22.1 through 22.8).(NJ)

Provisions for "registered muskrat marshes" and licensing details (11-1109).(NY)

Aquatic insect protection in trout streams, and prohibition on their sale as bait (11-1317).(NY)

Plumage, skin, body sale prohibitions for birds; exceptions for millinery and fly-tying purposes; license for fly-tying (11-1733).(NY)

Captivity license and pelting allowed of beaver, bobcat, coyote, raccoon, sable, skunk, otter, fisher, nutria, muskrat; other details (11-1907).(NY)

Duty of licensees to determine if private lands are posted against such activities, and provisions for landowner registration and posting of such lands, notice to law enforcement officers, and use of standardized entry forms to hunt or fish (113-282, -283 and -287).(NC)

Migrant farm worker resident privileges for fishing provisions (113-276).(NC)

Rules against spotlighting deer must be proposed at public hearing in local areas; provisions for setting no-shine-light periods (113-291.1).(NC)

Provisions for issuance and use of special landowner antlerless deer tags as a means of animal damage control, records, and investigation of deer populations on such lands (113-291.2).(NC)

Fox taking provisions for hunting, chasing, dog trials, and animal damage control (113-291.4; -291.4A).(NC)

Commission may not restrict the number or dogs nor breeds used in hunting, nor require leashing or confining of pet dogs (113.291.5).(NC)

Hunter Safety and Conservation course content and provisions (1533.10).(OH)

Requirement to wear license back tag on garment when hunting (1533.13; .14).(OH)

State-owned lands for conducting dog field trials in each conservation district, to be stocked with state game; propagation of game thereon; other provisions (1533.20; .22).(OH)

Fishing reciprocity with other states exempting state license requirements; details for reciprocal recognition of hunting, fishing licenses by other states or federal districts (1533.32.2; .3).(OH)

Restrictions on transportation of hunters other than to licensed public airports, records pilots must keep, and time limits within which hunters can take big game after such flights (498.126).(OR)

Landowner protection provisions; tree stands; driving on fields; other damages (34-2510; 2511).(PA)

Ammunition size restrictions (20-13-13).(RI)

Weapons restrictions for taking deer (20-15-1).(RI)

Foxhunting preserves (50-11-2580).(SC)

Mandatory jail term at hard labor or fine for using, possessing explosives on state waters (50-30-1440).(SC)

Restrictions on sale of bait and biological supply company specimens without a wholesale bait dealer license; other details of bait sales, transport, and taking (41-6-5).(SD)

Policy statement and procedures for setting open and closed seasons according to specified criteria, and publication of destructive and unprotected wildlife (70-4-107).(TN)

Conservation Passport Permit program requiring one person in each vehicle using Department lands to have a permit, whether using the land for consumptive or nonconsumptive purposes, as a fund raiser (5.43.521 through .525).(TX)

Conservation license or hunting, fishing or trapping license required when using identified Department lands or access facilities for any purpose (77.32.380).(WA)

Wildlife taken lawfully outside the state is subject to the same laws and rules as that taken as that taken within the state (20-2-4).(WV)

Trapper education program; details of course content; other provisions (29.224).(WI)

Hunter education program; course content details; uses of course fees; other provisions (29.226).(WI)

Back tag required when deer hunting (29.23; .22).(WI)

Group deer hunting for another person if all are licensed; details and requirements (29.405).(WI)

Right of Department to take fish privately caught to be stripped of eggs and milt; permits; other provisions (29.515).(WI)

Taxidermy school permit, purchase of fish for taxidermy; details for two-year taxidermy course (29.134 through .136).(WI)

Deer farm licensing; restrictions on breeding, killing, propagating and selling deer; facilities; other details (29.578).(WI)

Commercial deer farm provisions and venison retailer permits; restrictions; license details (29.58; 583).(WI)

Prohibitions on scent gland removal on skunks; restrictions on possession, sale, of live skunks; other skunk provisions (29.427).(WI)

Reciprocal enforcement powers for conservation officers; provisions of program; details of appointments of such officers (29.085).(WI)

Provisions regarding landowner's coupon which is part of big game, trophy animals or turkeys, which must be delivered to the Department who shall pay the landowner nine dollars per coupon (23-3-104 and -105).(WY)

No big game or trophy game hunting with bow and arrow or crossbow allowed without archery license plus hunting license (23-2-104).(WY)

Outfitter and Guide licensing provisions and qualifications of applicants (23-2-411 and 412).(WY)

ANIMAL DAMAGE CONTROL

All bounties are unlawful, except for taking on private lands (2019).(CA)

Metal trap restrictions for bears; trap restrictions for squirrels; provisions for release of squirrels in nonagricultural areas and parks; restrictions on bear permits for animal damage control; wild pig depredation permits (4181).(CA)

State liability for certain damages caused by wildlife and exceptions, and aid to landowners for animal damage (33-3-103).(CO)

Animal damage control permits for deer and landowner restrictions thereon (26-82).(CT)

Dogs as predators provisions and animal damage control (12-183D-65).(HI)

Policy on obligation of landowners to mitigate wildlife property damage and animal damage control provisions and restitution to landowners (36-1008).(ID)

The Department may not pay bounties for wildlife (10-207).(MD)

Animal damage control for deer, moose damage; appraisal procedure for claims (131-39).(MA)

Restrictions on use of poisons for animal damage control of various species (131-43).(MA)

Treatment of and restrictions on "ecologically harmful exotic species"; management plan; seeking grants through the federal Non-indigenous Aquatic Nuisance Prevention and Control Act (84.969).(MN)

Mitigation and animal damage control provisions for elk and non-native game animals, local panels to assess damage, and payments to landowners (504.175).(NV)

Killing of domestic cats found killing protected birds or with such in possession is allowed by licensed hunters and conservation officers (11-0529).(NY)

Wildlife Commission's powers to prohibit use of poison or pesticides after public hearing (113-300.2).(NC)

Killing of crippled or helpless wildlife for humane purposes; procedures and reporting requirements for (498.016).(OR)

Animal damage control provisions for landowners; reporting; carcass disposal (34-2121 through -2125).(PA)

Deer animal damage control; no permit issued unless actual damage is done and there is no alternative to shooting the deer (20-15-3).(RI)

Program for animal damage control by protected species involving notice by county judges and Department investigation, recommendations for mitigation by landowner, and issuance of permits for taking (5.43.151 through .153).(TX)

Animal damage control provisions, protection for endangered species, Department/landowner mitigation efforts for crop damage; Department must respond within 48 hours; provisions for arbitration of claims (77.12.265 through .300).(WA)

Animal damage control provisions; procedures for landowners; investigation; landowner reciprocation by opening lands to hunting and trapping; other details (29.59).(WI)

Liability of landowner who refuses consent to beaver damage abatement and who thereby allows damage to occur on public or private lands (29.59).(WI)

"Wildlife Damage Abatement" and "Wildlife Damage Claim" programs; provisions and requirements of each, including county and landowner and Department responsibilities (29.59).(WI)

Animal damage control provisions and basis for decisions regarding payments to landowners depending on animal type, crop or forage type; appeal procedures; arbitration (23-1-901).(WY)

ENFORCEMENT OF WILDLIFE LAWS

Member of Wildlife Violator Compact (17-501-503).(AZ)

Reciprocal enforcement provisions with other states; exchange of violators' records (391).(CA

Proceedings; penalties for accidental or negligent killing or wounding of humans (1250).(CA)

Soliciting for illegal taking for commercial or monetary gain, especially regarding endangered species, big game and eagles, and felony provisions (33-6-110).(CO)

Suspension of drivers' licenses for illegal taking of deer for one year (26-85).(CT)

Complaints of persons concerning alleged violations allowed in license suspensions and other suspension provisions (26-61).(CT)

Every license holder, landowner, family member or employee may arrest, without warrant, game and fish law violators (7-1301 and 1302).(DE)

In a prosecution for violation of wildlife laws, it is not a defense that the person taking, possessing, transporting wildlife was mistaken as to age, sex, size or other fact, as a purpose of wildlife laws is to penalize recklessness (27-1-34).(GA)

Reward payment provisions and one-half of fines to informants (187A-14).(HI)

Illegal taking a violation in Idaho as well as in state where it first occurred (36-504).(ID)

Civil actions for waste and chemical damage to lands and waters, uses of moneys, and procedures for habitat and animal recovery thereon (14-2-6-7). (IN)

Duty of Attorney General to give opinions in writing on questions of law under game and fish chapter, and right of any person to institute legal proceedings for any chapter provisions (109.35).(IA)

Court may impose any fine on children aged 16 or 17 charged with wildlife law violations, and may order child placed in juvenile detention facility (32-1040).(KS)

Commercialization of wildlife provisions, penalties, and wildlife values, and license revocations for illegal wildlife harvesting (32-1005).(KS)

Public display of coyote carcasses prohibited (32-1007).(KS)

No fines, penalty or judgment assessed or rendered under this chapter shall be suspended, reduced or remitted other than expressly provided by law (150.990).(KY)

Judges may adopt a schedule of fines and costs for wildlife law violations within limits, except for violations punishable by mandatory jail (56:9).(LA)

Jail sentences mandatory after second offense, and no sentence or fine shall be suspended or diminished for any cause (56:139).(LA)

Details of establishing civil penalties or restitution for illegal taking (56:40.1 through 56:45).(LA)

Injunction procedures for violation of endangered species laws and restoration of damaged areas (12-7758).(ME)

Penalties and mandatory license revocations provided for illegal taking of each game bird or mammal and other provisions (10-1101).(MD)

Suspensions and revocations of licenses for certain and subsequent offenses (131-34; -35).(MA)

Director or representative may make complaint against a person and may appear for the people and prosecute the case with same authority as the prosecuting attorney (300.12).(MI)

Mandatory vehicle seizure for spotlighting, transport of illegally taken big game, illegal minnows; provisions for sale of seized property (97A.225).(MN)

Concurrent court and enforcement jurisdiction in boundary waters by ND, SD, IA, WI, MI and MN (97A.235).(MN)

Appointment of conservation officers in other states or US as special conservation officers in MN, if reciprocity with US or other state exists (97A.241).(MN)

Penalty and fine provisions for gross misdemeanors for illegal sale of protected animals, intoxication, spotlighting poaching, and taking or possessing specified animals or fish (97A.335).(MN)

Mandatory civil liability for illegal taking provisions, and conservation work in lieu thereof (97A.341; .345).(MN)

Intoxication testing requirements for hunters; penalties; procedures (97B.065; .066). (MN)

Use of Hunter Safety Officer to investigate hunting deaths, injuries and accidents (49-4-31).(MS)

Mandatory license revocation for littering public lands (87-2-112).(MT)

Duty of Conservation Officers to investigate and make arrests for Game Law violations reported or observed by a person, and county attorney duties (37-603).(NE)

Nevada is a member of the Wildlife Violator Compact (506.010 through 506.020).(NV)

New Hampshire is a member of the Northeast Conservation Law Enforcement Compact (215:B:l).(NH)

Mandatory revocation and refusal to issue license for hunting, trapping, or guiding to person whose license for such activity has been suspended or revoked in any US or Canada jurisdiction (214:18-b).(NH)

Discretionary revocation of licenses of persons convicted in another state of specified offenses (spotlighting, intoxication, shooting/abandoning a person) and admissability of records to prove (214:20-b).(NH)

Trespassing on private lands restrictions, penalties, landowner arrest therefor (23:7-1; :7-2).(NJ)

Negligent weapon use provisions, penalties, license suspensions, mandatory "remedial sportsmen education program" (23:9A-2).(NJ)

License revocation provisions for license revocations for violation of NJ or any other state's fish and game laws (23:3-22.1).(NJ)

Intoxication while hunting provisions; testing, penalties, presumptions, license revocations (11-1201 through -1207).(NY)

"Levels of punishment" and penalties in the discretion of the court; subsequent violations (113-135).(NC)

Provisions and requirements before issuing permits or licenses to persons subject to administrative control, including those relating to special devices, captivity, collection, or various types of dealers (113-276.2).(NC)

Mandatory license suspension and revocation provisions (113-276.3).(NC)

Implied consent for intoxication testing for those afield with bow and arrow or firearm, testing of minors, and provisions of program and mandatory license revocations for refusal to comply (20.01-15-01 through -06).(ND)

Mandatory three year license revocation for violations relating to taking, possession, protection, propagation of wild animals and hunting or trapping violations; up to five years for negligent weapon use, felony violation, or taking an eagle (1533.13; .68).(OH)

Duty of Commission to initiate legal action in federal court, or through cooperation with other state wildlife commissions where actions of individuals, firms or corporations in other states are injurious to wildlife of Oklahoma (7-402).(OK)

Waste provisions and prohibition on mutilating living wildlife for their antlers, claws, teeth or other parts (7-205).(OK)

"Habitual Wildlife Violator" provisions; penalties; required restitution (1002; 7-207).(OK)

Wardens may arrest without warrant with visual or electronic perception, including aircraft, radio, night vision equipment; jurisdiction in either county if violation within 500 yards of boundary (3-205.2; -305.3).(OK)

Oregon is a member of the Wildlife Violator Compact (496.750).(OR)

Recreational value of "observing wildlife" recognized, other considerations in setting restitution values; "accidental taking" provisions (34-2306).(PA)

Penalties for spotlighting, illegal taking of endangered and other specified species (34-2310).(PA)

Prohibition on license issuance to those certified by court or medical authority to be mentally or physically unfit or addicted to alcohol or controlled substances (34-2741).(PA)

Persons convicted of crimes of violence, fugitives under the Firearms Act, those mentally incompetent, drug addicts or habitual drunkards may not obtain licenses until five years from being pronounced cured unless they have been pronounced criminally insane (20-13-5).(RI)

Point system for suspending/revoking hunting and fishing licenses; details (50-9-1020; -1030; -1040 through 1060; -1110; -1070).(SC)

Civil liability for illegal taking provisions to be printed on citations (41-1-5.6).(SD)

Provisions for court determined fines for corporations in violation of wildlife laws, up to $20,000 for a felony (2.12.410).(TX)

Provisions for payment of civil penalties in lieu of license suspensions after economic impact consideration by the Department, and minimum penalties (2.12.501 through .507).(TX)

Utah is a member of the Wildlife Violators Compact (23-25-1 through -13).(UT)

Disposition of illegal taking restitution moneys into the Wildlife Resources Account and the uses of such moneys for anti-poaching projects and other provisions (23-20-4.5).(UT)

Wanton destruction of protected wildlife provisions and penalties, including felonies, and fines for violation according to species of animals as listed (20-23-4).(UT)

Restriction on release of 50 or more nonbiodegradable balloons or other similar items within a one hour period; civil penalties; exceptions (29.1-556.1).(VA)

Mandatory reimbursement to the state for values as specified of animals illegally taken or possessed; prohibition against court suspending sentences or payments; other details and animal values (77.21.070).(WA)

West Virginia is a member of the Interstate Wildlife Violator Compact (20-2C-1 through -2C-3).(WV)

Penalties for illegal taking of bear; illegal bear possession; taking a hibernating bear (29.99).(WI)

Additional mandatory penalties if offender had prior convictions within specified periods; aiding and abetting; other details (29.995; .996).(WI)

Illegal taking of wildlife restitution provisions (29.998).(WI)

Toll free hotline number to report wildlife violations; confidentiality provisions for informants (29.055).(WI)

Mandate for justices of the peace or judges to keep records of every game and fish complaint, all court actions, and record of every conviction, acquittal and amount of fines or forfeitures for submission to the Department (23-6-108).(WY)

HABITAT PROTECTION

Policy statement under habitat on timber cutting and environmental impact statement required and citizen suits to enjoin cutting until compliance present (15-41-108).(AR)

"Adopt a Lake" volunteer program (2003.6).(CA)

Priorities in acquiring parcels of land containing endangered species and habitats, and obligation to acquire lands on which a species occurs, which has 20 or fewer world occurrences; other restrictions (2721 through 2733).(CA)

"Private Wildlife Habitat Enhancement and Management Program" provisions, purposes, licensing, benefits to landowners; other details (3401).(CA)

Protection of streams from stream bed modifications without approval, and policy statement (33-5-102 through -104).(CO)

Petition of landowners allowed to require fishways on dams (26-136 and -137).(CT)

Provisions for regulating draining water from streams and ponds and required notice period (26-138 and -139).(CT)

Commission and landowner agreements to restrict the operation of off-road and other vehicles on their lands to protect wildlife or habitat, and posting thereof (36-104).(ID)

Program for establishment of Wildlife Habitat Management Areas on private lands with landowner cooperation and reimbursement for leaving feed and cover strips on lands; limitation of hunters thereon ([61]219 through 233).(IL)

Provisions for Conservation Easements for recreational purposes given by landowners (58-3810 and -3811).(KS)

Creation of biologic station on Gulf coast to investigate problems of fish and fisheries (56:611 through :613).(LA)

Louisiana Acres for Wildlife cooperative environmental action program for private landowners, and assistance provided by state; purposes of program (56:191 through :193).(LA)

Parish game and fish preserves, parish commissions, levee boards and school board powers to establish preserves (56:721 through :728).(LA)

License fee increases used for feeding game birds and mammals, and Department contracts with farmers who plant and leave unharvested grains in the fields (10-301).(MD)

Waterfowl conservation program, ten-year licensing of private lands, advisory committee therefor, and other details (10-308.1).(MD)

Waterfowl feeding program to reduce crop depredations and extensive details and regulations of this program to ensure that hunters do not take advantage of feeding areas to attract birds for shooting (10-1002 through -1008).(MD)

Provisions for regulating industrial pollution of fisheries and compliance of state agencies with the state clean water act; liability for damages to fish; requirement of restitution for loss of fish and habitat (131-42).(MA)

Provisions and details of establishing Nature Preserves; membership of Nature Preserve Council; other details of program (131-10A through 131-10D).(MA)

Program for preservation of fresh water wetlands, coastal wetlands, beaches, flats, marshes, and swamps, and extensive details for establishing program, goals of program; purposes; Commission duties (131-40; -40A).(MA)

Procedure to be followed before a significant habitat can be altered under the Natural Heritage and Endangered Species Program; extensive details (131A-5).(MA)

Statement on preservation of biological diversity and habitat, consequences of loss of biological diversity, goals of state regarding same in the Biological Diversity Conservation Act (299.221 through .237).(MI)

"Native Prairie Bank" program, conservation easements therefor; management and land acquisition considerations to be observed (84.96; .961).(MN)

Designation of lands as state game refuges on petition of 50 residents; details thereof (97A.085).(MN)

Sharecrop agreements with landowners to grow wildlife food or habitat cover on state wildlife lands; services provided by Department (97A.135).(MN)

Wetlands acquisition procedures for water conservation relating to wildlife development (97A.145).(MN)

Declaration of all state lands to be forest reserves and wildlife refuges, including public parks and playgrounds, and leases of state lands for game and fish preserves (49-5-1).(MS)

Commission and Governor's responsibilities in establishing habitats for management of nongame and endangered wildlife, and use of other state programs in this effort (49-5-111).(MS)

Dedication of natural area preserves by landowners provisions, and declaration that such preserves are declared to be the highest use for the public (49-5-141 through 157).(MS)

Provisions for acquiring wildlife habitats through the Interlocal Cooperation Act and buying or leasing such habitat lands (37-109).(NE)

Provisions for posting and establishing every school section and every state-owned lake or pond as game and bird refuges and wildfowl sanctuaries, and for acquiring other such lands (37-401).(NE)

Provisions for landowners along both banks of rivers to petition that the river and adjacent lands in a one-half mile wide strip, at least five miles long, be made game and wild fowl sanctuaries (37-402).(NE)

State Wild Game Preserve provisions, and stocking of same with indigenous and historic wildlife, preserve to be 4,000 to 10,000 acres in size (37-415 through -417).(NE)

Nebraska Natural Areas Register provisions to protect endangered or relic species and other natural resources (37-1403).(NE)

Policy statement and provisions for use of abandoned railroad rights-of-way to develop a state trail system and to preserve wildlife habitats and create conservation corridors, and funding therefor (37-1502 and -1503).(NE)

Permit provisions for chemically or otherwise contaminated bodies of water which would kill wildlife, fees therefor, up to $10,000, and penalties (502.390).(NV)

Commission to determine necessity of fish ladder facilities, and provisions for cost sharing (211:8-a and :8-b).(NH)

Injunctive relief for water pollution, and recovery of value of fish, and procedure for calculating same, and collection of habitat and fish damages (211:71 through :74).(NH)

Policy statement on wetlands value, and that value exceeds private value of wetlands; provisions, purpose of "Freshwater Wetlands Protection Act" (13:9B-1 through -30).(NJ)

"Pinelands Protection Act" policy statement; threat of uncontrolled development (13:18A-1 through -49).(NJ)

Restrictions on cross-country vehicle use on private lands by Commission agreement with landowners; related provisions of "Habitat Protection Act" (17-6-3 through -9).(NM)

Littering, garbage disposal in state waters provisions (1531.29).(OH)

Establishment of fish sanctuaries on rivers on approval of county's legislative delegation and landowners; details (50-13-1960 through -2020).(SC)

Cooperation with landowners to acquire abandoned or unused section-line rights-of-way for game production areas; use of undeveloped roadways; other land acquisition provisions (41-5-7 through -11).(SD)

State system of scientific areas, details of funding, program objectives, and dedication of areas (5.81.501, .502, .503 and .506).(TX)

Department mandate, with county approval, to set aside parts of each public stream or river as fish sanctuaries for freshwater fish propagation, water flow provisions, restrictions on amount of sanctuary area allowed, and public notice requirements (5.81.201 through .207).(TX)

Department mandate to develop a State Wetlands Conservation Plan for coastal wetlands in cooperation with other designated agencies and provisions of plan (2.14.002).(TX)

Policy statement and procedures for doubling the state-wide game fish production by the year 2000, including methods and elements of the plan (77.12-710).(WA)

Details of projects under the Volunteer Cooperative Fish and Wildlife Enhancement Program, including habitat improvement projects and education projects (75.52.030).(WA)

Details and procedures for loans of equipment to volunteer groups for rearing of fish and game and providing expert advice to volunteer groups undertaking cooperative food fish, shellfish, and game and nongame projects (75.52.040).(WA)

Wildlife refuge creation provisions for landowners; stocking of same by department; procedures (29.57).(WI)

"Wisconsin Wildlife Exhibit"; establishment by Department; management details (29.565)(WI).

NATIVE AMERICAN PROVISIONS

Free, permanent state licenses for persons 1/16 Indian by blood (32-929).(KS)

INTERSTATE RECIPROCAL AGREEMENTS: WILDLIFE VIOLATORS COMPACT

OREGON REVISED STATUTES
TITLE 41 WILDLIFE
CHAPTER 496. APPLICATION, ADMINISTRATION AND ENFORCEMENT OF WILDLIFE LAWS
WILDLIFE LAW VIOLATOR COMPACT
COPR. (c)1991 by STATE OF OREGON Legislative Counsel Committee

496.750. Wildlife Law Violator Compact.
The Wildlife Violator Compact is hereby enacted into law and entered into on behalf of this state with all other states legally joining therein in a form substantially as follows:

ARTICLE I: FINDINGS, DECLARATION OF POLICY AND PURPOSE

(a) The party states find that:
  (1) Wildlife resources are managed in trust by the respective states for the benefit of all residents and visitors.
  (2) The protection of their respective wildlife resources can be materially affected by the degree of compliance with state statute, law, regulation, ordinance or administrative rule relating to the management of those resources.

Sample Statutes

(3) The preservation, protection, management and restoration of wildlife contributes immeasurably to the aesthetic, recreational and economic aspects of these natural resources.

(4) Wildlife resources are valuable without regard to political boundaries, therefore, all persons should be required to comply with wildlife preservation, protection, management and restoration laws, ordinances and administrative rules and regulations of all party states as a condition precedent to the continuance or issuance of any license to hunt, fish, trap or possess wildlife.

(5) Violation of wildlife laws interferes with the management of wildlife resources and may endanger the safety of persons and property.

(6) The mobility of many wildlife law violators necessitates the maintenance of channels of communications among the various states.

(7) In most instances, a person who is cited for a wildlife violation in a state other than the person's home state:
   (i) Must post collateral or bond to secure appearance for a trial at a later date; or
   (ii) If unable to post collateral or bond, is taken into custody until the collateral or bond is posted; or
   (iii) Is taken directly to court for an immediate appearance.

(8) The purpose of the enforcement practices described in paragraph (7) of this subdivision is to insure compliance with the terms of a wildlife citation by the person who, if permitted to continue on the person's way after receiving the citation, could return to the person's home state and disregard the person's duty under the   terms of the citation.

(9) In most instances, a person receiving a wildlife citation in the person's home state is permitted to accept the citation from the officer at the scene of the violation and to immediately continue on the person's way after agreeing or being instructed to comply with the terms of the citation.

(10) The practice described in paragraph (7) of this subdivision causes unnecessary inconvenience and, at times, a hardship for the person who is unable at the time to post collateral, furnish a bond, stand trial or pay the fine, and thus is compelled to remain in custody until some alternative arrangement can be made.

(11) The enforcement practices described in paragraph (7) of this subdivision consume an undue amount of law enforcement time.

(b) It is the policy of the party states to:
   (1) Promote compliance with the statutes, laws, ordinances, regulations and administrative rules relating to management of wildlife resources in their respective states.
   (2) Recognize the suspension of wildlife license privileges of any person whose license privileges have been suspended by a party state and treat this suspension as if it had occurred in their state.
   (3) Allow violators to accept a wildlife citation, except as provided in subdivision (b) of Article III, and proceed on the violator's way without delay whether or not the person is a resident in the state in which the citation was issued, provided that the violator's home state is party to this compact.
   (4) Report to the appropriate party state, as provided in the compact manual, any conviction recorded against any person whose home state was not the issuing state.
   (5) Allow the home state to recognize and treat convictions recorded for their residents which occurred in another party state as if they had occurred in the home state.
   (6) Extend cooperation to its fullest extent among the party states for obtaining compliance with the terms of a wildlife citation issued in one party state to a resident of another party state.
   (7) Maximize effective use of law enforcement personnel and information.
   (8) Assist court systems in the efficient disposition of wildlife violations.

(c) The purpose of this compact is to:
   (1) Provide a means through which the party states may participate in a reciprocal program to effectuate policies enumerated in subdivision (b) of this Article in a uniform and orderly manner.
   (2) Provide for the fair and impartial treatment of wildlife violators operating within party states in recognition of the person's right of due process and the sovereign status of a party state.

ARTICLE II: DEFINITIONS

As used in this compact, unless the context requires otherwise:

(a) "Citation" means any summons, complaint, ticket, penalty assessment or other official document issued by a wildlife officer or other peace officer for a wildlife violation containing an order which requires the person to respond.

(b) "Collateral" means any cash or other security deposited to secure an appearance for trial, in connection with the issuance by a wildlife officer or other peace officer of a citation for a wildlife violation.

(c) "Compliance" with respect to a citation means the act of answering the citation through appearance at a court, a tribunal or payment of fines, costs and surcharges, if any, or both such appearance and payment.

(d) "Conviction" means a conviction, including any court conviction, of any offense related to the preservation, protection, management or restoration of wildlife which is prohibited by state statute, law, regulation, ordinance or administrative rule, or a forfeiture of bail, bond or other security deposited to secure appearance by a person charged with having committed any such offense, or payment of a penalty assessment, or a plea of nolo contendere, or the imposition of a deferred or suspended sentence by the court.

(e) "Court" means a court of law, including Magistrate's Court and the Justice of the Peace Court.

(f) "Home state" means the state of primary residence of a person.

(g) "Issuing state" means the party state which issues a wildlife citation to the violator.

(h) "License" means any license, permit or other public document which conveys to the person to whom it was issued the privilege of pursuing, possessing or taking any wildlife regulated by statute, law, regulation, ordinance or administrative rule of a party state.

(i) "Licensing authority" means the department or division within each party state which is authorized by law to issue or approve licenses or permits to hunt, fish, trap, or possess wildlife.

(j) "Party state" means any state which enacts legislation to become a member of this Wildlife Compact.

(k) "Personal recognizance" means an agreement by a person made at the time of issuance of the wildlife citation that the person will comply with the terms of that citation.

(l) "State" means any state, territory or possession of the United States, the District of Columbia, Commonwealth of Puerto Rico, Provinces of Canada or other countries.

(m) "Suspension" means any revocation, denial or withdrawal of any or all license privileges, including the privilege to apply for, purchase or exercise the benefits conferred by any license.

(n) "Terms of the citation" means those conditions and options expressly stated upon the citation.

(o) "Wildlife" means all species of animals, including but not necessarily limited to mammals, birds, fish, reptiles, amphibians, mollusks and crustaceans, which are defined as "wildlife" and are protected or otherwise regulated by statute, law, regulation, ordinance or administrative rule in a party state. Species included in the definition of "wildlife" vary from state to state and determination of whether a species is "wildlife" for the purposes of this compact shall be based on local law.

(p) "Wildlife law" means any statute, law, regulation, ordinance or administrative rule developed and enacted to manage wildlife resources and the use thereof.

(q) "Wildlife officer" means any individual authorized by a party state to issue a citation for a wildlife violation.

(r) "Wildlife violation" means any cited violation of a statute, law, regulation, ordinance or administrative rule developed and enacted to manage wildlife resources and the use thereof.

ARTICLE III: PROCEDURES FOR ISSUING STATE

(a) When issuing a citation for a wildlife violation, a wildlife officer shall issue a citation to any person whose primary residence is in a party state in the same manner as if the person were a resident of the home state and shall not require the person to post collateral to secure appearance, subject to the exceptions contained in subdivision (b) of this Article, if the officer receives the person's personal recognizance that the person will comply with the terms of the citation.

(b) Personal recognizance is acceptable:
    (1)   If not prohibited by local law or the compact manual; and
    (2)   If the violator provides adequate proof of the violator's identification to the wildlife officer.

(c) Upon conviction or failure of a person to comply with the terms of a wildlife citation, the appropriate official shall report the conviction or failure to comply to the licensing authority of the party state in which the wildlife citation was issued. The report shall be made in accordance with procedures specified by the issuing state and shall contain the information specified in the compact manual as minimum requirements for effective processing by the home state.

(d) Upon receipt of the report of conviction or noncompliance required by subdivision (c) of this Article, the licensing authority of the issuing state shall transmit to the licensing authority in the home state of the violator the information in a form and content as contained in the compact manual.

ARTICLE IV: PROCEDURES FOR HOME STATE

(a) Upon receipt of a report of failure to comply with the terms of a citation from the licensing authority of the issuing state, the licensing authority of the home state shall notify the violator, shall initiate a suspension action in accordance with the home state's suspension procedures and shall suspend the violator's license privileges until satisfactory evidence of compliance with the terms of the wildlife citation has been furnished by the issuing state to the home state licensing authority. Due process safeguards will be accorded.

(b) Upon receipt of a report of conviction from the licensing authority of the issuing state, the licensing authority of the home state shall enter such conviction in its records and shall treat such conviction as if it occurred in the home state for the purposes of the suspension of license privileges.

(c) The licensing authority of the home state shall maintain a record of actions taken and make reports to issuing states as provided in the compact manual.

ARTICLE V: RECIPROCAL RECOGNITION OF SUSPENSION

All party states shall recognize the suspension of license privileges of any person by any state as if the violation on which the suspension is based had in fact occurred in their state and could have been the basis for suspension of license privileges in their state.

ARTICLE VI: APPLICABILITY OF OTHER LAWS

Except as expressly required by provisions of this compact, nothing herein shall be construed to affect the right of any party state to apply any of its laws relating to license privileges to any person or circumstance, or to invalidate or prevent any agreement or other cooperative arrangements between a party state and a nonparty state concerning wildlife law enforcement.

ARTICLE VII: COMPACT ADMINISTRATOR PROCEDURES

(a) For the purpose of administering the provisions of this compact and to serve as a governing body for the resolution of all matters relating to the operation of this compact, a board of compact administrators is established. The board shall be composed of one representative from each of the party states to be known as the compact administrator. The compact administrator shall be appointed by the head of the licensing authority of each party state and will serve and be subject to removal in accordance with the laws of the state the administrator represents. A compact administrator may provide for the discharge of the administrator's duties and the performance of the administrator's functions as a board member by an alternate. An alternate may not be entitled to serve unless written notification of the alternate's identity has been given to the board.

(b) Each member of the board of compact administrators shall be entitled to one vote. No action of the board shall be binding unless taken at a meeting at which a majority of the total number of votes on the board are cast in favor thereof. Action by the board shall be only at a meeting at which a majority of the party states are represented.

(c) The board shall elect annually, from its membership, a chairperson and vice-chairperson.

(d) The board shall adopt bylaws, not inconsistent with the provisions of this compact or the laws of a party state, for the conduct of its business and shall have the power to amend and rescind its bylaws.

(e) The board may accept for any of its purposes and functions under this compact all donations and grants of money, equipment, supplies, materials and services, conditional or otherwise, from any state, the United States or any governmental agency, and may receive, utilize and dispose of the same.

(f) The board may contract with or accept services or personnel from any governmental or intergovernmental agency, individual, firm, corporation or any private nonprofit organization or institution.

(g) The board shall formulate all necessary procedures and develop uniform forms and documents for administering the provisions of this compact. All procedures and forms adopted pursuant to board action shall be contained in the compact manual.

ARTICLE VIII: ENTRY INTO COMPACT AND WITHDRAWAL

(a) This compact shall become effective when it has been adopted by at least two states.

(b) (1) Entry into the compact shall be made by resolution of ratification executed by the authorized officials of the applying state and submitted to the chairperson of the board.

(2) The resolution shall be in a form and content as provided in the compact manual and shall include statements that in substance are as follows:

  (i)   A citation of the authority by which the state is empowered to become a party to this compact;

  (ii) Agreement to comply with the terms and provisions of the compact; and

  (iii) That compact entry is with all states then party to the compact and with any state that legally becomes a party to the compact.

(3) The effective date of entry shall be specified by the applying state, but shall not be less than 60 days after notice has been given by the chairperson of the board of the compact administrators or by the secretariat of the board to each party state that the resolution from the applying state has been received.

(c) A party state may withdraw from this compact by official written notice to the other party states, but a withdrawal shall not take effect until 90 days after notice of withdrawal is given. The notice shall be directed to the compact administrator of each member state. No withdrawal shall affect the validity of this compact as to the remaining party states.

ARTICLE IX: AMENDMENTS TO THE COMPACT

(a) This compact may be amended from time to time. Amendments shall be presented in resolution form to the chairperson of the board of compact administrators and may be initiated by one or more party states.

(b) Adoption of an amendment shall require endorsement by all party states and shall become effective 30 days after the date of the last endorsement.

(c) Failure of a party state to respond to the compact chairman within 120 days after receipt of the proposed amendment shall constitute endorsement.

ARTICLE X: CONSTRUCTION AND SEVERABILITY

This compact shall be liberally construed so as to effectuate the purposes stated herein. The provisions of this compact shall be severable and if any phrase, clause, sentence or provision of this compact is declared to be contrary to the constitution of any party state or of the United States or the applicability thereof to any government, agency, individual, or circumstance is held invalid, the compact shall not be affected thereby. If this compact shall be held contrary to the constitution of any party state thereto, the compact shall remain in full force and effect as to the remaining states and in full force and effect as to the state affected as to all severable matters.

ARTICLE XI: TITLE

This compact shall be known as the Wildlife Violator Compact.

[Oregon also provides for revocation of a violator's license for failure to comply with terms of a citation from a party state, or for conviction of a violation in a party state, in ORS (497.415).]

APPENDICES

DEFINITIONS

ALABAMA

Migratory waterfowl: a wild duck, wild goose, brant or coot (9-11-430.

Wildlife: For purposes of possession of wildlife for exhibition, wildlife is a wild mammal, wild bird, reptile or amphibian (9-11-320).

ALASKA

Domestic mammals: musk oxen, bison, elk and reindeer, if lawfully owned (16.05.940).

Fish: a species of aquatic finfish, invertebrate, or amphibian, in any stage of its life cycle, found in or introduced into the state, including any part (16.05.940).

Fish stock: a species, subspecies, geographic grouping or category of fish manageable as a unit (16.05.940).

Game: a species of bird, reptile, and mammal, including feral domestic animals, found or introduced in the state, except domestic birds and mammals; game may be classified by regulation as big game, small game, fur-bearers or other categories considered essential for carrying out the intention and purposes of 16.05 through 16.40 (16.05.940).

Game population: a group of game animals of a single species or subgroup manageable as a unit (16.05.940).

ARIZONA (Found in 17-101 and -296)

Aquatic wildlife: fish, amphibians, mollusks, crustaceans and soft-shelled turtles.

Big game: bear, wild turkey, deer, elk, antelope, bighorn sheep, bison (buffalo), peccary (javalina), mountain lion.

Candidate species: a species or subspecies of native Arizona wildlife for which habitat or population threats are known or suspected but for which substantial population declines from historic levels have not been documented.

Endangered species: a species or subspecies of native Arizona wildlife whose population has been reduced to such levels that it is in imminent danger of elimination, or has been eliminated, from its range in Arizona.

Fur-bearing animals: muskrats, raccoons, otters, weasels, bobcats, beaver, badgers and ringtail cats.

Game mammals: deer, elk, bear, antelope, bighorn sheep, bison (buffalo), peccary (javalina), mountain lion, tree squirrel and cottontail rabbit.

Nongame animals: all wildlife except game mammals, game birds, fur-bearing animals, predatory animals and aquatic wildlife.

Migratory game birds: wild waterfowl, including ducks, geese and swans; sand hill cranes; all coots; all gallinules; common snipe; wild doves; and bandtail pigeons.

Nongame birds: all birds except upland game birds and migratory game birds.

Nongame fish: all species of fish except game fish.

Predatory animals: foxes, skunks, coyotes, bobcats.

Small game: cottontail rabbits, tree squirrels, upland game birds and migratory game birds.

Threatened species: a species or subspecies of native Arizona wildlife that, although not presently in imminent danger of being eliminated from its range in Arizona, is likely to become an endangered species in the foreseeable future.

Trout: all species of family salmonidae, including grayling.

Upland game birds: quail, partridge, grouse and pheasants.

Wild: in reference to mammals and birds, those species which are normally found in a state of nature.

Wildlife: all wild mammals, wild birds and the nests or eggs thereof, reptiles, crustaceans and fish, including their eggs or spawn.

ARKANSAS: None.

CALIFORNIA

[Definitions usually are found in a particular chapter dealing with a certain species or group of animals, and most definitions begin with the words "as used in this chapter"].

Aquatic nuisance species: a nonindigenous species that threatens the viability or abundance of a native species, the ecological stability of waters inhabited by those species, or the viability of commercial, agricultural, aquacultural, or recreational activities which depend on those waters (-6431).

Candidate species: a native species or subspecies of a bird, mammal, fish, amphibian, reptile, or plant that the commission has formally noticed as being under review by the department for addition to either the list of endangered or threatened species, or a species for which the commission has published a notice of proposed regulation to add the species to either list (-2068).

Endangered animal: an animal of a species or subspecies of birds, mammals, fish, amphibia, or reptiles, the prospects of survival and reproduction of which are in immediate jeopardy from one or more causes, including loss of habitat, change in habitat, overexploitation, predation, competition, or disease (-2051).

Endangered species: a native species or subspecies of a bird, mammal, fish, amphibian, reptile, or plant which is in serious danger of becoming extinct throughout all, or a significant portion, of its range due to one or more causes, including loss or change in habitat, overexploitation, predation, competition, or disease (-2062).

Exotic nonresident game birds: birds of the order Galliformes (pheasant, grouse, quail) which are not established as a wild resident population in California (-3514).

Fur-bearing mammals: pine marten, fisher, wolverine, mink, river otter, gray fox, cross fox, silver fox, red fox, kit fox, raccoon, beaver, badger, and muskrat (-4000).

Game mammals: deer, elk, prong-horned antelope, wild pigs, including feral pigs and European wild boars, black and brown or cinnamon bears, mountain lions, jackrabbits and varying hares, cottontails, brush rabbits, pigmy rabbits, and tree squirrels. Nelson bighorn sheep are game mammals only for the purposes of sport hunting described in section 4902 (-3950).

Mammal: any wild animal of the class Mammalia as specified in Article 1 (commencing with Section 2116) or regulations adopted pursuant thereto which affects commerce (-2200).

Migratory game birds: ducks and geese, coots and gallinules, jacksnipe, western mourning doves, white-winged doves and band-tailed pigeons; "game birds" means both resident game birds and migratory game birds (-3500).

Native amphibians: salamanders, toads, or any other member of the class amphibia native to California (-6431).

Native reptiles: snakes, lizards, turtles, or any other members of the class reptilia native to California (-5060).

Rare animal: an animal of a species or subspecies of birds, mammals, fish, amphibia or reptiles that, although not presently threatened with extinction, is in such small numbers throughout its range that it may be endangered if its environment worsens (-2051).

Resident game birds: Chinese spotted doves, ringed turtledoves of the family Columbidae, California quail and varieties thereof, Gambel or desert quail, mountain quail and varieties, sooty or blue grouse and varieties, ruffed grouse, sage hens and sage grouse, Hungarian partridges, red-legged partridges including the chukar, ring-necked pheasants and varieties, and wild turkeys of the order Galliformes (-3500).

Shellfish: any bivalve mollusk (-5669).

Species: the fundamental biological unit of plant and animal classification that comprises a subdivision of a genus, also includes the unit of a subspecies (-2702).

Threatened species: a native species or subspecies of a bird, mammal, fish, amphibian, reptile, or plant that, although not presently threatened with extinction, is likely to become an endangered species in the foreseeable future in the absence of special protection and management efforts required (-2067).

Trout: includes steelhead trout (-1728).

Wild animal: any animal of the class Aves (birds), class Mammalia (mammals), class Amphibia (frogs, toads, salamanders), class Osteichtyes (bony fishes), class Monorhina (lampreys), class Reptilia (reptiles), class Crustacea (crayfish), or class Gastropoda (slugs, snails) which is not normally domesticated in this state as determined by the commission (-2116).

Wild pigs: free-roaming pigs not distinguished by branding, ear marking, or other permanent identification methods (-4650).

Wild rodents: wild ground squirrels, chipmunks, rats, mice or any other members of the order Rodentia native to California except muskrats and beavers (-2575).

Wildlife: all wild animals, birds, plants, fish, amphibians, and related ecological communities, including the habitat upon which the wildlife depends for its continued viability (-711.2).

COLORADO

Big game: elk, white-tailed deer, mule deer, moose, rocky mountain bighorn sheep, rocky mountain goat, pronghorn antelope, black bear, mountain lion, and all species of large mammals that may be introduced or transplanted into this state for hunting or are classified as big game (33-1-102).

Endangered species: native wildlife whose prospects for survival or recruitment within this state are in jeopardy as determined by the Commission (33-1-102).

Exotic aquatic species: species, subspecies, and hybrids of fish, mollusks, crustaceans, aquatic reptiles, and aquatic amphibians not originating naturally, either presently or historically, in Colorado and not currently found in the drainage in question, except those classified as native wildlife (33-1-102).

Fur-bearers: species with fur having commercial value and which provide opportunities for sport harvest, including badger, gray fox, kit fox, swift fox, opossum, hognosed skunk, spotted skunk, striped skunk, beaver, marten, mink, muskrat, ringtail, long-tailed weasel, short-tailed weasel, coyote, bobcat, red fox, and raccoon and all species of fur-bearers that may be introduced or transplanted into this state for commercial fur value and are classified as fur-bearers (33-1-102).

Game amphibian: species or subspecies of the class Amphibia classified as game amphibians (33-1-102).

Game crustacean: species or subspecies of the class Crustacea classified as game crustaceans (33-1-102).

Game fish: all species of fish which currently exist or may be introduced or transplanted into this state for sport or profit and which are classified as game fish (33-1-102).

Game mollusk: species or subspecies of the phylum Mollusca classified as game mollusks (33-1-102).

Game wildlife: wildlife species which may be lawfully taken for food, sport, or profit and which are classified as game wildlife (33-1-102).

Native wildlife: species and subspecies of wildlife which have originated naturally, either presently or historically, in Colorado; those which have been introduced into the wild by the Division; and those classified as native wildlife (33-1-102).

Nongame wildlife: all native species and subspecies of wildlife which are not classified as game wildlife (33-1-102).

Nonnative wildlife or exotic wildlife: species, subspecies, and hybrids of wildlife not originating naturally, either presently or historically, in Colorado, except those which have been introduced into the wild by the Division or classified as native wildlife (33-1-102).

Raptor: all birds of the order of Falconiformes or Strigiformes including falcons, hawks, owls, and eagles or such other birds classified as raptors (33-1-102).

Small game: game birds, including grouse, ptarmigan, pheasant, quail, partridge, wild turkey, wild ducks, wild geese, sora and virginia rails, coot, sandhill cranes, snipe, mergansers, band-tailed pigeons, doves, and crow; game mammals, including cottontail rabbit, snowshoe hare, fox squirrel, pine squirrel, Abert's squirrel, jackrabbits, marmot, and prairie dogs; and all species of small mammals and birds that may be introduced or transplanted into this state for hunting or are classified as small game (33-1-102).

Threatened species: any species or subspecies of wildlife which, as determined by the Commission, is not in immediate jeopardy of extinction but is vulnerable because it exists in such small numbers or is so extremely restricted throughout all or a significant portion of its range that it may become endangered.

Wildlife: wild vertebrates, mollusks, and crustaceans, alive or dead, including any part, product, egg, or offspring, that exist in a natural wild state in their place of origin, presently or historically, except species determined to be domestic animals by the Commission and the state agricultural commission (33-1-102).

CONNECTICUT (Found in 26-1 and -304)

Animal: birds, quadrupeds, reptiles and amphibians.

Bait: "bait species" fish, frogs, crustaceans and insects listed as bait in regulations.

Black bass: small and large mouth bass.

Endangered species: ★native species documented in danger of extirpation throughout all or a significant portion of its range and to have no more than five occurrences,★ and species determined to be endangered pursuant to the federal Endangered Species Act.

Grouse: ruffed grouse, partridge and spruce grouse.

Game bird: anatidae, or waterfowl, including brant, wild ducks and geese; raillidae, or rails, including coots, gallinules, sora and other rails; limicolae, or shore birds, including snipe and woodcock; gallinae, including wild turkeys, grouse, prairie chickens, pheasants, partridge and quail; corvidae, including crows (26-92).

Native: species indigenous to this state.

Occurrence: a population of a species breeding and existing within the same ecological community and capable of interbreeding. ★[Essential habitat, threatened continued existence, destruction/adverse modification of essential habitat are defined.]★

Pickerel: chain pickerel, not banded pickerel, grass pike, grass pickerel, mud pike or brook pickerel.

Quadruped: any four-legged animal wild by nature, although it may be enclosed and considered a pet or semidomesticated, but shall exclude purely domesticated animals.

Species: any species, subspecies, or variety of animal or plant, including any distinct population segment.

Species of special concern: native plant species or native nonharvested wildlife species having a naturally restricted range or habitat in the state, at a low population level, to be in such high demand that its unregulated taking would be detrimental to the conservation of its populations or has been extirpated from the state.

Threatened species: ★native species likely to become endangered within the foreseeable future throughout all or a significant portion of its range within the state and to have no more than nine occurrences in the state,★ and threatened species pursuant to the federal Endangered Species Act, except for such species determined to be endangered under 26-306.

Trout and Salmon: brook, speckled, brown, rainbow, and lake trout; Atlantic, kokanee or sockeye, coho, and chinook salmon; or any hybrid of two or more of these species.

Wildlife: invertebrates, fish, amphibians, reptiles, birds and mammals which are wild by nature.

DELAWARE

Protected Wildlife: all forms of game and wildlife except those not protected by Parts I and II of this title (7-101).

Nongame: fauna, including rare and endangered species, which are not commonly trapped, killed, captured or consumed, either for sport or profit (7-202).

Game animals: mink, snapping turtle, raccoon, opossum, gray squirrel, otter, muskrat, red fox, hare, rabbit, frog, deer and beaver. The Bryant fox-squirrel shall be protected wildlife (7-701).

Game birds: geese, brant and river and sea ducks; rails, coots, mudhens and gallinules; shorebirds, plovers, surf birds, snipe, woodcock, sandpipers, tattlers and curlews; wild turkeys, grouse, prairie chickens, pheasants, chukar partridges, partridges and quail; the reed bird of the Icteridae; and the dove (7-702).

DISTRICT OF COLUMBIA

Aquatic animals: animals which have typically lived in or otherwise established as a habitat the District waters (6-921).

Wild animals: mammals, birds, fish and reptiles not ordinarily domesticated (22-1628).

FLORIDA

Alligator: a member of the species of alligator but not its eggs (372.6671).

Alligator hatchling: a juvenile alligator as specifically defined by Commission rule (372.6671).

Endangered species: fish and wildlife naturally occurring in Florida, whose prospects of survival are in jeopardy due to modification or loss of habitat; over-utilization for commercial, sporting, scientific or educational purposes; disease; predation; inadequacy of regulatory mechanisms; or other natural or manmade factors affecting its continued existence (372.072).

Fish and game: fresh and saltwater fish, shellfish, crustacea, sponges, wild birds, and wild animals (372.001).

Fish and wildlife: a member of the animal kingdom, including, but not limited to, a mammal, fish, bird, amphibian, reptile, mollusk, crustacean, arthropod, or other invertebrate (372.072).

Freshwater fish: all classes of pisces that are indigenous to fresh water (372.001).

Fur-bearing animals: muskrat, mink, raccoon, otter, civet cat, skunk, red and gray fox, and opossum (372.001).

Game: deer, bear, squirrel, rabbits, and where designated by Commission rules, wild hogs, ducks, geese, rails, coots, gallinules, snipe, woodcock, wild turkeys, grouse, pheasants, quail and doves (372.001).

Nongame: all species and populations of indigenous wild vertebrates and invertebrates in the state that are not defined as game (372.001).

Threatened species: fish and wildlife naturally occurring in Florida which may not be in immediate danger of extinction, but which exists in such small populations as to become endangered if it is subjected to increased stress as a result of further modification of its environment (372.072).

GEORGIA

Alligator: any reptile commonly known or classified as an alligator or crocodile (27-1-2).

Big game: turkey, deer, bear (27-1-2).

Domestic species: those taxa of animals which have traditionally lived in a state of dependence on and under the dominion and control of man and have been kept as tame pets, raised as livestock or used for commercial breeding purposes, including, but not limited to, dogs, cats, horses, cattle and chickens. Captive or tame animals which lack a genetic distinction from members of the same taxon living in the wild are presumptively wild animals (27-1-2).

Feral Hog: any hog which is normally considered domestic but which is living in a wild state and cannot be claimed in private ownership (27-1-2).

Fur-bearing animals: mink, otter, raccoon, fox, opossum, muskrat, skunk, bobcat and weasel (27-1-2).

Game animals: bear, bobcat, deer, fox, opossum, rabbit, raccoon, sea turtles and their eggs, squirrel, cougar, and all members of the families Alligatoridae and Crocodylidae (27-1-2).

Game birds: turkey, quail, grouse, and all migratory game birds (27-1-2).

Game fish: Various listed species of: bass, trout (except as in 27-4-78), crappie, shad, sunfish or bream, perch, pickerel, catfish (except as in 27-4-78) (27-1-2).

Game species: all game animals, game birds and game fish (27-1-2).

Migratory game birds: brant, coots, cranes, doves, ducks, gallinules, geese, rails, snipe, swans and woodcock. Birds which are mutations of such birds and birds which are the result of hybridization are included as migratory game birds (27-1-2).

Mountain trout: rainbow, brook, brown trout (27-1-2).

Nongame fish: any fish not included within the definition of "game fish" in this code section and is synonymous with the term "rough fish" (27-1-2).

Pen raised game birds: game birds which are raised in captivity and are more than two generations removed from the wild (27-1-2).

Raptor: a migratory bird of the order Falconiformes or Strigiformes, other than the bald eagle or golden eagle (27-1-2).

Wild animal: any vertebrate or invertebrate of the animal kingdom which is not wildlife and is not normally a domestic species in this state. The term specifically includes any vertebrate or invertebrate of the animal kingdom which is a hybrid or cross between a wild animal and an animal of a domestic species (27-1-2).

Wildlife: any vertebrate or invertebrate animal life indigenous to this state or any species introduced or specified by the Board and includes fish, except domestic fish produced by registered aquaculturists, mammals, birds, fish, amphibians, reptiles, crustaceans and mollusks or any part thereof (27-1-2).

HAWAII

Aquatic life: a species of mammal, fish, amphibian, reptile, mollusk, crustacean, arthropod, invertebrate, coral, or other animal that inhabits the freshwater or marine environment, and includes any part, product, egg, or offspring; or freshwater or marine plants, including seeds, roots, and other parts (12-183D-1).

Endangered species: a species whose continued existence as a viable component of Hawaii's indigenous fauna or flora is determined to be in jeopardy and has been so designated pursuant to section 195D-4 (12-195D-2).

Game: birds and mammals designated by law or by rule for hunting (12-183D-1).

Game birds: birds designated by law or by rule for hunting (12-183D-1).

Game mammals: mammals designated by law or by rule for hunting (12-183D-1).

Indigenous species: aquatic life, wildlife, or land plant species growing or living naturally in Hawaii and not brought to Hawaii by man (12-195D-2).

Predators: animals destructive of wildlife by nature of their predatory habits, including mongooses, cats, dogs, and rats (12-183D-1).

Species: includes any subspecies or lower taxa of aquatic life, wildlife, or land plants (12-195D-2).

Threatened species: a species of aquatic life, wildlife, or land plant which appears likely, within the foreseeable future, to become endangered and has been so designated pursuant to section 195D-4 (12-195D-2).

Wild birds: birds, other than game birds, living in a wild and undomesticated state, and their young and eggs (12-183D-1).

Wild mammals: mammals, other than game mammals, living in a wild and undomesticated state, and their young (12-183D-1).

Wildlife: a nondomesticated member of the animal kingdom, including game, whether reared in captivity or not, including any part, product, egg, or offspring, except aquatic life as defined in this section (12-183D-1).

IDAHO

Domestic fur-bearing animal: fox, mink, chinchilla, karakul, marten, fisher, muskrat, nutria, beaver, and all other fur-bearing animals raised in captivity for breeding or other useful purposes (36-711).

Migratory waterfowl: members of the family Anatidae, including brants, ducks and geese (36-414).

Wildlife: any form of animal life, native or exotic, generally living in a state of nature (36-202).

ILLINOIS

Animal: those organisms commonly included in the science of zoology and generally distinguished from plants by possession of a nervous system and the ability to move from place to place, including all invertebrates such as sponges and mollusks and vertebrates such as fishes, amphibians, reptiles, birds, and mammals ([520]10.2).

Aquatic life: includes, all fish, reptiles, amphibians, crayfish, mussels, mollusks, crustaceans, algae, or other aquatic plants ([56]1-20).

Endangered Species: any plant or animal species classified as endangered under the Federal Endangered Species Act, plus other species which the Board may list as in danger of extinction in the wild in Illinois due to one or more causes including the destruction, diminution or disturbance of habitat, overexploitation, predation, pollution, disease, or other natural or manmade factors affecting its prospects of survival ([520]10.2).

Fur-bearing mammals: mink, muskrat, raccoon, striped skunk, weasel, bobcat, opossum, beaver, river otter, badger, red fox, gray fox, and coyote ([61]1.2).

Game mammals: cottontail, swamp and jack rabbit, white-tailed deer, fox squirrel, gray squirrel and ground hog ([61]1.2).

Minnow: any fish in the family Cyprinidae except carp and goldfish ([56]1-55).

Mussels: any freshwater mussel, or the shell of a mussel ([56]1-65).

Salmon: all the salmons and trouts ([56]1-85).

Threatened Species: any plant or animal species classified as threatened under the Federal Endangered Species Act plus other species which the Board may list as likely to become endangered in the wild in Illinois within the foreseeable future ([520]10.2).

Wild animal: any wild creature the taking of which is authorized by state fish and game laws ([61]301).

Wildlife: any bird or mammal living in a state of nature without the care of man including all species covered by this Act ([61]1.2).

INDIANA

Animal: all mammals, birds, reptiles, amphibians, fish, crustaceans, and mollusks (14-2-2-1).

Endangered species: any species or subspecies of wildlife whose prospects of survival or recruitment within the state are in jeopardy or are likely within the foreseeable future to become so due to: destruction, drastic modification or severe curtailment of its habitat; overutilization for scientific, commercial or sporting purposes; disease, pollution or predation; other natural or man-made factors affecting its prospects of survival or recruitment within the state; any combination of the foregoing factors. The term shall also include any species of fish or wildlife appearing on the US lists of endangered native or foreign fish and wildlife as modified (14-2-8.5-1).

Fur-bearing mammal: beaver, red fox, gray fox, long tailed weasel, mink, muskrat, raccoon, coyote, opossum, and skunk (14-2-2-1).

Migratory birds: brant, wild ducks, wild geese and swans; little brown, sandhill and whooping cranes; coot, gallinules, sora and other rails; avocets, curlews, dowitchers, godwits, knots, oyster catchers, phalaropes, plovers, sandpipers, snipe, tilts, surf birds, turnstones, willet, woodcock, tattlers, and yellow legs; doves and wild pigeons (14-2-2-1).

Migratory insectivorous birds: cuckoos; flickers and other woodpeckers; nighthawks or bull-bats, whippoorwills, swifts; hummingbirds and flycatchers; bobolinks, meadowlarks, and orioles; grosbeaks, tanagers; martins and other swallows; waxwings; shrikes and vireos; warblers; pipits; catbirds and brown thrashers; wrens; brown creepers; nuthatches; chickadees and titmice; kinglets and gnat catchers; robins and other thrushes; and all other perching birds which feed chiefly on insects (14-2-2-1).

Minnow: all fish of the minnow family (cyprinidae) and the young of all species of fish that are not protected by law (14-2-2-1).

Mollusk: one of the phylum mollusca (14-2-2-1).

Mussel: a mollusk possessing a hard, pearly, hinged shell completely encasing and protecting the living organism (14-2-2-1).

Wild animal: any animal whose species usually lives in the wild or usually is not domesticated (14-2-2-1).

Wildlife: any wild mammal, bird, reptile, amphibian, fish, mollusk, crustacean or other wild animal or any part, product, egg or offspring, or the dead body or parts thereof (14-2-8.5-1).

IOWA

Endangered species: any species of fish, plant life, or wildlife which is in danger of extinction throughout all or a significant part of its range. Endangered species does not include a species of insecta determined by the Commission or the US Department of Interior to constitute a pest whose protection would present an overwhelming and overriding risk to man (109A.1).

Fish or wildlife: any member of the animal kingdom, including any mammal, fish, amphibian, mollusk, crustacean, arthropod, or other invertebrate, and includes any parts, products, eggs, or offsprings, or dead bodies or parts. Includes migratory birds, nonmigratory birds, or endangered birds for which protection is afforded by treaty or other international agreement (109A.1).

Fur-bearing animals: beaver, badger, mink, otter, muskrat, raccoon, skunk, opossum, spotted skunk or civet cat, weasel, coyote, bobcat, wolf, groundhog, red fox, and gray fox, not domesticated fur-bearing animals (109.1).

Game: all of the animals below except those designated as not protected, and includes the heads, skins, and any other parts, and the nests and eggs of birds and their plumage: ▸ swans, geese, brant, and ducks; ▸ rails, coots, mudhens, and gallinules; ▸ shorebirds, plovers, surfbirds, snipe, woodcock, sandpipers, tattlers, godwits, and curlews; ▸ wild turkeys, grouse, pheasants, partridges, and quail; ▸ mourning doves and wild rock doves; ▸ gray squirrels and fox squirrels; ▸ cottontail rabbits and jackrabbits; ▸ deer and elk (109.1).

Migratory waterfowl: any wild goose, brant, or wild duck (110B.1).

Protected nongame species: wild fish, birds, reptile, and amphibians, and products, eggs, or offsprings, and dead bodies or parts. Nongame does not include game fish, fur-bearing animals, turtles, or frogs. Commission rule will designate species of nongame which by abundance or habits are declared a nuisance, and are not protected (109.42).

Threatened species: any species which is likely to become an endangered species within the foreseeable future throughout all or a significant portion of its range (109A.1).

KANSAS

Big game animal: antelope, deer, elk or wild turkey (32-701).

Endangered species: any species of wildlife whose continued existence as a viable component of the state's fauna is determined to be in jeopardy. The term also includes species of wildlife determined to be an endangered species pursuant to the Endangered Species Act of 1973 (32-958).

Fur-bearing animal: badger, beaver, black-footed ferret, bobcat, grey fox, lynx, marten, mink, muskrat, opossum, otter, raccoon, red fox, spotted skunk, swift fox or weasel (32-701).

Fur-harvest: to take any fur-bearing animal, or trap or attempt to trap any coyote (32-701).

Game animal: big game or small game animal (32-701).

Game bird: grouse, partridge, pheasant, prairie chicken or quail (32-701).

Game bird: pheasant, quail, partridge, turkey, hand-raised mallard duck, prairie chicken, grouse, exotic game bird or any other bird hunted by sportspersons (32-943).

Hunt: to take wildlife other than a fish, bullfrog, fur-bearing animal or coyote, or to take coyote other than by trapping (32-701).

Migratory birds: birds defined under the Migratory Bird Treaty Act (32-1008).

Migratory waterfowl: birds defined by the Migratory Bird Treaty Act (32-1008).

Migratory waterfowl: any wild goose, duck or merganser (32-939).

Nongame species: wildlife not legally classified as game, fur-bearer, threatened or endangered species by statute or rule/regulation (32-958).

Nongame wildlife: wildlife not legally classified as a game species or fur-bearer by statute or by rules and regulations (79-3221e).

Small game: any game bird, hare, rabbit or squirrel (32-701).

Species: subspecies of wildlife and other groups of wildlife of the same species or smaller taxa in common spatial arrangement that interbreed when mature (32-701).

Threatened species: wildlife which appears likely, within the foreseeable future, to become an endangered species. The term also includes threatened species of wildlife pursuant to the Endangered Species Act of 1973 (32-958).

Wildlife: any member of the animal kingdom, including any mammal, fish, bird, amphibian, reptile, mollusk, crustacean, arthropod or other invertebrate, and any part, product, egg or offspring thereof, or the dead body or parts thereof (32-701 and -958).

KENTUCKY

Minnows: fish under 6 inches in length, except basses, either largemouth, smallmouth or Kentucky; rock bass or goggle-eye; trout; crappie; walleye; sauger; pike; members of the striped bass family; and muskellunge (150.010).

Processed wildlife: wildlife specimen or part rendered into a permanently preserved state (150.010).

Protected wildlife: wildlife for which an open or closed season for taking has been designated (150.010).

Rough fish: all fishes other than those species designated by regulation as sport fishes (150.010).

Wildlife: any normally undomesticated animal, alive or dead, including any wild mammal, bird, fish, reptile, amphibian, or other terrestrial or aquatic life, whether or not controlled environment, bred, hatched, or born in captivity, including any part, product, egg, or offspring, protected or unprotected by this chapter (150.010).

LOUISIANA

Domesticated fish: fish that are spawned, grown, managed, harvested, and marketed in privately owned waters. Does not include bass, crappie, striped bass, bream, tetra, or other exotic fish unless approved by the Department (56:8).

Edible fish: commercial fish eaten as table food, including, but not limited to, sea bass, buffalo fish, bullfrog, catfish, crab, mullet, oyster, paddlefish, pompano, sheepshead, shrimp, spotted sea trout, white trout, gray trout, croaker, black drum, mackerel, shark, eel, and tuna (56:8).

Finfish: cold-blooded aquatic vertebrates that characteristically swim with fins, breathe with gills, and are covered with skin or scales (56:8).

Fish: all finfish, shellfish, crustacean, frogs, turtles, and other living aquatic resources which have sport or economic value (56:8).

Freshwater commercial fish: paddlefish, gar sturgeon, freshwater catfish; suckers, including buffalo fish of any species; carp; freshwater drum; bowfin; crayfish; bullfrogs; turtles; and all bait species taken for economic purposes (56:8).

Freshwater game fish: any species of fish found in state freshwaters taken for sport or recreation (56:8).

Game fish: species of freshwater and saltwater fish taken recreationally with the aid of a line, reel, rod, or bait (56:8).

Livestock: domesticated fish grown, managed, harvested, or marketed as a cultivated crop (56:8).

Migratory waterfowl: all species of wild ducks, geese, and coots (56:8).

Raptor: a live migratory bird which is a member of the Accipitridae, except the bald eagle; Falconidae; or great horned owl (56:8).

Shellfish: aquatic, invertebrate species having a shell, including oysters, clams, crayfish, shrimp, crabs, and other mollusks and crustaceans (56:8).

Threatened or endangered species: any species of wildlife determined by the Secretary or the USDI, with Commission concurrence, requiring protective regulation to prevent its extinction or destruction or deterioration of its economic usefulness, presently or in the foreseeable future (56:8).

Underutilized species: edible fish with commercial development potential not fully realized, including shark, clams, alligators, mullet, squid, gafftopsail catfish, hardhead catfish, spot, pinfish, silver eel, spanish mackerel, croaker, and black drum (56:8).

Wildbirds: migratory game birds: all species of ducks, geese, rails, coots, gallinules, snipe, woodcock, and wild doves. Resident game birds: wild turkey, black francolin, bobwhite quail, and all pheasants. Outlaw birds: crows, red-wing blackbirds, English sparrows, starlings, and when destructive to crops, grackles and blackbirds. Protected birds: all resident and migratory wild birds not game or outlaw birds. Does not include birds taken, possessed, or transported under game breeder or hunting preserve licenses (56:8).

Wild quadrupeds: Game quadrupeds: wild deer, bears, squirrels, and wild rabbits. Outlaw quadrupeds: coyotes and armadillos. Protected quadrupeds: wolves, cougars, bobcats, and foxes; except foxes and bobcats may be run with dogs. Nongame quadrupeds: mink, otter, muskrat, nutria, beaver, weasels, raccoons, skunks, opossum, alligator, and wild quadrupeds valuable for their skins or furs. Does not include those taken, possessed, or transported under game breeder license, nor buffalo, bison, or beefalo (56:8).

Wildlife: all species of wild vertebrates (56:8).

Wild animal: any wild creature, including fish, wild birds, and wild quadrupeds, the taking of which is authorized by provisions of this title (56:8).

MAINE

Baitfish: lake chub, silvery minnow, golden shiner, emerald shiner, bridled shiner, common shiner, blacknose shiner, spottail shiner, northern redbelly dace, finescale dace, fathead minnow, blacknose dace, longnose dace, creek chub, fallfish, pearl dace, banded killfish, mummichog, longnose sucker, white sucker, creek chubsucker, American eel (12-7001). [Scientific names are given.]

Endangered species: any species of fish or wildlife determined by the US Secretary of the Interior or by the Commissioner to be in danger of extinction throughout all or a significant portion of its range (12-7001).

Exotic: of foreign nature or character, not native, introduced from abroad, but not fully naturalized or acclimatized (12-7001).

Fish: any cold-blooded, completely aquatic vertebrate characteristically having gills, fins and an elongated streamlined body covered with scales, including parts of a fish. The term refers to fish living predominately in inland waters and anadromous and catadromous fish in inland waters (12-7001).

Migratory game birds: waterfowl, including brant, wild ducks, geese and swans; pigeons, including doves and wild pigeons; cranes, including little brown, sandhill and whooping cranes; shorebirds, including avocets, curlew, dowitchers, godwits, knots, oyster catchers, phalaropes, plovers, sandpipers, snipe,

stilts, surf birds, turnstones, willet, woodcock, and yellowlegs; rails, including coots, gallinules, and sora (12-7001).

Migratory waterfowl: waterfowl, including brant, wild ducks, geese and swans (12-7001).

Nongame species: any wild mammal, bird, amphibian, reptile, fish, mollusk, crustacean or other wild animal not otherwise legally classified by statute or regulation (14-2-8.5-1).

Nongame wildlife: all unconfined, terrestrial, freshwater and saltwater species which are not ordinarily collected, captured or killed for sport or profit (12-7757).

Raptor: birds of the order Strigiformes and of the families Accipitradae and Falconidae commonly called buteos, accipiters, falcons and owls (12-7001).

Threatened species: any species of fish or wildlife which is likely to become an endangered species within the foreseeable future throughout all of a significant portion of its range (12-7001).

Wild animal: a species of mammal, wild by nature, whether or not bred or reared in captivity, as distinguished from common domestic animals, including any parts. Use of a wild animal name, such as deer or bear, means the animal or its parts (12-7001).

Wild bird: a species of bird wild by nature, whether or not bred or reared in captivity, distinguished from common domestic birds, including parts. Use of a wild bird name, means the bird or its parts (12-7001).

Wildlife: any species of the animal kingdom, except fish, wild by nature, whether or not bred or reared in captivity; includes any part, egg or offspring; includes wild animals and birds (12-7001).

MARYLAND (Found in 4-101 and 10-101)

(Note: Definitions of classes of animals include "any part, egg, offspring, or dead body".)

Endangered Species: species whose continued existence as a viable component of the state's wildlife or fish resources is determined to be in jeopardy, or species determined to be "endangered species" pursuant to the Endangered Species Act (4-2A-01 and 10-2A-01).

Fish: finfish, crustaceans, mollusks and amphibians and reptiles which spend the majority of their life cycle in water.

Flighted mallard ducks: pen-reared mallard ducks banded by the licensee and released and shot immediately after release.

Forest game birds and mammals: forest game birds (ruffed grouse and turkey) and forest game mammals (black bears, deer, fox squirrels, excluding the Delmarva subspecies, and gray and red squirrels).

Fur-bearing mammal: raccoon, bobcat, opossum, beaver, mink, muskrat, otter, fox, skunk, fisher and long tailed weasel, (10-101).

Game and freshwater fish: fish found in nontidal water, including but not limited to a publicly or privately owned pond, lake, or canal (4-101).

Game birds or mammals: species defined as forest game birds and mammals, fur-bearing mammals, upland game birds and mammals, and wetland game birds (10-101).

Nongame birds and mammals: every wild mammal and bird not classified as game bird or mammal (10-101).

Nongame species: wildlife not classified as game birds or mammals, threatened or endangered species by state statute or regulation (4-2A-01 and 10-2A-01).

Protected birds: wild birds not included within the definition of "game bird" or "unprotected bird" (10-101).

Species: subspecies of fish and wildlife and other groups of fish or wildlife of the same species or smaller taxa in common spatial arrangement that interbreed when mature. Does not include fish bred or raised in authorized aquaculture operations in nontidal ponds, lakes or impoundments (4-2A-01 and 10-2A-01).

Threatened species: species of wildlife which appears likely, within the foreseeable future, to become endangered including species determined to be "threatened species" pursuant to the Endangered Species Act (4-2A-01 and 10-2A-01).

Unprotected birds: English sparrow and European starling (10-101).

Unprotected mammal: nutria and woodchuck (10-101).

Upland game birds and mammals: upland game birds (blackbirds, crows, pheasant, quail and woodcock) and upland game mammals (rabbit and hare) (10-101).

Wetland game birds: brant, coots, ducks, gallinules, geese, mergansers, rails, snipe and swan (10-101).

Wild birds: every bird wild by nature (10-101).

Wild mammal: every mammal wild by nature (10-101).

Wild quadruped: any species of wildlife having four feet (10-101).

Waterfowl: brants, coots, ducks, geese, mergansers and swans, including birds raised in captivity and released to the wild or otherwise used for hunting (10-101).

Wildlife: every living creature, not human, wild by nature, endowed with sensation and power of voluntary motion, including mammals, birds, amphibians and reptiles which spend a majority of their life cycle on land (10-101).

MASSACHUSETTS (Found in 131-1 and Found in 131A-1)

Animal: any member of the animal kingdom including a mammal, bird, reptile, amphibian, fish, mollusk, crustacean, arthropod or other invertebrate or part, product, egg or offspring, dead body or part.

Birds: wild or undomesticated birds.

Endangered species: a species of plant or animal in danger of extinction throughout all or a significant portion of its range including species listed as "endangered" under the Federal Endangered Species Act, and plants or animals in danger of extirpation, as documented by biological research and inventory.

Falcon: the female peregrine, and generally females of long-winged hawks and hawks trained to hunt game.

Fish: aquatic vertebrates of the osteichthyes class known as finny fish, found in inland waters.

Game: a wild bird or mammal commonly hunted for food or sport.

Horned pout: all fish in the family Ictaluridae.

Mammals: wild or undomesticated mammals.

Nongame wildlife: a nondomesticated animal not regulated as a game species and a plant, native to the commonwealth, not classified as domesticated.

Raptors: birds found in the wild that are members of the order Falconiformes or Strigiformes, including falcons, hawks, owls and eagles.

Species: a subspecies or variety of plant or animal and a distinct plant or animal population which interbreeds or cross pollinates when mature.

Species of special concern: a species of plant or animal which has been documented by biological research and inventory to have suffered a decline that could threaten the species if allowed to continue unchecked or that occurs in such small numbers or with such a restricted distribution or specialized habitat that it could easily become threatened.

Threatened species: a species of plant or animal likely to become endangered within the foreseeable future throughout all or a significant portion of its range including, but not limited to, species listed from time to time as "threatened" under the Federal Endangered Species Act, and any species declining or rare as determined by biological research and inventory and

likely to become endangered in the foreseeable future; provided that inclusion on the Federal threatened species list shall not limit the discretion of the Director to list species as "endangered".

MICHIGAN

Amphibian: any frog, toad, or salamander of the class amphibia (301.11).

Animals: wild birds and wild mammals (300.253).

Crayfish or crawfish: any arthropod of the decapoda family (304.1).

Crustacea: any freshwater crayfish, shrimp, or prawn of the order decapoda (301.11).

Endangered species: any species of fish, plant life, or wildlife which is in danger of extinction throughout all or a significant part of its range other than a species of insecta determined by the Commission or the Secretary of the USDI to constitute a pest whose protection would present an overwhelming and overriding risk to man (299.222).

Fish or wildlife: any member of the animal kingdom, including any mammal, fish, amphibian, mollusk, crustacean, arthropod, or other invertebrate, and includes any part, product, egg, or offspring, or body or parts. Fish or wildlife includes migratory birds, nonmigratory birds, or endangered birds for which protection is afforded by treaty or other international agreement (299.222).

Fur-bearing animals: badger, beaver, bobcat, coyote, fisher, fox, lynx, marten, mink, muskrat, opossum, otter, raccoon, skunk, weasel, and wolf (316.104).

Game: badger, bear, beaver, bobcat, brant, coot, coyote, crow, deer, duck, elk, fisher, Florida gallinule, fox, geese, hare, Hungarian partridge, marten, mink, moose, muskrat, opossum, otter, pheasant, quail, rabbit, raccoon, ruffed grouse, sharptailed grouse, skunk, snipe, sora rail, squirrels, weasel, wild turkey, woodchuck, woodcock, Virginia rail (300.254).

Game: game birds and game animals (316.105).

Game animals: includes bear, deer, elk, hares, moose, rabbits, fox squirrels, and black and gray squirrels (316.105).

Game birds: includes geese, brant, wild ducks, rails, coots, gallinules, shore birds, snipe, woodcock, plovers, sandpipers, pheasant, quail, Hungarian partridge, grouse, prairie chicken, sharptailed grouse, wild turkey, doves, pigeons, crows, ravens and jays (316.105).

Game fish: Mackinaw or lake trout; brook or speckled trout; brown and lock leven trout; rainbow and steelhead trout; landlocked salmon, grayling; largemouth and smallmouth black bass; bluegill, pumpkinseed or common sunfish; black crappie and white crappie, (calico bass and strawberry bass); yellow perch (perch); pike-perch (walleyed pike); northern pike (grass pike or pickerel); muskellunge; sturgeon (301.6).

Large game animal: bear, caribou, deer, elk, and moose (287.571).

Minnows: chubs, shiner, suckers, when of a size ordinarily used for bait in hook and line fishing, dace, stonerollers, muddlers, and mudminnows (304.1).

Mollusks: any mollusk of the classes bivalvia and gastropoda (301.11).

Mussel: pearly fresh-water mussel, clam, or naiad, and their shells (307.59).

Non-game fish: all kinds of fish, except game fish (301.7).

Nongame fish and wildlife: any fish or wild animals that are unconfined and not ordinarily taken for sport, fur, or food, and the habitat that supports them. Nongame fish and wildlife includes fish and wild animals designated as game species when located in an area of the state where the taking of that species of fish or wild animal is prohibited (299.152).

Reptiles: any turtle, snake, or lizard of the class reptilia (301.11).

817

Small game: all species of protected game birds and game animals except bear, deer, elk, and moose (316.108).

Species: any subspecies of fish, plant life, or wildlife and any other group of fish, plants, or wildlife of the same species or smaller taxa in common spatial arrangement that interbreed or cross-pollinate when mature (299.222).

Threatened species: any species which is likely to become an endangered species within the foreseeable future throughout all or a significant portion of its range (299.222).

Wild animal: a mammal, bird, or fish of a wild nature (316.109).

MINNESOTA

Big game: deer, moose, elk, bear, antelope, and caribou (97A.015).

Chub: shortnose cisco, and shortjaw, longjaw, blackfin and deepwater cisco; bloater and kiyi (97A.015).

Cisco: Coregonus artedii and includes lake herring and tullibee (97A.015).

Fur-bearing animals: mammals that are protected wild animals, except big game (97A.015).

Game: big and small game (97A.015).

Game birds: migratory waterfowl, pheasant, ruffed grouse, sharp-tailed grouse, Canada spruce grouse, prairie chickens, chukar partridge, gray partridge, quail, turkeys, coots, gallinules, sora and Virginia rails, American woodcock, and common snipe (97A.015).

Game fish: walleye, sauger, yellow perch, channel catfish, flathead catfish; members of the pike family, including muskellunge and northern pike; the sunfish family, including largemouth bass, smallmouth bass, sunfish, rock bass, white crappie, black crappie, members of the temperate bass family, including white bass and yellow bass; the salmon and trout subfamily, including Atlantic salmon, chinook salmon, coho salmon, pink salmon, kokanee salmon, lake trout, brook trout, brown trout, rainbow (steelhead) trout, and splake; the paddlefish family; the sturgeon family, including lake and shovelnose sturgeon. Includes hybrids of game fish (97A.015).

Migratory waterfowl: brant, ducks, geese, and swans (97A.015).

Minnows: members of the minnow family, except carp and goldfish; the mudminnow family; the sucker family, not over 12 inches in length; bullheads, ciscoes, lake whitefish, goldeyes, and mooneyes, not over 7 inches; and leeches (97A.015).

Predator: a timber wolf, coyote, fox, lynx, or bobcat (97A.015).

Protected birds: all birds except unprotected birds (97A.015).

Protected wild animals: big game, small game, game fish, rough fish, minnows, leeches, alewives, ciscoes, chubs, and lake whitefish, and the subfamily Coregoninae, rainbow smelt, frogs, turtles, clams, mussels, timber wolf, mourning doves, and wild animals that are protected by restriction in the time or manner of taking, other than a restriction in the use of artificial lights, poison, or motor vehicles (97A.015).

Rough fish: carp, buffalo, sucker, sheepshead, bowfin, burbot, cisco, gar, goldeye, and bullhead (97A.015).

Small game: game birds, gray squirrel, fox squirrel, cottontail rabbit, snowshoe hare, jackrabbit, raccoon, lynx, bobcat, red fox and gray fox, fisher, pine marten, opossum, badger, cougar, wolverine, muskrat, mink, otter, and beaver (97A.015).

Sunfish: bluegill, pumpkinseed, green sunfish, orange spotted sunfish, longear sunfish, and warmouth, including hybrids (97A.015).

Unprotected birds: English sparrow, blackbird, starling, magpie, cormorant, common pigeon, and great horned owl (97A.015).

Unprotected wild animals: wild animals that are not protected including weasel, coyote (brush wolf), gopher, porcupine, skunk, civet cat, and unprotected birds (97A.015).

Wild animals: all living creatures, not human, wild by nature, endowed with sensation and power of voluntary motion, including mammals, birds, fish, amphibians, reptiles, crustaceans, and mollusks (97A.015).

MISSISSIPPI

Endangered species: species or subspecies of wildlife whose survival or recruitment are in jeopardy or are likely within the foreseeable future to become so due to: destruction, modification or curtailment of its habitat; over-utilization for scientific, commercial or sporting purposes; the effect of disease, pollution, or predation; other natural or man-made factors affecting its prospects; and any combination of the foregoing factors. The term also includes species or subspecies of fish and wildlife appearing on the US Lists of Endangered Native or Foreign Fish and Wildlife (49-5-105).

Fur-bearing animals: muskrats, otters, skunks, weasels, minks, raccoons, nutria and bobcats; all others shall be deemed predatory animals (49-7-1).

Game: bear, deer, opossums, rabbits and squirrels (49-7-1).

Game birds: geese, brant and river and sea ducks, rails, coots, sora, snipe, woodcock, sandpipers, tattlers, plovers, wild turkey, quail and doves. All other species of wild resident or migratory birds shall be nongame birds (49-7-1).

Game fish: crappie (chinquapin perch, goggle eye, speckled perch), calico bass (red eyed, goggle eyed), breasted bream, long eared sunfish, blue gill (copper nosed sunfish), black bass (small mouthed black bass), straw bass (large mouthed black bass, green bass, bayou bass, club trout, green trout); jack perch, and walleyed pike and yellow perch (ringed perch); white bass, yellow bass, tabby cat and blue cat. However, the terms "tabby cat" and "blue cat" shall not apply to any class or classes of catfish taken from any navigable stream or lake (49-7-1).

Migratory waterfowl: wild goose, brant or wild duck (49-7-161).

Mussel: the pearly fresh water mussel, clam or naiad, and the shells thereof (49-9-1).

Nongame species: wild mammal, bird, amphibian, reptile, fish, mollusk, crustacean or other wild animal not otherwise legally classified by statute or regulation (49-5-105).

Wildlife: wild mammal, bird, reptile, amphibian, fish, mollusk, crustacean or other wild animal or any part, product, egg or offspring or the dead body or parts (49-5-105).

MISSOURI

Endangered species: species of fish and wildlife designated by the Department of Conservation, by rule filed with the Secretary of State and listed by the US Department of the Interior as threatened or endangered (252.240).

Wildlife: wild birds, mammals, fish and other aquatic and amphibious forms, and all other wild animals, regardless of classification, whether resident, migratory or imported, protected or unprotected, dead or alive, including parts of individual species (252.020).

MONTANA (Found in 87-2-101 and 87-5-102)

[For purposes of this summary: **"Game"** includes fish, game, fur-bearing animals and game and nongame birds; **"Take"** includes hunt, kill, shoot, capture, pursue or cause or attempt to do so.]

Endangered species: species or subspecies of wildlife threatened with extinction due to the following factors: destruction, drastic modification, or severe curtailment of habitat; overutilization for scientific, commercial, or sporting purposes;

the effect of disease, pollution, or predation; other natural or man-made factors affecting its prospects of survival or recruitment; or any combination of the foregoing factors.

Fur-bearing animals: marten or sable, otter, muskrat, fisher, mink, bobcat, lynx, wolverine, northern swift fox, and beaver.

Game animals: deer, elk, moose, antelope, caribou, mountain sheep, mountain goat, mountain lion, bear, and wild buffalo.

Game fish: chars, trout, salmon, grayling, and whitefish; sandpike or sauger and walleyed pike or yellowpike perch; northern pike, pickerel, and muskellunge; bass; paddlefish; sturgeon; burbot or ling; and the channel catfish.

Migratory game birds: waterfowl, including wild ducks, wild geese, brant and swans; cranes, including little brown and sandhill; rails, including coots; wilson's snipes or jacksnipes; and mourning doves.

Nongame wildlife: any wild mammal, bird, amphibian, reptile, fish, mollusk, crustacean, or other animal not otherwise legally classified by state statute or regulation. [In 87-5-102, it is added that animals designated as predatory are not nongame wildlife for purposes of that part.]

Predatory animals: coyote, weasel, skunk and civet cat.

Raptors: all birds of the orders falconiformes and strigiformes, commonly called falcons, hawks, eagles, ospreys and owls.

Upland game birds: sharptailed grouse, blue grouse, spruce (Franklin) grouse, prairie chicken, sage hen or sage grouse, ruffed grouse, quail, pheasant, Hungarian partridge, ptarmigan, wild turkey, and chukar partridge.

Wild buffalo: buffalo or bison not reduced to captivity.

Wildlife: any wild mammal, bird, reptile, amphibian, fish, mollusk, crustacean, or other wild animal or any part, product, egg, offspring or dead body or parts thereof.

NEBRASKA (Found in 37-101 and -431)

Endangered species: wildlife species whose continued existence as a viable component of wild fauna of the state is in jeopardy or which meets the criteria of the Endangered Species Act.

Extirpated species: wildlife species no longer found in Nebraska.

Fur-bearing animals: beaver, martens, minks, except mutation minks, muskrats, raccoons, opossums, and otters.

Game: game fish, bullfrogs, snapping turtles, tiger salamanders, mussels, crows, game animals, fur-bearing animals, game birds, and all other birds and creatures protected by the Game Law.

Game animals: antelope, cottontail rabbits, deer, elk, mountain sheep, and squirrels.

Game birds: coots, cranes, curlew, doves, ducks, geese, grouse, partridges, pheasants, plovers, prairie chickens, quail, rails, snipes, swans, woodcocks, wild turkeys, and all migratory waterfowl.

Game fish: fish except buffalo, carp, gar, quillback, sucker, and gizzard shad.

Migratory waterfowl: ducks, geese, coots, or brant upon which an open season has been established by the Commission (37-213).

Nongame species: mollusks, crustaceans, or vertebrate wildlife not classified as game, game bird, game animal, game fish, fur-bearer, threatened species, or endangered species by statute or regulation.

Raptor: Falconiforme or Strigiforme, except Golden and Bald eagles.

Species: subspecies of wildlife and any other group of wildlife of the same species or smaller taxa in common spatial arrangement that interbreed when mature.

Threatened species: species of wild fauna which appears likely to become endangered, either by determination of the Commission or by criteria provided by the Endangered Species Act.

Upland game: cottontail rabbits, squirrels, grouse, partridges, pheasants, prairie chickens, and quail (37-201).

Upland game birds: species and subspecies of quail, partridges, pheasants, wild turkeys, and grouse, including prairie chickens, on which an open season is in effect.

Wildlife: nondomesticated species, whether reared in captivity or not, including any mammal, fish, bird, amphibian, reptile, mollusk, crustacean, arthropod, or other invertebrate and any part, product, egg, offspring, or dead body or parts.

NEVADA (Found in 501.005 through 501.110 and 504.430)

Big game mammal, fur-bearing mammal, game mammal, game amphibian, game fish, migratory game birds, upland game birds: a game mammal, fur-bearing animal, amphibian, fish, or bird so classified by commission regulation.

Wild Horse: a horse, mare or colt which is unbranded and unclaimed and lives on public land.

Wildlife: a wild mammal, wild bird, fish, reptile, amphibian, mollusk or crustacean found naturally in a wild state, whether indigenous to Nevada or not, and whether raised in captivity or not.

NEW HAMPSHIRE

Aquatic species: all fish, crustacea, mollusks, invertebrates and aquatic plants which usually inhabit fresh water (211:62-e).

Endangered species: any species of native wildlife whose continued existence as a viable component of the state's wild fauna is determined to be in jeopardy and includes any species determined to be endangered pursuant to the Endangered Species Act (212-A:2).

Fin fish: all species and subspecies of fish listed under the definition of fish (207:1).

Fish: a member of the classes: Cyclostomata (hagfishes and lampreys); elasmobranchii (sharks, skates and rays); pisces (trout, perch, bass, minnows and catfish); including any part, product, egg or offspring, dead body or parts, excluding fossils (207:1).

Fur-bearing animals: beaver, otter, marten, sable, mink, fisher or fisher cat, raccoon, bobcat, fox, weasel, skunk and muskrat (207:1).

Game animals: moose, bear, caribou, elk, deer, wild rabbit, hare and gray squirrel (207:1).

Game birds: ruffed grouse or partridge, spruce grouse (spruce partridge), pheasant, quail, European partridge, chukar partridge and turkeys (207:1).

Migratory game birds: Anatidae or waterfowl (wild ducks and geese); Rallidae or rails (coot and gallinules); Limicolae or shore birds (plover, snipe and yellow legs); and Scolopacidae or woodcock (209:5).

Migratory birds: see federal regulations (207:1)

Nongame species: all wildlife, except those listed as fur-bearing animals, game animals, game birds, small game, unprotected birds, and fish under 207:1, and marine species regulated under 211:62 (212-B:3).

Protected birds: all wild birds not included within the terms game birds and unprotected birds (207:1).

Raptor: a live migratory bird of the family Accipitridae or Falconidae (209-A:1).

Small game: ruffed grouse or partridge, spruce grouse (spruce partridge), pheasant, quail, European partridge, chukar partridge, wild rabbit and hare, gray squirrel and migratory birds (subject to federal regulations) (207:1).

Threatened species: any species of wildlife which appears likely, within the foreseeable future, to become endangered. The term shall also include any species of wildlife determined to be a threatened species under the Endangered Species Act (212-A:2).

Unprotected birds: English sparrows, European starlings, and the common feral pigeon (rock dove), Colimba liva, except such birds as are protected by laws (207:1).

White deer: all deer which are primarily and predominantly white in color (207:1).

Wild animals: all animals other than domestic animals (207:1).

Wild birds: all birds other than domestic birds (207:1).

Wildlife: any member of any nondomesticated species of the animal kingdom, whether reared in captivity or not, including any mammal, fish, bird, amphibian, reptile, mollusk, arthropod or other invertebrate, and any part, product, egg or offspring, dead body or parts (212-A:2).

NEW JERSEY

Bait fish: all minnow, killifish and stone catfish species (23:9-5).

Endangered species: any species or subspecies of wildlife whose prospects for survival or recruitment are in jeopardy or are likely within the foreseeable future to become so due to any of the following factors: the destruction, drastic modification, or severe curtailment of its habitat; or its overutilization for scientific, commercial or sporting purposes; or the effect on it of disease, pollution or predation; or other natural or manmade factors affecting its prospects of survival or recruitment within the State; or any combination of the foregoing factors. The term shall be deemed to include any species or subspecies of wildlife appearing on any Federal endangered species list (23:2A-3).

Food fish: all other species or varieties of fish whatsoever (23:9-5).

Game bird: includes the anatidae, commonly known as geese brant, and river and sea ducks but excepting swans; rallidae, commonly known as rails, gallinules, coots and mud hens; limicolae, commonly known as shore birds, plovers, surf birds, snipe, woodcock, sandpipers, tattlers and curlews; and the gallinae, commonly known as wild turkeys, grouse, prairie chickens, pheasants, partridges and quails (23:4-49).

Game fish: any black bass or small-mouth bass; large-mouth bass, otherwise called Oswego or yellow bass; strawberry or calico bass; rock bass, known as redeye or goggle-eye; white bass; crappie; pike perch, otherwise called wall-eyed pike or susquehanna salmon; pike; pickerel; char, commonly called brook or speckled trout, or any form of trout (23:9-5).

Nongame species: any wildlife for which a legal hunting or trapping season has not been established or which has not been classified as an endangered species by statute or regulation of this State (23:2A-3).

Partridge: the species commonly known as Hungarian partridge and Chukar partridge (23:3-28).

Pheasant: the species commonly known as English Ringneck, Melanistic Mutant, Mongolian, Formosan, Chinese or artificially propagated variety thereof (23:3-28).

Quail: the species known as the "Bob White Quail" (23:3-28).

Wild bird: any bird other than a native, introduced, or feral game bird as defined in 23:4-49 and any other domesticated bird such as a chicken, turkey, guinea fowl, goose, duck, pigeon or peafowl and any egg of a wild bird (23:4-50).

Wildlife: any wild mammal, bird, reptile, amphibian, fish, mollusk, crustacean or other wild animal or any part, product, egg or offspring or the dead body or parts thereof (23:2A-3).

NEW MEXICO

Endangered species: a species of fish or wildlife whose prospects of survival or recruitment within the state are in jeopardy (group 1) or are likely within the foreseeable future to become so (group 2) due to any of the following factors: ▸ the present or threatened destruction, modification or curtailment of its habitat; ▸ overutilization for scientific, commercial or sporting purposes; ▸ the effect of disease or predation; ▸ other natural or man-made factors affecting its prospects of survival or recruitment within the state; or ▸ any combination of the foregoing factors. The term may also include any species or subspecies of fish or wildlife appearing on the US list of endangered native and foreign fish and wildlife provided that the State Game Commission adopts such lists in whole or in part (17-2-38).

Game mammals: javalina; non-domestic bison, ibex, bighorn sheep, aoudad, kudu and oryx; American pronghorn; elk and deer; pika; squirrels, marmots; bear, cougar (17-2-3).

Game birds: waterfowl; grouse and ptarmigans; quail, partridges, pheasants; wild turkey; francoli cranes; rails, coots gallinules; plovers, turnstones, surfbirds; shorebirds, snipe, sandpipers and curlews; avocets and stilts; phalaropes; wild pigeons and doves (17-2-3).

Game fish: trout; pike; catfish; sea bass and white bass; sunfish, crappie and bass; walleye pike and perch; introduced species of sargo, corvina, biardiella and redfish (17-2-3).

Fur-bearing and nongame animals: Muskrat, mink, weasel, beaver, otter, nutria, masked or blackfooted ferret, ringtail cat, raccoon, pine marten, coatimundi, badger, bobcat and all species of foxes (17-2-3).

NEW YORK

Big game: deer, bear, moose, elk, except captive bred and raised North American elk, caribou and antelope (11-0103).

Domestic game animal: white-tailed deer propagated under a domestic game animal breeder's license or on a preserve or island outside the state under a law similar to title 19 of this article (domestic game birds and shooting preserves) (11-0103).

Domestic game bird: ducks, geese, brant, swans, pheasants, quail, wild turkey, ruffed grouse, Chukar partridge and Hungarian or European gray-legged partridge, propagated under a domestic game bird breeder's or a shooting preserve license, or propagated on a preserve or island outside the state under a law similar to title 19 of this article (11-0103).

Endangered Species: species of fish, shellfish, crustacea and wildlife designated by the department as seriously threatened with extinction, including but not limited to those designated endangered by the US Secretary of the Interior (11-0535).

Fish protected by law: protected by law, regulations, by restrictions on seasons or size taken (11-0103).

Fish: all varieties of the super-class Pisces (11-0103).

Food fish: all species of edible fish and squid (11-0103).

Foreign game: pheasants of all species, Scotch grouse, Norwegian ptarmigan, Norwegian white grouse, European black game, European black plover, European gray-legged and European red-legged partridge, Egyptian quail, tinamou and species or subspecies of birds not native to this state, and European red deer, fallow deer and roebuck (11-0103).

Game birds: migratory game birds and upland game birds (11-0103).

Game: game birds; big game; small game (11-0103).

Migratory fish of the sea: catadromous and anadromous species that live a part of their life in salt water streams and oceans (11-0103).

Migratory game birds: waterfowl (geese, brant, swans and river and sea ducks); rails, American coots, mud hens and gallinules; shore birds (woodcock, snipe, plover, surfbirds, sandpipers, tattlers and curlews); jays, crows and magpies (11-0103).

Pacific salmon: coho, chinook and pink salmon (11-0103).

Protected birds: all wild birds except English sparrow, starling, pigeons and psittacine birds not domesticated (11-0103).

Protected wildlife: wild game, protected wild birds and endangered species designated by the Department pursuant to section 11-0535 or species listed in section 358a of the agriculture and markets law (11-0103).

Protected insect: any insect with taking restrictions imposed by Fish and Wildlife Law or Department regulations (11-0103).

Raptors: species of the orders Strigiformes and Falconiformes including falcons, hawks, owls and eagles except golden and bald eagles and peregrine falcons (11-1001).

Shellfish: oysters, scallops, and all clams and mussels (11-0103).

Small game: black, gray and fox squirrels, European hares, varying hares, cottontail rabbits, frogs, land turtles, box, wood and box turtles, coyotes, red and gray fox unless captive bred, raccoon, opossum, or weasel, skunk, bobcat, lynx, muskrat, mink unless captive bred, fisher, otter, beaver, sable and marten, not including coydogs (11-0103).

Threatened species: species of fish and wildlife designated by the Department as likely to become endangered within the foreseeable future throughout all or a significant portion of their range, including those designated threatened by the US Secretary of the Interior (11-0535).

Trout: includes brook, brown, red-throat and rainbow trout and splake (11-0103).

Unprotected wildlife: all wildlife that is not "protected wildlife" (11-0103).

Upland game birds: Wild turkeys, all grouse, pheasant, Hungarian or European gray-legged partridge and quail. Pheasant means ring-necked, dark-necked and mutant pheasants and all species and subspecies of the genus Phasianus representing true or game pheasants (11-0103).

Wild bird: birds which are wildlife (11-0103).

Wild game: all game, except domestic game birds and animals as defined; carcasses of foreign game as defined in section 11-1717, imported from outside the US and tagged under section 11-1721; game propagated or kept alive in captivity as provided; game imported alive under Department license, or artificially propagated when liberated for a field trial (11-0103).

Wildlife: wild game and all other animal life existing in a wild state, except fish, shellfish, and crustacea (11-0103).

NORTH CAROLINA

Animals: wild animals, except when clearly indicated otherwise (113-129).

Big game: bear, wild boar, wild turkey, and deer, not to include fallow deer raised for production and sale (113-129).

Birds: wild birds, except when clearly indicated otherwise (113-129).

Endangered Species: any native or once-native species of wild animal whose continued existence as a viable component of the state's fauna is determined by the Commission to be in jeopardy or any species determined to be "endangered" pursuant to the Endangered Species Act (113-331).

Fish; fishes: all marine mammals, shellfish, crustaceans, and other fishes (113-129).

Fur-bearing animals: beaver, mink, muskrat, nutria, otter, skunk, and weasel; bobcat, opossum, and raccoon when lawfully taken with traps.

Game: game animals and game birds (113-129).

Game animals: bear, fox, rabbit, squirrel, wild boar, and deer, except fallow deer raised for production and sale; bobcat, opossum and raccoon except when trapped in accordance with fur-bearing animals provisions (113-129).

Game birds: migratory game birds and upland game birds (113-129).

Game fish: inland game fish and game fish in coastal fishing waters regulated by the Department (113-129).

Inland game fish: species of freshwater fish, wherever found, and migratory saltwater fish, when in inland fishing waters, as to which there is an important element of sport in taking and which are denominated as game fish in Commission regulations (113-129).

Migratory birds: all birds, whether or not raised in captivity, included in the terms of conventions between the US and any foreign country for the protection of migratory birds and the Migratory Bird Treaty Act (113-129).

Migratory game birds: those migratory birds for which open seasons are prescribed by the USDI and belonging to the following families: Anatidae (wild ducks, geese, brant, swans); Columbidae (wild doves and pigeons); Gruidae (little brown cranes); Rallidae (rails, coots, gallinules); Scolopacidae (woodcock and snipe). The Commission is authorized to modify this definition by regulations only to keep it in conformity with federal laws and regulations pertaining to migratory game birds (113-129).

Nongame animals: all wild animals except game and fur-bearing animals.

Nongame birds: all wild birds except game birds (113-129).

Nongame fish: all fish found in inland fishing waters other than inland game fish (113-129).

Protected animal: a species of wild animal designated by the Commission as endangered, threatened or of special concern (113-331).

Raptor: a migratory bird of prey authorized under federal law and regulations for falconry (113-129).

Special concern species: any species of wild animal native or once-native to North Carolina determined to require monitoring but which may be taken under regulations (113-331).

Threatened species: any native or once-native species of wild animal likely to become an endangered species within the foreseeable future throughout all or a significant portion of its range, or one that is designated as a threatened species pursuant to the Endangered Species Act (113-331).

Upland game birds: grouse, pheasant, quail and wild turkey (113-129).

Wild animal: any native or once native nongame amphibian, bird, crustacean, fish, mammal, mollusk or reptile not otherwise classified by statute or regulation such as game and fur-bearing animals, except those declared to be pests under state pest control and pesticide acts (113-331).

Wild birds: migratory game birds, upland game birds and all undomesticated feathered vertebrates. The Commission may list specific birds or classes of birds excluded from the definition based upon the need for protection or regulation in the interests of conservation of wildlife resources (113-129).

Wildlife: wild animals, wild birds, all fish found in inland fishing waters, and inland game fish (113-129).

Wildlife resources: all wild birds; all wild mammals other than marine mammals; all fish found in inland fishing waters including migratory saltwater fish; all inland game fish; all uncultivated or undomesticated plant and animal life inhabiting or depending upon inland fishing waters; waterfowl food plants wherever found; all undomesticated terrestrial creatures, and the entire ecology supporting such birds, mammals, fish, plant and animal life, and creatures (113-129).

NORTH DAKOTA

Big game: deer, moose, elk, bighorn sheep, mountain goats, and antelope (20.1-01-02).

Endangered species: any species whose prospects of survival or recruitment within the state are in jeopardy due to any of the following factors: the destruction, drastic modification, or severe curtailment of its habitat; its overutilization for scientific, commercial or sporting purposes; the effect on it of disease, pollution or predation; other natural or manmade factors affecting its prospects of survival or recruitment within the state; any combination of the foregoing factors. The term also includes any species classified as endangered pursuant to the Endangered Species Act of 1973 (20.1-01-02).

Fur-bearers: mink, muskrats, weasels, wolverines, otters, martens, coyotes, bobcats, lynx, mountain lions, black bears, and red or gray foxes (20.1-01-02).

Game birds: all varieties of geese, brant, swans, ducks, plovers, snipes, woodcocks, grouse, sagehens, pheasants, Hungarian partridges, quails, partridges, cranes, rails, coots, wild turkeys, mourning doves, and crows (20.1-01-02).

Harmful wild birds: blackbirds, magpies, English sparrows and starlings (20.1-01-02).

Harmless wild birds: wild birds not defined herein as "harmful wild birds" (20.1-01-02).

Nongame wildlife: species of native animals not commonly taken for sport or commercial purposes and does not include animals determined by the Department to be harmful animals (20.1-01-02).

Raptor: any migratory bird of the family accipitridae, excluding bald and golden eagles, falconidae or strigidae (20.1-01-02).

Resident species: any species nearly all of whose individuals are located within this state for at least three-quarters of the annual cycle of the species (20.1-01-02).

Small game: all game birds and tree squirrels (20.1-01-02).

Species: any subspecies of wildlife and any other group of wildlife of the same species or smaller taxa in common spatial arrangement that interbreed when mature (20.1-01-02).

Threatened species: any species which is likely to become an endangered species within the foreseeable future and includes any species classified as threatened pursuant to the Endangered Species Act of 1973 (20.1-01-02).

Waterfowl: all varieties of geese, brant, swans, ducks, rails and coots (20.1-01-02).

Wildlife: any member of the animal kingdom including any mammal, fish, bird (including any migratory, nonmigratory, or endangered bird for which protection is also afforded by treaty or other international agreement), amphibian, reptile, mollusk, crustacean, or other invertebrate, and includes any part, product, egg, or offspring thereof, or the dead body or parts thereof. Wildlife does not include domestic animals as defined by the Board of Animal Health, or birds or animals held in private ownership (20.1-01-02).

OKLAHOMA (Found in 2-101 through 2-149)

Animal: an organism of the animal kingdom as distinguished from the plant kingdom, including any part, product, egg, or offspring, or dead body parts thereof, excluding fossils.

Endangered: wildlife species or subspecies in the wild or in captivity whose prospects of survival and reproduction are in immediate jeopardy and includes those species listed as endangered by the federal government, as well as species or subspecies identified as threatened by Oklahoma statute or Commission resolution.

Exotic wildlife: species of wildlife that are indigenous to, occur naturally, or are characteristic of another country other than the United States, its territories, commonwealths or possessions.

Fur-bearer: an animal whose fur or pelt has commercial value and includes beaver, badger, bobcat, fox, mink, muskrat, opossum, otter, raccoon, skunk, and weasel.

Gallinaceous game bird: heavy-bodied, short, broad winged, fowl-like bird, including pheasant, prairie chicken, quail and turkey.

Game: used alone, refers to mammals and birds and does not include fish.

Game bird: includes only all species of brant, cranes, doves, ducks, gallinules, geese, grouse, partridge, pheasant, pigeons, quail, prairie chickens, rails, snipes, swans, tinamous, wild turkeys, woodcock and any part.

Game fish: includes only largemouth bass, smallmouth bass, spotted bass, black crappie, white crappie, northern pike, trout, sauger, saugeye, stripped bass, walleye, blue catfish and channel catfish (defined to mean "forked tail" catfish).

Game mammal: mammalian species normally sought after by sportsmen and protected by this code, or any part.

Minnows: small nongame fish commonly used for bait, including bluntnose, bullhead minnows, chubs, dace, darters, fatheads, killifish, small carp, small goldfish, shiners and stonerollers.

Native wildlife: wildlife indigenous to or occurring naturally within the US, or any territory, commonwealth, or possession of the US.

Nongame birds: all birds not game birds.

Nongame fish: all fish not game fish.

Predatory bird: includes all eagles, falcons, hawks and owls.

Predatory mammal: includes only coyote and wolf.

Protected wildlife: wildlife which is accorded some measure of protection in the time or manner of taking other than restrictions in the use of artificial lights or poison.

Threatened: wildlife species or subspecies in the wild or in captivity that, although not presently threatened with extinction, is in such small numbers throughout its range that it may be endangered if its environment deteriorates. Includes those species and subspecies listed as "threatened" by the federal government as well as those identified as threatened by Oklahoma statutes or Commission resolution.

Upland game: game that does not normally live near water, including only squirrels, rabbits, quail, pheasant, partridge, grouse, prairie chicken, wild turkey, deer, elk and antelope.

Wild: wildlife, whether or not raised in captivity, that normally is found in a state of nature.

Wildlife: all wild birds, mammals, fish, reptiles, amphibians and other wild aquatic forms, and all other animals normally found in the wild state, regardless of classification, whether resident, migratory or imported, protected or unprotected, dead or alive, and includes every part thereof or produce, egg, or offspring, whether or not bred, hatched or born in captivity.

OHIO

Commercial fish: species permitted to be taken, possessed, bought or sold by the Code or regulation and are: alewife; american eel; bowfin; burbot; carp; small and big mouth buffalo; black, yellow, and brown bullhead; channel and flathead catfish; whitefish; cisco; freshwater drum or sheepshead; gar; gizzard shad; goldfish; lake trout; mooneye; quillback; smelt; sturgeon; sucker other than buffalo and quillback; white bass; and white and yellow perch [scientific names are given] (1531.01.).

Fish: cold-blooded vertebrates having fins (1531.01).

Fur-bearing animals: minks, weasels, raccoons, skunks, opossums, muskrats, fox, beavers, badgers, otters, coyotes and bobcats (1531.01).

Game: game birds, game quadrupeds, and fur-bearing animals (1531.01).

Game birds: pheasants; quail; ruffed, sharp-tailed, and pinnated grouse; wild turkey; Hungarian and chukar partridge; woodcocks; black-breasted and golden plover; Wilson's snipe or jacksnipe; greater and lesser yellowlegs; rail; coots; gallinules; duck; geese; brant; and crows (1531.01).

Game quadrupeds: hares or rabbits; gray, black, fox, or red squirrels; groundhogs or woodchucks; deer; wild boar and bears (1531.01).

Native wildlife: any animal species indigenous to this state (1531.01).

Nongame birds: all wild birds not defined as game birds (1531.01).

Raptor: a live migratory bird of the family Falconidae or of the family Accipitridae other than a bald eagle (1533.05).

Small game: pheasants; quail; ruffed, sharp-tailed, and pinnated grouse; Hungarian and chukar partridge; woodcocks; black-breasted and golden plover; Wilson's snipe or jacksnipe; greater and lesser yellowlegs; rail; coot; gallinules; ducks; geese, brant, crows, rabbits, gray squirrels, black squirrels, fox and red squirrels; and groundhogs or woodchucks (1531.01).

Wild animals: ★mollusks, crustaceans, aquatic insects, fish, reptiles, amphibians, wild birds, wild quadrupeds and all other wild mammals★ (1531.01).

Wild birds: game birds and nongame birds (1531.01).

Wild quadrupeds: game quadrupeds and fur-bearing animals (1531.01).

OREGON

Endangered species: native wildlife species determined by the Fish and Wildlife Commission to be in danger of extinction throughout a significant portion of its range, or a native wildlife species listed as an endangered species pursuant to the federal Endangered Species Act (496.004).

Fur-bearing mammal: beaver, bobcat, fisher, marten, mink, muskrat, otter, raccoon, red fox and gray fox (496.004).

Game bird: swans, geese, brant and river and sea ducks; mourning doves and bandtailed pigeons; grouse, ptarmigan and prairie chickens; pheasants, quail and partridge; wild turkey; snipe and woodcock; cranes; rails, gallinules and coots (496.007).

Game fish: trout, steelhead, char, grayling, Atlantic salmon and whitefish and salmon, when under 15 inches in length or when taken by angling; freshwater catfish; freshwater bass, sunfish and crappie; green sturgeon and white sturgeon, when taken by angling; yellow perch; walleye; mullet; striped bass; American shad, when taken by angling; bullfrog (496.009).

Game mammal: antelope, black bear, cougar, deer, elk, moose, mountain goat, mountain sheep and silver gray squirrel (496.004).

Native stocks: anadromous fish that naturally propagate in a given watershed (496.430).

Nongame wildlife: all wildlife species over which the Fish and Wildlife Commission has jurisdiction, except game mammals, fur-bearing mammals, game birds, and game fish (496.375).

Species: any species or subspecies of wildlife (496.004).

Threatened species: native wildlife species the Fish and Wildlife Commission determines is likely to become an endangered species within the foreseeable future throughout a significant portion of its range, or a native wildlife species listed as a threatened species pursuant to the federal Endangered Species Act (496.004).

Wildlife: fish, wild birds, amphibians, reptiles and wild mammals (496.004).

PENNSYLVANIA

Amphibian: cold-blooded, scaleless, vertebrates of the class amphibia, such as frogs, toads and salamanders (30-102).

Aquatic organism: a plant or animal that grows or lives in or upon the water (30-102).

Bait fish: unless otherwise provided, all forms of the minnow family except carp and goldfish; suckers, chubs, fallfish, lampreys and eels less than eight inches in length; and all forms of darters, killifishes and madtoms (stonecats) (30-102).

Big game: unless modified by regulation, includes elk, whitetail deer, bear and wild turkey (34-102).

Bird: a member of the class Aves, including any part, product, egg or offspring, dead body, or parts, whether or not included in a manufactured product or processed food product (34-102).

Endangered species: species and subspecies of fish and wildlife declared by the Secretary of the USDI to be threatened with extinction and appearing on the Endangered Species List or the Native Endangered Species List; or declared by the Directors of the Fish or Game Commissions to be threatened with extinction and appearing on the Pennsylvania Endangered Species List (30-102; 34-102).

Exotic wildlife: includes, but is not limited to, all bears, coyotes, lions, tigers, leopards, jaguars, cheetahs, cougars, wolves and any crossbreed thereof which have similar characteristics in appearance or features, whether or not the birds or animals were bred or reared in captivity or imported from another state or nation (34-2961).

Fish bait: unless otherwise provided, crayfish or crabs, mussels, clams and the nymphs, larvae and pupae of all insects spending any part of their life cycle in the water (30-102).

Fur-bearers: unless modified by regulation, includes badger, fisher, mink, muskrat, opossum, otter, pine marten, striped and spotted skunk, beaver, raccoon, all weasels, red and gray fox and bobcat (34-102).

Game: includes game animals and game birds (34-102).

Game animals: unless modified by regulation, includes geese, brant, wild ducks, mergansers and swans; coots, gallinules, rails, snipe, woodcock; turkeys, grouse, pheasants, Hungarian partridges, bobwhite quail and mourning doves (34-102).

Game fish: unless otherwise provided, the following fish: Brook trout, brown trout, and rainbow trout; the salmon family; walleye; chain pickerel; northern pike; muskellunge; fallfish; smallmouth, largemouth and rock bass; crappies; yellow and white perch; striped bass or rockfish; suckers; eels; chubs at least eight inches in length; sturgeon; and all other species or varieties of fish except bait fish (30-102).

Migratory waterfowl: all species so defined by the USFW

Protected birds: all wild birds not included within the term game bird (34-102).

Raptors: all eagles, falcons, hawks, and owls, individually or collectively, whether protected or unprotected (34-102).

Reptiles: any cold-blooded vertebrates of the Class Reptilia (30-102).

Small game: all species of game birds and game animals not classed as big game (34-102).

Threatened species: all species and subspecies of fish and wildlife declared by the Secretary of the USDI to be in such small numbers throughout their range that they may become endangered if their environment worsens and which appear on the Threatened Species List; or those declared by the Directors of the Fish or Game Commissions to be in such small numbers throughout their range that they may become endangered if their environment worsens and which appear on the Pennsylvania Threatened Species List (30-102; 34-102).

Wild animals: all mammals other than domestic animals as defined by law (34-102).

Wild birds: all migratory birds so defined by the USFW, game birds and any other birds designated by the Game Commission, including but not limited to grouse, partridge, pheasant, quail and wild turkey (34-102).

Wild resource: all fauna not commonly pursued, killed or consumed for sport or profit, but not including domestic fauna or domestic fauna that has reverted to a feral existence, and all flora not commonly considered an agricultural commodity (35-5303).

Wildlife: wild birds and wild mammals, regardless of classification, protected or unprotected, including any part, product, egg, offspring, dead body or parts (excluding fossils), whether or not in a manufactured product or processed food product (34-102).

RHODE ISLAND

Animal and plant: any living or dead organism(s) other than bacteria, or viruses or any part of such organism regardless of its age, condition, location or proximity to other parts or tissues of the same or similar organisms (20-37-2).

Deer: Virginia white tail deer (20-1-3).

Nongame wildlife: a member of the animal kingdom, which is a species neither harvested nor domesticated in Rhode Island. The Director has the power to promulgate lists of specific animals which are excluded from the category of nongame wildlife, in accordance with these criteria (20-18.1-2).

Endangered species: any animal or plant so declared by the US Endangered Species Acts of 1969 and 1973, or by the Director under chapter 34 of title 42 (20-37-2).

Migratory waterfowl: all waterfowl in the family anatidae including wild ducks, geese, brant and swans (20-2-34).

Protected Fur-bearers: Coyote, gray fox, red fox, raccoon, fisher, ermine, longtailed weasel, mink, striped skunk, river otter, bobcat, beaver, gray squirrel, muskrat, opossum, Eastern and New England cottontail, snowshoe hare (20-16-1).

Trout: a fish species in the family salmonidae including all species of trout, salmon and char (20-2-39).

SOUTH CAROLINA

Endangered Species: any species or subspecies of wildlife whose prospects of survival or recruitment within the state are in jeopardy or are likely within the foreseeable future to become so due to: destruction, drastic modification or severe curtailment of its habitat; overutilization for scientific, commercial or sporting purposes; effect on it of disease, pollution or predation; other natural or manmade factors affecting its prospects of survival or recruitment within the state or any combination of the foregoing factors; also includes any fish or wildlife species or subspecies appearing on US endangered native or foreign species lists as modified hereafter (50-15-20).

Fur-bearing animal: red and gray fox, raccoon, opossum, muskrat, mink, skunk, otter, bobcat, weasel, or beaver (50-11-2400).

Game animals: beaver, black bear, bobcat, white-tailed deer, fox, mink, muskrat, opossum, otter, rabbit, raccoon, skunk, squirrel, weasel (50-1-30).

Game birds: morning dove, bobwhite quail, ruffed grouse, wild turkey, Wilson snipe, woodcock, Anatidae (goose, brant, duck) and Rallidae (marsh hen, coot, gallinule, and rail)(50-1-30). All species of pheasants and francolins that have been stocked or may be released by the Wildlife and Marine Resources Department are classified as game birds, along with any other game bird species that the Division of Game Director may select for release; provided that any species that may not adapt itself to environmental conditions after extensive trial may be removed from the game bird list (50-1-40).

Game fish: bluegill, redear or shellcracker or government bream, copperface or bald bream, red breast, pumpkinseed or redeye bream, green sunfish, longear sunfish, orange-spotted sunfish, stumpknocker, warmouth or flyer; black bass, largemouth bass, smallmouth bass or coosae bass; striped bass or rockfish; white bass; hybrid striped bass-white bass; crappie; walleye or sauger; jackfish, pickerel or redfin trout; rainbow, brown or brook trout; yellow perch and Virginia or white perch (50-1-30).

Migratory waterfowl: the family Anatidae, including brants, ducks, geese and swans (50-9-155 and 50-11-20).

Nongame species: any wild mammal, bird, amphibian, reptile, fish, mollusk, crustacean, or other wild animal not otherwise classified by statute or regulation as a game species (50-15-20).

Protected wildlife: any wildlife, part, product, egg, offspring nest, dead body, or part which is managed or protected or the taking of which is specifically regulated by the Department (50-11-1180).

Small game: raccoon, opossum, rabbit, squirrel, fox, quail, bobcat, beaver, mink, muskrat, skunk, otter, grouse, weasel [for purpose of setting seasons and other restrictions] (50-11-110).

Unprotected birds: English sparrow, pigeon, starling (50-1-30).

Wildlife: a member of the animal kingdom including without limitation a mammal, fish, bird, amphibian, reptile, mollusk, crustacean, arthropod or other invertebrate (50-16-10). (Under 50-1-125, "wildlife" also includes any product, egg, offspring, or dead body parts.)

SOUTH DAKOTA

Bait: baitfish and other wild animal groups of amphibians (frogs and salamanders) (41-1-1).

Baitfish: fish of minnow family except carp and goldfish, fish of the sucker family except buffalofish and carpsucker, and fish of the stickleback family (41-1-1).

Big game: cloven-hoofed wild animals and wild turkey (41-1-1).

Biological specimens: wild nongame animals used for scientific study and collected for resale to biological supply companies (41-1-1).

Fur-bearing animals: opossum, muskrat, beaver, mink, marten, blackfooted ferret, skunks (all species), raccoon, badger, red, gray, and swift fox, coyote, bobcat, lynx, weasel and jackrabbit (41-1-1).

Game: wild mammals or birds (41-1-1).

Game fish: species belonging to paddlefish, sturgeon, salmon (trout), pike, catfish (including bullheads), sunfish (including black bass and crappies), perch (including walleye and sauger), and bass families. "Rough fish" shall include all species not included in the game fish families (41-1-1).

Migratory waterfowl: wild geese, brants or wild ducks (41-1-1).

Small game: anatidae (swans, geese, brants and river and sea ducks); rallidae (rails, coots, mudhens and gallinue); limicolae (shore birds - plover, surf bird, snipe, woodcock, sandpiper, tattler, curlews); gruidae (sandhill cranes); columbidae (mourning dove); gallinae (grouse, prairie chickens, pheasants, partridges, and quail, but shall not include wild turkeys; cottontail rabbit; fox, grey and pine squirrel (41-1-1).

Wild animal: a mammal, bird, fish or other creature of a wild nature endowed with sensation and the power of voluntary motion (41-1-1).

TENNESSEE

Big game: deer, bear, wild hog, wild turkey and all species of large mammals that may be introduced or transplanted into this state for hunting (70-1-101).

Bullfrog: jumbo frog (*Rana catesbiana*) (70-1-101).

Endangered Species: any species or subspecies of wildlife whose prospects of survival or recruitment within the state are in jeopardy or are likely within the foreseeable future to become so due to: the destruction, drastic modification, or severe curtailment of its habitat; its overutilization for scientific, commercial or sporting purposes; other natural or man-made factors affecting its prospects of survival or recruitment within the state; any combination of those factors. The term also includes any species or subspecies of fish or wildlife appearing on the US list of Endangered Native Fish and Wildlife or US list of Endangered Foreign Fish and Wildlife (70-8-103).

Fish: all species of trout, salmon, walleye, northern pike, bass, crappie, bluegill, catfish, perch, sunfish, drum, carp, sucker, shad, minnow, and such other species of fish that are presently found in the state or may be introduced or transplanted into this state for consumptive or nonconsumptive use (70-1-101).

Fur-bearer: beaver, raccoon, skunk, groundhog, coyote, gray fox, red fox, mink, muskrat, otter, weasel, bobcat and opossum, and all subspecies or variations of these, and any other animals that may be declared by the Commission to be a fur-bearer.

Game birds: all species of grouse, pheasant, woodcock, Wilson snipe, crow, quail, waterfowl, gallinules, rails, mourning dove, and all species of birds that may be introduced into this state for hunting (70-1-101).

Native wildlife: those species presently occurring in the wild in Tennessee and those extirpated species that could reasonably be expected to survive in the wild if reintroduced (70-4-402).

Nongame animals: all species of wild mammals not classified as big game, small game, or fur-bearers. Domestic dogs and cats running at large, apparently unclaimed and not under human control, whether licensed or unlicensed, come within these provisions for control and regulation by law or Commission regulation not inconsistent with Rabies Control Law, to the extent such dogs and cats are endangering or harassing wildlife (70-1-101).

Nongame birds: all birds not classified as game birds (70-1-101).

Nongame species: any wild mammal, bird, amphibian, reptile, fish, mollusk, crustacean or other wildlife not ordinarily taken for sport, fur, food or other commercial use (70-8-103).

Raptor: all birds found in the wild that are members of the order of falconiformes, strigiformes, and specifically, but not limited to, falcons, hawks, owls, and eagles, except the golden and bald eagle (70-1-101).

Small game: fur-bearers, game birds, swamp rabbits, bullfrogs, cottontail rabbits, fox squirrels, gray squirrels, red squirrels, and all species of small mammals and birds that may be introduced into this state for hunting (70-1-101).

Threatened: any species or subspecies of wildlife which is likely to become an endangered species within the foreseeable future (70-8-103).

Wild bird: all game birds, nongame birds, and raptors (70-1-101).

Wildlife: wild vertebrates, mollusks, crustaceans, and fish (70-1-101).

Wildlife in need of management: any species or subspecies of wildlife needing management to prevent it from becoming a threatened species within the foreseeable future (70-8-103).

TEXAS

Alligator: American Alligator (5.65.001).

Depredating animal: bobcats, feral hogs, red foxes, exotic animals, coyotes, and crossbreeds between coyotes and dogs, but does not include birds or fowl (5.43.103).

Endangered species: those species listed under 5.68.002 of this code (2.11.051).

Exotic animal: axis deer, fallowdeer, blackbuck antelope, sika deer, aoudad sheep, mouflon sheep, barbado sheep, European red

deer, Corsican sheep, four-horned sheep, sambar deer, eland antelope, sable antelope, white-tailed gnu, impala, greater kudu, blesbok, gazelle, oryx, guanaco, llama, thar, nilgai antelope, ibex (5.62.015). Term also includes wild animals nonindigenous to Texas (2.12.601).

Fish or wildlife: any wild mammal, aquatic animal, wild bird, amphibian, reptile, mollusk or crustacean, or any part, product, egg or offspring (5.68.001).

Fur-bearing animal: wild beaver, otter, mink, ring-tailed cat, badger, skunk, raccoon, muskrat, opossum, fox, nutria, or civet cat (5.71.001).

Game animals: Mule deer, white-tailed deer, pronghorn antelope, desert bighorn sheep, gray or cat squirrels, fox squirrels or red squirrels, collard peccary or javelina and in a few specified counties, elk and Aoudad Sheep (5.63.001).

Game birds: wild turkey, all wild ducks and geese, wild types of brant, grouse, prairie chickens, pheasants, partridge, bobwhite quail, scaled quail, Mearn's quail, Gambel's quail, red-belled pigeons, band-tailed pigeons, mourning doves, white-winged doves, white-fronted doves, snipe, plover and shorebirds of all varieties, chachalacas, sandhill cranes (5.64.001).

Migratory game birds: wild ducks, geese, and brant of all species; wild coot, rail, gallinules, plovers, Wilson's snipe or jack snipe, woodcock, mourning doves, white-winged doves, white-fronted doves, red-billed pigeons, band-tailed pigeons, all shorebirds and sandhill cranes (5.64.021).

Nongame: species of vertebrate and invertebrate wildlife not classified as game animals, game birds, game fish, fur-bearing animals, endangered species, alligators, marine penaeid shrimp, or oysters. Sections 5.67.001 and 5.67.0011 add "species of vertebrate and invertebrate wildlife indigenous to Texas, and elk east of the Pecos River," and exempt crayfish, other than in public water (2.11.051).

Pen-reared birds: bobwhite quail, pheasant, partridge, and mallard ducks propagated or acquired under chapter 45 (5.43.071).

Protected wildlife: game animals and birds and nongame animals and birds that are the subject of any protective law or regulation of this state or the US (5.62.031). Relating to scientific permits, "protected wildlife" means all animals, birds, fish, and other aquatic life the taking, possession, or propagation of which is regulated by law or by the Department and includes endangered species (5.43.021 and .022).

Trout: any species of the family Salmonidae, including but not restricted to rainbow trout, brown trout, and brook trout (5.43.501).

Waterfowl: wild ducks of all species, wild geese and wild brant of all species, and wild coot (5.43.301).

Wild: a species, including each individual of a species, that normally lives in a state of nature and is not ordinarily domesticated, not including exotic livestock defined by 161.001(a), Agriculture Code 1 (1.1.101).

Wildlife: any vertebrate species other than a domesticated animal (5.43.103).

Wildlife resource: an animal, bird, reptile, amphibian, fish or other aquatic life the taking or possession of which is regulated in any manner by this code (2.12.104). Under 5.61.005, the term is defined as all game animals, game birds, marine animals, fish and other aquatic life.

UTAH (Found in 23-13-2 and 23-17-11)

Aquatic wildlife: species of fish, crustaceans, aquatic insects or amphibians.

Big game: species of hoofed protected wildlife.

Fur-bearer: a species of the *Bassariscidae, Canidae, Felidae, Mustelidae* and *Castoridae* families, except coyote and cougar.

Game: a species of wildlife normally pursued, caught, or taken by sporting means for human use.

Protected aquatic wildlife: aquatic wildlife, including species of fish, crustaceans, or amphibians, but does not include aquatic insects.

Protected wildlife: crustaceans, including brine shrimp and crayfish; and vertebrate animals living in nature, except feral animals, but does not include coyote, field mouse, gopher, ground squirrel, jack rabbit, muskrat and raccoon.

Small game: species of protected wildlife commonly pursued for sporting purposes, and not classified as big game, aquatic wildlife, or fur-bearers.

Threatened or endangered: wildlife designated as such pursuant to Section 3 of the federal Endangered Species Act of 1973.

Upland game: pheasant, quail, partridge, Hungarian partridge, sage grouse, ruffed grouse, blue grouse, mourning dove, cottontail rabbit, or snowshoe hare.

Wildlife: crustaceans, including brine shrimp and crayfish, and species of vertebrate animals living in nature except feral animals.

VERMONT

Big game: deer, bear, moose, wild turkey, caribou, elk and anadromous Atlantic salmon taken in the Connecticut River Basin (10-4001).

Black bass: large mouth bass or small mouth bass (10-4001).

Endangered species: a species listed on the state endangered species list under this chapter or determined to be an "endangered species" under the federal Endangered Species Act. The term generally refers to species whose continued existence as a viable component of the state's wild fauna or flora is in jeopardy (10-5401).

Fur-bearing animals: beaver, otter, marten, mink, raccoon, fisher, fox, skunk, coyote, bobcat, and muskrat (10-4001).

Game: game birds or game quadrupeds, or both (10-4001).

Game birds: quail, partridge, woodcock, pheasant, plover of any kind, Wilson snipe, other shore birds, rail, coot, gallinule, wild ducks, wild geese and wild turkey (10-4001).

Game quadruped: caribou, elk, moose, deer, gray squirrel, rabbit and black bear (10-4001).

Nongame wildlife: members of nongame species which are native to this state, which are not classified as domesticated, and which are not commonly taken for sport or profit (10-4048).

Partridge: ruffed grouse (10-4001).

Pickerel: the great northern pike, chain pickerel or muskellunge (10-4001).

Pike perch: walleyed or yellow pike (10-4001).

Rabbit: includes wild hare (10-4001).

Small game: game birds except for turkeys; game quadrupeds except for big game; furbearers and other wild animals (10-4001).

Species: includes all subspecies of wildlife or wild plants and any other group of wildlife or wild plants of the same species, the members of which may interbreed when mature (10-5401).

Threatened species: a species listed on the state threatened species list under this chapter or determined to be a "threatened species" under the federal Endangered Species Act (10-5401).

Trout: brook, rainbow, and brown (10-4001).

Wild animals: all animals, including birds, amphibians and reptiles, other than domestic animals (10-4001).

Wildlife: any member of a nondomesticated species of the animal kingdom, whether reared in captivity or not, including without limitation, any mammal, fish, bird, amphibian, reptile, mollusk, crustacean, arthropod or other invertebrate, and also including any part, product, egg, offspring, dead body, or part of the dead body of any such wildlife (10-5401).

VIRGINIA (Found in 29.1-100 and 29.1-563)

Endangered species: any species in danger of extinction throughout all or a significant portion of its range.

Fish or wildlife: any member of the animal kingdom, vertebrate or invertebrate, except for the class Insecta, and includes any part, products, egg or dead body.

Fur-bearing animals: beaver, bobcat, fox, mink, muskrat, opossum, otter, raccoon, skunk, and weasel.

Game: wild animals and wild birds that are commonly hunted for sport or food.

Game animals: deer, bear, rabbit, fox, squirrel, bobcat and raccoon.

Game fish: trout (including all Salmonidae), all of the sunfish family (including largemouth bass, smallmouth bass and spotted bass, rock bass, bream, bluegill and crappie), walleye or pike perch, white bass, chain pickerel or jackfish, muskellunge, and northern pike, wherever such fish are found in Commonwealth waters and rockfish or striped bass where found above tidewaters.

Migratory game birds: doves, ducks, brant, geese, swan, coot, gallinules, sora and other rails, snipe, woodcock and other species of birds on which open hunting seasons are set by federal regulations.

Nonmigratory game birds: grouse, bobwhite quail, turkey and all species of birds introduced into the Commonwealth by the Board.

Nuisance species: blackbirds, crows, cowbirds, grackles, English sparrows, starlings, or species designated as such by Board regulations, and species found committing or about to commit depredation upon ornamental or shade trees, crops, wildlife, livestock or other property or when concentrated in numbers and manners as to constitute a health hazard or other nuisance. However, nuisance does not include: endangered or threatened species pursuant to 29.1-563, -564; and 29.1-566; game or fur-bearing animals; species protected by state or federal law.

Threatened species: any species which is likely to become an endangered species within the foreseeable future throughout all or a significant portion of its range.

Wildlife: all species of wild animals, wild birds and freshwater fish in the public waters.

WASHINGTON (Found in 75.08.011 and 77.08.010)

Big game: elk or wapiti; blacktail deer or mule deer; whitetail deer; moose, mountain goat; caribou; mountain sheep; pronghorn antelope; cougar or mountain lion; black bear; grizzly bear (77.08.030).

Deleterious exotic wildlife: species of the animal kingdom not native to Washington and designated as dangerous to the environment or wildlife of the state.

Endangered species: wildlife designated by the Commission as seriously threatened with extinction.

Food fish: species of the classes Ostiechthyes, Agnatha and Chrondrichthyes to be fished only by Director rule, and includes all states of development and parts.

Fur-bearing animals: game animals that shall not be trapped except as authorized.

Game animals: wild animals that shall not be hunted except as authorized [hereinafter by the Commission].

Game birds: wild birds that shall not be hunted except as authorized.

Game fish: species of the class Osteichthyes that shall not be fished for except as authorized by rule, including: rock bass; lake

826

white fish; blue catfish; black bullhead; yellow bullhead; brown bullhead; channel catfish; green sunfish; pumpkinseed; warmouth; bluegill burboth or freshwater ling; smallmouth bass; largemouth bass; kokanee or silver trout; yellow perch; white crappie; black crappie; mountain white fish; golden trout; cutthroat trout; rainbow or steelhead trout; Atlantic salmon; brown trout; eastern brook trout; Dolly Varden trout; lake trout; Walleye; arctic grayling (77.08.020).

Migratory waterfowl: the family Anatidae, including brants, ducks, geese and swans (77.08.045).

Predatory birds: wild birds that may be hunted throughout the year as authorized.

Protected wildlife: wildlife designated by the Commission that shall not be hunted or fished.

Salmon: the genus Oncorhynchus except species classified as game fish, including Chinook, Coho, Chum, Pink and Sockeye salmon.

Shellfish: marine and freshwater invertebrates to be taken only by Director's rule, including all stages of development and parts.

Wild animals: species of the class Mammalia existing in a wild state and the species bullfrog but does not include feral domestic mammals or old world rats and mie.

Wild birds: species of the class Aves existing in a wild state.

Wildlife: all species of the animal kingdom existing in a wild state, including but not limited to mammals, birds, reptiles, amphibians, fish and invertebrates; does not include feral domestic mammals, old world rats and mice, or fish, shellfish and marine invertebrates classified by the Director of Fisheries. "Wildlife" includes all stages of development and parts.

WEST VIRGINIA

Fur-bearing animals: mink, weasel, muskrat, beaver, opossum, skunk, civet cat (polecat), otter, red fox, gray fox, wildcat, bobcat or bay lynx, raccoon and fisher (20-1-2).

Game: game animals, game birds and game fish as herein defined (20-1-2).

Game animals: elk, deer, cottontail rabbits and hares, fox squirrels (red squirrels), gray squirrels and all their color phases--red, gray, black or albino, raccoon, black bear and wild boar (20-1-2).

Game birds: the Anatidae (swan, geese, brants and river and sea ducks); the Rallidae (rails, sora, coots, mudhens and gallinales); the Limicolae (shorebirds, plover, snipe, woodcock, sandpipers, yellow legs and curlews); the Galli (wild turkey, grouse, pheasants, quails and native and foreign species of partridges); the Columbidae (doves); and the Icteridae (blackbirds, redwings and grackled) (20-1-2).

Game fish: brook, brown, rainbow, and golden rainbow trout; Kokanee salmon; largemouth, smallmouth, Kentucky/spotted, striped, rock, and white bass; pickerel, muskellunge, walleye pike or pike perch, northern pike, white and black crappie, all sunfish, channel and flathead catfish and sauger (20-1-2).

Migratory birds: migratory game or nongame birds included in the terms of conventions between the US and Great Britain, and the US and United Mexican States, known as the "Migratory Bird Treaty Act," for the protection of migratory birds and game mammals. Under 20-2-63, the term includes wild geese, brant or wild ducks for purposes of the Migratory Waterfowl Stamp (20-1-2).

Protected birds: wild birds not included within the definition of "game birds" and "unprotected birds" (20-1-2).

Unprotected birds: English sparrow, European starling, cowbird and crow (20-1-2).

Wild animals: mammals native to the state occurring either in a natural state or in captivity, except house mice or rats (20-1-2).

Wild birds: birds other than domestic poultry (chickens, ducks, geese, guinea fowl, peafowls and turkeys); psittacidae (parrots and parakeets); other foreign cage birds such as the common canary, exotic finches and ring dove. All wild birds, either those occurring in a natural state in West Virginia or those imported foreign game birds such as waterfowl, pheasants, partridges, quail and grouse, regardless of how long raised or held in captivity, shall remain wild birds under the meaning of this chapter (20-1-2).

Wildlife: wild birds, wild animals, game and fur-bearing animals, fish (including minnows), frogs and other amphibians, aquatic turtles and all forms of aquatic life used as fish bait, whether dead or alive (20-1-2).

WISCONSIN

Bait: any species of frog, crayfish or minnow used for fishing (29.137).

Carcass: the dead body of any wild animal including head, hair, skin, plumage, skeleton or other part (29.01).

Endangered species: any species whose continued existence as a viable component of this state's wild animals or wild plants is determined by the Department to be in jeopardy on the basis of scientific evidence (29.415).

Fur-bearing animals: otter, beaver, mink, muskrat, marten, fisher, skunk, raccoon, fox, weasel, opossum, badger, wolf, coyote, wildcat and lynx (29.01).

Game: all varieties of wild mammals or birds; "game fish" includes all varieties of fish except rough fish and minnows; "rough fish" includes dace, suckers, carp, goldfish, redhorse, freshwater drum, burbot, bowfin, garfish, buffalo fish, lamprey, alewife, gizzard shad, smelt, goldeye, mooneye, carpsucker and quill back, in all waters and chub in inland waters only; "minnows" includes suckers, mud minnows, madtom, stonecat, killifish, stickleback, trout-perch, darters, sculpin and all minnow family cyprinids except goldfish and carp (29.01).

Game birds: the following aquatic birds: wild geese, brant, wild ducks, wild swan, rails, coots, gallinules, jacksnipe, woodcock, plovers and sandpipers; the following upland birds: ruffed grouse (partridge), pinnated grouse (prairie chicken), sharp-tailed grouse, pheasants, Hungarian partridge, Chukar partridge, bobwhite quail, California quail and wild turkey (29.01).

Hunt or hunting: ★includes shooting, shooting at, pursuing, taking, catching or killing any wild animal, except that for 29.1085, 29.1209 and 29.114; "hunt" or "hunting" does not include shooting, shooting at, taking, catching or killing any bear (29.01).★

Nongame species: any species of wild animal not classified as a game fish, game animal, game bird or fur-bearing animal (29.01).

Threatened species: any species of wild animal or plant which appears likely, within the foreseeable future, on the basis of scientific evidence to become endangered (29.415).

Waterfowl: wild geese, brant, wild ducks, rails, coots, gallinules, jacksnipe, woodcock, plovers, sandpipers and wild swan (29.27).

Wild animal: any mammal, bird, fish or other creature of a wild nature endowed with sensation and power of voluntary motion (29.01).

WYOMING

Big game animal: antelope, bighorn sheep, deer, elk, moose or mountain goat (23-1-101).

Exotic species: wild animals, including amphibians, reptiles, mollusks, crustaceans or birds not found in a wild, free or unconfined status in Wyoming (23-1-101).

Fur-bearing animal: badger, beaver, bobcat, marten, mink, muskrat or weasel (23-1-101).

Game bird: grouse, partridge, pheasant, ptarmigan, quail, wild turkey and migratory game birds (23-1-101).

Game fish: bass, catfish, crappie, grayling, ling, northern pike, perch, salmon, sauger, sunfish, trout, walleye or whitefish (23-1-101).

Migratory game bird: all migratory game birds defined and protected under federal law (23-1-101).

Predacious bird: English sparrow and starling (23-1-101).

Predatory animal: coyote, jackrabbit, porcupine, raccoon, red fox, wolf, skunk or stray cat (23-1-101).

Protected animal: black-footed ferret, fisher, lynx, otter, pika or wolverine (23-1-101).

Protected bird: migratory birds as defined and protected under federal law (23-1-101).

Small game animal: cottontail rabbit or snowshoe hare, and fox, grey and red squirrels (23-1-101).

Trophy game animal: black bear, grizzly bear or mountain lion (23-1-101).

Wildlife: all wild mammals, birds, fish, amphibians, reptiles, crustaceans and mollusks, wild bison designated by the Wyoming Game and Fish Commission and the Wyoming Livestock Board (23-1-101).

SUGGESTED READING

Animal Welfare Institute. *Animals and their Legal Rights*, 4th Ed. Washington, DC, 1990.

Animal Welfare Institute. "Congress Looks at Wildlife Law Enforcement." *The Animal Welfare Institute Quarterly*, 41(1):11.

Animal Welfare Institute and the Environmental Investigation Agency. *Flight to Extinction: The Wild-Caught Bird Trade*. Washington, DC, 1992.

Babbington, Charles. "Scandal in High Places." *Wildlife Conservation*, November/December 1990, pp. 88-93.

Balog, James. "A Personal Vision of Vanishing Wildlife." *National Geographic*, April 1990, pp. 84-103.

Bean, Michael J. *The Evolution of National Wildlife Law*, Revised Ed. New York: Praeger Publications, 1983.

Beattie, Kirk, Tech. Ed. *Proceedings of the International Conference on Improving Hunter Compliance with Wildlife Laws: The Roles of Management, Enforcement and Education, Reno, Nevada, 1992.* Stevens Point: University of Wisconsin.

Brinkley, John. "Wildlife Managers Claim Poaching is Out of Control." *Rocky Mountain News*, December 16, 1991.

Farnsworth, Carl L. "A Descriptive Analysis of the Extent of Commercial Poaching in the United States." Ph.D. dissertation, Sam Houston State University, 1980.

Favre, David S. *Wildlife Law*, 2d ed. Detroit: Lupus Publications, Ltd., 1991.

Gavitt, John D. *Unlawful Commercialization of Wildlife Parts*. Washington, DC: United States Fish and Wildlife Service Division of Law Enforcement, March 1989.

General Accounting Office. *Wildlife Protection: Enforcement of Federal Laws Could be Strengthened.* GAO/RCED-91-44. Washington, DC, 1991.

Glover, Ron. "Characteristics of Deer Poachers and Poaching in Missouri." Master's thesis, University of Missouri, Columbia, 1982.

Glover, Ron. "Locations and Timing of Closed-Season Deer Poaching Incidents in Missouri." In *Transactions, Missouri Academy of Science*, vol. 17, p. 88. Missouri Academy of Science, 1983.

Glover, Ron. "Sociological Profiles of Missouri Deer Poachers: Management Applications." In *Transactions of the Fifty-fourth North American Wildlife and Natural Resources Conference*, p. 108. Washington, DC: Wildlife Management Institute.

Hall, David L.; Bonnaffons, Gerald J.; and Jackson, Robert M. "The Relationship of Enforcement, Courts and Sentencing to Compliance with Waterfowl Hunting Regulations." In *Transactions of the Fifty-fourth North American Wildlife and Natural Resources Conference*, p. 342. Washington, DC: Wildlife Management Institute.

Jackson, Robert M.; Norton, Robert; and Anderson, Ray. "Improving Ethical Behavior in Hunters." In *Transactions of the Fifty-fourth North American Wildlife and Natural Resources Conference*, p. 27. Washington, DC: Wildlife Management Institute.

Littell, Richard. *Endangered and Other Protected Species: Federal Law and Regulation.* Washington, DC: Bureau of National Affairs, Inc., 1993.

Lund, Thomas A. *American Wildlife Law*. Berkeley: University of California Press, 1980.

Lyster, Simon. *International Wildlife Law*. Cambridge: Grotius Publications Ltd., 1985.

Mills, Judy A. and Servheen, Christopher. *The Asian Trade in Bears and Bear Parts*. Baltimore: World Wildlife Fund, Inc., Traffic USA, 1991.

Musgrave, Ruth S. and Dow, Mark, *Indian Wildlife Resources and Endangered Species Management*, 1991 A.B.A. Sec. SONREEL, paper no. 9.

Nilsson, Greta. *The Endangered Species Handbook*. Washington, DC: The Animal Welfare Institute, 1990.

New York Zoological Society. "Alaska: Walruses Killed for their Ivory Tusks." *Animal Kingdom*, November/December 1989, p. 18.

Petersen, David. *Racks: The Natural History of Antlers and the Animals That [sic] Wear Them.* Santa Barbara: Capra Press, 1991.

Poten, Constance J. "A Shameful Harvest:America's Illegal Wildlife Trade." *National Geographic*, September 1991, pp. 106-131.

Reisner, Marc. *Game Wars: The Undercover Pursuit of Wildlife Poachers.* New York: Penguin Books USA Inc., Viking Penguin, 1991.

Rohlf, Daniel J. The Endangered Species Act: *A Guide to Its Protections and Implementation.* Stanford: Stanford Environmental Law Society, 1989

Tennesen, Michael. "Poaching, Ancient Traditions, and the Law." *Audubon,* July/August 1991, pp. 90-97.

Thornton, Robert D. "Takings under Endangered Species Act Section 9." *Natural Resources and Environment* 4(4):7.

United States Fish and Wildlife Service. *Restoring America's Wildlife.* U.S. Department of the Interior, United States Fish and Wildlife Service, 1987.

United States Fish and Wildlife Service. *Digest of Federal Laws and Treaties of Interest to the U.S. Fish and Wildlife Service.* U.S. Department of the Interior, United States Fish and Wildlife Service, 1992.

United States Fish and Wildlife Service Division of Law Enforcement. *FY 1990 Annual Report.* Washington, DC: U.S. Department of the Interior, United States Fish and Wildlife Service.

United States Fish and Wildlife Service Law Enforcement Advisory Commission. *Report of Findings and Recommendations, June 1990.* Washington, DC: U.S. Department of the Interior, United States Fish and Wildlife Service.

WERNEKE © 1991

STATE FISH AND WILDLIFE AGENCIES

Alabama Division of Game & Fish
Dept. of Conser. & Nat. Resources
64 N. Union Street, Rm 728
Montgomery, AL 36130
205/242-3465

Alaska Dept. of Fish & Game
P.O. Box 25526
Juneau, AK 99802-5526
907/465-4100

Arizona Game & Fish Dept.
2222 W. Greenway Road
Phoenix, AZ 85023-4399
602/942-3000

Arkansas Game & Fish Commission
2 Natural Resources Drive
Little Rock, AR 72205
501/223-6300

California Dept. of Fish & Game
1416 Ninth Street-12th Flr
Sacramento, CA 95814
916/653-7664

Colorado Division of Wildlife
Dept. of Natural Resources
6060 Broadway
Denver, CO 80216-1000
303/297-1192

Connecticut Division of Wildlife
Dept. of Environmental Protection
165 Capitol Avenue - Rm 254
Hartford, CT 06106
203/566-4683 (Wildlife)
203/566-2287 (Fisheries)

Delaware Division of Fish & Wildlife
Natural Resources & Env. Control
P.O. Box 1401
Dover, DE 19903
302/739-5295

Florida Game & Freshwater
 Fish Commission
Farris Bryant Building
620 S. Meridian Street
Tallahassee, FL 32399-1600
904/488-1960

Georgia Game & Fish Division
Dept. of Natural Resources
205 Butler Street SE - Suite 1362
Atlanta, GA 30334
404/656-3523

Hawaii Division of Forestry & Wildlife
Land & Natural Resources Dept.
1151 Punchbowl Street
Honolulu, HI 96813
808/548-8850 (Wildlife)
808/548-4000 (Aquatic Resources)

Idaho Dept. of Fish & Game.
600 S. Walnut Street
P.O. Box 25
Boise, ID 83707-0025
208/334-3700
208/334-3736 (Enforcement)

Illinois Dept. of Conservation
Division of Wildlife Resources
600 N. Grand West
Springfield, IL 62701-1787
217/782-6384 (Wildlife)
217/785-8287 (Fisheries)

Indiana Fish & Wildlife Division
Dept. of Natural Resources
402 W. Washington Street - Room
W273
Indianapolis, IN 46204-2267
317-232-4080

Iowa Dept. of Natural Resources
Wallace State Office Building
East Ninth and Grand Avenue
Des Moines, IA 50319-0034
515/281-5145

Kansas Dept. of Wildlife and Parks
Box 54A, RR 2
Pratt, KS 67124-9599
316/672-5911

Kentucky Dept. of Fish &
 Wildlife Resources
#1 Game Farm Road
Frankfort, KY 40601
502/564-4406 (Wildlife)
502/564-3596 (Fisheries)

Louisiana Dept. of Wildlife
 & Fisheries
P.O. Box 98000
Baton Rouge, LA 70898-9000
504/765-2800

Maine Dept. of Inland Fisheries
 & Wildlife
284 State Street
State House Station #41
Augusta, ME 04333
207-289-3371

Maryland Dept. of Natural Resources
Tawes State Office Bldg.
Annapolis, MD 21401
410/974-3558

Massachusetts Dept. of Fisheries,
 Wildlife and Env. Law Enforcement
100 Cambridge Street, Rm 1902
Boston, MA 02202
617/727-1614

Michigan Dept. of Natural Resources
Division of Wildlife
P.O. Box 30028
Lansing, MI 48909
517/373-1263 (Wildlife)
517/373-1280 (Fisheries)

Minnesota Division of Fish & Wildlife
Dept. of Natural Resourcess
500 Lafayette Road
St. Paul, MN 55155
612/297-1308

Mississippi Dept. of Wildlife,
 Fisheries & Parks
P.O. Box 451
Jackson, MS 39205
601/364-2231, 601/364-2015

Missouri Dept. of Conservation
2901 W. Truman Blvd.
Jefferson City, MO 65109 (or)
P.O. Box 180
Jefferson City, MO 65102-0180
314/751-4115

Montana Dept. of Fish, Wildlife
 & Parks
1420 E. Sixth Avenue
Helena, MT 59620
406/444-2535

Nebraska Game & Parks Commission
2200 N. 33rd Street
P.O. Box 30370
Lincoln, NE 68503-0370
402/471-0641

Nevada Dept. of Wildlife
P.O. Box 10678
Reno, NV 89520-0022
702/688-1500

New Hampshire Fish & Game Dept.
2 Hazen Drive
Concord, NH 03301
603/271-3512

New Jersey Fish, Game &
  Wildlife Division
Environmental Protection Dept.
501 E. State Street - CN400
Trenton, NJ 08625
609/292-2655, 609/292-9430

New Mexico Game & Fish Dept.
Villagra Building
408 Galisteo Street
Santa Fe, NM 87503
505/827-7899

New York Dept. of Env. Conservation
Division of Fish & Wildlife
50 Wolf Road
Albany, NY 12233
518/457-5690

North Carolina Wildlife
  Resources Commission
Archdale Building
512 N. Salisbury Street
Raleigh, NC 27604-1188
919/733-3391

North Dakota Game & Fish Dept.
100 North Bismarck Expressway
Bismarck, ND 58501
701/221-6300

Ohio Dept. of Natural Resources
Division of Wildlife
1840 Belcher Drive, Bldg G-3
Columbus, OH 43224
614/265-6305

Oklahoma Dept. of Wildlife
  Conservation
1801 N. Lincoln Blvd
Oklahoma City, OK 73105
405/521-3851

Oregon Dept. of Fish & Wildlife
2501 SW First Avenue
P.O. Box 59
Portland, OR 97207
503/229-5406

Pennsylvania Fish Commission
P.O. Box 1673
Harrisburg, PA 17105
717/657-4518

Pennsylvania Game Commission
2001 Elmerton Avenue
Harrisburg, PA 17110-9797
717/787-3633

Rhode Island Division of Fish
  & Wildlife
Dept. of Environmental Management
4808 Tower Hill Road
Wakefield, RI 02879
401/789-3094

South Carolina Wildlife & Marine
  Resources Dept.
Rembert C. Dennis Building
P.O. Box 167
Columbia, SC 29202
803/734-3888, 803/734-4007

South Dakota Dept. of Game,
  Fish & Parks
Division of Wildlife
Joe Foss Building
523 E. Capitol Avenue
Pierre, SD 57501-3182
605/773-3381

Tennessee Wildlife Resources Agency
P.O. Box 40747
Ellington Agricultural Center
Nashville, TN 37204
615/781-6552

Texas Parks & Wildlife Dept.
4200 Smith School Road
Austin, TX 78744
512/389-4800

Utah Division of Wildlife Resources
Dept. of Natural Resources & Energy
1596 WN Temple
Salt Lake City, UT 84116-3195
801/538-4702

Vermont Dept. of Fish & Wildlife
Agency of Natural Resources
103 S. Main Street
Waterbury, VT 05676
802/244-7331

Virginia Dept. of Game &
  Inland Fisheries
4010 W. Broad Street
Richmond, VA 23230
804/367-1000

Washington Dept. of Fisheries
115 General Administration Building
MS 3141
Olympia, WA 98504-3135
206/586-8100

Washington Dept. of Wildlife
600 Capitol Way North
MS 3200
Olympia, WA 98501-1091
206/753-5700

West Virginia Division of Wildlife
  Resources
Dept. of Natural Resources
State Capitol Complex, Bldg. 3
1900 Kanawha Blvd E.
Charleston, WV 25305
304/558-2771

Wisconsin Dept. of Natural Resources
P.O. Box 7921
Madison, WI 53707
608/266-2193 (Wildlife)
608/267-0796 (Fisheries)

Wyoming Game & Fish Commission
5400 Bishop Blvd.
Cheyenne, WY 82006
307/777-4601

And

District of Columbia Dept. of
  Consumer and Regulatory Affairs
Environmental Regulatory
  Administration
Fisheries and Wildlife Division
2100 Martin Luther King Ave. SE
Suite 203
Washington, DC 20020
202/404-1155

Guam Dept. of Agriculture
P.O. Box 2950
Agana, Guam 96910
671-734-3941

Puerto Rico Dept. of Natural
  Resources
P.O. Box 5887
Puerta De Tierra
San Juan, PR 00906
809/723-3090

U.S. Virgin Islands Dept. of Planning
  & Resources
Nisky Center, Suite 231
St. Thomas, VI 00802
809/774-3320

WERNEKE © 1991

LEGISLATIVE SESSIONS: LEGAL PROVISIONS

State or other jurisdiction	Regular sessions				Special sessions		
	Legislature convenes			Limitation on length of session (a)	Legislature may call	Legislature may determine subject	Limitation on length of session
	Year	Month	Day				
Alabama	Annual	Jan. Apr. May	2nd Tuesday (b) 3rd Tuesday (c,d) 1st Tuesday (c)	30 L in 105 C	No	Yes (f)	12 L in 30 C
Alaska	Annual	Jan. Jan.	3rd Monday (c) 2nd Monday (c)	120 C (g)	By 2/3 vote members	Yes (h)	30 C
Arizona	Annual	Jan.	2nd Monday	(i)	By petition, 2/3 members, each house	Yes (h)	None
Arkansas	Biennial-odd year	Jan.	2nd Monday	60 C (g)	No	Yes (f,j)	(j)
California	(k)	Jan.	1st Monday (d)	None	No	No	None
Colorado	Annual	Jan.	Wednesday after 1st Tuesday	120 C	By request, 2/3 members, each house	Yes (h)	None
Connecticut	Annual (l)	Jan. Feb.	Wednesday after 1st Monday (m) Wednesday after 1st Monday (n)	(o)	Yes (p)	(p)	None (q)
Delaware	Annual	Jan.	2nd Tuesday	June 30	Joint call, presiding officers, both houses	Yes	None
Florida	Annual	Feb.	Tuesday after 1st Monday (d)	60 C (g)	Joint call, presiding officers, both houses	Yes	20 C (g)
Georgia	Annual	Jan.	2nd Monday (d)	40 L	By petition, 3/5 members, each house	Yes (h)	(r)
Hawaii	Annual	Jan.	3rd Wednesday	60 L (g)	By petition, 2/3 members, each house	Yes	30 L (g)
Idaho	Annual	Jan.	Monday on or nearest 9th day	None	No	No	20 C
Illinois	Annual	Jan.	2nd Wednesday	None	Joint call, presiding officers, both houses	Yes	None

See footnotes at end of table.

LEGISLATIVE SESSIONS: LEGAL PROVISIONS-Continued

| State or other jurisdiction | Regular sessions — Legislature convenes | | | | Special sessions | | |
	Year	Month	Day	Limitation on length of session (a)	Legislature may call	Legislature may determine subject	Limitation on length of session
Indiana	Annual	Jan.	2nd Monday (d,s)	odd-61 L or April 30 even-30 L or March 15	No	Yes	30 L or 40 C
Iowa	Annual	Jan.	2nd Monday	(t)	By petition, 2/3 members, both houses	Yes	None
Kansas	Annual	Jan.	2nd Monday	odd-None; even-90 C (g)	Petitions to governor of 2/3 members, each house	Yes	None
Kentucky	Biennial-even yr.	Jan.	Tuesday after 1st Monday (d)	60 L (u)	No	No	None
Louisiana	Annual	April	3rd Monday	60 L in 85 C	By petition, majority, each house	Yes (h)	30 C
Maine	(k, l)	Dec. Jan.	1st Wednesday (b) Wednesday after 1st Tuesday (n)	3rd Wednesday of June (g) 3rd Wednesday of April (g)	Joint call, presiding officers, with consent of majority of members of each political party, each house	Yes (h)	None
Maryland	Annual	Jan.	2nd Wednesday	90 C (g)	By petition, majority, each house	Yes	30 C
Massachusetts	Annual	Jan.	1st Wednesday	None	By petition (v)	Yes	None
Michigan	Annual	Jan.	2nd Wednesday (d)	None	No	No	None
Minnesota	(w)	Jan.	Tuesday after 1st Monday (m)	120 L or 1st Monday after 3rd Saturday in May (w)	No	Yes	None
Mississippi	Annual	Jan.	Tuesday after 1st Monday	125 C (g,x); 90 C (g,x)	No	No	None
Missouri	Annual	Jan.	Wednesday after 1st Monday	odd-June 30; even-May 15	By petition, 3/4 members, each house	Yes	60 C
Montana	Biennial-odd yr.	Jan.	1st Monday	90 L (g)	By petition, majority, each house	Yes	None

LEGISLATIVE SESSIONS: LEGAL PROVISIONS-Continued

State or other jurisdiction	Regular sessions – Legislature convenes			Limitation on length of session (a)	Special sessions – Legislature may call	Legislature may determine subject	Limitation on length of session
	Year	Month	Day				
Nebraska	Annual	Jan.	Wednesday, after 1st Monday	odd-90 L (g); even-60 L (g)	By petition, 2/3 members, each house	Yes	None
Nevada	Biennial-odd yr.	Jan.	3rd Monday	60 C (t)	No	No	20 C (t)
New Hampshire	Annual	Jan.	Wednesday after 1st Tuesday (d)	45 L	By 2/3 vote of members, each house	Yes	15 L (l)
New Jersey	Annual	Jan.	2nd Tuesday	None	By petition, majority, each house	Yes	None
New Mexico	Annual (l)	Jan.	3rd Tuesday	odd-60; even-30 C	By petition, 3/5 members, each house	Yes (h)	30 C
New York	Annual	Jan.	Wednesday after 1st Monday	None	By petition, 2/3 members, each house	Yes (h)	None
North Carolina	(w)	Jan.	Wednesday after 2nd Monday (m)	None	By petition, 3/5 members, each house	Yes	None
North Dakota	Biennial-odd yr.	Jan.	Tuesday after Jan. 3., but not later than Jan. 11 (d)	80 L (y)	No	Yes	None
Ohio	Annual	Jan.	1st Monday	None	Joint call, presiding officers, both houses	Yes	None
Oklahoma	Annual	Feb.	1st Tuesday after 1st Monday (z)	160 C	By 2/3 vote of members, each house	Yes	None
Oregon	Biennial-odd yr.	Jan.	2nd Monday	None	By petition, majority, each house	Yes	None
Pennsylvania	Annual	Jan.	1st Tuesday	None	By petition, majority, each house	No	None
Rhode Island	Annual	Jan.	1st Tuesday	60 L (t)	No	No	None
South Carolina	Annual	Jan.	2nd Tuesday (d)	1st Thursday in June (g)	No	Yes	None
South Dakota	Annual	Jan.	2nd Tuesday	odd-40 L; even-35 L	No	No	None

LEGISLATIVE SESSIONS: LEGAL PROVISIONS-Continued

State or other jurisdiction	Regular sessions				Special sessions		
	Legislature convenes			Limitation on length of session (a)	Legislature may call	Legislature may determine subject	Limitation on length of session
	Year	Month	Day				
Tennessee	(w)	Jan.	(aa)	90 L (t)	By petition, 2/3 members, each house	Yes	30 L (t)
Texas	Biennial-odd yr.	Jan.	2nd Tuesday	140 C	No	No	30 C
Utah	Annual	Jan.	2nd Monday	45 C	No	No	30 C
Vermont	(w)	Jan.	Wednesday after 1st Monday (m)	(t)	No	Yes	None
Virginia	Annual	Jan.	2nd Wednesday	odd-30 C (g); even-60 C (g)	By petition, 2/3 members, each house	Yes	None
Washington	Annual	Jan.	2nd Monday	odd-105 c; even-60 C	By vote, 2/3 members, each house	Yes	30 C
West Virginia	Annual	Feb. / Jan.	2nd Wednesday (c,d) / 2nd Wednesday (c)	60 C (g)	By petition, 3/5 members, each house	Yes (bb)	None
Wisconsin	Annual (cc)	Jan.	1st Tuesday after Jan. 8 (d,m)	None	No	No	None
Wyoming	Annual (l)	Jan. / Feb.	2nd Tuesday (m) / 2nd Tuesday (n)	odd-40; even-20 L	No	Yes	None
District of Columbia	(dd)	Jan.	2nd day	None			
American Samoa	Annual	Jan. / July	2nd Monday / 2nd Monday	45 L / 45 L	No	No	None
Guam	Annual	Jan.	2nd Monday (cc)	None	No	No	None
Puerto Rico	Annual	Jan.	2nd Monday	April 30 (g)	No	No	20C
U.S. Virgin Islands	Annual	Jan.	2nd Monday	75 L	No	No	15 C

LEGISLATIVE SESSIONS: LEGAL PROVISIONS

Sources: State constitutions and statutes.

Note: Some legislatures will also reconvene after normal session to consider bills vetoed by governor. **Connecticut**--if governor vetoes any bill, secretary of state must reconvene General Assembly on second Monday after the last day on which governor is either authorized to transmit or has transmitted every bill with his objections, whichever occurs first; General Assembly must adjourn *sine die* not later than three days after its reconvening. **Hawaii**--legislature may reconvene on 45th day after adjournment *sine die*, in special session, without call. **Louisiana**--legislature meets in a maximum five-day veto session on the 40th day after final adjournment. **Missouri**--if governor returns any bill on or after the fifth day before the last day on which legislature may consider bills (in even-numbered years), legislature automatically reconvenes on first Monday in September for a maximum 10 C session. **New Jersey**--legislature meets in special session (without call or petition) to act on bills returned by governor on 45th day after *sine die* adjournment of the first year of a two-year legislature; a special session may not be convened if the 45th day falls on or after the last day of the legislative year in which the second session occurs. **Virginia**--legislature reconvenes on sixth Wednesday after adjournment for a maximum three-day session (may be extended to seven days upon vote of majority of members elected to each house.) **Utah**--if 2/3 of the members of each house favor reconvening to consider vetoed bills,a maximum five-day session is set by the presiding officers. **Washington**--upon petition of 2/3 of the members of each house, legislature meets 45 days after adjournment for a maximum five-day session.

Key:

C -- Calendar day

L -- Legislative day (in some states, called a session day or workday; definition may vary slightly, however, generally refers to any day on which either house of the legislature is in session)

(a) Applies to each year unless otherwise indicated.
(b) General election year (quadrennial election).
(c) Year after quadrennial election.
(d) Legal provision for organizational session prior to stated convening date. **Alabama**--in the year after quadrennial election, on the second

Tuesday in January for 10 C. **California**--in the even-numbered, general election year, on the first Monday in December for an organizational session, recess until the first Monday in January of the odd-numbered year. **Florida**--in general election year, 14th day after election. **Georgia**--in odd-numbered year. **Indiana**--third Tuesday after first Monday in November. **Kentucky**--in odd-numbered year, Tuesday after first Monday in January for 10 L. **Michigan**--held in odd-numbered year. **New Hampshire**--in even-numbered year, first Wednesday in December. **North Dakota**--in December. **South Carolina**--in even-numbered year, Tuesday after certification of election of its members for a maximum three-day session. **West Virginia**--in year after general election, on second Wednesday in January.

(e) Other years.
(f) By 2/3 vote each house.
(g) Session may be extended by vote of members in both houses. **Alaska**; 2/3 vote for 10-day extension. **Arkansas**; 2/3 vote. **Florida**; 3/5 vote. **Hawaii**; petition of 2/3 membership for maximum 15-day extension. **Kansas**, 2/3 vote. **Maryland**; 3/5 vote for maximum 30 C. **Mississippi**; 2/3 vote for 30 C extension, no limit on number of extensions. **Nebraska**; 4/5 vote. **South Carolina**; 2/3 vote. **Virginia**; 2/3 vote for 30 C extension. **West Virginia**; 2/3 vote (or if budget bill as not been acted upon three days before session ends, governor issues proclamation extending session. **Puerto Rico**; joint resolution.

(h) Only if legislature convenes itself. Special sessions called by the legislature are unlimited in scope in **Arizona, Georgia, Maine, and New Mexico.**

(i) No constitutional or statutory provision; however, legislative rules require that regular sessions adjourn no later than Saturday of the week during which the 100th day of the session falls.

(j) After governor's business has been disposed of, members may remain in session up to 15 C by a 2/3 vote of both houses.

(k) Regular sessions begin after general election, in December of even-numbered year. In **California**, legislature meets in December for an organizational session, recesses until the first Monday in January of the odd-numbered year and continues in session until Nov. 30 of next even-numbered year. In **Maine**, session which begins in December of general the first Tuesday after the first Monday, in January and recessing not later than the first Monday in February of that year. Limited constitutional duties can be performed.

(aa) Commencement of regular session depends on concluding date of organizational session. Legislature meets, in odd-numbered year, on second Tuesday in January for a maximum 15 organizational session, then returns on the Tuesday following the conclusion of the organizational session.

(bb) According to a 1955 attorney general's opinion, when the legislature has petitioned to the governor to be called into session, it may then act on any matter.

(cc) The legislature, by joint resolution, establishes the session schedule of activity for the remainder of the biennium at the beginning of the odd-numbered year.

(dd) Each Council period begins on January 2 of each odd-numbered year and ends on January 1 of the following year.

(ee) Legislature meets on the first Monday of each month following its initial session in January.

---

election year runs into the following year (odd-numbered); second session begins in next even-numbered year.

(l) Second session limited to consideration of specific types of legislation. **Connecticut**--individual legislators may only introduce bills of a fiscal nature, emergency legislation and bills raised by committees. **Maine**--budgetary matters; legislation in the governor's call; emergency legislation; legislation referred to committees for study. **New Mexico**--budgets, appropriations and revenue bills; bills drawn pursuant to governor's message; vetoed bills. **Wyoming**--budget bills.

(m) Odd-numbered years.

(n) Even-numbered years.

(o) Odd-numbered years--not later than Wednesday after first Monday in June; even-numbered years--not later than Wednesday after first Monday in May.

(p) Constitution provides for regular session convening dates and allows that sessions may also be held "...at such other times as the General Assembly shall judge necessary." Call by majority of legislators is implied.

(q) Upon completion of business.

(r) Limited to 40 days if called by governor and 30 days if called by petition of the legislature, except in cases of impeachment proceedings.

(s) Legislators may reconvene at any time after organizational meeting; however, second Monday in January is the final date by which regular session must be in process.

(t) Indirect limitation; usually restrictions on legislator's pay, per diem, or daily allowance.

(u) May not extend beyond April 15.

(v) Joint rules provide for the submission of a written statement requesting special session by a specified number of members of each chamber.

(w) Legal provision for session in odd-numbered year; however, legislature may divide, and in practice has divided, to meet in even-numbered years as well.

(x) A 1968 constitutional amendment calls for 90 C sessions every year, except the first year of a gubernatorial administration during which the legislative session runs for 125 C.

(y) No legislative day is shorter than a natural day.

(z) Odd number years will include a regular session commencing on